James M. Burgin

STUDIES IN HITTITE ECONOMIC ADMINISTRATION
VOLUME I

Studien zu den Boğazköy-Texten

Herausgegeben im Auftrag
der Akademie der Wissenschaften und der Literatur, Mainz,
von Elisabeth Rieken und Daniel Schwemer
Band 70

James M. Burgin

Studies in Hittite Economic Administration

A New Edition of the Hittite Palace-Temple Administrative Corpus and Research on Allied Texts Found at Ḫattuša

Volume I: Background, Corpus Overview, Case Studies, Lexical Commentary, and Glossary

2022

Harrassowitz Verlag · Wiesbaden

Gefördert durch die Akademie der Wissenschaften und der Literatur, Mainz, im Rahmen des vom Bundesministerium für Bildung und Forschung, Bonn/Berlin, dem Ministerium für Bildung, Wissenschaft, Weiterbildung und Kultur Rheinland-Pfalz, Mainz, dem Hessischen Ministerium für Wissenschaft und Kunst, Wiesbaden, und dem Bayerischen Staatsministerium für Wissenschaft und Kunst, München, finanzierten Akademienprogramms.

Bibliografische Information der Deutschen Nationalbibliothek
Die Deutsche Nationalbibliothek verzeichnet diese Publikation in der Deutschen Nationalbibliografie; detaillierte bibliografische Daten sind im Internet über https://dnb.de/ abrufbar.

Bibliographic information published by the Deutsche Nationalbibliothek
The Deutsche Nationalbibliothek lists this publication in the Deutsche Nationalbibliografie; detailed bibliographic data are available on the Internet at https://dnb.de/.

For further information about our publishing program consult our website https://www.harrassowitz-verlag.de/

Printed on permanent/durable paper.
Printing and binding: Memminger MedienCentrum AG
Printed in Germany

ISSN 0585-5853 eISSN 2702-0002
ISBN 978-3-447-11929-0 eISBN 978-3-447-39350-8

CONTENTS

LIST OF TABLES AND FIGURES

Tables

Figures

ABBREVIATIONS

The bibliographic abbreviations follow in general those of the *Reallexikon der Assyriologie* (rla.badw.de/reallexikon/abkuerzungslisten/literatur-und-koerperschaften.html). Novel or especially pertinent sigla and bibliographical abbrevations are given below.

Sigla and Bibliographical Abbreviations

ABoT 1	Balkan, Kemal (1948). *Ankara Arkeoloji Müzesinde bulunan Boğazköy tabletleri.* Istanbul: Millî Eğitim Basımevi.
AnAr	Inventory number of the Anadolu Medeniyetleri Müzesi Ankara
Bo	Inventory numbers of Boğazköy tablets
CAD	*The Assyrian Dictionary.* Chicago: Oriental Institute, 1956–2010.
CHD	*The Hittite Dictionary.* Chicago: Oriental Institute, 1980–.
CTH	Laroche, Emmanuel (1971). *Catalogue des textes hittites.* Paris: Klincksieck. Supplements in *RHA* 30 (1972): 94–133 and *RHA* 33 (1975): 68–71. Maintained now as *Catalog der Texte der Hethiter* on the *Hethitologie-Portal Mainz* by Silvin Košak and Gerfried G. W. Müller (hethport.uni-wuerzburg.de/CTH/).
eDiAna	eDiAna (beta 0.2): Digital Philological-Etymological Dictionary of the Minor Ancient Anatolian Corpus Languages, at: https://www.ediana.gwi.uni-muenchen.de/dictionary.php.
EDHIL	Kloekhorst, Alwin (2008). *Etymological Dictionary of the Hittite Inherited Lexicon.* Leiden Indo-European Etymological Dictionary Series 5. Leiden: Brill.
EHS	Kronasser, Heinz (1962–1966). *Etymologie der hethitischen Sprache.* Wiesbaden: Harrassowitz.
GHL	Hoffner, Harry A., and H. Craig Melchert (2008). *A Grammar of the Hittite Language. Part I: Reference Grammar.* Winona Lake, Indiana: Eisenbrauns.
HED	Puhvel, Jaan (1984–). *Hittite Etymological Dictionary.* Trends in Linguistics. Documentation. Berlin; New York; Amsterdam: Mouton; De Gruyter.
HEG	Tischler, Johann (1983–2016). *Hethitisches Etymologisches Glossar.* Innsbrucker Beiträge zur Sprachwissenschaft, 20. Innsbruck: Institut für Sprachen und Literaturen.
HIT	Košak, Silvin (1982). *Hittite Inventory Texts (CTH 241–250).* Texte der Hethiter 10. Heidelberg: Winter.
HVP	Siegelová, Jana (1986). *Hethitische Verwaltungspraxis im Lichte der Wirtschafts- und Inventardokumente.* 3 vols. Praha: Národní muzeum v Praze.

HW²	Friedrich, Johannes, and Annelies Kammenhuber (1975–). *Hethitisches Wörterbuch. Zweite, völlig neubearbeitete Auflage auf der Grundlage der edierten hethitischen Texte.* Heidelberg: Winter.
HZL	Rüster, Christel, and Erich Neu (1989). *Hethitisches Zeichenlexikon. Inventar und Interpretation der Keilschriftzeichen aus den Boğazköy-Texten.* Wiesbaden: Harrassowitz.
IBoT	İstanbul Arkeoloji Müzelerinde bulunan Boğazköy Tabletleri(nden seçme metinler). Istanbul: Maarif Matbaası, 1944, 1947, 1954; Ankara: Türk Tarih Kurumu, 1988.
KBo	Keilschrifttexte aus Boghazköi.
Konkordanz	Košak, Silvin. Konkordanz der hethitischen Keilschrifttafeln, *Hethitologie-Portal Mainz*, at: http://www.hethport.uni-wuerzburg.de/hetkonk/.
KUB	Keilschrifturkunden aus Boghazköi.
MesZL	Borger, Rykle (2010). *Mesopotamisches Zeichenlexikon. Zweite, revidierte und aktualisierte Auflage.* Alter Orient und Altes Testament 305. Münster: Ugarit-Verlag.
RlA	*Reallexikon der Assyriologie.* Berlin, Leipzig: De Gruyter, 1920–2018.
VBoT	Götze, Albrecht, ed. (1930). *Verstreute Boghazköi-Texte.* Marburg: Selbstverlag des Herausgebers.

General Abbreviations

abl.	ablative	MH	Middle Hittite
acc.	accusative	mid.	middle voice
adj.	adjective	fn.	footnote
adv.	adverb	n.	neuter gender
all.	allative	NH	New Hittite
C	consonant (e.g., -*iC*-)	nom.	nominative
CLuw.	Cuneiform Luwian	obv.	obverse
col.	column	OH	Old Hittite
coll.	collective	PTAC	Palace-Temple Administrative Corpus
com.	common (gender)		
dat./loc.	dative/locative	ptc.	participle
DN	divine name	pl.	plural
gen.	genitive	pres.	present
GN	geographical name	pret.	preterit
imp.	imperative	ptc.	participle
infin.	infinitive	r. c.	right column
inst.	instrumental	rev.	reverse
iter.	iterative	sg.	singular
l. c.	left column	V	vowel (e.g., -*Vš*-)
lo. e.	lower edge	vb. subst.	verbal substantive
Luw.	Luwian		

Symbols and Transliteration Conventions

∢*	triple *Glossenkeil*
?	reading of a sign is uncertain
(?)	reading of reconstructed sequence of signs uncertain
!	abnormal or mistaken sign; designation of column or side of tablet varies from handcopy
[ ]	encloses reconstructed text
[( )]	encloses restorations according to duplicate text
⸢ ⸣	encloses damaged but legible signs
⟨ ⟩	mistaken omission by scribe
⟨⟨ ⟩⟩	mistaken inclusion by scribe
⟨⟨ ⟩⟩	encloses incompletely erased signs that are still legible
x	illegible sign (in transliteration)
[x x]	indicates amount of space in gaps; each x = space for one sign
+	fragments join directly; after reference to a single fragment adjoining other fragment(s) (listed elsewhere)
(+)	fragments join indirectly
//	duplicate text
*	reconstructed form
**	non-existent form for the sake of argument
...	encloses signs over erasure
=	separates morphological elements within words
[...]	indicates that some text is expected in break
( )	encloses words in translation which are understood but absent in the original language

Cursive text in translations indicates uncertain meanings of words, most of which are discussed in the respective entries of the *Lexical Commentary*.

Indentation at the beginning of a line in transliteration or translation indicates a matching indentation of arbitrary length on the original tablet.

PREFACE AND ACKNOWLEDGMENTS

The present book is the fruition of two undertakings: my dissertation, "Aspects of Religious Administration in the Hittite Late New Kingdom" (PhD Diss., University of Chicago, 2016), and the project "Critical Edition, Electronic Database, and Systematic Analysis of the Hittite Palace Administrative Corpus (CTH 240-250, 503, 504, 513)," funded by an Individual Research Grant (Project Number 382183667) from the *Deutsche Forschungsgemeinschaft* and conducted at the Lehrstuhl für Altorientalistik, University of Würzburg, from October 2017 to February 2021. The contribution of the dissertation is comprised by Chapters 1, 2 (in part), 4, 5, 6, and 8, with the dissertation material in every instance extensively revised, and in some cases, especially Chapter 2, greatly expanded with recent research. The remainder of the book, including the *Introduction*, Chapters 3 and 7, the *Summary and Conclusions*, and the *Lexical Commentary* and *Glossary* of Volume I, as well as the entirety of the text editions and philological commentary in Volume II, are the result of the above-named DFG project.

The book has received financial support at every stage. At the dissertation stage, I thank the Adolph Leo Oppenheim Fund for tuition assistance and the Franke Institute for the Humanities at the University of Chicago for a Dissertation Year Fellowship from 2015–2016. Beyond the stipend and tuition assistance by the fellowship, the semiweekly workshops and research facilities at the Franke Institute provided a stimulating and productive environment in which to finish the dissertation. For the project stage, I would like to thank the *Deutsche Forschungsgemeinschaft* for funding my employment as sole lead researcher on the project. I would also like to thank the University of Würzburg for the *Anschubförderung* ("Start-up Grant") that funded research assistants and proof-reading to mitigate the time lost preparing an application for my next research project.

A number of people have contributed to the successful completion of the present book. First, I extend my warmest gratitude to my dissertation advisors Theo van den Hout, Petra Goedegebuure, and David Schloen for their readings, comments, and guidance on the original disseration. I also thank Andreas Schachner for reading and commenting on portions of the dissertation. With equal warmth, I would like to thank the editors of the *Studien zu den Boğazköy-Texten* series, Daniel Schwemer and Elisabeth Rieken, for their heroic efforts in guiding the book to publication. I would also like to acknowledge and express my appreciation for research assistants Marie Klein and Stefano Aprà for their help in locating and scanning secondary literature and checking the book text for consistency, as well as Helen Young for reading portions of the book for style.

I am indebted to Michele Cammarosano for the many stimulating discussions we had concerning religious administrative texts, as well as his generous provision of preliminary transliterations for those administrative texts he determined ought to be excluded from the corpus of Hittite Local Cults. For their support and accomodation at the Hethitologie-Archiv at the Akademie der Wissenschaften und der Literatur, Mainz, I am grateful to Charles Steitler, who also identified and provided preliminary transliterations of some of the texts to be included in the administrative corpus, and Silvin Košak, who sadly passed away during the completion of this book. Silvin was, in addition to his more famous role as the author and tireless maintainer of the online *Konkordanz der hethitischen Keilschrifttafeln*, one of the pioneers of the study of Hittite administrative texts. It was a pleasure to be able to discuss these with him as I worked on the expanded corpus nearly forty years after his initial edition.

I also thank Oğuz Soysal for permission to use the relevant unpublished Boğazköy administrative texts from his upcoming *Chicago Hittite Dictionary Supplements 4*, and for his generously providing a preprint version of the texts with transliteration with philological commentary. I thank here as well Şafak Bozgun (Ankara University) and Hasan Peker (Istanbul University) for their generous permissions to provide provisional transliterations of the relevant unpublished Boğazköy administrative texts from their assigned lots of Bo texts based on the original excavation materials viewed at the Hethitologie-Archiv at the Akademie der Wissenschaften und der Literatur, Mainz.

Finally, I extend my sincerest thanks to the Anadolu Medeniyetleri Müzesi in Ankara for generous permission to examine the cuneiform tablet archives while preparing my dissertation, and to the Hethitologie-Archiv at the Akademie der Wissenschaften und der Literatur, Mainz, for access to the card files, *Grabungsumschriften*, and tablet photographs during preparation of the book. Last, but certainly not least, I express my sincere gratitude to Prof. Schwemer for the outstanding research environment furnished by the Lehrstuhl für Altorientalistik at the University of Würzburg, where I worked on this book for four years.

James M. Burgin
Würzburg, 2022

INTRODUCTION

When I began working on the dissertation that would become this book, it was with a feeling that Hittitology had neglected the administrative texts in favor of the more accessible genres of narrative, myth, and religion. By the end of the literature review for the dissertation, however, and even more so now after digesting the flurry of research that has appeared during the preparation of the book, I realized I had been wrong, or at least not fully correct. Hittitology has in fact been interested in texts of government and administration since its very beginning, with no signs of abating. Hittite socio-economic historiography comprehends a detailed and sophisticated literature, and one which has moreover generally kept pace with the intellectual currents of the 20th and 21st centuries.

If there is a shortcoming to be found with the discipline, it is perhaps that it has not had time to consolidate. Perhaps because the field is relatively small, with no more than a handful of scholars working on questions of administration at a time, the philological situation took time to mature. The bulk of the Hittite economic-administrative corpus was not edited until the mid-1980's, which meant that much of the previous research was based on prescriptive texts such as instructions and decrees, rather than the texts of the living administration itself. Then, even when the texts became widely available, it took still longer to bring them into conversation with the theory and archaeology necessary for their contextualization. This is now being corrected, much of it by research accomplished only in the last ten to fifteen years.

Nevertheless, there is little controversy in stating that Hittitology has not featured as frequently as it could among the comparative studies on Bronze Age administration. Fundamental differences between the Hittite economic administrative corpus and the corpora of its contemporaries contribute to the problem, not least of which is the difference in size. Unlike the vast troves of economic administrative documents recovered from the archives of Bronze Age Mesopotamia, Syria, and Egypt, where the challenge lies in managing the enormous, if sometimes repetitive, quantities of data contained within, a researcher can only be astonished by the meagre number of the same from the Hittite world. Fewer than 300 "living" economic records have been recovered in total across every Hittite period and site. A program of apparently assiduous recycling or destruction of obsolete tablets explains part of this small size, since the vast majority of the tablets – those that contain the texts that are the focus of this book – date to what was perhaps a single generation near the end of the Hittite Kingdom. Likewise, the handful of economic records recovered from one of the few published provincial archive outside of Ḫattuša all seem to date to a short time, perhaps even a single season, before the destruction of the site. But even projecting the number of preserved texts onto previous generations reveals a written economic administration that is vanishingly small for what is expected from a Bronze Age bureaucracy.

Unusual too is the fact that the Hittite texts tend to be larger in format, more detailed in description, but at the same time less prone to numeracy and abstraction than most of the records of contemporary kingdoms. Inventories of concrete, tangible objects predominate in the Hittite corpus. Records concerning the management of foodstuffs, grain, and livestock are almost completely absent, as are all private records. In fact, the absence of entire swathes of the Hittite economy from the administrative corpus led to the expectation, persisting as late as the 1970's, that the main economic archives of the Hittite capital were still to be uncovered. Now, with excavations at Ḫattuša having nearly exhausted the Hittite levels, this hope has been disappointed. As a result, the preserved corpus of Hittite economic administrative records is simply not commensurate in size or comparable in contents compared to the cuneiform and hieratic bureaucracies to the south, and this fact has remained probably the main impediment to its appreciation.

The greatest challenge, then, confronting the scholar of Hittite economic administration is explaining the dearth and differences of the texts compared to what is expected based on the archives of contemporary Bronze Age kingdoms. One popular explanation is that the Hittite Kingdom recorded most of its short-term economic records on perishable materials, which are now irretrievably lost thanks to the harsh environment of the Anatolian Plateau. It is unquestionable that wooden tablets, probably covered with wax to form a reusable writing surface, were used in Hittite Anatolia. However, estimating the extent to which wooden tablets were used to record economic matters is difficult. There is little evidence within the economic records preserved on clay for an interface with the wooden tablets, and indeed there are also preserved some quite preliminary texts written on clay, precisely the kind of temporary "rough drafts" that one would expect to be the domain of the wooden tablets. This suggests that the clay tablet administration and the wooden tablet administration, to whatever extent it existed, overlapped very little.

There is also a non-literate administrative medium to consider, namely the extensive system of seals, bullae (sealed lumps of clays attached to objects by a string), and *cretulae* (sealed lumps of clay applied directly to an object). Determining the extent to which this system overlapped with or complemented literate records is similarly difficult. Very few Hittite tablets were directly sealed, and none are preserved among the economic administrative records edited in this book. There are large numbers of bullae that were retained for generations in what appear to be dedicated archives, but these seem to have unfortunately been separated from the objects to which they were attached already in Hittite times. At least some of the bullae were probably once attached by strings folded into clay tablets, as evidenced by the string hole preserved in the edges of some tablets, including at least one economic administrative record. Other hypothesized uses for the bullae include being their being tied directly to objects as tags, wrapping locking mechanisms for doors and chests, and wrapping around and tying shut the leaves of folding wooden tablets. For the less frequent *cretulae*, impressions on their interior surfaces show that they were attached directly to bags and jars, confirming a non-literate use for the system. If an extensive economic administration on wooden tablets existed, then it would account for some of the bullae. At the same time, the fact that seals, bullae, and *cretulae* are richly attested in the archaeological record of pre-literate Anatolia is proof that they required no writing to be useful.

Given the uncertainties in the evidentiary basis of Hittite economic administration, the path of investigation chosen here is to focus on contextualizing the evidence that is actually at hand in the cuneiform texts on clay as they are preserved. For this reason, the book begins with a longitudinal historiographical study of previous and current models of the Hittite state. The intent of these chapters is to establish a framework in which the potential functions of the limited economic administration on clay tablets can be examined. The orientation of the introductory chapters is synoptic, building on the work of others, and occasionally trimming away old data and outdated assumptions, but for the most part letting the scholars speak for themselves.

Chapter 1, "History of Research (I): Past Models of the Hittite State," traces how the initial interpretation of the Hittite Kingdom as a feudal state was supplanted by a Marxist critique portraying the palace sector as an institution in parasitic dependence on the village communal sector. Western reception of this critique was initially mixed, but especially positive in Italy, but increasingly emphasized the roles of religion, ideology, and environment in explaining the structure of the Hittite state, which strained the traditional materialism of Marxist analysis. By the 1990's, a model was achieved whereby the combined institution of the Hittite palace and temple, with the latter fully subordinated to the former, stood at the center of a redistribution network erected in response the environmental challenges and historical situation of the Anatolia Plateau.

Redistribution, religion, and environment loom large in Chapter 2, "History of Research (II): Current Models of the Hittite State." Here, recent advancements in archaeology and theory provide support and vital clarifications to the palace-temple redistributive model. Archaeology has demonstrated that the Hittite state maintained its power on the Anatolia Plateau through a system of urban settlements newly founded at strategic locations. These settlements were endowed with a cultural-technological "package" in the form of walls, palace, and temples, and sustained by a system of grain silos and water features for local intensive agriculture and livestock that promoted the local, defensive accumulation of staple products. Theory suggests that states in environments such as the Anatolian Plateau, which combined an abundant mineral wealth, lack of navigable rivers, and proximity to civilizations with larger population bases, were maintained by control of trade in luxuries and exertions of ideological and military power over local elites. It is a central argument of this book that the relatively small corpus of written economic-administrative records, all of which concern the manipulation of wealth – above all religious wealth – in the form of metals, garments, and luxury objects, can be traced back to the needs of the Hittite state as it interacted with the conditions of the Anatolian environment. The economic-administrative records preserved on clay tablets concern precisely the sector of economy that the Hittite central state would have the most interest in dominating as it tied together the network of urban settlements on the Plateau. The defensive accumulation of staple resources was left to local authorities, who may or may not have employed wooden tablets in conjunction with a system of pre-literate seals and bullae to coordinate the agricultural life of their towns. These arguments are not necessarily new to this book, since, as will be seen, they build upon excellent previous research, but it is the first time they have been combined with an extensive philological reevaluation of the Hittite economic-administrative corpus. Suggestions for future research questions testing the hypothesis of a small, religiously focused Hittite economic-administration are then offered at the end of Chapter 2.

Having suggested a background for the texts, the corpus of economic-administrative documents as a whole is introduced in Chapter 3, "The Palace-Temple Administrative Corpus: Structure and Purpose." After reviewing its growth and revision of the criteria for inclusion, it is argued that the texts should be renamed the Palace-Temple Administrative Corpus. The renaming is necessary to reflect the redressed balance of what in previous editions of the Hittite economic texts was a decisive skew in findspots towards the palatial acropolis at Büyükkale. Now, with new finds, and the recognition that many of the temple inventories that were previously classified separately under religious administration cannot be separated from those of the palatial administration, the split between temple and palace is nearly even. A clear trend emerges, already observed based on the old editions and now further confirmed by the expanded corpus, where the documents discovered at Büyükkale involve the receiving tribute, manufacture, and distribution, while those found at temples involve storage and maintenance. The philological evidence for the limited interface of the corpus with other systems of administration, including the wooden tablets and seals and bullae, is also discussed at this point. The rest of Chapter 3 is devoted to the proposed internal divisions of the corpus. Here it must be emphasized that the contributions of previous editions have not been made obsolete. Much of the general outline of the Hittite economic administrative apparatus that can be recovered from the texts was already laid out in the previous edition of the texts by Jana Siegelová in her *Hethitische Verwaltungspraxis im Lichte der Wirtschafts- und Inventardokumente* (Prague, 1986) and expanded in subsequent studies. Every effort has been made to bring the philology up to date, but serious researchers must also consult the interpretation and arrangement of the texts by Siegelová.

The Chapters 4 through 8 of Volume I are devoted to case studies of economic-administrative documents, one within and the others without the Palace-Temple Administrative Corpus. The case studies are intended to serve as models for future research. Among other aims, it is hoped that they serve to demonstrate the benefits of quantification, however basic, when applied to the texts. Chapter 4 "Case Study: the KASKAL Series" examines the KASKAL Main Text, the largest and most complex text of the Palace-Temple Administrative Corpus. It is demonstrated that the text was constructed from a conscious editorial process of no less than four layers. In Chapter 5, "Quantifying the Contents of the KASKAL Main Text," it is demonstrated the objects of the KASKAL Main Text comprise the single largest collection of wealth known from the Hittite world. The value of the objects is compared to other sources of wealth available to the Hittites, namely tribute from international vassals and diplomatic gifts, in Chapter 6, "The Relative Value of the KASKAL Main Text." The destination and eventual recipient of the objects of the KASKAL Main Text cannot as of yet be determined, but a dowry for an unrecorded royal marriage is speculated in Chapter 7, "Concluding Remarks on the KASKAL Main Text."

Chapter 8, "The Hittite Votive Corpus as Economic Texts," provides an alternative perspective to the Palace-Temple Administrative Corpus, which can appear frustratingly timeless due to the almost complete absence of chronological markers, by examining the Hittite Votive Corpus. By correlating the expenditures recorded in the votive texts to the duration of the reign of queen Puduḫepa with which they coincide, it is shown that in the tenure of Puduḫepa at least half, if not two-thirds, of the regular gold income from foreign tribute and gift exchange were spent as votive gifts. This fact provides further, concrete support for the wealth-financed system of religious expenditure hypothesized in the introductory chapters as an explanation for the focus on religious wealth observed in in the Palace-Temple Administrative Corpus. A short recapitulation of the main ideas discussed in the book is then given in "Summary and Conclusions on Hittite Economic Administration."

The remainder comprises the philological portions of the book. The text editions of Volume II have as their aim a comprehensive update of the corpus, which has expanded by 113 texts and text fragments since the edition of Siegelová's *Hethitische Verwaltungspraxis.* Each text is prefaced with an introductory discussion designed to contextualize it in light of the new divisions of the corpus as well as the advances in archaeology, theory, and philology. The introductory analyses to the texts have attempted to diligently, responsibly, and critically incorporate the interpretations given in the previous editions and literature, but perhaps in no other genre of the Hittite corpus is interpretation of individual texts and their organization as a group so contestable. The serious scholar is invited to consult Silvin Košak's *Hittite Inventory Texts (CTH 241–250)* (Heidelberg, 1982) in addition to Siegelová's *Hethitische Verwaltungspraxis* for the interpretations of individual texts, as well as the various editions and commentaries given in the previous literature for each edition. Comments on the readings of individual lines are placed in the philological commentaries following each text. Discussion of individual words, including an impressive variety of technical terms and *realia* that are often or nearly unique to the Palace-Temple Administrative Corpus, is collected in the *Lexical Commentary* of Volume I. A *Glossary* of every word and word form appearing in the corpus is also included in Volume I. The placing of the *Lexical Commentary* and *Glossary* into a separate volume from the text editions is intended to allow for ease of simultaneous consultation.

It must be emphasized that despite its size, this book does not pretend to be a comprehensive study of Hittite economic administration. There are other text corpora, including the land grant documents, the instructions, and the few administrative texts found outside of Ḫattuša, that remain to be reinvestigated from fresh archaeological and theoretical perspectives. Then, establishing whether the focus on religious wealth in the cuneiform documentation is an artifact of preservation or evidence for a fundamentally different style of administration requires further research. This will include recourse to other genres, such as the festival texts and local cults, in order to establish the extent to which the program of religious intervention had purchase with the local populations and elites. Anthropological parallels must be consulted in conjunction with the latest archaeological research to determine whether it was possible for the Hittite state to sustain the exceptional level of urbanism on the Plateau without the use of an extensive literate administration of the staple economy. Finally, there is more work for philologists. Having brought the Palace-Temple Administrative Corpus to a level state, studies of individual texts, text groups, and themes on the model of the case studies presented in the book are waiting to be conducted. Indeed, it must be confessed that the truism that one does not begin to understand a corpus until after having fully edited it very much applies here: there is much information left in the texts. But I am inclined to say that future studies of Hittite administration should be motivated not by how far is left to go, but how close we are to a new level of understanding. If a few habits of mind – chiefly the over-expectation of bureaucracy crept in from modernity – are questioned, and complex questions reduced to testable hypothesis; and if the results are oriented in larger theories, the pieces of a new interpretation of the economic administration of the Hittite state will fall into place.

I will consider this book to be a success if it contributes to and further stimulates the ongoing conversation on the scale and disposition of bureaucracy in the Hittite state. While it would be delightful to find definitive proof that Hittite administration was more similar to Mesopotamian administration than it currently appears, or to the opposite, that the limited bureaucracy apparent in the texts was all there truly was, I do not see resolution of the problem happening until fresh evidence is discovered, perhaps in the archives of provincial capitals; and even so, the positive evidence of the enormous importance of religious administration in Ḫattuša would not be negated by such a discovery, only contextualized. Thus, this book should be taken as the beginnings of a new project to understand Hittite administration, not the final results. There is still an enormous amount of scholarship that can be gained from these administrative texts. I encourage readers and researchers, Hittitologists and Assyriologists alike, to mine, critique, and rearrange the texts edited in the Volume II of this book. Quantification, like that attempted in the case studies of Volume I, is certainly one way forward. The application of new theoretical models, the questioning and refinement of old ones, is also vital. This book is designed to provide a firm philological foundation for these endeavors.

1. HISTORY OF RESEARCH (I): PAST MODELS OF THE HITTITE STATE

1.1 Introduction

Since the beginning of studies in the postwar period, scholars of Hittite administration have been confronted by a basic problem: that Hittite bureaucracy looks very different from its ancient Near Eastern contemporaries. Previous solutions offered that the Hittite administrative corpus is incompletely preserved, and/or that the Hittite government only partially adopted Mesopotamian administrative practices (being held back by, i.a.: cultural feudalism, non-integrated elites, the environment, or unnatural urbanism on the Anatolian Plateau). The incomplete corpus hypothesis argues that a considerable portion of Hittite administration was written on the perishable medium of wooden tablets, but the philological situation of the wooden records is inconclusive: at a minimum, there is little perceptible interface of the wooden tablet economy with the administrative texts on clay under consideration in the present book. That the preserved cuneiform administration was sufficient to maintain a state the size of the Hittite Empire stretches the imagination, but, as will be seen, modern theoretical models can help close the gap. The arguments for the second solution to the problem of Hittite administration, the partial adoption of Mesopotamian administrative practices, have varied with historiographic trends: explanations have included the "Indo-Europeanness" of Hittite society, the origins of the state in a period of rapid conquest, the logistical difficulties of exploitation in a harsh environment, and the difficulties of maintaining an urban culture on the Anatolian Plateau. Factually, these arguments are not even necessarily untrue (the Hittite ruling class was indeed initially Indo-European, the state did arise from rapid conquest, etc.). But archaeological data, anthropological parallels, and philological case studies suggest that Hittite administration was not an incomplete imitation of bureaucracies to the south, but instead well-adapted to the geographical and human conditions of the Anatolian Plateau. And while the resulting bureaucracy is not as familiar to our modern eyes as those of Mesopotamia and Egypt, it is nonetheless an intelligible system when viewed through the correct historical and theoretical lens.

This chapter will review the previous literature on the Hittite state, presented in roughly chronological order from earliest to latest. For purposes of discussion, the literature should be divided into four major periods, which are labeled here the Early Western Consensus, Soviet Marxist Criticism, the Western Reaction, the New Western Consensus. These periods cover the literature from the 1950's to approximately the end of the 1990's. Scholarship from the turn of the millennium onward is saved for the next chapter, *2. History of Research (II): Current Models of the Hittite State.* As a principle the ideas discussed below can be considered additive, so that an interpretation stands if it is not contradicted by a later proposal. Additionally, while the chapter strives to be reasonably comprehensive with the overtly theoretical articles of the period, a number of studies of Hittite government, especially those which are primarily word-studies of titles or text editions of political documents, have been necessarily left out for sake of brevity.

1.2 Early Western Consensus (Culture-Historical)

Hittitology first emerged as an academic discipline in the period between World War I and World War II. With the Hittite language deciphered by Bedřich Hrozný in 1915, scholars began the work of analyzing the over 10,000 tablet fragments discovered during the first excavations at the Hittite capital of Ḫattuša-Boğazköy. The discovery of a hitherto unknown Indo-European language at the edge of the mostly Semitic ancient Near East led to a flurry of scholarship. Initial efforts focused on the accessible texts of state and society: political, literary, and historical documents, many of which were also written in the well-understood language of Akkadian. By 1933, Albrecht Goetze's volume on Asia Minor in the *Handbuch der Altertumswissenschaft* had synthesized a pioneering generation of Hittite scholarship into a remarkably complete outline of the Hittite state.[1]

The second generation of Hittite scholarship in the 1950's and 60's advanced into legal and administrative documents with numerous publications, seeing the appearance of Einar von Schuler on the instructions to royal officials (1957),[2] Kaspar Riemschneider's edition of the land-grant documents (1958),[3] Heinrich Otten on the Hittite Funerary Ritual (1958),[4] Johannes Friedrich's new edition of the Hittite Laws (1959),[5] Vladimir Souček's work on cadastral lists (1959),[6] and Rudolf Werner's work on Hittite court proceedings (1967).[7] The first taxonomy of the Hittite corpus was also published at this time by Emmanuel Laroche between 1956 and 1958.[8] There was throughout these new studies a question of whether the emerging Hittite state was better compared or contrasted to the Mesopotamian societies known from Assyriology. One strain of Hittitology emphasized the importance of Mesopotamian influences in

---

1 Albrecht Goetze, "Kleinasien," in *Kulturgeschichte des alten Orients, Abs. III, Lfg. 1*, eds. Albrecht Alt, Arthur Christensen, Albrecht Goetze, Adolf Grohmann, Hermann Kees, Benno Landsberger. HAW 3.1.3. (München: Beck, 1933). Revised edition: Albrecht Goetze, "Kleinasien," (2. neubearbeite Auflage), in *Kulturgeschichte des alten Orients, Abs. III, Lfg. 1*, eds. Albrecht Alt, Arthur Christensen, Albrecht Goetze, Adolf Grohmann, Hermann Kees, Benno Landsberger. HAW 3.1.3. (München: Beck, 1957).

2 Einar von Schuler, *Hethitische Dienstanweisungen für höhere Hof- und Staatsbeamte. Ein Beitrag zum antiken Recht Kleinasiens.* AfO Beiheft 10 (Graz: Weidner, 1957).

3 Kaspar Riemschneider, "Die hethitischen Landschenkungsurkunden," MIO 6 (1958): 321–81.

4 Heinrich Otten, *Hethitische Totenrituale* (Berlin: Akademie-Verlag, 1958).

5 Johannes Friedrich, *Die hethitischen Gesetze* (Leiden: Brill, 1959).

6 Vladimír Souček, "Die hethitischen Feldertexte," ArOr. 27 (1959): 5–43.

7 Rudolf Werner, *Hethitische Gerichtsprotokolle.* StBoT 4 (Wiesbaden: Harrassowitz, 1967).

8 Emmanuel Laroche, "Catalogue des Textes Hittites," RHA 14 (1956): 33–38, 68–116; RHA 15 (1957): 30–89; RHA 16 (1958): 18–64.

"sophisticating" Hittite culture – the adoption of cuneiform writing and Sumero-Akkadian literary traditions being the most visible example. The Code of Hammurabi and the Hittite Laws, being separated by only two to three centuries, were especially popular comparanda for these authors, not least because of the extensive use of Akkadian terminology in Hittite Laws. At the same time, the importance of Hittite as an Indo-European language compelled many Hittitologists to search for differences between the Hittites and their non-Indo-European neighbors. The tension between the "Indo-European" and "Oriental" aspects of the Hittites can be seen in nearly every research program of the first generations of Hittitologists.

1.2.1 Goetze: The Ethnogenesis of the Hittite State

It was clear from the first historical studies that the Hittite state and society had undergone a radical shift between its "Old" and "New Kingdom" periods. The reason for this change is still one of the outstanding questions of Hittite history, and the differing answers to it will often reveal a Hittitologist's school of thought. Most Western scholars came to a consensus by the postwar period that explained Hittite social and political changes in terms of the Indo-European/Oriental debate. For Goetze, as he argued in his revised edition of the Asia Minor volume in *Handbuch der Altertumswissenschaft*, the change in the Hittite state was an Orientalizing process. He hypothesized that Hittite government was the product of diverse ethnic influences, and wrote that the Hittites were

> to an extraordinary degree ... exposed to multifarious streams of influence during their whole existence. It goes without saying, that this shifting history must have left its imprint on the people. State and society of the Hittites are likely to reflect these changes even more than the other facets of Hittite civilization.[9]

Goetze divided Hittite history into four phases based on ethnicity: in the pre-Hittite phase, the Anatolian Plateau consisted of mostly Hattian city-states, with a sedentary lifestyle of palaces with possibly matriarchal elements. The Old Hittite Kingdom phase begins with the conquest and unification of the Plateau by the Indo-European Hittites under their first king, Labarna, and the intermixture of Hittite (or "Neshite," named after the dynasty's home city of Kaneš) and Hattian elements. To Goetze, the implantation of the kingdom's capital at the Hattian city of Ḫattuša suggests the intermixture was deliberate. After a poorly known "Middle Hittite Kingdom" period showing influence of the Luwians, a related Indo-European people of Anatolia, the New Hittite Kingdom (Empire) period reappears with a Hurro-Mesoptamian influenced ruling class.[10]

In Goetze's model, which can be called culture-historical since it emphasizes (cultural) ethnicity as the driver of change,[11] the Hittites began with an inherited non-

9 This quote (p. 25) and the following are taken from an updated English summary of the "Kleinasien" volume of the HAW, published as Albrecht Goetze, "State and Society of the Hittites," in *Neuere Hethiterforschung*, ed. Gerold Walser (Wiesbaden: Steiner, 1964), 22–33.

10 Goetze, "State and Society," 23–24.

11 The term "culture-historical" here is borrowed from a roughly contemporaneous movement in archaeology. For more, see Chapter 6: "Culture-Historical Archaeology" in Bruce Trigger, *A History of Archaeological Thought*, 2. ed. (Cambridge: Cambridge University Press, 1996).

divine, *primus inter pares* style of kingship from their Indo-European roots. Elements of the arrangement were still preserved in the Old Kingdom, in which government was essentially a power-sharing agreement between the king and the Neshite aristocracy, but were already being changed by the Hattian substratum of the region. Political documents of the Old Kingdom period readily attest to the importance of the Neshite aristocrats to the functioning of the state. The Political Testament of Ḫattušili I (CTH 6), one of the most debated political document of the Old Kingdom, shows the Hittite king appealing to an assembly of nobles called the *panku-* to witness his choice of successor. Side-stepping part of the debate, Goetze noted that regardless of whether Ḫattušili actually needed to consult the *panku-* on matters of succession, it is significant that he acted and wrote as if he did. A section in the Edict of Telipinu, the other pillar of documentary evidence for Old Kingdom politics, even suggests that the king could be tried by the *panku-* for "crimes of blood," further distancing the status of Hittite monarchy from the Mesopotamian god-kings.[12]

In the cultural-historical model, Hittite society was originally organized by clans, led by the "great clan" of the king's family. Most of the highest officials in the Hittite Kingdom were drawn from the king's or lesser Neshite clans, imparting an ethnic stratification to the Hittite state that probably lasted until its end. Oliver Gurney, Goetze's contemporary and author of one of the first rigorous popular histories of the Hittites in English, described the situation as "an exclusive caste superimposed on the indigenous population of the country ... [in] which a group of Indo-European immigrants became dominant over an aboriginal race of 'Hattians'."[13] The Neshite officials held large estates as fiefs stemming from the initial conquest, and would later provide chariot service to the state.[14] The ethnic separateness of the Neshite ruling class and the experience of conquest of the Hattian Plateau combined to give the Old Kingdom a supposed military vigor, an Indo-European *esprit de corps*, that propelled its armies to the gates of Babylon.

Non-Neshite populations in the Old Kingdom lived in the countryside and outlying towns where they were left to their own style of government, usually consisting of no more than a council of Elders. As Horst Klengel noted in his article about "Die Rolle der 'Ältesten'," the lack of documentary evidence produced by the Elders precludes determining whether they represented a sort of "primitive democracy" in Anatolia, or if they were a remnant of a tribal structure such as is attested in Syro-Mesopotamia.[15] From the documents of the Hittite central government it can be seen that power of the Elders grew with distance from the capital. In the heartland they were reduced to a religious and juridical function, while on the periphery they had administrative authority and even a political-military function (though always in conjunction with a

12 Goetze, "State and Society," 25–26. For a discussion by one of Goetze's contemporaries on the theocratic but non-divine nature of Hittite kingship, see Oliver R. Gurney, "Hittite Kingship," in *Myth, Ritual, and Kingship*, ed. Samuel H. Hooke (Oxford: University Press), 105–21.

13 Oliver R. Gurney, *The Hittites* (Baltimore: Penguin Books, 1961), 68–69.

14 Gurney, *The Hittites*, 69–70.

15 Horst Klengel, "Die Rolle der 'Ältesten' (LÚ.MEŠ ŠU.GI) im Kleinasien der Hethiterzeit," ZA 57 (1965): 225–26.

Hittite supervisor). In the most peripheral areas of Anatolia, such as among the Kaška and in Kalašma, there were no kings, only Elders.

Despite the separateness of the Neshite and Hattian populations, Hattian influence on Hittite government was not limited to the periphery or local levels. Most Hittite military and state officials had titles that originated in courtly life, and many with Hattian origins. Gurney takes this as evidence that the Hittites participated in a settled courtly life in the system of Anatolian palaces in the preexpansion period.[16] Furthermore, Goetze saw the political power of the Hittite *tawananna-*, a lifetime position held by the wife, mother, or even grandmother of the Hittite king, as evidence of a Hattian influenced matriarchy in Hittite government.[17]

The Old Kingdom ended in a period of strife that may have continued into the poorly documented "Middle Kingdom." By the time of the New Kingdom a new Hurrian-influenced ruling dynasty had recast the Hittite government according to Mesopotamian political ideals. The most prominent change was a growing feudal arrangement between the king and elites centered around chariot-service. By Goetze's account, the tribal relationships were replaced, as "[t]he state came more and more to depend on retainers of the king or the crown (palace) – not yet conceived of as distinct – to whom parcels of land were distributed in exchange for the obligation to serve the king as soldiers or in working the royal domains."[18] Among these retainers were the "knights," a class of professional chariot warrior drawn from the higher strata of society, but now directly dependent on the king and supported through endowments of state-owned land.[19] Below them were the LÚ ^{GIŠ}TUKUL ('men of the tool'), state craftsmen who manufactured goods in return for land tenure: according to Goetze, the LÚ ^{GIŠ}TUKUL furnished the Hittite state with a limited autarky, as "[t]heir production satisfied the needs of the country, both military and civilian; a surplus may have been handed over to "Merchants" ... for export and the import of necessary materials not available in the country itself."[20] Unlike in the Old Kingdom, the land tenure arrangements of both the knights and craftsmen depended on their continued service to the king. This arrangement also gave more opportunities to subaltern ethnicities, because as Goetze argued,

> [t]he parcels of land fiefed out remained, at least originally, the property of the king and he saw to it that the fiefs, when falling vacant, were assigned to new men. They seem to have come from the so-called NAM.RA people ... who were *glebae adscripti* and thus not allowed to move freely from town to town but who were shifted around by the authorities presumably as the needs of the state required.[21]

The Hittite Laws show that the status of these semi-slaves was fluid, and their economic importance increased as the feudal state matured.

---

16 Gurney, *The Hittites*, 67–68.

17 Goetze, "State and Society," 27.

18 Goetze, *op.cit.*, 28.

19 Goetze, *op.cit.*, 29–30.

20 Goetze, *op. cit.*, 28.

21 Goetze, *loc. cit.*

The *panku-* had disappeared as an organ of government by the start of the New Kingdom. The bodies of Elders, where they still existed, were reduced to juridical and religious responsibilities, except on the extreme periphery where they retained some administrative authority. Towns were now integrated through appointment of royal governors answering directly to the king, with larger territorial units becoming appanage kingdoms for members of the royal house. The federation of territories of the Old Kingdom was thus replaced by a "rigid structure," where high functionaries of state were given "instructions" and required to swear oaths to the king like the soldiers.[22] The use of direct personal oaths in the Hittite New Kingdom, an arrangement which only accelerated in reigns of the last kings, were reminiscent of the vassal treaties conducted between the Hittites and their client states, so that it appeared "that within the 'Hittite Land' the same principles were practiced that, outside, in the overall area subject to Hittite power, held the Empire together: in other words, that feudalistic ideas were all-pervasive and ruled internally as well as externally."[23]

There were no real alternatives to the culture-historical approach in Western Hittitology in the immediate postwar period. At most, scholars could limit themselves to pure descriptions: Hans Güterbock, for example, in his summarizing article of Hittite law and society, scrupulously de-emphasized the ethnic components of the Goetze–Gurney model, but in doing so forwent explanation for historical change.[24] The monopoly of the culture-historical approach among the scholars of the Early Western Consensus can be explained by its appeal in offering an easy equation between ethnicity and political structure. The seemingly transparent connection between ethnicity and politics was, and still is, especially seductive for philologists (that is to say almost every Hittitologist, given the many years of language training required for the field) because ethnicity is closely linked with language. The culture-historical approach tempts the researcher with the possibility that onomastics and etymologies reveal the deepest structures of politics and society; that if one could just trace the linguistic origins of government one could grasp its operation. Even more dangerously, such an approach is not completely wrong. There must certainly have been dimensions of the Hittite government in the Old Kingdom that changed with the influx of cosmopolitan ideas and people in the Empire period. But the danger is stopping at this, and being too reliant on linguistic thinking when political science and sociological theory are needed. The Soviet Marxist critique would serve as a corrective to the culture-historical approach (though possibly going too far in the other direction of over-relying on theory), but even the Marxist scholars did not entirely escape the Indo-European/Oriental tension in Hittite history. Today the question of whether the Hittites were Indo-European invaders, and to what extent this affected their society and government, remains unresolved. Most scholars, the present author included, choose to side-step the question in the absence of conclusive evidence. But the poverty of results does not mean that

22 Gurney, *The Hittites*, 72–73.

23 Goetze, "State and Society," 32.

24 Hans G. Güterbock, "Authority and Law in the Hittite Kingdom," JAOS Supplement 17 (1954): 16–24. Cf. however Güterbock's comment (p. 20) on Hittite feudalism being a result of the "Überlagerung" of a conquering people.

the questions are wrong, and thus the positive contributions of Goetze's theory of ethnic driven change should not be discarded. His ideas on the periodization of the Hittite state, and the correlation of these changes with an increasingly multi-ethnic and connected state, are still useful today, and reappear decades later in some of the most recent models of Hittite history.

1.3 Soviet Marxist Criticism (Historic-Materialist)[25]

Soviet scholarship of the Hittites and the ancient Near East remained largely unknown in the West until the post-Stalin period of the 1960's. In the pre- and postwar periods Marxist theoretical commitments had led most Soviet scholars to emphatically reject a feudal assessment for the Hittite New Kingdom, and indeed for any society in the ancient Near East. For them feudalism was a technical term, the name of a "mode of production," a stage of human development based on the social relationships arising from the evolving ways of manufacturing the means of life. In orthodox Soviet Marxist theory, history was divided into five modes of production, namely primitive-communal, ancient, feudal, capitalist, and socialist modes of production. In each stage there are economic contradictions that impel society to develop to the next, and ultimately towards the final mode of communism.[26]

Given that the ancient Near East was too early to be capitalist and too complex to be primitive-communalist, the question for early 20th century Marxist scholars was whether to describe the region as participating in the ancient (based on slavery) or feudal (based on serfdom) mode of production. The crucial distinction between the two is that, despite similar levels of non-market, extra-economic coercion, slaves do not own the means of production whereas serfs do. [27] In the ancient Near East, and indeed

25 The discussion and basic conclusions on the Marxist scholarship of the wider Ancient Near East found in this chapter are indebted to the analysis of David Schloen, *House of the Father as Fact and Symbol* (Winona Lake: Eisenbrauns, 2001), see especially pp. 187–94.

26 See the Soviet formulation in Joseph Stalin, "Dialectical and Historical Materialism," in *The Essential Stalin: Major Theoretical Writings, 1905–52*, ed. Bruce Franklin (Garden City, N.Y.: Anchor Books, 1972), 323.

27 As described by Igor M. Diakonoff, "Editor's Preface," in *Ancient Mesopotamia*, ed. Igor M. Diakonoff (Moscow: Nauka Publishing House, 1969), 15–16:

> A *slave* is a person being property of another person or body of persons, and thus forcibly subjected to exploitation. A slave does not own means of production, but can, in certain conditions, be in the possession of means of production not his property .... A *slave society* is a society where the antagonism between the class owning means of production (eventually including the producers themselves), and a socio-economic class devoid of means of production and forced to labour by non-economic means is the dominating force. The term does not necessarily imply that production in such society is exclusively the result of exploiting slave labour proper, or that there does not exist a mass of free or semi-dependent producers.

In contrast,

> A *serf* is a person owning means of production but personally dependent on another person (who usually belongs legally to another estate of society) or on a body, and subjected to exploitation, being coerced by non-economic means .... A *feudal society* is one based on the extra-

almost every economy prior to industrialization, the means of production was arable land. Though occasionally owning movable property, workers as a rule did not own the land, and were thus incapable of full economic independence in their agrarian societies: in other words, by Marxist logic they were slaves. Thus, despite superficial hierarchies of political power recalling the feudal societies of Medieval Europe, the socio-economic reality of the ancient Near East was in no way describable as feudal for Marxist scholars.

1.3.1 Struve: The Paradox of "Oriental Stagnation"

If the ancient Near East was a slave economic formation, then the next major task becomes reconciling the societies of the region, relatively alien to historians raised on Greece and Rome, with the better-known slave economies of the Classical world. In the highly influential view of Vasilii Struve, presented in his seminal article "The Problem of the Genesis, Development and Disintegration of the Slave Societies in the Ancient Orient," the Near Eastern world was substantially similar to the Classical, in that both exhibited a similar life-cycle of rise and fall, namely

1.) A concentration of power in hands of elites, especially in the "hydraulic societies" of Egypt and Lower Mesopotamia, leads to despotism
2.) Despotic militarism leads to the growth of a slave class through conquest
3.) Simultaneously, free communities are eroded through usury and debt slavery
4.) Societal decay, especially the decline of the freeholders forming the backbone of military power, leaves state vulnerable to barbarian conquest
5.) The foreign conquerors, often less developed than the conquered slave state, depend on slave holding elite for collaboration
6.) Captives and dissidents further enlarge the slave population, until the cruelty of the foreign rulers and slave holders inflames slave revolts to the point of societal collapse[28]

The divergent results of the Near East, which did not seem to embrace feudalism as fully as the West, were explained by the arrest of the disintegrative cycle, as slaves

---

> economic coercion of an exploited class of producers owning means of production but personally dependent on individual members of the governing class, or on a body representing it; typical of such a society is a division into estates (the members of each estate having a different degree of legal capacity), and ownership of the producers in at least some of the means production. The term does not necessarily imply a hierarchic structure of society based on vassalage, a phenomenon which occurs also in other socio-economic formations.

What made the choice between the categories slave and serf in the Ancient Near East mandatory, besides the period of world history, is that the dependent workers of the region were "owned" in part (through labor obligation) or in full (as chattel) by others. In contrast, the proletariat in the capitalist system, while also not owning the means of production, are nominally free to sell their work to whoever they want, whereas a serf or a slave cannot.

28 Vasilii V. Struve, "The Problem of the Genesis, Development and Disintegration of the Slave Societies in the Ancient Orient," in *Ancient Mesopotamia*, ed. Igor M. Diakonoff (Moscow: Nauka Publishing House, 1969), 17–69. This is a translation and digest (removing discussion of Egypt) of an earlier article: Vasilii V. Struve, «Проблема зарождения, развития и разложения рабовладельческих обществ древнего Востока», Известия Государственной Академии истории материальной культуры имине Н. Я. Марра, Вып. 77, 32–111, 157–81 (Ленинград: ИГАИМК, 1934). Citations for points 1–5 are: 22–23, 28–29, 53–54, 60, and 65–66.

were granted a more permanent attachment to the means of production.[29] In many parts of the Near East, both ancient and medieval, compromise situations were reached where slaves were granted limited rights (e.g., the ownership of movable property), so that the gap between the poor freeman and the slave was narrowed.[30] The resulting arrangement may have resembled an incipient feudalism, but paradoxically the better conditions lead to stagnation and slowed the growth of true feudalism. According to Struve, the later periods of the Near East saw the continuation of slavery as

> a powerful economic substructure within a society based on the feudal mode of production even when this society had consolidated; and it still permeated the entire social and state system .... The existence of slavery as a substructure within the feudal economic system was the cause of Oriental feudalism assuming a somewhat more stagnant form than Western feudalism, which [conversely] arose on the ruins of a thoroughly disintegrated slave socio-economic formation.[31]

With allowances for the mechanism of "Oriental stagnation," Struve was able to claim that the ancient Near Eastern and Classical worlds were substantially similar in their socio-economic foundations, and any differences explainable by time, culture, and the equilibrium of the East.

Struve's work dominated a generation of Soviet scholarship on the ancient Near East, but some scholars questioned his model as research progressed in the mid-20th century. At the time of Struve's death in 1965, coinciding with a renewed openness in the post-Stalin era, Igor M. Diakonoff was well-positioned to lead Soviet historiography in a new direction. For Diakonoff, despite the impressive Soviet achievement, which he found to have surpassed that of the West "due, to a great extent, to its theoretical base,"[32] scholarship had fallen into a rut, where

> studies in economic history in our country have been restricted mostly to attempts of discovering slaves in the various economic units or, at best, to establish the static class structure of society. No research has actually been carried out into the functioning of the social-economic mechanism; in particular, consumption and, especially circulation, have not been studied at all ....[33]

With Struve's passing, Diakonoff could advocate for more studies like the earlier works of Nikolai Nikolsky, those of contemporary scholars like Ninel Jankowska, and his own on Assyria[34] and southern Mesopotamia[35] focusing on communities outside the governing class. Diakonoff considered these studies, establishing "the extreme importance

29 Struve, "Slave Societies," 62.

30 Struve, *op. cit.*, 63–65.

31 Struve, *op. cit.*, 66–67.

32 Diakonoff, "Editor's Preface," *Ancient Mesopotamia*, 10.

33 Igor M. Diakonoff, «Проблемы экономики: О структуре общества Ближнего Востока до середины 2 тыс. до н. З.» *Вестник Древней Истории*,1968/3: 3–27, 1968/4: 3–40 [English translation: Igor M. Diakonoff, "The Structure of Near Eastern Society Before the Middle of the 2nd Millennium," *Oikumene* 3 (1982): 7–100]: 77.

34 Igor M. Diakonoff, Развитие земельных отношений в Ассирии (Ленинград: Издательство Ленинградского Государственного Ордена Ленина Университета им. А. А. Жданова, 1949) [English translation: Igor M. Diakonoff, "Agrarian Conditions in Middle Assyria," trans. G.M. Sergheyev, in *Ancient Mesopotamia*, ed. Igor M. Diakonoff (Moscow: Nauka Publishing House, 1969), 204–34].

35 Igor Diakonoff, "The Rise of the Despotic State in Ancient Mesopotamia," trans. G.M. Sergheyev, in *Ancient Mesopotamia*, ed. Igor M. Diakonoff (Moscow: Nauka Publishing House, 1969), 173–203.

of the rural and the family community in the third and second millennia B.C., as distinct from temple (or royal) land,"[36] to be the most important achievements of the post-war era. Diakonoff and like-minded scholars now had the opportunity to promulgate their views, many of which had been opposed by Struve.

1.3.2 Diakonoff: The "Two-Sector" Model

Diakonoff's model, published in a ground-breaking article in 1968,[37] postulated an irreducible tension between a state-sponsored slave mode of production in the cities and a communalist mode of production in the countryside of the ancient Near East. Every Bronze Age state was a composite, distinguished by two features, specifically:

> 1.) co-existence of state property in land and other means of production, and of private property; that is, not unlimited private property but as allowed for the members of certain communal bodies ...
>
> 2.) employment of the free labour of the citizens-proprietors – alongside of the exploitation of persons devoid of property in means of production and made to work by direct extra-economic coercion.[38]

The "state sector" in Diakonoff's model shared its etiology with the first two points of Struve's slave model, i.e., concentration of power in the hands of elites and enslavement through foreign conquest. It is in proposing the continued existence of a "private/communal" sector, evolved from the remnants of the primitive-communal mode of production from Near Eastern prehistory, that Diakonoff diverged from Struve. For Diakonoff, the king, instead of being a supremely powerful "Oriental despot" who might occasionally extend limited property rights to his slaves, was circumscribed in his power, and there were places in his country that the state did not reach. The majority of the population in most periods of the ancient Near East may have belonged to the communal sector. But, according to Diakonoff, in times of strong central authority "this class was constantly eroded by either upwards mobility or enslavement/dependency."[39] The state sector expanded at the expense of the private/communal as wealthy villagers were absorbed into royal service as "king's men" and the poorer villagers fell victim to debt-slavery or offering to serve as royal helots. The "king's men" entered the state sector on better terms, enticed by land grants that allowed property and status in addition to their government allotment, while the royal helot received only the inducement of security while laboring under the king's protection.

Throughout his work on the two-sector model Diakonoff was careful not to suggest that the socio-economic formation of the ancient Near East was unique. This would be too like the "Asiatic" mode of production (abbrev. AMP), a term mentioned by Marx in his personal notebooks (only recently published at the time of Diakonoff's writing) but deemed ideologically unacceptable in Soviet academia.[40] Rather, Diakonoff borrowed

36 Diakonoff, "Editor's Preface," *Ancient Mesopotamia*, 12.

37 Diakonoff, "Structure of Near Eastern Society."

38 Diakonoff, *op. cit.*, 90.

39 Diakonoff, *op. cit.*, 96.

40 Karl Marx, *Grundrisse der Kritik der politischen Ökonomie (Rohentwurf). 1857–1858, Anhang 1850–1859*, ed. Marx-Engels-Lenin-Institut, Moskau (Moskau: Verlag für fremdsprachige Literatur, 1939–41).

the intellectual maneuver of Struve's "stagnation" theory, though with the change that the region was stuck between the primitive-communal and slave modes instead of the slave and feudal modes of production. In Diakonoff's model all slave-holding societies had gone through this period of incomplete transition, including the Classical world, with most societies eventually differentiating along an axis of private/communal versus state-sector dominance depending on the locus of slave exploitation. Earlier societies were less differentiated and clustered in the middle of the axis, so that:

> [t]he Asiatic states of the 3rd and 2nd millennia B.C., especially the city-states, just because of their 'two-sector economy', belong[ed] to an early stage of a society type which, as it were, was intermediary between Sparta and Doric Crete on the one hand [i.e., state-sector dominant], and Athens, Corinth, Republican Rome, etc., on the other [i.e., private/communal sector dominant].[41]

In most of the ancient Near East, especially by the Iron Age, the growth of enslavement through conquest or domestic impoverishment had benefited the state. In the Classical world, which arose after the collapse of the statist societies of the Mediterranean Bronze Age, the private/communal sector, especially the wealthy citizens of the *polis*, became the primary exploiter of slaves.

The Hittites, even among the state-sector dominant ancient Near East, were by Diakonoff many times as one of the most state-oriented and hierarchical societies of their era, and appear his discussion of the "two-sector" model as an outlier. The reason for the strong state-sector orientation of the Hittite economy was a result of the history of the Hittites as a conquering people – a story familiar from the Western culture-historical model – whose state grew rapidly from the single city of Kaneš to controlling the entire Anatolian Plateau. Because the Neshite speakers who controlled the Hittite state were an ethnic minority within the Plateau, Diakonoff considered that "the conquering community constituted nearly in its entirety the governing group of the serving aristocracy of the Hittite kingdom – [...] the so-called 'lord[s] of (the community of) Hatti'."[42] In Diakonovian terms, this means that the entirety of the original private/communal sector of Kaneš was recruited into the state sector as "king's men," who, due to ethnic difference and economic incentive readily undermined the communal ownership of property in the conquered villages. Thus, a state-dependent governing class, whose property rights were defended solely by the king and not by family or community ties, emerged among the Hittites with artificial rapidity when compared to the strong civic societies of Mesopotamia and Syria.[43]

---

41 Diakonoff, "Structure of Near Eastern Society," 93–94. Diakonoff considers the *polis* of the Classical world to be another form of communalism, albeit with an increased scope for individualism as a result of "the decline of the hierarchic agnatic structures which were so typical of all early societies ..." and a strong Mediterranean world-market which encouraged export production (*ibid.* 93).

42 Diakonoff, *op. cit.*, 95. Typos emended.

43 Diakonoff, *loc. cit.*:

> The base of riches of the Hittite aristocracy were either lands allotted from the royal fund on condition of service, or royal grants which had become private property of the grantees (or of their family communes). In the synchronous Assyria and Arrapha one can observe a process developing in the opposite direction, viz., the separation of an aristocracy from among that part of the citizens of the territorial community which had grown affluent through trade and especially through usurious operations, and then got hold also of the state offices.

The great tracts of conquered land gave the Hittite king a large land fund with which to reward his kith and kin. The abundance of land and relative poverty of labor led to two distinguishing features of the Hittite system. First, because of the need for physically occupying and pacifying the land outweighed the need for taxation, the land grants were often given without service obligations and thus became unconditional property of the grantee (something that was strongly resisted by kings to the south).[44] Second, the relative shortage of labor led to the furnishing of both royal and "private" estates with royal laborers captured in battle. From these two features a category of "*muškēnūtu* (helot) of a private person" emerged unique to the Hittite cultural sphere, so that by Diakonoff's account,

> [i]f we add that in the Hittite kingdom many noblemen were local royal deputies of different ranks, or even vassal kinglets, it will be clear that the land was covered, alongside the royal domains, by manifold estates which also constituted, as it were, royal economies on a small scale.[45]

From this description, it is perhaps easy to forgive a non-Marxist scholar for having mistook Hittite society as feudal.

Despite the enormity of the Hittite state sector and the power of the state land fund, Diakonoff argued in a separate article against the claim that the Hittite king was the *de jure* proprietor of all the land within his kingdom.[46] His principle objection was that the monarch lacked the power to enforce such a claim. Even in the New Kingdom, when royal power seemed strongest, the king was limited by the religious strictures of cult and ritual and dependence on the servant-aristocracy and priesthood.[47] The economic situation was also tilted against centralization, as the king often received only indirect economic benefits from the land grants. He could grant income from the royal estates to servants, artisans, and priests, in return for service and gifts from his royal officials. But, in contrast to the *latifundia* of the Classical world worked by chattel slaves, Diakonoff argued that in the Hittite state economy,

> gab es kein System der Bearbeitung des Landes durch Sklaventrupps, ja auch das Einkommen floß dem König, so muß man annehmen, nicht so sehr durch das Einsammeln der Ernte von den unmittelbar königlichen Domänen als vielmehr infolge der Einnahme der verschiedenen Steuern und Abgaben zu.[48]

And so, despite the greater state-sector orientation of the Hittites, the state collected its revenue in much the same way as its ancient Near Eastern contemporaries through a distributed and diversified system of service and taxation.

In other words, Hittite officials became wealthy because they were connected to the government, while Syro-Mesopotamian became government officials if and when they were already wealthy.

44 Diakonoff, "Structure of Near Eastern Society," 87–88.

45 Diakonoff, *op. cit.*, 88.

46 Igor M. Diakonoff, "Die hethitische Gesellschaft," MIO 13/3 (1967): 313–66. This article was nominally a book review of Eduard Menabde, *Хеттское общество: экономика собственность, семья и наследование* (Тбилиси: Издат. Мецниереба, 1965).

47 Diakonoff, "Hethitische Gesellschaft," 316. Moreover, as Diakonoff noted in "Structure of Near Eastern Society," 15–16, if the king were the ultimate and perpetual proprietor of the land, he would not be able to grant land to his servants, an act which is well attested in the Hittite corpus.

48 Diakonoff, *op. cit.*, 339.

While Diakonoff stuck to his Marxist credentials by rejecting the feudal description of the ancient Near East, he did offer a conciliatory note in labeling the disagreement as a miscommunication rather than a misinterpretation of the evidence. He was willing to accept that although "one can often encounter the statement that while the Soviet scholars see in the Eastern antiquity a slave-holding society, the Western scholars see in it feudalism ... [t]his, however, is not quite correct." Rather,

> the Soviet scholars usually find in the Ancient Orient an economic structure of the *society* based on slavery, and Western scholars find that the Ancient Oriental society was in certain periods of its history characterized by a feudal structure of the *state*. Western historiography mostly puts the main stress on the problem of state power, ignoring its being conditioned by socio-economic relations. But it is well known that entirely different forms of state structure can evolve on the basis of one and the same socio-economic formation.[49]

The distinction between socio-economic formation and state structure served Diakonoff's own ends as well. While acknowledging that some states could look more "feudal" than others, the hierarchy of status observed among the slaves of the ancient Near East does not vitiate a description of these societies as "slave-holding." Just as quasi-capitalist merchant republics could exist in the feudal world of the Middle Ages, so too quasi-feudal federations could exist in the slave world of the Bronze Age. Indeed, according to Diakonoff:

> [C]hattel slavery ... [is] just another sub-type of the exploitation of the ancient type, to which a very numerous class of persons was subject. Characteristic of this class as a whole was the absence of property in means of production and exploitation by extra-economic (non-market) coercion. To this class belonged the 'dependent labourers of the helot type', the 'dependent labourers of the patriarchal slave' and of the 'chattel slave type' and, generally, all kinds of ancient 'slave-type' dependent labourers.[50]

Ancient Near East society was thus still describable as a "slave society" if, and only if, the term is broadened to include all forms of dependent labor, and if in analogy to "feudal society," where not everyone is a lord or serf, the term slavery is only evocative and not definitive of every member of society.[51]

Diakonoff's work had a profound impact on the development of ancient Near Eastern studies in the following decades. A formulation of his model, though based mostly on research from the 1980's, even appeared as late as 1991 in Gregor Giorgadze's article on "The Hittite Kingdom" in *Early Antiquity*, an English language volume of Soviet scholarship edited by Diakonoff.[52] Perhaps because of the global intellectual currents of the mid to late 20th century, a period of intense decolonization in Europe, the focus on "subaltern" classes and ethnicities found a very receptive audience in the West. The

---

49 Diakonoff, "Structure of Near Eastern Society," 91.

50 Diakonoff, *op. cit.*, 99. Typos emended.

51 Diakonoff, *op. cit.*, 100.

52 Gregor Giorgadze, "The Hittite Kingdom," in *Early Antiquity*, ed. Igor M. Diakonoff (Chicago: University of Chicago Press, 1991), 266–85. Giorgadze is mostly summarizing, providing a brief narrative and social history of Hittites, with comments about social structure. Interestingly, Diakonoff intervened with extensive commentary in editorial notes (authoring fourteen out of the twenty-two total footnotes). The editor's preface to *Early Antiquity*, pp. 6–13, provides a good history of the discussion of the Asiatic Mode of Production in the 20th century.

ready-made program of research implied by Diakonoff's model also helped the uptake, as the relationship and relative strengths of the two sectors in a given society was an attractive target for typologization.

1.4 Western Reaction

The initial response in the West to Soviet criticism of the feudal designation for the Hittites was mixed. Some Western scholars celebrated confirmation of their preexisting suspicions of Hittite feudalism. Richard Haase had critiqued Hittite feudalism from a socio-legal standpoint already around the same the time of publication of Diakonoff's "Die hethitische Gesellschaft." Haase, who was a lawyer by trade, specifically the *Amtsgerichtsdirektor* for the city of Leonberg in Baden-Württemberg, made his Hittitological career publishing a number of articles on the Hittite Laws. His initial work was very much part of the proliferation of philological studies on the Hittite Laws undertaken by the Western scholars in the postwar period. But in 1968 he incorporated Soviet and Western theory in an analysis of "Herrscher und Beherrschte im Hatti-Reich."[53] The results, which he read against François-Louis Ganshof's work on feudalism in Medieval Europe,[54] ultimately led him to argue against a feudal designation of the Hittite state.

In "Herrscher und Beherrschte," Haase blended a Western and Soviet bibliography and often sided with the analysis of the latter. The first half of his article consisted of a schematization of Hittite society by social class. He accepted the existence of state slavery at the bottom of society in the form of the ᴸᵁ́*ḫippara-*, but argued, contra Gurney, that slaves owning a small amount of property were not semi-free "muškênu" serfs, as their master still held the power of life and death over them.[55] The true "muškênu" were rather drawn from the middle ranks of society, in the form of the ᴸᵁ́NAM.RA captives and possibly the LÚ ᴳᴵˢ̌TUKUL craftsmen, and these were the groups living most nearly to the *glebae adscripti* serfs of the Western sense. At the top of society were the members of the *panku-*, whom Haase described in the Soviet tradition as the remnants of a family originated assembly, and not the "cream of society" as Goetze calls them. While not explicitly claiming an Indo-European origin for the group,

53 Richard Haase, "Herrscher und Beherrschte im Hatti-Reich," *Recueils de la Société Jean Bodin* 23 (1968): 87–100. Given the frequent citation of Eduard Menabde on Hittite slavery (but no later than 1963), the article seems to have been composed prior to Diakonoff's work.

54 François-Louis Ganshof, *Qu'est-ce que féodalité?*, 3é ed. rev. et augm. (Bruxelles: Office de publicité, 1957). Haase cites the corresponding German edition, François-Louis Ganshof, *Was ist das Lehnwesen?* (Darmstadt: Wissenschaftliche Buchgesellschaft, 1961).

55 Haase, "Herrscher und Beherrschte," 90; contra Gurney, *The Hittites*, 72. Haase sidestepped the philological question of the *MUŠKĒNU* in the Hittite context, noting only that they are connected with the palace and mostly restricted to cadastral lists (Haase, "Herrscher und Beherrschte," 87). He deferred to Vladimír Souček, ("Randnotizen zu den hethitischen Feldertexte," MIO 8 [1963]: 368–82), who considered the Hittite Laws as lacking the three-fold terminological distinction between *awīlum*, *muškēnum*, *wardum* (free, dependent, slave) found in Hammurabi's code. Rather, in Hittite texts, the term *MUŠKĒNU* generally means "poor" (although certain examples, such as *MUŠKĒNU* "of the Palace," and *MUŠKĒNU* appearing as providers of last resort for festivals, are enigmatic in this definition).

Haase drew parallels between the balance of power between the *panku-* and the Hittite king and the Germanic practice of elective kingship. The *tawananna-* was accepted as a vestige of Hattian matriarchy.[56]

The most enduring contribution of Haase's article was to remove *šaḫḫan*, a service obligation translatable by the archaic English term 'socage' that applied almost universally to members of Hittite society, from the discussion of feudalism in the Hittite state. His principal objection was that *šaḫḫan* lacked military connotations, unlike for example the similar service arrangements of Medieval Europe and Hammurabi's Babylon. Instead, *šaḫḫan* was a "service-tax for land tenure," i.e., a form of rent in a non-market economy based on agriculture. If *šaḫḫan* was not linked to military service, then the largest piece of evidence for Hittite feudal society was removed, and with it would leave the attendant sociological and juridical structures of feudalism, such as a specialized warrior-caste, extreme fragmentation of authority, and a hierarchy of titles.[57] Haase did accept, while advocating for further research, that feudalism could be found at the apex of the Hittite state, between the Hittite king and government "dignitaries" (^{LÚ}DUGUD) and foreign vassals, but these relations were in no way the organizing principle of Hittite society.[58]

Haase was for the most part vindicated by subsequent scholarship, but other Western scholars reacted to Diakonoff's work by doubling down on the feudalism label. Friedrich Cornelius in 1972 wrote a short article entitled "Das Hethiterreich als Feudalstaat," probably aimed as a rebuttal to Haase (though without citing him or any other anti-feudal authors!), which argued that the parallels between the Hittite state and Medieval Europe were too numerous to warrant any other designation ("das Hethiterreich gleicht in allen Zügen, die wir feststellen können, dem mittelalterlichen Feudalstaat.").[59] Crucially, Cornelius considered feudalism to rest not on "economic matters," but rather the institution of equestrian military service common to both

56 Haase, "Herrscher und Beherrschte," 98–99.

57 Haase, *op. cit.*, 94–95, citing François-Louis Ganshof, *Was ist das Lehnwesen?*, 13–14. The exact citation is as follows:

> 'Lehen' bedeutet im Mittelalter: (a) soziologisch 'stark ausgeprägte Abhängigkeitsverhältnisse zwischen den einzelnen, eine *spezialisierte Kriegerkaste*, äußerste Zerstückelung der Eigentumsrechte, eine aus dieser Zerstückelung hervorgegangene Hierarchie der Grundbesitzrechte, die der ebengenannten Hierarchie der persönlichen Abhängigkeitsverhältnisse entspricht; dann eine Aufspaltung der öffentlichen Gewalt, aus der in jedem Lande eine Hierarchie autonomer Instanzen hervorgeht, die in eigenem Interesse jene Gewalten ausübt, die normalerweise dem Staat zugeordnet sind und oft aus dem Machtbereich des Staates einer vorangegangenen Zeit stammen', (b) juristisch 'eine Gesamtheit von Institutionen ..., die zwischen einem Freien, genannt 'Vasall' (*vassal*), und einem anderen Freien, genannt 'Herr' (*seigneur*), Verbindlichkeiten zweifacher Art schaffen und regeln: der 'Vassal' ist dem 'Herrn' gegenüber zu Gehorsam und Dienst – *vor allem zum Waffendienst* – verpflichtet und der 'Herr' dem 'Vassal' gegenüber zur Gewährung von Schutz und Unterhalt.

58 Haase, *op. cit.*, 95.

59 Friedrich Cornelius, "Das Hethiterreich als Feudalstaat," in *Gesellschaftsklassen im Alten Zweistromland und in den angrenzenden Gebieten; XVIII. Rencontre assyriologique internationale, München, 29. Juni bis 3. Juli 1970*, ed. Dietz O. Edzard (München: Verlag der Bayerischen Akademie der Wissenschaften, 1972), 33.

periods of history. The lords of Ḫatti were defined as those who had the means to own and train a warhorse, and were lords because they were professional soldiers, and not vice versa. The reliance on skilled horsemen, and the resulting social status of "knights," explained the similarities of the Hittites and Medieval European states. In fact, Cornelius considered that the only major difference was the absence, and even prohibition, of subinfeudation, i.e., the unsupervised creation of lower-ranked vassals, in the Hittite state.[60] However, most later Western scholars, if they accepted feudalism at all, gravitated towards Haase's thesis of a "shallow feudalism" affecting only the highest reaches of Hittite society.

1.5 The Italian School

Diakonoff's challenge to the Western culture-historical model was taken up most fully in Italy, where in the 1970's and 80's a number of scholars undertook an immensely productive project of explaining ancient Near East society in neo-Marxist terms. The Italian scholars, perhaps because they were free to work outside the Stalinist orthodoxy, took Diakonoff's work to its logical conclusion and embraced the Asiatic Mode of Production as a description for the societies of the ancient Near East.

The Italian School began with the two-sector premise of co-existing palatial and communal modes of production. Unconstrained by rigid historical materialism, the Italians mooted the question of slavery that wracked Soviet literature and simply accepted the gradations of dependency as a sociological fact of the region. They shifted the research questions instead to the interaction of the two sectors, how they were integrated, and the specialization of production between them, on which there was a spectrum of results. One side, led by Mario Liverani, a specialist on Syria and pioneering literary critic of ancient Near Eastern sources, emphasized the strong political and productive divide between the palace and communal sectors. The other side, led by Nuzi specialist and historian Carlo Zaccagnini, focused on the parasitic dependency of the palace sector on the communal sector.[61] The work of Liverani, Zaccagnini, and their many collaborators framed the discussion of ancient Near Eastern and Hittite history well into the 1990's and even today.

1.5.1 Liverani: A Strongly Dichotomous Two-Sector Model

Mario Liverani wrote for the first time on the "Two-Sector" model in 1975, using it to describe the relationship between village and palace in Late Bronze Age Syria.[62]

60 Cornelius, "Das Hethiterreich als Feudalstaat," 34.

61 Prior to his work on the Asiatic Mode of Production, Zaccagnini was probably best known for his study of gift exchange, one of the primary drivers of the palatial economy in the Ancient Near East: see Carlo Zaccagnini, *Lo scambio dei doni nel Vicino Oriente durante i secoli XV–XIII*. OrAntColl. 11 (Rome: Centro per le antichità e la storio dell'arte del Vicino Oriente, 1973).

62 Mario Liverani, "Communautés de village et palais royal dans la Syrie du IIème millénaire," JESHO 18 (1975): 146–64. For a succinct English summary of his model, see Mario Liverani, "Economic and Socio-

Lieverani's interest in Soviet historical materialism can be traced back to at least 1969, when he edited a volume on Syria with a contribution from Michael Heltzer, and to a review of an edited volume of Diakonoff's on Mesopotamian history.[63] In his own first article on the topic, Liverani used Diakonoff's model to explain the erosion of the communal sector in Syria, but with a refined description of the role of land grants in the process.

According to Liverani, it was the innovation of heritable land grants – and not just the skimming off of the talented or ambitious villagers and enslavement of the poor – that undermined village communalism by creating social stratification.[64] In essence, the introduction of non-communal private property corrupted a system of inheritance ill-equipped to handle it. The transformation was for the most part unintentional: land grants were initially not heritable, but social pressure and human nature pushed the recipients to make them so, often against the wishes of the palace. The traditional Syrian practice was for divided inheritance, where each child received more or less equitable shares and the property stayed within the village community. However, the conditions of land grants were often indivisible, linked to a specific service or profession required by the palace. Parents now had to pick and choose among their children who would inherit the grant, oftentimes based on ability. Sometimes the eldest son was not the best suited to his father's profession, and other times a son-in-law was adopted if the grantee only had daughters. In extreme cases, the grantee could attempt to sell his office through an adoption of convenience. Over time, the effect of undivided inheritance and notions of private property was to sort the communal sector into "winners" and "losers," transforming the village, as Liverani argued, "d'une communauté organique de travail à un endroit où chacun poursuit sa propre politique d'affirmation personelle."[65] The palace benefited from the changing social structure in that it sapped the independence of the villages and colonized the communities with loyal servants. The outcome of communal erosion was the same Struvean rebellion, leading to the final collapse of the two-sector structure into the single mode of production of generalized slavery.[66] Though Liverani did not explicitly explore the topic, it can be deduced that the same general process should have occurred in the other societies of the ancient Near East.

In the same article Liverani also argued for a strongly dichotomous Two-Sector Model, when he parsed the division of production between the palace and communal sectors in terms of an urban revolution, writing that

> Au point de vue de la réparation du travail, il est bien connu que dans les villages la population 'libre' se consacre presque exclusivement à la production primaire de nourriture (agriculture et

Political Developments," in *History of Humanity, Volume II, From the Third Millennium to the Seventh Century B.C.*, eds. Ahmed H. Dani, Jean-Pierre Mohen (New York: Routledge, 1996), 130–36.

63 Michael Heltzer, "Problems of Social History," in *Syria nel tardo bronzo*, ed. Mario Liverani (Roma: Ipocan, 1969), 31–46. Mario Liverani, "Review of Igor Diakonoff, *Ancient Mesopotamia: Socio-Economic History (Moscow, 1969)*," OrAnt. 11 (1972): 226–29.

64 Liverani, "Communautés de village," 157–59.

65 Liverani, *op. cit.*, 158.

66 Liverani, *op. cit.*, 162–63

élevage); tandis que le travail de transformation (artisanat) et d'échange (commerce) est concentré dans le secteur palatin, avec les "services" de nature cultuelle, militaire, d'administration et d'organisation de la production. On peut dire – pour simplifier – que les communautés de village n'ont pas participé à la 'révolution urbaine' en ce qui concerne leur structure interne (réparation spécialiste du travail), mais qu'elles l'ont seulement subie, car le palais prélève le surplus des villages pour entretenir ses spécialistes.[67]

Liverani's language is striking, even if he does qualify the description as a simplification ("pour simplifier"), and later acknowledged in an article from 1978 that, despite the human and spatial continuities between Neolithic and Bronze Age villages, the socio-economic trajectory of a community is not always linear and village life not necessarily fossilized. Nevertheless, he argued in the same article that villages in the Bronze Age Near East were marked by undiversified economies, dependence, and technological stagnation, and completely subjected to the palatine cities, compelling him to use a biological metaphor to describe the villages as "cellule produttive subalterne del sistema socio-economico complesso centrato sul palazzo."[68]

1.5.2 Zaccagnini: The Neo-"Asiatic Mode of Production" Model

In 1981, Carlo Zaccagnini penned a large article which attempted to synthesize the Western Marxist discussion of the Asiatic Mode of Production.[69] The article was aimed at two different audiences. To non-theoretical orientalists, or those who might be less informed about Marxist and socio-economic methodologies in general, Zaccagnini offered an intellectual history of the Asiatic Mode of Production that is still an extremely useful discussion for anyone wishing to know more about the historiography of the period. For this audience Zaccagnini also provided analysis of land grant use in the major Bronze Age states in the second half of the article. For the Marxist historian,

67 Liverani, "Communautés de village," 148.

68 Mario Liverani, "Sulle tracce delle comunità rurali. In margine ai lavori della Société J. Bodin," OrAnt. 17 (1978): 71.

Ed essendo la città palatina dell'antico Oriente la sede del potere politico, il rapporto di contrapposizione è un rapporto di subordinazione della comunità rurale e di inserimento di essa quale cellula di un organismo più vasto, unificato dalla città palatina. Il primo tratto strutturale della comunità rurale è dunque il suo carattere subalterno. Il secondo tratto strutturale è il persistere nelle comunità rurali di un modo di produzione non basato sulla differenziazione specialistica delle attività lavorative, che invece caratterizza le unità produttive proprie del palazzo anche quando si dedichino alla stessa produzione di cibo cui si dedicano le comunità rurali. Le comunità rurali sono cioè unità produttive internamente indifferenziate che si situano però quali unità costitutive di un processo produttivo differenziato, controllato dal palazzo. Al tratto dell'indifferenziazione produttiva se ne connettono strettamente altri: il ristagno tecnologico, l'ideale della sussistenza (e non dell'accumulo come a palazzo), l'autosufficienza (con un livello di scambi estremamente ridotto), e così via. Tutto può confluire nella definizione delle comunità rurali come cellule produttive subalterne del sistema socio-economico complesso centrato sul palazzo.

69 Carlo Zaccagnini, "Asiatic Mode of Production and Ancient Near East, Notes Towards a Discussion," in *Production and Consumption in the Ancient Near East*, ed. Carlo Zaccagnini (Budapest: Chaire d'Egyptologie de l'Université Eötvös Loránd de Budapest, 1989), 1–126 (translation of Carlo Zaccagnini, "Modo di produzione asiatico e Vicino Oriente antico. Appunti per una discussione," *Dialoghi di archeologia*, NS 3/3 (1981): 3–65).

who reflexively rejected the Asiatic Mode of Production because of the after-effects of Stalinist orthodoxy, he attempted to fashion a new version of the model that was consistent with the theoretical framework, if not the exact contents, of the canonical Marxist texts. For convenience, Zaccagnini's model will be designated here as the "neo-AMP" to distinguish it from Marx's aborted "(paleo-)AMP."[70]

Zaccagnini found much inspiration in Liverani's work: after a thorough evaluation of recent Marxist literature, he chose Liverani's interpretation of the Two-Sector Model as the basis for his own reformulation of the Asiatic Mode of Production (Zaccagnini's choice to extensively study the land grants is direct evidence of his debt to the former). But unlike Liverani's "strong" version, the key feature of the model for Zaccagnini was the *relationship*, not the division, between the sectors. He argued that

> the functional nexus that binds the village m.o.p. to the palatial m.o.p. in such a way that the 'combination' of the two m.o.p.s figures forth one mode of production, the asiatic mode .... [I]t is just this 'dominance' (in Liverani's meaning) of the palatial m.o.p. – which represents an evolution of the village m.o.p. – and the functionality of the relation that binds it to the 'subaltern' m.o.p. (the village one), that brings out the structural features of an asiatic form.[71]

The "superordinate" relationship of a palace sector directly over a village sector ("village+palace" in Zaccagnini's notation), with no intervening levels, was the *sine qua non* of the Asiatic economic formation. Formations not based on this dominance, the recognition of which Zaccagnini credits to Liverani, are not "Asiatic"; so too, economic formations lacking a communal/village element (thus "slave latifundia+palace" or "feudal estates+palace" would not qualify).[72] Turning to Marx's original texts, Zaccagnini recovers the following features of the Asiatic Mode of Production:

1.) Common ownership of the land, based on the villages. The individual, as member of the community, is only a possessor (1st level of mediation).
2.) In its turn, the presupposition for (communal) ownership of the land is the superior authority (the "despot," the State), which claims to be the unique and higher owner of all the land (2nd level of mediation).
3.) The superior unit demands and receives a surplus quota of the product and of the work of the community in the form of tribute and corvée.[73]

Thus far Liverani and Zaccagnini agreed. But in the next two points, on the economic disposition of the villages, their models diverged to an extent that has not been sufficiently recognized:

4.) The individual productive units (= the village system). This characteristic seems, for Marx, to apply not only to individual village communities ... but to the Asiatic system as a whole, that is to say, to the combination: city + country: ... [in which] 'the unification of manufacture and agriculture, of city (village) and country' is emphasized. This statement probably refers to a higher level of historiographic abstraction, [because] in reality it is only the second term in the equation that has the decisive role in the process of production and transformation (manufacturing) of the primary product, and the superior unit defines itself – apart from its 'fiscal'

70 Zaccagnini, "Asiatic Mode of Production," 6–14.
71 Zaccagnini, *op. cit.*, 22.
72 Zaccagnini, *loc. cit.*
73 Zaccagnini, *op. cit.*, 26. Formatting changed.

activity – by its responsibility for the celebratory and the ostentatious (pyramids, etc.) achievements.

5.) Undifferentiated unity of the city and the country: the city does not exist (or exists as a superfetation),[74] or it identifies itself with the villages.[75]

The last two points minimize the economic impact of the urban/rural dichotomy by locating all productive power within the village. The results of the "urban revolution" – economic specialization, industry, social hierarchy – that Liverani ascribed to the palatine cities are in Zaccagnini's model diffused into the countryside, reducing the palatine city to a locus of expenditure in the form of royal monuments and propaganda.

The main implication of Zaccagnini's "neo-AMP" model is to make the control of villages by the palatial sector even more important. Instead of being benighted, agricultural backwaters serving only to power the urban sector, they become the fundamental units of production for ancient states. Thus, when Zaccagnini finished his article with a thirty-page excursus on land grants and the transfer of villages in the ancient Near East, it was more than just homage to Liverani; it was in fact the axis of his own project aimed at showing how the palace sector managed economic units that were in many ways greater than themselves. The results of the project were ambiguous in the Hittite case. On the one hand, Zaccagnini concluded from the *Landschenkungsurkunde* of Kuwatalla and the Šaḫurunuwa grant discussed in the article that the Hittite king could transfer full ownership of villages and households, even those not already belonging to the palace, to individuals or institutions. In comparative terms this is a remarkable level of power for any monarch to wield in the ancient Near East. It also speaks to the relative weakness of the Hittite nobility, further undermining the feudal thesis of Hittite society. On the other hand, because the king would sometimes compensate the land-stripped third party with grants of palace land, the king's justification for transferring property lay, according to Zaccagnini, not "in some supposed 'eminent right' of the sovereign over all landed-property, but rather in a *de facto* power of widespread intervention even where the property is that of third parties ...."[76] Of course, *de facto* power changes with the facts. The king's power was naturally limited by the

---

74 The unusual term "superfetation" (*Superfötation*), meaning here a useless outgrowth or artifice, comes from a passage at the very end of Notebook IV of Marx's *Grundrisse der Kritik der politischen Ökonomie (Rohentwurf)*, where Marx refers to the indifferent unity of town and country in Asiatic cities, which tend to have the function of "royal camps."

75 Zaccagnini, "Asiatic Mode of Production," 26–27. Formatting changed.

76 Zaccagnini, *op. cit.*, 86. See further Gregor Giorgadze, "Zum Kauf und Verkauf von Grund und Boden in der hethitischen Gesellschaft," AoF 25 (1998): 57:

> In der hethitischen Gesellschaft bestand kein umfassendes und ausschließliches Eigentum des Staates am gesamten Land, weil in einem Staat, der seiner Bevölkerung als Gegenleistung für den Besitz von Land bestimmte Pflichten auferlegte, Bedingungen für die Entstehung eines nichtstaatlichen, privaten Eigentums geschaffen wurden. Die Quellen für die Entstehung von Privateigentum an Land waren folgende: königliche Landschenkungen, besonders solche mit Immunität; Aufteilung von Wirtschaften, wenn sich ein Teil des nicht mit Verpflichtungen verbundenen staatlichen Landes bei einer Privatperson mit Verfügungsrecht befand; Kauf und Verkauf des Landes unter der Bedingung, dass die Erfüllung der staatlichen Verpflichtungen auf den Käufer übergeht. In diesen Fällen gab der Staat sein Recht auf das Eigentum am Land auf, das nach dem Verkauf in das Eigentum einer Privatperson übergehen mußte.

opportunity for later kings to overturn the arrangements of their predecessors; though, as seen in the Šaḫurunuwa donation, the king could try to prevent this by writing clauses explicitly prohibiting revocation by future kings. It also is worth recalling here Ḫattušili III's perhaps hyperbolic claim to have accepted being stripped of every title but his last. It is remarkable that this supposedly happened even under a very weak king dealing with an exceptionally strong vassal, but in this case the king, Urḫi-Teššub, overestimated his strength and lost his throne to rebellion.

1.6 Neo-Marxism and the "New Humanities"

The other implication of the Zaccagnini's neo-AMP Model is to cause the historian to take more seriously the monuments and propaganda, which far from being secondary products of government become the prime industry of the palatial sector. Zaccagnini did not explore the production of monuments in the scope of his article, perhaps out of a Marxist habit of mind to consider these "superfetations" of the city as less important than the material products of the village. However, the intellectual trends of the period were against Zaccagnini as more emphasis came to be placed on the "New Humanities," a set of intellectual approaches which arose out of the neo-Marxist embrace of culture.

In an introduction to a collection of essays on the ancient economy (including one on the ancient Near East by Liverani), the Classicists Ian Morris and Joseph Manning explained the concept of "New Humanities" as arising from the struggles of Marxist intellectuals in the 1950's to 1970's to escape the purely economic determinism of orthodox Marxism, which lead them to embrace diverse philosophies such as "existentialism, psychoanalysis, structuralism, poststructuralism, and feminism"; as a result,

> Rather than seeing culture as an epiphenomenon, legitimating the economic infrastructure and institutional structure, some Marxist humanists argued that these structures were culturally constituted .... [These] new humanists pay great attention to economics but generally argue that economic categories are culturally constructed as merely one dimension of the creation of a new set of subjectivities, narratives, and gender relations.[77]

While no Hittitologist advanced so bold an argument for the economy (though Mario Liverani came closest in certain literary analyses of ancient sources),[78] the field could not help but be influenced by emerging new humanistic studies.[79] A year after the

77 Ian Morris and Joseph G. Manning, "Introduction," in *The Ancient Economy: Evidence and Models*, eds. Joseph G. Manning, Ian Morris (Stanford: Stanford University Press, 2005), 28.

78 The most important in the Hittite context are Mario Liverani, "Storiografia politica hittita – I. Šunaššura, ovvero: della reciprocità," OrAnt. 12 (1973): 267–97, and Liverani, "Storiografia politica hittita – II. Telipinu, ovvero: della solidarietà," OrAnt. 16 (1977): 105–31. Liverani outlined his methodology in Mario Liverani, "Memorandum on the approach to historiographic texts," Or. 42 (1973): 178–94.

79 To the great lament of Itamar Singer, who railed against the corrupting influence of Liverani's approach (variously described as "pessimistic," "hyper-critical," and, most damningly, "postmodern"). Against the proponents of Liverani's "semiological revolution," who claimed it had not received the attention it deserved, Singer argued its outsized impact on the field:

appearance of Zaccagnini's neo-AMP model, Fiorella Imparati wrote an article pleading for the expansion of historical research to consider also the cultural products of the Hittite state. In it she gave a description of the erosion of the communal sector and village life in Hittite Anatolia that is in practice almost identical to Liverani's account for Syria, but with the caveat that the loss of village autonomy was not uniform but disproportionally greater in the political and economic spheres.[80] Because a purely economic typology of Hittite society would fail to capture the continued independence of law and religion in the communities, she argued for increased attention to the cultural side of Hittite history, or as she phrased it: "des ainsi-dites 'super-structures' (religieuses, juridiques, idéologiques, linguistiques, etc.), qui exerçaient une fonction très considerable dans les sociétés à économie pré-capitaliste."[81] This decidedly new humanistic approach risks stretching the definition of Marxism so as to become unrecognizable (indeed, a page later she went so far as to suggest that different periods of

---

> My own impression is that Liverani's influence on ancient Near Eastern studies has been far more decisive than it may appear on the face of it. As noted by the renowned French historian Marc Bloch, co-founder of the Annales School, 'for a philosophy to impregnate an entire age, it is not necessary that it should act precisely in accordance with a prescribed formula nor that the majority of minds should come under its influence except by a sort of osmosis of which they are often only half aware.'

(Itamar Singer, "Between Scepticism and Credulity: In Defence of Hittite Historiography," in *Diversity and Standardization: Perspectives on Social and Political Norms in the Ancient Near East*, eds. Eva Cancik-Kirschbaum, Jörg Klinger, Gerfrid G.W. Müller [Berlin: Akademie Verlag, 2013], 178).

As of 1973, Liverani was not poststructuralist. His focus was: "the text as source of knowledge of its author, and not {or previously to being} source of knowledge of narrated events" (p. 198). The poststructuralist criticism would be that the text is not even a source of knowledge of its author, but can only be interpreted as an object in and of itself; that the difficulties experienced in recovering narrated events from the text are the same as recovering knowledge of the author – i.e., both impossible. The tendency of structuralism to lead to poststructuralism, and from there to "a conspicuous transformation in scholarly focus, namely a decreasing interest in political history and a rush towards other historical sub-disciplines, such as socio-economic, cultural and intellectual histories," (Singer, "Between Scepticism and Credulity," 179) was the thrust of Singer's criticism of Liverani. Others, such as Gary Beckman ("The Limits of Credulity," JAOS 125 (2005): 343–52), riposted that traditional scholars (cf. William Hallo, "The Limits of Skepticism," JAOS 110 (1990): 187–99) ignore the internal structure of the text.

80 Fiorella Imparati, "Aspects de l'organization de l'État Hittite dans les documents juridiques et administratifs," JESHO 25 (1982): 260–61:

> Il me semble donc qu'on puisse conclure en remarquant que, avec le temps, le secteur communautaire tendait de plus en plus à être subordonné au pouvoir central. Et même si certaines compétences continuaient à être attribuées à ce secteur et à ses représentants, les Anciens et l'inspecteur de ville ou de village, cela semble avoir eu lieu surtout pour les institutions liées à certaines traditions, comme les institutions juridiques et religieuses. Mais tout ce qui concernait le secteur politique et économique était contrôlé par la vaste organisation bureaucratique du Palais.

Compare also Imparati, "Die Organisation des hethitischen Staates," in *Geschichte des Hethitischen Reiches*, by Horst Klengel, contribs. Fiorella Imparati, Volkert Haas, Theo van den Hout. HdO 1/34 (Leiden: Brill, 1998), 320–87, which contains the most mature version of Imparati's AMP-influenced model of the Hittite state.

81 Imparati, "Aspects de l'organization," 263.

Hittite society could have different Modes of Production, a proposition that is categorically impossible in orthodox Marxism),[82] but looking ahead to Hittitological research in the 1990's and 2000's, the renewed appreciation for culture was useful in explaining the monumental yet under-inhabited urban plan of Ḫattuša, or the recognition of the importance of religious institutions to the state economy.

In retrospect, the main contribution of Italian Neo-Marxism to the discussion of Hittite and Near Eastern history was to create testable hypotheses for the archaeological and textual data of the different cultures and periods of the region (cf. the second half of Zaccagnini, "Asiatic Mode of Production," 56–58, on the transfer of villages in the ancient Near East). The political subordination of village to city, for example, while unremarkable given the natural tendency to centralize power in human government, becomes a productive statement when it makes specific claims of where certain economic activities took place, i.e., agrarian villages and industrial cities for Liverani, versus diversified villages and monumental cities for Zaccagnini. Comparing such claims to the much less testable hypothesis of Orientalization in the culture-historical model demonstrates the welcome scientific rigor brought to the study of Hittite history by the neo-Marxists. The results of their approach can and should be contested, but the questions and method are still useful to modern attempts to model the Hittite state.

1.7 New Western Consensus

The new Western consensus on the Hittite state emerged as an adaptation to the Marxist critiques of the 1970's. Its earliest stages were prefigured by Richard Haase's article on feudalism; that is to say, scholars were willing to entertain (neo-)Marxist ideas without adopting the theoretical apparatus itself. However, the rapprochement between East and West quickly faded as the study of religion, a topic famously ill-suited to historical materialist explanation, grew in importance for modeling the Hittite state. A slew of articles published in the 1980's began the immense and still ongoing task of untangling the Hittite religious-administrative corpus. By the mid-1980's Western scholars achieved the framework of a consensus that remains stable into the 21st century: a paradigm firmly rooted in a centralized temple and palatial infrastructure, but with a growing awareness of regional difference and impact of the Anatolian environment on the Hittite government (the implications of which will be discussed in Sections *2.2 The Hittites and Their Environment* and *2.3 Political Integration on the Anatolian Plateau*).

1.7.1 The End of Hittite Feudalism as a Theoretical Model

At the same time as Liverani and Zaccagnini were drawing attention to the differences between palaces and villages in the ancient Near East, the Italian Hittitologist Alfonso Archi was attempting to put Hittite society back together amidst the disintegration of feudalism as a useful model. His major insight was to focus research on the palatial

82 Imparati, "Aspects de l'organization," 264.

(and later temple) infrastructure as the premier site of integration for the Hittite state. When he began modeling the Hittite state in a pair of articles from 1973, two years before the publication of Liverani's study on two-sector Syria, the question of Hittite feudalism was still alive and well. Haase's debunking (1968) and Cornelius' defense (1972) were still recent, and it remained to be seen which direction the new generation of Hittitologists would go with the controversy. Archi for his part rejected the feudal label from the standpoint of Diakonoff's Two-Sector Model, but used the intellectual space created by feudalism's demise to craft his own alternative interpretation of the Hittite state.

Archi was perhaps the first Western Hittitologist to positively cite Diakonoff's Two-Sector Model, when he used it to side with the anti-feudalists in his 1973 article on "Bureaucratie et communautés d'hommes libres dans le système économique hittite."[83] At this time Archi was in general agreement with Diakonoff's assessment of the nature of power in the Hittite state; that is, observing a two-sector division in Hittite society while acknowledging a much more limited economic role for the Hittite state sector than its Mesopotamian contemporaries. In practical terms this meant that while the Hittite palace had the usual responsibilities for defense, religion, justice, and basic infrastructure, it lacked the decisive control over the means of production needed to create the grand public works observed to the south. Anatolian villages, like their counterparts everywhere in the ancient Near East, were essentially economically self-sufficient; however Archi argued that in contrast to other societies they had a relatively open membership, being composed of essentially anyone who could afford land. The Hittite Laws recorded that landowners, state tenants, and even deportee "serfs" could freely buy and sell land so long as the general service-tax on land was paid, and there was thus very little evidence for the persistence of communal ownership in Hittite Anatolia.[84] Though the Hittite palace lacked decisive economic control, it paradoxically may have had a broader base of interaction with the village sector than its Mesopotamian and Syrian counterparts. Land grants, often with attendant serfs, were the primary currency of the Hittite state, and were used for everything from the maintenance of temples, the salary of state officials large and small, and even purchasing services from craftsmen. Archi agreed with Haase's earlier argument that the land grants were no evidence for a feudal relationship, because the beneficiaries enjoyed the use of the land only as result of their continuing participation in the state bureaucracy. But he improved the argument with respect to Diakonoff's Two-Sector Model by claiming that the serf-like condition of the deportees was an anomaly in Hittite society, and arose only in the specific moment in Hittite history when the kingdom was consolidating its conquests into empire. For Archi, Hittite serfdom was only a phenomenon that "vint s'insérer dans une situation essentiellement 'asiatique', puisque, à la base du système, il y a contraste entre les communautés et la bureaucratie."[85] This sentence marks the high point of Archi's commitment to (neo-)Marxist theory, which he seems

83 Alfonso Archi, "Bureaucratie et communautés d'hommes libres dans le système économique hittite," in *Festschrift Heinrich Otten*, eds. Erich Neu, Christel Rüster (Wiesbaden: Harrassowitz, 1973), 17–24.

84 Archi, "Bureaucratie et communautés," 18–22.

85 Archi, *op. cit.*, 21–22.

to tacitly abandon after the late 1970's, but the general conclusion of a Hittite society defined by a broad, direct interface between palace and community remains remarkably durable.

Archi returned to the topic of feudalism in 1977 with the publication of "Il 'feudalismo' ittita," an article which more than any other can be credited with permanently ending the debate on the term in Hittite society. Living up to the categorical promise of its title, the work began with a deep Soviet and Western bibliography of the use (and misuse) of the feudal designation in studies of the Hittite and ancient world.[86] Archi's method of attacking the label was the same as Haase's ten years earlier, namely stripping the "benefices" normally cited as evidence of their feudal characteristics ("La concessione di tali benefici è un tratto comune a molti stati antichi e dell'Oriente medievale, e non costituisce di per sé un elemento feudale ...").[87] Archi expanded the philological foundations for rejection by showing that the service obligations of the LÚ^{MEŠ} ^{GIŠ}TUKUL and LÚ^{MEŠ} *ILKI*, and not just *šaḫḫan*, must be disqualified from feudal evidence.[88] Previously, the LÚ^{MEŠ} ^{GIŠ}TUKUL (lit. 'men of the weapon/tool'[89]) were mostly thought of as "free men," i.e., those entitled to bear arms, and the LÚ^{MEŠ} *ILKI* (lit. 'men of the soke') as the palace dependents. A sharp distinction between these two groups had been assumed by both the feudal and two-sector models of the Hittite state: the former because it postulated a class of armigerous freemen in voluntary service to the state, and the latter because it needed contrasting groups of autonomous villagers and palace dependents. Archi showed that in practice the distinction between TUKUL-men and *ILKU*-men was not exact: rather, both groups held land tenure agreements that could be freely bought and sold, with the distinction being that TUKUL-tenure was on land that belonged to a village, and *ILKU*-tenure on land belonging to the palace. Holders of TUKUL obligations were taxed indirectly under the system of *luzzi* 'corvée', which was the

86 Alfonso Archi, "Il 'feudalismo' ittita," SMEA 18 (1977): 7–18.

87 Archi, "Feudalismo," 16. Archi seems to have reached this conclusion through the works of Paul Garelli, "Le problème de la 'féodalité' assyrienne du XVe au XIIe siècle av. J.-C.," *Semitica* 17 (1967): 5–21; and Richard Haase, "*Einführung in das Studium keilschriftlicher Rechtsquellen.* Rezension von G. Cardascia," *IVRA* 17 (1966): 325–28. However, Haase's "Herrscher und Beherrschte" was overlooked.

88 It is not the intention to present here a comprehensive discussion of the LÚ ^{GIŠ}TUKUL and LÚ *ILKI*. The nebulous socio-economic status of these persons has tended to evolve with the theoretical models imposed on them. For recent discussion, see Taifun Bilgin, *Officials and Adminstration in the Hittite World.* SANER 21 (Berlin: De Gruyter, 2018), 444, and especially Lorenzo d'Alfonso, "'Servant of the King, Son of Ugarit, and Servant of the Servant of the King'. RS 17.238 and the Hittites," in *Pax Hethitica. Studies on the Hittites and their Neighbours in Honour of Itamar Singer*, eds. Yoram Cohen, Amir Gilan, Jared L. Miller. StBoT 51 (Wiesbaden: Harrassowitz, 2010), 71–80, with previous literature.

89 On the ambiguous etymology of ^{GIŠ}TUKUL, Richard Beal ("The ^{GIŠ}TUKUL-institution in Second Millennium Hatti," AoF 15 [1988]: 304) concluded that the military implications were negligible by the historical period of the Hittite Kingdom:

> In summary ^{GIŠ}TUKUL-men appear to have been men who worked for the government or others and received their pay in the form of land who produce supported them. This type of pay seems to have originally been introduced to pay for army troops, hence the title 'weapon-man' for those paid in this way. However, already in the Old Hittite Period, it had been extended so as to provide pay for a vast number of different types of civilian employees, who, since they were paid in the same way as their military counterparts, were also called 'weapon-men.'

collective responsibility of the village, while *ILKU*-holders paid taxes directly to the palace as *šaḫḫan* 'socage'. Individuals, even "muškēnu" who were bound to their *ILKU*-land, could simultaneously hold TUKUL and *ILKU* land, provided they could meet the tax obligations.[90] Archi thus did for the LÚ^{MEŠ} ^{GIŠ}TUKUL and *luzzi-* what Haase did for *šaḫḫan*, that is, showed the terms to be another variety of land-tax, and not permanent social categories, meaning neither term could be used as evidence for feudalism in the Hittite state. This interpretation, with some refinement, still has currency to the present day.[91] But by demonstrating the free mixing of palace and village service obligations, Archi also undermined the validity of the Two-Sector Model for the Hittites – a trend that would continue in his later articles.

Archi concluded his dismantling of Hittite feudalism with what was perhaps his most innovative contribution to Hittite political theory. He began with the premise, going back to Goetze, that external Hittite political relationships should homologize internal political relationships. While Goetze used the link to argue that the seemingly feudal vassal treaties reflected the feudalism of Hittite society, Archi turned the conclusion on its head: he argued that the internal political documents, especially the instruction and loyalty oath genre that regulated the relationship of the king and palace dependents, had a non-feudal, contractual arrangement that is also observed in the vassal treaties.[92] The language shared by the instructions and treaties revolves around clearly defined obligations (*išḫiul-*) that bind (*lengai-*) the two parties before the gods.[93] While mutual protection (*paḫš-*) and homage[94] can be part of the treaty/instructions, they are only two stipulations among the many which can appear. The instruction genre prescribed the responsibilities, schedules, and even hygiene of palace officials, and treaties could include stipulations ranging from the exact number of troops to be contributed by a village (CTH 133 "Treaty between Arnuwanda I and the Men of

90 Archi, "Feudalismo," 13–15.

91 See Massimiliano Marazzi, "Messa a coltura e procedure di gestione e controllo dei campi nell'Anatolia hittita: caratteristiche della documentazione e stato della ricerca," in *The Management of Agricultural Land and the Production of Textiles in the Mycenaean and Near Eastern Economies*, eds. Massimo Perna, Francesco Pomponio. Studi egei e vicinorientali 4 (Paris: De Boccard, 2008), 63– 65; Jürgen Lorenz, "Sahhan und luzzi," in *Private and State in the Ancient Near East. Proceedings of the 58th Rencontre Assyriologique Internationale at Leiden 16– 20 July 2012*, eds. Rients de Boer, Jan G. Dercksen (Winona Lake: Eisenbrauns, 2017), 193– 202; Lorenzo d'Alfonso and Alvise Matessi, "Extracting Cohesion: Fiscal Strategies in the Hittite Staple Economy," in *Ancient Taxation. Mechanics of Extraction in Comparative Perspective*, eds. Jonathan Valk, Irene Soto Marín. Institute for the Study of the Ancient World Monographs (New York: New York University Press, 2021): 132–34.

92 Archi, *op. cit.*, 16–18.

93 Here Archi built on the work of Einar von Schuler, "Staatsvertäge und Dokumente hethitischen Rechts," in *Neuere Hethiterforschung*, ed. Gerold Walser (Wiesbaden: Steiner, 1964), 34–53; von Schuler, "Sonderformen hethitischen Staatsverträge," in *Anadolu Arastırmaları. Helmuth Bossert'in Hatırasına Armağan* (Fs. H. Th. Bossert) (Istanbul: Istanbul University, 1965), 445–64; and von Schuler, *Hethitische Dienstanweisungen für höhere Hof- und Staatsbeamte. Ein Beitrag zum antiken Recht Kleinasiens.* AfO Beiheft 10 (Graz: Weidner, 1957).

94 There is no direct Hittite translation for the concept of homage, but a number of vassal treaties, including all of the Syrian treaties beginning with Šuppiluliuma I and Aziru of Amurru (CTH 49), require the appearance of the vassal in person at the Hittite court at least once a year.

Išmerikka") to the sexual behavior of the vassal when he visits the Hittite court (CTH 42 "Treaty between Šuppiluliuma I and Ḫuqqana of Ḫayaša"). Despite the loyalty and mutual protection undergirding the stipulations (such as the responsibility of vassals and officials to report malicious gossip and curses to the king), Archi argued that the treaties and instructions cannot be considered in feudal terms. The missing feature of both the vassal treaties and the instructions was the element of subordination – political, financial, cultural, or otherwise.[95] Referring to Hittite vassals as protectorates or even confederates, as the Egyptians did in the propaganda surrounding the battle of Qadeš, is entirely inappropriate, as even the smallest cities and village groups were generally free from Hittite interference in their internal matters. While Archi conceded that "vassalage" may be the least worst term to describe the network of treaties binding the Hittite Kingdom with its allied states, care must be taken not to confuse the situation with Medieval Europe.[96]

Archi came very close to banishing feudalism completely from the Hittite state. He still considered the "loyalty oaths," decrees requiring an unlimited and personal allegiance from all senior officials and vassals to the Hittite king, to be evidence of a growing feudal tendency at the very end of the Hittite New Kingdom.[97] But as Fiorella Imparati pointed out in her article from 1982, these oaths are better read as symptoms of the difficulties of the last days of the Hittite New Kingdom.[98] While Imparati attributed the troubles of the Hittite state to the Kaška and Assyrians, her view was confirmed by the discovery of the Bronze Tablet and rereading of the Ulmi-Teššub treaty, which laid bare the extent of the political fractures resulting from Ḫattušili III's usurpation. With the discarding of the loyalty oaths as evidence, there is very little reason today to find feudalism anywhere in Hittite society.[99]

The disposal of feudalism as a valid model left the question of the identity and historical origin of the Hittite state apparatus open. The earlier idea (presented in, e.g., Goetze, "State and Society," 25–26, as discussed in *1.2.1 Goetze: The Ethnogenesis of the*

95 Archi did not explicitly define a sociologically typical feudal society, but he could have referenced here the analysis of Marc Bloch on the personal locus of feudalism as a relationship of subordination. Bloch found the feudal relationship in Medieval Europe to be illustrated best not by oaths of fealty or law codes, but the act of homage between two free men: where one man places his clasped hands between the hands of another as a gesture of submission, and declares himself to be the "man" of the person facing him, and they kiss each other on the mouth in a gesture of friendship (Marc Bloch, *Feudal Society*, trans. L.A. Manyon (Chicago: University of Chicago Press, 1961), 145–46). From everything we know as Hittitologists, such a scene would be entirely alien to Hittite culture and completely insufficient as a contract between the king and his vassal, which had to be defined and then sworn before the assembled gods.

96 Archi, "Feudalismo," 17.

97 Archi, *op. cit.*, 18.

98 Imparati, "Aspects de l'organization de l'État Hittite," 257.

99 As Fiorella Imparati ("Lehenswesen s. a. Feudalismus, *ilku*. A. Bei den Hethitern," RlA 6 [1980–83]: 547) concluded after a review of arguments in favor and against the feudal interpretation of the Hittite state:

> We can conclude, therefore, that the divergences in the structure of Hittite society and that of feudal societies seem to prevail over certain similarities which can be observed. It ensues that the adoption of a typically feudal terminology to designate certain institutions of the Hittite state may misrepresent the features proper to this society.

Hittite State) that there existed a deliberative body called the *panku-* drawn from the free-men of the realm survived in some permutation until the early 1980's. Clelia Mora approached the topic from a philological perspective to demonstrate that *panku-* indicated only a generic term for "the community, the entire population," a group that could informally called to assembly (*tuliya-*) when needed to witness or reinforce the ruling monarch's decisions.[100] Gary Beckman, in his article on the "The Hittite Assembly,"[101] demonstrated that the *panku-* was composed of the court officials and high-level servants resident at the palace, and "[n]ot a gathering of a class, but rather primarily a judicial body, subject even in this area to the will of the monarch" (p. 435). Fiorella Imparati agreed with Beckman's interpretation of the *panku-* as palace officials, and considers this an attempt by the kings of the Hittite Old Kingdom to create a centralized power base to counterbalance the power of local potentates.[102]

From later periods, it is clear that royal family members received many positions of power, including most of the internal governorships in Hittite Anatolia and many of the high-level positions in the palace bureaucracy.[103] While there was a terminological distinction between the *panku-* and the royal family (*šalli ḫaššatar*) (Beckman, "The Hittite Assembly," 442), prosopography shows there was at least a partial overlap between the two groups. However, as Beckman noted at the time, "the extent to which the higher bureaucracy was coterminous with what indeed might be called the Hittite 'ruling class' is a question which awaits further study" (p. 442, fn. 91), which, as will be discussed next chapter in *2.5 Current Models of the Hittite State: Conclusions and Next Steps*, the book of Taifun Bilgin, one of his students, would accomplish.[104]

100 Clelia Mora, "Il ruolo politico-sociale di *pankus* e *tulijas*: revision di un problema," in *Studi orientalistici in ricordo di Franco Pintore*, eds. Onofrio Carruba, Mario Liverani, Carlo Zaccagnini. StMed. 4 (Pavia: GJES, 1983), 159–84. See especially review of previous literature pp. 161–65, and conclusions 179–80.

101 Gary Beckman, "The Hittite Assembly," JAOS 102 (1982): 435–42.

102 Fiorella Imparati, "Autorità centrale e istituzioni collegiali nel regno ittita," in *Esercizio del potere e prassi della consultazione. Atti dell'VIII Colloquio internazionale romanistico-canonistico (10–12 maggio 1990)*, eds. Americo Ciani, Giovanni Diurni. Utrumque ius 21 (Rome: Libreria editrice vaticana, 1991), 161–81; also Imparati, "Die Organisation des hethitischen Staates," 345–48. See also Franca Pecchioli Daddi, "The System of Government at the Time of Tuthaliya IV," in *The Life and Times of Hattušili III and Tuthaliya IV. Proceedings of a Symposium Held in Honour of J. de Roos, 12–13 December 2003, Leiden*, ed. Theo van den Hout. PIHANS 103 (Leiden: Nederlands Instituut voor het Nabije Oosten, 2006), 121-25.

103 Archi, "Feudalismo," 18.

104 Bilgin, *Officials and Administration.* Ironically, in discussing the socio-economic structure of the Hittite state in terms of Weberian ideals, Bilgin also took a step towards resurrecting feudalism as an analytic category when he suggested (pp. 445–46) that the benefices and land-grants which seemed to have constituted the primary means compensation of Hittite high officials were in essence fiefs. Bilgin was cautious due to the lack of information concerning the rights and services attached to these parcels, but it will be interesting to see if future discoveries from provincial towns and the periphery confirm Bilgin's statement (p. 446) that "as we move away from the center of the empire towards its edges, the territorial organization of the administration starts to appear more feudal."

1.7.2 Archi: The Palace Network Model

Archi's second article from 1973, "L'organizzazione amministrativa ittita e il regime delle offerte cultuali,"[105] was a philological study of the administrative units of the Hittite Kingdom. The article formed the foundation of what can be called the "Palace Network" model of the Hittite state, and would have a profound impact on future studies of the Hittite state by emphasizing the importance of redistribution, not just extraction as did the Italian neo-Marxists, in the palatial-communal interface. Archi's argument was that the Hittite state functioned as a redistributive apparatus, physically manifested in the palatial infrastructure, and operating through the "regimen of cultic offerings." The very first sentence of the article offered a powerful reappraisal of the Hittite state, described as

> organizzato su una rete di cosiddetti palazzi, É.GAL, dislocati in numerose città, anche di non primaria importanza, che non solo servivano al re come residenze durante i suoi spostamenti, ma costituivano i centro da dove i funzionari controllavano i possedimenti statali, detti appunto del palazzo.[106]

The "palaces" were full-service administrative centers implanted in the local communities, accompanied by storehouses and seal houses, and governed by superintendents who distributed taxes and labor to state and especially temple institutions. Finished goods and foodstuffs were supplied to government workers through the system of cults, and members of local communities received ration supplements at festivals. Archi argued that there was neither a distinction between state and royal property, nor a functional difference between the palace and temple: all were aspects of the same redistributive system of the Hittite state.[107]

Archi returned to his Palace Network model in 1984 to provide a historical account of its development out of the pre-Hittite political infrastructure.[108] The article can in many ways be read as a counterpart and corrective to Goetze's culture-historical description of Hittite government, sharing the basic details and periodization as the earlier model, but explained from a resolutely economic and administrative perspective. Epigraphic and archeological evidence agree that pre-Hittite Anatolia was composed of multiple principalities, based around cities mentioned in the Old Assyrian trade documents such as Purušḫanda, Ankuwa, Kaneš, and Ḫattuša, each with dependent towns and hinterland. Besides the Assyrian trade network, the Anatolian principalities had independent contacts with the kingdoms of Syria, as evidenced by ivories, lapis lazuli, and seals with the name of Mari kings at Acem Höyük.[109] The conquest of the Anatolian Plateau by the Hittites changed this by cutting off the lateral contacts of the former

---

105 Alfonso Archi, "L'organizzazione amministrativa ittita e il regime delle offerte cultuali," OrAnt. 12 (1973): 209–26.

106 Archi, "L'organizzazione amministrativa," 209.

107 Archi, *op. cit.*, 218–20.

108 Alfonso Archi, "Anatolia in the Second Millennium B.C.," in *Circulation of Goods in Non-Palatial Context in Ancient Near East*, ed. Alfonso Archi (Roma: edizioni dell'Ateneo, 1984), 195–206.

109 Archi cited Kurt Bittel, *Die Hethiter* (München: Beck'sche Verlag, 1979), 64–66 for a general overview of trade relations, and Machteld Mellink, "Archaeology in Asia Minor," AJA 81 (1977): 295 for Acem Höyük specifically.

principalities and routing all trade through Ḫattuša. The newly centralized taxation system provided, perhaps by political design, an insufficient economic stimulus to maintain the population base of the large cities. The diminishing of the principalities meant local government could flourish: while the large urban centers were systematically disadvantaged compared to Ḫattuša, Archi argues that the villages, "favoured by the morphology of the largely mountainous and hilly territory," were privileged with new autonomy.[110] A tangible result of the autonomy was the system of local Elders in unmediated contact with the central government observed in the Old Kingdom period.[111]

While echoes of the pre-Hittite "urban+hinterland" organization persisted into the time of Ḫattušili I and Muršili I, by the reign of Telepinu central Anatolia was reorganized into 100 or so administrative centers centered on the É ^{NA_4}KIŠIB 'seal-house'. The seal-houses were outposts of central authority in the now largely rural Plateau, and were staffed by the LÚ^{MEŠ} AGRIG, local authorities who acted as liaisons between the villages and Ḫattuša. In later times the É ^{NA_4}KIŠIB network was supplemented by strategically placed É.GAL 'palaces' that served as extensions of the palace in Ḫattuša.[112] The palaces collected metals and wool as taxes (compared to the agrarian responsibilities of the É ^{NA_4}KIŠIB and ^{LÚ}AGRIG), with some evidence for the existence of dependent craftsmen such as weavers.[113] Temples were planted along with the palaces as extensive land-owners and self-sufficient centers of production.[114] In the absence of local dynasties and urban conglomerations, Hittite state officials, who were often members of the royal family, accumulated scattered estates and governorships; but Archi, ever watchful for misconstruings of feudalism, emphasized that their individual power never supplanted or constituted the state.[115]

Taken together, Archi's two articles from 1973, and their descendants of 1977 and 1984, erased the feudal interpretation of the Hittite state and in its place offered a new evaluation focused on the role of palace infrastructure in uniting the Anatolian Plateau in a redistributive scheme. Much of the philological detail is shared with the consensus

---

110 Archi, "Anatolia," 198.

111 It should be noted here that the prohibition of the Elders speaking to the king in the Political Testament of Ḫattušili I (CTH 6) (LÚ^{MEŠ} ŠU.GI *uddār lē memieškanzi* ... 'let the Elders not speak words ...' KUB 1.16 obv. ii 59), interpreted by Güterbock, "Authority and Law," 19 as evidence for the Elders' impotence, actually signifies its opposite: Ḫattušili is advising his successor *not* to be swayed by the Elders seeking favors (see CHD M *s.v.* **mi(ya)ḫu(wa)nt-* 3. 4′ [pp. 225–26]). It is in fact a classic example of an "exception proving (the existence of) a rule," where Ḫattušili's warning shows that the Elders normally had a potentially dangerous amount of influence.

112 Archi, *op. cit.*, 199.

113 Archi, *op. cit.*, 201–2.

114 Archi, *op. cit.*, 204–5.

115 Archi, *op. cit.*, 205–6. Emmanuel Laroche came to the same assessment in "Pouvoir central et pouvoir local en Anatolie hittite," in *Les Pouvoirs locaux en Mésopotamie et dans les régions adjacents: colloque organisé par l'Institut des Hautes Études de Belgique 28 et 29 janvier 1980.* ed. André Finet (Bruxelles: Institut des hautes études de Belgique, 1982), 138–43. He noted (p. 139) that the recently discovered Maşat letters show that local officials behaved as executors of the king's will, not independent rulers, though this might be a special case only applying to the northern frontier.

of Goetze and Gurney, but presented with a finer appreciation of socio-economic power thanks to the Marxist literature published in the intervening decades. It should be stressed, though, that Archi was not a theoretician. He was comfortable with using theory to contextualize his source material, but did not feel compelled to develop theory for its own sake. Thus, his articles from 1973 were perhaps the high point of his engagement with neo-Marxist interpretations of Hittite history. From this point on, Archi abstained from engaging directly with the neo-Marxists, even after the work of Liverani and Zaccagnini in the late 1970's and early 1980's. Nevertheless, his model evolved to be tacitly incompatible with the strong divisions of Liverani's Two-Sector Model. There is evidence that Archi was aware of this, as his later work includes commentary that contradicts two of the main pillars of Liverani's model, namely the internal colonization of the communal sector by the palatial and the impoverishment of the village at the expense of the city. To wit, Archi found in his study of the LÚ^{MEŠ} TUKUL and LÚ^{MEŠ} *ILKI* a muddling of the two social categories, and noted that "Tra i due gruppi, gli uomini dipendenti dal Palazzo e i membri delle comunità, non esisteva una separazione netta e definitiva."[116] And in his assessment of the historical development of the palace administrative system, Archi argued that the decline of Anatolian regional centers actually favored the growth of the villages, so that the region was on the whole not impoverished by Ḫattuša's new preeminence as capital city.[117] At the same time Archi did not embrace Zaccagnini's neo-AMP. Perhaps at the time of its publication in 1981 Archi was already contemplating the "religious turn," incompatible with Marxist analysis, that would define his work and others' into the 1980's and 1990's. Indeed, it was only when the Palace Network Model shifted its focus to emphasize the temple and performative religious experience in the Hittite state that it truly escaped co-option by the neo-AMP.

1.7.3 Klengel: The Palace-Temple Synthesis

By the 1970's the Hittite Laws had been well-studied, and it became clear that advances in understanding the Hittite state would have to come from elsewhere. Investigating the administrative corpus led Hittitologists to realize that the living bureaucracy of the Hittite state was confined almost exclusively to the religious sphere, though it was not yet known if this was an accident of preservation or a fundamental feature of Hittite society.[118] In 1975, Horst Klengel provided the first investigation of the economic role of the Hittite temple, a topic which, as he noted in his introductory footnotes, had previously received attention only in passing.[119] His article was not concerned with

116 Archi, "Feudalismo," 14. An antagonism to a strong two-sector division can also be read in Haase's remarks on the thematic unity of the Hittite Laws: "Hier wie überall findet man ein einheitliches Recht für Stadt und Land. Das zeigt sich auch daran, daß gewisse Vorschriften für die Hauptstadt Ḫattuša in die Rechtssammlung übernommen und damit verallgemeinert worden sind." (Richard Haase, "Die ländliche Gemeinschaft im Hethiterreich," in *Les Communautés rurales, Deuxième partie: Antiquité = Rural Communities, Second Part: Antiquity*, ed. Société Jean Bodin pour l'histoire comparative des institutions [Paris: Desain et Tolra, 1983], 201).

117 Archi, "Anatolia," 204.

118 Archi, "Bureaucratie et communautés," 23.

119 Horst Klengel, "Zur ökonomischen Funktion der hethitischen Tempel," SMEA 16 (1975): 181–200.

theory, but on the inapplicability of models of the Mesopotamian temple to the Hittite situation. For Klengel, the differences between the Hittite and Mesopotamian systems was most revealed by the absence of independent "temple cities" in Anatolia. All temples in Hittite lands functioned as part of the palace system outlined by Archi: physically, the temples were built proximate to palaces and in the same "government style" of architecture, and administratively no distinction can be found in the Hittite state archives between temple and state property.[120] Unlike in Mesopotamia, Hittite temples did not seem to conduct activities to accumulate wealth, using their benefices only to serve their cult obligations.[121] As such they played no role as workshops or engines of economic innovation. Klengel suspected that Hittite temples failed to innovate because there was no money economy in which to exchange their products; similarly Gregor Giorgadze traced the dearth of hired labor – a key driver of a monetized economy – to the prevalence of corvée in the Hittite economy.[122] Combining these two points suggests a vicious equilibrium where the Hittite economy was too dependent on compulsory labor to innovate. Land transferred to temples remained state land. It was worked to provide offerings for the gods, but any surplus production was sent back to the state palace/temple complex. Thus, unlike the situation in Mesopotamia, there was a complete identification between the interests of the temple and state in Anatolia, unified in the person of the king.[123]

For Klengel, the unity of palace and temple in Anatolia resulted from its pre-Hittite history. The geography of the Anatolian Plateau encouraged scattered local com-

120 Klengel, "Zur ökonomischen Funktion," 181–83. On the architecture of Hittite temples, see recently Dirk P. Mielke, "Hittite Cities: Looking for a Concept," in *Insights into Hittite History and Archaeology*, eds. Hermann Genz, Dirk P. Mielke (Leuven: Peeters, 2011), 167–70, where he notes that later Hittite temples look like compact, stylized palaces. Both structures tended to be built in prominent, artificially elevated areas of landscape within a city and are difficult to distinguish because of their similar economic functions.

121 Klengel, *op. cit.*, 191.

122 Gregor Giorgadze, "Two Forms of Non-Slave Labour in Hittite Society," in *Labor in the Ancient Near East*, ed. Marvin A. Powell (New Haven, American Oriental Society: 1987), 251–55.

123 Klengel, *op. cit.*, 199. In 1979, Vladimír Souček examined KBo 19.28, a list of temple personnel probably belonging the Temple 1 in Ḫattuša, in which 205 administrative personnel (singer, priests, seers, musicians, and nineteen scribes and thirty-three "scribes on wood") are mentioned. Emphasizing the role of the state in managing the temple, Souček notes that at least some of the temple personnel were NAM.RA "deportees" assigned to the temple by the king. (Vladimír Souček, "Soziale Klassen und Schichten in der hethitischen Tempelwirtschaft," ArOr. 47 [1979]: 78–82.) Alfonso Archi in 1989 penned a short article confirming in philological detail Klengel's assessment of the temple as an arm of the Hittite government. Archi's main argument is that the temples, while possessing economic-administrative structures of their own, were fully integrated and subordinate to the king, and act as centers of redistribution and royal ideology (Alfonso Archi, "Funzioni economiche del tempio ittita," Sc. Ant. 3–4 [1989–90]: 119–25). It should be noted that the English abstract of the article is somewhat misleading when it says "The Hittite temple has 'Oriental' features, in the sense that the important economic-administrative structures were autonomous of the Palace." The structures, i.e., the economic apparatus that allowed the temple to provision its cultic activities, while separate from the Palace were subordinate to it in every way. Finally, Klengel's model was adopted (pp. 327–39) in the overview of the Hittite state in Fiorella Imparati, "Die Organisation des hethitischen Staates," 320–87.

munities and did not permit large collective institutions like the Mesopotamian temples (see discussion of the impact of geography in *2.2.2 Geography of the Anatolian Plateau*). On the positive side, this meant that when the Hittites united Anatolia, they did not have to contend with powerful and independent urban institutions (which would have necessitated a different response, as seen with their later conquests in Syria).[124] The negative side was there was no preexisting system for coordinating the economic surplus of the Anatolian region, and the temple system was an attempt to create one *ex novo*.[125] This description of the Hittite temple as an extractive/redistributive unit resulting from the environmental and political history of the Anatolian Plateau can be called the Klengel hypothesis. It remains the foundation for the current understanding of the role of temples and religion in the Hittite state.

1.8 Conclusions

Klengel refined his model over the next two decades and along with Archi lead a theoretical shift away from the old feudal/two-sector binary to a new discussion based on redistribution, patrimonialism, and bureaucracy.[126] At the same time, Hittite administrative philology enjoyed its second great flourishing with the publication of the Hittite

124 Cf. Gary Beckman, "Hittite Administration in Syria in Light of the Texts from Ḫattuša, Ugarit, and Emar," in *New Horizons in the Study of Ancient Syria*, eds. Marc W. Chavalas, John L. Hayes (Malibu: Undena, 1992), 41–49.

125 Klengel, "Zur ökonomischen Funktion," 200:

> Dem Herrscher der zugewanderten Hethiter, der die politische Gewalt an sich zu bringen vermochte, standen diese Einzelwirtschaften der Leute von GN gegenüber sowie wohl Grosswirtschaften lokaler Dynasten, jedoch, soweit man sehen kann, keine Tempelwirtschaften mesopotamischen Typs. Auf der Grundlage eines Unterwerfungsverhältnisses entstand ein Herrschaftssystem, das im Wesentlichen auf der Nutzung intakter Wirtschaftseinheiten beruhte, deren Leistungsfähigkeit im Interesse des Staates lag und daher von ihm kontrolliert wurde. Die Veränderungen lagen vor allem im Bereich der Distribution; die Existenz der Tempel wurde dabei umso mehr von dem Herrscher abhängig, desto umfangreicher ihre kultischen Aufgaben und damit die kultische Konsumtion wurden. Die Tempel wurden als vorgefundene oder neu gegründete lokale Zentren in dieses Herrschaftssystem voll einbezogen und erfüllten darin eine Funktion.

While Klengel's description is difficult to confirm in the absence of historical sources, the Hittite king's self-promotion as priest of the land very much recalls Max Weber's definition of a "Caeseropapist" society, where the religious structure is fully subordinated to the ruler.

126 See Horst Klengel, "Naturbedingungen und Produktivkraftentwicklung im alten Vorderasien," *Ethnographisch-Archäologische Zeitschrift* 23 (1982): 33–44, in which Klengel grounds his focus on the environment in Marxist materialism; Klengel, "Aspetti dello sviluppo dello stato ittita," in *Stato Economia Lavoro nel Vicino Oriente antico: Atti del convegno promosso dal Seminario di orientalistica dell'Ist. Gramsci Toscano* (Milan: Franco Angeli, 1988), 183–94, where he extends his hypothesis to include an imported, Mesopotamian influenced bureaucracy in the later Hittite state. Finally, Klengel, "Einige Bemerkungen zur Struktur des hethitischen Staates," AoF 30 (2003): 281–89, and Klengel, "Studien zur hethitischen Wirtschaftsgeschichte: Einleitende Bemerkungen," AoF 32 (2005): 3–23, represent the final recapitulations of his thesis, with the latter intended as the introduction to a monograph on Hittite economy that unfortunately was never to appear.

inventory texts[127] and the ration lists of the KI.LAM-festival,[128] among others, as well as the discovery and publication of the Maşat Höyük texts, the first major collection of Hittite texts found outside the capital, which contained a number of local administrative documents.[129] Finally, new archaeological evidence from around the Anatolian Plateau, including many smaller sites, expanded understanding of the conditions of Bronze Age life outside of Ḫattuša. The three trends – theoretical, philological, and archaeological – combined to usher in the current, redistribution-centered era of study of the Hittite state that forms the subject of the next chapter.

127 Silvin Košak, *Hittite Inventory Texts (CTH 241–250)* (Heidelberg: Winter, 1982); Jana Siegelová, *Hethitische Verwaltungspraxis im Lichte der Wirtschafts- und Inventardokumente* (Praha: Národní muzeum v Praze, 1986).

128 Itamar Singer, *The Hittite KI.LAM Festival (Part Two)*. StBoT 28 (Wiesbaden: Harrassowitz, 1984), 139–70.

129 For the letters, which contain interesting evidence of royal intervention in local affairs, see Sedat Alp, *Hethitische Briefe aus Maşat Höyük* (Ankara: Türk Tarih Kurumu, 1991). For the local administrative texts, see Giuseppe del Monte, "I testi amministrativi da Maşat Höyük/Tapika," OrAntMisc. 2 (1995): 89–138.

2. HISTORY OF RESEARCH (II): CURRENT MODELS OF THE HITTITE STATE

2.1 Introduction

Just as "feudalism" was the theme of postwar scholarship on the Hittite state, "redistribution" can be considered the theme of studies today. The terms feudalism and redistribution both serve as convenient lables to explain the system of Hittite government, but on closer analysis both are found to have limitations. Feudalism neglects the importance of slavery to the Hittite economy and assumes sociological features of personal dependence that were not there; redistribution neglects communal self-sufficiency and assumes a level of state economic intervention that is unattested outside of the core regions. But whereas the critique of feudalism ended with a complete rejection of the model no later than the 1980's, perhaps because the Marxist wing of Hittitology that existed at the time would have brooked no less, the concept of redistribution, arising as it does from the more ecumenical fields of anthropology and archaeology, seems to be undergoing a progressive refinement rather than outright rejection (though as will be discussed, the explanatory capacities of redistribution might also be reaching their limits). So, although Hittitologists today no longer speak of feudalism, redistribution is still regarded as a perfectly acceptable function of the Hittite state, if care is taken to specify the *kind* of redistribution, and to what end.

Because the gradual awakening to the limits of an intellectual trend (redistribution) is unfortunately not nearly as compelling a narrative as a clash between political philosophies of East and West (feudalism), the present chapter must eschew the chronological and character-driven structure of the previous chapter. Instead, discussion will proceed topically. Since the influence of the Anatolian environment looms large over modern research on the Hittite state, the sections are organized following the propositions of the Klengel Hypothesis. To recap from the last chapter, these were that the environment of the Anatolian Plateau conditioned a system of weak political integration in the Hittite state based on a redistributive network of palaces and temples. Accordingly, the chapter will be divided into discussions of the current understanding of the interaction of the Hittites with their environment (*2.2 The Hittites and Their Environment*), the resulting impact on political integration (*2.3 Political Integration on the Anatolian Plateau*), and the kinds of redistribution used in the Hittite heartland (*2.4 The Wealth-Financed State*). Finally, a brief overview of the current trends in understanding of the Hittite state and possible future questions will be presented in *2.5 Current Models of the Hittite State: Conclusions and Next Steps.*

The ultimate goal of the chapter is to navigate from the environment and geography of Anatolia to the limited Hittite economic administration reflected in the textual evidence. It will be suggested that the limited scale of direct economic intervention attested can be interpreted as an appropriate response to the geographical conditions in which the Hittite state developed, and not a deficiency in economic-administrative sophistication or evidence for an extensive hidden bureaucracy conducted on a perishable medium.[130] Since a single book chapter is insufficient to discuss a topic as complex and evolving as the impact of environment and geography on the Hittite state, and since so much of the information on the early state in Anatolia is archaeological, and hence beyond the philological scope of the present book, an effort is made instead to direct the reader to the recent literature on the topic. The present chapter cannot of course aspire to contribute to the developing archaeological understanding of the Hittite state, only to serve as a preface to encountering the administrative texts that are the focus of the remainder of the book.

2.2 The Hittites and Their Environment[131]

2.2.1 History of Research

For most of the history of Hittite studies, whenever Hittitologists acknowledged the influence of the Anatolian environment (if they did at all), it was in the negative sense: usually how the unfavorable geographical conditions retarded the growth of a centralized state that could compete with those found in the rest of the ancient Near East. Anatolia is generally lacking in navigable rivers and deep alluvial soils. As has been noted, this puts the Hittites at odds with other "first-wave Old World civilizations" that developed in major river valleys in climatic zones dependent on irrigation.[132] Whereas conditions in Mesopotamia and Egypt promoted centralized, interconnected city-states sustained by irrigation and bureaucracy, "second-wave civilizations" such as Hittite Anatolia were relegated to a precarious existence as dispersed, territorial states

130 That some administration was conducted on perishable (waxed) wooden tablets is not contested, only the assumption that it must have matched the bureaucracy known from Mesopotamia and Egypt.

131 The reader is encouraged to reference Andreas Schachner, "Geographical Prerequisites versus Human Behavior: Settlement Geography, Rural Economy, and Ideological Aspects of Anthropogenic Relations with the Natural Environment during the Second Millennium BC in Central Anatolia," in *Handbook of the Hittite Empire. Power Structures*, ed. Stefano de Martino. Empires through the Ages in Global Perspective 1 (Oldenbourg: De Gruyter, 2022), 159–202, for the most recent comprehensive overview of the topics discussed in the present section.

132 Neil Roberts, "The Land of the Hittites: Airs, Waters and Places," in *Hittite Landscape and Geography*, eds. Mark Weeden, Lee Z. Ullmann, HdO 1/121 (Leiden: Brill, 2017), 17, referencing the earlier "hydraulic civilization" hypothesis of Karl Wittfogel. Although the explanatory power of Wittfogel's theory was challenged (see, among many others, Robert McCormick Adams, "Historic Patterns of Mesopotamian Irrigation Agriculture," in *Irrigation's Impact on Society*, eds. Theodore E. Downing, McGuire Gibson. Anthropological Papers of the University of Arizona 25 [Tucson: University of Arizona Press, 1974], 1–6, who argued that the rigidly bureaucratic state dependent on control of the Mesopotamian alluvium for its existence is not evident in the earliest polities of the ancient Near East), the impact of irrigation on human and state organization in the region is undeniable (see Chapter 5 "Landscapes of Irrigation" in Tony J. Wilkinson, *Archaeological Landscapes of the Ancient Near East* [Tucson: University of Arizona Press, 2003], 71–99, for an impressive guide to the daunting literature on the subject in 20th century archaeology).

dependent on trade with their more established neighbors. Advantages to low centralization can sometimes be acknowledged. For example, Viktor Korošec attributed the comparatively better legal situation of the Hittite slave at least partially to the impossibility of extreme economic concentration and exploitation on the Anatolian Plateau.[133] But, in general, the Hittite Empire's geographic location was seen in past research as perhaps its greatest misfortune.

For decades, from the 1970's to the 90's and early 2000's, Horst Klengel was one of the few Hittitologists to examine the potentially positive impact of the Anatolian environment on the Hittite state, even if his valiant attempt to connect Marxist materialism and environmental studies failed to elicit further work on the environment from other Marxist Hittitologists.[134] Nonetheless, Klengel's earliest work on the topic still emphasized the negative effects of low-density settlement patterns. In his 1975 study on the economics of Hittite temples, for example, Klengel posited that the great difference between the Mesopotamian and Hittite religious systems was the comparative absence of independent "temple-cities" in Anatolia. Whereas Mesopotamia possessed the advantages of economically active religious institutions throughout its history, Hittite temples were mere extensions of the central government. As such, they played no independent role in economic accumulation or innovation, which limited the formation of non-governmental capital and credit. Klengel attributed the absence of temple-cities to the dispersed population of the Plateau, which inhibited the formation of large collective institutions.[135] Klengel's view of an economically inert system of local temples fully subordinate to the central government might be challenged today (temples were in fact vital economic organs of the state),[136] but it must be admitted that the Hittite temple was by no means as independent, as influential, or simply as large as the massive temples of the Mesopotamian world.[137]

The first hint of a positive role for the Anatolian environment came in 1988 in a short article by Klengel on the development of the Hittite state. He argued that the

---

133 Viktor Korošec, "Einige Beiträge zur gesellschaftlichen Struktur nach hethitischen Rechtsquellen," in *Gesellschaftsklassen im Alten Zweistromland und in den angrenzenden Gebieten; XVIII. Rencontre assyriologique internationale, München, 29. Juni bis 3. Juli 1970*, ed. Dietz O. Edzard (Munich: Verlag der Bayerischen Akademie der Wissenschaften, 1972), 111.

134 Horst Klengel, "Naturbedingungen und Produktivkraftentwicklung," 33–44.

135 Horst Klengel, "Zur ökonomischen Funktion der hethitischen Tempel," SMEA 16 (1975): 199–200. See *1.7.3 Klengel: The Palace-Temple Synthesis* in previous chapter for main discussion of this article.

136 Cf. Chapter 6, *Economics of the Local Cults: Offerings and Participants*, in Michele Cammarosano, *Hittite Local Cults*. WAW 40 (Atlanta: Society for Biblical Literature, 2018). For an archaeological perspective, see Suzanne Herbordt, "Die Tempelinventare aus der Oberstadt von Boğazköy/Hattusa: hethitische Tempelanlagen als Kultstätten und Wirtschaftseinheiten," in *Ancient Near Eastern Temple Inventories in the Third and Second Millennia BCE: Integrating Archaeological, Textual, and Visual Sources*, eds. Jean M. Evans, Elisa Roßberger. Münchener Abhandlungen zum Alten Orient 4 (Gladbeck: PeWe-Verlag, 2019), 175–87.

137 On the subordination of the Hittite temple to the Hittite state, see Amir Gilan, "Formen der Transaktion im hethitischen 'Staatskult' - Idee und Wirklichkeit," In *Geschenke und Steuern, Zölle und Tribut*, eds. Hilmar Klinkott, Sabine Kubisch, Renate Müller-Wollermann. CHANE 29 (Leiden: Brill, 2007), 314–18.

short growing season and rich mineral wealth of the Plateau encouraged a focus on metallurgy, and that the scattered communities were conducive to the establishment of local aristocracies specialized in the exchange of accumulated wealth.[138] The influence of metallurgy on Anatolian history had been recognized since the beginnings of Hittitology, at which time metal was identified mostly as a source of trading wealth and military technology.[139] Klengel, however, was the first to argue for a direct link between the environment, metallurgy, and political structure of Anatolia (an argument that would later be developed by K. Aslıhan Yener in expanded and greatly amplified form into her "highland production model").[140] Thus, instead of being a simple brake on the growth of complex states, the environment was depicted as a positive factor insofar as it promoted an alternate, indigenous form of political hierarchy. Klengel still acknowledged an important role for Mesopotamian influence on Anatolian history, in that the Old Assyrian trade colony network accelerated the formation of native competing principalities on the Plateau. Mesopotamia also offered a model for the Hittites on how to break the power of the Anatolian local nobility, most notably when Ḫattušili I's conquests of Syria allowed to him acquire the booty, the alternative religious cults, and a new bureaucracy staffed by Syrian scribes necessary to centralize the state.[141]

Since the 1990's much of the progress in understanding the Hittite state can be attributed to archaeologists. Studies such as Andreas Schachner's systematic investigation of the interaction of the Hittites with their environment, Jürgen Seeher's work on the grain silos of Ḫattuša, Claudia Glatz's work on the archaeological markers of empire, Ulf-Dietrich Schoop and Dirk Paul Mielke and others on Hittite pottery, and Marcella Frangipane on the finance of the Hittite state (all of which, along with others, will be discussed below), have made the 21st century an "archaeologist's century" thus far in the field of Hittitology. The basis of much of the archaeological insight in Anatolia has been the anthropological consequences imposed by the environment: a sort of "history from below" beginning with the land itself. This section will follow the archaeologists' lead, and now begin with a description of the Anatolian Plateau and its anthropological impact.

2.2.2 Geography of the Anatolian Plateau

The landscape of the Anatolian Plateau offers a mosaic-like habitat ranging from semi-arid steppe with hills and scrubby forest, to open parklands, to dense coniferous and

---

138 Horst Klengel, "Aspetti dello sviluppo dello stato ittita," in *Stato Economia Lavoro nel Vicino Oriente antico: Atti del convegno promosso dal Seminario di orientalistica dell'Ist. Gramsci Toscano* (Milan: Franco Angeli, 1988), 184–85.

139 The study of Anatolian metal production goes back at least to Stefan Przeworski, *Die Metallindustrie Anatoliens in der Zeit von 1500–700 v.Chr.: Rohstoffe, Technik, Produktion* (Leiden: Brill, 1939); for a history of the importance of iron in Hittitology, see the introductory chapter of Silvin Košak, *Hittite Inventory Texts (CTH 241–250)*. THeth. 10 (Heidelberg: Winter, 1982); for Hittite metallurgy in general, see Andreas Müller-Karpe, *Altanatolisches Metallhandwerk*. Offa-Bücher 75 (Neumünster: Wachholz, 1994).

140 K. Aslıhan Yener, *The Domestication of Metals: The Rise of Complex Metal Industries in Anatolia* (Leiden: Brill, 2000).

141 Klengel, "Aspetti dello sviluppo," 186–87.

broadleaf forests in the surrounding mountain ranges.[142] Archaeologist Jak Yakar, in his overview of the growth of ancient Anatolian society, divided the area into three zones based on agricultural potential (cf. the illustration *Abb. 44: Karte und Profile der potenziellen natürlichen Vegetation* in Hütteroth and Höhfeld, *Türkei*, 96). To the north, the Plateau contains "a narrow discontinuous belt" along the inner arc of the Pontus Mountains that contains soils and precipitation levels favorable to agriculture.[143] In Hittite times, this fertile zone lay just north of Ḫattuša and seems to have been one of the few regions directly managed by the Hittite state. This fertile area was often contested between the Hittites and Kaška tribesmen because of its agricultural potential and proximity to the refuge of the Pontus Mountains. To the south of the farming belt lay a region, including Ḫattuša itself, defined by moderate rainfall in the fall and spring allowing for the dry farming of various cereals.[144] In Hittite times most of what was designated the "Upper Land" belonged to this region. Archaeological excavations have shown that small-scale irrigation was used in this region to supplement rain-fed agriculture in areas of artificially high population, above all the capital city.[145] Then, beginning with the Kızıl Irmak valley and continuing south and west to the center of the Plateau, the climate becomes arid and the land steppe-like. Agriculture within this zone is precarious, with the land having saline soils that are suitable for wheat and barley if there is sufficient rain for the year, but prone to exhaustion from over-cultivation or over-grazing.[146] The pastures of the region, especially in the colder but wetter higher elevations to the east, support seasonal semi-nomadism.[147] The Hittite "Lower Land" encompassed most of this region. In total, about one-third of the Anatolian Plateau was

---

142 Perhaps the best general overview of the (modern) Anatolian landscape remains the chapter "Klima und Vegetation" (pp. 73–114) in Wolf-Dieter Hütteroth and Volker Höhfeld, *Türkei* (Darmstadt: Wissenschaftliche Buchgesellschaft, 2002). Description of the geographic conditions on the Anatolian Plateau forms something of a genre within Hittitology. In addition to the work of Jak Yakar discussed in this section, the reader can compare Neil Roberts, "The Land of the Hittites: Airs, Waters and Places," in *Hittite Landscape and Geography*, eds. Mark Weeden, Lee Z. Ullmann. HdO 1/121 (Leiden: Brill, 2017), 17–27 for an overview of the central Anatolian environment and its impact on the state during the Hittite period, as well as the relevant portions of Schachner, "Geographical Prerequisites versus Human Behavior." For the economic considerations imposed by central Anatolian environment, cf. also Klengel, "Studien zur hethitischen Wirtschaft," 7–14.

143 Jak Yakar, *Reflections of Ancient Anatolian Society in Archaeology: From Neolithic Village Communities to EBA Towns and Polities* (Istanbul: Homer Kitabevi, 2011), 345. This region corresponds to the *(eu)mediterrane Trockenwälder* (dark blue) and *submediterrane Trockenwälder* (medium blue) patches immediately south of the Pontus range in the map of Hütteroth and Höhfeld, *Türkei*, 96, *Abb. 44.*

144 Yakar, *Reflections*, 345, corresponding to the *supramediterrane Trockenwälder – Waldkiefer, Schwarzkiefer, Flaumeiche* (medium green) region that dominates the map of inland Anatolia in Hütteroth and Höhfeld, *Türkei*, 96, *Abb. 44.*

145 Andreas Schachner, "Hattusa and its Environs: Archaeology," in *Hittite Landscape and Geography*, eds. Mark Weeden, Lee Z. Ullmann. HdO 1/121 (Leiden: Brill, 2017), 40.

146 See Hütteroth and Höhfeld, *Türkei*, 110–11 for description of the mechanism of over-grazing in this region.

147 Roberts, "The Land of the Hittites," 19.

suitable for agriculture and horticulture in ancient times – enough to sustain a good-sized, but dispersed population.[148]

In prehistoric times most of the Plateau was covered by pine forests (*Pinus brutia, P. nigra, P. halepensis*) with interspersed deciduous oaks (mostly *Quercus pubescens*) and junipers (*Juniperus oxycedrus, J. excelsa, J. feotidissima*). Pollen samples found in sedimentary layers of ponds demonstrate that central Anatolia was, on the whole, wetter and more wooded and ecologically diverse than it is today.[149] The forests helped store precipitation and supported a diverse range of wildlife, including game animals such as roe (*Capreolus capreolus*), fallow (*Damus damus*), and red (*Cervus elaphas*) deer (the latter, thanks to its size and impressive antlers, being a popular subject in Anatolian art). Although studies of faunal remains have shown that wild game did not form a significant part of the diet of urban ancient Anatolia,[150] remains of game animals are found at Hittite sites, where they were perhaps regularly delivered to temples to be sacrificed,[151] and one can imagine that Hittite city dwellers would not have rejected wild game as a potential food source during periods of famine.

In terms of settlement patterns, prior to the urbanization and then territorialization of the region during the late 3rd/early 2nd millennium BC as a result of the intensification of trade contacts with Mesopotamia, the Plateau was covered with small settlements. Yakar described these towns as

> hardly more than villages with small residential areas .... The spacing of villages, usually no closer than ca. 4–5 km from each other, would have allowed each small community to develop separate tracts of land for cultivation and pasturage .... According to a rough estimate of 4–5 ha of cultivatable land per household and judging from the spacing of most small EBA sites, it is reasonable to suggest that an average-sized farming village consisted of less than 50 or 40 households.[152]

---

148 Yakar, *Reflections*, 345, corresponding to the *Steppen – winterkühl bis kalt* (dark brown) region in Hütteroth and Höhfeld, *Türkei*, 96, *Abb. 44*.

149 Walter Dörfler, Reinder Neef, and Rainer Pasternak, "Untersuchungen zur Umweltgeschichte und Agrarökonomie im Einzugsbereich hethitischer Städte," MDOG 132 (2000): 367–80.

150 According to Walter Dörfler, Christa Herking, Reinder Neef, Reiner Pasternak, and Angela von den Driesch, "Environment and Economy in Hittite Anatolia," in *Insights into Hittite History and Archaeology*, eds. Hermann Genz, Dirk Paul Mielke (Leuven: Peeters, 2011), 117:

> Hunting contributed insignificantly to the diet of the inhabitants of the different Hittite sites. It can be assumed that hunting was primarily an amusement of the kings and their courtiers, as shown in Hittite and post-Hittite iconography .... This general observation does not rule out the existence of professional hunters who, from time to time, sold game to households, to the court or to the temples (where such meat was part of the offering ceremonies to the gods).

151 For overview of the consumption of wild game in the Hittite world, see Horst Klengel, "Studien zur hethitischen Wirtschaft, 3: Tierwirtschaft und Jagd," AoF 34 (2007), 168–70. For the archaeological presence of wild game in the Lower City of Ḫattuša, including large numbers of red deer (*C. elephas*), but also lions, leopards, and bears, see Angela von den Driesch and Joachim Boessneck, *Reste von Haus- und Jagdtieren aus der Unterstadt von Boğazköy-Ḫattuša. Grabungen 1958–1977.* BoḪa. 11 (Berlin: Mann, 1981).

152 Yakar, *op. cit.*, 436.

The overall effect of the numerous hills, hollows, and original forests of the landscape was to create a dispersed and isolated human geography across the ancient Anatolian Plateau.[153]

2.2.3 Climate of the Ancient Anatolian Plateau

With much of the region under conditions of marginally sufficient rainfall, year-to-year survival on the Anatolian Plateau was sensitive to short- and long-term variations in climate. In modern time, the region has experienced a pattern of drought that leads to poor or catastrophically poor harvests almost every ten years.[154] Although this specific pattern of decadal drought in Turkey dates back probably only to the 18th century AD,[155] there is evidence that ancient Anatolia experienced similar climatic conditions, especially during the Hittite period. Based on sedimentary cores recovered from lake beds at various sites on the Anatolian Plateau, environmental archaeologist Catherine Kuzucuoğlu was able to conclude that:

> the climate in central Anatolia during the whole period of Hittite rise and expansion remains dry, with only three short humid phases between 1650–1550 BC, 1450–1400 BC and 1350–1300 BC. Thus, the central Anatolian regions lived under dry conditions during most the IInd mill. BC, with a few decades-long additional droughts *ca* 1680–1650 BC, 1530–1490 BC, 1380–1350 BC. The longest dry phase is bracketed *ca* 1250 and 1050 BC.[156]

Recognition of the cyclical nature of drought and crop failure in ancient Anatolia is a recent phenomenon. As late as 2005, even Klengel, perhaps the Hittitologist most sensitive to the effects of the environment on the Hittite state, wrote that "Trockenjahre, Dürrekatastrophen oder Schädlingsbefall konnten *zuweilen* [emphasis added] die Ernteerträge beträchtlich mindern und zu Notzeiten führen."[157] Now, however, it is apparent that drought was a *regular* occurrence on the Anatolian Plateau in Hittite times, especially in the latter phases of the kingdom.

---

153 On the tendency of the Anatolian Plateau to produce a diversity and regionalization of political and economic entities, see Ulf-Dietrich Schoop, *Das anatolische Chalkolithikum. Eine chronologische Untersuchung zur vorbronzezeitlichen Kultursequenz im nördlichen Zentralanatolien und den angrenzenden Gebieten* (Remshalden: B. A. Greiner, 2005); also Bleda S. Düring, *The Prehistory of Asia Minor: From Complex Hunter-Gatherers to Early Urban Societies* (Cambridge: Cambridge University Press, 2011).

154 Hütteroth and Höhfeld, *Türkei*, 86–90 (esp. Tab. 1 showing the frequency of crop failure in Turkey from 1928–1961, and Abb. 36 showing the geographical extent of drought and near-drought conditions in Turkey from 1930–1947).

155 Hütteroth and Höhfeld, *op. cit.*, 93–94.

156 Catherine Kuzucuoğlu "The Rise and Fall of the Hittite State in Central Anatolia: How, When, Where, did climate intervene?" in *La Cappadoce méridionale de la Préhistoire à l'époque byzantine: 3e Rencontres d'archéologie de IFEA, Istanbul 8–9 novembre 2012*, eds. Dominique Beyer, Olivier Henry, Aksel Tibet (Istanbul: Institut français d'études anatoliennes, 2015), 27.

157 Klengel, "Studien zur hethitischen Wirtschaftsgeschichte," 13. Earlier, Klengel ("'Hungerjahre' in Ḫatti," AoF 1 [1974]: 165–74) had already argued that "hunger years" were a regular occurrence in Hittite Anatolia, such that mention of crop failure in a Hittite text could not date it to a particular year. Crucially, however, he did not tie the phenomenon to the underlying climatological conditions of Anatolia.

Against the backdrop of drying and drought-prone climatic conditions, an anthropogenic phenomenon known as the Beyşehir Occupation Phase (BOP) spread across Anatolia beginning around 1500 BC.[158] Beginning on the inner slopes of the Taurus mountains in central and southern Anatolia, the BOP is the archaeological signal of an economic system in which forest was cleared from most of Anatolia to make way for cereal, livestock, and tree crop production,[159] and was subsequently kept clear by the intensive grazing of sheep and goats.[160] The overall effect of widespread deforestation was to make the region more susceptible to the long-term patterns of cyclical drought, though the impact varied according to local climatic conditions and agricultural practices. It is tempting to draw a connection between the introduction of the BOP economic system, subsequent environmental degradation, and the eventual collapse of the Hittite state at the end of the Bronze Age (ca. 12th century BC). However, caution is warranted, since other regions of Anatolia continued to employ and even expand upon the BOP well into the Iron and Classical Ages. As Kuzucuoğlu emphasized:

> This 1500 yr-long continuity [of the BOP] demonstrates the capacity of this production system to resist to climatic change. It also shows that the impacts of climate changes on a production system depend on the organization and technics of the rural management. It also evidences the importance of the maintenance of resources diversity. When dependent on a large centralized political authority (in a "capital" such as Hattusa for example), the centralization would have reverse impacts on this sustainability in case climate change modifies the availability vs. types of resources.[161]

Kuzucuoğlu instead argued that it was what she perceived as the rigidity of the Hittite centralized management of food resources and its failure to adapt to changing climatic conditions by taking advantage of new or diversified agricultural resources that resulted in the collapse of the Hittite state. However, there may also have been some bad luck involved, in that the Hittite imperial heartland lay in the north of the Plateau, where the drought was not only the most intense and longest, but also the environment

---

158 For the Beyşehir Occupation Phase in Anatolia in general, see Willem van Zeist, Henk Woldring, and Dick Stapert, "Late Quaternary Vegetation and Climate of Southwestern Turkey," *Paleohistoria* 17 (1975): 55–143; Sytze Bottema and Henk Woldring, "Late Quaternary Vegetation and Climate of Southwest Turkey II," *Paleohistoria* 26 (1984): 123–49; Sytze Bottema, Henk Woldring, and Burhan Aytuğ, "Palynological Investigations on the Relations Between Prehistoric Man and Vegetation in Turkey: The Beyşehir Occupation Phase," *Proceedings of the 5th Optima Congress, Sept. 1986* (Istanbul: İstanbul Üniversitesi, Fen Fakültesi, 1993), 315–28; Sytze Bottema and Henk Woldring, "Anthropogenic Indicators in the Pollen Record of the Eastern Mediterranean," in *Man's role in the shaping of the Eastern Mediterranean Landscape*, eds. Sytze Bottema, Gertie Entjes-Nieborg, Willem van Zeist (Rotterdam: Balkema, 1990), 231–64; Warren J. Eastwood, Neil Roberts, and Henry Lamb, "Paleoecological and Archaeological Evidence for Human Occupance in Southwest Turkey: The Beyşehir Occupation Phase," AnSt. 48 (1998): 69–86.

159 Ünal Akkemik, Hülya Caner, Grace A. Conyers, Matthew J. Dillon, Nurgül Karlıoğlu, Nicholas K. Rauh, and Lawrence O. Theller, "The Archaeology of Deforestation in South Coastal Turkey," *International Journal of Sustainable Development and World Ecology* 19/5 (2012): 1–11. For deforestation during the Hittite period see Nathan J. Wright, Andrew S. Fairbairn, J. Tyler Faith and Kimiyoshi Matsumura, "Woodland Modification in Bronze and Iron Age Central Anatolia: An Anthracological Signature for the Hittite State?," JArS 55 (2015): 219–30.

160 von den Driesch and Pöllath, *Vor- und frühgeschichtliche Nutztierhaltung*, 37.

161 Kuzucuoğlu, "The Rise and Fall of the Hittite State," 35.

was least amenable to the required agricultural flexibility. It would have been furthermore ideologically impossible, or at least very difficult, to move the Hittite capital, as Andreas Schachner's research on the aggrandizement of Old Kingdom Ḫattuša suggests (see *2.3.3.1 Anatolian Regionalism – Hittite Identity à la carte* below). In contrast, the ecologically and hydrologically diverse southern Plateau – which included, crucially, mountain streams running on to the plains and depositing alluvial fans that stored water in easily accessible soil – allowed for a greater continuity of political-economic structures.[162]

2.2.4 Modes of Subsistence on the Anatolian Plateau

Because of the uneven productivity of the soil and the precariousness of rain-fed agriculture, survival for the populations that dwelled on the Plateau prior to industrialized agriculture required a diversified and extensive, as opposed to specialized and intensive, approach to food resources.[163] One way to diversify was to place equal emphasis on herding and farming, i.e., the so-called agropastoral mode of subsistence, named after the two loci of production, that survived with remarkable continuity in the region from the Neolithic to Ottoman times.[164] In the agropastoral system, in good years, grain provides the higher return on investment. In drought years, livestock can be driven to regions of higher precipitation, which often lay in the neighboring highlands. Agropastoralism often goes hand-in-hand with seasonal semi-nomadism, whereby almost entire villages will summer in mountain pastures (Turkish *yayla*), a practice which survived in Anatolia until recent time.[165] Then, in worst case scenarios, such as when a landscape becomes unproductive, whether through seasonal variation, soil exhaustion,

162 Kuzucuoğlu, "The Rise and Fall of the Hittite State," 37. For an alternate summary of the impact of climate in the Hittite period, see the section "Climate Change and its Consequences" in Roberts, "The Land of the Hittites," 22–25. Note that Roberts (p. 24) situates the introduction of the BOP into most of Anatolia *after* the collapse of the Hittite Kingdom, seeing the Hittite state instead as the final, and ultimately unsustainable, stage of a Bronze Age economic system. In Roberts' interpretation, the Hittites maintained an artificially high population in central Anatolia through military coercion, which overtaxed the environment in the drought period at the end of the Kingdom. Although not an implausible component of what was a multi-causal chain of events, the interpretation misses the fact that the BOP signal is observable at almost every Hittite site during the Late Bronze Age (see Fig. 8: "The Beyşehir Occupation Phase (BOP) in Turkey" in Kuzucuoğlu, *op. cit.*, 30–31), possibly – or even probably – due to promotion of the economic system by local elites (Kuzucuoğlu, *op. cit.*, 29).

163 See Chapter 3 "Ein Leben auf des Messers Schneide: die naturräumlichen Bedingungen Zentralanatoliens" in Andreas Schachner *Hattuscha. Auf der Suche nach dem sagenhaften Großreich der Hethiter* (München: Beck, 2011).

164 On methods for measuring the importance of agropastoralism for a given era, see Naomi Miller, "From Food and Fuel to Farms and Flocks: The Integration of Plant and Animal Remains in the Study of Ancient Agropastoral Economies at Gordion, Turkey," CA 50 (2009): 915–24; Naomi Miller and John Marston, "Archaeological Fuel Remains as Indicators of Ancient West Asian Agropastoral and Landscape Use Systems," *Journal of Arid Environments* 86 (2012): 97–103.

165 See Hütteroth and Höhfeld, *Türkei*, 146–48 for the ethnographic perspectives on *Yaylabauerntum*. For the practice of this form of seasonal nomadism to the Hittite period, see Jak Yakar, *Ethnoarchaeology of Anatolia. Rural Socio-Economy in the Bronze and Iron Ages*. Tel Aviv Mon. Ser. (Jerusalem: Emery and Claire Yass Publ. in Archaeology, 2000), 276–78.

or a catastrophe such as a multi-year drought, populations in the marginal landscapes of central Anatolia could pick up and move to a better location.[166]

Here it is important to keep in mind that the needs of the Hittite state and the needs of the Anatolian people did not always coincide. In contrast to the state, which aimed to maximize the extraction and mobilization of resources, preindustrial "peasant economies" – to use the term employed by Marshall Sahlins in his book *Stone Age Economics* – such as would have dominated the Hittite hinterlands (i.e., what the Marxist Hittitologists discussed in *1.5 The Italian School* would call the communal sector), placed the self-sufficiency of the household unit first and foremost as the goal of production. According to Sahlins, peasant economy households tend to strive towards what he termed the Domestic Mode of Production, where households grow or manufacture as many of the necessities of life as possible using the skills and labor of the immediate family.[167] Although it is most readily observed in "traditional" societies, the Domestic Mode's mindset of self-sufficiency is not in itself innate or traditional, but a calculated reaction to the high transaction costs of infrequent interactions with a market economy. While there is no direct data for private households during the Hittite period,[168] the slim agricultural margins of the landscape, low population density, and the lack of navigable rivers that precluded the development of a robust market economy such as occurred in Mesopotamia in some periods would all have favored the Domestic Mode of

166 Here Andreas Schachner ("Das 16. Jahrhundert v. Chr. – eine Zeitenwende im hethitischen Zentralanatolien," IstM 59 [2009]: 20–21), in an intentional echo of Hütteroth, has the turn of phrase to describe the relation of the Hittite Anatolian peasant to the state:

> Da Landwirtschaft fast überall in Anatolien möglich war, bestand nur eine vergleichsweise schwache Bindung des Bauern an seine Scholle. Bei mangelnder Fruchtbarkeit konnte man leicht neue Flächen in anderen Regionen urbar machen. Gleiches gilt für politischen Druck oder staatliche Ausbeutung, denen man sich durch Umsiedlung oder eine Rückkehr zu nomadischen Lebensformen relativ leicht entziehen konnte. Dies bedeutet für einen Staat, daß er die Balance zwischen der Produktivität des Landes, dessen Ausbeutung und der Kontrolle über die Bauern halten mußte.

In this geographic reality, it is no wonder that the Hittites were, as will be discussed, so sensitive to emigration and population movement.

167 See Chapters 2 and 3 in Marshall Sahlins, *Stone Age Economics* (New York: Aldine De Gruyter, 1972).

168 For indirect evidence of the economic disposition of the Hittite household, see Horst Klengel, "The Economy of the Hittite Household (É)," *Oikumene* 5 (1986): 23–31, which draws from Hittite government sources to confirm a picture of the Anatolian household as a diversified, agropastoral economic unit with distributed fields and a basic household size of 7–10 people. Klengel argued that the household structure predated Hittite expansion and was co-opted relatively intact by the state. For further thoughts on the private Anatolian household in Hittite times, see also Jörg Klinger, "Hittite Economics," in *Handbook of the Hittite Empire. Power Structures*, ed. Stefano de Martino. Empires through the Ages in Global Perspective 1 (Oldenbourg: De Gruyter, 2022), 609–619. Cf. also the comments of archaeologist Christoph Bachhuber on the agrarian focus of Anatolian life, noting that "Assyrian trading enterprise was brought to a standstill during the cereals harvest in the summer and the grape harvest in the fall .... Similarly, nearly all references to property in the Hittite laws are farm-related and rural .... The Hittite laws were meant to govern the farming hinterland" (Christoph Bachhuber, "The Anatolian Plateau," in *A Companion to the Archaeology of the Near East*, ed. Daniel T. Potts [Oxford: Wiley-Blackwell, 2012)], 577).

Production in Hittite Anatolia.[169] It is not impossible that Bronze Age households and villages participated in some sectors of the interregional economy, especially metallurgy;[170] but these were the exceptions, rather than the rule, at the domestic level.

2.2.5 Strategies for Communal Self-Sufficiency

The drive for self-sufficiency in ancient peasant economies was not restricted to the household unit, but also extended to long-standing relationships beyond the immediate family, i.e., to the community. Communal survival strategies were especially important in marginal landscapes like Anatolia, where households pool resources with neighboring villagers – who, given the stability of village life, were probably related by blood anyhow – in order to mitigate risk. The resulting interdependence can often be observed in the architectural record, tending to generate nucleated settlement patterns such as the compact, agglutinated villages attested in ancient Anatolia. Communal interdependence also creates an economy at least partially regulated by social norms. In other words, self-sufficiency at the village level implies the use of social currency in addition to market resources. The social dimensions of communal exchange allow for behaviors like altruism that were vital for survival in times of disaster. But socially regulated exchange is permeated by politics to a far greater extent than exchange conducted within a market economy, so that power and coercion were implied by the survival strategies of even the smallest village. As was discussed in the previous chapter on the origins of the economic inequality that in the Bronze Age led to the rise of the Palace sector (see *1.5.1 Liverani: A Strongly Dichotomous Two-Sector Model*), neighbors borrowing in times of need may incur debt, social or otherwise, that can never be repaid, leading to ties of semi-feudal dependence or debt-slavery *in extremis*. In short, it can be assumed that there was already a link between environment, communal survival strategies, and the expression of political power in ancient Anatolia at the level of subsistence.

The relationship between food production and political power is one of the central questions pursued by Timothy Earle, an economic anthropologist who studies subsistence, specialization, and exchange in early complex societies. Earle is best known for his work on the Incan Empire and Hawaiian chiefdoms, but his theoretical insights apply just as well to the Hittites (as recognized by Marcella Frangipane, who used an article of Earle's on Incan finance strategies in discussing the Hittite state – see *2.4.1*

169 For examples of a market economy in the Neo-Babylonian periods based on date production – and the vital importance of rivers for transporting bulk goods to large urban markets –, see especially Chapter 4 of Michael Jursa, *Aspects of Economic History of Babylonia in the First Millennium BC*. AOAT 377 (Münster: Ugarit-Verlag, 2010).

170 It has long been thought that a reference in an Egyptian-Hittite letter to seasonal iron production is result of cottage industry economics: see KBo 1.14, a letter from Ḫattušili III to an Assyrian king, and background discussion of Hittite metal industry in Jana Siegelová and Hidetoshi Tsumoto, "Metals and Metallurgy in Hittite Anatolia," in *Insights into Hittite History and Archaeology*, eds. Hermann Genz, Dirk P. Mielke (Leuven: Peeters, 2011), 282. As discussed in *2.4.2 Wealth Finance and Hittite Metal Production* below, the work of Yener and Lehner, among others, suggests that the extreme localization of primary metal production can be traced back to regional, even village-level traditions of metallurgy.

Staple Finance, Wealth Finance below). In his book *Bronze Age Economics*, based on three decades of case studies and theory and titled as a conscious reference to Sahlins' *Stone Age Economics*, Earle endeavors to explain the connection between village economies and chiefdoms/early kingdoms.[171] He began by outlining three common strategies for self-sufficiency at the village/community level: diversification, overproduction, and communal storage. Diversification includes not only flexibility in the choice of plant varieties to cultivate, but also a drive to exploit a range of different geographies. In a case study from precolonial Hawaii, Earle showed that communities will try to control, exploit, and defend the full range of ecological niches in their vicinity rather than attempting to specialize. Thus, the same village will be involved in growing cereals and catching fish in nearby rivers, herding livestock at higher altitudes, and hunting game and gathering plants in the forest. This drive towards diversification contradicts a previous anthropological model that posited community specialization – e.g., pure pastoralists trading with pure farmers – as the catalyst for the evolution of social complexity. Earle notes that local specialization is not impossible, since a community will take advantage of an especially abundant local resource for trade purposes (indeed, this seems to be exactly the case for certain Middle Bronze Age Anatolian villages located near tin mines, where surplus levels of tin were produced for export without any need for a central state).[172] But in general, and returning to the principle of self-sufficiency, villages (strive to) trade for luxuries and not necessities.

In addition to diversification, the two other strategies for self-sufficiency discussed by Earle are overproduction and communal storage. Villages will strategically overproduce more foodstuffs than needed for survival in order to increase the margin for error. In good years, the surplus above that needed for storage could be consumed in communal feasts. In bad years, the extra food is consumed right away to make up for caloric shortfalls and the remainder put into storage. Storage can be private or communal (and usually a mix of both), but communal storage has the advantage of sharing risk and minimizing conflict between the have and have-nots of a particular year's harvest. Communally stored food will be placed in a central and defensible location where many observers can keep watch.

All three strategies of diversification, overproduction, and communal storage were present in Anatolia at the time of the Hittites. For evidence of nutritional diversification, paleobotanical research at Boğazköy-Ḫattuša,[173] Kuşaklı-Šarišša,[174] Kaman-Kale-

171 Timothy Earle, *Bronze Age Economics: The Beginnings of Political Economies* (Boulder, Colorado: Westview Press, 2002).

172 Yener, K. Aslıhan, Fikri Kulakoğlu, Evren Yazgan, Ryoichi Kontani, Yuichi S. Hayakawa, Joseph W. Lehner, Gonca Dardeniz, Güzel Öztürk, Michael Johnson, Ergun Kaptan, and Abdullah Hacar, "New Tin Mines and Production Sites Near Kültepe in Turkey: A Third-millennium BC Highland Production Model." *Antiquity* 89 (345) (2015): 596–612.

173 Rainer Pasternak, "Vorbericht über die archäobotanischen Arbeiten in Ḫattuša 2009–2011," ArchAnz. 1/2012 (2012): 110–14.

174 Rainer Pasternak, "Übersicht über die Ergebnisse der archäobotanischen Arbeiten in Kuşaklı 1994–1997 und ein Interpretationsansatz zu den Befunden," MDOG 130 (1998): 160–170. Also: Pasternak, "Archäobotanische Arbeiten 1999: Die Bearbeitung eines Massenfundes von Gersten im Nordflügel des Gebäudes C," MDOG 132 (2000): 348-351.

höyük,[175] Gordion,[176] and elsewhere show that, over and above the general principles of agropastoralism, inhabitants of the Anatolian Plateau also hedged against the decadal droughts through a diversification of cereals (reliable barley besides high-yield but fragile wheat) and pulses (bitter vetch besides lentils).[177] Diversification is also observed in faunal remains (mostly sheep, goat, and cattle).[178] Here, as might be expected, relative levels of economic security played a role in choice of diet. At Ḫattuša, the provisional picture of the spatial, temporal, and socio-economic distribution of faunal remains shows that goats were consumed in larger numbers by the poorer segments of the city, probably as a result of their relatively low investment costs.[179] In contrast, sheep and cattle were consumed by the rich, with prize rams and bulls kept for religious sacrifice and festival consumption.[180] Data from smaller settlements, such as Kaman-Kalehöyük, Lidar Höyük, and Çadır Höyük, which perhaps better reflect the pre-Hittite milieu of diversification, show pigs being raised, while the big cities such as Ḫattuša were fed by a centralized sheep/goat/cattle economy.[181]

---

175 Andrew Fairbairn, "Crop Storage at Kaman-Kalehöyük. Some Preliminary Observations," *Kaman-Kalehöyük* 14 = *Anatolian Archaeological Studies* 14 (2005): 129-135.

176 John Marston, "Agricultural Strategies and Political Economy in Ancient Anatolia," AJA 116/3 (2012): 387–90.

177 For textual evidence of the diversity of Hittite plant-based foodstuffs, see Harry A. Hoffner, Jr., *Alimenta Hethaeorum. Food Production in Hittite Asia Minor.* AOS 55 (New Haven: American Oriental Society, 1974); Hoffner, "Alimenta Revisited," in *Akten des IV. Internationalen Kongresses für Hethitologie: Würzburg, 4.–8. Oktober 1999*, ed. Gernot Wilhelm. StBoT 45 (Wiesbaden: Harrassowitz, 2001), 199–212; and Klinger, "Hittite Economics," 611–12.

178 Dörfler et al., "Environment and Economy in Hittite Anatolia," 115–17. A list of primary studies of zooarchaeological data from the Hittite period may be found in Rémi Berthon, "Herding for the Kingdom, Herding for the Empire. The contribution of zooarchaeology to the knowledge of the Hittite economy," in *Innovation versus Beharrung: Was macht den Unterschied des hethitischen Reichs im Anatolien des 2. Jahrtausends v. Chr.? Internationaler Workshop zu Ehren von Jürgen Seeher, Istanbul, 23–24. Mai 2014*, ed. Andreas Schachner. Byzaz 23 (Istanbul: Deutsches Archäologisches Institut, 2017), 182.

179 Daria Hollenstein and Geraldine Middea, "The Faunal Remains from the Square Building Horizon in the Valley West Sarıkale, Boğazköy-Ḫattuša, Turkey (16th/15th Century BC)," in *Ausgrabungen und Forschungen in der westlichen Oberstadt von Ḫattuša I*, eds. Andreas Schachner, Jürgen Seeher. BoḪa. 24 (Berlin: De Gruyter, 2016), 178–80.

180 Angela von den Driesch and Nadja Pöllath, *Vor- und frühgeschichtliche Nutztierhaltung*, 18; Dörfler et al., "Environment and Economy in Hittite Anatolia," 116. Whereas the ram was the sacrificial animal most favored in Hittite temples, cattle are also attested at elevated concentrations compared to the general archaeological context.

181 Berthon, "Herding for the Kingdom," 180. Cf. also the "ethnographic" disparagement of the Kaška as "swineherds," as discussed in Claudia Glatz and Roger Matthews, "Anthropology of a Frontier Zone: Hittite-Kaška Relations in Late Bronze Age North-Central Anatolia," BASOR 339 (2005): 57; cf., however, the interpretation of N. İlgi Gerçek, "The Kaška and the Northern Frontier of Ḫatti" (PhD diss., University of Michigan, 2012), 41–42, that the reference to the Kaška as swineherds in Muršili II's Hymn and Prayer to the Sun-goddess of Arinna (CTH 376) emphasizes only their role as suppliers of agricultural and animal products as tribute to the Hittite state, and by extension, the cult of the Sun-goddess of Arinna. Such an interpretation better matches the archaeological data for a rural/urban, rather than ethnic, divide for the consumption of pork in the Anatolian hinterlands.

Nutritional diversification was also responsive to climatic and political changes in ancient Anatolia. It seems that a more drought-tolerant breed of cattle spread across the region during the drought period at the end of the Late Bronze Age.[182] It has also been noted in excavations at Kaman-Kalehöyük that animal consumption patterns adapted to the economic insecurity after the end of the Hittite Empire, with low-investment animals such as goats becoming preferred over sheep and cattle.[183] If, as the evidence suggests, this trend towards low-investment animals was resisted at Ḫattuša, it may be due to the special importance placed on cattle by the remaining Anatolian elites in the city, and no doubt the remaining concentration of religious institutions at Ḫattuša, where cattle were valued as sacrificial animals.[184]

Geographical diversification, where a village seeks to dominate multiple ecological niches, is more difficult to estimate for ancient Anatolia. The range of biomes exploited by a settlement can ideally be estimated by floral and faunal remains, but it is difficult to distinguish between food acquired by cultivation and that obtained through trade (which, if improbable for bulky cereals, is more conceivable for the more mobile livestock "on the hoof"). Future studies based on GIS surveys might be able to better determine boundaries of settlements and agricultural exploitation in Anatolia.

Overproduction, as reflected in the form of feasting, was also prevalent in Hittite society. Whereas the best evidence for feasting comes from the state festivals, there also exists a stratum of Anatolian local cults recorded in the Hittite archives in which feasting and celebration were, if anything, even more important. As shown by Michele Cammarosano, these indigenous, non-state festivals were distinguished by joy and communal celebration to a greater degree than the more grandiose and spectacular state festivals.[185] It is also hypothesized that they functioned at least in part as "work feasts" for the local communities.[186] That the local cults reflect pre-Hittite customs is almost certain given their highly individualized rites: it is unlikely that a such a varied

182 For evidence of the introduction of zebu cattle, see Glatz and Matthews, "Anthropology of a Frontier Zone," 58.

183 Hitomi Hongo, "Continuity or Changes: Faunal Remains from Stratum IId at Kaman-Kalehöyük," in *Identifying Changes: The Transition from Bronze to Iron Ages in Anatolia and Its Neighbouring Regions. Proceedings of the International Workshop, Istanbul, November 8–9, 2002*, eds. Bettina Fischer, Hermann Genz, Éric Jean, Kemalettin Köroğlu (Istanbul: Türk Eskiçağ Bilimleri Enstitüsü, 2003), 257–69. See also Salima Ikram, "A Preliminary Study of Zooarchaeological Changes between the Bronze Age and Iron Ages at Kinet Höyük, Hatay," in the same volume, pp. 283–94.

184 Benjamin S. Arbuckle, "The Rise of Cattle Cultures in Bronze Age Anatolia," *Journal of Eastern Mediterranean Archaeology & Heritage Studies* 2/4 (2014): 277–97. For the persistence of cattle culture at Ḫattuša, see Angela von den Driesch and Nadja Pöllath, "Changes from Late Bronze Age to Early Iron Age Animal Husbandry as Reflected in the Faunal Remains from Büyükkaya/Boğazköy-Ḫattuša," in *Identifying Changes: The Transition from Bronze to Iron Ages in Anatolia and Its Neighbouring Regions. Proceedings of the International Workshop, Istanbul, November 8–9, 2002*, eds. Bettina Fischer, Hermann Genz, Éric Jean, Kemalettin Köroğlu (Istanbul: Türk Eskiçağ Bilimleri Enstitüsü, 2003), 295–99; von den Driesch and Joachim Boessneck, *Reste von Haus- und Jagdtieren aus der Unterstadt*; and von den Driesch and Pöllath, *Vor- und frühgeschichtliche Nutztierhaltung*.

185 Michele Cammarosano, *Hittite Local Cults*. WAW 40 (Atlanta: Society for Biblical Literature, 2018), 103–5.

186 Cammarosano, *Hittite Local Cults*, 155–58.

set of practices would have been invented by the Hittite state, given the marked tendency towards regularization otherwise observed.

2.3 Political Integration on the Anatolian Plateau

2.3.1 Basis of the Hittite State in Communal Antecedents

Having traced the connection between the Anatolian environment and communal self-sufficiency, the interaction of the Hittite state with the subsistence practices of the Anatolian village remains to be explored. Here it is useful to consider that the "high" economic features of a given society tend to reflect, consciously and unconsciously, the conditions of its basic economic unit. This point was made in detail by David Schloen, an archaeologist specializing in Bronze and Iron Age Syro-Palestine, who argued that for much of Mesopotamian history the patriarchal extended household, what he called "the house of the father," was not only the economic basis of the state but also the conceptual and symbolic model for legitimate authority – what in Weberian terms is referred to as patrimonialism.[187] Mesopotamian rulers used the language of patrimonialism because it took advantage of a potent symbol of authority familiar to every Assyrian, Amorite, or Canaanite in their land. Moreover, Schloen argued, it was more than just a metaphor, but quite simply the only language available at the time to describe a position of compassionate-but-absolute authority.

The heart of Schloen's thesis, and what distinguishes "the house of the father" from earlier Weberian patrimonialism, is the hermeneutic-phenomenological observation that ancient states did not just reflect the economic conditions of their subjects, but also reshaped them by symbolically and factually amplifying the inherited activities useful to the state and suppressing (or monopolizing) activities that are threatening. This matches exactly the selective manipulation of the communal survival strategies observed in the case of the Hittite state. As will be shown, the Hittites adapted the village-level subsistence strategies of communal storage and overproduction to a state-wide scale, resulting in a peak of civilizational complexity on the Anatolian Plateau that was not achieved again until perhaps the Ottoman period. At the same time, population movement was strictly controlled and necessary agricultural diversification was suppressed (see above Kuzucuoğlu's assessment of the effects of the Beyşehir Occupation Phase in northern Anatolia), leading to regional resistance and ecological fragility that ended in the complete disappearance of the Hittite economic system within two to three generations after the fall of the Kingdom. These two outcomes of Hittite state intervention, namely economic boon and regional resistance, are presented below.

2.3.2 Hittite State Intervention as a Necessity: The Schachner Thesis

The current director of excavations at the Hittite capital of Ḫattuša-Boğazköy, Andreas Schachner, has postulated that Hittite state intervention on the Anatolian Plateau did

187 David Schloen, *House of the Father as Fact and Symbol* (Winona Lake: Eisenbrauns, 2001).

not just control preexisting settlements, but actually increased the urban population of the region above what could have been sustained without it. According to Schachner, Hittite state intervention took the form of a threefold cultural-technological "package" that is observable at almost every urban site on the Plateau during the Hittite period: grain silos, artificial dams and ponds, and monumental architecture, most visibly in the form of temples and settlement walls.[188] The purpose of these urban elements was to encourage the concentration of the Anatolian population into controllable settlements,[189] and indeed the combination was so ubiquitous that Schachner has suggested it may very well have constituted what the Hittites considered a city.[190]

The technological innovations of large-scale grain silos and dam building during the Hittite period, coupled with long-term trends that predated or coincided with the establishment of the Hittite state, namely the development and increasing sophistication of Anatolian hieroglyphics, the wide-spread use of stamp seals, the development of Hittite ceramics, art, and monumentality, the introduction of cuneiform, religious centralization, and finally the "peace dividend" earned by the unification of central Anatolia in the Old Hittite period, led to an increase in population and production surplus on the Anatolian Plateau.[191] Whereas it had long been recognized that the Hittites built upon the Anatolian basis which they inherited through unification and conquest, it is what may be called the *Schachner Thesis* that the Hittites did not just harness, but in fact created the Anatolian efflorescence observed in the Late Bronze Age. As Schachner wrote:

> so wird eine deutliche Steigerung der gesamtgesellschaftlichen und wirtschaftlichen Effizienz und Integration in ein einheitliches politisches und kulturelles System erkennbar, die offensichtlich durch den Staat implementiert wurde. Diese Entwicklung ist jedoch nicht monokausal auf die Verbesserung in einem bestimmten Bereich zurückzuführen. Vielmehr ermöglichte erst das Zusammenwirken technischer, sozialer und organisatorischer Innovationen sowie die Kontrolle von deren Umsetzung diese Steigerung der gesamtgesellschaftlichen Effizienz, die die Grundlage für den

188 See now Andreas Schachner, "Building for King and Country: Architecture as a Symbol of the Hittite Empire," in *Handbook of the Hittite Empire. Power Structures*, ed. Stefano de Martino, Empires through the Ages in Global Perspective 1 (Oldenbourg: De Gruyter, 2022), 421–66, for the most recent discussion of Hittite monumental architecture as a cornerstone of power.

189 Andreas Schachner, "Das 16. Jahrhundert v. Chr. – eine Zeitenwende," 18–21.

190 Andreas Schachner, "Von einer anatolischen Stadt zur Hauptstadt eines Großreichs – Entstehung, Entwicklung und Wandel Hattušas in hethitischer Zeit," *Mesopotamia* 46 (2011): 98. Schachner considered that:

> ist noch unklar, ob sich die hethitische Stadt durch eine festgelegte Kombination bestimmter Bauwerke auszeichnete .... Doch deuten die überregional einheitlichen Bauformen der Tempel, der Befestigungsanlagen und anderer offizieller Gebäude ebenso wie die Existenz von Wasserreservoiren und Getreidespeichern in den meisten der im 16. Jahrhundert v. Chr. neu gegründeten Siedlungen auf einen vergleichbaren Kanon und einen bis dato unbekannten zentralisierten Urbanismus in der hethitischen Großreichszeit hin, demzufolge bestimmte Gebäudeensembles im hethitischen Sinne eine Stadt ausgemacht haben könnten.

191 Schachner, "Das 16. Jahrhundert v. Chr. – Eine Zeitenwende," 25.

kulturellen Höhepunkt bildete, den die hethitische Großreichszeit in der Kulturgeschichte Zentralanatoliens darstellt.[192]

This model of a Ḫattušan urbanism leading and stimulating the development of the Anatolian Plateau stands in stark contrast to earlier models.[193] Schachner went on to describe Hittite efforts at cultural and economic centralization as a kind of "nation building" (p. 26) that allowed the Plateau to escape, for a period of time, the low population density and regionality conditioned by its climate and topography. As Schachner concluded in a separate article, the fact that architectural changes in Hittite Anatolia are only observable in monumental or representative buildings, while being hardly perceptible in the buildings of day-to-day life, makes it clear that the changes were driven by the ideology of the Hittite ruling dynasty and imposed from Ḫattuša.[194]

The three economic elements of the Hittite cultural/technological package proposed by Schachner, namely the grain silos, dams, and feasting (as a proxy for temples), will now be briefly presented in more detail.

2.3.2.1 Food Storage and Grain Silos

Food storage changed greatly in Anatolia in the transition from the Middle to Late Bronze Age. Private household storage was reduced, while institutional storage at temples and palaces using pithoi was amplified. Excavations of private residences are limited, but both Middle Bronze Age (MBA) Kültepe-Kaneš and MBA Boğazköy-Ḫattuša show evidence of extensive household storage,[195] whereas private storage in the Late Bronze Age (LBA) Hittite period is limited in volume and extent.[196] Conversely, the

192 Schachner, "Das 16. Jahrhundert v. Chr. – Eine Zeitewende," 26. See further Schachner, "Motor oder Bremse? Die Rolle der hethitischen Hauptstadt Hattuša für die Transformation des hethitischen Reichs," in *Innovation versus Beharrung: Was macht den Unterschied des hethitischen Reichs im Anatolien des 2. Jahrtausends v. Chr.? Internationaler Workshop zu Ehren von Jürgen Seeher, Istanbul, 23–24. Mai 2014*, ed. Andreas Schachner. Byzas 23 (Istanbul: Deutsches Archäologisches Institut, 2017), 220–21. Here, Schachner described the process as an economic and social system that for four centuries was capable of overcoming the "glass ceiling" (a term borrowed from Ian Morris) imposed by the Anatolian environment on population density and social complexity.

193 Cf. e.g., Horst Klengel, "Hattuša: Residence and Cult-Centre," in *Towns as Regional Economic Centre in the Ancient Near East (10th International Economic History Congress)*, eds. Erik Aerts, Horst Klengel (Leuven: Leuven University Press, 1990), 45-50, where Ḫattuša is a locus of consumption and religious/ideological production. This perspective of ancient Near Eastern urbanism is very much in line with Carlo Zaccagnini's neo-Asiatic Mode of Production discussed in Section 1.5.2 above.

194 Schachner, "Motor oder Bremse?," 234.

195 For Kültepe-Kaneš, see Tahsin Özgüç, *Kültepe. Kaniş/Neşa: The Earliest International Trade Center and the Oldest Capital City of the Hittites* (Ankara: The Middle East Culture Center in Japan, 2003), 88–90. At Boğazköy-Ḫattuša, see Andreas Schachner, *Von der Rundhütte zum Kaufmannshaus: Kulturhistorische Untersuchungen zur Entwicklung prähistorischer Wohnhäuser in Zentral-, Ost- und Südostanatolien* (Oxford: Oxford University Press, 1999), 116; and Néhémie Strupler, "Vorratshaltung im mittelbronzezeitlichen Boğazköy – Spiegel einer häuslichen und regionalen Ökonomie," IstM 63 (2013): 21–30.

196 It has been noted at Ḫattuša that large household pithoi, well-attested from EBA to the early Hittite Old Kingdom, are replaced by a kind of medium-sized storage jar (Ulf-Dietrich Schoop, "Indication of Structural Change in the Hittite Pottery Inventory," in *Central-North Anatolia in the Hittite Period: New Perspectives in Light of Recent Research (Acts of the International Conference Held at the University*

system of institutional pithoi and sealing bullae discovered at MBA Acemhöyük,[197] Kültepe-Kaneš,[198] and Boğazköy-Ḫattuša[199] was greatly expanded in the LBA, as is demonstrated by the over 100 pithoi, ranging in size from 900 to 1750 liters, discovered at LBA Boğazköy-Ḫattuša.[200]

The principal marker of institutional storage in LBA Anatolia is the grain silo. Archaeological evidence shows that the massive subterranean grain silo complex at Boğazköy-Ḫattuša dating to the Old Hittite Kingdom period could have fed up to 20,000–30,000 people for a year.[201] The silo complex represented the apex of Hittite grain storage techniques and was perhaps intended to show off royal wealth. Ironically, the great size of the silo complex may also have been its weakness, since it was replaced by a series of dispersed, smaller silos after it burnt down in a catastrophic fire the 16th cent. BC.[202] Similar, though proportionally smaller, grain silos were also found at Alacahöyük,[203] Kaman-Kalehöyük,[204] Kuşaklı-Šarišša,[205] and Oymaağaç-Nerik.[206] It has been observed that the grain silos were unlikely to have been entirely filled and emptied every year: the grain was kept in sealed pits, creating a cool, low-oxygen environment that facilitated conservation for at least ten to fifteen years – a period that recalls exactly the pattern of decadal drought observed for Anatolia.[207] The long-term

---

of Florence (7–9 February 2007)), eds. Franca Pecchioli Daddi, Giulia Torri, Carlo Corti (Roma: Herder, 2009), 151–52). Schoop interprets this as reflecting "a change in household economy from bulk storage to middle-range storage. The situation implies that there must have existed a now secure and permanent supply from a more central source .... It is tempting to see a connection with the large grain silos identified as such in Hattuša and other Hittite centres recently, even if most of these will have played a role outside daily supply in Hittite economy" (Schoop, "Structural Change," 152).

197 Nimet Özgüç, "Seal Impressions from the Palaces at Acemhöyük," in *Ancient Art in Seals*, ed. Edith Porada (Princeton: Princeton University Press, 1980), 6–100 (discussion of bullae pp. 61–69).

198 Cf. the discovery of three large pithoi announced in a news article, "Giant amphoras unearthed in Kültepe," Hurriyet Daily News, last modified September 24, 2015, https://www.hurriyetdailynews.com/giant-amphoras-unearthed-in-kultepe--88905.

199 Strupler, "Vorratshaltung im mittelbronzezeitlichen Boğazköy," 31–39.

200 Peter Neve, "Der Große Tempel und die Magazine," in *Boğazköy IV: Funde aus den Grabungen 1967 und 1968*, ed. Kurt Bittel. ADOG 14 (Berlin: Mann, 1969), 12–17.

201 Jürgen Seeher, "Getreidelagerung in unterirdischen Großspeichern: Zur Methode und ihrer Anwendung im 2. Jahrtausend v. Chr. am Beispiel der Befunde in Hattuša," SMEA 42/2 (2000): 261–301; Reinder Neef, "Getreide im Silokomplex und der Poternenmauer (Boğazköy) – erste Aussagen zur Landwirtschaft," ArchAnz. 2001/3 (2001): 335–41; Jürgen Seeher, "Der althethitische Getreidekomplex," in *Ergebnisse der Grabungen an den Ostteichen und am mittleren Büyükkale-Nordwesthang in den Jahren 1996–2000*, ed. Jürgen Seeher. Boğazköy-Berichte 8 (Mainz: von Zabern, 2006), 45–84.

202 Charlotte Diffey, Reinder Neef, Jürgen Seeher, Amy Bogaard, "The Agroecology of an Early State: New Results from Hattusha," *Antiquity* 94/377 (2020): 1220.

203 Seeher, "Getreidelagerung," 291. See also Aykut Çinaroğlu and Elif Genç, "Alaca Höyük ve Alaca Höyük hitit barajı kazıları, 2002," *Kazı Sonuçları Toplantısı* 25/1 (2003): 279–88.

204 Andrew Fairbairn and Sachihiro Omura, "Archaeological Identification and Significance of É.SAG (agricultural storage pits) at Kaman-Kalehöyük, Central Anatolia," AnSt. 55 (2005): 15–23.

205 Walter Dörfler, Reinder Neef, and Rainer Pasternak, "Untersuchungen zur Umweltgeschichte und Agrarökonomie im Einzugsgebiet hethitischer Städte," MDOG 132 (2000): 367–78.

206 Jana Richter, "Spätbronzezeitliche Bebauung: das Silo," MODG 148 (2016): 38–42.

207 Seeher, *op. cit.*, 268.

storage provided by the grain silos suggests that they were used for emergencies, and not for the regular provisioning of the state apparatus as was previously thought, this being perhaps the function of the institutional pithoi and the smaller storage pits.[208]

Contrary to previous assumptions that the enormous silos of Ḫattuša were filled using an extensive extractive network,[209] it now seems more likely that Ḫattuša's grain silos were filled using local sources for local purposes, especially if the grain was intended as an emergency reserve. It has been estimated that the 7000–9000 m^3 of storage space in the Old Hittite silo complex at Ḫattuša could have stored between 5512 and 7087 tons of cereal grain.[210] Using yields of 1200 kg/ha barley based on early 20th century data from Çorum province in Turkey, where Ḫattuša is located, this volume could have been be filled using grain from just one year's cultivation of 46–59 km^2 of land,[211] i.e., in ideal terms, a circle of land around Ḫattuša with a radius of no more than 4.33 km. Of course, not all land around Ḫattuša can be farmed, but even doubling the radius of cultivation to a still modest 8.66 km requires only one quarter of the area to be arable. Moreover, archaeobotanical research on the carbonized mixture of grains and weeds recovered from the burnt silos has shown that the grain must be of local, Anatolian origins.[212] The general impression given by the contents of the silos is that the silos were filled with grain produced through extensive, but low-intensity local agriculture from a wide variety of sources in the hinterland of Ḫattuša, i.e., either from taxes on small farmers,[213] or from compulsory labor on dispersed crown estates.[214]

Despite their ubiquity in the Hittite period, large grain silos are unattested in the MBA period, at least on a scale detectable in the archaeological record. Nevertheless, it is clear that the Hittite subterranean silos developed from preexisting Anatolian technology. Anthropological parallels discussed by Seeher suggest that the storage of grain in cool, hypoxic conditions was a relatively widespread ancient technology,[215] and Ulf-Dietrich Schoop has noted that storage in subterranean pits predates even pithoi technology in EBA Anatolia,[216] with excavations at, e.g., Resuloğlu showing that modestly sized, defensible grain silos were placed in the center of the settlement in the EBA.[217] What changed was that a previously modest practice was enlarged and institution-

---

208 Charlotte Diffey, Reinder Neef, and Amy Bogaard, " The Archaeobotany of Large-scale Hermetic Cereal Storage at the Hittite capital of Hattusha," in *Innovation versus Beharrung: Was macht den Unterschied des hethitischen Reichs im Anatolien des 2. Jahrtausends v. Chr.? Internationaler Workshop zu Ehren von Jürgen Seeher, Istanbul, 23–24. Mai 2014*, ed. Andreas Schachner. Byzas 23 (Istanbul: Deutsches Archäologisches Institut, 2017), 195–97.

209 Cf. Bachhuber, "The Anatolian Plateau," 580: "By the late Early Hittite period most of the AP had become a kind of farming hinterland of the capital Boğazköy-Hattusha."

210 Seeher, "Der althethitische Getreidekomplex," 49.

211 Diffey, et al. "The agroecology of an early state," 1219.

212 Diffey, et al. "The archaeobotany of large-scale hermetic cereal storage," 191.

213 Diffey, et al. "The agroecology of an early state," 1219–20.

214 Klinger, "Hittite Economics," 624.

215 Seeher, "Getreidelagerung", 261–68.

216 Schoop, "Structural Change," 151–52.

217 Tayfun Yıldırım and Aslı Kısa, "Çorum/Resuloğlu 2014 yılı kazıları," *Çorum Kazı ve Araştırmalar Sempozyumu* 5 (2015): 97–104.

alized. As succinctly expressed by Jürgen Seeher: "Das Wissen um die Vorteile dieser Methode der Vorratshaltung stammt zwar aus sehr viel früherer Zeit, aber der Wille, Großspeicher anzulegen, muß aus der Entwicklung komplexerer Gesellschaftsformen und der ersten größeren Herrschaftsgebiete hervorgegangen sein."[218] The institutionalization of the grain silos on the Anatolian Plateau seemingly ended with the Hittite state, with the silos at Boğazköy-Ḫattuša filled in and built upon in the immediate post-Hittite period before the final abandonment of the city.[219]

2.3.2.2 Dams and Artificial Ponds

Dams or artificial ponds represent a second form of communal storage sponsored by the Hittite state, with examples found outside the walls at Boğazköy-Ḫattuša, Kuşaklı-Šarišša, and Ortaköy-Šapinuwa.[220] There is some evidence that smaller-scale water management systems such as cisterns and water pipes were used in Anatolia prior to the Hittites.[221] However, unlike the grain silos, the dams and artificial ponds seemed to have been a pure innovation of the Hittite state, with the first sophisticated clay-core dam appearing no earlier than the 16th cent. BC.[222] The clay-core dams were used to create artificial ponds that stored large volumes of non-potable water. Experimental archaeology has shown that the ponds filled gradually with groundwater seeping from wells cut into shallow aquifers.[223] The ponds were primarily used to water gardens and orchards, to support the intensive cultivation of nearby meadows, and to supply drinking water for livestock, especially cattle and horses.[224] In non-urban contexts, such as Yalburt and Eflatun Pınar, ponds with adjacent monuments were established at key locations for the dual purposes of providing water reserves for livestock and laying

218 Seeher, "Der althethitische Getreidekomplex," 81.

219 Seeher, "Getreidelagerung", 298. See also Jürgen Seeher, "Die Zerstörung der Stadt Ḫattuša," in *Akten des IV. Internationalen Kongresses für Hethitologie. Würzburg, 4.-8. Oktober 1999*, ed. Gernot Wilhelm. StBoT 45 (Wiesbaden: Harrassowitz, 2001), 62–64.

220 See literature in Andreas Schachner and Hartmut Wittenberg, "Zu den Wasserspeichern in Boğazköy/Hattuša und der Frage ihrer Befüllung," in *Wasserwirtschaftliche Innovationen im archäologischen Kontext: Von den prähistorischen Anfängen bis zu den Metropolen der Antike*, eds. Florian Klimscha, Ricardo Eichmann, Christof Schuler, Henning Fahlbusch (Rahden/Westf.: Leidorf, 2012), 245–56.

221 Andreas Hüser, *Hethitische Anlagen zur Wasserversorgung und Entsorgung* (Rahden/Westf.: Leidorf, 2007), 176 (cisterns), 209 (water pipes).

222 Hüser, *Hethitische Anlagen zur Wasserversorgung und Entsorgung*, 148.

223 Kutlu Emre, "The Hittite Dam of Karakuyu," in *Essays on Anatolian Archaeology*, ed. H. I. H. Prince Takahito Mikasa, (Wiesbaden: Harrassowitz, 1993), 1–42; Hartmut Wittenberg, "Capture and Management of Ground and Stratum Water in the Hittite Empire – Technology and Cultural Significance," in *Innovation versus Beharrung: Was macht den Unterschied des hethitischen Reichs im Anatolien des 2. Jahrtausends v. Chr.? Internationaler Workshop zu Ehren von Jürgen Seeher, Istanbul, 23–24. Mai 2014*, ed. Andreas Schachner. Byzas 23 (Istanbul: Deutsches Archäologisches Institut, 2017), 167.

224 Jürgen Seeher. "Die hethitischen Ostteiche," in *Ergebnisse der Grabungen an den Ostteichen und am mittleren Büyükkale-Nordwesthang in den Jahren 1996–2000*, ed. Jürgen Seeher. Boğazköy-Berichte 8 (Mainz: von Zabern, 2006), 1–23; Wittenberg, "Capture and Management of Ground and Stratum Water," 170.

ideological claim to the surrounding landscape.[225] In urban contexts, it has been demonstrated that at the provincial center of Kuşaklı-Šarišša, the dams and pipes were constructed as a unified water management system at the same time that the city was founded.[226] The dams needed to create the large artificial ponds were essentially coterminous with the Hittite state, and fell out of use in Anatolia after its collapse, presumably due to the loss of the technical knowledge necessary to construct and maintain the dams.[227]

2.3.2.3 Festival and Feasting

Like the grain silos, religious festivals also show evidence of being a preexisting Anatolian practice greatly amplified in service of the state. Judging from administrative records, feasting was a cornerstone of the Hittite state.

The Hittite archives abound in festival texts scripting the performance and provisioning of religious ceremonies carried out as part of the state cult, and describe large quantities of foods being distributed to the participants.[228] The festival participants were at least in part local Anatolians drawn from towns across the Anatolian Plateau and were supplied food and presumably lodging for the duration of the celebrations.[229] State festival texts are among the most numerous genres in the Hittite corpus: Theo van den Hout has counted twenty-two festival texts out of the total of forty-nine compositions with duplicates (i.e., the "permanent records" of the Hittite chancery) written

---

225 At Yalburt, see the work of the Yalburt Yaylası Archaeological Landscape Research Project (website: yalburtproject.org), including Ömur Harmanşah, et al. "Lake-Places, Local Hydrology, and the Hittite Imperial Projects in the Ilgın Plain: Yalburt Yaylası Archaeological Landscape Research Project 2015–2016 Seasons," in *The Archaeology of Anatolia Volume II. Recent Discoveries (2015–2016)*, eds. Sharon R. Steadman, Gregory McMahon (Newcastle upon Tyne: Cambridge Scholars Publishing, 2017), 302–320, where it is established that the pool at Yalburt Yaylası was part of a larger, locally sponsored but imperially managed regional hydrological project that included a clay-core dam at Köylütolu Yayla and a fortress supplied by a canalized spring at Kale Tapesi. For Eflatun Pınar, see Martin Bachmann and Sırrı Özenir, "Das Quellheiligtum Eflatun Pınar," ArchAnz. 2004/1 (2004): 85–122, for the consolidation of decades of research on the monument.

226 Hüser, *Hethitische Anlagen zur Wasserversorgung und Entsorgung*, 134–47.

227 Hüser, *op. cit.*, 148.

228 See the discussion of the *MELQĒTU* lists in Itamar Singer, *The Hittite KI.LAM Festival* (Part Two). StBoT 28 (Wiesbaden: Harrassowitz, 1984), 157–70. See now also James M. Burgin, "Hittite Ration Lists Revisited: The Old and Middle Hittite Ration Text Corpus," in *Proceedings of the 10th International Congress of Hittitology, August 28–September 1, 2017, Chicago* (Chicago: Oriental Institute, forth.), and Jana Siegelová, "Naturalabgaben für den Kult und für Kulteinrichtungen des hethitischen Reiches," in *Economy of Religions in Anatolia: From the Early Second to the Middle of the First Millennium BCE. Proceedings of an International Conference in Bonn (23rd to 25th May 2018)*, eds. Manfred Hutter, Sylvia Hutter-Braunsar. AOAT 467 (Münster: Ugarit-Verlag, 2019), 103–12.

229 For discussion of one such example of religious "draft," see Ian Rutherford, "Women Singers and the Religious Organisation of Hatti. On the Interpretation of CTH 235.1&2 and Other Texts," in *Offizielle Religion, locale Kulte und individuelle Religiosität*, eds. Manfred Hutter, Sylvia Hutter-Braunsar. AOAT 318 (Münster: Ugarit-Verlag, 2004), 377–94. The women singers were usually daughters or servants of well-connected men living in or within a short journey Ḫattuša. Rutherford suspects that the presence of stereotyped personnel lists indicated Hittite religious festivals were not celebrated by permanent temple staff but rather by local citizens fulfilling obligatory religious service.

in the New Script of the Hittite Empire period,[230] and it has been estimated that festival texts and fragments comprise up to 40% of the entire Hittite corpus.[231]

In the absence of written records it is impossible to estimate the frequency and economic burden of religious festivals in the earlier trade colony period (and its immediate aftermath), but the local nature of the appropriately named "local cults" attested in Hittite records, which were possessed of innumerable minor gods and geographical hypostases, suggests that the festivals were inherited from diverse and preexisting Anatolian traditions.[232] The system of cultic provisioning for *state* festivals, however, was deemed by Itamar Singer, in a 1984 article stemming from his work on the KI.LAM festival, as unlikely to have predated the Hittite state.[233] Hittite festival texts show that food supplies for many of the festivals were managed by the ^{LÚ}AGRIG. The ^{LÚ}AGRIG was a palace servant and nominal member of the royal household, classified in the younger Laws as a slave, albeit with additional rights.[234] The ^{LÚ}AGRIG-s were not normally appointed from members of the nobility or royal family, and rather seem to have been drawn from among important local Anatolians, who, based on the Telepinu Edict, accumulated considerable economic power in the countryside in the exercise of their office.[235] The ^{LÚ}AGRIG was responsible for maintaining two storehouses: one in his home town (some forty "AGRIG towns" are recorded, all within the Hittite heartland), and one in Ḫattuša. Singer hypothesized that the twinned storehouses were the basis of an extractive system, with the ^{LÚ}AGRIG collecting and storing foodstuffs in the local storehouse before importing it to Ḫattuša, where the ^{LÚ}AGRIG features in many festival

230 Theo van den Hout, "Administration in the Reign of Tuthaliya IV and the Later Years of the Hittite Empire," in *The Life and Times of Ḫattušili III and Tuthaliya IV. Proceedings of a Symposium Held in Honor of J. de Roos, 12–13 December 2003*, ed. Theo van den Hout. PIHANS 103 (Leiden: NINO, 2006), 83.

231 Gerfrid G. W. Müller, *apud* Daniel Schwemer, "Quality Assurance Mangers at Work: The Hittite Festival Tradition," in *Liturgie oder Literatur? Die Kultrituale der Hethiter im transkulturellen Vergleich. Akten eines Werkstattgesprächs an der Akademie der Wissenschaften und der Literatur Mainz, 2.–3. Dezember 2010*, ed. Gerfrid G. W. Müller. StBoT 60 (Wiesbaden: Harrassowitz, 2016), 7.

232 See Michele Cammarosano, "Hittite Cult Inventories – Part Two: The Dating of the Texts and the Alleged 'Cult Reorganization' of Tudḫaliya IV," AoF 39/1 (2012): 16–21 and Cammarosano, *Hittite Local Cults*, 111–14 ("5.3 Unity and Diversity: Antiquity of the Festivals, Cult Evolution and Transformation").

233 Itamar Singer, *The Hittite KI.LAM Festival*. StBoT 27–28 (Wiesbaden: Harrassowitz, 1983–84). Itamar Singer, "The AGRIG in the Hittite Texts," AnSt. 34 (1984): 97–127. See also Stefano de Martino, "Hatti: From Regional Polity to Empire," in *Handbook of the Hittite Empire. Power Structures*, ed. Stefano de Martino, Empires through the Ages in Global Perspective 1 (Oldenbourg: De Gruyter, 2022), 221–22, for the contextualization of the AGRIG-system in the reign of Telipinu. Although it is impossible to prove, the same may be assumed to apply to the local cults in which the Hittite state took interest, where the intervention and systemization of the state was not always in harmony with local needs (see "6. Economics of the Local Cults: Offerings and Participants," in Cammarosano, *Hittite Local Cults*, 139–58, esp. 155–59).

234 Singer, "The AGRIG in Hittite Texts," 100–1.

235 Singer, *op. cit.*, 105–6.

texts as distributing foodstuffs for the participants.[236] According to Singer, the AGRIG-system was not a remnant of Hattian administration, but rather an innovation of an expanding Hittite state: his reasoning turns on the philological grounds that while the ^{LÚ}AGRIG is always named by his hometown and the Hattian gentilic suffix *-il*, the AGRIG towns are also found outside the Hattian linguistic area; the "Hattianness" of the AGRIG system is in other words only a by-product of its being set up early in the Hittite Kingdom's history.[237] The presumed absence of a preexisting *regional* system of religious festivals is consistent that fact that temples in MBA Anatolia are not attested as owning land or accumulating the large agricultural surpluses of the LBA period.[238]

In sum, the grain silos and religious festivals suggest that the Hittite state adapted local survival strategies, either attested in pre-Hittite Anatolia or recognizable from anthropological parallels, or amplified them, as with the new technologies of clay-core dams and artificial ponds vis-à-vis the earlier cisterns and water pipes, as part of government programs designed to further the economic and ideological integration of the state. Thus, some of the most conspicuous features of what it meant to be "Hittite" in day-to-day life, i.e., the intense and diverse calendar of festivals, the massive grain storage silos and large artificial ponds, stem directly from the environment of the Anatolian Plateau. However, despite its recognizably Anatolian character, the Hittite state was not the inevitable apotheosis of the Anatolian way of life. Rather, it was selective in the strategies it appropriated and those which it suppressed, and as will be seen, regionalism remained a problem within the confines of the Plateau.

2.3.3 Anatolian Regionalism and Resistance: The Glatz Corollary

Anatolian archaeologist Claudia Glatz, in an innovative research program on the Hittite state culminating in a recent book on Hittite imperialism,[239] has taken as her central argument that Hittite control of the Anatolian Plateau was an ongoing, contested project throughout Hittite history. Her thesis measured Hittite domination of Anatolia and Syria using a set of imperial markers, namely a particular settlement pattern, a style of pottery, Anatolian glyptics, and landscape monuments, that were simultaneously imposed by imperial agents and selectively adopted by imperial subjects.[240] The

236 Singer, "The AGRIG in Hittite Texts," 111–13. Singer cautioned that only the distributive, and not extractive, responsibilities of the ^{LÚ}AGRIG are recorded in the Hittite archives. It seems that taxation occurred at the local level.

237 Singer, *op. cit.*, 126–27. Singer considered his point proved by attestations of AGRIG's with Hattian gentilics coming from towns far outside of the Hattian cultural area. This shows that the "Hattianness" of the AGRIG's resulted from their appearance in the Hattian liturgy of the early Hittite festivals.

238 See Bachhuber, "The Anatolian Plateau," 578 ("... temples appear to have been marginal in most aspects of the productive and commercial life of Kanesh."), also citing Jan G. Dercksen, *Old Assyrian Institutions*. PIHANS 98 (Leiden: Nederlands Instituut voor het Nabije Oosten, 2004), 139, for absence of MBA temple land ownership.

239 Claudia Glatz, *The Making of Empire in Bronze Age Anatolia. Hittite Sovereign Practice, Resistance, and Negotiation* (Cambridge: Cambridge University Press, 2020).

240 Claudia Glatz, "Empire as Network: Spheres of Material Interaction in Late Bronze Age Anatolia," *Journal of Anthropological Archaeology* 28 (2009): 129.

core of Anatolia was defined by the presence of all four markers, whereas peripheral regions such as Kizzuwatna (Cilicia), Išuwa (eastern Anatolia), and the Near West of Anatolia (the Luwian vassal-states) lacked the particular settlement pattern, despite experiencing an intensive hegemony. Ugarit and Amurru showed indirect control, adopting glyptics, while coastal western Anatolia exhibited a limited veneer of control of marked only by outposts of landscape monuments in the form of rock reliefs.[241]

2.3.3.1 Anatolian Regionalism – Hittite Identity à la carte

While the Hittite imperial project was negotiated between rulers and subjects, the terms could vary from imposition to free adoption. The clearest case of imposition is the change in settlement pattern between Middle Bronze and Late Bronze Age Anatolia. This took the form of a network of cities newly founded (or refounded) at strategic sites across the Plateau during the transition from the Old to Middle Hittite period.[242]

At the center of the network of Hittite cities stood Ḫattuša. The capital vastly differed in size and quality from the other cities on the Plateau. While others have argued that the Hittite "capital" followed the king to wherever he temporarily resided,[243] Andreas Schachner has persuasively shown that the varied and unique monumental architecture of Ḫattuša, found nowhere else in the Hittite world, incontrovertibly marked the city out as the center of kingly legitimation.[244] According to Schachner, Ḫattuša was reshaped during the 16th century, and aggrandized "von einer bis in alt-hethitische Zeit organisch gewachsenen, anatolischen Stadt zu einer nach ideologischen Vorstellungen gestalteten Metropole."[245] Schachner connected this to the rise of the Hittite dynasty, noting that:

241 See especially figs. 9 and 10 in Glatz, "Empire as Network," 137–38.

242 See Dirk Paul Mielke, "Hittite Settlement Policy," in *Places and Spaces in Hittite Anatolia I: Hatti and the East. Proceedings of an International Workshop on Hittite Historical Geography in Istanbul, 25th–26th October 2013*, ed. Metin Alparslan (Istanbul: Türk Eskiçağ Bilimleri Enstitüsü, 2017): 13–27. Mielke described (p. 18) a general trend of fewer but larger settlements sites in the Middle and Late Bronze Age compared to before and afterwards on the Anatolian Plateau. Some settlements such as Kuşaklı-Šarišša were founded in new, strategically defensible but economically marginal locations that could not have sustained urbanism without the "cultural package" of water storage, grain silos, city walls, and temples identified by Schachner ("Das 16. Jahrhundert v. Chr. – eine Zeitenwende," 16–18). As Mielke concluded (p. 21) concerning Hittite settlement policy: "Trying a characterization, we can attest a massively state-controlled settlement policy, which was extremely engaged in the lives and the existence of the population."

243 See most recently Piotr Taracha, "The Capital Hattuša and Other Residential Cities of Hittite Great Kings," in *Belkıs Dinçol ve Ali Dinçol'a Armağan. VITA: Festschrift in Honor of Belkıs Dinçol and Ali Dinçol*, eds. Metin Alparslan, Meltem Doğan-Alparslan, Hasan Peker (Istanbul: Ege Yayınları, 2007), 755–59.

244 Andreas Schachner, "Von einer anatolischen Stadt zur Hauptstadt eines Großreichs – Entstehung, Entwicklung und Wandel Hattušas in hethitischer Zeit," *Mesopotamia* 46 (2011): 99.

245 Schachner, "Das 16. Jahrhundert v. Chr. – eine Zeitenwende," 16. On the novelty of Hittite representative architecture in general vis-à-vis earlier Anatolian traditions, see Andreas Schachner, "Auf welchem Fundamenten? Überlegungen zum Stand der Erforschung der hethitischen Architektur," in *Strukturierung und Datierung der hethitischen Archäologie: Voraussetzungen – Probleme – Neue Ansätze. Internationaler Workshop Istanbul, 26–27. November 2004*, eds. Dirk Paul Mielke, Ulf-Dietrich

> bereits im ausgehenden 17. Jh. v. Chr. mit einer ideologischen Kriterien unterworfenen und großräumig angelegten Umgestaltung der Stadt begonnen wurde. Die textlichen Belege für diese Zeit sind nur schwach, können aber als Indiz dafür gewertet werden, daß diese bewußt gesetzten Veränderungen der bis dahin traditionellen städtebaulichen Entwicklung mit der sich in dieser Zeit neu etablierenden, hethitischen Dynastie und deren Institution zu verbinden ist.[246]

Although all Hittite cities shared an architectural palette, Ḫattuša was at this time endowed with monumental architecture that differentiated it even from other Hittite cities, and with the close identification of Ḫattuša with the Hittite dynasty, the capital became ideologically indispensable.[247]

The importance of this new style of urbanism to Hittite control of Anatolia should not be underestimated. As observed by Gary Beckman, "the network of cities with Ḫattuša at its head constituted the armature of the Hittite state in Anatolia," and further: "If the system of cities was constitutive of state power, a lack of cities indicated the absence of control."[248] Beckman went on to note that Hittite cities were planned or refounded by the state, and pointed out:

> We might also recall in this regard that the Kaškaean chieftain Piḫḫuniya sought to eradicate Hittite influence in territory he had conquered by reducing the captured town of Ištitina to his 'grazing ground' (*wišiyaūwaš pēdan*). Conversely, when a Hittite ruler such as Šuppliluliuma I wrested a region from the barbarians, his first act was to re-establish state authority through the (re-)settling of *ḫappiriya*-'s. An interesting fragment of an instruction deals with the engineers who are commanded by the king to construct a city 'in the foremost march'. Through such activity the authority of Ḫatti would be restored or extended.[249]

The function of these new Anatolian cities seems to have been at least in part to establish a capillary system of extraction, above all of mineral wealth and other trade goods such as wool, but also the mobilization of manpower, as discussed by Jana Siegelová in her analysis of Hittite local palaces in the textual sources.[250]

At the same time, Glatz's survey of archaeological sites suggested a concerted program of de-urbanization on the Anatolian Plateau at the beginning of the Hittite Empire, and possibly progressing by stages to peripheral areas with the growth of the

---

Schoop, Jürgen Seeher. Byzas 4 (Istanbul: Deutsches Archäologisches Institut, 2006), 149–66; and again most recently, Schachner, "Building for King and Country."

246 Andreas Schachner, "Die Ausgrabungen in der Unterstadt von Ḫattusa (2009–2014): erste vorläufige Ergebnisse," in *Sacred Landscapes of Hittites and Luwians. Proceedings of the International Conference in Honour of Franca Pecchioli Daddi. Florence, February 6th–8th 2014*, eds. Anacleto D'Agostino, Valentina Orsi, Giulia Torri. St. Asiana 9 (Firenze: Firenze University Press, 2015), 73.

247 In addition to Büyükkale ("Der königliche Palast auf Büyükkale" in Schachner, *Hattuscha*, 136–53), see the collection of *sui generis* structures such as Yerkapı, the gates and city walls, and the numerous built-up rocky outcroppings throughout the city discussed in "Weitere repräsentative, staatliche Gebäude in Hattuscha" in Schachner, *Hattuscha*, 153–72. See further discussion in Schachner, "Motor oder Bremse?," 226–32.

248 Gary Beckman, "The City and the Country in Hatti," in *Landwirtschaft im Alten Orient. Ausgewählte Vorträge der XLI. Rencontre Assyriologique Internationale Berlin, 4.–8.7.1994*, eds. Horst Klengel, Johannes Renger (Berlin: Reimer, 1999), 168.

249 Beckman, "The City and the Country in Hatti," 168–69.

250 Jana Siegelová, "Der Regionalpalast in der Verwaltung des hethitischen Staates," AoF 28/2 (2001): 193–208.

state. Reductions in settlement sizes had been observed by earlier archaeologists (Ron Gorny had even speculated that destruction of walls and reduction in size in the Middle Bronze to Late Bronze Age transition at Alişar Höyük was a direct consequence of Hittite rule),[251] but Glatz argues that the phenomenon was a regionally significant trend. Cities that were the seats of principalities in the Assyrian Trade Colony period were reduced in size and systematically demoted in the settlement hierarchy in favor of secondary sites. The new centers of administration were smaller, ranging between 10 and 20 ha in size, e.g., Kuşaklı-Šarišša (18.2 ha intramural) and Maşat Höyük-Tapikka (ca. 8 ha), compared to MBA Karahöyük-Konya (39 ha) and Acemhöyük (44 ha). Only five Anatolian settlements "transgressed" the 20 ha threshold in the Hittite period: their size was presumably limited by comparison to Ḫattuša, which had only 30 ha of inhabited space, the remaining 120 being for monumental purposes.[252] At the same time there was a corresponding increase in the number of small rural settlements. Glatz considered the reasons for the break-up of the urban settlements to have been as much symbolic as practical, and to have been used by the Hittites to send "a strong symbolic message of the shift of power from a local to a spatially more extensive polity."[253] The program of "ruralization" was restricted to the Anatolian Plateau, but Hittite imperial influence affected settlement patterns also in neighboring areas. Kizzuwatna and Išuwa, while not showing the same restriction on large settlements, demonstrated an increase in the number of small, unwalled settlements during the Hittite period, perhaps as a result of improved regional security.[254] Conversely, the Kaškaen frontier in the Pontic zone was severely depopulated and settlements reduced to a line of compact fortified towns.[255]

A more ambiguous case of imperial imposition is the case of Anatolian pottery during the Hittite period. The interpretation of the Hittite ceramic tradition has been one of the most controversial topics of Anatolian archaeology in the past two decades.[256] The basic problem is explaining the relationship between the remarkable uniformity of the Anatolian ceramic assembly and the growth of the Hittite state. By the time of the Hittite New Kingdom, Anatolian pottery was restricted to utilitarian assemblage sometimes called "Gray Drab Ware" that showed almost no regional or chronological variation. The periodization of Anatolian pottery is similarly unusual, showing two discontinuities. Ceramicist Ulf-Dietrich Schoop describes the situation thus:

> Following up a line of essentially unbroken cultural continuity, we are able to observe the transformation of a comparatively simple late Early Bronze Age society into an urban civilisation within a territorial state. Within this general movement towards increasing complexity, two emergent

251 Ronald Gorny, "Hittite Imperialism and Anti-Imperial Resistance as Viewed from Alishar Höyük," BASOR 299–300 (1995): 74–76.

252 Glatz, "Empire as Network," 132.

253 Glatz, *op. cit.*, 133.

254 Glatz, *loc. cit.*

255 Glatz, *op. cit.*, 134.

256 See the overview of this topic in Dirk Paul Mielke, "Hittite Pottery: Research, Corpus and Social Significance," in *Handbook of the Hittite Empire. Power Structures*, ed. Stefano de Martino, Empires through the Ages in Global Perspective 1 (Oldenbourg: De Gruyter, 2022), 649–90, esp. 676–82, where the social significance of Hittite pottery assemblage is discussed.

> patterns appear to be of special significance. The first would be that the Assyrian Colony period and the early part of the Old Hittite period seem to belong together and to be set apart from later times by a set of changes in the 16th century. The second would be the rapid formation of what we could call an Empire Period pattern of (pottery) economy around 1400 BC and the subsequent slackening of further change.[257]

In the Early Bronze Age, prior to the Assyrian Trade Colony period, Anatolian pottery was handmade and probably produced at the household level. The wares were carefully burnished, decorated with ornaments and colored slips (mostly red, sometimes white), and sometimes with painted motifs.[258] The Assyrian Trade Colony period (Middle Bronze Age) introduced the potter's wheel, but otherwise the pottery was the same (as Schoop the change as "a strong cultural continuity combined with technological discontinuity").[259]

Pottery seems to have changed little between the end of the Assyrian trade colony period and the beginnings of the Hittite state in the 17th century, but by the 16th century there is a significant winnowing of the ceramic assemblage as formal variations are rationalized to single types.[260] Decorative slips became rare, and where present, reduced to single bands instead of covering the vessel. Large storage pithoi become prevalent for the first time.[261] Already the pottery of the 15th century can be described, as Schoop phrased it, as "bland outputs of an industry of mass production," and older types of pottery, especially the more elaborate, mostly disappeared.[262] By the 14th century, Hittite pottery was "typologically dead," and showed very little development until the end of the empire, and all ornamentation is purged from the assemblage.[263] Almost all pottery in the Hittite Empire period was utilitarian and mass-produced. Two exceptions are locally produced "Eggshell Ware" in the form of a small hemispherical bowl with extremely thin walls and a blade-like lip, and Red Lustrous Wheelmade Ware, a prestige good imported from Cyprus, usually in the form of a spindle bottle thought to contain perfume and well known from other palace contexts in the ancient Near

257 Ulf-Dietrich Schoop, "Indications of structural change in the Hittite pottery inventory at Boğazköy-Hattuša," *Central-North Anatolia in the Hittite Period: New Perspectives Light of Recent Research, Acts of the International Conference held at the University of Florence (7–9 February 2007)*, eds. Giulia Torri, Carlo Corti, Franca Pecchioli Daddi (Rome: Herder, 2009), 155. See also Ulf-Dietrich Schoop, "Hittite Pottery: A Summary," in *Insights into Hittite History and Archaeology*, eds. Hermann Genz, Dirk Paul Mielke (Leuven: Peeters, 2011), 241–73.

258 Schoop, "Structural Change," 149.

259 Schoop, *op. cit.*, 150.

260 For this process, see Dirk Paul Mielke, "From 'Anatolian' to 'Hittite'. The Development of Pottery in Central Anatolia in the 2nd Millennium BC," in *Innovation versus Beharrung: Was macht den Unterschied des hethitischen Reichs im Anatolien des 2. Jahrtausends v. Chr.? Internationaler Workshop zu Ehren von Jürgen Seeher, Istanbul, 23–24. Mai 2014*, ed. Andreas Schachner. Byzas 23 (Istanbul: Deutsches Archäologisches Institut, 2017): 121–44.

261 Schoop, *op. cit.*, 151.

262 Schoop, *op. cit.*, 153.

263 Schoop, *op. cit.*, 154. See also p. 155, where Schoop explicitly links the lack of change and ornamentation to "industrialization" of pottery production.

East.[264] Pottery development in the last 200 years of Hittite history is almost imperceptible, and most changes are only in the statistical distribution of forms.[265] Just prior to the abandonment of Ḫattuša the assemblage is increasingly restricted, but still recognizably Hittite, with a noticeable decline in quality in some pieces.[266] Then in the Early Iron Age, pottery at Ḫattuša reverted to a plain, handmade style reminiscent of the Early Bronze Age and Chalcolithic, offering the possibility that pre-Hittite Anatolian ceramic traditions had been preserved all along,[267] perhaps among the Kaška.[268]

At present there are four major theses on how the Hittites achieved such a remarkably uniform pottery style during their reign.[269] An early thesis by Günther Korbel linked the spread of Hittite pottery with the forced resettlement of deportees (NAM.RA) on the Plateau[270] (though this fails to explain the adoption of elements of the Hittite assemblage outside of the Hittite heartland pointed out by Glatz below). The second thesis by Marie-Henriette Gates argued that, based on similar or even identical potter's marks found at Ḫattuša and the town of Kinet Höyük (Hitt. Izziya, Classical Issus), Hittite pottery was part of a consciously controlled imperial economic system, which she described as "an economic program overseen by direct government regulation."[271] A third thesis proposed by Uwe Müller[272] and Nicholas Postgate[273] considered it more

---

264 Schoop, "Structural Change," 155; Dirk Paul Mielke, "Red Lustrous Wheelmade Ware from Hittite Contexts," in *The Lustrous Wares of Late Bronze Age Cyprus and the Eastern Mediterranean, Papers of a Conference, Vienna 5th–6th of November 2004*, ed. Irmgard Hein. Contributions to the Chronology of the Eastern Mediterranean 13 (Wien: Österreichische Akademie der Wissenschaften, 2007), 155–68.

265 Ulf-Dietrich Schoop, "Pottery Traditions of the Later Hittite Empire: Problems of Definition," in *Identifying Changes: The Transition from Bronze to Iron Ages in Anatolia and Its Neighbouring Regions. Proceedings of the International Workshop, Istanbul, November 8–9, 2002*, eds. Bettina Fischer, Hermann Genz, Éric Jean, Kemalettin Köroğlu (Istanbul: Türk Eskiçağ Bilimleri Enstitüsü, 2003), 168.

266 Schoop, *op. cit.*, 172–73.

267 Hermann Genz, "Früheisenzeitliche Keramik von Büyükkale in Boğazköy/Hattuša," IstM 53 (2003): 113–29; also Jürgen Seeher, "After the Empire: Observations on the Early Iron Age in Central Anatolia," in *ipamati kistamati pari tumatimis. Luwian and Hittite Studies presented to J. David Hawkins on the Occasion of his 70th Birthday*, ed. Itamar Singer, Tel Aviv Mon. Ser. 28 (Tel Aviv: Tel Aviv University, 2010), 220–29.

268 Claudia Glatz and Roger Matthews, "Anthropology of a Frontier Zone: Hittite-Kaška Relations in Late Bronze Age North-Central Anatolia," BASOR 339 (2005): 57–58.

269 See Dirk Paul Mielke, *Die Keramik vom Westhang*, KuSa. 2 (Rahden/Westf.: Leidorf, 2006),13–23, for a history of research on Hittite pottery. The conventional term "Hittite pottery" will be adopted here, while acknowledging with Glatz ("Empire as Network," 129–30) that a more neutral term such as "North-central Anatolian-style" might be more appropriate.

270 Günther Korbel, *Die spätbronzezeitliche Keramik von Norşuntepe* (Hannover: Institut für Bauen und Planen in Entwicklungsländern, 1985), 117–20.

271 Marie-Henriette Gates, "Potmarks and Kinet Höyük and the Hittite ceramic industry," in *La Cilicie: espaces et pouvoirs locaux (2e millénaire av. J.-C. – 4e siècle ap. J.-C.)*, eds. Érik Jean, Ali M. Dinçol, Serra Durugönül (Istanbul: Institut français d'études anatoliennes Georges Dumézil, 2001), 141.

272 Uwe Müller, " Norşun Tepe and Lidar Höyük. Two Examples for Cultural Change During the Early Iron Age," in *Anatolian Iron Ages* 5, eds. Altan Çilingiroğlu, Gareth Darbyshire (London: British Institute of Archaeology at Ankara, 2005), 107–14.

273 J. Nicholas Postgate, "The Ceramics of Centralization and Dissolution: A Case Study from Rough Cilicia," AnSt. 57 (2007): 141–50.

likely that standardized pottery resulted from the presence of Hittite administrative officials. Instead of intervention of the central administration in the daily economic life of local towns, the similarity in pots stemmed from Hittite governors and soldiers wanting to (or being expected to?) live in the style of Ḫattuša, which they demanded from local craftsmen. Postgate reasoned that,

> from Assyria in the 13th century we have extensive documentary evidence of the tight control exercised by the state over industrial production, in the shape of a system of work-assignment .... All the signs are that in other respects the Late Bronze Age kingdoms operated along very similar lines to each other, and it would be no surprise if in Hittite territories similar tight administrative control was exerted from the centre at Ḫattuša.[274]

Unfortunately, there is very little evidence, outside of perhaps goldsmithing[275] and the supply of ritually pure products for the king's sacred person,[276] of industrial intervention by the Hittite state. This makes the last thesis on Hittite pottery, offered by Claudia Glatz, attractive. Glatz argues that uniform pottery was not imposed at all (except perhaps at the very center of the kingdom), but rather adopted selectively by local elites emulating the Hittite court style. Evidence for adoption is best at the periphery of the Anatolian Plateau, where elements of the Hittite assemblage begin to appear at different dates, but never in their entirety as would be expected in an imposed ceramic regime.[277] However, caution must be used in order not to over-interpret the limited evidence. As concluded by Dirk Paul Mielke, we can at present only state that an increasing association of pottery production with the Hittite state is the probable cause of the standardization, with the larger central towns progressively taking over production for the villages in their regions.[278]

The last two features of Glatz's model of regionally differentiated responses to Hittite imperialism, landscape monuments and glyptics, are clearer cases of adoption by regional elites. Glyptics, i.e., Anatolian Hieroglyphs, were the most extensive and least regulated marker of the Hittite world: indeed, their "classical" period of use is only after the fall of the Hittite Empire and at its former periphery in the Neo-Hittite king-

---

274 Postgate, "Ceramics of Centralization," 145.

275 See discussion of the goldsmiths Zuzu(l)i and Palla in Giulia Torri, "The Goldsmith Zuzu(l)li and the Find-spots of the Inventory Texts from Ḫattuša," AoF 43 (2016): 147–56. See also the gathered attestations of state production in "4.3.1 Smiths and Craftsmen" in Tayfun Bilgin, *Officials and Administration in the Hittite World.* SANER 21 (Berlin: De Gruyter), 391–92.

276 See KUB 13.3 iii 10, where leatherworkers are instructed to only use hides obtained from the palace kitchen when crafting leather for the king's chariot.

277 Glatz, "Empire as Network," 138: "ceramic similarities in [the peripheral] regions differ in terms of their chronology of introduction and intensity, [which suggests] a series of local processes of adoption rather than the deliberate imposition of imperial cultural elements on surrounding territories." See now also Glatz, *The Making of Empire*, 255–63, where it is further suggested that "plain, monochrome, and visually homogenous pottery" (p. 262) was an areal feature of imperial states and their emulators in the Late Bronze Age Near East.

278 Dirk Paul Mielke, "Produktion und Distribution von Keramik im Rahmen der hethitischen Wirtschaftsorganisation," in *Wirtschaft als Machtbasis. Beiträge zur Rekonstruktion vormoderner Wirtschaftssysteme in Anatolien: drittes wissenschaftliches Netzwerk der Abteilung Istanbul des Deutschen Archäologischen Instituts*, ed. Katja Piesker. Byzas 22 (Istanbul: Deutsches Archäologisches Institut, 2016): 175–81; Mielke, "From 'Anatolian' to Hittite'," 138–40; Mielke, "Hittite Pottery," 678–79.

doms of Syria. As for "Hittite" landscape monuments, Glatz points out that more were created by local elites, some of whom were antagonistic to the Hittites, than were commissioned by the royal family.[279] It seems that Hittite-style landscape monuments were less markers of the Hittite state than a shared visual language for settling local scores. As Glatz writes:

> In view of both the large number of monuments apparently commissioned by princes and local kings as well as textual references to incessant upheavals and subsequent military campaigns across Anatolia, I propose that despite potentially close familial and/or contractual ties with the Hittite core, representations or inscriptions of princes and local rulers [i.e., landscape monuments] should be seen as evidence for power-political discourses among local factions as well as with central forces.[280]

Monuments were claims to territory rather than manifestations of control, and more concerned with defining an interior that subjugating a boundary.[281] They were thus placed where political competition was most intense: western Anatolia and the border between Tarḫuntašša and the Lower Lands were especially popular sites, and it is no surprise that landscape monument building became popular in the political upheaval of the last stages of the Empire.[282]

In sum, research suggests that the Anatolian Plateau was a patchwork of competing political and cultural elements during the Hittite Kingdom. Even at the height of Hittite power in the ancient Near East, the Hittite king would have had full control over a very small part of the Empire, perhaps even just Ḫattuša and the Upper Land, marked by the quadruple overlap of political markers discussed above. Although Glatz, as an archaeologist, does not speculate on the textual-historical aspect of Anatolian regionalism, the administrative records found at Ḫattuša are also seemingly restricted to the core region in which the king had full control.[283] Conveniently, as discussed in *2.2.2 Geography of the Anatolia Plateau*, this area under direct control contained the richest farmlands of the kingdom. Thus, the intense micromanagement observed in, e.g., the Maşat Höyük-Tapikka letters, where the king takes personal interest in repelling a

---

279 Claudia Glatz and Aimée Plourde, "Landscape Monuments and Political Competition in Late Bronze Age Anatolia: An Investigation of Costly Signaling Theory," BASOR 361 (2011): 57. For further reading on the function of Hittite landscape monuments, see Jürgen Seeher, "Der Landschaft sein Siegel aufdrücken – hethitische Felsbilder und Hieroglypheninschriften als Ausdruck des herrscherlichen Macht- und Territorialanspruchs," AoF 36 (2009): 119–39; and Seeher, "Natürliche und künstliche, unbewusste und beabsichtige Landmarken: Menschliche Wahrnehmung und herrscherliche Betonung der Besetzung von Landschaft und Territorien," in *Manifestation von Macht und Hierarchien in Stadtraum und Landschaft*, ed. Felix Pirson. Byzas 13 (Istanbul: Deutsches Archäologisches Institut, 2012), 25–42. See now also Glatz, *The Making of Empire*, 152–74.

280 Glatz, "Empire as Network," 136. Glatz, *The Making of Empire*, 153: "Landscape monuments are one of the hammers in Bronze Age political toolkits that were deployed in the hope of chiseling out new spheres of authority where they were previously lacking, tenuous, or claimed by others."

281 Glatz, "Empire as Network," 137.

282 Glatz and Plourde, "Landscape Monuments," 58–60.

283 This point could use further research, but it can be seen at a glance that most of the place names in the Palace-Temple Administrative Corpus, but especially the sources of taxes/tribute in the form of raw materials (see comments on geography in Siegelová, *Hethitische Verwaltungspraxis*, 548–51), are in central and northern Anatolia.

Kaškaen incursion into what is otherwise an insignificant frontier town, should neither be generalized to the remaining areas of the Hittite Kingdom,[284] nor should it be interpreted as a symptom of a government "incapable of delegation" (a phrase used by Glatz and Matthews to describe the king's military responsibilities, prior to her dissertation ironically revealing the unique position of the northern frontier in Anatolia).[285] Rather it was the king exercising the responsibilities of a regional lord in his personal "royal demesne."[286]

2.3.3.2 Anatolian Resistance

Given the regionalization of Anatolia, it is no surprise that the Hittites faced resistance to their rule. Regional lords, vassals, and (most dangerously) other members of the royal family were threats to the state, though in general all of these groups sought to usurp rather than to dismantle Hittite power (cf. Ḫattušili III, Kuruntiya, and the political aspirations of the Arzawa confederacy in contacting Egypt). True resistance to Hittite rule also came from substate actors in two directions: from outside in the form of tribal entities who did not recognize Hittite governance, and possibly from within in the form of passive resistance by Hittite subjects.

The tension between the Hittite state and the Anatolian populace can in many ways be traced to the landscape. Not every element of pre-Hittite lifestyle discussed in *2.2.4 Modes of Subsistence on the Anatolian Plateau* was in harmony with the needs of the Hittite state. The semi-nomadism used as a survival strategy for Anatolian populations was discouraged by the Hittites, and population movement in any form was inimical to the Hittite state: almost every one of their treaties with neighboring states includes stipulations concerning the return of migrant Hittite subjects,[287] and, despite zooarchaeological evidence for intensive pastoralism supplying the major urban centers of

---

284 Thus, statements such as "There is absolutely no evidence for the participation of the local population in the government of [Maşat Höyük-]Tapikka" (Gary Beckman, "Hittite Provincial Administration in Anatolia and Syria: the View from Maşat and Emar," in *Atti del II Congresso Internazionale di Hittitologie*, eds. Onofrio Carruba, Mauro Giorgieri, Clelia Mora. StMed. 9 [Pavia: Gianni Iuculano Editore, 1995], 26), must not be applied to all of "Hittite provincial administration." The fact that Tapikka, a frontier farming village assigned a modest but direct administration due its strategic importance, lacked a council of elders, whereas Emar, a prosperous city-state with its own king, possessed one, does not allow one to make a strong claim about the difference in administrative styles between Anatolia and Syria.

285 Claudia Glatz and Roger Matthews, "Anthropology of a Frontier Zone: Hittite-Kaška Relations in Late Bronze Age North-Central Anatolia," BASOR 339 (2005): 54. Compare earlier the faintly stated caveat of Emmanuel Laroche that the servile nature of the Maşat Höyük administrators might only have been "un aspect des dispositions prises par quelque souverain hittite ... pour contrôler la frontière en pleine crise d'invasion gasga" (Laroche, "Pouvoir central et pouvoir local en Anatolie hittite," in *Les Pouvoirs locaux en Mésopotamie et dans les régions adjacentes: colloque organisé par l'Institut des Hautes Études de Belgique 28 et 29 janvier 1980*, ed. André Finet [Bruxelles: Institut des hautes études de Belgique]: 140).

286 The subsistence of the ruler in the same way as his followers is a well-recognized feature of vertically oriented, or tributary societies (see Frangipane's discussion below).

287 See the introduction to Gary Beckman, *Hittite Diplomatic Texts*. 2 ed. WAW 7 (Atlanta: Society for Biblical Literature, 1999).

Anatolia, the state seems to have taken comparatively little interest in herding livestock.[288] Of resistance to these infringements on the Anatolian way of life, none is better known than that of the Kaška, a tribal group often described as semi-nomadic who lived to the immediate north of the Hittite heartland in the Pontic region.[289] Historically, it appears the Kaška did not emerge as a distinct group until the Middle Hittite Kingdom, since they are not attested until the reign of Tudḫaliya I, despite frequent campaigns by Ḫattušili I in northern Anatolia.[290] Like the *foederati* of Imperial Rome, there seems to have been considerable social mobility between the Kaška and the Hittite state,[291] which is sometimes difficult to trace due to the fact that Kaškaen names are oftentimes indistinguishable from the Hattic or "Cappadocian" stratum of Hittite onomastics.[292] This lends credence to the possibility that the Kaška were not necessarily even ethnically or religiously distinct from the original Hattian population of northern Anatolia.[293] And while it is conventional to refer to the Pontic zone as a frontier, archaeologist Paul Zimansky has suggested that there were no "hidden Kaška" beyond the boundaries of the Hittite state, and instead that the Kaška were endemic to the hills and valleys of the area and just too expensive for the Hittite state to fully and continuously pacify.[294] This fits well with the archaeological picture of a relatively stable and peaceful Pontic region in the Middle Bronze Age, which only later changed to the fortified zone of the Hittite Period.[295] If it were indeed the case that the Kaška were

288 The interaction of the Hittite state with pastoralism, pastoralists, and the population movement required by that lifestyle probably warrants renewed investigation from a combined textual/archaeological perspective. For the moment, see Gary Beckman, "Herding and Herdsmen in Hittite Culture," in *Documentum Asiae Minoris Antiquae. Festschrift für Heinrich Otten zum 75. Geburtstag*, ed. Erich Neu (Wiesbaden: Harrassowitz, 1988), 33–44. See also Horst Klengel, "Studien zur hethitischen Wirtschaft. 3: Tierwirtschaft und Jagd," AoF 34 (2007): 155–61, and Gerçek, "The Kaška and the Northern Frontier of Ḫatti," 37–41.

289 For a comprehensive treatment of the interactions of the Hittite state with the Kaška of this region, see also Gerçek, "The Kaška and the Northern Frontier of Ḫatti." On the ascription of semi-nomadism to the Kaška, see Gerçek, "The Kaška and the Northern Frontier of Ḫatti," 30–31, and Glatz and Matthews, "Anthropology of a Frontier Zone," 57. See earlier the mostly philological treatment of Jörg Klinger, "Zalpa, Nerik und Hakmiš - Die Bedeutung der nördlichen Peripherie Zentralanatoliens in hethitischer Zeit," in *Hattuša-Boğazköy. Das Hethiterreich im Spannungsfeld des Alten Orients. 4. Internationales Colloquium der Deutschen Orient-Gesellschaft 22.-24. März 2006 in Würzburg*, ed. Gernot Wilhelm. CDOG 6 (Wiesbaden: Harrassowitz, 2008), 277–90.

290 Itamar Singer, "Who were the Kaška?," *Phasis* 10/2 (2007): 167–68.

291 Glatz and Matthews, "Anthropology of a Frontier Zone," 54.

292 As noted by Klinger, "Zalpa, Nerik und Hakmiš," 279. See especially HKM 102, Giuseppe del Monte, "I testi amministrativi da Maşat Höyük/Tapika," OrAntMisc. 2 (1995): 103–111, a list naming Kaškaen prisoners from the Maşat Höyük-Tapikka dossier.

293 A hypothesis going back to foundational study of the Kaška by Einar von Schuler, *Die Kaškäer: Ein Beitrag zur Ethnographie des alten Kleinasiens* (Berlin: De Gruyter, 1965), 89–91; see also von Schuler, "Kaškäer," RlA 5 (1976–80): 460–63.

294 Paul Zimansky, "The Lattimore Model and Hatti's Kaska Frontier," in *Settlement and Society: Essays Dedicated to Robert McCormick Adams*, ed. Elisabeth C. Stone (Los Angeles: Cotsen Institute of Archaeology, 2007), 157–72.

295 Claudia Glatz and Robert Matthews, "The Historical Geography of North-central Anatolia in the Hittite Period: Texts and Archaeology in Concert," AnSt. 59 (2009): 55–56.

neither ethnically distinct (being Hattian) nor geographically separate (dwelling within the nominal boundaries of the Hittite Kingdom) from other Hittite subjects, then they are better defined as Anatolians living a lifestyle that rejected the political legitimacy of the Hittite state – or better, given their semi-nomadism, Anatolians living in a Hittite state that rejected their lifestyle.

Evidence of internal resistance is more difficult to measure. The poor-to-indifferent quality of grain and high proportion of weeds recovered from the silos at Ḫattuša has been offered as additional evidence for passive rural resistance in Glatz's model (although alternative interpretations are possible). As was touched upon in *2.3.2.1 Food Storage and Grain Silos* above, archaeobotanical research has shown that the silos of Ḫattuša were filled by grain likely coming from a variety of local sources, probably representing a system of taxation rather than direct cultivation. The granaries contained a high proportion of undersized grains, either indicating a bad harvest or cultivation on unfavorable soil, and were mixed with a high proportion of weeds.[296] A similar quality of grain seems to be found at Kuşaklı-Šarišša.[297] Researchers have suspected that the indifferent quality of the grain and admixture of weeds indicates that the contents of the silos reflected the banal incentive for farmers to pay their taxes whenever possible with the least desirable part of their harvest.[298] A variation of this thesis is that the low average quality stemmed from the fact that the fields were cultivated for the state by compulsory labor, and hence received less care and maintenance than fields in private hands.[299] Glatz suggested as an alternative that the poor quality and admixture of weeds in the grain at Kuşaklı-Šarišša was possible evidence for active rural resistance to state control.[300]

2.4 The Wealth-Financed State

2.4.1 Wealth Finance, Staple Finance

In spite of the difficulties of regionalism and resistance, the Hittite state survived for over 400 years while contending with environmental factors that seemingly should have limited its economic power vis-à-vis its competitors in the ancient Near East. But as Horst Klengel (and others) have argued, there are advantages to the Anatolian Plateau, principally in mineral resources and the administrative capacities stimulated by

296 Walter Dörfler, Christa Herking, Reinder Neef, Reiner Pasternak, and Angela von den Driesch, "Environment and Economy in Hittite Anatolia," in *Insights into Hittite History and Archaeology*, eds. Hermann Genz, Dirk P. Mielke (Leuven: Peeters, 2011), 99–124.

297 Rainer Pasternak, "Übersicht über die Ergebnisse der archäobotanischen Arbeiten in Kuşaklı 1994–1997 und ein Interpretationsansatz zu den Befunden," MDOG 130 (1998): 160–70.

298 Pasternak, "Übersicht über die Ergebnisse," 163–64, followed by Andreas Müller-Karpe, *Sarissa: Die Wiederentdeckung einer hethitischen Königsstadt* (Darmstadt: von Zabern, 2017), 78–80.

299 Jörg Klinger, "Hittite Economics," 624.

300 Claudia Glatz, "The Hittite State and Empire from Archaeological Evidence," in *The Oxford Handbook of Ancient Anatolia*, eds. Sharon R. Steadman, Gregory McMahon (Oxford: Oxford University Press, 2011), 881–82.

the extraction, trade, and taxing of metals, that allowed the nascent Hittite state to quickly adapt when it came into contact with Mesopotamian models of government.[301]

Marcella Frangipane revisited and greatly expanded Klengel's thesis in a pair of articles comparing the growth of administration in Anatolia and Mesopotamia, giving both anthropological and historical reasons for the differing, but potentially equally viable trajectories. As Frangipane noted, southern Mesopotamia had a head start on urbanized society due to its highly productive land and competitive household units, which encouraged a naturally stratified society.[302] The necessity of legitimate inequality for civilizational growth is a classic concept (cf. Weber's essay on the "The Social Causes of the Decay of Ancient Civilizations" that rooted Roman and Athenian economic success in slave holders concerned with maximizing profit for competitive consumption),[303] but also somewhat unnatural to develop, as shown in the above discussion of peasant economies where countervailing forces of communalism and autarky are encouraged as survival strategies. Overcoming the communalist inertia requires a specific set of factors: as Frangipane wrote,

> The discriminating factors for the formation of highly urbanised society and centralised systems appear to be mainly of two types: 1) environmental: the growth of large concentrations of people in urban settlements is only possible if there are conditions for a highly productive agriculture, generating large and continuously increasing surpluses; 2) social: a system of social and kinship relations emphasising the separate and competitive role of individual household units, fostering the legitimation of differences within which higher status members of the society can emerge.[304]

The floodplains of lower Mesopotamia are a high risk/high reward environment that rewarded the competing large family units of the original Mesopotamian societies. Minor differences in initial competitive success led to a "feedback circuit," where families would spend the increased surplus of goods to enhance prestige, which allowed them to attract more dependent labor. As Frangipane described it, this encouraged "a 'dynamic' wealth, consisting of the capacity to reproduce itself through very strict control over the labor force."[305] The system rewarded efficient and publicly minded householders, which resulted in a strong public sphere which did not at the same time restrict private economic activity.[306] According to Frangipane, Mesopotamian society was marked by:

---

301 This being roughly the conclusion of Klengel's article on "Aspetti dello sviluppo dello stato ittita" discussed in Section *2.2.1 History of Research* above.

302 Marcella Frangipane, "Different Models of Power Structuring at the Rise of Hierarchical Societies in the Near East: Primary Economy Versus Luxury and Defense Management," in *Development of Pre-state Communities in the Ancient Near East: Studies in Honour of Edgar Peltenberg*, eds. Diane Bolger, Louise C. Maguire (Oxford: Oxbow, 2010), 79–81.

303 Max Weber, "The Social Causes of the Decay of Ancient Civilizations," in Essays in Economic Sociology, by Max Weber, ed. R. Swedburg (Princeton: Princeton University Press, 1999), 138–53.

304 Frangipane, "Different Models of Power Structuring," 79.

305 Marcella Frangipane, "The Evolution and Role of Administration in Anatolia: A Mirror of Different Degrees and Models of Centralisation," in *Archivi, depositi, magazzini presso gli ittiti: nuovi materiali e nuove ricerche*, eds. Maria E. Balza, Mauro Giorgieri, Clelia Mora. StMed. 23 (Genova: Italian University Press, 2012), 113.

306 Frangipane, "Evolution and Role of Administration," 113.

> elites who centralised primary goods and labour, accumulated wealth in the form of staple products, and established a system of regular reinvestment in various activities by redistributing these staple products, or part of them, to increasingly broader sections of the population in the form of remuneration for their labour. The centralised organisation in this case became almost an 'entrepreneurial' system, creating a very close interdependency between all of its social components. The consequences of this system were (conditions permitting) urbanisation, the emergence of sophisticated administrative procedures, and bureaucracy. The origin of the elites and their privileges were usually deeply entrenched in the socio-economic system. It was this model that led to the birth of the state.[307]

The accumulation of luxury goods and land rights was only a later outcome of the Mesopotamian system, and durable goods were used for a long time primarily as markers of prestige rather than storable wealth.[308]

Anatolia adopted an urbanized, stratified social organization only later through contact and emulation of their neighbors to the south, which by virtue of its being borrowed was shallowly rooted and maintained only by the continuous exertion of political, military, and administrative power.[309] Whereas the original role of the Mesopotamian state was to regulate the mutual exchange of service and benefits, in Anatolia the state focused on protecting the populace and defending trade routes, with results measured by the hoarding and display of luxury goods, accumulation of which preceded urbanization.[310] Anatolian societies were in Frangipane's model thus led by:

> political/military type leaders who seem to have managed small territories and who were probably viewed ideologically in terms of their role as defenders and representatives of the community. Interference by these elites in the basic production system of the general population appears to have been virtually non-existent, whereas elites may have played a very important role in protecting the trading routes for raw materials and in supporting craftsmen. Their financial system was therefore based essentially on handicraft items and luxury goods, above all metals, and their political role was probably linked to their ability to guarantee access to the supply of raw materials in a weakly hierarchical society made up of small territorial units in a basically mountainous environment.[311]

---

307 Frangipane, "Different Models of Power Structuring," 84.

308 Frangipane, "Evolution and Role of Administration," 114.

309 Frangipane, "Different Models of Power Structuring," 81–82. For evidence in the architectural record of the (surprisingly late) rise of an elite class disconnected from the agrarian economy at Ḫattuša, see Schachner, "Das 16. Jahrhundert v. Chr. – eine Zeitenwende," 25: "Diese Entwicklung ist textlich zwar nicht genau nachvollziehbar, findet aber z. B. in der Entwicklung neuer Hausformen ihre Bestätigung. Diese neuen Wohnformen sind spätestens seit dem 15. Jh. in Ḫattuša belegbar und weisen im Gegensatz zu den in der anatolischen Tradition stehenden Häusern keinen architektonischen Bezug zur Subsistenzwirtschaft mehr auf."

310 Frangipane, "Evolution and Role of Administration," 116–17. See also Gary Beckman, "Hittite Administration in Syria in Light of the Texts from Hattusa, Ugarit, and Emar," in *New Horizons in the Study of Ancient Syria*, eds. Mark W. Chavalas, John L. Hayes (Malibu: Undena, 1992), 41, for the view that Hittite activities in Syria revolved around the strategic control of trade routes. For Hittite military campaigns as a quest for exotic trades goods, see Bilgin, *Officials and Administration*, 15: "The main purpose of such incursions was not the expansion of state territory, but rather the collection of spoils and tribute to increase royal prestige, as well as the distribution of these riches to followers in order to consolidate power."

311 Frangipane, "Different Models of Power Structuring," 84.

Anatolian society can be described as vertical in that its members had limited dependence on others of the same social class and participated in a hierarchical chain of economic obligations. The Anatolian-type societies did not naturally develop an indigenous urbanism and bureaucracy, but selectively appropriated its advantages after contact with Mesopotamia.

As recognized by Frangipane, the two types of society, Anatolian and (southern) Mesopotamian, have strong anthropological parallels, falling respectively into the complementary "Wealth Finance" and "Staple Finance" categories first described in a study of the Incan state by anthropologists Terence D'Altroy and Timothy Earle (the latter of whom incorporated the ideas into his *Bronze Age Economics* discussed above).[312] Wealth finance, based on control of trade routes and production of prestige objects, and staple finance, based on ownership of land and control of foodstuffs, refer to different forms of redistribution, defined by Earle as "[s]urpluses ... mobilized and distributed centrally to finance institutional apparatuses of power (e.g., warriors, managers, and craftsmen of wealth items and weapons) with the goal to expand political reach."[313] Redistribution is present in any sufficiently centralized state, but elites have multiple strategies to convert dependent relationships into the reinforcement of political hierarchy through finance. Earle described the distinction and relationship between the two systems as follows:

> Based on ownership of productive facilities, staple finance involved the mobilization of staples, their storage, and redistribution to support ruling institutions. These systems were difficult to control at any distance, because heavy staples were impractical to move far. Based on control over valuables, wealth finance involved the production and/or procurement of special objects to mark status, which were therefore useful as payment. Staple and wealth finance could often be joined. Staples were used to support attached specialists, who converted the staples into the more easily moved valuables that would allow for a centralized political economy over a greater distance.[314]

The choice between staple and wealth finance was often environmental. In Anatolia, the difficulties of moving bulk items over long distances and the abundant mineral wealth of the region made it naturally suited to wealth-financed states. Anatolia's proximity to the population centers of Mesopotamia was also a factor: Earle notes that while wealth-financed states are difficult to control and comparatively rare, they tend to arise secondarily to the neighboring agrarian states with which they trade.[315] William Parkinson and Michael Galaty have argued that this is precisely the situation that gave rise to the Minoan and Mycenean states of the Bronze Age Aegean.[316] An argument could be made that the scenario of wealth-financed secondary state formation

312 Terence D'Altroy and Timothy Earle, "Staple finance, wealth finance and storage in the Inka political economy," CA 26/2 (1985): 187–206.

313 Timothy Earle, "Redistribution and the Political Economy: The Evolution of an Idea," AJA 115/2 (2011): 237–38.

314 Earle, "Redistribution," 241.

315 Earle, *loc. cit.*

316 William Parkinson and Michael Galaty, "Primary and Secondary States in Perspective: An Integrated Approach to State Formation in the Prehistoric Aegean," *American Anthropologist* 109 (207): 113–29.

might also describe what is observed in Anatolia, certainly no later than the Assyrian trade colony period.[317]

2.4.2 Wealth Finance and Hittite Metal Production

As might be expected on the mineral-rich Anatolian Plateau, the premier marker of wealth finance in the Hittite state lay in the organization of the production of metal. Since metal production has been extensively discussed in Hittitology, both from philological and archaeological perspectives, the topic will only be outlined here with references to the main sources. The principal conclusion of current research is that copper, silver, some tin, and perhaps iron, were produced in Anatolia by local communities in dispersed locations and according to a diverse variety of metallurgical techniques – a situation that can be directly tied to the diverse and highly regionalized landscape of the Anatolian Plateau.[318] In the Hittite period, processed ingots stemming from dispersed and disparate local primary production sites were gathered at urban centers for secondary production into alloys and finished goods. Here, an interesting and not necessarily expected phenomenon can be observed. As noted by Joseph W. Lehner and Andreas Schachner:

> Absent from most texts are the actual production strategies and technologies associated with primary and secondary metallurgy during this time period. This leaves the possibility that access to processed raw materials at Hattuša was only partially controlled by state institutions, and the organization of production and metallurgical knowledge was outside the immediate domain of the palace and temples.[319]

Once noticed, the absence of detailed records of metal production in the texts of the Palace-Temple Administrative Corpus is remarkable. In spite of the archaeological evidence that a great amount of Hittite secondary metallurgical production was spons-

---

317 See thoughts on the political consolidation in this period in the chapter "Political History" in Gojko Barjamovic, Thomas Hertel, Mogens Trolle Larsen, *Ups and Downs at Kanesh. Chronology, History and Society in the Old Assyrian Period.* OAAS 5 (Leiden: Nederlands Instituut voor het Nabije Oosten, 2012), 43–52. The causal direction of the impact Assyrian trade colonies on the Middle Bronze age polities of central Anatolia is unclear. As concluded in Maryanne W. Newton and Peter Ian Kuniholm, "A Dendrochronological Framework for the Assyrian Colony Period in Asia Minor," TÜBA-AR 7 (2004): 175, "observations still do not tell us whether the karum buildings or the palaces came first. Was the prosperity obvious in the palatial structures [at Kanesh] on the mound above a by-product of the commercial activities in the karum below? Or did the merchants come to an already prosperous center?"

318 See K. Aslıhan Yener, *The Domestication of Metals: The Rise of Complex Metal Industries in Anatolia* (Leiden: Brill, 2000); see esp. pp. 30–66, where it is shown that the shared trans-regional material culture of Anatolia, e.g., sealing practices, ceramics, architecture, starkly contrasted the metallurgical practices, which remained hyper-regional and distinctive, even in Hittite times. For the Hittite period, see Joseph W. Lehner and Andreas Schachner. "The Organization of Metal Production at Hattuša: A First Assessment," in *Overturning Certainties in Near Eastern Archaeology: A Festschrift in Honor of K. Aslıhan Yener*, ed. Çiğdem Maner, Mara T. Horowitz, Allan S. Gilbert. CHANE 90 (Leiden: Brill, 2017), especially pp. 404–8 for the theoretical underpinnings of the development of primary production of metal in the highland environment of Anatolia.

319 Lehner and Schachner, "The Organization of Metal Production at Hattuša," 409.

ored on site at Ḫattuša,[320] almost all objects appearing in the administrative texts found at the capital are finished objects (or at least preformed tokens, depending on how the copper axes and sickles are interpreted). Evidence for smelting and reforging of the objects is indirect, except in the case of gold, and seems to have been conducted outside of workshops directly controlled by the palace (see discussion in *2.4.2.1 Copper, Tin, and Bronze* immediately below). From this combination of archaeologically provable diversity in primary metallurgy but textual silence on secondary production, Lehner and Schachner concluded that:

> One of the most prominent features of metallurgical production at Boğazköy-Hattuša is that secondary metallurgy seems to be sponsored indirectly by state institutions at least during the Late Bronze Age .... This degree of sponsorship allowed for workshops to be relatively autonomous in production, though textual evidence does suggest that the metal supply was controlled through redistribution and taxation ... .[321]

Against this general rule of indirect sponsorship of production, the various metals and alloys were handled by the state very differently based on value and domestic availability; these different patterns will be discussed below.

2.4.2.1 Copper, Tin, and Bronze

For copper, the dissertation of Joseph Lehner has shown that, in accordance with K. Aslıhan Yener's highland production model of diverse and autochthonous metallurgical development, the copper used by the Hittite state came from a kaleidoscope of sources on the Anatolian Plateau, each defined by its own techniques for smelting and refining.[322] Prior to the Hittite imperial expansion at the end of the Late Bronze Age, when copper tribute from Ugarit and Cyprus was introduced, metallurgical analysis shows that central Anatolian copper was entirely natively sourced.[323] As discussed by Lehner, building on the earlier data and observations of Jana Siegelová and Andreas Müller-Karpe, a comparison of metal income from tax with metal output in the form of finished goods stored in the Hittite inventory texts reveals that copper predominated in the tax lists but is rarely attested in "inert" inventories, implying that the rate of circulation of copper through the inventory texts was fairly high.[324]

Whereas primary production of metals in Anatolia, i.e., the mining, smelting, and refining, was carried out in rural areas at or near the mines, secondary production, the

320 Lehner and Schachner, "The Organization of Metal Production at Hattuša," 410, with references to archaeological evidence for storerooms and metal workshops near temples and royal and elite residences at Ḫattuša.

321 Lehner and Schachner, *op. cit.*, 416.

322 Joseph W. Lehner, "Cooperation, the Craft Economy, and Metal Technology during the Bronze and Iron Ages in Central Anatolia" (PhD diss., University of California Los Angeles, 2015). For the highland production model, see Yener, *The Domestication of Metals.*

323 Joseph W. Lehner, "Cooperation, the Craft Economy, and Metal Technology," 184–92.

324 See "Figure 3.6: (Top) Relative frequency of metal commodity types for all different objects compared against tax and palace/temple inventory lists; (Middle) primary metal commodity types; and (Bottom) metal commodity types for finished goods," in Lehner, *op.cit.*, 88. See similar conclusion in Jana Siegelová, "Anwendung von Kupfer und Bronze in Anatolien anhand der hethitischen Texte," in *Handwerk und Technologie im alten Orient: Ein Beitrag zur Geschichte der Technik im Altertum. Internationale Tagung Berlin, 12.–15. März 1991*, ed. Ralf-Bernhard Wartke (Mainz: von Zabern, 1994): 119–24.

alloying and actual smithing of items, took place in urban centers. This pattern predates the Hittite Kingdom, having emerged already by the EB II period.[325] Anatolian urban centers supported detached specialists who were provisioned with metal that stemmed, at least in part, from the temples and palaces which constituted the state.[326] This scenario applied especially to the prestige product of tin bronze, which had a major center of production at Ḫattuša. As Lehner discussed,

> we can be certain that tin bronze production was a central activity of metal producers at Hattuša. This further suggests that these producers focused on a metal type that held a more interregional quality, which is somewhat contradictory to the known compositional data from finished objects at Hattuša. Tin bronze production at Hattuša therefore lends credence to the value and prestige of this metal type.[327]

Tin bronze, as opposed to the other frequently encountered alloy of arsenic copper, is archaeologically associated with elite and religious contexts, suggesting that its sponsored production and control was a component of state power.[328] And although it seems now that the tin necessary for bronze production was produced at least in some quantities in Anatolia,[329] it is known from textual and archaeological evidence that the metal was also imported in order to fill an elite demand that was greater than the native supply, thus further implicating the state through trade in the process of bronze production.

In terms of textual evidence, the intake of copper especially, but even tin, as tribute from various Anatolian localities is well attested in the Palace-Temple Administrative Corpus (see texts 3.1.1–9 in *3.1 Domestic Tribute in* the Form of Metals and Durable Goods in Vol. II). In contrast, as was already mentioned, copper and bronze secondary

---

325 Lehner, "Cooperation, the Craft Economy, and Metal Technology," 179:

> By the EB II in Anatolia ca. 2600-2300 BC, metal production activities exhibit significant degrees of labor specialization, where primary and secondary production activities were spatially discrete. Commodity chains at this point witnessed bottlenecks of control at the point of secondary production, whose activities were largely held within regional centers and in relative proximity to elite members of society.

326 Lehner, *op. cit.*, 89, also 177–95.

327 Lehner, *op. cit.*, 92.

328 Lehner, *op. cit.*, 188.

329 As discussed in Jana Siegelová, "Metals in Hittite records," in *Ancient Mining in Turkey and the Eastern Mediterranean*, eds. Ünsal Yalçın, Hadi Özbal, A. Günhan Paşamehmetoğlu (Ankara: Atılım University, 2008): 50–51, limited quantities of tin are present in domestic tribute records. It is conceivable that some of this came from low-level, capillary trade. On the other hand, potentially exploitable sources of tin have been discovered for Middle and Late Bronze Age Anatolia: at Kayseri-Hisarcık, Ünsal Yalçın and Hadi Özbal, "Ein neues Zinnvorkommen in Kayseri-Hisarcık – Ein Vorbericht," TÜBA-AR 12 (2009): 117-122; at Kültepe, K. Aslıhan Yener, et al.," New Tin Mines and Production Sites Near Kültepe in Turkey: A Third-millennium BC Highland Production Model," *Antiquity* 89 (345) (2015): 596-612. It is not clear whether the tin exploitation at these sites was meaningful in the Old Assyrian and Hittite periods, although the isotopic signature of a tin ingot found in a grave at Alacahöyük was found to match the Kayseri-Hisarcık data (Ünsal Yalçın, "Zinn für die Königin. Ein Barrenfragment aus Alacahöyük und seine Deutung," in *From Bright Ores to Shiny Metals. Festschrift for Andreas Hauptmann on the Occasion of 40 Years Research in Archaeometallurgy and Archaeometry*, eds. Gabriele Körlin, Michael Prange, Thomas Stöllner, Ünsal Yalçin. Der Anschnitt, Beiheft 29 [Rahden/Westf.: Leidorf, 2016]: 69–74).

production is attested only sparingly. Evidence for the manufacture of copper objects is limited to only three representative texts plus a few fragments of less-than-secure classification edited under 4.1.2 Coppersmithing Texts in Vol. II, as well as some scattered references to copper processing and manufacture in the 5. Extramural Allocations genre. The main text pair of the coppersmithing text group, 4.1.2.1 and 4.1.2.2, appear to document an allotment of raw materials to groups of non-palace craftsmen in 4.1.2.1, which was subsequently returned as finished objects as a kind of tribute in 4.1.2.2 (see reconstruction presented in the introductory Analysis to 4.1.2.1). The same arrangement is hypothesized for 4.1.2.3, which seems to be issuing raw materials as in 4.1.2.1, although the text is broken at the crucial part where the responsible parties would be named and the counterpart text where the items are returned is lost. A more indirect line of evidence for the copper secondary production comes from the so-called "īde texts," a set of texts edited under 5. Extramural Allocations in Vol. II that are named after the operative verb "he knew" that invariably follows the name of the supervisor who approved the disbursements recorded within. Here are found occasional references to quantities of raw copper owned by the palace being distributed to outside smiths for processing, including five instances where copper ingots are broken down into smaller pieces,[330] and two instances where copper is manufactured into modest numbers of blades and vessels.[331] It is not clear if either the broken-down copper pieces or the manufactured items are to be returned to the palace, especially since the other items in the *ĪDE* texts are seemingly issued with no implied promise of return. Outside of the limited evidence from the *4.1.2 Coppersmithing Texts* and the *5. Extramural Allocations* cited above, coppersmithing is not directly attested in the texts of the PTAC.

For bronze, the evidence is even slimmer. Surprisingly, perhaps even astonishingly given the rich attestation of finished bronze objects in the texts and the archaeological record, the manufacture of bronze objects is nowhere directly attested in the Palace-Temple Administrative Corpus. In fact, there are only two attestations in total that may be plausibly interpreted as involving even sponsored bronze production. The first comes from the *ĪDE* text 5.2, where in obv. ii 6–8 three talents of copper and at least one talent of tin, along with various copper vessels are issued to the "king's *parwala*-men." Unlike the copper ingots discussed above, which were explicitly issued for processing and manufacture, no hint is given as to intended use of the copper and tin. If it is assumed that the metals were destined for transport to crafting workshops somewhere in Ḫattuša (there being otherwise little reason to possess so much raw metal, and the "king's *parwala*-men" not being craftsmen themselves), then this passage constitutes the only attestation in the administrative corpus of the Hittite palace issuing copper and tin for bronze production. Even so, as with the other *ĪDE* texts, it is never actually stipulated that the metal be returned to the palace. The second attestation for possible bronze acquisition comes from the tribute text 3.1.12. Although very broken, the text lists a grand total of over 1,000 unknown items described as "tribute of the smiths" (3.1.12 4′: [*MA*]*N-TA-TUM* LÚ.MEŠSIM[UG.A). Following a double paragraph line, the text then lists a number of objects, including 2,000 blades (3.1.12 8′: 2 *LI-IM* EME [ZABAR) that

330 See 5.1 rev. iv 2–4, 5.2 obv. ii 13 and rev. iii 4′, 5.5 rev. iii 5′, and 5.7 rev.? iii 10′ in Vol. II.

331 See 5.2 obv. ii 13–18 and 5.7 rev. iii? 9′–10′ in Vol. II.

are almost certainly of bronze (bronze being the only material that is both written after its head noun and common enough for such a large number of blades). The double paragraph line suggests that these blades are not part of the tribute of the smiths, but if, as seems not unlikely, the blades were tribute from another domestic or professional group, then it would confirm another source of bronze for the Hittite palace, which was perhaps even produced from some of its own raw materials.[332] Next to this meager textual evidence for sponsored bronze manufacturing by non-palace-dependent craftsmen, the administrative texts also show that the Hittite palace could acquire finished bronze items directly as tribute (see, e.g., 3.1.1.A_2 rev. vi 3′), although this is not nearly as well attested as one might expect for a mature state of the eponymous Bronze Age.

In summary, the textual evidence strongly suggests that most non-precious metal objects used by the Hittite state were manufactured by external craftsmen who were not directly dependent on the state. This is in constrast to the gold- and silversmiths, as will be discussed immediately below. The pattern of diverse local sources of copper processed into bronze at the urban centers continued up to the end of the Hittite state. Returning to the general observations of Lehner and Schachner on Hittite metal production, the pattern of diverse local sources and sponsored urban production seems to be part of a conscious imperial strategy: one that weighed the advantages and disadvantages of intervention at different stages of production, before settling on indirect control through state-sponsored craftsmen at select urban sites.[333] Moreover, this economic-administrative configuration matches many other systems modeled for the Hittite state, such as the ceramic production and the implantation of defensible urban centers discussed in *2.3.3.1 Anatolian Regionalism – Hittite Identity* à la carte.

2.4.2.2 Gold and Silver

Perhaps more than any other metal, gold had a special place in the Hittite world. Anatolia, while blessed with deposits of copper, iron, and silver, was poor in exploitable gold during Hittite times. There is no evidence of large-scale mining of the metal in the region during the Bronze Age, save for a few sites in far western Anatolia along the Aegean (and thus beyond regular Hittite control).[334] Due to its rarity, gold was

---

332 See the discussion of "value-added" tribute in the introductory *Analysis* to text 3.2.1 in Vol. II, an arrangement in which the Hittite palace apparently outsourced the manufacture of some of its resources, with the returned products described as tribute.

333 Lehner and Schachner, "The Organization of Metal Production at Hattuša," 418:

> The varied range of alloy types at Hattuša reflects not only access to a range of different materials deriving from separate regions under the patronage of the Hittite state, ... but more importantly, this variability reveals the cultural knowledge associated with generations of technological adaptation in these distinctive highland zones. These data are therefore consistent with an imperial strategy that adopts redistributive control of resources as a way to integrate regions and labor. This evidence for integration should not undermine the possibility that many producers were in fact independent of state institutions, as we see in the Kültepe texts for earlier periods.

334 See Bülent Bayburtoğlu and Selahattin Yıldırım, "Gold and Silver in Anatolia," in *Anatolian Metal IV*, ed. Ünsal Yalçın. Der Anschitt 21 (Bochum: Deutsches Bergbau-Museum, 2008), 43–51; see also map in Lehner and Schachner "The Organization of Metal Production at Hattuša," 428, Fig. 22.1, where

seldom used for purely economic purposes, and the substance is in fact not attested at all in the Hittite Laws, which regulated the Hittite domestic economy.[335]

As was already observed by Andreas Müller-Karpe in his study of Anatolian metalworking, the lack of domestic sources of gold is confirmed by the Hittite texts, where the substance is nearly (or completely) absent from the taxation lists.[336] Conversely, in the temple inventory texts known to Müller-Karpe at the time, over 60% of the objects are described as made of gold, a percentage that has not much changed with the updated corpus, as a cursory glance at the attestations of KÙ.SI$_{22}$ – which in absolute terms far outnumber copper, bronze, and even silver, if not in actual number of objects – in the *Glossary* of the present volume will attest.[337] Gold also appears in fifty-five of the 160 standardized "minor" vows that will be analyzed in *8. The Hittite Votive Corpus as Economic Texts*, showing that the precious metal was vital to the palace religious economy. In logical terms, if the gold filling the Hittite coffers did not come from domestic sources, it must have come from abroad; and given Hittite state silence on private commerce this must have meant the well-attested channels of diplomatic gifts and tribute,[338] which were possibly supplemented by state-sponsored merchants who would have supplied the metal.[339]

It will be shown in *6.3 Tribute from Hittite Vassals* that during the reign of Ḫattušili and Puduḫepa the Hittite palace could expect a minimum yearly tribute of at least twenty-one minas of gold (thirteen and one-half minas from Ugarit and seven and one-

---

gold is only present on Aegean coast and by Ugarit. It is still not clear how intensively these sources were exploited in the Bronze Age.

335 As noted by Harry A. Hoffner, *The Laws of the Hittites: A Critical Edition*. DMOA 23 (Leiden: Brill, 1997), 11. See general overview of Hittite use of gold in Jana Siegelová, "Metals in Hittite records," 44–47. See also comments of Metin Alparslan and Meltem Doğan-Alparslan, "Symbol der ewigen Herrschaft: Metall als Grundlage des hethitischen Reiches," in *Anatolian Metal V*, ed. Ünsal Yalçın. Der Anschnitt 24 (Bochum: Deutsches Bergbau-Museum, 2011), 81, who rightly ascribe a "sacral" character to gold.

336 Müller-Karpe, *Altanatolisches Metallhandwerk*, 73–78. See now also the similar conclusions in Lehner, "Cooperation, the Craft Economy, and Metal Technology," 85–88. The sole example of gold in the tribute texts comes from 3.1.8.A obv. 8′, where a number of gold necklaces are produced by smiths. Previous interpretations have taken the text as a *Sammeltafel*, in which case the jewelry on the obverse was probably not tribute at all, or as is argued in the introductory *Analysis* to 3.1.8 in Vol. II, the obverse concerns value-added tribute produced for various groups for the palace, in which case the jewelry was produced from palace supplies. In either interpretation, it is highly unlikely that the gold necklaces were produced from Anatolian gold.

337 Müller-Karpe, *op. cit.*, 78 Abb. 53.

338 The same can be said for any of the exotic materials appearing in the Hittite religious economy, including the seven lapis lazuli objects in the votive texts, which probably came from Egypt, and any mention of ivory and ebony elsewhere in the inventories. On the ultimate central Asian origin of many of the semi-precious stones in Hittite texts see Horst Klengel, "Handel mit Lapislazuli, Türkis und Karneol im alten Vorderen Orient," in *Anatolian Metal V*, ed. Ünsal Yalçın. Der Anschitt 24 (Bochum: Deutsches Bergbau-Museum, 2011), 69–77.

339 Harry Hoffner, "Some Thoughts on Merchants and Trade in the Hittite Kingdom," in *Kulturgeschichten: Altorientalistische Studien für Volkert Haas zum 65. Geburtstag*, eds. Thomas Richter, Doris Prechel, Jörg Klinger (Saarbrücken: Saarbrücker Druckerei und Verlag, 2001), 179–89.

half minas from Amurru). This total would have been augmented by the incidental diplomatic gifts accompanying letters between kings. The gold was referred to by weight in the vassal treaties, suggesting it was shipped in bullion form, in contrast to the finished objects appearing as gifts in the diplomatic texts. It is probable that the bullion did not stay this way for long: Müller-Karpe found within the Hittite inventory texts that in contrast to the raw silver, which probably came from a domestic source, gold tended to be stored as finished objects.[340] The relative lack of unfinished gold suggests a high turnover in the gold economy, with the yearly tribute being processed into objects fast enough by the palace workshops (see texts 4.1.1.1, 4.1.1.2, and 4.1.1.8 edited in *4.1.1 Silver- and Goldsmithing Texts* in Vol. II) that bullion was the exception rather than the rule in the palatial storehouses.

As described by Jana Siegelová, gold was treated with painstaking exactness in the inventory texts, including measurements noting the exact denominations of weights used to measure each quantity, perhaps as a way to prevent debasement or fraud.[341] In addition, gold seems to have been one of the few commodities that retained information on its geographic origins even in later stages of processing and inventory (see attestation in the KASKAL Main Text, 8.1.A obv. ii 18′–27′, where gold from Egypt, Babylon, and the Lukkā-lands of western Anatolia is recorded; since the KASKAL Main Text can in no way be interpreted as a tribute or manufacturing text, it can only be assumed that this gold had been stored with the labels of its geographic origins for some time). Prosopographical studies also show that the palace goldsmiths were no mere craftsmen, but were also entrusted the with functions of high-level administrators.[342] They were closely bound to the state apparatus, since the material they worked with would have been almost exclusively supplied by the state.[343]

In contrast to gold, silver was comparatively plentiful in Anatolia.[344] Elisabetta Floreano, in her analysis of the very interesting domestic tribute text KBo 18.155 (edited in Vol. II as text 3.1.10; see also the very similar 3.1.11), suggested that the Hittite state acquired silver from taxation directly at the mines, in addition to indirect or capillary mechanisms.[345] Like gold, silver was crafted by palace dependent smiths – apparently the same ones who handled the gold (see *4.1.1 Silver- and Goldsmithing Texts*). However, unlike gold, the texts of the PTAC show that silver was retained in ingot form for

---

340 Müller-Karpe, *Altanatolisches Metallhandwerk*, 75 Abb. 50b. See the same conclusion in Lehner, "Co-operation, the Craft Economy, and Metal Technology," 88, where the prevalence of gold finished objects in the inventories is taken as evidence that gold stayed in the Palace-Temple sphere longer, where it was stored as finished objects.

341 Siegelová, *Hethitische Verwaltungspraxis*, 294–95.

342 The privileged status of the goldsmith being the outstanding conclusion of Giulia Torri, "The Goldsmith Zuzu(l)li and the Find-spots of the Inventory Texts from Ḫattuša," AoF 43 (2016): 147–56.

343 Lehner, "Cooperation, the Craft Economy, and Metal Technology," 184; Lehner and Schachner, "The Organization of Metal Production at Hattuša," 409.

344 On silver in the Hittite economy, see Jana Siegelová, "Metalle und Metallurgie in den hethitischen Texten," RlA 8 (1993): 117; Lehner, "Cooperation, the Craft Economy, and Metal Technology," 81–82; and especially Elisabetta Floreano, "The Role of Silver in the Domestic Economic System of the Hittite Empire," AoF 28 (2001): 209–35.

345 Floreano, "The Role of Silver," 232.

seemingly long periods of time and in quantities far greater that could have been recently gathered as tribute, suggesting that ingots of silver were kept for use as a cash reserve by the Hittite state.[346] Instances of the palace tapping into this reserve are encountered in the PTAC (e.g., the 100 minas of silver brought by the Hittite king to the AN.DAḪ.ŠUM-Festival at Arinna in text 6.1 rev. A 6″–lo. e. 10″) and the Votive Corpus (e.g., 100 minas of silver for Ḫepat of Kummanni in KUB 15.29 obv. i 2′–3′), demonstrating that one of the main uses of bulk silver was to transfer wealth between regions for the endowment of temples and festivals. Silver was used as a medium of exchange in the Hittite domestic economy, being attested in the Hittite laws for the payment of fines, suggesting it was also used as a currency by the general population – though as Floreano noted, silver would have been too value-dense for daily use, at which scale trade in kind (especially grain) would have taken over.[347]

A brief remark must be added regarding the exchange rate of silver to gold in Hittite texts. Although suspiciously low ratios of two-to-one (also four-to-one) for exchange rates of silver to gold have been proposed,[348] these ratios seemed to be based on a misinterpretation of the vow genre, and specifically the text KUB 48.123 obv. i 18′. Instead, the ratio of two-to-one in KUB 48.123 obv. i 18′ reflects the expected proportions of silver and gold in the standard international "diplomatic gift" of the period (see *6.2.1.1 Commentary: The Standard Diplomatic Gift Package* and also *8.14 Average Value and Significance of the Vow Objects* for the reflex of this standard in the votive corpus), with the relative abundance of gold reflecting, if anything, the concern of the palace economies of Syria, Mesopotamia, and Anatolia to diplomatically prise of gold out of Egypt, which controlled access to the productive mines of Nubia. In pure economic terms, the exchange rate of silver to gold was probably closer to the ratio of eight-to-one attested in Anatolia in the Assyrian trade colony texts, with the true ratio of course varying based on the purity of the gold.[349]

2.4.2.3 Iron?

For the problematic role of iron in the Hittite Palace-Administrative Corpus, see the discussion in *Lexical Commentary s.v.* AN.BAR (GE_6). The essential problem is that the term AN.BAR, which certainly designated metallic iron in 1st millennium cuneiform texts, appears with a frequency and in quantities in Hittite cuneiform sources that cannot be corroborated by the restricted archaeological evidence for metallic iron in Late Bronze Age Anatolia. Already the term AN.BAR GE_6, which was earlier translated as meteoritic iron, was suggested to actually refer to an iron ore such as hematite based on its excessive frequency in the inventory texts. Since AN.BAR is used in essentially

346 See again Figure 3.6: "(Top) Relative frequency of metal commodity types for all different objects compared against tax and palace/temple inventory lists; (Middle) primary metal commodity types; and (Bottom) metal commodity types for finished goods (data from Siegelová 1986 and Müller-Karpe 1994: 75–76)" in Lehner, "Cooperation, the Craft Economy, and Metal Technology," 88.

347 Floreano, "The Role of Silver," 212.

348 Siegelová "Metalle und Metallurgie," 117, and Siegelová, "Metals in Hittite Records," 47, respectively.

349 Jan G. Dercksen, "Metals According to Documents from Kültepe-Kanish Dating to the Old Assyrian Colony Period," in *Anatolian Metal III*, ed. Ünsal Yalçın. Der Anschnitt 18 (Bochum: Deutsches Bergbau-Museum, 2005): 26–27.

the same quantities and applications as AN.BAR GE$_6$ in the PTAC (see *Table 59: Attestations of* AN.BAR *in the PTAC* [p. 367] and *Table 60: Attestations of* AN.BAR GE$_6$ *in the PTAC* [p. 368]) – including in applications that would be metallurgically difficult with early ironworking techniques – there is a chance that, pending the discovery of new archaeological evidence, AN.BAR in Hittite texts also referred to iron ore.

There is no firm textual evidence in the PTAC for how the Hittite palace acquired iron (or iron ore, as the case may be), nor how it produced objects made from the material.[350] Iron/iron ore does not regularly appear in the tribute lists. For acquisition, there is only a single appearance in the metal tribute text 3.1.7 of 26 shekels of iron (ore) (3.1.7.A$_1$ l. e. 3: 26 GÍN AN.BAR). The context is broken, but it would be very surprising if this amount was part of the tribute, based both on its location on the left edge of the tablet seemingly as part of a note unconnected to the main tribute, as well as its very small amount compared to the other metals in the text, which are measured in the dozens and hundreds of minas. For production, there is the broken context of 4.1.1.1.B$_1$ rev. iv$^?$ 3–4. Here, all that is preserved is what is probably a small amount of iron (rev. iv$^?$ 3: n+]1 MA.NA 30 GÍN AN.BAR) and then a verb (rev. iv$^?$ 4: *p*]*í-i-e-er* "they gave"). Since the previous uses of *piyēr* in the text involved disbursements of metal for the plating of divine statues (4.1.1.1.A$_1$ rev. 6′; 4.1.1.1.B$_1$ rev. iii$^?$ 12′–13′), it is probable that the AN.BAR was also being distributed for manufacture, though to whom and for what purpose are unknown. In this way, AN.BAR as a material fits better among the non-metallic luxury materials in the PTAC, such as the semi-precious stones and ivory and ebony – these also received no documentation on their origins (the ivory and ebony must have been imported, but at least some of the semi-precious stones must have been native) or their manufacture, despite being amply attested among the finished objects of the inventories.

2.4.3 Wealth Finance and Textiles

Although archaeologically nearly invisible, textual evidence shows that textiles were a major component of the Hittite wealth-financed state. Garments are on the whole at least as numerous as metallic objects in the PTAC, and wool, along with limited numbers of finished garments, forms the other major category of domestic tribute recorded in the cuneiform records (see *3.2. Domestic Tribute in the Form of Wool and Garments* in Vol. II). Dyed wool and luxury garments in the form of foreign tribute and international gifts are also attested as income of the Hittite state.[351] In terms of manufacture, administrative records also show that the Hittite state could engage in more or less

350 Nevertheless, see Violetta Cordani, "The Development of the Hittite Iron Industry. A Reappraisal of the Written Sources," WO 46 (2016): 162–76, with extensive previous literature, for the Hittite iron from a philological perspective. As discussed above and in the *Lexical Commentary s.v.* AN.BAR (GE$_6$) (see especially Enrico Lehnhardt, "The Introduction of Iron in the Old World as a Research Problem," in *Time and Materiality: Periodization and Regional Chronologies at the Transition from Bronze to Iron Age in Eurasia (1200-600 BCE)*, eds. Elke Kaiser, Wolfram Schier. Prähistorische Archäologie in Südosteuropa 31 [Rahden/Westf.: Leidorf, 2021], 19–60), the archaeological evidence for Hittite iron use, much less production, is negligible.

351 See the dyed wool in *6.3.1 Tribute from Ugarit*, and the garments in *6.2 Gifts in the Egyptian-Hittite Correspondence*.

direct sponsorship of wool processing and some textile production.[352] However, the number of garments attested in storage and static inventories far exceed the textual basis for production, suggesting that non-palace workshops were also engaged to process the wool tribute.

Garments are favored handouts in the PTAC, to both elites and lower-ranking dependents of the Hittite state.[353] The nature of textiles make them an ideal gift for influencing stakeholders in a wealth-financed state: they fashionably mark status as a member of an in-group, while at the same time they are less permanent, less fungible, and as a result less easily repurposed than metal wealth. It is more difficult for potentially dangerous local elites to hoard gifted garments for the purpose of building a rival powerbase than it is to do the same with gold and silver, or more directly, with bronze weapons. It was perhaps for this reason that garments predominate among the direct handouts by the Hittite state, while gold and silver were expended in the potentially less hazardous realm of religious donations (see further in *2.5.2 Future Research Questions* below).

The economic importance of the textile industry to the Hittite state is difficult to measure. Unlike some detailed records from Mesopotamia,[354] which in addition to the raw materials also document the man-hours necessary to produce a textile (and thus provide an approximate value), the few Hittite texts concerning textile production only list weights of dyed wool and linen. The Hittite Laws give prescriptive values for garments,[355] but garments in real-world conditions would have varied wildly in worth depending on their quality of materials, skill in construction, rarity of dyes, and level of finishing. Some terminological distinction between garments is available in the PTAC (e.g., *iyatnaš* 'luxurious', SIG 'thin, fine', *MAŠLU* 'patterned'), but there is no way to convert such terms to an absolute value, or even to gauge the relative values of the garments. Coupled with the enormous range of often opaque terminology for garment types and styles, and the unknown premium attached to exotic or imported textiles,[356] it is difficult to assess the amount of wealth represented by the textiles of the PTAC.

352 For wool processing, see 4.1.3.1–5 and possibly 4.1.3.7. For garment manufacturing, see under *4.1.4 Textile Manufacturing Texts* in Vol. II.

353 See texts 4.1.4.1–5, which involve the production of belts for named elite individuals, as well as the texts edited under *6. Gifts and Handouts* in Vol. II, especially the handouts to the garrison troops at Nerik in 6.1.

354 Here Hittitology can only look on with envy at the bountiful documentation of the Ur III period: see Hartmut Waetzoldt, *Untersuchungen zur neusumerischen Textilindustrie.* Studi economici e tecnologici 1 (Roma: Centro per le antichità e la storia dell'arte del Vicino Oriente, 1972).

355 See "Table 2: Prices" in Hoffner, *The Laws of the Hittites*, 7–10; cf. also Siegelová, *Hethitische Verwaltungspraxis*, 23–25, for a comparison of these figures to a living sales text.

356 It would be surprising if the appreciation for imported textiles had much abated since the trade colony days, where Assyrian textiles were, next to tin, the premier imported good; see Cécile Michel and Klaas R. Veenhof, "The Textiles Traded by the Assyrians in Anatolia (19th–18th centuries BC)," in *Textile terminologies in the ancient Near East and Mediterranean from the third to the first millennia BC*, eds. Cécile Michel, Marie-Louise Nosch (Oxford: Oxbow, 2010), 210–71; more generally, Klaas R. Veenhof, "Ancient Assur: The City, its Traders, and its Commerical Network," JESHO 53 (2010): 39–82.

Suffice it to say that judging by their frequency and complexity of description in the administrative corpus, textiles were extremely important, and served alongside metals as the second workhorse, as it were, pulling the yoke of the Hittite wealth-financed state.[357]

2.4.4 Staple Finance (and its Near Absence in Hittite Textual Sources)

The management of staple finance, i.e., grain and livestock, is barely attested in the "living" economic-administrative records of the Hittite state outside of a handful of field texts (CTH 239)[358] and some documents of the (potentially) exceptional Maşat Höyuk–Tapikka corpus.[359] In the Palace-Temple Administrative Corpus, foodstuffs are almost completely absent. Some staples appear in the more distantly administrative, prescriptive genres of the land grant documents (CTH 222),[360] the Vow of Puduḫepa (CTH 585),[361] and the provisioning documents for the state[362] and local cults,[363] but not nearly to the extent one would expect from a mature Bronze Age state. As such, the topic of staple finance remains problematic from a philological point of view and will only be discussed here briefly. Fortunately, an article by Lorenzo d'Alfonso and Alvise

---

357 The role of textiles in the Hittite luxury economy deserves a book-length treatment of its own. Despite much appreciated advances brought by recent research (e.g. Matteo Vigo, "Linen in Hittite Inventory Texts," in *Textile terminologies in the ancient Near East and Mediterranean from the third to the first millennia BC*, eds. Cécile Michel, Marie-Louise Nosch. Ancient Textiles Series 8 [Oxford: Oxbow, 2010], 290–322, and Giulia Baccelli, et al., "Elements for a Comparative Study of Textile Production and Use in Hittite Anatolia and in Neighbouring Areas," in *Prehistoric, Ancient Near Eastern and Aegean Textiles and Dress*, eds. Mary Harlow, Cécile Michel, Marie-Louise Nosch [Oxford: Oxbow, 2014], 97–142), it may be seen from the various entries on garments and textiles in the *Lexical Commentary* of the present volume that Hittite textual terminology is in dire need of a modern philological reassessment. This reassessment must take into account not only the Hittite texts, but also the terminologies of neighboring cultures (especially of the Syrian city-states such as Ugarit and Mari), as well as the latest archaeological and experimental archaeological data.

358 Vladimír Souček, "Die hethitischen Feldertexte." ArOr. 27 (1959): 5–43; *id.*, "Randnotizen zu den hethitischen Feldertexte," MIO 8 (1963): 368–82.

359 See editions in Giuseppe del Monte, "I testi amministrativi da Maşat Höyük/Tapika," OrAntMisc. 2 (1995): 89–138; and discussion in Beckman, "Hittite Provincial Administration," 19–37. The administrative documents from Maşat Höyük–Tapikka record inventories of around one hundred pieces of agricultural equipment as well as modest amounts of seed grain. However, it is not clear how much of the textual record concerning agricultural activities at Maşat Höyük-Tapikka is due to the exceptional circumstances surrounding the archive, which was found in the destruction layer following a Kaškaen raid and records defensive preparations, including coordination of the relief forces and garrison for the early taking in of the wine and grain harvest. A second provincial archive recording *regular* grain storage and distribution, not in the context of an emergency, would allow for much firmer conclusions.

360 Christel Rüster and Gernot Wilhelm, *Landschenkungsurkunden hethitischer Könige*. StBoT Beiheft 4 (Wiesbaden: Harrassowitz, 2012).

361 See below *8.13 The Vow of Puduḫepa (CTH 585) and Vow Fulfillment in Practice.*

362 See again Singer, *The Hittite KI.LAM Festival*, 157–70; *id.* "The AGRIG in the Hittite Texts," 97–127; Burgin, "Hittite Ration Lists Revisited"; and Siegelová, "Naturalabgaben für den Kult," 103–12.

363 See again "6. Economics of the Local Cults: Offerings and Participants," in Cammarosano, *Hittite Local Cults*, 139–58.

Matessi has ably consolidated recent research on the topic.[364] Their basic conclusions are thus: the Hittite state managed control of the land indirectly through the imposition of service obligations (the *šaḫḫan*, *luzzi-*, LÚ^MEŠ^ *ILKI*, and LÚ^MEŠ^ TUKUL discussed already in *1.7.1 The End of Hittite Feudalism as a Theoretical Model*) of indeterminate scope, which implied a range of relationships to the Hittite state, but probably did not imply a universal service obligation levied on the general population.[365] More direct control of land resources can be seen in the land grants, which established *latifundia* under the control of Hittite elites dependent on the royal family. As d'Alfonso and Matessi described it, the dependence of the land grants on the Hittite king prevented elites from becoming "decentralized regional potentates," and the documents testify to "robust intervention by the state to keep the land productive and thus to maintain the inflow of state revenues through the allotment of resources to various stakeholders and through the distribution of manpower"[366] – or, as summarized by d'Alfonso and Matessi, "Hittite political institutions directly regulate rural life only in order to keep non-private land productive."[367] Even so, while the Hittite state directed what seems to have been a considerable amount of administrative effort to documenting the condition of estate at the time of handover, the day-to-day and year-to-year administration of the land was left to the possessing elite. There is no evidence for any follow-up audits of productivity.[368]

D'Alfonso and Matessi also discussed the absence of textual documentation related to the staple Hittite economy.[369] Although many have assumed that wooden writing boards must have been used for the management of the complex system of extraction

364 Lorenzo d'Alfonso and Alvise Matessi, "Extracting Cohesion: Fiscal Strategies in the Hittite Staple Economy," in *Ancient Taxation. Mechanics of Extraction in Comparative Perspective*, eds. Jonathan Valk, Irene Soto Marín. Institute for the Study of the Ancient World Monographs (New York: New York University Press, 2021), 128–59; cf. also the brief summarizing overview of Matteo Vigo, "Staple and Wealth Finance and the Administration of the Hittite Empire," in *Economy of Religions in Anatolia: From the Early Second to the Middle of the First Millennium BCE. Proceedings of an International Conference in Bonn (23rd to 25th May 2018)*, eds. Manfred Hutter, Sylvia Hutter-Braunsar. AOAT 467 (Münster: Ugarit-Verlag, 2019), 141–51. For a perspective on the agricultural management of the Hittite state which is more critical of the Wealth Finance/Staple Finance model, see Klinger, "Hittite Economics," 609–30.

365 See d'Alfonso and Matessi, "Extracting Cohesion," 132–36.

366 See d'Alfonso and Matessi, *op. cit.*, 136.

367 See d'Alfonso and Matessi, *op. cit.*, 137.

368 The point in Klinger, "Hittite Economics," 618, emphasizing the administrative capacities necessary to generate the land-grant documents is well taken, as is the suspicion that the Hittite state would be loath to abandon this lever of control over the elite after the Old Kingdom, but the size of the bureaucracy should not be overestimated. The survey of a granted estate would have required only a single literate individual plus perhaps a few assistants visiting the site for interviews and measurements. Nor should the quality and precision of the land grants be assumed to be uniform in all periods of Hittite history, since the level of information in the existing land-grant documents varies greatly. In the absence of standardization, and without the pressure of regular updates and audits, the administrative burden would be comparatively light, and perhaps require the dedication of only one or two officials tasked with the portfolio of "land management" per generation.

369 See also here Klinger, *op. cit.*, 609–11.

and accumulation of agricultural resources observed in the archaeological record,[370] d'Alfonso and Matessi presented the cogent argument that impressive amounts of accumulation and storage of agricultural products are also attested in Early Bronze Age III and Middle Bronze Age Anatolia, where the process was managed with non-literate technologies, including, above all, the use of seals and bullae, themselves inherited from the Chalcolithic.[371] As d'Alfonso and Matessi concluded:

> Given their persistence from the fourth to the early second millennium BCE, methods of recordkeeping by means of seals and *bullae* may have been such an integral part of the administrative *modus operandi* in Anatolia that writing was simply deemed unnecessary even after the Hittite court definitively adopted cuneiform beginning in the Old Hittite Kingdom. ... recording of staple finance transactions on perishable materials, namely wooden tablets, cannot be ruled out ... . But it is also possible that non-literate recordkeeping traditions did survive in this sector of Hittite administration. [372]

Independent of how agricultural surpluses were coordinated, whether with literate or with non-literate administrative techniques, d'Alfonso and Matessi ultimately concluded that state intervention functioned to accumulate emergency reserves, rather than as a redistributive network.[373] Symbolic redistribution is observed in the rations of the state cult and the provisions of the local festivals, but the true economic scale of these measures is currently unknown.[374]

---

370 See d'Alfonso and Matessi, "Extracting Cohesion," 143, for citations, to which may be added Willemijn Waal, "They Wrote on Wood. The Case for a Hieroglyphic Scribal Tradition on Wooden Writing Boards in Hittite Anatolia," AnSt. 61 (2011): 21–34, and Michele Cammarosano, et al., "They Wrote on Wax. Wax Boards in the Ancient Near East," *Mesopotamia* 54 (2019): 121–80.

371 See the 4th millennium administrative system at Arslantepe reconstructed in Marcella Frangipane and Enrica Fiandra, "Chapter VII: Arslantepe: A Complex Administrative System before Writing," in *Arslantepe* Cretulae*: An Early Centralised Administrative System Before Writing*, by Marcella Frangipane, et al., Arslantepe 5 (Rome: Ed. CIRAAS, 2007), 415–68.

372 See d'Alfonso and Matessi, *loc. cit.* See similar conclusions already in Theo van den Hout, "Administration and Writing in Hittite Society," in *Archivi, depositi, magazzini presso gli Ittiti: nuovi materiali e nuove ricerche / Archives, Depots and Storehouses in the Hittite World: New Evidence and New Research (Proceedings of the Workshop held in Pavia, June 18, 2009)*, eds. Maria Balza, Mauro Giorgieri, Clelia Mora. StMed. 23 (Genoa: Italian University Press, 2012), 53–54, and van den Hout . Contrast the views of Massimiliano Marazzi, "Sigilli, sigillature e tavolette di legno: alcune considerazioni alla luce di nuovi dati," in *Belkıs Dinçol ve Ali Dinçol'a Armağan. VITA: Festschrift in Honor of Belkıs Dinçol and Ali Dinçol*, eds. Metin Alparslan, Metlem Doğan-Alparslan, Hasan Peker (Istanbul: Ege Yayınları, 2007), 465–74, with previous literature; and Suzanne Herbordt, *Die Prinzen- und Beamtensiegel der hethitischen Grossreichszeit auf Tonbullen aus dem Nişantepe-Archiv in Hattusa*. BoḪa. 19 (Mainz: von Zabern, 2005), 36–39, where it is argued that the bullae were principally used to secure wooden diptych-style tablets.

373 See d'Alfonso and Matessi, *op. cit.*, 147. See also similar conclusions in Klinger, "Hittite Economics," 619–22, under "Funding the State: Levies and Duties," where Klinger rightly raised suspicion against assuming the regular contribution of agricultural products from the private rural sector to the Hittite state, and vice-versa, the extensive dependence of the rural population on the Hittite urban economy for crafted products.

374 See d'Alfonso and Matessi, *op. cit.*, 148–49. See similar conclusion in Klinger, "Hittite Economics," 614–15, with fn. 38.

Even though almost no traces of the staple economy, including the grain silos, the water reservoirs, and the actual living provisioning records for the feasts are documented in the cuneiform administrative records that are the focus of the present book, it is still vital that these elements of the Hittite state be kept in mind. It is important to realize that these areas of massive state intervention, which for most Anatolians almost certainly constituted the Hittite state as they encountered it, stand in the silent background of every discussion of Hittite administrative power. Although arguments can be presented for and against the existence of an extensive administration recorded on perishable materials that was used to coordinate the efforts of building and maintaining these power structures, the topic as a philological research question is moot: these records are by definition lost and they have moreover left only tangential traces in the cuneiform records.[375] Instead, as this chapter has shown, investigation of what must have constituted a considerable expenditure of Hittite administrative power – the building, the maintenance, the stockpiling, the provisioning – must defer to archaeology and anthropological models.

2.4.5 Wealth Finance, Staple Finance Conclusions

Bringing the evidence together, it can be seen that the Hittite state intervened at different levels of the wealth and staple economies. In the case of wealth, indirect control was exercised over the secondary production of metals and textiles, supplemented by the production of certain prestige goods, and control over trade in exotic materials and luxury goods. In theory, the Hittite state could have also chosen to intervene at the level of primary production of metal, but it instead chose to rely a system of coercive extraction (taxation) for silver, copper, and possibly tin, that drew on a network of localized and diverse regional sources rather than direct management of government mines. Textile production seems to have occurred under similar conditions: there is no textual evidence for state-owned flocks of sheep supplying state-owned textile workshops. Gold is the major exception to the pattern of indirect control. Gold was acquired exclusively through international trade, which, to judge from the texts, was an extension of state diplomacy. As such, it was carefully controlled and used in the production of jewelry and especially religious figurines and paraphernalia by state craftsmen.

For staples, state intervention was also indirect, but at the level of primary production: the Hittite state intervened at the fields, either by taking a portion of the harvest, or through the induction of labor to state-controlled fields managed by elites. In either scenario, the harvest was put aside for long-term storage as emergency reserves in silos. Thus, in contrast to the coercive system of taxation, the villages who tithed the grain or worked the fields as corvée had some expectation of seeing their grain again, specifically at the next decadal crop failure. Evidence for large-scale rationing, where the state provided the *daily* bread or meat for large numbers of workers, is lacking,

375 See *3.1.2 On the Interface of the PTAC with Other Systems of Administration* below, although discussion is the limited there to the only interface of the luxury economy recorded in the Palace-Temple Administrative Corpus with the wooden tablets and *cretulae*/bullae; evidence for the staple economy in the *cretulae*/bullae system is even slimmer, although this could change with future studies on the impressions left by substrate materials on the back of the *cretulae*.

except for perhaps the closest of palace dependents (but this distribution was probably portrayed as household dependence). Festivals could be seen as an exception, since large amounts of food were consumed, but these were "feast" situations, where the ceremony and pageantry of food distribution was more important than the caloric contents. In addition, local feasts were supplied from local agricultural products: the villages were essentially celebrating with their own bread, meat, and cheese.

The Hittite administrative record as it is preserved shows a distinct focus on the acquisition, production, curation, and distribution of luxury goods, including metals and textiles from both foreign and domestic sources. This apparent focus on a wealth-financed model of political economy helps explain some of the more unusual features of the Hittite state compared to its contemporaries. The seeming lack of private foreign trade and independent merchants in the Hittite Kingdom has long been noticed by Hittitologists (in Goetze's original description of the Hittite state, merchants were state employees tasked with acquiring raw materials not domestically available).[376] In what is still the most recent overview of the merchant as a profession in Hittite society, Harry Hoffner concluded that Hittite merchants were state-sanctioned purveyors of foreign goods for the king, with the primary responsibility of conveying tribute and loot to Ḫattuša, though they were permitted to conduct their own business on the side.[377] Otherwise, foreign trade appears to have been severely restricted.[378] This is confirmed by the archaeological record, as attested by the astonishingly limited

---

376 Albrecht Goetze, "State and Society of the Hittites," in *Neuere Hethiterforschung*, ed. Gerold Walser (Wiesbaden: Steiner, 1964), 28.

377 See now text 1.5 in Vol. II, for what is perhaps the first confirmation of this arrangement from an administrative text.

378 Hoffner, "Some Thoughts on Merchants," 181–82, 189. However, cf. Klinger, "Hittite Economics," 634–36, where doubts are expressed about the exclusively "merchant envoy" model reconstructed by Hoffner: as Klinger noted (p. 634)

> It seems inconceivable, to me personally, that an authority such as that of the Hittite kings with their profound relationships to northern Syria especially, but also beyond, should have been otherwise completely self-sufficient and not had any interest in products and goods "from abroad," even if, and this has to be conceded without doubt, no tangible material evidence can be quoted.

As Klinger discussed, the comparative paucity of precious metal luxury goods of any type, Hittite or otherwise, in the archaeological record makes it difficult to assess the frequency of imported luxury wares. Nevertheless, what does remain among the *Kleinfunde*, shows no perceptible admixture of clearly identifiable foreign items, including among hoards of metal objects, where one would logically expect to find high-value international goods (see Tayfun Yıldırım, et al., "Symbolism in 13th-century BC Hittite Metallurgy: The Kastamonu-Kınık (Turkey) Metal Hoard, Again," JNES 80 (2021): 32 for a current list of metal *Sammelfunde* from the Hittite period). Even the seeming exception to the trend, namely the Mycenaean pattern swords, of which three are currently known (Ahmet Ünal, "A Hittite Mycenaean Type B Sword from the Vicinity of Kastamonu, Northwest Turkey," in *Essays on Ancient Anatolia*, ed. H. I. H. P. Takahito Mikasa. BMECCJ 11 [Wiesbaden: Harrassowitz, 1999], 207–26), appear to have been locally manufactured in Anatolia (see Yıldırım, et al., "Symbolism in 13th-century BC Hittite Metallurgy," 40–43, for metallurgical analysis, where the Kastamonu-Kınık sword falls squarely among the other high-tin content items, especially the juglets of the hoard, which seemed to have been intentionally crafted as *objets d'art* selected for their silvery sheen).

assemblage of foreign goods found in Ḫattuša (including a complete absence of Mycenaean/Aegean material, even in Hittite-controlled Tarsus, which given the proximity and well-attested contact between the regions would be improbable absent political interference with trade).[379] While severe restrictions on foreign trade seem economically disastrous in today's globally connected world, in a wealth-financed state which relied on the ability to control the distribution of prestige objects as the basis for power, discouragement of, or at a minimum, a failure to encourage, private merchants venturing abroad makes perfect sense. Likewise, the focus of the Palace-Temple Administrative Corpus on durable goods to the exclusion of staples (as was discussed, there are almost no "live" records of grain administration in Ḫattuša, and the agricultural records at Maşat Höyük-Tapikka may be a result of the circumstances surrounding the archives), is appropriate for a state focused on the production, management, and circulation of luxury goods among elites.[380]

In closing, it can be noted that the Hittite state also seems to have applied its wealth-financed model to its interactions with the parts of Syria it governed. As Gary Beckman found in a pioneering study comparing the administrative archives of the Syrian city of Emar to those found at the (admittedly much smaller) Anatolian town of Maşat Höyük-Tapikka, the foremost concerns of the Hittite authorities at Emar were military matters, the collections of taxes, and religion, with the agricultural sphere left to the locals.[381] Beckman's observation of Emar can be applied to other parts of the Hittite Empire in northern Syria, where, as Elena Devecchi has outlined in a recent contribution synthesizing decades of research, the Hittites were content for the most part to leave in place the local dynasties (diplomatic relationships with which were intensively managed) and economic structures (which were left comparatively alone) in exchange for luxury goods and military support.[382] What slim evidence exists for intervention at

379 Ekin Kozal and Mirko Novák, "Geschenke, Tribute und Handelswaren im Hethiterreich. Eine archäologische Bestandsaufnahme am Fallbeispiel Ḫattuša," in *Geschenke und Steuern, Zölle und Tribute: Antike Abgabenformen in Anspruch und Wirklichkeit*, eds. Hilmar Klinkott, Sabine Kubisch, Renate Müller-Wollermann. CHANE 29 (Leiden: Brill, 2007), 340–41. See also Hermann Genz, "Anatolien als Landbrücke in der späten Bronzezeit? Kommentare zu den hethitischen Fernbeziehungen aus archäologischer Sicht," in *Interkulturalität in der Alten Welt. Vorderasien, Hellas, Ägypten und die vielfältigen Ebenen des Kontakts*, eds. Robert Rollinger, Birgit Gufler, Martin Lang, Irene Madreiter. Philippika 34 (Wiesbaden: Harrassowitz), 13-22.

380 This being the purpose of the Hittite state archives as concluded by Mauro Giorgieri and Clelia Mora, "Luxusgüter als Symbole der Macht: Zur Verwaltung der Luxusgüter im Hethiter-Reich," in *Organization, Representation, and Symbols of Power in the Ancient Near East. Proceedings of the 54th Rencontre Assyriologique Internationale at Würzburg 20–25 July 2008*, ed. Gernot Wilhelm (Winona Lake: Eisenbrauns, 2012), 654–57.

381 Beckman, "Hittite Provincial Administration," 26–27:

> Here [*scil.* at Emar] defense against enemy incursions was also a primary concern of the local authorities .... To be noted too is a strong interest in the collection of local and imperial revenues and in the supply of the regional cult with offering materials. Agricultural production, on the other hand, seems to have been left largely to the individual household, judging from the hundreds of sale documents dealing with fields, gardens, and orchards.

382 Elena Devecchi, "The Governance of Subordinated Countries," in *Handbook of the Hittite Empire. Power Structures*, ed. Stefano de Martino. Empires through the Ages in Global Perspective 1

the level of staple products in the region by the Hittites, which comprises essentially the well-known letter RS 20.212 concerning the grain shipments from Mukiš to Ura, the letter Bo 2810 concerning a grain shipment from Syria possibly to Ḫatti, and now the new evidence from the House of Urtenu in Ugarit concerning the circulation of grain among Hittite vassals in Syria,[383] all comes in the context of grain shortages and famine – i.e. the exact same kind of "defensive" intervention observed with the Hittite state in Anatolia.

2.4.6 Patrimonialism, Bureaucracy, and the Elites

If the economic basis of the Hittite state can be archaeologically traced in staples and wealth, the social basis must be recovered from texts. Here, a patrimonialist interpretation of the Hittite state has lately found an audience in Hittitology. Amir Gilan was perhaps one of the first to encourage turning away from the dominance of the Italian School, which in 1998 had reached what was probably its high-water mark in Fiorella Imparati's masterful overview of the organization of the Hittite state.[384] Gilan argued that David Schloen's model (discussed in *2.3.1 Basis of the Hittite State in Communal Antecedents*) of a Weberian patrimonialism mixed with the hermeneutic-phenomenologic interpretation of the state predicated on the manipulation of inherited symbols and structures was a better alternative to what Gilan considered the artificial divisions of the Two-Sector/neo-AMP models.[385] For Gilan, the greatest advantage of the patrimonialist system was that it unifies the systems of cultic supply and universal corvée labor into a single organic, manorial economy pervading Hittite society.[386]

(Oldenbourg: De Gruyter, 2022), 271–312. See especially, sections "Military Contribution and Hittite Military Presence in the Subordinated Countries" (281–86) and "Economic Exploitation of the Subjugated Countries" (287–98).

383 Devecchi, "The Governance of Subordinated Countries," 295 fn. 113 with literature; on Ugarit's role as an entrepôt for the emergency grain shipments of the period, see also Elena Devecchi, "A Reluctant Servant: Ugarit under Foreign Rule during the Late Bronze Age," in *A Stranger in the House – The Crossroads III: Proceedings of an International Conference on Foreigners in Ancient Egyptian and Near Eastern Societies of the Bronze Age held in Prague, September 10–13, 2018*, eds. Jana Mynářová, Marwan Kilani, Sergio Alivernini (Prague: Charles University, 2019), 131.

384 Fiorella Imparati, "Die Organisation des hethitischen Staates," in *Geschichte des Hethitischen Reiches*, by Horst Klengel, contribs. Fiorella Imparati, Volkert Haas, Theo van den Hout. HdO 1/34 (Leiden: Brill), 320–87.

385 Amir Gilan, "Formen der Transaktion im hethitischen 'Staatskult' - Idee und Wirklichkeit," in *Geschenke und Steuern, Zölle und Tribut: Antike Abgabenformen in Anspruch und Wirklichkeit*, ed. Hilmar Klinkott, Sabine Kubisch, Renate Müller-Wollermann. CHANE 29 (Leiden: Brill, 2007), 293–322.

386 Amir Gilan, "'Ist denn der Sinn von Menschen und Göttern irgendwie verschieden?' – Zur Ökonomie, Religion (und Herrschaft) im hethitischen Anatolien," in *Das Heilige und die Ware. Zum Spannungsfeld von Religionen und Ökonomie*, ed. Martin Fitzenreiter (Düsseldorf: Golden House Publications, 2007), 57–65. Although Hittite manorialism is difficult to directly measure, given the lack of private administrative records – or even the administrative records of the large, state-owned *latifundia* – and the paucity of archaeological data for Hittite rural settlements and farmsteads, traces of the manorial system are best visible in the land-grant documents, which organized estates into multiple households of dependent and unfree artisans and laborers – see Klinger, "Hittite Economics," 615–19 for the latest thoughts on the economics of the estates in these documents, including calculation of the

Tayfun Bilgin has since grappled with the question of Hittite patrimonialism in detail at the end of his book-length study of the administrators who ran the Hittite state. Bilgin found that there was a continuous, organic growth in number and hierarchy of offices, as well as evidence for the increased importance of officials observable in the witness lists of treaties and grants over history of kingdom.[387] Both factors were taken as evidence of a native impulse towards bureaucratization, born out of a rational response to the increased administrative burdens of empire, and thus not necessarily adopted from Mesopotamia.[388] Nevertheless, a tension existed between a rationalized bureaucracy on the one hand and the "family business" of the Hittite state on the other for the duration of Hittite history. It seems that the hierarchy at the Hittite court was only weakly determined by the office one held: using evidence from the witness lists, Bilgin demonstrated that the particular office held by a high official was largely irrelevant to his actual status. This observation is in partial agreement with an earlier thesis of Frank Starke.[389] However, contrary to Starke, Bilgin argued that the irrelevance of office for rank does not mean that all Hittite high officials were equal. Rather, a strong hierarchy predicated on external factors existed that was mostly independent of a particular official's office of the moment.[390] Relationship to the royal family was a major contributing factor to status, but also not the sole determining factor, since favoritism and one's political star were also decisive.[391] The specifics of the hierarchy of Hittite administration were also not static: Bilgin presented a historical interpretation whereby a great and increasing percentage of officials were members of the extended royal family (though the apparent increase may be due only to the extension of the DUMU.LUGAL title to the wider male kinship group), who dominated the highest levels of the administrative hierarchy in the Empire Period.[392] The one exception to this trend is the increase in prominence of the non-royal LÚ^{MEŠ} SAG officials in the reign of Ḫattušili III and Tudḫaliya IV, individuals proximate to the king who, according to Bilgin, "became his confidants and advisors, and thereby formed a buffer zone around the king against

potential agricultural surplus they were capable of producing, and also again d'Alfonso and Matessi, "Extracting Cohesion." The pervasivess of manorialism as an economic system in Hittite government and society deserves a dedicated investigation in the near future.

387 See "5.2 Continuity and Discontinuity in Hittite Offices," in Bilgin, *Officials and Administration*, 407–13.

388 Bilgin, *op. cit.*, 412–13.

389 Frank Starke, "Zur 'Regierung' des hethitischen Staates," ZABR 2 (1996): 140–82.

390 Theo van den Hout ("Elites and the Social Stratification of the Ruling Class in the Hittite Kingdom," in *Handbook of the Hittite Empire. Power Structures*, ed. Stefano de Martino. Empires through the Ages in Global Perspective 1 [Oldenbourg: De Gruyter, 2022], 328–29) has pushed back against Bilgin's interpretation of a full disconnect between status and office, with the argument that the best offices were reserved for the most powerful individuals, and some princes would prefer to be temporarily without office if a suitable position was not available for them at the moment, than to take a "real job" in one of the technical, administrative positions.

391 Bilgin, *op. cit.*, 419–22.

392 See "5.4 Kinship, DUMU.LUGAL, and the Rise of the LÚ.MEŠ SAG" in Bilgin, *op. cit.*, 423–36.

threats."[393] With the disruption of administrative documents at the end of the Hittite New Kingdom, it is not possible to tell whether the LÚ^{MEŠ} SAG continued to enjoy a high status after Tudḫaliya IV, but any diminution of the power of the extended royal family would have certainly been contested.

In his concluding assessment of the Hittite administrative system, Bilgin argued for a limited bureaucracy attached to a patrimonial system.[394] After discussing the features of a bureaucracy vis-à-vis a patrimonial system (specialization vs. generalized and overlapping responsibilities, impersonal rules vs. special treatment based on personal connections, deep vs. flat hierarchy, technical training vs. lack thereof, fixed payment vs. compensation via benefices and privileges), Bilgin suggested that evidence can be found for bureaucracy only among the lowest-ranking, and hence non-royal, state officials.[395] In the schema of elite stratification recently put forth by Theo van den Hout, these officials occupied the fourth and lowest tier of elites, composed of "hard working" retainers promoted for nothing more than their technical competency and loyalty to the crown.[396] In contrast, the upper administrators displayed all of the features of a patrimonial system, and were drawn from the hereditary, temperamental, and potentially dangerous class of the extended royal family of the Hittite king.[397] Ultimately, however, Bilgin conceded that problems of documentation make proving the existence of rational and bureaucratic features even at the lower administrative levels impossible, and it may be wondered how truly meritocratic membership among the subelites of the Hittite state was.

2.4.7 Mesopotamian Influence on the Hittite State?

In Frangipane's original account of wealth finance and staple finance in the Hittite and Mesopotamian contexts, the Hittite state inherited its government from the highly localized, wealth-financed Anatolian principalities, upon which the growing Hittite Kingdom grafted a Mesopotamian-inspired (but as Bilgin established, locally-grown) bureaucracy that aspired to control at least the defensive accumulation of staple products. Frangipane's model left open the motivations for the Hittite adoption of Mesopotamian practices, noting only that all mature states of the ancient Near East eventually adopted a hybrid system of finance,[398] but Klengel's original thesis in which the imported governmental practices were used to break the power of the Anatolian nobility rings true, especially in light of Glatz's research underlining the historical destruction

393 Bilgin, *Officials and Administration*, 435–36. See also van den Hout, "Elites and the Social Stratification," 337–40, 348–49, for thoughts on the dangers of granting power to extended royal family, and the "solipsistic paranoia of the thirteenth century" (p. 351) triggered by the coup of Ḫattušili III.

394 "5.5 Hittite Administration as a Patrimonial Organization," Bilgin, *op. cit.*, 473–51.

395 Bilgin, *op. cit.*, 440–45; *ibid.* 445: "This brief survey suggests that any indication of a bureaucratic system is only visible at the lower levels of administration. The higher we move, the more patrimonial the organization appears."

396 See van den Hout, "Elites and the Social Stratification," 347–50.

397 These comprising tiers two (the immediate family, including in-laws, of the royal couple and the king's full brother) and three (the king's half-brothers, sons of concubines, and the extended royal family) in the system of van den Hout, *loc. cit.*.

398 Frangipane, "Evolution and Role of Administration," 122.

or reduction of any urban competitors to Ḫattuša. Frangipane is correct in describing the continued focus on wealth finance in the Hittite state as a source of strength, even if the wealth brought by the burgeoning empire strained the traditional verticalism of Anatolian society.[399]

In light of Mesopotamian influence on the formation of the Hittite state, it is useful to query the "Anatolianess" of the Hittite state. For some, such as archaeologist Christoph Bachhuber, the Hittites were essentially foreigners in their own land. Bachhuber observed that urbanism is not natural to the Anatolian Plateau, with cities only created and maintained there in exceptional circumstances.[400] In the Middle Bronze Age, the circumstances sustaining urbanization were the intensified contact and commerce with Assyrian merchants, and in the Late Bronze Age it was the ambition and resources of the Hittite Empire. In both cases foreign contacts and exotic materials were the key to urbanization.[401] Bachhuber's thesis interpreted the cities of the Anatolian Plateau, the same settlement pattern observed by Glatz, as the Hittites building monumental "shell towns" to dominate rural inhabitants of Anatolian Plateau. Even the significant swathes of the pantheon of the Hittite state was foreign, incorporated into the temples of Ḫattuša (and elsewhere)[402] in order to overawe the locals.[403] As Bachhuber concluded,

> much of the ideological core of Hittite urbanism was indeed foreign and ad hoc, as well as parasitic. Like those of the elites of the MBA, the urbanizing and imperial ambitions of the Hittites had become over-reliant on their acquisitions from foreign people and foreign lands. And as in the MBA, the urbanism of Hittite society was too shallowly rooted to survive the socioeconomic quakes that ended the Bronze Age in western Asia and the eastern Mediterranean.[404]

Bachhuber may be correct in arguing that urbanism is unnatural to the Anatolian Plateau. But it is better, I think, to appreciate just how Anatolian the mature Hittite state was. The regional religious calendar, the grain silos, the wealth-financed administration can all be traced directly to the Anatolian environment, and, as elucidated in the "Schachner Thesis" of the Hittite state, resulted from long-term indigenous development, punctuated by significant but self-explicable changes.

By time span the Hittite Kingdom is the most successful state by far to have existed with a power base situated exclusively on the Anatolian Plateau (the Ottomans eventually moved their capital to the coast after the conquest of Constatinople in the process of transforming into a multi-continental, Mediterranean empire). The state could not have survived long without considerable adaptation to the region: so let it be said

---

399 Frangipane, "Evolution and Role of Administration," 121–22.

400 Bachhuber, "The Anatolian Plateau," 593–95.

401 Again, emphasis should be placed on "materials" here: as shown by the archaeological record, the Hittites did not seem to want finished goods (except perhaps linens, which have not been preserved), but rather raw materials which they could transform into culturally and religiously appropriate luxury items.

402 See Jared Miller, "Setting up the Goddess of the Night Separately," in *Anatolian Interfaces: Hittites, Greeks and their Neighbours*, eds. Billie J. Collins, Mary R. Bachvarova, Ian Rutherford (Oxford: Oxbow, 2008), 67–72.

403 Bachhuber, *op. cit.*, 594.

404 Bachhuber, *op. cit.*, 595.

that, rather than parasitic, the Hittite state gathered what advantages it could from the human and physical geography given to it.

2.5 Current Models of the Hittite State: Conclusions and Next Steps

2.5.1 Summary of Current Research

Combining the theories, archaeology, and textual evidence discussed in the preceding chapter yields the following model as one possible understanding of the Hittite state. Although all sufficiently complex ancient states exhibit aspects of wealth and staple finance, there is good reason to believe that the Hittites ruled over what would be considered a primarily wealth-financed state. Features of wealth-financed states include a focus on the acquisition, production, curation, and distribution of luxury good among its elites and the control of trade routes – both of which are attested in the Hittite context. In contrast, states that are primarily staple-financed focus on the ownership of land and the control of the food surpluses for large sectors of the population. This is not attested for the Hittites, where archaeological evidence and textual evidence suggest that the management of agriculture was focused on building emergency reserves and the provisioning of feasting at religious events using local resources.

The proportions of effort dedicated to wealth finance and staple finance is influenced by state complexity, cultural contact, and especially environment. For the Hittites, the mosaic pattern of local ecologies on the Anatolian Plateau, the dispersed populations, the lower potential for high agricultural yields, the difficulty of conveying bulk goods over distances, combined with the inherited trade networks of the *kārum* period and the proximity of the population centers of Mesopotamia, all encouraged a focus on value-dense, transportable goods. In Anatolia these consisted above all in items produced from the region's ample mineral wealth. In the case of the Hittites, a mixture of direct and indirect control of the exploitation of mineral wealth is observable. Metals were principally controlled at the level of secondary production, with primary production left to decentralized and local actors. Copper, tin, and silver were extracted from villages as taxes and tribute in the form of refined ingots and token objects and conveyed to major urban sites for processing. Most metallurgical knowledge was not directly controlled by the state, but in the case of copper and bronze was left in the hands of craft specialists indirectly associated with the state. Gold- and silversmithing, on the other hand, was sponsored directly by the state due to its value and not least the fact that gold could only be acquired through international trade. The mineral wealth resulting from taxes and trade and the combination of direct and indirect sponsored production was converted to both utilitarian and luxury products. These were used to incentivize elites, mobilize manpower, finance warfare and – as is lavishly attested in the text sources – to produce religious paraphernalia and endow religious activities.[405]

---

405 See Theo van den Hout, "Hittite Society, Economy, and Ritual," Orient 55 (2020) for a recent discussion of wealth finance and the expenditure on religious activities in the Hittite state. The comparative

Concerning staple finance, current research suggests that the Hittite state did not intervene directly except to build up defensive reserves against crop failure and drought and to encourage the continued productivity of the land managed by an invested elite. To this may be added that staples were almost certainly accumulated for the regular provisioning of palace dependents. In addition, feasting scenarios were decreed using local resources for the celebration of the various local and state festivals that filled the Hittite calendar. There is, however, no evidence yet for large scale redistribution of staple products to large segments of the population. This does not mean that the defensive agricultural infrastructure (i.e. the grain silos and artificial ponds), was in any way superfluous or secondary to the Hittite state. Combined with the Hittite local palaces and temples to physically and ideologically claim the landscape, the mobilization of the elite and military power through wealth finance, and the promulgation of local and state festivals to bind it all together, the agricultural infrastructure was indispensable for sustaining urbanism against the backdrop of not-infrequent failures of crops and livestock that afflicted central Anatolia during most the 2nd millennium BC.

In spite of extensive intervention in the wealth economy and (to a lesser extent) the staple economy of Anatolia, limitations to Hittite central authority are also apparent. This was not least because aspects of Hittite control required changes to the diversified and extensive approach to food resources necessary for village-level survival in Anatolia. Urban concentration posed inherent problems in a such an environment, requiring the erection of comparatively intensive (for Anatolia) agricultural and pastoralist systems to feed the cities. In addition, the population movement necessary during times of drought or soil exhaustion was inimical to a Hittite state that was ever short on manpower. Tribal and possibly local passive resistance grew, and the Hittite state, unable to govern absolutely, resorted to tiered regions of control. At the center of the tiered network of control stood Ḫattuša, raised already in the Old Kingdom period to a true imperial city that was visually and morphologically different from other Anatolian cities. Surrounding Ḫattuša was an unfortified, lightly settled area given over entirely to intensive agriculture or religious sanctuaries. Moving outwards, the tiered levels of control are then traceable from center to periphery by four elements, namely settlement patterns, with the Anatolian Plateau reconfigured into a new pattern of urbanism consisting of smaller settlements placed at defensible, if sometimes economically less-than-ideal, locations; pottery, which was highly standardized in the Hittite core territory; glyptics, which spread wider to include the use of Anatolian Hieroglyphs across the Taurus; and landscape monuments, which marked important internal boundaries, such as that with Tarḫuntašša, as well as the limits of Hittite influence in western Anatolia. Finally, there is evidence that the Hittite Empire also applied a model of indirect rule through wealth finance balanced with attention to staples during periods of emergency at the extremes of its reach, in the viceregencies and vassal states of northern Syria.

---

lack of military propaganda produced by the Hittites suggests that, in the Anatolian heartland at least, the religious-oriented strategy of legitimation was quite successful.

In terms of the mixture of elites and subelites who ran the Hittite state, recent research has suggested that a patrimonialist interpretation is appropriate for most of the administrative apparatus, which perhaps gave way to a more rationalized bureaucracy at the lower levels. Historically, the Hittite administrative class grew in number, complexity, and importance over the course of the history of the kingdom, probably driven by the needs of the expanding state rather than because of Mesopotamian influence. The Hittite extended royal family seems to have grown in importance until it dominated almost all important offices in the New Kingdom, although the most technically demanding (and hence lower ranked) positions were still occupied by professionals. An exception to the trend of the expanding power of the extended royal family may be observed in the reign of Tudḫaliya IV with the increased importance of non-royal courtiers, but the disruption caused by the end of the Hittite Kingdom does not allow for determination of whether this trend continued.

2.5.2 Future Research Questions

Having come to the end of this two-chapter survey on the history of research on the Hittite state, it can be seen that Hittitologists have produced a mature and sophisticated literature over the now 100 years of the field. The recent contributions of Anatolian archaeologists have been especially enlightening, and continuing collaboration between the philological and archaeological wings of Hittitology will be vital for advancing the field. A few thoughts can be offered here on what research questions might be answered by this collaboration in the near future.

As has been noted on a number of occasions in the preceding chapter, the extant Hittite economic administrative documentation deals almost exclusively with luxury goods. This leads to what is perhaps currently the main, outstanding question on Hittite administration. Some scholars have argued for a separate system of wooden tablets,[406] possibly supplemented by the *cretulae* and bullae system discovered at Hattuša,[407] that was perhaps especially dedicated towards, but not limited to, the control of staple goods. However, the function of the system of *cretulae* and bullae is still contested, and decisive evidence for an extensive administration of staple goods on wooden tablets is currently absent.[408]

In the absence of finding a preserved wooden tablet, resolution of the question of the existence of separate administration of staple goods on wood will turn on three points. The first is to confirm that there is no archaeological evidence for the regular

406 See again d'Alfonso and Matessi, "Extracting Cohesion," 143 for citations, along with Waal, "They Wrote on Wood," and Cammarosano, et al., "They Wrote on Wax."

407 Cf. Frangipane, "Evolution and Role of Administration," 118–20.

408 See Chapter 10, "The Wooden Writing Boards" in Theo van den Hout, *A History of Hittite Literacy. Writing and Reading in Late Bronze-Age Anatolia (1650–1200 BC)* (Cambridge: University Press, 2020), 184–217 for a skeptical view of the extensive use of wooden tablets by the Hittites. Based on the unequivocal use of clay for ephemeral records and the limited overlap of the wooden administrative corpus with the clay economic-administrative corpus (see Section 3.1.4 in the next chapter), the present book is inclined to agree van den Hout's conclusion (p. 218) that "[w]ithin the Hittite administration clay tablets remained the primary and default script carriers with wooden tablets coming in a probably distant second."

transportation, storage, and redistribution of grain and foodstuffs. As discussed above, the silos at Ḫattuša were filled with low quality grain from local sources, conceivably from the immediate hinterland of Ḫattuša. The quality and storage method of the grain, which because of the need for hypoxic conditions did not allow for frequent access, suggest that the silos operated as an emergency supply in case of drought, or perhaps fodder for animals; what they do not suggest is the regular income and distribution of grain rations as would be expected in a primarily staple-financed state. The current state of research strongly suggests that the grain silos were used primarily as hedges against drought. The definitive tests for the "defensive hypothesis" of grain storage will be future archaeobotanical research on other pithoi and grain silos on the Anatolian Plateau, or the discovery of an archive referencing the distribution of grain, be it for planting or consumption.[409] If it continues to be confirmed that the grain silos operated as an emergency reserve, as opposed to a center of redistribution, and that the pithoi stored economically negligible amounts of foodstuffs at Hittite sites, this would suggest a lower administrative burden: for the silos perhaps as simple as requiring local farmers each year to bring in carts of left-over grain until the silo is full, or alternatively, requiring villages to contribute labor to state fields until they are harvested; for the pithoi, agricultural products drawn from local and perhaps state-owned farms. A diachronic perspective is also necessary to see if this arrangement is true for all periods of the Hittite Kingdom, and to compare it to the periods immediately preceding the Hittites.[410] If it can be confirmed that grain storage was in all periods defensive in nature, and thus staple finance was not a priority of the Hittite New Kingdom, then the need for an extensive, literate administration on wood for this sector of the economy is obviated, and the *cretulae* and bullae might be sufficient.[411]

The second point is a philological version of the first. It is widely acknowledged that the Hittite state cult must have had an economic impact on the Anatolian population, but the nature and scale of the impact is currently unknown.[412] The primary expenditure on foodstuffs attested in the Hittite state archives relates to the religious

---

409 As was discussed in *2.4.4 Staple Finance (and its Near Absence in Hittite Textual Sources)*, written sources for grain storage are few in the Hittite corpus. The handful of administrative documents from Maşat Höyük-Tapikka proves an exception, but this may be due to the circumstances surrounding the archive, which concerns defensive preparations, including an early harvest, in the face of Kaškaen raids. The location of Tapikka in the tightly administered "royal demesne" of the Hittite king is also a mitigating factor. A second provincial archive recording *regular* grain storage and distribution, not in the context of an emergency, would allow for much firmer conclusions.

410 As pointed out in d'Alfonso and Matessi, "Extracting Cohesion," 143, agricultural products were accumulated and stored in preliterate Anatolia, admittedly on a smaller scale, probably with the help of *cretuale* and bullae.

411 The word extensive should be emphasized here, since it is of course possible and even likely that wooden tags were sometimes used for labeling storage containers or taking a tally. But short-term uses like these are different from the shadow administration being proposed by wooden tablet proponents.

412 See investigations of this topic in the recent volume of Manfred Hutter and Sylvia Hutter-Braunsar (eds.), *Economy of Religions in Anatolia: From the Early Second to the Middle of the First Millennium BCE. Proceedings of an International Conference in Bonn (23rd to 25th May 2018)*. AOAT 467 (Münster: Ugarit-Verlag, 2019).

festivals. An enormous variety of breads and cuts of meat, as well as specialty foods like honey, fruits, and cheeses, appear in the festival descriptions. Yet living administrative documents for provisioning these festivals, such as flour expenditures on bread loaves, distribution of livestock, and lists of attendees, are completely absent.[413] In their place are stereotyped lists prescribing the delivery of goods from specific groups and villages that seemed to have changed little since the establishment of the festivals in the time of the Hittite Old Kingdom. One must wonder if these lists were created to address the needs of a specific period of the Hittite state when the festivals were used to bind together the societies, ideologies, and also the economies of the newly conquered Plateau, but had outlived their economic usefulness by the time of the New Kingdom, becoming a dead letter of sorts as a tool of Hittite state policy.[414] If the Hittite festivals as recorded in the corpus had become economically moribund by the end of the Empire, it should be revealed in the philology. Other religious practices, such as local cults (which, coincidentally, because they use state-supplied metal objects but depend on local food supplies fit much better with the "traditional Anatolian verticalism" discussed by Frangipane) and votive offerings (see *8. The Hittite Votive Corpus as Economic Texts* below), underwent continuous updating and revision in the New Kingdom period, and one would expect the economic components of a living Hittite Festival corpus to have done the same.[415] There is evidence that festivals could be checked and corrected for accuracy with older records, and in some cases updates made by process of oracle.[416] This makes sense for texts of tradition, the liturgy and rites of which were endowed with all the more meaning on account of their antiquity. But the detailed economic records associated with the festivals, such as the *MELQĒTU*-lists or isolated finds such as the intriguing grain-management tablet KUB 31.57(+), are also in almost every case older compositions that were copied with their festivals.[417] On the one hand,

413 The possible exception to this are two texts, edited in Vol. II as 12.3.4 and 12.35, consisting respectively of seven short lines concerning the distribution of a total 210 loaves of bread to named individuals and the two lines preserving mention of flour and beer. Such transactions must have occurred weekly, if not daily, in a city the size of Ḫattuša, given the number of palace dependents, bureaucrats, priests, and soldiers resident in the capital – and this before taking into account festival events. It seems improbable to the point of impossible that these two documents, which give no context, would be all that remains of four centuries of redistribution if such redistribution were regularly recorded.

414 This is in line with Singer's conclusion on the LÚAGRIG, (Singer, "The AGRIG in Hittite Texts," 126–27), but I wonder if it might apply to the whole festival supply system.

415 For the most recent discussion and bibliography of Hittite festivals, understanding of which, it must be emphasized, is continuously growing and changing with the ongoing Academy project *Das Corpus der hethitischen Festritualen (HFR)* (www.hethport.uni-wuerzburg.de/HFR/), see the section "Providing for the Deities, Celebrating Festivals," in Daniel Schwemer, "Religion and Power," in *Handbook of the Hittite Empire. Power Structures*, ed. Stefano de Martino. Empires through the Ages in Global Perspective 1 (Oldenbourg: De Gruyter, 2022), 387–91.

416 Daniel Schwemer, "Quality Assurance Managers at Work: The Hittite Festival Tradition," in *Liturgie oder Literatur? Die Kultrituale der Hethiter im transkulturellen Vergleich. Akten eines Werkstattgesprächs an der Akademie der Wissenschaften und der Literatur Mainz, 2.–3. Dezember 2010*, ed. Gerfrid G. W. Müller. StBoT 60 (Wiesbaden: Harrassowitz, 2016), 13–24.

417 For this text, which has been extensively treated, Carlo Corti, "The Grain of the King. Agricultural Landscape of the Hittite Festival and Land Management in Late Bronze Age Anatolia and the

it is possible to interpret the copying of these economic texts as evidence that the economic-administrative conditions supporting the festivals were highly stable: in other words, that the stereotyped cultic supply records of the festival were recopied because they were still valid.[418] On the other hand, it seems almost inconceivable that the towns, villages, and population bases supporting the expenditures attested in the texts did not show any fluctuation in the 400 year timespan of the Hittite Kingdom – especially given the well-documented disasters of wars, droughts, and plagues that not infrequently swept the Anatolian Plateau. If it were found that the administration implied by the Hittite state festival corpus was economically inert, then it would again reduce the need for assuming a large staple-oriented Hittite bureaucracy.

The third and last point is to ask whether the wealth-financed administration attested in the clay tablet archives was sufficient to maintain an empire the size of Ḫatti. In terms of communications and logistics, the smallness of the administrative archives, when allowing for attrition and recycling between generations,[419] poses little problem: after all the Incan Empire spanned the length of the Andes with nothing more than messengers and *qipu* knots used as memory-aides. But the question is much more pertinent on the ideological level, and tied to the fate of the Hittite festival and cultic traditions. As Earle noted, wealth-financed states are inherently unstable because they are essentially sustained by strong-arming trade routes and continuous bribery of local elites. Moreover, wealth is portable, fungible, and reproduces itself through conquest, which means that a local warlord can rise to threaten the state in a way that a successful farmer or merchant cannot. From the state's perspective, wealth can be made less fungible and reproducible in two ways: by controlling the means of acquisition (as the Hittites did by monopolizing foreign trade), and by making the most prestigious gifts exotic and unique (cf. the *spondylus* shells used by the Incan Empire, the purple *murex* dye of Rome, or any of the innumerable preciosities fashionable throughout history). The ideal luxury good for the ruler of a wealth-financed state would be a highly desirable object which only he could obtain and give, and once given could never be regifted.[420] The closest object to this description in the Hittite world are the religious idols, figurines, and symbols so amply attested in the archives. The idols were a low

---

Northern Levant," in *Cult, Temple, Sacred Spaces. Cult Practices and Cult Spaces in Hittite Anatolia and Neighbouring Cultures*, eds. Susanne Görke, Charles W. Steitler. StBoT 66 (Wiesbaden: Harrassowitz, 2020), 231–51, with bibliography of previous editions.

418 See conclusion of Corti, *op. cit.*, 244: "I believe that the copying of the festival tablets by the scribal schools of the Empire period was strictly linked to reasons that were not only liturgical but also economical and administrative. It is my belief that these texts were copied because the control of the territory and the administrative management (with the AGRIG 'administrator') of these 'peripheral' areas did not undergo any fundamental changes throughout the course of the Hittite kingdom."

419 See thoughts on the recycling of short-term clay tablets in Theo van den Hout, *A History of Hittite Literacy*, 167–68. As van den Hout concluded, although recycling can partly explain the reduced quantity of economic-administrative records, it cannot explain why certain genres of economic administration are entirely missing.

420 Cf. the prohibitions against unauthorized resale of royal gifts in the "Instruction for Priests and Temple Personnel" (CTH 264). It is, of course, one thing to forbid re-gifting and another to make it categorically impossible through selection of specific gifts.

risk/high reward strategy for the Hittite state: they are inalienable gifts that cannot easily be repurposed by the village (melting down the statue of a local god is not a good start for a potential usurper!), and, if the propaganda was believed that the king was the human interface with the divine world, the idols could not be acquired from an alternate source. Thus, the king was able to safely spend wealth in the provinces and trust that it would remain sequestered there. However, a system of ideologically restricted gifting only works among believers, and makes those who do not participate in the ideology (usually designated "barbarians" with the full cultural force of the word, such as the Kaška to the Hittites), or those who can usurp the ideology (i.e., those who also possess the necessary traditional legitimation, such as other members of the royal family), all the more dangerous.

To strengthen the argument that a relatively compact, wealth-financed administration was sufficient to bind together the otherwise highly-regionalized Hittite Kingdom, it would have to be shown that the wealth circulating in the religious system had purchase with the local Anatolian populace. Local cults and festivals are the best attested route in the Hittite archives for luxury objects to filter into the villages, but what is needed is a better sense of the level of popular and local elite participation in the celebrations. If it can be confirmed that local gods continued to be worshipped, presumably allowing for a more intimate connection between worshiper and god, and that a broad spectrum of Anatolians participated in state-sponsored festivals, with the Hittite government endowing the celebrations with luxury and majesty and the people responding with contributed food and enthusiasm, then the clay administration preserved in the Hittite state archives was sufficient. If not, that is, if Hittite religious experience was aimed primarily at the elites or consisted of imposed foreign gods, then an alternative explanation for the coherence of the Hittite state must be sought, and perhaps staple finance managed by wooden tablets is the best alternative. As was mentioned at various points in the preceding chapter, much progress has been made towards understanding the popular dimension of the Anatolian local cults thanks to the work of Michele Cammarosano,[421] but the relative economic weights accorded by the Hittite administration to the state cult, promulgated through the grand festivals of the Hittite calendar and marked by spectacle and display, and the local cults, which were celebrated by the more humble means of communal rejoicing, have not yet been measured. The continued work of the ongoing Academy project *Das Corpus der hethitischen Festritualen (HFR)* will go a long way towards solving this problem, but it will probably require the discovery and publication of the administrative records of a major urban center outside of Ḫattuša to lay the matter to rest. If it is shown that regional celebrations of the great festivals of the state cult were endowed with riches to an extent comparable to the festivals at Ḫattuša, and if broad participation of the local potentates

421 See again Cammarosano, *Hittite Local Cults*, also Cammarosano, *At the Interface of Religion and Administration: The Hittite Cult Inventories*, with a contribution by Adam Kryszeń. StBoT 68 (Wiesbaden: Harrassowitz, 2021), and especially Cammarosano "Rejoicing in the Gods: the Verb *dušk-* and Hittite Cheese Fighting," in *Proceedings of the Eighth International Congress of Hittitology, Warsaw, 5–9 September 2011*, ed. Piotr Taracha (Warsaw: Agade, 2014), 138–70, for popular participation in the local cults.

and urban citizenry were documented, then a wealth-financed state that buttressed military domination and control of trade with religious experience is feasible.

It is taken here as a methodological axiom that an extensive economic administrative bureaucracy, whether written on clay or wood, that is now lost should not be assumed unless it is absolutely necessary. An argument can be made that the Hittite economic administration as it is preserved on clay is sufficient for the Hittite state reconstructed using the theory of a wealth-financed state outlined above – especially when allowance is made for the loss of the single-column draft tablets, of which only a fraction are still preserved. This is not to say that enormous amounts of effort and manpower were not dedicated to the management of agriculture and pastoral herding by the Anatolian populace; only that the Hittite state need not have intervened on a day-to-day basis using literate administrative techniques to extract the foodstuffs necessary to sustain itself. If a cache of wooden tablets or short-term clay records managing the staple economy of the Hittite state were discovered tomorrow, it would be a cause for celebration and the stimulus for many articles among Hittitologists concerned with economic matters. But it would not change the fact that the large and comparatively detailed economic records that form the remainder of this book almost exclusively document the manipulation of wealth, above all religious wealth.

3. THE PALACE-TEMPLE ADMINISTRATIVE CORPUS: STRUCTURE AND PURPOSE

3.1 Introduction

The Palace-Temple Administrative Corpus currently consists of approximately 252 texts discovered at Ḫattuša. The texts contain mostly inventories of relatively small numbers of precious goods, which documented in a correspondingly high level of detail. Almost all of the texts seem to come from the late reign of Ḫattušili III and early reign of Tudḫaliya IV, i.e., from the early second-half of the 13 cent. BC. Inventories mentioning foodstuffs are exceedingly rare, and are limited to only five texts.[422] Texts concerning real estate or land tenure agreements are nearly absent, with only two stray texts from the Middle Hittite period.[423] Even bolstered by the arguments of the previous chapter for an economic administration focused on wealth-finance, it must be admitted that this corpus is small compared to the economic administrative corpora of the contemporary powers of the late Bronze Age.[424] In fact, the paucity of texts led the first assessments of the corpus to assume that "real" archives of the Hittite administration were yet to be found. As was opined by Aharon Kempiński and Silvin Košak:

> [i]t is quite certain that the fragments discussed here have nothing in common with the royal inventories from Nuzi (...), Alalakh (...), or Ugarit (...). Our documents do not show large quantities of materials; the fact that they were all found outside the main archives would suggest that we are not dealing with taxation lists of the imperial system which recorded the annual tributes of the entire empire, but rather with private and somewhat peculiar lists of presents and personal tributes

---

422 These are KUB 31.65+(+) (Vol. II, 1.1), which concerns what are probably market purchases for a palace institution, in which brewing ingredients owned by estates attached to the institution are mentioned; KUB 38.12 (Vol. II, 10.1.1.1) and KUB 38.17 (Vol. II, 10.1.1.2), which are general temple inventories that included stock-taking of what were probably the monthly rations of the temple; and KBo 18.189 (Vol. II, 12.3.4), which is a tiny *Etikett*-style tablet containing baker's receipt for 210 bread loaves to be distributed to various institutions, and KBo 32.134 (Vol. II, 12.3.5), which is a fragment of an *Etikett*-style tablet preserving only a mention of flour and beer.

423 These are KBo 55.4 (Vol. II, 12.3.1) and KBo 13.254 (Vol. II, 12.3.2). Since, as will be discussed, the remainder of the PTAC date to the early second-half of the 13th cent. BC, these texts can technically be excluded from the PTAC proper. As is discussed in the introductory *Analysis* to 12.3.1 in Vol. II, it is possible they should be classified under CTH 229 "Sales Agreements." This category is currently occupied by only one other Hittite text, KBo 62.32, but it is unfortunately too damaged to permit conclusive comparison with KBo 55.4 and KBo 13.254.

424 See discussion of this fact in Section 8.7 "Booking and Socio-Economic and Legal Administration" in Theo van den Hout, *A History of Hittite Literacy. Writing and Reading in Late Bronze-Age Anatolia (1650–1200 BC)* (Cambridge: University Press, 2020), 165–69, esp. Table 8.1 "Hittite lists and bookkeeping texts" (p.165), which arrives a grand total of only 538 administrative texts and fragments out of the approximately 30,000 recovered from Ḫattuša.

> to high-ranking officials and members of the royal family; it must be concluded that the official archives of Hattuša, providing information on the state economy are still to be found.[425]

Sadly, with the dwindling of yearly finds from excavations at Boğazköy, it seems that fragments of the PTAC are indeed the totality of economic records in the official archives Ḫattuša, or at least the only ones that survived to be recovered. However, Kempiński and Košak were perceptive in their assessment that the scope of the corpus is much more personal and detailed than other administrations of the period. This has held true even as the textual basis of the corpus has improved thanks to further work on the corpus by Košak himself,[426] as well as by Jana Siegelová.[427] But the focus of the texts on persons and individual objects, as opposed to totals and abstracts, should not be surprising, since, as will be shown in the divisions of the corpus, the administration was keenly interested in influencing elites and subelites (see especially *6. Gifts and Handouts*) as much as it was the gods (see *7. Votive Texts* as well the relevant texts of *4.1 Manufacturing Allocations*, especially the *4.1.1 Gold- and Silversmithing Texts*).

Although the Palace-Temple Administrative Corpus has expanded considerably since its last edition by Siegelová, from 138 to 252 (much of the growth coming admittedly from new fragments), much of what she established concerning the format and composition, findspots, and dating of the corpus still holds. These topics can thus be touched upon more briefly here than they would otherwise warrant, since the work of the present book is supplementary to the analyses of Siegelová (and subsequent scholars) on these points. A fourth topic, that of the interface of the PTAC with other administrative systems, will then be discussed in more depth.

3.1.1 Format and Composition

In terms of format and composition, Siegelová noted a relationship between the number of columns and contents of a tablet: to the three-column tablets belonged "Dokumente von umfassenden, gewissermassen resümierendem bzw. rekapitulierendem Charakter,"[428] whereas the one-column tablets were "primäre, vielleicht unmittelbar mit dem Transfer des ausgeführten Materials, evtl. mit dessen vorhergehender physischen Kontrolle und Aufnahme verknüpfte Rechnungsbelege."[429] This assessment is still accurate for the updated corpus. It is only to be clarified to the unwary reader that almost none of the one-column tablets seem to have *conferred* the transfer of material, only to have documented the process, as Siegelová elsewhere clarified.[430]

---

425 Aharon Kempiński and Silvin Košak, "Hittite Metal 'Inventories' (CTH 242) and their Economic Implications," Tel Aviv 4 (1977): 91–92.

426 Silvin Košak, *Hittite Inventory Texts. (CTH 241–250)*. THeth. 10 (Heidelberg: Winter, 1982).

427 Jana Siegelová, *Hethitische Verwaltungspraxis im Lichte der Wirtschafts- und Inventardokumente* (Praha: Národní muzeum v Praze, 1986).

428 Siegelová, *Hethitische Verwaltungspraxis*, 1.

429 Siegelová, *op. cit.*, 4.

430 See Siegelová, *op. cit.*, 567, where it is emphasized that the one-column records were the hastily written notes, recorded in the moment, from which later administrative records were compiled. One of the few exceptions to the formatting trend is perhaps KUB 42.59, edited in Vol. II as text 6.5, which is a large, handsomely written, one-column tablet preserving string holes for attached bullae that lists jewelry, garments, and the names of the women who presumably received them.

In a ratio that still holds for the updated corpus, the three- and one-column tablets were found by Siegelová to have comprised a sixth of the corpus each, with the remaining two thirds being two-column tablets of various contents. The format of the texts closely corresponded to their stages of administration. To quote Theo van den Hout's paraphrase of the stages established by Siegelová:

1.) The initial receipt of tax goods was mostly recorded on one-column tablets in hasty handwriting, betraying its preliminary and temporary character;
2.) a full inventory of received goods was then made recording place and manner of storage, whether they were sealed or not and whether any transport documents were present; or an inventory was made recording the receiving institution, the provenance of the goods, and the correctness of the tax amount. These texts are to be seen as ledgers, combining many smaller inventories of phase 1 into larger and more permanent records. They are mostly recorded on large three-column (per side) tablets;
3.) a new phase starts with the redistribution of the goods of phases 1 and 2; carefully checked, raw materials are either assigned to various workshops for further treatment or finished products are given as gifts to temples or for remuneration of persons for services rendered; and finally
4.) there were inventories of finished products received back from workshops to whom the raw materials had been redistributed in phase 3.[431]

The model established by Siegelová remains significantly valid for the expanded corpus. If there is a criticism to be raised, it is that the model perhaps over-emphasized production and redistribution, when many of the new texts, the greater part of which come not incidentally from Temple 1, belong to genres better classified as "maintenance and management."[432] It seems now that the Hittite administration took as much interest in the control and curation of its religious luxury assets as it did in their production.

3.1.2 Findspots

It was noted by Siegelová that the outsized majority of the texts with known findspots in her corpus came from Büyükkale, with only a limited number of texts coming from the area around Temple 1.[433] In contrast to the texts of Büyükkale, which concerned intake, processing, and redistribution, as well as some storage, Siegelová observed that the texts of Temple 1 were predominantly concerned with storage.[434] The inventories of Temple 1 constituted what van den Hout later described as "lists of mostly valuable

431 Theo van den Hout, "Administration and Writing in Hittite Society," in *Archivi, depositi, magazzini presso gli Ittiti: nuovi materiali e nuove ricerche / Archives, Depots and Storehouses in the Hittite World: New Evidence and New Research (Proceedings of the Workshop held in Pavia, June 18, 2009)*, eds. Maria Balza, Mauro Giorgieri, Clelia Mora. StMed. 23 (Genoa: Italian University Press, 2012), 45–46; van den Hout's paraphrase was based on Siegelová, *op. cit.*, 547–68.

432 See especially *9. Complex Inventories* and *10. Inventories Connected with the Regular Management of the State Cult* below.

433 Siegelová, *Hethitische Verwaltungspraxis*, 7–10. Counting the texts with known findspots discussed by Siegelová yields 20 (or 21, depending on a join) texts from Büyükkale and 11 from Temple 1.

434 Siegelová, *op. cit.*, 10, also p. 440, regarding the findspots of the "true inventories" (*Inventarverzeichnisse*), of which the great majority for which the findspots are known were found in and around Temple 1.

objects that represented the end of the economic chain."[435] Thus, even with the smaller corpus available to Siegelová, it was already apparent that the endpoint for a not-inconsiderable amount of taxation and production recorded in the inventory texts lay in the temple storerooms of Ḫattuša.

The expanded corpus redresses the balance between Büyükkale and Temple 1. In the updated count, 85 of 252 texts have known findspots, with 41 coming from Büyükkale and 35 coming from the area of Temple 1. Confirming the observations of Siegelová and van den Hout, the new fragments from Temple 1 fall overwhelmingly (although not exclusively) into what can be called the "static inventories," which record objects in storage, as opposed to the "dynamic inventories" of Büyükkale, which concern intake, production, and redistribution. In addition, a total three texts come from the *Haus am Hang* and five texts from the Upper City, including three found at Temple 2 and one at Temple 12. There is also one stray find comes from the Lower City. The texts of the *Haus am Hang* and the Upper City seem to group with the static inventories of Temple 1, but the dataset is too small to draw firm conclusions.

Using the functional categories that will be defined below in *3.3.2 Division of the Corpus in the Present Book*, the findspots and classifications of the tablets are:

Texts found at Büyükkale (41×)

- *2. Inventory Records Connected with Intake and Storage.* (4×) 2.3, 2.5, 2.12, 2.16
- *3.1 Domestic Tribute in the Form of Metals and Durable Goods.* (7×) 3.1.5, 3.1.6, 3.1.7, 3.1.8, 3.1.9, 3.1.10, 3.1.12
- *3.2 Domestic Tribute in the Form of Wools and Garments.* (2×) 3.2.4, 3.2.5[436]
- *4.1.1 Silver- and Goldsmithing Texts.* (2×) 4.1.1.1, 4.1.1.5
- *4.1.2 Coppersmithing Texts.* (1×) 4.1.2.1
- *4.1.3 Wool and Hide Processing Texts.* (3×) 4.1.3.4, 4.1.3.5?,[437] 4.1.3.6
- *4.1.4 Textile Manufacturing Texts.* (4×) 4.1.4.1, 4.1.4.2, 4.1.4.3, 4.1.4.7
- *4.2 Equipment Allocations.* (1×) 4.2.9
- *5. Extramural Allocations.* (3×) 5.1, 5.5, 5.6
- *6. Gifts and Handouts.* (3×) 6.2, 6.7, 6.12
- *7. Votive Gifts.* (2×) 7.1, 7.2
- *8. Transportation Texts.* (2×) 8.5, 8.8.B[438]
- *9.1 Named Complex Inventories.* (1×) 9.1.5
- *9.2 Other Complex Inventories.* (1×) 9.2.3

---

435 Theo van den Hout, "Administration in the Reign of Tutḫaliya IV and the Later Years of the Hittite Empire," In *The Life and Times of Ḫattušili III and Tutḫaliya IV: Proceedings of a Symposium Held in Honor of J. de Roos, 12–13 December 2003*, ed. Theo van den Hout. PIHANS 103 (Leiden: Nederlands Instituut voor het Nabije Oosten, 2006), 86.

436 As noted by Siegelová, *Hethitische Verwaltungspraxis*, 10, this fragment (KBo 7.26) listed as being found at Büyükkaya possibly came instead from Büyükkale, since KBo 7.25 (Vol. II, 8.8.B), found in the same area, is a direct join to KBo 31.52, which comes from the debris fallen from Büyükkale Building A.

437 Since this fragment (KBo 42.23) would otherwise be the only text from the PTAC found on Büyükkaya, one wonders if it was secondarily deposited there.

438 See fn. 436.

10.2.2 Votive Objects in Storage. (1×) 10.2.2.2
11.1 Fragments of Mixed Inventories. (1×) 11.1.7
11.3 Inventory Fragments of Jewelry. (1×) 11.3.2
11.5 Inventory Fragments of Ivory Objects. (1×) 11.5.1
11.6 Inventory Fragments of Cloths and Garments. (1×) 11.6.7

Texts found at Temple 1 (35×):

2. Inventory Records Connected with Intake and Storage. (1×) 2.17
4.1.1 Silver- and Goldsmithing Texts. (1×) 4.1.1.6
4.1.2 Coppersmithing Texts. (1×) 4.1.2.6
4.2 Equipment Allocations. (2×) 4.2.6, 4.2.11
8. Transportation Texts. (1×) 8.2
9.1 Named Complex Inventories. (3×) 9.1.3, 9.1.10, 9.1.13
9.2 Other Complex Inventories. (3×) 9.2.9, 9.2.10, 9.2.14
10.1.2 Other General Temple Inventories. (2×) 10.1.2.3, 10.1.2.4
10.2.1 Cult Image Descriptions ("Bildbeschreibungen"). (1×) 10.2.1.5
10.2.2 Votive Objects in Storage. (1×) 10.2.2.1
10.3 Inventories Concerned with Condition and Maintenance. (4×) 10.3.6, 10.3.7, 10.3.8, 10.3.14
11.1 Fragments of Mixed Inventories. (5×) 11.1.1, 11.1.2, 11.1.4, 11.1.5, 11.1.6
11.2 Inventory Fragments of Cult Images, Animal Figurines, and Model Objects. (3×) 11.2.1, 11.2.3, 11.2.6
11.3 Inventory Fragments of Jewelry. (1×) 11.3.3
11.5 Inventory Fragments of Ivory Objects. (1×) 11.5.3
11.6 Inventory Fragments of Cloths and Garments. (4×) 11.6.2, 11.6.8, 11.6.9, 11.6.11
11.7 Unclassified Inventory Fragments. (1×) 11.7.4

Texts found at the *Haus am Hang* (3×):

7. Votive Gifts. (1×) 7.3
9.1 Named Complex Inventories. (1×) 9.1.2
10.2.1 Cult Image Descriptions ("Bildbeschreibungen"). (1×) 10.2.1.7

Texts found in the Upper City (1×), Lower City (1×), Temple 2 (3×), and Temple 12 (1×):

9.1 Named Complex Inventories. (1×) 9.1.4 (Temple 2)
9.2 Other Complex Inventories. (1×) 9.2.8 (Temple 2)
10.1.2 Other General Temple Inventories. (1×) 10.1.2.5 (Temple 2)
11.6 Inventory Fragments of Cloths and Garments. (1×) 11.6.10 (Upper City)
12.3 Other Miscellaneous Texts. (2×) 12.3.4 (Lower City), 12.3.5 (Temple 2)

No attempt has been made here to distinguish between the various buildings of Büyükkale, nor the different storerooms of Temple 1. Although this information, when available, has been duly recorded in the *Catalog Information* of the editions of the individual texts in Vol. II, the uneven quality of data stemming from early excavations, and the fact that the findspots for two-thirds of the texts are irretrievably lost, renders any closer analysis of the findspots beyond what was observed by Siegelová and van den Hout futile, and risks projecting a veneer of certainty onto a fundamentally uncertain substrate. None of the tablets were discovered, e.g., collected into pithoi or segregated into small storerooms or houses, so it is impossible to engage in the kind archives analysis common to studies of Syro-Mesopotamian texts.

3.1.3 Dating of the Corpus

The texts of the PTAC contain no internal dating system, and thus the corpus can only be dated inferentially based on prosopography and paleography. In this regard, nothing has come to light to overturn the assessment of Siegelová that the texts stem from the late reign of Ḫattušili III and early reign of Tudḫaliya IV, i.e., somewhere in the early second-half of the 13th cent. BC.[439] The only significant update to the prosopography comes from two complex inventories, VBoT 97 (Vol. II, 9.1.9) and KBo 18.170(+) (Vol. II, 9.1.10), which might respectively name the two sons of Tudḫaliya IV, Arnuwanda III and Šuppiluliuma II/Šuppiluliama, during their tenures as crown princes (or at least potential successors to the throne).[440] Even so, given that both might have been adults at the time their father took the throne, these texts do not necessarily push the corpus any further into the reign of Tudḫaliya IV than was already suspected. Likewise, a new paleography study of the corpus, while a desideratum, since one was not undertaken in the present book due to time constraints, is anticipated only to reveal nuances in scribal hands rather than a change in chronology.

It may be pointed out here that the seemingly simultaneous end of the cuneiform records of the PTAC and the Hittite Votive Corpus (see *8. Dating Criteria of the Vows in Detail* in the present volume) is remarkable. But whereas the end of the votive corpus can be perhaps explained by a shift in religious practice (see discussion under *8.12 Vows of Tudḫaliya IV*), no explanation for the economic administrative records of the PTAC presents itself on internal grounds at the moment. The current understanding of an orderly abandonment of the Hittite capital sometime at the very beginning of the 12th cent. BC explains why permanent records such as sensitive letters and treaties ought to be missing, since these would have presumably been taken by a retreating regime, but offers no motivations for why ephemeral records such as those found in the PTAC, which would have presumably been left behind, are not found dating to the final years of Ḫattuša.[441] It could be that the records were considered valuable enough that they were taken with the evacuation or intentionally destroyed. It could also be that a major shift in administrative practice occurred, or that administration had already broken down before the final abandonment of the capital, but if this is the case, the reasons are not perceptible from the corpus itself.

439 See "Datierung der Texte" in Siegelová, *Hethitische Verwaltungspraxis*, 535–46.

440 See respective introductions to the texts in Vol. II. See also Burgin 2022 for the hypothesis that the named complex inventories were authored by crown princes. Cf. also the introductory *Analysis* to 9.1.1 "The Inventory of Manninni" in Vol. II, where it the possibility is raised that Manninni might have been the second name of Šuppiluliama, and that the heavy Luwianization observed in the Inventory of Manninni and 9.1.10 and its proposed indirect joins 9.1.11–15, might place these texts among the latest records in the entire PTAC.

441 See Jörg Klinger, "Šuppiluliuma II. und die Spätphase der hethitischen Archive," in *Saeculum. Gedenkschrift für Heinrich Otten anlässlich seines 100. Geburtstags*, eds. Andreas Müller-Karpe, Elisabeth Rieken, Walter Sommerfeld. StBoT 58 (Wiesbaden: Harrassowitz, 2015), 87–111, for the paradoxically poverty of records from the Hittite archives in the last phase of the Hittite Kingdom.

3.1.4 Interface of the PTAC with Other Systems of Administration

One of the more important reevaluations of the Hittite economic-administrative corpus since its last edition by Siegelová has come from Clelia Mora, who, in a series of articles, explored the possible relationship of the clay tablets of the Palace-Temple Administrative Corpus to the *cretulae* (pieces of clay bearing seal impressions applied directly to an object) and bullae (lumps of clay bearing seal impressions attached by a string to an object) discovered at Ḫattuša.[442] As Mora noted, in contrast to the economic administrative records of other ancient Near Eastern archives, the Hittite texts are as a rule not sealed.[443] Indeed, only one record, KUB 42.59 (Vol. II, 6.5), a list of garments and jewelry handed out to named women, shows evidence of attached bullae in the form of holes for the attached strings preserved on the tablet's edge. While it is of course possible that some of the other texts originally had attached bullae, and that the traces of the string holes have been lost, the edges of enough tablets are sufficiently preserved to suggest that the feature was exceedingly rare.

In the absence of physical evidence for the interaction of the Hittite economic administrative texts with the system of seals, *cretulae*, and bullae, Mora turned to the written evidence of the texts themselves. Here, Mora took IBoT 1.31 (Vol. II, 2.7.A), a record of incoming chests, as an exemplary text, finding in her analysis that it revealed a three step administrative process. First, the chests of the text were received at a temporary storage location, where, as a second step, their contents were provisionally recorded on wooden tablets, followed by third step where they were dispatched to their final storage location and the provisional records transferred to clay tablets. Mora's reconstruction is generally sound, and IBoT 1.31 does indeed confirm the existence of temporary intake location, after which the chests were sent to storage (in the case of IBoT 1.31, to the É ^{NA_4}KIŠIB) and provided with an additional layer of documentation. However, some details of the reconstruction unfortunately cannot be sustained. The

442 See Clelia Mora, "Riscossione dei tribute e accumulo dei beni nell'impero ittita," in *Fiscality in Mycenaean and Near Eastern Archives. Proceedings of the Conference held at Soprintendenza Archivistica per la Campania, Naples, 21–23 October 2004*, ed. Massimo Perna. Studi egei e vicinorientali 3 (Paris: De Boccard, 2006), 133–46; Mora, "I testi ittiti di inventario e gli archive di *cretule*. Alcune osservazioni e riflessioni," in *Tabularia Hethaeorum. Hethitologische Beiträge Silvin Košak zum 65. Geburtstag*, eds. Detlev Groddek, Maria Zorman. DBH 25 (Wiesbaden: Harrassowitz, 2007), 535–50; Mora, "The Enigma of the 'Westbau' Depot in Ḫattuša's Upper City," in *Archivi, depositi, magazzini presso gli Ittiti: nuovi materiali e nuove ricerche / Archives, Depots and Storehouses in the Hittite World: New Evidence and New Research (Proceedings of the Workshop held in Pavia, June 18, 2009)*, eds. Maria Balza, Mauro Giorgieri, Clelia Mora. StMed. 23 (Genoa: Italian University Press, 2012), 59–76; Mauro Giorgieri and Clelia Mora, "Luxusgüter als Symbole der Macht: Zur Verwaltung der Luxusgüter im Hethiter-Reich," in *Organization, Representation, and Symbols of Power in the Ancient Near East. Proceedings of the 54th Rencontre Assyriologique Internationale at Würzburg 20–25 July 2008*, ed. Gernot Wilhelm (Winona Lake: Eisenbrauns, 2012), 647–65; and Clelia Mora and Matteo Vigo, "Attività femminili a Ḫattuša. La testimonianza dei testi d'inventario e degli archivi di *cretulae*," in *Centro Mediterraneo Preclassico. Studi e Ricerche III. Studi vari di egeistica, anatolistica e del mondo mediterraneo*, ed. Natalia Bolatti-Guzzo, Silvia Festuccia, Massimiliano Marazzi, 173–223. Serie Beni culturali 20 (Napoli: Suor Orsola Benincasa nell'Università, 2012).

443 Mora, "I testi ittiti di inventario," 537.

GIŠ.ḪUR referred to in the text, regardless of whether they were wooden tablets or not, were official documents that quite likely came with, or were supposed to come with, the chests (see *Lexical Commentary s.v.* GIŠ.HUR, especially the travelling GIŠ.ḪUR of the Kayalıpınar texts). In this way they are similar to another, apparently less-detailed, provisional record, the *lalami-* (see *Lexical Commentary s.v. lalami-*), which Mora discussed as having a close association with chests.[444] Second, even if the GIŠ.HUR of IBoT 1.31 were produced at the temporary intake location, they would probably have been written on clay: the text effectively identifies itself a temporary record when it is explicitly stated in obv. 11 it is stated that the goods newly added by the queen have not yet been officially inventoried (see further *Lexical Commentary s.v. ḫatiwita(i)-* for the significance of the *ḫatiwi*-inventory), and again in obv. 15 that a tablet will be created only when accomplished when the goods have reached the É ^{NA_4}KIŠIB. Thus, the interpretation of Mora that IBoT 1.31 is itself the final tablet referred to in the text seems improbable.[445]

That temporary records were produced on clay tablets, presumably written at the temporary location where chests were received and processed, is furthermore suggested by the partial duplicate of IBoT 1.31, KUB 42.65 rev.? (Vol. II, 2.7.B), the existence of which Mora omitted from her analysis. As is discussed in the introductory *Analysis* to 2.7 in Vol. II, it can be discerned that KUB 42.65 rev.? was written on a reused tablet (the obv.? concerns wool allotments, which seem to be unrelated and do not appear in IBoT 1.31). It seems that administrative complications arising from the queen's intervention during the original composition of the tablet caused the scribe to start a fresh tablet, since KUB 42.65 rev.? ends on the exact line before the queen intervenes. It must be presumed that the reason why more reused tablets like KUB 42.65 do not exist is because they were recycled shortly after copying (cf. the other texts with duplicates in the PTAC, which also show an evolution from rough, temporary records to more polished permanent records). If there is good evidence for temporary records on clay tablets that were produced close to the time and the location at which the chests were received (see Siegelová's original analysis on this point, as well as the "preliminary inventories," many of which were written on single-column tablets, edited under *2. Inventory Records Connected with Intake and Storage* in Vol. II), then the assumption of an additional, primary layer of wooden tablet administration seems unnecessary.

However, the question of wooden tablets was not the primary focus of Mora's research, this being instead the question of seals and sealing practices. The administrative stages reconstructed by Mora,[446] in which sealed chests were ultimately stored with sealed packing lists, is almost certainly correct, even if all of the details proposed cannot be confirmed at the moment by the cuneiform evidence. Whether, as was proposed by Mora, the *cretulae* and bullae discovered at the archives of Nişantepe and elsewhere in Ḫattuša are the remnants of this administrative process of sealed administrative texts on wooden tablets is uncertain, and alternative explanations have been

444 Mora, "I testi ittiti di inventario," 537.

445 Mora, *op. cit.*, 538.

446 Mora, *op. cit.*, 539–41.

proposed for the collection.[447] Yet the centerpiece of Mora's argument for a textual interface between the *cretulae* and bullae system of the Nişantepe *Westbau* and the PTAC, the so-called *ĪDE* texts (edited under *5. Extramural Allocations* in Vol. II), named after the Akkadian verb 'he knows/he knew' appearing after named supervisors, cannot be taken as evidence. As is discussed in the introductory *Analysis* to 5.1 in Vol. II, the interpretation that the *ĪDE* texts were the textual counterparts of the *cretulae*/ bullae system,[448] and that the *ĪDE* phrase was an "idiomatic expression" for the act of sealing,[449] is reliant on problematic interpretations of key points of the texts, as well as an unfounded assumption that the partial overlap between the names of the supervisors in the texts and the *cretulae* and bullae of Nişantepe signified anything more than the fact that the supervisors, many of whom were princes, were important enough to be attested in multiple genres and media.

In summary, the thesis of Mora that the cuneiform records of the PTAC must have had some relationship to the extensive collections of *cretulae* and bullae found at Ḫattuša, especially the archives of Nişantepe, is attractive, but the details of the interaction of the two administrative systems remain frustratingly elusive. Here it must be emphasized just how narrow the attested interface between the clay tablet administration and the system of seals and bullae actually is: of the 252 texts edited in Vol. II of the present book, only eleven (which is reduced to nine, if duplicates are counted together) contain a term that is plausibly related to sealing or sealed (wooden) tablets.[450] Thus, it cannot be confirmed from textual evidence that the administration of the luxury economy recorded in the PTAC commanded any significant percentage of the sealing remains recovered at Ḫattuša. Indeed, there are other administrative systems that can be imagined to have produced these.[451] For the moment, pending further proof, which must almost certainly await the excavation and publication of an extensive provincial archive, it seems prudent to avoid reconstructing an extensive interface of between the

447 Cf. the presentation of the Nişantepe and Büyükkale materials and review of previous interpretations in van den Hout, *A History of Hittite Literacy*, 218–225. Van den Hout (*op. cit.*, 225–27) convincingly critiqued the earlier interpretations of the Nişantepe and Büyükkale bullae and *cretulae* as remnants of an archive of sealed permanent records on wooden tablets, and suggested instead (*op. cit.* 227–33) that the bullae and cretulae were preserved as a reference collection of seal impressions for purposes of verification. Given the historical parallels cited by van den Hout, including examples from Medieval Europe as well as the ancient Near East, and given the absence of any significant material finds in the Nişantepe archives outside of seals and seal impressions, van den Hout's interpretation seems the most plausible at this point in time.

448 Mora, "The Enigma of the 'Westbau'," 64–65.

449 Giorgieri and Mora, "Luxusgüter als Symbole der Macht," 656.

450 These are: 2.7.A (GIŠ.ḪUR: obv. 3, 13); 2.7.B (GIŠ.ḪUR: rev. 1′, 7′); 2.9.A_3 ($^{(GIŠ.ḪUR)}$(<)*parzaki-*: obv. ii 13′); 2.12 ($^{(GIŠ.ḪUR)}$(<)*parzaki-*: obv.$^!$ ii 9′); 4.1.1.1.A_1 (*lalami-*: obv. 4′, 14′, 15′, 16′; GIŠ.ḪUR: obv. 17′); 4.1.1.1.B_2 (*lalami-*: obv. i$^?$ 2′; GIŠ.ḪUR: obv. i$^?$ 6′); 4.1.1.9 (*lalami-*: 8′); 4.1.3.2 (GIŠ.ḪUR: rev. 2′; ^{NA_4}KIŠIB: rev. 4′); 4.2.6 (GIŠ.ḪUR: rev.$^?$ 8′), 4.2.9 (^{GIŠ}LE.U_5: obv. 15, rev. 30′); 6.1 (*lalami-*: up. e. 1, obv. 5, 11, 15, 19). Note that the $^{(GIŠ)}$LE.U_5 of 3.1.1.A_1 rev. v 15 and 8.1.A obv. ii 3′ seem to be physical objects (perhaps even just 'wooden boards') cataloged within the respective inventories, not administrative instruments.

451 See again discussion in *2.4.4 Staple Finance (and its Comparative Absence in the Hittite Textual Sources)* of the hypothesis of Lorenzo d'Alfonso and Alvise Matessi that the staple sector of the Hittite economy might have been managed using bullae and possibly wooden tablets.

cuneiform texts of the PTAC and a submerged administrative system conducted via wooden tablets, seals, *cretulae*, and bullae.

3.2 Division of the Corpus by CTH Number

Having established the basic parameters of the Palace-Administrative Corpus, including its scope and composition, findspots, dating, and potential interface with other administrative systems, it is now possible to examine the divisions of the corpus, beginning with formal criteria and corresponding CTH Numbers.

3.2.1 Growth of the Corpus, and Its Division

The first classification of the Hittite administrative texts was undertaken by Emmanuel Laroche in his *Catalogue des textes hittites*. The text were classified into the range CTH 241–250 based on their contents, with a total 140 texts and fragments identified. Laroche's original categories appeared almost unchanged in the successor to his work, the online *Catalog der Texte der Hethiter* (CTH).[452] These are, at the time of writing:

240 "Purchase Lists" (CTH: *Kauflisten*)
241 "Inventories of Chests" (CTH: *Inventare von Truhen*)
242 "Inventories of Metals, Utensils, and Weapons" (CTH: *Inventare von Metallen, Geräte und Waffen*)
243 "Inventories of Textiles and Garments" (CTH: *Inventare von Kleidern und Stoffen*)
244 "Inventories of Tribute (*MANDATTU*)" (CTH: *Inventare von Tributen (MANDATTU)*)
245 "Inventories of Gems and Jewelry" (CTH: *Inventare von Juwelen und Schmuckstücken*)
246 "Inventories of Furniture" (CTH: *Inventare von Möbeln*)
247 "Statements of Receipt" (CTH: *Empfangsbescheinigungen*)
248 (unassigned)
249 (unassigned)
250 "Fragments of Inventories" (CTH: *Inventarfragmente*)

The texts were first comprehensively edited by Silvin Košak in his *Hittite Inventory Texts (CTH 241–250)* (Heidelberg, 1982). Their organization was almost unchanged from their original groupings in Laroche's *CTH*, with only a few minor adjustments and the suggestion that CTH 504 "The Inventory of Manninni" be classified among the administrative texts.[453] With the addition of the Inventory of Manninni and additional fragments brought to light in the intervening years, and subtracting the joins discovered between existing texts, the total of administrative texts stood at 153.

With the publication four years later of Siegelová's *Hethitische Verwaltungspraxis im Lichte der Wirtschafts- und Inventardokumente* (Prague: 1986), the corpus was again updated with new finds. Siegelová included CTH 504 "The Inventory of Manninni," the one-text category of CTH 503 "Inventar des Siegelhauses (É.^{NA_4}KIŠIB)," and one text from CTH 522 "Fragmente der Beschreibungen von Götterstatuen und verschiedenen

452 Silvin Košak – Gerfrid G.W. Müller – Susanne Görke – Charles W. Steitler, hethiter.net/: CTH (2022-02-17).

453 Košak, *Hittite Inventory Texts*, 2.

Objekten" (KBo 18.166 = CTH 522.4) as administrative texts, but the CTH numbers were again left virtually untouched. Instead, as will be discussed in the next section, Siegelová spent her effort on classifying the texts according their function. With the joins discovered among the existing texts by Siegelová and sixteen texts and fragments removed from corpus, the number of administrative texts was consolidated to 138.[454]

3.2.2 Proposed New Categories for CTH 240–50

The number of administrative texts has grown considerably since the last edition of the corpus by Siegelová. As mentioned at the beginning of the chapter, the present book edits a total of 252 texts as part of what is now called the Palace-Temple Administrative Corpus.[455] Most of the growth in this number has come from the appearance of small fragments that had escaped the notice or interest of the earlier publications, supplemented by a small but steady stream of new discoveries. The recent reorganization of the cult inventories by Michele Cammarosano has in addition expanded the corpus by almost a dozen texts and fragments.[456]

With a new edition of the corpus, it is a good time to reevaluate the existing CTH numbers. Some of the current CTH categories are overloaded, especially CTH 242 "Inventories of Metals, Utensils, and Weapons" (55 texts), CTH 243 "Inventories of Textiles and Garments" (35 texts), and CTH 250 "Inventory Fragments" (127 texts), and combine texts of very different formats and functions.[457] Other categories are underutilized: CTH 240 "Purchase Lists" (3 texts), 245 "Inventories of Gems and Jewelry" (9 texts), 246 "Inventories of Furniture" (4 texts), and 247 "Statements of Receipt" (5 texts). A number of texts that have been accepted as part of the administrative corpus by previous editions, namely the "Inventory of Manninni," included by both Košak and Siegelová, and the other religious administrative documents added by Siegelová, remain classified outside of the CTH 240–50 range. Then there is the problem that some generally accepted divisions of the corpus have not been incorporated (e.g., CTH 244 "Inventories of Tribute (*MANDATTU*)," which should be sub-divided into metal and wool tribute, since these are never mixed and come from different sources). Finally, some categories, but not all, number the texts according to the arbitrary system inherited from Laroche's initial division of the corpus. The numbering system does not give any useful information, since almost none of the administrative documents have any perceptible sequential relationship, and in some cases combines very different texts under

454 For the concordance of edited texts by CTH number, see "Konkordanz (3)" in Siegelová, *Hethitische Verwaltungspraxis*, 576–78. For excluded texts, see *op. cit.*, 579–80, though note that one of these, KUB 42.41 (= 10.2.1.7 in Vol. II), has been reincluded in the PTAC.

455 This number includes duplicates as separate texts. The number would be reduced to 227 in the improbable event that all of the less-secure indirect joins proposed in the present book but edited separately are correct.

456 These are: 9.1.9 (formerly CTH 503), 7.3 (formerly CTH 512), and 9.1.7, 10.1.1.1, 10.1.1.2, 10.2.1.2, 10.2.1.4, 10.3.2, 11.2.2, and 11.2.5 (all formerly CTH 522). Note that 10.2.2.1 (formerly CTH 513), which was tentatively reclassified by Cammarosano as CTH 210 "Miscellaneous Letter Fragments," is taken here as an administrative document.

457 All data taken from Silvin Košak, hethiter.net/: hetkonk (2.0), accessed August 2022.

the same overly specific number (cf. the seven texts of CTH 242.12 for an egregious example).

In light of the problems outlined above, a new division of CTH 240–250 is proposed here. The categories are the following:

240 "Texts Concerning Sales, Purchases, and Exchange"
241 "Inventories of Chests (.I Inventories, .II Transportation Texts (*ŠA KASKAL*))"
242 "Texts Concerning the Crafting of Metal Objects (.I Gold and Silver, .II Copper)"
243 "Texts Concerning Textile and Leather Production (.I Wool and Hide Processing, .II Textile Manufacture)"
244 "Inventories of Domestic Tribute (*MADDATTU*) (.I Metals and Durable Goods, .II Wool and Garments)"
245 "Texts Concerning Distributions and Handouts (.I Under Supervision (*ĪDE*), .II To Named Individuals, .III Other)"
246 "Complex Inventories (.I Named, .II Fragments)"
247 "Inventories Concerned with Condition and Maintenance"
248 "Inventories Connected with the State Cult (.I Temple Inventories with Comment on Provisioning, .II Detailed Descriptions of Cult Images, .III Texts Concerning Votive Objects, .IV Inventory Fragments of Cult Images and Figurines)"
249 "Inventories and Inventory Fragments (.I Mixed Inventories, .II Textiles and Garments, .III Precious Metal and Stone Objects and Jewelry, .IV Ivory and Ebony Objects, .V Weapons and Tools)"
250 "Miscellaneous Inventories and Administrative Fragments"

The above categories comprise all of the texts currently classified under CTH 240–250 in the online CTH (minus the reclassifications that will be suggested below), the religious administrative texts reclassified by Košak, Siegelová, and Cammarosano, as well as a few additional texts, also mostly religious-administrative, reclassified and edited as administrative documents in the present book.[458] Effort has been made to retain as many of the old categories of the CTH 240–250 range as possible. Unfortunately, the smallest of the old categories, namely CTH 245, 246, and 247, needed to be dissolved to make room for new categories. This leaves eighteen texts that will now be classified under an obsolete CTH number in older literature, but allows the remaining 243 texts (233 in the PTAC, plus 10 found outside of Ḫattuša) to be accurately classified with minimal disruption. A concordance of the texts can be found in the concordance of Vol. II of the present book under *Concordance by New CTH Number* and *Concordance by Old CTH Number.*

The new CTH categories have been kept intentionally broad and based as much as possible on formal features, since, as will be discussed in *3.3 Division of the Palace-Temple Administrative Corpus by Purpose and Function*, the classification of administrative texts is an interpretive task. A description of each category and criteria for inclusion are given below.

458 These are: 4.1.2.4 (CHDS 4.46), CTH 832 > 242.II; 9.2.11 (CHDS 3.142), CTH 470.2188 > 246.II.?; 10.2.1.1 (KUB 38.21), CTH 527.52 > 248.II; 10.2.2.1 (KBo 61.9), CTH 210.? > 248.III; 10.2.2.2 (KUB 38.8), CTH 527.52 > 248.III; 10.2.2.3 (KUB 38.9), CTH 527.52 > 248.III; 10.2.2.4 (Bo 9419), CTH 527.52 > 248.III; 12.3.2 (KBo 13.254), CTH 239.? > 240.?; 12.3.3 (Bo 7969), CTH 233.? > 250.

CTH 240 "Texts Concerning Sales, Purchases, and Exchange"

The new CTH 240 "Texts Concerning Sales, Purchases, and Exchange" (7 texts) comprises all of the texts from the obsolete CTH 240 "Purchasing Lists." The title has been changed to reflect that the category includes one text, 1.3 (Bo 5168), that seems to involve a scenario of barter or exchange in which no sales price in silver is mentioned. Two Middle Hittite texts, 12.3.1 (KBo 55.4) and 12.3.2 (KBo 13.254), which seem to concern real-estate transaction, are also tentatively included. The main criterion for classification in CTH 240 is the presence of a sales transaction, especially the mention of a sales price (ŠÀM), but any future text discovered to record barter or compensated exchange should be included.

CTH 241 "Inventories of Chests (.I Inventories, .II Transportation Texts (ŠA KASKAL))"

CTH 241 "Inventories of Chests" (42 texts) can be carried over mostly unchanged from the previous category. The primary criterion for inclusion is the presence of a container, usually GI/GIŠPISAN or GIŠ*tuppaš*, in which items are stored. This formal criterion leaves the category intentionally broad, so that it includes texts from what must have been different stages of administration (income, circulation, storage). However, because these different administrative stages are difficult to differentiate, and must be argued on a text-by-text basis, no finer classification has been attempted.

CTH 241 is divided into two subcategories: 241.I "Inventories" (27 texts), which have no additional criteria, and 241.II "Transportation Texts" (15 texts). The diagnostic feature for inclusion in the Transportation Texts category is the presence of a "KASKAL-formula" (see further discussion in *4.2 Defining the KASKAL Series*), of which the nominal variant *ŠA* KASKAL is the most common. The largest of the transportation texts, the KASKAL Main Text, is given its own number in the category, CTH 241.II.1, with the various witnesses of the text receiving a further letter designation. It is possible that other transportation texts without the KASKAL-Formula will be discovered, since there is one text, 8.5 (KBo 18.160), that seems to concern a military expedition (*laḫḫa-*), but does not use the Sumerogram KASKAL. Due to the fragmentary nature of the text, which is damaged at the crucial line mentioning the military expedition, 8.5 (KBo 18.160) is for the moment classified in the present edition under the generic CTH 249.V "Inventories of Weapons and Tools."

CTH 242 "Texts Concerning the Crafting of Metal Objects (.I Gold and Silver, .II Copper)"

Most of the texts in the new CTH 242 "Texts Concerning the Crafting of Metal Objects" (20 texts) come from the old CTH 242 "Inventories of Metals, Utensils, and Weapons," with the name updated to reflect the fact the texts are not just inventories, but involve the production of metal objects. Criterion for inclusion in the category is the recording of any stage of metal crafting, which is most often the smithing of an object with the verb *iye/a-* 'to make', but also includes other stages such as *zanu-* 'to smelt'. When a verb is not preserved, the presence of a weighed quantity of metal followed by one or more finished objects is sufficient to classify a text here through inference. The category is subdivided into 242.I "Gold and Silver" (13 texts) and 242.II "Copper" (7 texts), since these metals are always treated separately in the crafting texts.

CTH 243 "Texts Concerning Textile and Leather Production (.I Wool and Hide Processing, .II Textile Manufacture)"

CTH 243 "Texts Concerning Textile and Leather Production" (17 texts) is the textile (and leather) counterpart to the metal crafting texts of CTH 242. Analogous to the metal crafting texts, most of the texts in this category come from the corresponding older CTH number, in this case CTH 243 "Inventories of Textiles and Garments," with the name updated to reflect the emphasis on production and the inclusion of texts involving animals hides. The two subcategories are 243.I "Wool and Hide Processing" (8 texts) and 243.II "Textile Manufacture" (9 texts). The "Wool and Hide Processing" texts record the distribution of lots of raw wool and animal hides to named individuals. There is often no explicit verb of transaction, nor are any verbs of dyeing or processing mentioned, and so most of the texts can only be inferentially identified by quantities of wool or numbers of hides followed by named individuals. In the case of wool, these are usually women. The "Textile Manufacture" subcategory comprises texts related to any stage of the manufacture of finished textiles. These may be identified for the most part by quantities of dyed wool followed by one or more finished garments, but texts involving other stages, including embellishing (*MAŠLU*), washing or walking (depending on how A-*za arnu-* is interpreted in 4.1.3.8) and cutting (*iškallai-*), are also included.

*CTH 244 "Inventories of Domestic Tribute (*MADDATTU*) (.I Metals and Durable Goods, II. Wool and Garments)"*

The old CTH 244 "Inventories of Tribute (*MANDATTU*)" has been divided into two categories, CTH 244.I "Metals and Durable Goods" (14 texts) and 244.II "Wool and Garments" (4 texts). Since all preserved texts involve domestic tribute, the name of the category has been changed accordingly. The spelling has also been changed to standard Akkadian form *MADDATTU* according to modern Hittitological convention. The primary criterion for classification of a text in CTH 244 is the description of an item as *MADDATTU*, though the highly standardized format of the *MADDATTU* texts allows for inferential classifications to be confidently included. Since copper and wool tribute are never mixed, texts concerning the materials are segregated into two subcategories. Under CTH 244.I are texts recording the delivery of metals, which thus far consist exclusively of copper and tin, in the form of ingots and token objects (axes, sickles, arrowheads). Chariots and weapons are also listed in some of these texts as tribute, hence the inclusion of durable goods in the title. Under CTH 244.II are texts recording the delivery of dyed wool and small numbers of garments.

*CTH 245 "Texts Concerning Distributions and Handouts (.I Under Supervision (*ĪDE*), .II To Named Individuals, .III Other)"*

Most of the texts of the new CTH 245 "Texts Concerning Distributions and Handouts" are drawn from the old CTH 242 "Inventories of Metals, Utensils, and Weapons" and CTH 243 "Inventories of Textiles and Garments," respectively, depending on contents. The criterion for inclusion is the recording of any instance of unremunerated distribution or granting of goods. Three subcategories can be discerned. The first are the so-called "*ĪDE* texts," a well-defined group identified by a sequence of large amounts of metals and finished goods followed by groups of recipients identified by town name or profession and the name of a high-ranking official as the subject of the Akkadian verb

ĪDE 'he knew'. These texts are labeled here CTH 245.I "Under Supervision (*ĪDE*)" (8 texts). A more heterogenous group of texts involving handouts to named persons is placed under CTH 245.II "To Named Individuals" (7 texts). These consist of lists of items followed by a personal name. Because the personal names appear in dative case with a preceding *ANA* only sometimes, classification can be difficult, so that four of the seven texts are classified here only tentatively. All other scenarios of handout or distribution, including a list of items to be handed out at a festival (6.1), a chest described as containing handouts (6.3), a list of garments and jewelry which might be a diplomatic gift (6.12), and an individual collection of complete outfits with accessory (6.2), which is tentatively interpreted as a handout, are placed under CTH 245.III "Other" (5 texts). The distribution and handout texts from Maşat Höyük–Tapikka (Mşt. 75/48, Mşt. 75/75, Mşt. 75/92, Mşt. 77/7), which are not edited in the present volume, should also be categorized here.

CTH 246 "Complex Inventories (.I Named, .II Fragments)"
The new category CTH 246 "Complex Inventories" (30 texts) designates inventories distinguished by the regular use of explicit syntax, including sentence particles and clitic chains, and a higher level of detail than normal inventories. Some of the texts also include the name of the official responsible for the inventory, either in the colophon or at the end of a section. Texts of this group are classified under the subcategory CTH 246.I "Named" (13 texts). Since the named complex inventories are large, complicated texts that can span more than one tablet, the individual inventories are assigned numbers. The premier example of a named complex inventory, the old CTH 504 "Inventory of Manninni," is designated here as 246.I.1. Other texts classified among the Named Complex Inventories are CTH 246.I.2 "Inventory of Tudḫaliya," CTH 246.I.3 "Inventory of Arnuwanda," and CTH 246.I.4 "Inventory of Šuppiluliuma (II)," which is preserved in two copies, 246.I.4.A and .B. Inventories that show unusually high detail and/or explicit syntax but do not preserve a name are placed under CTH 246.II "Fragments" (17 texts). Since three of the named complex inventories are only identifiable as such by their colophon (only 246.I.4 "Inventory of Šuppiluliuma (II)" has a name at a section end), it is possible that many of the complex inventory fragments are joins to the existing named inventories, or to other named complex inventories now lost.

CTH 247 "Inventories Concerned with Condition and Maintenance"
The primary criterion for inclusion in the new category CTH 247 "Inventories Concerned with Condition and Maintenance" (11 texts) is the regular presence of a notes on the conditions of the items. Usually this is in the form of damage, such as plating that is *arḫa arrirant-* 'scraped away' or stones that are *arḫa išḫūwant-* 'removed, fallen out', but some texts (10.3.1 and 10.3.2) also mention a process of repair. While other categories of texts can have isolated comments on condition, especially CTH 246 "Complex Inventories" (e.g. 9.1.1, 9.1.6, 9.2.5) and CTH 248.II "Detailed Description of Cult Images" (e.g. 10.2.1.2), the notes on condition in these texts are infrequent enough to be considered incidental to their main classification. Most of the texts in the new CTH 247 are drawn from the old CTH 250 "Fragments of Inventories" category, with the old CTH 246 "Inventories of Furniture" being also well represented.

CTH 248 "Inventories Connected with the State Cult (.I Temple Inventories with Comment on Provisioning, .II Detailed Descriptions of Cult Images, .III Texts Concerning Votive Objects, .IV Inventory Fragments of Cult Images and Figurines)"

Almost all of the texts in the new category CTH 248 "Inventories Connected with the State Cult" are drawn from the old 250 "Fragments of Inventories." Included are all of the texts recently reclassified by Cammarosano from the cult inventories, as well as four texts currently classified under CTH 527 "Cult Inventories with Cult Image Descriptions." The category is divided into four subcategories. The first is CTH 248.I "Temple Inventories with Comment on Provisioning" (2 texts), which classifies comprehensive inventories showing a wide variety of temple goods (cult images, ornaments, textiles) and also including documentation of offering rations. The second category, CTH 248.II "Detailed Descriptions of Cult Images" (7 texts), contains texts characterized by detailed, paragraph-length descriptions of cult images, which describe each body part by material and often include measurements. The third category, CTH 248.III "Texts Concerning Votive Objects" (8 texts), includes both descriptions of the production of votive objects for deities and also inventories of objects in storage inscribed with the names of what must be presumed to be the donating king. Finally, CTH 248.IV "Inventory Fragments of Cult Images and Figurines" (6 texts) contains inventories of cult images and figurines that are not detailed enough to be included among CTH 248.II and too fragmentary to be classified elsewhere in CTH 248.

CTH 249 "Inventories and Inventory Fragments (.I Mixed Inventories, .II Textiles and Garments, .III Precious Metal and Stone Objects and Jewelry, .IV Ivory and Ebony Objects, .V Weapons and Tools)"

Under CTH "Inventories and Inventory Fragments" (50 texts) are inventories that do not fall under any of the above categories. These are often simple lists of items that lack the explicit syntax and detail that would otherwise classify them under CTH 246 "Complex Inventories" and do not include the votive objects or cult images that would place them among CTH 248 "Inventories Connected With the State Cult." Nevertheless, the fact that many of the texts categorized in CTH 249 were found at Temple 1 suggests that many, if not most, of the inventories are records of temple property. The category is subdivided by the contents. Under CTH 249.I "Mixed Inventories" (23 texts) are simple inventories containing more than one type of item: these almost always contain garments plus additional amounts of precious metal, ivory, or wooden objects. Under "CTH 249.II Textiles and Garments" (13 texts) are fragments only showing textiles and/or garments. The categories CTH 249.III "Precious Metal and Stone Objects and Jewelry" (6 texts) and CTH 249.IV "Ivory and Ebony Objects" (5 texts) likewise show only items made of gold, silver, and precious stones (which are almost always set in precious metal) and ivory and ebony, respectively. It is almost certain that most of the fragments themed by material in the categories of CTH 249.II, .III, and .IV would be moved to CTH 249.I "Mixed Inventories" if they were better preserved. In contrast, the few texts under CTH 249.V "Weapons and Tools" (3 texts) would probably remain separate, since these record functional items made of wood and base metal that were probably part of a single packing list for a military expedition.

CTH 250 "Miscellaneous Inventories and Administrative Fragments"
The final category, CTH 250 "Miscellaneous Inventories and Administrative Fragments" (19 texts), is reserved for texts that cannot be classified into any of the other categories. In some cases this is because the fragments are too small, but any texts that are distinct without warranting their own category (e.g. the copying exercises), span more than one classification (e.g. KUB 42.65, which contains a wool processing text on the obv.?, and an inventory of chests the rev.?), or are otherwise difficult to classify (e.g. the lists of precious metal and stone objects that may in fact be equipment for use in rituals) are also included. Some texts found outside Ḫattuša should also be included here (see *3.2.3 Texts not Edited in Present Book* immediately below).

3.2.3 Texts not Edited in Present Book

A number of texts are currently misclassified as administrative texts. Some of these, including a number of chemical and glass recipes, were already noted by Siegelová in her *Hethitische Verwaltungspraxis* but never reclassified in the online CTH. The number of chemical and glass recipes has only since grown, so that the creation of a new CTH category for these texts now seems prudent. It can be suggested here that under the CTH division "II. Administrative und fachliche Texte" a new sub-category "F. Rezepte" be created, to be filled by taking the currently unassigned CTH 289 and 290 from "E. Hippologie." The texts to be assigned can be provisionally placed under a new category CTH 289 "Chemical and Glass Recipes" until the next time they are studied and sorted out.[459] The chemical and glass recipes are not edited in the present book.

Other misclassified texts that should be reclassified include those from coming related economic or administrative genres,[460] from rituals,[461] from festivals,[462] as well as a few random texts.[463] These are not edited here.

The few administrative texts that have been found outside of Ḫattuša are also not edited in the present book since they belong to archives that are geographically and chronologically distinct from the PTAC. However, these can still be classified according to the new CTH numbers. The seven administrative texts from Maşat Höyük–Tapikka that fall into the old CTH 240–50 range should be recategorized according to the new system,[464] while the one text from Tell Afis (TA.10.E.187) and the one text from Kayalıpınar, DAAM 1.26, can remain under CTH 250. The one text from Oymaağaç, OyT 09/1, should be moved to CTH 241.I since it explicitly refers to inventories

459 The texts to be assigned to the new CTH 289 are: Bo 5555, Bo 6001, Bo 6356, Bo 6889, ABoT 2.9, AMUM 2433, HT 3, KBo 31.55, KBo 8.65 + 18.201, KUB 42.74, KUB 43.74, Privat 13.

460 These are: Bo 5985 (to the Egyptian correspondence, CTH 170.?, based on the non-Hittite form of the GÍN 'shekel'), KBo 67.245 (a list of men, thus to CTH 234).

461 To CTH 470: CHDS 2.127, HT 69, KBo 18.182, KBo 18.185, KBo 18.200, KBo 22.160, KBo 48.205, KUB 12.37, KUB 42.45, KUB 58.100.

462 To CTH 670: IBoT 4.3, KBo 18.191, KBo 18.192, KBo 31.60, KBo 64.334, KUB 54.83.

463 KUB 7.26 (contains Hattic, thus to CTH 745.?), KBo 37.143 (unclassified, to CTH 832).

464 Giuseppe del Monte, "I testi amministrativi da Maşat Höyük/Tapika," OrAntMisc. 2 (1995): 89–138. The suggested recategorizations for these texts are: Mşt. 75/7 (old 244.? > new 250), Mşt. 75/48 (old 242 > new 245.III), Mşt. 75/54 (old 250 = new 250), Mşt. 75/75 (old 244.? > new 245.III), Mşt. 75/92 (old 242 > new 245.III), Mşt. 75/119 (old 242 > new 249.V), Mşt. 77/7 (old 243 > new 245.III).

of chests.[465] The one text from Emar, RE 70, should be removed entirely from the *Konkordanz* and online CTH, since it has no appreciable connection to the Hittite world.

3.3 Division of the Corpus by Purpose and Function

Perhaps the most important innovation of Siegelová's edition of the administrative texts was to divide the corpus according to "Zweck und Bestimmung," as opposed to just the formal criteria of the CTH numbers.[466] It is only through attempting to reconstruct the original function of the texts that the underlying administrative can be revealed. However, as recognized by Siegelová, the sparse amounts of contextualizing information in the documents – what one might call in modern terms their "metadata" – and the incomplete preservation of most texts make the reconstruction of the administrative corpus' structure, purpose, and meaning a debatable task. This does not make the task any less worthwhile. Indeed, perhaps more so than any other genre of Hittite texts, it is the task of each new generation of Hittitologists to reevaluate the Hittite administrative corpus in light of new finds and new theories. The difficulty of the task also means that previous interpretations, when well-constructed, are not necessarily superseded. As will be seen, for some scholars the division of the inventory texts by complexity, as was done by Siegelová among, e.g., the *Systematische Inventuren*, the *Inventurprotokolle verbunden mit einer Ermittlung*, and the *Dokumente, verbunden mit der Zuweisung von Rohstoffen an Verarbeitungswerkstätten*, might be more useful than a division by perceived administrative stage, as is done in the present book. It is therefore incumbent on researchers of Hittite administrative texts to be more assiduous than usual in recognizing the results of their predecessors. Thus, the current section will proceed with a critical overview of the divisions in the Siegelová's *Hethitische Verwaltungspraxis* and an explanation of how the texts correspond to the categories of the present book.

3.3.1 Division of the Corpus in Siegelová's *Hethitische Verwaltungspraxis*[467]

Siegelová divided her corpus of 138 texts into eleven chapters. As will be recognized, a number of these chapters serve as the bases for the chapters of the present book. The eleven chapters are the following.

465 This important text deserves a full edition. For the moment, see discussion in Theo van den Hout, "^{LÚ}DUB.SAR.GIŠ = 'Clerk'?," in *Studi di Ittitologia in onore de Alfonso Archi*, ed. Rita Francia, Giulia Torri. Or. 79 (2010): 264, and discussion and photograph in Jörg Klinger, "Ein Einblick in die bisherigen Texfunde," MDOG 143 (2011): 222–23.

466 Siegelová, *Hethitische Verwaltungspraxis*, vi.

467 In order to avoid confusion between the numbering system of the texts used in Vol. II of the present book and that of Siegelová's *Hethitische Verwaltungspraxis*, texts in this section will be referred to by their publication or excavation number, with the numbers used in Vol. II and in *Hethitische Verwaltungspraxis* (HVP) added in parentheses. The full concordance of texts can be found in Vol. II, under *Concordance with J. Siegelová,* Hethitische Verwaltungspraxis *(Prague, 1986).*

1. "Acts of Purchase" (Der Kaufakt)

Siegelová classified two documents under the heading "Kaufakt." The first, KUB 31.65++ (HVP 1.1; Vol. II, 1.1), records a number of transactions involving local Anatolians, though the fragmentary preservation of the tablet prevented any conclusions on the state's involvement. With the join of Bo 9280 + 10306 (Vol. II, 1.1.A_1), it now seems that the text is a record of market purchases for the queen's household (see introductory *Analysis* to Vol. II, 1.1). The other text classified as a *Kaufakt* was Bo 6606 (HVP 1.2; Vol. II, 1.2), though as recognized by Siegelová, the description of the sales price as "compensation" (*šarnikzēl*) means that no sale needs to have actually taken place.[468] Unfortunately, no joins or parallels have come forth to allow for further interpretation of the text.

The category of *Kaufakt* is adopted with little change in the present book. The only caveat is that all extant texts seem to involve only transactions in which the Hittite state administration had a material interest. The records produced by general duty of administrative personnel to retain receipts when selling gifts discussed by Siegelová as a possible motivation for sales records were apparently not retained by the palace, or at least have not been recovered.[469]

2. "Inventory Records" (Inventurprotokolle)

The *Inventurprotokolle* are records of items seemingly as they are found, usually described as belonging to chests and other containers, and often noting the origins of the items and any primary records attached. According to Siegelová, the inventories arose out of the duty described in royal edicts to regularly inventory temple and palace property.[470] Siegelová divided the *Inventurprotokolle* into two major groups: "Systematic Inventories" (*systematische Inventuren*), which give the impression of a systematic recording and regular stock-taking and tend to be written on three-column tablets; and "Inventory records connected with an investigation" (*Inventurprotokolle verbunden mit einer Ermittlung*), which give the impression of a one-time, purposeful inspection.[471] These are often written on one-column tablets, and tend to note missing objects, the disposition of materials, and any further manipulations of the objects, often while naming and quoting the individual now responsible for the objects. Siegelová further divided the "Inventory records connected with an investigation" into two broad categories: inventories of stored goods and inventories concerned with the management of precious metals.[472]

The *Inventurprotokolle* formed a large category in *Hethitische Verwaltungspraxis*, comprising twelve systematic inventories and ten inventories connected with an investigation. Since most of the texts categorized by Siegelová as systematic inventories record incoming shipments of goods, these are now edited under *2. Inventory Records*

468 Siegelová, *Hethitische Verwaltungspraxis*, 22.

469 Siegelová, *op. cit.*, 12–13, citing KUB 13.4 obv. ii 40′ (CTH 246 "Instructions for Priests and Temple Personnel").

470 Siegelová, *op. cit.*, 29.

471 Siegelová, *op. cit.*, 30–31.

472 Siegelová, *op. cit.*, 96.

Connected with Intake and Storage in Vol. II of the present volume, where they have been organized by their relative stage in the process. Some of the systematic inventories also appear elsewhere, e.g., under *4.2 Equipment Allocations* when it is clear that the inventoried goods had been gathered for distribution. Three of the systematic inventories (HVP 2.1.10, 2.1.11, 2.1.12: = Vol. II, 10.3.12, 10.3.10, 10.3.5) are categorized under *10.3 Inventories Concerned with Condition and Maintenance*, since their focus is on documenting item conditions as part of a process of repair. Siegelová's second category, the "inventory records connected with an investigation," combined texts of various different functions based on the particulars of the matters they investigated. These texts have been reassigned by function, and so have been distributed to a number of different categories. The most significant of these is the *4.1.1 Silver- and Goldsmithing Texts*, to which most of the investigative inventories concerned with precious metals have been assigned.

*3. "Intake Receipt" (*Einnahmebeleg*)*
Siegelová's category of *Einnahmebeleg* contained only a single text, KUB 42.21 (HVP 3.; Vol. II, 4.2.1). The highly preliminary nature of this one-columned inventory of chests led her to hypothesize that it recorded the first layer of documentation of a set of goods being received by the palace.[473] Now, with an all-but-direct join of Bo 6911 (Vol. II, 4.2.1.A_2) to the tablet, it may be seen that the direction of travel is reversed: the objects are leaving the palace control and being placed into the trust of a palace official, Tarḫuntamanadu. The text is hence reclassified here under *4.2 Equipment Allocations*. The function imputed to the *Einnahmebeleg* category in documenting the first intake of goods is now taken over by the preliminary inventories of the *2. Records Connected with Intake and Storage*.

*4. "Tribute Lists" (*Abgabenlisten*)*
In the analysis of Siegelová, the *Abgabenlisten* represented the summarizing, systematic documentation of tribute income, analogous in administrative stage to the "Systematic Inventories."[474] She astutely divided the tribute lists into two categories by material received, namely metals (copper, tin, and silver) and wool and garments. It was noted that the texts can be organized by the locations where the tribute was received ("Einnahmestelle"), with all tribute delivered to that location listed in one paragraph or section. According to Siegelová:

> Bei diesen Einnahmestellen handelte es sich um Institutionen, die verschiedene Formen der staatlichen Verwaltung und der Kulteinrichtungen, auf zentraler wie auch regionaler Ebene, darstellten. Auf sie zielten wohl die Steuern aus den – wahrscheinlich durch Entscheidungen von längerer Gültigkeit – festgesetzten Bezirken direkt ab. Dabei ist bemerkenswert, dass die zentrale Administration auch dann eine detaillierte, zusammenfassende Buchhaltung führte, wenn die Lieferungen an verschiedene Stellen, auch ausserhalb von Ḫattuša, gingen.[475]

Whereas the point was left somewhat ambiguous in *Hethitische Verwaltungspraxis*, Siegelová clarified in a later article that the "Einnahmestellen," regional or otherwise,

473 Siegelová, *Hethitische Verwaltungspraxis*, 137.

474 Siegelová, *op. cit.*, 141. See also recapitulation of the analysis of the tribute texts in Siegelová, *op. cit.*, 556–60.

475 Siegelová, *op. cit.*, 207.

were mere entrepôts for the tribute, which belonged ultimately to the central administration.[476] Now, with the recognition that not just some, but all of the "regional" palaces and institutions attested in the tribute texts were located at Ḫattuša (see *Lexical Commentary s.v.* É(.GAL) [(URU)]...), the problem of the detailed bookkeeping by the central administration at regional locations is removed, since it now seems that the tribute is being distributed from the central administration to these institutions at Ḫattuša for use and storage, and not the other way around.

As was also recognized by Siegelová, the regular *MADDATTU* tribute could also be accompanied by IGI.DU$_8$.A "compulsory gift" (*Pflichtgeschenk*). The latter is always a smaller amount of tribute of the same type as the *MADDATTU*. Siegelová proposed that since the two types of tribute were physically indistinguishable and apparently delivered at the same time, the difference must lie in their intended use and function in the redistributive system: *MADDATTU* was intended for immediate use in the redistributive system, whereas IGI.DU$_8$.A was set aside as a "reserve fund" and for gifts."[477] However, as is discussed in the respective entries of the *Lexical Commentary*, the distinction between *MADDATTU* and IGI.DU$_8$.A almost certainly has nothing to do with the intended use of the tribute, but rather the circumstances of its origins: the *MADDATTU* being the fixed regular tribute, and the IGI.DU$_8$.A being an additional compulsory gift of customary minimal size but no upper limit.

Although some of the interpretation of the texts has changed, the tribute lists as a category was well constructed in *Hethitische Verwaltungspraxis* and has been adopted here almost without change as *3.1 Domestic Tribute in the Form of Metals and Durable Goods* and *3.2 Domestic Tribute in the Form of Wool and Garments*. Even the order of texts has been retained, with newly discovered fragments inserted after the texts they most resemble. These categories have also been proposed as the respective titles for the new CTH numbers 244.I and 244.II.

*5. "IGI.DU$_8$.A-Income" (IGI.DU$_8$.A-*Einkommen*)*

The category IGI.DU$_8$.A-*Einkommen* is somewhat confusingly labeled, since none of the texts classified there in *Hethitische Verwaltungspraxis* actually concern the income or receipt of IGI.DU$_8$.A, but rather the production of belts. As was discussed under *3.3.1.4 "Tribute Lists" (*Abgabenlisten*)* immediately above, Siegelová proposed two main uses for IGI.DU$_8$.A: to be kept as a reserve fund, or to be handed out as personal gifts or rewards at festivals. The texts she classified under IGI.DU$_8$.A-*Einkommen* were intended to bridge these uses, since they recorded, according to Siegelová, the production of belts from reserves of IGI.DU$_8$.A wool that were intended to be handed out as gifts to named persons and institutions.[478] However, since IGI.DU$_8$.A does not appear in every text (sometimes the belts are followed immediately by the name or institution, as expected in a handout text), and since, when it does, the IGI.DU$_8$.A appears between the belts and the recipient, the natural reading of the texts suggests that the IGI.DU$_8$.A

476 Jana Siegelová, "Der Regionalpalast in der Verwaltung des hethitischen Staates," AoF 28/2 (2001): 203, in reference to the É.GAL [URU]*ḫāriyaša* (3.1.1.A$_1$ rev. v 2′).

477 Siegelová, *Hethitische Verwaltungspraxis*, 246–56, esp. 249–50.

478 Siegelová, *op. cit.*, 238–39.

designates the relationship between the belts and the recipients, not the origin of the wool (see further discussion in introductory *Analysis* to 4.1.4.1 in Vol. II). Rather, as is discussed in the *Lexical Commentary s.v.* IGI.DU$_8$.A, the term is more simply interpreted as a "gift" in every context, whether a customary or compulsory contribution, a votive donation, or a handout or reward. Therefore, the IGI.DU$_8$.A-*Einkommen* category is dissolved in the present edition and, based on the detail with which the weights and colors of wool are recorded compared to the inconsistency of the IGI.DU$_8$.A label, the texts are classified under *4.1.4 Textile Manufacturing Texts* instead of *6. Gifts and Handouts.*

*6. "Distributions Taking Place Under Official Supervision" (*Unter amtlicher Aufsicht stattfindende Ausgaben*)*

Siegelová's "Unter amtlicher Aufsicht stattfindende Ausgaben" comprise the *ĪDE* texts, a group of documents distinguished by the presence of high-ranking officials in charge of supervising or witnessing the withdrawal of goods by named individuals from palace control. As observed by Siegelová, the texts contain a regular formula consisting of object or materials, the name of individual or his town, and the name of supervising officials, followed by the Akkadian verb 'he knew'.[479] The supervising officials all belonged to the highest level of the Hittite state, and many were princes of the first-rank.[480] Occasionally, further remarks on the character or disposition of the disbursed items may follow. The purposes of the disbursements are varied. In some cases, it seems to be for manufacture, in others for handouts or gifts, and in yet others, the temporary withdrawal of equipment for official business. As with the *Kaufakt* category, Siegelová related the purpose of the supervised disbursements to the obligation described in the "Instructions for Temple Personnel" for royal gifts to temple staff to be witnessed and registered, although admitting in these texts the disbursements apparently took place at more mundane, quotidian level.[481]

The *Unter amtlicher Aufsicht stattfindende Ausgaben* form another well-constructed category that has been adopted in the present book with little change. Because it is not clear, and in fact unlikely, that any of the materials or goods issued by the central administration in the "*ĪDE* texts" were to be returned, the name of the category has been changed to *5. Extramural Allocations* in order to distinguish the category from the *4. Intramural Allocations*, which concern property of the central administration either temporarily entrusted to named personnel or raw materials issued with an expectation of return in the form of manufactured objects.

*7. "Documents Connected with the Allocation of Raw Materials to Processing Workshops" (*Dokumente, verbunden mit der Zuweisung von Rohstoffen an Verarbeitungswerkstätten*)*

Siegelová defined the *Dokumente, verbunden mit der Zuweisung von Rohstoffen an Verarbeitungswerkstätten* as texts issuing specific, weighed amounts of raw materials to named groups for the purpose of production. For Siegelová, the texts were dist-

479 Siegelová, *Hethitische Verwaltungspraxis*, 257, 283–91.

480 Tayfun Bilgin, *Officials and Administration in the Hittite World.* SANER 21 (Berlin: De Gruyter, 2018), 392–95.

481 Siegelová, *op. cit.*, 285.

inguished from the similar *Inventurprotokolle verbunden mit einer Ermittlung* by their being "primary acts" (*primäre Akten*), recorded closer to the moment of distribution.[482] The category was not subdivided by material, which in fact forms what is the main criticism of the category: due to the functional and sometimes formal overlap between the *Dokumente, verbunden mit der Zuweisung von Rohstoffen an Verarbeitungswerkstätten* and the *Inventurprotokolle verbunden mit einer Ermittlung*, it seems more sensible to group the texts of both categories together and subdivide them instead by material. For this reason, the "Zuweisung von Rohstoffen" category has been dissolved in the present book and the texts distributed among *4.1.1 Silver- and Goldsmithing Texts, 4.1.2 Coppersmithing Texts*, and *4.1.3 Wool and Hide Processing Texts*, where they appear alongside their counterparts from the erstwhile *Inventurprotokolle verbunden mit einer Ermittlung* category.

8. "Allocations for Personal Use" (Zuweisungen für den persönlichen Gebrauch)
Under Siegelová's *Zuweisungen für den persönlichen Gebrauch* were categorized documents issuing modest numbers of finished products to named groups or individuals.[483] The category was functionally well-defined and, the reinterpretation of a few individual texts aside, most of the texts have been placed in the essentially identical *6. Gifts and Handouts* category in the present book.

9. "Textiles from Personal Property" (Textilien aus persönlichen Besitz)
Under the category *Textilien aus persönlichen Besitz*, Siegelová tentatively classified five texts as concerning collections of personal property, while admitting the fundamental uncertainty of the purpose of the texts in the category.[484] The lead text of the group, KBo 18.181 (HVP 9.1; Vol. II, 4.2.9), had been interpreted in the earlier edition of Silvin Košak as an inventory divvying out booty to the various individuals named within.[485] However, based on the phrase *ŠA* ŠU PN, interpreted by Siegelová as "of the property of PN,"[486] Siegelová cautiously suggested instead that the items were gathered for an offering, or perhaps represents a confiscation of goods.[487] Scholarly discussion of KBo 18.181 has since favored Košak's interpretation (see introductory *Analysis* to 4.2.9 in Vol. II). More significantly, reinterpretation of the term *ŠA* ŠU PN – including the crucial passages from the oracle text KUB 22.70 upon which Siegelová's interpretation of the phrase rested – as meaning "entrusted to PN" (see *Lexical Commentary*, *s.v.* ŠU PN), strongly suggests that KBo 18.181 be reclassified. As such, it is placed in the

482 Siegelová, *Hethitische Verwaltungspraxis*, 292.

483 Siegelová, *op. cit.*, 328.

484 Siegelová, *op. cit.*, 363 (formatting changed): "Der Erhaltungszustand und die Knappheit der Dokumente erlauben nicht zu klären, ob das Eigentumsverhältnis eben eingetreten (und dadurch einfach die Zweckbestimmung der Kollektion ausgedrückt) ist, als bestehend konstatiert wird oder, ob der Besitz soeben entzogen (und so lediglich die Quelle der Kollektion präzisiert) wurde."

485 Košak, *Hittite Inventory Texts*, 122, translating obv. 15: *A-NA* LE.U$_5$ *i-pu-ra-u-*[*aš* "on the record of booty." Note that based on the phrase *A-NA* LE.U$_5$ *ipurawaš* is translated in the present edition more literally as "per the writing board (recorded at) the ramparts" (see *Lexical Commentary s.v. ipurawa-*).

486 Siegelová, *op. cit.*, 364, with fn. 2.

487 Siegelová, *op. cit.*, 366–67.

present edition among the other texts with the ŠU PN phrase under *4.2 Equipment Allocations*.

With the removal of KBo 18.181 from consideration, there are no other texts from Siegelová's *Textilien aus persönlichen Besitz* category that explicitly refer to personal possessions, since these texts were only inferentially categorized based on their similarity to KBo 18.181. One other text, KUB 42.106 (HVP 9.3; Vol. II, 4.2.6), has also been classified as an equipment allocation, while the others have been left as *11.6 Inventory Fragments of Cloths and Garments*.

10. "Transport Registries" (Transportverzeichnisse)

The texts of Siegelová's *Transportverzeichnisse* are identical in form to the *systematische Inventuren*, being essentially distinguished only by an appended note *ŠA* KASKAL "of the caravan" or similar. It was Siegelová's great discovery compared to previous editions to establish that the first eleven texts of the category constituted a single, extended text, present in no less than four copies, which, as observed by Siegelová, treat its contents "auf eine systematische und gründliche Weise, als ob sie auf ein einmaliges, bedeutsames Geschehen zurückginge."[488] Since Siegelová's edition, further analysis and the important join of KUB 60.112 (Vol. II, 8.1.E(A_3)) now strongly suggest that the "KASKAL Main Text," as it is referred to in the present book, records a single, large outgoing caravan.[489]

The *Transportverzeichnisse* was another well-formed category, and the KASKAL Main Text and most of the other texts of Siegelová's *Transportverzeichnisse* category have been retained here under *8. Transportation Texts*. At the same time, emphasizing how difficult classification can be in absence of a preserved KASKAL formula, it was necessary to move four of the more fragmentary and questionable texts of the *Transportverzeichnisse* to other categories, and then also to recategorize three texts edited elsewhere in *Hethitische Verwaltungspraxis* under the transportation texts of the present book.

11. "Inventory Registries" (Inventarverzeichnisse)

Siegelová's final category was the *Inventarverzeichnisse*. These are the inventories that were for the most part not otherwise classifiable, most often on account of their fragmentary preservation. The items of the texts are rarely in chests, are only sometimes grouped by material, and have no notes concerning manufacture or transfer of control. They are, as Siegelová accurately described them, inventories in the truest sense of the word, and were interpreted by Siegelová as representations of what the scribe found in the storerooms as they were encountered.[490] As noted by Siegelová, many of the *Inventarverzeichnisse* come from Temple 1.[491]

Siegelová divided the *Inventarverzeichnisse* into seven unlabeled categories, organized roughly by complexity and level of preservation. At the head of the category stood the "Inventory of Manninni" (HVP 11.1.1.: Vol. II, 9.1.1), a highly detailed and well-preserved text, and one of the few that explicitly identifies itself as an inventory.

488 Siegelová, *Hethitische Verwaltungspraxis*, 397.
489 See Chapters 4 and 7 of the present volume.
490 Siegelová, *op. cit.*, 439–40.
491 Siegelová, *op. cit.*, 440.

Siegelová placed an additional eight texts in the same category as the Inventory of Manninni based on similarities in language and detail. Almost all of these texts are categorized in the present book as complex inventories, either under *9.1 Named Complex Inventories* or *9.2 Other Complex Inventories*. The next unlabeled category (HVP 11.2) was reserved for what appear to be other detailed inventories that could not be directly related to the Inventory of Manninni. Most of these texts are also retained as complex inventories in the present book, although one, KBo 18.187 (HVP 11.2.4; Vol. II, 4.2.7) has been tentatively reclassified as an equipment allocation. The theme of Siegelová's next category (HVP 11.3), which contained only two texts, was weapons. The first text, KUB 42.81+ (HVP 11.3.1; Vol. II, 2.17) has been reassigned in the present book to the *2. Inventories Concerned with Intake and Storage*, where it is classified as a digest of preliminary inventory records based in part on the highly variable level of detail with which the items are inventoried and the fact that some of the items had apparently not yet been received (see introductory *Analysis* to 2.17). The other text, KUB 42.36 (HVP 11.3.2; Vol. II, 9.1.14), was assigned as a possible indirect join to a named complex inventory, the "Inventory of Šuppiluliuma (II)" (Vol. II, 9.1.10) based on its contents and ductus. The remaining unlabeled categories of Siegelová contained progressively smaller fragments of inventories grouped by theme: inventories of mostly precious stones and jewelry (HVP 11.4), mixed inventories of textiles and precious metal objects and jewelry (HVP 11.5), inventory fragments of mostly textiles (HVP 6.1), and finally uncategorized inventory fragments (11.7). Most of the texts from these final categories have been assigned to their respective thematic category in the *11. Inventory Fragments* of the present book, though a few were successfully reclassified under other headings, including the *9.1 Named Complex Inventories* and the *10.1.2 Other General Temple Inventories.*

3.3.2 Division of the Corpus in the Present Book

The present book organizes the 252 texts of its remit into twelve categories and five broad groups. Four of the groupings are based on their stage of economic administration, with a fifth reserved for texts not otherwise classified. The groupings are:

> *I. Income*, containing three categories: *1. Texts Concerning Sales, Purchases, and Exchange*, *2. Inventory Records Connected with Intake and Storage*, and *3. Domestic Tribute*. These represent the records connected with the acquisition and documentation of incoming goods by the palace administration.
>
> *II. Circulation*, containing two categories: *4. Intramural Allocations* and *5. Extramural Allocations*. These are texts concerned with the processing and distribution of materials and goods for palace business.
>
> *III. Expenditure*, containing three categories: *6. Gifts and Handouts*, *7. Votive Gifts*, and *8. Transportation Texts*, which document goods leaving palace control (though with the votive gifts, the administration still had a responsibility for curation and maintenance).
>
> *IV. Storage*, containing three categories: *9. Complex Inventories*, *10. Inventories Connected with the Regular Maintenance of the State Cult*, and *11. Inventory*

Fragments, representing the various records of goods that have been enrolled in the palace and temple storehouses of Ḫattuša.

V. Miscellaneous, containing one category: *12. Miscellaneous Texts*. Here are placed suspected ritual lists, copying exercises, other texts that do not fit into the other categories.

Since they serve mainly as an organizing principle, and not classificatory criteria, the five broad groupings are as a rule not referred to in citation (so *1. Texts Concerning Sales, Purchases, and Exchange*, not *I. Income: 1. Texts Concerning* ..., or *I.1. Texts Concerning* ...). The categories used to classify the texts are given below in detail with criteria for inclusion and notable results.

1. Texts Concerning Sales, Purchases, and Exchange

The "Texts Concerning Sales, Purchases, and Exchange" category contains texts showing evidence of compensated exchange. Criteria for inclusion are almost exactly the same as that discussed in *CTH 240 "Texts Concerning Sales, Purchases, and Exchange"* above, with the mention of a sales price (ŠÀM) being decisive. However, two of the new CTH 240 texts, KBo 55.4 (Vol. II, 12.3.1) and KBo 13.254 (Vol. II, 12.3.2), both of which are Middle Hittite texts involving real estate transactions, are placed in the present volume under *12. Miscellaneous Texts*. This is primarily because they are from a different time period to the rest of the texts edited, but also because the topic of real estate does not appear elsewhere in the PTAC corpus.

The major difference of interpretation between the *1. Texts Concerning Sales, Purchases, and Exchange* category compared to the Siegelová's *Kaufakt* category is that a material interest of the palace can be discerned in most of the texts, rather than the neutral recording of sales transactions proposed by Siegelová. That the palace had interests in the transactions of the texts in fact better explains why these limited numbers of sales records appeared in cuneiform archives of Ḫattuša at all. Highlights include the reinterpretation of KUB 31.65+(+) (Vol. II, 1.1) thanks to a new join as market purchases for the queen's household, which adds another source of income to the queen's household beyond tribute, gifts, war spoils, and its own estates;[492] and the interpretation of KUB 42.84 (Vol. II, 1.5) as a list of diplomatic gifts with an appended commercial transaction, which adds further textual evidence supporting the interpretation of merchant-envoys as purveyors of foreign goods to the Hittite court.

2. Inventory Records Connected with Intake and Storage

The "Inventory Records Connected with Intake and Storage" is a new category that draws mostly from texts classified as *Inventurprotokolle* by Siegelová, both from the *Systematische Inventuren* and *Inventurprotokolle verbunden mit einer Ermittlung* subcategories. As might be expected from a category concerned with incoming goods, almost all of the texts in the category, except for some of the more tentatively classified fragments, come from the new "I. Inventories" subdivision of CTH 241 "Inventories of

492 Jana Siegelová, "Die hethitische Königin und die Wirtschaft der Krone," in *Saeculum. Gedenkschrift für Heinrich Otten anlässlich seines 100. Geburtstags*, eds. Andreas Müller-Karpe, Elisabeth Rieken, Walter Sommerfeld. StBoT 58 (Wiesbaden: Harrassowitz, 2015), 243–45.

Chests." Yet the "Inventory Records Connected with Intake and Storage" is not coextensive with CTH 241.I, and an argument must be made on a text-by-text basis that a particular record represents an early administrative stage when the goods were first being enrolled in the inventories of the central administration, and not, e.g., an inventory of chests in long-term storage. As such, one of the most important criteria for classification in the "Intake and Storage" category is the level of detail with which the contents of the chests are recorded. The most distinct are the "preliminary inventories" of chests. These are often written on one- and two-column tablets and crucially present only generic, unenumerated descriptions of chest contents for some of their entries (in this, the lead text of the category, KUB 42.18//KUB 42.20 = Vol. II, 2.1.A, .B, is exemplary). Sometimes additional comments, such as descriptions of chests being "cleared out" (*arḫa u(n)ḫ-*) in Vol. II, 2.1, 2.2, and 2.5, or the mention that chests are in the process of being inventoried (*ḫatiwita(i)-*) in 2.7 and 2.8, can help secure classification in the "Intake and Storage" category. When the contents of the preliminary inventories show evidence of being tribute, e.g., in Vol. II, 2.1, 2.2, 2.5, 2.6, and 2.7, it can be assumed that the texts are recording incoming goods (note that the *MADDATTU* tribute records are classified separately, since, as already noted by Siegelová, these are much more detailed). Sometimes this income is directly forwarded to other parts of the palace administration, e.g., in 2.2 where some of the precious metal is sent directly to the smiths, where its appears again in paragraphs quoted nearly verbatim in the manufacturing text 4.1.1.1. There are also preliminary inventories that seem to describe chests that been retrieved from long-term storage (Vol. II, 2.9–2.14), including chests described as containing tribute received when the king and queen were enthroned (2.9 and 2.12). A subset of these (2.9, 2.10, and 2.11) are recognizable by the mention of bolts (^{GIŠ}SAG.KUL), which are apparently part of a locking mechanism for the chests (see also 2.12, a slightly more detailed, near-duplicate of 2.9 in which the chests have been freed of their bolts). Texts showing preliminary inventories (Vol. II, 2.15 and 2.18) that cannot be securely classified into the intake or the retrieval-from-storage administrative stages and texts showing what appear to be three-column digests of preliminary inventories (Vol. II, 2.16 and 2.17) are placed towards the end of the category.

3. Domestic Tribute

As was discussed in *CTH 244 "Inventories of Domestic Tribute (*MADDATTU*) (.I Metals and Durable Goods, .II Wool and Garments)"* and *4. "Tribute Lists"* (Abgabenlisten), the tribute lists are a stable and well-defined category that has been carried over almost without change from Siegelová's *Hethitische Verwaltungspraxis*. The tribute lists are recognizable by the characteristic feature the presence of the Akkadogram *MADDATTU*. The tribute texts can be divided by material into two subcategories. The first, edited under *3.1 Domestic Tribute in the Form of Metals and Durable Goods*, records tribute mostly in the form of large amounts of copper and sometimes smaller amounts of tin (Vol. II, 3.1.5, 3.1.6, and 3.1.7). The copper is very often delivered as finished objects of standardized weight. The tribute is checked and any deficiencies or shortfalls noted (e.g. 3.1.1.A_1 obv. ii 10′–16′). The fact that tin is included provides evidence that the tribute was partly commodified (i.e., that the towns did not themselves produce all of the tribute they sent, but also acquired some of it through trade), since the tin is listed as being sent from more towns in Anatolia than would have been capable of producing it (see introductory *Analysis* to 3.1.5). Silver, on the other hand, appears separately in two dedicated texts (Vol. II, 3.1.10 and 3.1.11), where it was probably sent from a town connected with mining. AN.BAR 'iron/iron (ore)' is encountered only once in unclear circumstances (Vol. II, 3.1.7.A_1 l. e. 3), and gold not at all. Small numbers of chariots are encountered in two texts (Vol. II, 3.1 and 3.8) and weapons in three (3.1.1, 3.1.8, and 3.1.9). One text, KBo 18.158 (Vol. II, 3.1.12), describes a "tribute of the smiths" ([*MA*]*N-TA-TUM* $^{\text{LÚ.MEŠ}}$SIM[UG.A in 3.1.12 4′). It is hypothesized that the objects recorded in the text, which include a large number of bronze implements, were a form of value-added tribute, whereby the smiths contributed their labor to craft objects from palace-supplied materials. The curious text KBo 18.161 (Vol. II, 3.1.8.A), which contains a crafting text on its obverse and a tribute text on its reverse, adds further to the impression that manufacturing could be a form of tribute.

Texts of the second category, *3.2 Domestic Tribute in the Form of Wools and Garments*, are fewer in number. They contain tribute mostly in the form wool delivered at various stages of production (perhaps as yarn, either natural or dyed) and modest numbers of finished garments. The text NBC 3842 (Vol. II, 3.2.1) provides a second instance of value-added tribute, since it is matched by a near-duplicate text among the manufacturing texts (Vol. II, 4.1.3.1), where individuals and institutions produced garments and dyed wool from what were apparently palace supplies.

In both the metals and durable goods and the wool and garments tribute texts, the tribute may be listed as contributed by a town, by an individual representing a town, by an individual without town name, by a professional group (see Vol. II, 3.1.6), or by an institution. The tribute can be described as loose, in chests, some of which were sealed, or in leather bags. With containers, a GIŠ.ḪUR 'list' or *lalami-* 'accounting receipt' was often, but not always, included. In some texts, the tribute is already divided into sections by the government institutions (Vol. II, 3.1.1 and 3.1.7) or deities (Vol. II, 3.1.11) that will receive the objects for use and storage.

4. Intramural Allocations

One of the major changes from Siegelová's organizational scheme in the present book is the creation of a new category of "Intramural Allocations." This category contains texts dealing with the internal distribution of materials and objects for what can broadly designated "palace business." The intramural allocations have two divisions: *4.1 Manufacturing Allocations* and *4.2 Equipment Allocations.*

4.1 Manufacturing Allocations

The manufacturing allocations combine texts from three main categories in *Hethitische Verwaltungspraxis*, namely the *Inventurprotokolle*, the *Dokumente, verbunden mit der Zuweisung von Rohstoffen an Verarbeitungswerkstätte* and the IGI.DU_8.A-*Einkommen* – which, as was discussed above, concern production rather than income. With the increase in texts concerned with crafting, it seems more sensible to combine the texts, some of which are formally dissimilar, by function. As such, the texts were organized by their contents along with the addition of a number of texts and fragments that were not available to Siegelová into four divisions: *4.1.1 Silver- and Goldsmithing Texts*, *4.1.2*

Coppersmithing Texts, 4.1.3 Wool and Hide Processing Texts, 4.1.4 Textile Manufacturing Texts.

Under *4.1.1 Silver- and Goldsmithing Texts* are grouped texts concerned with the distribution of precious metals to palace-dependent smiths for the manufacture and repair of luxury items. The first text of the category, appearing in two copies as KBo 18.153(+) and KUB 26.66(+) (Vol. II, 4.1.1.1.A and 4.1.1.1.B), provides an important link between the *2. Texts Concerned with Intake and Storage* and the *4.1 Manufacturing Allocations*, since, as mentioned, the text contains two paragraphs repeated almost verbatim from the intake text VSNF 12.116 (Vol. II, 2.2). 4.1.1.1 is also a liminal text, in the sense that only some of the lots of precious metals in the text are destined for manufacture, with some also destined distribution to local temples and perhaps a foreign country. The other major contribution of 4.1.1.1 is that it reveals evidence for what seems to be small amounts of gold (in this case, a copper-gold alloy) in semi-private possession. Four short paragraphs in 4.1.1.1.A" obv. i 6′–12′ note quantities of copper-gold alloy as *IŠTU ŠA* ᵐ... 'from the lot of ᵐ... ', after which, in three of the paragraphs objects, are described as EGIR-*anda* ... [*d*]*āš* (or perhaps [*ped*]*āš*) "subsequently he took/carried off ... ." It is hypothesized in the introductory *Analysis* to 4.1.1.1 that the copper-gold alloy was taken by the palace smiths from the stores of semi-private individuals (i.e., important officials connected with the palace) who then took the objects as compensation. A similar arrangement might have obtained in 4.1.1.6. The careful recording of the variety of sources and destinations of gold in 4.1.1.1 testifies to the fine-grained administrative documentation and control the Hittite palace exercised over its precious metal supplies.

The remaining texts under *4.1.1 Silver- and Goldsmithing Texts* are proper crafting receipts, in which carefully weighed quantities of precious metals are distributed to smiths for the production of specified items. The actions to be accomplished are described by the appropriate verb (e.g. DÙ 'to make' for crafting new objects, *ḫališši(ya)-* 'to plate' for plating existing objects in metal, *zanu-* 'to smelt' for processing metal into ingots, etc.). A number of the texts are single-column tablets (Vol. II, 4.1.1.2.B, 4.1.1.3, 4.1.1.5) that seem to have been recorded close to the administrative action, although one text, KBo 18.159 (Vol. II, 4.1.1.6), is a multicolumned tablet accounting for objects that have already been produced (see also 4.1.1.7). Finally, there are two texts (Vol. II, 4.1.1.9) involving the production of divine figurines and/or votive objects that provide a link between the manufacturing texts and the *10.2.1 Cult Image Descriptions ("Bildbeschreibungen")* or *7. Votive Gifts* genres.

Under *4.1.2 Coppersmithing Texts* are texts concerned with processing of bulk copper and the production of copper items. The lead texts of the category, KBo 18.163 (Vol. II, 4.1.2.1) and KUB 42.71 (Vol. II, 4.1.2.2), form an important example of value added tribute. In 4.1.2.1 weighed quantities of copper are distributed to named individuals and groups belonging to government institutions. The same individuals and institutional groups then return finished objects in 4.1.2.2, which in its format is most similar to the domestic tribute texts. It seems that the distribution of copper to external smiths was one of the ways in which the palace processed the copper it received as domestic tribute. The use of external smiths perhaps also explains the comparatively patchy records for the rest of the category, since only two other texts (Vol. II, 4.1.2.3 and 4.1.2.4) can be confidently identified as crafting receipts, with the assignments of the remaining three (Vol. II, 4.1.2.5, 4.1.2.6, and 4.1.2.7) to the category becoming progressively more tentative.

4.1.3 Wool and Hide Processing Texts contains texts recording the various stages of the processing of animal products into useable materials for textiles and leather goods. As with *4.1.2 Coppersmithing Texts*, the lead text of the category, Bo 6489 (Vol. II, 4.1.3.1), which can be paired with the domestic tribute text 3.2.1, involves value added tribute, demonstrating that the labor involved in the processing of wool received as tribute by the palace was itself a form of tribute. Most of the remaining texts of the category also involve the issuing of wool from palace supplies to various groups and individuals, including many named women (Vol. II, 4.1.3.4 and 4.1.3.5), for processing. One text (Vol. II, 4.1.3.6) involves an analogous scenario with animal hides instead of wool. The final two texts of the category (Vol. II, 4.1.37 and 4.1.3.8) are fragmentary, but seem to mix both raw wool and small numbers of garments, and might represent a bridge to the next category of textile manufacturing.

Under *4.1.4 Textile Manufacturing Texts* are placed texts concerning the actual manufacture of garments. As was discussed in *5. "IGI.DU$_8$.A-Income" (IGI.DU$_8$.A-*Einkommen*)*, the majority of these texts concern the production of belts described as gifts (IGI.DU$_8$.A) for various individuals and institutions. Since the handful of belts produced in these texts represent a vanishingly small proportion of the total number of garments recorded in the PTAC, which taken together number into the thousands, it is clear that direct textile production was not a major concern of the palace administration. It does indicate that handouts, specifically of belts, which are encountered again most prominently as handouts to the garrison at Nerik in KBo 9.91 (Vol. II, 6.1), were an exception. This in turn suggests that the palace took production of material tokens of in-group status, which the belts may be assumed to represent, seriously. The few remaining the textile manufacturing texts indicate that textile ornamentation was accomplished by dedicated craftsmen (Vol. II, 4.1.4.8), and that the finishing and refurbishing of cloths for chariot and furnishing coverings, including for diplomatic gifts, was also recorded in palace records (Vol. II, 4.1.4.9).

4.2 Equipment Allocations

The other category of intramural allocations is *4.2 Equipment Allocations*. These are texts in which various pieces of equipment, including drinking vessels, jewelry, garments, furniture, etc., are entrusted to named individuals or professional groups (e.g., the $^{LÚ.MEŠ}$*šalašḫa-* MUNUS.LUGAL "queen's footmen" in Vol. II, 4.2.6). The hallmark of the category is the appearance of the ŠU PN phrase (see *Lexical Commentary s.v.*), indicating that the items have been temporarily placed in the trust of the person named. Although the intended use of the entrusted goods is rarely given, and sometimes difficult to perceive (except in cases where precious metal items are entrusted to smiths for repair), it can be assumed that the items were being used for various officially sanctioned events, such as festivals, rituals, and feasts, after which they would be returned to palace control (hence the classification as intramural allocations, since the goods never left the control of the palace or temple). A special case is the already discussed KBo 18.181 (Vol. II, 4.2.9) (see *9. "Textiles from Personal Property" (*Textilien aus persönlichen Besitz*)* above), which seems to record the division of booty among three individuals, who were possibly temporary caretakers of the goods during their transport back to Ḫattuša.

5. Extramural Allocations
As discussed in *6. "Distributions Taking Place Under Official Supervision" (*Unter amtlicher Aufsicht stattfindende Ausgaben*)*, the "ĪDE texts" are a formally well-defined category consisting of quantities of objects and materials followed by groups of recipients and a named supervisor and the Akkadian verb for 'he knew'. If easy to classify, the function of the texts is more open to interpretation (see discussion in the introductory *Analysis* to Vol. II, 5.1 for previous theories), but are most simply interpreted as distributions to individuals outside of direct palace control for various aspects of palace business. However, in contrast to the *4. Intramural Allocations*, it is not certain in every case that the objects distributed in the *5. Extramural Allocations* were to be returned. For some of the smithing operations, such as those involving the breaking up of copper talents, the expectation of return is made more-or-less explicit, With other operations, such as the distribution of large quantities of copper and tin, a return in the form of bronze can be seen as implied – indeed, the "ĪDE texts" may record the main avenue for the acquisition of bronze by the palace (see Vol. II, 5.2). But in other instances, such as the distribution of tools and weapons, or even figurines and furniture, it can only be surmised that the objects were to be employed in the accomplishment of palace aims, perhaps being consumed or permanently given away in the process. The distribution of items to individuals of humble rank and groups from obscure Anatolian towns furthers this impression of permanent, extramural redistribution.

6. Gifts and Handouts
As discussed in *8. "Allocations for Personal Use" (*Zuweisungen für den persönlichen Gebrauch*)*, the *6. Gifts and Handouts* are another category that has been adopted with little change from *Hethitische Verwaltungspraxis*. Most of the texts categorized there are also edited here, with adjustments based on reclassification of individual texts rather than any major changes in classificatory criteria. Notable results include the reinterpretation of the phrase *para* SUM-*uaš* appearing in two texts (Vol. II, 6.1 and 6.3) as meaning 'handouts' (see *Lexical Commentary s.v.* SUM *(para* SUM-*uaš)*), granting the category a welcome emic validity, and the addition to the category of a very interesting text, KUB 31.24 (Vol. II, 6.4), that appears to record the distribution of gifts in the form of decorative lion's heads by princes of the royal family to governors in a possibly Syrian context.

7. Votive Gifts
The category of *7. Votive Gifts* is unusual in that none of four texts classified within were edited in *Hethitische Verwaltungspraxis*. This is perhaps because the grouping is a bit of an "in-between" category: the texts placed here concern votive objects which have been promised, but probably not yet produced (which would have classified them under *4.1 Manufacturing Allocations*) or placed in storage (which would make them *10.2.2 Votive Objects in Storage*). Nevertheless, the inventory-like descriptions of the objects and subject matter qualify them for inclusion in the present book. The genre forms a crucial link between the Hittite Votive Corpus (see Chapter 8 in the present

volume) and the texts of the PTAC. As discussed in the introductory *Analysis* to Vol. II, 7.1, it is possible that the entries in the *7. Votive Gifts* were extracted from the texts recording the vows.

8. Transportation Texts
The *8. Transportation Texts* are also carried over mostly unchanged from Siegelová's *Transportverzeichnisse.* As was discussed under *CTH 241 "Inventories of Chests (.I Inventories, .II Transportation Texts (*ŠA *KASKAL))"*, the texts of this category are fundamentally inventories of chests, distinguished only by the addition of a "KASKAL-Formula" (see *4.2 Defining the KASKAL Series*), as encountered in Vol. II, 8.1 and 8.4, or by some other mention of a caravan or campaign, as might be the case in Vol. II, 8.5. Since the KASKAL-formula in 8.4 only comes at the very end of the text, an area of the tablet that is often damaged or lost, it is possible that other transportation texts are hidden among the other inventories of chests. The most notable result of the new edition was to establish that that 8.1, the "KASKAL Main Text," records the largest single collection of wealth from the Hittite world thus far discovered (see Chapters 5 and 6 in the present volume), and that a new join suggests that the text may have been a dowry for an unknown royal marriage (see Section *7.3 Evidence for a Royal Marriage?*).

9. Complex Inventories
The *9. Complex Inventories* are a new category that carries over most of the texts that were edited in the first two unlabeled categories of Siegelová's *Inventarverzeichnisse.* The criteria for inclusion among the complex inventories has already been discussed under *CTH 246 "Complex Inventories (.I Named, .II Fragments)"* above. The category was subdivided into *9.1 Named Complex Inventories* and *9.2 Other Complex Inventories* based on whether the name of the administrator responsible for their authorship is preserved. A notable new result was to establish to a high degree of probability that the "authors" of the named complex inventories (at least those in whose names the inventories were conducted) were all crown princes, revealing a hitherto unexpected level of familiarity and direct involvement of the male members of the Hittite royal family in the economic administration of the state.[493]

10. Inventories Connected with the Regular Management of the State Cult
The new category of "Inventories Connected with the Regular Management of the State Cult" records what is reconstructed as the regular inventory and maintenance cycle of the temples and other organs of the state cult located at Ḫattuša. These are similar in contents to what was recorded in the *9. Complex Inventories*, but with less detail and probably anonymously (no colophons), suggesting they were more regular, quotidian inventories. The category contains the largest number of texts of any category that were not edited in *Hethitische Verwaltungspraxis.* This is because many of the texts were classified as part of the religious administration (Laroche: *Chapitre VIII. Administration religieuse*; CTH: *VIII. Kultinventare*) in earlier editions of the *Catalogue des textes hittites/Catalog der Texte der Hethiter.* A number of these were edited by Liane

493 See James M. Burgin, "A Hands-Off Administrator? The Absence of the King, but Presence of the Crown Prince, in the Hittite Palace-Temple Administrative Corpus," WO 52/1 (2022): 112–35.

Jakob-Rost.[494] However, as was recognized early on with the Inventory of Manninni, and then with the many economic-administrative texts edited by Siegelová found at Temple 1, there is little reason to separate the palace and temple administrations since they formed a single, extended economic unit.[495] It is in fact difficult to distinguish the "Inventories Connected with the Regular Management of the State Cult" from other inventories in formal terms, especially since the texts of this category contain non-religious items, and the texts of other inventories contain many pieces of religious paraphernalia. And while most of the "Inventories Connected with the Regular Management of the State Cult" with known findspots come from Temple 1, at least one, the detailed description of inscribed animal figurines KUB 38.8 (Vol. II, 10.2.2.2 – see also probable join 10.2.2.3 and 10.2.2.4), was found at Büyükkale.[496] Perhaps if more findspots of the tablets were known, or were more precise for the early excavations, the nuances of the relationship between the palace and temple economic administrations could be better differentiated. But under the present conditions it is best to edit the texts together.

The *10. Inventories Connected with the Regular Management of the State Cult* are subdivided into three groups: *10.1 General Temple Inventories*, *10.2 Detailed Inventories of Cult Images and Votive Objects*, and *10.3 Inventories Concerned with Condition and Maintenance*. It is of course possible that many, if not most of the *9. Complex Inventories* were also connected with management of the equipment and paraphernalia of the state cult, but since these seem to have occasioned by special events, rather than the regular stock-taking exemplified by the texts categorized here, they are classified separately. It can be further surmised from the contents of the texts categorized under *11. Inventory Fragments* that many, and certainly all with known findspots from Temple 1, were part of the same management of the extensive material possessions of the state cult.

10.1 General Temple Inventories

The "General Temple Inventories" contains texts that by virtue of their comprehensiveness or by explicit self-identification (see Vol. II, 10.1.1.2 and 10.1.2.8) instantiate what appear to be general inventories of a temple's possessions. The category has two

---

494 Liane Rost, "Zu den hethitischen Bildbeschreibungen (I. Teil)," MIO 8 (1961–63): 161–217. Liane Jakob-Rost, "Zu den hethitischen Bildbeschreibungen (II. Teil)," MIO 9 (1963): 175–239.

495 See again, as mentioned in Chapter 2 under *2.2.1 History of Research*, Amir Gilan, "Formen der Transaktion im hethitischen 'Staatskult' - Idee und Wirklichkeit," In *Geschenke und Steuern, Zölle und Tribut*, eds. Hilmar Klinkott, Sabine Kubisch, Renate Müller-Wollermann. CHANE 29 (Leiden: Brill, 2007), 314–18; and Suzanne Herbordt, "Die Tempelinventare aus der Oberstadt von Boğazköy/Hattusa: hethitische Tempelanlagen als Kultstätten und Wirtschaftseinheiten," in *Ancient Near Eastern Temple Inventories in the Third and Second Millennia BCE: Integrating Archaeological, Textual, and Visual Sources*, eds. Jean M. Evans, Elisa Roßberger. Münchener Abhandlungen zum Alten Orient 4 (Gladbeck: PeWe-Verlag, 2019), 175–87.

496 Since it is suspected that the inscribed animal figurines are votive objects, this text could prove to be further documentation of the palace's role in endowing the state cult through votive gifts, thereby explaining its find location on Büyükkale. See also KUB 42.41 (Vol. II, 10.2.1.7), a detailed description of cult images found at the *Haus am Hang*, halfway between Büyükkale and the Lower City temple district, as possible further evidence of the circulation of texts concerned with the economic administration of the state cult between the palace and temple sectors.

subdivisions: *10.1.1 General Temple Inventories with Comment on Provisioning* and *10.1.2 Other General Temple Inventories*. The first are distinguished by recording over-and-above the statues, garments, ornaments, religious paraphernalia, and furniture of the other general temple inventories what appear to be the food rations of the temple. As discussed in the introductory *Analysis* to 10.1.1.1, the amount of roasted grain, emmer, barley-mash, and beer recorded in the text could satisfy the full caloric requirements of between 20 to 30 people for a month. Of course, there is no indication of a time frame, nor the designated recipients of the food rations, so a scenario of longer-term storage is also possible. The other text in the category, 10.1.1.2, is an omnibus or digest of temple inventories offering the same combination of items and provisions. It offers the important information that the temples were located in "the city" (URU-*ri*, 10.1.1.2 rev. iv 15′), which, appearing as it does without further qualification, is presumably Ḫattuša.

The second subcategory, *10.1.2 Other General Temple Inventories*, contain inventories that through their range and numbers of objects (sometimes in the dozens for statues and figurines or hundreds for cloths, instead of the single-digits of other inventories) and complex formatting (double paragraph lines, use of totals), and similarities in language to the "General Temple Inventories with Comment on Provisioning" suggest the stock-taking of entire temples or, at the very least, large temple-storerooms. Many of the texts are admittedly inferentially classified, but this is preferable to leaving what recommends itself as a natural class of texts among the undifferentiated inventory fragments.

10.2 Detailed Inventories of Cult Images and Votive Objects

Distinguished from the "General Temple Inventories" are inventories that seem to specialize in the detailed description of cult images and votive objects. The category of *10.2 Detailed Inventories of Cult Images and Votive Objects* has two subdivisions: *10.2.1 Cult Image Descriptions ("Bildbeschreibungen")* and *10.2.2 Votive Objects in Storage*. The first contain detailed description of statues, often of divine subjects. The text genre is often referred to as "Bildbeschreibungen" thanks to the early edition of the texts (when compared to other inventories) by Liane Jakob-Rost in the 1960's. Many of these texts come from Temple 1. Except for their thematic focus on the description of cult images, which is not unique to this genre, since such descriptions are also found inserted into other inventories, the *Bildbeschreibungen* are almost indistinguishable from the other inventories. Only the occasional use of linear measurements of height and length are unique to the genre. Thus, as discussed above, there is no reason to keep them separate from the other inventories of Temple 1, and indeed the Palace-Temple Administrative Corpus at large. Rather, they should be taken as just another form of detailed inventory, probably tied to the maintenance cycle of the temples (see 10.2.1.2 for an example of a *Bildbeschreibung* with notes on condition).

The second subcategory, *10.2.2 Votive Objects in Storage*, contains inventories of votive gifts that have been produced (see *7. Votive Gifts*) and reached storage. The category is small, consisting of only four texts, which might be reduced to only two if the suggested indirect joins are correct. However, it may be suspected, if it cannot be proven, that many of the other objects attested in the general temple inventories, *Bild-*

beschreibungen, and the inventory fragments were also in origin votive gifts. In the texts of the *10.2.2 Votive Objects in Storage*, the fact that the objects, mostly animal figurines, are inscribed with the names of Hittite kings, and in one instance explicitly labeled as a gift (*ŠULMAN* ᵐZAG-ŠEŠ "gift of Bentešina" in 10.2.2.4 obv. r. c. 5′), is taken as proof they were donated. In some cases, it seems the votive objects have been in storage for quite some time, as the antiquity of the names Muršili (probably Muršili II, or possibly Muršili III, i.e. Urḫi-Teššub) and Muwatalli II (if correctly restored in 10.2.2.1 3′) reveal. In format, the closest genre are the *Bildbeschreibungen*, with the difference that most of the votive objects seem to be animal figurines rather than anthropomorphic divinities. Also, although the votive objects are described in considerable detail, the description never rises to the meticulous level of detail found in the *Bildbeschreibungen*.

10.3 Inventories Concerned with Condition and Maintenance

The last subcategory of the "Inventories Connected with the Regular Management of the State Cult" is *10.3 Inventories Concerned with Condition and Maintenance*. These texts are distinguished by a focus on evaluating the condition of the items they inventory. Whereas other categories contain occasional notes on damage, e.g. the complex inventories and the *Bildbeschreibungen*, here the damage is systematically noted. Two of the texts, Bo 3826 (Vol. II, 10.3.1) and KUB 58.9 (Vol. II, 10.3.2), go a step further and also contain what seem to be notes on where the item is in the process of repair (see the mention of the smiths in 10.3.1 rev. iii 7′, the description of an object as "finished/complete" in rev. iii 13′, and the mention of replating in 10.3.2 obv. i(?) 4″). The remainder of the texts in the category record only damage. Furniture is unusually well-represented among the objects of the inventories concerned with condition and maintenance, with the tables and chairs of 10.3.4–10.3.9, and especially 10.3.4 and 10.3.5, where the tables and chairs appear next to cutlery and dining equipment, serving as internal evidence of the kind of equipment kept on hand by the temples for ritual feasting (10.3.5 and 10.3.6 were found at Temple 1).

11. Inventory Fragments

The category *11. Inventory Fragments* is reserved for fragments that are too small to otherwise classify. They are separated into seven subcategories: *11.1 Fragments of Mixed Inventories*, which show a mixture of textiles and durable goods, but cannot be further assigned by form or function to the other classes of inventories categorized above; *11.2 Inventory Fragments of Cult Images, Animal Figurines, and Model Objects*, which contain descriptions of images and figurines not detailed enough to be classified among the *Bildbeschreibungen*; *11.3 Inventory Fragments of Jewelry*, which show precious metal and stone jewelry; *11.4 Inventory Fragments of Gold and Silver Objects*, which show gold and silver objects; *11.5 Inventory Fragments of Ivory Objects*, which show ivory objects; *11.6 Inventory Fragments of Cloths and Garments*, which show only textiles; and *11.7 Unclassified Inventory Fragments*, which contain texts that are too fragmentary to classify. Due to the size of the fragments and the fact that most inventories show some tendency to separate objects by material, usually into paragraphs, it is almost certain that most, if not all, of the inventory fragments classified here by material were parts of larger mixed inventories. Only two of the texts from among the

11.3 Fragments of Jewelry, KUB 42.38 (Vol. II, 11.3.1) and KBo 9.92 (Vol. II, 11.3.2), perhaps one text from the *11.4 Inventory Fragments of Ivory Objects*, KBo 18.152 (Vol. II, 11.5.1), and two of the texts from among the*11.6 Inventory Fragments of Cloths and Garments*, KUB 42.56 (Vol. II, 11.6.1) and KBo 18.186 (Vol. II, 11.6.2), preserve enough text to suspect that they may have been parts of inventories dedicated exclusively to their respective themes.

12. Miscellaneous Texts

The final category of *12. Miscellaneous Texts* contains texts of tangential connection to the main Palace-Temple Administrative Corpus. These are divided into *12.1 Ritual Lists*, *12.2 School Texts*, and *12.3 Other Miscellaneous Texts.*

12.1 Ritual Lists

Here are classified four texts that in formal terms are inventories, but the contents of which suggest a ritual list, either because of the token-like nature of the objects or the explicit mention of apparently ritual activity. A highlight of this category is KBo 18.165++ (Vol. II, 12.1.1), previously classified as a list of jewelry (HVP 11.4.3). However, joins to the text reveal it to be a list of figurines of mostly aquatic creatures required for a ritual stemming from perhaps the Kizzuwatnean cultic sphere that involved the king and the sea.

12.2 School Texts

Three texts seem to be copying exercises, presumably for scribal training. The focus of the texts seems to be sign forms and vocabulary, since no evidence for mathematic calculation is preserved.

12.3 Other Miscellaneous Texts

The other miscellaneous texts include two examples of real-estate transactions (Vol. II, 12.3.1 and 12.3.2), which, judging from their script and prosopography, come from the Middle Hittite period. This provides further evidence alongside the *Landschenkungsurkunden* for palace interaction with land tenure in this period, a topic which is nearly absent in the cuneiform texts of the New Hittite period. The other miscellaneous texts include a list of equids and personnel (Vol. II, 12.3.3), a baker's receipt for the production and distribution of 210 loaves of bread (Vol. II, 12.3.4), a receipt mentioning flour and beer (Vol. II, 12.3.5), a difficult-to-interpret fragment involving animal hides (Vol. II, 12.3.6), and what might be a fragment from a court proceeding involving some garments and necklaces (Vol. II, 12.3.7).

3.4 Conclusions on the Hittite Palace-Temple Administrative Corpus

The evolution of the Hittite economic-administrative corpus from what was originally called the "inventory texts" by Košak to the "Wirtschafts- und Inventardokumente" by Siegelová to what is named here the Palace-Temple Administrative Corpus reflects a growth in understanding of the function of the texts. Inventorying was certainly part of the corpus, and the predominance of inventories of concrete, tangible objects as opposed to, e.g., shipments of grain is one of the remarkable features of the corpus vis-à-vis its Mesopotamian contemporaries. But the corpus is more than just inventories, and bears witness to a system of intake, circulation, expenditure, and storage that required participation of the Hittite palace and temple institutions, internal as well as external craftsmen, and the central and local religious and administrative elites.

The mechanics of how the texts of the corpus worked together will not be repeated here, since it would be difficult to summarize the process any more succinctly than was done in the just-completed Section 3.3.2. Rather, a general remark will be made. The texts of the PTAC are not illocutionary: they are not legal instruments and do not effect a change of ownership. With the exception of one text, KUB 42.59 (Vol. II, 6.5), which preserves evidence of attached bullae, there is no evidence that the tablets were sealed. What legal authority existed in the transactions was vested outside of the texts, either in supervisors who "knew" (*ĪDE*) of them, or in sealed documents that were given into the possession of the recipients. Instead, the texts of the PTAC served to document the day-to-day business of the palace and temple organizations that created them. Perhaps they were to be retained for later use as evidence in case of problems, or perhaps they were the personal records of the administrators in whose remit the activities took place. In the terminology set out by Nicholas Postage in his *Bronze Age Bureaucracy*, most of the texts are *descriptive*, in that they record past events (although portions of the texts under *4.1 Manufacturing Allocations* are prescriptive when they specify the objects to be made from the disbursed materials); most are *internal*, in that the transmission of commodities occurs within the Palace-Temple organization (the texts under *I. Income*, which record the entrance and enrollment of the commodities into the organization, and *5. Extramural Allocations* and *6. Gifts and Handouts*, which record commodities leaving Palace-Temple control, being the exceptions); almost all of the texts are *unilateral*, in that all of the texts seem to be for the internal records of the palace and temple administrations (the above-mentioned KUB 42.59 being the only probable exception, since it might have been intended to be retained by the collective recipients); and the corpus is universally *administrative* and *public*, in that they are records generated as part of the functioning of government institutions.[497] This constellation of attributes, especially the frequency of internal documents, makes the authority of the texts of the Palace-Temple Adminstrative Corpus dependent on the individual scribe who created them. The poverty of "metadata" in the texts, i.e., the dates, locations, and other bits of essential information that were elided, conspires to prevent even another cuneiform-literate individual from being able to properly interpret the records. The presence of the scribe who authored the text, who could literally point to the chest that a particular paragraph referred to, was required for its valid use.

It must be emphasized how different the personal, indexical records of the Hittites are in comparison to those of contemporary Bronze Age kingdoms. In Mesopotamia and Egypt, the bureaucracy wrestled with staples of grain and livestock, sometimes measuring in the tons. Their documents conform to more modern conceptions of 'paperwork': figures and sums. The scribes who recorded the economic activity were often removed at a distance from the event itself, because their job was to *abstract* the bulk

497 J. Nicholas Postgate, *Bronze Age Bureaucracy. Writing and the Practice of Government in Assyria* (Cambridge: Cambridge University Press, 2014), 79–80.

into manageable numbers.[498] When an Assyrian scribe wrote down an amount of grain, the nominal measurement might be 81,000 liters, but in practice, depending on atmospheric humidity, how much the grain settled during storage, and human error, the grain could never be measured the same way twice. But the Hittite government was concerned with recording utensils, ingots, and precious goods, not staple products, so that a Hittite scribe recording "81 complete knives, of which 57 are cook's knives" would always mean just that. The reduced bulk of the luxury objects, and the specificity needed in recording them, allowed the Hittite scribe to take a hands-on approach to his work, yielding a decidedly concrete, even "artisanal" bureaucracy. This approach can be seen everywhere in the administrative genres, and confirms the larger point set out in *2.5.1 Summary of Current Research*: the Hittites had different economic needs and opportunities compared to their contemporaries, and this created a different kind of bureaucracy, which resulted in a different kind of record. There was an immanence to the Hittite bureaucracy that is revealed in the concrete, indexical nature of its written products. Thus, it can be seen that the specificity of the descriptions in the inventories that dominate the Hittite economic-administrative corpus, far from being superfluous, reflects a way of thinking that is at the core of the entire Hittite political economy.

498 See Piotr Steinkeller, "The Function of Written Documentation in the Administrative Praxis of Early Babylonia," in *Creating Economic Order: Record-Keeping, Standardization, and the Development of Accounting in the Ancient Near East*, eds. Michael Hudson, Cornelia Wunsch (Bethesda, Maryland: CDL, 2004), 65–88. Here, the scribe was not proximate to the administrative action itself, but recorded the events after the fact. See also the description of the chronological metrological capabilities of the Middle Assyrian scribe under "Time and Measure" in Postgate, *Bronze Age Bureaucracy*, 51–56.

4. CASE STUDY: THE KASKAL SERIES

4.1 Introduction

The KASKAL series is a subset of the Hittite administrative documents dealing with the transportation of durable goods and textiles edited under the *8. Transportation Texts* in Vol. II. In the Main Text of the series, 8.1.A–K, each paragraph begins with a container followed by a list quantities of objects. The objects are described in the modest but not exceptional level of detail typical of a regular inventory text (i.e., not a preliminary inventory, where only classes of objects are described, nor a complex inventory, where subsets and individual pieces can receive extra description). The distinguishing feature of the KASKAL series, and what sets it apart from other inventories of chests, is the fact that almost every paragraph in the case of the Main Text, or just the final line of the text in the outlier 8.4, closes with an appearance of the Sumerogram KASKAL in a characteristic formula.[499] The basic variations of the formula describe the chest and items as either *ŠA* KASKAL 'of the way/journey/road' or *INA* KASKAL *NAŠÛ* 'to be carried on the way/journey/road'.

Scholarly investigation of the KASKAL series began piecemeal: the frequent appearance of Egyptian goods (or perhaps goods in the Egyptian style) was the first point of interest in the texts, garnering the attention of Pierre Cornil and René Lebrun in 1976.[500] The texts were then edited as a series of separate documents interspersed among other texts of CTH 241 "Inventories of Chests" by Silvin Košak in 1982.[501] It was only in 1986, when Jana Siegelová addressed the Hittite administrative corpus as an object of study in and of itself, that the separate tablets of the KASKAL series were classified as a separate group within the administrative texts.[502] Siegelová brought together seventeen fragments, lettering them A through Q, and labeled the group as *Transportverzeichnisse* ('Transport Registers') based on the closing KASKAL formula. She established that the first eleven fragments, A through K, were witnesses to a single extended text – the aforementioned "Main Text" – standing at a minimum in four

---

499 KASKAL is the Sumerographic writing for Hittite *palša-* 'road, path; way, behavior; journey, campaign, expedition; caravan, transport' (CHP P *s.v. palša-* [p. 66]; Mark Weeden, *Hittite Logograms and Hittite Scholarship*. StBoT 54 [Wiesbaden: Harrassowitz 2011], 529). The other Hittite word for 'campaign, journey', *laḫḫa-*, which can have a military connotation, also appears once in the PTAC, if the reading proposed in 8.5 rev. iv(?) 6′: *l*]*a*?-*aḫ-ḫi* 'for [the ca]mpaign/[jo]urney(?)' is correct.

500 Pierre Cornil and René Lebrun, "Fragments hittites relatifs à l'Égypte," OLP 67 (1976): 83–108.

501 Silvin Košak, *Hittite Inventory Texts (CTH 241–250)*. THeth. 10 (Heidelberg: Winter, 1982). See "Previous Editions" under *Catalog Information* in the edition of 8.1 *The KASKAL Main Text* in Vol. II for page numbers.

502 Jana Siegelová, *Hethitische Verwaltungspraxis im Lichte der Wirtschafts- und Inventardokumente* (Praha: Národní muzeum v Praze, 1986), 388–438.

copies.[503] The remaining texts L through Q (of which only text L, edited in Vol. II as the aforementioned outlier 8.4, bears a KASKAL formula) were considered to be unrelated, smaller documents from the same genre.[504]

Siegelová left the interpretation of the KASKAL series' purpose and meaning to future scholars, observing only that the unity of the KASKAL Main Text suggests it recorded a single event.[505] A cursory glance at the contents of the text confirms already that this event must have been of enormous economic importance – though just how important only becomes obvious after calculation and comparison with other texts outside of the PTAC. The present chapter is thus part of a case study aimed at contextualizing and hopefully answering some of the questions surrounding the KASKAL Main Text. The first part, undertaken here, examines the philological context of the KASKAL series and establishes the structure and relationship of the witnesses of the Main Text. It is shown through a reevaluation of the text's editorial history that the four copies of the Main Text were not duplicates, but rather the result of a concerted effort at producing a "final" draft. Then, in *5. Quantifying the Contents of the KASKAL Main Text* and *6. The Relative Value of the KASKAL Main Text* it will be demonstrated that the Main Text recorded an economic event of extra-ordinary magnitude, certainly the largest recorded in the Palace-Temple Administrative Corpus. Finally, in *7. Concluding Remarks on the KASKAL Main Text*, it will be suggested that the economic event concerned the outbound shipment that traveled to, or through, south-central Anatolia, perhaps as part of a royal dowry for an unknown diplomatic marriage conducted in the reign of either Ḫattušili III or Tudḫaliya IV.

4.2 Defining the KASKAL Series

Except for the characteristic formula, the KASKAL series are difficult to distinguish from other inventories of chests, especially those coming from the later administrative stages of the texts edited in Vol. II under *2. Inventory Records Connected with Intake and Storage* (e.g., 2.12–2.16), and also some of those in *6. Gifts and Handouts* (e.g., 6.11–6.13). These inventories display many of the same features as the KASKAL series: they are mostly two- to three-column tablets composed of lists of chests, quantities of objects described in moderate detail, and very little extra information. They rarely contain personal names indicating possession or responsibility, a trait also shared with the KASKAL series. The surest definition, therefore, of a KASKAL text is the presence of the above-mentioned KASKAL formula, which appears usually as either *ŠA* KASKAL 'of the way/journey/road' or *INA* KASKAL *NAŠÛ* 'to be carried on the way/journey/road'.

503 Siegelová, *Hethitische Verwaltungspraxis*, 393–96.

504 Emphasizing the difficulties of classification, of Siegelová texts M–Q, only Text M (edited as 8.8 in Vol. II) is still classified as transport text in the present edition, while the others have been reassigned to various other categories (see *Concordance with J. Siegelová,* Hethitische Verwaltungspraxis *(Prague, 1986)* in Vol. 2).

505 Siegelová, *op. cit.*, 397.

The corpus of the KASKAL series as it stands today can be divided into three parts. The first, comprising Siegelová's *Transportverzeichnisse* texts A through K, and edited in Vol. II as 8.1.A–K, are labeled here as the "Main Text." The Main Text has grown by two fragments since Siegelová's edition: a direct join of the tiny fragment KBo 18.175d to KBo 18.175 (8.1.F), with KBo 18.175d 1′ = KBo 18.175 rev. vi 8, and a more substantial indirect join of KUB 60.112 (8.1.E(A_3)) with KUB 42.16 (8.1.E(A_1)), for which see introductory *Analysis* to 8.1 in Vol. II. All tablets belonging to the Main Text contain the tripartite scheme of container, contents, and KASKAL formula. The second group of the series comprises two fragments, edited as 8.2 and 8.3, both of which are related to the KASKAL Main Text. The first of these, 8.2, is a tiny fragment which might be an indirect join to 8.1D. The join by itself would add a negligible amount of information to the contents of the Main Text, but if valid, would place the find spot of at least one of the drafts of the KASKAL Main Text at Temple 1, in addition to the already known find spots on Büyükkale. The second, larger fragment 8.3 is a possible forerunner to 8.1.E(A_1), although it cannot be determined with certainty if the text is a duplicate or just a description of similar items. The third part of the KASKAL series, and the only one with no perceptible relationship to the Main Text, is represented by the single isolate text 8.4.

Although the contents of the possible join 8.2, the precursor 8.3, the isolate text 8.4 will not be tabulated in the portion of the case study conducted in *5. Quantifying the Contents of the KASKAL Main Text* due to the uncertainty of their relationship to the Main Text, the texts are nevertheless useful for the present task of elucidating the editorial process behind the KASKAL Main Text. For 8.2, the fact that some stage of the editorial process might have taken place in Temple I, an area administratively associated primarily with long-term storage,[506] suggests that the preparation of the text took cooperation from multiple institutions. For 8.3, the fact the text contains a near-duplicate list of items to 8.1.E(A_1) obv. ii 4–14, but in a slightly different order (see introductory *Analysis* to 8.3 in Vol. II), combined with the extensive erasures and uninscribed space on the reverse of the text, makes it possible that 8.3 was a two-column predecessor to 8.1.E(A_1). This would add a third attestation of the editorial step represented by 8.1.C and 8.1.D vis-à-vis 8.1.A (see *4.7 Editorial Layers in the KASKAL Main Text* below).

8.4, in contrast, has no parallels within the KASKAL Main Text. The text is a one-sided, single-column tablet with very sloppy formatting, containing many open spaces towards the end and skewed paragraph lines. It was almost certainly a temporary record, intended as a rough draft or a note taken by the scribe. Its entries lack the tripartite structure defined above: each of its eight preserved paragraphs starts without mention of a container, and ends without a KASKAL formula, meaning that 8.4 technically does not even meet the criteria for belonging to CTH 241 "Inventory of Chests" (it is presently classified under CTH 245 "Inventory of Jewels and Jewelry"). Indeed, the text

506 Siegelová, *Hethitische Verwaltungspraxis*, 9, 440. Also Theo van den Hout, "Administration in the Reign of Tutḫaliya IV and the Later Years of the Hittite Empire," in *The Life and Times of Ḫattušili III and Tutḫaliya IV: Proceedings of a Symposium Held in Honor of J. de Roos, 12–13 December 2003*, ed Th. van den Hout, PIHANS 103 (Leiden: Nederlands Instituut voor het Nabije Oosten, 2006), 85–86.

would be impossible to identify as a KASKAL text were it not for the last line, spaced far below the body of the text at the lower edge of the tablet, which reads EGI]R KASKAL-*NI*. The tablet would have little use as a shipping manifest: lacking a description of the containers the reader cannot find the goods listed without opening each chest or finding the label and comparing the contents. One must instead imagine that the items have not yet been packed into their respective containers – these being perhaps the four chests in 8.4 rev. 19′. Thus, 8.4 represents the stage when the scribe was working in a storeroom, gathering the goods to be packed up. This makes the text a strong candidate for the type of the primary documentation from which it is hypothesized the KASKAL Main Text was assembled: the single-column precursor inventory, of which no examples for the Main Text have been preserved. The careless formatting of 8.4 suggests that the KASKAL precursor inventories were meant for almost immediate recycling, going a long way to explain their non-existence for the Main Text. However, since 8.4 is identifiable as a transport text only by its very last line on the tablet edge – the most fragile and least likely part of the tablet to be preserved – the format of 8.4 also reveals that there is every chance that a number of other transport text precursors could be lurking unidentified among the other inventories, even those that do not mention chests.

4.3 Structure of the KASKAL Main Text

In the KASKAL Main Text every paragraph begins with a container, usually either ^{GIŠ}*tuppaš* 'chest' or $^{\text{GI/GIŠ}}$PISAN (Sumerian for 'basket', though in Boğazköy it can signify any kind of container made of GI 'reed' or GIŠ 'wood'), and every paragraph ends with the formula *ŠA* KASKAL or *INA* KASKAL *NAŠÛ*, translated as 'of the road' or '(to be) carried on the road'. Thus, a typical entry will look like:

8.1.A (KUB 42.11)
Transliteration
rev. v
23′ 1 ^{GIŠ}PISAN SA_5 KUR *mi-iz-ri ša-ra-*⸢*a*⸣ [*wa-aš-ša-an-za*
24′ 13 GÚ GU_4 KÙ.BABBAR 3 GÚ UR.[MAḪ KÙ.BABBAR
25′ 5 GÚ $\text{TI}_8^{\text{MUŠEN}}$ KÙ.BABBAR 2 ŠU.[SI KÙ.BABBAR
26′ 14 GAL KÙ.BABBAR *an-da ŠA* [KASKAL

Translation
rev. v
23′ 1 red chest of the land of Egypt, [upholstered] on top. [
24′ 13 silver ox protomes, 3 [silver] li[on] protomes, [
25′ 5 silver eagle protomes, 2 [silver] fin[gers
26′ 14 silver cups (are) inside. Of [the caravan.

A single tablet contains many such entries, one after the other, separated by paragraph lines, with a general rule of one container per paragraph. If a paragraph does describe more than one container at a time, more detail is added to clarify the situation (e.g., the two chests in 8.1.A obv. ii 8′–17′, and especially 14′–17′ which describes how the items are distributed in the two chests). Depending on the contents of the container, the entries can be as long as twenty-four lines (8.1.A obv. i 1′–24′) or as short as one line (8.1.A rev. v 28). Finally, the KASKAL formula can be in-line with the last item of the contents, or given a line of its own depending on the formatting of the particular tablet and the length of the formula. Regardless of variations, the tripartite structure of 'Container', 'Contents', and 'KASKAL Formula' is the defining feature of the series.

If one takes seriously the tripartite structure of the entries of the KASKAL series, so that the contents of the paragraph are the contents of one chest (unless otherwise marked), then some of the containers must have been huge. One chest held twelve articles of clothing, a total of 125 KÙŠ of *parna*-cloth (approximately 62.5 meters in total length, unknown width),[507] and a gold-ornamented ivory bed (presumably disassembled) and bed sheets.[508] Another container apparently held six subcontainers, one of which contained at least 41 minas and 4 (Hittite) shekels of gold (8.1.A obv. ii 18′–23′). The twenty-four-line entry mentioned previously had each line filled with unknown quantities of gold, iron, and stone implements and jewelry (8.1.A obv. i 1′–24′).

Though the entries have a clear structure, the rest of the text does not. The beginning of the KASKAL Main Text is not preserved, but it would not be surprising if it began *in media res* like other inventory texts.[509] The body of the text is a series of self-contained entries, usually filling a three-column tablet. One can occasionally discern an attempt to group the entries by contents. Within 8.1.A there is a progression of materials: first gold, then *iron (ore)*, then precious stones and ivory, and then more *iron (ore)* objects and silver implements. Then, within the extended text 8.1.A–K, there is a division by material: fragments 8.1.A, B, C, and J record durable goods like metals and stone, and 8.1.E, F(+)G(+)H, I, and K record textiles. Only fragment 8.1.D, which is unusual in other respects, has both durable goods and textiles.

507 See Marvin Powell, "Masse und Gewichte," RlA 7 (1987–90): 462, where the Sumero-Babylonian "30 finger" cubit (Sum. KÙŠ, Akk. *ammatu*) in use before the Neo-Babylonian period is estimated at about 50 cm in length.

508 8.1.F rev. v 3–16. To give an idea of weight of the cloth, there are two gifts of linen in the Egyptian gifts that are 5 *ammatu* (KBo 28.32 [ÄHK 94] obv. 5′) and 6 *ammatu* (KUB 3.63 [ÄHK 51] rev. 6′) in width, so between 2.5 and 3 meters wide. Most modern linen is sold in 56″-60″ width (~1.5 meters). With these two data points in mind, one might guess that a 2-meter width for the Hittite cloth would not be far from the mark. A decent quality, modern flax linen cloth used for clothing and bed sheets weighs about 265 g/m^2, though a tapestry might use a heavier, canvas-like cloth. Putting this all together gives 62.5m x 2m x 265g ≈ 33kg of cloth. The weight estimated for the Hittite *parna*-cloth could vary depending on the width of the cloth and its quality, but one can at least say that along with the bed frame and other linens in the container, the chest would be at the upper limit of size and weight that two people could comfortably carry.

509 Finding any administrative text with its first line intact is uncommon, but see 1.5, 2.7.A, 2.8, 3.2.1, 4.1.1.2.B, 4.1.1.3, 4.1.4.9, 4.2.2, 4.2.4, 4.2.9, 6.1, and 9.1.6, all of which start *in medias res* with inventoried goods. The sole exception to this trend seems to be 4.1.1.5, which has a preserved upper edge bearing what seems to be a label repeating the first line of obv. 1.

Finally, of the two tablets, 8.1.A and 8.1.E, preserving the end of a text, only 8.1.A has a colophon:

8.1.A (KUB 42.11)
Transliteration
rev. vi
1′ [… *ŠA*(?)] KASKAL-*ni-kán*
2′ [*A-NA ṬUP-PÍ* (*IŠ-TU* GIŠ.ḪUR$^{\text{ḪI.A}}$)(?) …] ⌜*a*⌝*-ni-ia-an*
[ ] uninscribed
3′ [DUB n^{KAM}(?) …] ⌜*Ú*⌝*-UL QA-TI*

Transliteration
rev. vi
1′ [(Chests) of(?)] the caravan,
2′ written/copied [on a tablet (from the GIŠ.ḪUR$^{\text{HI.A}}$)(?) …
[ ]
3′ [nth tablet(?)] (Series) not complete.

8.1.E, on the other hand, has a postscript written in a smaller script below the final entry and seemingly continued onto the edge. The postscript concerns the behavior of a certain ^{f}*Ḫentī* that is difficult to relate to the rest of the text (but see Section *7.3 Evidence for a Royal Marriage?*). Since 8.1.E is an unusual text, and hypothesized to be prior to the final editorial layer to which 8.1.A belongs (see *4.7 Editorial Layers in the* KASKAL *Main Text*), the addition of a true colophon could be a feature of the finalized tablet series. It is thus probable that the other final drafts of the KASKAL Main Text, i.e., 8.1.B, F(+)G(+)H, I, and J also had colophons.

An important inference can be made from the structural simplicity of the KASKAL series. The regular and monotonous nature of the entries was a result of their completeness, because the work of discovering and sorting the contents of the chest, which sometimes requires extra comment, has been done elsewhere. Such work was probably recorded on more temporary records, perhaps single-column tablets of the type represented by the transport text 8.4 (see above), where the incidentals of the inventory process would have been dealt with: whether tags had been made for the chests, or if the Hittite queen wanted to look through the items first.[510] Such comments are almost completely lacking in the KASKAL series. Even when a KASKAL tablet shows physical evidence of being a rough draft, with erasures and mistakes, the information within is complete. In other words, the information recorded in the KASKAL Main Text is the culmination, not the beginning, of an administrative process.

---

510 For a fuller treatment of the involvement of the queen in Hittite administrative texts, see Jana Siegelová, "Die hethitische Königin und die Wirtschaft der Krone," in *Saeculum. Gedenkschrift für Heinrich Otten anlässlich seines 100. Geburtstags*, eds. Andreas Müller-Karpe, Elisabeth Rieken, Walter Sommerfeld. StBoT 58 (Wiesbaden: Harrassowitz, 2015), 239–50.

4.4 Editorial Relationship of the Tablets of the KASKAL Main Text: 8.1.A–K

The KASKAL Main Text consists of twelve fragments: eleven fragments edited by Siegelová as texts A through K (= 8.1.A–K in Vol. II of the present book), plus a twelfth fragment, 8.1.E(A_3), which is a newly proposed indirect join to Siegelová's E (+) E_a (relabled here as 8.1.E(A_1)(+)E(A_2)). In addition to 8.1.E(A_1)(+)E(A_2)(+)E(A_3) (which will be referred to simply as 8.1.E unless further specification is needed), three of the other fragments, 8.1.F(+)G(+)H, form indirect joins.[511] 8.1.A–H can be connected with each other through overlaps, where the same text is replicated on multiple tablets. Only J and K cannot be securely joined to the main body, but their contents are very similar to the other tablets and their ductus and format suggest they were written by the same scribe. If J and K are included in the total, there were thus originally at least nine tablets bearing witness to the extended text. The find-spots of the tablet fragments hint that the Main Text may have been associated with the Hittite palace. Five text fragments came from Büyükkale, the acropolis of Ḫattuša and location of the Hittite palace: the tablet F(+)G(+)H has a secure find-spot in Büyükkale Building D, and tablets B and C were found in secondary deposits also on Büyükkale. The remaining tablets have no find-spot listed on the *Konkordanz*. While the association with Büyükkale does not rule out temple involvement (indeed, if the indirect join of 8.2 to 8.1.D is accepted, then at least some of the drafts were composed or stored at Temple 1),[512] it does indicate the palace was an important partner in the economic event recorded in the KASKAL Main Text.

There was a strong thematic division between the tablets, with 8.1.A, B, C, J, and K recording durable goods, and 8.1.E, F(+)G(+)H, and I recording textiles. Only tablet D stood apart, with its obverse containing durable goods and its reverse textiles. The modern scholar is exceedingly fortunate for the preservation of tablet D, as it is the philological linchpin uniting the two halves of the Main Text. Without text D, which duplicates information from both the durable goods and textile tabet groups, it would be impossible to prove the Main Text of the KASKAL series recorded a single economic act, and the series would most likely have been treated like the rest of the administrative texts, as a category of disparate economic records.

The editorial relationship between the nine tablets of the Main Text is tangled, and may be impossible to fully resolve. Siegelová seems to assume a flat editorial hierarchy between the tablets, that is to say, she does not acknowledge that one copy might be an earlier or later draft.[513] But it is difficult to accept that all nine tablets were contemporary duplicates, as there are significant differences in style and composition between

511 See Siegelová, *Hethitische Verwaltungspraxis*, 391. Although Siegelová did not make her reasoning explicit, the fragments are placed in what must the correct order based on space considerations: fragment G, based on the incommensurability of its paragraph lines with F obv. i/ii, must be in the upper half of obv. i/ii, and H must for the same reason be in the lower half of rev. iv.

512 A split of the drafts across multiple composition sites would also be further support for the argument of Theo van den Hout, "On the Nature of the Tablet Collections at Ḫattuša," SMEA 47 (2005): 289, that the archives of Ḫattuša openly circulated between the temple and palace.

513 See Siegelová, *op. cit.*, 394 for a graphic representation of the tablet overlaps.

the tablets. Siegelová does note some of these differences in her editions, such as the variations in KASKAL formulas between the tablets. In the following sections, the differences between the tablets will be examined in more detail, with the results suggesting that a more nuanced relationship mapping the evolution of the series can be recovered.

4.5 Variation in the KASKAL Main Text: Systematic Differences

Variation between the tablets of the KASKAL Main Text can be approached in two ways: through a comparison of systematic differences in formatting and style and through examination of particular differences in content when the texts overlap. The systematic differences will be addressed first, since they are in many ways the more useful. Systematic differences are those features that consistently pertain to an entire text, meaning that they can be recovered from any sufficiently large tablet fragment. An example of a systematic difference is the different styles of KASKAL formulas. From the evidence available, if a text uses one variation, e.g., *ŠA* KASKAL-*NI*, in one place, it will use it everywhere. Thus, one need only find the KASKAL formula once and it can be safely assumed that the whole fragment, and the joining fragments, used the same formula. In contrast, particular differences can only be observed where texts overlap. An example is when one text has a sentence that the duplicate text does not. Without the overlap, there would be no way to know that a sentence was missing.

The ultimate goal in examining the differences among duplicates is to identify the stages of the editing process. This is done by correlating particular differences with systematic differences, and then based on certain assumptions such as "tablets with sloppy or inconsistent formatting and/or lots of erasures are likely to be earlier drafts," associating systematic differences with stages of the editing process.

In this section, the systematic differences among the tablets of the Main Text will first be identified and briefly discussed, with a comprehensive analysis postponed until *4.7 Editorial Layers in the KASKAL Main Text.*

4.5.1 Columns and Dividers

Siegelová observed a larger pattern in the Hittite administrative corpus concerning columns and column dividers.[514] About two-thirds of the corpus consists of three-column tablets, often divided by simple vertical lines (a feature heavily overrepresented among the inventories of the PTAC).[515] The three-column tablets tend to contain texts of a "recapitulatory" type – inventories and summaries. In the remaining third of the corpus, one half consists of two-column tablets with wide intercolumnia, and which can have any variety of contents, and the other half is single-column tablets, which tend to contain notes and first-drafts of the inventory process. This pattern applies remarkably well to the KASKAL series. The inchoate disposition of the one-column 8.4

514 Siegelová, *Hethitische Verwaltungspraxis*, 1–6.

515 Willemijn Waal, *Hittite Diplomatics. Studies in Ancient Document Formant and Record Management.* StBoT 57 (Wiesbaden: Harrassowitz, 2015), 92–93, with Appendix I.3 (197–98).

has already been discussed above. In the Main Text, at least one (probably two or three) tablets have two columns, but most of the tablets have the three columns befitting their systematic nature.

8.1.D is the only clear example of a two-column tablet. Although it has fewer columns, it appears to have been similar in size to the other tablets. Thus, each column is wider, so that together they accommodate the same total of information as a three-column tablet. The three-column tablets in the KASKAL series share not just the number of columns, but also the lineation, so when the same text appears on more than one tablet, duplicate lines begin and end with the same words. But where 8.1.D overlaps with a three-column tablet, one line of D corresponds to one-and-a-half or even two lines of a three-column tablet. Thus, two-column tablets had longer lines. If the contrapositive is true, and longer lines in the KASKAL series mean a two-column tablet, then 8.1.D is not alone: 8.1.C, a fragment which is otherwise too small to identify as a two-column tablet, also shows "two-for-one" lineation. Because 8.1.C and 8.1.D themselves overlap, this means there are at least two examples of two-column tablets. 8.1.K should also be added to the two-column group, based on its broad intercolumnium and its similarity in ductus to 8.1.D.[516] Outside of the tablets belonging securely to KASKAL Main Text, the differing lineation of 8.3 2′–7′, which was suspected to be a possible forerunner, vis-à-vis the duplicate or parallel text of 8.1.E(A_1) obv. ii 4–14 suggests that 8.3 was also a wide, two-column tablet.

The column dividers of the KASKAL series follow the pattern established by Siegelová: single lines for three-column tablets and a wide intercolumnium for two-column tablets. Text E is an exception, having what can be described as either a "double vertical line" divider, or a very narrow intercolumnium.

Columns and Dividers
Three-column tablet with simple intercolumnia: 8.1.A, B, F(+)G(+)H, I, J
Three-column tablet with narrow intercolumnia: 8.1.E
Wide, two-column tablet with broad intercolumnia: 8.1.C, D, K; also 8.3(?)

4.5.2 Space at End of Paragraphs

A readily observable feature of certain tablets of the KASKAL Main Text is the inclusion of a significant amount of uninscribed spaces between the final line of text in a paragraph and the subsequent paragraph line. These spaces are in fact peculiar to "administrative" texts – only inventories and oracle question texts seem to regularly have them (perhaps due to the temporary and businesslike nature uniting the two genres). The purpose of the uninscribed space is unclear, though it may have allowed entries to be distinguished at a glance, which would be useful for frequently consulted administrative texts. One can at least observe a great internal consistency in their usage. When a text has an uninscribed space after one paragraph, it has it everywhere. The

---

516 A join between these two tablets was already ruled out by Siegelová, *Hethitische Verwaltungspraxis*, 392, based on the differences in writing certain key terms, including the KASKAL formula.

one exception to this is in 8.1.E obv. iii 1′–4′ (which will be discussed in *4.6.4 Nexus 4* below), which has an unexpected uninscribed space that was perhaps erased.

Space at End of Paragraph
Uninscribed-space: B, F(+)G(+)H, I
No space: A, C, D, J, K
Mostly no space: E

4.5.3 KASKAL Formula

The variations in KASKAL formulas were already systematically recorded by Siegelová in her introduction to the KASKAL series,[517] although state of affairs in texts 8.1.D and 8.1.E were somewhat simplified.

KASKAL *Formula Type*

a.) Majority *ŠA* KASKAL

8.1.A:	*ŠA* KASKAL in body
	ŠA KASKAL-*NI* in colophon
8.1.D:	*ŠA* KASKAL (6 attestations), *anda* KASKAL (1 attestation)
8.1.J:	*ŠA* KASKAL

b.) Majority *ŠA* KASKAL-*NI*

8.1.F(+)G(+)H:	*ŠA* KASKAL-*NI*
8.1.I:	*ŠA* KASKAL(-*NI*?)
8.1.K:	*ŠA* KASKAL-*NI* (1 attestation), *ŠA* KASKAL-*NI* EGIR-*anda* (1 attestation)

c.) Other

8.1.B:	not preserved
8.1.C:	*anda* KASKAL (1 attestation)
8.1.E:	KASKAL (1 attestation), *I-NA* KASKAL *NA-ŠU-Ú* (3 attestations), *ŠA* KASKAL *I+NA* É.GAL-*LIM* (1 attestation), *ŠA* KASKAL *I+NA* ⟨⟨*NA*⟩⟩ É$^{!?}$ ^{N}[^{A_4}KIŠIB(?)

Despite their variability, there is no observable difference in meaning between the KASKAL formulas.

The *anda* KASKAL (lit.) "in the path" in 8.1.D obv. i 3′ is possibly an influence from 8.1.C, since it occurs right before an interpolation that only these two texts share. One would have expected here the *ŠA* KASKAL 'of the path' that appears in the duplicate portion of 8.1.A, and which 8.1.D consistently uses elsewhere.

The *ŠA* KASKAL-*NI* EGIR-*anda* 'of the path, after(wards)' in K rev. vi$^{?}$ (probably rev. iv if it considered a two-column tablet), line 10′ has the *ŠA* KASKAL-*NI* written normally and the EGIR-*anda* running over into the intercolumnium. Either the scribe did not

517 Siegelová, *Hethitische Verwaltungspraxis*, 388–92.

budget enough space, or the EGIR-*anda* was added later. Because the right-dislocation of the EGIR-*anda* is unexpected in Hittite syntax, the later addition is more likely. The meaning of the addition is unclear. Since the text immediately breaks of, it could be that additional items were recorded in the next line. This interpretation would fit with an argument made further below, that the KASKAL Main Text documents an administrative event in revision and flux.

As with the previous two categories, 8.1.E is again an outlier, being almost experimental in its use of KASKAL formulas. In E(A_1) obv. ii 7–8, there appears the phrase GIŠPISAN(?)] É.GAL*karupaḫiaš=kan* 8[ ] *danza* KASKAL "Chest(?)] of the palace *karupaḫi*-house, 8taken. Caravan." The *danza* is graphically aligned to the right, which is not uncommon in the final word in the last line of a paragraph. However, in this case the *danza* is not the last word of the line, since it is followed immediately by KASKAL. The lone KASKAL is a conundrum. It cannot be read as part of the previous sentence, but at the same time it is the only example of a one-word KASKAL formula. In contrast, E(A_1) obv. ii 15 – the same column, only seven lines later – has a similar phrase fully spelled out:] *karupaḫi I-NA* KASKAL *NA-ŠU-Ú*.

As for the location of the KASKAL formulas in the texts, certain texts seem to prefer them in-line with the last entry of the paragraph (e.g., 8.1.A), while others prefer to place them on their own line after the last entry (e.g., 8.1.F(+)G(+)H), but there are too many exceptions within each text to consider this a systematic feature.

4.5.4 Uncorrected Erasures

Some texts have more erasures than others. Usually when a scribe has more than just a sign to erase and correct, he will smooth out the signs to be deleted with his stylus and write over it. But certain texts have erased spaces that have not been written over. One might assume that these uncorrected erasures indicate an earlier draft of the text.

Uncorrected Erasures
8.1.D
8.1.E (very frequent)

It is entirely possible that some of the smaller fragments do not show erasures because of an accident of preservation. Nonetheless, the positive results of the larger fragments because mostly erasure-free should not be ignored.

4.5.5 Other Features

A few texts contain graphical oddities that cannot be explained as part of the content. Most notable are certain numbers appearing at the end of paragraphs in texts 8.1.F(+)G(+)H and 8.1.D, for example:

8.1.D[518]

Transliteration

obv. i

6′	[1 ^{GIŠ}*tup*]-*pa-aš* ⟨^{GIŠ}⟩EREN erasure ^{NA_4}KÁ.DINGIR.RA ^{NA_4}T[I]
7′	[^{NA_4}*mu*]-*uš-nu-wa-an-ti-iš* ŠÀ 1 ^{GIŠ}*tup-pa* SIG$_5$ ⌜*ŠA*⌝ [KASKAL]
7a′	[ ] 11

Translation

obv. i

6′	[1] cedar [che]st. erasure Babylon-stone, "li[fe]"-stone
7′	[*m*]*ušnuwanti*-stone, inside 1 good chest. Of [the caravan.]
7a′	[ ] 11

In every case, the numbers appear right above the paragraph line, and are often faintly impressed, as if they had been added after the clay had hardened, or as if the scribe had written them very lightly. Siegelová was able to explain some of them away: the "2" in F obv. i 19′ she read as the end of a KI].MIN 'ditto', and the "16" in D obv. i 10′ was interpreted as the misplaced quantity for the preceding entry. But the uniformity of style and placement of these numbers argue instead a common phenomenon, the meaning of which is elusive. It is possible the numbers are related to a system van den Hout has proposed for the oracle questions.[519] Here he guessed that small tablets containing a single question to be answered by oracle were given a number to keep them in order. Because the oracle process was procedural, certain questions could only be asked after others. The numbering system allowed the questions to be answered piecemeal and remotely, probably at the site of the animal sacrifice or observation, and then reconstituted later on a summary tablet. Unfortunately, there were not enough numbered tablets preserved to confirm his system for the oracle texts. Perhaps the numbers in the KASKAL Main Text, which are similarly too few to test, represent a similar editorial system. It is possible they refer back to a single-column precursor tablet, or a paragraph within the tablet, or even label on a chest.

Post-paragraph Numbers

8.1.F(+)G(+)H:	F obv. i 2′: "1"
	F obv. i 19′: "2"
	G obv. r. col, 7′: "9"
8.1.D:	D obv. i 7a′: "11"
	D obv. i 10′: "16"

518 See fuller discussion of this passage in *4.6.2 Nexus 2* below.

519 Theo van den Hout, "Bemerkungen zu älteren hethitischen Orakeltexten," in *Kulturgeschichten: Altorientalistische Studien für Volkert Haas zum 65. Gerburtstag*, eds. Thomas Richter, Doris Prechel, Jörg Klinger (Saarbrücken: Saarbücker Druckerei und Verlag, 2001), 423–40.

Another graphical oddity occurs in text 8.1.A in the form of three diagonal wedges, provisionally transliterated here as ≮*, grouped next to each other at the beginning of the line in A obv. ii 5′. Siegelová noticed this in her edition, and even had the feature printed.[520] Siegelová did not comment on the triple *Glossenkeil*, perhaps since it was ostensibly unique. However, checking the photograph of the tablet shows the same glyph appears again in the following line at beginning of A obv. ii 6′, something which was not recorded in the handcopy of the cuneiform. The wedges are smaller in size and impressed faintly but clearly to the left of the margin, and were either added by the scribe after the fact or incompletely erased. There is not enough context to determine what the glyph means. One immediately thinks of a *Glossenkeil* which usually precedes a translation of a foreign word, or identifies an untranslated word as non-Hittite, but is also sometimes used for punctuation.[521] The same triple *Glossenkeil* apparently also appears in 4.1.4.1 A$_1$ rev. vi 10′, where it might mark an indented line, which is obviously not the case in 8.1.A obv. ii 5′ and 6′. As for the form, the typical *Glossenkeil* is a diagonally oriented triangle (known as a *Winkelhaken* in German) or a wedge. Its Mesopotamian form is normally a single wedge, but there is a Syrian and Hittite regional variant with two wedges.[522] The glyph was perhaps a further, "northern" elaboration of the *Glossenkeil*, but it is just as likely to be a scribal "one off" or idiosyncracy (cf. now also a "quadruple" *Glossenkeil* in 2.2 rev. 12).

4.6 Variations in the KASKAL Main Text: Particular Differences

There are four overlaps among the witnesses of the Main Text allowing for particular differences to be observed. The overlaps have been labeled Nexuses 1–4, and are discussed below.

4.6.1 Nexus 1

Transliteration

8.1.A obv. ii 18′–26′

18′ 1 ^{GIŠ}PISAN SA$_5$ GIŠ$^{HI.A}$ GAM ^{G}[^{IŠ}ESI(?)

19′ ŠÀ-*ŠU* 2 ^{GIŠ}PISAN DUḪ.ŠÚ.A [*ŠA* NUNUZ

20′ 2 ^{GIŠ}PISAN DUḪ.ŠÚ.A *MI-IZ-R*[*I-I*

21′ 2 ^{GIŠ}PISAN ⸢DUḪ⸣.ŠÚ.A KÙ.[SI$_{22}$] 3[8 MA.NA

22′ 4 KI.LÁ NA$_4$ 3 MA.NA 4 [GÍN KÙ.SI$_{22}$

23′ 1 KI.LÁ NA$_4$ [*ŠA* KASKAL

24′ 1 ^{GIŠ}PISAN SA$_5$ TUR UGU *wa-aš-š*[*a-an-za*

520 Note, however, that Siegelová's printing of the glyph is slightly inaccurate: the heads of the three wedges should be aligned in an ascending diagonal line.

521 The recent work of Valerio Pisaniello, "Glossenkeil and Indentation on Hittite Tablets," AoF 47/1 (2020): 125 fn. 15 explicitly excluded the the triple *Glossenkeile* of 8.1.A obv. ii 5′, 6′ from comment.

522 See Pinhas Artzi, "The Glosses in the El Amarna Tablets," *Sefer Bar Ilan* 1 (1963): 33–35. English summary: XIV-XVII.

25′ 4 MA.NA 7 GÍN KÙ.SI$_{22}$ KUR *kar-*[^{D}*du-ni-aš*
26′ 2 MA.NA 2 GÍN KÙ.SI$_{22}$ KUR *lu-uk-k*[*a$_4$-a*
27′ *Š*[*A* KASKAL

8.1.B rev. 1′–10′

1′ [1 ^{GIŠ}PISAN SA$_5$ GIŠ$^{\text{ḪI.A}}$ GAM ^{G}]^{IŠ}E[SI$^{?}$
2′ [ŠÀ-*ŠU* 2 ^{GIŠ}PISAN DUḪ.Š]Ú.A *ŠA* NUN[UZ
3′ [2 ^{GIŠ}PISAN DUḪ.ŠÚ.A KU]R *mi-iz-ri* x[
4′ [2 ^{GIŠ}PISAN DUḪ.ŠÚ.A K]Ù.SI$_{22}$ 38 MA$^{!}$.[NA
5′ [4 KI.LÁ NA$_4$] ⌜3⌝ MA.NA 4 GÍN KÙ.SI$_{22}$ x[
uninscribed
7′ [ ] *Š*[*A* KASKAL
uninscribed

8′ [1 ^{GIŠ}PISAN SA$_5$ TUR U]GU *wa-aš-ša-an-za* [
9′ [4 MA.NA 7 GÍN K]Ù.SI$_{22}$ ^{URU}*kar-*^{D}*du-n*[*i-aš*
10′ [2 MA.NA 2 GÍN KÙ.S]I$_{22}$ KUR *lu-uk-ka$_4$-a* [
uninscribed
[ ] *Š*[*A* KASKAL

8.1.A obv. ii 18′–26′//B rev. 1′–10′
Translation

1* 1 red chest (made of various) woods, below is e[bony(?)
2* inside which 2 yellow chests [of *malachite* (objects)
3* 2 yellow Egypti[an] chests [
4* 2 yellow chests, 3[8 minas of] go[ld
5* 4 stone weights (of) 3 minas, 4 [shekels of gold
6* 1 stone weight. [Of the caravan.

7* 1 small, red chest, upho[lstered] on top [
8* 4 minas, 7 shekels of gold: land of Bab[ylon
9* 2 minas, 2 shekels gold: land of Lukk[a
O[f the caravan.

Discussion

The differences between 8.1.A and 8.1.B are minor. The phrase 1 KI.LÁ NA$_4$ ‘one stone weight’ which appears in A obv. ii 23′ is not found in B. The sign traces at the end of B rev. 5′ do not permit restoring the phrase, and there is no room to do so afterwards. It is not clear if the omission in B is significant.

A second difference is KUR *Karduniaš* in A obv. ii 25′ versus ^{URU}*Karduniaš* in B rev. 9′. The latter geographical description is more correct, since “Karduniaš” was the Kassite name for the city (URU) of Babylon, not the name of the territory controlled by the Babylonians. The final discrepancy of *MI-IZ-R*[*I-I* in A obv. ii 20′ versus ^{KU}]^{R}*Mi-iz-ri* in B rev. 3′ is not a problem, since the form *MIZRĪ* ‘Egyptian’ substitutes freely with KUR

Mizri 'Land of Egypt' in the KASKAL series.[523] The plene *-ī* in *MIZRĪ* is probably an Akkadian *nisbe* formation, indicating appurtenance ("of or belonging to Egypt"), and thus should be properly read as an Akkadogram.

4.6.2 Nexus 2

Transliteration

8.1.A rev. v 4–11

4 ⸢5 EME GÍR.TUR⸣ AN.BAR GE$_6$ 6 GÍR.TUR AN.BAR
5 10 EME GÍR AN.BAR 6 EME GÍR ZABAR
6 18 EME GÍR.GAL ŠÀ.BA 2 TUR
7 7 *pal-za-ḫa-aš* AN.BAR ŠÀ 1 LIBIR
8 81 NÍG.GÍD.DA AN.BAR GE$_6$ 3 *pu-ri-aš* ŠÀ.BA 1 AN.[BAR SIG$_5^{?}$]
9 [n] *pal-za-ḫa-aš* AN.BAR SIG$_5$ erasure[524] *ŠA* KASKAL [

---

10 [1 ^{GI}]^{Š}⸢*tup*⸣*-pa-aš* SA$_5$ 81 GÍ[R] *GÁM-RU* [ŠÀ.BA
11 [...]x GÍR ^{LÚ}[MUḪALDIM
A rev. v 12–13 broken away
14′ [1 ^{GI}]^{Š} *tup-pa-aš* SA$_5$ ⸢TUR AN.BAR GE$_6$⸣ [*ki-i-na-a-an-ta-aš*
15′ 16 NÍG.GÍD.DA AN.BAR GE$_6$ ŠÀ.BA 1 ŠU.U [
16′ *ŠA* KASKAL

8.1.C 1′–5′

1′ [6 GÍR.TUR AN.BAR 10 EME GÍ]R AN.BAR 6 [EME GÍR ZABAR
2′ [18 EME GÍR.GAL ŠÀ.BA 2 TU]R 7 *pal-*⸢*za-ḫa-aš*⸣ [AN.BAR ŠÀ 1 LIBIR
3′ [81 NÍG.GÍD.DA AN.BAR G]E$_6$ 3 *pu-ri-aš* ŠÀ 1 *[A]N.BAR SIG$_5^{?*}$ x[
4′ [n *pal-za-ḫa-aš* AN.BAR] SIG$_5$ *an-*⸢*da*⸣ KASKAL

5′ [1 ^{GIŠ}*ḫu-u-up-pár-al-liš* SA$_5$ 27] ^{KU}[^{Š}*MAR-Š*]*UM* *an-da* [

8.1.D obv. i 1′–12′ (D obv. i 1′ = A rev. v 6′/C 2′)

1′ [ŠÀ.BA 2 *T]UR* 7 *pal-z*[*a-ḫa-aš* AN.BAR ŠÀ 1 LIBIR]
2′ [81 NÍ]G.GÍD.DA AN.B[AR GE$_6$ 3 *pu-ri-aš* ŠÀ.BA 1 AN.BAR SIG$_5^{?}$]
3′ [n *pal*]*-za-ḫa-aš* AN.BAR SIG$_5$ ⸢*an-da*⸣ [KASKAL]

4′ [1 ^{GIŠ}*ḫ*]*u-u-up-pár-al-liš* SA$_5$ 27 ^{KUŠ}*MAR-Š*[*UM an-da*]
5′ [ ] erasure *ŠA* [KASKAL]

6′ [1 ^{GIŠ}*tup*]*-pa-aš* ⟨^{GIŠ}⟩EREN erasure ^{NA_4}KÁ.DINGIR.RA ^{NA_4}T[I]
7′ [^{NA_4}*mu*]*-uš-nu-wa-an-ti-iš* ŠÀ 1 ^{GIŠ}*tup-pa* SIG$_5$ ⸢*ŠA*⸣ [KASKAL]
7a′ [ ] 11

---

523 Only one exception to this pattern occurs, in text D rev. iv$^{?}$ 7′ (and probably the duplicate line in H rev.$^{?}$ r. c. 5′), which has a non-plene *Mizri* without a KUR determinative.

524 The erased sign looks very much like an *a-* or maybe a warped *an-* given the context. See discussion below.

8′ [1 ^{GIŠ}PISAN] SA$_5$ ^{SÍG}*pít-tu-la-aš* ŠU-*aš* *ŠA* KASKAL

9′ [1 ^{GIŠ}*tup-p*]*a-aš* SA$_5$ 81 GÍR *GÁM-RU* ŠÀ.BA 57 GÍR ^{LÚ}MUḪALDIM
10′ [o o 24] GÍR *gi-im-ra-aš* 16 *ŠA* KASKAL

11′ [1 ^{GIŠ}*tup-pa-a*]*š* SA$_5$ TUR AN.BAR GE$_6$ *ki-i-na-a-an-*[*ta-aš*
12′ [16 NÍG.GÍD.DA AN.BAR] G[E$_6$] ŠÀ.B[A 1 ŠU.U

Translation

1* 5 black *iron (ore)* small-knife blades, 6 *iron (ore)* small-knives,
2* 10 *iron (ore)* knife blades, 6 bronze knife blades,
3* 18 sword blades, of which 2 small,
4* 7 *iron (ore)*statue bases, among (which) 1 old,
5* 81 black *iron (ore)* rods, 3 *trays*, among which 1 [good?] *ir*[*on (ore)*
6* [n] good *iron (ore)* statue bases. erasure Of the caravan (A) / In the caravan (C, D).

C and D have an interpolation not found in A

7* [1] red [*ḫ*]*ūpparalli*-container. 27 leather straps (are) inside.
8* [ ] erasure Of [the caravan.]

9* [1] cedar [che]st. erasure Babylon-stone, "li[fe]"-stone,
10* [*m*]*ušnuwanti*-stone, inside 1 good chest. Of [the caravan.]
11* [ ] 11

12* [1] red [chest.] Woolen hand loops. Of the caravan.

end interpolation, D and A resume

13* [1] red chest. 81 complete kniv[es, among which 57 cook's knives,]
14* [24] field knives. 16 Of the caravan.

15* [1] small, red chest. Black *iron (ore)* [assortment.
16* 16 black *iron (ore)* rods, among which 1 (with) basalt [
17* Of the caravan.

Discussion

As discussed under the Systematic Differences, 8.1.D certainly and 8.1.C probably are two-column tablets. 8.1.C is a smaller fragment that does not preserve a column divider or tablet edge, but based on the restorations, it must have either had wide columns characteristic of a two-column tablet, or consistently had extensive overruns at the end of its lines.

In addition to their format, 8.1.C and 8.1.D also share an interpolation of five lines, starting in 8.1.D obv. i 4′–8′ and duplicated in C 5′ that is not found in 8.1.A (if these lines had appeared in A, they would have been inserted between lines A rev. v 9′ and 10′). Interestingly, this interpolation is the only known instance in the KASKAL Main Text. That is to say, while other texts may differ by a word or sign from each other, or (as will be seen in *4.6.3 Nexus 3*) miss a couple lines at the end of a paragraph, no other text overlap has an insertion of this size.

The contents of the interpolation are thematically different from the surrounding metal implements, being leather, precious stones, and wool. The format of the entries is also unusual. Only the first has all the expected features, with both the number and type of contents listed (twenty-seven leather straps). The second entry contains an unspecified quantity of gems. The last entry also has an contents without quantity, containing an unspecified number of woolen carrying straps.

It is clear that 8.1.C and 8.1.D, by their number of columns and inserted text, stand at a different editorial level than A. Is there a way to tell which came first? One possible interpretation comes from the last common line in 8.1.A, C, and D before the interpolation. Text A rev. v 9′ ends with *ŠA* KASKAL and the equivalents lines in C and D end with *anda* KASKAL. As a formula, *anda* KASKAL is doubly unique: it appears only in C and D, and within D it appears only once, compared to six instances of *ŠA* KASKAL. This unusual formula might have caused the scribe some difficulty. Immediately before *ŠA* KASKAL in text A, precisely where the first difference between A and C/D is encountered, there is an erasure. In this erasure, there are traces of a sign that could plausibly read as an *an-* (though given the displacement of clay caused sometimes by erasure, this is by no means certain). It is imaginable that the scribe was copying 8.1.A from 8.1.C or D and, reaching the unusual phrase *anda* KASKAL, wrote the first sign without thinking, erased it and then corrected it to *ŠA* KASKAL in line with the rest of text A. He then also removed the five interpolated lines, which were thematically out of place (perhaps these entries were moved to another tablet, since text 8.1.A is concerned exclusively with durable goods). The direction of copying should thus be reconstructed as going in the expected direction from two-column tablets to three-column tablet. This fits well with Siegelová's observation that the three-column tablets tend to be retrospective and summarizing, qualities one might expect in the "final" products in the administrative chain.

4.6.3 Nexus 3

Transliteration

8.1.D rev. iv 1′–13′

1′ [n GADA(?) *ŠU*]-⸢*U*⸣-*RU* 2 ⸢^{TÚG}*ku-ši-ši*⸣ [n ^{TÚG}*ku-uš-ša-di* 1 ^{TÚG}GÚ *ḪA-ŠÁR-DI*(?)]
2′ [n ^{TÚG}ḪI.Ḫ]I-*na-tar* *ḪAŠ-MAN-NI* 1 ^{TÚG}⸢ḪI.ḪI⸣-*na-tar* x[
3′ [n TÚG *ta*]-*piš-pa* 1 GADA *ŠU-U-RU* 1 TÚG *ka-pí-t*[*a-šàm-na*]
4′ [1 BAR].SI 1 ^{TÚG}*ma-za-ga-an-ni-iš* TUR SA$_5$ [uninscribed]
5′ [5 ^{TÚG}*i*]*r-ḫi-iš* 14 GAD.DAM ŠÀ 4 ⸢*ḪAŠ*⸣-*MA*[*N-NI*
6′ [6 Z]A.GÌN 4 SA$_5$ *ŠA* KASKAL [

7′ [1] ^{GIŠ}PISAN SA$_5$ *MI-IZ-RI* UGU *wa-aš-*⸢*ša-an*⸣-[*za*
8′ [TÚG^{M}]^{EŠ} ^{D}*ḫé-pát* *Ù* ^{D}LUGAL-*ma an-d*[*a*
9′ [1 TÚG] ⸢SIG⸣ *HAŠ-MAN-NI* *ka-pí-it-ta-šàm-*[*na*
10′ [1 TÚG Z]A.GÌN *ka-pí-it-ta-šàm-na* [
11′ [1 ^{TÚG}GÚ] ⸢*ḪUR.*⸣ BABBAR 1 TÚG *ta-piš-pa* BABBAR 1 x[
12′ [... 1] ^{TÚG}GÚ *ḪUR-RI* *ḪA-ŠÁR-DI* x[
13′ [...]x *ŠA* KAS[KAL

8.1.E(A$_1$) rev. v 6′–12′

6′ [...]x GIBIL ^{TÚG}NÍG.LÁM^{MEŠ} MUNUS.LUGAL *an-da*
7′ [n GADA(?) *ŠU-U-RU* 2 ^{TÚG}*ku-ši-ši* n ^{TÚ}]^{G}*ku-uš-ša-di*
8′ [1 ^{TÚG}GÚ *ḪA-ŠÁR-DI*(?) n+]1 ^{TÚG}ḪI.ḪI-*na-tar* *ḪAŠ-MAN-NI*
9′ [1 ^{TÚG}ḪI.ḪI-*na-tar* ... n TÚG *ta-piš-p*]*a* 1 GADA *ŠU-U-RU* 1 ^{TÚG}*ga-pí-ta-šàm-na*
10′ [1 BAR.SI GADA 1 ^{TÚG}*ma-za-ga-an-ni-iš* TUR] SA$_5$ 5 ^{TÚG}*ir-ḫi-iš*
11′ [14 GAD.DAM ŠÀ 4 *ḪAŠ-MAN-NI* 6 ZA.G]ÌN 4 SA$_5$
12′ [*I-NA* KASKAL] *NA-ŠU-Ú*

E(A$_1$) rev. v ends. Text continues in E(A$_3$) rev. vi with contents unrelated to D, H, I

8.1.H rev. r. c. 1′–10′

1′ ⸢2⸣ ^{TÚG}*k*[*u-ši-ši* n ^{TÚG}*ku-uš-ša-di*
2′ 1 ^{TÚG}GÚ ⸢*ḪA-ŠAR*⸣-[*TI* 1 ^{TÚG}ḪI.ḪI-*na-tar* ... (?) 1 ^{TÚG}ḪI.ḪI-*na-tar* *ḪAŠ-MAN-NI*(?)]
3′ 1 ^{TÚG}*ka-pár-ta-šà*[*m-na* n TÚG *ta-piš-pa*(?) 1 GADA *ŠU-U-RU*(?)]
4′ 1 BAR.SI GADA [*ŠA* KASKAL(?)

two lines uninscribed

5′ 1 ^{GIŠ}PISAN SA$_5$ *MI-IZ-RI* [UGU *wa-aš-ša-an-za*
6′ TÚG$^{\text{MEŠ D}}$*ḫé-pát* *Ù* ⸢^{D}⸣[LUGAL-*ma an-da*
7′ 1 TÚG SIG *ḪAŠ-MAN-NI* *k*[*a-pí-it-ta-šàm-na*
8′ 1 TÚG ZA.GÌN *ka-pí-ta-*[*šàm-na* 1 ^{TÚG}GÚ *ḪUR-RI* BABBAR
9′ 1 TÚG *tap-pa-aš-pa* BABBAR 1 [
10′ 1 ^{TÚG}GÚ *ḪUR-RI* *ḪA-*[*ŠÁR-DI*

two lines uninscribed before H rev r. c. breaks off

8.1.I rev. r. c. 1′–7′

1′ [1 ^{TÚG}G]Ú ⸢*ḪA-ŠÁR*⸣-*D*[*I*? 1 ^{TÚG}ḪI.ḪI-*na-tar* ... (?) 1 ^{TÚG}ḪI.ḪI-*na-tar* *ḪAŠ-MAN-NI*(?)]
2′ 1 *ka*⸣-*pár-ta-aš-š*[*àm-na* n ^{TÚG}*ta-piš-pa*(?) 1 GADA *ŠU-U-RU*(?)]
3′ 1 BAR.SI GADA *Š*[*A*[525] KASKAL(?)

two lines uninscribed

4′ 1 ^{GIŠ}PISAN SA$_5$ *MI-IZ-R*[*I* UGU *wa-aš-ša-an-za*
5′ [T]ÚG$^{\text{MEŠ D}}$*ḫé-pát* *Ù* [^{D}LUGAL-*ma an-da*
6′ [1 T]ÚG SIG *ḪAŠ-MAN-NI* [*ka-pí-it-ta-šàm-na*
7′ [1 TÚG] ZA.GÌN *ka-*[*pí-it-ta-šàm-na*

I rev. r. c. breaks off

Translation

translation after text E

1* [ ]... new. Splendid garments of the queen inside.
2* [n *dark-brown* linens(?), 2 *kušiši*-garments, n] *kuššati*-[garm]ents,

---

525 The sign traces show the clear beginnings of two horizontal wedges, which exclude a restoration "1 ^{TÚG}*mazaganniš*" from texts D and E. The traces should probably be interpreted as the start of a *ŠA* sign based on the expectation of a KASKAL formula at the end of the paragraph.

3* [1... blended(-wool) garment, n Tapašp]an garments, 1 *dark-brown* linen, 1 Kapitašamnan garment
4* [1 linen head band, 1 small,] red [*mazakanni*-garment], 5 *belts*,
5* [1 linen head band,
the following items only appear in D and E
1 small,] red [*mazakanni*-garment], 5 *belts*,
6* [14 *leggings*, among (which) 4 (red-)purple, 6 bl]ue, 4 red.
7* [ ] Transported [in the caravan.
$E(A_1)$ rev. v ends

---

translation after D
8* [1] red, Egyptian chest. Upholstere[d] on top. [
9* [Garment]s of Ḫepat and Šarruma (are) insid[e.
10* [1] thin, (red-)purple, Kapitašam[nan garment
11* [1 b]lue Kapitašamnan [garment
12* [1] white Hurrian tunic, 1 white Tapašpan garment, 1 ... [
13* [... 1] green, Hurrian tunic ...[
14* [...] ... Of the cara[van.

Discussion
In addition to what must have been a different order of contents between the manuscripts (the restorations in H rev. r. c. 2′–3′//I rev. r. c. 1′–2′ presented here are uncertain), D rev. iv 4′–6′//$E(A_1)$ rev. 10′–12′ contain an interpolation of items which are absent in H and I. Thus, a decision must be made between D/E and F(+)G(+)H/I as to which version came first. In the previous interpolation, it was decided that the extra lines in D and C belonged to an earlier editorial level than A, with the fact that D and C were both two-column tablets, as well as the fact that the interpolation was thematically out of place, adduced as evidence. This time 8.1.D is backed by the three-column 8.1.E. But despite E's three-column format, the text contains a number of problematic features that argue against it being any kind of finished draft. As noted in *4.5 Variation in the Main Text: Systematic Differences*, 8.1.E is a consistent outlier in every category. It contains many erasures (see further *4.6.4 Nexus 4*), uses an unparalleled variety of KASKAL formulas, and has a unique type of column divider. Compared to the consistency of the three-column 8.1.F(+)G(+)H, it is 8.1.E and again 8.1.D which must be considered the earlier drafts.

The anteriority of 8.1.D and 8.1.E can mean two things for the extra contents. On the one hand, it is always possible the items were listed by mistake, and were never in fact in the chest at all (perhaps the scribe's eyes strayed to the wrong column of the tablet he was copying, and the mistake was not immediately discovered until the next draft). On the other hand, since cataloging of the chests must have involved a physical element, it is possible that the extra contents were physically removed from the chest before H and I were written, either removed completely or perhaps placed in a different chest.[526] If this is so, then an important inference can be made about the organization of the contents within the chests. In unpacking a chest, the first items to be removed are the ones in the topmost layer. In every case that items are present in one draft and absent in another (observed in Nexuses 1, 3, and 4), the removed items come from the final line, and not the beginning or middle, of the entry. If one assumes that the order of the text roughly matches the physical order in the chest, this means the last entries in a paragraph represent the topmost layers of the chest. Such a paragraph orientation gives a clue as to the direction of movement of the chests in the KASKAL series. The order of the entries, recording the bottom layers first and finishing with the top, is the order that a scribe would record while *packing* the chests, not unpacking, where the top layers would be written first. This can be taken as evidence that the chests originated in Ḫattuša, where they are being prepared to be shipped out of the capital, and not being received from elsewhere to be unpacked and processed.

4.6.4 Nexus 4

Transliteration

8.1.E(A$_1$) obv. iii 1′–10′

0′ [1 ^{GIŠ}PISAN SA$_5$ LÚGUD.DA 40 ^{TÚG}GÚ *ḪUR-RI* GADA][527]

1′ ⸢39⸣ [^{TÚG}GÚ GADA 2 GADA SA$_5$ 1 GADA *ŠU-UḪ-U-RU*]

2′ 8 GADA ⸢SIG⸣ ⸢5⸣ [GÚ GADA ^{URU}*a-la-ši-ia*]

3′ 5 GADA LÚGUD.DA [*ka-a-aš* ^{GIŠ}PISAN]

three lines erased and left uninscribed

4′ *ŠA* KASKAL *I+NA* É.GAL-*LIM* [*ŠA* KASKAL-*NI*

uninscribed

5′ 1 ^{GI}PISAN SA$_5$ LIBIR.RA [uninscribed?][528]

6′ 5 TÚG GAL BABBAR 7 ^{TÚG}*maš-ši-aš* BABB[AR]

7′ 4 TÚG *ŠU-U-RU* 17 TÚG SIG BABBAR x[

8′ 2 TÚG SIG ZA.GÌN 5 ^{TÚG}*ku-uš-š*[*a-di*]

9′ 2 ^{TÚG} SAG.DUL 1 TÚG ⸢*ḫur-li*⸣-[*ša* SA$_5$]

10′ ⸢2 ^{TÚG}GÚ *ḪUR*⸣-*RI* BABBAR 1 ^{TÚG}G[Ú

E(A$_1$) obv. iii breaks off

8.1.F obv. i 3′–11′

3′ [1 ^{GIŠ}PI]SAN SA$_5$ LÚGUD.DA 40 ^{TÚ}[^{G}G]Ú *ḪUR-RI* GADA [

4′ 39 ^{TÚG}GÚ GADA 2 GADA SA$_5$ 1 GADA *ŠU-UH-U-RU*

5′ 8 GADA SIG 5 GÚ GADA ^{URU}*a-la-ši-ia*

6′ 5 GADA LÚGU[D.D]A *ka-*[*a-aš*] ^{GIŠ}PISAN *ŠA* É.GAL-*LIM*

---

526 If the deletion of items from the tablets indeed indicates their removal from chests, my guess is that what is being observed is a normal repacking and rebalancing process, where a few items are removed from the top layers of overloaded chests and transferred to lighter chests. This would make sense for chests that are being prepared for transportation.

527 This line is lost in break before start of 8.1.E, and is restored here based on 8.1.F.

528 Following the contents of 8.1.F, the remainder of 8.1.E(A$_1$) obv. iii 5′ must be uninscribed. Perhaps the line was erased in E?

7′ ˹*ŠA*˺ KASKAL-*NI*

two lines uninscribed

8′ [1 ^{GI}PISAN SA$_5$ LIBIR.RA 5 TÚG GAL BABB]AR 7 ^{TÚG}*maš-ši-aš* BABBAR
9′ [4 TÚG *ŠU-U-RU* 17 SIG BABBAR ...]x 2 TÚG SIG ZA.GÌN
10′ [5 ^{TÚG}*ku-uš-ša-di* 2 ^{TÚG}SAG.DU]L 1 TÚG ˹*ḫur-li-*˺*š*[*a* S]A$_5$
11′ [2 ^{TÚG}GÚ *Ḫ*]*UR-R*[*I* BABBAR 1 ^{TÚG}GÚ

Translation

1* [1] short, red [ch]est. 40 linen Hurrian [tu]nics [
2* 39 [linen tunics, 2 red linen, 1 *dark-brown* linen,]
3* 8 thin linen, 5 [tunics of Cypriot linen,]

E {4* 5 short linens. [This chest]
{5* of the caravan (is) in the palace [

F {4* 5 sho[r]t linens. Th[is] chest (is) of the palace.
{5* Of the caravan.

6* 1 old, red chest.
7* 5 large, white cloths, 7 whi[te] *shawls*,
8* 4 *dark-brown* cloths, 17 thin, white cloths ...[
9* 2 thin, blue cloths, 5 *kušš*[*ati*-garments]
10* 2 head coverings, 1 [red] *Ḫurli*[*š(š)an*]-garment,
11* 2 white Hurrian tunics, 1 tu[nic

Discussion

In the above transliteration, the entry in 8.1.E displays three unparalleled oddities. First, in no other text in the PTAC are so many lines of erasure left in the middle of a paragraph, and second, in no other text of the KASKAL series does information stand after the KASKAL formula. Third, and perhaps because of the erasure, the uninscribed line after the KASKAL formula in 8.1.E(A$_1$) obv. iii 4′ is the only example of a space before the paragraph line in a text that normally lacks them. All this confirms the impression gained from *4.5 Variation in the KASKAL Main Text: Systematic Differences* that 8.1.E is an unusual tablet.

In constrast, the same entry in 8.1.F takes a very different appearance. Gone are the erased lines and the atypical single uninscribed space, and the KASKAL formula becomes the *ŠA* KASKAL-*NI* typical of 8.1.F(+)G(+)H. The phrase *I+NA* É.GAL-*LIM* appended to the end of the entry in E in now replaced by *k*[*āš*] ^{GIŠ}PISAN *ŠA* É.GAL-*LIM* 'Th[is] chest (is) of the palace' in the body of the entry in F. The meaning is now slightly revised: the chest being prepared for transportation is no longer in the palace, but is now (only) of the palace. What exactly this means is not clear. Describing a container as being "of" an institution is itself unparalleled in the KASKAL series. It seems that whatever situation led to the erasures and abnormalities in E required the use of unprecedented phrasing in F. In any event, the standardized, erasure-free composition of F makes it clear that it is a more finished draft than E.

4.7 Editorial Layers in the KASKAL Main Text

With the preceding analysis in mind, a new overview of the tablets of the KASKAL Main Text is now possible. One of the first conclusions is that the continuity of the text across drafts needs to be reevaluated. The graphical depiction of the relationship between the texts given by Siegelová (*Hethitische Verwaltungspraxis*, 394) assumes that the textual archetype, the ideal document behind all of the textual witnesses, was transcribed continuously without break or rearrangement within the tablets. But the interpolations, additions, and erasures found in the overlaps analyzed in the preceding section cast doubt on this assumption. Instead, it appears that tablets of the KASKAL Main Text drew on an evolving source. As a consequence, the length of the Main Text can no longer be confidently fixed. At a minimum, the text filled two three-column tablets, with texts 8.1.A and 8.1.F(+)G(+)H probably representing the first and last. But there is no way to tell how many tablets lay between these endpoints. At the very least, it can be observed that 8.1.E begins approximately one and two-thirds of a column before 8.1.F(+)G(+)H.[529] Was the extra material at the beginning of 8.1.E removed to the end of F(+)G(+)H, or was there another tablet of textiles before 8.1.F(+)G(+)H, the only evidence of which has been preserved in 8.1.E? It will be assumed for the sake argument that tablets 8.1.A and 8.1.F(+)G(+)H contained the entirety of the KASKAL Main Text (there is a pleasant symmetry to having one tablet devoted to durable goods and one to textiles), while conceding that a third tablet could be discovered to fit in between.

The evolving nature of the source text for the various witnesses can be explained in two ways: either the differences are scribal errors or they are conscious revisions. The former would be explained by human error, the usual culprit in textual criticism. The more times a manuscript is copied, the more chances there are for mistakes to be introduced, especially when the instances of copying are separated by time or done by different hands. But this explanation fits better with "texts of tradition," like political or literary documents which are disseminated widely or retained across generations. The KASKAL Main Text is not this. It has an administrative nature, and as such is constrained by a need to function within an administrative reality. Discrepancies between tablets in the KASKAL series would have more consequence than just a mistransmission of esoteric knowledge. They would mean that certain valuable goods might disappear or be left behind, and that is not something a scribe would want to confess to the palace.

If instead the differences among the tablets are conscious revisions reflecting a changing administrative reality (i.e., goods being assembled, packed, moved), this means that the texts have a chronological and editorial relationship to each other. Some drafts must be earlier and less correct drafts and others later and more definitive drafts. By making use of the particular differences at the overlaps in the text, some tablets can be established as coming earlier in this editorial process than others. Then comparing the systematic differences of the earlier tablets with those of the later tablets demonstrates that editorial levels exhibited certain features, presented below.

529 For points of overlap between 8.1.E and 8.1.F(+)G(+)H, see discussion of 8.1.E in Section 5.3.1 below.

4.7.1 Single-column tablet

Exemplars: None (but compare 8.4)

Features: (Using 8.4 as model:) single-column tablet, messy writing and sloppy formatting, no space before paragraph lines, no mention of chests, no mention of KASKAL until colophon.

Comments: As discussed in *4.2 Structure of the* KASKAL *Main Text*, 8.4 represents a probable KASKAL precursor text, albeit one which cannot be conclusively connected to the Main Text.

4.7.2 Two-column tablet

Exemplars: 8.1.C, D, (K?)

Features: Two-column tablet, heterogeneous contents, interpolations, erasures, no space before paragraph lines, some variation in KASKAL formulas.

Comments: This level represents what was probably the first gathering together of the single-column drafts and attempt to segregate the chests by contents, though this process is incomplete. It is interesting that 8.1.D contains the second half of 8.1.A and the first half of 8.1.F(+)G(+)H. Does this mean that 8.1.D was the middle of a three-part series of two-column tablets? Alternatively, 8.1.D could have been the unitary core from which the later KASKAL revisions grew and diversified.

4.7.3 Three-column tablet: first draft

Exemplar: 8.1.E

Features: Three-column tablet, thematic division of contents, space before most paragraph lines, erasures, experimental KASKAL formulas, odd column divider, note at end.

Comments: 8.1.E is included in the three-column "first draft" category because while it displays the formatting qualities of final drafts, it has too many idiosyncrasies to be considered anywhere near complete. It can be hypothesized that this draft was used by the scribe to resolve the outstanding questions about the contents and dispositions of the chests, which would explain the erasures, the verbosity of the KASKAL formulas (see the discussion of the phrase *ŠA* KASKAL *I+NA* É.GAL-*LIM* in *4.6.4 Nexus 4*), and the unusual note after the final entries at the end of E(A_3) rev. vi.

4.7.4 Three-column tablet: intermediate draft?

Exemplars: 8.1.A, J

Features: Three-column tablet, thematic division of contents, no space before paragraph line, consistent KASKAL formulas (*ŠA* KASKAL). 8.1.A attests a colophon.

Comments: At this level the Main Text has assumed its final shape, with a thematic division of contents into durable goods and textiles. Extraneous items have been removed (see *4.6.2 Nexus 2*). 8.1.A would for all intents and purposes function as a final draft. The only major difference between

8.1.A and what are considered here to be the actual final drafts (8.1.B, which overlaps 8.1.A, 8.1.F(+)G(+)H, and 8.1.I) is the lack of space before paragraph lines in 8.1.A. Since this feature is also not present in the earlier two-column drafts, it is tentatively assumed that space before paragraph lines was characteristic of later drafts. The alternative is to assume that space was added during the first assembly of the three-column tablets and then removed again in the finalized versions, in which case, the "three-column tablet: intermediate draft?" and "three-column tablet: final draft?" categories should be reversed. The fact that the unusual 8.1.E also space before paragraph lines could be taken as evidence for this second scenario.

4.7.5 Three-column tablet: final draft?

Exemplars: 8.1.B, F(+)G(+)H, I

Features: Three-column tablets, thematic division of contents, space before every paragraph line, consistent KASKAL formulas (*ŠA* KASKAL-*NI*), final trimming of contents.

Comments: The final drafts of KASKAL series are very consistently formatted and with perfect thematic division of contents. A final inventory of the chests might have been performed, and the items which had been erroneously included in the earlier drafts, or since removed (see *4.6.3 Nexus 3*), are now pared from the tablets. It is probably just an accident of preservation that tablet B is the only representative from the durable goods half of the series to be found at this final editorial level.

4.8 Conclusions on the Structure of the KASKAL Main Text

Two trends can be observed in the editorial history reconstructed above. First, there is a growth from single to triple columns, which matches Siegelová's proposal for the editorial flow of the rest of the palace administrative corpus. Second, there is a consistent winnowing of complexity: from heterogeneous to homogeneous contents and from a variety of KASKAL formulas to a single type. The final product is a standardized, three-column tablet with generous spaces between paragraphs that allow for distinguishing entries at a glance. Such spacing and three-column format with simple dividers is rarely found elsewhere, and so it is a convincing result that the most finished tablets exhibit the features most unique to the administrative genre.

The implications of such an editorial history are subtle but important. A flat editorial hierarchy, where every copy was a "final" copy, would have demanded multiple end users of the documents. This would in turn imply the involvement of several cuneiform-literate professionals. And if the texts were not revisions of each other, the radically different styles would suggest several different authors. The end result would match a "classical" view of Bronze Age territorial states: big projects carried out by big bureaucracies.[530] But the deep editorial hierarchy recovered alleviates the need for such a reconstruction. The multiple revisions show a development and pruning that suggest the craft of a small group of scribes, perhaps only two individuals.

The structure of the text also constrains its possible uses. The KASKAL Main Text is insufficiently abstract to be an account or ledger, where one would expect to find sums and totals. Instead it is resolutely particular throughout its multiple revisions.[531] The chests and contents are recorded in concrete detail, and never combined or quantified. This makes sense if the document was an index, a tool to help the user find a real object in a real place. Most probably the KASKAL series was created to keep the objects, many of which were both small and expensive, under administrative control while they were being prepared for transport. Thus, an inference can also be made about the physical disposition of the chests and contents of the KASKAL Main Text. If the scribe used no explicit organizational scheme (and even if their meaning could be deciphered, the "postparagraph numbers" in texts D and F(+)G(+)H are too infrequent to form a useful filing system), it means an implicit one was already available. The only solution is to assume the order of the chests on the tablet must have reflected the order of the chests in the storeroom; otherwise the scribe would have to keep a mental concordance between the dozens of chests on the tablets and their location the real world. As a consequence, any revisions must have been matched by or followed a physical reorganization of the chests. The editorial process, with its layers of drafts, was therefore a physical as well as a textual process. This means that the production of the KASKAL Main Text must have been an event that took weeks, maybe months, with goods packed into chests and gathered into one place where they were recorded in an evolving inventory. The scribe, no doubt assisted by laborers, would organize and reorganize these chests

530 This view finds its home especially in the (truly) massive administrations of Egypt and Mesopotamia. For an introduction to administration in contemporary Egypt, see Chapter 4 "The Bureaucratic Mind" and Chapter 6 "New Kingdom Egypt: the mature state" in Barry J. Kemp, *Ancient Egypt: Anatomy of a Civilization (2nd ed.)* (New York: Routledge, 2006). In Pierre Grandet, "The Ramesside State," in *Ancient Egyptian Administration*, ed. Juan Carlos Moreno García (Leiden: Brill, 2013), 863, to the Egyptian state is ascribed an " ... ambition to monitor all human activities, and the concomitant need to record all acts for purposes of periodical verification by a higher authority." This included the requirement that each administrative agency keep a daily log, a journal, of its activities (*ibid.*, 864). For the impressively literate bureaucracies of contemporary Assyria and the Syrian city-states of Nuzi, Alalaḫ, and Ugarit (as well as comparative view of Mycene), see J. Nicholas Postgate, *Bronze Age Bureaucracy. Writing and the Practice of Government in Assyria* (Cambridge: Cambridge University Press, 2014); further Stefan Jakob, *Mittelassyrische Verwaltung und Sozialstruktur: Untersuchungen*. CM 29 (Leiden: Brill, 2003). Contemporary Babylon has yet to receive such attention, though some 12,000 administrative tablets from Nippur (of which 15% have been published) and a few hundred from Babylon, Dur-Kurigalzu, and Ur are known to exist (Jonathan S. Tenney, *Life at the Bottom of Babylonian Society* (Leiden: Brill, 2011), 139). A comprehensive comparison of Late Bronze Age bureaucracies in the Ancient Near East has yet to emerge, primarily due to the enormity of the task but also the need for more primary research for many of the states.

531 Siegelová, *Hethitische Verwaltungspraxis*, 397 already noted, in the context of arguing against reading the KASKAL texts as a ledger of tax incomes, that "Die Urkunde behandelt ihren Stoff auf eine systematische und gründliche Weise, als ob sie auf ein einmaliges, bedeutsames Geschehen zurückginge." She does not go so far as to speculate what these meaningful events might be.

by contents, and remove (or note the removal of) articles of goods and metal as needed. The standardization of form in the tablets thus reflects a similar growing tidiness in the real world.

Yet even as an index corresponding roughly to a real-world arrangement of chests, the KASKAL Main Text is not self-sufficient. There is no perceptible system of numbering or location, and the descriptions of the containers are generic enough that even if a person – say, the modern scholar – could read the cuneiform, he or she would still be unable to recover the original organization of the chests. The arguments for a personal, deictic system of record-keeping in the larger PTAC apply especially so to the KASKAL Main Text: for the text to fulfill its administrative function, the author's presence was required. The importance of the scribe to the undertaking of the the text elevates him to something more than just an observer/recorder. Instead, he was an indispensable interpreter and maybe even the chief administrator of the chests in the KASKAL series. Even if the scribe was not in charge of the chests, and instead only assisting the actual administrator, he would still need to be present anytime the KASKAL Main Text needed to be consulted. Deciding between the titles "administrator" and "assistant" depends on how one wishes to view the social importance of the scribe.

5. QUANTIFYING THE CONTENTS OF THE KASKAL MAIN TEXT

5.1 Introduction

The first step towards establishing the value of the contents of the KASKAL Main Text is to quantify the contents by number, material, and weight. Herein lies a methodological difficulty. As argued in the *4.8 Conclusions on the Structure of the* KASKAL *Main Text*, the KASKAL texts are primarily concerned with *indexing*: the purpose of the tablets was to recover real objects from real chests and to keep them under administrative control. The written structure reflected this being more concerned with recording the visually identifying features of the objects rather than their weights or values. Many other contemporary documents, such as other inventories in the Palace-Temple Administrative Corpus and the lists in the Egyptian-Hittite marriage correspondences, differ from the KASKAL series in that their purpose is *evaluation* – that is, to provide a value for the recorded objects for accounting (internal administration) or politics (foreign gift-exchange). The evaluative documents give information like amounts of gold or silver weighed out in shekels, or a final total number of textiles. Because of the differences in purpose and structure, the indexical KASKAL series is not directly commensurable with the evaluative inventories. The task of this chapter is to try to make the KASKAL comparable to the other inventories by grouping the items of the former into intelligible categories and quantifying them, in essence converting the indexical text into an evaluative one, and doing so without the categories to become projections onto, and not reflections of, the data at hand.

Despite the cross-purposes of the original scribe and the modern scholar, the text fortunately offers some help. A basic categorization by material is available in the text itself: in addition to the major division between textiles and durable goods, the durable goods tend to cluster into groups of gold, iron, silver, etc., revealing that the scribe, even as he was concerned with indexing, applied an organizational structure to the chests around him. While the scholar might wish for more weights and measures, adopting the material categories at least has the advantage that the objects are easy to count. In many cases, even when the meaning of the Hittite word for an object is imprecisely known, the material of the objects is quite clear due to the use of a Sumerographic determinative.

Even without precise measurements, the materials are decent proxies for determining the value of the entries because the size of the objects is fairly constant. From the preserved text it can be seen that most objects are "people-sized": they are personal objects like knives, jewelry, cups, and shirts, and thus constrained in size by human needs. Though their exact dimensions are rarely given, the goods will all be roughly "hand-held" for durable goods and "body-covering" for cloths. And because the objects are all of a similar size, the material will determine most of the difference in value. To put it another way, when comparing one-hundred copper knives of varying size with one-hundred pieces of assorted silver jewelry, the length and weight of the knives will matter far less than the fact they are made of base metal. The outsized objects in the KASKAL series, which do have their dimensions preserved, such as the forty-seven minas of gold ingots and 125 cubits of *parna*-cloth, are few enough to be considered separately. Thus, while the reconstruction of the wealth documented in the KASKAL series makes use of broad categories, the large quantities and personal-sized nature of the objects allow these categories to be sufficient for a basic comparison with the evaluative inventories.

Beyond the lack of precise measurements, the major challenge in evaluating the contents of the KASKAL series is the incomplete preservation of the tablets. It is not just that columns are broken and lines are missing, but sometimes individual entries are broken away just where a vital number or item would be. Thus the information preserved in the tablets is only a fraction of what was originally there. Determining the size of this fraction, and presenting a coherent estimation, is the first step towards evaluation of the tablet contents.

It will assumed that the original text was two tablets long in its final form, with no "hidden" tablets in between.[532] Every durable good had its home in the first tablet, and every textile in the second. The best representatives of the tablet archetype are text 8.1.A for durable goods and 8.1.F(+)G(+)H for textiles. When an entry is attested in another text and does not also appear in these two tablets, it must be assumed that the entry was located in a portion of 8.1.A and 8.1.F(+)G(+)H now broken away. In principle, this means that the number of missing lines can be estimated by reconstructing the total number of lines on the original undamaged tablets 8.1.A and 8.1.F(+)G(+)H, subtracting the preserved lines on these tablets, then subtracting the unduplicated lines from the rest of the tablets of the main text.[533]

In this chapter, the preserved contents will be presented in tables divided into categories by material. An estimate of the completeness for each tablet will be made based on the number of preserved lines of text. The estimate will then be combined with the tabulated data to offer a calculation of the amount of objects originally contained in the KASKAL Main Text. The final result will be a reconstructed quantity of objects which will form the basis for comparison with other collections of wealth mentioned in texts of the ancient Near East.

532 See discussion of a potential third tablet in Section *4.7 Editorial Layers in the KASKAL Main Text*.

533 The texts 8.1.J and 8.1.K, two small fragments that due to their brevity and poor state of preservations cannot be securely located within the two original tablets, are not included in the reconstruction. The details they provide, even if included, would not much affect the reconstructed total number of objects provided at the end of this chapter.

5.2 Durable Goods in the KASKAL Main Text

The durable goods in the KASKAL Main Text include items made of gold, silver, *iron (ore)*, precious stones, copper, and bronze. The only raw material preserved is gold, with silver, bronze, and copper present only as finished objects. The finished objects cover the breadth of objects known from the PTAC: jewelry, statues, drinking vessels, decorations, offering equipment, and knives. The only category missing compared to the rest of the PTAC is military equipment such as bows and arrows and chariots and horse tack. Quantities range from items in the single digits to the low hundreds in the case of rings, drinking straws/tubes, and rods/wires.

5.2.1 Items in the Preserved Portions of the Durable Goods Tablet

Notes on format: a pair of brackets [] indicates the information is broken away on the tablet. For calculating quantities, an empty bracket [1] is given a value of 1 to represent the minimal restoration possible. When subtotals are added, the value of the empty brackets is given after the total (e.g., 5 *iron (ore)* knives + [1] bronze knife + [1] copper knife = 5 + [1] + [1] = 5+[2]). An uninscribed space means it was not included in the original text. Because many of the items have no translation, they are presented in transcription with translations added in parentheses where possible. The materials and colors, the meanings of which are better known, are presented in translation.

8.1.A is the largest and most well-preserved exemplar of the Durable Goods tablet and therefore comprises the lion's share of the total attested durable goods in the KASKAL Main Text.

Table 1: Durable Goods in Preserved Portions of 8.1.A

Gold			
Item	Description	Quantity	Citation
[]	NUNUZ KÙ.SI$_{22}$ *ipulliyaš* "*malachite* (and) gold *on the wraps/covers*"	[1]	A obv. i 5′
p]*enki* 'knob'	KÙ.SI$_{22}$ *ištarna* ZA.GÌN "gold, blue in the middle"	[1]	A obv. i 6′
BURU$_5$ 'locust'	KÙ.SI$_{22}$ 'gold'	1	A obv. i 10′
[]	K]Ù.SI$_{22}$ GAR.RA 'gold-inlaid'	[1]	A obv. i 15′
-*t*]*aš*	KÙ.SI$_{22}$ GAR.RA 'gold-inlaid'	[1]	A obv. i 16′
AL]AM 'statue'	KÙ.SI$_{22}$ 'gold'	[1]	A obv. i 18′
^{M}]^{EŠ}	KÙ.SI$_{22}$ 'gold'	[2]	A obv. i 19′
tiyawa[*ra*(?)	ŠÀ.BA 5 KÙ.S[I$_{22}$ "of which 5 gold"	5	A obv. ii 4′–5′

(ingots)	KÙ.[SI$_{22}$] 'gold'	3[8 MA.NA]	A obv. ii 21′
(ingots)	[KÙ.SI$_{22}$] 'gold'	3 MA.NA, 4 [GÍN]	A obv. ii 22′
(ingots)	KÙ.SI$_{22}$ 'gold'	4 MA.NA, 7 GÍN	A obv. ii 25′
(ingots)	KÙ.SI$_{22}$ 'gold'	2 MA.NA, 2 GÍN	A obv. ii 26′
[NÍG.GÍD.DA] 'wire/rod'	[KÙ.SI$_{22}$] 'gold'	(182(?) - 2) = 180(?)[534]	A obv. ii 29′
	Subtotal	186+[6] pieces; 47 minas, 13 shekels ingots	
Silver			
Item	Description	Quantity	Citation
^{TÚG}BAR.DUL$_8$ 'robe'	KÙ.BABBAR G[AR.RA 'silver-inlaid'	1	A obv. ii 7′
GÚ GU$_4$ 'ox protome'	KÙ.BABBAR 'silver'	13	A rev. v 24′
GÚ UR.[MAḪ] 'lion protome'	[KÙ.BABBAR][535] 'silver'	3	A rev. v 24′
GÚ TI$_8^{\text{MUŠEN}}$ 'eagle protome'	KÙ.BABBAR 'silver'	5	A rev. v 25′
ŠU.[SI] 'finger'	[KÙ.BABBAR][536] 'silver'	2	A rev. v 25′
GAL 'cup'	KÙ.BABBAR 'silver'	14	A rev. v 26′
ŠU[L.PÁT] '(drinking) straw/tube'	[KÙ.BABBAR][537] 'silver'	200	A rev. v 27′

534 A obv. ii 28′–29′: 1 *ME* ⌜82⌝(?) [NÍG.GÍD.DA KÙ.SI$_{22}$(?) ŠÀ.BA(?)] $^{29'}$ NÍG.GÍD.DA KÙ.SI$_{22}$ *wa-ak-š*[*i?-at*(?) "182(?) [gold wires/rods(?), of which(?)] $^{29'}$ 2 gold wires/rods [are] abs[ent(?)." As discussed in the *Commentary* to the text edition of these lines, the 100(+) objects in 28′ are probably NÍG.GÍD.DA 'wires/rods'. Although it cannot be determined with certainty that all of the wires/rods in the chests were gold, spacing considerations (there is not much room to expect a full breakdown by material type, e.g., *1 *ME* ⌜82⌝(?) [NÍG.GÍD.DA ŠÀ.BA n KÙ.SI$_{22}$ n KÙ.BABBAR ... etc., at the end of A obv. ii 28′), and the general rule of items of homogeneous material being stored together in the KASKAL series (cf. also the NÍG.GÍD.DA in A rev. v 3, 8, 15′, all of which are AN.BAR GE$_6$), make it not unlikely.

535 Material inferred from neighboring items, viz. rhyta.

536 Material inferred from the neighboring items.

537 The PTAC has one other text in which ŠUL.PÁT are mentioned along with the material of their construction, where they are mostly made of silver (5.1 obv. i 3′; obv. ii 4′, 6′, 8′ (2×), 9′; rev. iii 11), with one gold example attested (5.1 obv. i 4′). The silver ŠUL.PÁT of 5.1 and the appearance of the line between two other paragraphs of silver items argue for the 200 ŠUL.PÁT of A rev. v 27′ also being made of silver.

^{GIŠ}*ḫūpparalliš* '(a container)'	KÙ.BABBAR 'silver'	1	A rev. v 28′
	Subtotal	239 pieces	
Iron (ore)			
Item	Description	Quantity	Citation
[]	AN.BAR GE_6 'black *iron (ore)*'	[1]	A obv. i 2′
ḪAR.GÚ 'torc'	AN.BAR GE_6 'black *iron (ore)*'	8	A obv. i 2′
pe]*ran pēdumaš* '"fore-carrier"'	AN.BAR GE_6 'black *iron (ore)*'	[1]	A obv. i 3′
INṢABTUM 'earring'	AN.BAR GE_6 'black *iron (ore)*'	[1]	A obv. i 4′
UNQU 'ring'	AN.BAR GE_6 'black *iron (ore)*'	[1]	A obv. i 11′
^{GIŠ}TUKUL 'mace'	A[N.BAR (GE_6) '(black) *iron (ore)*'	3	A rev. v 1
[]	ŠÀ.BA 1 AN.BAR G[E_6] "of which is 1 black *iron (ore)*"	1	A rev. v 2
[]	[AN.BA]R GE_6 'black *iron (ore)*'	[1]	A rev. v 3
NÍG.GÍD.DA 'rod'	AN.BAR G[E_6] 'black *iron (ore)*'	5	A rev. v 3
EME GÍR.TUR 'small-knife blade'	AN.BAR GE_6 'black *iron (ore)*'	5	A rev. v 4
GÍR.TUR 'small-knife'	AN.BAR '*iron (ore)*'	6	A rev. v 4
EME GÍR 'knife blade'	AN.BAR '*iron (ore)*'	10	A rev. v 5
palzaḫaš 'statue base'	AN.BAR '*iron (ore)*'	7	A rev. v 7
NÍG.GÍD.DA 'rod'	AN.BAR GE_6 'black *iron (ore)*'	81	A rev. v 8
puriaš '*tray*'	ŠÀ.BA 1 AN.[BAR SIG_5? … [538] "of which 1 [excellent? *iron (ore)* … "	3	A rev. v 8
palzaḫaš 'statue base'	AN.BAR SIG_5 '*iron (ore)*, excellent'	[n]+1	A rev. v 9

538 Since all surrounding items are made of *iron (ore)*, the line presumably continues: 2 AN.BAR (GE_6).

NÍG.GÍD.DA 'rod'	AN.BAR GE$_6$ ŠÀ.BA 1 ŠU.U "black *iron (ore)*, among which 1 (with) basalt"	16	A rev. v 15
	Subtotal	145+[16] pieces	
Precious Stone or Ivory			
Item	Description	Quantity	Citation
[]	^{NA_4}GU]G *išgarān* "carnelian, pierced"	[1]	A obv. i 8′
[^{NA_4}*IZZIḪU*(?)]	^{N}]^{A_4}*ḪALTI* 'of *ḪALTU*-stone'	[1]	A obv. i 9′
^{NA_4}*IZZIḪU*	*KIBŠI* 'of *variegated* stone'	1	A obv. i 9′
[]	^{NA_4}G]UG(?) 'carnelian'	[1]	A obv. i 10′
UNQU 'ring'	^{NA_4}GUG *MIZRĪ* 'Egyptian carnelian'	26	A obv. i 13′
tiyawa[*ra*(?)	ZU$_9$ AM.SI 'ivory'	8	A obv. ii 4, 6′
[]	^{NA_4}ZA.G[ÌN 'lapis lazuli'	28	A obv. ii 9′
SAG.DU *kinuḫi*[*š* 'pommel of a *kinuḫa*-knife'	[precious stone?][539]	1	A obv. ii 10′
šūtariš G[IŠ.INANNA(?) '*šūtari*-piece (for a) lyre'	[precious stone?][540]	1	
AŠ.ME '(sun) disk'	ZA.GÌN 'blue (stone)'	16	A obv. ii 12′
UNQU 'ring'	^{NA_4}Z[A.GÌN] 'lapis lazuli'	178	A obv. ii 13′
[]	*ŠA* NUNUZ '*malachite*'	[2][541]	A obv. ii 19′
[]	*^{NA_4}*ZA.GÌN 'lapis lazuli'	179	A rev. v 19′
	Subtotal	438+[5] pieces	
Base Metal			
Item	Description	Quantity	Citation
EME GÍR 'knife blade'	ZABAR 'bronze'	6	A rev. v 5

539 Material inferred from surrounding items. Cf. also the dagger pommel in 6.1 obv. 9, which is made out of ^{NA_4}DU$_8$.ŠÚ.A 'rock crystal(?)'.

540 Material inferred from surrounding items. See further *Lexical Commentary s.v. šūtari-*.

541 Given the color designation of the chests, the 2 ^{GIŠ}PISAN DUḪ.ŠÚ.A [(*ŠA* NUN[UZ) in A obv. ii 19′//B rev. 2′ is probably to be interpreted as "2 yellow chests of (= containing) *malach*[*ite* objects," rather than "2 yellow chests (made) of *malach*[*ite*.

EME GÍR.GAL 'sword blade'	⟨ZABAR?⟩[542] 'bronze'	18	A rev. v 6
GÍ[R] *GAMRU* 'complete knife'	(copper?)[543]	81[544]	A rev. v 10
GIŠBÚGIN 'trough'	AN.NA GAR.RA 'tin-inlaid'	40	A rev. v 22′
[URU]DU*ANKURINU* '*lampstand*'	URUDU, GAL AMAR 'copper', "large (and) (in the form of a) calf"	2	A rev. vi 4′, 5′
	Subtotal	147 pieces	
Cloth			
Item	*Description*	*Quantity*	*Citation*
Ḫ]AR.ŠU KUR *Mizri* 'Egyptian bracelet'	*ṬURRI* GADA SA₅ "red linen for the band"	[1]	A obv. i 7′
	Subtotal	[1] piece	
Miscellaneous			
Item	Description	Quantity	Citation
GIŠLE.U₅ 'wooden writing board'		2	A obv. ii 3′
Unclassified			
Item	Description	Quantity	Citation
kuwalamaš '(a decoration)'		1	A obv. ii 2′

The contents of 8.1.B are completely duplicated by 8.1.A, and are accounted for in Table 1. The contents of 8.1.C are completely duplicated by 8.1.A and 8.1.D, and are accounted for under Table 1 and Table 2, respectively.

With the exception of a five-line interpolation (see discussion in *4.6.2 Nexus 2*), the durable goods on the obverse of 8.1.D tablet are duplicated in 8.1.A, and have therefore been tabulated under Table 1. The contents of the five-line interpolation that were not included there are presented below.

542 No material given. Since the immediately preceding EME GÍR are described as ZABAR, it is possible that same should be emended for the EME GÍR.GAL.

543 No material given. Since there are no surrounding objects from which to restore the material, it is assumed that the knives are made of copper, the default material for cutting instruments in the PTAC.

544 This number includes fifty-seven GÍR LÚMUḪALDIM (cook's knife) and an unknown number of GÍR *gimraš* (field knife).

Table 2: Durable Goods in Preserved Portions of 8.1.D

Precious Stone or Ivory			
Item	Description	Quantity	Citation
	^{NA_4}KÁ.DINGIR.RA '"Babylon-stone"'	[1]	D obv. i 6′
	^{NA_4}T[I] '"life"-stone'	[1]	D obv. i 6′
	^{NA_4}[*m*]*ušnuwantiš*	[1]	D obv. i 7′
	Subtotal	[3] objects	
Miscellaneous			
Item	Description	Quantity	Citation
^{KUŠ}MAR.Š[UM] 'leather strap'		27	D obv. i 4′
^{SÍG}*pittulaš* ŠU-*aš* 'woolen hand loops'			D obv. i 8′

The preserved portions of 8.1.A, 8.1.B, 8.1.C, and 8.1.D attest to a total of: 192 or more gold objects (of which 180 are gold wires/rods), 47 minas and 13 shekels of gold ingots, 239 silver objects (of which 200 are silver drinking straws/tubes), 161 or more *iron (ore)* objects (of which 81 are rods), 446 or more objects made of precious stone or ivory (of which 179 are rings), 147 base metal objects, 1 or more pieces of cloth, and a few miscellaneous items, including 2 wooden writing tablets, a piece of a musical instrument, 27 leather straps and some woolen carry straps.

5.2.2 Items in the Missing Portions of the Durable Goods Tablet

In the calculations below, each recoverable line has been weighted with a value of either full (= 1) or half (= .5). A line is valued at "half" when it preserves at least one entry which appears in the above table, but is otherwise only partially complete (that is, there is a high probability that another entry was lost in the break). A line is valued at "full" when an entry can be recovered and a lost entry is unlikely. Uninscribed lines at the end of paragraphs, which are often not given line numbers in the hand-copies, are noted separately and added to the total of full-lines. The weighted values have been added for each column to give an idea of the tablet's completeness.

Note: when restored lines are cited that fall outside of the handcopy's numbering range, they will be prefixed by a superscripted negative $^{-}$ if they are before the first line, or a positive $^{+}$ if they are after the last line. So $^{-}$4′ would be the fourth line before the start of line 1′ in the handcopy, and $^{+}$2 would be two lines after last numbered line in the handcopy.

Approximately four lines are completely missing at the beginning of the tablet of 8.1.A. Most of the objects in the first half of the tablet, including 8.1.A obv. i, are of *iron (ore)*, so one might safely assume the first lines also contain *iron (ore)* implements. The last eight lines of the tablet of 8.1.A are also completely missing. The lines immediately before the break at the end of 8.1.A obv. i mention golden statues and a number of inlaid objects, including something inlaid with carnelian. The first lines preserved after the break at the beginning of 8.1.A obv. ii contain gold, silver, and precious stones. It is sensible then to restore objects of precious materials in the last eight lines of 8.1.A obv. i. In later calculations, the weighted value of these lines will be split evenly between the gold and precious stone categories.

Table 3: 8.1.A obv. i

Level of preservation	Citation		Weighted value
reasonably complete (full line)	A obv. i 2′–9′		8
partially complete (half line)	A obv. i 10′–13′, 15′, 16′, 18′, 19′, 24′		4.5
	Subtotal		12.5
Missing lines (by material)	Full lines	Half lines	Weighted value
Iron (ore)	A obv. i (⁻4′)-1′		5
gold/precious stones	A obv. i 14′, 17′, 20′–23′, (⁺25′–⁺32′)	A obv. i 10′–13′, 15′, 16′, 18′, 19′, 24′	18.5

The first five lines of 8.1.A obv. ii are also broken away. Given the contents of the end of obv. i and the rest of obv. ii, these lines probably contained gold items accompanied by precious stones. Most of the middle of obv. ii contains precious stones, but there could be some gold mixed in (see. obv. ii 5′). Starting at obv. ii 18′, the text can be partially restored from text B.

Table 4: 8.1.A obv. ii

Level of preservation	Citation		Weighted value
reasonably complete (full line)	A obv. ii 18′–29′		12
partially complete (half line)	A obv. ii 2′–17′		8
	Subtotal		20
Missing lines (by material)	Full lines	Half lines	Weighted value
gold/precious stones	A obv. ii (⁻5′)-1′	A obv. ii 2′–17′	14

8.1.A obv. iii and rev. iv are completely broken away. There is no clue as to the material of the objects they contained. In order to provide the most conservative valuation possible, these lines will be arbitrarily considered to have contained base metal objects.

8.1.A rev. v is almost completely preserved. One or two lines are broken away in the middle, which, judging by the surrounding lines, probably contained *iron (ore)* objects. The final lines of the column concern small containers of silver objects.

Table 5: 8.1.A rev. v

Level of preservation	Citation	Weighted value
reasonably complete (full line)	A rev. v 4–11, 14–29	24

partially complete (half line)	A rev. v 1–3, 30, 31		2.5
	Subtotal		26.5
Missing lines (by material)	Full lines	Half lines	Weighted value
Iron (ore)	A rev. v 12–13	A rev. v 1–3	3.5
Silver	A rev. v 32–33	A rev. v 30–31	3

For 8.1.A rev vi, only the last few words of five lines, appearing about three-quarters of the way down the tablet, are preserved. These five lines seem to contain the colophon of the tablet, so no further text is expected. One could guess that about fifteen preceding lines are lost, but there is no clue as to the quality of their contents, so I will again assume a default of base metal items.

Table 6: 8.1.A rev. vi

Level of preservation	Citation		Weighted value
reasonably complete (full line)	A rev. vi 1′–3′[545], 4′– 5′ (+2 uninscribed)		7
	Subtotal		7
Missing lines (by material)	Full lines	Half lines	Weighted value
base metal	A rev. vi (⌈1′–⌈15′)		15

The contents of the five lines unique to 8.1.D (and 8.1.C) deviate from the theme of the surrounding text in 8.1.A. The first entry (obv. i 4′–5′) and third entry (obv. i 8′) describe containers of fastening or carrying supplies: ^{KUŠ}MAR.ŠUM "leather straps" and ^{SÍG}*pittulaš* ŠU-*aš* "woolen hand loops (= carrying straps?)." Because of their utilitarian nature, these have been categorized as durable goods and not textiles.

Table 7: 8.1.D obv. i 4′–8′

Level of preservation	Citation		Weighted value
reasonably complete (full line)	D obv. i 4′–8′		5
	Subtotal		5
Missing lines (by material)	Full lines	Half lines	Weighted value
Precious Stone or Ivory Objects	D obv. i 6′–7′		2
Miscellaneous	D obv. i 4′–5′, 8′		3

5.2.3 Reconstructed Total of Items in the Durable Goods Tablet

There is no way to know for sure if the interpolation recorded in 8.1.C and 8.1.D was completely removed from the later draft represented by 8.1.A, or if it was relocated to a part of that tablet that is now broken away. But as explained in the section

545 Lines rev. vi 1′–3′ are part of the colophon, and can be considered "reasonably complete" because one can predict that they do not contain any objects.

introduction, the latter will be assumed. Thus, the total number of lines preserved can be found by adding the lines in 8.1.A to the interpolation of 8.1.D.

Judging by 8.1.A obv. ii and rev. v, the tablet's most completely preserved, a full column in this text would contain around thirty-four lines of text. Column A obv. i is slightly longer at thirty-six lines because it has no paragraph breaks. Column A rev. vi ends about two-thirds of the way down the tablet, at around line 20′ of rev. v. These numbers can be used to estimate how much of the tablet is missing:

Table 8: Percentage of Missing Lines in Durable Goods Tablet

Text	Column	Preserved/Total
8.1.A	obv. i	12.5/36 lines
	obv. ii	20/34 lines
	obv. iii	0/29[546] lines
	rev. iv	0/34 lines
	rev. v	26.5/33 lines
	rev. vi	7/22 lines
8.1.D	obv. i	5/5 lines
	Total	71/188 (= 38%)

While not all of the lines missing would have contained entries of durable goods (as can be seen in the preserved portion of 8.1.A, some lines were KASKAL formulas or extended descriptions of certain objects), and some lines would have contained more entries than others, this does not diminish the conclusion that the goods tabulated above represent considerably less than half the durable goods originally recorded in the KASKAL main text.

Having tabulated the preserved entries, and estimated the percentage of preserved lines, the next step is to extrapolate the total number of objects once contained in the KASKAL main text. More so than the previous steps, this is fraught with caveats and uncertainty because of the "lumpy" nature of the data: one entry may contain a few pieces of bronze, and the next forty pounds of gold. If the data were more easily quantifiable, that is, if the objects could be reduced to integers that measure the same thing, the best statistical practice would be to account for the "lumpiness" using standard deviation. Standard deviation is a way of measuring the volatility of a data set, how close or far the data points are from the average. If the contents of the KASKAL series could be converted into the same units of measurement (for example, value in shekels of silver), one would see that some items were worth a lot more than others, and thus

546 The extra five lines from 8.1.D are arbitrarily placed into 8.1.A obv. iii for the purposes of calculation. Hence, the reconstructed total number of lines for A obv. iii appears as if it were five lines shorter, i.e., 29 instead of 34. As was argued in the introduction to this chapter, it is assumed that the extra materials in tablets like 8.1.D and 8.1.E were not removed, but shifted elsewhere in later drafts. The placement of 8.1.D obv. i 4′–8′ into 8.1.A obv. iii was made so as to not double-count these items.

its data would be said to have a high standard deviation.[547] But since the data for performing standard deviations is lacking, crude averages and common sense will have to suffice. Below will be presented the total number of objects for each material, divided by the number of lines they occupy (using the full/half line weighted method), yielding an average number of objects per line. The anomalously large or valuable entries will be excluded from this calculation. The resulting average will be applied to the number of missing lines estimated for each class of material.

The precise numbers offered throughout this chapter are ultimately educated guesses. Nevertheless, full appreciation of the KASKAL Main Text requires an honest attempt to restore its contents, so that if restoration requires guesses, they should be as educated as possible. Hence the exactness of the calculations: because even if the results are speculative, starting with rounder numbers will not improve them.

Below is the total number of objects preserved in the durable goods tablet, with anomalously large entries noted separately:

Objects in Preserved Portion of KASKAL Durable Goods Tablet

Gold:	6+[6] objects, 180 gold wires/rod, 47 minas 13 shekels gold ingots
Silver:	39 objects, 200 drinking straws/tubes
Iron (ore):	64+[16] objects, 81 rods
Stone and ivory:	81+[5] objects, 178 rings, 179 (more rings?)
Base metal:	147 objects

Dividing the preserved objects by the number of lines they are observed to occupy yields an estimated average density of objects of that material per line. To put it another way, reading through the Durable Goods section of the KASKAL Main Text, one notices that gold objects receive more description that, say, silver or *iron (ore)* objects. This in turn means that an equal number of lines spent describing gold objects should ultimately contain a lower number of individual items than an equal number of lines describing silver or *iron (ore)* objects. The "Observed Obj./Weighted Line" column in the table below is a way of enumerating this impression. Multiplying the observed obj./weighted line by the reconstructed total of missing lines for each material (which is in turn gained from adding up the *Missing lines* sections of the tables for each column by material) should therefore yield an educated guess about how many objects of that material are missing.

Setting aside the anomalously large entries, the following estimations of the missing objects can be made:

547 More advanced statistical methods could also be applied, allowing one to estimate e.g., how likely it is that a very valuable entry (such as forty minas of gold) was lurking in a broken portion of the text. Breaks of a few lines would not be likely to contain these large entries, while in the cases like A obv. iii and rev. iv, where two consecutive columns are missing, the broken portions would have a chance to contain at least one or two of these anomalously valuable entries.

Table 9: Total Missing Objects by Material in Durable Goods Tablet

Material	Observed Obj./Weighted Line	Obv. Obj./Weight. Line x total reconstr. missing lines	Est. total of missing objects.
Gold	6+[6] obj. / 5 lines = 2.4	2.4 obj./line x 16.25 lines[548]	≈ 39 missing objects
Silver	39 obj. / 7.5 lines = 5.2	5.2 obj./line x 3 lines	≈ 16 missing objects
Iron	64+[16] obj. / 11.5 lines = 7.0	7.0 obj./line x 8.5 lines	≈ 60 missing objects
Stone and ivory	81+[5] objects/6 lines	14.3 obj./line x 16.25[549]	≈ 232 missing objects
Base metal	147 objects/6.5 lines	22.6 obj./line x 78 lines	≈ 1,763 missing objects

The biggest contributor to the missing totals is the base metal category. This is because it was arbitrarily assumed that the broken columns A obv. iii, rev. iv, and the first half of rev. vi contained base metals. The intention was to restore base metals so as not to inflate the value of the columns, but the base metal goods turned out to have the densest entries. Yet substituting another material, or any combination of materials, would not lessen the value of the two-and-a-half missing columns, because by the ratios found for the density of objects per line correlates inversely with the preciousness of the material. The results should not be surprising: the more expensive objects will appear in fewer numbers,[550] and the wealth contained in two-and-a-half columns will be very great. Thus, the 1,763 missing base metal objects are placeholders representing one possible distribution of goods for the missing columns, with other distributions of durable goods at their appropriate densities also allowed.

Combining the preserved objects, including the anomalously large entries, and the reconstructed missing objects gives the following final estimate of the total contents of the durable goods tablet:

Reconstructed Total of Objects in KASKAL Durable Goods Tablet

Gold:	231 objects (inclusive of 180 gold wires/rods), plus 47 minas and 13 shekels in ingots
Silver:	255 objects (inclusive of 200 silver (drinking) straws)
Iron (ore):	221 objects (inclusive of 81 iron (ore) rods)
Stone and ivory:	675 objects (inclusive of 178–357 rings)
Base metal:	1910 objects

548 This figure taken from half of the total of the gold/precious stone missing lines from 8.1.A obv. i and ii (18.5 + 14) / 2 = 16.25. See commentary under discussion of 8.1.A obv. i in Section *5.2.2.*

549 Same as above.

550 Or maybe better, the more expensive objects receive a more thorough and individualized description, yielding fewer objects per line. This is probably the case in 8.1.A, where the entirety of obv. i, which records iron, gold, and precious stone jewelry, is devoted to a single container. This would make the container impossibly large if one does not assume a high detail/low density description. Alternatively, one could also say that highly individualized "show pieces," which merit detailed description, are more likely to be made of precious materials than the utilitarian, base metal objects.

There were additionally some miscellaneous objects like the leather straps, woolen hand loops, and wooden writing boards – and of course the chests themselves, which were not inexpensive items.[551]

5.3 Textiles in the KASKAL Main Text

The same process as above can be applied to the textile tablet, with the difference that there will be no attempt to discriminate by material category. Any arguments for this approach are moot: almost all of the textiles are listed without material. It is possible that the default material was wool (as it is never explicitly mentioned, yet the Hittite palace was known to receive vast quantities as tax and tribute), with a few linen garments mentioned by name. In any case the material of the textiles is mostly irrelevant. Textiles are premier examples of high value-added products, and what determines their worth is not so much their material, but the skill and quality of their manufacture.[552] For example, in the texts to be discussed in *6.2. Gifts in the Egyptian-Hittite Correspondences*, each piece of linen is graded on a scale from "kingly" quality at the top, then *miku* (meaning unknown), and afterwards "fine" and normal quality at the bottom. Unfortunately, gradations in the KASKAL texts are almost completely absent. While some cloths are occasionally noted as "thin/fine" (SIG) or "excellent" (SIG_5), such descriptors occur too infrequently to be of systematic use in assigning value in the text. One can assume that the cloths of the KASKAL series existed on a spectrum of quality and value, but the specifics remain unknown. Suffice it to say that the preserved textiles are all finished goods, many of them dyed and patterned, and worthy of being contained in a royal storehouse, and thus not inexpensive items.

5.3.1 Items in the Preserved Portions of the Textiles Tablet

Almost all of the textiles of the KASKAL Main Text are contained in its second half, as represented by tablets 8.1.D, 8.1.E(A_1)(+)E(A_3)(+)Ea, the group 8.1.F(+)G(+)H, and 8.1.I.

551 For the Hittites, living in an era prior to cheap, mass-produced containers that could withstand the rigors of overland transport, a well-made chest was a valuable commodity in and of itself.

552 It is impossible to reconstruct exact values of garments in the Hittite context due to a paucity of data and uncertain terminologies, but cf. Matteo Vigo, "Linen in Hittite Inventory Texts," in *Textile terminologies in the ancient Near East and Mediterranean from the third to the first millennia BC*, ed. C. Michel, M.-L. Nosch (Oxford: Oxbow, 2010), 290–322. The Hittites clearly calculated how much raw material was necessary for a finished garment, as can be seen by the "recipes" for manufacturing belts in the texts 4.1.4.1–4.1.4.5 edited in Vol. II, where weights of wool and linen are allotted for specified numbers of garments. Looking further afield, Old Assyrian merchants were keenly concerned with the variables of weight and quality in the textiles they imported (see Cécile Michel and Klaas R. Veenhof, "The Textiles Traded by the Assyrians in Anatolia (19th-18th centuries BC)," in *Textile terminologies in the ancient Near East and Mediterranean*, 210–71). Finally, texts from the Ur III period show that pieces of cloth could take anywhere from five to one hundred-and-fifty(!) workdays to manufacture (Hartmut Waetzoldt, "Leinen (Flachs)," RlA 6 [1980–83]: 586). The point is that there are many variables determining a garment's worth, and material is only one of them.

Since the reverse of 8.1.D is entirely duplicated in 8.1.E and 8.1.H, the contents will be respectively tabulated in Table 10 and 13 .

The best preserved exemplars of the KASKAL Textiles Tablet tablets are represented by the partial duplicates 8.1.E(A_1)(+)E(A_2)(+)E(A_3) and 8.1.F(+)G(+)H. The contents of the tablets mostly overlap, but 8.1.E seems to have contained an additional one and two-thirds columns of text, now lost, at its beginning compared to 8.1.F(+)G(+)H, whereas 8.1.F(+)G(+)H had an additional one and two-thirds column at its end.[553] The editorial relationship of the two tablets is further complicated by the fact that the inventory on 8.1.E(A_3) rev. vi ends after only four lines, with the rest of the column and left edge occupied by an obscure scribal note. It is always possible that the contents of the two tablets nonetheless overlapped, with the missing contents from the beginning of 8.1.E appearing at the end of 8.1.F(+)G(+)H. However, if the extra columns of information were not the same, then the KASKAL Main Text almost certainly contained an additional, "hidden" tablet devoted to textiles, essentially doubling the final total that will be calculated. The first scenario will be assumed here, if only to avoid overestimation of the contents of the tablets. But as will be seen, the text is rich enough without positing additional tablets.

Table 10: Durable Goods and Textiles in 8.1.E(A_1)(+)E(A_2)(+)E(A_3)[554]

Gold			
Item	Description	Quantity	Citation
DÙG.GAN 'sheath'	KÙ.S[I$_{22}$] 'gold'	[1]	E(A_1) rev. iv 16′
[]	[*t*]*ittali* KÙ.SI$_{22}$ SAG.KI "(with) gold edging (and) a frontlet"	[1]	E(A_1) rev. v 4′
	Subtotal	[2] objects	
Base Metal			
Item	Description	Quantity	Citation
GÍR g[*imraš*] 'field knife'		1	E(A_1) rev. iv 15′
	Subtotal	1 object	

553 The first overlap occurs at 8.1.F obv. i. 4′ = 8.1.E(A_1) obv. iii 1′. At this juncture, 8.1.E(A_1) obv. iii 1′ has two lines lost before the top of the tablet, whereas 8.1.F obv. i 1′ is at least a third of the way down the tablet. This leaves about one and two-thirds of a column in 8.1.E unaccounted for at the beginning of 8.1.F(+)G(+)H. The final overlap occurs at the end of 8.1.E rev. v (8.1.E(A_1) rev. v 12′ = 8.1.H rev. r. c. 4′). It can be established that 8.1.H, the last point of contact between 8.1.E and 8.1.F(+)G(+)H, should be placed in the lower half of 8.1.F rev. iv, which means that 8.1.F(+)G(+)H had at least an additional one and two-thirds of a column beyond 8.1.E.

554 Excluding information that is duplicated in 8.1.F.

Precious Stone or Ivory			
Item	Description	Quantity	Citation
]...-*iš*	$^{\text{NA}_4}$ZA.GÌN 'lapis lazuli'	[1]	E(A$_1$) rev. v 3′
	Subtotal	[1] object	

Cloth			
Item	Description	Qty.	Cit.
[]	*iyatnaš 'luxurious'*	[1]	E(A$_3$) obv. i 3′
TÚG *ikkuwaniy*]*a*(?) 'Ikkuwanian garment'	BABBAR 'white'	[1]	E(A$_1$) obv. ii 2
TÚG *ikkuwaniya* 'Ikkuwanian garment'	*marušam*[*eiš*] 'blackened'	2	E(A$_1$) obv. ii 2
[$^{\text{(TÚG)}}$BAR.S]I(?) 'head band'		[1]	E(A$_1$) obv. ii 3
^{TÚG}*maššiaš 'shawl'*	*ḪAŠMANNI* '(red-)purple'	2	E(A$_1$) obv. ii 3
[]	[*maruš*]*ameiš* 'blackened'	[1]	E(A$_1$) obv. ii 4
^{TÚG}*puššaimeiš 'felted-*cloth'		6	E(A$_1$) obv. ii 4
[]	SIG 'thin'	[1]	E(A$_1$) obv. ii 5
^{TÚG}GÚ 'tunic'	SIG SIG$_5$ "thin, excellent"	2	E(A$_1$) obv. ii 5
[TÚG *i*]*kkuwaniya šarrumaš* 'Ikkuwanian garment "of dividing"'		[1]	E(A$_1$) obv. ii 9
^{TÚG}GÚ.È.A *ḪURRI* 'Hurrian tunic'		4	E(A$_1$) obv. ii 10
^{TÚG}GABA 'breast cloth'	BABBAR 'white'	1	E(A$_1$) obv. ii 11
^{TÚG}E.ÍB 'belt'	*MAŠLU* SIG$_5$ "patterned, excellent"	[1]	E(A$_1$) obv. ii 12
[^{TÚG}*pušš*]*aimiš 'felted-*cloth'		[1]	E(A$_1$) obv. ii 13
TÚG 'cloth'	GAL ŠÀ 1 *marušameš* "large, of which 1 blackened"	2	E(A$_1$) rev. iv 2′
TÚG 'cloth'	(various types)	12	E(A$_1$) rev. iv 2′
^{TÚG}*kapitašamna* 'Kapitašamnan garment'		1	E(A$_1$) rev. iv 4′
TÚG 'cloth'	SIG BABBAR "thin, white"	2	E(A$_1$) rev. iv 4′
TÚG 'cloth'	[]	2	E(A$_1$) rev. iv 4′

TÚGGÚ *ḪURRI* 'Hurrian tunic'	*ḪAŠARDI* 'green'	1	E(A_1) rev. iv 5′
TÚGGÚ *ḪURRI* 'Hurrian tunic'	*mar*[*ušameš*] 'blackened'	1	E(A_1) rev. iv 5′
TÚGGABA 'breastcloth'	*QADU* GADA *ḪAŠMANNI* "with linen, (red-)purple"	2	E(A_1) rev. iv 6′
TÚGGABA 'breastcloth'	*mar*[*ušameiš*] 'blackened'	2	E(A_1) rev. iv 6′
TÚGGÚ *anduriaš* 'domestic(-styled) tunic'	BABBAR 'white'	3	E(A_1) rev. iv 7′
TÚGSAG.[DUL] 'head covering'	[]	7	E(A_1) rev. iv 7′
TÚGSAG.DUL 'head covering'	GADA 'linen'	5	E(A_1) rev. iv 8′
TÚGE.ÍB 'belt'	[*MAŠ*]*LU* SI[G_5] "patterned, excellent"	4	E(A_1) rev. iv 8′
TÚGBAR."TE" 'cloak'	*ḪAŠMAN.* '(red-)purple'	2	E(A_1) rev. iv 9′
TÚG 'cloth'	[]	1	E(A_1) rev. iv 9′
TÚGBAR."TE" 'cloak'	BABBAR 'white'	2	E(A_1) rev. iv 10′
[]	[]	1	E(A_1) rev. iv 10′
KARKU '"twined"-cloth'	*ḪAŠMANNI* '(red-)purple'	1	E(A_1) rev. iv 11′
[]	*ḪAŠMANNI* '(red-)purple'	2	E(A_1) rev. iv 12′
[]	[]	2	E(A_1) rev. iv 12′
TÚGE.Í[B] 'belt'	[]	6	E(A_1) rev. iv 13′
TÚG*ḫapu*[*šammi*(-) '*fulled*-cloth'	[]	1	E(A_1) rev. iv 14′
[]	*MAŠL*[*U*] 'patterned'	4	E_a 4′
[]	[]	4	E_a 5′
[]	[*ma*]*rušama* 'blackened'	[2][555]	E_a 6′
TÚGGÚ 'tunic'		20	E_a 8′
TÚGGÚ 'tunic'	*maru*[*šama*] 'blackened'	[2][556]	E_a 9′
[]	SA_5	[1]	E(A_1) rev. v 1′
[]	*ḪAŠMANNI* '(red-)purple'	2	E(A_1) rev. v 2′
[GADA?] 'linen'	*Š*]*ŪRU* '*dark brown*'	[1]	E(A_1) rev. v 7′
TÚG*kušiši* '*kušiši*-garment'		2	E(A_1) rev. v 7′
[TÚ]G*kuššadi* '*kuššati*-garment'		[1]	E(A_1) rev. v 7′

555 The explicit pl. nom.-acc. n. implies that more than one item is described.
556 See fn. above.

[^{TÚG}GÚ] 'tunic'	[*ḪAŠARDI*] 'green'	1	E(A_1) rev. v 8′
^{TÚG}ḪI.ḪI-*natar* 'blended(-wool) garment'	*ḪAŠMANNI* '(red-)purple'	[n+1]	E(A_1) rev. v 8′
^{TÚG}ḪI.ḪI-*natar* 'blended(-wool) garment'		1	E(A_1) rev. v 9′
[TÚG *ta*]*pišpa* 'Tapašpa garment'		[1]	E(A_1) rev. v 9′
GADA 'linen'	*ŠŪRU* '*dark brown*'	1	E(A_1) rev. v 9′
^{TÚG}*gapitašamna* 'Kapitašamnan garment'		1	E(A_1) rev. v 9′
BAR.SI 'head band'	GADA 'linen'	1	E(A_1) rev. v 10′
^{TÚG}*mazaganniš* '*ma-zakanni*-garment'	TUR SA_5 'small, red'	1	E(A_1) rev. v 10′
^{TÚG}*irḫiš* '*belt*'		5	E(A_1) rev. v 10′
GAD.DAM 'leggings'	(various colors)	14	E(A_1) rev. v 11′
[]	SÍ]G *ḪAŠM*[*AN(-)* "(red-)purple wool"	[1]	E(A_3) rev. vi 2
[]	S]ÍG ZA.[GÌN "blue wool"	[1]	E(A_3) rev. vi 3
	Subtotal	136+[20]	

All items attested in 8.1.F, including the those duplicated by 8.1.E, are accounted for in Table 11.

Table 11: Durable Goods and Textiles in 8.1.F

Gold			
Item	Description	Quantity	Citation
GÌR UR.MAḪ 'lion's feet'	KÙ.SI_{22} GAR.RA 'gold-inlaid'	4	F rev. v 14
	Subtotal	4 objects	
Base Metal			
Item	Description	Quantity	Citation
^{URUDU}*ḪAṢṢINU* 'copper axe'		1	F rev. vi 5
	Subtotal	1 object	
Precious Stone or Ivory			
Item	Description	Quantity	Citation
^{GIŠ}NÁ 'bed frame)'	ZU_9 AM.SI 'ivory'	1	F rev. v 13
	Subtotal	1 ivory bed frame	

Cloth			
Item	Description	Quantity	Citation
^{TÚ}[^{G}G]Ú *ḪURRI* 'Hurrian tunic'	GADA 'linen'	40	F obv. i 3′
^{TÚG}GÚ 'tunic'	GADA 'linen'	39	F obv. i 4′
GADA 'linen'	SA$_5$ 'red'	2	F obv. i 4′
GADA 'linen'	*ŠUḪURU* '*dark brown*'	1	F obv. i 4′
GADA 'linen'	SIG 'thin'	8	F obv. i 5′
GÚ 'tunic'	GADA ^{URU}*Alašiya* "Cypriot linen"	5	F obv. i 5′
GADA 'linen'	LÚGU[D.D]A 'short'	5	F obv. i 6′
TÚG 'cloth'	GAL BABB[AR] "large, white"	5	F obv. i 8′
^{TÚG}*maššiaš* '*shawl*'	BABBAR 'white'	7	F obv. i 8′
TÚG 'cloth'	*ŠŪRU* '*dark brown*'	4	F obv. i 9′
TÚG 'cloth'	SIG BABBAR "thin, white"	17	F obv. i 9′
TÚG 'cloth'	SIG ZA.GÌN	2	F obv. i 9′
^{TÚG}*kušš*[*adi*] '*kuššati*-garment'		5	F obv. i 10′
^{TÚG}SAG.DUL 'head covering'		2	F obv. i 10′
TÚG *ḫurliš*[*a*] '*Ḫurliš(š)an*-garment'	[S]A$_5$ 'red'	1	F obv. i 10′
^{TÚG}GÚ *ḪURRI* 'Hurrian tunic'	BABBAR 'white'	2	F obv. i 11′
^{TÚG}G[Ú 'tunic'	[]	1	F obv. i 11′
[]	ZA.GÌN 'blue'	[1]	F obv. i 12′
[^{TÚG}*lu*]*panni* 'cap'	ZA.GÌN 'blue'	[1]	F obv. i 16′
[]	ZA.GÌN TUR "blue, small"	[1]	F obv. i 17′
^{TÚG}*kuššadi* '*kuššati*-garment'		10	F obv. i 20′
TÚG ÉRIN^{MEŠ} '"army"-cloth'		9	F obv. i 21′
^{TÚG}GÚ [*ḪUR*]*RI* 'Hurrian tunic'	ḪI.ḪI 'multi-hued'	1	F obv. i 21′
[]	*šar*[*ḫanuwamiš*(?)	3	F obv. ii 2′

E.ÍB	[]	16[557]	F obv. ii 4′–5′
BAR."TE" 'cloak'	ḪI.ḪI 'multi-hued'	2	F obv. ii 5′
[]	[]	10	F obv. ii 5′
GAD.DAM '*leggings*'	*ḪAŠMAN.* '(red-)purple'	3	F obv. ii 6′
GAD.DAM '*leggings*'	SA_5 'red'	2	F obv. ii 7′
SAG.DUL 'head covering'	*QA*[*DU* "with ..."	2	F obv. ii 8′
KARKU '"(inter)twined"-cloth'	BABBAR 'white'	5	F obv. ii 9′
[TÚ]GGÚ *ḪURRI* 'Hurrian tunic'	[]	[1]	F obv. ii 10′
TÚG⌈GÚ⌉['tunic'	[]	9	F obv. ii 11′
TÚGGÚ 'tunic'	[]	6	F obv. ii 12′
TÚGGÚ 'tunic'	S[A_5 'red'	3	F obv. ii 13′
TÚG 'cloth'	GA[L 'large'	5	F obv. ii 17′
TÚG*kiša*[*meiš* 'carded (wool) garment'	[]	8	F obv. ii 18′
TÚ[G 'cloth/garments'	[]	39	F obv. ii 19′
TÚGGUZ("SIG_4").Z[A] '*guzza*-cloth'	[]	6 sets	F rev. v 6
TÚG *parnaš* '*parna*-cloths'	multiple colors	14 (125 cubits total)	F rev. v 7–11
TÚG *tappāšpa* 'Tapašpan garment'	SA_5 *QADU* GADA "red, with linen"	1	F rev. v 11
ÍB.LÁ 'belt'	*MAŠLU* 1-*ŠU kitkar* ḪI.ḪI-*natar* "patterned one time at the head"	1	F rev. v 12
TÚGGÚ 'tunic'	SA_5 *QADU* GADA "red, with linen"	2	F rev. v 13
lakkušanzanienzi 'bed clothes'	BABBAR GADA-*ia* "white and linen"	1 set	F rev. v 15
TÚG*ip*]*u*[*l*]*i* 'shroud'		[1]	F rev. vi 9
KUŠN[ÍG.BÀ]R 'leather curtain'		1	F rev. vi 9
TÚG *ta*[*pišpa*(?)] 'Tapašpan garment'	[]	1	F rev. vi 9
TÚG ÉRINMEŠ '"army"-cloth'		5?	F rev. vi 13

557 It is assumed that the ŠU.NÍGIN 16 includes the 9 E.ÍB of 8.1.F obv. ii 4′.

TÚG ÉRIN^MEŠ '"army"-cloth'	*maššayaššiš* 'of *shawl-cloth*'	7	F rev. vi 15
[TÚ]G ÉRIN^MEŠ '"army"-cloth'	^LÚ.MEŠ^ḪU[B.B]I-*aš* 'of acrobats'	[1]	F rev. vi 17
[TÚG ÉRI]N^ME[Š '"army"-cloth'	[]	[1]	F rev. vi 19
	Subtotal	303+[7] objects; 125 cubits of *parna*-cloth; 1 set of bed sheets, 1 leather curtain	

The tablet fragment 8.1.G should be located in the top half of tablet 8.1.F, with 8.1.G obv. l. c. = 8.1.F obv. i, and 8.1.G obv. r. c. = 8.1.F obv. ii. The information in 8.1.G obv. l. c. would thus duplicate what would have been the lower half of 8.1.E(A_1) obv. ii.

Table 12: Textiles in 8.1.G

Cloth			
Item	Description	Quantity	Citation
^TÚG^*maš-ši-aš*	BABBAR 'white'	27	G obv. l. c. 2′
[]	*and*]*a appanta* "with appurtenances"	[1]	G obv. l. c. 3′
[G]ADA 'linen'		[1]	G obv. l. c. 4′
[GA]D.DAM 'leggings'	BABBAR 'white'	[1]	G obv. l. c. 5′
[^TÚG^*karkiši*]*liš*(?) 'Karkišan garment'	*MAŠLU* 'patterned'	[1]	G obv. l. c. 7′
^TÚG^['cloth/garment'	[]	1	G obv. r. c. 1′
^TÚG^x['...-cloth/garment'	[]	1	G obv. r. c. 2′
GAD.DA[M 'leggings'	[]	2	G obv. r. c. 3′
^TÚG^GÚ *adu*[*pli* '*adupli*-tunic'	[]	10	G obv. r. c. 5′
[TÚG] 'cloth'	[GA]L BABBAR "large, white"	[1]	G obv. r. c. 9′
TÚG 'cloth'	GAL ḪI.ḪI "large, multi-colored"	2	G obv. r. c. 9′
T[ÚG? 'cloth/garment'		1	G obv. r. c. 9′
[^TÚG^*maš*]*šiaš* '*shawl*'	*ḪAŠMAN*. '(red-)purple'	[1]	G obv. r. c. 10′
^TÚG^x['...-cloth/garment'	[]	2	G obv. r. c. 10′
[]	*ḪAŠAR*[*TI*] 'green'	[1]	G obv. r. c. 11′
	Subtotal	46+[7] objects	

8.1.H rev. r. c. is partially duplicated by 8.1.D, 8.1.E, and 8.1.I. Lines 8.1.H rev. r. c. 1′–4′ have already been tabulated under 8.1.E(A_1) rev. v 6′–10′. The remaining lines (with restorations from 8.1.D), and the unique contents of 8.1.H rev. l. c., are presented below.

Table 13: Textiles in 8.1.H

Cloth			
Item	Description	Quantity	Citation
TÚG *kapittašam[na]* 'Kapitašamnan garment'	SIG *ḪAŠMANNI* "thin, (red-)purple"	1	H rev. r. c. 7′
TÚG *kapittašamna* 'Kapitašamnan garment'	ZA.GÌN 'blue'	1	H rev. r. c. 8′
[^{TÚG}GÚ *ḪUR.*] 'Hurrian tunic'	[BABBAR] 'white'	1	H rev. r. c. 8′
TÚG *tappašpa* 'Tapašpan garment'	BABBAR 'white'	1	H rev. r. c. 9′
[]	[]	1	H rev. r. c. 9′
^{TÚG}GÚ *ḪURRI* 'Hurrian tunic'	*ḪAŠARDI* 'green'	1	H rev. r. c. 10′
[^{TÚG}G]Ú *ḪURRI* 'Hurrian tunic'		[1]	H rev. l. c. 1′
SÍG 'wool'	*ḪAŠARTI* 'green'	[1]	H rev. l. c. 4′
[SÍ]G *šarḫanuwamiš* '*šarḫanuwam(m)a/i*-wool'	*ḪA-ŠÁR-TUM* 'green'	[1]	H rev. l. c. 5′
GADA 'linen'		[1]	H rev. l. c. 6′
	Subtotal	6+[4] objects	

The contents of the fragment 8.1.I is entirely duplicated by 8.1.D, 8.1.E, and 8.1.H, with the exception of a few traces at the end of 8.1.I rev. l. c., which are not presented here.

5.3.2 Items in the Missing Portions of the Textiles Tablet

As with the Durable Goods Tablet, the number of items lost in the missing portions of the textiles tablet can be approximated, with the simplification that all missing lines can be assumed to have contained textiles.

8.1.E(A_3) obv. i contains the final lines of the missing obv. i of 8.1.E(A_1)(+)E(A_2).

Table 14: 8.1.E(A_3) obv. i

Level of preservation	Citation	Weighted value
reasonably complete (full line)	(2 uninscribed)	2
partially complete (half line)	obv. i 1′–6′	3
	Subtotal	5

Table 15: 8.1.E(A_1) obv. ii

Level of preservation	Citation	Weighted value
partially complete (half line)	obv. ii 1–16	8
	Subtotal	8

8.1.E(A_1) obv. iii is entirely duplicated by 8.1.F obv. i, so its contents will be tabulated there.

Table 16: 8.1.E(A_1) rev. iv

Level of preservation	Citation	Weighted value
reasonably complete (full line)	rev. iv 1′–8′	8
partially complete (half line)	rev. iv 9′–16′	4
	Subtotal	12

The fragment 8.1.E(A_2) can be placed at the beginning of 8.1.E(A_1) rev. v. 8.1.E(A_1) rev. v can be partially restored from 8.1.D, 8.1.H, and 8.1.I.

Table 17: 8.1.E(A_1)(+)E(A_2) rev. v

Level of preservation	Citation	Weighted value
reasonably complete (full line)	E(A_1) rev. v 6′–12′	6
partially complete (half line)	E(A_1) rev. v 1′–5′; E(A_2) 2′–4′, 6′, 8′–10′	6
	Subtotal	12

8.1.E(A_3) rev. vi represents the top of the missing rev. vi of 8.1.E(A_1)(+)E(A_2).

Table 18: 8.1.E(A_3) rev. vi

Level of preservation	Citation	Weighted value
partially complete (half line)	E(A_3) rev. vi 1–4	2
	Subtotal	2

The tablet fragments constituting 8.1.F(+)G(+)H were heavily damaged by fire in ancient times. The top-half of the tablet shows evidence of having exploded from the heat: the clay is vitrified and peels outwards at the top edges, and small tablet fragments were found nearby, giving a complicated join schematic. At the middle of the tablet, the clay is five to six centimeters thick and still expanding. One side of the tablet is mostly intact, but the other, apparently closer to the heat source, is heavily damaged by swelling and bubbling. This state of preservation makes it impossible to determine the original dimensions of the tablet. The curvature of the reverse which would have normally indicated the mid-point of the tablet is gone. For this reason, no complete column can be reconstructed, and hence the number of lines per column cannot be calculated. It will be assumed that the textiles tablet was roughly the same size as the durable goods tablet, that is, about thirty-four lines to a column. The obv. i of 8.1.F is partially duplicated by 8.1.E(A_1) obv. iii.

Table 19: 8.1.F obv. i

Level of preservation	Citation	Weighted value
reasonably complete (full line)	obv. i 2′–12′ (+2 uninscribed), 19′–21′ (+1 uninscribed)	17
partially complete (half line)	obv. i 16′–18′	1.5
	Subtotal	18.5

Table 20: 8.1.F obv. ii

Level of preservation	Citation	Weighted value
reasonably complete (full line)	(1 uninscribed)	1
partially complete (half line)	obv. ii 2′–19′	9
	Subtotal	10

8.1.F obv. iii is completely broken away, while 8.1.F rev. iv preserves only the very beginnings of three lines, from which no items can be recovered.

Table 21: 8.1.F rev. v

Level of preservation	Citation	Weighted value
reasonably complete (full line)	rev. v. 5–16 (+4 uninscribed)	16
	Subtotal	16

Table 22: 8.1.F rev. vi

Level of preservation	Citation	Weighted value
reasonably complete (full line)	(5 uninscribed)	5
partially complete (half line)	rev. vi 5′, 9′, 10′, 13′, 15′–18′	4
	Subtotal	9

Table 23: 8.1.G obv. l. c.

Level of preservation	Citation	Weighted value
reasonably complete (full line)	(2 uninscribed)	2
partially complete (half line)	obv. l. c. 2′, 4′, 5′, 7′	2
	Subtotal	4

Table 24: 8.1.G obv. r. c.

Level of preservation	Citation	Weighted value
reasonably complete (full line)	obv. r. c. 7′	1
partially complete (half line)	obv. r. c. 1′–3′, 5′, 6′, 8′–11′	4.5
	Subtotal	5.5

Table 25: 8.1.H rev. r. c.

Level of preservation	Citation	Weighted value
reasonably complete (full line)	rev. r. c. 5′–10′ (+2 uninscribed)	8
	Subtotal	8

Table 26: 8.1.H rev. l. c.

Level of preservation	Citation	Weighted value
reasonably complete (full line)	(4 uninscribed)	4
partially complete (half line)	rev. l. c. 1′, 4′–6′	2
	Subtotal	6

5.3.3 Reconstructed Total of Items in the Textiles Tablet

Because of the problems involved in relating tablets 8.1.E and 8.1.F(+)G(+)H, as well as the inability to reconstruct a complete column from the latter, the estimation of the original contents of the textiles tablet will be less precise than that of the durable goods. For lack of alternative, it will be assumed that the textiles tablet had the same number of lines as the durable goods tablet: 188. Adding together the weighted values of the preserved lines yields 116 recoverable lines, and thus a percentage of 62%, which matches well the impression gained from collating the tablets that a bit over half of the text has been preserved.

Objects in Preserved Portions of the KASKAL Textile Tablet
Gold: 4+[2] objects
Stone and ivory: [1] object, 1 ivory bed frame
Base metal: 2 objects
Textiles: 491+[38] garments, 125 cubits of tapestry, 1 set of bed sheets, 1 leather curtain

If this represents 62% of the total, the original contents of the textiles tablet would have been around 853 textiles, plus perhaps 10 gold and 3 base metal objects, as well as a collection of bulky household objects like bed frames, tapestries, and curtains. With the possibility of an extra column of contents lost from 8.1.E (see discussion under Section 5.3.1 above), or even an entire missing second textiles tablet, the true number of textiles could have been considerably larger.

5.4 Grand Total of Items in Reconstructed KASKAL Main Text

Using the reconstructions and estimates from the preceding sections, and adding the subtotals of the objects in the durable goods tablet and the textile tablet, the grand total of everything in the original KASKAL Main Text would have been:

Reconstructed Total of Objects in KASKAL Main Text

Gold:	241 objects (inclusive of 180 gold wires/rods), plus 47 minas and 13 shekels in ingots
Silver:	255 objects (inclusive of 200 silver drinking straws/tubes)
Iron (ore):	221 objects (inclusive of 81 *iron (ore)* rods)
Stone and ivory:	676 objects (inclusive of 178–357 rings), 1 ivory bed frame
Base metal:	1913 objects
Textiles:	853 textiles, 125 cubits of *parna*-cloth, 1 set of bed sheets, 1 leather curtain
Miscellaneous:	Dozens of wooden and wicker chests, leather and wool carrying straps, wooden writing tablets, etc.

It can be seen from this estimated total that the wealth of the KASKAL Main Text would have filled a large storeroom and required many wagons – plus a suitably large contingent of armed guards – to transport.

6. THE RELATIVE VALUE OF THE KASKAL MAIN TEXT

6.1 Introduction: Finding Suitable Comparisons

There are a number of sources extrinsic to Hittite administration that can be used to illustrate the value of the wealth in the KASKAL Main Text, including gifts from Egypt listed in the Egyptian-Hittite correspondence, and levies of tribute from certain Hittite vassals. These sources contain many of the same materials, gold and cloth especially, which enable a direct comparison with the KASKAL series. But the similarity of contents, while necessary, is not sufficient alone to contextualize the wealth of the Main Text; rather, the most valuable feature of the extrinsic sources is that they are, in addition, political documents.

Why is the political nature of these documents so important? The answer is one of hermeneutic need. The modern scholar lacks enough hard data about the Hittite economy to estimate the impact of the KASKAL wealth in absolute terms. There is no way to tell if the amounts reconstructed in the previous section were small or a lot in relation to the yearly income of the Hittite palace. But the *relative* impact of the wealth can be gauged by comparing the amounts to other politically significant exchanges of wealth involving the Hittites. If the contents of the main text are near the same size as, say, the bridal gifts of Ramses II to Ḫattušili III – part of a marriage negotiation that bound two superpowers of the ancient Near East into a long-lasting friendship – then one can be assured that the beneficiary of the KASKAL text was of similar importance to the Hittite palace. The operative concept is opportunity cost, that whatever the value of the wealth in the KASKAL main text, it could have been used for, and was thus "worth," a royal marriage, or the wartime contributions of a vassal, or a similar political statement. By measuring against a contemporary benchmark, the modern scholar can translate the numbers of the KASKAL texts into meaning.

6.2 Gifts in the Egyptian-Hittite Correspondences

The most comparable texts to the KASKAL series in terms of contents (gold and textiles), time period (Late New Hittite), and size (roughly speaking), are the Egyptian-Hittite correspondences of Ḫattušili III/Puduḫepa and Ramses II.[558] There are two major

558 These have been edited by Elmar Edel, *Die ägyptisch-hethitische Korrespondenz aus Boghazköi in babylonischer und hethitischer Sprache.* 2 vols. (Opladen: Westdeutscher Verlag, 1994), and translated by Violetta Cordani, *Lettere fra Egiziani e Ittiti.* TVOA 5 (Torino: Paideia, 2017). In the following discussion, these will be referred to by publication number and then the number under which they were edited in Edel's book (e.g., ÄHK 1 for the first letter of his book). For further consideration of the economic aspects of the Egypitan-Hittite gift exchanges, see Jana Siegelová, "Geschenk oder

dossiers that will be examined. The first comprises the letters of the "Eternal Treaty" negotiations, which secured peace between the Hittites and Egyptians in the 21st year of Ramses II, and the second are the marriage correspondence accompanying a Hittite bride to Egypt in the 34th year of Ramses II. A third dossier, which will not be considered here, consists of the isolated gift inventories KBo 7.10 (ÄHK 93) and KBo 28.32 (ÄHK 94). These were sent to the Hittite court on unknown and perhaps unrelated occasions, and contain much smaller sets of gifts compared to the Eternal Treaty and Marriage correspondences.[559]

Within these two dossiers, there are multiple passages mentioning gifts. The passages can be broken down into three types. The first are general descriptions, such as in KUB 3.51 (ÄHK 2) obv.? 16′–21, 31′–35′, rev.? 2′–8′ and KUB 3.52 (ÄHK 3) obv. 1′–8′. These are usually located towards the beginning of the texts, and seem to be part of the diplomatic formula of royal letters, serving as an overview of the gifts and signaling that a detailed inventory will follow. The second type of gift passage occurs at the very end of a letter and describes the routine gifts that seem to have accompanied most diplomatic exchanges. The quantities are usually very small, and in some cases could be quite cursory. The last and largest type is the gift inventory. These can occupy entire letters and analytically detail the entire shipment of gifts accompanying a major diplomatic embassy. They seem to be used especially when dowries or bride-prices are involved, as can be seen in letter KBo 28.33 (ÄHK 92) of the marriage correspondence dossier from the 34th year of Ramses II, but also in the Amarna letters such as EA 22[560] recording the gifts of Tušratta of Mittani to Amenhotep III.

Geschäft? Wovon zeugt die ägyptisch-hethitische Korrespondenz," in *Times, Signs and Pyramids: Studies in Honour of Miroslav Verner on the Occasion of His Seventieth Birthday*, ed. Vivienne Gae Callender, et al. (Prague: Faculty of Arts, Charles University of Prague, 2011), 323–34.

559 See commentary of Edel, *Die ägyptisch-hethitische Korrespondenz*, vol. 2, 301–5. For KBo 7.10 (ÄHK 93), the only solid data point is the 25 garments given by Ramses to Ḫattušili in obv. 1′. Compare this to the 72 garments reconstructed in *6.2.1.2 Lacuna 1: The Gift of King Ramses to Ḫattušili* for the same in KBo 28.47 (ÄHK 7). The single gold object weighing 60 shekels given by Šutuḫapšap? to Ḫattušili in KBo 7.10 (ÄHK 93) rev. 7′ is likewise modest. It may thus be suggested that the diplomatic gift in KBo 7.10 (ÄHK 93) was less than half, and perhaps even only a third, as large as that of the Eternal Treaty dossier – which, as will be shown in *Figure 1: Comparison of Gold in KASKAL Main Text, Gifts, and Tribute* and *Figure 2: Comparison of Textiles in KASKAL Main Text, Gifts, and Tribute* below, was the smallest of the one-off economic acts under comparison.

KBo 28.32 (ÄHK 94) is more fragmentary than KBo 7.10 (ÄHK 93), but the gift of a necklace and pair of earrings of unknown weight, and the cup of 21½ shekels of gold of the Egpytian queen to Puduḫepa (KBo 28.32 [ÄHK 94] rev. 18′–22′), together with the modest gift received by the Hittitie princes (1 cup and 2 textiles apiece in KBo 28.32 [ÄHK 94] rev. 23′–25′, 26′–28′, and 29′–31′) suggests a size similar to a diplomatic gift. Thus, it may be said that the gift inventories KBo 7.10 (ÄHK 93) and KBo 28.32 (ÄHK 94) record gifts that are considerably larger than the standard diplomatic gift of forty-eight shekels of gold and four garments accompanying regular letters (see *6.2.1.1 Commentary: The Standard Diplomatic Gift Package* below), but somewhat below the magnitude of the gifts found in the gift inventories of other major diplomatic events.

560 William L. Moran, *The Amarna Letters* (Baltimore: Johns Hopkins, 1992), 51–61; Anson F. Rainey, *The El-Amarna Correspondence*. 2 vols. HdO 1/110 (Leiden: Brill, 2015), 160–83.

In terms of usefulness for comparison with the KASKAL series, the letter inventories are the most desirable, followed by the routine gift lists. The general descriptions at the beginning of letters can be used to aid restorations, but otherwise will not be included in the tables presented below.

Note: when number for objects can safely be restored, either because of a close parallel, or because it can be subtracted from a total, or because the object is grammatically singular, it will be placed in parentheses inside brackets [( )] instead of the brackets [ ] used for less certain restorations. These numbers will be added as if they were fully preserved numbers to the totals calculated at the end of each section. Less secure restorations will be kept separate from the final totals.

6.2.1 Gifts in the "Eternal Treaty" Dossier

The letters concerning the "Eternal Treaty" are mostly complete, with the exception of three major lacunae to be addressed below.

Table 27: Gifts in the Eternal Treaty Dossier (21st year of Ramses II)

Durable Goods				
Recipient	Item	Material	Qty./Wt.	Citation
Ḫattušili	[*kāsu*] 'cup'	[good gold]	[(1 / 48 s.)]	KBo 28.47 (ÄHK 7) rev. [⌈1′]
"	*kāsu* 'cup'	[good] g[old]	1 / [(48 s.)]	KBo 28.47 (ÄHK 7) rev. 4′
"	[GAL] ... *ša šetê* [*ina p*]*āni* GU₄.MAH "drinking cup with the face of a bull)"	good gold (with) inlay, white and black stone	[1] / 93 s. of good gold	KUB 3.70 (ÄHK 9) rev. 11
"	*kāsu* 'cup'	[good] gold	1 / [(48 s.)]	KUB 34.2 (ÄHK 10) rev. 3′
Puduḫepa	*ša tikki* ... *ša* 12 *ṭurri* "necklace 'for the neck', with 12 strands"	good gold, very colorful (*ṣubbuʾu*)	1 / 88 s.	KBo 1.29+ (ÄHK 12) obv. 25
(A Hittite Prince?)	[ ]	[gol]d inlai[d]	[1? / 48 s.?]	KBo 28.36 (ÄHK 15) rev. 1′
Teššub-Šarruma	GAL ... [*ša šetê*] ... GU₄ ... [*rāṭu*] *ina šapti*=[*šu*] "drinking cup with a cow (face?), and a spout on its lip"	good gold, inl[aid], [stone]-encrusted	1 / [(93 s.)][561]	KUB 4.95+ (ÄHK 16) obv. 12–14
"	GIŠGIGIR *ša* GIŠ ... "chariot made of x-wood"	[inlaid with gold]	1 / [96 s.?][562]	KUB 4.95+ (ÄHK 16) obv. 15–16

561 Weight restored after the bull rhyton given to Ḫattušili.

562 It is difficult to guess how much gold was inlaid on the chariot. One point of comparison comes from a chariot found in an inventory of gifts from the Mittanian King Tušratta to Amenhotep III (EA 22 i 2–3; see Moran, *The Amarna Letters*, 51; Rainey, *The El-Amarna Correspondence*, 160–61). The letter comes from the Amarna correspondence, some three-generations prior to the correspondences between Ramses II and Ḫattušili III. The chariot sent by Tušratta, a *quadriga*, is quite literally the

"	*ṣi*[*mittu ša* ANŠE.KUR.RA^{MEŠ}] "team of horses"		1	KUB 4.95+ (ÄHK 16) obv. 17
Tašmi-Šarruma	*kāsu* 'cup'	good gold	1 / 49 s.	KBo 28.44 (ÄHK 17) obv. 13
Textiles				
Recipient	Item	Material/Quality	Quantity	Citation
Ḫattušili	[^{GADA}TÚG *maklalu*]	[kingly] linen	[(1)]	KBo 28.47 (ÄHK 7) [0′]
"	^{GADA}TÚG G[UD.DU] (tunic)	[kingly] linen	[(1)]	KBo 28.47 (ÄHK 7) rev. 1′
"	^{GADA}TÚG *mak*[*lalu*]	[kingly] linen	1	KBo 28.47 (ÄHK 7) rev. 5′
"	^{GADA}TÚG GUD.[DU] (tunic)	[kingly] linen	1	KBo 28.47 (ÄHK 7) rev. 6′
"	]-*ti* ⟨⟨GU⟩⟩	fine [linen], good, new	[(1)]	KUB 3.70 (ÄHK 9) rev. 15
"	[^{GADA}TÚG *t*]*unsu* ... [*ša* ^{GIŠ}NÁ] *ša* 2 *pānu=šu* "bed blanket with two sides"	fine [linen], good, new	[(1)]	KUB 3.70 (ÄHK 9) rev. 16
"	^{GADA}TÚG *lubult*[*i*] (cloth)	[kingly] linen, colorful]	1	KUB 34.2 (ÄHK 10) rev. 4′
"	^{GADA}TÚG GÚ.UD.DU$^{⟨⟨MEŠ⟩⟩}$ (tunic)	[kingly] linen, colorful]	1	KUB 34.2 (ÄHK 10) rev. 5′
Puduḫepa	^{GADA}TÚG$^{⟨⟨MEŠ⟩⟩}$ *maklalu lubul*⟨*ti*⟩	kingly linen, colorful	1	KBo 1.29+ (ÄHK 12) obv. 27
"	^{GADA}TÚG^{MEŠ} GÚ.UD.DU *lubulti* (tunic)	kingly linen, colorful	1	KBo 1.29+ (ÄHK 12) rev. 1
"	^{GADA}TÚG (garment)	fine linen, good, colorful	5	KBo 1.29+ (ÄHK 12) rev. 2
"	^{GADA}TÚG GÚ.UD.DU (tunic)	fine linen, good, colorful	5	KBo 1.29+ (ÄHK 12) rev. 3
(A Hittite Prince?)	[^{GADA}TÚG GÚ.UD.D]U *lubulti* (tunic)	kingly [linen], [good, colorful]	[(1)]	KBo 28.36 (ÄHK 15) rev. 3′
"	[^{GADA}TÚG GÚ.UD].DU *lubulti* (tunic)	kingly [linen], [c]ol[orful]	[(1)]	KBo 28.36 (ÄHK 15) rev. 4′

headline item to the entire letter, being the first object (along with the team of four swift horses that draw it) mentioned. It was described as covered all over with 320 shekels of gold (= 5⅓ minas, or around 2.6 kg). One might suspect that Prince Teššub-Šarruma received a more modestly appointed chariot from Ramses. The horses and construction of the chariot would have been very expensive by themselves, and even without 320 shekels (more than six times the weight of the "standard" gold gift: see below) attached. Perhaps a guess of 96 shekels (a double standard gold gift) would be more in line with the twelve textiles also received by Teššub-Šarruma.

"	[^{GADA}TÚG *bi*]*rmu* (garment with multi-colored trim)	fine [linen], good	[2+]	KBo 28.36 (ÄHK 15) rev. 5′
"	[^{GADA}TÚG *tu*]*nsu* (cloak)	fine [linen], good, two-[sided]	[(1)]	KBo 28.36 (ÄHK 15) rev. 6′
"	[^{GADA}TÚG] (garment)	[fi]ne [linen], good, colorful	[2+]	KBo 28.36 (ÄHK 15) rev. 7′
"	[^{GADA}TÚG x]-*ta*^{MEŠ}	fine [linen], good, colorful	[2+]	KBo 28.36 (ÄHK 15) rev. 8′
Teššub-Šarruma	[^{GADA}TÚG^{MEŠ}] (garment)	[kingly linen, colorful]	[(4)]	KUB 4.95+ (ÄHK 16) rev. [0′]
"	$^{\text{G[ADA}}$TÚG *maklalu lubulti*]	[kingly linen, colorful]	4	KUB 4.95+ (ÄHK 16) rev. 1′
"	^{GADA}TÚG GÚ.UD.[DU^{MEŠ}] (tunic)	[kingly] linen, [colorful]	4	KUB 4.95+ (ÄHK 16) rev. 2′
Tašmi-Šarruma	^{GADA}TÚG *maklalu lubulti*	kingly linen, [c]olorful	2	KBo 28.44 (ÄHK 17) obv. 15
"	^{GADA}TÚG GÚ.UD.DU [*lub*]*ulti* (tunic)	kingly linen, colorful	2	KBo 28.44 (ÄHK 17) obv. 16

6.2.1.1 Commentary: The Standard Diplomatic Gift Package

Judging by the letters of the Eternal Treaty Dossier, the standard diplomatic gift package seemed to have been one cup made of gold, weighing about 48 shekels, and at least two garments of linen (and sometimes as many as four garments per gold object).[563] This was the size of gift given by Egyptian Queen Mother Tūya to Ḫattušili (KUB 34.2 [ÄHK 10] rev. 3′–5′), and by Prince Šutaḫapšap (KBo 28.47 [ÄHK 7] rev. ˉ3′–1′) and Prince Ramses (KBo 28.47 [ÄHK 7] rev. 4′–6′) to Ḫattušili. In other letters not related to the Eternal Treaty, sometimes the cup or the garments would be omitted: see KUB 3.62 (ÄHK 29) rev. 5′, a letter about the Urḫi-Teššub affair, where Ramses sends only a cup with a spout of good gold (*kāsu rāṭu ina šaptišu ša* KÙ.SI$_{22}$ SIG$_{5}$), and KBo 28.13+ (ÄHK 76) rev. 7′, where Ramses sends four garments but no gold.

More important diplomatic exchanges involved multiples of the standard gift formula. Within the Eternal Treaty dossier, Prince Šutaḫapšap sends a letter to Ḫattušili as sole author, and with it a gold rhyton with the face of a bull containing approximately twice as much gold as the usual cup (KUB 3.70 [ÄHK 9] rev. 11). Compare this to the separate letters King Ramses sent to the Hittite princes Teššub-Šarruma and Tašmi-Šarruma: the former (the senior of the two brothers?) received a gold rhyton of a cow, a chariot and team of horses, and a total of twelve garments (KUB 4.95+ [ÄHK

563 For the weight of the cup, see KBo 28.44 (ÄHK 17) obv. 13 (49 shekels), KBo 28.5(+)6 (ÄHK 45) rev. 5′ (ten cups weighing 480 shekels total), KBo 28.4 (ÄHK 46) rev. 15′ (two cups weighing 96 shekels total). Other sizes are mentioned in a few cases: two cups weighing 60 shekels apiece in KBo 7.10 (ÄHK 93) rev. 7′ and 10′, and 21½ shekel cup (given by Naptera to Puduḫepa) in KBo 28.32 (ÄHK 94) 21′.

16] obv. 12–rev. 3), while the latter received only a standard-sized cup and four garments (KBo 28.44 [ÄHK 17] obv. 13–17). Finally, Queen Naptera sent to Puduḫepa a gold necklace weighing eighty-eight shekels and twelve garments (KBo 1.29+ [ÄHK 12] obv. 25–rev. 4). The pattern of gifts between forty-eight and ninety-six shekels of gold and two to twelve garments is well-established, with the ideal ratio seeming to be about four garments per one forty-eight-shekel cup.

6.2.1.2 Lacuna 1: The Gift of King Ramses to Ḫattušili

The letter KBo 28.47 (ÄHK 7) is addressed from King Ramses and his sons, Prince Šutaḫapšap and Prince Ramses, to Ḫattušili. The gifts from the princes are preserved on the tablet's reverse, but the gifts from King Ramses are lost in the break at the end of the obverse and beginning of the reverse. Fortunately, the diplomatic gifts in the Egyptian-Hittite correspondence are fairly formulaic, and with a few reasonable assumptions a restoration can be attempted.

Because this was a gift between kings, one can assume that the size of the gift must have exceeded those given by the Egyptian princes to Ḫattušili in letter KUB 3.70 (ÄHK 9). The gift must also have been on par with or greater than the gifts of the Egyptian queen Naptera to her counterpart Puduḫepa in letter KBo 1.29+ (ÄHK 12). The contents would also have been more diversified: Ramses states in the introductory letter to the Eternal Treaty dossier that he is sending gifts of gold, silver, and linens to the Hittite court, ported by ninety Nubian men and ninety Nubian women,[564] as well as eye balm for Ḫattušili (KUB 3.51 [ÄHK 2] obv.$^{?}$ 25′–35′, rev.$^{?}$ 1′–12′). The silver and eye balm are not attested in the preserved portions of any of the letters, so they might have been located in the broken portion of KBo 28.47 (ÄHK 7).

It is possible to derive a ratio of gifts for the Hittite royal couple from the isolated gift text dossier KBo 7.10 (ÄHK 93) and KBo 28.32 (ÄHK 94) that in turn aids the restoration in the Eternal Treaty dossier. In the isolated gift text dossier, Puduḫepa receives one gold object, one ebony chest, and twelve linens from Ramses (KBo 28.32 [ÄHK 94] obv. 1′–11′), and two gold objects and two linens from Naptera (KBo 28.32 [ÄHK 94] rev. 18′–22′). Ḫattušili receives twenty-five linens, forty ebony logs, and five boxes and twenty tubes of medicine from Ramses (KBo 7.10 [ÄHK 93] obv. 1′),[565] and one gold necklace and eight linens from Naptera (KBo 28.32 [ÄHK 94] obv. 12′–rev. 17′). Thus, it seems that Ramses gives at least three times the gifts as his queen Naptera, and Puduḫepa receives half as many gifts as Ḫattušili. Using the linens as a guide, this gives ratios of around $1_{\mathrm{N>P}}$: $3_{\mathrm{R>P}}$: $2_{\mathrm{N>H}}$: $6_{\mathrm{R>H}}$. To put it in words, Ḫattušili receives twice as many gifts as Puduḫepa, three-quarters of which come from Ramses, and one-

564 There is no clear indication whether these individuals were meant to stay permanently. The Nubians are probably meant to correspond to the five-hundred Kaška plus livestock sent by the Hittites to Ramses: see KUB 3.24+ (ÄHK 53) rev 8′. It seems that Ancient Near Eastern rulers attempted to maintain at least a fictive parity in the types of gifts they exchanged, so even when the Hittites exported slaves and livestock for gold they also sent some gold, and when the Egyptians exported gold for slaves they also sent some slaves.

565 There are probably also some gold items in this gift that are broken away. For the restoration of letters KBo 28.5(+)6 (ÄHK 45), KBo 28.4 (ÄHK 46), and KBo 28.33 (ÄHK 92), which all seem to be referring to the same gifts, see the section on the marriage correspondence below.

quarter from Naptera. If this ratio is applied to the 12 garments and 1 gold object of Naptera to Puduḫepa in the fully preserved Eternal Treaty letter KBo 1.29+ (ÄHK 12) – the only point of comparison since Ramses did not give directly to Puduḫepa – the result would be around six gold objects and seventy-two linens (or the equivalent value) given by Ramses to Ḫattušili. This is the amount that will be added to the total calculated below.

6.2.1.3 Lacuna 2: The Gift of Vizier Pašiyara and the Egyptian Grandees to Ḫattušili
The letter KBo 28.48 (ÄHK 8) is addressed from the Egyptian Vizier Pašiyara and the "Grandees" ($^{\text{LÚ.MEŠ}}$GAL.MEŠ) to Ḫattušili. The gift section begins at the bottom of the obverse, but the last line of the obverse and first three lines of the reverse are damaged. Additionally, the reverse breaks off at what would have been line fourteen, leaving an unknown number of lines missing at the end of the tablet. Again, it is necessary to make an educated estimation of the missing gifts. All told there are around nine lines listing gold items (obv. 27 to rev. 2′). Elsewhere in the Egyptian-Hittite correspondences, outside of the letters devoted exclusively to gift-lists, it can be seen that there is usually one gold item per line, and sometimes multiple lines for a single item. So as not to exceed King Ramses' gift to Ḫattušili, where six gold items were estimated, no more than six gold items in the nine lines of KBo 28.48 (ÄHK 8) should be restored. For the textiles, lines rev. 4′–11′ preserve only fragments of garment names which continue into the tablet break. There must have been a fairly large number of textiles to match the nine lines of gold objects, and using again Ramses' gift to Ḫattušili as the upper bound, a number near seventy-two can be guessed.[566]

6.2.1.4 Lacuna 3: Gifts to the Wives(?) of the Hittite Princes
The letter KBo 28.36 (ÄHK 15) is poorly preserved, with only part of the reverse legible. On the reverse is a list of goods, sender and recipient of which are unknown, followed by the beginning of another list naming the (Egyptian) queen as the sender. Edel restored Ramses sending gifts to a Hittite prince for the first list (KBo 28.36 [ÄHK 15] rev. 1′–9′), and Naptera sending gifts to the wife for the second (KBo 28.36 [ÄHK 15] rev. 10′–12′ and continuing into the break; see commentary in Edel, *Die ägyptisch-hethitische Korrespondenz*, vol. 2, 69). Another letter, KUB 4.95+ (ÄHK 16), also contains gifts for a Hittite prince, Teššub-Šarruma, and his wife. Here the prince receives gold objects, a chariot, and twelve textiles, while the wife receives only textiles (Edel restored a minimum of eight). In other words, the prince receives twelve textiles to his wife's eight, a ratio of three to two. Applying this logic to letter KBo 28.36 (ÄHK 15), where the prince received nine textiles, the wife would receive approximately six textiles. The eight textiles of KUB 4.95+ (ÄHK 16) and six textiles of KBo 28.36 (ÄHK 15) will be added to the total given below.

566 I think it is no coincidence that the space on the tablet should suggest a gift of the same size as Ramses'. There is a potent political statement in the fact that Ramses' resources are equivalent to the rest of his court combined.

6.2.1.5 Total Gifts Received by the Hittite Court in the Eternal Treaty Dossier

Adding the restorations discussed above and the amounts in the tables, the total wealth gifted in the Eternal Treaty dossier was:

Gifts Received by the Hittites in the Eternal Treaty Dossier	
Gold:	attested: 9+[1] objects, weighing around 562 shekels restored: 12 objects, at 48 s. per "standard" gift = 576 shekels total: 1,138 shekels = 18 minas, 58 shekels gold
Textiles:	attested: 39+[6] textiles restored: 158 textiles total: 193 textiles
Other:	1 team of horses, 180 Nubian servants, unspecified quantity of eye balm and silver

These numbers are broad estimates, but it can be stated with confidence that the gifts accompanying the formalization of the Eternal Treaty were at least between 150 and 250 textiles and 15 to 20 minas of gold, plus servants, horses, and an unspecified quantity of silver and eye balm.

6.2.2 Gifts from the First Hittite-Egyptian Royal Marriage

Calculating the gifts exchanged in the letters surrounding the Hittite-Egyptian royal marriage (34th year of Ramses II) is a more straightforward exercise. In the previous section, the goal of the letters surrounding the Eternal Treaty was to establish a diplomatic relationship between the Egyptian and Hittite courts, and this required the creation of as many bilateral connections as possible. The newfound relationship between the Hittite and Egyptian courts was constructed in kinship terms – gifts of the king to his "brother," the queen to her "sister-in-law," princes to their "cousins," and every combination in between.[567] The merging of two families into one was expressed by a web of binding gifts: there was no room, or no need, for a unitary gift celebrating the treaty itself. In contrast, the marriage letters have the concentrated goal of securing a Hittite bride for Ramses, transplanting her from her father's house to her new home in Egypt. The political impact is expressed through a large compensatory gift: the bride-price.

Dynasties in the ancient Near East were keenly aware of the convertibility of gifts and diplomatic power in the context of marriage, both for their own children and those of competing courts.[568] In practice this means that the strongest political signal of the marriage negotiations was the size of the bride-price. In this case, for the purposes of

567 If this feels dissatisfying to the modern reader, that such a momentous occasion as the first major treaty between equals regulating the peacetime interactions between two countries is commemorated with such piecemeal gift giving, one must keep in mind that precedent, language, and protocol, for such an event were lacking. See David Schloen, *House of the Father as Fact and Symbol* (Winona Lake: Eisenbrauns, 2001) for the phenomenological-hermeneutical explanation behind this use of family language.

568 Cf. EA 1 (Moran, *Amarna Letters*, 1–5; Rainey, *El Amarna Correspondence*, 58–65), esp. rev. 50–61.

comparison to the KASKAL Main Text, the usual diplomatic gifts accompanying the marriage letters are meager enough be ignored, and will not be included in the total.[569] This makes the calculations of the total significantly easier: unlike the small gifts of the Eternal Treaty, which appeared in separate letters and in single copy, the bride-price was recorded in triplicate, appended to two parallel letters to Ḫattušili and Puduḫepa, and once as a separate gift list. Between these three sources there is very little left to reconstruction. Moreover, and further underlining the importance of the bride-price to the negotiations, the gifts are presented analytically and with subtotals. Thus, calculating the total amount of gold or textiles in the list is as simple as finding the relevant lines in the text and adding them up.

The letters concerning the bride-price sent by Ramses begin with the near identical pair, sent to Ḫattušili and Puduḫepa respectively. These letters record Ramses' joyous response on hearing that his marriage proposal has been accepted, and end with a promise of a large gift to be sent to Ḫattuša.[570] The follow-up letters KBo 28.5(+)6 (ÄHK 45) and KBo 28.4 (ÄHK 46) deal with roughly the same topic, recycling much of the phrasing from KBo 1.9+ (ÄHK 42) and KBo 28.23 (ÄHK 43) on their obverses. The reverses of the letters then continue with a large gift-list, providing the first two attestations of the bride-price. The gift-lists of the follow-up letters are supplemented by a separate letter KBo 28.33 (ÄHK 92), which consists entirely of a gift-list which parallels almost word for word the ends of the lists in KBo 28.5(+)6 (ÄHK 45) and KBo 28.4 (ÄHK 46), but then begins a new list of near identical value naming the children of the Hittite king and queen as the recipients.

Following Edel's analysis, it seems that three editions of the bride-price letters were sent out: the "diplomatic" version of letters KBo 1.9+ (ÄHK 42) and KBo 28.23 (ÄHK 43), which is devoted to the full expression Ramses' joy, with the bride-price discussed in only general terms; the "condensed" versions of KBo 28.5(+)6 (ÄHK 45) and KBo 28.4 (ÄHK 46), which combine celebratory language and a gift-list into one tablet; and the "analytical" version of KBo 28.33 (ÄHK 92), which enumerates the total gift to the Hittite court, including the gift to the children of the Hittite king and queen (and thus the siblings of the bride) who collectively received a gift equal to their parents.[571] It may be assumed that the royal children also received "diplomatic" and "condensed" letters that are now lost. It can thus be reconstructed that a single gift of two halves was sent to the Hittite court: this first half to be shared by Ḫattušili and Puduḫepa, as attested in KBo 28.5(+)6 (ÄHK 45) rev. 1′–16′ and KBo 28.4 (ÄHK 46) rev. [⸢7′]–18′, and KBo 28.33 (ÄHK 92) [⸢2′]–5a′, and a second half of approximately equal contents to be shared by the children of the Hittite king and queen, as attested in the remainder of KBo 28.33 (ÄHK 92) 6′–21′.

---

569 Though I do not tabulate these gifts, which are few by comparison, I have included them for reference in Appendix II. They include, for example, two golden cups (96 shekels) and 12 linens to the Chiefs of the Bodyguards of the Right and Left, and 2 leather cuirasses and a bronze helmet to an unnamed palace official. These are probably unrelated to the marriage, and perhaps belong instead to the topic of the sons of Mašniyalli which was also being discussed in the body of the letter.

570 See KBo 28.23 (ÄHK 43) obv. 30–43 for Ramses' reaction, and rev. 76–79 for the promise of gifts.

571 See Edel, *Die ägyptisch-hethitische Korrespondenz*, vol. 2, 300.

Table 28: The First Hittite-Egyptian Royal Marriage (34th year of Ramses II)

Recipient	Item	Amount
Ḫattušili and Puduḫepa	Gold	1779 shekels
"	Silver	17 shekels
"	hawk(?) statues of precious stone	2
"	rings of precious stone	10
"	various fine linens	207
"	ebony logs	40
"	*kukubu*-containers of excellent eye medication	5
"	reeds of excellent eye medication	20
Children of Hittite King and Queen	Gold	1779 shekels
"	various fine linens	207
"	ebony logs	40
"	ebony chest	1

Combining the two halves of the gift attested in the correspondence surrounding the first Hittite-Egyption royal marriage gives a total of:

Gifts Received by the Hittites from the First Hittite-Egyptian Royal Marriage

Gold:	3558 (Babylonian) shekels (= 59 minas, 18 shekels)
Silver:	17 shekels
Textiles:	414 textiles
Stone and ivory:	2 stone statues, 10 stone rings
Other:	80 logs of ebony, 1 ebony chest, 25 containers of eye medications

As can be seen, the gifts of the Marriage Correspondence were at least twice as large as those of the Eternal Treaty. This goes to show how the two diplomatic interactions were valued by the ancient parties involved: the innovative treaty establishing a *modus vivendi* between equals, stimulated a respectable exchange of wealth; but a diplomatic marriage, built on the time-honored practice of exchanging a bride for a dowry, garnered a much larger gift.

6.3 Tribute from Hittite Vassals

Another source of wealth with political connotations comes from tribute imposed on international Hittite vassals. Yet, although one might expect a rich corpus of texts regulating the flow of economic obligations to the Hittite court, treaties listing tribute from vassals are surprisingly rare in the Hittite corpus.[572] Most treaties instead concern mutual military support, either defensive or offensive. Vassal contributions were usually described in terms of manpower and loyalty, especially reporting of sedition and extradition of fugitives, but rarely required a financial contribution.[573] In the treaties preserved, only two Hittite vassals stand out for being required to send gold: Ugarit and Amurru.[574]

6.3.1 Tribute from Ugarit

Ugarit stands among the most well-documented vassals of the Hittites. This is undoubtedly due in part to the importance of the Levantine city-state within the empire, but also not the least because the palace of the city of Ugarit has been discovered, excavated, and well published and discussed. The importance of Ugarit's contribution to understanding the Hittite vassal system cannot be overstated, since the city's palace archives provide a view on the vassal relationship from the perspective of the lesser partner. What is revealed is a relationship more fluid and negotiable than the stipulations of the treaties would suggest.

---

572 See the overview of these treaties in Elena Devecchi, "The Governance of Subordinated Countries," in *Handbook of the Hittite Empire. Power Structures*, ed. Stefano de Martino. Empires through the Ages in Global Perspective 1 (Oldenbourg: De Gruyter, 2022), 287–95.

573 For a schematic overview of such treaties, see "La contribution financière" in Guy Kestemont, *Diplomatique et droit international en asie occidentale (1600–1200 av. J.C.)*. PIOL 9 (Louvain: Institut orientaliste, 1974), 353–60.

574 Two other vassals are known to have been levied gold, but the amounts are broken away. A treaty between Šuppiluliuma I and Tette of Nuhašše contains a clause concerning tribute (presumably gold) "weighed in the Hittite fashion" (KBo 1.4 obv. ii 1–3. Edition: Giuseppe del Monte, *Il trattato fra Muršili II di Ḫattuša e Niqmepa' di Ugarit*. OrAntColl. 18 [Rome: Centro per le antichita e la storia dell'arte del Vicino Oriente, 1986], 142–55. English translation: Gary Beckman, *Hittite Diplomatic Texts*. 2 ed. WAW 7 [Atlanta: Society of Biblical Literature, 1999], 54–58). The land of Alašiya, located on or possibly comprising the island of Cyprus, was also tasked in the time of Tudḫaliya IV and Šuppiluliuma II with delivering a fixed amount of gold, as well as a very large amount of copper (4 talents = 240 mina) and a token amount of grain, to Ḫattuša to be distributed to various deities. Again, the amounts of gold are broken away, so there is no way to directly compare the tribute to the KASKAL series (estimating the exchange rate of copper would be difficult). The document listing the tribute, KBo 12.38+, is not a treaty or letter, but rather a cuneiform copy of a monumental inscription, and has its own complicated history: see *editio princeps* in Hans Güterbock, "The Hittite Conquest of Cyprus Reconsidered," JNES 26 (1967): 73–81; also Stefano de Martino, "Relations Between Ḫatti and Alašiya, According to Textual and Archaeological Evidence," in *Ḫattuša–Boğazköy. Das Hethiterreich im Spannungsfeld des Alten Orients. 6. Internationales Colloquium der Deutschen Orient-Gesellschaft, 22–24 März 2006 in Würzburg*, edited by Gernot Wilhelm, 247–63. CDOG 6 (Wiesbaden: Harrassowitz, 2008). The "earmarking" of tribute for specific gods in this text is also unprecedented, and might indicate a non-standard political relationship between Ḫatti and Cyprus. Fragments of a treaty between Šuppiluliama II and Alašiya (CTH 141) confirm the relationship, but are too broken to clarify the matter; see the edition of Matteo Vigo, "'Tradurre e non tradire' il problema delle integrazioni. Il caso di KBo XII 39," in *Traduzioni di tradizioni e tradizioni di traduzione. Atti del quarto incontro "Orientalisti" (Pavia, 19–21 aprile 2007)*, eds. Benedetta Bellucci, Elio Jucci, Alfredo Rizza, Bianca Maria Tomassini Pieri (Milan: Qu.A.S.A.R S.r.l., 2008), 191–248.

Even without the perspective afforded by the Ugarit archives, it is clear from the evidence in the Hittite chancery at Hattuša that the city-state occupied a special place in the system of vassals. Along with Amurru, its neighbor to the south, Ugarit elected more or less voluntarily to come under Hittite rule during Šuppiluliuma's Great Syrian War, and for its compliance was rewarded with territory and favor.[575] Also like Amurru, it retained its native dynasty until the end, and intermarried extensively with the Hittite royal family. In economic terms, Ugarit took advantage of its position on the coast to become a center of maritime trade in the northern Levant. Many documents recovered from the site show a deep involvement by the ruling family in trade agreements and disputes, including the famous edict concerning the Hittite merchants of Ura,[576] and the provisioning of grain to Ḫattuša.[577] Reflecting its commercial importance to the Hittites, Ugarit was at least in one case granted the privilege of contributing gold instead of troops to a campaign (see below). The impression given is Ugarit as a wealthy vassal kingdom trading in luxury goods, sheltered from the border conflicts that plagued the Hittite Empire, and profiting handsomely from the protection of its Hittite overlord – a captive maritime trading power serving a continental master.

As memories of Šuppiluliuma's conquest faded, there is evidence that Ugarit became less content with its tributary status to Ḫatti. Prior to the (re)assertion of Hittite power in Syria, Ugarit was nominally under the protection of Egypt, though able to maintain an independent existence due to the distance between the two countries.[578] Ugarit was removed from Egypt's influence with the coming of the Hittites and bound to a formal relationship and heavy tribute with its new overlord. This change in status was compensated for by expansion of Ugaritic territory to the east at the expense of the kingdoms of Mukiš, Nuhašši, and Niya.[579] When a portion of Ugarit's territory was removed by Muršili II, the tribute was reduced. But by the time of Ḫattušili III and Tudḫaliya IV it seems even the lighter tribute was resented, and the Hittites had a recurring problem of securing tribute payments.

A series of four documents traces the evolution of the status of Ugarit. The first three concern the yearly tribute: its establishment by Šuppiluliuma I, a voluntary augmentation of the amount by Ugarit, and a downwards revision by Muršili II. The fourth

575 For a general overview of Ugarit's history, see Itamar Singer, "A Political History of Ugarit," in *Handbook of Ugaritic Studies*, ed. Willfred G. E. Watson, Nicolas Wyatt (Leiden: Brill, 1999), 603–733. See also Elena Devecchi, "A Reluctant Servant: Ugarit under Foreign Rule during the Late Bronze Age," in *A Stranger in the House – The Crossroads III: Proceedings of an International Conference on Foreigners in Ancient Egyptian and Near Eastern Societies of the Bronze Age Held in Prague, September 10–13, 2018*, eds. Jana Mynářová, Marwan Kilani, Sergio Alivernini (Prague: Charles University, 2019), 121–36.

576 CTH 93 (RS 17.130, 17.461, 18.003, 34.179). Edition: RS 17.130 = Nougayrol, PRU IV, 103–5; RS 17.461 = *ibid.*, 154; RS 18.003 = *ibid.*, 102; RS 34.179 = Pierre Bordrueil and Daniel Arnaud, *Une bibliothèque au sud de la ville. Les textes de la 34ᵉ campagne (1973).* RSOu. 7 (Paris: Éditions Recherche sur les civilisations, 1991), 15. English translation: Beckman, *Hittite Diplomatic Texts*, 177.

577 RS 20.212. Edition: Nougayrol, Ugaritica V, 105–7.

578 Singer, "A Political History of Ugarit," 621–27.

579 Confirmed in the treaty between Šuppiluliuma I and Niqmaddu II (CTH 46). Edition: Nougayrol, *PRU IV*, 51–52. English translation: Beckman, *Hittite Diplomatic Texts*, 34–36.

document is a letter sharing formal characteristics with a treaty or legal case, in which Tudḫaliya IV accepts a payment in lieu of Ugarit's participation in a war against Assyria. This arrangement of contributing gold instead of troops is unparalleled in the Hittite corpus. But while the letter confirms Ugarit's place as a commercial power in the Hittite Empire, it is not necessarily proof of an economic exceptionalism for the city. In light of Ugarit's lukewarm loyalty, increasingly courted by Assyria and Egypt, and given Tudḫaliya's abandonment by another vassal at the battlefield of Niḫriya, the Hittites might have specifically requested hard cash instead of unreliable troops from Ugarit, reasoning that at least gold cannot flee if the tide of battle turns.

On the eve of the Hittite Empire's fall and the end of the Bronze Age, letters show that Ugarit needed constant encouragement to fulfill their yearly obligations to the Hittite court. A veritable subgenre of complaints from the Hittite overlords has been discovered in Ugarit: cheap or unsatisfactory gifts; failure to visit the Hittite court for one, even two years; failure to visit the queen when visiting the king; snubbing particular officials with unsatisfactory gifts; delays in shipping grain to Ḫattuša – all in spite of the clear stipulations in the treaties.[580] More worrisome was Ugarit's solicitation of gifts from foreign powers. The city is found resuming trade and political ties with Egypt, harking back to their days of semi-independence, and requesting and receiving gifts from the Pharaoh for the restoration of a temple of Baʿal.[581] The quantities for the restoration are impressive: 102 linen garments, 50 logs of ebony, 1000 tiles (*lēḫu*^{MEŠ}) of colored stone, 800 whips (whisks?), 1200 cubits of rope, and various other items. The Ugaritic king even requested Egyptian sculptors be sent to carve a statue of the Pharaoh to be placed in front of the image of Baʿal in recognition of the donation (which, probably sensing the effrontery this would cause towards Ugarit's Hittite overlords, the Egyptian king politely declined).[582] The political implications of these gifts are more important than their amount. They show Ugarit negotiating for independence well before the Hittite Kingdom collapsed, and seeking at the very least normalized relations with other great powers, and perhaps even a return to the Egyptian protection. The gifts also confirm that luxury goods could be freighted with political importance in excess of their material value.

The evolution of Ugarit's yearly tribute obligations, with tabulation and commentary, are now presented below. These documents (along with parallels from Amurru, Cyprus, and Emar) provide a glimpse into the yearly income of the Hittite palace, and deepen understanding of the wealth of the KASKAL main text by permitting its conversion into a period of time.

---

580 For the citation, discussion, and scholarly apparatus of the specific letters (some of which have contested translations) see Singer, "A Political History of Ugarit," 693–96; 707–19.

581 RS 88.2158. Edition: Sylvie Lackenbacher, "Une lettre d'Égypte (nº 1)," in *Études ougaritiques: I. Travaux 1985–1995*, eds. Marguerite Yon, Daniel Arnaud. RSOu. 14 (Paris: Éditions recherche sur les civilisations, 2001), 239–48. Earlier discussed in Sylvie Lackenbacher, "Une correspondance entre l'administration du pharaon Merneptah et le roi d'Ougarit," in *Le Pays d'Ougarit autour de 1200 av. J.-C.: Historie et archéologie. Actes du Colloque International; Paris, 28 juin-1er juillet 1993*, eds. Marguerite Yon, Maurice Sznycer, Pierre Bordreuil. RSOu. 11 (Paris: Éditions recherche sur les civilisations, 1995), 77–83.

582 RS 88.2158 obv. 10′–16′.

6.3.1.1 Edict of Šuppiluliuma I concerning Tribute of Ugarit (CTH 47)[583]

Table 29: Edict of Šuppiluliuma I concerning Tribute of Ugarit (CTH 47)

Recipient	Durable Goods	Textiles
King	12 minas, 20 great (=Hittite) shekels of gold 1 gold cup (1 mina)	4 linen cloths 1 large linen cloth 500 shekels blue-purple wool 500 shekels red-purple wool
Queen	1 gold cup (30 shekels)	1 linen cloth 100 shekels blue-purple wool 100 shekels red-purple wool
LÚ*tartenu* (crown prince)	1 gold cup (30 shekels)	1 linen cloth 100 shekels blue-purple wool 100 shekels red-purple wool
LÚ*tuppalanuri* (chief scribe)	1 gold cup (30 shekels)	1 linen cloth 100 shekels blue-purple wool 100 shekels red-purple wool
LÚ*ḫuburtanuri*	1 gold cup (30 shekels)	1 linen cloth 100 shekels blue-purple wool 100 shekels red-purple wool
LÚ*ḫuburtanuri šanû* (2nd *ḫuburtanuri*)	1 gold cup (30 shekels)	1 linen cloth 100 shekels blue-purple wool 100 shekels red-purple wool
LÚSUKKAL (vizier)	-	1 linen cloth 100 shekels blue-purple wool 100 shekels red-purple wool
LÚ*antubšalli*	1 gold cup (30 shekels)	1 linen cloth 100 shekels blue-purple wool 100 shekels red-purple wool

CTH 47, a single document present in multiple copies, was appended to the first Hittite treaty with Ugarit[584] and establishes the details of Ugarit's tribute to the Hittite court. It is stipulated that Ugarit is not obligated to provide any other gifts. As clarified in the subsequent Edict of Muršili II (CTH 65), this was probably designed to prevent visiting Hittite dignitaries from demanding extra gifts at the Ugaritic court. Additionally, the king of Ugarit is required to visit Ḫattuša once a year.

The tribute list shows structural parallels with the Egyptian diplomatic gifts discussed in the previous sections, specifically that the goods are not presented as a lump

583 Edition: Nougayrol, PRU IV, 40–44. English translation: Beckman, *Hittite Diplomatic Texts*, 166–67. French translation: Lackenbacher, *Textes akkadiens d'Ugarit*, 73–75 (written as CTH 46).

584 Beckman, *Hittite Diplomatic Texts*, 34–36.

sum to the Hittite court, but rather designated for distribution to individual officials. Note that even the weights of the cups are roughly the same: 30 Hittite shekels would weigh about 45 Babylonian shekels, which is very close to the 48 shekel "standard diplomatic cup" given in the Egyptian gifts of the previous section. Besides recognizing and confirming the idealized composition of power in the Hittite court, the gifts also open a line of communication between the king of Ugarit and the Hittite ministers who held so much power over his state.[585] The ratios of gifts are also the same as those seen in the Egyptian gifts: roughly one half goes to the king and queen, and the other half is divided among everyone else.

Total Yearly Tribute of Ugarit under Šuppiluliuma I

Gold:	28 minas gold (14¼ minas to royal couple, 13¾ minas to officials)[586]
Textiles:	12 textiles
Raw Materials:	2400 shekels dyed wool (1200 to royal couple, 1200 to officials)

6.3.1.2 Inventory of (Revised) Ugaritic Tribute (CTH 48)[587]

Table 30: Inventory of (Revised) Ugaritic Tribute (CTH 48)

Recipient	Additional Durable Goods	Additional Textiles
[King]	(same gold, plus) 1 gold cup (weighing 50 shekels, instead of 40)	(unchanged)
[Queen]	(same gold cup, plus) 1 silver cup (30 shekels)	2 linen cloths, 400 shekels of dyed wool (= double amount)
[LÚ*tartenu*] (crown prince)	(same gold cup, plus) 1 silver cup (30 shekels)	2 linen cloths, 400 shekels of dyed wool (= double amount)
LÚ*tuppanuri*[588] (chief scribe)	(same gold cup, plus) 1 silver cup (30 shekels)	(unchanged)
[LÚ*ḫ*]*uburtanuri*	(same gold cup, plus) 1 silver cup (30 shekels)	(unchanged)
LÚ*ḫuburtanuri*	(same gold cup, plus) 1 silver cup (30 shekels)	(unchanged)
LÚSUKKAL (vizier)	1 silver cup (30 shekels) (new)	(unchanged)

585 The LÚ*tuppalanuri* 'Chief of Scribes' in particular seemed to have an outsized influence on Ugarit's finance, controlling as he did the tolls of the caravans from Egypt through Hittite Syria (Singer, "A Political History of Ugarit," 708). The king of Ugarit complains in at least one case that the caravans were avoiding his state, instead traveling through inner Syria (*ibid.*, 694). Perhaps this is why the LÚ*tuppalunuri* was snubbed with substandard gifts on at least two occasions.

586 All shekels are assumed to be "great" (= Hittite) shekels.

587 Edition: Nougayrol, PRU IV, 47–48. English translation: Beckman, *Hittite Diplomatic Texts*, 168. French translation: Lackenbacher, *Textes akkadiens d'Ugarit*, 75–76.

588 A variant spelling of *tuppalanuri*, see Nougayrol, PRU IV, 42 fn. 1.

LÚEN É-*ti abusi* ('lord of the storehouse' = *andubšalli?*)[589]	(same gold cup, plus) 1 silver cup (30 shekels)	(unchanged)
LÚGAL LÚ.MEŠ*qardabbi* (commander of the charioteers)	1 silver cup (30 shekels) (new)	1 linen cloth, 200 shekels of dyed wool (new)

In CTH 48, an internal document from Ugarit from some period after the first treaty with Šuppiluliuma I but before the revision by Muršili II, one finds the curious case of Ugarit voluntarily exceeding its treaty obligations. This is strong support for an argument by Mario Liverani that the origins of tribute lay in voluntary gifts, designed to court favor, that become habitual and eventually mandatory.[590] The mandatory nature of the extra gifts will be confirmed in the next text from the Ugarit tribute dossier, where Muršili II levies a reduced tribute composed not from a return to the original, but by picking and choosing from among the original and voluntary contributions.

The distribution of the extra gifts suggests that Ugarit had a different reading of the power structure of the Hittite court than Ḫattuša. The LÚSUKKAL (vizier) receives an a silver cup like the rest of the high officials, even though he was not entitled to a gold cup in the original treaty. A new official, the LÚGAL LÚ.MEŠ*kartappī* (commander of the charioteers), receives gifts equal to the vizier despite not being mentioned in the first treaty at all. Finally, the queen and the LÚ*tardennu* (crown prince) are given double amounts of textiles, elevating them above the other court officials, who were previously their equals in received gifts.

Total Yearly Revised Tribute of Ugarit

Gold:	28¼ minas gold (14½ minas to royal couple, 13¾ minas to officials)
Silver:	6 minas silver (¾ mina to queen, 5¼ minas to officials)
Textiles:	15 textiles
Raw Materials:	3000 shekels dyed wool (1400 to royal couple, 1600 to officials)

589 See Nougayrol, PRU IV, 79 who only notes that the *BĒL* É*ABŪSI* (= LÚEN É*ti* *abūsi*) has replaced the *andubšalli*. The two titles are equated by Manfried Dietrich and Oswald Loretz, "Der Vertrag zwischen Šuppiluliuma und Niqmaddu: Eine philologische und kulturhistorische Studie," WO 3 (1964–66), 240.

590 Mario Liverani, *Prestige and Interest* (Padova: sargon srl, 1990), 267–73. It should be noted that Liverani on pp. 269–70 followed the original translation of Nougayrol, PRU IV, 41, of the *Edict of Šuppiluliuma concerning the Tribute of Ugarit (CTH 47)*, discussed above, leading him to transliterate 12 MA.NA 20 GÍN KÙ.SI$_{22}$MEŠ 20 *at-ru* (RS 17.227 obv. 21), translated as "12 minas and 20 shekels of gold – the 20 being a supplement (*atru*)." Instead, with Beckman, *Hittite Diplomatic Texts*, 185 note 3, the 20 is probably a *Glossenkeil*, indicating the shekels are "great" shekels, i.e., Hittite shekels (corresponding to Ugaritic *ṯql kbd* 'heavy shekel': see Dietrich and Loretz, "Vertrag zwischen Šuppiluliuma und Niqmaddu," 210).

6.3.1.3 Edict of Muršili II concerning Tribute of Ugarit (CTH 65)[591]

Although also present in multiple copies, the edict classified under CTH 65 is preserved in a fragmentary state, with the beginning of the tribute list being damaged. In the preamble, Muršili recounts how the service of the king of Šiyannu, formerly a vassal of the king of Ugarit, has been transferred to the Hittite viceroy at Carchemish. Niqmepa complains that his land has been reduced to two-thirds its former size and now the yearly tribute is too heavy. Muršili agrees, and the remainder of the text concerns the adjusted amount of tribute. What is interesting from the historical perspective is that the result is not a reduction of the gifts back to the original treaty (perhaps that was still too burdensome), but instead a hybrid list incorporating the voluntary gifts found in the internal Ugaritic documents. Some of the original gifts (the gold cups) are discarded from the treaty in favor of the voluntary gifts (silver cups), and some recipients keep their gains (the vizier keeps his silver cup, though his wool allotment is reduced by half), whereas others lose their status as gift recipients (the commander of the chariots is not mentioned at all).

Enough figures can be recovered from the broken text to reconstruct a trend. The king probably receives the same amount of gold ingots given the mention of 500 Hittite shekels of gold, which is equal to the 12½ minas originally prescribed.[592] One might imagine he kept his 40-shekel gold cup too. The gifts of the queen and crown prince are broken away (it will be assumed here that they were returned to a state of equality with those of the other officials). For the palace officials, insofar as they are preserved, the gold cups of the original treaty have been dropped, and the silver cups are now mandatory. The list ends with the vizier, so that the chief of the chariots is not mentioned. Muršili affirms that the king of Ugarit does not have to provide for other officials, saying that he may give gifts to Hittite nobles who come to Ugarit "if it pleases him" (*ša ḫadê libbi*) but it is not an obligation (*lā rikiltu šūtu*).[593]

Revised Total Yearly Tribute of Ugarit under Muršili II

Gold:	13½ minas gold (to king)
Silver:	5¼ minas silver (¾ mina to queen, 4½ minas to officials)
Textiles:	12 textiles
Raw Materials:	2300 shekels dyed wool (1200 to royal couple, 1100 to officials)

If these numbers are accurate, then given the reduction in gold Ugarit is probably paying considerably less than two-thirds of its original tribute obligations, suggesting a weakening grip of Hittite power in Syria after the terror of Šuppiluliuma's conquests had passed.

591 Edition: Nougayrol, PRU IV, 80–83. English translation: Beckman, *Hittite Diplomatic Texts*, 175–76. French translation: Lackenbacher, *Textes akkadiens d'Ugarit*, 135–37.

592 Following Beckman, *Hittite Diplomatic Texts*, 175.

593 RS 17.382+380 rev. 52–59.

6.3.1.4 Edict of Tudḫaliya IV Releasing Ammištamru II of Ugarit from Participation in War with Assyria (CTH 108)[594]

CTH 108 comprises a short statement written in the presence of the viceroy of Carchemish, wherein Tudḫaliya IV states that he does not require Ammištamru II of Ugarit to bring troops and chariots to his aid, and that he will not bring a suit against the king of Ugarit for this after the war is finished. Then it is declared that the king of Ugarit has paid 50 minas of gold in ten shipments to Tudḫaliya (RS 17.59 rev. 1–3), which, by the assessment of Muršili II, would be the equivalent to just under four years worth of gold tribute.

6.3.2 Tribute from Amurru

Amurru also occupied a special place in the constellation of Hittite vassals, having voluntarily sought Hittite vassalage as a way of breaking away from Egypt, and as a reward being permitted to maintain a native dynasty until the end. Unfortunately, the palace archives of Amurru have not been discovered, so its history can only be reconstructed from texts preserved in Ḫattuša, Egypt, and Ugarit. Two treaties from the archives of Ḫattuša stand out for reconstructing its economic relations with Ḫatti. The first, between Šuppiluliuma I and Aziru of Amurru (CTH 49),[595] sets a tribute of "300 shekels [gold, refined], first-class, and good," weighed in the Hittite manner, to be delivered each year to Ḫatti.[596] A yearly appearance at the Hittite court in Ḫattuša is also required. The same amount is set in a later treaty between Muršili II and Tuppi-Teššub of Amurru (CTH 62): "300 shekels gold, refined and first-class."[597] Amurru was not required to present other diplomatic gifts like cups and textiles to other officials in the Hittite court. This is perhaps because Amurru already hosted a number of Hittite officials directly: the treaty stipulates that the king is to graciously provide for nobles and soldiers garrisoned in his territory, which must have given the king of Amurru opportunities to make connections with important Hittite officials.[598] Any further details of Hittite-Amurru tribute will have to wait until the discovery of Amurru's palace archives.

Total Yearly Tribute of Amurru

Gold:	300 Hittite shekels (7.5 mina) gold

594 RS 17.59. Edition: Nougayrol, PRU IV, 150–51. English translation: Beckman, *Hittite Diplomatic Texts*, 182–83. French translation: Lackenbacher, *Textes akkadiens d'Ugarit*, 101–2.

595 Edition: del Monte, *Il trattato fra Muršili II*, 116–41. English translation: Beckman, *Hittite Diplomatic Texts*, 36–41. See now the recent Italian translation: Elena Devecchi, *Trattati internazionali ittiti*. TVOA 4 (Brescia: Paideia, 2015), 203–12.

596 KBo 10.12+, obv. 9–13 (Hittite version). KUB 3.19 + 48.71, obv. 9′–10′ (Akkadian version).

597 KBo 50.26(+), obv. 9–12 (Hittite version). KUB 3.14, obv. 9–11. Edition: del Monte, *Il trattato fra Muršili II*, 156–77. English translation: Beckman, *Hittite Diplomatic Texts*, 59–64. Italian translation: Devecchi, *Trattati internazionali ittiti*, 212–20.

598 KBo 5.9, obv. ii 30′–37′.

6.3.3 Tribute from Emar

Emar (modern Tell Meskene) was an economically important city-state with its native dynasty/local government, under the suzerainty of the viceroy of Carchemish, during the Hittite New Kingdom.[599] Its archives were discovered in the 1970's and excavated and published by a team of French archaeologists.[600] A pair of tablets from the archives, published as *Texte 14* and *Texte 15* in Daniel Arnaud, *Textes syriens de l'âge du Bronze récent*,[601] record the collection of a large amount of gold and silver, apparently as a one-time levy of tax intended for the "king."

TBR 14: 19–24

19 *i-nu-ma ana a-ra-*[*na* LUGAL]
20 3 SIG$_7$ KÙ.BABBAR 7 *me-tì* KÙ.SI$_{22}$
21 URU^{KI} *i-ri-šu*
22 ^{KI}*er-ṣe-tu ù* É$^{\text{ḪI.A}}$
23 *a-na* KÙ.BABBAR *ù* KÙ.SI$_{22}$
24 *id-di-nu-ma*
25 KÙ.BABBAR *ù* KÙ.SI$_{22}$ *a-na a-ra-na* LUGAL
26 *id-di-nu*

> When for the *tribu*[*te*[602] of the king] they asked the city for 30,000 (shekels of) silver and 700 (shekels of) gold, they sold *ruined houses*[603] and houses for silver and gold and gave the silver and gold for the *tribute* of the king.

---

599 For the relationship of Emar to the territorial states, see *The City of Emar among the Late Bronze Age Empires: History, Landscape, and Society (Proceedings of the Konstanz Emar Conference, 25.–26.04.2006)*, eds. Lorenzo d'Alfonso, Yoram Cohen, Dietrich Sürenhagen. AOAT 349 (Münster: Ugarit-Verlag, 2008).

600 The results of the original excavations are published in Daniel Arnaud, *Recherches au Pays d'Aštata: Emar.* Emar VI (Paris: Editions Recherches sur les Civilisations, 1985–87).

601 Daniel Arnaud, *Textes syriens de l'âge du Bronze recent.* AulaOr. Suppl. 1 (Barcelona: Editorial AUSA, 1991).

602 For *arana* as a Hurrian term meaning "gift, tribute," see Aaron Skaist, "A Hurrian Term at Emar," in *General Studies and Excavations at Nuzi 10/2*, eds. David I. Owen, Gernot Wilhelm. SCCNH 9 (Bethesda, Md.: CDL Press, 1998), 169–71. Skaist's interpretation has received widespread acceptance: see bibliography *s.v. arana* in Thomas Richter, *Bibliographisches Glossar des Hurritischen* (Wiesbaden: Harrassowitz, 2012), 43. Compare earlier translation "*trésor*," from a conjectured extended sense of Akk. *arānu* 'chest, cashbox, coffin', given in Arnaud, *Textes syriens de l'âge du Bronze recent*, 16. Cf. Masamichi Yamada, "The Arana Documents from Emar Revisted," *Orient* 52 (2017): 121–33, who interprets Arana as the name of an Emariote king, while acknowledging (p. 124 fn. 12, with literature) the popularity of Skaist's interpretation.

603 For the frequent appearance of ^{KI}*erṣetu*, or *kirṣitu*, a type of old or ruined house, among the real estate transactions at Emar, see Lena Fijałkowska, "Politics and Socials Needs in 2nd Millennium Syrian Sale Formularies: the Case of Emar," in *Sale and Community Documents from the Ancient World. Individuals' Autonomy and State Interference in the Ancient World. Proceedings of a Colloquium supported by the University of Szeged. Budapest 5-8.10.2012, Trieste*, ed. Éva Jakab, (Trieste: EUT Edizioni Università di Trieste, 2015), 36, with *ibid.* fn. 34 for previous literature on discussion and translation of the term.

TBR 15: 5′–9′ (cf. ASJ 12 2, Emar VI 153)[604]

[4′ … 3 SIG$_7$ KÙ.BABBAR]
5′ 2 *li-mi* KÙ.SI$_{22}$ ^{URU}*e-mar*^{KI}
6′ *i-ri-šu-ma* DU$_6$-*la*$^{!ḪI.A}$ A.ŠÀ$^{ḪI.[A]}$
7′ *a-na* KÙ.BABBAR KÙ.SI$_{22}$ *id-di-nu-ma*
8′ KÙ.BABBAR KÙ.SI$_{22}$ *a-na-ra-na*[605] *ub-lu*

> … they asked Emar for [30,000 (shekels of) silver and] 2,000 (shekels of) gold and they sold ruin mounds and field[s] for silver and gold and brought the silver and gold for the *tribute*.

The dating of the texts and identity of the king are disputed. Initial scholarship considered the ultimate recipient to be the Hittite viceroy at Carchemish.[606] Later analysis has pushed the dating of the texts back to an earlier period, possibly predating Hittite hegemony of the region, and hence suggesting that the recipient was a Mittanian king.[607] Thus, although TBR 14 and TBR 15 (and related texts) are not direct comparisons to the Ugarit and Amurru tribute, since there is no possibility in either scenario that any part of the tax ended up directly in Ḫattuša's coffers, the *arana* levies of Emar are useful points of indirect comparison for wealth in Late Bronze Age. In this case, the 500 minas silver, 11⅔ minas of gold and 500 minas silver, 33⅓ minas of gold, respectively, demonstrate what the citizenry of a wealthy Syrian city-state could come up with when pressed. That such one-off events, the historical context of which is still murky, but which may have involved compulsion or extortion by a foreign power, still

604 Notwithstanding the interpretation of *arana* as a personal name, see Masamichi Yamada, "'ARANA-Documents' from Emar," *Orient* 29 (1993): 140–42, for the philological reconstruction of TBR 15, ASJ 12 2, and Emar VI 153.

605 Arnaud, *Textes syriens*, 44: "Ecriture en sandhi pour *a-na a-ra-na*."

606 Arnaud, *op. cit.*, 16 ("sans aucun doute du roi de Karkamis"). Gary Beckman, "Hittite Provincial Administration in Anatolia and Syria: the View from Maşat and Emar," in *Atti del II Congresso Internazionale di Hittitologie*, eds. Onofrio Carruba, Mauro Giorgieri, Clelia Mora. StMed. 9 (Pavia: Gianni Iuculano Editore, 1995), 27, fn. 51: "It is uncertain whether the lugal in this context refers to the King of Karkamiš or to the local monarch, but even in the later case such an enormous sum of precious metals was probably intended for the payment of the imperial tribute."

607 Aaron Skaist, "The Chronology of Legal Texts from Emar," ZA 88/1 (1998): 62: "It is against this historical background that we gain a better understanding of four Ninurta sales texts that are dated to *Irib*-IŠKUR and *Igmil-Dagan*, the immediate predecessors of *Limi-šarra*. The texts contain a clause noting that a large sum of silver and gold were to be paid *ana arana* LUGAL 'as tribute to the king'. … The king to whom all these payments were made was the king of Mittani." See also Fijałkowska, "Politics and Socials Needs," 30 fn. 8, for a proposed 14th century dating for TBR 14, ASJ 12 2, and Emar 153 – with due caution surrounding the dating of the Emar sales contract corpus cited by Fijałkowska, *loc. cit.*, fn. 6. For Mittanian influence and/or domination of Emar in this period, for which no incontrovertible evidence exists, see now John Tracy Thames, Jr., *The Politics of Ritual Change. The* zukru *Festival in the Political History of Late Bronze Age Emar*. HSM 65 (Leiden: Brill, 2020), 236–39, with lit., where the contribution of the *arana* texts to the question is discussed.

do not rise to the level of wealth observed in the KASKAL Main Text is further testimony to the latter's richness.[608]

6.4 Comparative Magnitude of the KASKAL Main Text

Comparing the totals extracted from the above documents and converting them to common units is no easy task. The differing levels of preservation, curt descriptions, and variety of materials are all complicating factors. Yet each of these have been more or less satisfactorily addressed: The levels of preservation were discussed in the individual subsections, where philological analysis revealed patterns in the texts that allow for educated restorations. For the brevity of descriptions, an argument was made that in large enough quantities the units of textiles and weights of gold are commensurable across texts. And for the variety of materials, the following section limits itself to presenting only the two most common categories, gold and textiles, with the caveat that the reader should return to the individual discussions to appreciate the true extent of the wealth. Admittedly this undervalues documents with a high diversity of durable goods, primarily the KASKAL Main Text, with the Egyptian marriage gifts a distant second. But in spite of this, a clear fact emerges in Figures 1 and 2 below: the KASKAL Main Text is unquestionably the largest single collection of movable wealth known in the Hittite world by gold and textiles alone, before even taking into consideration the hundreds, if not thousands, of *iron (ore)*, stone and ivory, and base metal objects. In gold ingots and objects alone, even using the conservative estimation of ¼ mina (10 Hittite shekels) per object, and discounting the 180 gold wires/rods of 8.1.A obv. ii 29′, the KASKAL text is equal to or greater than the marriage gifts of the Hittite-Egyptian royal marriage. It can be suspected that the true value of the durable goods in the KASKAL text was actually in line with its advantage in textiles – that is, over twice as much as the nearest comparandum.

608 The combined amount of 45 minas in gold is only three-quarters of what is reconstructed for the KASKAL Main Text. The combined 1000 minas of silver does not have a direct comparison since no bulk silver is recorded in the preserved portions of the KASKAL Main Text, but it can safely be assumed that the nearly 900 luxury textiles, the hundreds of silver, *iron (ore)*, stone, and ivory objects, and nearly 2000 copper and bronze objects reconstructed far exceeded that value in silver.

Table 31: Comparison of Gold in the KASKAL Main Text, Gifts, and Tribute[609]

Document	Amount of Gold	Notes
KASKAL Main Text	62 minas, 23 Hittite shekels	47 m. 13 Hitt. s. gold ingots, plus 61 gold objects (estimated at ¼ mina per object)[610]
Marriage Gifts	59 minas, 18 shekels	
Treaty Gifts	18 minas, 58 shekels	
Ugarit Tribute (Šuppiluliuma)	28 minas	yearly
Ugarit Tribute (Muršili)	13 minas, 20 Hittite shekels	yearly
Amurru Tribute	7 minas, 20 Hittite shekels	yearly

Figure 1: Comparison of Gold in KASKAL Main Text, Gifts, and Tribute

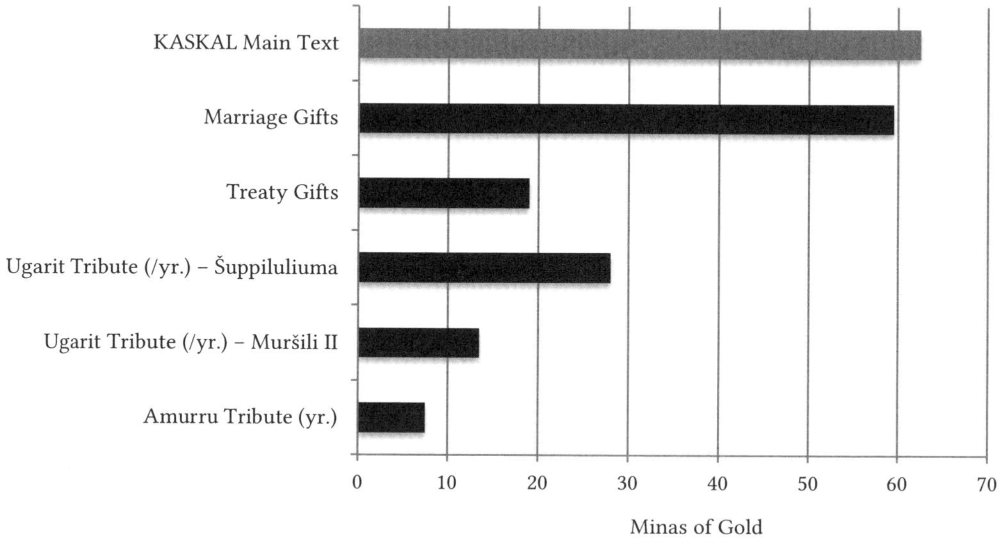

609 The tax levy of Emar is not included in the following tables and graphs because, as discussed above, it was not directly given to the central administration in Ḫattuša.

610 The 180 gold wires/rods are not included since it cannot be estimated how much they weighed. Even at 1 Hittite shekel a piece, they would add another 4.5 minas to the total.

Table 32: Comparison of Textiles in the KASKAL Main Text, Gifts, and Tribute

Document	Textile Pieces	Notes
KASKAL Main Text	853	plus 125 cubits of *parna*-cloth, 1 set of bed sheets, 1 leather curtain
Marriage Gifts	414	
Treaty Gifts	193	
Ugarit Tribute (Šuppiluliuma)	92	12 garments, plus 2400 shekels dyed wool (= raw material for 80 garments, at 3 minas wool per garment)
Ugarit Tribute (Muršili)	88	12 garments, plus 2300 shekels dyed wool (= 76 garments, at 3 minas wool/garment)
Amurru Tribute	0	

Figure 2: Comparison of Textiles in KASKAL Main Text, Gifts, and Tribute

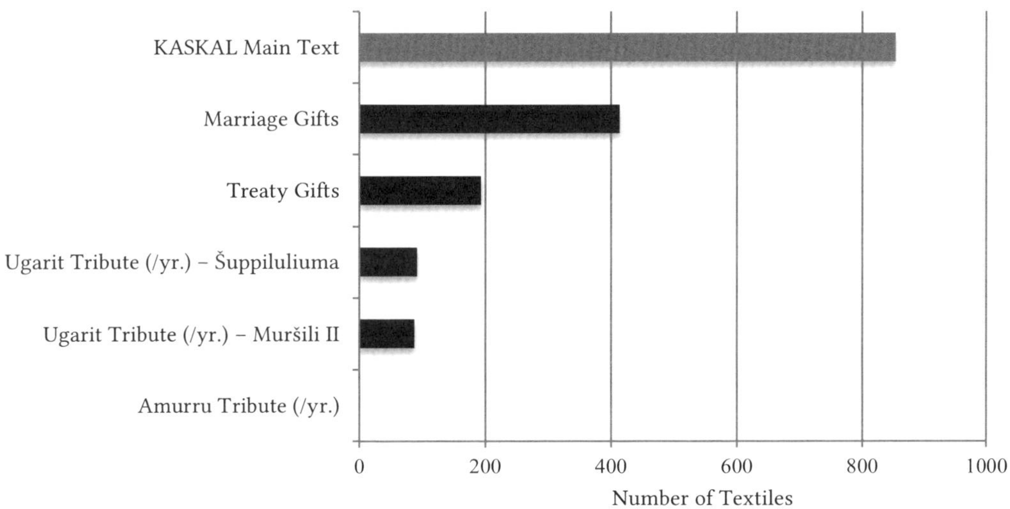

6.5 Conclusions on the Relative Value of KASKAL Main Text

So how great was the wealth contained in the KASKAL Main Text? In the time of Ḫattušili III and Tudḫaliya IV, it could have paid the bride-price of one, if not two daughters of Great Kings. It could have been used to secure six peace treaties with other great powers. It was equal to six years of revenue from the contemporary tribute of Ugarit and Amurru in gold, and ten years in textiles. The KASKAL Main Text contained enough in gold ingots alone (47.25 mina) to pay double the blood price (1400 Babylonian shekels = 23.3 mina) given by Ammištamru of Ugarit so that he could take vengeance on his disgraced wife, a sister of king Šaušgamuwa of Amurru and possible member of the Hittite royal family, whose actions nearly brought the two vassals to war in the reign of Tudḫaliya IV.[611]

It is certain that the wealth of the KASKAL text was designed to influence someone: the movement of so many finished goods from one place to another is unlikely without a transfer of ownership (or at the very least without redistribution at the new location). Returning to the discussion at the beginning of this chapter, political documents offer a way to gauge the relative impact of the wealth in the KASKAL Main Text by rephrasing it in terms of contemporary acts. But caution should also be used with this approach, as the opportunity costs revealed by the rephrasing are meaningless if the opportunities were not there. Royal marriage with another Great King may not have possible at the end of the Hittite Kingdom, and peace treaties might have been elusive. The Babylonians were too weak at that point to invest in, Aḫḫiyawa was too fractious, and Egypt already satisfied. If the wealth of the KASKAL Main Text could have secured long-term peace along the Assyrian border, Tudḫaliya IV would surely have considered it a bargain at twice the amount. The possibility of royal marriage will be discussed in the next chapter, but as will be seen, even with the new join of 8.1.E(A_3) suggesting a southern destation for the caravan, no firm conclusions are yet available.

611 RS 17.228, Nougayrol, *PRU IV*, 141–43. See also Itamar Singer, "A Concise History of Amurru," in *Amurru Akkadian: A Linguistic Study, vol. 2*, ed. Shlomo Izre'el (Atlanta: Scholars Press, 1991), 174–75. There is a question as to which wife of Ammištamru this document refers. Beckman (*Hittite Diplomatic Texts*, 180) was not convinced that this letter must be connected to the *Edict of Tudḫaliya IV concerning the Divorce of Ammištamru II of Ugarit (CTH 107).*

7. CONCLUDING REMARKS ON THE KASKAL MAIN TEXT

7.1 Remaining Questions

The outstanding question of the KASKAL Main Text is to where and for whom the luxury goods were meant to be transported. The incomplete preservation of the text, its telegraphic style, meager "metadata," the lack of references to any historical act or contingent event such as a festival, and the absence of an obvious destinations make a definitive answer impossible. This does not mean that a few final words cannot be said about the possible scenarios of use for the text.

The range of objects of the KASKAL Main Text span the luxury, sumptuary, and religious spheres – military items and raw materials are noticeably absent. The text was not the record of supplies for a military campaign. The contents are also far too numerous to be intended for an individual, or even a large group of individuals, meaning the items were probably not meant for immediate redistribution. Instead, an institutional context must be assumed. Since the goods are in motion, the transfer took place from one institution to another, meaning that many eyes and hands would have passed over the chests – including at the very least a person authorized to move them, the scribe(s) to record them, the workers to stack and arrange them, the teamsters to transport, and the soldiers to guard the caravan itself. Such an immense undertaking would require a level of royal initiative and supervision that must have exceeded the typical activities recorded in the Palace-Temple Administrative Corpus. Taking all of this into account, this final chapter of the case study will make a few brief concluding remarks on the time frame and direction of shipment for the text and will tentatively suggest based on the additional information added by the indirect join 8.1.E(A_3) that the items were intended to endow a palace, perhaps as part of a dowry.

7.2 Time Frame and Direction of Shipment for the KASKAL Main Text

The most important constraint on the possible uses of the KASKAL Main Text is the administrative time frame of the text and the direction of the shipments recorded within. The time frame covered by the KASKAL texts was left unstated by the scribe: it is not indicated whether the chests are being received or sent all at once, or if they are being accumulated and recorded in a ledger over a period of time. Here it is unfortunate that none of the actual precursor inventories to the KASKAL Main Text have been discovered, which might have given more insight on the origins of the items encountered in the text. The difficulty posed by the unspecified time frame is compounded by the fact that the direction of travel of the chests is not given: neither origins nor destinations are given for the chests (unless this information is lost in the colophons), meaning the only certainty is that the chests have, or will soon be, moved. Because they are not directly stated, the time frame and direction must be inferred.

It can be confidently stated that the wealth of the KASKAL Main Text is too large to be tribute or taxes, unless representing a total collected over many years and/or from multiple vassals. This was in fact the initial hypothesis presented by Silvin Košak, namely that the KASKAL texts were records of incoming shipments.[612] But, as was discussed already in *4.1 Introduction* at the beginning of the case study, the unity of the text observed by Siegelová makes the interpretation of the text as running account difficult. The additional fact that the tablets of the text are not duplicates, but show a concerted effort to produce a final version (as concluded in *4.7 Editorial Layers in the KASKAL Main Text*) further solidify the impression that a single economic act is recorded. Instead, it was suggested in the first chapter of the case study (*4.1. Introduction*) that the KASKAL Main Text recorded a single, large shipment of wealth originating in Ḫattuša: the present chapter section will make the argument for a short time frame and outgoing direction explicit.

7.2.1 Time Frame

The proposed solution to the administrative time frame is straightforward: the same lack of "metadata" in the Main Text which hinders the modern scholar in determining the text's time frame must also have limited the usefulness of the text as a long term reference tool for the ancient scribe. As discussed in *4.8 Conclusions on the Structure of the KASKAL Main Text*, the relative absence of quantitative measurements in the KASKAL Main Text meant that it was intended as an indexical rather than evaluative inventory, meaning its purpose was not to abstract the goods by value, but rather to establish their location, and presumably order, in a particular chest. Yet, although the contents of the chests can be considered organized, being indexed to the container within which they are recorded, the chests themselves are not. In the absence of a numbering system or other organizational scheme, the text is too vague to function as an information retrieval system without the help of the scribe who created it. The Main Text could therefore have only functioned as an *aide-mémoire* of the contents of the chest for use by its scribal author. Even so, unless the scribe kept a continuously updated mental concordance of the chests' physical locations with their order on the tablet, it must be deduced that the order of the text followed an implicit organizational scheme, which was probably the physical arrangement of the chests within the storeroom. This fact, and the relative ordering of the chest contents, limits the possible administrative time frame of the text, as any change in the physical disposition of the chests would require changes on the tablet to keep it up to date, and vice-versa.

It was suggested that the multiple editorial layers observed in the Main Text reflected a process of physical rearrangement and textual updating. Under these conditions, the final draft preserved in 8.1.B, F(+)G(+)H, and I, would only remain valid so long as the arrangement of the chests remained intact. This in turn implies that the chests were either destined for long-term storage – which is improbable, since there

612 Silvin Košak, *Hittite Inventory Texts (CTH 241–250)*. THeth. 10 (Heidelberg: Winter, 1982), 13.

would then be no reason to label the items as being "of the caravan"–, or, more likely, were soon to be shipped away, so that their organization in the storeroom would no longer matter. In short, the KASKAL Main Text is most logically interpreted as a packing list for a punctual event.

7.2.2 Direction of Shipment

The argument for the direction of shipment in the KASKAL Main Text is more complicated. As with the time frame, the direction of shipment is not made explicit in the text. As discussed in *4.2 Defining the KASKAL Series*, the only evidence that the chests are even being shipped at all comes from the KASKAL formula at the end of each paragraph, and these only confirm that the goods are in motion. The most common formula used, *ŠA* KASKAL(-*NI*) 'of the road', is completely ambiguous as to direction, and the few variant formulas also offer no help. In 8.1.E, the phrase *INA* KASKAL *NAŠÛ* 'carried on the road' appears three times can be interpreted as a stative 3 pl. (as is done in the text edition) or as an infinitive. If taken as a stative, then the goods are either in transit or already transporte, at least as of the draft of 8.1.E. If an infinitive, then it could be that the transportation was to still happen in the future (the Akkadian infinitive has a jussive force [GAG §150I*], but it is unclear if a bare infinitive would be used this way in a Hittite administrative text, rather than in a construction with *ANA*). The single occurrence of *ŠA* KASKAL EGIR-*anda* 'of the path, after(wards)' appearing in 8.1.K (rev. vi? 10′) was discussed under the KASKAL formula subheading in *4.5 Variation in the KASKAL Main Text: Systematic Differences*, but it was concluded that the EGIR-*anda* was a syntactically disjointed, late addition by the scribe and its meaning unclear. Thus, the entries of the KASKAL Main Text are grammatically ambiguous as to direction of shipment. Deciding the direction of shipment for the Main Text must instead be deduced from the text.

The first piece of evidence in favor of an outgoing shipment direction is the fact that there is no hint that the goods of the KASKAL Main Text changed ownership as part of the administrative process recording them. Quantification and summarization is a vital administrative step when transferring ownership of items between two parties. While a few items are precisely quantified in the KASKAL Main Text (such as the bars of gold and the cubits of *parna*-cloth), the overwhelming majority are not. This is in great contrast to, e.g., the Egyptian correspondences, and the vassal treaties discussed in *6. The Relative Value of the KASKAL Main Text*, where individual cups and quantities of wool, etc., were weighed out. Unless a final quantification was located on a broken portion of the text, or composed on a separate tablet, the indexical nature of the Main Text makes it improbable that the text recorded a recent change in ownership. Thus, the text was not a final ledger of a recently received shipment of diplomatic or tributary goods.

The second piece of evidence for an outgoing direction of shipment is an extension of the first, and comes from the almost complete absence of identifiers of personal or geographic origin in the text. For a final layer of documentation prior to transfer of ownership, who sent the items and where they are from are perhaps the only two vital pieces of information, even above quantification. The only personal names in the KASKAL Main Text come in A rev. vi 4′ and 5′, where they are attached to two items listed after the colophon. This *unicum* was interpreted in the *Commentary* to these lines in the edition in Vol. II as a gift or spontaneous personal contribution tacked on to the already packed and organized caravan, but the situation is unclear. The only items bearing a clear geographic origin in the KASKAL Main Text are the bars of gold in A obv. ii 25′ and 26′. It can be hypothesized that the gold uniquely retained its geographic origins due to the extreme value and rarity of the metal in the Hittite economy, which could only be acquired from foreign sources. The designation of a number of chests as KUR (URU)*Mizri* or *MIZRI/Ī*,[613] although initially promising, must be interpreted as referring to the style of construction of the containers, not their immediate origins. The geographic appellation appears immediately after the chests, occupying the same slot as the other adjectives describing the appearance of the chest. Moreover, no other country is mentioned in connection to the chests, and many chests have no geographic designation. It is possible, even probable, that the chests designated as KUR (URU)*Mizri* or *MIZRI/Ī* had their ultimate origins in the Egypt and were perhaps being reused, but there is no evidence that the items within these particular chests came from Egypt. The absence, then, of regular personal and geographic identifiers in the KASKAL Main Text stands in marked contrast to other texts where an incoming shipment can be assured, such as 2.7, where the geographic origin appears immediately after the description of the items, and the tribute texts edited under *3. Domestic Tribute* in Vol. II, where the contributing towns as a rule occupy the final line of the paragraph.

The complex editorial history of the KASKAL Main Text as a whole, and the indexical specificity with which the items of the chests are individually described and rearranged, means that the objects were assuredly physically present in Ḫattuša. Since there is no evidence for a recent change of ownership in the form of quantification or personal or geographical origin, and since the goods are in motion, then the chests of the text can only have an outgoing direction. This conclusion finds possible confirmation also in the editorial history of the individual entries. As discussed in *4.6.3 Nexus 3*, any items removed from a chest between drafts always came from the final lines of the paragraph, which, assuming the order of writing matched the order of packing, would represent the last items to be packed and hence the first to be unpacked if the chests were reopened for any adjustment to their contents.

7.3 Evidence for a Royal Marriage?

Having established the deep editoral hierarchy of the KASKAL Main Text, having calculated the economic magnitude of the contents, which appear to rival anything known from the Hittite world, and having argued for a punctual event with an outgoing direction of shipment, the significance of the indirect join 8.1.E(A_3) can now be properly discussed.

613 *MIZRI* 8.1.D rev. iv 7′//8.1.H rev. r. c. 5′//8.1.I rev. r. c. 4′. *MIZRĪ* 8.1.A obv. ii 17′, 20′. KUR *Mizri* 8.1.A obv. ii 8′; rev. v 21′, 23′. KUR URU*Mizri* 8.1.B rev. 3′. Note the duplicate lines *MIZRĪ* 8.1.A obv. ii 20′ = KUR URU*Mizri* 8.1.B rev. 3′.

8.1.E(A_3) (= KUB 60.112) is a modestly sized fragment from a multi-column tablet preserving an inventory of items in chests. The inventory portion of the text is followed by two non-inventory notes appearing respectively in the final column after the main text and on the tablet edge. The fragment was not included in either Košak's *Hittite Inventory Texts* or Siegelová's *Hethitische Verwaltungspraxis*, and was not published until 1990. The text initially received no comment in the *Inhaltsübersicht* of KUB 60, but was recognized as an inventory text in the review of the volume by Košak, who suggested a classification under CTH 241 "Inventories of Chests."[614] Later, Siegelová suggested that the fragment contained vocabulary appropriate for an *Inventarverzeichnis* of objects in storage.[615] A finer point can now be put to these classifications: 8.1.E(A_3) contains a KASKAL formula (obv. i 4′–5′), and moreover, not just any KASKAL formula, but the formula *ŠA* KASKAL-*NI* ... *INA* ..., which is attested elsewhere only in 8.1.E (A_1 obv. iii? 4′). Further examination shows that 8.1.E(A_3) is almost certainly an indirect join with 8.1.E(A_1)(+)E(A_2), sharing peculiarities in handwriting (e.g., the idiosyncratic SA$_5$ with extremely tall verticals in 8.1.E(A_3) obv. i 2′ and traces of the same 8.1.E(A_1) obv. iii 5′) and word-forms (the ligature *I+NA*, which is attested in 8.1.E(A_1) obv. iii? 4′ and 8.1.E(A_3) obv. i 5′ and nowhere else in the PTAC), and fitting the gap left by missing columns obv. i/rev. vi of 8.1.E. The fact that curious notes appear after the inventory portion of 8.1.E(A_3) only amplifies the preexisting impression that 8.1.E is the most unusual manuscript of the KASKAL Main Text (see discussions *6.4 Nexus 4* and *4.7.3 Three-column tablet: first draft*).

The join of E(A_3) to E(A_1)(+)E(A_2) provides little in the way of contents to the inventory section of the text, but adds two potentially important pieces of non-administrative information. The first is a note appearing after the final line of the inventory in E(A_3) rev. vi 4, written in a smaller, lightly impressed, and more cursive script, concerning a certain ᶠ*Hentī*, who is prohibited from eating under unclear conditions.[616] As discussed already by Stefano de Martino, the particular Ḫenti here should be identified not with the Early New Kingdom Ḫenti, wife of Šuppiluliuma I, but rather with a daughter of the royal family in the Late New Kingdom.[617] She is almost certainly the same Ḫenti who appears in 6.6 rev. 1′ ("Fragment of a List of Garments Handed Out to Members of the Royal Family," edited in Vol. II) among her siblings in a list of garments handed out to members of the royal family. There is no reason to assume that the note represents a reuse of 8.1.E(A_3) to record other information, since, as observed by Willemijn Waal in her study of Hittite diplomatics, unrelated or discontinuous information

614 Silvin Košak, Review of *Keilschrifturkunden aus Boghazköi, Heft LX: Texte verschiedenen Inhalts*, by Horst Klengel, ZA 94 (1994): 289.

615 Jana Siegelová, "Der Regionalpalast in der Verwaltung des hethitischen Staates," AoF 28/2 (2001): 198 fn. 26.

616 See publication of the prohibition portion in translation in Yoram Cohen, *Taboos and Prohibitions in Hittite Society*. THeth. 24 (Heidelberg: Winter, 2002), 170.

617 Stefano de Martino, "The Wives of Šuppiluliuma I," in *New Results and New Questions on the Reign of Šuppiluliuma I*, ed. Stefan de Martino, Jared L. Miller (Firenze: Elite, 2013), 70.

is usually inserted upside down to the main text.[618] Since in the PTAC this usually takes the form of single-column texts with either non-continuous obverses and reverses (e.g., 2.5 and 4.1.1.2.B in Vol. II) or upside-down paragraphs (e.g., 4.1.1.3, 4.1.3.8, 6.1, 6.3 in Vol. II), there is probably a non-trivial relationship of Ḫenti to the caravan recorded in the text.

The second piece of non-administrative information comes in a second note found on the left edge of 8.1.E(A_3).[619] The note preserves mention of a "Palace of Ḫupišna" (l. e. 1: É.GAL ^{URU}[*Ḫ*]*upišn*[*a*]), and two personal names: a "son/child of Muḫunawi[ya" (l. e. 2: DUMU ^{*f*}*mu-*⌜*ḫu*$^{?}$⌝*-na-wi*$_5$*-*[*ia*(?)]) and a "Marianni" (l. e. 3: ^{m}*ma-ri-an-ni*). The personal names are unfortunately not securely connectable to any known Late New Kingdom individuals. The Palace of Ḫupišna, on the other hand, is comparatively well-attested.

As discussed by Siegelová in her study of Hittite regional palaces, the É(.GAL) ^{URU}*Ḫupišna* seemingly referred to two institutions: an administrative building or storehouse located at Ḫattuša and an actual palace located in the regional city of Ḫupišna.[620] The storehouse, written É ^{URU}*Ḫupišna,* is attested as a source of cult provisions in the KI.LAM Festival (KBo 10.24 rev. v 11) and in the ritual context of KBo 39.155 obv. i 2,[621] and also by implication with the ^{LÚ}AGRIG ^{URU}*Ḫupišna* in the AGRIG-list KUB 26.2 rev. 3′.[622] Attestations of cult provisioning written with É.GAL ^{URU}*Ḫupišna* are more ambiguous,[623] but at least some may be suspected as referring to an actual regional palace, especially when the provisions are for the cult of Ḫuwaššana, the patron deity of Ḫupišna.[624] Independent of these attestations in the cultic sphere, the fact that the town of Ḫupišna is continuously attested throughout Hittite history, favors the continued existence of a regional palace located there: the other regional palaces which continued on only as storehouses in Ḫattuša belonged almost exclusively to minor towns that disappeared from Hittite geography after the Old Hittite period (see discussion of the "palaces" of Ḫāriyaša, Gazzimara, and Šulupašši in *Lexical Commentary s.v.* É(.GAL) $^{(URU)}$...).

In terms of location, it is generally agreed that Ḫupišna can be associated with Classical Kybistra – Herakleia,[625] with recent research arguing for a placement at the site of Tont Kalesi, located some 13 km southeast of Ereğli (Konya).[626] The geographic

618 Willemijn Waal, *Hittite Diplomatics. Studies in Ancient Document Formant and Record Management.* StBoT 57 (Wiesbaden: Harrassowitz, 2015), 77.

619 It is possible that the second note is simply a continuation of the first, but this would make the first note, which starts approximately seven lines from the top of rev. vi, very long.

620 Siegelová, "Der Regionalpalast in der Verwaltung des hethitischen Staates," 197–98.

621 Siegelová, *op. cit.*, 197.

622 Itamar Singer, "The AGRIG in the Hittite Texts," AnSt. 34 (1984): 114.

623 See Siegelová, *op. cit.*, 198 fn. 28, 29 for list.

624 Hans G. Güterbock, "Rituale für die Göttin Ḫuwaššanna," *Oriens* 15 (1962): 345–51.

625 See literature in Giuseppe Del Monte and Johann Tischler, *Die Orts- und Gewässernamen der hethitischen Texte.* RGTC 6 (Wiesbaden: Reichert, 1978), 118.

626 Çiğdem Maner, "Searching for Ḫupišna. Hittite Remains in Ereğli Kara Höyük and Tont Kalesi," in *Places and Spaces in Hittite Anatolia I: Hatti and the East. Proceedings of an International Workshop on Hittite Historical Geography in Istanbul, 25th–26th October 2013*, ed. Metin Alparslan (İstanbul: Türk Eskiçağ Bilimleri Enstitüsü, 2017), against earlier identification with Ereğli Kara Höyük.

importance of Ḫupišna in Hittite times was two-fold. First, it was perhaps one of the last major administrative centers of Hittite power in the Lower Lands before the border with Tarḫuntašša.[627] Second, and the probable geo-political explanation for why Ḫupišna was kept by Ḫatti and not ceded to Tarḫuntašša, the town was one of two major settlements, along with Tuwanuwa (Classical Tyana), that controlled passage from inner Anatolia to Cilicia in Hittite times.[628] Whereas Tuwanuwa was the last major city in the direction of travel from Ḫattuša before the Cilician Gates, Ḫupišna, some 70 km further southwest, was the last major city before another passage through the Bolkar Dağları, which followed a road ultimately ending at the coast near modern Mersin.[629] Indeed, recent research has suggested that in contrast to their great importance in the Classical period, the Cilician Gates were hardly used during the Hittite period, with most traffic following the Bolkar Dağları route.[630]

As with the note on Ḫenti, there is no reason to assume that the note referring to the Palace of Ḫupišna was unrelated to the main text of 8.1.E. A connection between the Palace of Ḫupišna with the caravan must therefore be entertained. The context of the KASKAL Main Text favors interpretation of the palace as the actual regional palace, rather than the Ḫattušan storehouse, since unlike the broad economic footprint of the other storehouses named after towns, the storehouse of É(.GAL) [URU]*Ḫupišna* is only attested with festival provisioning. The items of the KASKAL Main Text are drawn from many economic spheres, but festivals provisions are not one. Since there are at present no other hints for the destination of the shipment recorded in the KASKAL Main Text, then it is not unreasonable to assume that the city formed the destination for the caravan, either as an end-point or as a point of transshipment. If interpreted as an end-point, there is not much further that can be said: it would seem the authorities at Ḫattuša had some reason to ship what is the single largest collection of wealth in the Hittite corpus to a minor regional palace in the Lower Lands. However, if taken as a transshipment point, then the town offers two possibilities: from Ḫupišna, the shipment could have either continued on to Tarḫuntašša or crossed the Taurus into Kizzuwatna and probably onwards to the coast.

The focus of the KASKAL Main Text on personal items, such as garments and jewelry, and on feasting items, such as cutlery, drinking vessels, troughs, and straws; the large numbers of similar objects, such as 178 lapis lazuli rings (8.1.A obv. ii 13′), 81 knives (8.1.A rev. v 10), 200 drinking straws (8.1.A rev. v 27′), and 40 Hurrian tunics and 39 linen tunics in a single chest (8.1.F obv. i 3′–4′); the inclusion of precious raw materials, such as raw gold (8.1.A obv. ii 18′–27′) and loose stones (8.1.D obv. i 6′–7′);

627 Massimo Forlanini, “South Central: The Lower Land and Tarḫuntašša,” in *Hittite Landscape and Geography*, eds. Mark Weeden, Lee Z. Ullmann, HdO 1/121 (Leiden: Brill, 2017), 250 with fn. 112 and 133, citing Jacques Freu, “Quatre-vingts ans d’histoire hittite (1320–1240 av. J.-Chr.),” in *L’apogée du nouvel empire hittite*, eds. Jacques Freu, Michel Mazoyer. Les Hittites et leur histoire 3 (Paris: L’Harmattan, 2008), 174–75, for analysis of the city in the Šaḫurunuwa grant.

628 Forlanini, *op. cit.*, 240–42.

629 Forlanini, *op. cit.*, 242 with fn. 40.

630 See Alvise Matessi, “The Ways of an Empire: Continuity and Change of Route Landscapes across the Taurus during the Hittite Period (ca. 1650–1200 BCE),” *Journal of Anthropological Archaeology* 62 (2021) *101293*, especially pp. 10–14 with previous literature.

and the comparative rarity (relative to the remainder of the PTAC) of religious items such as divine figurines and offering equipment, all suggest that the text contained the necessities for setting up and staffing a palatial household. A temple could also be considered, since these would also host feasts, but more emphasis on religious equipment might be expected. Returning to Ḫenti, since royal daughters are not attested as administrators, it can safely be assumed that Ḫenti was probably not involved with the planning and packing of the caravan. Therefore, she probably accompanied the caravan as a passenger, and further she was meant to be one of the occupants of the household at its destination. This in turn suggests two imaginable scenarios. On the one hand, if Ḫenti was just one of many family members accompanying the caravan, then the text might record the journey or temporary relocation of the Hittite royal household. Although the KASKAL Main Text represents a significant logistical burden, it is perhaps not so extraordinary if one imagines that a caravan involving the king and queen would contain dozens, if not hundreds, of accompanying officials, servants, and bodyguards. In this scenario, the goods of the KASKAL Main Text represent the partial transposition of the existing royal palace from one location to another. On the other hand, the mention of a royal daughter in a text that was established to be similar in contents and comparable, if not greater, in magnitude to the largest of known royal dowries, naturally suggests the possibility of a royal marriage. In this scenario, the goods would represent the foundation of a new palace: namely that of Queen Ḫenti. The principal challenge to this scenario is that there are no known royal marriages in the age of Ḫattušili III/Tudḫaliya IV, although it is not impossible that the records surrounding negotiation of the marriage were not preserved.[631]

7.4 Conclusions on the KASKAL Main Text

The case study conducted in the three preceding chapters has advanced understanding of the KASKAL Main Text in three main ways. First, philologically, the detailed investigation of the editorial history of the text in *4. Case Study: the KASKAL Series* revealed that the document was the product of an extended process of revision, beginning with what were probably hastily written, single-column tablets and ending with three-column tablets with standardized formatting and homogenous contents. The deep editorial hierarchy was taken as evidence that only a small group of scribes, perhaps as few as two, were tasked with the production of the text, which in turn was taken as confirmation of the suspected state of a fairly limited cuneiform scribal bureaucracy in the

631 Here, the possibility that Assyria and Hatti were negotiating a royal marriage in the reign of Tudḫaliya IV is intriguing (Itamar Singer, "A Hittite-Assyrian diplomatic exchange in the Late 13th Century BCE," SMEA 50/2 (2008): 713–20), but there is insufficient information, and the date is in any event perhaps too late. Closer to the time period of the PTAC is the mention in the Bronze Tablet (Bo 86/299 obv. ii 84–94) that Puduḫepa had chosen a wife for Kuruntiya in a previous treaty. Apparently, Kuruntiya had not yet taken her in marriage, and indeed by the terms of the treaty of the Bronze Tablet was no longer bound to accept her, hinting at what may be an immensely intriguing reference to an aborted royal marriage between Tarḫuntašša and Ḫattuša.

Hittite world. It was further demonstrated that the text was insufficiently abstract to be an account or ledger, and that it should be interpreted as an index corresponding to a real-world arrangement of chests, one which moreover required the presence of the scribe to interpret.

Second, in terms of contents, it was estimated in *5. Quantifying the Contents of the KASKAL Main Text*, based on the items in the preserved text that the KASKAL Main Text originally contained hundreds of precious metal objects, hundreds of *iron (ore)*, stone, and ivory objects, perhaps thousands of base metal objects (or their equivalent in value), and nearly one thousand textiles. In raw terms, this is by far the largest collection of wealth in the Palace-Temple Administrative Corpus. Further, in *6. The Relative Value of the KASKAL Main Text*, it was demonstrated that this estimate exceeded any single collection of wealth known from anywhere in the Hittite world. In gold and textiles alone, the KASKAL Main Text was shown to be greater than the dowry given in the first Hittite-Egyptian royal marriage in the 34th year of Ramses II, to be almost six times the size of the gifts given in connection with the fashioning of the "Eternal Treaty" conducted in the 21st year of Ramses II, and to equal a combined six years of gold and ten years of textiles received as tribute from Ugarit and Amurru.

Third and finally, in terms of possible purpose, it was argued in the preceding chapter that the timeframe and direction of shipment match that of a single, punctual, outgoing shipment. The indirect join of 8.1.E(A_3) suggests the destination was to or through the Palace of Ḫupišna in south-central Anatolia. The presence of Ḫenti, daughter of Ḫattušili III and Puduḫepa and sister of Tudḫaliya IV, confirms at the very least an interest of the royal family in the caravan. It was only the absence of a known royal marriage in the era of Ḫattušili III/Tudḫaliya IV that prevented a firm conclusion that the text concerned the dowry for a royal marriage for Ḫenti herself. The endowment of a palace, or less likely a temple, or the temporary transfer of the royal court, were also considered as possible uses.

As it stands, more evidence will need to be discovered if the purpose of the KASKAL Main Text is to be revealed. A personal preference can be stated here for the dowry hypothesis, but closer examination of the contents might suggest other possibilities. Regardless of the outcome, be it a dowry, a packing list for a royal journey or the temporary relocation of the Hittite court, a palace or temple endowment, or even something else entirely, uncovering the circumstances behind the creation of the KASKAL Main Text, if ever revealed, would clarify one of the most impressive and intriguing economic acts of the Late New Kingdom period.

8. THE HITTITE VOTIVE CORPUS AS ECONOMIC TEXTS

8.1 Introduction to the Hittite Votive Corpus

The Hittite vow corpus (CTH 58–90) discussed in this chapter consists of eighty-eight texts of varying size, almost all of which have been edited in Johan de Roos' *Hittite Votive Texts*.[632] The detail with which the votive obligations are recorded, including the not-infrequent description of the promised votive objects according to weight and dimension, allows the vows to be considered from an economic-administrative standpoint.[633] Estimating the yearly vow obligations, which will be undertaken below in *8.15 Reconstructing the Vow Schedule of Ḫattušili and Puduḫepa*, allows an alternative glimpse into Hittite state expenditure that is not captured by the Palace-Temple Administrative Corpus.

The Hittite vows treated in this chapter usually take the form of a condition, termed the protasis, which the god can affect, and a promised action, called the apodosis, which the human supplicant offers as inducement for the god's favor. A typical vow looks thus:

KUB 15.1+ obv. i 3–11
obv. i

3 *nu-za-kán* MUNUS.LUGAL ŠÀ Ù-*TI*
4 *A-NA* ^{D}*ḫé-pát* ^{URU}*u-da ki-iš-ša-an IK-RU-UB*
5 *ma-a-an-wa* DINGIR-*LUM* GAŠAN-*IA* ^{D}UTU-*ŠI* TI-*nu-an ḫar-ti*
6 ḪUL-*u-i-wa-ra-an pa-ra-a Ú-UL tar-na-at-ti*

(Protasis:) The queen in a dream to Ḫepat (of) Uda vowed thus: "If you, the goddess, my lady, keep His Majesty alive, (and) do not deliver him to evil,

7 *nu-wa A-NA* ^{D}*ḫé-pát* ALAM KÙ.SI$_{22}$ *i-ia-mi*
8 *A-IA-RU* KÙ.SI$_{22}$-*ia-wa-aš-ši i-ia-mi*
9 *nu-wa-ra-at-za ŠA* ^{D}*ḫé-pát A-IA-RU ḫal-zi-iš-ša-an-*[*z*]*i*
10 ^{UZU}GABA-*aš-ma-wa-du-za TU-DÌ-TUM* KÙ.SI$_{22}$ *i-ia-mi*
11 *nu-wa-ra-at-za TU-DÌ-TUM* DINGIR-*LIM ḫal-zi-iš-ša-an-zi*

---

632 Johan de Roos, *Hittite Votive Texts*. PIHANS 109 (Leiden: Nederlands Instituut voor het Nabije Oosten, 2007). Note that since the present chapter is primarily concerned with the evaluation of the vows from an economic perspective, full editions of the vows are not given. Instead, the texts are presented in the author's own translations, with only significant differences with de Roos noted.

633 James Burgin and Theo van den Hout, "Weihgaben. B. Bei den Hethitern," RlA 15 (2016): 32–35.

(Apodosis): I will make for Ḫepat a gold statue. And I will make a gold rosette for it; they will call it the rosette of Ḫepat. And I will make a (toggle-)pin for your breast; they will call it the deity's (toggle-)pin."

More or less contextual information, such as the location where the vow was made, or the general topic, can be written before the protasis. The weights of the objects to be given, the location where they will be donated, and whether or not the promised donation has been fulfilled can appear in the apodosis. In some vows, probably from the later stages of the administrative process, only the name of the deity and the action promised by the human supplicant is written. Many of the vows appear in the context of a recounted dream, and some vows were modified or confirmed by oracles.[634]

The most salient feature of the genre from a historical viewpoint is that almost all the vows come from the era of Ḫattušili III and Puduḫepa. The dating began as a circumspect observation by Leo Oppenheim based on KUB 15.1–30, who placed these texts broadly in the period from Muwatalli II to Ḫattušili III.[635] It was followed by Heinrich Otten and Vladimir Souček in the introduction to their 1965 edition of the Vow of Puduḫepa (CTH 585, an unusual text that goes into much more detail than is typical of the vow corpus).[636] In a review of Otten and Souček's work, Annelies Kammhuber was the first to suggest that the dating of the vows was more than just coincidence: she argued rather that the vow-genre was an *innovation* of Ḫattušili III, or more specifically his wife Puduḫepa.[637] Her view finds confirmation in de Roos' comprehensive edition of the votive texts, which shows that there are at most one or two vow texts, atypical in form, that can be dated prior to their reign. The last major tranche of votive texts was published in 1986,[638] and all were confined to the same the time period.

The significance of the vow genre's association with Ḫattušili and Puduḫepa is still debated. The most recent discussions of the genre as a whole, in de Roos' edition and Alice Mouton's work on Hittite dreams,[639] emphasize the continuity of the vows with previous traditions. The origins of the vows were traced by de Roos to the Hittite practice of the *malteššar* offering, a kind of thanksgiving celebrated by Hittite kings at the

634 An example of oracle text dealing with vows is found in KUB 56.24. Following the oracle topics of *arkamman* 'tribute', *maškan* 'propitiatory gift', and *šarnikzil* 'compensation', a vow appears in rev. 17, where it is determined that a *tiwatašša-* (= *šittar* 'sundisk(?)', with Richard Beal, review of *Hittite Votive Texts*, by Johan de Roos, JNES 73/2 [2014]: 344), weighing 5 shekels silver should be given.

635 A. Leo Oppenheim, *The Interpretation of Dreams in the Ancient Near East, with a Translation of an Assyrian Dream-Book* (Philadelphia: American Philosophical Society, 1956), 193.

636 Heinrich Otten and Vladimir Souček, *Das Gelübde der Königin Puduḫepa an die Göttin Lelwani*. StBoT 1 (Wiesbaden: Harrassowitz, 1965), 1.

637 See Annelies Kammenhuber, Review of *Das Gelübde der Königin Puduḫepa an die Göttin Lelwani*, by Heinrich Otten and Vladimir Souček, ZA 60 (1970): 222, and *ead.*, *Orakelpraxis, Träume und Vorzeichenschau bei den Hethitern*. THeth. 7 (Heidelberg: Winter, 1976), 25–26.

638 Horst Klengel, *Hethitische Gelübde und Traumtexte sowie Rituale und Festbeschreibungen*, KUB 56 (Berlin: Akademie-Verlag, 1986).

639 De Roos, *Hittite Votive Texts*, and Alice Mouton, *Rêves hittites: Contribution à une histoire et une anthropologie du rêve en Anatolie ancienne*. CHANE 28 (Leiden: Brill, 2007).

conclusion of military campaigns.[640] Mouton saw in KUB 15.5+, one of the anomalous texts dating to the period before Ḫattušili and Puduḫepa, demonstration of a widespread, possibly popular, practice of vow-making in the Hittite court.[641] Their arguments suggest that the genre had antecedents in Hittite culture and the votive texts were not foreign introductions.

The dwindling of the vow genre in the reign of Tudḫaliya IV is made even more surprising if, as seems to be the case, the vows are accepted as a native tradition. The votive corpus is administrative in nature in that it records obligations that require timely responses from a network of people associated with Hittite central government. The great majority of Hittite administrative documents come from the very end of the Empire: it is assumed that the chronological distribution of the administrative documents is due to the fact that the tablets were recycled or destroyed when their information was no longer current.[642] The presence of votive administrative texts from the time of Ḫattušili and Puduḫepa, and the relative absence of the same texts from the reign of Tudḫaliya IV, is opposite to the expected distribution. It suggests two things: one, the vows were kept because they were useful for a longer period of time than most administrative documents, and two, the distribution of vow texts is probably not an accident of preservation. It seems the practice of vow-making that Tudḫaliya inherited from his parents was changed or abandoned during his reign, though the records were kept intact.

Since there is no perceptible discontinuity at the Hittite court at the end of Ḫattušili's reign, the rise and subsequent disappearance of the vows from the Hittite corpus should be seen as a shift in emphasis rather than a rupture of tradition. Tudḫaliya had been well groomed for succession, and Puduḫepa outlived her husband and remained influential in her role as *tawananna-* and almost certainly continued to sponsor votive texts during the early years of her son's reign. By her royal intervention, vow-making had been elevated from a personal act familiar to the Hittite court to an instrument of *government policy* under Ḫattušili and Puduḫepa, whereby the vows commanded, as will be seen, the resources of the Hittite state in their fulfillment. With the change in king then came a change in policy, evidencing the great latitude afforded to the royal person in how he chose to combine religious obligation with the running of the state. Rulers had different solutions, from the literature of Muršili II, to the moving of the Hittite capital by Muwatalli II to his god's city of Tarḫuntašša; from the vows of

640 De Roos, *Hittite Votive Texts*, 38–41.

641 Mouton, *Rêves hittites*, 24–26.

642 For the proposed life-cycle of administrative documents, see Theo van den Hout, "Administration and Writing in Hittite Society," in *Archivi, depositi, magazzini presso gli Ittiti: nuovi materiali e nuove ricerche / Archives, Depots and Storehouses in the Hittite World: New Evidence and New Research (Proceedings of the Workshop held in Pavia, June 18, 2009)*, eds. Maria Elena Balza, Mauro Giorgieri, Clelia Mora (Genoa: Italian University Press, 2012), 46–48. It is a matter of definition whether festival texts and their provisioning lists, which verge on texts of tradition, should be included as administrative documents. While the festival texts were used to coordinate government activity, they were (in theory) timeless and prescriptive as opposed to the short-term and descriptive texts of e.g., the Palace-Temple Administrative Corpus.

Ḫattušili and Puduḫepa, to the greater focus on local cults of Tudḫaliya IV.[643] Modern scholars might see ulterior motives – a literary bent for Muršili or geopolitical strategy/religious reform for Muwatalli;[644] or centralization and decentralization for Ḫattušili and Tudḫaliya, respectively – but it should be remembered that from the emic viewpoint these are secondary to the enormous spiritual burden borne by the Hittite king as he guided the land of Ḫatti, and was guided in turn by the gods.

If the votive texts are to be interpreted in the context of governance, then an investigation of the economics of the vows is paramount. The remainder of this chapter will undertake this by first examining the dating criteria of the texts in detail, and then offering a method for estimating and restoring the magnitude of wealth expended on votive offerings during the reign of Ḫattušili and Puduḫepa. The vows will be divided into categories by subject and discussed. Finally, an attempt will be made to situate the vow corpus historically, and with regard to Palace-Temple Administrative Corpus in general.

8.2 Dating Criteria of Vows in Detail

Because economic analysis of the vows depends so heavily on their belonging to a specific time period, it is useful to present a detailed account of the criteria by which the texts are dated.[645] Most of the vows are anonymous, with the identity of the persons involved concealed behind generic titles of MUNUS.LUGAL 'queen' and ᴰUTU-*ŠI* 'His Majesty (i.e., the reigning king)', but there are certain criteria that can link the vast majority of the vows with Ḫattušili and Puduḫepa, making them contemporary to at least part of the Palace-Temple Administrative Corpus.

It can be inferred that vows on the same tablet belong to roughly the same chronological stratum, so that the dating of one vow can be applied to the whole tablet. The

643 However, see 2.3 "The Dating of the Texts and the Question of the 'Cult Reform' of Tudḫaliya IV" in Michele Cammarosano, *Hittite Local Cults.* WAW 40 (Atlanta: Society for Biblical Literature, 2018), 20–23, with previous literature, for the argument that the practice of monitoring local cults was not restricted to Tudḫaliya's reign, but reflected an abiding interest of the central government at Ḫattuša in the cultic practices of the Anatolian hinterlands. Nevertheless, as discussed under *8.12 Vows of Tudḫaliya IV* below, the genres of votive texts and local cult reports show a complementary distribution of texts, with vows restricted to Ḫattušili III and Puduḫepa and local cult reports confined to Tudḫaliya IV. At a minimum this suggests that Tudḫaliya IV intentionally turned away from the vow system of his parents, and may even reveal a shift in policy where religious wealth was redirected to the countryside through the local cults instead.

644 For a discussion of the domestic, religious, and geopolitical considerations of Muwatalli II's move to Tarḫuntašša, see Itamar Singer, "The Failed Reforms of Akhenaton and Muwatalli II," *British Museum Studies in Ancient Egypt and Sudan* 6 (2006): 37–58.

645 This account is intended as a supplement to, not a replacement of, de Roos' work in *Hittite Votive Texts*, 30–38 (see especially pp. 37–38 for his breakdown of reasoning by text). Note that de Roos' list is not comprehensive of the texts edited in the book: the book was based on his dissertation written in 1984, and was revised and expanded in the version published in 2007 (completed with the assistance of Alice Mouton). However, while the number of texts was increased, the expositive portions of the introduction, including the discussion on dating, consider only the texts from the dissertation.

votive corpus was the culmination of an administrative process that recorded the pronouncement and fulfillment of vow obligations. Vows could have very different time frames for their completion, sometimes measured in years, being ultimately dependent on the will of the gods. If it had been the case that only vows with outstanding obligations were kept in the corpus, regular recopying the tablets would be needed to prune the finished vows and consolidate the current vows. Unless the scribes were scrupulous to make a new tablet as soon as even one vow on it was fulfilled, and fastidious in discarding every old tablet, then the votive corpus would contain vows that appear multiple times. This is not so, and there are very few instances of repeated vows.[646] Rather, the votive corpus was likely an archive with low turnover, as demonstrated by the many vows present in the corpus that must have been completed (for example all of the illness vows, and vows explicitly marked as "already done," as discussed in the next section). Records of every vow pronounced were kept, even after they were fulfilled: the royal couple were saving all of their receipts as it were. Given the low amount of recopying implied in the system, and the seemingly unsystematic mixture of topics and gods within a tablet, vows were likely written down near the time they were made, and thus vows on the same tablet come from the same time.

8.2.1 The Illness Vows

The premier dating criterion for the corpus comes from the so-called "illness vows," in which the queen pleads for the life and health of the king, often mentioning specific ailments and body parts. While in theory it could be any (New Hittite) queen making these vows for any king, Puduḫepa and Ḫattušili are almost surely the only candidates. No other queen is known to have been as powerful as Puduḫepa, and certainly none were as prolific in producing texts. She produced many prayers, many for the health of Ḫattušili, and authored numerous letters and diplomatic communications. Such was her influence that she is in fact the last Hittite queen to be known by name. All of this makes her *prima facie* the likeliest candidate for any time the queen appears in the votive corpus. At the same time her husband Ḫattušili was probably the New Hittite king most needing of divine intervention for his health. He was given as a sick child to the care of Ištar and prone to malady all his life.[647] Illnesses of the eyes seemed especially to have plagued him, as evidenced by Puduḫepa's prayers and the numerous containers of eye medicine sent from Egypt as diplomatic gifts. Thus, when His Majesty's eyes appear as one of the most frequent topics in the votive corpus, it is likely that Ḫattušili is the king in question.

646 There are only four cases of vows being repeated twice, and never exactly the same. These "doublets" are: the matter of the *auli-* in the town of Zitḫara (KUB 15.28 + IBoT 3.125 obv. ii 2′–5′ and KUB 48.123 obv. i 8′–11′); the statues of the king and queen for their lives (KUB 15.28 + IBoT 3.125 obv. ii 6′–10′ and KBo 55.217 4′–8′); the illness of the son of the king of Išuwa (KUB 15.1 rev. iii 48′–53′ and KUB 15.3 rev. iv 5′–9′); and the matter of the eagle (KUB 31.77+ obv. i 30–36 [= KUB 48.126 3′–9′] and KBo 64.338 obv. 9–14). There are no cases of a vow being repeated three times.

647 De Roos, *Hittite Votive Texts*, 37 implies that the succession of illnesses for his different body parts makes multiple illnesses likely, whereas Ünal's viewpoint is that Ḫattušili suffered the same chronic illness since his youth (Ahmet Ünal, *Ḫattušili III. Teil I. Ḫattušili bis zu seiner Thronbesteigung. Band 1: Historischer Abriß*. THeth. 3 [Heidelberg: Winter, 1974], 45).

It has been remarked that Puduḫepa's unparalleled involvement in the Hittite state was perhaps due to her husband's chronic ill health, but her position was precarious and dependent on the continued support of her husband.[648] She had ample opportunity and motive to make vows for Ḫattušili, and his need was greater than most kings, and so it can be said following de Roos that "[e]very time a vow is made in a text by the queen for the life or health of the king we may assume that that text dates from the reign of [Puduḫepa and Ḫattušili]."[649] Indeed whenever an illness vow can be dated by independent criteria, all date to theirs and no other reign. Therefore, de Roos' criteria for dating the illness vows will be adopted here, and those involving eye illnesses will be considered especially secure.

8.2.2 Ištar of Lawazantiya

The mention of Ištar of Lawazantiya, the personal goddess of Puduḫepa (for whom she was a priestess before her marriage), can also be used as evidence for dating a text to her reign.[650] The Lawazantiyan hypostasis of Ištar was obscure before Puduḫepa came to the throne, with only a single attestation in the middle of a long list of regional gods of Kizzuwatna written during the reign of Muwatalli II (KUB 48.87 rev. iii 6),[651] compared to the dozens of attestations under Puduḫepa.

8.2.3 Military Campaigns

There is an "Arzawa dossier" recording vows made in connection with Ḫattušili's historically attested military campaign to the west. Five of the texts (KUB 15.6, KUB 31.69, KUB 48.123(?),[652] KUB 56.15, KUB 56.27, KUB 56.31) can be positively dated to Puduḫepa and Ḫattušili, and the sixth (KUB 56.18) should also be dated to this time based on the shared theme. Another subset of vows (KUB 15.21, KUB 48.119) deals with a campaign (or campaigns) in the north of Anatolia, a region which formed the historic and religious power base of Ḫattušili, yet was regularly threatened with violence by Kaškaen tribesmen during his reign.

648 Cf. Heinrich Otten, *Puduḫepa: Eine hethitische Königin in ihren Textzeugnissen*. AbhMainz 1975/1 (Wiesbaden: Steiner, 1975).

649 De Roos, *Hittite Votive Texts*, 37.

650 Following de Roos, *Hittite Votive Texts*, 33, and Otten, *Puduḫepa*, 13.

651 For attestations, see entry in Ben van Gessel, *Onomasticon of the Hittite Pantheon*. HdO 1/33 (Leiden: Brill, 1998). For primary edition and discussion of KUB 48.87, see Itamar Singer, *Muwatalli's Prayer to the Assembly of Gods through the Storm-God of Lightning (CTH 381)* (Atlanta: American School of Oriental Research, 1996), 165–67. It is unclear exactly when in the reign of Muwatalli the prayer and god-list was composed. It is possible that Ḫattušili had already married Puduḫepa, affording her and her father, a priest of Ištar of Lawazantiya, the influence necessary for the goddess' inclusion.

652 Attribution is based on appearance of INIM KUR ^{URU}*A*[*r*- 'matter of the land of A[r- ... ' (obv. ii 13′). The text can be positively dated to Ḫattušili by the illness vows and mention of Ḫešni (a son of Ḫattušili who was implicated in a plot to usurp Tudḫaliya's throne). While it is conceivable that the military campaigns on rev. iv of the tablet could date to the Northern Campaign instead of Arzawa, the INIM KUR ^{URU}*A*[*r*- tips the balance towards the latter.

8.2.4 Tudḫaliya IV

The length of Ḫattušili's reign is fairly well known (about thirty years, c. 1267–37),[653] but Puduḫepa survived her husband for many years. How long did she continue to produce vows in an official capacity after her husband's death? She remained politically active for some time, being likely attested in a letter at the time of the Battle of Niḫriya (c. 1234), and possibly still communicating with vassals as late as the reign of Niqmaddu III (c. 1220).[654] Opaque terminology hinders an exact dating. Puduḫepa continued to use the title MUNUS.LUGAL, while her daughter-in-law, the wife of the reigning king, was referred to as DUMU.MUNUS GAL 'great princess.'[655] Because Puduḫepa's title did not change with her husband's death, it may be that some of the vows made by the queen date from the reign of Tudḫaliya.

Tudḫaliya used the title ᴰUTU-*ŠI* upon his father's death (and perhaps in co-regency before),[656] but whether Puduḫepa called him by this is an open question. Because the name Tudḫaliya appears in the votive corpus, there are three possibilities: either she used his name and his title interchangeably when he became king; or she continued to refer to him as Tudḫaliya even when he became king; or she referred to him in the vows as Tudḫaliya when he was prince and ᴰUTU-*ŠI* while king.[657] The first nomenclature is unlikely given her consistency in using ᴰUTU-*ŠI* for vows concerning Ḫattušili (she did not mix the name and title of her husband, so why for her son?), and the fact that no votive text can ᴰUTU-*ŠI* be independently proven to refer to Tudḫaliya. There is also no evidence for the second pattern of naming, since the four texts that mention Tudḫaliya by name all seem to date to his time as prince:

1.) KUB 56.31 has a string of six vows (rev. iv 8′–22′) in which the queen asks for the gods to militarily support His Majesty. The queen makes one of these vows in rev. iv 13′ in the town of Yalanda, which if it is the same as the town of Iyalanda would put

653 All dates after those used in Trevor Bryce, *The Kingdom of the Hittites* (Oxford: Oxford University Press, 1999).

654 Itamar Singer, "The Battle of Niḫriya and the End of the Hittite Empire," ZA 75 (1985): 116–18 saw Puduḫepa as the queen addressed in a letter concerning betrayal of Išuwa in the events surrounding the battle of Niḫriya. The text RS 17.434 was assumed by Nougayrol to have been written by Puduḫepa to Niqmaddu III. Itamar Singer, "Dating the End of the Hittite Empire," *Hethitica* 8 (1987): 415 placed this around 1220 BC. Bryce, *Kingdom of the Hittites*, 289 supposed that she might have lived to the age of 90.

655 Itamar Singer, "The Title 'Great Princess' in the Hittite Empire," UF 23 (1991): 327–38.

656 See Theo van den Hout, "Hethitische Thronbesteigungsorakel und die Inauguration Tudḫalijas IV," ZA 81 (1991): 277–79.

657 The matter is further confused by the existence of Tašmi-Šarruma as a by-name for Tudḫaliya, as demonstrated by J. David Hawkins in his discussion of the Tašmi-Šarruma seals ("Seals type 3"), where the hieroglyphic names of MONS+*TU* (= 'Tudḫaliya') and L.418(I)-*ŠARMA* (= 'Tašmi-Šarruma') appear together. See J. David Hawkins, "VI. The Seals and the Dynasty," in *Die Siegel der Grosskönige und Grossköniginnen auf Tonbullen aus dem Nişantepe-Archiv in Ḫattuša*, by Suzanne Herbordt, Dahlia Bawanypeck, J. David Hawkins. BoḪa. 23 (Mainz: von Zabern, 2011), 95, 99, 101–2; after the original proposal equating the two names by Sedat Alp, "Zur Datierung des Ulmitešup-Vertrages," AoF 25 (1998): 54–60.

her in western Anatolia and thus in the context of Ḫattušili's Arzawa campaign.[658] The next paragraph is separated by a double paragraph line (which usually indicates a change of topic), and Tudḫaliya's name appears in a broken context, indicating at least that he was receiving vows already by the time of the Arzawa campaign.

2.) KUB 15.23 has a vow mentioning the title ^{D}UTU-*ŠI* and the city of Nerik (obv. 3′), and then asking for military support for Tudḫaliya (obv. 8′). It is unlikely Puduḫepa would use both the title and name within the same vow separated only by five lines. An 'illness vow' on the tablet's reverse (17′–21′) further confirms that Ḫattušili is probably still alive. It is possible they are on a joint campaign: Tudḫaliya was appointed governor of the region of Ḫakmiš and Nerik in Ḫattušili's lifetime and gained military experience fighting the Kaška there, often in coordination with his father (see discussion under *8.5 Vows Concerning Military Matters* below).

3.) KUB 56.30 also has the queen requesting military support for Tudḫaliya (KUB 56.30 rev. 14′–24′). The obverse of the KUB 56.30 contains an extremely interesting but fragmentary set of vows involving a number of palace officials (obv. 4′–5′) and large gifts of silver given by His Majesty (obv. 19′–22′, 23′–26′). The appearance of the title ^{D}UTU-*ŠI* in obv. 20′ and 24′ in contrast to the name Tudḫaliya in rev. 15′ and 21′ should indicate that Ḫattušili is still king.

4.) The fourth text, KUB 56.28 obv. 5′–11′ has apparently conflicting criteria. On the obverse is an 'illness vow' relating to His Majesty's eyes (or possibly nose), which would place it strongly in the time of Ḫattušili:

KUB 56.28 obv. 5′–8′
obv.
5′]⌈^{D}⌉*IŠTAR* ^{URU}*ša-mu-ḫa* ⟨*I-NA*⟩ ^{URU}*u-ri-k*[*i-na*
6′]x-*at nu-za-kán* [MUNUS].LUGAL *A-NA* ^{D}*IŠ*[*TAR* ^{URU}*ša-mu-ḫa*
7′] *ma-a-an-mu-kán* DINGIR-*LUM* GAŠAN-*IA* x[
8′] IGI ^{D}UTU-*ŠI* ≮*ti-ti-ti-in* [
9′ -*š*]*i* ^{DUG}*ḫar-ši-ia-al-li* x[
10′] *ku-uš* UD.KAM *šar-la-at-t*[*a*
11′]x UD-*ti* ^{DUG}*ḫar-ši-ia-a*[*l-li*

658 It is quite possible that the spelling Yalanda is simply a scribal error. See de Roos, *Hittite Votive Texts*, 283 fn. 736, who guessed it is a "[c]urious spelling of Iyalanda located in the lands of Lukka?" The town of Iyalanda was where Ḫattušili arranged to meet Piyamaradu (see "the Tawagalawa letter" KUB 14.3) and was the location of an ambush and a resulting battle that ended in a reported Hittite victory (as recounted in KBo 28.28, Ramses quoting a letter from Ḫattušili). Puduḫepa took a keen interest in this campaign, especially in capturing Piyamaradu (cf. KUB 56.15 obv. ii 15–29; note the use of the first person in line 19: "he will not escape me"). Her presence in Yalanda indicates she may have followed Ḫattušili on campaign.

> [...] Ištar of Šamuḫa ⟨in⟩ Urik[ina ...] The [qu]een to Iš[tar of Šamuḫa vowed thus: I]f the goddess, my lady, for me [...] the eye (of) His Majesty, (its) pupil[659] [you heal? ...] a *ḫaršiyalli*-vessel [I will institute? ...] these[660] daily praise offeri[ngs ...] on the day a *ḫaršiya*[*lli*-vessel ...

The reverse of the tablet contains four vows (rev. 5′–28′) concerning a military campaign in which the queen asks the gods to support Tudḫaliya. The mention of the king of Išuwa in Kizzuwatna in rev. 6′ suggests a specific historical context, since it was possibly this vassal who failed to support Tudḫaliya against Assyria at the Battle of Niḫriya.[661] Unfortunately, the lines are broken and it cannot be determined whether the king of Išuwa is part of the topic or the context of the vow. But like many vassals and officials, the king of Išuwa's importance bridged the reigns of Ḫattušili and Tudḫaliya – a certainty in his case since he was married to Puduḫepa's sister (or daughter, cf. commentary to the illness vows KUB 15.1+ rev. iii 48′–53′ and KUB 15.3 rev. iv 5′–9′ below) – and so his presence is not decisive for the purposes of dating. The highly stylized phrasing of the vow, where the gods are asked to "deliver the lands of the enemy to him" (rev. 9′), to "place in [Tudḫaliy]a's hand" the enemy (rev. 14′), and to "spread a net for the enemies" (rev. 16′), furthermore suggests a campaign of conquest. Such rhetoric fits the Northern Campaigns to recover holy sites from the Kaška, but seems out of place in a war to preserve the status quo of some Hurrian buffer states against Assyrian aggression.

The third possible nomenclature, that Puduḫepa referred to Tudḫaliya by his name as prince and by his title as king, is the most difficult to assess, but the distribution of vows made for Tudḫaliya by name offers a possible avenue of interpretation. Of the twelve vows made for his name, eleven are for his military success and one is for good tidings (Tašmi-Šarruma, if he is to be included, appears once in KUB 48.123 obv. i 19′–22′ where it is determined for him to perform a certain ritual, but the context and purpose are unclear). In contrast, the vows for ᴰUTU-*ŠI* tend overwhelmingly to be illness vows (55), with vows for military matters a distant second (13) followed by the topics of calamity (5), dreams and omens (3), and good tidings (2). It can be assumed that Tudḫaliya garnered the same kinds of vows as prince as he would as king, since there is no reason to suppose Puduḫepa would be any less concerned for the well-being of Tudḫaliya before his enthronement. He was the chosen successor for most of Ḫattušili's reign, and the only prince to merit regular mention in the votive corpus even

659 Against de Roos' translation (*Hittite Votive Texts*, 271), I prefer to read the word ⸗*tititin* as coming from Luw. *titit-* 'pupil' and not Hitt. *titita-* 'nose': see discussion of this passage in HEG T/D *s.v.* ⁽ᵁᶻᵁ⁾*titita-* (p. 394), where both possibilities are acknowledged. This would allow the sign IGI 'eye', which is transliterated but left untranslated by de Roos, to be read in apposition to ⸗*tititin* in the double case construction of inalienable possession expected for body parts.

660 Contra CHD Š *s.v.* ⁽ˢᴵˢᴷᵁᴿ/ˢÍˢᴷᵁᴿ⁾*šarlatta-*⁽ˢᴵˢᴷᵁᴿ⁾ 2 a (p. 276), under discussion of KUB 58.73 iii 14–16, the presence now of a third example of *ku-uš šar-la-at-ta* (IBoT 3.148 rev. iv 48, KBo 17.65 rev. 14, and the present KUB 56.28 obv. 10′, which seems to have been overlooked in the CHD entry) suggests that Beckman's dismissed interpretation of the form as an uninflected pl. acc. com. is correct.

661 Though the vassal is not mentioned by name, Bryce, *Kingdom of the Hittites*, 318 considers it "almost certainly the king of Isuwa," following Singer, "The Battle of Niḫriya," 110–18.

as other princes risk their lives in battle. His older brother Nerikkaili was *tuḫ(u)kanti*, a title translated as 'heir designate' or 'crown prince' and which carried significant military responsibilities,[662] during earliest years of Ḫattušili's reign and was perhaps the same one found in the Tawagalawa letter in the Arzawa campaign.[663] If Tudḫaliya had needed an illness vow as prince, Puduḫepa would hardly have denied him these (there does not seem to be a prohibition against making illness vows for others beside the sitting king, since vows for the son of the king of Išuwa are recorded, as will be seen in KUB 15.1+ rev. iii 48′–53′and KUB 15.3 rev. iv 5′–9′). Because Tudḫaliya did not need illness vows as prince, being blessed perhaps with a stronger constitution than his father, it is unlikely he required many as king.

Thus, all of the vows by Puduḫepa mentioning Tudḫaliya by name come from his time as prince, and none of the vows for ᴰUTU-*ŠI* can positively be assigned to him as king. This makes it unlikely that any of the vows for ᴰUTU-*ŠI* date to Tudḫaliya as king. Few, if any, of the illness vows refer to Tudḫaliya, given his seeming healthiness as prince. Most of the military vows are also accounted for: Tudḫaliya is not known to have campaigned in western Anatolia, making it unlikely any of the Arzawa vows are for him. Among the texts containing vows for northern Anatolia, KUB 48.119 can safely be assigned to Ḫattušili based on an illness vow for the eye, and KUB 15.21 mentions the town of Ḫatenzuwa, which was captured by Tudḫaliya prior to kingship.[664] This leaves few opportunities in the remainder of the votive corpus for ᴰUTU-*ŠI* to refer to Tudḫaliya. It is possible some of the vows with damaged contexts could date to his reign, but given what seems to be a marked lack of enthusiasm on his part for making vows, with only one or maybe two attributable to him, the better explanation is that the votive program went into swift decline with his ascension to the throne.

8.2.5 Conclusions on Dating

8.2.5.1 Useable Texts

Based on the above criteria, the ninety useable vow texts have the following breakdown: two from the reign of Urḫi-Teššub, one from Ḫattušili III's time as king in Hakmiš, forty-six from the reign of Ḫattušili III and Puduḫepa as king and queen in Ḫattuša, nine dateable only to Puduḫepa, two from the reign of Tudḫaliya IV, and thirty of insufficient context to date. There are an additional nine texts edited in de Roos' volume that do not yield vows and are excluded from the total.

---

662 Cf. Oliver R. Gurney, "The Hittite Title *tuḫkanti*-," AnSt. 33 (1983): 97–101.

663 It has been suggested that Nerrikaili may only be Tudḫaliya's half-brother, and thus Puduḫepa would be favoring her biological son. Cf. Bryce, *Kingdom of the Hittites*, 272 fn. 37 for the literature cited for and against this view. If so, this would only further emphasize Tudḫaliya's importance to Puduḫepa.

664 See de Roos, *Hittite Votive Texts*, 38. The minor settlement of Ḫatenzuwa was claimed by Ḫattušili to have been captured for him by a young Tudḫaliya, who was perhaps only twelve years old at the time (see KUB 19.8//9 rev. iii 25–31), which should likely be read as propaganda designed to solidify Tudḫaliya's position as successor. Given the size of gifts it is unlikely that the author of the vows in KUB 15.21 was anyone besides the king.

Table 33: Dating of the Vow Corpus by Text and Dating Criteria

Text	Dating Criteria
a) Vows dateable to reign of Urḫi-Teššub	
KUB 15.5 + 48.122+ KBo 43.66	(see discussion of de Roos)[665]
Merzifon 3	(possible indirect join to KUB 15.5+?)
b) Vows dateable to reign of Ḫattušili III in Ḫakmiš	
KBo 9.96 (+) KBo 41.60	campaign against Egypt and Amurru[666]
c) Vows dateable to reign of Ḫattušili III (and Puduḫepa) in Ḫattuša	
(CTH 585)	“The Vow of Puduḫepa”
FHL 186	(topic of É ^{D}10 ^{URU}Manuziya parallel to KUB 15.11+ obv. 2, 12)
IBoT 3.123	illness vow
KBo 8.61	illness vow (eye)
KBo 27.60	illness vow (eye)
KBo 55.208	illness vow (probable eye illness)
KBo 55.213	queen interceding for His Majesty
KBo 55.217	illness vow
KBo 55.221	illness vow (eye)
KBo 55.223	illness vow (eye)
KBo 64.338	Ištar of Lawazantiya, eagle statue parallel to KUB 31.77+ obv. i 30–36 (= KUB 48.126 3′–9′)
KUB 15.1 + DBH 43/2.14 + CHDS 2.145	illness vow
KUB 15.3	illness vow
KUB 15.4	illness vow
KUB 15.6	illness vow (eye), Arzawa campaign
KUB 15.8	illness vow (probable eye illness)[667]
KUB 15.9	illness vow
KUB 15.11 + KBo 60.99	illness vow
KUB 15.18	illness vow (eye)[668]
KUB 15.19	illness vow

665 See de Roos, *Hittite Votive Texts*, 33–36 for dating and discussion of this interesting text, and again Mouton, *Rêves hittites*, 24–26 for its implications.

666 See de Roos, *op. cit.*, 31–33. See now comments of Petra Goedegebuure, *The Hittite Demonstratives: Studies in Deixis, Topics and Focus*. StBoT 55 (Wiesbaden: Harrassowitz, 2014), 158, confirming Ḫattušili III as the speaker of this vow.

667 Based on the donation of “eyes” as votive objects.

668 Illness mentioned in a fragmentary context in rev. iii 9′–14′.

KUB 15.21	capture of Ḫatenzuwa
KUB 15.22	illness vow (though queen not preserved)
KUB 15.23	illness vow, Tudḫaliya
KUB 15.24	illness vow
KUB 15.28 + IBoT 3.125	illness vow
KUB 15.30	illness vow
KUB 31.69	illness vow, Ištar of Lawazantiya, Arzawa campaign
KUB 31.77 + 48.126	mention of Puduḫepa by name, queen vowing for His Majesty
KUB 48.119	illness vow (eye)
KUB 48.123	illness vow, Ištar of Lawazantiya, Arzawa campaign?
KUB 56.12	illness vow
KUB 56.13	illness vow (eye)
KUB 56.15	Arzawa campaign (Piyamaradu)
KUB 56.18	Arzawa campaign
KUB 56.20	prayer of the king for the queen in childbirth?[669]
KUB 56.21	illness vow (eye)
KUB 56.23	illness vow
KUB 56.27	Arzawa campaign (town of Waliwanda)[670]
KUB 56.28	queen, Tudḫaliya, Northern Campaign?
KUB 56.30	queen, Tudḫaliya
KUB 56.31	Arzawa campaign, Tudḫaliya
Liv. 49-47-42	illness vow
d) Vows probably dateable to Ḫattušili but too fragmentary to use	
Bo 6102	illness vow
KBo 27.25	illness vow (eye)
KBo 53.112	mention of Babylonian doctor makes dating to Ḫattušili probable[671]
KBo 55.219	illness vow (eye)

669 There are two possibilities for the king and queen, either Ḫattušili and Puduḫepa or Tudḫaliya and his unnamed wife. Since Tudḫaliya does not seem to make vows independent of Puduḫepa, and since Puduḫepa retained the title of queen her whole life, and since Puduḫepa is unlikely to be giving birth to children after her husband's death, the king should be identified with Ḫattušili III.

670 The town of Waliwanda appears in the Tawagalawa Letter (KUB 14.3 obv. i 16) as a place where Ḫattušili stopped to arrange a meeting with Piyamaradu (in Iyalanda) during his campaign to the west. The appearance of this town in the context of a campaign to Arzawa makes it almost certain KUB 56.27 belongs to the reign of Ḫattušili III.

671 Following de Roos, *Hittite Votive Texts*, 154 fn. 345.

e) Vow dateable only to Puduḫepa (but likely also Ḫattušili)[672]	
KBo 8.63	Ištar of Lawazantiya
KBo 34.145	queen$^{?}$ interceding for His Majesty (12′)
KBo 55.216	queen
KUB 15.10	queen
KUB 15.15	queen
KUB 15.26	Ištar of Lawazantiya
KUB 15.29	queen
KUB 56.25 + 60.118	Ištar of Lawazantiya
VBoT 75	queen
f) Vows dateable to reign of Tudḫaliya IV	
KBo 33.216	campaign against Assyria
KUB 56.19	(see historical discussion)[673]

8.2.5.2 Vows of Insufficient Context to Date

The following votive texts cannot be dated and so will not be used here (interesting features noted in parentheses): HT 33, KBo 3.51, 8.62, 13.72 (temple reorganization, including implements and personnel), 13.80 (temple reorganization and endowment, compensating (*šarni(n)k-*) the gods), 34.143, 41.59, 55.207, 55.222, 55.225, 55.226, 64.38; KUB 15.7, 15.13 (condition involves lunar eclipse), 15.14 (involves festivals and temple restoration), 15.20, 15.25, 15.27, 44.27, 48.120, 55.224, 56.16, 56.22, 56.26, 56.29, 57.109, 60.60, 60.86, 60.95.

8.2.5.3 Texts Excluded from Consideration

The following texts were edited in de Roos, *Hittite Votive Texts*, but excluded from the present study:

Dreams with no vow preserved: KUB 15.12, 31.67, 48.118, 48.121, 48.124, 48.125, 56.14.

Other: KUB 48.117 (a list of households, reminiscent of a *Landschenkungsurkunde*), 56.24 (oracle text mentioning vows)

672 Three texts (KUB 15.10, 15.29, and VBoT 75) contain vows made by an anonymous queen for matters other than the health of His Majesty. Though they cannot be corroborated by other criteria to the time of Puduḫepa, they will also be dated to her reign given the absence of any other viable candidates.

673 For dating, see discussion in the section *8.12 Vows of Tudḫaliya IV* below.

8.3 Using the Vows as Economic Documents

The condition of the votive texts, individually and as a corpus, precludes an exhaustive understanding of their economic impact. As ever in the field of Hittitology, fully intact tablets are a luxury and the state of preservation of the votive corpus leaves too many unknowns. Most of the texts yield only a fraction of their original lines. There is no good way to estimate how many vows should be restored in the broken portions of tablet. Unlike with "pure" economic texts that record large volumes of goods (e.g., the KASKAL Main Text), the variable levels of detail and discourse of the vows make an estimation of average entries per line impossible. There is no perceptible correlation between the length of the vow and the value of the gift. One entry can stretch for eleven lines and yield a single modest gift (e.g., KUB 15.1+ obv. ii 13–24), while the next entry has a comparable gift in only three lines (KUB 15.1+ obv. ii 25–27). There are also dependent entries in which a topic is resumed in an abbreviated form, usually with the phrase *kēdani=pat* INIM-*ni šer* 'because of precisely this matter'. This can lead to chains of dependent entries with unpredictably high concentrations of gifts per line (see e.g., KUB 15.21 1′–17′ for an extreme example).

Even if the individual tablets were restored, the dynamics of the corpus as an administrative archive remain unknown. The very fact the vows are written down means that they were mediated by a scribal bureaucracy (there is no evidence for actively literate Hittite rulers, even one as involved as Puduḫepa). But it is impossible to reconstruct a division of labor for the vows between the scribes of the temple and palace because, as de Roos noted in his introduction to the votive texts, most of the tablets were recovered in the early excavations of Hugo Winckler and the findspots are now lost.[674]

As with all administrative documents there is also the question of how many were retained and how many were discarded. The lack of an internal dating system in Hittite documents is again keenly felt. On the one hand, vows could be kept for some time: at least one text dates from when Ḫattušili was a local king in Hakmiš (KBo 9.96(+)), with the tablet presumably carried with him to Ḫattuša or recopied. But are these old vows the exception or the rule? Scribal remarks suggest that the survival of older vows was probably not an isolated incident. Some vows are marked as completed (*karū* 'already'), instead of being erased, which means the administration had reasons for maintaining a record even after the transaction with the gods was fulfilled,[675] and the very fact that

674 De Roos, *Hittite Votive Texts*, 6–7.

675 De Roos, *op. cit.*, 7 fn. 16, 17 provided a discussion and list of the attestations of *karū* (SUM-*an*/*piyan*) and its counterpart *nāwi* 'not yet (fulfilled)', but the list is not complete, having not been updated to include the vows newly edited in the book, and does not include line numbers. Below is presented the full list:

karū: KBo 8.61 (4′). KBo 55.208 (obv.? 9′). KBo 55.221 (5′). 55.226 (7′). KUB 15.4 (obv. i 11′). KUB 15.11+ (obv. ii 4; rev. iii 18′, 25′). KUB 15.15 (rev. iv 9′). KUB 15.19 (obv. 10′; rev. 4′). KUB 15.20 (obv. ii 11′). KUB 15.23 (rev. 22′). KUB 15.29 (obv. i 8′, 11′, 13′). KUB 56.12 (2′, 10′). KUB 56.22 (2′)

nāwi: KBo 9.96 (obv. i 6′, 15′) (+) KBo 41.60 (obv. i? 7′, 8′, 11′)

the corpus survived to be buried with the fall of the Empire also makes it likely that votive texts were not assiduously recycled. However, the survival of some of the vows does not guarantee that more were not lost, nor can every older vow be identified by internal criteria.

If exhaustive analysis is made impossible by the corpus' state of preservation, an episodic approach organizing vows by events or episodes in historical context can yield better results. Instead of estimating that a specific amount of vows was made during Ḫattušili's reign, one would say that "during Ḫattušili's reign, a military campaign would precipitate this amount of vows, and his periodic illnesses would trigger that amount of vows by Puduḫepa," and so forth. From the wealth expended on certain episodes one can get an idea of the *potential* vow budget for any given year in which similar events took place. This can then be measured against the other economic data points discussed in *6. The Relative Value of the* KASKAL *Main Text*: see esp. *Figure 1: Comparison of Gold in* KASKAL *Main Text, Gifts, and Tribute* and *Figure 2: Comparison of Textiles in* KASKAL *Main Text, Gifts, and Tribute.* The result is a series of relative comparisons, where one can weigh, for example, the wealth expended on the illness vows against the yearly tribute from Hittite vassals.

Though the episodic approach simplifies the problem of chronology, there still remains the question of measuring the wealth of the vows themselves. The uneven level of detail in the apodoses makes direct comparisons between vows difficult. Few of the objects mentioned are given with weights and dimensions that would allow for quantification of value. It is possible to see that in general terms gifts come in two sizes, "major" and "minor." Minor gifts usually consist of one or two votive objects made of precious metal and sometimes an offering of livestock amounting to one ox and six to eight sheep. When the dimensions of the votive objects are preserved, they are generally smaller than expected, perhaps being models rather than functioning items.[676] The majority of the vows have apodoses belonging to the minor gift category. Major gifts are a much more heterogeneous group, ranging from the inauguration of a new festival, to the creation of a life-sized statue of the god, to a gift of 100 minas of precious metals, and they are less frequent than the minor gifts.[677]

---

both: KBo 34.145 (*karū*: 9′; *nāwi*: 6′). KBo 55.219 (*karū*: 8′; "*nāwi awan arḫa*": 5′). KUB 31.69 (*karū*: rev.? 9′; *nāwi*: rev.? 6′). KUB 48.119 (*karū*: obv.? 13′; *nāwi*: obv.? 19′)

It may be observed that the "*nāwi*" are far fewer than the "*karū*," placing the votive texts towards the end of the economic-administrative cycle, at the level of audit and control, rather than promise and production. This "production" level of vow fulfilment is probably captured by the few PTAC texts edited under *7. Votive Gifts* in Vol. II. As discussed in *8.13 The Vow of Puduḫepa (CTH 585) and Vow Fulfillment in Practice*, discerning an interface of the votive corpus with any written system of production and control remains a problem.

676 See de Roos, *Hittite Votive Texts*, 42–48 for discussion of the weights, and the comment that the objects seem to be smaller than those from the Egyptian correspondences.

677 Outside of the Illness Vows of Puduḫepa for Ḫattušili, where they are treated separately, major and minor gifts will be presented in the same tables, with the major gifts distinguished by having their citations in bold. The criteria for a major gift is inexact, and the reader is invited to make their own evaluation, but in general festivals (but not rituals) are included, as are any large quantities of silver, gold, livestock or deportees, and objects with exceptional dimensions, such as statues which are

The size of the gifts is unpredictable from the protases, but in the following analysis of the vows it will be shown that Puduḫepa tends to offer many minor gifts while Ḫattušili gives fewer but larger major gifts, and that the distribution has implications for the economic sectors of the Hittite state.

8.4 Vows Concerning Health and Wellness (The "Illness Vows")

There are a total of fifty-five vows recoverable from the votive corpus in which Puduḫepa pledges on behalf of Ḫattušili's health. Most of the vows ask the gods to keep His Majesty alive. Some concern specific body-parts such as the ear (KUB 15.9 rev. iii 6′–8′; KBo 55.208 obv.? 6′–7′), the feet (KUB 15.3 obv. i 17–21), the neck (KUB 15.28+ obv. ii 2′–5′; KUB 48.123 obv. i 8′–11′), the head (KBo 55.208 rev.?), and very frequently the eyes (KBo 8.61 6′–8′; KBo 27.60 5′–10′; KBo 55.223 6′–15′ ; KUB 15.6 obv. i 17′–19′; KUB 48.119 obv.? 9′–13′, rev.? 8–10; KUB 56.13 obv. 11′–14′, 15′–17′, rev. 9′–13′, 19′–22′; KUB 56.21 7′–10′; KUB 56.23 obv. 1–16; KUB 56.28 obv. 6′–11′). Other ailments include fever (KUB 48.123 rev. iv 1–3) and the demon DÌM.NUN.ME (KUB 15.11+ rev. iii 13′–18′, 19′–25′). In one case the topic is "the illness of this year" (KBo 55.221 3′–5′).

8.4.1 Vows by Puduḫepa for Ḫattušili (Minor Gifts)

Of the fifty-five total "illness vows," forty-three contain what will be classified as "minor gifts." Most of these gifts consist of one or two objects of metal or stone. Some include livestock, usually one ox and eight sheep. Where weights of the objects are specified, they are modest amounts.

Table 34: Illness Vows: Minor Gifts (Puduḫepa for Ḫattušili)

Protasis	Apodosis
1. IBoT 3.123 1–5	
The queen to Kun[iyawanni thus vowed:] If you Kunniyawanni [...] (and) for him that illness you the goddess, my lady, [...] (and) you the goddess, my lady, justic[e ...,] (1–4)	1 head of lapis lazuli, 1 soul [of ... I will give.] (5)
2. KBo 8.61 6′–8′	
[...i]f the god [heals(?)] His Majesty's eyes, (6′)	[...] I will [g]ive, and to the god [... 1 p]air of eyes, silver, (weighing) 2 minas [...] (7′–8′)
3. KBo 27.60 5′–10′	
[The queen(?) in the to]wn of Utruna in a dream to Ištar of the *ḫašta*[*ri*- vowed: "If you, the goddess, my lady,] rev[eal] (your divine) rule [to me, and	for the goddess 6 oxen [...] inlaid, 1 silver axe of Iš[tar ...] 1 ox, 8 sheep for the women I will give [...] (8′–10′)

described as life-sized or wearing jewelry of their own; normal statues, which could be as small as 1 mina of silver (KBo 34.145 6′), are excluded.

the eye]s of His Majesty you make fast [... and] you [...,] (5′–8′)	
4. KBo 55.208 obv.? 6′–7′	
When [His M]ajesty had an illness of the ear, (obv.? 6′)	[1 s]ilver ear, 1 gold ear, weight [not specified ... to t]his god for H[is Majesty (obv.? 7′)
5. KBo 55.208 rev.? 11′–15′	
When His Majesty's he[ad was ill. The queen(?)] thus vowed: "If [...] goes healthily, (and) the illn[ess...,] (rev.? 11′–13′)	eyes of gold (weighing) 1 mina, eye[s of silver(?) weighing 1(?) mina], 1 soul of lapis lazuli, eyes [of ....]" (rev.? 14′–15′)
6. KBo 55.208 rev.? 16′–18′	
[The que]en for the life [of His Majesty made a vow,] (rev.? 16′)	[...] harv[est] festival [...] sheep [I will g]ive. (rev.? 17′–18′)
7. KBo 55.217 4′–8′	
[The queen(?) to Ištar] of Šamuḫa thus vowed: [If the king] and queen (stay) living, (4′–5′)	before [the goddess s]tatues of silver of the king and queen we will make. [...] its eyes (and) its hands of gold [...] the doctor knew. (5′–8′)
8. KBo 55.221 2′–5′	
[The queen(?) in the town of ... to] NIN.GAL (of) Kumma[nni thus vowed: ...] the illness of this year [...] (2′–3′)	for the sake of His Majesty 2 years of silver, 3 statues of silver [...] in their temple I will bring. Alre[ady (done). (4′–5′)
9. KBo 55.223 6′–15′	
[... i]n the town of Ušša to the god [... i]f this which [...] in which month [...] I will see. But the Moon-god [...] If in whi[ch ...] of His Majesty, of the right eye [... i]f whichever matter down [...] but if it for me [...] (6′–14′)	I will decorate [...] 1 ox, 2 sheep for *ambašši-*, 1 [...] (14′–15′)
10. KUB 15.1+ obv. ii 13–24	
Concerning [t]hese oaths determined for me, each by oracle – since I am at present not able to undo them by offering[678] – until thereafter, until I undo them by offering, if you, Šarruma, my lord, [keep] His Majesty [from] evil [... and i]f to Ḫepat, your mother, [you ... and for] His [Majesty] nothing evil reaches hi[s] body [...] (and) in no way does it go badly for us, (obv. ii 13–23)	for Šarruma, my lord, I will make [1 sh]ield of silver with gold inlay, weight unspecified. (obv. ii 23–24)

678 For *arḫa šippanda-* in sense of "to undo (the consequences of a broken oath) by offering," see CHD Š *s.v. šip(p)a(n)d(a)-* 3 e 2′ (p. 395).

11. KUB 15.1+ obv. ii 25–27	
(continuing above) And [i]f Šarruma, my lord, lends his [ear] to this word of mine, (and) hears me, (obv. ii 25–27)	[1] ear weighing 10 shekels of gold, 1 ear weighing 1 mina of silver I will [gi]ve to Šarruma. (obv. ii 27)
12. KUB 15.1+ obv. ii 28–36	
(see above) And if for me you two Šarrumanni deities and one Allanzunni deity who are sprung from the loins of the god, if you hear this my word, and you mention it across to Šarruma, and no evil word finds His Majesty, while he fulfills these oaths, (obv. ii 28–34)	to the two Šarrumanni deities and one Allanzunni deity, for each I will make 1 gold ear (and) 1 silver ear. Weight [not speci]fied. (obv. ii 35–36)
13. KUB 15.3 obv. i 17–21	
Dream of the queen. "In a dream someone is saying to me: 'vow thus to NIN.GAL: "If for His Majesty that fire of his feet becomes well soon, (obv. i 17–19)	for N[IN.GAL] I will make a [*t*]*alla*- of gold inlaid with lapis lazuli, a w[hole] *talla*-."'" [T]o the l[and] of Egypt [they] will send true words. (obv. i 19–21)
14. KUB 15.4 obv. i 1′–11′	
[... the queen(?)] vowed: "If [...] you do not deliver, [...] I will make. But that later [....] If you [keep] His Majesty alive, (obv. i 1′–4′)	[...] strong [weapon]s for him/her/it [....] But in the tower [...] I will make. [...] I will make." [...] Already (given). (obv. i 5′–11′)
15. KUB 15.6 obv. i 17′–19′	
If [...] you make the eyes live, (obv. i 17′)	[... al]ready standing [... a *ḫaršiy*]*alli*-vessel of silver I will make. (obv. i 18′–19′)
16. KUB 15.8 obv. i 4′–7′	
The queen to the Storm-god of Heaven, (according to) Ms. Zamuwa[tti's advice thus] vowed: If the god, my lord, [keeps His] Maj[esty alive], (obv. i 4′–5′)	for the god 1 soul of gold, 3 shekels [... 1 p]air of silver eyes of 6 sh[ekels I will make.] (obv. i 6′–7′)
17. KUB 15.9 obv. ii 1′–11′	
[If ... you keep him] alive [...] (obv. ii 1′)	[...] and strong weapons [I will make ...] he will sate himself [...] because of *ušantarai* [...] from the borders [...] but of that for him [...] And for the god, my lord, [...] for 1 sun-disk [...] but [for 1] sun-disk [...] But that then [... for the go]d, my lord, 1 bord[er ... (obv. ii 2′–11′)
18. KUB 15.9 rev. iii 6′–8′	
[...] the ear [... became s]ick. The queen [vowed thus: "If you heal his ear ... "] (rev. iii 6′)	1 gold ear weighing 10 shekels, [...] and a gold [ear]ring weighing 3 shekels. (rev. iii 7′–8′)
19. KUB 15.11+ obv. ii 1–4	
[... the queen(?) v]owed [...] I [...f]or the life of His Majesty ⟨⟨His Majesty⟩⟩ (obv. ii 1–2)	1 pair of (female) breasts, gold [... weighing] 1 mina, vowed. Already (given). (obv. ii 3–4)

20. KUB 15.11+ rev. iii 6′–7′	
[The queen for] the life of His Majesty to (the goddess) Išḫara [...] (rev. iii 6′)	[... , its we]ight not specified, vowed. Already (given). Kat[apaili ...] (rev. iii 7′)
21. KUB 15.11+ rev. iii 13′–18′	
The queen in town of Ḫurma to the deity DÌM.N[UN.ME of] Kumman(ni) vowed: If DÌM.NUN.ME [...] does not seize His Majesty, (rev. iii 13′–15′)	1 silver *ḫuganni-*, 1 go[ld] *ḫutanni-*, filled with fine oil [...] His Majesty[...] of gold, 1 mina I will make beforehand. Al[ready] gi[ven.] (rev. iii 16′–18′)
22. KUB 15.11+ rev. iii 19′–25′	
[I]f DÌM.NUN.⟨ME⟩ does not further [seize] His Majesty, and does not [r]eturn to him, (rev. iii 19′–20′)	I will come [to] Kummanni, and [...] offer to the god. With a finger [...] And His Majesty for you gold [...] I will make beforehand. [...] Already (given). (rev. iii 21′–25′)
23. KUB 15.19 obv. 3′–5′	
[Šaumat]ari of Kaittana. The queen to Šaumatari [of Kaittana vowed thus: If the go]d, my lord, will keep His Majesty alive, while [...,] (obv. 3′–4′)	I will come and [give] to the god, my lord, 1 soul of gold weighing 1 mina. (obv. 5′)
24. KUB 15.23 rev. 17′–22′	
The queen to the Sun-god of Heaven of Ḫuḫana [th]us vowed: If the god, my lord, makes His Majesty live for [year]s, (rev. 17′–19′)	I will invoke the god, and for him a [gold/silver(?)] statue [o]f His Majesty [...] I will make, its weight not specified. [...Al]rea[dy given.] (rev. 19′–22′)
25. KUB 15.28+ obv. ii 2′–5′	
[... the queen(?) vowed concerning the *a*]*uli-* in the town of Zitḫar[a ... if] the *auli-* is fixed, [...] (obv. ii 2′–3′)[679]	[...] of silver (and) gold I will make. [...] its weight I will take to heart. (obv. ii 4′–5′)
26. KUB 15.28+ obv. ii 6′–10′	
[... for Ištar of] Šamuha (he/she) vowed: [if the king and queen(?)] are alive, [...] (obv. ii 6′–7′)	[... for the goddess(?)] statues of silver [of the king and queen(?) I will make. Their eye]s (and) their hands [will be made of gold(?), and] it for Ištar of Šamuha [...] (obv. ii 8′–10′)[680]
27. KUB 15.28+ obv. ii 11′–15′	
[The queen(?) for] Ištar of Šamuha vowed thus: [if the goddess, my lady, f]or His Majesty on this journey/ campaign [...,] (obv. ii 11′–12′)	[...] for the goddess, my lady, a hand [...] I will give. The great assem[bly ...] they will give. (obv. ii 13′–15′)

679 Cf. KUB 48.123 obv. i 8′–11′ (Table 34, no. 32).

680 Cf. KBo 55.217 4′–8′ (Table 34, no. 7) for a similar apodosis.

28. KUB 15.30 rev. iii 1′–7′[681]	
[...]	"[...] silver [...] comes. [A breas]t/pectoral of lapis lazuli and [...]-es of lapis lazuli for the Goddess of the Night [...] they will make in it." Thus Tatti to the queen: "Walwaziti said to me: 'I hope His Majesty recovers: give this breast/pectoral, as is, to Ištar of Šamuha.'" (rev. iii 1′–7′)
29. KUB 31.69 rev.? 6′–9′	
[The queen(?) i]n the town of Uda to Ištar of [Lawazantiya thus vowed: If Hi]s Majesty the illness of this year [...] (rev.? 6′–7′)	[for the godde]ss 1 year of silver, 1 silver statue (of the) king [I will give. ... Al]ready (given). The year (and) statue (of the) ki[ng] no[t yet]. (rev.? 8′–9′)
30. KUB 48.119 obv.? 9′–13′	
And [if] now they bring the god, my lord, [awa]y from Utruna to Nerik, they will offer [fort]h 1000 sheep to him in the *daḫanga-*. And on whichever day for His Majesty the *kammara-*disease departs from [the eyes], (obv.? 9′–12′)	(on that day) I will offer to the god 1 fat ox (and) 8 sheep. [...] Already (given). (In(?)) the town of Partaparta. (obv.? 12′–13′)
31. KUB 48.119 rev.? 7–10	
[...] after the *purulliya-*[fe]stival [...] he/she will make healthy, and the right eye, when [...] likewise becomes healthy, (rev.? 7–9)	for the god 1 lion rhyton of gold, [its weight n]ot specified I will make. (rev.? 9–10)
32. KUB 48.123 obv. i 8′–11′	
[Whe]n in the town of Zitḫara (it) struck the *auli-*. [The queen] vowed to Ištar of Lawazantiya: [If the goddess,] my [lady,] makes soft the hand of Piḫatarḫunta, the doctor, (obv. i 8′–10′)[682]	for the goddess, my lady, [a ..., its we]ight not specified, I will make. (obv. i 10′–11′)
33. KUB 48.123 obv. ii 18′–25′	
The queen in the t[own of ... vowed: If you keep] His Majesty alive [...] (obv. ii 18′–19′)	1 cow of/and si[lver/gold (obv. ii 25′)
34. KUB 48.123 rev. iii 14–18	
The queen in the town of Ḫasa-[...] to Ištar of Lawazan[tiya vowed thus: "If His Majesty] becomes healthy, (rev. iii 14–16)	then t[o ...] desired. Now it [...] separately a *kušiši-*garment [....]" (rev. ii 16–18)

681 That the queen is the probable author of this vow can be inferred from the apodosis. Lines 1′–3′ contain the end of an offering for the Goddess of the Night. Lines 4′–7′ contain a message from Tatti, on behalf of Walwaziti, asking the queen to donate a breast or pectoral (GABA) to Ištar of Šamuḫa for the sake of His Majesty's recovery. There is no paragraph line between lines 1′–3′ and 4′–7′, so all seven lines probably concern the same topic, namely His Majesty recovering from an illness. The first three lines contain the end of an offering by the main author of the vow, who is probably the queen. The last four lines can be read as a supplementary gift that Walwaziti asked Tatti to pass on to the queen.

682 Cf. KUB 15.28+ obv. ii 2′–3′ (Table 34, no. 25).

35. KUB 48.123 rev. iv 1–3	
[... y]early the fever [...] (rev. iv 1)	[...] 1 soul of gold [and ... so much will be] its weight, I will give. (rev. iv 2–3)
36. KUB 56.13 obv. 5′–7′	
[...] (obv. 5′)[683]	[1 pa]ir of eyes of lapis lazuli weighing 1 mina, [...] of gold and lapis lazuli *ḫurlaimant-* [...] (obv. 5′–7′)
37. KUB 56.13 obv. 8′–10′	
The queen(?) to [...] for His Majesty (in) Tarḫuntašša vowed: (obv. 8′)	[...] of silver, 1 *uppiya-* of gold [...] I will [gi]ve. (obv. 9′–10′)
38. KUB 56.13 obv. 11′–14′	
[The queen fo]r the sickness of the eyes for the sake of His Majesty vowed: (obv. 11′)	[...] I myself will bring [...] I will [ma]ke, and him first [...] for him/her 1 oil-loaf I will begin to give regularly. (obv. 12′–14′)
39. KUB 56.13 rev. 1′–8′	
[...] "And [...] if for that [... for the god Piḫas]ašši of Tarḫuntašša vo[wed ...] you will make(?) [... i]f for His Majesty [...] (rev. 1′–5′)	[...] 1 dream of silver, weighing 2 minas [... an object of go]ld, and breads of gold [...]-ed in [...] 1 night of gold, its weight not specified, to the god I will give. (rev. 6′–8′)
40. KUB 56.13 rev. 9′–13′	
"[... on the advice of(?)] Tuttu, lord of the É *ABUSI* [...] is sick. For his eye [....]" If that dream the kneeling [...] (rev. 9′–12′)	[... 1] dream of silver weighing 2 minas, 1 dream of gold weighing 1 mina I will give. (rev. 13′)
41. KUB 56.13 rev. 16′–17′	
[...] but if for His Majesty [...] (rev. 16′)	[1 ox(?)] and 8 sheep(?) of silver I will give. (rev. 17′)
42. KUB 56.13 rev. 19′–22′	
[... a]rrived at. The queen [vowed thus: If] the gods, my lords make better His Majesty's eyes, (rev. 19′–20′)	[...] 1 pair of eyes of silver (of?) the king [I will make]. (rev. 21′–22′)
43. KUB 56.21 7′–10′	
[...] for His Majesty's life [... if his] eyes become well, (7′–8′)	[... a *ḫutl*]*a-*, ornament[ed ...] I will give [...] (9′–10′)

8.4.2 Illness Vows: Puduḫepa for Ḫattušili (Major Gifts)

Eleven illness vows by Puduḫepa for Ḫattušili contain larger gifts. The protases of these "major vows" are not discernably different from the minor vows, save for the

683 From the gift of a pair of eyes in the apodosis it can be inferred the topic is probably an eye illness of His Majesty.

possibility that they are perhaps skewed towards general prayers for His Majesty's long life and rather than specific illnesses.

Table 35: Illness Vows: Major Gifts (Precious Metals)

Protasis	Apodosis
1. KUB 15.1+ obv. i 5–10	
Ḫepat (of) Uda. Dream of the queen. The matter of the neck [she] deliver[ed], while in (the dream).[684] The queen in the dream to Ḫepat (of) Uda vowed thus: "If you, the goddess, my lady, keep His Majesty alive, (and) do not deliver him to evil, (obv. i 5–6)	I will make for Ḫepat a gold statue. And I will make a gold rosette for it; they will call it the rosette of Ḫepat. And I will make a gold pectoral for your breast; they will call it the god's pectoral." (obv. i 7–10)
2. KUB 15.1+ rev. iii 32′–35′	
The q[ueen for her(?) p]erson vowed thus: "I[f ... in] a dream already forth [...] my l[ady] in a house [...] you make (and) His Majesty lives, (rev. iii 32′–35′)	f[or] Iš[tar a stat]ue of gold I will make. The statue will be [equ]al to Ištar of Šaḫpina.[685] I will plate the weapons for her, either in silver or in gold." (rev. iii 36′–38′)
3. KUB 15.3 obv. i 5–16[686]	
[The q]ueen to the Moon-god for the recovery thus vowe[d: "If] you, the Moon-god, my lord, [giv]e to His Majesty long years, (so that) [His Majesty] achieves the years which are promised by the god, (obv. i 5–8)	to the god, my lord, in a year 1 silver cup, and in a year to him 1 gold cup, its weight not specified, I will give. And because there are 12 months in a year, yearly I will begin making 1 year and 12 months of silver and gold. I will determine the weight by heart and commence giving them to the god. But whatever is willed (by) the Moon-god, according to that I will be giving the months of silver and gold, whether (in) Urikina or wherever." (obv. i 8–16)

Three of the major vows by Puduḫepa for the health of Ḫattušili contain large gifts of precious metals. Among these, KUB 15.3 obv. i 5–16 stands out as one of the few examples of an open-ended or continuous gift. Presumably the queen would give the silver cup, the gold cup, and the year and month symbols (models of the Anatolian hieroglyphic signs? Cf. suggestion of same for the "souls" appearing in the votive texts in de Roos, *Hittite Votive Texts*, 99 fn. 130) for as long as Ḫattušili lived. It is surprising

684 As de Roos, *Hittite Votive Texts*, 97 fn. 118 notes, the translation of this line is difficult. I have interpreted the phrase *kuwapi anda* "while in (the dream)" as right-dislocated from the main clause INIM GAM *maniyaḫta* "she delivered the matter" (in the sense of entrusting the goddess with a petition), emphasizing that the entrusting took place within the dream. This is confirmed by the next clause that specifies the vow also took place within the dream.

685 With de Roos, *op. cit.*, 95, the statue will be life-sized?

686 See also Jürgen Lorenz, "'Lange Jahre' und Lebenszeit bei den Hethitern," in *Time and History in the Ancient Near East: Proceedings of the 56th Rencontre Assyriologique Internationale at Barcelona 26–30 July 2010*, eds. Lluis Feliu, Jaume Llop, Adelina Millet Albà, Joaquin Sanmartín (Winona Lake: Eisenbrauns, 2013), 174–75, for transliteration and translation of this passage.

that more vows for the health of His Majesty do not adopt this contractual arrangement, since it seems a good way to guarantee the continued interest of the gods. It could be that the problem lay with the attention span of mortals, and not the divine: in KUB 15.11+ obv. ii 13–19 Puduḫepa offers a compensatory gift for neglecting the conditions of a similar yearly vow, and promises to begin the regular offerings forthwith. There are other examples in the vows and oracles of divine wrath at forgotten promises, so a pattern of frequent "one-off" gifts might have been safer for the devotee.

The two other vows promise substantial statues made of precious metal, both of divine images. Dimensions for these statues are not given, but in KUB 15.1+ rev. iii 32′–35′, the phrase ALAM *ŠA* ᴰ*IŠTAR* ᵁᴿᵁ*šaḫ-pí-na* [*ma-ši*]-*wa-an* "a statue [equ]al to Ištar of Šaḫpina" might indicate a life-sized (i.e., human-sized?) object.[687] A life-size gold statue, even if plated or made of lower quality gold, would be an immensely expensive undertaking. The other statue received a rosette and pectoral as decoration, which means that even if it turned out not to be as large as the other statue it must also have commanded an extra level of time and resources than the typical votive gift. Judging by the paucity of examples in the votive corpus, they were not lightly promised.

Table 36: Illness Vows: Major Gifts (Festivals and Rituals)

Protasis	Apodosis
1. KUB 15.1+ rev. iii 7′–16′[688]	
[Dream of the quee]n, the matter (of) the god Gurwašu, when [.... Gu]rwašu while in the dream spoke [t]o the queen: "That matter of your husband which you hold in your heart – he will live, and I will give him 100 years." (rev. iii 7′–12′)	The queen in the dream vowed thus: "If you do thusly for me, and the king, my husband, lives, for the god I will establish three *ḫaršiyalli*-vessels, 1 of oil, 1 of honey, 1 of fruit." (rev. iii 12′–16′)
2. KUB 15.24 obv. i 1–6	
His Majesty [...] when from the land of Ḫatti [goes(?) ...,] and for them [...] regular festivals [celebrates(?) ...] On whic[h da]y there was the great assembly, [on that day] (the queen) vowed to the Storm-god of Ḫatti thus: if you, [the god, my lord,] cause [His Majesty] to live. (obv. i 1–5)	[I will honor] the Storm-god of Ḫatti in the *ḫal*[*entuwa*-structure]. But a gate the *ḫazqaraya*-women [...] (obv. i 5–6)
3. KUB 15.24 obv. i 7–8	
(see above)	And the Storm-god of Ḫatti for precisely that mat[ter ...] and [I] will invoke the *kaliman*. (obv. i 7–8)

687 See entry *mašiwant*- in the CHD, especially citation of KUB 21.27 rev. iii 39–41 (CTH 384, Prayer of Puduḫepa to the Sun-goddess of Arinna) where a silver statue "as big as Ḫattušili, its head, hands, and feet of gold" is promised. The interpretation of "a statue [equ]al to Ištar of Šaḫpina" is not clear. Perhaps it meant a copy of another, preexisting statue of the goddess?

688 See also transliteration and translation in Goedegebuure, *The Hittite Demonstratives*, 234.

4. KUB 56.28 obv. 5′–11′[689]	
[...] Ištar of Šamuḫa ⟨in⟩ Urik[ina ...] The [qu]een to Iš[tar of Šamuḫa vowed thus: I]f the goddess, my lady, for me [...] the eye (of) His Majesty, (its) pupil [you heal(?) ...] (obv. 5′–8′)	[...] a *ḫaršiyalli*-vessel [I will institute(?) ...] these daily praise-offeri[ngs ...] on the day a *ḫaršiya*[*lli*-vessel ...] (obv. 9′–11′)
5. Liv. 49–47–42 5′–6′	
And [i]f you the god, my lord, keep His Majesty alive, (his) healt[h f]ull good, (5′–6′)	for the god a ritual [...] (6′)

The establishment of *ḫaršiyalli*-vessels ("pithoi") in KUB 15.1+ rev. iii 7′–16′ (and possibly KUB 56.28 obv. 5′–11′) implies a commitment of resources beyond the supply of oil, fruit, and honey. The filling of the *ḫaršiyalli*-vessel in the fall and opening in the spring was a vital component of the Hittite cultic calendar, and Puduḫepa's gift would probably entail compensation for temple staff to carry out the ritual. The verb *dai-/tiya-* 'to set, place, establish' suggests a long-term (yearly?) commitment to the vow.

In KUB 15.24 obv. i 1–6 it is unclear what honoring the Stormgod in the *ḫalentuwa*-structure (which was probably the "(great) hall" of a building – see *Lexical Commentary s.v.* ^{É}*ḫalentu(wa)-*) means in terms of labor. As pointed out by both Michele Cammarosano and Gary Beckman, taking obv. i 5: *nu=za* ^{D}10 ^{URU}*ḫatti* ^{É}*ḫal*[*entūwa* DÙ-*mi*] as a promise to build a *ḫalentuwa*-structure is grammatically impossible, since the construction *iya-* + *-za* with a divine name has a technical sense of 'to honor a god' (HW^{2} I *s.v. iya-/iye-* I.3.2 [p. 13]).[690] Thus, KUB 15.24 obv. i 3–5 should be interpreted as a vow to honor the Storm-god in the *ḫalentuwa*-structure. The fact that the vow was made during a great assembly means that the particular *ḫalentuwa*-structure in question is probably the very same where the vow was made. The invoking of the *kaliman* in obv. i 7–8 would at least require the personal time and attention of the queen, a precious resource in and of itself.

Table 37: Illness Vows: Major Gifts (People and Settlements)

Protasis	Apodosis
1. KUB 15.11+ obv. ii 12–19	
And to (the goddess) Allani because of the House of the Storm-god of Manuziya, 6 [...] for the sake of His Majesty's life I have vowed: (obv. ii 12–13)	"I have begun to give [it t]o the goddess yearly, but now, because of that [...] I have never given it. But now [...] I have sent 25 people for the goddess. More[over] I already placed [7] people [here] and 7 people there. I will send it [...] to the goddess.

689 See discussion of this passage under *8.2.4 Tudḫaliya IV* above.

690 Michele Cammarosano, "Kultinventare aus Kayalıpınar (Šamuḫa)," in *Keilschrifttafeln aus Kayalıpınar 1. Textfunde aus den Jahren 1999–2017*, ed. Elisabeth Rieken. Documenta Antiqua Asiae Minoris 1 (Wiesbaden: Harrassowitz), 78, against Piotr Taracha, "Hittite ^{É}*ḫalentuwa-* Revisited," AoF 44 (2017): 106 and de Roos, *Hittite Votive Texts*, 185–86. See earlier same point in Gary Beckman, Review of *Beiträge zur Erforschung des hethitischen Tempels: Kultanlagen im Lichte der Keilschrifttexte*, by Sedat Alp, JAOS 104/3 (1984): 583.

	Le[t] it be for the goddess a propitiation." (obv. ii 13–19)
2. KUB 15.11+ obv. ii 19–23	
(cont. from previous vow without break) "And if His Majesty comes up well from campaign, and it is completely compl[ete] for him, (obv. ii 19–20)	then too I will [s]end 6 pe[ople] to the goddess [...] 1 fat ox, 6 sheep, 1 golden soul for kings[hip], for the sake of His Majesty's life I will se[nd.]" (obv. ii 21–23)
3. KUB 56.13 obv. 15′–17′	
[The queen thus] vowed: If for the eye of His Majesty [...] the vows [...] (obv. 15′–16′)	[...] I will, and with 1000 sheep. (obv. 17′)
4. KUB 56.23 obv. 1–16	
[The dream of the queen. ... the queen] saw [a dream] in the town of Šaḫḫaniya, and the Mother Goddess spoke to her b[y dream]. The queen to the Mother Goddess (of) [Š]aḫḫaniya thus v[owed: If His Majes]ty's eyes you cool(?), and my son and daughters who were (there), [you ... it ...] (obv. 1–4)	I will invoke the goddess to an offering table, [...] inlaid with stone I will make. I will p[late] a column with silver for you, and I will plate an offering table with silver for you. And sons [...] I will [make], or I will make for all of them offerings therein, and a column for you above [...] I will restore back. [...] the gods Ummeda, Kattarala, Tarumma, O Goddess [...,] if they are determined for plating it, [...] (for/in) the town of Šiyatta (behind its) *walla-*, 20 horses, 300 deportees I will set[tle ....][691] Who for you (or: who belonging to you) [...] they are [op]pressing [...] with silver, gold, *iron (ore)*, copper, bronze [...] and for you a [...] statue of the queen [...] they will finish. (obv. 4–16)

Deportees (^{LÚ}NAM.RA, lit. 'booty') were civilian prisoners captured by the Hittite army.[692] They were semi-free persons whose fate was solely determined by the king. Often, they were used to endow temples with servants, work royal estates, or settle new towns. From the above vows it appears that Puduḫepa was granted control of at least some of His Majesty's deportees. Although KUB 15.11+ obv. ii 13–23 uses the euphemistic term SAG.DU^{MEŠ} 'persons', their being sent and placed with the goddess leaves no doubt as to their origins.

691 De Roos, *Hittite Votive Texts*, 261 translated the passage [...] ^{URU}*Ši-ia-at-ta* BÀD 20 ANŠE-*ma*$^{?}$ 3 ME NAM.RA *a-še-š*[*a-nu-mi* as "(In) Šiyatta [I] will (build) a surrounding wall ... (and) settle (there) 300 civilian prisoners [" relying on a different parsing of the signs constituting "20 ANŠE-*ma*" for recovering a verb of building. My translation attempts to read BÀD 'wall' with the city of Šiyatta, perhaps in partitive apposition: "the city of Šiyatta, (its) wall, I will settle ...," i.e., settling the deportees within the walls of Šiyatta and not the surrounding countryside. In the Middle Hittite Instructions to the *BĒL MADGALTI* (CTH 261), concerning the management of settlements on the Kaška frontier, every deportee settler is required to be within the walls by nightfall, and remain there until morning.

692 For an overview of this topic, see Harry A. Hoffner, "The Treatment and Long-Term Use of Persons Captured in Battle according to the Maşat Corpus," in *Recent Developments in Hittite Archaeology and History*, eds. Harry A. Hoffner Jr., K. Aslıhan Yener (Winona Lake: Eisenbrauns, 2002).

Perhaps because it involves not only Ḫattušili, but also children of Puduḫepa, the apodosis of KUB 56.23 obv. 4–16 contains possibly the most impressive vow of the entire votive corpus: it entails nothing less than the foundation or enhancement of a community with 300 souls, an endowment of multiple offering tables, columns, quantities of various metals, and a statue of the queen. The settlement seems to be walled for defense, and the twenty horses are presumably destined for military service.

8.4.3 Other Illness Vows by Puduḫepa

There are five vows concerning health made by Puduḫepa for someone other than Ḫattušili (note: in this and the remaining sections, major and minor gifts will not be treated separately, and instead major vows will be distinguished by having their citations in bold).

Table 38: Illness Vows: Puduḫepa for Herself

Protasis	Apodosis
1. KUB 15.1+ obv. ii 2–4	
[The queen(?)] in a drea[m to ...] Zababa (of) Urikina thus vowed: "If you, the god, my lord, cause me to live, (obv. ii 2–3)	I will plate for you a stele and an offering table." (obv. ii 3–4)
2. KUB 48.119 obv.? 3′–8′[693]	
[If] you, o god, make good this unknown disease this year, (obv.? 3′)	for the god I will institute some new festival, and I will celebrate a *purulliya*-[fes]tival for you in Ḫakmiš, and also [i]n Nerik I will celebrate you separately. And [i]f it is determined for me to celebrate it in one place in Nerik, just there I will celebrate [i]t. (obv.? 4′–8′)
3. KUB 56.15 obv. ii 7–14	
And if the deity DÌM.NUN.ME [does not seize] me fu[rther ...] (obv. ii 7)	for the [...] and for the goddess, my lady, 1 ox, 8 sheep [as *ambašši*-offering], and 1 ox, 8 sheep as *keldi*-offering I will give [...] which place with oil fill[ed ...] for the goddess, my lady, erected [...] (weighing) 1 mina I will make. I will [es]tablish it with fine oil [filled], and I will give it to the goddess [(obv. ii 8–14)

Puduḫepa seems to have experienced fewer illnesses than her husband, and only three vows are preserved where she prays for her own health. KUB 48.119 obv.? 3′–8′ would be classified as a "major vow," since it promises the establishment of a new festival (again with yearly connotations?) and the celebration of a *purulliya*-festival. The deity DÌM.NUN.ME in KUB 56.15 obv. ii 7–14 is considered to be a demon of some sort, often

693 For newer transliteration and translation, see Goedegebuure, *The Hittite Demonstratives*, 409.

associated with the difficulties of childbirth.[694] However, this same demon also afflicts His Majesty in KUB 15.11+ rev. iii 14′–25′.

Table 39: Illness Vows: Puduḫepa for Other Family Members

Protasis	Apodosis
1. KUB 15.1+ rev. iii 48′–53′	
[The queen(?)] for the [sake of the] son of the king of Išuwa vowed [thu]s: "If the son [...] comes alive from the [...] illness, (rev. iii 48′–51′)	I [will .... For the sake of the son] of the king of Išuwa I will give a [da]gger, a spindle, and 1 soul of silver, [its weight not sp]ecified, to the god." (rev. iii 51′–53′)
2. KUB 15.3 rev. iv 5′–9′	
The queen on which day [...] The queen [made an oath on behalf of] the son of the king of [Išuwa.] "If from that il[lness he comes out alive] (rev. iv 5′–7′)	[...] he will clothe. And for the god [...] I will give." Its weight no[t specified.] (rev. iv 8′–9′)

Surprisingly, the only child attested as receiving attention in Puduḫepa's illness vows was not her own. Perhaps her children were exceedingly lucky in avoiding the frequent illnesses of childhood, or perhaps her children had grown to adulthood before she was in a position to make vows on their behalf. The "son of the king of Išuwa" would have been important to the Hittite court, being a member of the extended royal family (if the child's mother was Kilušḫepa, who was either the sister or daughter of Puduḫepa, he was thus a grandson or nephew of the royal couple),[695] and thereby a living link between the Kingdom of Ḫatti and a crucial vassal. Ironically, if the "son of the king of Išuwa" and Eḫli-Šarruma, last king of Išuwa and contemporary of Tudḫaliya IV, were the same person, Puduḫepa's vows might not have been enough to ensure his full loyalty (see discussion of the Assyrian campaign below).

694 Emmanuel Laroche, *Recherches sur les noms des dieux.* (Paris: Maisonneuve, 1947). See also Volkert Haas, "Das Ritual gegen den Zugriff der Dämonin ᴰDÌM.NUN.ME und die Sammeltafel KUB XLIII 55," OrAnt. 27 (1988): 85–104. Although often assumed to be a Lamaštu-demon based on Mesopotamian equivalences, is is not clear that a Mesopotamian deity stood behind the Sumerogram DÌM.NUN.ME in Hittite texts (Birgitte Christiansen, *Die Ritual Tradition der Ambazzi: eine philologische Bearbeitung und entstehungsgeschichtlische Analyse der Ritualtexte CTH 391, CTH 429 und CTH 463.* StBoT 48 [Wiesbaden: Harrassowitz, 2006], 134–35). On the other hand, adaptations of Akkadian medical knowledge in Hittite language texts provide at least one example, KBo 21.20 obv. 16–18′, in which a man seized by ᴰDÌM.NUN.ME is treated by Hurrian recitations and Mesopotamian therapetuic techniques (Valeria Zubieta Lupo, "Foreign Medical Knowledge in Ḫattuša," in *Hrozný and Hittite: The First Hundred Years. Proceedings of the International Conference Held at Charles University, Prague, 11–14 November 2015*, eds. Ronald I. Kim, Jana Mynářová, Peter Pavúk. CHANE 107 [Leiden: Brill, 2020], 613), suggesting that ᴰDÌM.NUN.ME here was a Mesopotamian *lamaštu.* A new comprehensive study of ᴰDÌM.NUN.ME in the Hittite context would seem to be a desirable.

695 See de Roos, *Hittite Votive Texts*, 60–65, for discussion of this name as it appears in the votive corpus and elsewhere, and see Bryce, *Kingdom of the Hittites*, 268, for historical context.

8.4.4 Illness Vows: Ḫattušili for Puduḫepa

There are only two illness vows by Ḫattušili, both for Puduḫepa. The mention of the son in KUB 56.20 10 and the Mother Goddess in lines 17 and 21 suggest a topic of childbirth, but this would be difficult to square with chronology implied by the absence of vows against childhood illness by Puduḫepa. Perhaps the queen and one of the adult royal children have been struck by the same illness. As one would expect in a vow made by the sovereign himself, the gifts offered for their recovery are rich and numerous, involving multiple votive objects, livestock, and the performance of a sacrifice or ritual: KUB 56.20 7–16 certainly qualifies as a major vow.

Table 40: Illness Vows: Ḫattušili for Puduḫepa

Protasis	Apodosis
1. KUB 56.20 7–16	
When [His Majesty] in Uššа for the queen [...] offered a propitiatory gift. His Majesty [thus vowed: If the quee]n comes away well ...] the son (is) well, (7–10)	1 sun-[disk of gold ...] ox statue of gold, 1 day of gold [... fo]r the queen. 1 day of silver, 1 soul of g[old ...,] 1 ox, 8 sheep for the Storm-god of Heave[n ...] he/she tended to [...] the god, an offer[ing ...] he will fulfill. (10–16)
2. KUB 56.20 17–22	
[... i]n Uššа the Mother Goddess of the person of the queen [...] "but if the *pur*[*ulli*]-festival [...] I omit, for me of the soul [...] if/when she c[omes] away well (17–20)	[...] which [...] the Mother Goddess o[f the person of the queen ....]" (21–22)

8.4.5 Illness Vows: Conclusion

The similarity in size between the diplomatic gifts and the minor vows would allow Puduḫepa to use her own funds for at least some of the vows. But the larger gifts, especially the ones involving deportees, show that Ḫattušili must have been aware of and even complicit in his wife's 'vow habit'. One might wonder why the royal couple persisted in making vows despite the recurrence of Ḫattušili's illnesses. Confirmation bias, which can still affect medical treatment today, must have had some role: when Ḫattušili recovered, the positive result would be attributed to the god's intervention. It would be imprudent in any case to withhold gifts to the gods if there was any chance it would help, and there was always the chance that *this* time the illness would be gone for good. Perhaps the many objects with weights described as "not given" at the time of the vow or "to be taken to heart" were enticements to the gods for exceptional and/or permanent results.

8.5 Vows Concerning Military Matters

The second most common topic in the votive corpus is war. Persons and place names furnish a historical background for most of the military vows and the limited possibilities allow the location of the remainder to be deduced. Ḫattušili III was an experienced commander, but commitments on the home front led him to pursue diplomacy abroad, as evidenced by his peace treaty with Egypt. A secure southern border allowed him to concentrate on stabilizing Anatolia during his reign. His campaigning was restricted to two theaters. In the Lukka lands of western Anatolia, an area referred to somewhat anachronistically by the Hittites as Arzawa (named after a kingdom which had once threatened to supplant Hittite power in Anatolia), Ḫattušili moved to restore Hittite authority and quell the violence against Hittite subjects. He contested a long tradition of rebellion in the area where local rulers often accepted Hittite vassalage only to pursue their own interests with the collusion of outside powers. Ḫattušili's Arzawa campaign had a major goal of bringing one such provocateur, the notorious Piyamaradu, to justice. In northern Anatolia dwelled the Kaška, a dangerous population group Ḫattušili knew all too well from his time as ruler of Hakmiš. He took propagandistic pride in wresting from them the holy city of Nerik, proof of his fitness to be Great King of Ḫatti, and control of the region became a matter of dynastic honor. He assigned a young Tudḫaliya to gain experience by governing the area, and undertook frequent police actions together with his son against the remaining unsubdued Kaškaen tribes. These actions can be referred to collectively as the Northern Campaigns.

Ḫattušili is well represented in the military vows, authoring a total of eight vows (compared to the meager two he made for his wife's illnesses), but Puduḫepa is deeply involved as well, actually exceeding this number with thirteen vows for her husband. She may have even accompanied her husband on his campaign to Arzawa (see discussion of the town of Yalanda, KUB 56.31 rev. iv 14′–16′, under *8.2.4 Tudḫaliya IV* above). Despite comparable representation in the military vows, the types of gifts promised by the royal couple are different. Puduḫepa offers gifts similar to her illness vows, i.e., products of the palace economy: many objects of precious metals (KUB 15.23 obv. 8′–11′, 12′–16′; KUB 48.119 obv.? 15′–19′; KUB 48.123 obv. ii 11′–17′, rev. iv 23–25, 26–28; KUB 56.15 obv. ii 25–29, 30–31; KUB 56.28 rev. 5′–12′, 13′–15′, 16′–20′; KUB 56.30 rev. 4′–7′; KUB 56.31 rev. iv 14′–16′), some celebrations (KUB 31.69 obv.? 4′–11′; KUB 48.119 rev.? 11–18; KUB 56.15 obv. ii 15–24), and the rare livestock (KUB 48.119 obv.? 15′–19′). Most of these offerings would be minor gifts in the classification scheme used for the illness vows. In contrast, Ḫattušili's offerings are what would be expected from the fruits of a successful campaign: deportees (KUB 15.21 4′–6′, 7′–8′), large numbers of livestock (KUB 56.18 obv. 1′–7′, 12′–14′), the restoration of festivals and cults in conquered areas (KUB 15.21 1′–3′, 4′–6′, 9′–11′, 12′–14′, 15′–17′; KUB 56.18 obv. 1′–7′), along with some precious objects (KUB 56.18 obv. 1′–7′; KUB 56.27 3′–10′). Ḫattušili's gifts resonate with the classic *malteššar* offering of thanks for a safe return from war, where gifts from the spoils were presented to the gods. In rural Anatolia this would overwhelmingly mean deportees, livestock, and land, but little in the way of gold and silver.

8.5.1 The Arzawa Campaign

The Arzawa campaign is primarily reconstructed from the "Tawagalawa Letter" (CTH 181) and the fragments of Ḫattušili's Annals (CTH 82).[696] In these sources a Luwian

696 For a history of scholarship concerning the connection of these two texts, see Oliver R. Gurney, "The Annals of Ḫattušili III," AnSt. 47 (1997): 132–38; for the Tawagalawa letter, see *Der "Tawagalawa-*

westerner named Piyamaradu establishes a power base in the lawless and peripheral Lukka lands of Anatolia (classical Lycia, and possibly parts of Caria, Psidia, and Lycaonia). With the encouragement of the Greek kingdom of Aḫḫiyawa in the Aegean he conducted raids in Hittite territory and captured many prisoners and livestock. Ḫattušili made an expedition to capture Piyamaradu, and his excursion to Arzawa had the useful effect of reassuring the vassal states and reaffirming Hittite sovereignty in the region. Piyamaradu evaded capture after some treacherous diplomacy and fled to the Aegean islands. Ḫattušili lacked a navy and could only compose a frustrated letter to the king of Aḫḫiyawa whom he believed to be complicit in the whole affair. The campaign was thus a mixture of success and failure. One the one hand, it stopped the raids and stabilized the Hittite vassal system in western Anatolia (Tudḫaliya would not need to campaign here during his reign). On the other hand, it also left Piyamaradu a free man and failed to recover the people and booty he seized.

Table 41: Military Vows: Puduḫepa (Arzawa Campaign)

Protasis	Apodosis
1. KUB 15.6 obv. ii 10′–13′	
The queen in the town of Kat[apa to the god ...] thus v[owed]: "If [...] for the campaign to the land of [A]rzaw[a ...] the land of [...] (obv. ii 10′–13′)	[...]
2. KUB 31.69 obv.$^{?}$ 4′–11′	
[If you, Išt]ar of Lawazantiya, my lady, [r]un [before] His Majesty in the l[and of Arzawa], (if) you dress your clothing like a man, [or if like a woman] you dress, your clothing on hi[s] body [...] (if) before His Majesty you strike the land of Arzawa, (obv.$^{?}$ 4′–7′)	when/if [a ...][697] they begin to dress, for you they will begin to dress your [...,] and as a woman for you [...] they will begin to [...,] and a festival for you a man [...,] or a ritual I will take to heart. (obv.$^{?}$ 8′–11′)
3. KUB 48.123 obv. ii 11′–17′	
The qu[een ...] your [...] matter of the land of A[rzawa(?) ...] tended to[698] [...] (obv. ii 11′–14′)	[...] and weapons [of/to him ...] a statue of silver [...] Piḫatarḫunta [...] (obv. ii 15′– 17′)
4. KUB 48.123 rev. iv 12–22	
[... the town of Manay]ara away, in the land of Kudupšašši [...] the queen in the town of Manayara [dreamed] an evil dream. [...] arrived. [The queen to Ištar of Lawaz]antiya vowed thus: If [you, the goddess, my lady, a bad death for His Majesty] and for the armies do not [allow, (and) in th]at	[...] I will enact, [and ...] I will [make]. (rev. iv 20–22)

Brief." Beschwerden über Piyamaradu. Eine Neuedition, eds. Susanne Heinhold-Krahmer, Elisabeth Rieken. UAVA 13 (Berlin: De Gruyter), especially Heinhold-Krahmer, "I. Einleitung" (1–22) and *id.*, "VIII. Zur Datierung von VAT 6692 in die Regierungszeit von Ḫattušili III. (ca. 1265–1237)" (366–76).

697 Contra de Roos, *Hittite Votive Texts*, 203, the traces in the photo show a vertical wedge preceding the -*LUM*, thus ruling out a reading LÚ]-*LUM*.

698 Or perhaps the literal meaning of "he went forth and back" in this case?

field before His Majesty [you will run, and for him the enemy] you will slay. His Majesty and the armies [...] in front good fortune [...] (rev. iv 13–20)	
5. KUB 48.123 rev. iv 23–25	
[... if in the midst of] the armies an ev[il deat]h [...] a shield [...] (rev. iv 23)	[...] for the god(dess) a shield, a lion [of gold on it I will em]boss [... (rev. iv 24–25)
6. KUB 48.123 rev. iv 26–28	
If [...] the armies of Ḫ[atti] and His Majesty [...] you [protect(?)], (rev. iv 26–27)	fo[r the god(dess) a ...,] its weight n[ot specified] I wi[ll make.] (rev. iv 27–28)
7. KUB 56.15 obv. ii 15–24	
[Whe]n [the queen] in the town of Izziya to the sea [....] The queen to the sea thus [vowed: ...] if you the sea, my lord, for me to the gods [intercede(?)], you [...] Piyamaradu for me [...,] he does not escape me [...][699] (obv. ii 15–19)	[...] which offering they are giving [...] which river is designated for the offering [...] and for which gods [...] was alive. For those ones [...] he/she will grind a thick bread of [...] (obv. ii 20–24)
8. KUB 56.15 obv. ii 25–29[700]	
[...of] Kummani: If Piyamara[du ...] from the region you seiz[e ...] (obv. ii 25–26)	[...] of gold, a bird of gold, perio[d of gold ...] and Piyamaradu [...] (obv. ii 27–29)
9. KUB 56.15 obv. ii 30–31	
(see above) [If ... for the] s[ake] of [t]his matter precisely [...] (obv. ii 30)	[...] a period of gol[d...] (obv. ii 31)
10. KUB 56.31 rev. iv 8′–11′	
[The quee]n to the goddess GAZ.BA.A.A [th]us vowed: [If you, the goddess, my l]ad[y], run before His Majesty, because I have already vowed to the goddess, (and) I have been seeing the goddess by dream (about(?)) the matter ... (text unintelligible for one line) (rev. iv 8′–11′)	[...]
11. KUB 56.31 rev. iv 13′–16′	
The qu[een] in the town of Yalanda to the River Š[etarpu thus] vowed: If you, the River Šetarpu, for me for [...] approach the god (and) [you] run before His Majesty [...,] (rev. iv 13′–15′)	a silver statue (of) the god, its weight not specified, I will make [...] (rev. iv 16′)

Puduḫepa's vows for the Arzawa campaign are divided between those wishing for the general good fortune of the army (victory over the enemy, avoidance of camp pestilence, etc.) and vows for a specific result: the capture of Piyamaradu. The success of

699 It is surprising that the queen uses the first-person construction in "he does not escape me" (*UL-aš=mu=kan išparzazi*). Could this be a nested quotation with the speaker actually the king?

700 Although it is likely the queen is still the speaker, KUB 15.1+ rev. iii 18′–31′ demonstrates that the king and queen can make vows, one after the other, on the same topics.

vows wisihing for general good fortune is difficult to measure. How many soldiers can get sick, or how many can be lost to the enemy before a vow has failed? The vow maker would probably be hesitant to withhold gifts and risk the god's anger in the case of mixed results. However, the capture of Piyamaradu presents a clear binary: he was either caught or he was not by the end of the campaign. Given the historical evidence (it seems the Aḫḫiyawan king never bothered to get back to Ḫattušili), KUB 56.15 obv. ii 15–24 and KUB 56.15 obv. ii 25–29 were unambiguous failures. Of course, the Hittites might have been hesitant to take these vows "off the books." Gods can work in mysterious ways, and there was always the chance Piyamaradu would fall into Hittite hands at a later time.

Table 42: Military Vows by Ḫattušili (Arzawa Campaign)

Protasis	Apodosis
1. KUB 56.18 obv. 1′–7′[701]	
[...] (obv. 1′)	[... in the lan]d of Arzawa for me [... the land] of Ḫatti the temp[les(?) ...] but the city of Ḫupišna [...] that much gold [...] and the land of Arzawa for you [....] Yearly 10 oxen, 100 sheep [...] (obv. 2′–7′)
2. KUB 56.27 3′–10′	
[... to the Sun-goddess o]f Ari[nna ...] His Majesty [...] of the offering table [...] you hear (of?) the campaign of the land of Arzawa [...] I, His Majesty, will arrive in the town of Waliwanda [...] they do not find [...] who is [...] (3′–9′)	[...] I will give, but a horn which is inlaid with stone [...] I will give. (9′–10′)

KUB 56.18 obv. 1′–7′, if it can be assigned to Ḫattušili, seems to involve the endowing of temples, possibly in Ḫupišna. The phrase "that much gold" (KÙ.SI$_{22}$ *apinišuwanda*) in obv. 5′ is a correlative, referring to an amount probably discussed in the break of the previous line. Given the military context, a reasonable restoration might be: "[however much gold I seize], that much gold [I will give to the temples/gods]." The gold, the mention of "the land of Arzawa for you," and the yearly gifts of livestock fit the hypothesis that Ḫattušili is promising offerings of thanks after campaign.

8.5.2 Northern Campaign(s)

After Ḫattušili pacified northern Anatolia during his brother's reign, he began a program of resettlement of the towns with loyal Hittite subjects (cf. the settlement of Tiliura, CTH 89) and refurbishment of the temples, especially at Nerik (CTH 90). This process was likely incomplete by the time he took the throne in Ḫattuša, and so he assigned his son, Tudḫaliya, to finish the task. Regular campaigns were necessary to subdue the Kaška and secure the borders, and Ḫattušili probably accompanied his son

701 The assignment of this vow to Ḫattušili is based on his being the author of the next vow starting in KUB 56.18 obv. 8′.

on these campaigns during the early years, though he was careful to ascribe the military victories to Tudḫaliya.[702]

Table 43: Military Vows by Puduḫepa (Northern Campaign)

Protasis	Apodosis
1. KUB 48.119 obv.$^{?}$ 14′–19′	
[...] dying was established. The queen to the Storm-god of Nerik [thus vowed: If] you, the god, my lord, listen to me, (and) in the midst of the army [there is no dying ...$^{?}$,] (obv.$^{?}$ 14′–15′)	[...fo]r the god, my lord, 1 silver shield [... and another object of s]ilver, its weight not specified, 1 ox (and) 8 sheep I will give. [... in whi]chever place the queen wishes [.... The in]voking is not yet (given). (obv.$^{?}$ 16′–19′)
2. KUB 48.119 rev.$^{?}$ 11–18	
But [no]w, those armies which Šaḫurunuwa and LUGAL-*aš*-^{D}LAMMA lead, if they [subsequently] come back safely, even if they do (i.e., accomplish) absolutely nothing, [...] but if they come back safely, (rev.$^{?}$ 11–13)	Šaḫurunuwa will invoke separately the Storm-god of Nerik of the Campaign,[703] and LUGAL-*aš*-^{D}LAMMA will invoke (him) separately while stopped.[704] But which officers and armies (are there), they will divide equally, and half will step behind Šaḫurunuwa, and half will step behind LUGAL-*aš*-^{D}LAMMA. (rev.$^{?}$ 13–18)

Most of Puduḫepa's vows involving the Northern Campaigns concern her son Tudḫaliya in a separate section below. Two military vows that do not specify Tudḫaliya appear in KUB 48.119, a tablet with a strong northern Anatolian context. The appearance of illness vows in KUB 48.119 obv.$^{?}$ 3′–8′ and 9′–13′, the former promising the celebration of a festival in Hakmiš and Nerik and the latter referring to the transplantation of a god from Utruna to Nerik, show that Nerik is fully under Hittite control, thus dating the text Ḫattušili's reign as Great King (the appearance of Šaḫurunuwa, a well attested figure who spanned the reigns of Ḫattušili and Tudḫaliya,[705] in KUB 48.119 rev.$^{?}$ 11–18 confirms the dating). The first military vow on the tablet is unremarkable: KUB 48.119 obv.$^{?}$ 15′–19′ asks for protection against illness and offers a minor gift of silver objects and livestock. But the second vow, KUB 48.119 rev.$^{?}$ 11–18, has Puduḫepa promising what is in essence a military parade. There is no indication that the speaker has changed between this vow and previous, which was authored by the queen, but can it be the case that Puduḫepa was capable of so much involvement with the army that she could orchestrate a martial display, down to the

702 Cf. Bryce, *Kingdom of the Hittites*, 296 and his discussion of KUB 19.8//9 and the conquest of Ḫatenzuwa, which had eluded Ḫattušili.

703 De Roos, *Hittite Votive Texts*, 212 translates "then for the sake of the campaign shall [Ša]ḫurunuwa the Stormgod of Nerik invoke separately ... ," whereas van Gessel, *Onomasticon (Part II)*, 783 has ^{D}10 ^{URU}Nerik *ŠA* KASKAL-*NI* as a separate entry (only occurring in this text).

704 GUB-*za* is translated here as "stopped," i.e., when the army is at a standstill, versus de Roos, *op. cit.*, 212 ("after his arrival"), who read GUB-*za* as ablative.

705 For prosopography, see introductory materials to Fiorella Imparati, *Una Concessione di Terre da Parte di Tudhaliya IV*. RHA 32 (Paris: Klincksieck, 1974), especially pp. 11–14.

grouping of the officers and the disposition of the troops? If so, taken with her presence deep in western Anatolia during the Arzawa campaign, and her request that the gods "not allow Piyamaradu to escape *me*" (KUB 56.15 obv. ii 15–24, if it is not a nested quote), it seems Puduḫepa was indispensable to her husband in more than just the realm of diplomacy and religion.

Table 44: Military Vows by Ḫattušili (Northern Campaign)[706]

Protasis	Apodosis
1. KUB 15.21 1′–3′	
Because of precisely [this] matter: If I[štar ...] (1′)	[...] I will make. I will establish festivals for you. [...] festival of autumn, festival of spr[ing.] (2′–3)
2. KUB 15.21 4′–6′	
Because of precisely [thi]s matter: If [I conquer] the enemy, (4′)	[for you statu]es I will make. Festivals of ol[d I will re]est[ablish, and de]portees for you I will give. (5′–6′)
3. KUB 15.21 7′–8′	
[Because] of precisely [this] matter: [...] (7′)	[...] and a deportee [I will give to you.] (7′–8′)
4. KUB 15.21 9′–11′	
[If] because of precisely [t]his matter: will I conquer the enemy(?) (9′)	[...] and the statue of the god I will restore. [...] I will [a]sk. They will make it so. (10′–11′)
5. KUB 15.21 12′–14′	
And [if] because of precisely this [matte]r: will I conquer the enemy(?) (12′)	[a statue of the god] I will make. 1 ox, 1 sheep, 1 he-goat, ½ *SUTU* porridge [I will give. A festival of a]utumn and festival of spring th[us ...] (13′–14′)
6. KUB 15.21 15′–17′	
[If in the town of] Ḫatenzuwa, [because of] precisely this matter: (15′)	[a statue of the go]d I will make good, [...] I will make. For you festivals [I will] es[tablish.] (16′–17′)

It is unclear whether the mention of Ḫatenzuwa as the possible location of festivals means that the vows of KUB 15.21 postdate the town's capture. Ḫattušili again offers celebrations, renovations, and deportees. The general theme of creating new festivals and resurrecting the old is especially poignant in the context of northern Anatolia. The region was the heartland of Hattian religion in the Old Hittite Kingdom and its loss in the Middle Hittite period was still keenly felt two centuries later.

706 The vows of KUB 15.21 1′–17′ are linked together by the phrase "because of precisely this matter" (*kedani=pat* INIM-*ni šer*). The identification of the speaker as the Hittite king is based on the first person use of "will I conquer the enemy?" ([LÚ]KÚR-*za tarḫmi*) in 9′ and 12′. The identification of the king as Ḫattušili is based on mention of the town of Ḫatenzuwa (see introduction to *8.5.2 Northern Campaign(s)*).

8.5.3 Military Vows mentioning Tudḫaliya

The distribution of Tudḫaliya's name in the votive corpus was remarked upon in the discussion of dating criteria. If the dating is correct, the twelve vows concerning Tudḫaliya (and certainly the extra two concerning Tašmi-Šarruma) come from before he was king. All were made for him by Puduḫepa and almost all concern military matters.[707] He is the only prince to receive military vows, confirming his unique importance to Ḫattušili and Puduḫepa. The vows are of the "minor gift" types offering small objects of precious metal.

Table 45: Puduḫepa's Military Vows Mentioning Tudḫaliya

Protasis	Apodosis
1. KUB 15.23 obv. 8′–11′	
If you, the god, will run before Tudḫaliya, (obv. 8′–9′)	for the god I will make a Hurrian shirt of copper and gold, and later a golden earring. (obv. 10′–11′)
2. KUB 15.23 obv. 12′–16′	
(see above)	For the priestess of Kuššara [...] for precisely that matte[r], for the sake of [...] a gold wreath I will make. (obv. 12′–16′)
3. KUB 56.28 rev. 5′–12′	
[Dream of the queen.] "In a [d]ream the queen in the town of Anašip[a ...] the king of the land of Išuwa in Kizzuwatna [...] I will be vowing for that one: [if the goddess, my la]dy, for Tudḫaliya you [run in front], (and) give over the lands of the enemy [... if you(?) ...] the lands of the enemy (as if they were) 𒑱*tuwanta*-s of bees [...] (rev. 5′–10′)	for the goddess silver 𒑱*tuwanta*-s [... and] a 𒑱*ḫelwati*- of gold, its weight not specified, I will make. (rev. 11′–12′)
4. KUB 56.28 rev. 13′–15′	
[If the goddess, my lady,] for the enemies you set a (limited) term, [and in Tudḫaliy]a's hand you place (them), (rev. 13′–14′)	[for the goddess 1 t]erm of silver (and) a bird of gold, its weight not specified, I will give. (rev. 15′)
5. KUB 56.28 rev. 16′–20′	
[If the goddess, my lady,] for the enemies you place a net, [and the enemie]s as if with a net [... and if the goddess,] my lady, for Tudḫaliya [you run in front,] (rev. 16′–19′)	[for] the goddess a net of silver [...] I will give. (rev. 19′–20′)
6. KUB 56.30 rev. 1′–3′	
[If ... you] ru[n in front ...] the god [...] good [...] (rev. 1′–2′)	[... *kunz*]*ikannaḫiša*- and implemen[ts I will give. (rev. 3′)

707 The exception is KUB 56.31 rev. iv 23′–26′, in which Puduḫepa seems to ask to hear good tidings about Tudḫaliya. However, it cannot be ruled out that these tidings are related to a military campaign.

7. KUB 56.30 rev. 4′–7′	
(see above) [T]o Šarruma of Urikina [for the sake of precisely this matter(?)] (rev. 4′)	1 hand of gold I will make [....] I will fasten it on the breast [...] for the god an offering [...] (rev. 5′–7′)
8. KUB 56.30 rev. 10′–11′	
(see above) [...] (rev. 10′)	[...] *kun[zikan]na[ḫiša- ...*] (rev. 11′)
9. KUB 56.30 rev. 12′–13′	
(see above) For Šar[rum]a of [...] (rev. 12′)	*kunzikanna[ḫiša- ...*] (rev. 13′)
10. KUB 56.30 rev. 14′–19′	
The queen to [... thus vowed:] If Tudḫali[ya ...] on which campaign [...] you run [in front], (rev. 14′–17′)	[I will] offer [...] and for him anoth[er ...] (rev. 18′–19′)
11. KUB 56.30 rev. 20′–24′	
(see above) To Ištar the (morning) star [for the sake of precisely] t[his matter:] If Tudḫali[ya ...] of the queen [...] (rev. 20′–22′)	[I will] offer [...] and for him anoth[er ...] (rev. 23′–24′)

8.5.4 Other Military Vows of Puduḫepa

There is one military vow that cannot be securely assigned to a specific campaign. The type of gift suggests Puduḫepa as its author.

Table 46: Other Military Vows of Puduḫepa

Protasis	Apodosis
1. KUB 15.15 rev. iv 4′–9′	
[... in the m]idst of the army [...] vowed: If [... the bad] dying does not occu[r ...] (rev. iv 4′–6′)	[...] 1 soul of silver, 1 justice [of silver ...] and I will invoke the god, for who[m ...] 1 ox, 8 sheep, (and) silver (and) gold.[708] Already (given). (rev. iv 7′–9′)

8.5.5 Military Vows: Conclusion

The gift pattern seen in the illness vows is strengthened by the more numerous military vows by Ḫattušili. The king is quick to offer the products of the land and the results of its manpower to the gods, while Puduḫepa deals in gold and silver. It was suggested that the source of these precious objects was her diplomatic and tributary income, but the large number of vows stretches credulity that her personal funds were sufficient. It seems she was placed in charge of her husband's diplomatic income too, regularly and not just for the major vows. If so, then Ḫattušili's offering of livestock and festivals are perhaps no coincidence, but evidence of a conscious division of resources between

708 De Roos, *Hittite Votive Texts*, 172 translated "1 ox (and) 8 sheep (of) silver (and) gold," but I am not sure that the silver and gold must modify the ox and sheep, considering that an offering of 1 (living) ox and 8 (living) sheep is a customary gift in so many vows.

the king and queen. Whether this division was traditional and/or associated with the gender roles of the king and queen, or whether the arrangement was a historical feature of the relationship of Ḫattušili and Puduḫepa is unclear.

8.6 Vows Concerning Dreams and Omens

Dreams were a way of receiving direct communication from the gods, especially for requests or warnings, and were not just welcome but sought in rituals designed to encourage "good dreams" (a process termed incubation after parallels from the Classical world).[709] Incubation rituals for the queen are evidenced in two vows, one in which she asks for the god to cause her to sleep in bed (KUB 48.123 rev. iii 19–21), and another in which (probably) Ḫattušili asks for a "pure bed" for the queen (KUB 15.15 obv. i 3–7).[710] The latter vow is in the context of "the seventh day," which taken with the mention of EZEN_4 in the next vow means it probably belongs to a festival (fitting well with de Roos' suggestions that stimulated dreams were a component of the festival calendar for the Hittite royals). Another pair of dreams in KUB 15.1+ obv. ii 47–52 and KUB 15.19 obv. 11′–13′ come from the "days of the Festival of the Torch." In the vows, Puduḫepa asks that His Majesty not come to misfortune on her account. Was she afraid of making a mistake during the ritual?

In terms of gifts, Puduḫepa again promises votive objects of precious metal and Ḫattušili offers deportees and buildings in addition to any gold and silver. Noteworthy are Puduḫepa's gift of a statue of His Majesty "under the wings of an eagle" (KUB 31.77+ obv. i 30–36//KUB 48.126 3′–9′); KBo 64.338 obv. 9–14: does this phrase refer to the winged sun-disk found above kings in Hittite iconography?) and the building and endowing of a temple(?) with forty deportees by Ḫattušili.

Table 47: Vows Concerning Dreams and Omens (Puduḫepa)

Protasis	Apodosis
1. KUB 15.1+ obv. ii 5–10	
Šarruma of Urikina. When in a dream some young men were confining the queen in Iyamma in the back of the *tarnu*-house. (obv. ii 5–8)	The queen in the dream vowed 1 *tarnuza*-house of gold to Šarruma of Urikina. (obv. ii 8–10)
2. KUB 15.1+ obv. ii 37–41	
Šarruma of Layuna. When in a dream some young men were confining the queen in Layuna in the back of the *tarnu*-house. (obv. ii 37–40)	The queen in the dream vowed 1 *tarnuza*-house of gold to Šarruma of Layuna. (obv. ii 40–41)

709 Cf. de Roos, *Hittite Votive Texts*, 19–21. For all things dream-related, see introductory chapters and editions of Mouton, *Rêves Hittites*. Almost all of the passages in the votive texts involving dreams are discussed therein.

710 See the term *šuppa šeš-* 'pure sleep' in Mouton, *Rêves Hittites*, 27–28 and discussion of therapeutic incubation *ibid.* 70–74.

3. KUB 15.1+ obv. ii 45–53[711]	
In a [d]ream, the [qu]een in the days of the Festival of the Torch made a prayer [t]o Šarru[m]a! of Tarḫuntašša [th]us: "If His Majesty does not come to misfortune by anything on my account, (obv. ii 47–48)	I will look with favor(?) […] (at) Šarruma of Tarḫuntašša. I will make [n lamb(s)] of lapis lazuli for Šarruma. 1 silver day, 1 gold day, [1] silver [night(?), 1 gold night(?), (their) w]eight not (specified). And wh[at] of the lamb […]…[…, l]ambs (for) Šarruma I will make. […] Concerning (the fact that) the brother of His Majesty it down?/with? [….]" (obv. ii 48–53)
4. KUB 15.19 obv. 11′–13′	
[In a dream] the queen for the days of the Festival of the Torch, to Šaumatar[i] made [a prayer thus]: "If for His Majesty from nowh[ere] on my part [does it go unfavorably,] (obv. 11′)	[t]o Šaumatari I will give 1 soul of gold weighing 20 shekels." (obv. 13′)
5. KUB 31.77+ obv. i 30–36 (= KUB 48.126 3′–9′)[712]	
[Dream] of the queen, matter of the eagle […] while in (the dream). […] "If for His Majesty […]	with *mušnuwanti*-stone […] I will place, and which eagles […] under wings (of an) eagle, and a

711 A transliteration is provided here to include new fragments (DBH 43/2.14 + CHDS 2.145) which have been joined since the edition of de Roos. Differences with transliteration given in CHDS 3, p. 263 are noted below. Lines KUB 15.1+ obv. ii 49–53 can be partially restored from the duplicate in KUB 15.18 obv. ii 1′–4′.

KUB 15.1+ DBH 43/2.14 + CHDS 2.145 obv. ii 45–53

obv. ii

45 [*z*]*a-aš-ḫi-ia-za* [MUN]US.LUGAL *A-NA* UD.KAM$^{\text{ḪI.A}}$ EZEN$_4$ ^{GIŠ}*zu-up-pa-ri*

46 [*A-N*]*A*$^{?}$ $^{\text{D!(text: MUNUS)}}$LUGAL-⸢*ma*?⸣ $^{\text{URU.D}}$10-*aš-ša ar-ku-wa-ar*

47 [*kiš*]*-an e-eš-*⸢*še*⸣*-eš-ta ma-a-an-wa* ^{D}UTU-*ŠI am-*[*me*]*-e-da-*⸢*az*⸣

48 [*Ú-U*]*L ku-*⸢*e-ez*⸣*-qa* GÙB-*li-iš-zi* *⟨⟨MUNUS⟩⟩* *^{D}LUGAL!(text: ANŠE)*⸣-[*m*]*a* $^{\text{URU.D}}$10-*aš-ša-wa*

49 [ ]x S[I]G$_5$?-*it u-uḫ-ḫi nu-wa A-NA* ⸢^{D}⸣LUGAL-⸢*ma*⸣

50 [n SILA$_4$ ^{N}]$^{\text{A}_4}$ZA.GÌN DÙ-*mi* 1 ⸢UD⸣ KÙ.BABBAR 1 ⸢UD⸣ KÙ.SI$_{22}$ [1 GE$_6$(?)] KÙ.BABBAR

51 [1 GE$_6$ KÙ.SI$_{22}$(?) K]I.LÁ.BI NU.GÁL *ŠA* ⸢SILA$_4$⸣*-ia-wa k*[*u-*]*x*(-)⸢*ga*⸣*-an*(-)[

52 [SIL]A$_4$^{MEŠ} ^{D}LUGAL-*ma* DÙ-⸢*mi*⸣

53 [ ]x ŠEŠ ⸢^{D}⸣UTU-⸢*ŠI*⸣*-wa-ra-at ku-it* GAM?(-)[

Commentary:

obv. ii 46 With revised reading of CHDS 3, 263 for obv. ii 48: (erasure) ^{D}LUGAL-[*m*]*a* $^{\text{URU.D}}$10-*aš-ša*, and the non-existence of a "^{D}MUNUS.LUGAL *ŠA* $^{\text{URU D}}$10-*aš-ša*," there is no longer a translation available for obv. ii 46 without emendation. Apparently, the scribe did not erase and replace the MUNUS in obv. ii 46 as he did in obv. ii 48.

49 CHDS 3, 263 proposed ⸢Ù⸣-*it* instead of the S[I]G$_5$?-*it* given here. However, the alleged Ù does not match the Ù in e.g., KUB 15.1+ obv. ii 42, and appears instead to end with a broken vertical.

51 Contra CHDS 3, 263: SILA$_4$-*ia-wa-m*[*a*(?), the final sign cannot be -*m*[*a*, unless -*ia-wa-* are taken as phonetic complements to SILA$_4$. This seems less probable than interpreting a sentential clitic chain. The suggestion of CHDS 3, 263 to take]x-⸢*ga*⸣*-an*(-)[as a form of (*arḫa*) *gangan-* 'to weigh (out)' is not implausible, although the specific form is unclear.

712 Cf. KBo 64.338 obv. 12–14 (Table 47, no. 9).

which ones the deity Pirinkira [...] (obv. i 30–33)	statue of the king [I will make.]" (obv. i 34–36)
6. KUB 48.123 rev. iii 9–13	
The queen in the town [of ... vowed:] If Talm[i-Teššub ...] and the statue of Urḫi-Teššu[b ...] made. (obv. ii 9–12)	But now [...] of silver I will make, and [...] (obv. ii 12–13)
7. KUB 48.123 rev. iii 19–21	
And if you, the goddess, my lady, for me [...] you cause to sleep in bed [...,] (obv. ii 19–20)	then (in the) bedroom bed[s they will ...] (obv. ii 21)
8. KUB 56.31 obv. i 3′–7′	
[... for the divine] Earth-roads, for the sake of precisely this matter [...] (obv. i 3′)	[...] I will give. To the male god (and) female god of the divinity [... an object of] colorful[713] gold I will make. At which moment [...] he begins to march [...] they will put in order, then [...] (obv. i 4′–7′)
9. KBo 64.338 obv. 9–14[714]	
[Dream of the queen(?)] in a sitting bed [... the queen in the dre]am vowed thus: "If [... Iš]tar of Lawazantiya which [...,] (obv. 9–11)	with *mu*[*šnuwanti*-stone ...] I will place, and whi[ch] eagles [... under the w]ings of an eagle, [and] a statue of the k[ing I will make.]" (obv. 12–14)

Table 48: Vows Concerning Dreams and Omens (Ḫattušili)

Protasis	Apodosis
1. KBo 8.63 obv. i 3′–8′	
Which matter His Majesty kne[w ...] for the gods Ea and Al[- ....] But they will determine a place by oracle, and in which plac[e that is designated(?),] (obv. i 3′–5′)	[there(?)] I will build, and then it with deportee[s I will endow ...] 1 silver rhyton weighing 1 mina, 1 li[on] rhyton [...] 40 deportees I will give. I will ask the great *tapir*-. (obv. i 6′–8′)
2. KBo 8.63 obv. i 9′–15′	
Which matter of the town of Šapla His Majesty knew, wh[ich ...,] that matter he will administer to. Ištar of La[wazantiya ...] you will arrange (it) well, (obv. i 9′–11′)	for Ištar of Lawaz[antiya ...] I will build, and then with silv[er ...] the *purapši*-priest I will compensa[te ....] determined [...] (obv. i 11′–15′)
3. KUB 15.15 obv. i 2–7	
[To] the Storm-god of Nerik thus [vowed:] for the queen [...] a pure be[d ... ,] (obv. i 2–4)	on the 7th day, [Išta]r, my lady, [...] and a statue of the queen [...] to the god(dess) [I] will g[ive.] (obv. i 5–7)

713 The reading GÙN.A 'speckled, colorful' (see Mark Weeden, *Hittite Logograms and Hittite Scholarship*. StBoT 54 [Wiesbaden: Harrassowitz, 2011], 506) instead of DAR.A = DAR.RA 'reduced', contra de Roos, *Hittite Votive Texts*, 282.

714 Cf. KUB 31.77+ obv. i 34–36 (= KUB 48.126 7′–9′) (Table 47, no. 5).

8.7 Vows Concerning Calamity

Some of the vows in the corpus concern calamities such as "dying" (probably from a plague: KUB 15.1+ obv. i 19–28, 29–37; KUB 56.12 5′–10′), fire (KUB 15.1+ rev. iii 18′–21′, 23′–26′, 27′–31′), famine (KUB 15.11+ obv. ii 5–9), and the hazards of travel (KUB 15.11+ rev. iii 1′–5′, 8′–12′; KUB 56.25+ rev. iv 1′–7′, 8′–9′, 10′–13′). Instead of being general requests for protection against famine or fire (which can threaten any time), the vows seem to be reactions to specific events or warnings, possibly from oracles, and are thus fewer in number than one might otherwise expect for such dire matters.

There is a strong connection between the topic and gifts in the vows – a model of a city if Ankuwa is spared full destruction, a model of a team of horses and a chariot if the horses avoid damage, a *ḫaršiyalli*-vessel ("pithos") of grain if the earth is productive, and a shield for protection against illness and invasion. It is noteworthy that the gifts from the king and queen for the city of Ankuwa in KUB 15.1+ rev. iii 18′–31′ are exactly the same, and do not observe the usual distribution of precious metals and products of the land.

Table 49: Vows Concerning Calamity (Puduḫepa)

Protasis	Apodosis
1. KUB 15.1+ obv. i 19–28	
The queen to Šarruma (of) Uda [t]hus vowed: "If the mountain [...,] my lord, holds His Majesty alive, (and) life [...] (and) later nothing [...] in the midst of the lands, in the midst of the army, in the mi[dst of ...] the dying becomes better, (and) you do not allow the bad dea[th,] (obv. i 19–25)	for [Šarruma] *ḫarnai*-[715] in Uda [....] Either *ḫarnai*- of [...] or of (temple) person[nel ....]" (obv. i 25–28)
2. KUB 15.1+ obv. i 29–37	
The queen for the sa[ke] of the dying [to the god ... thus vowed:] "If [...] in the midst of the land [of ..., and in the midst of the light troops] and the midst of the heavy troops [...] the prince, the lord [there is no dying(?) ...] if of [...] arrives. But if [...] the evil death [...] nothing [...] (obv. i 29–37)	[...]"
3. KUB 15.1+ rev. iii 23′–26′	
The queen vowed thus to the Storm-god of Heaven: "If the city of Ankuwa escapes, and does not burn down completely, (rev. iii 23′–24′)	for the Storm-god of Heaven I will make 1 silver city, its weight not specified. I will (also) give 1 cow and 8 sheep." (rev. iii 25′–26′)
4. KUB 15.11+ obv. ii 5–11	
[... the queen(?)] to (the goddess) Allani vowed: O goddess, my lady, because the [dark] earth is	for the goddess I will pour a *ḫaršiyalli*-vessel in Ḫattuša and Ḫakmiš. "But the storage vessel I will

715 See HW² Ḫ *s.v. ḫarnai-*² (p. 316) "gegorene Flüssigkeit" with literature. The *ḫarnai*-substance is obtained from aromatic woods and used for purification purposes in ritual contexts – a usage that makes sense in a prayer against plague in the army camp.

arrested, and the grain is bound, [i]f you, my lady, loose the dark earth (and) the grain becomes good, (obv. ii 5–7)	take to heart," (i.e., determine) whether they should open from the palace, or they should send some lord. (obv. ii 8–11)
5. KUB 15.11+ rev. iii 1′–5′	
[...] Fo[r (the goddess)] Allaziyaš[i ... vowed: If] the children from the land of Kummann[i ... ar]rive, (rev. iii 1′–3′)	for the goddess, my lady, 1 *pul[puli-* of silver, 1] *pulpuli* of gold, its weight not specified [I will give ...] already (given). Katapaili. (rev. iii 3′–5′)
6. KUB 15.11+ rev. iii 8′–12′	
[If/when(?)] we, His Majesty (and) the queen, from the land of Kummanni [...] arrive, (rev. iii 8′–9′)	for the goddess because [...] I was an *allinarali*-woman, [...] *allina(ra)li*-women I will designate, [... to the godd]ess, my lady, I will give. (rev. iii 9′–12′)
7. KUB 15.22 3′–11′	
[... the queen(?)] in the town of Arinna to make a prayer [... thu]s vowed: Wanza, my lady, the [matter(?)] of taking to heart [...] you are taking to [h]eart. If for me for the Sun-goddess of Arinna, my lady, [in the land]s of Ḫatti you do not allow the weapon of the enemy, (and) for the lands of Ḫatti [... by no such ev]ent arrives, and for them by no such event upend[s ...] for the person of His Majesty the matter of dying comes no further, if the land [of ...] the lands of Ḫatti, in the heart of the palace and for the person of His Majesty health [is allotted(?) ... (and) if you the god]dess, my lady raise a shield against evil, (3′–10′)	for the goddess, my lady, a sh[ield of silver(?)], (and) a gate of silver I will make. Its weight I will take to heart. (10′–11′)
8. KUB 56.12 3′–10′	
[The queen(?) to L]elwani thus v[owed: ...] down from Ḫattuša [... if you, the goddess, hold up a] shield [agai]nst illness, (5′)	[for] the goddess a shield of silver I will make. [...] 8 sheep in the temple [I will] purify. [...] likewise I will libate. [...] the *upititalla*-men a second time afterwards [.... The shield(?) is] already (given). The sheep and *upatitalla*-men [not yet(?)] (6′–10′)
9. KUB 56.25+ rev. iv 1′–7′[716]	
[... concerning the matter(?)] of the 'misdeed of the horses' [....] The queen to the god [...] of Arušna [vowed thus: "I]f you, the g[od], my [lor]d, cause me to live, [and] the 'misdeed of the hors[es]'[717] for His Majesty goes [...] far away, (rev. iv 1′–5′)	for [the god] my lord a harnessed (team) of silver, [its weight] not specified, in [Aru]šna I will give. [Alo]ngside I will [gi]ve 1 ox, 8 sheep." (rev. iv 5′–7′)

716 The join with KUB 60.118 was mentioned, but neither transliterated nor translated, in de Roos, *Hittite Votive Texts*, 265 fn. 701. See transliteration of join in Beal, review of *Hittite Votive Texts*, 345.

717 Beal, review of *Hittite Votive Texts*, 345, translated *ḪI-IṬ-ṬÌ* ANŠE.KUR.RA^{MEŠ} here as "road accident (lit. misdeed of horses)" (see further discussion of the term, *id.* "Assuring the Safety of the King During the Winter (1.79) (KUB 5.4 + KUB 18.53 and KUB 5.3 + KUB 18.52)," Context 1, 209 fn. 29). Beal's

10. KUB 56.25+ rev. iv 8′–9′	
(see above) But [i]f for them (*scil.* the king and queen) there is health (and) for the sake of precisely this matter of the campaign [you ...] (rev. iv 8′)	[...] I will give. (rev. iv 9′)
11. KUB 56.25+ rev. iv 10′–13′	
(see above) [... the queen to Iš]tar of Lawazantiya for precisely [th]is matter, (rev. iv 10′)	[...] (of) gold, weighing 1 mina, 1 chariot (and) [harne]ssed (team) of silver [its weight] not specified, 1 ox and 8 sheep i[n] Lawazantiya [...] I will [gi]ve on the spot (or: I will give in its place). (rev. iv 11′–13′)

Table 50: Vows Concerning Calamity (Ḫattušili)

Protasis	Apodosis
1. KUB 15.1+ rev. iii 18′–21′	
His Majesty vowed thus to Kataḫḫa: "If the city of Ankuwa escapes, and does not burn down completely, (rev. iii 18′–19′)	for Kataḫḫa I will make 1 silver city, its weight not specified. I will (also) give 1 cow and 8 sheep." (rev. iii 20′–21′)
2. KUB 15.1+ rev. iii 27′–31′	
[His Majesty(?) vo]wed [thus] to the Storm-god of Zippalanda: "If the city of Ankuwa e[scapes, and does n]ot burn down completely, (rev. iii 27′–29′)	[for the Storm-god of Z]ippalanda [I will make] 1 silver city, [its weight not specified.] I will (also) give 1 cow and 8 sheep." (rev. iii 30′–31′)

8.8 Vows for Good Tidings

Similar to the Illness Vows, and perhaps even a subtype, are a number of vows offered for good fortune and averting evil. The royal children make one of their few appearances in KUB 48.123 obv. i 12′–18′, and Tudḫaliya specifically in KUB 56.31 rev. iv 23′–26′. In KUB 15.28+ rev. iii 6′–12′ Ḫattušili makes the offer to invoke the "ancient" (*annalli-*) Sun-goddess of Arinna if he hears no evil words for a year (i.e., the time it takes to celebrate the autumn and spring festivals). The significance of offering to invoke a god is unclear, but a year free of bad news was probably no light favor to ask.

translation is technically correct, but at the same time not specific enough. KUB 5.4+, after raising the question of the "misdeed of the horses" (obv. ii 30–36b), places places the grooms under special obligation the next paragraph (obv. ii 37–42) to prevent a *ḪI-IṬ-ṬÌ* ANŠE.KUR.RA^{MEŠ}. This implies that the horses themselves were the source of the threat to His Majesty, whether indirectly by road accident or directly by kicking or trampling, and the grooms could be reasonably expected to prevent this. The silver models of a harnessed team offered in the protasis of KUB 56.25+ rev. iv 5′–7′ further suggests that the horses were expected to be the instrument of harm: perhaps Puduḫepa was warned of this in a dream, and these were offered as a substitute or appeasement.

Table 51: Vows for Good Tidings (Puduḫepa)

Protasis	Apodosis
1. KUB 48.123 obv. i 12′–18′	
[The queen] to [Išt]ar of Alwazantiya(sic) [vowed thus: …] who(ever) the evil [dreams …] thus for the dreams back to His Majesty […] good. You, the goddess, are for me turning up […] nothing of His Majesty and of the children, (and) you, the goddess, are not allowing for His Majesty [… e]vil to come near, (obv. i 12′–17′)	[for the goddess] 1 Ištar of silver (weighing) 1 mina, 1 Ištar of gold (weighing) 20 shekels I will make. (obv. i 18′)
2. KUB 48.123 obv. i 23′–27′	
[The queen to Ištar of Lawa]zantiya vowed: [If you, the goddess, my lady,] protect well [His Majesty,] (obv. i 23′–24′)	[… for the goddes]s, my lady, 1 tabl[e …] they will […] (obv. i 25′–27′)
3. KUB 48.123 obv. ii 2′–10′	
[…] evil […,] and it for me […,] (obv. ii 2′–3′)	fo[r …] 3 pitchers […] he will coun[t …] for Iš[tar …] 2 breasts of go[ld …] for the b[ody …] fo[r …] (obv. ii 4′–10′)
4. KUB 48.123 rev. iv 4–10	
[The queen in the town of … to] Ištar of Lawazantiya [vowed thus: If you from the s]oul the evil words [… and i]f you, the goddess, my lady, the *zarantiya-* of the soul [… and if the ev]il words no longer […] (rev. iv 4–7)	[… for the go]ddess 2 souls of gold joined together [… the ba]ck I will pierce, [… to the godd]ess I will give. (rev. iv 8–10)
5. KUB 56.31 rev. iv 17′–18′	
To Ḫ[epa]t of Aleppo: If for the goddess […] I hear good (things), (rev. iv 17′)	for the goddess a festival […] I will make. (rev. iv 18′)
6. KUB 56.31 rev. iv 23′–26′	
[The queen(?)] to Ištar of Dūpa thus [vowed: If …] Ištar for Tudḫaliya [… and good things] I hear, (rev. iv 23′–25′)	fo[r …] (rev. iv 25′–26′)

Table 52: Vows for Good Tidings (Ḫattušili)

Protasis	Apodosis
1. KUB 15.28+ rev. iii 6′–12′	
[… His Majesty(?) to the ancient Sun-goddess of Ar]inna of His Majesty. [… t]o the ancient Sun-goddess of Arinna, he vowed: [if] because on my behalf vowing was determined, [… un]til the festivals of autumn and [of spring(?)] I complete, if no [evi]l word at all finds us, (rev. iii 6′–11′)	I will [inv]oke the ancient [Sun-goddess of A]rinna of His Majesty. (rev. iii 12′)

8.9 Vows Concerning Political Matters

There are only two vows which deal with matters of the Hittite court, and both are of murky context. The protasis of the first vow is missing a crucial adjective (KUB 15.19 obv. 6′–7′): *A-NA* ᴰUTU-*ŠI* *ku-i-e-eš* [... *-u*]*š* UN^{MEŠ}*-uš na-aš-kán pé-an ar-ḫa du-wa-ar-na-at-ti* "whoever for His Majesty (are) [...] men, you break them up." This vow is immediately followed by another from "the days of the Festival of the Torch" (cf. KUB 15.1+ obv. ii 47–52). The verb (*peran arḫa duwarna-*) and its object (UN^{MEŠ}) are without parallel in the votive texts, and do not seem to be the typical language for success against an external enemy.[718]

The second political vow (comprising the obverse of KUB 56.30) contains a broad spectrum of the Hittite court officials and the verb 'oppressing/suppressing' (*tamaš-*). Four dependent vows are attached, all by His Majesty, that include some of the most expensive gifts in the votive corpus: two gifts of 100 minas of silver and a collection of other votive objects for ᴰNIN.GAL and ᴰ30 are promised. Whatever event occasioned the vows concerning the Hittite court and oppressing, it was of great personal importance to the king. The mention of an "eighth day" in KUB 56.30 obv. 13′ suggests a festival context for the delivery of the gifts. The promise of silver recalls a similar passage from the Palace-Temple Administrative Corpus in a packing list for festival in Arinna:

KBo 9.91 (= 6.1) rev. A 6″–lo. e. 10″
rev. A
6′ ḪAR.ŠU KÙ.BABBAR *A-NA* ᴰ10 ^{URU}PÚ*-na*
7′ ᴰUTU⟨⟨*ŠI*⟩⟩ ^{URU}PÚ*-na* $^{\text{LÚ.MEŠ}}$KÙ.DÍM
8′ KASKAL*-aḫ-ḫa-an-zi*
lo. e.
9′ 1 *ME* GÍN KÙ.BABBAR ᴰUTU-*ŠI*
10′ EZEN$_4$ AN.DAḪ.ŠUM ^{URU}PÚ*-na pé-da-i*

> A silver bracelet for the Storm-god of Arinna (and) the Sun-goddess of Arinna. The smiths will dispatch (it). 100 shekels of silver His Majesty will bring (to) the spring festival (at) Arinna.

It would appears that a king's gift of silver bullion and some votive objects to a festival was a not unprecedented event. In another vow, KUB 15.9 rev. iii 1′–5′ (with an unfortunately damaged protasis), Ḫattušili promises 100 minas of silver and 100 minas total of a miscellany of other metals for a god. KUB 15.29 obv. i 2′–3′ also has a promise of 100 minas of silver to Ḫepat of Kummanni, but it is not clear whether the king or queen is making the gift. Thus, both the votive and administrative corpora demonstrate that Ḫattušili could donate large amounts of (unfinished) precious metals, always in the

718 The verb *arḫa duwarna-* is encountered in the disbursement texts 5.2 obv. ii 13, rev. iii 4′ and 5.5 rev. iii 5′, where it seems to be a technical term for "breaking down" a large ingot of copper into smaller pieces for further processing (see Vol. II, *Commentary* to 5.2 obv. ii 13). It is unclear if the additional *pe(r)an* in KUB 15.19 obv. 7′ significantly changes the meaning.

context of festivals or temple endowments, but seemingly at a less frequent rate compared to the steady stream of votive objects offered by Puduḫepa.

Table 53: Vows for Political Matters (Ḫattušili)

Protasis	Apodosis
1. KUB 15.19 obv. 6′–10′	
[If] you the [g]od, my lord, stand beside (me) well, (and) whoever for His Majesty (are) [...] men, you break them up, and [...] (obv. 6′–7′)	[if the weapons/statue(?)] of the god is established to be sufficient, then I will plate it complet[ely (with precious metal) ...] but if it is not established, (then) for Šaumatar[i ...] the plated (object) I will build up.[719] Already (given). (obv. 8′–10′)
2. KUB 56.30 obv. 12′–26′	
Note: the obverse of this tablet begins with fragments of what looks to be a substantial vow condition involving multiple actors (including a scribe, a "scribe on wood," a treasurer, and a table servant, obv. 4′–5′). The vow obligations include [1] ox and 8 sheep (3′), suppressing/oppressing something (6′), invoking (8′), and a golden hand (11′). The remainder of the obverse contains dependent vows naming a god and with the "for the sake of precisely this matter" formula, which are listed here (with format of recipient / gift): obv. 12′–13′: For the Great God / Him on the eight day ... obv. 16′–18′: For ... / ... and a mother's breast obv. 19′–22′: For NIN.GAL / His Majesty, with 100 min[as silver[720]] 1 silver hand weighing 5 minas, 1 [hand of gold(?)] to the god I will give obv. 23′–26′: For ^{D}30 / His Majesty, with 100 minas s[ilver] 1 silver hand weighing 5 minas, 1 ha[nd of gold(?)] to the god [I will give]	

8.10 Unconditional Vows

Not every vow was conditional. Some were in response to direct requests from the gods, which were then usually confirmed by oracle, or promises seemingly volunteered outright. In most cases it was the queen who is contacted by the gods, but KUB 15.1+ obv. i 15–18 offers the possibility that others could be contacted (see discussion in fn. 721 below).

719 As de Roos, *Hittite Votive Texts*, 178 fn. 406 notes, the meaning of *awan šarā* DÙ is not clear. He translates the phrase as "make famous," but I prefer a more literal translation of "make (very) high," or "build up," referring to the improvement of the cultic object which was established as insufficient. Alternatively, as noted in Beal, review of *Hittite Votive Texts*, 343, the CHD Š *s.v. šara* B 1 c 3′ (p. 222) suggested: "I will make [...-s] plated from the sides up(?)."

720 It is assumed silver should be restored here, since 100 minas of gold would be an improbably large amount. Cf. also KUB 15.29 obv. i 2′–3′.

Table 54: Unconditional Vows

Protasis	Apodosis
1. KUB 15.1+ obv. i 12–14	
Dream of the queen. (obv. i 12)	"Through a dream Ḫepat requested of me a necklace of sun disks and lapis lazuli." We took an oracle. Ḫepat (of) Uda was determined. (obv. i 12–14)
2. KUB 15.1+ obv. i 15–18	
Dream (of) ...[721] (obv. i 15)	"By dream the king said to me: 'Ḫepat is saying: "[In] the land of Ḫatti let them prep[are] *zizzaḫi*-beverage for me, in the land of Mukiš let them prepare wine for me."'" They will take [an oracle.] (obv. i 15–18)
3. KUB 15.1+ obv. ii 11–12	
N/A	The queen to Šarruma of Urikina vowed 1 soul of gold, its weight not specified, (and) 1 soul of silver weighing 10 shekels. (obv. ii 11–12)
4. KUB 15.1+ obv. ii 42–44	
Dream of the queen. (obv. ii 42)	"Šarruma spoke to me in a dream: 'Up in the mountains in twelve places give me to eat.'" They will take an oracle. (obv. ii 42–44)
5. KUB 31.77+ obv. i 42–45 (= KUB 48.126 15′–18′)	
Ištar of Šamuḫa through a dream to the queen [...] (obv. i 42)	"Behold, for you a breastplate [...] I will offer, and you will come somewhere [...] and gold [I will] br[ing ...]" (obv. i 43–45)
6. KUB 56.31 rev. iv 19′	
N/A	For Ištar of Aleppo 2 maces I will plate in gold. (rev. iv 19′)
7. KUB 56.31 rev. iv 20′	
N/A	For Ištar of Mušunipa 2 maces I will plate in gold. (rev. iv 20′)

721 De Roos, *Hittite Votive Texts*, 89 fn. 73: "Ù.NUN mentioned by ŠL II/3, 880 no. 53 without further explanation. As translation: 'Traum'." HZL no. 36 (p. 107) suggested a translation for NUN "'Fürst'?" in this passage, leading to the tempting interpretation "dream of the prince." However, a free-standing NUN is exceedingly rare, and consultation of the card files at the *Hethitologie Archiv* at the Akademie der Wissenschaften und der Literatur, Mainz, shows only one additional attestation, KBo 41.170 rev. iv 1: NUN KUR *mi*-[(kindly checked by Daniel Schwemer), which can be confirmed in the photographs of the tablet. Besides being exceedingly rare, NUN necessarily means 'prince' in sense of ruler, rather than a royal son (this being expressed by DUMU.LUGAL), so it is not clear whom the "ruler" referred to would be. As such, the term will be left untranslated here.

8. KUB 56.31 rev. iv 21′–22′	
N/A	And whichever Ištars of the Land of Ḫurri there are all together, each of them I will give 1 ox and 1 sheep. (rev. iv 21′–22′)

8.11 Vows with Damaged or Lost Conditions

There are unfortunately many vows in which the protasis has been damaged to the extent that they cannot be classified into any of the categories discussed above. These are included here for reference. Notable major gifts include KUB 15.6 obv. ii 5′–9′ (construction of a temple) KUB 15.9 rev. iii 1′–5′ (100 minas of silver, 100 minas of other precious metals), KUB 15.29 obv. i 2′–3′ (100 minas of silver), and FHL 186 2′–7′ (construction and endowment of a temple with linens, gold, and an offering table).

Table 55: Vows with Damaged or Lost Conditions

Protasis	Apodosis
1. FHL 185 2′–7′	
[... for] the Storm-god of Manuziya [...] you will not deliver [...] (2′–3′)	[...] a temp[le] I will make. The god [...] of him, his linens, gold [...] moun[tain ... of]fering table [...] (4′–7′)
2. IBoT 3.123 6–7	
And if for him for thi[s ...] (6)	1 sheep of silver, its weight not [specified, I will give.] (7)
3. KBo 8.61 3′–4′	
[...] (3′)	[... l]ion statue, silver, of 1 m[ina ...] a sheep I will give. Already (given). (3′–4′)
4. KBo 27.60 11′–13′	
[...] (11′)	[...] gold from here [... go]ld *wantiant-* ('glowing?'), 1 [...] 1 ox, 8 sheep to the gods [I will give.] (11′–13′)
5. KBo 34.145 1′–3′	
[...] (1′)	[...] a rhyton of gol[d ... to] the Sun-goddess of Arinna he/she prom[ised.] (2′–3′)
6. KBo 34.145 4′–5′	
For the sake of [...] (4′)	to the Storm-god of Lightning [... its h]ead gold he/she promised. (4′–5′)
7. KBo 34.145 6′	
[...] (6′)	[...] 1 statue of silver weighing 1 mina he/she promised. Not yet (given). (6′)

8. KBo 34.145 7′–9′	
[...] (7′)	[... for] the Storm-god of Kummanni 1 Morning Star of silver (weighing) 15 shekels, [...] in Zanzara he/she promised. [...] it is already given. (7′–9′)
9. KBo 55.208 obv.? 1′–2′	
[...] (obv.? 1′)	[... an object of] gold (weighing) 5 shekels [...] (obv.? 2′)
10. KBo 55.208 obv.? 10′–15′	
[The que]en to the god [... "I]f the god (for) His Majesty [... ,] (obv.? 10′–11′)	[f]or the god 1 set of [... a b]ad [...] and the king will [...] a st[atue] for him, its [weig]ht [I will take] to heart." (obv.? 12′–15′)
11. KBo 55.208 rev.? 6′–10′	
Dream of the queen. By a dream [...] (rev.? 6′)	"[...] 60 *PARĪSU* of barley, 1 *ḫarš*[*iyalli*-vessel] make. Bar[ns ....] For two jugs [...] let them bring [...]" (rev.? 7′–10′)
12. KBo 55.213 5′–10′	
[...] Ḫepat His Majesty [... they] lick away [...] the god will unlucky [...,] (5′–7′)	for Ḫepat, my lady, 2 o[x ... 1] of the right, one of the left [...] for the mountain sheep of the offering tab[le ...] (8′–10)
13. KBo 55.213 11′–12′	
[...] The queen to Ḫepat [... v]owed: (11′–12′)	1 silver soul, weighing 2 mi[nas ....] (12′)
14. KBo 55.216 1′–5′	
[...] for Tuttu [... for] His [Majesty you do] no[t allow in ...] Ištar of Šamuḫa in [...] hang[s] from [...] (1′–4′)	[...] and a statue of silver before [the god(dess) ....] (5′)
15. KBo 55.217 1′–3′	
[... Ištar of Ša]muḫa, my lady, [...] (1′)	[... I will g]ive, and before the goddess a silver statue [...] (of) silver I will make. (2′–3′)
16. KBo 55.219 7′–8′	
[...] (7′)	[...gol]d inlay, [... (of) ston]e(?) I will pierce/thread (on a string). [A]lready (done).[722] (7′–8′)
17. KBo 55.223 1′–3′	
[...] for the goddess NI[N. ... vo]wed: If [...] (1′–2′)	[...] of silver, its weigh[t not specified, I will give.] (3′)
18. KBo 64.338 obv. 4–8	
[...] to me someone sa[id ...] "and thu[s ...] his/her female servants has[ten(?) ... ,] (obv. 4–6)	[for Ištar of Lawa]zantiya 1 *talla*- [of gold(?) I will give ...] as in Egypt [....]" (obv. 7–8)

722 Contra de Roos, *Hittite Votive Texts*, 305 fn. 815, a [*k*]*a*-⌜*ru-ú*⌝ is clearly visible.

19. KUB 15.1+ rev. iii 2′–3′	
[...] (rev. iii 2′)	[for a deity] of L[ayuna ... 1] soul of silver weighing 10 shekels [vowed (rev. iii 2′–3′)
20. KUB 15.1+ rev. iii 4′–6′	
[...] (rev. iii 4′–6′)	[for Ša]nda of Layu[na ... f]or the sake of [...] 1 statue of the god [...] vowed. (rev. iii 4′–6′)
21. KUB 15.1+ rev. iv 18′–22′	
And if [to me ... you lend] an ear [and hear me,] (rev. iv 18′–19′)	1 silver ear [...] for which [...] I will give. (rev. iv 20′–22′)
22. KUB 15.6 obv. ii 5′–9′	
The queen in the town [of ... to Ḫurri] and to Šeri [... if(?)] all nig[ht ...] remained, (obv. ii 5′–8′)	for them [...] they will make a temple. Whe[re/which ... (obv. ii 8′–9′)
23. KUB 15.9 rev. iii 1′–5′	
[...] you will let [...] (rev. iii 1′)	His Majesty, with 100 minas [...] silver, gold, *iron (ore)*, black *iron (ore)*, tin [...] all. Its weight is 100 minas. [...] to the god I will give. (rev. iii 2′–5′)
24. KUB 15.18 obv. ii 1′–2′	
[...] (obv. ii 1′)	1 s[ilver] day, 1 gol[d] day [...] (obv. ii 2′)
25. KUB 15.18 obv. ii 6′	
[... in the town of] Tarḫuntašša, (obv. ii 6′)	1 gol[d] soul [...] (obv. ii 6′)
26. KUB 15.18 obv. ii 7′–11′	
[...] in the town of Uda for [...] thus vowed: Whil[e ...] you will fear nothing [...] inside him [...] (obv. ii 7′–10′)	[...] I will give, and additionally 1 bull [...] he will [...] (obv. ii 11′)
27. KUB 15.18 rev. iii 2′–3′	
[... t]o the god, m[y] lord, [...] (rev. iii 2′)	[... (of) si]lver to the god [I will] g[ive]. (rev. iii 3′)
28. KUB 15.18 rev. iii 6′–8′	
[...] they came forward favorably. [...] determined for goodness by the god [...] (rev. iii 6′–7′)	[...] I will give, and I will invoke the god. (rev. iii 8′)
29. KUB 15.22 1′–2′	
[... thus v]owed: If [for me ...,] (1′)	1 ox and 8 sheep I will give. (2′)
30. KUB 15.26 7′–10′	
And [i]f you, Ištar of Lawa[zantiya, ...] come for me and this *iparwaš*[*ḫa*- do not(?)] throw [away,] (7′–9′)	for the goddess [... 2] *iparwašḫa*-s, 1 of silver, 1 of gol[d I will make.] (9′–10′)
31. KUB 15.28+ rev. iii 2′–5′	
[...in the city of] Šamuḫa for Išt[ar of the field ...] if Ištar of the Field, my lady, [...] (rev. iii 2′–3′)	[... the goddess,] my [lad]y I will invoke. [...] I will [g]ive, and the queen [...] (rev. iii 4′–5′)

32. KUB 15.29 obv. i 2′–3′	
[... gui]ded favorably, and made it good for me [...] (obv. i 2′)	[... Ḫepat of] Kummanni, with 100 minas of silver. (obv. i 3′)
33. KUB 15.29 obv. i 4′–8′	
[... Ša]ušgaziti went. The queen [... , and vowed:] If the goddess, my lady, for Šaušgaziti [...] Ḫuwaza downwards [...he/she/they x]-s, (obv. i 4′–6′)	for the goddess a silver period and a silver city, [its weight not sp]ecified, I will give. Already (given). (obv. i 7′–8′)
34. KUB 15.29 obv. i 9′–11′	
[... to Ḫe]pat of Kummanni vowed: [...] (obv. i 9′–10′)	[...] for the goddess dreams of silver and gold [I will give. Al]ready (given). (obv. i 10′–11′)
35. KUB 15.30 obv. ii 1–7	
"Or His Majesty [...,] and by dream for me $^{f.D}$10-IR [...] sent favor. Clothing for me [...] she brought, and for His Majesty a bronze *UDDALU* [....] And if Kilušḫepa later [...,] (obv. ii 1–5)	a *ḫarnašalla*-container [...] I will enclose." (obv. ii 6–7)
36. KUB 31.69 rev.$^{?}$ 1′–5′	
[...] (rev.$^{?}$ 1′–3′)	[...] birds of silver and gold, [its weight n]ot specified, I will give. (rev.$^{?}$ 4′–5′)
37. KUB 31.77+ obv. i 46–50 (= KUB 48.126 19′–23′)	
[The king(?)] to Ištar of Šamuḫa [... thu]s vo[we]d: "If you for m[e ...] run [in front,] (obv. i 46–48)	for I[štar ...] 1 lion of silver weighing 20 shek[els ...] 1 ox, 8 sheep before the god [....]" (obv. i 48–50)
38. KUB 48.119 rev.$^{?}$ 1–6	
[...] His [M]ajesty [... i]f for me, (you) the god, [my] lo[rd ... he/she x]-s, for the god(dess) [...] I have been [x]-ing, but now [...] (rev.$^{?}$ 1–4)	[I will] give [...] (and) 8 sheep, 1 ox (and) 8 sheep, [... an object] of silver, weight not specified. (rev.$^{?}$ 5–6)
39. KUB 48.123 obv. i 19′–22′	
[...] (obv. i 19′)	[...] of a lion, Ḫešni and Tašmi-Šarruma did [...] And for [Ta]šmi-Šarruma [... for the goddess,] my [lad]y, the ritual of the weapon (of) the goddess, (and) the ritual of the bee [...] it was determined he perform on the [sp]ot. (obv. i 19′–22′)
40. KUB 48.123 rev. iv 11–12	
[...] (rev. iv 11)	[... Ištar of Lawa]zantiya, a *pattankuran*-heart [... of g]old, weight not specified, I will give. (rev. iv 11–12)
41. KUB 56.13 obv. 1′–4′	
[...] (obv. 1′)	[... to the go]d I will give. [...] for the sake of [... Tašmi(?)]-Šarruma [...] 1 silver sun disk weighing 20 shekels, [... and an object, its weight]

	not specified, 1 cow (and) 8 sheep I will give. (obv. 1′–4′)
42. KUB 56.13 obv. 18′–19′	
[... if(?)] you remove [awa]y, (obv. 18′)	that *uppiya-* of his [... an object] of lapis lazuli I will give. (obv. 18′–19′)
43. KUB 56.13 rev. 18′	
For the sake of [...] (rev. 18′)	1 ox, 8 sheep I will give. (rev. 18′)
44. KUB 56.13 rev. 23′–26′	
[...] for the Moon-god (of) Tarḫuntašša vowed: [if ...] you remove back [...] (rev. 23′–24′)	[...] 1 ox protome of silver, its weight not specified, [and(?) ...] I will start [to give regularly.] (rev. 25′–26′)
45. KUB 56.25+ rev. iv 14′–19′	
[...] the goddess, my lady, manfully [...] the person [...] for [...] in the time I am destroying [...] and if he/she does not say [...] (rev. iv 14′–17′)	[...] but I will dress myself manfully[723] [...] I will destroy [...] (rev. iv 18′–19′)
46. KUB 56.28 obv. 1′–4′	
[...] in front [...] (obv. 1′–2′)	[... a]n *uppiya-* of gold, its weight [not specified ...] I will [ma]ke, whether of gold [or of silver.] (obv. 3′–4′)
47. KUB 56.28 rev. 1′–4′	
[...] (rev. 1′–2′)	[...] of silver for Iš[tar ...] I will make. (rev. 3′–4′)
48. KUB 56.31 obv. i 8′–10′	
[...] for the seed [...] ditto. [...] back [...] (obv. i 8′–9′)	[... and object of] silver (and) [co]lorful go[ld] I will make. (obv. i 10′)
49. KUB 56.31 obv. i 11′–12′	
[... for the sake of] precisely that m[atter ...] (obv. i 11′)	[the hous]es (of) the gods I will build. (obv. i 12′)
50. KUB 56.31 rev. iv 2′–7′	
[...] (rev. iv 2′–5′)	[...] 1 rhyton of gold f[or ... its weig]ht no[t specified, I will make.] (rev. iv 6′–7′)
51. Liv. 49-47-42 1′–4′	
[... Šar]ruma requeste[d ...] the town of Gallazz[uwa ...] (1′–2′)	for you they will begin to give regularly [... , fo]r you, the god, also I will make a statue of the king. (3′–4′)

723 Cf. dressing like a man, cf. KUB 31.69 obv.? 4′–11′ (Table 41, no. 2).

52. Liv. 49–47–42 7′–9′	
[The q]ueen to Šarumma (of) [Ga]llazzuwa th[us vowed: If …] and if you the god, my lord, it for me […,] (7′–8′)	[…] I will make. A *ḫarnai-* of the hea[d] for you […] (9′)
53. Liv. 49–47–42 10′–12′	
[The queen(?)] in the town of Alalaḫ to Ištar [vowed thus: If you] the goddess, my lady, […] back what is covered, […] (10′–11′)	[… w]ith bread I will cover, and later […] (12′)
54. Liv. 49–47–42 13′–16′	
[… the go]ddess, my lady, for His Majesty […] where […] broken away in front […] (13′–15′)	[… for the god]dess weapons of […] (16′)
55. VBoT 75 2′–8′	
[…]	[…] came in […] the queen for/to the Storm-god (and) Ḫepat […] heaven [….] By humanity [… 1] ox, 8 sheep for a *keldi*-offering, [… to(?)] Ḫepat 1 ox, 8 sheep for an *ambašši*-offering [… to] the Sun-god of Heaven I will give […] (2′–8′)

8.12 Vows of Tudḫaliya IV

In striking contrast to the bounty left by the Royal Couple, there are only two texts in the votive corpus that can be assigned to Tudḫaliya as king. Both are atypical in form and contents. KUB 56.19, the longer of the two, is written almost entirely in first-person and has a substantial non-votive interlude. Mention of "His Majesty" in obv. ii 8 shows the author is a king, but it is not immediately obvious whether the text should be ascribed to Ḫattušili or Tudḫaliya (the only two real possibilities given the general dating of the votive corpus). A lengthy historical passage in the non-votive interlude, in which the king asks for guidance from the Storm-god regarding a matter of a *tapri(tašši)*-woman (a kind of religious functionary), decides the matter:

> And because my father had placed his daughter for the Storm-god, my lord, as a *tapritaš*[*ši*]-woman, then [in] the matter for one god right there[724] […], some say: "For the Storm-god she was a hierodule," but others say: "For Šarruma she wa[s] a hierodule." Then my father sent me to the land of Ḫurri to ask the elders again, and (even) they did not resolve the matter. Because my father died, the matter of the *tapri*-woman continues to be investigated by oracle, but in no way will it descend to a matter of presumptuousness (on my part). (KUB 56.19 obv. ii 13–21[725])

724 The translation given here of KUB 56.19 obv. ii 14 is based on my reading: *nam-ma me-mi-*[*ni*] *A-NA* 1 DINGIR *a-pí-ia-pát* ≮*l*[*a-*. Cf. Johann Tischler, *Hethitische Texte in Transkription: KUB 56 und KUB 57.* DBH 49 (Wiesbaden: Harrassowitz, 2016), 28: *nam-ma me-*⸢*mi-ia-na*⸣ x x *a-pí-ia-pát* x x[.

725 For KUB 56.19 obv. ii 13–16, see also translation of Gary Beckman, *Hittite Birth Rituals.* StBoT 29 (Wiesbaden: Harrassowitz, 1983), 256–58; Ahmet Ünal, "Word Play in Hittite Literature?" in *Hittite Studies in Honor of Harry A. Hoffner Jr. on the Occasion of His 65th Birthday*, eds. Gary Beckman,

The speaker then continues by promising to respect the word of the god and asks that the Storm-god enlighten him by speaking through a dream or letting it be determined by oracle. The fact that the matter is still unresolved at the time the text was written suggests that the father's death was recent and the newly crowned king is affirming an inherited obligation to the Storm-god. Since the father of Ḫattušili III, Muršili II, passed away some twenty-five years prior to Ḫattušili's inauguration, and twenty years prior to the appearance of the first votive texts in Urḫi-Teššub's reign, Tudḫaliya IV is almost certainly the only candidate for author.[726]

The vows of KUB 56.19 are all of a single, stylistically unusual type. They use sympathetic magic similar to the vows against catastrophe, but instead of offering imitative objects as geld for sparing the victim, they promise celebrations of an aspect of the god's beneficence. Here, festivals were the preferred pledge. Thus, cleansing of evil was rewarded with a Festival of Purity, and hearing of a petition (lit. "words") yielded a Festival of Justice. Only one vow (obv. i 28–30) offers a material reward in the form of a statue. The *topos* of every vow is the person of the king. They ask for subjective, even psychological outcomes, such as expelling evil from the body, illumination of the mind, and purity. With the exception of a good campaign (obv. i 15–16) the results cannot be objectively measured.

It is clear from KUB 56.19 that Tudḫaliya had a very different idea of vow-craft from his parents. Although it has been argued that the restoration of local cults was not an innovation of Tudḫaliya, despite the dating of the overwhelming majority of texts to his reign,[727] it cannot be denied based on the present distribution of texts that the votive genre was neglected in the same period. Thus, of the two systems of distributing religious wealth, it seems that Tudḫaliya in his mature kingship chose to express piety through investment into the local cults and festivals rather than votive gifts to the gods. If so, then KUB 56.19 might represent a transitional text, where Tudḫaliya still used the votive system inherited from his parents, but with a focus on festivals that anticipated the religious shift in his later reign.

Richard H. Beal, J. Gregory McMahon (Winona Lake: Eisenbrauns, 2003), 384–88; and Goedegebuure, *The Hittite Demonstratives*, 464–65.

726 De Roos, *Hittite Votive Texts*, did not offer a dating in his introduction for this or any of the texts that were published after his dissertation, but cf. Theo van den Hout, *The Purity of Kingship: An Edition of CTH 569 and Related Hittite Oracle Inquiries of Tudḫaliya IV*. DMOA 25 (Leiden: Brill, 1998), 139, who also dated this text to Tudḫaliya.

727 See Michele Cammarosano, "Hittite Cult Inventories – Part Two: The Dating of the Texts and the Alleged 'Cult Reorganization' of Tudḫaliya IV," AoF 39/1 (2012): 3–37, and again Cammarosano, *Hittite Local Cults*, 20–23.

Table 56: Personal Vows of Tudḫaliya[728]

Protasis	Apodosis
1. KUB 56.19 obv. i 11–12	
If [...] you will, and for me this [ev]il [you expel,] (obv. i 11)	[for you the Fes]tival of the Soul I will celebrate. (obv. i 12)
2. KUB 56.19 obv. i 13–14	
[If ... with a s]ubstitute you take, [and] you illuminate [and ...] you do, (obv. i 13–14)	I will celebrate the Festival of Illumination for you. (obv. i 14)
3. KUB 56.19 obv. i 15–16	
If you allot for me a good campaign, and you support me well, (obv. i 15)	I will celebrate the Festival of the Campaign for you. (obv. i 16)
4. KUB 56.19 obv. i 17–18	
And [i]f whichever evils of mine, you, the Storm-god, my lord, [...,] (obv. i 17–18)	I will [ce]lebrate separately this festival too for you. (obv. i 18)
5. KUB 56.19 obv. i 19–20	
But the Storm-god, my lord, because I have grasped the knee, if you, the Storm-god, my lord, cause me to live, (obv. i 19)	I will celebrate the Festival of the Grasping of the Knee for you. (obv. i 20)
6. KUB 56.19 obv. i 21	
And if you, the Storm-god, my lord, purify me from evil, (obv. i 21)	I will celebrate for you the Pure Festival. (obv. i 21)
7. KUB 56.19 obv. i 22–25	
And if you, the Storm-god, my lord, [...] my evil, and all these evils you expel completely, (obv. i 22–23)	for you this festival too I will establish, and which house [...] I have [...]-ed, I will take even from there and I will establish it f[or the Storm-god]. (obv. i 23–25)
8. KUB 56.19 obv. i 26–27	
But if for me [...] ... (*too fragmentary for translation*) ... (you), the Storm-god, my lord, draw away ... (obv. i 26–27)	I will celebrate a festival. (obv. i 27)
9. KUB 56.19 obv. i 28–30	
But like a bird the god [...] I have gras[pe]d. If you, the Storm-god, my lord, cause me to live, (obv. i 28–29)	the right(hand side) [... for the Storm-god], my [lord], a sta[tue] I will make. For him a window [...] festival [...] I will establish. (obv. i 29–30)

728 As with almost all the votive texts, some vows are too damaged to include. Only the clearest have been included here. The absence of KUB 56.19 obv. i 33–41 is especially regrettable, since it is a complex vow that is unfortunately missing key words. In it Tudḫaliya seems to be praising the gods' attentiveness to his well-being and offering the celebration of the Festival of Invoking.

10. KUB 56.19 obv. i 31–32	
And if you, the Storm-god, my lord, for me to these word[s ...,] (obv. i 31)	for you [I] will celebrate the Festival of Justice. (obv. i 32)

The only other votive text dateable to Tudḫaliya as Great King is KBo 33.216.[729] It contains a single military vow, written in first-person, concerning success against the king of Aššur (KBo 33.216 obv.? i 5′–9′). This vow, and possibly one other in the preceding paragraph (obv.? i 2′–4′), are the only vows on the tablet. The remainder of the text concerns obligations towards the gods and an oracular inquiry, also written in first-person. The gift of the vow follows the *malteššar* format of livestock, festivals, and infrastructure. The disaster at the Battle of Niḫriya presumably meant that the vow was never fulfilled.

Table 57: Assyrian Campaign of Tudḫaliya

Protasis	Apodosis
1. KBo 33.216 obv.? i 5′–9′	
[I]f you, Ninurta, Kumarbi [...] give me, (and) [I] conquer the king of Aššur, (obv.? i 5′–6′)	3 steles I will erect. [To each] god 1 ox, 8 sheep I will give. [Festivals] I will establish, and [...] (obv.? i 7′–9′)

KBo 33.216 obv.? i 5′–9′ is the latest vow by any author that can be positively dated. Did the defeat in the Battle of Niḫriya, which was the largest known loss of Hittite prestige since the "concentric invasion" suffered by Šuppiluliuma I, cause Tudḫaliya to become disenchanted with the votive system? The aftermath of the battle saw an inward turn in Hittite policy as Tudḫaliya struggled with the fallout among his vassals and the ever-present threat posed by Kuruntiya, brother of the rightful king deposed by Ḫattušili and now ruler of Tarḫuntašša. In this light, Tudḫaliya's discovery of a passion for cult restoration and the consensual and redistributive process it implies was well-timed.

Tudḫaliya's treaties with Kuruntiya and Tarḫuntašša (CTH 106) show a profound ambiguity and maybe even guilt about Ḫattušili's usurpation, and it might be that the transition away from the votive system was a rejection in part of his parents' legacy. Palace intrigue might also have been at work. Puduḫepa, the votive system's greatest proponent, fell out of favor sometime early in Tudḫaliya's reign, and a loss of access to palace funds would account for her subsequent silence in the vows. It appears the votive system was dismantled in her absence, and even when she returned to the court later in Tudḫaliya's reign the vows did not resume. The fact of the matter was that Ḫattušili and Puduḫepa's inclination for "endowment by fiat," emanating from the political center through vows that quite literally came to them in dreams, might have become out of place in the new political order.

729 Also edited by de Roos, but in a separate article: Johan de Roos, "*KBo* 33.216. A Votive Text of Tutḫaliaš IV," JAC 4 (1989): 40–48.

8.13 The Vow of Puduḫepa (CTH 585) and Vow Fulfillment in Practice

There is very little evidence of vow fulfillment attested in the votive texts themselves, beyond the occasional admission of a neglected vow (e.g., KUB 15.11+ obv. ii 13–19), and the sparse notation of *karū* and *nawi* (discussed in *8.3 Using the Vows as Economic Documents*).[730] Yet the objects and actions promised by the vows must have imposed a substantial administrative and logistical burden on the Hittite palace, and it must be reckoned that the monitoring of vow fulfillment took place outside the clay tablet administration. Whether the compliance process was monitored with wooden tablets or oral communication is a moot point, since there is no evidence for substantial interface with either in the votive corpus: there are no names or seal impressions of individuals responsible for the manufacture and delivery of the promised goods, nor any reference to the numerous terms for lists, inventories, or tags associated with wooden tablets. The interface with the Palace-Temple Administrative Corpus is also disappointingly slim. Besides four texts edited under Vol. II, *7. Votive Gifts*, which record the production of votive objects, and two to four texts (depending on indirect joins) edited in Vol. II, *10.2.2 Votive Objects in Storage*, which inventory objects – mostly animal figurines – inscribed with the names of the Hittite kings who presumably donated them, items identifiable as votive gifts are almost non-existant. Of course, it could be that votive gifts lurk unnamed and unrecognized elsewhere among the manufacturing and inventorying texts, but uncovering these would pose a speculative, if not impossible, task.

The near absence of formal feedback between the systems of vow creation and vow fulfillment suggests that the systems interfaced along a narrow front, probably in the person of the scribe who produced the votive texts. As with the KASKAL Main Text, the lack of metadata (names, dates, locations, stages of completion) in the votive corpus means that the documents would circulate poorly among multiple users, especially if the vows were not rigorously updated to record new administrative action. Without well developed administrative controls, the fewer users involved with the votive corpus, the less chance for error – which, in the context of the vow administration, would mean either an expensive duplication of efforts or the potentially disasterous neglect of a votive promise. A single scribe directly answerable to the queen, with precise records and encyclopedic familiarity of the vows that he himself had recorded, could do the job that an army of administrators, each working at a different pace and in different locations, might fail.[731] Such a reconstruction again raises the implication that the size

730 The notations appear in eighteen texts, as presented in fn. 675 above. However, some of these texts are very small, and even in the larger ones the notations usually appear only once or twice. It can be estimated that less than 10%, and perhaps closer to 5%, of all vows were thus annotated. This seems far too small a number to constitute a working system of monitoring vow fulfillment.

731 Deference must be shown to the old saw that "absence of evidence is not evidence of absence." But if evidence for a substantial body of coordinate administrative documents on wood or otherwise were to be discovered for the votive corpus, it would not change the peculiar lack of logistical feedback within the votive texts themselves. If it were proven that an administration on wood existed for vow fulfillment, explaining the poor interface between vow promise and fulfillment would require a transference of authority from the scribe to the votive texts. The texts would effectuate, but not be affected by, administrative action, and the authority of the votive texts would be such that when their vows

of the bureaucracy is to be reduced and the authority and prestige of the scribes correspondingly increased in the model of Hittite government.

There is a single exceptional text, the Vow of Puduḫepa (CTH 585),[732] which must be weighed against the "single scribe" hypothesis, since it appears to be an example of exactly the kind of sustained, written-on-clay description of vow compliance that is argued to be missing from the corpus. The Vow of Puduḫepa is a year-by-year review of the fulfillment of a major vow, preserved in multiple copies overlapping as many as six layers deep in some places. The multiple copies might be explained by the episodic nature of the review: earlier years were created first then copied into each subsequent draft (by Year Five the overlaps are reduced to three copies, and it is always possible that later years might have been lost). But the fact that the earlier drafts were kept suggests that the Vow was not written down solely for the scribe's own use, but intended for perusal or review by multiple, cuneiform-literate individuals. The exact editorial history of the text, whether it yielded more than one finished "presentation" copy, would require a philological reevaluation that is beyond the scope of the present work. However, a few useful considerations on the Vow of Puduḫepa's administrative context may still be presented.

The Vow begins with a formal version of the vows found in the rest of the votive corpus:

CTH 585.A = KUB 15.17+ obv. i 1–9

Thus Puduḫepa, Great Queen, queen of the l[and of] Ḫatti, daughter of the city of Kummanni: to Lelwani, my lady, for the sake of the life of the person of His Majesty I have vowed. "If you the goddess, my lady, keep His Majesty alive and healthy for long years, (and) he tends to you, goddess, for long years, for you the goddess yearly [I will give] years of silver and years of gold, months of silver and gold, days [of silver and days] of gold, a cup of silver and a cup of gold, one (statue of the) person of His Majesty of gold [and one of silver.[733] And year]ly if it is 100, (or) if it is 50 sheep, I will be giving (them), it [does not] matter.

Its topic and contents are recognizable from the Illness Vows: the gold and silver "years," "months," and cups are exactly paralleled by the vow to the Moon-god for the health, life and long years of His Majesty in KUB 15.3 obv. i 5–16,[734] and the person (or literally "head") of His Majesty in gold recalls the offer of a statue for long years of His Majesty to the Sun-god of Heaven of Ḫuḫana in KUB 15.23 rev. 17′–19′. Thus, although the Vow of Puduḫepa is substantial – one of the largest besides KUB 56.23 obv. 1–16 (which offered a walled settlement with 300 deportees, 20 horses, quantities of metal, temple appointments made of precious materials, and a statue of the queen) – it is nonetheless not an unprecedented votive act.

---

were fulfilled and the texts were no longer administratively active, they would be kept as a historical archive. Would the votive corpus be classified as "texts of tradition" in this scenario?

732 For the principal edition, see again Otten and Souček, *Das Gelübde der Königin Puduḫepa.*

733 Otten and Souček do not restore the silver statue, but the gold/silver pairing of every other object, and the appearance of four statues in KUB 31.53 obv. 2 (instead of the expected two) and five statues in KUB 31.54 rev. 16′ (instead of two or three), make the restoration probable.

734 The "days" promised in the Vow of Puduḫepa are not the days of the month, but the ten or so extra ("epagomenal") days it takes to reconcile a lunar calendar with a solar year. It is quite possible these days were implicit in KUB 15.3 obv. i 5–16.

After the introduction the text proceeds with a description of the gifts actually given each year, for a total of five years. Surprisingly, the practice of the vow diverges considerably from its description. Year One begins with a description of named households, formally recalling the Hittite land-grant documents (CTH 222), given into the service of Lelwani. Many of these households are headed by women, all contain small children and at least one deportee, and most are assigned economic specialties like milking (KUB 15.17 obv. i 16), baking (rev. iii 39), and beekeeping (rev. iii 50). The households are reported on again in later years with updated demographics. The legal status and relationship of the persons in the households are unclear,[735] but they were apparently counted as part of the Puduḫepa's fulfillment of her vow to Lelwani, despite not appearing in the original apodosis: see KUB 31.51 obv. i 8′–9′ "These person(s)[...] he/she gav[(e)] from the palace," and KUB 56.10 + 4.33 (= CTH 585.P) obv. ii 3′–5′ "Grand total: 48 persons, whom Queen Puduḫepa to Le[(lwani)], her lady, for the sake of the life of Ḫattušili, the Great King, her husband, each has given."

Why were these extra people given, and why did they not appear in the original vow? The simplest explanation, and one preserving the integrity of the original vow, is that they were implicit with the livestock. After all, sheep and goats need shepherds to tend them and households to process their secondary products. The livestock promised in the vow are not given until the third year, at which point some 412 are given all at once (KUB 31.53 obv. i 4–10 has 8 cattle, 6 horses, 387 sheep, 11 goats). Of these only 1 cow, 5 sheep, and 3 goats seem to be explicitly designated for slaughter. The details of the Vow of Puduḫepa thus suggest that offerings of livestock elsewhere in the votive corpus (such as the 1,000 sheep in KUB 56.13 obv. 15′–17′) should be reassessed: it seems very few of the animals were meant to be slaughtered, and that the vast majority were intended instead as capital for the god. Moreover, the gift of livestock might also have implied a substantial gift of people to put that capital to work.

The silver and gold gifts are delivered irregularly and in amounts that only approximate the promises of the vow. The first mention of the silver and gold calendar objects come in Year Two, where a double amount appears to make up for the first year. The gift in this case is even more generous than necessary, perhaps because of the delay. Everything is delivered as prescribed, except instead of two statues of the person of His Majesty of gold and two of silver, all four are of gold, as are the four years (KUB 31.53 obv. 2). The next delivery of gold and silver comes in Year Five, which judging by the amounts given might be better described as "Year Four-and-a-Half." Here there are three gold cups given but no silver cups, five (out of expected six) statues of the person of His Majesty, again all of gold, and thirty months (out of thirty-six) of silver and thirty (of thirty-six) of gold (KUB 31.54 rev. 16′–17′; the silver and gold days may be lost in the break at the end of 17′).

The final revelation of the text concerning vow fulfillment in practice is that it was not only Puduḫepa who contributed to the gift, but also individuals who hailed among the "lords of Ḫatti." Twenty-three persons "of the campaign against the city of Zikeššara" are given to Lelwani by Á^{MUŠEN}-LÚ-*iš* (KUB 31.51 obv. ii 6), and smaller contrib-

735 See discussion of Otten and Souček, *Das Gelübde der Königin Puduḫepa*, especially 42–43.

utions of six to eight persons were made by AMAR^MUŠEN^-*iš* the *urayanni*, by Pinaura, and by Alalimi the governor of Kaneš (KUB 31.51 obv. ii 7–18). The only parallel to these (seemingly unforced) contributions to the queen's vow was the single, modest gift of a lapis lazuli model of a breast for the king's health by Walwaziti (KUB 15.30 rev. iii 1′–7′). There is no way to know how common such additional gifts actually were, given that the contributions of the nobles could not be guessed from the preamble of the Vow of Puduḫepa, but the possibility of economic coercion should not be discounted for the votive system. Even if the coercion was only a pressure to impress the king and queen, it fits well with the centralizing tendencies of the ruling couple.

The Vow of Puduḫepa records one of the largest and most complex votive offerings in the corpus, and the only one containing evidence of major contributions to fulfillment by multiple parties. Its complexity may explain in part why both the vow promise and fulfillment were committed to writing, but if complexity and size were the only criteria for extra administrative attention then one might expect other vows to have received similar treatment. The conundrum of the Vow of Puduḫepa's uniqueness is not unprecedented. There is a pattern of exceptional "capstone" texts in the administrative corpus, which appear as mirages to tempt the modern reader to reconstruct such regularity everywhere in the corpus. The *9.1 Named Complex Inventories* edited in Vol. II do this for the inventory texts, the KASKAL Main Text for shipment records, and the Vow of Puduḫepa for the votive texts. These special texts are too infrequent to be constitutive of the regular Hittite bureaucracy, and it must be assumed they originated from extraordinary administrative situations no longer perceptible. The capstone texts are in other words the limit cases of a minimalist Hittite bureaucracy: they do not define the bureaucracy, but can be appreciated as brief glimpses into processes otherwise undocumented on the preserved clay tablets of Hittite administration.

The divergence between promise and delivery on display in the Vow of Puduḫepa shows that there was some flexibility to vow fulfillment. While the sample size of one text does not allow for firm conclusions, the late delivery of the livestock, the gift of unpromised deportees, and the irregularity in the gifts of precious metal suggest that the administration of vows was perhaps more *ad hoc* than one might have expected based on the regular votive texts. The conspicuous gap between prescription and practice in the only preserved record of vow compliance must serve as a caution to the present study's attempt to reconstruct the economics of the votive system.

8.14 Average Value and Significance of the Vow Objects

Counting all of the vows presented in the tables above (including the Vow of Puduḫepa and excluding the vows of Tudḫaliya) gives a total of 164 minor vows and 30 major vows attested from the reign of Ḫattušili and Puduḫepa.

Vow Totals by Category

Type	Minor	Major
Illness Vows:	48	14
Military Vows:	26	7

Other Vows:	36	6
Vows w/ Lost Conditions:[736]	50	5
Total:	160	32

The minor vows, as was discussed in section *8.3 Using the Vows as Economic Documents*, tend to be similar in the quantity and size of gifts, while major vows varied enormously in size and contents. Because the minor vows are fairly uniform, consisting usually of one or two votive objects made of precious metal or stone and the occasional livestock, it is possible to reconstruct the amount of gold and silver in a "standard" minor gift by averaging the objects with known weights. Conversely the major gifts must be treated separately.

Table 58: Objects with Preserved Material and Weights in Minor Vows

Text	Object	Material	Weight
KUB 15.1+ obv. ii 12	soul	silver	10 shekels
KUB 15.1+ obv. ii 27	ear	gold	10 shekels
KUB 15.1+ obv. ii 27	ear	silver	1 mina
KUB 15.1+ rev. iii 3′	soul	silver	10 shekels
KUB 15.8 obv. i 6′	soul	gold	3 shekels
KUB 15.8 obv. i 7′	pair of eyes	silver	6 shekels
KUB 15.9 rev. iii 7′	ear	gold	10 shekels
KUB 15.9 rev. iii 8′	earring	gold	3 shekels
KUB 15.11+ obv. ii 4	pair of breasts	gold	1 mina
KUB 15.19 obv. 5′	soul	gold	1 mina
KUB 15.19 obv. 13′	soul	gold	20 shekels
KUB 31.77+ obv. i 49	lion figurine	silver	20 shekels
KUB 48.123 obv. i 18′	Ištar figurine	silver	1 mina
KUB 48.123 obv. i 18′	Ištar figurine	gold	20 shekels
KUB 56.13 obv. 3′	sun disk	silver	20 shekels
KUB 56.13 rev. 6′	dream	silver	2 minas
KUB 56.13 rev. 13′	dream	silver	2 minas
KUB 56.13 rev. 13′	dream	gold	1 mina
KUB 56.25+ rev. iv 11′	[an object]	gold	1 mina

736 Because of the state of preservation, these vows are classified as minor unless there is compelling evidence otherwise, which is why there are relatively few major vows compared to the ratios in other categories.

KBo 8.61 3′	lion figurine	silver	1 mina
KBo 8.61 8′	eyes	silver	2 minas
KBo 34.145 6′	statue	silver	1 mina
KBo 34.145 7′	Morning Star	silver	15 shekels
KBo 55.208 obv.? 2′	[an object]	gold	5 shekels
KBo 55.208 rev.? 14′	eyes	gold	1 mina
KBo 55.213 12′	soul	silver	2 minas

From the attested object weights in minor vows, it can be estimated that an average gold votive object weighed 26 Hittite shekels (a little over half a mina) and an average silver votive object weighed 40 Hittite shekels (exactly one mina).

Of the 160 minor vows attested in the corpus, there are 151 with sufficiently preserved apodoses to determine the nature of at least some of the gifts. Of the 151 preserved apodoses, 129 show evidence of votive objects. Due to the poor state of preservation for many vow texts, the construction material of the objects cannot be determined in every case. Of the 133 instances where the material is known (some apodoses contain multiple objects), there are 55 attestations of votive objects made of gold (= 41.4%),[737] 65 of silver (= 48.9%),[738] and 13 of other materials (= 9.8%).[739] Problems of preservation also makes it difficult to determine the average number of votive objects for a given vow. Some apodoses have only one, whereas others have three or four. For the convenience of calculation, it can be assumed that there was an average of two objects per minor vow apodosis.

Restricting calculations to the objects made of precious metal, a combination of the ratios (41.4% gold / 48.9% silver) and average weight (26 s. gold / 40 s. silver) of the gold and silver objects in the minor vows gives an average value of 10.8 shekels gold and 19.6 shekels silver per one composite votive object. If there were two votive objects in a minor gift, then the "standard" minor vow contained 21.6 shekels of gold and 39.1 shekels of silver, or to put in rounder terms, a minor vow contained on average of one-half mina of gold and one mina of silver. Although it is only a very rough estimation, it is promising that this figure matches the one-to-two ratio of gold to silver observed in three of the vows with known weights (KUB 15.8 obv. i 6′–7′; 48.123 obv. i 18′; 56.13 rev. 13′).

737 Gold in Minor Gifts, listed by Table (T.) and Vow number: T.34: 4, 5, 7, 10, 11, 12, 13, 16, 18, 19, 21, 22, 25, 26?, 31, 35, 36, 37, 39, 40. T.41: 11. T.45: 1, 2, 3, 4, 7. T.46: 1. T.47: 1, 2, 3, 4, 8. T.49: 5, 11. T.51: 1, 3, 4. T.54: 3, 5, 6, 7. T.55: 4, 5, 6, 9, 16, 18, 24, 30, 34, 36, 40, 46, 48, 50.

738 Silver in Minor Gifts, listed by Table (T.) and Vow number: T.34: 2, 3, 4, 5, 7, 8, 10, 11, 12, 15, 16, 21, 25, 26, 29, 37, 39, 40, 41, 42. T.39: 1. T.41: 3, 5?, 8, 9. T.43: 1. T. 45: 3, 4, 5. T.46: 1. T.47: 3, 6. T.49: 3, 5, 7, 8, 9, 11. T.50: 1, 2. T.51: 1. T.54: 3. T.55: 2, 3, 7, 8, 13, 14, 15, 17, 19, 21, 24, 27, 30, 33, 34, 36, 37, 38, 41, 44, 46, 47, 48.

739 Other materials, listed by Table (T.) and Vow number: Precious stone (T.34: 1, 5, 13, 28, 36. T.42: 2. T.47: 3, 5, 10. T.54: 1. T.55: 16, 42). Copper (T.45: 1). The small number and relative lack of known weights excludes these objects from further discussion.

It is remarkable just how close in value the half mina of gold and mina of silver of the average minor gift is to the "standard" diplomatic gift of the Egyptian correspondences (48 Babylonian shekels gold = .8 mina) and the gold cups of the Ugaritic tribute (30 Hittite shekels gold = .75 mina) discussed in *6.2.1.1 Commentary: The Standard Diplomatic Gift Package*. The similarity cannot be a coincidence. In theory, the Hittite palace could have had considerable flexibility in choosing the schedule and size of votive offerings. Even if the royal couple were committed to a certain value of yearly gifts, the gifts could have been presented as a lump sum once or twice a year, perhaps coinciding with the Autumn and Spring Festivals. But it seems that the king, and especially the queen, were habituated to make votive offerings of a value nearly identical to the international diplomatic gifts of the day. Mechanically, it seems not unlikely that the frequency of votive gifts was a by-product of the "vow budget" having its source, at least in part, in the diplomatic gifts themselves – trade being the only regular source of gold in the Hittite lands (see *2.4.2.2 Gold and Silver*). But there is also a potent symbolism in the congruence of diplomatic gifts and votive offerings of Puduḫepa. As Gary Beckman noted in his work on Hittite diplomatic texts, "In times of good relations among the great powers, there was a constant exchange of messengers among their courts."[740] With these messengers came a steady stream of diplomatic gifts. By giving a votive gift that echoes the form and value of a standard diplomatic gift – from vassal to master and from king to allied king – Puduḫepa signaled her commitment to maintain a regular, loyal, and in the language of Bronze Age diplomacy, affectionate relationship with the gods. One might indeed wonder how many of the vows were occasioned by a crisis such as severe illness, and how many were simply intended to keep open the lines of communication (cf. the many vows for His Majesty's long life).

The votive texts can be perceived as a redistributive system of prestige and material when seen as a link between the diplomatic and the religious worlds. The king and queen transferred the diplomatic income accorded to their political station to the gods in approximately the same dimensions as it was received. In real terms this meant that wealth was invested into the temples of Ḫattuša and provincial Anatolia. In symbolic terms Ḫattušili and Puduḫepa piously situated the Hittite Kingdom, one of the great powers of the ancient Near Eastern world, as vassal and tributary to the divine.[741]

8.15 Reconstructing the Vow Schedule of Ḫattušili and Puduḫepa

Given the state of preservation, it can be cautiously estimated that tablets of the corpus retain around half of their original text, so the 160 minor vows and 32 major vows represent a reconstructed total of 320 minor and 64 major vows. It can be assumed that

740 Gary Beckman, *Hittite Diplomatic Texts.* WAW 7 (Atlanta: Society of Biblical Literature, 1999), 5, quoting further from KBo 1.10 + KUB 3.72 obv. 50–54, a letter from Ḫattušili III to Kadashman-Enlil II, "'[Only if two kings] are hostile do their messengers not travel continually between them.'"

741 Such a mindset was not at all unique to Ḫattušili and Puduḫepa, but stood rather at the center of Hittite royal ideology. See Fiorella Imparati, "Die Organisation des hethitischen Staates," in *Geschichte des hethitischen Reiches*, by Horst Klengel, contribs. Fiorella Imparati, Volkert Haas, Theo van den Hout. HdO 1/34 (Leiden: Brill, 1998), 323, 327–28.

most of the vows were distributed evenly across the reign of Ḫattušili and Puduḫepa. The military vows are an exception, since these were triggered by specific, historically compact events. If the reign of Ḫattušili and Puduḫepa lasted about thirty years (ca. 1267–37), and the reconstructed total for non-military vows are divided evenly across thirty years, the results are:

Reconstructed Vow Obligations per Year (over 30 years, excluding Military Vows)

For Illness:	3.2 minor / 0.9 major
For Other Topics:	2.4 minor / 0.5 major
Unknown Topics:	3.3 minor / 0.3 major
Total:	8.9 minor / 1.7 major per year

The vows for "Unknown Topics" reflect the vows with lost or damaged conditions. If the conditions could be recovered, the topics would probably show a distribution similar to the undamaged vows, with the exception that it is probable they would skew towards the "Other Topics" (of omens, calamity, etc.), since many damaged vows have already been identified as dealing with illness and war (these topics being easier to identify, since it only takes the discovery of a single word in the damaged text, e.g., a body part or mention of healthiness, or a campaign or mention of the enemy, to assign the vow to the illness vows or military vows, respectively).

The military vows probably clustered into a few short years. The campaigns themselves were fairly brief (the Arzawa campaign took place in a single season) and the preparation was most likely accomplished in the preceding winters, which leaves a small window of time for military vows to be made. There is a reconstructed total of 52 minor and 14 major military vows (doubled from the 26 minor / 7 major counted at the beginning of section *8.14 Average Value and Significance of the Vow Objects*) to be divided across the thirty years of Ḫattušili's reign. The outstanding question is: how many years did the Hittites spend in campaigns against the Kaška? The preserved portions of Ḫattušili's Annals unfortunately do not allow a continuous narrative to be reconstructed for his kingship. In the votive texts, the single-year Arzawa campaign garnered thirteen vows in seven texts. The Northern Campaigns, which include the vows of Puduḫepa for Tudḫaliya, have nineteen vows in five texts. Even allowing that the Arzawa campaign was much more of a formal military expedition compared to the police actions against the Kaška, it seems the Northern Campaigns, at least those significant enough to appear in the vows, were not exceedingly frequent. Let it be assumed for convenience's sake that the total number of years during Ḫattušili's reign spent on military campaigns was around five years. The 52 minor and 14 major military vows, divided over 5 years, yields a total of 10.4 minor vows / 2.8 major vows per year. When added to the normal obligations, this average means the total number of vows was effectively doubled during war years.

Thus, during the reign of Ḫattušili III the Hittite palace could typically expect to offer nine to ten minor gifts and one to two major gifts per year, with campaign years seeing perhaps as many as twice this amount. Of every ten minor vows offered, nine of them would be authored by Puduḫepa and one by Ḫattušili, except for military vows, when the ratio would be closer to seven to three, but still in the queen's favor. For the major vows the distribution is almost even, with half given by Puduḫepa and half by Ḫattušili.

Ḫattušili gave far less frequently than Puduḫepa but his gifts could be very large. In the vows from KUB 56.30 obv. 19′–22′, 23′–26′ and KUB 15.9 rev. iii 1′–5′ he offered a total of 300 minas of silver and 100 minas of mixed precious metals, though it also possible that the 100 minas of silver from KUB 15.29 obv. i 2′–3′ should also be added to this total. By these three vows alone it is thus conceivable that despite the queen being the more frequent user of the votive system, the total value of Ḫattušili's gifts equaled or exceeded the gifts of Puduḫepa.

8.16 Source and Destination of the Votive Objects

It was estimated at the beginning of the previous section that a the gift of a minor vow was roughly equal in value to a standard diplomatic gift, suggesting there was a symbolic link between diplomacy and devotion in the Hittite court. Because large quantities of gold could only be acquired through trade for the Hittites, the link was also practical.

As discussed in *8.14 Average Value and Significance of the Vow Objects*, an average minor vow contained about one-half mina of gold and one mina of silver. Combining this with an estimated rate of ten minor vows per year means that around five minas of gold was consumed by minor votive gifts each year. It is not possible to estimate how much gold was consumed by the major gifts in a year because the major gifts could vary so greatly in size. It is clear that the palace would need to build up a "strategic gold reserve" so that they could deliver on promises like the life-size golden statue in KUB 15.1+ rev. iii 32′–35′ and the recurring yearly gifts in KUB 15.3 obv. i 5–16 and in the Vow of Puduḫepa. Let it be assumed that somewhere between five and ten minas of diplomatic gold was saved for major gifts each year, which would allow for a very substantial statue weighing between twenty-five and fifty minas to be produced every five years. With the estimates of minor and major gifts in mind, it can be said in very general terms that between a half and a three-quarters of the gold from the known yearly tribute was earmarked for votive objects during the reign of Ḫattušili and Puduḫepa. Some of the remaining gold income must have been returned to the diplomatic economy through out-going gifts, and some of it designated for the maintenance of cult objects around the countryside. Judging by the jewelry attested in the inventory texts, some gold was also turned into objects for use in the ritual vestments and perhaps also for the personal wardrobe of the royal family.[742]

---

742 See discussion of Hittite use of precious metals in Jana Siegelová and Hidetoshi Tsumoto, "Metals and Metallurgy in Hittite Anatolia," in *Insights into Hittite Archaeology and History*, eds. Hermann Genz, Dirk P. Mielke (Leuven: Peeters, 2011), 277–78: "The precious metals were controlled by the administration offices and hoarded as an accumulation of capital, but were also spent: for temples (regular maintenance of for votives), for furnishing palaces (insignia, emblems, prestige weapons and jewellery), or as remuneration or reward (all metals, but predominantly silver)."

It is necessary for the modern observer to break out of the mindset of seeing gold simply as a marker of wealth in the Hittite context. The only attested expenditures of gold during the Hittite Late New Kingdom were for votive gifts, the restoration of cult objects domestically, and diplomatic gifts abroad. There is no evidence for large-scale distribution of gold in the form of non-religious prestige gifts to local elites.[743] It was too precious and exotic for mundane use, and altogether too value-dense for most transactions, so that, unlike silver, there is no evidence of its use for exchange or currency. Gold's import, manufacture, and emplacement in the form of religious objects was almost certainly centrally controlled. Because of its restricted source and utility, gold must be seen in the Hittite context not so much as a marker of wealth but of prestige connected to the central government. Viewed this way, the votive system was a program of redistribution, or perhaps better curation of wealth gained through foreign contacts, since the objects were inalienable to the temple and did not circulate.[744]

8.17 Conclusions on the Votive Corpus

All evidence from the votive texts suggests that the vows were completely centered on the psyche of the royal persons of Ḫattušili and Puduḫepa, either occasioned by dreams or in response to an event impacting a member of the royal family. It seems that the vows were pronounced solely at the discretion of the king or queen, with apparently little to no consultation with the local temples. In terms of the operative chain behind the gifts, the items promised by the vows were centrally manufactured in the workshops of the capital from gold and other exotic materials acquired through diplomatic trade. It is not clear in every case where the gifts ended up. Some of the offerings were surely given in Ḫattuša, which is known to have contained many temples of different gods transplanted to the capital. But others must have been distributed across temples in land of Ḫatti. A number of the vows are prefaced by the location where they were made or where the dream occurred, and it is not unreasonable to assume that the location where the vow was promised was in many cases where the gift was intended to be given.[745] Sometimes it is explicitly stated that the gifts will be given in a specific location, as in KUB 15.3 obv. i 15–16: "But whatever the Moon-god wills, according to that I will be giving the months of silver and gold, whether (in) Urikina or wherever"; cf. also KUB 48.119 obv.[?] 3′–8′ where the possible sites of Nerik and/or Hakmiš are offered. Additional evidence for the dispersal of votive gifts comes from the various

743 Although elites besides the immediate royal family could acquire and accumulate gold, as is evidenced by the diplomatic gifts from Ugarit sent to important officials discussed in *6.3.1 Tribute from Ugarit*, as well as the intriguing case of copper-gold alloy taken from the "lot of …" various individuals, including possibly the high official Lupakki, in 4.1.1.1, edited in Vol. II.

744 The display and limited distribution of wealth obtained through foreign contacts is a time-honored and anthropologically sound way of cultivating legitimacy, and one of the main factors for secondary state formation of wealth-financed states, as discussed by Earle, Galaty, and others (see Section *2.4.1 Wealth Finance, Staple Finance*).

745 De Roos, *Hittite Votive Texts*, 22–26, provides a discussion and list of the locations of the vows, almost all of which are confined to central Anatolia.

geographical hypostases of the gods in the vows.[746] In some cases the human suppliant cycles through the different hypostases of a single godhead, raising doubt that the gifts will be distributed to all of the locations mentioned, but most of the time the god appears only once, identified by a specific town suggesting that the vow might be connected to that location.

The votive system as a government institution was coincident with Puduḫepa's tenure as *tawananna-* at the Hittite court. While there are clear precedents for vows in Hittite culture, only under Puduḫepa was vow-making a tool of state. Though she pioneered and largely ran the votive system, she relied on the full support and participation of her husband Ḫattušili. Puduḫepa's share of the votive gifts comprised nine out of ten of the minor vows and half of the major vows, greatly exceeding the number of gifts she is recorded to have personally received in yearly tribute. It must be concluded that she was explicitly tasked by Ḫattušili with spending a large portion of the combined diplomatic income of the Palace. The importance of the consent of the king to the votive system can be seen in its abrupt collapse when Puduḫepa fell out of favor with Tudḫaliya, which presumably resulted in a loss of access to diplomatic income.

Ḫattušili III was also an active participant in the votive system, but his gifts seem to have drawn on a different source of income than Puduḫepa's, as evidenced by the strong distribution in the kinds of gifts given by the king and queen. Ḫattušili's gifts tend towards deportees, livestock, and large amounts of raw silver, all of which are obtainable within Anatolia. Puduḫepa's gifts contain most of the gold and lapis lazuli objects attested in the corpus, which could only be obtained from her diplomatic contacts abroad. This division fits well with the image of Puduḫepa as a political driving force and diplomatic doyenne in the Hittite court, and confirms that she had great influence not only in the crafting of foreign diplomacy, but also in the spending of its tangible rewards.

The preceding economic analysis suggests that the votive texts constituted a symbolic link between the diplomatic and religious spheres for the Hittite court. It is possible that the vows can be interpreted as more than expressions of piety: by their very nature of arising from the dreams and emotional states of the king and queen, the vows and the wealth they promised served to centralize power in the royal persons. Given the complementary distribution of the votive corpus and the Hittie local cult reports, it is possible that this centralizing aspect of Ḫattušili and Puduḫepa should be constrasted to a more consensus-based approach of Tudḫaliya, who distributed the diplomatic wealth of his reign in conversation with local temples.[747]

A brief closing remark can be made on the (limited) connections between the votive texts and the Palace-Temple Administrative Corpus. As alluded to at the beginning of the chapter, the Hittite Votive Corpus allows for an alternate view on expenditure to

746 As also discussed and listed by de Roos, *Hittite Votive Texts*, 26–30.

747 For the administrative/ideological impact of the Hittite local cults, and Tudḫaliya IV's role in promoting them, see Michele Cammarosano, "Hittite Cult Inventories – Part One: The Hittite Cult Inventories as Textual Genre," WO 43 (2013): 63–105; Cammarosano, "Hittite Cult Inventories – Part Two: The Dating of the Texts and the Alleged 'Cult Reorganization' of Tudḫaliya IV," AoF 39/1 (2012): 3–37; and Cammarosano, *Hittite Local Cults*.

that found in the Palace-Temple Administrative Corpus. In the PTAC, the votive objects are encountered in only a handful of texts. These fall into three main categories: the manufacturing texts (cf. 4.1.1.8 and 4.1.1.9), the inventories of votive gifts (7.1–4), and scattered references among the other inventories, where they can be difficult to distinguish from the other religious imagery and paraphernalia stored in the temple storehouses (but see especially 10.2.2.1–4). If one were constrained to only the texts of the PTAC, there would be no way to guess the origins or events that occasioned the votive objects crafted and stored there. Without the extensive records of the Votive Corpus, fortuitously contemporary to the PTAC in stemming also from the reign of Ḫattušili III and Puduḫepa and the early years of Tudḫaliya, there would be no way to estimate how often votive objects were dedicated and produced. And, without comparison to the diplomatic texts discussed in *6. The Relative Value of the* KASKAL *Main Text* and the stream of gold recorded therein, there would be no way to link the votive objects to the diplomatic income of the Hittite court. Thus, the Hittite Votive Corpus provides an important counter-perspective compared to the static and often frustratingly timeless – since very few relative and fully no absolute chronological references are ever given – inventories of the PTAC. The value of the votive texts in providing an alternative glimpse into the living, dynamic economic administration of the Hittite state should not be underestimated.

SUMMARY AND CONCLUSIONS ON HITTITE ECONOMIC ADMINISTRATION

It has been suggested in this book that the most important aspects of Hittite economic administration, or at least the aspects considered by the central elites as the most important for maintaining legitimate power, rested on a small, personalized, and "hands-on" bureaucracy marked by a limited number of scribes utilizing a compact-but-efficient cuneiform corpus to control the production and manipulation of wealth, especially religious wealth. An extensive administration on wooden tablets, insofar as it existed, may or may not have been used to maintain other aspects of the Hittite economy, but no new evidence for its interface with the administration on clay has emerged. The background on which these conclusions were based was as follows.

In Chapter 1, "History of Research (I): Previous Models of the Hittite State," it was argued that the literature on Hittite state should be divided into four major periods, which were labeled the Early Western Consensus, Soviet Marxist Criticism, the Western Reaction, and the New Western Consensus. The Early Western Consensus emphasized cultural ethnicity as the organizing factor and driver of change in the Hittite state. In this model, Hittite society was originally organized in the Old Kingdom by clans, led by the "great clan" of the king's family, supposedly reflecting a non-divine, *primus inter pares* style of kingship inherited from Indo-European roots. Most of the highest officials in the Hittite Kingdom were drawn from the king's or lesser Neshite clans, imparting a supposed ethnic stratification to the Hittite. By the time of the New Kingdom a new Hurrian-influenced ruling dynasty had recast the Hittite government according to Mesopotamian political ideals. The most prominent change was what was interpreted as a growing feudal arrangement between the king and elites centered around chariot-service. The clan system disappeared and towns were now integrated through appointment of royal governors answering directly to the king. The federation of territories of the Old Kingdom was replaced by a rigid administrative structure predicated on feudalistic ideals.

Soviet Marxist, historic-materialist critique challenged the culture-historical approach of early Western Hittitology. Marxist scholars rejected a feudal assessment for the Hittite New Kingdom, because feudalism was for them a technical term, the name of a "mode of production," constituting one of the evolving ways of manufacturing the means of life. In orthodox Soviet Marxist theory, history was divided into five modes of production, namely the primitive-communal, ancient, feudal, capitalist, and socialist modes of production. For Marxist scholars, the question was whether to describe the ancient Near East as participating in the ancient mode of production based on slavery or the feudal mode of production based on serfdom. Since in the ancient Near East workers as a rule did not own the land, they were inevitably slaves by Marxist logic. Thus, despite hierarchies of political power superficially recalling the feudal societies of Medieval Europe, the ancient Near East could not be described as feudal in the historic-materialist critique. However, the clear differences between the trajectories of the slave societies of the Classical world, which led to European feudalism, and the ancient Near East, which supposedly stagnated at slavery, remained to be explained. A "two-sector" or Asiatic mode of production was proposed whereby the ancient Near East remained stuck in a transition between the primitive-communal and slave modes of production. State-sponsored slave exploitation dominated in the cities and royal estates, while private individuals in the countryside, although also exploiting dependent labor, retained more connections with the primitive-communalist mode of production. The Hittites were considered in this model to be one of the most state-oriented and hierarchical societies of their era, in that access to slave labor was almost exclusively dependent on connections with the state.

The Western Reaction to the Marxist analysis of the ancient Near East was mixed, but led most Western scholars to reject feudalism in the Hittite state. The reception of Marxist thought was especially positive in Italy, where a neo-Marxist analysis of the ancient Near East emphasized the strong political and productive divide between the palace and communal sectors. Two poles of interpretation emerged: one emphasizing the primacy of the urban palatial sector in driving political and technological development and the other emphasizing the village communal sector as the site of primary economic production, which was coordinated and co-opted by a parasitically dependent state sector. The ascendance of the latter interpretation, supported by the rise of the "New Humanities" that encouraged a turn away from pure economic determinism in favor of the investigation of ideologies and mentalities, stimulated a greater focus on the production of propaganda and monuments as the key industry of the palatial sector.

The New Western Consensus of the Hittite state that emerged from the adaptation to the Marxist critiques of the 1970's resulted in a paradigm rooted in a centralized palace and temple infrastructure, but with a growing awareness of regional differences and the impact of the Anatolian environment. Feudalism was banished almost completely from discussion of the Hittite state, and society was defined instead by a broad, direct interface between palace and community. In this model, the Anatolian Plateau was controlled by a network of palaces implanted in the local communities. Controlling the palaces were often members of the royal family, who occupied many positions of power, including most of the internal governorships in Hittite Anatolia and many of the high-level positions in the palace bureaucracy. The palace institutions were full-service administrative centers accompanied by storehouses and governed by superintendents who distributed taxes and labor to state institutions, which included temples. Finished goods and foodstuffs were supplied directly to government workers, and members of local communities received ration supplements at festivals. There was little functional difference between the palace and temple: both were aspects of the same redistributive system of the Hittite state. The importance of the temple as an extension of the palace economy came increasingly to be recognized, and the explanation of this arrangement for coordinating regional economic surpluses as arising from the specific environmental and political history of the Anatolian Plateau remains the foundation for the current understanding of the role of temples and religion in the Hittite state.

Chapter 2, "History of Research (II): Current Models of the Hittite State," explored the increasing emphasis on redistribution and its interaction with the Anatolian environment in the modern understanding of the Hittite state. In newer models, instead of being a simple brake on the growth of complex states, the Anatolian environment has been depicted as a positive factor insofar as it promoted an alternate, indigenous form of political hierarchy. The short growing season, lack of navigable rivers, and rich mineral wealth of the Anatolian Plateau encouraged a focus on local metallurgy, with the scattered communities conducive to the establishment of local aristocracies specialized in the exchange of accumulated wealth. Mesopotamian influence on Anatolian history came later in the form of trade networks that accelerated the formation of competing principalities on the Plateau. Interaction with Mesopotamia also offered the growing Hittites the means to break power of the Anatolian local nobility through a fund of conquered wealth and novel bureaucratic techniques necessary to centralize the state.

At the same time, the Anatolian environment provided less-than-benign incentives for increasing political, technological, and administrative sophistication. It has only been recently recognized that ancient Anatolia experienced a cycle of drought and crop failure during the Hittite period, which necessitated a series of adaptations at the communal and state levels that were sometimes in tension with each other. At the communal level, the precarity of the environment encouraged a diversified and extensive, as opposed to specialized and intensive, approaches to food resources. These communal approaches included a reliance on an agropastoral system, optional semi-nomadism with the possibility of full relocation, diversification of crops and livestock, overproduction, and communal storage. At the state level, a system of cultural and technological innovations, including grain silos, artificial dams and ponds, and monumental and defensive architecture was designed to encourage concentration of population into more easily controllable urban settlements. The cities were supported in part by unfree labor on royal estates, and political and military pressure was exerted to suppress population movements. However, despite their Anatolia-wide scale of impact, the cultural and technological interventions of the Hittite state were aimed only achieving a defensive, local changes. Contrary to previous assumptions that the silos were filled by an extensive extractive network, it now seems more likely that grain silos were filled using local sources as an emergency reserve. The large artificial ponds were likewise designed for intensive local horticulture near cities and watering of livestock in the countryside. Religious festivals were used in major and minor urban settlements to redistribute foodstuffs in an ideological context, but the economic impact of the festivals, and hence the amount of redistribution that took place, remains elusive. In sum, recent research suggests that the Hittite state adapted local survival strategies, either attested in pre-Hittite Anatolia or recognizable from anthropological parallels, and amplified them with the new technologies and political innovations as part of government programs designed to bolster local economic resiliency while furthering the political and ideological integration of the state. Undergirding this state was an extractive network focused on the mobilization of labor and the taxation of mineral wealth.

Hittite control of the Anatolian Plateau did not go unchallenged, and the administrative reach of the state was contested both externally and internally throughout Hittite history. The extent of the Hittite imperial project can be seen in a set of identity markers, namely a particular pattern of settlement, a style of pottery, the adoption of Anatolian glyptics, and the building of landscape monuments, that was simultaneously imposed on and selectively adopted by imperial subjects. The clearest case of imposition is the change in settlement pattern between Middle Bronze and Late Bronze Age on the Anatolian Plateau, where certain preexisting cities were diminished or destroyed, certain regions depopulated, and a network of cities was newly founded at strategic sites during the transition from the Old to Middle Hittite period. A more ambiguous case of imposition is the change in pottery style during the Hittite period, which was reduced with few exceptions to a utilitarian and mass-produced assemblage. It is possible that the pottery assemblage was sometimes voluntarily adopted by local elites, rather than centrally imposed, but for the moment it can only be confirmed that larger central towns progressively took over production for the villages in their regions. Anatolian glyptics and landscape monuments are clearer cases of adoption by regional elites. The glyptics, which evolved into the Anatolian Hieroglyphs that spread across the Anatolian Plateau and well into Syria and the Levant, where they flourished after the fall of the Hittite Kingdom. Hittite-styled landscape monuments, which also made use of Anatolian glyptics, were erected or carved at strategic locations by local elites, some of whom were at odds with the Hittite central government. Active internal resistance to the Hittite state can also be observed at the tribal level, most notably in the form of the Kaška, and passive internal resistance might explain low-quality grains recovered from some of the grain silos.

In spite of regionalism, resistance, and an environment that seemingly should have limited its projection of power, the Hittite state endured for over 400 years as a major player in the ancient Near East. However, whereas the high risk/high reward environments of Mesopotamia naturally encouraged a stratified society and large-scale urbanism, the Anatolian environment encouraged vertically oriented societies focused on protecting small territories and population groups and defending trade routes. It has been observed that Anatolian and Mesopotamian societies have strong anthropological parallels, falling respectively into the complementary redistributive categories of "Wealth Finance," based on control of trade routes and production of prestige objects, and "Staple Finance," based on ownership of land and control of foodstuffs. Although all mature ancient states show both forms of finance, the Hittite state seems to have shown a marked predilection throughout its history for wealth finance due to its origins and continued existence on the mineral-rich but agriculturally precarious Anatolian Plateau.

The primary sector of wealth finance in the Hittite state lay in metal production. Although there was general rule of indirect sponsorship of production, with the Hittite state controlling trade routes and taxation, the various metals and alloys were handled by the state very differently based on value and domestic availability. Archaeological research has shown that the copper used by the Hittite state came from a kaleidoscope of sources on the Anatolian Plateau, each defined by its own techniques for smelting and refining, while secondary production, including the alloying and smithing of the copper, took place in urban centers. The copper was combined with tin, which was mostly imported in order to fill an elite demand that was greater than the native supply, in order to produce bronze. Bronze production was also indirectly sponsored by the

Hittite state, since there is no textual or archaeological evidence for its production in palace or temple workshop. In contrast to copper and bronze, gold, which could not be acquired from domestic sources in the Hittite period, was tightly controlled by palace workshops. Silver presented a hybrid case, in that primary production took place in villages near the mines of rural Anatolia, though with perhaps increased state supervision, but at least some secondary production took place in palace workshops. The origins and manufacturing process for the other metals and luxury materials used by the Hittite state, including iron (or iron ore), remain mysterious, since these are not attested in the tribute texts nor sufficiently studied in the archaeological records. Ebony and ivory, as well as some semi-precious stones such as lapis lazuli, must have been imported, but iron/iron ore and at least some of the semi-precious stones should have had domestic sources.

Although archaeologically nearly invisible, textual evidence shows that textiles were also a major component of the Hittite wealth-financed state. Garments are at least as numerous as metallic objects in the PTAC, and wool and limited numbers of finished garments are a major category of domestic tribute. Dyed wool and luxury garments were also acquired from foreign tribute and international gifts. The Hittite state engaged in at least some direct sponsorship of wool processing and textile production, but the number of garments attested in storage far exceed the textual basis for production, suggesting that non-palace workshops were also engaged to process the wool tribute into textiles.

In contrast to the metals and garments dominating the economic-administrative texts, the management of staple finance is barely reflected in the written administrative records of the Hittite state. Textual and archaeological evidence suggest that Hittite intervention in the staple economy functioned primarily to accumulate emergency reserves, rather than as a redistributive network. The Hittite state managed control of the land indirectly through the imposition of service obligations, while more direct control came in the form of estates granted to Hittite elites in order to keep state land productive. Symbolic redistribution is observed in the rations of the state cult and the provisions of the local festivals, but the true economic scale of these measures is currently unknown. At the very least, evidence for large-scale rationing, where the state provided the daily bread or meat for large numbers of workers, is absent.

The wealth-financed interpretation of the Hittite state helps explain some of its unusual features. First and foremost, a limited economic-administrative corpus focused on utensils, garments, and luxury goods, including metals and textiles from both foreign and domestic sources, is more appropriate for a state focused on controlling the production, management, and circulation of luxury goods among elites. Even if a separate literate administrative system on wooden tablets existed, the fact that all of the records placed on durable clay – the same material used for composing religious festivals, historical compositions, treaties, and other texts of tradition – concern wealth demonstrates the importance placed by the Hittite administration on this sector of the finance. The seeming lack of private enterprise and independent merchants in the Hittite Kingdom, with foreign trade appearing to have been severely restricted, as the limited assemblage of foreign goods in the archaeological record corroborates, can also be possibly traced to the wealth-financed orientation of the Hittite state. Control of foreign trade would be necessary to the control of the distribution of prestige objects as a basis for power.

In terms of the social structure of Hittite administration, recent research has suggested there was continuous, organic growth in number and hierarchy of offices, and evidence for the increased importance of officials over history of the Hittite Kingdom. The gradual nature of the growth has been taken as evidence of a native impulse towards bureaucratization in response to the increased administrative burdens of empire, rather than pure adoption from Mesopotamia. Nevertheless, a tension existed between the growing rationalized bureaucracy and the traditional "family business" of the Hittite state for the duration of Hittite history. Hierarchy at the Hittite court was only weakly determined by the office one held, and other factors, including relationship to the royal family and favoritism were important. Historically, an increasing percentage of officials were members of the extended royal family who came to dominate the highest levels of the administrative hierarchy in the Empire Period. Current knowledge suggests that the Hittite state consisted of a limited rational bureaucracy attached to a largely patrimonial system. The relative smallness of the rational bureaucracy, and the reduced cadre of cuneiform-literate individuals who ran it, might also be a feature of a wealth-financed state, and help explain why the written economic-administrative documentation is so light.

In conclusion, Hittite economic administration as it is preserved was a hands-on, small-scale affair focused on the management of luxury goods. This style of administration was sufficient for the Hittite Empire because the state was maintained primarily by the manipulation of wealth, i.e., by the acquisition of metals for trade, tools, and weapons, the production of garments for influence, and the control of prestige objects and exotic materials acquired from foreign trade for expenditure in the religious sphere. Thus, in spite of clear Mesopotamian influences on the Hittite state, much of its organization and most of its power structures, including the regional religious calendar, the grain silos, the wealth-financed administration, can be traced directly to the Anatolian environment, and resulted from long-term indigenous development, punctuated by significant but self-explicable changes.

A future program of research on Hittite administration is needed to deepen understanding of especially the interface of religion, economy, and political legitimation in the Hittite state. The study of the Hittite Votive Corpus undertaken in Chapter 8 of this book is a step in this direction, in that it substantiates a direct link between the income of foreign luxury goods acquired by the royal family and the Hittite religious system. But there is more to discover, especially in the economics of the popular aspects of religious experience in the Hittite Kingdom. Then, tracing the economic administration of the Hittite state back to its antecedents in the Anatolian principalities in a detailed, methodical way is another avenue for future research. Although the texts produced by the merchants of the Old Assyrian trade network were written in a different language and from a completely different perspective, in addition to being separated by 500 years from those of the PTAC, the environment of the Anatolia Plateau was fundamentally the same, so that a comparison of Anatolian economic administration in the Hittite New Kingdom and *kārum* periods is desirable. Finally, the most realistic next step for research is to compare Hittite economic administration with its

Syrian and Mesopotamian contemporaries. Since so many of the luxury objects in the corpus are international, and since the theoretical chapters explicitly invoke comparison with Mesopotamia, it is a sincere hope that this book will prove both enticing and accessible enough that Assyriologists will feel inspired to critically incorporate the texts and the model of Hittite state presented here into future comparative studies of economic administration.

In closing, it should be noted that while a comprehensive book on "Hittite Economic Administration" may someday exist – which must necessarily include evidence from the cult inventories, festival texts, land tenure agreements, court proceedings, archaeology, and so on –, one on "Hittite Economy" will not, and cannot, ever be written. The reason is that the evidence for such a study does not exist. Estimating the "Gross Domestic Product" for the Hittite Kingdom would require the kind of history from below that is simply impossible in the Hittite world. Private economic documents, census data, and records of large-scale taxation are all missing, and were probably never recorded. Only the very narrow portion of the economy that the Hittite central government was able to cream off for financial purposes has been preserved. But I hope to have shown that studying even this narrow interface between government and economy, i.e., finance, is a worthwhile goal, because it gives a glimpse into the motivations of the Hittite ruling class as it sought legitimacy. It is by understanding the human response to the environmental constraints of Anatolia, the economic and ideological motivations of the religious system, and the political importance of acquiring foreign luxury goods that the modern scholar can better access the often alien world of Hittite history.

APPENDIX I. GIFTS FROM THE ETERNAL TREATY DOSSIER IN THE 21ST YEAR OF RAMSES II

The lists of gifts presented here are dependent on the editions of Elmar Edel, *Die ägyptisch-hethitische Korrespondenz aus Boghazköi in babylonischer und hethitischer Sprache*. 2 vols. (Opladen: Westdeutscher Verlag, 1994), with consultation of the new translations of Violetta Cordani, *Lettere fra Egiziani e Ittiti* (Torino: Paideia, 2017).

ÄHK 7 (KBo 28.47)

ÄHK 7 (end of obv., beginning of rev.)[748]
King Ramses to King Ḫattušili:
[6 gold objects]
[48 linens]

ÄHK 7 rev. -3′–1′
Prince Šutaḫapsap to Ḫattušili:
[1 cup of good gold]
[1 *maklalu* garment of kingly linen]
[1] tuni[c of kingly] linen

ÄHK 7 rev. 4′–6′
Prince Ramses to Ḫattušili:
1 cup of [good] g[old]
1 *mak*[*lalu* garment of kingly] linen
1 tuni[c of kingly] linen

ÄHK 8 (KBo 28.48)

ÄHK 8 obv. 27–rev. 11′[749]
Vizier Pašiyara and the "Grandees" of Egypt to King Ḫattušili:
[2(?)] containers (made of) good gold

748 See *6.2.1.2 Lacuna 1: The Gift of King Ramses to Ḫattušili* for the reasoning behind the restoration of King Ramses' gift to Ḫattušili.

749 There are a minimum of four lines of gifts lost (one line at the end of obv., three lines at beginning of rev.). The reverse of the column breaks off at line 11′ (= line 14 if beginning three lines restored), leaving a maximum of fifteen or so lines possibly broken away. See *6.2.1.3 Lacuna 2: The Gift of Vizier Pašiyara and the Egyptian Grandees to Ḫattušili* for reasoning behind restorations.

[3 additional gold objects(?)]
[1(?)] small [...] of good gold
[48 linens]

ÄHK 9 (KUB 3.70)

ÄHK 9 rev. 11–17
Prince Šutaḫapšap to King Ḫattušili:
[1] drinking [cup] of good gold (with) inlay [with of the fac]e of a bull, its horns of white stone, [and its eyes(?)] of black stone. [Its weight] 93 shekels of good gold.
[1] ... of fine [linen], good, new
[1] fine [linen b]lanket, good, new, [for the bed] with two-sides

ÄHK 10 (KUB 34.2)

ÄHK 10 rev. 3′–5′
Queen Mother Tūya to King Ḫattušili:
1 cup of [good] gold
1 [colorful] garment of [kingly] linen
1 [colorful] tunic⟨⟨s⟩⟩ of [kingly] linen

ÄHK 12 (KBo 1.29 + KBo 9.43)

ÄHK 12 obv. 25–rev. 4
Queen Naptera to Queen Puduḫepa:
1 very colorful necklace of good gold, of 12 strands, weighing 88 shekels
1 colorful *maklalu* garment of kingly linen
1 colorful tunic of kingly linen
5 colorful garments of fine linen, good
5 colorful tunics of fine linen, good

ÄHK 15 (KBo 28.36)

ÄHK 15 rev. 1′–9′[750]
King Ramses(?) to a Hittite Prince(?):
[1(?) gol]d-inlai[d object]
...
[1 colorful tuni]c [of kingly linen, good]

750 See *6.2.1.4 Lacuna 3: Gifts to the Wives(?) of the Hittite Princes* for restorations.

[1 c]ol[orful tun]ic of kingly [linen]
[2+ garments with colorful t]rim of fine [linen], good
[1 clo]ak of fine [linen], good, two-[sided]
[2+] colorful [garments of fi]ne [linen], good
[2+] colorful [ ]-*ta* [garments] of fine [linen], good

ÄHK 15 rev. [10′–12′]
Queen Naptera to a Wife of a Hittite Prince(?):
[4 linens]

ÄHK 16 (KUB 4.95 + KBo 28.45)

ÄHK 16 obv. 12–rev. 3′[751]
King Ramses to Prince Teššub-Šarruma:
1 [drinking] cup of good gold, inl[aid, stone]-encrusted, a cow o[f good gold … a spout] on [its] lip
1 chariot of [ ]-wood, [inlaid with gold]
1 t[eam of horses]
[4 colorful garments of kingly linen]
4 [colorful *maklalu* garments of kingly] li[nen]
4 [colorful] tuni[cs of kingly] linen

ÄHK 16 rev. 6′–13′
King Ramses to Teššub-Šarruma's Wife(?):[752]
1 [colorful *m*]*a*[*klalu*] ga[rment of kingly] linen
[1(?) colorful tunic of kingly linen]
[1(?) colorful garment of *miku* linen]
[1(?) colorful *maklalu* garment of *miku* linen]
[1(?) colorful tunic of *miku* linen]
[1(?) colorful garment of fine linen, good]
[1(?) c]olorful [*maklalu* garment of fine linen, good]
[1(?) colorful tunic of fine linen], good

ÄHK 17 (KBo 28.44)

ÄHK 17 obv. 13–17
King Ramses to Prince Tašmi-Šarruma:
1 cup of good gold, weighing 49 shekels.
2 [c]olorful *maklalu* garments of kingly linen
2 colorful tunics of kingly linen

---

751 See *6.2.1.4 Lacuna 3: Gifts to the Wives(?) of the Hittite Princes* for restorations.
752 With the exception of the first and last garments, this set is entirely restored by Edel.

APPENDIX II. GIFTS FROM THE HITTITE-EGYPTIAN ROYAL MARRIAGE IN THE 34TH YEAR OF RAMSES II

The lists of gifts presented here are dependent on the editions of Elmar Edel, *Die ägyptisch-hethitische Korrespondenz aus Boghazköi in babylonischer und hethitischer Sprache*. 2 vols. (Opladen: Westdeutscher Verlag, 1994), with consultation of the new translations of Violetta Cordani, *Lettere fra Egiziani e Ittiti* (Torino: Paideia, 2017).

ÄHK 45 (KBo 28.5(+)6) and ÄHK 46 (KBo 28.4)

ÄHK 45 rev. 1′–[20′] (// ÄHK 46 rev. [-7′]–13′)[753]
Ramses (and Naptera) to Ḫattušili and Puduḫepa:
[765 shekels] good [gold] in ingots.
[1 ... of good gold, in]laid with precious stones, weighing 234 she[kels].
[1 ... of] good gold, inlaid with precious stones, weighing 83 [shekels].
[10 drinking cups of] good [gol]d, weighing 480 shekels.
[1 *kaptukû* jar of goo]d [gold], weighing 96 shekels.
[2+ ... variegat]ed [eyes] of good gold, with inlay, weighing 36 shek[els].
[1 very colorf]ul [necklace] of good gold, weighing 26 shekels.
[(1 pai)r of earrings of] good [g]old, weighing 22 shekels.
[(11 rin)gs of] good [gol]d, weighing 12 shekels.
[(2 arm-clasps o)f g]ood [gold], encrusted with various stones, weighing 5½ shekels.
[(1 casket o)f goo]d [gold], in the Hittite style, weighing 19½ shek[els].
(sum of gold: 1779 shekels)
(sum of silver: 17 shekels)
[(2 hawks(?) of p)reciou(s stone)], their [c]opies of gold encrusted with stones
[(10 rings of precious stone)]
[(69)] vari[ous (garments of ki)]ngly [(linen)]
[(11 various garments of *miku* linen)]
[(127 vario)us (garments of good fine linen)]
(Sum of linens: 207)
[(40 good logs of ebony)]
[(5 *kukubu* containers) o(f excellent eye medication)]
[(20 reeds of excellent eye medication)]

753 These texts record gifts from Ramses to Ḫattušili (ÄHK 45) and Puduḫepa (ÄHK 46), and are near duplicates. They can also be partially restored from a gift summary tablet ÄHK 92. For the relationship between these texts, see Edel, *Die ägyptisch-hethitische Korrespondenz*, vol. 2, 180–97, and especially the useful table summarizing gifts in *ibid.*, 190–91.

ÄHK 46 rev. 14′–16′ (recapitulated in ÄHK 92 [-2]–5a′)
Ramses (and Naptera) to "two Grandees" of Ḫatti, i.e., the Chief of the Guards of the Right (GAL LÚ.MEŠ*redî* ZAG), *and the Chief of the Guards of the Left* (GAL LÚ.MEŠ*redî* GÙB):
[2 drink]ing [cup]s of good gold, weighing 96 shekels
[6 *maklalu* garments of kingly linen]
[6 tun]ics of kingly! linen[754]

ÄHK 46 rev. 17′–18′ (recapitulated in ÄHK 92 18′–19′)
Ramses (and Naptera) to a palace official:
[1 leather cuirass f]or a man
1 br[o]nze helmet with leaves of tin
[1 leather c]uirass with bronz[e] inlay

ÄHK 92 (KBo 28.33)

ÄHK 92 6′–17′[755]
Ramses and Naptera to Hittite Princes and their wives:
se[ven hundred and 65 shekels of good gold i]n ingots
13 im[plements of good gold, weighing] 893 shekels of gold
100[+] [jewelries of good gold, weighing 121 shekels]
(sum of gold: one thousand, sev[en hundred and 79 shekels of gold])

A number of garments are listed in 13′–15′, including 9[3] garments of miku *linen. I will assume there is a sum of 207 garments to parallel the gift given to the Hittite royal couple.*

[40] good [logs of] ebony
1 [casket of ebony, in the Hittite fashion]

754 As noted in Edel, *Die ägyptisch-hethitische Korrespondenz*, vol. 2, 195, ÄHK 46 and ÄHK 92 differ at this juncture. The former has the "two grandees" receiving only "[x] tunics of good fine linen," whereas the latter has the two men, who are named as the Chiefs of the Guards, each receiving "3 colorful *maklalu* garments of good kingly linen, and 3 colorful tunics of good kingly linen." Edel takes this discrepancy as an accidental omission of the *maklalu* garments, and notes that there is a difference in quality. For my purposes, I will err on the side of Ramses' generosity, and restore the richer gift amount described in ÄHK 92.

755 This section is restored on the assumption that the gifts given to the Hittite princes are perfectly parallel to the gifts given to the Hittite royal couple in ÄHK 45 and ÄHK 46. Also see Edel's arguments for this interpretation in *Die ägyptisch-hethitische Korrespondenz*, vol. 2, 189–92.

ÄHK 44 (KBo 28.14)

ÄHK 44 rev. 3′–14′[756]
King Ramses to Queen Puduḫepa:
1 *kapt*[*ukû* jar of goo]d [gold], weighing 96 shekels.
1 *ḫagar*[*abaš* container o]f good gold, weighing 36 shekels.
(sum of [gold: 1]32 shekels)
2 large colorful cloths of [kingly] linen, 15 cubits in length, brea[dth o]f 5½ cubits
2 [col]orful *maklalu* garments of king[ly] linen
2 co[lorf]ul tunics of king[ly] linen
3 [color]ful garments of fine linen, g[ood]
3 colorful tun[ics of fine linen, g]ood
(sum of l[inens: 12 garments])
1 cas[ket of ebony, inlaid with gold, its feet ...]

ÄHK 47 (KUB 28.10)

ÄHK 47 rev. 33′–34′
Ramses to Ḫattušili:
2 [colorful] *maklalu* garments [of kingly] linen
2 [colorful] tunics [of kingly] linen

ÄHK 49 (FHL 98)

ÄHK 49 rev. [0′]–4′:
Ramses to Ḫattušili:
[1 drinking cup of good gold, its weight ...]
3 [colorful *maklalu* garments of kingly linen]
[3 colorful tunics of kingly linen]
4 [colorful] *ma*[*klalu*] garments of [*miku*] linen
[4 colorful tunics of *miku* linen]
2 *mak*[*lalu*] garments [of fine] linen, [good[
[2 tunics of fine linen, good]

ÄHK 49 rev. 5′–16′:
Ramses to Puduḫepa:
1 very co[lorful] necklace [of good gold, its weight ...], a flower blossom motif on it
2 rings of [good] gold [its weight ...]
6 rings of [good] gold [its weight ...]
1 ring of good gold [its weight ...], his/its booty

756 This letter is fairly well preserved, but there may be five or six lines at the end of obverse and beginning of reverse containing gifts.

7 collars with gra[nulations ... of good gold, their weight ...]
[2 *maklalu* garments of kingly linen]
2 tunics [of kingly] linen
[2 *maklalu* garments of fine linen, good]
[2 tunics of fine linen, good]
10 rings of bronze
10 r[ings of ...]

ÄHK 51 (KUB 3.63)

ÄHK 51 rev. 4′–8′[757]
King Ramses to Queen Puduḫepa:
[4] rings [of] good [gol]d, [t]he[ir] we[eight] 4 shekels of refined gold[758]
1 linen [...]
1 [large colorful cloth of kingly] lin[en, its length x c]ubits
4 [large colorful] linen cloth[s, t]he[ir le]n[gth] 6 cubits
5 very good [bed] b[lankets of kingly linen]
[1 ... g]arment of ⟨kingly⟩ [linen], good
1 sto[rage jar of gold(?) with excel]lent [eye medicine]
10 lar[ge *ku*]*k*[*u*]*bu* containers [of gold(?)] fill[ed] with medicine

757 It is difficult to guess how much is missing at the beginning of this letter. There could easily have been another 10–15 lines of gifts before what is preserved.

758 Cf. ÄHK 45 rev. 10′, where 11 rings weigh a total of 12 shekels of gold

LEXICAL COMMENTARY

The following commentary contains notes on lexemes encountered in the texts of the Palace–Temple Administrative Corpus edited in Volume II. For Hittite words, the dictionaries are assumed as the defaults: HW^{2} for words beginning with A–K, CHD for L–Š, EDHIL, HED, and HEG for T–Z. The online eDiAna (www.ediana.gwi.uni-muenchen.de) should also be consulted for any entries with Luwian origins. Weeden 2011 and MesZL serve as the basis for the Sumerograms, and CAD and AHw for Akkadograms. Words appearing in these sources for which there is general agreement are not discussed. Disagreements among the reference works, relevant outside literature, and new forms and interpretations based on discoveries in the PTAC are discussed where pertinent.

Note that macrons are not indicated in Hittite lemmas, but are used when citing passages in bound transcription. Thus, the lemma *aška-* 'gate' is cited as pl. dat./loc. *āšgaš* in 4.1.1.1.B_2 obv. i$^{?}$ 6′.

Hittite

aḫḫuwatar/aḫḫuwatn-

aḫḫuwatar are discrete, countable objects that can be attached to linen garments (9.1.1 rev. iv 9′), and can be made of silver (2.14 13′) or gold (9.1.1 rev. iv 9′). In 2.17 obv.$^{?}$ r. c. 2′–3′ a container is described as being "filled" with *aḫḫuwatar*-objects, next to a container that is filled with silver. Starke 1990, 509–10 connected *aḫḫuwatar* with CLuw. *āḫḫuwāḫḫuwai-*, which is attested in participle form modifying 'earth' (*taganzipa-*), based on interpreting *āḫḫuwāḫḫuwam(m)a/i-* as "encircled, constrained by an *āḫḫuwa*(?)." Rieken, eDiAna, *s.v. aḫḫūwattar/-t(t)an-* (= lemma 2351) suggested a meaning 'ring(?)' for *aḫḫuwatar.* A piece of jewelry is quite plausible, since it is possible that *aḫḫuwatar* is further attested as a personal name in the cadaster list KBo 60.7+(+) r. c. 8′: *ŠA* ^{m}*a-ḫu-u-wa-t*[*a*]*r*$^{?}$ and 9′: *ŠA* ^{m}*a-ḫ*[*u-u-wa-tar*(?). If the non-geminate spelling *aḫuwatar* can be accepted, this invites comparison to other personal names based on precious objects, cf. ^{m}*Manninni*, and possibly ^{m}*Ḫuwarlu*/^{m}*Ḫurlu* – see *ḫu(wa)rlu-* in Lexical Commentary below – and ^{m}*Tarzu.*

ayakki-

The emendation *a-ia-ak-ki*$^{!}$ in 9.1.5 rev.$^{!}$ 5′ (final sign appears in photo as -⌜*du*⌝ or -*uš*) follows the transliteration of the passage in CHD Š, p. 458. With HW^{2} *s.v. aịakki* (p. 47) and contra Hoffner 1978, 244, *ayakki-* should be considered a loanword appearing in Hittite as an *i*-stem, and not an Akkadogram. As noted by HW^{2} (*loc. cit.*), the form *a-ia-ak-ki-in-na* in KBo 13.114 rev. iii 2–3 indicates a probable Hurrian intermediary. The meaning of Akkadian *ayakku* is itself unclear. It seems that the *ayakku*, a loanword from Sum. É.AN.NA, was the part of the temple in which the god dwelt: see CAD A_1 *s.v. ajakku* '(a structure in a temple)' (p. 224); AHw *s.v. ajja(k)ku(m)* 'Heiligtum, Hochtempel(?)' (p. 24). In Hittite, the mention of bronze figurines in the above-cited example from KBo 13.114 rev. iii 2–3 (*nu* ⸢4⸣ ALAM ZA[BAR ...] ⸢GU$_4$⸣ ZABAR *a-ia-ak-ki-in-na išḫarnūmaizzi* "4 figures of br[onze ...], a steer of bronze, (and) the *ayakki*-s he smears with blood"), combined with a passage from 9.1.5 rev.! 5′ (20 *a-ia-ak-ki*! ŠÀ-*ŠÚ* ... "twenty *ayakki*, inside of which ... ") where the *ayakki* appear among a list of other portable containers, suggests that the *ayakki* was, in the Anatolian context, a portable shrine or reliquary for divine statues.

URUDU*akutalla-*

Outside of 3.1.7.A_1 obv. i 11′, this lexeme is attested elsewhere only in two duplicate texts: *a-ku-ta-al-li-it* (KUB 9.20 5′) and *a-ku-ga-al-li-it* (KUB 2.13 obv. i 8), where silver examples of the vessel are used in a ritual to carry water. EDHIL *s.v. akutalla-* 'container of water' (p. 169) preferred *akutalla-* as the correct form, deriving the word from *eku-/aku-* 'to drink' plus instrument suffix *-talla-* (PIE **-d^{h}lo-/*-tlo-*): thus, "thing for drinking with."

aniya-

See now van den Hout 2016 for discussion of *tuppiyaz aniya-* 'record via tablet'.

andur(ri)a-

Within the PTAC, *andur(ri)a-* 'inner; native, domestic' is applied exclusively to cloths and shirts. It is not clear whether these cloths are 'inner' garments, i.e., for wearing under other clothes or for use indoors, or if they are 'native', i.e., not of foreign or exotic design. If the latter, the domestic garments can be contrasted to the TÚGGÚ.E.A *ḪURRI*, TÚG *ikkuwaniya-*, and other "ethnic" shirts. In 9.1.11 obv.? 4′, *anduraš* appears to be functioning as a substantivized adjective. The form *anduraš* has thus far escaped inclusion in the dictionaries (HW^2 A *s.v. anturii̯a-* [p. 122]; HED I/II *s.v. anturii̯a-* [p. 83] – though see the *addenda et corrigenda* in HED III, 445; EDHIL *s.v. anturii̯a-* [p. 188], where an original stem *andur-* is reconstructed). Berman 1982, 125 cited the form *an-dur-aš*, found in 6.9 obv. 7, as well as KUB 50.48 rev. iii 2′ and KUB 50.22 6′. To these may be added 9.1.11 obv.? 4′. Thus, *anduraš* must be taken seriously as a distinct form, either the sg. nom. of an adjective *andura-* or genitive of the stem *andur-*, also attested in the ablative adverb *andurza* 'indoors' (EDHIL, 188).

annutaim(m)a/i-

HW^2 A *s.v. annutaima*[(-) (p. 124) and HIT (p. 148) treated *annutaim(m)a/i-* as a single word of unknown meaning. In contrast, HVP (p. 428) and HEG T/D *s.v. taimant-* (p. 27) interpreted the word as a supposed Akkadogram **ANNU* 'tin' plus a participle *taimant-* 'montiert, befestigt (?)' (HEG, *loc. cit.*). Both HVP (p. 496 fn. 1) and HEG T/D considered *annutaim(m)a/i-* to be another example of "Akkadogram + Partizip" formation, analogous to *PÉ-EN-KI taiman* in 11.3.1 11′. However, cf. now discussion in *Lexical Commentary s.v. penki(t)-* and *penkitaim(m)a/i-* below, where *penki(t)-* was shown by Starke

1990, 217–18 to be a loanword instead of an Akkadogram. Thus, *annutaim(m)a/i-* should be interpreted, with CLL *s.v. annutaima/i-* (p. 19), as "fitted with **annuta-*." Whether this **annuta-* was a loanword **annu(t)-* cannot be determined. The proposed connection of HEG with supposed *anu(m)* 'tin' is highly unlikely, since this form is attested only in a lexical list, against the regular Akkadian *annaku* (CAD A_2 s.v. *annaku* [p. 127]).

appanziya-

Given the comparative frequency of words based on the lexeme *tuppa-* 'chest, container' in the PTAC, the previous readings of this lexeme as *tuppanziya-* (HW² A *s.v. appanzii̯a-* "Evtl. *tup-* zu lesen" [p. 165]; HEG T/D *s.v. tupanzi-* [p. 447]: "Wegen der Doppelschreibung *-pp-* ist fraglich, ob auch das in einem heth. Inventartext bezeugte XIV *tup-pa-an-zi-i̯a-aš* ... hierher gehört."; cf. also Miller 2010, 513 fn. 14, where the attestations from 9.2.3 obv. (ii) 5″ and 9.2.2 rev.! iii 10′ are included in spite of their being the only examples with geminate *-pp-*) are not impossible. However, the attestation in 9.2.2 rev.! iii 10′ of the *appanziya-* as attachments or modifications of a sun-disk makes a derivation from *epp-/app-* 'to take, seize, grab' more plausible. Perhaps the sixteen *appanziya-* in 9.2.2 rev.! iii 10′ were "grabbers," i.e., brackets used to mount attachments onto the sun-disk, and thus the mounting surface for the pearls, gold, and stones described as *išgarān* 'threaded, bored, stuck (on)' in 9.2.2 rev.! iii 9′, 12′, and 17′.

apupi-

See Richter 2012 *s.v. abubi* for bibliography. For the meaning, see HW² *s.v. apupi* '(Kultgegenstand)' (p. 192) and Wegner 2004, 12 "vielleicht eine Waffe oder Attribut einer Waffe." Wegner 1981, 85 considered Hittite *abubi* to be a loanword from Akk. *abūbu* 'deluge, storm surge', providing another example of a Hurrian-/Luwian-mediated Akkadian loanword in Hittite. It seems that there are two variants in Hittite: an *apupiš* showing a 'Hittitized' common gender *i*-stem, and *abubi*, which is probably an original Luw. neuter *i(t)*-stem: see Starke 1990, 152–53; GHL §4.16, p. 86. See also van Gessel 1998, 383, *s.v.* Šauri for forms such as ᴰ*ša-a-ú-ri a-bu-ú-bi* (KUB 27.16 rev. iv 13).

aramni-

For a discussion of *aramni-* and the related *aramnant*-bird attested in ornithomantic contexts, see Sakuma 2009, 373–74 (with previous literature). After a discussion of the evidence for and against an identity of the *aramni*-objects and the *aramnant*-birds, Sakuma concurred (p. 374) with HED I/II *s.v. aramni-* (p. 127) and HEG A–K *s.v. aramni-* (p. 53) in suggesting both were a type of falcon or hawk, predicated on the original observation of Laroche 1961, 83 that the H. Luw. sign *ara/i* (H.H. 134), which depicts a bird of prey, was acrophonic for *aramni-*. The translation "falcon" will be preferred here to maximize contrast with the eagle, on the basis that falcons have a distinctive appearance and hunting style, being small, lightly built raptors that hunt by steep dives and kill with their beaks, whereas hawks and eagles differ only in size (both are large, sturdy raptors that hunt by swooping from a concealed perch followed by a short pursuit and kill with their talons).

LÚ*araunna-*

The translation of HIT (pp. 26–27, with previous literature) of LÚ.MEŠ*araunna-* as 'yeomen', connected with *aruwan(n)i-* 'free, non-slave', was rejected by Beal 1992, 83 fn. 296 based on the lack of non-*i*-stem forms of the adjective and the existence of geographical name of URU*araunna*. As explained by Klinger 2008, 285–86, the Araunna-men were northern Anatolian tribal levies who were apparently employed as garrison troops when they were not raiding livestock or being captured in raids. In this respect, the Araunna-men of the Hittite Kingdom are reminiscent the social morphology of the Medjay of New Kingdom Egypt.

arkamma(n)-

As the regular Hittite reading behind *MADDATTU*, *arkamma(n)-* 'tribute' is itself a *Wanderwort* of uncertain etymology current to Bronze Age Syro-Mesopotamia (see also HED I/II, 145–46; HEG A–K, 59–60; Mankowski 2000, 38–39 for bibliography). Singer (2010, 22–23, 29–30) noted that despite the interchangeable use of *argamannu* and *ḫašmānu* in Akkadian to designate 'red-purple', in Hittite *arkamma(n)-* seems only ever to be attested in the meaning 'tribute'. However, compare now 3.2.5 r. c. 2′. Here *ar-kam-ma-aš* appears in the middle of a broken list of garments. It would be unusual for *MADDATTU* to appear in the middle of a list – the term usually appears at the beginning or end of a paragraph. The intermittent occurrence of color names written out in Hittite (see *ḫarki-* 'white' and *maruša-* 'black') means that reading *arkammaš* '(red-)purple' (sg. gen.) instead of 'tribute' is not impossible for 3.2.5 r. c. 2′.

armannaim(m)a/i-

As pointed out in Hoffner 1983, 411, this is a Luw. participle comparable to Hitt. *armannant-* 'ornamented with lunulas'. Both are derived from a *arman-* 'moon' plus a direct possessive formation with *-aim(m)a/i-* and *-ant-*, respectively.

arwanal(l)i-

Whereas Rost 1961–63, 199 expressed doubt about a reading *arwanalli-* in 10.3.3 obv.? 13′ as a type of bird because of a missing MUŠEN determinative it may be noted that: 1.) MUŠEN is a postdeterminative, 2.) non-heterographic bird names in any case tend to omit the MUŠEN (cf. the *aramni-* bird, *passim*, and the sequence of Hurrian bird names in 12.1.1 r. c. 3′). Also, contra the transliteration and comment of HW² A *s.v.* [*ar*??]-*wa-na-al-la* (p. 349) – "Nicht dazu]x-*ar-wa-na-li* KÙ.BABBAR" –, the spacing between the initial *ar-* and the preceding sign traces, which apparently constitute the numeral ⌜2⌝, indicates they are separate words. Finally, it is not unexpected that *arwanali* in 10.3.3 refers to a bird, given the appearance of other animals in the previous lines.

arumu-x[

This fragmentary word only occurs in the combination "n ½ GÍN ½ *arumu*-x[" in 12.2.3 and 12.2.2, most logically suggesting it designated a weight measurement smaller than a half-shekel.

ašanni-

The interpretation "[v]ielleicht ein Sattel(teil)?" offered by HVP (p. 487 fn. 14) for *ašanni-* is presumably based on the qualification of this item being made of *taḫapši*-cloth in 9.1.10.A_2 rev. 3′. However, as discussed in the *Lexical Commentary, s.v. taḫapši-*, the understanding of HVP (p. 704) of *taḫapši* as "'eine Decke für Pferde' (auch anstelle des Sattels genutzt)" is too narrow, and misses the use of *taḫapši-* to describe objects and materials with no relation to horses. It is therefore prudent to leave *ašanni-* in 9.1.10.A_2 rev. 3′ untranslated for now.

ašara-

As discussed by HED IV *s.v. kasi-* (p. 119), *ašara-* was possibly a "bright white" in contrast to *gaši-* "off-white" since only the former is attested as a the basis for a denominative verb (see Lexical Commentary to *gaši-* below). See HVP (pp. 312–13) for earlier discussion of *ašara-* as a *terminus technicus* in the PTAC to describe a quality of white wool; Christiansen 2006, 99–101 (with bibliography) provides complementary history of interpretation for the term outside of PTAC, especially ritual texts. Contra the discussions of *ašara-* and *gaši-* in Mora – Vigo 2012, 179–80, Bacelli et. al 2014, 113, and Vigo 2016, 342, in which the crucial contribution of Christiansen 2006, 99–101 is overlooked, the meaning of the terms as shades of white wool is now settled (insofar as the meanings of ancient color terms can ever be). See also the suggestion of Christiansen (2006, 101) that the *ašara-* could be used as a nominal adjective to refer to wool itself ("white [stuff]"), and possibly woolen garments ("the whites"). This reverses the emphasis in Riemschneider's original definition of *ašara-* as "'(weißer?) Wollfaden'" (1957, 145 fn. 26) to now: "weiß(er Wollfaden)." In terms of wool processing, since natural wool is rarely bright white, *ašara-* could refer to wool that has already been cleaned and perhaps bleached.

^{DUG}*aššauwaš*

The appearance of ⌜^{DUG}⌝*aš-šu-w*[*a-* in DBH 46/2.45 obv. 8 confirms the reading $^{DUG!}$*aš-ša-u-wa-aš* by HIT (p. 117) (so Akdoğan 2016a, 25 fn. 65; the reading *gaššauwaš* in HVP, p. 458, and the otherwise unattested verbal stem *gašš(a)-* adduced by Neu 1983b, 303, should be rejected). Contra HED I/II *s.v. ass-, assiya-* (p. 197), 3 DUG *aš-ša-u-wa-aš* KU.SI_{22} NA_4 in 9.2.1 rev. iii 6′ should not be translated adjectively "three vessels of good gold [and] stone[s]," but rather as a free-standing genitive: '(vessel) of well-being, favor', comparable (or identical?) to the *aššuzeri-* '"good" cup' attested elsewhere in Hittite rituals.

aška-

4.1.1.1.B_2 obv. i$^?$ 6′ provides the fourth known attestation of pl. dat./loc. *āšgaš*. The three previously known attestations show both "direction to" (pl. *āšgaš* in KUB 33.121 rev. iii 13 // sg. *āški* in KUB 17.1 obv. ii 12) and "location in/on" (*āšgaš* in KUB 30.27 rev. 8, 15) usages. All three attestations are conventionally interpreted as taking *aška-* in its concrete sense: "at the gate(s)" (though KUB 30.27 rev. 8, 15 could conceivably also mean "outside"). In contrast, as discussed in the *Commentary* to 4.1.1.1 13, 20, 24, the new attestation from 4.1.1.1.B_2 obv. i$^{?}$ 6′ must be interpreted as "location in/on" and in the abstract sense "outside."

ašku-

If the reading **aš*$^{?}$*-*ku-uš* in 9.1.11 obv.$^{?}$ 8′ is correct (the photo suggests that what is drawn as surface damage in the handcopy below the *aš-* is a clearly perceptible *Winkelhaken*, but *nu-ku-uš* yields nothing recognizable), then 1-*NUTUM aškuš* AN.BAR GAR.RA '1 set of *ašku-*, inlaid with *iron (ore)*' appearing among garments and horse tack offers a new lexeme. The word is almost certainly not related to *ašku-*, a small animal attested in ritual texts as an ill omen (HW^2 A *s.v. ašku-* [p. 424], HED I/II *s.v. asku-* [p. 215]).

ašuša-

Güterbock's original identification (1983, 208) of *ašuša-* as 'earrings' remains the best, though cf. HW^2 A *s.v. ašuša-*^{2} (p. 537) for reservations (and Ünal 1994, 214, for reservations about these reservations). The argument of Starke 1990, 552 fn. 2044 that the *Bildbeschreibung* of Pirwa (KUB 38.4 obv. i 6), the god of horses and equestrianism, holding a whip in one hand and "2 *ašuša-*" in the other, rules out the *ašuša-* being 'earrings' is not decisive: cf. the denominative verb *ašuša(i)-* 'to install an (ear)ring' applied to the ears of a bull in KBo 15.1 obv. i 24 (see HED I/II *s.v. asusa-* [p. 221] for citation). Thus, it seems that the objects in Pirwa's hands represented two methods of controlling large domesticated animals, viz. a whip, and a set of ear hoops for attaching restraining ropes. In the human context, then, *ašuša-* would be large "hoop" earrings (Ünal 1994, 214), such as those seen on the jesters of the Alaca Höyük orthostats (*op. cit.*, Plate XLVII (c)).

(-)a]ddannaim(m)a/i-

A word fragment of unknown meaning. Based on analogy with, e.g., *armannaim(m)a/i-* 'ornamented with lunulas', one would expect a Luwian direct possessive formation in *-aim(m)a/i-*, though a concrete object ending in (-)*a*]*ddan-* is for the moment elusive.

$^{\text{(TÚG)}}$*adupli(t)-*

See HW^2 A *s.v.* ^{TÚG}*adupli-* (p. 571) 'ein Teil des (königlichen) Festgewandes im Kultus'. *Pace* HW^2 A, 572 (followed by HEG A–K, 94; HED I/II, 229), ^{TÚG}*atupli(t)-* is almost certainly a Hurrian- or Luwian-mediated loanword from Akk. ^{TÚG}*ATUPLU/UTUPLU*: see Hoffner 1989, 89, most probatively the pl. nom.-acc. n. form *aduplita* in Bo 2839 [= KUB 58.33] iii 25′–27′ cited there (see also Starke 1990, 207–8, GHL §4.16, p. 86, and Dardano 2018, 367). As discussed in Starke 1990, the neuter *i(t)*-stem declension pattern was applied to both native (pp. 176–209) and loaned words (pp. 210–21) in CLuw., and appeared frequently among Luwian borrowings in Hittite. The same CLuw.-derived dental stem is found on neuter nouns elsewhere in the PTAC, in, e.g., *penki(t)-* and $^{\text{(GADA)}}$*zazzi(t)-*, as well as being the source of certain common gender *i*-stem nouns, such as *apupi-*, $^{\text{NA}_4}$*kibši-*, etc.

awiti-

For discussion of identification of *awiti-* as a "sphinx," i.e., a winged lion with a human head, see most recently Cammarosano 2018, 300–301 (with previous literature). According to Cammarosano (p. 301), while the *awiti-* can be positively identified with the sphinx, it cannot be ruled out that the term also comprised the other leonine *Mischwesen* attested in Hittite art, such as the 'gryphon' or 'winged lion' figures. In Hittite art, the *awiti-* was most closely associated in with the goddess Ištar/Šauška.

$^{(\text{NA}_4)}$*eḫlipak(k)i-*

See Polvani 1988, 13–14 (with previous literature) where it is argued that *eḫlipakku/eḫlipak(k)i* referred to either a stone or type of glass. It had been earlier suggested in Bottéro 1949, 18 that the stone was amethyst, leading Vigo 2010, 295 to translate *eḫlipak(k)i* as "amethyst, shiny bright purple" when used as a color. However, see now Thavapalan 2020, 271–74, following Black 2001, where amethyst is identified with Akkadian $^{(\text{NA}_4)}$*ḫašmānu* / Sumerian $^{\text{na}_4}$sag-gil-mud, leaving the stone and color referents of *EḪLIPAKKU/eḫlipak(k)i* again unknown. The sg. gen. ending in *-iyaš* in 10.1.2.7 obv. 3, 6 shows that the word was treated synchronically as a Hittite *i*-stem and not a Luwoid *i(t)*-stem (cf. Starke 1990, 153), despite its certain origins as a loanword.

^{TÚG}*e/itriwa-*

A connection with *etri-* 'food, fodder' and *etri(ya)-* 'to feed' was rejected without explanation by HW^2 E *s.v. etri̯a-* (p. 140): "[s]icher nicht dazu ... ^{TÚG}*it-ri-u̯a-aš* in einer Aufzählung von Kleidungsstücken"; see also HW^2 *s.v.* ^{TÚG}*itriwaš*[(-) oder *itriwa-* (p. 307), where no mention of *etri-* is made. Given the existence in the PTAC of other cloth names in genitive (cf. $^{(\text{TÚG/GADA})}$*parna-*, GADA *arrumaš*, etc.), a *^{TÚG}*etri(ya)waš* 'cloth of/for feeding/foddering' should not be dismissed out of hand. The syncope of *-(i)ya-* > *-i-* (see GHL §1.76, p. 32) is also attested in KBo 23.65 11′ *e-et-ri-wa-aš* EZEN 'festival of foddering$^{?}$'. What a "feeding cloth" actually meant in practice remains unknown: perhaps it was a kind of bib?

^{É}*ḫalentuwa-*

The complicated secondary literature on the ^{É}*ḫalentuwa-* was recently revisited in Taracha 2017, which should now be taken as the starting point for discussion of this word rather than the entry of HW^2 Ḫ *s.v.* ^{É}*ḫalentuwa-* "der Hauptkultraum des Tempels, 'Cella'," which carries over the disputed interpretation of Alp 1983. In Taracha's summary (p. 101), the structure was "a gathering hall for cultic purposes" which functioned as "the cultic-residential nucleus connected with the family identity and ancestor cult in the palace, or as the meeting place of mortals and gods in the temple." As he discussed, buildings of different functions and sizes could have a ^{É}*ḫalentuwa-* (see Taracha 2017, 102 for the ^{É}*ḫalentuwa-* of the *ḫuwaši*-sanctuary at Šarišša, which Wilhelm 1997 14, fn. 16; *id.* 2015, 94 considered to be something close to a "guesthouse"), including both palaces and temples. The list of features of the ^{É}*ḫalentuwa-* included a dais, a hearth, windows, pedestals for cult images, mobile tables to be set for feasting, a curtain for creating privacy in one corner or end of the room, adjacent private rooms, including a wash room and bed room (Taracha 2017, 104; note, however, that the king never seems to explicitly sleep *in* the ^{É}*ḫalentuwa-*, but in an adjoining É.ŠÀ = *tunakkeššar* 'inner room': cf. KBo 52.111+ obv. i 21′–24′). Although Cammarosano (2019, 78) rightly rejected the specific connection of the ^{É}*ḫalentuwa-* with the ancestry cult, his argument (*loc. cit.*) that the term designated a structure or room with a primarily ritual function undervalued, in my opinion, the evidence that stands in favor of Taracha's "hall" interpretation. If anything, the sacralized nature of the ^{É}*ḫalentuwa-* should be de-emphasized, since it can be argued that the seeming primacy of the ritual function of the ^{É}*ḫalentuwa-* is a product of the fact that those sources that give the most detailed, particular, and spatially precise descriptions are primarily festival and ritual tablets. Moreover, one learns that ^{É}*ḫalentuwa-* are directly accessible from the courtyard (the *ḫalentuwa-* mentioned in IBoT 1.36, the Instructions for the Royal Bodyguard, formed the back wall opposite the main gate of the 'guard's courtyard' at the royal palace: see the discussion of the physical ^{É}*ḫalentuwa-* structure by Güterbock in Güterbock – van den Hout 1991, 59–60), and that it is indeed possible to drive a chariot up to one (see the list of citations in Beckman 1984, 583–84; see also KUB 7.25 obv. 1–14 in Taracha 2017, 102, where the king steps from the ^{É}*ḫalentuwa-* to his chariot, and vice versa). Then, as amply attested in the festival texts, it is the opening of this room, and no other, that starts the day: it signals the palace or temple is "open for business." Thus, it seems better to interpret ^{É}*ḫalentuwa-* architecturally as the main hall or greatroom of a building, whether it be a palace or temple, and whether it be sacralized or not. As the heart of a building complex it served as the location for public cultic activities, especially those involving a meal, with more intimate rites were reserved for temple adyta (see discussion in Taracha 2017, 105–7). By translating *ḫalentuwa-* as "hall, greatroom" instead of the very specific "cultic-residential nucleus" of a palace or temple, all the denotations of the term are covered. The definition also grasps the connotation of the main room of a structure functioning as the seat of the householder, whether he be the king in his palace or the god in his temple, the opening and closing of which mark the beginning and end of that building's public business for a day. In this way, the ^{É}*ḫalentuwa-* resembles a "great hall" found in various forms throughout history and cultures. It is assumed here that when the *ḫalentuwa-* occurs in texts from Boğazköy without further qualification, as in 2.2 rev. 8, where items are taken *ANA* $^{\text{LÚ.MEŠ}}$KÙ.DÍM ŠÀ ^{É}*ḫal*[*(intūwaš* ^{URU}*Ḫadduši=kan)* "to the smiths in the h[all in at Ḫattuša" (restored from 4.1.1.1A_1 rev. 5′//B_1 obv. ii$^?$ 11′), the term refers to "*the* hall", i.e., the great hall of the king's palace.

$^{\text{(TÚG)}}$*ḫamankant-*

HVP (p. 588) suggested ^{TÚG}*ḫamankant-* = "Band$^{(?)}$," but Hittite grammar does not allow for a decision between an active or passive participle for *ḫamankant-*, i.e., if the garment is a "binding cloth" or a "bound (i.e., tied or knotted) cloth." On the one hand, $^{\text{(TÚG)}}$*ḫamenkant-* invites comparison with KEŠDA(*-m(m)a/i-*), which HVP (p. 64 fn. 1) suggested to be a *terminus technicus* for a type or treatment of fabric. The lexical list KBo 1.38 rev. 3–7 (CTH 304 – Kagal), where KEŠDA is glossed by both Akk. *rakāsu* ≈ Hitt. *išḫai-/išḫi(ya)-* and Akk. *karāṣu* ≈ Hitt. *ḫamenk-* (see discussion of HW^2 *s.v.* *ḫamank-/ḫamenk-*, *ḫami(n)k-* 0.1 [p. 111]), also speaks in favor of a semantic equation of KEŠDA(-*m(m)a/i-*) and *ḫamankant-* (cf. *ḫulpanzinant-/ḫulpanzinaim(m)a/i-* and TÚG*ḫapušant-/*TÚG*ḫapušam(m)a/i-* for other examples of a Hitt./Luw. participial or possessive suffix doublets in the PTAC), and thus in favor of a "bound" cloth. On the other hand, passages such as KBo 2.18 obv. 27′, 28′ // KUB 41.31 obv. ii 13, where ritual practitioners "tie" (*ḫamenkanzi*) red and white garments, demonstrate that the verb *ḫamank-* could also be applied to garments in a non-technical sense, thus allowing for a "binding cloth."

ḫant-

Previous editions have offered neutral translations for *ḫant-* as it appears in the PTAC: Košak 1978, 113 "fronts"; HVP (p. 463) "Frontteile"; cf. the "frontlets" of HED III *s.v. hant-* (p. 89) and HW^2 Ḫ *s.v. ḫant-* 5. "Stirnen" (p. 160). The context of *ḫant-* and its Sumerographic equivalent SAG.(DU.)KI as free-standing objects in lists of ornaments and attachments for clothing, as well as the absence of further qualification, such as its forming part of a larger object or its attestation as a technical term, suggest *ḫant-*/SAG.(DU.)KI should instead be interpreted in the PTAC as a concrete object, i.e., an ornament named "front, brow, forehead" that was used in some cases as a garment decoration, like the AŠ.ME 'sun-disk' and *armanni-* 'lunula' of 9.2.2 rev.! iii 8′–17′ (cf. lunula attached to leggings in 2.7.A obv. 26).

ḫapalki-

See Weeden 2011, 152 for literature on the communis opinio that AN.BAR is read *ḫapalki-* in Hittite texts. It is probable that Hitt. *ḫapalki-* and Hurr./Akk. *ḪAPALKIN(N)U* represent a common borrowing from Hattic (Laroche 1957b, 9–15; Kammenhuber 1969, 436–37; Schwemer 2005/2006, 222; Richter 2012, 127–28 with recent literature). Outside of the PTAC, the simultaneous use of Hurro-Akkadian *ḫapalkinnu* and Sumerogram AN.BAR (Akk. *parzillu*) in the "Inventory of Gifts from Tušratta" (EA 22 obv. i 32; obv. iii 7) has led to the suggestion that *ḫapalkinnu*, and therefore *ḫapalki-*, must refer to another ferrous product such as 'steel' (cf. earlier literature rejected in Reiter 1997, 393 fn. 171), or an iron ore such as magnetite (Reiter 1997, 392–400). However, as already pointed out by Hoffner (1968, 43), AN.BAR is nowhere equated with or spelled out as *parzillu* in the El Amarna texts, and there is every possibility that the reading behind AN.BAR was, at least in texts originating from the Syro-Hurrian world, *ḫapalkinnu* (see Cordani 2016a, 3 for a different phrasing of the same argument).

As discussed below, *s.v.* AN.BAR (GE_6), it is possible with the scarcity of metallic iron and its production by-products in the archaeological record of the Late Bronze Age, that AN.BAR/*ḫapalki-*/*ḪAPALKI(N)NU*, regardless of its hetereographic writings, might have instead designated iron ore of any of the common types (hematite, goethite, magnetite), which are impossible to macroscopically distinguish (Melein 2018, 5–12).

ḫapuna-

HVP (p. 588) translated "ein Gefäß," based on a reference (p. 278 fn. 3) to Bo 3303 7′:]x(-)*ḫa-pu-na-ia ši-pa-an-ti*. However, Bo 3303 6′–7′ is actually an offering sequence to DZa(š)ḫapuna, goddess of the city of Kaštama and consort to Mt. Zaliyanu (Haas 1994 446; Popko 1995, 114), and not a description of a vessel. Thus Bo 3303 6′–7′ should be read: ^{D}*mi*]*-iz-zu-ul-la* ḪUR.SAG *ḫu-ul-la* 7′ [… ḪUR.SAG *za-li-ia-nu* ^{D}*z*]*a-ḫa-pu-na-ia ši-pa-an-ti* (for another example of the sequence of Mt. Ḫulla and Mt. Zaliyanu, cf. KUB 21.1++ rev. iv 24, CTH 76 – Treaty between Muwatalli II and Alakšandu of Wiluša). With *ḫapuna-* again a *hapax*, the definition of HW^2 *s.v. ḫapuna-* "ein Material(?)" (p. 255) remains the best that can be done.

^{TÚG}*ḫapušam(m)a/i-*

With HED III *s.v. hap(p)us(s)-* (p. 134), ^{TÚG}*ḫapušam*[- in 8.8.B r. c. 3′ is the Luwian participial equivalent (*-m(m)a/i-*) of ^{TÚG}*ḫapušant-*. While HED III (*loc. cit.*) gave the interpretation of "reclaimed, previously used" or "second-hand dress," HW^2 Ḫ *s.v. (:)ḫap(p)uš(š)-* I.2.2 (p. 259) cited the comparatively high price of ^{TÚG}*ḫapušant-* in the Hittite Laws as evidence against its being a recycled cloth, and offered instead a meaning "nochmals behandeln," i.e., a "'gewalktes(?) Gewand'," which fits better with the other names for garments in the PTAC based on their construction (cf. (TÚG) *ḫamakant-* above).

ḫara(n)-

See the translations of HVP (p. 589) "ein geschmückte Gegenstand" and HW^2 *s.v. ḫarant-* (p. 272) "Gegenstand, der mit Gold verziert kann," superseding translations of Košak 1978, 104 "damaged (piece)" (participle from *ḫarr-*) and Starke 1990, 424 fn. 1532 "Silber." Contra the common gender *nt*-stem given by HW^2 (*loc. cit.*), the following Luwian sg. nom.-acc. n. participle *šakantamanza* in 9.1.1 rev. iii 20′ indicates that *ḫaranza* must also be Luwian sg. nom.-acc. n., i.e., either an *n*-stem *ḫaran-* or a vocalic stem *ḫara-* plus case ending *-n* and neuter particle *-ša/-za* (van den Hout 1984, Melchert 2003, 186–87, Jasanoff 2010, Simon (forth.)). While HVP and HW^2 offered no further interpretation, the presence of *aramni*-bird ("falcon, hawk(?)") figurines in the following paragraph (9.1.1 rev. iii 22′) suggest that the *ḫara(n)-* might also refer to animal figurine. Although the CLuw. word for eagle is currently unknown, since passages such as KUB 18.5 + 49.13 obv. i 28: Á^{MUŠEN} *ḫarraninn=a* "(we saw) the eagle and the *ḫarrani*-bird," (see EDHIL *s.v. ḫarrani-* [pp. 302–3]; further HW^2 Ḫ *s.v. ḫarrani-* [pp. 271–72]) show that the previous candidate *ḫarran(i)-* cannot mean eagle in CLuw., and although it is tempting, given the copious amount of Luwianisms in the Inventory of Manninni and the superficial similarity to Hitt. *ḫaran-* 'eagle', to entertain *ḫaranza* as the CLuw. word for the eagle, such a derivation is unlikely. In addition to historical linguistic difficulties in deriving *ḫara(n)-* from Indo-European, one would have to explain the scenario of 'eagle', being both naturally animate and attested as a common gender noun in Hittite, being classed as neuter in Luwian.

$^{\text{(GIŠ)}}$*ḫa/urnašal(l)a-*

See main discussion under ^{GIŠ}DUB.ŠEN.

ḫatiwi-

A loanword of certain Luwian and possible Hurrian origins. Earlier literature (CLL, 66; EHS 1, 191–93 [§108.5], 476; HEG A–K *s.v. ḫatiu̯i-* [p. 224]; HED III *s.v. hatiwi-* [p. 266]; HW^2 Ḫ *s.v. ḫatiwi-* [p. 510]) considered the seemingly inserted *-t-* in the denominative verb *ḫatiwita(i)-* to be a vestige of the Hurrian directional ending *-ta*. However, Starke (1990, 184) explained the *-t-* as a remnant of the CLuw. *i(t)*-stem declension pattern (*ibid.*, 176–221) that is frequently observed among borrowings from Luwian into Hittite (GHL §4.15, p. 86). Although many of the CLuw. *i(t)*-stem borrowings into Hittite have ultimate Hurrian or Akkadian origins (Simon 2020, esp. 416 fn. 21), there is thus far no independent evidence linking *ḫatiwi-* to either language (Oettinger 1981, 387). At present, it can only be said that the Hittite word for "inventory" was borrowed at some point from Luwian, though an ultimate origin in Hurrian cannot be ruled out.

See *ḫatiwita(i)-* immediately below for discussion of semantics of inventories and inventorying in the PTAC

ḫatiwita(i)-

Evidence from the PTAC suggests that the verb *ḫatiwita(i)-* has a technical meaning within the corpus more specific than the simple recording of contents on a clay tablet. It seems that "to *ḫatiwita(i)-*" represented an administrative stage in which items have been received within the relevant processing facility (probably the É ^{NA_4}KIŠIB in most texts) and have been enrolled with detailed descriptions (i.e., descriptions that in theory allow an item to be identified individually, and not just generically). In addition, both preserved examples of texts explicitly identified as *ḫatiwi*-s (9.1.1 rev. iv 45′–46′; 9.1.9 rev. iv 4′–5′) are large, multi-column inventory tablets that were authorized by a high-level administrator, though it is not clear whether all *ḫatiwi*-s had this format.

The specific, technical sense of the verb *ḫatiwita(i)-* rests mostly on interpretation of 2.7. As discussed in the introductory *Analysis* to 2.7, the duplicate texts 2.7.A and 2.7.B record what seems to be a preliminary inventory of incoming chests, some of which bear attached GIŠ.ḪUR-schedules, and some of which are described as "not (yet) inventoried" (*UL/nawi ḫatiwitān*). Each chest is given a brief, usually one-line description of its generic contents regardless of whether a GIŠ.ḪUR is noted as present (e.g., 2.7.B rev. 6′–7′; cf. 2.7.B rev. 1′–2′ in broken context), and regardless of whether it is explicitly described as not inventoried (e.g., 2.7.A obv. 18: 1 ^{GI}PISAN SA$_5$ *BI-IB-RI*$^{\text{ḪI.A}}$*=kan anda nawi ḫatiwitān* "1 red chest. Rhyta (are) inside. Not yet inventoried."). Most entries contain neither a GIŠ.ḪUR nor mention of an inventory status. However, two curious entries involving the queen contain both. The first of these is 2.7.A obv. 2–11:

2.7.A obv. 2–11 (A obv. 2–3//B rev. 6′–7′)

Transcription

Obv.

2 1 ^{GI}PISAN SA$_5$ GAL GÌR UR.MAḪ IGI.DU$_8$.A *ŠA* KUR *A-MUR-RI-kan*

3 GADA$^{\text{ḪI.A}}$ *anda IŠ-TU* GIŠ.ḪUR GUL-*aššan* (2.7.B rev. ends here)

4 EGIR-*anda=ia=kan* …

5–10 (2.7.A obv. 4–10 continues with a list of individual items)

11 MUNUS.LUGAL *anda dāiš kūn* ^{GI}PISAN *nāwi ḫatiwitanzi*

Translation
Obv.

2 1 large, red, reed chest (with) lion-feet. A gift-payment of Amurru
3 (consisting of) linens (is) inside. Marked down by GIŠ.ḪUR-schedule.
4 And later, ...
5–10 (a number of luxury items) ...
11 the queen placed in. They have not yet inventoried this chest.

As can be seen, 2.7.B ends with the description of the chest as "A gift-payment of Amurru (consisting of) linens (is) inside. Marked down by GIŠ.ḪUR-schedule." 2.7.A then begins at roughly where B leaves off, duplicating only one single-line entry (B rev. 5′) and the two lines of B rev. 6′–7′ before continuing with a description of items added by the queen. Since 2.7.B ends with an erasure that corresponds exactly to the point of intervention by the queen, it may be suspected that royal presence, and not just the fact that the scribe was running out of space, required a new, presumably more official tablet (cf. the continued presence of the queen in the very next paragraph of 2.7.A obv. 12–15). Alternatively, it may be that some period of time had elapsed between the tablets: as argued in the *Commentary* to 2.7 8–15, the (EGIR-*anda*) must be interpreted as "later," with the syntax of 2.7.A obv. 3–11 suggesting one continuous sentence: "Later (these items) the queen added in."

Previous interpretations have focused on the distinction in finality or completeness implied by GIŠ.ḪUR and *ḫatiwi-* (and *ḫatiwita(i)-*). As Goetze (1959, 32 fn. 4) remarked in the *editio princeps* of 2.7.A, " we observe a contrast between the (final) *tuppi* and the (temporary) GIŠ.ḪUR on which the objects have been jotted down (*gulšan*)." Goetze's explanation was picked up in the translations of HIT (p. 6: "jotted down on the wooden board" vs. "not yet inventorized") and HVP (p. 81: "Auf der Holztafel notiert" vs. "noch nicht inventarisiert") for 2.7.A obv. 2–11. But while it is probable, and perhaps even near certain, that there was a difference in administrative finality between GIŠ.ḪUR and *ḫatiwi-* (and *ḫatiwita(i)-*), it is not necessarily proved by this passage (nor is the construction of Mora 2007, 538 of a three-phase system of registration consisting of reception, preliminary GIŠ.ḪUR registration at site of reception, and final *ḫatiwi-* registration at site of storage warranted based on 2.7.A). Goetze's and the subsequent editions have assumed that both the GIŠ.ḪUR and the *ḫatiwi-*s were produced by the administration at Ḫattuša, when it is more likely that the documents came with the chests that were being unpacked. Such a scenario is seemingly confirmed by the administrative text OyT 09/1, which records an inventory of chests that were presumably being packed and sent from Oymaağaç-Nerik, each of which had a *ḫatiwi-* included within (see discussion in van den Hout 2010a, 264; Klinger 2011, 222–23). Such a reconstruction also better explains the patchy availability of the GIŠ.ḪUR for the chests (some had already been removed, or had been lost in transit, or were never there). The presence or absence of GIŠ.ḪUR was therefore incidental to the process of *ḫatiwita(i)-*.

At the same time, if the detailed listing of objects in 2.7.A obv. 3–10 does not count as an inventory, one is left to wonder what does. An interpretation can be offered that the original contents of the chest, the "linens" labeled as the gift-payment of Amurru without further description of the contents, had not yet been examined by the scribe beyond reading the GIŠ.ḪUR attached to the chest. Before he could perform a proper inventory, or at least assess that one was needed, the queen, who, judging by the direct speech A obv. 12–15, was at this point present in the storeroom, added a number of loose items to the chest. These items were recorded on clay while they were being added, but the original contents, now likely buried underneath the new additions, still needed their official reckoning. Given that the remainder of the chests in 2.7.A were also not inventoried (this seems to be the theme of the tablet) and received only one or two line entries, it is not improbable that the scribe wanted to indicate that in spite of the detailed listing of items, the assessment of the chest in paragraph obv. 2–11 was unfinished. Thus, *kūn* ^{GI}PISAN *nāwi ḫatiwitanzi* in obv. 11 should be read "this chest (i.e., its original contents; or perhaps, its newly combined total) they have not yet inventoried." Confirmation of this interpretation, namely that an exhaustive listing of objects does not in and of itself constitute an inventory, might be found later in the text in 2.7.A obv. 23–24. Here, a chest apparently containing a single gold-inlaid Hurrian tunic is also described as *UL ḫatiwitān* (obv. 24). If the single Hurrian tunic is not a mistake for multiple tunics, so that it was indeed the only object in the chest (conceivable for such a rare item), then the chest has had its contents completely recorded on clay, and yet was also considered not inventoried.

The only items which can certainly be classified as inventoried in the PTAC are those appearing on the Named, Complex Inventories of 9.1.1 ("The Second Tablet of the Inventory of Manninni") and 9.1.9 ("Fragment of the Second Tablet of the Inventory of Arnuwanda of the *UNŪT* É $^{\mathrm{NA_4}}$KIŠIB 'Equipment of the Seal House'"), since the colophons of both texts identify their tablets as *ḫatiwi*-s. However, it is possible that other texts described only as *tuppa-* '(clay) tablet', e.g., 11.1.3 12′: [*t*]*uppiš* ^{TÚG}*šašš*[*anaš* ... "[T]ablet of sleep[ing clothes ... ," were also *ḫatiwi-* inventories. In 2.7.A obv. 14–15, the queen states regarding a chest that: GIM-*an=ma=wa* ŠÀ É $^{\mathrm{NA_4}}$KIŠIB *teḫḫi nu=war=at tuppiaz* 15 *aniyanzi* "'When I place (it) in the seal house, they will record it using a tablet'." Although Mora (2007, 538) suggested that the tablet promised by the queen in this passage was in fact 2.7.A itself, this seems improbable. Since the theme of 2.7 seems to be chests in the first stages of administrative processing, it is better to assume that that the passage records another variety of administrative shortcoming or interruption with respect to the chest (again) due to the actions of the queen. A simple *UL ḫatiwitān* would not suffice in this instance, since the chest had apparently left the control of the administrators and been turned over to the queen. The fact that the location of the Inventory of Arnuwanda and the final destination of the queen's chest are one and the same, suggests that "making a tablet (in the É $^{\mathrm{NA_4}}$KIŠIB)" was equivalent to or a circumlocution for *ḫatiwita(i)-*.

^{GIŠ}***ḫatuli-***

With HW^2 Ḫ *s.v.* ^{GIŠ}*ḫatuli(š)-* (p. 536) "Bez. einer Waffe(?)," and further in reference to 9.1.10.A$_2$ rev. 6′–11′ (*loc. cit.*), "Da ^{GIŠ}*ḫ.* innerhalb einer strukturierten Aufzählung in der Sektion Waffen begegnet, liegt es nahe, hierin ebenfalls die Bezeichnung einer zum

Kampf vom Wagen geeigneten Fernwaffe zu sehen." However, it may pointed out that the position of ^{GIŠ}*ḫatuli-* in the list between the bows at the end of 9.1.10.A$_2$ rev. 6′ and the quivers of arrows at the end of 9.1.10.A$_2$ rev. 7′, combined with the fact that the traces of a single horizontal wedge before the word rule out a numeral (attestations of *ME* 'hundred' elsewhere on 9.1.10.A$_1$ and 9.1.10.A$_2$ look very different) but suggest instead a sg. gen. *-aš* of a preceding noun, hints that the ^{GIŠ}*ḫatuli-* was not a separate weapon, but rather a subcomponent of a bow or other piece of archery equipment.

$^{\text{(NA}_4\text{)}}$*ḫekur-*

See the discussion of van den Hout 2002, 74–80, who concluded that the $^{\text{(NA}_4\text{)}}$*ḫekur* referred originally to any natural rock outcropping, which could become divinized for use as a sanctuary for the gods or a memorial for dead kings. The $^{\text{(NA}_4\text{)}}$*ḫekur* could then also refer metonymically to the cult institution and buildings surrounding the rock outcropping. *Ḫekur*-sanctuaries/monuments did not necessarily have to be in remote locations, though there is evidence that the extramural rock-reliefs of Fraktın and Sirkeli could have served as such (van den Hout 2002, 90), but could also be within settlements, e.g., on Nişantepe in Ḫattuša itself (*ibid.*, 80, 88). In the context of the PTAC, the attestations from 3.1.7.A$_2$ rev. v 4′ ($^{\text{NA}_4}$*ḫekur*) and probably 3.1.1.A$_2$ rev. vi 2′ (É.GAL *ḫekur* ^{D}LAMMA in a broken context) reveal that the *ḫekur*-institutions could receive tribute dispatched from the central administration for storage and use.

ḫešḫa-

With HW^2 Ḫ *s.v. ḫešḫa-/ḫešḫiša-* (p. 572) (commenting on 9.1.4.A$_1$ obv. ii 19): "vielleicht … t[erminus] t[echnicus] für Nacken/Rand einer Protome (unterschieden vom *puri-* 'Lippe, Rand' in [9.1.4.A$_1$ obv.] ii 20, 25)." Other suggestions include Singer 2011, 465 fn. 40: "some part of the vessel (rim$^?$, handle$^?$) or perhaps some sort of application" and Tischler 2013, 253: "Seitenflach$^?$." The attestation in 9.1.5 rev.$^!$ 13′, which was overlooked by the HW^2, should probably be interpreted as sg. dat./loc.: 3 ŠU.ŠÈ.LÁ KÙ.BABBAR ŠÀ.BA 1 *ḫe-eš-ḫi* KÙ.SI$_{22}$ "3 silver *kraters*, of which 1 (is) gold on (its) *ḫešḫa-*" (see *Commentary* to this line in edition of 9.1.5; alternatively to be taken as a stem form, as implied in Singer, *loc. cit.*, "one with a 'golden *ḫešḫi*'"). This confirms that *ḫešḫa-* (less likely *ḫešḫi-*) is the correct form of the lemma, and that it is indeed some integral part of a drinking vessel.

ḫuḫḫurtalla/i-

Translated correctly by HIT (p. 215) and HVP (p. 591) as 'necklace', the intervening proposal by Erkut 1997 to equate *ḫuḫḫurtalla-* with ŠEN 'tube, (drain)pipe, gutter' was based on an etymological relationship with ^{UZU}*ḫuḫḫurta/i-* 'throat, windpipe.' The etymology is not incorrect, but as HW^2 Ḫ *s.v. ḫuḫ(ḫ)urtalla-*, ↖ *ḫuwaḫḫuwartalla-* (p. 645) demonstrated: "*ḫ.* is ein *nomen instrumenti* abeleitet von ↗^{UZU}*ḫuḫḫarta/i-* 'Kehle/Luftröhre' + *-ala* (bildet eigentl. *nomina actoris*). Die Trilingue [RS 25.421 obv. 24] und die Belegstellen (Gegenstand, *pl. tantum*, aus Gold und Edelstein) verweisen auf die Bedeutung 'Halskette'…." As discussed in GHL §2.21 (p. 55), the *-alla/i-* suffix creates a secondary noun of flexible semantics whose identity is predicated upon its relationship with the base noun. Thus while the *ḫuḫḫurtalla/i-* could in theory have been a "throat-like thing" – i.e., some sort of tube – it in practice designated a "throat-thing" – i.e., a necklace that was defined by its proximity to the throat.

^{NA_4}*ḫulali-*

See Schuster-Brandis 2008, 436 (with previous literature, including Polvani 1988, 16–17 for Hittite) for identification of Akk. *ḫulālu* as a black-and-white banded agate, possibly onyx. For the argument that ^{NA_4}*ḫulali-* is a true loanword (not an Akkadogram) in Hittite, see HW² *s.v.* ^{NA_4}*ḫulali-* (p. 690):

> ^{NA_4}*ḫulali-* wird als die hethitisierte Form von akkad. *ḫulālu* (CAD Ḫ 226f.; Ahw. 353) betrachtet, die, wie viele akkad. Lehnwörter, als *i*-Stamm ins Heth. aufgenommen worden sei (vgl. H.A. Hoffner/H.C. Melchert, GHL 86). Die für einen *i*-Stamm ungewöhnliche Form des Pl.N.-A.n. ^{NA_4}*ḫu-u-la-la* kann wegen der Pleneschreibung von *-u-* wohl kaum (analog zu *ṬUP-PA*$^{ḪI.A}$ von akkad. *ṭuppu*, Hoffner/Melchert l.c. 90) als Akkadogr. ^{NA_4}*ḪU-U-LA-LA* aufgefaßt werden.

ḫuli-

This word is a hapax to 6.5 rev. 9′: 1 ^{TÚG}*lupanniš ḪAŠ-MAN-NI ḫu-liš šarianza* […. The translations of HW² *s.v. ḫuli-* (p. 700): "1 blau-grüne Kappe, *ḫ.*, bestickt(?)" and CHD Š *s.v. šariya-* B 1.b (p. 258): "1 cap: *ḪAŠMANNI*-colored, *ḫuliš*, and embroidered(?)" treat *ḫuliš* as a modifier of the *lupanni-* 'cap', i.e., as a cap that is *ḫuli-* or made of *ḫuli-*. The obvious similarity of *ḫuli-* with *ḫuliya-* 'wool', *ḫulana-* 'id.', and ^{GIŠ}*ḫulali-* 'distaff', makes it attractive to take *ḫuli-* as another word for 'wool'. It could either be a graphically abbreviated form of Hittite *ḫuliya-*, or, if the etymological concerns of EDHIL *s.v. ḫulana-* (p. 358) are justified, another borrowed form (in the expected *i*-stem, per GHL §4.16, p. 86) from Hurrian noun **ḫul(a)-* 'wool' (Kronasser 1967, 45 for reconstruction). Alternatively, due to the peculiarities of the text, it could be that *ḫu-liš* was simply a mistake or an abbreviation, with some sign or string of signs missing in the middle (cf. ^{TÚG}*i⟨-pu⟩-li* in 6.5 obv. 11′).

ḫulliya-

The attestation in 3.1.1.A$_1$ of pret. pl. 3 *ḫullier* with bulk copper (obv. ii 10′) and a copper adze (obv. ii 11′) was not discussed by HW² Ḫ *s.v. ḫulla/e-, ḫulliya-* (p. 686), but presumably demonstrates a technical sense for the verb, perhaps with a meaning "to break up, chop into pieces," i.e., a stage of cold processing of metal that does not involve smelting it. The technical relationship of *ḫulliya-* to the other term attested for "breaking" metal in the PTAC, *(arḫa) duwarna-*, which is also applied to bulk copper (*arḫa duwarner*, 5.2 obv. ii 13) and tools (*ḪAṢṢ*]*INNU duwarnaš*, 5.1 rev. iv 2), is unclear: Note, however, the appearance of EGIR-*pa laḫuwāer* 'they poured back' one line later in 5.1 rev. iv 3, suggesting *duwarna-* might have immediately preceded smelting (*zanu-*).

ḫulpanali-

HW² *s.v. ḫulpanali-* (p. 701) ("u.B.; vielleicht ein Tuch oder Kleidungstück") suggested a connection of this garment with **ḫu(wa)lpa-* 'hump', *ḫulpara-* 'hillock, knoll' (see Lorenz – Rieken 2007, 480–81 for the reconstruction of this root), and by extension *ḫu(wa)lpazi/ana-* '(decorative) stud, knob(?)', which are attested as clothing embellishments elsewhere in the PTAC. The absence of metal in connection to the attestations of *ḫulpanali-* in 4.1.4.1.A$_1$ rev. vi 13′ and 11.6.1 6′ unfortunately precludes their identification as studded garments, since *ḫu(wa)lpazi/ana-* are always described as being made of precious metal in the PTAC. One could speculate instead that the *ḫulpanali-* was a "humped" or "hillocky" garment, perhaps a quilted garment stuffed with padding. If the *ḫulpanali-* was not actually worn on the body, which is possibly indicated by the absence of the TÚG determine, they could have perhaps been instead 'pillows'. Regardless of their form or function, the large number of *ḫulpanali-* in 11.6.1 6, numbering 130 when the other items in the text are restricted to the teens and single digits, suggests that the *ḫulpanali-* could be relatively small.

^{TÚG}*ḫunipala(za)-*

HW^2 *s.v.* $^{\text{(TÚG)}}$*ḫunipala(za)*$^?$- (p. 724) "eine Art Decke oder Tuch" gives only three attestations, including 6.1 from the PTAC. Of the other two, KBo 30.164+ (CTH 666 'Texts from the Cult of Arinna') rev. iv 6–7, has the king sitting on a *ḫunipalaza*-cloth while he receiving the lituus and scepter. KUB 51.77 (CTH 666) provides only a fragmentary context, but the presence of the cloth in obv. 4′ and *eša* 'he sits down' in obv. 7′ might indicate that the *ḫunipalaza-* was again sat upon. It may also be observed that all three attestations of the word come from a northern Anatolian context (6.1 is a list of gifts to be distributed at the AN.DAḪ.ŠUM-festival in Nerik), suggesting the item was a regional term for a kind of seat cover.

ḫudanni-

While *ḫudanni-* is classified HW^2 *s.v. ḫud/tanni-* (p. 790) as common gender based on attestations of sg. acc. *ḫūtannin* in KUB 15.11+ rev. iii 16′ (CTH 583 'Vow of Puduḫepa'), the existence of *ḫu-u-da-an-ni* in 9.1.15 5′ – which is probably not stem form, since the other nouns in the text, both Hittite and Akkadian, are consistently declined – together with the form *ḫu-da-an-ni* in the festival fragment KUB 10.91 rev. iii 2′ suggest the existence of a neuter gender variant.

$^{\text{(GADA)}}$*ḫu(wa)ndar(a)-*

The suggestion of Starke 1990, 371 to define $^{\text{(GADA)}}$*ḫu(wa)ndar(a)-* as a very fine, "airy-thin" linen fabric is attractive, though HW^2 *s.v.* ^{GADA}*ḫuwand/tar(a)-* (p. 816) is more cautious about etymological connection with *ḫuwant-* 'wind'. The sg. nom. form $^{\text{GADA!}}$*ḫuntaraš* in 2.11 obv.$^?$ 4′ (pl. gen. or dat./loc. is very unlikely here), which has thus far escaped remark, probably represents a reanalysis of the word from the original neuter abstract suffix *-ar-* borrowed from CLuw. (Starke 1990, 370–84) to a common-gender *r*-stem Hittite noun, which was subsequently thematized (see GHL §4.83, p. 116).

ḫu(wa)rtiyal(l)a/i-

Previous editions read in 11.1.9 7′ *ḫuwarti[š*, either as coming from *ḫuwartiš* 'extract, concoction' (HIT, p. 175) or as a homophonous noun with an unknown meaning (HVP, p. 530 fn. 2, 593), leading HW^2 *s.v. ḫuwarti-* "Absud$^{(?)}$, Gebräu$^{(?)}$" (p. 823) to cautiously include 11.1.9 7′ among the unclear attestations of the entry. However, consulting the photo for 11.1.9 shows that the close spacing and relatively low placement of the two horizontals suggest instead a reading -*a*[*l*- instead of -*i*[*š*. This suggests that 11.1.9 7′ actually records the *ḫurtiyal(l)a/i*-vessel (HW^2 *s.v.* $^{\text{(DUG)}}$*ḫurtiyal(l)a/i*- [p. 773]) instead, i.e., the vessel for preparing infusions/concoctions, which would much better fit the theme of metallic vessels and objects in 11.1.9, rather than the infusion/concoction itself. If so, *ḫu-u-wa-ar-ti-a*[*l-li-iš* would then represent a hitherto unattested form of the lemma, which retained the -*uwa*- semi-vowel of the base noun *ḫuwarti*-.

ḫurli-

The appearance of 33 *ḫur-li-eš* KÙ.SI$_{22}$ "33 gold *ḫurli*-" in 10.1.2.8 r. c. 2′ in the context of implements and temple furnishings makes it unlikely they belong to the lemma $^{\text{(UZU)}}$*ḫu(wa)rla/i*-, a body part in the head or neck region (see discussion under *ḫu(wa)rlu*- immediately below). Neither would an adjective "Hurrian" be appropriate here. One must therefore assume the existence of a third lemma *ḫurli*-. It is possible another example of this *ḫurli*- (sg. acc. *ḫur-li-in*) is attested among a fragmentary list of votive objects in Bo 5801 rev. (iv) 3′.

ḫu(wa)rlu-

The attestations given under HW^2 Ḫ *s.v.* *ḫurli*- (/*ḫurla*$^?$-) (p. 758) and *s.v.* $^{\text{(UZU)}}$*ḫuwarla*- (p. 822) should be reorganized into two new lemmata: $^{\text{(UZU)}}$*ḫu(wa)rla/i*-, a body part in the head or neck region that is attested as both an *a*-stem and *i*-stem (probably as a result of *i*-mutation), and *ḫu(wa)rlu*-, a metallic object or subcomponent that is attested only as a *u*-stem. All attestations currently listed under HW^2 Ḫ *s.v.* *ḫurli*- (/*ḫurla*$^?$-) – including the suspected form *ḫur-lu-uš*, which must be pl. acc. according to the syntax of KUB 7.55 obv. 5′ – should be assigned to $^{\text{(UZU)}}$*ḫu(wa)rla/i*-, together with all *a*-stem attestations currently under HW^2 Ḫ *s.v.* $^{\text{(UZU)}}$*ḫuwarla*- (see already Soysal 2016, 423 no. 86 for the proposal of combining $^{\text{(UZU)}}$*ḫu(wa)rla/i*- and *ḫurli* (/*ḫurla*$^?$-)). Then, the attestations ending in -*uš* in HW^2 Ḫ *s.v.* $^{\text{(UZU)}}$*ḫuwarla*- currently classified as pl. nom. should be reclassified as *u*-stem sg. nom. and moved to the new lemma *ḫu(wa)rlu*-. The personal name ^{m}*Ḫuwarlu*/^{m}*Ḫurlu* probably also belongs here (compare ^{m}*Manninni* and ^{m}*Aḫuwatar* for other "jewelry names").

The precise meaning of the newly found *u*-stem lemma *ḫu(wa)rlu*- hinges on interpretation of 9.1.5 rev.$^!$ 15′. Here, the transliteration given by HW^2 Ḫ *s.v.* $^{\text{(UZU)}}$*ḫuwarla*- (p. 822) (written obv. 15′ for rev.$^!$ 15′): GIŠ.ḪUR$^{\text{ḪI.}}$]⌜$^{\text{A?}}$⌝ KÙ.BABBAR GIŠ.ḪUR$^{\text{ḪI.A}}$ KÙ.GI *nu* 1-*edani* 1 GIŠ.ḪUR SA$_5$/DIRI-*ri*/-*RI* 1-*edani=ma ḫu-wa-ar-lu-uš* SI.GAR *dupiya*[*ḫ*-$^?$, can be improved in multiple ways. First, given that the context of the paragraph 9.1.5 rev.$^!$ 13′–18′ is an inventory of ornamented weapons, it is nearly certain that the end of rev.$^!$ 15′ reads "4 *dupiyali*[*š*" 'four *sledg*[*es*' and not "SI.GAR *dupiya*[*ḫ*$^?$-" 'necklace ....' This is confirmed in the photos of the tablet, where the numeral "4" is clearly differentiated from the GAR-sign in, e.g., obv. 14′. Second, the reading GIŠ.ḪUR 'sketch, plan' should be discarded for GIŠ.(BAR.)KÍN 'covering, overlay', as attested elsewhere in the PTAC (see *Lexical Commentary, s.v.* GIŠ.(BAR.)KÍN below). Third, SA$_5$/DIRI-*ri*/-*RI* can be conclusively read in this context as DIRI-*ri* '(it) remains/(it) is left'. The resulting transliteration,]x KÙ.BABBAR GIŠ.KÍN$^{\text{ḪI.A}}$ KÙ.SI$_{22}$ *nu* 1-*edani* 1 GIŠ.KÍN DIRI-*ri* 1-*edani=ma ḫuwarluš* DIRI$^!$(text: SI) 4 *dupiyali*[*š*, may be translated: "(a number of weapons made of)] silver (with) golden overlays. On one (weapon), one overlay remains, but on (the other) one, the *ḫuwarlu-* remains. 4 *sledg*[*es* ....” The emendation DIRI$^!$ is demanded by context: the contrastive enclitic *-ma* and the parallel structure of the preceding clause suggest that some comment is being made on the state of the weapon’s overlay (cf. also 9.1.5 rev.$^!$ 16′: 2 ^{GIŠ}*ŠU-RE-EN-NU* ŠÀ.BA 1 2 GIŠ.KÍN KÙ.BABBAR 1-*e-ma* 1 GIŠ.KÍN KÙ.BABBAR). Without emendation, the translation ‘on one (weapon), one overlay remains, but on (the other) one, the *ḫuwarlu-* is horn’ not only lacks contrast, but makes no sense since the overlays at the beginning of 9.1.5 rev.$^!$ 15′ are described as made of gold. By emending SI to DIRI$^!$ (DIRI being a composition SI×A, meaning the scribe simply forgot to add the ligatured *a*-sign), parallelism is restored to the clauses: “on one (weapon), one overlay remains, but on the (other) one, the *ḫuwarlu-* remains.” The clause suggests that the *ḫuwarlu-* must somehow contrast to the golden overlay, and yet still be related. One can propose that the *ḫuwarlu-* perhaps refers to a setting, mount, substrate, or bracket for the overlay on the weapon. The close connection of *ḫu(wa)rlu-*s and overlays is affirmed by the two other attestations in the PTAC, namely 2.17 obv.$^?$ r. c. 18′: *A-NA* 1]-*EN* GIŠ.BAR.KÍN KÙ.SI$_{22}$ *ḫur-lu-uš* x[and obv.$^?$ r. c. 19′: *nu A-NA* 3 GIŠ.BAR.KÍN KÙ.SI$_{22}$ *ḫ*[*ur-lu-uš* (in light of the present discussion, these latter are not “Hurrian” overlays, contra HVP, 493 and HW^2 Ḫ *s.v.* $^{\text{(URU)}}$*ḫurla-* 1.4 [p. 757]).

iyata(r)-/iyatn-

With HW^2 I *s.v. iyat/da(r), iyata-/iyatn-* 4. (pp. 30–31), the form *iyatnaš* attested modifying a variety of garments in the PTAC must be treated as either a determinative-less, sg. gen. form of ^{SÍG}*iyatna-* ‘wool felt(?)’ or as a sg. gen. from *iyatar* ‘plenty’. The latter option is preferred here, with a translation of sg. gen. *iyatnaš* “of plenty” = “luxurious,” since it does not require an explanation of the missing determinative.

iya- (šer arḫa iya-)

For the verb and preverb combination *šer arḫa iya-*, see the previous discussions of Rost 1953, 373 (“fertigmachen,” with reservations); HVP (p. 219, with fn. 3 “oben abgeschlossen$^{(?)}$”); Miller 2004, 72 (to “*make up*”; also p. 115 with commentary), HW^2 I *s.v. iya-*^{1}*/iye-*, ... I.1.5 “(Kleid/Stoffbahn) abschließen(?)” (p. 10). The main problem of interpreting the collocation *šer arḫa iya-* is the tension between its usage as a participle with garments, and the single active use attested in a ritual. As a participle, the phrase appears as an attribute of garments (within the PTAC in 4.1.4.1.A$_1$ obv. i 4′–7′, rev. vi 8′–12′; 11.6.1 7, 8; outside of the PTAC in KBo 40.114 6′:]x GADA *še-er ar-ḫa i-ia-*[, and in broken contexts of KBo 46.255 4′–6′; KBo 21.30 obv. i 3′). In its active use, the phrase refers to some process of manufacture of objects from raw material: see KBo 39.8 obv. ii 15–17: *nu* EGIR-*a*[(*nd*)]*a* [(^{MUNUS}ŠU.G)I IM$^?$-*a*]*n dāi nu=ššan šer* [(*arḫa* 7 EME$^{\text{ḪI.A}}$)] ^{16} *iyazzi n=aš=kan katta tarmāizzi n=*[*aš=(kan)*] ^{17} *A-NA* 2 *BE-EL* SÍSKUR *šer arḫa waḫnuz*[*i*, which Miller 2004, 72 translated: “Then afterwards she takes clay$^{(?)}$, whence she *makes up* seven tongues, and she *secures them to the ground.* Then she waves them over the two ritual patients ....” In contrast, the CHD Š *s.v. šēr, šer* 7 b 2′ b′ 4″ (p. 430) chose to leave out the clay$^{(?)}$ restored by Miller, and translated: “Afterwards the Old Woman takes [...], and models seven tongues all over on (it). She secures them to (it), and swings [them] over the two ritual patrons (and) away.” With the minor change of “modeled” to "finished (vel. sim.)," the translation of the CHD has the advantage of being usable for both the ritual and garment contexts.

For the syntax of the term, according the schema observed in GHL §20.10 (p. 297) for dual preverbs, the first adverb should be treated as a locational specifier for the action indicated by the interior preverb/verb combination, which in the case of *arḫa iya-* is "to make/carry out to completion" (ḪW² I *s.v. iya-*¹/*iye-*, ... III [p. 15]: *arḫa i. "vollständig machen/ausführen"*). As already suspected by HVP (p. 523 fn. 4: "Wahrscheinlich ein Terminus technicus der Textilienverarbeitung."), the sense of *arḫa iya-* in the context of garments must surely have a technical meaning, since almost all the garments described in the inventories were finished products, "on top" or otherwise (note, however, that the further hypothesis of HVP, *loc. cit.*, of an opposition between *šer arḫa iya-* and TÚG UGU SUD-*an* relating the respective direction of selvedge for the cloth edges seems excessively specific – and in fact, the terms are not comparable since the TÚG UGU SUD-*an* was probably another of the functionally designated garments, in this case a cloth that was "spread over", i.e., a cloth cover, whereas *šer arḫa iya-* could be applied attributively to any garment). Fortunately, an English translation "finished (on top)," or even "top-finished" captures the ambiguity of the participle form, since it can describe either a product that was finished at its top, or one that had a "finish," i.e., an extra level or step of detailed work, applied to it. In either interpretation, the specifics of the finishing must remain unknown barring further evidence.

ipeššar (or: *ipa/i*-^{SAR}, *ipi*-^{SAR})

In the context of the 1 GURUN KÙ.SI$_{22}$ "1 (model) golden fruit" in the preceding line, the otherwise unknown lemma found in 10.3.13 5′: 3 *i-pé-eš-šar* KÙ.S[I$_{22}$ may just as easily be read *i-pí-eš*^{SAR}, i.e., as either a sg. nom. of **ipi-* or a pl. nom. of **ipa-*, with the SAR 'plant' as postdeterminative. Although semantically attractive, further connection with the word group $^{\text{(GIŠ/Ú)}}$*ippi(y)a-* 'grape vine', *ippi(y)ant-*$^{\text{(SAR)}}$ 'grape leaves' is made difficult by the lack of gemination.

ipurawar

The twice occurring designation *A-NA* LE.U$_5$ *i-pu-ra-u-*[*aš* (4.2.9 obv. 15), *A-NA* LE].U$_5$ *i-pu-r*[*a-u*]*-aš* (4.2.9 rev. 30′) was translated "on the record of booty" in HIT (p. 122), with *ipurawaš* taken as sg. gen. verbal noun of "*epurai-* 'to besiege, to storm, to tear down'" (*ibid.* 124, with earlier literature). HW² E *s.v epurai- (ipurai-)* (p. 89) later stressed that the exact meaning of the verb is not 'to besiege, to storm, etc.', but rather a technical term for the act of moving earth in the construction of, e.g., siege ramps and dams. This led Singer (2011, 463) to hypothesize instead a meaning "stockpile" for *ipurawar*, based on a radical sense of 'piling up', whether of earth or otherwise, which he attributed to the verb. Questions aside of whether it is appropriate for luxury goods to be "piled up" (the items of the PTAC give the impression of being carefully sorted in chests, and no other goods are described as being in or from an *ipurawar*), choosing between the interpretations "ramparts" and "stockpile" depends mostly on how one interprets the context of 4.2.9. The presence of three groups of objects of roughly equal value and contents, each of which was then given to a different individual, suggests the division of a single preexisting pile of goods – a scenario consistent with dividing up the spoils of war (see further introductory *Analysis* to 4.2.9 and *Commentary* to 4.2.9 lo. e. 33′–34′). Thus, the translation "ramparts" will be retained here.

$^{(TÚG)}$***irḫi-***

Based on the context of the garments mentioned in 4.1.4.1.A$_2$ obv. ii – as well as 4.1.4.4 and 4.1.4.5, if these are indeed indirect joins per HVP (p. 240) – HVP (p. 214) plausibly considered that the $^{(TÚG)}$*irḫi-* was a kind of belt, i.e., either a variety of, if not the reading behind, the Sumerogram ^{TÚG}E.ÍB. Note that the argument of HIT (p. 44) that the $^{(TÚG)}$*irḫi-* needed only one shekel of material to manufacture, and therefore was a garment of very light construction such as a "shawl," must be discarded since it was based on a misinterpretation of the syntax of the numeral "1" in 4.1.4.1.A$_2$ obv. ii 6′. Instead of the number of shekels of wool required for the garment, "1" was the number of $^{(TÚG)}$*irḫi*-s to be made from the minimum 48 shekels of wool listed in 4.1.4.1.A$_2$ obv. ii 4′–5′.

iššar(a)l(l)ad(d)ar

See now Simon, eDiAna, *s.v. iššaralladar-* (= lemma 265) for discussion and literature (earlier HW^2 *s.v. iššaralladdar* [p. 99]). As widely recognized, the first element *iššr(i)-*, CLuw. for 'hand', indicates that the object must have some relationship with the hand or arm, suggesting a kind of bracelet. Despite the misgivings of Simon 2020b due to non-geminate spelling, note the correct reading by Starke (1990, 471 fn. 1714) of 4.1.1.1.A$_1$ obv. 7′ as a pl. gen. *iššaralatanaš* belonging to this lemma, and not as an otherwise unattested lemma *iššarattana-* given by HIT (p. 75), HVP (p. 100), and Simon, eDiAna, *s.v. iššarattanaš* (= lemma 266). See now also the previously unrecognized form *iš-šar-la-at-ta-aš* in 4.1.1.3 rev. B 6, which must be pl. gen. from context, for an additional variation of this graphically unstable lexeme: here, *iššarlattaš* is either a mistake for *iš-šar-la-at-ta-⟨na-⟩aš* (see 4.1.1.1.A$_1$ obv. 7′ for the correct form with unassimilated *-t(a)n-*), or else shows an alternative stem in *-att(i)-* or *-att(a)-*.

išḫuwant-

With HW^2 I *s.v. išḫuwa(i)-* 3.3 and 3.4 (pp. 161–62), *arḫa išḫuwa-* has a technical sense in the context of cult inventories and statue descriptions: "to separate, remove, scrap." The "scrapping" can apply to cult images as a whole (e.g., the nine statues to be replaced in KUB 38.12 rev. iii 10–11, as quoted by HW^2, pp. 161–62) or in part, such as in 10.2.1.2 obv. 13′ and 15′ where only the stone was removed, or in 9.1.1 rev. iv 22′ where only the stone portion of the rim decoration (*tit(ta)li-*, see Lex. Comm. further below) was removed. The distinction of HW^2 between senses 3.3 "(Statue) aussondern" and 3.4 "(Edelmetall, -steine, Perlen etc.) (vom damit verzierten Gegenstand) entfernen, herausbrechen" seems unnecessary: in both cases the object or its components are removed from circulation, whether it be for refurbishment or recycling. In this way a technical distinction can be drawn between *arḫa išḫuwant-* 'removed (for recycling)' and *arḫa arrir(r)ant-* 'scraped away, effaced': the former is used when the disposition of the removed precious material was known (i.e., it is being recycled, and so has not left the statue production and maintenance system), whereas the latter is reserved for when the material was accidentally lost or destroyed. Compare this distinction to another lexical pair in the PTAC, *wakš-* ('absent, not presently at hand') and *wak(k)-* ('missing, no longer extant').

iššera-

One wonders if 9.1.13 5′:] 1 *iš-še-ra* UL [represents a new form of CLuw. *išš(a)ra-* 'hand', perhaps a hybrid writing influenced by Hitt. *keššar/kiššer-/kiš(ša)r-* 'hand' (note that Rieken 1999, 280 considers that the second *-e/i-* of form *kiššer-/kiššir-* "lediglich graphischen Ursprungs" while Kloekhorst 2008, 472 reconstructs an "original hysterodynamic paradigm *$\acute{g}^h$és-r, *$\acute{g}^h$s-ér-m, *$\acute{g}^h$s-r-ós, etc."). There is otherwise insufficient context to determine the meaning or even class of object of this hapax in 9.1.13.

TÚG*iškalleššar*

The neutral translation "'slitted' garment" used here follows HIT (p. 217) "slit garment" and HVP (p. 595) "geschlitztes Kleid," although as pointed out by HW^2 I *s.v.* TÚG*išk/galleššar* (p. 178): "Auf Grund seines Preises und der Verteilung an verschiedene Funktionäre (KUB 57, 71:2ff.) ist *i*[*škalleššar*] kein zerrissenes oder zerlumptes Gewand, sondern eher ein spezielles Kleidungsstück besonderer Machart (z.B. wie Spitze, Lochmuster etc.), Trageform (Art Pareo) bzw. Aussehens (z.B. Schlitzrock)."

išgapuzzi-

According to HW^2 I *s.v.* *išg/k$^?$ap(p$^?$)uzzi-* (p. 179): "Nach KUB 12, 9+ i 16f. und KUB 42, 34 Vs. 12 ist *i*[*šgapuzzi*] ein kleiner Gegenstand (3 Schekel, ca. 36–40g) aus Bronze, wegen des möglichen Zusammenhangs mit Duftöl (VSNF 12, 70 Rs. 9ff.) und mit dem Ledersack eines Wagenlenkers (KUB 42, 34 [=9.2.6] Vs. 11ff.) vielleicht mit der Körperreinigung verbunden?" It can be noted that the hypothesis of HW^2 is bolstered by the appearance of *warpuzi* (EDHIL *s.v.* *u̯arpuzi-* "object used by bathing?" [p. 965]) in KUB 12.8 obv. i 17 as the next item in the list after the *išgapuzzi*, as well as the *warpal*-object in 9.2.6 obv. i 13′, which is probably also be related to the same root *warp-* 'to wash, bathe'.

išgaratar

The multiple uses of the derivational suffix *-ātar* in Hittite have led to a variety of translations of *išgaratar* (see HW^2 *s.v.* *išgaratar* [p. 184] for literature). The suffix *-ātar* in the sense of "a designation for concretes instances of the status" (GHL §4.105, p. 127) is most promising, but the exact countable, concrete object that instantiates the piercing or boring promised by the root (*išgar-*) has not yet been identified. The attribution of gold and stone to the *išgaratar* in 9.1.10.B 4′ rules out a sense of a hole or other modification resulting in negative space on an object implied by the translation 'piercings' in HIT (p. 218). The translation "Brosche" – presumably from an etymological sense "piercer" – given in HVP (p. 595) requires the development of the abstractum formation in *-ātar* into a "nomen instrumenti," which is normally expressed by the *r*-stem suffix *-tar(a)-*. Instead, it may be suggested here that based on the association with GÚ.ḪAL 'neck piece' in 11.3.2 r. c. 2′, 3′, 6′ (e.g., r. c. 3′: 1-*NU* GÚ.ḪAL KÙ.SI$_{22}$ 8 *iš-ga-r*[*a-tar*), that the *išgaratar* was, at least in some instances, a necklace component. Since the participle *išgarant-* 'pierced, bored' often describes objects attached to necklaces and bracelets (8.1.A obv. i 7′–8′; 9.2.4 obv. i 7′–8′), including beads (9.2.2 rev.[!] iii 12′: NUNUZ KÙ.SI$_{22}$ NA$_4$ *iš-ga-ra-a-an* 'bead(s) of gold and stone, pierced'; 11.3.1 12′: ^{NA_4}NUNUZ-*ia išgarānta* 'pierced beads'), the *išgaratar* was perhaps a type of bead or pendant, i.e., a thing that was defined by its being bored through, and hence able to be strung on a necklace or bracelet.

kallaratar

See main discussion under DIRI.

$^{(TÚG)}$*kalup(p)a-*

See HW^2 K *s.v.* $^{(TÚG)}$*kalup(p)a-*, $^{(TÚG)}$*galup(p)a-* 'ein Kleidungstück für Frauen' (p. 47). The older translation of HW Erg. 1 *s.v.* ^{TÚG}*kaluppa-* (p. 355) "'Unterkleid' (inneres Kleidungstück der Frauen)," which has been repeated in various forms (HED IV *s.v. kaluppa-* "'petticoat' (vel sim.)" [p. 32]; HIT, p. 219 "(female) undergarment, vest"; HVP, p. 597 "ein Kleidungstück, 'Unterkleid'$^{(?)}$"), goes back to a comment by Goetze (1955, 61), who based on their positions in stereotyped lists of men's and women's clothing, saw a connection between the female *kariulli-* and *kalup(p)a*-garments on the one hand, and their ostensible male counterparts, the ^{TÚG}GÚ.È.A and ^{TÚG}GÚ.È.A *ḪUR-RI*, on the other. For the *kariulli*-garment Goetze proposed "a garment which drapes the head of women and covers their whole figure to the feet" (p. 61). The meaning "hood" is secured by the use of the verb *šai-/ši(ya)-* for donning the garment, though ascribing floor-length to the covering rests only on Goetze's suggestion that women's cloaks depicted on the reliefs at Carchemish were *kariulli*-garments (*loc. cit.*). With the *kariulli-* being the outer garment, Goetze then considered that the *kalup(p)a-* "may be the inner garment worn underneath the *kariulli-*, presumably the one in which women would appear while at home and among themselves" (*loc. cit.*). Three pieces of evidence from the PTAC modify, at the very least, Goetze's description. First, the *kalup(p)a-* had a specific metal attachment, the *kalupašša/i-* (HIT, p. 219 "toggle(?)"; HVP, p. 597 "zum *kalupa*-Kleid gehörige Nadel"), which was presumably used to fasten the garment. Second, the *kalup(p)a-* itself could be modified with gold (see 8.4 rev. 17′; 9.1.1 rev. iii 39′), indicating they were meant for display. Third, the *kalup(p)a-* is attested in the PTAC not with the *kariulli-* hood, but rather with the *lupanni-* (see e.g., 2.7.A obv. 9; 11.6.4 obv. 7′–8′), a covering that is suspected to be only shoulder- or back-length. Taken together, the presence of precious metal fasteners, precious metal appliqués, and the association with less-than-body-length hoods suggest that the *kalup(p)a*-garment was, at a minimum, not the most intimate or innermost garment of the female wardrobe, but rather a normal, everyday dress that was meant to be seen, and which could be supplemented, as needed, by an outer coat or mantle.

kalup(p)ašša/i-

A Luwian adjectival genitive form of $^{(TÚG)}$*kalup(p)a-*. The identification of the *kalup(p)ašša/i-* as fastener goes back to Košak 1978, 114: "kalupašši-, genitival adj. of kaluppa- 'undergarment, vest', made of gold; perhaps a toggle or a similar device to keep the garment in place?" Given the complete absence of toggle-pins at Boğazköy in the Hittite period (Andreas Schachner, Suzanne Herbordt, pers. comm.), another type of fastener must be supposed. Although the “zum *kalupa*-Kleid gehörige Nadel” of HVP (p. 597) is one such possibility, it seems that the *kalup(p)ašša/i*- was apparently made of more than one component: as was noted by HIT (pp. 150, 156), the *kalup(p)ašša/i*- appears in frequent combination with *lalini*- or its possessive construction *lalin(n)aim(m)a/i*-. Unfortunately, the meanings of *lalini*- and *lalin(n)aim(m)a/i*- are also uncertain – though *Lexical Commentary, s.v.* (𒑱)*lalini*- below for a suggested interpretation “tonguelet.”

kanduna-

The *kanduna*- has thus far escaped inclusion in the dictionaries. However, contra HVP (pp. 490, 491 fn. 4) “GÁN.DU.NA,” there is no reason to consider the word a Sumerogram (which would have no recognizable meaning). Based on context of 2.17 obv.[?] r. c. 10′–13′, the *kanduna*- designates a component or decoration of a bow. Whether *kanduna*- is Hittite or from another ancient Near Eastern language cannot be determined, though the latter is favored since weapon terminology, like other traded goods and technology, could be notoriously international.

(TÚG)*kaparzu*-

Although HED IV *s.v. kapartas(s)amna-, kapittas(s)amna-, kapitasamna-* (p. 60–61) suggested that “*kaparzu* … has the looks of actual ‘short form’ for **kapartsamna*- …,” the appearance of the two garments within two lines of each other in 8.8.A 3′–5′//8.8.B l. c. 3′–6′ and the unexplained *u*-stem argue against this.

(NA4)*kabši*-

The form ⌜NA4⌝*kab-ši-iš* in 9.2.4 obv. i 4′ should probably be interpreted here as another Hittite *i*-stem borrowing, in this case from NA4*KIBŠU*. The different vocalization of *kab*- vs. *kib*- may be explained as a variant pronunciation of the name of the stone, or simply as another example of an unstable middle vowel in the Hittite use of CVC signs (GHL §1.20, p. 18). Cf. earlier readings NA4 KAB-*ši-iš* in HVP (p. 470, fn. 1: “evtl. (LÚ)KAB.SAR, ‘Graveur’ … zu vergleichen?”; p. 656: “KAB ‘graviert’(?)”), and HIT (p. 57) NA4SÁD-*ši-iš*.

(GIŠ)*karnaš(š)a*-

The semantics of the (GIŠ)*karnaš(š)a*- are fairly straightforward, the item being another of the many varieties of Hittite chairs and seats (Soysal 2016, 424). The earlier suggestion of HED IV *s.v. karnasa-/karnasi-* (p. 91): “a wooden base for setting down (and drawing along?) heavy objects …” relies on a misinterpretation of 4.2.9 rev. 5′, where the GAM-*an* SUD-*uaš* modifies not the *karnaššaš*, but represents rather what is almost certainly a linen or cloth name lost in the break at the beginning of the line. Dispensing with the attestation from 4.2.9 leaves the sense “tray, wooden base” unsupported, since it is quite possible to lay a variety of symbolic objects on a chair in a ritual context, suggesting that the translation “Schemel, Holzsockel” in HW^2 K *s.v.* GIŠ*karnaš(š)a(/i)-*, GIŠ*karna*- [p. 167] can thus be reduced to just the first: “Schemel.”

As for the stem and gender of the word, Klinger 1996, 448 presented evidence for both *a*-stem and *i*-stem attestations. The *i*-stem attestation may now be discarded, since his citation of GIŠ*karnaši* in KUB 42.96 (= 4.1.4.9) obv. 3 as sg. nom.-acc. n. is better interpreted as a Hittite sg. dat./loc. based on the *A-NA* 2 ^{GIŠ}ŠÚ.A in the following line (4.1.4.9 obv. 3: 2 ^{GIŠ}*karnaši karū* 1 TÚG *iškallanzi* "they have already slit 1 cloth for two *karnaš(š)a*-chairs," vs. obv. 4–5 "*A-NA* 2 ^{GIŠ}ŠÚ.A *karū* [5] 1 ^{TÚG}GUZ("SIG$_4$").ZA *iškallanzi* "they have already slit 1 *guzza*-cloth for two chairs"). This leaves the lemma without a clear attestation of an *i*-stem or *i*-mutation (despite the choice of lemma names, only *a*-stems are presented in HW^2 K *s.v.* ^{GIŠ}*karnaš(š)a(/i)-*, ^{GIŠ}*karna-* [p. 167]). In addition, the examples of *karnaš(š)a* in 4.2.9 rev. 6′, 7′ (and KBo 55.133 rev.$^?$ 10′) should not be interpreted with HW^2 K (p. 167) as Luw. pl. nom.-acc. n., but taken instead as common gender collective plurals in *-a*: cf. ^{GIŠ}*šarpa-*, a type of cross-legged chair or stool (CHD Š *s.v.* $^{(GIŠ/KUŠ)}$*šarpa-* A [p. 287]), for another example of a common gender sitting implement with collective plural in *-a*. Without *i*-mutation or Luwian declension patterns, there is little evidence to support the supposition offered in HW^2 K (p. 168) that *karnaš(š)a-* contained a Luwian adjectival suffix *-ašša/i-*.

^{TÚG}*karupalani-*

Although thus far attested only in two texts (6.10 and almost certainly 10.1.2.6, unless another garment beginning in "*karu-*" is discovered), the ^{TÚG}*karupalani-* exhibits a seemingly transparent morphology of TÚG plus *karupa-* 'granary, storehouse' (a loanword from Hurrian that is also found in Hittite as the basis of *karupaḫi-* 'storehouse'), the *-ala-* nomen actoris suffix, and *-n-* infix before the *i*-stem: thus "garment of the granary-/storehouse-workers." The morphology of *karupalani-* is thus very similar to *TUPPALANURU*/*tuppalanura/i-* 'chief of the storehouse-workers/administrators' (van den Hout 2010a, 266–67; against earlier 'chief of scribes'). However, the analysis of *TUPPALANURU*/*tuppalanuri-* as a compound word *tuppalan* 'of the administrators' (Hitt. pl. gen.) + *ura/i-* 'great' (Giorgieri – Mora 2012, 651–52) is not be possible for *karupalani-*. Instead, a suffix chain of *-ala-* + *-ann(i)-* seems more probable, although the non-geminate writing of *-ann(i)-* is problematic, and perhaps defective in 6.10 7′ (Elisabeth Rieken, pers. comm.).

gaši-

Per HED IV *s.v.* *kasi-* (p. 119) and HW^2 K *s.v.* *kaši-* (p. 244), *gaši-* is a shade of white. The suggestion of HED IV that *gaši-* represented "off-white" (p. 120) in contrast to *ašara-* 'bright white', is made even more attractive when it is considered that only the latter, more visually salient shade of white is used to form a denominative verb, *ašariya-* 'to whiten'.

$^{(GADA)}$*gaz(z)arnul-*

See Rieken 1999, 467: "Tuch zum Abtrocken$^?$" based on etymological reconstruction. Despite phonological doubts in EDHIL *s.v.* ^{GADA}*kazzarnul-* (p. 466), the use of the cloth in the Hittite Funerary Ritual to clean the bones of the deceased (see HED IV *s.v.* *kaz(z)arnul-* [p. 141] for citations), together with its appearance among other dining and washing cloths in the PTAC in 6.5 rev. 21′, supports the interpretation of Rieken. Other attestations in PTAC clarify that the cloth must have been very small or very compactable given the collection of at least 108 *gazzarnul*-cloths, plus other garments, into a single chest (see 9.2.9 rev.$^?$ 4′), as well the comparatively high number, 10, compared to the single cloths in 6.5 rev. 21′–22′. The $^{(GADA)}$*gaz(z)arnul* will thus be translated here as a 'drying swatch' to emphasize its small size.

kiklibaim(m)a/i-

See Starke 1990, 421–24 for discussion of the word group **kiklubaššar-* 'Eisen', *kiklubaššari-* (RS 25.421 obv. iv 22′) 'eisern', and *kiklibaim(m)a/i-*, which he defined as "möglicherweise eine bestimmte Technik der Metallbearbeitung" (p. 423), from an etymon **kikli/uba-* of questionable origins (see Starke 1990, 423 fn. 1528 for discussion of interchanging vowel; see also Richter 2012, 201 for literature on possible attestation in Hurrian PN ^{m}*Kiklib-adalli*). Puhvel 1996, 64–65 posited an areal connection with Gk. *χάλυβος/χάλυψ* 'steel'; see further HED IV *s.v. kikluba-, kikliba-* "inferentially 'iron, steel'" (p. 174). The earlier proposal of Melchert 1983, 139–41 to derive *kiklibaššari-* from an Indo-European root **kiklu-* 'iron' in compound with *paššari-* 'ring' required an emendation of 9.1.1 rev. iv 26′ to *ki-ik-li-ma*!*-i-me-en-zi* 'plated with iron' (pp. 140–41). HVP (p. 448) followed Melchert in reading *kiklimaimenzi*, but without translation. The earlier interpretation of Košak 1978, 110 of *kiklimai-* 'fashioned in a leaf shape', related to *kikla-* 'leaf(?)' can be discarded. With the suggestion now that AN.BAR (GE_6), **parza-*, and *ḫapalki-* might all have referred to iron ore (see respective entries in the present *Lexical Commentary*) based on their impossibly high frequency and technical applications vis-à-vis the archaeological record, the rare **kikli/uba-* is left as the best current lexical candidate for metallic iron.

kikpaniš

Per KBo 71, viii (Nr. 46): "[4.1.1.5 obv. 3] klärt den lexikalischen Ansatz der in *HHw* 87 als *kikpani-* oder *ikpani-* angesetzten Bezeichnung eines Metallgegenstands (wohl eines Gefäßes), der bislang nur in [1.2 rev. 8′] belegt war; das Wort lautet sicher auf *k*- an und ist wohl ein neutraler *s*-Stamm ...." The presence now of the *kikpani-* among other vessels in 4.1.1.5 obv. 2–3 suggests that it is also a container or vessel of some sort.

kinant-

Morphologically *kinantaš* is a participle in sg. gen. from *kinae-* 'to (as)sort'; thus "(thing) of assorting = assortment." HVP (p. 83) translated *kinantaš* as "(Kleider)kollektion" in the context of 2.7.A obv. 21, 22, and suggested (*loc. cit.* fn. 13) a meaning of "Ausgesuchte, ausgewählte Kleider, vielleicht im Sinne einer kompletten, untereinander abgestimmten Garderobe, so wie man ihr in Kleiderverzeichnissen ... begegnet." See also HIT (p. 9) "assorted, choice," with earlier literature. The sense 'choice' (perhaps an adverbial formation in sg. gen., like TUŠ-*aš*, Elisabeth Rieken, pers. comm.) works well for the other attestations of *kinantaš* in the PTAC: In 8.1.A rev. v 14′//8.1.D obv i 11′, a chest containing a small collection of *iron (ore)* implements described as *kinantaš* follows a larger chest of *iron (ore)* implements without this designation (8.1.A rev. v 1–9). It can be inferred that the smaller collection was specially selected, either for its coherence as a group or its excellence. Note that this interpretation is contra Siegelová 1984, 160, where the *kīnān*-[in 8.1.D obv i 11′ is taken to refer to a preliminary stage of metallurgical preparation, i.e., the sorting of the iron ore (HVP, 405 fn. 16: "(mit) sortiertem Meteoreisen"). Questions of the metallurgy of AN.BAR GE_6 aside (see *Lexical Commentary, s.v.* AN.BAR (GE_6)), there is no reason to supposed that 'sorted, choice' meant anything different in the context of implements and garments.

(𒑱)*kinzalpa-*

See now Busse, eDiAna, *s.v. kinzalpa-* (= lemma 1002) and *ead.*, eDiana, *s.v.* 𒑱?*kinzalpašša/i-*. The question mark after the *Glossenkeil* 𒑱? in the eDiAna entry represents only the uncertainty that the lemma is actually a "gloss word" based on the observation (Košak 1978, 107) that the form 𒑱*kinzalpaššiš* (9.1.1 rev. iii 5′) is the only word in the Inventory of Manninni marked with a *Glossenkeil*; the presence of the wedge in text is paleographically uncontested.

(NA₄)(𒑱)*kirinni-*

Previously misidentified as an Akkadogram, see HED IV *s.v. girenni-, kirinni-* (p. 188) for citations of fully inflected Hittite forms. The appearance of sg. acc. *ki-ri-in-ni-in* (KUB 34.71 obv. i 35) in contrast to *ki-ri-in-na* (8.4 rev. 8′) and 𒑱*ki-ri-in-na* (1.5 obv. 7) suggest the latter two forms should be considered common gender collective plurals in *-a*. To the bibliography of interpretations found in HED IV (p. 189) may be added Schuster-Brandis 2008, 414, where the GUG *gi-rin-na* is translated "*girinnu*-(Frucht)-Karneol," after an apparently red fruit or berry.

kukupalla(nt?)-

Previous lexical discussions of this vessel were based on the incomplete edition of Rost 1961–63, 199, which preserves only DUG*ku-ku-pa-al-l*[*a-* (10.1.1.1 obv.? 11′). Thus, HEG A–K *s.v.* DUG*kukupalla-* (p. 618), HED IV *s.v. kukupalla-* (p. 234) and all discussions dependent on these dictionaries have assumed an *a*-stem for the word. However, the very next line, 10.1.1.1 obv.? 12′, preserves a full DUG*ku-ku-pa-al-la-an*. A sg. acc. would be highly unusual in the context of a list, suggesting the word might have instead been an *nt*-stem. An *-alla/i-* derivation from with Akk. *ku(k)ku(b)bu* and Sum. dugḫab.ḫab remains probable.

gul(aš)šant-

The Hittite reading *gul(aš)šant-*, particple of a verb *gul(aš)ša-* 'to engrave, inscribe, mark, draw', as opposed to a Sumerographic reading GUL-*š-* follows Yakubovich 2013–14 and Melchert 2016 against Waal 2014 and Waal 2019. However, as noted by van den Hout 2020a, 197, the exact reading of the word has little effect on its meaning, so a future decisive argument one way or the other should not change the understanding of the texts much (note, however, that the specific meaning of 'to write in hieroglyphics' proposed by Waal 2014 should probably be rejected). The translations of GUL-*aššan* in HIT (p. 6) "jotted down" and HVP (p. 81) "notiert" are semantically attractive for implying a brevity of contents, but are perhaps too interpretive. *gul(aš)šant-* will instead be translated here as "marked down," with "down" included only for ease of reading in English, and not reflecting directional or local sense in the Hittite.

kurupšini-

With HED IV *s.v. kurupsini, kurupzina* (p. 279), this lemma has previously been interpreted as either a shape or type of theriomorphic rhyton or, based on the Old Assyrian lexeme *kupuršinnum/kuruš⟨p⟩inam* (a designation of gold) from Kaneš, a quality of metal. The Hittite passages previously cited in discussions of the term have been ambiguous, although the existence of the $^{LÚ.MEŠ}$*kurupzina* (HED IV, *loc. cit.*) points towards an animal name, since animal imitators are well attested in Hittite sources and since a place name *^{URU}*kurupzina* is non-existent (Schwemer 2005/2006, 222 fn. 24). The previously unrecognized attestations of the word in 2.2 rev. 6 and 10.1.2.5 3′, where the *kurupšini-* appear among other theriomorphic rhyta depicting beasts and monsters, add additional evidence that the term designated, in Hittite times, a particular terrestrial predator which stood on four feet (2.2 rev 6: *kur*]*upšiniš* KÙ.BABBAR 4 *aranteš*).

$^{(TÚG)}$***kuššati-***

Two points must be made about this garment. First, contra previous editions, $^{(TÚG)}$*kuššati-* is probably a Hurrian-mediated loanword from Akk. ^{TÚG}*KUŠŠATU* (see GHL §4.16, p. 86 for other examples of Hurrian loanwords in *-i-*; see also ^{TÚG}*atupli(t)-*), and thus should not be treated as an Akkadogram (which would be everywhere in sg. gen.!), but as a Hittite *i*-stem. Second, if $^{(TÚG)}$*kuššati-* is not an Akkadogram, then the original suggestion of Goetze (1956, 36 fn. 2) that the "^{TÚG}*KU-UŠ-ŠA-DI*" represented the plural form of "^{TÚG}*KUŠIŠI*," the allegedly Anatolian version of ^{túg}*kusītu* (see objection to this equation in *Lexical Commentary, s.v.* $^{(TÚG)}$*kušiši-* below), does not work. This is in addition to the fact that, as Veenhof 1972, 162–63 demonstrated, the Akkadian garments are independent, since ^{túg}*kusītu* and ^{túg}*kuššatu* (written *kuš(š)utum* due to expected Old Assyrian vowel harmony) are already attested simultaneously in the Kaniš *kārum* texts, with attestations from OB Mari providing further evidence for the independent existence of a ^{túg}*kuššatu*-garment (Veenhof 1972, 163; now Durand 2009, 54 with complete list).

Unfortunately, little can be said about the nature of the Hitt. $^{(TÚG)}$*kuššati-*/Akk. ^{túg}*kuššatu-* garment. On the one hand, Durand (2009, 55) suggested that the *kuššatu* designated a garment shape, and not a fabric, since a form *^{gú}*kuššatum* is not attested at Mari. On the other hand, examples from Ḫattuša in which the *kuššati* must designate a type of cloth or construction, such as ^{TÚG}*i*]*šgalleššar kušš*[*ati* (4.2.7 5′), [4 ^{T}]^{ÚG}GÚ ŠÀ.BA 2 *kišama* 2 *kuššati* (11.6.5 obv.$^{?}$ 6′), and ^{TÚG}GÚ *kuššati* (11.6.7 5′), abound.

$^{(TÚG)}$***kušiši-***

Since Goetze's original discussions of the term (1947, 177–79; 1955, 51, 57), three facts have generally been accepted concerning the ^{TÚG}*kušiši-*: that it is a royal or priestly garb, that it is a borrowing from Akkadian ^{TÚG}*kusītu*, and that its Sumerographic equivalent is ^{TÚG}BAR.DUL$_5$/"TE". Of these, only the first holds up to scrutiny: the ^{TÚG}*kušiši-* is indeed a priestly garb, and is intimately associated with Hittite kingship. The list of attestations provided by Goetze 1947, 177 remains sufficient demonstration of the kingly nature of the garment. Whether the ^{TÚG}*kušiši-* was worn "only by kings" (Goetze 1955, 51; p. 57 also "gods, kings, and priests"; *id.* 1947, 179 "both queen and king") is still to be proved, but a mundane usage of the garment has yet to be discovered. In KUB 17.21+ obv. ii 15′–16′, a passage from a prayer of Arnuwanda I and Ašmunikkal (CTH 375.1.A) concerning the depredations of the Kaška, TÚG.GÚ.È.A *kušišiyaš* 'shirt(s) of *kušiši*-(fabric)' are listed among the fine garments and divine symbols plundered from the Sun-goddess of Arinna. This could indicate a somewhat wider distribution of the ^{TÚG}*kušiši*-, but extending its use to include the high priests of the Hittite Kingdom does not much affect Goetze's original assessment.

For the second point, that of the word's borrowing from Akkadian, despite the mostly uncritical repetition in the dictionaries (HEG A-K *s.v.* $^{(\text{TÚG})}$*kušiši*- [p. 674] with previous literature; also HED IV *s.v. kusisi*- [p. 295]; CAD K *s.v. kusītu* [p. 585]; AHw *s.v. kusītu(m)* [p. 514]), Goetze's suggestion to derive *kušiši*- from *kusītu* (Old Assyrian *kušītu*) is impossible in the current understanding of Hittite historical phonology. Goetze proposed an original *i*-stem borrowing **kušiti* in Hittite, which he supposed "should, with the customary assibilation, almost automatically yield **kušizi*-," with assimilation thence from **kušizi*- to *kušiši*- (1947, 179). While Goetze was correct that historic *V*ti* yielded V*zi* (/t^{s}i/) in Hittite (GHL §1.90, p. 37), this process occurred at a much earlier period, in the transition from Proto-Anatolian to Proto-Hittite (see Table 2 in Kloekhorst 2020, 168). There are no known Akkadian loanwords in Hittite that show this sound change (see list in Schwemer 2005/2006; including assessment [p. 226] that ^{TÚG}*kušiši*- < ^{TÚG}*kusītu* "bleibt nach wie vor fraglich"). The existence of other loanwords preserving Akkadian -V*ti*, including $^{(\text{TÚG})}$*kuššati*- (see *Lexical Commentary, s.v.* $^{(\text{TÚG})}$*kuššati*- above), prove that assibilation did not occur "automatically." Conversely, all loanwords from Hittite into Old Assyrian already demonstrate V*zi* from historical *V*ti*: e.g., *išpuruzzinnum*, *luḫuzzinnum*, **ekuzzinnum* (Dercksen 2007, 34–35), and *tuzzinnum* (Dercksen 2004, 147–50; Giusfredi 2020), all of which demonstrate the Hittite instrumental suffix -*uzzi*- from PA *-*uti*- (from *-*u*- + *-*ti*-, Melchert 1984, 166; *id.* 1994, 97, 188; *id.* 1999c, 368; EDHIL *s.v. tuzzi*- [p. 905]; cf. Benveniste 1962, 105–6; Kronasser 1966, 240–41 for doubts of IE origins, but without contesting a PA preform *-*uti*-). Thus, a borrowing of $^{(\text{TÚG})}$*kušiši*- from Akkadian ^{túg}*kusītu* seems impossible.

Goetze's third point, that Hitt. $^{(\text{TÚG})}$*kušiši*- = ^{TÚG}BAR.DUL/DUL$_5$/"TE" via Akk. ^{TÚG}*kusītu* is made *a priori* unlikely if $^{(\text{TÚG})}$*kušiši*- cannot be derived from Akk. ^{TÚG}*kusītu*. As for a direct equation of ^{TÚG}BAR.DUL$_5$/"TE" and $^{(\text{TÚG})}$*kušiši*-, there are three points against this. First, there are no direct substitutions of the terms. Bacelli et al. 2014, 122 offered the "strange form ^{TÚG}*kušiši*(-)DUL quoted in a Hittite palace inventory" as proof of $^{(\text{TÚG})}$*kušiši*- = ^{TÚG}BAR.DUL/DUL$_5$/"TE" (= ^{TÚG}*kusītu*), but this form does not seem to actually exist (although Bacelli et al. did not give a citation for the inventory text in question, it can be deduced from their further description that they refer to 4.1.1.1.A$_1$ obv. 9′; however, as discussed in the Phil. Comm. to this line, the reading DUL is impossible based on the preserved sign traces). Second, the ^{TÚG}BAR.DUL$_5$/"TE" in Hittite sources seems to be a mundane cloak or mantel, by no means restricted the king and priests: cf. 4.2.6 and 4.2.9 where ^{TÚG}BAR.DUL$_5$/"TE" are among the possessions divvied up among non-royal individuals. The mundane nature of the ^{TÚG}BAR.DUL$_5$/"TE" is confirmed in the texts of the PTAC, where the ^{TÚG}BAR."TE" is most often listed, in rough order of frequency, with $^{(\text{TÚG})}$GAD.DAM 'gaiters, leggings(?)', $^{(\text{TÚG/GADA})}$GÚ(.È.A) 'shirt', $^{(\text{TÚG})}$E.ÍB 'belt', and $^{(\text{TÚG})}$SAG.DUL '(a head covering)'. With Bacelli et al. 2014, 122, it may be seen that these form a mostly complete outfit (though contra Bacelli et al. 2014, *loc. cit.*, the ^{TÚG}BAR."TE" is *not* "almost always listed together with shoes ... ;" in fact, ^{TÚG}BAR."TE" and $^{\text{(KUŠ)}}$E.SIR co-occur in only a single PTAC text, 4.2.6, and then on opposite ends of the tablet: ^{TÚG}BAR."TE" in obv.$^{?}$ 10′, 13′, $^{\text{(KUŠ)}}$E.SIR in rev.$^{?}$ 7′). However, the cloak, gaiters, shirt, belt, and non-*lupanni*- head-covering do not necessarily evince the Hittite priestly outfit as it is described in texts or depicted on reliefs.

The explanation of Durand (2009, 55) deriving Hittite $^{\text{(TÚG)}}$*kušiši*- as a borrowing from a form of Akkadian ^{túg}*kuššatu* "sans la désinence féminine" (so presumably **kuššu* > **kušišu*) seems unlikely.

Concerning the distribution of the $^{\text{(TÚG)}}$*kušiši*- in the PTAC, the statement of Bacelli et al. 2014, 123 that the $^{\text{(TÚG)}}$*kušiši*- "is always listed together with other festive-garments (TÚG NÍG.LÁM^{MEŠ}) like head-bands (*lupan*(*n*)*i*-) and *kureššar*" is only partly true. Although 8.1.D rev. iv 1′//8.1.H rev. r. c. 1′ records $^{\text{(TÚG)}}$*kušiši*-s in a chest labeled ^{TÚG}NÍG.LÁM^{MEŠ} MUNUS.LUGAL (8.1.E(A_1) rev. v 6′), the contents of the chest are not otherwise recognizable as ceremonial or royal, suggesting that a translation "splendid garments of the queen" rather than "festive/ceremonial garments ..." is appropriate here. Moreover, contra Bacelli et al., there seem to be no actual attestations of the $^{\text{(TÚG)}}$*kušiši*- appearing with the *lupan(n)i*- or *kureššar*. The $^{\text{(TÚG)}}$*kušiši*- appears instead in the PTAC with a completely different set of items, most prominently the ^{TÚG}*kuššadi*- (8.1.D rev. iv 1′; 11.6.1 7: 6.5 rev. 16′). In 6.5, two passages reveal the *kušiši*- could also be a type or style of cloth. In 6.5 rev. 10′–11′ one finds the sequence: 4 TÚG SIG 1 *ḪAŠMANNI* 1 *ŠUḪR*[*U* 1 ...] $^{11′}$ 1 *kušiši* "4 fine cloths (among which) 1 red-purple, 1 dark-brow[n, 1 ...], 1 *kušiši*-," and in 6.5 rev. 16′: 5 TÚG ŠÀ.BA 1 GADA *ŠUḪRU* 1 *tapašpa* 2 *kuššadi* 1 *kuši*[*ši* "5 cloths, among which 1 is dark-brown linen, 1 (in the) Tapašpan(-fashion), 2 *kuššadi*-, (and) 1 *kuši*[*ši*-." It is possible that these passages from 6.5 confirm Goetze's original interpretation (1947, 179) that the $^{\text{(TÚG)}}$*kušiši*- was a type of "gown," rather than a close-cut garment, but definitive evidence of the garment's style and construction remains wanting.

$^{\text{(GADA/TÚG)}}$*lakkušanzani*-

A cloth closely associated with beds (with beds in 4.2.9 rev. 1′, 9′, 23′; 8.1.F rev. v 15; 9.1.10.A_1 obv. 8′//9.1.10.B 12′; 11.1.3 8′; 11.1.4 5′ – only 9.1.10.A_2 rev. 10′ and the broken 10.3.14 l. c. 9′ without), the $^{\text{(GADA/TÚG)}}$*lakkušanzani*- are attested both as single items, e.g., sg. nom. 1 ^{TÚG}*lakkušanzaniš* (4.2.9 rev. 23′), and as sets, e.g., pl. acc. 1-*NU* ^{GADA}*lakkušanzaniuš* (10.3.14 l. c. 9′). The assertion of Vigo 2010, 297 that "the most viable hypothesis is that the expression $^{\text{TÚG/GADA}}$*lakkušanzani*- refers to a canopy" is difficult to sustain. The translation "canopy" goes back to a suggestion by HIT (p. 17), where it was noted that while the $^{\text{(GAD/TÚG)}}$*lakkušanzani*- is most obviously interpreted as 'sheets', "because they also come in sets, the meaning 'canopy' can be considered." The reasoning here is opaque, since there seems to be no special reason why canopies should be counted in sets, nor why sheets could not be counted so. At the very least, no new evidence has been discovered in favor of a meaning 'canopy' for $^{\text{(GADA/TÚG)}}$*lakkušanzani*-, leaving 'bed sheet(s), bed clothes' as the most likely option.

lalami-

With CHD L–N *s.v.* (:)*lalami-* (p. 26), this term refers to an itemized list (see also Billing, eDiAna, *s.v.* 𒑱*lalam(i)-* [= lemma 2562] for etymology, derivation, and bibliography of interpretations), especially in the context of a sealed receipt that indicates a legitimate transfer of possessions from an institution to an individual (HVP, 98–99; see also citations in CHD L–N, *loc. cit.*, of KUB 13.35 obv. i 1–6; rev. iv 35–40, etc.). The presence of *lalami-* in 4.1.1.1.A_1 obv. 4′, 14′, 16′, 18′ immediately before instructions for the processing of the contents of the chests is enticing, but possibly coincidental (see *Commentary* to 4.1.1.1 4, 14, 16, 18), since there is no other evidence that *lalami*-receipts also noted, e.g., the purpose of or conditions attached to the transfer of items, or indeed anything beyond the items and (presumably) the recipient.

lalin(n)aim(m)a/i-

See main discussion under (𒑱)*lalini-* below. Note that though the adjective *lalin(n)aim(m)a/i-* 'set/endowed with a *lalini-*' most often modifies *kalup(p)ašša/i-* (perhaps a kind of fastener; see *Lexical Commentary* above), it is also attested with a SAG.DU.KI 'frontlet' in 9.1.1 rev. iv 44′.

(𒑱)*lalini-*

While appearing more often in a denominal possessive stem *lalin(n)aim(m)a/i-* modifying the *kalup(p)ašša/i*-fastener, the (𒑱)*lalini-* is also sometimes described as a separate object appearing next to the *kalup(p)ašša/i-* (1.5 obv. 6; 8.4 rev. 6′). If *kalup(p)ašša/i-* was a kind of fastener, then one could speculate, based on the superficial similarity to the Anatolian lexeme *lala-* 'tongue', that the *lalini-* was a subcomponent in the form of a "tonguelet."

Note that the alleged root **lalinit-* was based on the previous readings of 8.4 rev. 6′ as *la-li-ni-tạ*! (Starke 1990, 208) or *la-li-ni-*[*š*]*a*(?) (CLL *s.v.* *lalinit-* [p. 123]) instead of the correct *la-li-ni* ^{*NA_4*} (see *Commentary* to 8.4 rev. 6′). An original *i*-stem, as opposed to an *i(t)*-stem, is further supported by the fact that the denominal form *lalin(n)-aim(m)a/i-* shows no evidence of an intrusive *-t-*, in contrast to, e.g., *penki(t)-*, *penkitaim(m)a/i-*. Note also that the comment of Starke 1990, 208 that the *lalini-* formed "ein eventuell Bestandteil des *kalupašša(/i)*-Gewandes" is based on a misreading of 1-*š*]U? *galupaššiš* in 1.5 obv. 6 as TÚ]G*galupaššiš*, presumably following the identically mistaken transliteration of CHD L–N *s.v.* (:)*lalin(n)aimi-* (p. 28). As discussed in the *Lexical Commentary, s.v. kalup(p)ašša/i-*, the *kalup(p)ašša/i-* designates an accessory to the *kalup(p)a*-garment, not the garment itself.

lammam(m)a/i-

CHD L–N *s.v.* *lammami-* (p. 30) offered only "(an object made of precious metal)," whereas Starke 1990, 423 fn. 1524 considered the form to be a Luw. participle meaning 'soldered', based on etymological connection with a putative Hittite **lam-* 'to be mixed together' (CHD L–N *s.v.* [*lam-*] [p. 30] and HED V *s.v.* *lam-* [p. 50] do not recognize existence of this verb). The paucity of attestations does not allow for a closer definition, but the spellings and distribution of the term in the PTAC is at least not inconsistent with Starke's interpretation as an Luwian adjectival participle.

lapattašši-

There is no existing commentary on this hapax legomenon appearing among a list of equipment belonging to the temple of the town of Alatarma. Although an etymological connection with Hittite *lappa-* 'tong(?)' is attractive, it would require emendation to geminate *-pp-*, which is improbably given the presense of 𒑱*lapiya-* in the previous line of the same text.

𒑱*lapiya-*

Another hapax legomenon, to be connected with *lapattašši-* of the same text.

lup/wan(n)i-

The core meaning of the *lup/wan(n)i-* lexeme seems to have simply been "cap," i.e., anything that covered the top or terminating point of an object or person. As a garment, the $^{\text{(TÚG/GADA)}}$*lup/wan(n)i-* was probably the close-fitting skullcap found in the many depictions of the Hittite king as priest (see *Lexical Commentary, s.v.* $^{\text{(TÚG/GADA)}}$*lup/wan(n)i-* below). As an object, the *lup/wan(n)i-* is found most often as a component of a knife – the "cap" likely being equivalent to or a type of pommel (SAG.DU) – but also once seeming to occur as part of a rhyton (9.1.15 6′). Note that the argument in Vigo 2010, 308–9, that the appearances of EME, GABA, and *lupanni-* together in, e.g., 9.1.1 rev. iii 8′, 9′, 10′, 12′, refer to metal headbands that were apparently sometimes attached to the *lupan(n)i*-cap relies on a loose interpretation of syntax in the cited attestations and is unfortunately incorrect (cf. 9.1.1 rev. iii 13′ for the unambiguous 1-*EN šikkiš* AN.BAR GE$_6$ GABA *lupanneš* $^{\text{NA}_4}$Z[A.GÌN "1 *šikki(š)-knife* of black *iron (ore)*, the guard (and) pommel of lapis l[azuli"). Rather, reverting to the earlier interpretations of HVP (p. 443), CHD L–N *s.v.* $^{\text{(TÚG/GADA)}}$*lupan(n)i-, luwanni* 2. (p. 86), and HED V *s.v. lupan(n)i-, luwanni-* (p. 119), the EME 'tongues' in the contexts cited are the knife blades, the GABA 'fronts' or 'breasts' are the guards, and the *lup/wan(n)i-* 'caps' are the pommels or handle caps.

$^{\text{(TÚG/GADA)}}$*lup/wan(n)i-*

See Vigo 2010, 303–14 for disussion with previous literature. The $^{\text{(TÚG/GADA)}}$*lup/wan(n)i-* is identifiable as a cloth headdress for both sexes, possibly the same as the 'priest's cap' depicted on Hittite rock reliefs and seals, that was associated with members of the nobility and especially the king and queen.

malwi-

The direct join now of KUB 42.81+ with Col. Univ. Lib. (see 2.17) confirms that the lemma is *malwi-* and not *alwi-*; cf. discussion of CHD L–N *s.v. malwiš* (p. 137). Unfortunately, the join does not elucidate the meaning of the word, other than demonstrating that in both instances the *malwi*-objects appear grouped with *uraki(t)-* 'rods, wires' of the same material at a ratio of approximately one *malwi-* to two *uraki(t)-*.

mannaiya/i-

Melchert (forth.) suggests a meaning “bulging” for *mannaiya/i-*. Cf. earlier CHD L–N *s.v. mannai-* (p. 161) “(describing a reed basket or box)” and Rieken 2021, 466–67 “seed basket.”

^{GIŠ}*manzari-*

With CHD L–N *s.v.* ^{GIŠ}*manzari, :manzari* (p. 179), the attestation in KUB 49.97 7′ with *Glossenkeil* shows the word is not to be treated as an Akkadogram. HVP (p. 281 fn. 7) suggested a connection with Akkadian *massaru* ‘saw(?)’, but the fact that the Akkadian word is only attested in Late Babylonian (CAD M_1 *s.v. massaru* [p. 326]), and the fact that Hittite ^{GIŠ}*manzari-* takes a ^{GIŠ} determinative, not URUDU, makes such an equation improbable, if not impossible. If a borrowing is nonetheless to be sought, a better option could be the equally obscure *maṣarru* (CAD M_1 *s.v. maṣarru* [p. 329]), which has the advantage of being attested from Old Babylonian onwards and being made of wood (among other materials). The *maṣarru* is attested in a Neo-Assyrian inventory as a wooden object among trays and potstands (CAD M_1, *loc. cit.*), and, if it is the same object, as a kind of bronze vessel attested at Mari (e.g., ARM XXII 332 rev. 34: *ma-ṣa-ar-ru* zabar // ARM XX 20 obv. 16: *mu-ṣa-ri-*[*ir*]*-tum*, translated “aiguière” – ‘ewer’ – by Guichard 2005, *s.v. maṣarrum* = *muṣarritum* = aiguière [233–34], *mušarritum* = aiguière [241–43]). The two known attestations of Hittite $^{\text{(GIŠ)}}$*manzari-*, namely in KUB 49.97 7′–8′ as an object carried into a bedchamber, and in 5.7 rev. iii$^{?}$ 27′, if connected with the copper cups in the next line, do not rule out the semantic field of vessel, though the connection with *maṣarru* remains conjectural.

$^{\text{NA}_4}$*marruwašḫa-*

Per CHD L–N *s.v.* $^{\text{NA}_4}$*ma(r)ruwašḫa-* (p. 202), a mineral imported from Cyprus. Outside of the PTAC, the mineral is attested as an ingredient in a medicinal preparation for the eye (Polvani 1988, 65–67 with previous literature). Despite the frequent need for eye medication at the Hittite court, at least in the time of Ḫattušili III (cf. the shipments of eye medication in ÄHK 45 (KBo 28.5(+)6) and ÄHK 46 (KBo 28.4) in *Appendix II. Gifts From The Hittite-Egyptian Royal Marriage in the* 34th *Year of Ramses II*), the appearance of the $^{\text{NA}_4}$*marruwašḫa-* among containers of other stones in 2.1.A obv. ii(?) 4′–8′ suggests it had no special medicinal connotation in that context.

maruša-

For the semantics of the set of color words beginning **maru-*, see main entry of CHD L–N *s.v. marwai-* (p. 201) and EDHIL *s.v. maru̯āi-* (p. 562). For form and meaning, superseding earlier entry of CHD L–N *s.v. marušaš(a)-* (p. 203), see Rieken 1999, 195 fn. 908: “Kein *s*-Stamm ist dagegen das im CHD L–N, 203 als *marušaš(a)-* angesetzte *ma-ru-ša-ša-aš* (IBoT I 31 Vs. 16), sondern der heth. Gen. Sg. eines luw. Adj. gen. zu **maruš-* ‘Schwärze’ (parallel zu *ḫarkiaš* ‘des weißen …’ in der gleichen Zeile) ….” See similar conclusions of Zinko 2001, 421 fn. 69 (‘black, dark blue’).

marušam(m)a/i-

See above discussion of *maruša-* for semantics. The form *marušam(m)a/i-* is transparently a Luwian particple (perhaps from Luw. *marruwa-* 'to blacken' plus imperfective verbal suffix *-šša-*), and therefore to be translated as 'blackened, darkened' (vel sim.) instead of a color 'black'.

maššayašša/i-

A Luwian adjectival genitive of $^{\text{(TÚG)}}$*maššia-*, *maššayašša/i-* is hapax, appearing only once in the phrase: 7 TÚG ÉRIN^{MEŠ} *maššiyaššiš* (8.1.F rev. vi 15). Since the $^{\text{(TÚG)}}$*maššia-* seems also to have designated a type of fabric (see *Lexical Commentary, s.v.* $^{\text{(TÚG)}}$*maššia-* below) the "7 'army'-cloths of *maššia-*" probably refers to the fabric from which the "'army'-cloths" were made.

$^{\text{(TÚG)}}$*maššia-*

The $^{\text{(TÚG)}}$*maššia-* was originally equated by Goetze 1955, 54 with ^{TÚG}ŠÀ.GA.DÙ (*ibid.*, 55: "waist-band," but cf. now discussion in *Lexical Commentary, s.v.* ^{TÚG}ŠÀ.GA.DÙ below) based on distribution of the terms in similar lists. Although the CHD L–N *s.v.* ^{TÚG}*maššiya-* (p. 205) questioned the similarity of the lists cited by Goetze, an equation of the two terms still seems possible. The cognate terms of Hittite $^{\text{(TÚG)}}$*maššia-* in Akkadian ^{túg}*maššiyannu*, Ugaritic *mṯyn*, both analyzable as *maššia-* plus what is probably the Hurr. derivational suffix *-(n)ni-*, seem to represent some sort of shawl, scarf, or possibly sash of a light and costly construction (see Vita 2010, 331 with literature). In Hittite texts, the designation of "sash" is covered by ^{TÚG}ÍB.LÁ, and indeed, in 4.2.9, the ^{TÚG}ÍB.LÁ and $^{\text{(TÚG)}}$*maššia-* occur twice in the same paragraph, suggesting they are different garments. The order of clothing in 4.2.9 is roughly head-to-toe for a given paragraph, and in both instances the $^{\text{(TÚG)}}$*maššia-* (4.2.9 obv. 1, rev. 11′) comes before ^{TÚG}ÍB.LÁ (4.2.9 obv. 5, rev. 13′). Thus, the comparative evidence, the distinctness from the ^{TÚG}ÍB.LÁ 'sash', and the fact that the garment was worn higher up on the body, suggests that the Hittite $^{\text{(TÚG)}}$*maššia-* was probably a scarf or shawl. Such a translation also works well for ^{TÚG}ŠÀ.GA.DÙ, especially in KUB 45.32 rev. iii 6′, where the queen performs a ritual dance with a ^{TÚG}ŠÀ.GA.DÙ on her shoulders (see *Lexical Commentary* to ^{TÚG}ŠÀ.GA.DÙ below).

As with many garments in the PTAC, it is possible, based on passages such as 6.5 rev. 11′: 2 GÚ ŠÀ.BA 1 *maš-ši-aš* 1 GADA, that *maššia-* also designated the type of cloth from which the garment was constructed, i.e., a light and costly "shawl-cloth."

nurima(nt)-

The use of model fruits as jewelry on necklaces and garments in the PTAC suggests that *nu-úr-i-ma-an-za* was a Luw. word meaning either *nuriman-* 'pomegranate' (Akk. *NURMÛ*, Hurr. *nurati*) or **nurim(m)a/i-* 'set with pomegranates', with the fairly rare *úr-* sign and the broken syllabification attesting to what looks to be an (pseudo-)etymological spelling influenced by the Akkadogram *NU-ÚR-MU* (see 9.1.1 rev. iii 19′ for occurrence in the PTAC). Note that the remark of the CHD L–N (p. 476) comparing the unusual syllabification of *nu-úr-i-ma-an-za* to *nuḫalim(m)a/i-* can no longer be sustained if the revised reading *nu-ḫa-*⌜*li*?⌝*-i-*⌜*me*⌝*-iš* (see *Commentary* to 10.1.2.1 rev.? l. c. 4′) is accepted, leaving the orthography of *nu-úr-i-ma-an-za* all the more strange. For the analysis of the form as a Luwian sg. nom.-acc. n. ending in *-an* + particle *-ša/-za*, see HEG N *s.v. nuriman-* (p. 351) (also van den Hout 1984, Melchert 2003, 186–87, Jasanoff 2010, Simon (forth.)). A sg. nom.-acc. of an *nt*-stem might also be considered.

(GI)*nutaršat(t)ena-*

The new restoration in 2.15 l. c. 2′ means that the obscure (GI)*nutaršat(t)ena-* is now potentially attested thrice, every time at the beginning of a paragraph: 1 *nu-tar-ša-at-te-na* ZU₉ AM.SI (11.5.2 rev.? r. c. 1′), 1 GI*nu-ta*[*r-ša-at-te-na*(?) (2.15 l. c. 2′), [n *nu-tar-ša-t*]*i*(?)*-na* ZU₉ AM!.SI *QA-DU NA-A*[*K-DAM-MI*(?) (10.3.10 r. c. 11′). The consistent presence at the beginning of the paragraph and the explicit mention of a lid (*NAKTAMU*) in 10.3.10 r. c. 11′ strongly suggest the object was a container of some sort. The fact that it was in two instances made of ivory would classify it among the luxury containers, although versions made of reed (2.15 l. c. 2′) were also possible.

baluga-

This previously unrecognized word is attested in two texts, and in all three instances shows the comparatively rare use of *ba-* in a non-heterographic context, which in the PTAC, at least, mostly occurs with loanwords, e.g., *kiklibaim(m)a/i-*, NA₄*p/baraššu-*, (≮)*bašta-*/*baštaim(m)a/i-*. The attestation *ba-lu-ga-aš* in the context of a list in 11.1.1 r. c. 8′ suggests that the word is a common gender *a*-stem. Note that the *-ú-* (instead of *-lu-*) shown in the handcopy of 11.1.1 r. c. 8′ is contradicted by the photo and now the *-lu-* in the example from 11.2.5 3′. No further definition of the object can be given, save that it can be made from gold (11.1.1 r. c. 8′), and appears among models and figurines (11.2.5 3′).

NA₄*paraššu-*

Although HVP (p. 610) treated the hapax NA₄*paraššu-* (9.2.5 obv. i(?) 8′) as a variant of Hitt. NA₄*parašḫa-*/NA₄*parušḫa-*/NA₄*parašḫi-*, Akk. *marḫušu/marḫašû*, a kind of semi-precious stone, this identification was ignored by CHD *s.v.* NA₄*parašḫa-* (p. 139), which seems appropriate given the strong articulation of *ḫ* in Hittite (a consonant that if anything tends to strengthen to a full stop *k* rather than assimilate; see GHL §1.131, pp. 47–8). However, the implicit rejection by CHD *s.v. paraššuwant-* (p. 141) of HVP (p. 610) "*paraššuwant-* 'mit (Stein) *p.* versehen'(?)" (10.3.11 l. c. 6′) is unwarranted: the *paraššu*-stone could be both different from the *parašḫu*-stone and also the nominal base for *paraššuwant-*.

≮*pariyašša/i-*

A quality or treatment of hide or leather, the specifics of which cannot be further discerned. See ≮*pariyaššam(m)a/i-* below.

∡*pariyaššam(m)a/i-*

With HVP (p. 610) and Melchert 1993, 169, the ∡*pariyaššaima* 3.1.1.A_1 rev. v 4′ (and 9′) are to be analyzed as sg. nom.-acc. n. derived them from a Luw. participle *pari-yaššam(m)a/i-*. The analysis of CHD P *s.v.* *:pariyašši-* (p. 153) of the forms as *pari-yaššai=ma*, i.e., as an *i*-stem pl. nom.-acc. n. plus enclitic contrastive conjunction *-a/-ma*, can be dismissed, since an appearance of the relatively rare Hittite sg. nom.-acc. n. *i*-stem adjective ending *-ai* on a Luwian *Glossenkeil* word is unexpected. In the context of chariots mentioned in 3.1.1.A_1 rev. v 4′, 9′, a translation "upholstered with *pariyašši*-leather" seems appropriate.

$^{\mathrm{(TÚG/GADA)}}$*parna-*

CHD P *s.v.* $^{\mathrm{TÚG/GADA}}$*parna-* (p. 176) described the $^{\mathrm{(TÚG/GADA)}}$*parna-* as "an article made of linen cloth, occasionally decorated with gold and gems, sometimes associated with royalty" (note, however, that the translation in the CHD, *loc. cit.*, as "kilim" seems excessively interpretative, since it refers to a specific style of Turkish or Persian flat-woven blanket or rug, often with geometric designs). The *parna*-cloth can be used as a seat-covering (compare also the ^{TÚG}*ḫunipala-*), can be associated with chariotry, and appears among valuable objects associated with a royal coronation. The fact that a ^{TÚG}*parna-* in KUB 44.60+ rev. iii 12–13 is waved by the king to cut a calf from a herd should not lead one to assume a utilitarian value for the cloth, but rather the opposite, since each item mentioned in the ritual seems to have been selected for a close association with its wielder: hence, the $^{\mathrm{TÚG/GADA}}$*parna-* was evidently emblematic of the king and kingship. As for the etymology of the word, regardless of whether $^{\mathrm{TÚG/GADA}}$*parna-* was an original sg. gen. from *per/parn-* 'house', the existence of forms like accusative ^{TÚG}*pár-na-an* and ablative ^{TÚG}*pár-na-az* (see CHD *loc. cit.* for citations) shows the word was synchronically treated as a common gender *a*-stem.

parta-

See CHD P *s.v.* *parta/i-* "(an item associated with beds, bed linens and eagles), leg(?), talon(?)" (p. 197) for reading *pár-ta-aš*, based on a connection with Luwian *pārta/i-* (Melchert 1993, 171), against earlier *maš-ta-aš* (HIT, p. 56) and *maš/pár-ta-aš* (HVP, p. 58). According to the CHD P (*loc. cit.*): "If this word is related to Luw. *parta/i-*, a body part of which a sheep [in KUB 35.43 obv. 12] has four ... , then perhaps the above texts refer to furniture legs or to the carved hooves, paws, or talons at the bottom of a furniture leg." Alternatively, HED VIII *s.v.* *parta(i)-* (p. 174) argued that the attestation of *partianza* with an eagle belonged to a separate lemma, and proposed that the four *pārta/i-* KUB 35.43 obv. 12 referred instead to the four sides or directions of the sheep. The evidence from the PTAC is inconclusive: although the *parta-* belong in every instance to the wooden structure of a bedstead, no context demands they be interpreted as feet or legs. Indeed, the concept of furniture legs and feet, e.g., in the detailed descriptions of table components (10.3.10, etc.) and the numerous examples of chests with lion's feet, is already covered in the PTAC by the Sumerogram GÌR (Hittite, like e.g., Russian нога́, did not seem to have a strong distinction between [FOOT] and [LEG]) and the *Glossenkeil* word ∡*patialli-* (10.3.2 obv. i(?) 13″. The appearance of GÌR in 8.1.F rev.

v 13–14 – 1 ^{GIŠ}NÁ ZU$_9$ AM.SI 4 GÌR UR.MAḪ KÙ.SI$_{22}$ GAR.RA "1 ivory bed-frame (with) 4 gold-inlaid lion's feet" – suggests that the scribes of the PTAC also described "bed-feet/-legs" with GÌR. Thus, if *parta-* was a leg/foot, and hence the reading behind GÌR, one wonders why it appears only with beds (in three different texts!) in the PTAC, and not with the numerous tables, figurines, rhyta, chests, or any of other objects bearing GÌR 'feet/legs'. On this evidence it will be assumed instead that the term designated a special feature unique to beds. Thus, the inferential translation "sideboard(?)," in the sense of the board forming one side of the bedstead, offered by HED VIII (p. 173) is provisionally adopted, with the caveat that the term might have referred to another part of a bedstead.

$^{(GIŠ.ḪUR)}$(𒑱)*parzaki-*

With the CHD P *s.v.* (:)*parzaki-* (p. 202), this term must refer to "clay label or bulla, attached to the chest;" i.e., an externally visible item. The passage in 2.12 obv. ii$^!$ 9′: 1 ^{GIŠ}*tuppaš* GAL *KÁN-KU* $^{GIŠ.ḪUR}$*parzakiš* NU.GÁL "1 large wooden chest, sealed. There is no $^{GIŠ.ḪUR}$*parzaki*-bulla" reveals that the $^{(GIŠ.ḪUR)}$*parzaki-* was not constitutive of the sealing mechanism itself. In spite of the missing *parzaki-*, the lock or physical seal of the chest was intact, since the scribe was not able to open it to check the contents. And, on the assumption that the physical seal on the chest was intact, or otherwise the scribe would have simply checked inside to summarize the contents as he did with other chests in the texts, this further suggests that the *parzaki-* was a free-hanging bulla attached by a string. Finally, note also that the $^{GIŠ.ḪUR}$ in the cited example is a determinative, not a separate noun 'outline, list' in asyndeton, as was taken by HIT (p. 50) and HVP (p. 40) (see *Lexical Commentary, s.v.* GIŠ.ḪUR for further examples of the term used as a determinative). Thus, although the determinative implies that the $^{GIŠ.ḪUR}$*parzaki-* contained an "outline" of information – in this case probably the geographic origins and/or chain of personal responsibility for the chest – it apparently did not identify the contents inside, since none are listed (cf. also the single line in 2.9.A$_1$ obv. ii 13′: 2 ^{GIŠ}*tuppaš* TUR.TUR 𒑱*parzak*[*iš* NU.GÁL(?), which might show two small chests also missing their tags).

parzagulliya-

See Valério – Yakubovich 2010, 111 for the interpretation of *parzagulliya-* as "(an object) having loops (made) of hematite/magnetite," from Luw. **parza-* 'iron ore' + Akk. loanword *qullu* 'loop'. Cf., however, discussion in *Lexical Commentary s.v. parzašša/i-* and AN.BAR (GE$_6$) for uncertainty over identity of **parza-* as a substance.

(𒑰)*parzam(m)a/i-*

A hitherto unrecognized lemma. The clearly attested *kat-ta* 𒑰*pár-za-ma-an* in 11.2.2 7′ now suggests that 9.2.2 rev.$^!$ iii 8′ should be read *katta pár-z*[*a-ma-an* against the previous restorations *katta parz*[*a* "downwar[ds(?) ...]" in Košak 1978, 111, CHD P *s.v. paršza, parza, pirza*(?) a 4′ (p. 197), and HVP (p. 462), or the suggestion of a form of (𒑱)*parzakiš* 'seal, bulla' in Melchert 1993, 171. The preverb, *Glossenkeil*, and ending virtually demand that 𒑰*pár-za-ma-an* is a Luwian participle from a verb **parza-*. CHD P records a verb *parzai-* (p. 202), which is unfortunately a hapax with unknown meaning. The appearance of *katta* (𒑱)*parzam(m)a/i-* after two unrelated objects – a gold and stone sun disk in 9.2.2 rev.$^{!}$ iii 8′ and a stone and gold ox figurine (or a subcomponent thereof) in 11.2.2 7′ – suggests that the term referred to a treatment of metal or stone or a style of ornamentation.

parzašša/i-

parzašša- is formally a Luwian genitival adjective that Valério – Yakubovich 2010 would derive from **parza-* 'iron ore', i.e., an iron-bearing mineral such as magnetite or hematite, with preference for the latter (*op. cit.*, 112 fn. 10) based on that mineral's widespread use in Bronze Age Anatolia. Their further equation of **parza-* = AN.BAR GE$_{6}$ (*op. cit.*, 110–13) was congruent with the identification in Maxwell-Hyslop 1980, 87–88, of AN.BAR GE$_{6}$ as magnetite or another ferrous mineral of similar blackness. However, see now main discussion in *Lexical Commentary*, *s.v.* AN.BAR (GE$_{6}$), where it is argued that both AN.BAR and AN.BAR GE$_{6}$ must refer to the same substance, although whether that substance is iron or iron ore is a matter of ongoing archaeological debate. The interpretation of *parzašša/i-* has a stake in this debate, since the identification of **parza-* with iron ore is dependent on AN.BAR = (Akk.) *parzillu* < (Luw.) **parzil(i)-* being iron in the 2nd millennium. If **parzil(i)-* were itself iron ore, then the derivational relationship of **parzil(i)-* ⟵ **parza-* would require a different explanation than a metal and its ore. This in turn opens the possibility that the lexeme **parza-* might not inherently belong to the semantic field of minerals.

baššu-

Both HIT and HVP declined to assign the hapax *baššu-* (11.2.4 3′) to a lemma (contra HIT, 182, neither the photograph nor handcopy support for a reading *ba-aš-t*[*u*]*-uš*). *Pace* Kloekhorst 2010, 225 (with fn. 81), the context and position of the term in 11.2.4 makes an association with *paššu-* 'pedestal' highly improbable, though Kloekhorst's larger argument (*loc. cit.*) that the initial grapheme *ba-* suggests a borrowing *baššu-* still stands. Rather, its position at the end of a subclause (… ZU$_{9}$ S]I *baššuš*) in the middle of a list of figurine and offering equipment suggests that *baššuš* described the material of the preceding item. Its position after ivory further specifies it was probably a type of wood (cf. 11.2.4 6′: KÙ].SI$_{22}$ ZU$_{9}$ SI ^{GIŠ}ESI).

(𒑱)*bašta-*

Previous interpretations of (𒑱)*bašta-* have included CHD P *s.v. bašta-* "trim(?), filigree(?), embroidery(?)" (p. 209); Rieken and Yakubovich 2020 "Schmuck, Verzierung"; and HED VIII *s.v. basta-* 'clasp, buckle' (vel sim.) (p. 192). The translation of clasp or buckle suggested by HED seems difficult in light of 9.2.2 rev.$^{!}$ iii 11′: 1-*EN* AŠ.ME ^{NA_4}ZA.GÌN *araḫzanda b*[*āštan*, where a translation "1 sun-disk of lapis lazuli, 'set with clasps/buckles' around the outside" would be semantically difficult. For the form of the word, note that if the reading 𒑱*pa-aš-*⸢*ta*$^{!?}$⸣*-aš* in 12.3.7 4′ is correct, and not an otherwise unattested lemma 𒑱*pa-aš-*⸢*ša*⸣*-aš*, then the *Glossenkeil* at least confirms the Luwian origin (or intermediary) of the *bašta-/baštaim(m)a/i-/baštant-* group hypothesized by HED VIII (p. 163). Most promising now is the highly plausible theory in Rieken and Yakubovich 2020, 219–21 of the word's ultimate origin in Akkadian *bāštu (bāltu)*, in the sense "pride, ornament, characteristic feature" (CAD B *s.v. baštu* 3. [p. 142]). It is not clear whether (𒑱)*bašta-* was the generic word for decorations, or referred to a specific kind of decorative element.

(TÚG)*patalla-*

As discussed in the CHD P *s.v.* (TÚG)*patalla-* (p. 238), the presence in the same paragraph in 8.8.B of both TÚG*patalla-* (r. c. 5′) and (TÚG)GAD.DAM (r. c. 8′) implies that the two items should be distinguished from one another. Further attestation of the TÚG*patalla-* being used in a ritual to tie the feet of oath breakers led the CHD to suggest (*loc. cit.*) that the TÚG*patalla-* was a 'puttee', i.e., a long strip of fabric wrapped around the lower legs and fastened at the end, leaving the TÚGGAD.DAM to be interpreted as 'gaiter', i.e., a solid piece of cloth covering the shin, calf, and ankle.

paddaniyaš(š)a/i-

The attestation of 2 *gur-zi-ip pát-tar* "two hauberks *pattar*" (KUB 17.35 obv. ii 35′; see CHD P *s.v. pattar* C [p. 242]) in an inventory of cult symbols belonging to the war-god Yarri of Guršamašša makes it almost certain that the *GUR-SÍ-PU pád-da-ni-ia-ša* in 2.8 3 contains a form of *pattar*. If the sequence is a Hitt./Luw. denominal adjective in *-ašša/i-* (GHL §2.28, p. 56), then based on other heteroclitic *r/n*-stems the expected form would be **padd(a)naššа/i-*; compare, however, the appearance of *-iya/i-* in CLuw. *wattani(ya)-* 'country, land' and the derivation of PAnat. *udnéi̯h_2 'land' (eDiAna, lemma 1886) from PAnat. *u̯ód-r̥/u̯éd-n- 'water' (eDiAna, lemma 1883). In terms of semantics, although the CHD P (*loc. cit.*) was uncertain as to whether the word was related to *pattar* 'feather', *pattar* 'basket', or to a third lexeme, one may suggest that a "'feather(y)' corselet" would be an apt visual description of scale armor of the type found at Ḫattuša (see the "Panzerplättchen" in Boehmer 1972, 102–4; also the collected illustrations of scale armor in Lorenz – Schrakamp 2011, 129 and discussion *ibid.* 140, with literature). Thus, the 2 *GURSIPU paddaniyaš* will be translated here "'feather(y) corselets'/'corselets of feather(-like items)' = scale corselets."

𒑱*patialli-*

The entry in CHD P *s.v.* GIŠ*patialli-* (p. 244) can now be updated to include the attestation from 10.3.2 obv. i(?) 13″, which both supplies the first attestation in sg. nom. and the first form with a *Glossenkeil*. The *-iya/i-* and *-alla/i-* suffixes suggest that the translation "leg, foot (of furniture)" given by the CHD is not entirely adequate: the term meant something of or related to the foot, and would not have been confused with the actual body part. There is unfortunately no easier way to translate this distinction in English than the somewhat awkward "foot/leg (piece)," or perhaps "footlet."

penki(t)-

With Starke 1990, 217–18, *penki(t)-* is to be interpreted as a Luwian borrowing via a Hurrian intermediary of Akkadian *pinku(m)* 'knob, pommel', against previous interpretations as either an unrelated Hittite word (HIT p. 232 "an ornament") or an Akkadogram (HVP p. 699). Attestations of pl. nom.-acc. n. forms 𒑱*pí-in-ki-ta* (KUB 22.70 obv. 20), *pé-en-ki-ta* (*ibid.* obv. 25), *pí-in-ki-ta* (*ibid.* obv. 71), together with the possessive derivative form *penkitaim(m)a/i-*, establish that *penki(t)-* is another example of a CLuw. *i(t)*-suffix (GHL §4.16, p. 86) attached to a loanword.

penkitaim(m)a/i-

A Luwian possessive derivative of a denominative verb **penkitai-* 'set with knobs' (see *Lexical Commentary* immediately above; see *Lexical Commentary, s.v. annutai-m(m)a/i-*). In the PTAC the term is only attested twice, both times applied to ḪAR.ŠU 'arm ring'. It is not clear whether these knobs were somehow functional on the arm ring, for, e.g., hanging additional decorations.

peri-

Although CHD P *s.v. peri-* (p. 312) considered the meaning of *peri-* to be unknown, HED IX *s.v. peri-* (p. 23, with prev. lit.) posited a connection of *peri* with Akkadian *pīru* 'elephant', suggesting the Hittite word designated both elephant and ivory. In addition to the appropriateness of the *i*-stem for a loanword, see now also Soysal 2009, 301 (no. 120), for a possible attestation of AM.SI as an independent logogram meaning 'elephant' in KBo 53.120 obv. 8′, which Soysal considered to support the existence of a Hittite *peri-* 'elephant/ivory' alongside *laḫm/pa* 'ivory'. In the PTAC, the interpretation 'ivory' works well for the pair of attestations 9.2.1 obv. ii(?) 7′: *a-r]a-am-ni-iš* KÙ.SI$_{22}$ NA$_4$ and 9.2.1 obv. ii(?) 10′: *a]-ra-am-ni-iš pé-e-ri-iš*, where *peri-* is most logically interpreted as a material.

pulpulumi-

In addition to the discussion of CHD P *s.v. pulpulumi-* (p. 376), see now the translation "hand-saw" in Beal 2014, 344. Beal's observation that the *pulpulumi-* object is counted among other cutting implements in 10.3.5 6′ is possibly correct (the entry occurs at the juncture between razors and knives in the preceding lines and drinking vessels in the following lines), but the larger part of his interpretation of a forestry tool rests on a connection with the *pulpuli-* attested in the Hittite Gilgamesh. However, translations of the relevant passage in KUB 8.53+ rev. iv 33′ (CHD P *s.v. pulpuli-* [pp. 375–76], cited as "KUB 8.53:25"; Beckman 2019, 39, 42) have traditionally interpreted *pulpuli-* as a direct object of the *karašmi* in the next line – thus, KUB 8.53+ 33′–34′: *daššaⅰ〈m〉uš pulpuli[uš ...]* 34′ *karašmi* "I will cut [...] strong *pulpuli*-s," and hence the usual translation of *pulpuli-* as "beam." While Beal's point (*loc. cit.*) that *pulpuli-* never appears with a GIŠ determinative still stands, it seems better for now to avoid a connection between the *pulpuli-* of the Hittite Gilgamesh and the *pulpulumi-* of the PTAC. Likewise, the same connection advocated by HED IX *s.v. pulpulā, :pulpulī, pulpulumi-* (p. 118), but with the meaning "beam, bar," should be set aside.

(≮)*puriyalla/i-*

While CHD P *s.v. puriyalli-, puriyalla-* 3. (p. 388) is uncertain, the context of the term among cutlery, cups, and containers in 2.16 obv. i 7′ confirms that (≮)*puriyalla/i-* is here (and 4.1.1.1.A$_1$ obv. 13′) probably a type of drinking vessel distinguished by its lip or rim, and not a 'muzzle', as the term means when found in hippological contexts.

$^{\text{(TÚG)}}$*puššaim(m)a/i-*

See CHD P *s.v.* $^{\text{(TÚG)}}$*puššaimi-* (p. 399), which suggested a Luwian participle from *puššai-* "to chop up, crush"; hence the ^{TÚG}*puššaim(m)a/i-* is a "felted" garment. If so, the ^{TÚG}*puššaim(m)a/i-* seems to have been functionally different from *taḫapši-*, the other kind of felt attested in the PTAC: the ^{TÚG}*puššaim(m)a/i-* is attested only as a garment, whereas *taḫapši-*, perhaps being much thicker, appears only as a material for bags, barding, and seat covers.

^{GIŠ}*šalašturi-*

See Hoffmann 2004 for previous discussion of this item. Contra Hoffmann, the identification of the ^{GIŠ}*šalašturi-* as a comb, based solely on the passage from 9.1.1 rev. iv 28′–29′ (Inventory of Manninni), cannot be sustained, since previous transliterations of this passage, including hers, have been incorrect. Rather than 2, there are actually ⸢22⸣ ^{GIŠ}*šālašturi-* (traces of both preceding *Winkelhaken* are visible in the photos, and the spacing also demands that something must be restored before the two verticals of the 2). Thus, instead of 2 ^{GIŠ}*šālašturi* ... ŠÀ.BA 7 SAG-*SÚ* ZU$_9$ AM.SI, based on which Hoffman supposed that the 7 SAG-*SÚ* must be a component of the ^{GIŠ}*šālašturi*, reasoning that a subset of a group cannot exceed its total, there are in fact ⸢22⸣ ^{GIŠ}*šālašturi* ... ŠÀ.BA 7 SAG-*SÚ* ZU$_9$ AM.SI "22 *šālašturi-* ... of which 7, their (lit. its) head(s) (are) ivory." The passage thus reveals itself to be the normal construction for specifying certain items for further description: "{n}, of which {< n} are ...." Hoffmann's argument that the ^{GIŠ}*šalašturi-* was an implement with seven "teeth" was in any event always problematic: The literal and technical meaning of SAG(.DU)-*SÚ* 'its head' in the PTAC is the exact opposite of 'tine, tooth'. The term is found describing the pommel of a dagger (6.1 obv. 9; 9.1.4.A$_1$ obv. ii 17), the head of a mace (9.1.14 obv. r. c. 6′), the head of a zoomorphic rhyton (9.1.5 obv.$^{!}$ 2) and, only a few lines later in the Inventory of Manninni, the head of pegs or pins (9.1.1 rev. iv 4′). From the revised transliteration, it can be interpreted that the ^{GIŠ}*šalašturi-* is not an implement with multiple "heads," but rather an implement with a single head that sometimes could apparently be made of ivory. The material indicates the heads here are probably pommels or caps, since ivory is a poor material for the working end of a tool or weapon. Other attestations in the PTAC, namely 2.17 obv.$^{?}$ r. c. 17′ and 2.18 7′, show a close association of the ^{GIŠ}*šalašturi-* with bows and arrows, suggesting the item was a piece of archery equipment. This fits well with the citation outside of the PTAC given by Hoffmann, where in KBo 39.98+ obv. iii 5′–15′ (CTH 626: *nuntarriyašḫaš*-Festival) the king is presented successively with a quiver, a bow, and a ^{GIŠ}*šalašturi-*. As Hoffmann herself remarked (p. 381) at the time, "Es fragt sich natürlich, was der König mit dem Kamm tut" – to which the best answer is that there was no comb.

šaluwa-

CHD Š *s.v.* *šaluwa-* B (p. 107) suggested a connection between *šaluwa-*$^{\text{(MUŠEN)}}$, an oracle bird, and the *šaluwa-* in 9.1.8 obv. 13′, the latter supposedly being statuettes of the same. However, the context of 9.1.8 obv. 12′–15′, beginning with the phrase *Ú-NU-UT*^{MEŠ}-*ma-kán* ... (obv. 12′), combined with the utilitarian nature of the following the items, suggests the *šaluwa-* is here instead a tool or utensil of some sort, apparently commonly made of ivory (see now 4.2.8 5′: *ša*]*l*$^{?}$*-u-wa-aš* ZU_9 A[M.SI, appearing on the same tablet as adzes and axes). A firmer connection might be with *šalwan-* (CHD Š *s.v.* [p. 108]), a silver object placed on an altar in a ritual, and further with the verb *šalwai-* "to penetrate(?), stick(?)" (CHD Š *s.v.* [p. 107]), making the *šaluwa-/šalwan-* a sort of 'sticker, skewer'. If a connection between the bird and the *šaluwa-/šalwan-*objects is to be retained, it is conceivable that the *šaluwa*$^{\text{(MUŠEN)}}$- was a bird that perhaps had a spear- or skewer-like bill (the stabbing motion of a heron striking its prey comes to mind).

šap(a)ra-

The previous translations of HVP (p. 339 fn. 4) "Kleidungstück" and CHD Š *s.v. šap(p)(a)ra-, šipart(a?)* ("part of a person's garment") (p. 204) were non-specific. However, based on its position among the garments listed in 6.5, where it alternates with ^{TÚG}E.ÍB, the *šap(a)ra-* should be a type of belt. This interpretation fits well with the attestation from KBo 12.96 obv. i 18′: [*i*]*šḫuzziyanteš=ma=at=kan šapparit* "But they (*scil.* the [$^{\text{LÚ.MEŠ}}$M]UŠEN.DÙ of obv. i 16′) are girt with *šap(a)ra*-s."

šappi[*š*(-)

The CHD Š *s.v. šapp-* 'to hit, to churn' (p. 201) lists 4.2.4 obv. 13: *ša-ap-*⌜*pí*⌝*-i*[*š(-)* as an iterative form of the verb. This is not impossible, if the form is taken as an otherwise unattested participle **šappi*[*škant-* meaning perhaps 'hit, scraped, knocked off', analogous to other descriptions of item conditions in the PTAC (e.g., *arḫa ḫarrant-*, *arḫa duwarnant-*), but the context of 4.2.4 in no way demands this interpretation. Considering the abundance of hapax words in the PTAC, it seems best to leave 4.2.4 obv. 13 untranslated.

šarganiant-

CHD Š *s.v. šargan(n)iya-, šarqanae-, šarkaliya-* (p. 264) proposed a meaning "to tear apart(?), destroy(?)," against previous suggestions "sich erheben, sich überheben" (cf. literature in CHD *loc. cit.*). The interpretation of the CHD is preferable in the context of 9.1.6 obv. 7, since incidental descriptions of damage are a feature of the complex inventories (cf. the same 9.1.5 rev.$^{!}$ 15′, a tablet which was hypothesized to be a possible indirect join to 9.1.6). Thus, *arḫa šarganiant-* should be classed among the other verbs for indicating damage to inventoried items: cf. *arḫa ḫarrant-*, *arḫa duwarnant-*, and maybe *šappi*[*š-* (see above).

šarlanni-

HEG S *s.v. sarlanni-* '(ein Schmuckgegenstand)' (p. 914) justified its translation by pointing out the appearance of the word in 10.1.2.1 rev.$^{?}$ r. c. 3′ after earrings (r. c. 2′). With the addition of 10.3.4 8′, where *šarlanna* also appears among a list of earrings (7′, 9′), it is now almost certain that the *šarlanni-* is a wearable piece of jewelry, or jewelry subcomponent (if *šarlanna* NU.GÁL "the *šarlanni-* are not there" in 10.3.4 8′ is still referring to the item broken away at the beginning of the line).

šašanna-

Contra HVP (p. 617), it is not necessary to take 2 *ša-ša-an-na-a*[*š* in 11.1.3 9′ as a pl. nom., which would be morphologically unexpected (pl. nom. *-aš* is usually restricted to *i*-stems GHL §3.16). Although according to the rules of numerical congruence with cardinal numbers in Hittite (Rieken 2013), a common gender, semantically inanimate noun such as *šašan(n)a-* should technically be declined as a plural after the numbers two through four (and as a singular after the number five or greater), the rule is sensitive to genre, and list enivironments more often than not trigger a use of the singular (Rieken, *op. cit.*, 331). If the form in 11.1.3 9′ is indeed in sg. nom., it would be the first known Hittite attestation of $^{(DUG)}$*šašan(n)a-*, *šaša-* 'lamp' (CHD Š *s.v.*, p. 304) in that case and number.

***šikki-* (or: *šikkiš*?)**

See discussion in CHD Š *s.v. šikki-/šikkiš* (p. 359) for interpretations of this hapax. There is little to add, save that the *šikki-* or *šikkiš* was almost certainly a type of knife, since the description in 9.1.1 rev. iii 13′ mentions it having a "guard" (GABA) and a "pommel" (*lupannieš*) (see *Lexical Commentary, s.v. lup/wan(n)i-*).

šittar-, šittara-, šittari-

Although Starke 1990, 408–9 (further EDHIL *s.v. šittar(a)-* [p. 761]) argued against the traditional interpretation '(sun) disk' in favor of a sharp, pointed object, see the pertinent criticism under CHD Š *s.v. šittar(a/i)-* (pp. 460–61) that Starke's translation was based primarily on etymological considerations. Furthermore, any translation that does not treat *šittar-, šittara-, šittari-* as a celestial phenomenon fails to explain the amply documented complementary relationship of the lexeme with (^{D})U$_4$.SAKAR/*armanni-* 'lunula'.

šertappila-

The attestation of this term in 9.1.4.A$_1$ obv. ii 40 is the first example of this lemma in sg. nom. Although the majority of the examples cited in CHD Š *s.v. šertappila-* (p. 438) are made of wood, the presence now of *šertappilaš* KÙ.[in 9.1.4.A$_1$ suggests that the citation in the CHD entry (*loc. cit.*) of KBo 38.93 rev. 4: *še-er-tap-pí-la-az ap*[*piškizzi*(?) is better read instead *še-er-tap-pí-la-az* ⌈URUDU⌉ [.

****šumra(i)-/*šumriya-***

In addition to the fact that the traces in the photograph suggest a single horizontal intersecting the mid-point of a vertical, i.e., a *ḫ*[*u-*, *z*[*i-*, *g*[*i-*, or *r*[*i-*, the previous transliterations of 8.1.F obv. ii 15′ as HIT (p. 11) *an-da* ŠUM-*š*[*U* and HVP (p. 414) *an-da* ŠUM-*a*[*n* are problematic in their own rights. Against both translations (HIT, 13 "His name is therein"; HVP, 415 "darin der Nam[e") it may be objected that *anda* rarely occurs as a postposition or free-standing adverb at the beginning of a line (the only other example in the PTAC would be 9.1.1 rev. iii 19′, where it is part of a string of clauses ending in *anda*), and also that when something is "inside," the arrangement in the PTAC is always with *anda* as the final word of the clause (to pick among the many example, e.g., 2.17 obv.? r. c. 5′ 1-*EN duppaš* 4 *BIBRU* KÙ.SI$_{22}$[*a*]*nda* "1 chest, 4 gold rhyta (are) inside"). Thus, *anda* is probably here a preverb, which is made all the more likely by the fact that preverbs often occur at the beginning of lines immediately followed by their verbs (4.1.1.2.B rev. 4; 8.1.A obv. ii 14′, 15′, rev. v 20′; 9.1.1 rev. iii 41′). A preverb + verb combination **anda* ŠUM/*lamni(ya)*- is unattested (the semantics of which would be anyhow unclear). There is, however, a rare verb *šumreške*- 'to become pregnant', which the CHD Š *s.v. šumreške*- (p. 591) suggested, following others (see prev. lit.), is derived from an unattested verb **šumra(i)*-, **šumriya*-, or **šumrešš*- (form uncertain), connected to **šumar* 'being full', emphasizing the fullness or heaviness of pregnancy. Whereas in other circumstances it would be overly bold to restore an unattested root of an already rare verb, the semantics fit the context perfectly: One of the obvious actions that can be done to a chest is to fill or load it, and 8.1.F obv. ii 14′–15′ can be interpreted as a scribal comment describing the condition of the chest cataloged in the preceding lines. Thus, one can plausibly reconstruct for the lines: "in this chest ... (they will) load/fill in/(they have) load(ed)/filled in" or a particple "loaded/filled in."

šutari-

See CHD Š *s.v. šutari*- "(a part of a lyre)" (p. 657), to which a few pieces of additional information can be added. First, it may be noted that all of the other objects in the paragraph in which *šutari* is attested in the PTAC (8.1.A obv. ii 8′–17′) are made of semi-precious stone. This fact, together with the fact that the *šutari*- never appears with a GIŠ determinative in its three attestations (despite being part of a musical instrument that is by definition made of wood), strongly suggests the part was also made of stone, and thus not part of the resonant body of the instrument. It can be additionally garnered from the other attestations given by the CHD (*loc. cit.*) that the *šutari*- was 1.) separable from the lyre, 2.) large enough to be smeared with oil "in front on one side" (KUB 47.34+ 8), but 3.) small enough to be shipped in a box that also contained other items (8.1.A obv. ii 11′), and 4.) only attested as a single piece and not in pairs or multiples, ruling out, e.g., the arms of the lyre or the tuning pegs. This leaves one to imagine some sort of decorative element "in the round" attached to the body of the lyre, perhaps similar to the highly figured protomes attested on the lyres of Ur. Although the 2 ^{GIŠ}PISAN KUR *mi-iz-r*[*i* in 8.1.A obv. ii 4′ does not demand that the contents of the chest originated in Egypt (the chests could be "in the Egyptian style," or simply reused for storage), the presence of lapis lazuli and sun-disks described as "blue" (perhaps faience) pushes the balance of interpretation towards the objects in the paragraph being imported, leading to the final piece of information is that a *šutari*- was apparently precious enough to be classed among the luxury goods traded between royal courts. With the anointing of the *šutari*- with oil in a ritual context, an interpretation of a decorative protome, perhaps representing the divine voice of the instrument, becomes quite plausible for the item.

taḫapši-

Evidence from Akkadian and especially Assyrian sources conclusively demonstrate that the *taḫapšu*-material was a type of felt (Cancik-Kirschbaum 1999, 85–87; Postgate 2000, 213–27 and 2014, 406–7; Zawadzki 2006, 134–35 and 2013, 562–63), i.e., "a solid, elastic and insulating material that is suitable for a variety of purposes" (Gaspa 2018, 90–91) produced by the application of heat, pressure, and moisture to a mixture of wool with goat and sheep hair recovered from leather-processing. Contra HIT (p. 294), HVP (p. 704), and CAD T *s.v. taḫapšu* (p. 40), the Hittite form *taḫapši* is unlikely to be an Akkadogram, rather a direct borrowing from Hurrian or Hurro-Luwian intermediary in the expected *i*-stem. A borrowing scenario is supported by the reflexes of the term widely attested in the languages of the LBA Near East (Akk. *taḫapšu*, Ug. [*bʿl*] *tǵpṯm*, Egypt. *tḫbś.t*). *Taḫapšu* in these languages denotes both the material, but also by semantic extension, a range of objects (a horse blanket, barding, or saddlecloth and a covering for a sedan chair in Akkadian; a covering for a chariot and a type of belt in Hittite; a type of plaited basket in Egyptian: see CAD T *s.v. taḫapšu*, and Richter 2012, 425–26 for bibliography). In Hittite, *taḫapši-* as a material often appears with leather, either in contrast, as in 9.1.11 obv.? 9′, 10′, where pairs of objects, ŠÀ.BA 1 *ta-ḫap-ši* 1 KUŠ "of which one is *taḫapši-*, one is leather," are listed, or in combination, as in 2.7.A obv. 5, 6: 1 KUŠA.GÁ.LÁ *taḫapši* "1 (leather) bag (made with) *taḫapši-*." It can thus be seen that the definition in HVP (p. 704) of *taḫapši* as "'eine Decke für Pferde' (auch anstelle des Sattels genutzt)" is not incorrect, but in light of the use of the term in contemporary languages, it omits the core meaning of the term as 'felt'.

KUŠ*taḫapši-*

See immediately above for main discussion. The only assured use of *taḫapši-* as an object, rather than material, in the PTAC comes in 9.1.1 rev. iii 4′: 1-*EN* KUŠ*taḫapši* "1 (leather) felt (horse blanket/barding)." There is just enough space between the signs in the photo to consider a transliteration KUŠ *taḫapši* instead, i.e., a "skin (= sheet?)" of felt, which may have been the same in practice. For the frequent association of leather and felt in horse barding and chariot equipment, see already Postgate 2000, 2015–16.

tayašša/i-

A hapax that describes a set of cups in 9.1.4.A_1 obv. ii 38. While clearly a derived adjective in *-ašša/i-*, the identity of the first element is not clear. The verb *taya/e-* 'to steal' is a candidate, but the semantics would be unexpected. A relationship to **da-* 'two' is more likely, perhaps with the same *-(i)ya-* suffix found on the multiplicative 4-*yaḫḫ-* (**mewiyaḫḫ-*) 'to quadruple' (GHL §9.59, p. 170). Perhaps a GAL *tayašša/i-* was a "double cup," i.e., either twice normal size/capacity, or with some other doubled element, such as spouts or handles.

tak(ka)p(p)i-

From Schwemer 2019, viii (Nr. 46): "In [4.1.1.5 obv. 4] genanntes *tág-ga-pí-iš* ist zu dem in [4.1.1.3 obv. 15] belegten *ták-pí-iš* zu stellen. Beide Belege können mit der in KUB 56.32 Vs. III 21 bezeugten Gefäßbezeichnung DUG*ta-kap-pí-iš* verbunden werden, zu der eine thematisierte Variante DUG*taggapišša-* mehrfach belegt ist." No information on the qualities of the (DUG)*tak(ka)p(p)i-* can be discerned.

talla-

For discussion of *talla-* 1. 'unguentarium' (an oil- or perfume-container), 2. '(a body part) heel?', see now Pecchioli Daddi 2010. All of the examples in the PTAC seem to belong to the first lemma, i.e., a small container for scented oil.

$^{\text{(GI)}}$*damalanga-*

The appearance of $^{\text{(GI)}}$*dam*]*alangaš* in 4.2.3 would be the first attestation of this object outside of the *nuntariyašḫaš*-festival (CTH 626: KBo 24.67 obv. i 5; KBo 30.96 + 39.68 rev. iv 2′; KBo 39.66 + 24.85 obv. i 7′), and the first indication that it could be fitted with overlays (GIŠ.KÍN$^{\text{ḪI.A}}$ AN.BAR(?)). Otherwise, its qualities and function remain mostly unknown. The fact that the *damalanga-* can be made of reed, combined with fact that it appears in the first line of a paragraph of drinking veessels in 4.2.3 l. c. 3′–7′, could suggest that it was a serving tray or table of some sort.

dammel-

If the attestation in 8.1.E(A_1) rev. iv$^{?}$ 3′ and the frequently attested *dammel pedan* share a lemma (HEG T/D, 77 is skeptical), then a meaning 'unworked, unprocessed, uncultivated' (Güterbock 1964, 103–4; Hoffner 1997, 172–73 with attestations, commentary and literature) seems preferable to a derivation from *tamai-* 'other' (notwithstanding the arguments of Puhvel 2012). As pointed out by HIT (p. 43), the context of 8.1.E(A_1) rev. iv$^{?}$ 3′ demands *dammeluš* be treated here as a color term, translatable as 'natural', 'dun', or some other such description of the color of unbleached, undyed woolen or linen cloth.

^{GADA}*tanipu-*

The passage VSNF 12.2 obv.$^{!}$ iii 7′–8′: GAL DUMU^{MEŠ} É.GAL ^{GADA}*ta-ni-pu-un pa-a-i* $^{8'}$ *QA-TI-ŠU-NU a-an-ši-an-zi* "The chief of the palace attendants gives a handtowel (to the king and queen). They wipe their hands" cited by HVP (p. 377) demonstrates that the meaning of the common gender *u*-stem ^{GADA}*tanipu-* should be "handtowel" or some sort of cloth for wiping the hands. In light of this, together with the fact that 11.6.2 otherwise carefully marks its case endings, the attestation ^{GADA}*ta-ni-pu-ú* in 11.6.2 l. e. 1 must be taken as a collective plural of a common gender noun, and not a stem form.

taptappa-

See HEG T/D *s.v.* ^{GIŠ}*taptappa-* (p. 135) for discussion and literature. Interpretation has been based on a proverb-like remark in Muršili's plague prayer (KUB 14.8 rev. 22) that a bird returns to the *taptappa-* for safety, stated as an analogy for the supplicant seeking divine mercy. Although it is unclear what "nests" are doing among lists of metal objects in the inventory texts (10.1.2.2 2′; 10.1.2.1 rev.$^{?}$ r. c. 8′), a literal interpretation as "(model) bird nests" should not be discounted: given the GURUN 'fruit' listed in the vicinity in both attestations (10.1.2.2 3′, 4′; 10.1.2.1 rev.$^{?}$ r. c. 6′), it could be that the passages describe votive dioramas, especially in light of the Hittite penchant for thematic instantiation in their votive objects.

tarna- (anda tarna-)

With the discussion of HVP (p. 520 fn. 6), whereas the particple TÚG *anda tarnanza* is unique to 9.1.6, the conjugated verbal phrase is well attested with the manipulation of wool, e.g., in KUB 9.31 obv. ii 46–48, where wool threads of different colors are braided (*anda tarna-*) into a garland. It is if anything unusual that the TÚG *anda tarnanza* does not appear more frequently in the PTAC, since a "braided/interwoven cloth" seems like it should be a not-uncommon form of textile. If the Hittite phrase was concealed under a Sumerogram, it is not clear which one.

taruppenza

As already pointed out by HEG T/D *s.v. tarupp-* (p. 243) and EDHIL *s.v. tarupp-*^{zi} (p. 852), the lack of a convincing morphological derivation, combined with the broken context of 9.2.4 obv. i 10′, prohibit a confident connection of the form *taruppenza* with the verb *tarupp-*.

tarzu-

It being the case that *tarzu* in 11.1.3 4′ seems to be neuter, this hapax cannot be immediately the same as the common gender ^{GIŠ}*tarzu-*, a small piece of a door-closing mechanism, perhaps constituting a latch (HEG T/D *s.v.* ^{GIŠ}*tarzu-* [p. 251]). The presence of the *tarzu-* in a list of bedroom items immediately after a bed-frame (11.1.3 2′) and set of gold-inlaid pegs (3′), which are presumably part of the bed, suggest it could also have been a component of a bed. Cf. *tarzuda-* in *Lexical Commentary, s.v. tarzuda-* immediately below.

tarzuda-

The conflicting readings of HEG T/D, 252 *tar-zu-ú-dạ-ạš*[and CHD Š, 458 *tarzūda*[*n* cannot be resolved by the photos or handcopy, so the final traces of 9.1.5 rev.[!] 3′ will be left untransliterated. The word is a *dis legomenon* with no identifiable properties. The suggested connection (HEG loc. cit) with *tarzidu-* 'raw glass' seems improbable. A closer etymon would no doubt be *tarzu-* (see *Lexical Commentary, s.v. tarzu* immediately above), which has the benefit of at least also being attested in the PTAC.

tiyalant-

Contra Vigo 2010, 296–97, there is no evidence for a GADA *tiyalant-* as a special type or workmanship of linen cloth (p. 296 fn. 60), much less for a translation as specific as "a type of cloak for special occasions worn as an over-garment" (p. 296). Whereas Vigo gave two attestations of *tiyalant-* with GADA (4.2.9 rev. 11′, 14′), and one attestation of *tiyalant-* without GADA (4.2.6 obv.[?] 4′, also purportedly a cloak), three are an additional three attestations (4.2.9 obv. 2, 29; 9.1.8 obv. 7′) of the cloth, also without GADA. From these six attestations in total, all that may be said of *tiyalant-* is that it can be applied to a range of garments, mostly shirts (^{TÚG}GÚ *ḪUR-RI* 'Hurrian shirt' of different varieties in 4.2.9 obv. 2, 29; rev. 11′; 4.2.6 obv.[?] 4′; ^{TÚG}GÚ.È.A 'shirt' in 9.1.8 obv. 7′; and the *adupli(t)*-garment in 4.2.9 rev. 14′), and that it was an art, addition, or treatment of fabric (two attestations with linen, four attestation with wool) that was noteworthy enough to distinguish a garment from a group: see 11 *TA-PAL* ^{TÚG}GÚ.È.A *nu* 1-*NU-TI* *ti-ia-la-an* in 9.1.8 obv. 7′.

tiyawara-

See HEG T/D *s.v.* *tiyawa*[(p. 371) for discussion. As pointed out there, a connection with the ^{GIŠ}*ti-ia-wa-ra* found among items in a Hurrian offering list (KBo 33.157 obv. i 6′) seems more promising than a form of GAM-*an tiyawa(š)*.

tit(ta)li(t)-

Assuming a connection between 1 ^{TÚG}*lupanniš* *ḪAŠMANNI* 1 *titli* KÙ.SI$_{22}$ "1 *lupanni*-head-dress, 1 gold *titli*-" (6.5 rev. 12′, 15′), *t*]*ittali* KÙ.SI$_{22}$ SAG.KI "*t*]*ittali* (of) gold (and) a frontlet" (8.1.E(A$_1$) rev. v$^?$ 4′), and the possessive formation *tittalitaim(m)a/i-*, which, as discussed in *Lexical Commentary*, *s.v.* *tittalitaim(m)a/i-* below, can be interpreted as 'endowed with *tit(ta)li(t)-*' on analogy with *penki(t)-* 'knob', *penkitaim(m)a/i-* 'set with knobs', then it may be possible to elucidate the meaning of all three terms. As discussed by Vigo 2010, 303–14, iconography shows that the *lupanni*-cap often came with a decorative metal band affixed to its front. Contra the proposal of Vigo (*loc. cit.*), these cannot be identified with the "EME ... *lupanni*-s" found in the PTAC (see *Lexical Commentary*, *s.v.* *lup/wan(n)i-* above, where it is argued that the EME 'blade' and *lupanniš* '(pommel-)cap' refer in these instances to parts of a knife). Instead, the above-mentioned attestations in 6.5, where a *tit(ta)li(t)-* is attached to a *lupanni*-cap, and 8.1.E(A$_1$), where it appears in proximity to a "frontlet" attached to what was presumably another piece of headgear, suggest that the *tit(ta)li(t)-* is a better match for the metal band observed in the iconography. Moreover, attestations of the possessive formation *tittalitaim(m)a/i-* where it is used to describe the fringes of garments (e.g., 9.1.1 rev. iv 43′; 9.2.1 obv. ii 22′) as well as the lips or edges of drinking vessels (9.1.4.A$_1$ obv. ii 20; 9.1.1 rev. iv 21′–22′), suggest that the *tit(ta)li(t)-* was a general word for a decorative metal element applied as edging, whether it be to caps, textiles, or cups.

tittalitaim(m)a/i-

This lexeme, which is attested as being applied to the fringe of textiles and the rim of drinking vessels, has been uncritically translated since Goetze 1951, 72 as 'damaged, frayed, chipped' (see HEG T/D *s.v.* *tittalitaimi-* [p. 384] for prior literature). Goetze's interpretation was based primarily on 9.1.1 rev. iv 21′–22′: ŠÀ.BA 3 KÙ.SI$_{22}$ NA$_4$ 1-*EN* KU.SI$_{22}$ *pūrin* [*ti*]*ttalitaimeš* NA$_4$ *arḫa išḫūwan*, where the concatenation of the two clauses *pūrin tittalitaimeš* "*tittali*-ed with respect to the lip" and NA$_4$ *arḫa išḫūwan* "the stone (is) removed (for recycling)" was taken to indicate that both described damage to the rhyton. However, if the change in gender between *tittalitaimeš* (common gender, agreeing with an implied *BIBRU*) and *arḫa išḫūwan* (neuter) is taken seriously, then the second clause must refer to an implied neuter noun, for which *tit(ta)li(t)-* is the best candidate. This yields the translation: "of which 3 (are) gold (and) stone, 1 (is) gold (and) [*ti*]*ttali*-ed with respect to the rim, (but) the stone (on the *tit(ta)li(t)-* is) removed." With the recognition of the lexeme *tit(ta)li(t)-* as a tangible metal object, possibly designating a decorative metal band (see *Lexical Commentary*, *s.v.* *tit(ta)li(t)-* above), it seems more likely that *tittalitaim(m)a/i-* described a treatment whereby a decorative edging was applied to the lip or fringe of objects. Indeed, this interpretation fits better with the attestations of the lexeme found outside of 9.1.1, none of which appear in contexts where damage to the objects would be expected to be described.

tuk(k)anzi-

See Melchert 1999b for discussion of etymology and meaning of *tuk(k)anzi* 'breeding, cultivation' and its verb *tuk(k)-* 'to breed, cultivate'. The verb and noun can be used with both grain and livestock. With grain, the letter HKM 18 obv. 23–25 shows that "grain held for cultivation" was stored in granaries, presumably for next year's sowing (see discussion in Melchert, *ibid.*, 19), which is probably the context of both attestations in 1.1.

^{URUDU}*dupiyali-*

Whereas HIT (p. 89: "javelin"), HVP (p. 265: "Wurfspieß"), and HEG (T, D *s.v.* ^{URUDU}*dupiyali-* [p. 452]: "Art Speer?") interpret *dupiyali-* as a pointed object, others have suggested a blunt striking instrument such as a hammer or mace on etymological grounds: see HEG *loc. cit.*, and Simon – Busse, eDiAna, *s.v. dupiyal(a/)i-* (= lemma 344) for literature. If the restoration now of 11.1.7 4′: *intal*]*uzziš*(?) AN.BAR 4 *du*[*piyališ* is accepted (there are no other objects beginning with *du-* in the PTAC, except for *du-up-pa-aš* 'chest', which would be unexpected in this context), this would be the second instance in the PTAC of exactly four *dupiyali-* appearing in a list following potential digging tools: compare 9.1.5 rev.$^{!}$ 14′–15′, where the *dupiyali-* come after the ŠAḪ.TUR(-*anza*) "piglet" (a digging tool?) (see *Lexical Commentary*, *s.v.* ŠAḪ.TUR below). Compare also 5.3 r. c. 7′, where an ^{URUDU}*d*[*upiyališ* is now restored in a manufacturing receipt among common agricultural tools. While previous commenters have suggested a martial or cultic role for the *dupiyali-* (Simon – Busse, *op. cit.*, 3. Meaning '(a weapon)'), its context in the PTAC suggests that the item probably had in addition a utilitarian role as a sledge or maul.

ulip(a)na-

See now Rieken, eDiAna, *s.v. ulipn(i)-/walipn(i)-* 'wolf' (= lemma 1593) for review of evidence in favor of equating *ulip(a)na* with UR.BAR.RA 'wolf'. As noted (Rieken, *loc. cit.*) under *2. Forms*, the *ú-li-ip-ni-eš* in 9.2.1 obv. ii 12′ can be either sg. nom. of a Luwian form with *i*-mutation or a Hittite pl. nom. of a borrowed *a*-stem *ulip(a)na-*; since the other nouns in the text seems to sg. nom. (cf. 9.2.1 obv. ii 11′: *a-ú-wi*$_5$*-ti-iš*), the same is assumed here.

uluppanni-

Based on the context of 9.1.7, the *uluppanni-* could be a silver component or attachment to a statue or rhyton (see HEG U *s.v. uluppanni-* (Kultgegenstand aus Silber) [p. 43]). The connection implied by Rost 1961–63, 213 between *uluppanni-*, ^{TÚG}*ulipali-*, and *ulipna-* 'wolf' (also cited by HEG U, p. 44) has yet to be sustained by evidence. Rather, if an etymological connection is to be sought, one wonders if the originally Hattic *lup/wa(n)ni-* 'cap' forms a better comparison.

u(n)ḫ-

See Lorenz and Rieken 2011 for discussion of etymology and meaning.

uraki-

See main discussion in *Lexical Commentary, s.v.* NÍG.GÍD.DA. Given the paucity of true Akkadograms ending in *-I* for pl. nom. in the PTAC, it is more probable that the *ú-ra-ki* of 2.17 obv.? r. c. 1′, 2′ represents *i*-stem borrowing, i.e., *uraki-*. This is supported by the fact that the only two other attestations of *uraki-/URĀKU* present in the files of the Hethitologie Archiv in Mainz also show an *i*-stem: 1-*EN ú-ra-ki* KÙ.SI_{22} (KBo 31.43 rev. 4′; CTH 294.4 "Court Proceedings of Kuniyapiya") and especially *ú-ra-ki-ia ḫar-zi* (KUB 60.60 l. c. 6′; CTH 590 "Fragments of Dreams and Vows"), which may be interpreted as pl. nom.-acc. n. (and which also demonstrates that the borrowing was a true *i*-stem, and not an *i(t)*-stem).

ušimašša/i-

A hapax to 10.3.4 5′, *ušimašša/i-* is transparently a Hitt./Luw. denominal adjective in *-ašša/i-* (GHL §2.28, p. 56). Consulting the photograph shows that word is clearly written, and there is no reason to suspect reading with other sign values, e.g., ***šam-ši-ma-aš-ša* or ***ú-lim-ma-aš-ša*. The *šarlanna* in pl. nom.-acc. n. in 10.3.4 8′ indicates *ušimašša* is probably also pl. nom.-acc. n. Although a reading ^{NA_4}*ušimašša* cannot be ruled out, the context of 10.3.4 suggests that the preceding NA_4 describes the material of the preceding item (probably an earring), making *ušimašša* a quality or classifier of jewelry.

wak(k)-

The verbs *wak(k)-* and *wakši(ya)-* share approximately the same meaning, 'to be missing, absent' (HEG W–Z *s.v. wakk-* 'ermangeln, fehlen' [p. 215]; *op. cit. s.v. wakšiya-* 'fehlen, abwesend sein' [p. 227]), but seem to exhibit a distinct pattern of usage in the PTAC, with the former used to describe items that are "missing" or "lacking," in the sense of not being extant, and the latter items that are "absent," but the whereabouts of which are known. This most frequent use of *wak(k)-* is to describe a number or quantity missing from a nominal amount. See, for example, 3.1.1 *passim*, where *wak(k)-* is used to record the amount of copper missing from a total, e.g., in 3.1.1.A_1 obv. ii 13′–16′, where 100 axes are weighed at 199 minas, 12 shekels, and 28 shekels are noted as *wakari* (implying that each axe was supposed to weigh 2 mina). In 3.1.1.A_1 obv. ii 10′–12′, it is explained that a large copper adze has been accidentally "broken up" (*ḫullier*) during the processing of the tribute, with the result that "1 large copper adze of [tri]bute is [lac]king." Another example where *wak(k)-* is shown to have a clear meaning of "missing, lacking" comes in 10.1.2.8, a temple inventory of the town of Alatarma, where in rev. r. c. 4–5 one gold hand belonging to the statute of the deity Āla is noted as *wakkari* "missing" (if the hand were only temporarily missing, say if it had been sent out for refurbishing, the priests in charge of the temple would surely have given a statement to this effect). The remaining examples of *wak(k)-* in the PTAC are of single items in lists, usually at the end, which are "missing."

The verbs *wak(k)-* and *wakši(ya)-* only appear in the same text once in the PTAC, in 4.1.1.3 rev. B 3–5, where at first glance they seem to be used interchangeably: [n MA.NA/GÍN KÙ.BABBAR 1 KI.LÁ] TI$_{8}$$^{M[UŠ]EN}$ *ŠA* ^{TÚG}E.ÍB *wakšiat* [4] *ANA EPIŠ MAŠLU* [5] [n MA.NA/GÍN KÙ.BABBAR 1 KI].LÁ TI$_{8}$^{MUŠEN} *ŠA* ^{TÚG}E.ÍB *ANA* $^{LÚ.MEŠ}$KÙ.DÍM *wakkari* "[n mina(s)/shekels silver, 1] eagle [weight], of a belt *wakšiat* – for making embellishment. [n mina(s)/shekels silver, 1] eagle [we]ight, of a belt, for the smiths *wakkari*." Here, it is *wakkari* that initially seems to be a mistake, or at least an imprecision in language, since *wakšiat* is attested again in the next entry of 4.1.1.3 rev. B 7. Moreover, unlike the typical usage of the verb when it is encountered with metal quantities in the PTAC, there does not seem to be a nominal amount from which the silver of 4.1.1.3 rev. B 5 is missing. However, as is noted in the edition, 4.1.1.3 rev. B 5 is written in a very cramped style, coming immediately after rev. B 4. It also appears that the paragraph line between rev. B 4 and 5 was added after the fact, since both lines lack the noticeable spacing found in the rest of the texts before the paragraph lines. The positioning and shared contents of rev. B 4 and 5, in which both refer to silver *ŠA* ^{TÚG}E.ÍB 'of a belt', suggest that rev. B 5 is dependent on the context of rev. B 4, i.e., that the quantity of silver given in the break at the beginning of rev. B 4 is in fact the nominal amount from which the silver of rev. B 5 is missing. 4.1.1.3 rev. B 3–5 would thus seem to act as a limit case confirming the semantic distinction of the verbs, in which from a certain portion of "silver of a belt" (KÙ.BABBAR ... *ŠA* ^{TÚG}E.ÍB) that was temporarily "absent" (*wakšiat*) for the making of embellishment" (rev. B 3–4), a subportion of that silver is found to be "missing" (*waqqari*) for the smiths (*ANA* $^{LÚ.MEŠ}$KÙ.DÍM) (rev. B 5).

wakši(ya)-

As discussed in *Lexical Commentary*, *s.v. wak(k)-* immediately above, *wakši(ya)-* is the other verb of missing or absent items in the PTAC. Unlike *wak(k)-*, which occurs in the context of nominal quantities of metals, on the one hand, and individual items in a list on the other, *wakš-* is appears in every instance with metal. The precise details of the metal are known, namely its quantity, how it was weighed, and its purpose or destination (2.2 rev. 5: *ANA* GAL$^{ḪI.A}$ "for cups"; 4.1.1.3 rev. 3, 7: *ANA EPIŠ MAŠLU* "for making embellishment"). The examples from 2.2 rev. 10//4.1.1.1.A$_{1}$ rev. 7′ (30 GÍN KÙ.BABBAR-*ma ANA BIBRI*$^{ḪI.A}$ *wak*[*šiyat* (EGIR-*anda* 1$^{?}$ GAL) DÚ-*zi*] "But 30 shekels of silver for the rhyta are abs[ent. (Later they will make 1$^{?}$ cup)]) and 4.1.1.1.A$_{1}$ rev. 2′ (KÙ.BABBAR-*ma* ... *wakšiat* EGIR-*anda* ... ŠUL.PÁT *udai* "But the silver ... is absent. Later ... (drinking) straw(s) he will bring") confirm that the contexts of the absent metal was for crafting. This suggests that *wakši(ya)-* had a technical sense referring to the status of metals during the period of time when they were being processed according to the crafting receipt and hence were not physically present for the inventories represented by the preserved tablets. In contrast to *wakk-*, items described as *wakš-* were not irretrievably lost, but rather temporarily "absent" or even "checked out" from the storehouse that served as the inventory's frame of reference (the one possible counter-example for this technical distinction of *wak(k)-* and *wakš-* might come in 8.1.A obv. ii 29′: 2 NÍG.GÍD.DA KÙ.SI$_{22}$ *wakš*[*iat*(?) "2 gold wires/rods [are] abse[nt(?)," but the broken context of the preceding line prevents a firm interpretation).

$^{\text{(URUDU)}}$*wakšur-*

Against earlier HVP 53, fn. 1 “Messgefäss,” HIT 38 “clepsydra” (with previous literature), see now Blažek 2012 for proposal to derive *wakšur-* from the numeral “six.” Blažek’s interpretation has the advantage of uniting the disparate uses of the *wakšur-* as a liquid measure, a vessel or container of this size, a unit of time (possibly derived from use of the *wakšur*-vessel as a clepsydra or water clock; see Christman-Franck 1971, 105), and a unit of length. Thus, the *wakšur*-vessel was a ‘one-sixth’-vessel – though a sixth of what measurement remains unclear. According to 3.1.1.A_3 obv. iii 9′ (1 ^{URUDU}*ANKURINNU ANA* 4 ^{URUDU}*wakšur* “one copper *lampstand* for 4 copper *sixth*-vessels”) the *wakšur*-vessel could also serve as a lamp.

warḫueššar

The “shagginess” ascribed to the ^{URU}*kummanni warḫueššar* in 8.8.B l. c. 7′ should not be interpreted as ‘coarse, rough-spun’, since there garment is numbered as one among a set of ten garments described as SIG ‘fine’. The translation of HVP (p. 627) “‘Zottenkleid’$^{(?)}$,” i.e., a “shaggy” cloth, is not inappropriate, but perhaps carries unwanted connotations of a connection with the Mesopotamian “Zottenrock, Zottenstoff,” for which there is no evidence.

warpal-

Cf. previously HEG W–Z *s.v. warpal-* (p. 347): “Möglicherweise eine morphologisch unklare Ableitung von *warpa-* ‘Kreis’ …,” and Sasseville, eDiAna, *s.v. warpal-* ‘(a tool)’ (= lemma 2192), with tentative suggestion of a connection with Luwian /warp(i)-/ ‘weapon, tool’. However, given the context of the paragraph 9.2.6 obv. i 11′–16′ in which the term appears in (see discussion in *Lexical Commentary*, *s.v. išgapuzzi-* above), a possible derivation from *warp-* ‘wash, bathe’ might be entertained instead.

watarma-

See HEG W–Z *s.v. watarma-* (no translation) (p. 441) for main discussion, where a Hattic origin for the word is confirmed in spite of the superficial similarity to Hittite *watar* ‘water’. It may be proposed here based on the similarity of 4.2.9 obv. 17: ^{TÚG}*parnaš watarmaš* and 4.2.9 rev. 24′: ^{TÚG}*parnaš tapriaš*, that the *watarma-* should be a type of chair. This translation might work with the other passage pointed out by HEG, KBo 14.116 rev. iv 7′–8′: [*A-NA* MUNUS(?)].LUGAL *wattarma ḫalziya nu* ^{NINDA}*miumiuda* $^{8'}$ [… *IŠ-TU*] É ^{LÚ}NINDA.DÙ.DÙ *udanzi* “He calls ‘*wattarma*’ [to] the king/[qu]een(?), and they bring *miumiu(t)*-bread […] from the bakery.” Since the previous lines in KBo 14.116 involve the tablemen bringing out the other components of the meal (rev. iv 3′–5′) and showing the dishes before the god (rev. iv 6′), while the following line (rev. iv 9′) has the first breaking of the bread, it seems quite plausible that the “*wattarma*” called out in rev. iv 7′ was meant to mark the start of the meal, in which case a translation “(take your) seat” would not be inappropriate. This would imply that the *watarmašši*-breads discussed by HEG (*loc. cit.*), then, would be another variety of model or figure breads so loved by the Hittites (see also Burgin 2019, 75 and Hoffner 1974, 188), in this case shaped like a chair.

The suggestion in HED VIII *s.v. parna-* (p. 148) of *watarmaš* "toponym$^{?}$," presumably based on similar ^{URU}*alatarma*, is not impossible, but does not explain the use of the word as an exclamation in the example from KBo 14.116 rev. 7′ discussed above.

wilan-, wilana-

As already recognized in HEG W–Z *s.v. wilan- (welin-) /wiln-* (n.), *wilana-* (c.) (p. 565–67), but missing from GHL §4.69 (p. 108), *wilan-*, *wilana-* 'clay' is apparently attested in two stem forms: a neuter *wilan-/wilna-* showing syncope *-lan-* > *-ln-* in the oblique cases, and a common gender *wilana-* that does not show syncope. Thus far, the *wilana-* stem has only been attested in acc. pl. (KBo 8.74+ obv. ii 16; see HEG W–Z, 567), but see now 10.1.1.2 rev. iv 7′: ŠÀ.BA 2 *ú-i-l*[*a-*... , which can only be interpreted as a genitive construction from the non-syncopated stem: ŠÀ.BA 2 *ú-i-l*[*a-na-aš* 'of which 2 [of] cla[y]' (this passage was already correctly transliterated by CHD L–N, p. 80, but without commentary on spelling *-l*[*a-* vs. *-i*[*l-*).

zaima-, zaimi-, zaimiya-

Hitherto a hapax to 6.1 obv. 6, it is now possible, based on the traces and the context of other shirts and garments in 11.1.7 6′–8′, that *zaima-* should also be restored in 11.1.7 7′ (as with 6.1 obv. 6, also modifying a Hurrian shirt): ^{TÚG}GÚ *ḪUR-R*]*I za-i-ma-aš*. The sg. nom. form *za-i-ma-aš* precludes interpreting *zaima-*, *zaimi-* as a Luwian participle **zaim(m)a/i-*.

zakkit(ta)r-

Contra HEG W–Z, p. 628, the suggested reading (following comment of D. Groddek) of 9.1.11 obv.$^{?}$ 3′ as ^{GIŠ}NÀGA-*r*]*a-aš zakkit* RA AN.BAR GAR[.RA "ein Mörs]er mit Stößel, mit Eisen beschlagen", taking *zakkit* as either an instrumental of *zakki-* or a sg. nom. of Luw. *zakki(t)-* "in Verbindung mit RA 'schlagen' in der Bedeutung 'Stößel'," is syntactically suspect: one would expect the required genitive case of RA to be somehow marked (*RA-*aš*, *RA-*uwaš*, **ŠA* RA). A more plausible parsing would be to read *zakkitra* as a pl. nom.-acc. n. of an unknown noun **zakkit(t)ar-*: one could suspect a further relationship between this and Luw. *zakki(t)-* 'bolt, latch' (see Simon, eDiAna, *s.v. zakkit-* [= lemma 409]), but the morphological details are unclear.

$^{\text{(URUDU)}}$*z/šap(p)eškur-*

See HEG W–Z *s.v.* $^{\text{(URUDU)}}$*zapiskur-* (p. 668), with previous literature. No new information has come to light regarding the meaning of *z/šap(p)eškur-*, except to note that the context of the *šapešgur* in 9.1.4.A_1 obv. ii 2 in a paragraph labeled *UNŪT* ^{LÚ}ŠÀ.TAM "equipment of the treasurer" (obv. ii 6) and among "*waršanaim(m)a/i*-stoves," a statue, and the divinized throne of the treasurer does not necessarily promote the specific interpretation of the items as a shaving razor.

zarat(t)a-

A previously unattested *dis legomenon* with no obvious etymology. Context demands it be a kind of vessel or container.

(GADA)*zazzi(t)-*

See HEG W–Z *s.v.* (GADA)*zazzi-* (p. 682), where attestations reveal the *zazzi(t)-*linen to be a type of cloth suitable for dedicatory offerings and delicate tasks such as wiping a newborn baby's head. The inserted *-t-* in the ablative form *zazzitaz* indicates the lemma was originally a Luwian *(i)t*-stem, possibly borrowed from Hurrian.

zingi-

This lemma is unattested outside of 9.1.5 rev.! 13′ and a single enigmatic context in KBo 59.218 obv. 13′, where it appears (if the same lemma) as UZU*zi-in-gi-i*[*a*. Based on context in 9.1.5, the *zingi-* is a component of a bow, or perhaps another piece of archery equipment.

zuḫati-

This hapax should probably be connected with the equally obscure *t/suḫatu*, an item attested as a covering or piece of armor at Nuzi (CAD S *s.v.* *suḫatu* [p. 346]). If, as suggested by the CAD (*loc. cit.*), the item is the same as the Neo-Babylonian *suḫattu* (CAD S *s.v.* *suḫattu* [p. 346]), then the *suḫatu* was a cloth used as padding for neck/throat armor, i.e., a gorget. The Hurro-Akkadian context at Nuzi, the semantic field, and the otherwise unexplained *-ti* ending in 9.1.11 obv.? 9′ suggest that *zuḫati-* is yet another Hurro-Luwian borrowing in *i-* or *i(t)-*.

Sumerograms

AN.BAR (GE_6)

It is argued in Lehnhardt 2021 that AN.BAR cannot refer to metallic iron in the Hittite period due to the vanishing rarity of the substance in the archaeological record prior to the $13^{th}/12^{th}$ centuries – and then only in small pieces of jewelry, such as rings and clothing pins (see the latest overview of the archaeological evidence of Anatolian iron in Pare (forth.); earlier Yalçın 2005 and Jean 2001). As emphasized by Lehnhardt (2021, 41), almost none of the iron objects recovered from Bronze Age Anatolia come from securely dated contexts (see similar conclusions concerning the evidence from Ḫattuša in Herbordt – von Wickede 2021, 24–25), and the waste products expected from iron industry are likewise missing. The dearth of archaeological evidence for large-scale iron production in the Hittite Kingdom is thus difficult to square with not only the philological plentitude of "iron" objects, including knife-blades, in the PTAC, but also with the statues, models, and figures described as AN.BAR, which would have been impossible to produce with early wrought-iron techniques (Lehnhardt 2021, 26, 29–30). Lehnhardt suggested that AN.BAR was instead iron ore, i.e. an iron oxide such as hematite or magnetite, which are both well-attested archaeologically and as well as eminently carvable into the decorated objects attested in the texts. Acceptance of Lehnhardt's proposal would thus reopen the philological relationship of AN.BAR,

AN.BAR GE_6, *ḪAPALKINNU*, *ḫapalki-*, and **parza-* (attested as *parzašša/i-* and *parzagulliya-* in the PTAC and in Akkadian *parzillu*).

The current *communis opinio* is that AN.BAR meant '(metallic) iron' in all stages of cuneiform. The Sumerographic lexeme AN.BAR displaced earlier KÙ.AN over the course of the 2nd millennium, and was matched by the similar displacement of Akkadian *amūtu, aši'u* with *parzillu* (Maxwell-Hyslop 1974, 162; see Dercksen 1992, 798b fn. 3 for the suggestion that AN.BAR was itself a Sumerographic back-formation from *parzillu*). According to Valério – Yakubovich 2010, 113, *parzillu*, and by extension AN.BAR, derives from Luwian **parzil(i)-* 'iron' ⟵ **parza-* 'iron ore', and the terms spread with the import of iron smelting from Anatolia into Mesopotamia, apparently under Luwian influence (the Hittite word for iron, *ḫapalki-*, is Hattic in origin; see Weeden 2011, 152, with previous literature). Under the assumption that AN.BAR = (Akk.) *parzillu* and (Luw.) **parzil(i)-* referred to metallic iron, Valério – Yakubovich (*loc. cit.*, fn. 13) were required in their analysis to reconstruct the spread of iron smelting technique out of Anatolia at least as early as the 17th century, since the Alalaḫ text AT 410 (Wiseman 1953, 107) refers to 400 spearheads made of AN.BAR – an impossibly high number of utilitarian objects to have been made of meteoritic iron.

For AN.BAR GE_6, Maxwell-Hyslop 1980, 87–88, argued after a suggestion of Ronald Tylecote (*apud loc. cit.*) that AN.BAR GE_6 referred to iron which had oxidized to magnetite, based on the supposed observation that AN.BAR GE_6 was restricted to decorative contexts, where the black mineral would be valued for its contrastive color. Valério – Yakubovich 2010, 111–13 reprised the argument of Maxwell-Hyslop that AN.BAR GE_6 was an iron ore, which they extended to include **parza-*, thus, introducing a contrast: AN.BAR = Luw. **parzil(i)-* 'iron', and AN.BAR GE_6 = Luw. **parza-* 'iron ore'. Other interpretations of AN.BAR GE_6 include Siegelová 1984, 159, where it was proposed that AN.BAR meant 'smelted iron' and AN.BAR GE_6 was 'meteoritic iron'; and Košak 1986, 125–26, where an inversion of the equations was argued, reasoning that the Anatolians would have named the metal they first encountered, i.e., meteoritic iron, as "iron," and appended the modified name of "black iron" to the smelted version only after the technology was developed to produce it. Reiter 1997, 394, accepted Maxwell-Hyslop's argument of that AN.BAR GE_6 = magnetite, but attempted to equate AN.BAR GE_6 with Hittite *ḫapalki-* based on a supposed equation of AN.BAR = **kelku-* after Melchert 1983, 139–41 (this interpretation is no longer philologically tenable: see the argument of Starke 1990, 423–24 that **kelku-* is in fact **kikli/uba-*, with the argument Puhvel 1996, 64–65 that this substance was perhaps an improved ferrous alloy; see further *Lexical Commentary s.v. kiklubaim(m)a/i-* above). More cautiously, Tsumoto in Siegelová – Tsumoto 2011 (296–97) considered that the large quantities of AN.BAR GE_6 attested in the Hittite corpus preclude its identification with meteoritic iron (Tsumoto did not comment on the yet more frequently attested AN.BAR, but it must be assumed that his logic rules out meteoritic iron for this substance as well). However, Tsumoto did not offer an alternative for AN.BAR GE_6, considering (p. 296) that "[t]he archaeological finds do not allow any conclusions to be drawn about the nature or origin of this material."

The alleged philological fact on which the arguments of Maxwell-Hyslop 1982 and Valério – Yakubovich 2010 hinged, namely that both AN.BAR GE_6 and the reflexes of **parza-* (*parzagulliya-* and *parzašša/i-*) are restricted to decorative contexts, breaks down upon closer observation. AN.BAR and AN.BAR GE_6 are used in substantially the same contexts, both in the general corpus (the list of attestations in Košak 1986, 125–33 is still relatively complete) and certainly within the PTAC:

Table 59: Attestations of AN.BAR in the PTAC

Knife blades		
56 EME GÍR AN.BAR	56 AN.BAR knife blades	3.1.12 5′
20 E[ME GÍR A]N.BAR	20 [A]N.BAR [knife blades]	4.2.2 obv. 1
6 GÍR.TUR AN.BAR	6 AN.BAR small-knives	8.1.A rev. v 4
10 EME GÍR AN.BAR	10 AN.BAR knife blades	8.1.A rev. v 5
6 EME AN.BAR	6 AN.BAR blades	9.1.5 rev.! 14′
6 EME ZABAR KÙ.SI_{22} AN.BAR	6 blades of bronze, gold, (and) AN.BAR	9.1.5 rev.! 14′
Jewelry and Decorative Elements		
⟨n⟩(?) *TU-TI-IT-TUM*! TUR.TUR A[N.BAR]	⟨n⟩(?) very small A[N.BAR] toggle-pin(s)	4.2.1.A_1 obv. 4
[n?] **TU-TI-IT-TUM* GAL AN.BAR*	[n?] large AN.BAR toggle-pin(s)	4.2.1.A_1 obv. 5
GABA *lu-pa-an-ni-eš* AN.BAR	(n knives, of which) the guard(s) (and) pommel(s) (are) AN.BAR	9.1.1 rev. iii 12′
1-*E*]*N*(?) EME ZABAR *lu-pa-an-ni-eš* AN.B[AR]	1(?) (knife with a) bronze blade (and) AN.B[AR] cap	9.2.4 rev. iv 6
Statues and Figurines		
3 ᴰU_4-*aš*.SAKAR ŠÀ ... 1-*EN* ⌜KÙ.SI_{22}⌝ NA_4 AN.BAR	3 divinized crescent moons, of which ... 1 (with?) gold, stone, (and) AN.BAR	9.1.4.A_1 obv. ii 7–8
1 GU_4.MAḪ AN.[BAR	1 AN.[BAR] bull (figurine)	10.1.1.1 rev.? 6′
1 ALAM LÚ AN.[BAR	1 AN.[BAR] man (figurine)	10.1.1.1 rev.? 7′
1 ḪUR.SAG AN.BAR	1 AN.BAR mountain (figurine)	10.1.1.1 rev.? 11′
1 ALAM MUNUS AN.BAR	1 AN.BAR statue (of a) woman	10.1.1.2 rev. iv 4′
2 ḪUR.SAG AN.BAR	2 AN.BAR mountain (figurines)	10.1.1.2 rev. iv 4′
1 *ḪI-IN-ZU* AN.BA[R	1 AN.BA[R] (model of a) *ḪINZU*-weapon	11.1.9 6′
Vessels and Implements		
ŠU-ŠI AN.BAR *pal-za-ḫa-aš*	60 AN.BAR statue bases	4.2.1.A_1 obv. 7
1 MÁ AN.BAR	1 AN.BAR (vessel in the shape of a) boat	4.2.1.A_1 obv. 10
1 ᵁᴿᵁᴰᵁ⌜NÍG.ŠU⌝.LUḪ.ḪA AN.BAR	1 copper (and) AN.BAR wash basin	4.2.9 rev. 31′
7 *pal-za-ḫa-aš* AN.BAR ŠÀ 1 LIBIR	7 AN.BAR statue bases, among (which) 1 old	8.1.A rev. v 7
[n] *pal-za-ḫa-aš* AN.BAR SIG_5	[n] good AN.BAR statue bases	8.1.A rev. v 9

3 *pu-ri-aš* ŠÀ 1 *[A]N.BAR SIG$_5$$^{?}$*	3 *trays*, among (which) 1 [A]N.BAR, excellent$^{?}$	8.1.C 3′
za-ak-ki-it-ra AN.BAR GAR.[RA]	AN.BAR-inlai[d] *zakkit(t)ar*-s ("bolts?")	9.1.11 obv.$^{?}$ 3′
1-*NU-TUM* **aš* $^{?}$*-*ku-uš* AN.BAR GAR.RA	1 set AN.BAR-inlaid *ašku-* (a piece of horse tack?)	9.1.11 obv.$^{?}$ 8′
1 GAL AN.BAR	1 AN.BAR cup	11.1.7 2′
n *in-ta-lu*]-*uz-zi-iš*(?) AN.BAR	[n] AN.BAR [scoo]p(s)(?)	11.1.7 4′
Other		
26 GÍN AN.BAR	26 shekels of AN.BAR	3.1.7.A$_1$ l. e. 3
n+]1 MA.NA 30 GÍN AN.BAR	n+]1 mina(s), 30 shekels of AN.BAR	4.1.1.1.B$_1$ rev. iv$^{?}$ 3
ŠU-ŠI 6 AN.BAR SIG$_5$	66 AN.BAR (objects), excellent	4.2.1.A$_1$ obv. 6
22 AN.BAR *ŠA* GUNNI	22 AN.BAR (objects) "of the hearth"	4.2.1.A$_1$ obv. 6
25 AN.BAR	25 AN.BAR (objects)	4.2.1.A$_1$ obv. 8
⸢30 AN.BAR⸣ S[I]G$_5$$^{?}$	30 AN.BAR (objects), ex[cell]ent$^{?}$	4.2.1.A$_1$ obv. 12
3 PAD AN.BAR	3 AN.BAR bars	4.2.2 obv. 1
... Š]À.BA 1 AN.BAR 1 ^{URUDU}DUG.SAGI.A AN.BAR	... o]f which 1 (is) AN.BAR, 1 copper (and) AN.BAR cupbearer's vessel	4.2.9 lo. e. 32′

Table 60: Attestations of AN.BAR GE$_6$ in the PTAC

Knife blades		
⸢15 EME⸣ [G]ÍR AN.BAR GE$_6$	15 AN.BAR GE$_6$ [kn]ife blades	4.2.2 obv. 2
[n GÍR(MEŠ) ŠÀ(.BA) 1]-*EN* EME AN.BAR	[n knives, of which] 1 (with) AN.BAR GE$_6$ blade	4.2.2 rev. iv 5
⸢5 EME GÍR.TUR⸣ AN.BAR GE$_6$	5 AN.BAR GE$_6$ small-knife blades	8.1.A rev. v 4
2 EME AN.BAR GE$_6$	2 AN.BAR GE$_6$ blades	9.1.1 rev. iii 8′
1-*EN* *ši-ik-kiš* AN.BAR GE$_6$	1 AN.BAR GE$_6$ *šikki(š)-knife*	9.1.1 rev. iii 13′
Jewelry and Decorative Elements		
1 *KÍ-RI-SÚ* AN.BAR GE$_6$ KÙ.SI$_{22}$	1 gold (and) AN.BAR GE$_6$ hair clasp	4.2.4 obv. 10
8 ⸢ḪAR.GÚ⸣ AN.BAR GE$_6$	8 AN.BAR GE$_6$ torcs	8.1.A obv. i 2′
IN-ṢA-AB-TUM AN.BAR GE$_6$	AN.BAR GE$_6$ earring(s)	8.1.A obv. i 4′
UN-QÚ AN.BAR GE$_6$	AN.BAR GE$_6$ rings	8.1.A obv. i 11′
E]ME ZABAR *lu-wa-an-ni-eš* GABA AN.BAR G[E$_6$	(knife with a) [b]lade of bronze, cap (and) guard of AN.BAR G[E$_6$	9.1.10.A$_1$ rev. 2′
Statues and Figurines		
UDU AN.BAR GE$_6$	AN.BAR GE$_6$ sheep (figurine)	2.3 1
1 GÚ GU$_4$ AN.BAR GE$_6$	1 AN.BAR GE$_6$ ox protome	2.13 obv.$^{?}$ 4′
4 *a-ra-am-ni-uš* KÙ.SI$_{22}$ NA$_4$ AN.BAR GE$_6$	4 gold, stone, (and) AN.BAR GE$_6$ *falcons*	9.1.1 rev. iii 22′

3 ^{D}U$_4$-*aš* SAKAR ŠÀ 2 KÙ.SI$_{22}$ AN.BAR GE$_6$ ^{8} GAR-*ri*	3 divinized lunulas, of which 2 gold- (and) AN.BAR GE$_6$-inlaid	9.1.4.A$_1$ obv. ii 7–8
3 *BI-IB-RU* UR.MAḪ ŠÀ 1-*EN* 4 GÌR^{MEŠ} GUB-*za* ^{17} SAG.DU-*ŠÚ* GABA ⸢KÙ.SI$_{22}$⸣ AN.BAR GE$_6$	3 lion rhyta, of which 1 standing onfour legs, its head (and) breast of gold (and) AN.BAR GE$_6$	9.1.4.A$_1$ obv. ii 16–17
1-*EN* *ar-ma-an-ni-eš* AN.BAR GE$_6$	1 lunula of AN.BAR GE$_6$	9.1.10.B 5′
1-*EN* AŠ.ME ^{NA_4}ZA.GÌN AN.BAR GE$_6$ KÙ.SI$_{22}$ GAR.R[A	1 lapis lazuli (and) AN.BAR GE$_6$ sun disk, gold-inlai[d	9.2.2 obv. ii(?) 13′
[1] ⸢GU$_4$$^{?}$⸣ ^{NA_4}ZA.GÌN AN.BAR GE$_6$	[1] lapis lazuli (and) AN.BAR GE$_6$ ox$^{?}$	11.2.2 4′
Vessels and Implements		
16 ^{GIŠ}TUKUL AN.BAR G[E$_6$	16 AN.BAR G[E$_6$] mace(heads)	3.1.12 7′
pé]-*ra-an pé-e-du-ma-aš* AN.BAR GE$_6$	AN.BAR GE$_6$ ["f]ore-carriers"	8.1.A obv. i 3′
1 ⸢*pé*⸣-*an* ⸢*pé*⸣-*dum-ma-aš* AN.BAR GE$_6$ KÙ.SI$_{22}$	1 AN.BAR GE$_6$ (and) gold "fore-carrier"	8.4 rev. 16′
Other		
5 NÍG.GÍD.DA AN.BAR G[E$_6$]	5 AN.BAR G[E$_6$] rods	8.1.A rev. v 3
81 NÍG.GÍD.DA AN.BAR GE$_6$	81 AN.BAR GE$_6$ rods	8.1.A rev. v 8
16 NÍG.GÍD.DA AN.BAR GE$_6$ ŠÀ.BA 1 ŠU.U	16 AN.BAR GE$_6$ rods, among which 1 (with) basalt	8.1.A rev. v 15′

Given the similar applications of AN.BAR and AN.BAR GE$_6$ in the PTAC and elsewhere, it is difficult to make a philological argument that the two substances referred to substantially different materials. One is faced with the choice of either making both terms refer to variants of metallic iron (this is the preferred solution of Pare (forth.)), or to consider both to be varieties of iron ore (the solution preferred in Lehnhardt 2021). Deciding between these two interpretations is not a straightforward task. On the one hand, the inappropriateness of iron ore for some the applications attested in the Hittite corpus (it is unclear how useful an iron ore blade would be) favors the metallic iron interpretation. On the other hand, the rarity of metallic iron in the archaeological record before the 13th/12th century BC, including the near complete absence of utilitarian iron ore implements everywhere in the ancient Near East until the late 12th century BC (see discussion of the 13th/12th century BC "ring horizon," where iron rings began to appear in the archaeological record of the ancient Near East, versus the "knife horizon" of the late 12th/early 11th century BC, with utilitarian objects appearing at the same time), combined with the apparent inadequacy of early metallurgy for some of the other applications attested in the corpus (primarily the figurines and vessels), favors an interpretation of both AN.BAR and AN.BAR GE$_6$ as iron ore. To reflect the current uncertainty while retaining a connection to the traditional interpetation, a translation "*iron (ore)*" for AN.BAR as is chosen here as a compromise.

As for AN.BAR GE$_6$, the common variants of iron ore are macroscopically indistinguishable from one another, and indeed often mixed in the same objects (Melein 2018,

5–12). Natural iron ore varies in color from black to dark-chocolate brown, with gray, yellow-brown, or red flecks possible from various inclusions (Melein 2018, 8). If AN.BAR and AN.BAR GE$_6$ are interpreted as iron ores, AN.BAR GE$_6$ might therefore only refer to a chromatic difference among the natural varieties of ore. In the metallic iron interpretation, Pare (forth.) suggests that AN.BAR GE$_6$ might refer to iron that has received a surface treatment designed to induce a black oxide corrosion layer. This layer can in turn be treated with oil to provide to protection against further corrosion. Since it possible in both the iron ore and the metallic iron interpretations that the distinction between the terms AN.BAR and AN.BAR GE$_6$ was one of color, and since the textual record preserves no evidence for a difference in substance, a literal translation "black *iron (ore)*" will be used here for AN.BAR GE$_6$.

AN.BAR (*ŠA*) GUNNI

For the much discussed AN.BAR *ŠA* GUNNI '*iron (ore)* "of the oven"', see Cordani 2016b, 171–72 (with previous literature). With the indirect join of 4.2.1.A$_2$, the erstwhile hapax of *ŠU-ŠI* 6 AN.BAR SIG$_5$ 22 AN.BAR *ŠA* GUNNI in 4.2.1.A$_1$ obv. 6 is now matched by 55 AN.BAR SIG$_5$ 10 AN.BAR GU[NNI in 4.2.1.A$_2$ rev. 12′, which at least confirms the validity of the phrase, even if it does not allow for much further understanding of the meaning. Cordani offered the interpretation (p. 172, following original interpretation of Siegelová 1984, 158) that AN.BAR *ŠA* GUNNI represented iron from the first stages of production (Siegelová 1984, 158: "die qualitativ noch minderwertigen, dem Ofen bloss entnommenen Stücke"), in contrast to the more refined AN.BAR SIG$_5$ 'good iron' of the same line. Such an interpretation is problematic for a number of reasons, not the least of which is the thus far archaeologically unconfirmed assumption that the Hittites possessed the technology for smelting metallic iron (see main discussion *s.v.* AN.BAR (GE$_6$) above). There is also the question of whether a scribe would be conscious of, or able to visually determine, the stage of iron processing for the purposes of an inventory text. Questions of metallurgical development aside, the interpretation of AN.BAR *ŠA* GUNNI as 'iron "of the oven"' founders on the assumption that the objects of 4.2.1.A$_1$ obv. 6 and 4.2.1.A$_2$ rev. 12′ are chunks or ingots of iron (ore), which is not at all certain. Were it to be the case, the chunks or ingots would be the only pieces of raw iron (ore) in the whole of the PTAC that are not accompanied by a weight measurement. One wonders if instead of iron (ore) lumps or ingots, the enumerated but unweighed AN.BAR SIG$_5$ and AN.BAR (*ŠA*) GUNNI are just "iron (ore)s," i.e., iron (ore) objects or implements, leaving 4.2.1.A$_1$ obv. 6 to be read: "66 good *iron (ore)* (objects), 22 (regular) *iron (ore)* (objects) of the hearth," i.e., either components of a hearth such as andirons or firedogs, or tools for manipulating objects in a hearth. This interpretation is supported by the appearance two lines later (4.2.1.A$_1$ obv. 8) of the label 1 ^{GIŠ}*tuppaš* 2 ^{KUŠ}A.GÁ.LÁ 25 AN.BAR *anda* "1 chest: a leather bag (with) 25 *iron (ore)* (objects) inside," and other equally elliptical container descriptions, where only the material but not the form of the objects is named; cf. 8.1.D obv. i 6′–7′: [1 ^{GIŠ}*tup*]*paš* ⟨^{GIŠ}⟩EREN erasure $^{\text{NA}_4}$KÁ.DINGIR.RA $^{\text{NA}_4}$T[I] $^{7'}$ [$^{\text{NA}_4}$*m*]*ušnuwantiš* ŠÀ 1 ^{GIŠ}*tuppa* SIG$_5$ *ŠA* [KASKAL] "[1 che]st of cedar. erasure Babylon-stone, 'li[fe]'-stone, [*m*]*ušnuwanti*-stone, inside 1 good chest"; or even more elliptically: 2.7.A obv. 16 1 ^{GI}PISAN SA$_5$ GÌR NU.GÁL *ḫarkiaš marušašaš* "1 red chest, no feet. (Things) of white (and) of black".

BAL-*uwaš*

If 11.1.9 4′: 3 *ḫūpparaš* BA[L-*ūwaš* ‘3 vessels [of] lib[ating’ is restored correctly, then this attestation would constitute one of the few examples of $^{\text{(DUG)}}$*šip(p)anuduwa-* used in its original *genitivus quasi gerundivalis* form, and provide confirmation for the proposed reading of DUG *išpanduwaš* in KBo 21.1 obv. ii 5 as a genitival construction, as discussed in CHD Š *s.v.* $^{\text{(DUG)}}$*šip(p)anduwa-*, $^{\text{(DUG)}}$*išpand/tuwa-* (p. 396).

$^{\text{(TÚG)}}$BAR.“TE”

See HZL no. 20 (p. 100) and Weeden 2011, 170–71 for discussion of the reading “TE,” which may simply be a Hittite form of DUL. Weeden (p. 170) considered that the DUL and “TE” were interchangeable (“Hittite texts also know the ^{TÚG}BAR.DUL, sometimes even in the same text as the ^{TÚG}BAR.TE”). However, the ^{TÚG}BAR.DUL cited by Weeden from 8.1.F rev. vi 1–2 is based on the faulty reading of HIT (p. 12); see now the *Commentary* to 8.1 290–91, where the “BAR.DUL” are in both cases ⸢^{D}⸣*IŠTAR*. With the removal of the alleged attestations in 8.1.F rev. vi 1–2, there are no certain examples of ^{TÚG}BAR.DUL in any Hittite text, eliminating Weeden’s argument (p. 171) that “Garments known as ^{TÚG}BAR.TE are only ever qualified by their colour in Hittite texts, whereas the $^{\text{[TÚG]}}$BAR.DUL is qualified by its place of origin, perhaps indicating exoticism.” Instead, it seems that, whatever the origins of the practice, ^{TÚG}BAR.DUL was simply written ^{TÚG}BAR.“TE” at Ḫattuša (cf. ^{GIŠ}“NUNUZ” for ^{GIŠ}ÉRIN, where the NUNUZ sign substitutes for ÉRIN only in the context of this logogram – see further *Commentary* to 5.5 obv. ii 5).

Baccelli et al. 2014, 122 considered the ^{TÚG}BAR.DUL/^{TÚG}BAR.“TE” to be equivalent to Hitt. ^{TÚG}*kušiši-* based on their appearance in similar contexts and the supposed derivation of ^{TÚG}*kušiši-* from Akk. ^{túg}*kusītu* (= ^{TÚG}BAR.DUL), but this is no longer tenable: Instead, the ^{TÚG}BAR.“TE” appears to be a mundane piece of outerwear, perhaps a cloak or mantle, while the ^{TÚG}*kušiši-* is a type of fine gown (see further under *Lexical Commentary s.v.* ^{TÚG}*kušiši-*).

DIRI

To my knowledge, the equation DIRI = *(W)ATĀRU* = *kallar(a)-*, *kallareš-*, *kallareške/a-* has previously not been made explicit (though HW^2 K *s.v. kallaratar*, ⸗*gallaratar* [p. 24] proposed *kallaratar* = *ĀTRU*, and then CAD A$_2$, p. 487, DIRI = *(W)ATĀRU*). The Hittite lexeme *kallar(a)-* and its derivatives seems to have an original sense ‘badness’ (Starke 1990, 357–59; Rieken 1999, 367), which still appears in its usage in oracles as a technical term for an unfavorable oracle result. From this a secondary sense of ‘excess, enormity’ developed in the derivatives of *kallar(a)-*, such as *kallaratti-* ‘enormity, monstrosity, wonder(?)’ (defined as *ša at-ra-a-ti* in lexical list KBo 1.30 obv. 11′; see HW^2 *s.v. kallaratti-* [p. 24]), and also *kallaranni* ‘in excess’ (sg. dat./loc. of *kallaratar*) (see citations from “Instructions of the *BĒL MADGALTI*” in HW^2 *s.v. kallaratar*, ⸗*gallaratar* 2. “Übermaß(?)” [p. 24]). The Hittite writing of the lexeme *kallaratar* appears once in the in PTAC, as *kallaranni* ‘in excess’ in 4.1.1.1.B$_1$ rev. iv$^?$ 8. The Akkadogram *A-AT-RU* ‘excess, surplus’ likewise appears only once, in a tally of breads in 12.3.4 6. Most instances of excess or surplus items are instead expressed in the PTAC by the Sumerogram DIRI. In most cases, DIRI appears alone, presumably reflecting an underlying *kallaranni*.

However, in a few cases the term is written DIRI-*ri*. While it is possible to imagine that the *ri*-sign functioned here as a disambiguating Sumerian phonetic complement (thus **DIRI^{RI}), the more natural interpretation is to take the form as Hittite phonetic complement indicating a medio-passive pres. sg. 3 verbal ending: cf. the pair of clauses *ANA* $^{\text{LÚ.MEŠ}}$KÙ.DÍM *wakkari* 'it is lacking for the smiths' (4.1.1.3 rev. B 5) and *ANA* ^{m}*Mutta* DIRI-*r*[*i* 'it is surplus for Mutta' (4.1.1.3 rev. B 8) in the same text. It may be proposed here, then, that the underlying verb of DIRI-*ri* is *kallareške/a-* (imperfective of a denominal verb *kallareš-*), which is attested exclusively in medio-passive (see HW^2 *s.v. kallareš-, gallareš-* [p. 25]).

^{LÚ}DUB.SAR.GIŠ

See van den Hout 2010a for translation 'clerk, administrator', against earlier 'scribe on wood'.

^{GIŠ}DUB.ŠEN

With Steinkeller 1981, the ^{GIŠ}DUB.ŠEN is not just a tablet container, but also a box for treasures in general that, in Mesopotamia, often appeared among temple furnishings. This description fits well with the use of the term in the Hittite PTAC, where ^{GIŠ}DUB.ŠEN are found containing a variety of precious objects. HIT (p. 190) proposed an equation of the terms $^{\text{(GIŠ)}}$*ḫa/urnašal(l)a-*, ^{GIŠ}*KANḪANNU*, and ^{GIŠ}DUB.ŠEN, on the basis that all three terms are recapitulated in 4.2.4 rev. 8′ with ^{GIŠ}DUB.ŠEN – although cf. the pertinent objection of HIT (*loc. cit.*) and HW^2 Ḫ *s.v.* $^{\text{(GIŠ)}}$*ḫa/urnašal(l)a-* (p. 321) that the ^{GIŠ}*KAN-ḪA-AN.* of 4.2.4 rev. 7′ is made of silver, whereas the ŠU.NÍGIN 7 ^{GIŠ}DUB.ŠEN in rev. 8′ only mentions ivory, ebony, and gold. If the equation ^{GIŠ}DUB.ŠEN with ^{GIŠ}*KANḪANNU* is accepted, then the appearance of $^{\text{(GIŠ)}}$*KAN-Ḫ*]*A-AN-NU* DUB.SAR in 8.5 rev. iv(?) 5′ confirms – the exception proving the rule – Steinkeller's point that unmodified ^{GIŠ}DUB.ŠEN/*KANḪANNU* was a generic treasure box, since its use as a scribal or tablet container required further specification.

DUG.KA.GAG

See Weeden 2011, 258–59 for discussion, and earlier del Monte 1995b, 219–24 with observation of close association of the DUG.KA.GAG vessel with beer.

$^{\text{(URUDU)}}$DUG.$^{\text{(LÚ)}}$SAGI(.A)

See Siegelová 1984, 108 fn. 9 for the argument for translating $^{\text{(URUDU)}}$DUG.$^{\text{(LÚ)}}$SAGI(.A), lit. 'cupbearer's vessel', as perhaps also 'scoop, ladle' based on its combination with a wash basin NÍG.ŠU.LUḪ(.ḪA). In addition to the two cases with NÍG.ŠU.LUḪ(.ḪA) she cited (4.1.1.3 obv. 6; 3.1.1.A$_3$ rev. iv 12′), Siegelová's observation is further borne out by the appearance of $^{\text{(URUDU)}}$DUG.$^{\text{(LÚ)}}$SAGI(.A) in other contexts with articles of toiletry (and not drinking vessels) in 4.2.6 rev.$^{?}$ 5′ and 4.2.9 lo. e. 32′.

$^{\text{(GIŠ)}}$DÙG.GAN

In Mesopotamia ^{kuš}dùg.gan = *tukkannu* 'leather bag' (see CAD T *s.v. tukkannu* [pp. 456–57]), but at Boğazköy the ^{KUŠ}DÙG.GAN (note the obligatory ^{KUŠ} determinative!) and $^{\text{(GIŠ)}}$DÙG.GAN seem to be two completely different objects, with the latter inferentially translated as 'sheath' since Güterbock 1973, 83. Only the $^{\text{(GIŠ)}}$DÙG.GAN appears in the PTAC, where it is in every instance found in the context of knives or blades, suggesting that the additional meaning 'Behälter$^{?}$' suggested by HZL no. 335 (p. 259) for $^{\text{(GIŠ)}}$DÙG.GAN is unnecessary. The $^{\text{(GIŠ)}}$DÙG.GAN in the PTAC are described as being made of leather/having leather components (9.2.4 rev. iv 4), made of wood overlaid with gold (9.1.1 rev. iii 7′), or just made of gold, which might also be overlay on an unspecified substrate (8.1.E(A_1) rev. iv$^{?}$ 16; 6.2 obv. 2′).

^{LÚ}DUGUD

From Burgin 2019, 47:

> On the reading $^{\text{LÚ.MEŠ}}$DUGUD = Akk. *kabtūti* = Hitt. $^{\text{LÚ.MEŠ}}$*nakkieš* 'important ones, dignitaries', Weeden (2011, 198–99) concluded that the logogram DUGUD designates the adjective *daššu-* 'heavy' when suffixed with phonetic complement *-u-*, and *nakki-* 'important' when uncomplemented. The ^{LÚ}DUGUD is normally a military title with courtly functions (cf. von Schuler 1956: 209–223; Beal 1992: 488–504). Through the DUGUD = *nakki-* equation, it can also refer to the $^{\text{LÚ.MEŠ}}$*nakkieš* 'dignitaries' found in the manuscripts of the KI.LAM Great Assembly. Weeden left open the (admittedly slim) possibility that the military title ^{LÚ}DUGUD and the civilian(?) $^{\text{LÚ.MEŠ}}$*nakkiš* were originally one and the same, or at least homophonous titles.

In 3.1.10, a domestic tribute list, it is impossible to tell whether the ^{LÚ}DUGUD are attested in their military capacity, or as civilian dignitaries. In contrast to the military title, the civilian ^{LÚ}DUGUD does not have a clearly defined administrative role. Some hint of their importance, however, comes from the KI.LAM Great Assembly, where the ^{LÚ}DUGUD 'dignitaries' described attending the meal were probably visiting and local grandees invited to partake of a feast with the king (Burgin 2019, 28–29). In CTH 272 – 'A Royal Reprimand of the Dignitaries' (see edition of J. Miller 2013, 73–77; also comments of Bilgin 2018, 365–66), the $^{\text{LÚ.MEŠ}}$DUGUD are reprimanded for taking advantage of $^{\text{LÚ.MEŠ}}$TUKUL 'socagers' who held land for agricultural rent, implying the dignitaries had some sort of economic authority over workers in their region. If the ^{LÚ}DUGUD in 3.1.10 are local civilian potentates, and not military officers, then it seems one of their tasks was also to escort tribute from towns in their regions to Ḫattuša. It could be that the ^{LÚ}DUGUD were assigned to these otherwise unknown mining towns (see introductory *Analysis* to 3.1.10) because the settlements were too small to have official governors (LÚ ^{URU}GN), or alternatively, if the ^{LÚ}DUGUD were natives of the towns, they were not important enough to be designated as governors.

DUḪ.ŠÚ.A

See now Thavapalan 2020, 244–63 for comprehensive discussion, with previous literature, of the color term DUḪ.ŠÚ.A (also written DUḪ.ŠI.A, Hurr. *tuḫšiwa/tuḫšuwa*, Akk. *duḫšu/dušû*, Heb. *taḥaš*). The term is applied to various materials, but was perhaps originally the designation for a variety of stone, specifically a type of yellowish banded calcite (*op. cit.*, 260). Thus, the original translation of HIT (p. 249) of ^{GIŠ}PISAN DUḪ.ŠÚ.A as "orange-yellow chest" is substantially correct.

$^{\text{(TÚG)}}$E.ÍB.KUN

See Baccelli et al. 2014, 124 for the suggestion that a "belt with tail" might be represented on the figure found on the King's Gate relief at Ḫattuša.

^{KUŠ}E.SIR $^{\text{(URU)}}$*ḫat(t)a/ili*

Contra the translation 9.2.6 obv. i 9′: ^{KUŠ}E.SIR ^{URU}*ḫattal*[*i* "Schuhe hethitische[r Art" in HVP (p. 57), the existence of the spelling variations ^{URU}*ḫattali*/^{URU}*ḫatili* and the fact that the other type of shoes in the PTAC designated by geographic origin, namely the ^{KUŠ}E.SIR ^{URU}*kašipura*, appears without the adverbial suffix *-ili* suggest that the ^{KUŠ}E.SIR ^{URU}*ḫat(t)a/ili* were named after a separate town, ^{URU}*ḫat(t)a/ili*, which was apparently known for a style of shoe.

É(.GAL) $^{\text{(URU)}}$...

See Siegelová 2001 for discussion of the economic and administrative functions of the regional palaces (with Kryszeń 2016, 179, the list of known regional palaces can now be updated to include the É.GAL *tak-ki-pu-ut-ta* in KUB 46.17 rev. iv 1 [CTH 529], a cult inventory in which the palace at Takkiputta supplies livestock and grain to the Spring Festival at Zipplanda). As Siegelová (p. 207) concluded from the textual evidence, the regional palace:

- ... sorgt für die Steuererhebung in seinem Umkreis und leitet die eingezogenen Abgaben (wenigstens teilweise) an zentrale Thesaurierungs- und Redistributionseinrichtungen weiter
- dient als eine Redistributionseinrichtung in seinem Umkreis (gegebenenfalls mit Akzent auf gewisse Warenarten)
- übt eigene Wirtschaftstätigkeit aus und kontrolliert den Produktionsverlauf in seinem Bereich
- verfügt über Personal und NAM.RA; die Letzteren stellt er nach Weisung der Zentralmacht auch für regionübergreifende Aufgaben zur Verfügung
- sorgt für Kultverpflegung – entweder auf Palastkosten, meistens jedoch auf Kosten der Leute des Palastes.

The best illustration of the functions of the regional palace in practice comes from the Maşat-Tapikka archives, a town of the lowest administrative rank (see Imparati 1997, 201–6 for an overview of the interactions of the palace at Ortaköy-Šapinuwa with the town of Maşat-Tapikka).

As may be expected in a "wealth-financed" model predicated on the control of international luxury goods, while many regional palaces are found supplying festivals and cults in their hinterland, very few are found supplying luxury objects to Ḫattuša. Hence, very few true regional palaces (as distinguished from "regional" palaces that were actually government offices – see below) appear in the PTAC:

É.GAL ^{URU}*Ḫupišna*	8.1.E(A_3) l. e. 1
É.GAL ^{URU}*Šapinuwa*	3.1.5.A_2 obv. ii(?) 10′
É.GAL ^{URU}*Kašaya*	5.1 obv. ii 4′

The first of these, the palace at Ḫupišna, lies outside of discussion of a redistributive model. The enormous shipment of goods documented in the KASKAL-series directed from Ḫattuša to, or through, the palace at Ḫupišna is a one-off event of national importance (see introductory *Analysis* to 8.1), which by its magnitude stands too far outside any normal instance of redistribution to illuminate the system.

The mention of the É.GAL ^{URU}*Šapinuwa* in 3.1.5, in contrast, seems at first glance to be exactly the kind of record of tribute that Siegelová supposed when she described the regional palaces as responsible for collecting and shipping the tribute from their regions to Ḫattuša. The text records tribute in the form of bulk amounts of tin and copper in the approximate ratios needed to make bronze, received from locations spanning Anatolia, from Kizzuwatna in the southeast (3.1.5.A_2 obv. ii(?) 6′) to Awana (= Auna by Tumana(?)) (3.1.5.A_1 obv. ii(?)5′) in the far northwest. The positioning of the É.GAL ^{URU}*Šapinuwa* at the head of a new section in 3.1.5.A_2 obv. ii(?) 10′, would seem to confirm Siegelová's assessment of Šapinuwa as an entrepôt for tribute to be sent to Ḫattuša. However, the closest analogue to 3.1.5, where tribute received from local towns is divided into sections headed by an institution, comes from 3.1.1. Here, all of the institutions were located at Ḫattuša and must be interpreted as the receiving or storage institutions (see introductory *Analysis* to 3.1.1) for the tribute. Thus, the role of the "Palace at Šapinuwa" in 3.1.5 cannot be decided: On the one hand, if it were the actual local palace, it would be the sole textual attestation of a regional palace interfacing with the tribute system of the central administration. This might be conceivably due to the relative proximity of Šapinuwa to Ḫattuša, which would allow for more direct administrative control. On the other hand, the É.GAL ^{URU}*Šapinuwa* could refer to an institution at Ḫattuša itself, which, given the continued importance of Šapinuwa, might have continued to retain the hypothesized original function of the "regional" palaces as economic-administrative embassies for their respective cities.

The third mention of a regional palace, the É.GAL ^{URU}*Kašaya* in 5.1, appears not as the institution itself, but as part of a personal name. In 5.1 obv. ii 4′–5′, Ḫešmi-Šarruma, who is almost certainly the member of the extended royal family (DUMU.LUGAL) of the same name (Bilgin 2018, 394), supervised the issuance of a small number of silver items (at least one silver cup and one silver drinking straw) to a certain ^{m}*Wattiḫaḫla* ^{LÚ}SIPA É.GAL ^{URU}*Kašaya*. As discussed in the introductory *Analysis* to 5.1, the *ĪDE*-texts are a sort of running account of distributions for palace business distributions. In the case of the Wattiḫaḫla, the small numbers of items suggests a personal gift or handout, rather than a transfer of material from the central administration to the palace at Kašaya.

As also discussed by Siegelová (2001, 203–7), there are also "regional" palaces named after locations in the northern heartland that seem to have become fully centralized institutions. These are the É(.GAL) $^{(URU)}$*Ḫariyaša*, the É(.GAL) $^{(URU)}$*Gaz(zi)mara*, and the É.GAL *Šulupašši*. All three appears in the PTAC:

É.GAL ^{URU}*Ḫariyaša*	3.1.1.A_1 rev. v 2′
É *Gazzimara*	4.1.3.1 6′; 3.2.1 rev. 11′
É.GAL *Šulupašši*	4.1.4.6 obv. 12′

As explained by Siegelová (p. 203), these palaces were "drei Zentren, die weder in der alten Tradition stehen noch bis jetzt in der Gebietsaufteilung richtig verankert werden können." Since Siegelová's article, Kryszeń 2016, 179 added to this group the É(.GAL) $^{(URU)}$*Takkiputta*, which like the others, occasionally appears without its geographic determinative. These regional palaces are attested almost exclusively as economic-administrative institutions, to the point that their original geographical location is difficult to determine: only Šulupašši can be confidently placed, and then only in the broad region somewhere between Ḫattuša, Šamuḫa, and Šarišša (Hazenbos 2012, 289).

For the É.GAL URU*Ḫariyaša*, note that contra Siegelová (*op. cit.*, 203), comparison with the other institutions appearing at the ends of sections in 3.1.1 indicates that it was the recipient of or storage point for tribute already located in Ḫattuša, and not an intake point for the tribute (see introductory *Analysis* to 3.1.1).

For the É (URU)*Gazzimara-*, as Siegelová described (*op. cit.*, 205), the institution was intimately associated with the other "houses" of the central government apparatus, and is found providing foodstuffs, wool, and deportees, often for cult and festival provisioning purposes. In the PTAC the institution is attested twice, in both cases with wool products. As Siegelová (*loc. cit.*) noted, a representative of the É *Gazzimara*, certain m*Mašidu*, is listed after a quantity of fine wool in 4.1.3.1 6′, and then a m*Makarduwaš* of the same institution (3.2.1 rev. 11′) gives as *MADDATTU*-tribute a quantity of dyed wool and two belts. As is argued in the introductory *Analysis* to 3.2.1, while not necessarily a workshop in its own right, the exchange of unfinished wool for finished wool products indicates that the É *Gazzimara* was, along with other palatial institutions, responsible for the delivery of "value-added tribute" to the central palace storehouses.

Finally, the É.GAL *Šulupašši* is attested only once in the PTAC, where it appears at the end of a paragraph listing an amount of dyed wool followed by a modest number of finished belts. Whereas Siegelová 2001, 206–7, assumed that the Šulupašši-palace mentioned in the texts was located in the town itself, Bilgin 2018, 397 fn. 141, noted that: "considering that all other institutions mentioned in KUB 42.48 [= 4.1.4.6] obv. 12′ are probably part of the palace complex on Büyükkale, it is likely that Šulupašši-house also refers to a building in the same complex or somewhere nearby within the city of Ḫattuša." It is hypothesized in the introductory *Analysis* to 4.1.4.6 that the institutions named in the text are receiving the belts as gifts as handouts, rather than being the sources or sites of production.

É *ḫarwašiaš*

The É *ḫarwašiaš*, lit. "house of secret (things)" was translated "secret house" in HIT (p. 7). Concerning the meaning of the term in practical terms, HVP tentatively hypothesized (p. 75 fn. 3):

> É *ḫarwašiaš*, abgeleitet von *ḫarwaši-* "geheim", im Sinne von besonders gesichertem, verborgenem Ort der Reservenaufbewahrung? Vgl. dazu 1251/z, 11′ *n*]*a-at-kán* LÚE.DÉ.A *an-d*[*a* (12′)]x-*e ḫar-wa-ši* É-*ir*[(13′)-]*e an-da pí-da*[*-an-zi* und Bo 7953 II 7′: É *ḫar-wa-ši-ia-aš ku-it* (8′) *ar-ḫa šar-ra-aḫ-ḫu-un*

HVP (p. 85) then translated the IGI.DU$_8$.A É *ḫarwašiaš* of IBoT 1.31 rev. 5 as "Pflichtgeschenk der Reservenkammer," and the same translation was also adopted in HW^2 Ḫ *s.v. ḫarwaši-* (p. 384). While a translation "reserves chamber" is perhaps the best that can be done based on the limited attestations of the term, three further philological points may be added.

First, the fragment 1251/z (= KBo 35.92) 11′–13′ cited by HVP (*loc. cit.*) is Copy F of the first tablet of the "Ritual of Allaituraḫ(ḫ)i" (CTH 780.II.Tf01.F), the much better preserved duplicate of which, VSNF 12.57+ (CTH 780.II.Tf01.G) obv. i 10′–12′, shows the connection of *ḫarwaši* É-*ir* with É *ḫarwašiaš* to be illusory. The transliterations VSNF 12.57+ obv. 10′: "*nu* GIŠPISAN *ḫar-wa-*[(*ši*)] ⌜É⌝-*ir*" and KBo 35.92 12′: "G]IŠPISAN (Autographie: E) *ḫar-wa-ši* É-*ir*" given in the most recent edition by Haas (2007, p. 14, with translation: "Und an einem geheimen Platz im Haus (ist) ein Korb") are based on a mistake in the handcopy of VSNF 12.57+. As Groddek et al. 2002, 94 fn. 6 noted in their transliteration of VSNF 12.57 obv. 10′: "Die Autographie Weidners bietet ein deutliches, unbeschädigtes GIŠ, worauf ebenfalls ein klares E folgt." This led them to read GIŠPISAN!, which was adopted, without exclamation mark, by Haas. Consulting the photos, however, shows the handcopy to be incorrect. The alleged undamaged GIŠ is in fact ⌜*ku*⌝-, with the head of the lowest horizontal visible in the photograph; cf. also the different shape of the sign compared to the GIŠ/*iz*-signs elsewhere in the text, e.g., *ḫandaizzi* (obv. 13′) and *paizzi* (obv. 14′), which show the heads of the horizontals stacked evenly, whereas the ⌜*ku*⌝- in obv. 10′ matches the indented middle horizontal of the *ku*-sign in *ekuzi* in obv. 14′. Together with the fact that both VSNF 12.57+ obv. 11′ and KBo 35.92 12′ show a clear -*e*, which need not be emended to PISAN!, the text should thus read:

VSNF 12.57+ (= CTH 780.II.Tf01.G)
obv. i
11′ *na-at pár-na pé-e-da-i nu* ⌜*ku*⌝*-e ḫar-wa-*⌜*ši* É⌝*-ir*
12′ *na-aš-ta* MUNUSŠU.GI SÍSKUR *a-pí-ia an-da da-a-i*

> "He brings it (*scil.* the supplies purchased from the smith) to the buildings/rooms. Which(ever) secret buildings/rooms (there are), in there the Old Woman places the ritual (supplies)."

The main translation difficulty comes from *kue*, which can only be a pl. nom.-acc. n. indefinite pronoun, forcing *ḫarwaši* and É-*ir* to also be plural. Morphologically this is no problem: CHD P *s.v. per/parn-* (p. 274) lists É-*er* without allographic plural markers as a viable form of the pl. nom.-acc. n., and as a non-ablauting *i*-stem adjective, the form *ḫarwaši* can also be a pl. nom.-acc. n. Semantically one must imagine that a collective "structure" is intended, either a group of nearby buildings or connected rooms (the distinction being blurry in the agglutinative architecture of the Hittite world). The phrase *nu kue ḫarwaši* É-*ir* 12′ *n=ašta* MUNUSŠU.GI SÍSKUR *apiya anda dāi*, then, may be interpreted as preposed non-specific relative construction (GHL §30.59, pp. 424–25). The Old Woman's setting up of the ritual in the secret rooms of the building is intended to mirror and counteract the deeds of the unknown evil magician, who later in the text (VSNF 12.57+ obv. ii 23′–24′) is accused of having done or made something in the steppe (LÍL-*ri*), brought it into the city (URU-*ia*), and once in the city, set it in an inner room (ŠÀ É.ŠÀ, Hittite *tunakkešni*) in a hidden place (*ḫarwaši pedi*). Thus, despite the appearance of a smith (LÚSIMUG.A) within a few lines of a "hidden house" (*ḫarwaši* É-*ir*), closer examination shows that VSNF 12.57+ and KBo 35.92 have little to contribute to understanding the É *ḫarwašiaš* in the PTAC. It may only be deduced that common households could also have secret places in their inner rooms. Whether this location was the domestic analog to the É *ḫarwašiaš* of the Hittite state remains to be seen.

Second, HVP (*loc. cit.*) also cited unpublished Bo 7953 obv. ii 7′–8′: É *ḫarwašiyaš kuit arḫa šarraḫḫun*, translated in HW² Ḫ (p. 385): "weil ich (den Anteil?) der Reservenkammer abgetrennt habe ...." Bo 7953 belongs to a *Sammeltafel* concerning inquiries into spiritual misdeeds committed during the time of Ḫattušili III and Tudḫaliya IV (see edition and discussion of partial duplicate KUB 56.19 in Ünal 2003, 380–88 and de Roos 2007, 247–55). The context of Bo 7953 obv. ii is that the king is trying to determine why the god is angry. One of the self-suggested causes is "dividing the É *ḫarwašiaš*." As the king explains (translation here following the *Grabungsumschrift*):

Bo 7953 obv. ii 3′–27′

> "But [I took(?)] nothing for myself, and I destroyed nothing. Before the Storm-god my lord, I confessed the matter! Given that I divided the É *ḫarwašiaš* (É *ḫarwašiyaš* 8′ *kuit arḫa šarraḫḫun*) – if you, the Storm-god my lord, are an[gry] with me on account of that matter – now you, the Storm-god my lord, speak to me by oracle in divine guidan[ce]! When I handed it (*scil.* the É *ḫarwašiaš*) over, I had also already (at that time) brought it back together (EGIR-*pa=ya=t anda* 16′ *karū arnunun*). Be not angry with me in any way, O Storm-god my lord, on account of the matter of the É *ḫarwašiaš*! I confessed the matter. But now, to whomsoever at all (*kuedani=pat kuedani=pat*) you, the Storm-god my lord, assign the É *ḫarwašiaš* – show it to me, [Storm-god] my [lord], by oracle, [or] speak it to me by dream – [and] I will hand [it] over to that one (*apedani parā peḫḫi*)."

There are two translational difficulties in this passage. The first is the sense of *parā pai-* in obv. ii 14′ and 27′. The combination can mean to "hand over" in the literal sense, but also figuratively to give up a claim or control of, e.g., tribute, prisoners, etc., and to dedicate things to gods. While not certain, since *kuedani=pat kuedani=pat* in obv. ii 22′ mentions no god, it is safer to assume that *parā pai-* is used in its mundane sense of handing over claim or control. The second crux is the meaning of the phrase pair *arḫa šarra-* (obv. ii 8′) and *anda ... arnu-* (obv. ii 15′–16′). The structure of the passage indicates that the actions must be the opposites of each other. The separation of *anda* from the verb shows that it is not a preverb, and so must be taken as a free-standing adverb in the sense of either "in" or perhaps "together." The pair of actions may thus be interpreted as the king reversing his division of the É *ḫarwašiaš* by bringing it back together prior to handing it over. As a matter between the king and his god, the narration of the state of affairs behind this passage is elliptical. It may be reconstructed that the king at some point held responsibility for the É *ḫarwašiaš*. Since it is known that members of the royal family were entrusted with responsibility over various palatial institutions, perhaps this occurred when he was still a prince. During his superintendence of the institution he did no damage to it (obv. ii 3′–4′). He did, however, "divide it," which he suspects is what angered the god. The division of the É *ḫarwašiaš* may refer to separating its contents over two locations, or to splitting responsibility for the institution (the two might be the same in effect). In either case, contents and/or responsibility were reunited prior to the king handing back the institution for the first time (obv. ii 14′). At some point the king came into possession of the É *ḫarwašiaš* again, perhaps in the sense of his assuming ultimate authority for the palace upon becoming king, and he asks the god to designate who should hold the institution henceforth. If nothing more, it may be learned from the passage that the É *ḫarwašiaš* was a palatial institution that could command the direct attention of the king and that apparently was disturbed at great spiritual risk.

Third, in its single attestation in the PTAC, 2.7.A rev. 5′, the É *ḫarwašiaš* is the origin(?) of a small quantity of heterogenous items given as IGI.DU$_8$.A-tribute. Since IGI.DU$_8$.A is to be understood as a customary gift of variable size, rather than a fixed tribute (see *Lexical Commentary*, *s.v.* IGI.DU$_8$.A below), then coupled with the previous point that the É *ḫarwaši* should not be "divided" lightly, it can be suggested that the É *ḫarwašiaš* did not participate in the normal circulation of the palace economy.

The three points discussed, namely that private houses could also have hidden areas, that the É *ḫarwašiaš* could command the direct attention of the king, and that the institution was involved with IGI.DU$_8$.A gifts, generally support the interpretation of HVP of the É *ḫarwašiaš* was a "Reservenkammer," but also suggest connection with the idea of a "hoard" in the historical sense of a collection of valuables cached in a hidden or guarded location. Prior to the advent of reliable lock-boxes and safes, the only recourse for long-term storage of valuables for most households was hiding or burying them, with only state institutions able to afford permanent guards for their hoards. It can be imagined, then, that the É *ḫarwašiaš* was originally the hoard of the king's household, which later developed into a government institution in its own right that could be asked for occasional (value-added) tribute.

É(.GAL) *tuppaš*

Discussion of the É(.GAL) *tuppaš* has proceeded along two lines of interpretation: morphological and functional. Functionally, the institution was established as meaning "seat of administration" as early as Imparati 1969, 157, with the major disagreement being over whether it was the seat of administration of the central government in a vassal state (so Imparati, *op. cit.*, also Imparati 1982, 259) or the representative of a vassal administration in Ḫattuša (Archi 1973, 213–14). Morphologically, the name of the institution was interpreted as "tablet house" (see Neu 1983a, 201 fn. 586 for previous literature) until HIT (pp. 63–64) showed it must be "house of chests, i.e., storehouse" (followed by Neu 1983a, 201 fn. 586; HVP 198–99, with an overview of its economic functions; Otten 1988, 40). Further discussion of its function ensued (Beal 1992, 53, pointed to evidence from the Bronze Tablet, Bo 86/299 rev. iii 32–33 and KBo 4.10 obv. 42–44 to argue that: "some É *tuppa*-s were barracks for troops from the provinces;" Beckman 1999a, 120 translated the term as "armory" in the same passages, whereas van den Hout 1995, 66; Klinger 2005, 135; and Devecchi 2015, 178 maintained the neutral "Verwaltung"/"amministrazione," though with continued disagreement over whether it is the central administration at Ḫattuša or the local administration in the Ḫulaya-River-land that is meant), but without explicit discussion or incorporation of the updated morphological interpretation. To my knowledge, no explicit explanation has been given why the "house of chests" should also be a "seat of administration" in the Hittite world, but see implicitly van den Hout 2010a, 266–67, who discusses the hapax *tupalān* and the related **tuppalanura/i-*, deriving both from ^{GIŠ}*tuppa-* 'chest', with a meaning **tup(p)ala* = "administrator, clerk" and *tuppalanura/i-* "chief of the administrators" (against the usual translation "scribe" and "chief of the scribes": cf. also the objections of Giorgieri – Mora 2012, 651, to the derivation of *tuppala-* from *tuppi* 'tablet'). This forms a simple syllogism: É *tuppaš* 'house of chests = seat of (economic) administration', **tup(p)al(l)a* 'men of the chests = (economic) administrators'.

One further philological point can be made about the É(.GAL) *tuppaš*. First, the connection of the institution with wool processing in HVP (198–99) based on the attestations in 3.2.1 rev. 8′ and 4.1.3.1 5′ (which are, in fact, the only attestations of the institution in the PTAC) is probably a mirage. As discussed in the introductory *Analysis* to 3.2.1, the individuals and institutions contributing the garments were not necessarily themselves the manufacturers. Rather, the conversion of the raw wool into finished products was a type of "value-added" tribute for which many government institutions were responsible (cf. also 4.1.2.1 and 4.1.2.2). That the institution appears in the text makes it no more a wool processing site than the É *Gazzimara* or the various towns attested in the texts. The other economic interactions of the É(.GAL) *tuppaš* outside of the PTAC cited by HVP (*loc. cit.*) come from ritual contexts, where the institution delivers token offerings (an unspecified quantity of tin and copper in KUB 30.32 obv. i 5, followed by a handful of garments in obv. i 18–19; a club in Bo 3459 1′) alongside other non-economic institutions (Bo 3459 2′: É MUNUS.LUGAL; 3′: É.GAL ^{LÚ}SANGA). In short, there is no evidence that the É(.GAL) *tuppaš* operated as a manufacturing facility.

É GIŠ.KIN-*TI*

See Gordin 2010 and Weeden 2011, 85–89 (with previous literature) for discussions of this institution, which was a kind of workshop (employing at least 205 persons, according to KBo 19.28), which produced, among other things, inscribed metal and stone objects. Note that the difficulties discussed in Gordin 2010 in connecting the 33 $^{LÚ.MEŠ}$DUB.SAR.GIŠ (KBo 19.28 obv. 5) of the É GIŠ.KIN-*TI* with the prosopography of known scribes are obviated if the ^{LÚ}DUB.SAR.GIŠ is taken, with van den Hout 2010a, as a (not necessarily literate) "clerk, administrator." In the context of the PTAC, the É GIŠ.KIN-*TI* is attested once in 4.1.4.9 obv. 7 as the destination for *guzza*-cloths to be cut and tailored for various applications.

É ^{D}UTU-*ŠI*

See Cammarosano 2019, 64, for a list of attestations of É.GAL É ^{D}UTU-*ŠI* (KUB 5.9+ obv. 9; KpT 1.36 obv. i 43, obv. ii 15, rev. iv 45), to which 4.1.4.6 obv. 4′ may be added. The context of the É.GAL É ^{D}UTU-*ŠI* in 4.1.4.6 obv. 4′ is among other organs of the palace, namely the É.GAL É ŠÀ.TAM (obv. 6′), É.GAL É ^{NA_4}KIŠIB GÍD.DA (obv. 8′), É.GAL *šu-lu-pa-aš-ši* (obv. 12′), and É.GAL MUNUS.LUGAL (lo. e. 16′). Since the otherwise superfluous É.GAL before the entries in 4.1.4.6 probably specifies their location on Büyükkale, the É.GAL É ^{D}UTU-*ŠI* might have been the main economic household or estate of the king.

É-*TUM* GAL/*RABÛ*

The two main interpretations of the É-*TUM* GAL/*RABÛ* have been on the one hand that of Güterbock (1970, 180; 1974, 305), who argued that the term designated the main temple of a city, and specifically the Great Temple (Temple 1) in the context of Ḫattuša, and on the other hand that of Otten (1971, 22–23; followed by Weeden 2011, 473), who argued that the term was equivalent to É.GAL, the palace. Both interpretations have their problems, and unfortunately no clarifying attestations have been forthcoming. Note that the equation É-*TUM* GAL/*RABÛ* = É.GAL = [É]*ḫalentuwa* in Weeden 2011, 473, is not necessarily proved by the passage cited from KBo 19.128, a tablet from the second day of the AN.DAḪ.ŠUM-festival, the opening paragraph of which reads (obv. i 1–5): *mān* [É]*ḫalentūwa* [2] *ḫaššanzi* LUGAL-*uš uizzi* [3] *naššu padait našma* [4] [GIŠ]*ḫulugannit I-NA* É-*TIM* GAL [5] *paizzi* "When they open the *ḫalentuwa*, the king comes and goes either by foot or by carriage into the 'Great House'." Instead, all that may be inferred is that the É-*TIM* GAL was within walking distance of the *ḫalentuwa*-, i.e., the "(great) hall" (see *Lexical Commentary, s.v.* [É]*ḫalentuwa*- above), in this case probably the hall of the main palace in Ḫattuša, where the day's activities presumably begin. A new study of the word is no doubt desirable.

In the context of the PTAC, the attestation in 3.1.1.A_1 shows the É-*TUM RABÛ* to be among the many institutions receiving tribute for use and storage (note that the attestation in 3.1.1.A_1 rev. v 3′: É-*TUM RA-BU-Ú* also emends the observation of Güterbock 1974, 305, that the institution only ever appears in genitive É-*TIM* GAL). The institution appears late in the text, in rev. v 3′–7′, where it receives in total only two chariots. This is by far the smallest amount of tribute handed out in the text, and suggests that the É-*TUM RABÛ* was not the (main) palace or the great temple.

É.GAL *ḫekur* [D]LAMMA

See *Lexical Commentary, s.v.* [NA₄]*ḫekur* for main discussion. The É].GAL *ḫekur* [D]LAMMA in 3.1.1.A_2 rev. vi 2′ was probably located on Nişantepe in Ḫattuša (van den Hout 2002, 88). Being located in Ḫattuša, [D]LAMMA should probably be interpreted here as Inar, the tutelary deity of that city.

É.GAL *karupaḫi*-

Contra HED IV *s.v. karupahi* (p. 115), an improved reading of 4.1.3.2 rev. 9′ (see *Commentary*) now confirms that *karupaḫi* never occurs without an É(.GAL) determinative. The sense of "granary," as opposed to generic "storehouse," recoverable from the etymology of É(.GAL) *karupaḫi* (Hoffner 1974, 37) is not perceptible in the PTAC. In 8.1.E(A_1) obv. ii 7, 15, the É.GAL *karupaḫi*- provides chests of garments, which is not an obvious function of a granary.

É.NA_4

The translation of É.NA_4 (and É.ŠÀ *ḫaštiyaš*) as "royal funerary structure" follows Miller 2013, 369 n. 284. See Miller 2013, 209 for previous literature on the É.NA_4 institution, which was a specific cultic building within the larger royal cemetery (Singer 2009, 171), supported by dedicated staff and land-grants, and tasked with housing the mortal remains of the Hittite royal family.

É.ŠÀ *ḫaštiyaš*

See *Lexical Commentary, s.v.* É.NA_4 above. If the É.NA_4 is the institution, then the É.ŠÀ *ḫaštiyaš*, lit. "the inner room of bones", was the ossuary or inner sanctum of the structure that contained the actual bones.

EGIR-*anda*

Although sporadically translated in the editions of HVP as 'back, in return' (see especially 4.1.1.1, HVP 100–8, esp. 101 fn. 5: "EGIR-*an(da) uda-* ... 'zurückbringen, (nach geleisteter Arbeit) liefern'"), there are no examples for EGIR-*anda* in the PTAC where EGIR-*anda* must form a semantic unit with a verb to give a sense "to give in return, to give back," nor indeed anywhere else (cf. CHD P *s.v. pai-* B, *pe-*, *piya-* k 6′ [p. 52] where EGIR-*anda pai-* has only a temporal sense "to give afterwards"). Such a translation would need to rely on the infrequently attested confusion of EGIR-*an(da)* = *appan(da)* 'behind (location where)' with *appa* 'back (location to)' in New Hittite (HW^2 A *s.v. appa*[3], *a-ap-pa* = (jheth.) EGIR-*pa* V. Kontamination *appa/appan* im Jheth. [p. 151]), which should not be forced unless the context clearly demands it. Instead, EGIR-*anda* can be interpreted in its temporal sense 'afterwards' in every attestation in the PTAC, save for 9.1.5 rev.[!] 14′, where it has a locational sense. The sense of '(to bring/give) back, in return' is expressed in 4.1.1.1 by the expected EGIR-*pa*, e.g., 4.1.1.1.A_1 rev. 6′: (They gave it to them for replating), *karū* EGIR-[*pa*] *uter* "they have already brought (it) back here" (cf. 4.1.1.1.B_2 obv. i[?] 7′:]x-*aš* EGIR-*pa uter*). Indeed, the example cited by HVP (101 fn. 5) in support of the interpretation "zurückbringen, (nach geleisteter Arbeit) liefern" for EGIR-*anda uda-*, namely KUB 13.35 rev. iv 4, is actually EGIR-*pa uda-*, preserving the EGIR-*anda* vs. EGIR-*pa* distinction observed in 4.1.1.1.

EN ŠU-*TI*

EN ŠU-*TI* is presumably identical with EN *QA-TI* (see Weeden 2011, 483). With d'Alfonso (2010, 78–80), identification of the EN ŠU-*TI*/*QA-TI* as 'craftsman, handworker' in Hittite against Akkadian *bēl qātāti* 'guarantor' is secured by the passage KBo 5.4 obv. 39′ (CTH 67 – Treaty of Muršili II with Targašnalli of Ḫapalla): [LÚ]APIN.LÁ-*ma našma=aš* [LÚ][UŠ.BAR?] [LÚ]NAGAR [LÚ]AŠGAB *kuiš=aš imma kuiš* EN *QA-TI* "but [if] he is a ploughman, or a [weaver?], carpenter, or leatherworker – whatever handworker he is ...." As emphasized by d'Alfonso in discussion of this passage, these craftsmen were among the "low-ranking state dependents, who were assigned by the king to a high-ranking royal dependent and fulfilled a given task under his control" (*op. cit.*, p. 80). The EN *QA-TI*/EN ŠU-*TI* is thus atypical compared to other constructions with EN + x in Hittite cuneiform, which connote an elevated or supervisory function.

EN *UNŪTI*

An infrequently attested title for which there is little information. Bilgin 2018, 328–29 debated between assigning the [m]*pí-ḫa*-[D]10 EN *Ú-NU-TI* "Piḫa-Tarḫunta, lord of the implements" (5.1 rev. iii 1) to Piḫa-Tarḫunta [LÚ]SAG/EUNUCHUS$_2$, a high official and perhaps an augur, or to Piḫa-Tarḫunta, son of Upparamuwa and thus scion of the royal family, before eventually deciding for the former (*op. cit.*, 394). However, the improved reading

^{m}*pí-ḫa-*^{D}10 EN *Ú-NU-TI* ⸢*I*⸣-[*DE* in 5.1 rev. iii 1 now suggests that Piḫa-Tarḫunta was a supervisor, and thus probably the son of Upparamuwa and member of the royal family. If nothing more, this same passage at least also suggests that the *EN UNŪTI* was a high-level title.

^{GIŠ}ESI

Ebony was well known in Egypt and the ancient Near East as a decorative wood, where it often contrasted with ivory. According to Van Lerberghe 1979, 46–47, the ^{GIŠ}ESI/*ušû*-tree referred to two species: African ebony (*Dalbergia melanoxylon*) and Indian ebony (*Diospyros melanoxylon*). In the periods up to and including the Old Babylonian period, when trade with Meluḫḫa was still active, most attestations of the *ušû*-tree referred to the Indian species. Afterwards, in the Kassite period and beyond, most of the ebony attested in Mesopotamia was of the African variety, originating in Sudan and imported through Egypt. Other varieties of 'ebony', all in the *Diospyros* genus, were intermittently available, such as the 'true ebony' (*Diospyros ebenum*) from southern India and Ceylon, and *Diospyros tomentosa*, another type of ebony grown in northern India and similar to the *D. melanoxylon* variety. Besides its decorative use, Goetze 1956, 36–37 noted that ebony seeds were valuable commodities and had medicinal uses in Mesopotamia. Concerning the seeds of the "Hurrian ebony" attested in 2.7.A obv. 9, Van Lerberghe (*op. cit.*, 48) wrote that

> the seed of the 'Hurrian' *ušûm*-tree ... possibly refers to the *Diospyros lotus L.*, a tree which is native to the Anti-Taurus and which is still growing in the region of Maraş (Ahir Daği, Dereköy, alt. 1110 m.). Its *fruit* is globose, 1,5 - 2 cm. in diameter, yellowish or bluish black. Fresh or dried, this berry is edible. When eaten fresh, it is very astringent due to the presence of tannin. This astringency disappears on maturing. All of these characteristics of the fruit are comparable with those of *Diospyros melanoxylon* [Indian Ebony] discussed above.

The *Diospyros lotus*, known as the date-plum or Caucasian persimmon, has a fruit very similar to that of *D. melanoxylon*, which, as Van Lerberghe wrote, "was famous for its medical use," including its use in a dilute extract as "an astringent lotion for the eyes" (*ibid.* 37; according to Van Lerberghe, *ibid.* 43, the ophthalmic properties of ebony were also shared with African/Egyptian variety). The use of ebony as eye medicine is especially relevant as it would fit with the dating of the text to Ḫattušili and Puduḫepa, and the chronic eye ailments of the former, for which queen was constantly seeking a cure. Thus, while 'ebony' seeds, in all their botanical varieties, were a valuable commodity in the ancient Near East, they would have been especially valuable to the court of Ḫattušili III.

GADA *anda damaššuaš*

In the PTAC, the GADA *anda damaššuaš* tends to be listed with other "functional" linens of the construction GADA + vb. subst. (gen.), or GADA + item (gen.). The item appears at the head of the list in 4.2.9 rev. 25′–lo. e. 34′, which appears to record implements necessary for washing, setting a table, and waiting upon a king:

washing: GADA *arrumaš* 'washcloth' (rev. 25′) (cf. ^{URUDU}*warpuaš* 'washbasin' in rev. 30′)

setting: GADA *genuwaš* 'lapcloth' (rev. 27′), ^{GADA}*tanipuš* 'hand towel' (rev. 28′), GADA ^{GIŠ}ŠÚ.A 'chair linen' (rev. 28′), GADA ^{GIŠ}BANŠUR 'tablecloth' (rev. 28′)
waiting: GADA IGI ŠÀ.BA 2 ^{LÚ}SAGI "'eye cloths', of which two are (of the) courtier (type)" (4.2.9 rev. 27′) (cf. ^{URUDU}DUG.SAGI.A 'cupbearer's vessel' in lo. e. 32′)

Paragraphs with similar themes are found in 4.2.6 rev.$^{?}$ 9′–11′, which contain a GADA *genuwaš* (9′), GADA *anda damaššuwaš* (9′), GADA EGIR *arḫa ḫūittiyauwaš* (10′), and GADA *ḫapšaliaš* (11′), and 6.5 rev. 20′–22′, which contain a GADA *arrumaš* 'washcloth' (rev. 20′), GADA IGI 'eye cloth' (rev. 20′), ^{GADA}*gazarnul* 'drying swatch' (rev. 21′), and GADA *ḫapšalliaš* '*ḫapšalli*-chair linen' (rev. 21′, 22′). Unfortunately, the position of the GADA *anda damaššuaš* is not consistent among the lists of 4.2.6, 4.2.9, and 6.5, so no specific function can be assigned. It may at least be confirmed that by the association with the above "functional cloths," it is almost certain that the GADA *anda damaššuaš* was not worn on the body, but was probably either placed on something as covering, or used for a task, such as washing or drying. The motion or activity expressed by *anda damašš*- "pressing/pushing in" is not clear. Previous translations have included Neu 1982, 133: "'Tücher' zum 'Aneinander-Drücken' ('zum Hineinzwängen'$^{?}$);" HIT (p. 123): "Linen of pressing down;" HVP (p. 621) "'Leinen (zum) Aneinander-Drücken', eine Art 'Hülle, Verband'$^{(?)}$."

GADA EGIR*(-an) arḫa* SUD*-uaš*

Another of the "functional" linens (see *Lexical Commentary, s.v.* GADA *anda damaššuaš* above), the GADA EGIR*(-an) arḫa* SUD*-uaš* appears in the context of linens using table service: 4.2.6 rev.$^{?}$ 9′–11′; 4.2.9 rev. 25′–lo. e. 34′; 11.3.6 obv.$^{?}$ 6′ (note the ^{GIŠ}BANŠUR in obv.$^{?}$ 7′). The textile should be translated as something like 'linen for "spreading out (on the) back," but the exact function is unclear.

GADA SU$_6$

Read literally, the GADA SU$_6$ is a "beard-linen." HIT (p. 188), following Güterbock 1971, 5, translated it as "lip(-)cloth," without comment. The translation "Lippentuch" was explained in HVP (p. 65 fn. 2) thus: "KA×SA (SU$_6$) entspricht üblicherweise akkad. *ZIQNU*, 'Bart'. Das Zeichen kann jedoch auch für NUNDUN = *ŠAPTU*, 'Lippe' stehen .... Ein 'Lippentuch' scheint zweckdienlicher als ein 'Tuch (für den) Bart' zu sein." However, as pointed out in Haroutunian 2002, 47 fn. 29, 4.2.4 obv. 1 clearly shows KA×SA (SU$_6$) 'beard' and not KA×NUN (NUNDUN) 'lip', a sign that is also attested at Boğazköy, with Haroutunian's implicit argument being that Hittites would not use KA×SA (SU$_6$) to mean lip when they had the proper sign KA×NUN (NUNDUN) available to them. The best argument is made, again implicitly, by HZL no. 173 (p. 174) with the translation "GADA.SU$_6$ 'Serviette' (wörtlich: Barttuch)," followed without comment by Haroutunian 2002, 47: "'napkin' (lit. 'cloth for beard')." The implication of HZL's definition being that while GADA SU$_6$ is etymologically a linen used to wipe the beard, or at least the area of the face which is covered by a beard on unshaven adult men, in practice it referred to a generic napkin. Since the Hittite men were notoriously clean-shaven vis-à-vis their Near Eastern counterparts (Haroutunian 2002), the word underlying GADA SU$_6$, if it calques the Sumerian signs, was probably borrowed from a bearded culture. As for the function of the GADA SU_6, since the items in the first paragraph of 4.2.4 represent a suite of libation equipment, this napkin/"beard-cloth" may not have been used to wipe faces at all, but rather to dab liquids from the offering implements (though the GA.ZUM 'comb' in obv. 1 leaves open the possibility of a role in maintaining standards of the personal hygiene of the offering king).

$^{(\text{TÚG})}$GAD.DAM

Weeden 2011, 226–27 *s.v.* $^{(\text{TÚG})}$GAD.DAM presented two interpretations for this garment: Read as a true Sumerogram, GAD.DAM must mean 'cloth of the wife', but this is problematic for two reasons, since the word seems to have no intrinsic connection with women or wives in its usage, and according to Weeden the word would be "the only example of a genitive construction using GAD which is additionally determined by TÚG" (p. 226). This led Weeden (p. 227) to suggest that the GADA element was insufficient to identify the object as cloth, raising a possible second interpretation of the word as a pseudo-Sumerogram for a reconstructed Hittite word **kattama(n)* 'low(est) (things)'; hence the interpretation 'leggings'. The 'leggings' interpretation of Weeden was accepted in CHD P *s.v.* $^{(\text{TÚG})}$*patalla-*, with modification that the garment was a type of 'gaiter' in contradistinction to the $^{(\text{TÚG})}$*patalla-* 'puttee'.

^{LÚ}GAD.TAR

See the discussion in Weeden 2011, 227–29 of this logogram, which has received two radically divergent interpretations. On the one hand, according to lexical equation KBo 1.30 obv. 8′–9′, ^{LÚ}GAD.TAR = Akk. *nûʾu* 'foreigner, ignorant man' = Hitt. *dampupi-* 'unskilled man, barbarian(?)' = ^{LÚ}AŠ.ḪAB 'rogue, knave', which Weeden (p. 229) would see as potential evidence that ^{LÚ}GAD.TAR was a pseudo-Sumerogram related to Hittite *kattera-*. On the other hand, KBo 5.11 gives the pair of Hattic correspondences LÚ ^{GIŠ}GIDRU = ^{LÚ}***tanišawa*** (obv. i 16), and ^{LÚ}GAD.TAR = ^{LÚ}***tušḫawadun tanišawe*** (obv. i 17), which according to Nakamura 2002, 56, means the "***tanišaue***(-Mann) der (Gottheit) Tušḫawadu," in effect making ^{LÚ}GAD.TAR a variety of LÚ ^{GIŠ}GIDRU 'staff bearer, herald'. Since heralds were of a high status (see Bilgin 2018, 302–3 for the office), and, even if not a variety of herald, since KBo 5.11 lists functionaries "who sleep up at the palace" (rev. iv 26′: DUB.1^{KAM} ***šer šēšuwaš*** 'first tablet of (those) 'sleeping up (there)'; KBo 5.11 obv. 5–6 ***nu*** *INA* É.GAL-*LIM* ***kuieš šēšanzi n=at parā tianzi*** "those who sleep in the palace, they take up their position"), this indicates a higher status for the ^{LÚ}GAD.TAR than should be allowed by the equations of the lexical list KBo 1.30. The higher status of the ^{LÚ}GAD.TAR better fits the context in the PTAC, where in 6.1 rev. B 5, the ^{LÚ}GAD.TAR is found in a list of important cultic officials (including the priests and great priest of Arinna, the mayor of the town of Ḫallapiya, and the winner of the horserace) who are gifted knives at a celebration of the AN.DAḪ.ŠUM-festival in Arinna. The observation of Weeden (p. 229) that the $^{\text{LÚ.MEŠ}}$GAD.TAR offer an ox at their own expense, instead of sheep, in KUB 25.27 rev. iii 13–16 also in fact speaks to the relative wealth of the group, since oxen were worth multiples of sheep. Nevertheless, the unresolved conflicts between the lexical list KBo 1.30 and the usage in the texts make it safer to conclude with Weeden (*loc. cit.*) that "the logogram must remain ultimately unclarified."

GAM-*an tiyawa(š)*

The GAM-*an tiannaš* and GAM-*an tiyawa(š)* are nearly identical in morphology and pattern of attestations, both being verbal substantives in sg. gen. of *dai-/ti(ya)-* 'to put, place' = "that of setting down," and both being included among offering equipment. The attestation twice now of GAM-*an tiyawa* (2.14 4′; 10.3.12 obv. i 11′) means the form must be taken seriously and not emended. One could imagine that the name of this not-infrequently attested cultic object could have been reinterpreted as univerbation **kattantiyawaš* in free-standing sg. gen., and then from there to a sg. nom. common gender *a*-stem, suggesting that *tiyawa* could be interpreted as an *a*-stem pl. coll. Exactly what the GAM-*an tiannaš/tiyawaš* was used to set down remains unclear.

GIŠGIGIR *weraš*

See EDHIL *s.v.* GIŠ*u̯era-, ura-* 'plate, tray' (p. 1002). Since GIŠ*wera-* is attested as a type of carrying tray upon which food, beverages, and utensils may be placed, a "chariot of a tray" might be a type of open cart or wagon consisting of a platform without any sides.

GÍR *kinuḫi(ya)-*

As discussed in Rieken, eDiAna, *s.v. kinuḫi(ya)-* 'related to kinuḫi-' (= lemma 1016) and *ead.*, eDiAna, *s.v. kinuḫaimma/i* '(adjective qualifying swords or sword-parts)' (= lemma 1015), *kinuḫi(ya)-* is an adjective of unknown meaning modifying GÍR 'dagger, knife' (6.2 obv. 5′; 6.13 5′) and SAG.DU 'pommel' (8.1.A obv. ii 10′). Since an adjective that could modify both the pommel of a dagger and the weapon in its entirety must be of the generic type, it may be suggested that *kinuḫi(ya)-* referred to a style or type of dagger or knife. There is little that can be said about the knife, except to note that a certain *kinuḫuš*, presumably a pl. acc. of an *a*-stem form of the substantive *kinuḫa-*, appears in a sword-swallowing scene in KBo 32.106 rev.? 7′–8′ (*namma=at kinuḫuš* EGI[R ... 8′ ... *išg*]*āri*) (see Ünal 1994, 214). This means that the SAG.DU *kinuḫiš* in 8.1.A obv. ii 10′ was not a pommel that was itself *kinuḫi(ya)-*, but instead a pommel of a *kinuḫa*-style dagger or knife.

GIŠ.(BAR.)KÍN

See Güterbock 1973 for the original discussion of the logograms GIŠBAR.KÍN = *SIḪPU* 'covering, overlay; inner bark (bast) of the *kiškanû*-tree' (p. 79) and GIŠ.KÍN '*kiškanû*-tree; (also, by synecdoche) its fruit/nut' (p. 84) in the Hittite context. After comparing the attestations of GIŠ.KÍN in the administrative texts to a passage KBo 10.34 obv. i 24, where cracked and roasted "GIŠ.KÍN" are listed among other cracked and roasted seeds and grains, Güterbock concluded (p. 86) that GIŠ.KÍN in the Hittite context "handelt es sich anscheinend um eine Frucht, die man knacken und rösten, aber auch in Edelmetall als Ornament nachbilden kann ...." Although Güterbock's original definition of "covering, overlay" works well for every attestation of GIŠ.BAR.KÍN in the PTAC, the proposed translation '(ornament in the shape of a) *kiškanû*-tree-fruit/nut ornament' for GIŠ.KÍN is more problematic. Compare the following attestations of GIŠ.KÍN and GIŠ.BAR.KÍN in the PTAC:

(1) 2.17 obv.[?] r. c. 11′–13′, 17′
obv.[?] r. c.
11′ 43 ^{GIŠ}PAN *A-NA* 4 *kán-du-na* KÙ.SI$_{22}$ GAR.RA *A-NA* 4[+n n GI]Š.BAR.KÍN [
12′ *A-NA* 2 3 GIŠ.BAR.KÍN KÙ.SI$_{22}$ *A-NA* 1-*EN* 2 GIŠ.BAR.KÍN KÙ.[S]I$_{22}$ *A-NA* 1-*E*[*N* n GIŠ.BAR.KÍN
13′ *A-NA* 1-*EN* 2 GIŠ.BAR.KÍN KÙ.SI$_{22}$ *A-NA* 2 2 GIŠ.BAR.KÍN KÙ.S[I$_{22}$] ⸢*A*⸣-*NA* 1-*EN* 6 G[IŠ.BAR.KÍN
...
17′ 2 ^{GIŠ}*ša-la-aš-du-ri* ŠÀ.BA 1-*E*[*N*] *ḪUR-RI* 4 GIŠ.BAR.KÍN KÙ.SI$_{22}$ 1-*EN* [

"43 bows: on 4, the *kanduna-* (are) gold-inlaid, on 4[+n (are) n GI]Š.BAR.KÍN [...], on 2 (are) 3 gold GIŠ.BAR.KÍN, on 1 (are) 2 go[l]d GIŠ.BAR.KÍN, on 1 [(are) n GIŠ.BAR.KÍN ...], on 1 (are) 2 gold GIŠ.BAR.KÍN, on 2 (are) 2 gol[d] GIŠ.BAR.KÍN, on 1 (are) 6 G[IŠ.BAR.KÍN
...
2 *šalašturi-*, of which 1 (is) Hurrian (with) 4 gold GIŠ.BAR.KÍN, 1 (is) [...]"

(2) 9.1.5 rev.[!] 16′
obv.
16′ ... 2 ^{GIŠ}*ŠU-RE-EN-NU* ŠÀ.BA 1 2 GIŠ.KÍN KÙ.BABBAR 1-*e-ma* 1 GIŠ.KÍN KÙ.BABBAR ...
"... 2 (divine) emblems, of which 1 (with) 2 silver GIŠ.KÍN, but 1 (with) 1 silver GIŠ.KÍN ..."

(3) 10.3.14 l. c. 3′
l. c.
3′ K]Ù.BABBAR *A-NA* 1-*EN* ⸢1⸣-*EN* GIŠ.KÍN KÙ.BABBAR
"s]ilver, on 1, 1 GIŠ.KÍN of silver."

Consulting these and the other attestations of GIŠ.KÍN and GIŠ.BAR.KÍN in the PTAC reveals three points: first, in a corpus almost completely devoid of model images of fruits and/or nuts (the *NU-ÚR-MU* 'pomegranate' attested as cloth appliqué in 9.1.1 rev. iii 19′ and the *nu-úr-i-ma-an-za* 'decorated with pomegranates(?)' in 9.2.2 rev.[!] iii 23′ being the only other examples) the GIŠ.KÍN-fruit/nut would be an excessively popular decoration. Second, the GIŠ.KÍN appears on a wide array of wooden objects, such as the ^{GIŠ}*damalanga-* '?' (4.2.3 3′), ^{GIŠ}PAN 'bow' (9.1.5 rev.[!] 9′), ^{GIŠ}*šarpa-* 'chair, stool' (9.1.5 rev.[!] 10′), and ^{GIŠ}*ŠURĪNU* '(divine) emblem' (9.1.5 rev.[!] 16′), none of which one would expect to have an especially close association with fruits or nuts. Third, as demonstrated by the examples cited above, the GIŠ.KÍN and GIŠ.BAR.KÍN appear in a special construction that is unique to the two terms: *A-NA* n (objects) n GIŠ.KÍN/GIŠ.BAR.KÍN. It may thus be suggested here that, in palace administrative texts from Boğazköy at least, the two Sumerograms were interchangeable, both with the meaning 'covering, overlay'. For other cases of deletion of elements of Sumerograms in Hittite texts without an apparent change in meaning, cf. ^{LÚ}(E.)DÉ.A, $^{(KUŠ/GIŠ)}$(É.)MÁ.URU.URU$_{6/7}$, $^{GI/GIŠ}$GAG.(Ú.)TAG(.GA), IGI.DU$_8$.(LIŠ.)A, $^{(DUG)}$IM.ŠU.(NÍG.)RIN.NA, ^{TÚG}ŠÀ.GA.(AN.)DÙ. See also the comments of Weeden 2011, 258–

59 on DUG.KAB.KA.GAG/DÙ vis-à-vis DUG.KA.GAG/DÙ and DUG.KAŠ.Ú.SA.KA.GAG (del Monte 1995b, 220).

GIŠ.ḪUR

Discussion of the term GIŠ.ḪUR in Hittite has an extensive history and no doubt a vibrant future. Earlier research focused on GIŠ.ḪUR as a free-standing noun, with the conclusion that it was a record of a more-or-less temporary or preliminary nature: see Starke 1990, 459 "(Vor-)Zeichnung, Entwurf, Planung" (also "kein Wort für 'Holztafel'," *loc. cit.*); Marazzi 1994, 142–51, esp. 148–49 "piano, organizzato, scritto," secondarily "tavoletta (cerata) lignea." Van den Hout 2010a, 261 (GIŠ.ḪUR = "outline, plan, schedule") emphasized that the GIŠ.ḪUR referred to the style of text, and was ambiguous as to the material on which it was written. Waal 2015, 165–67 in discussion of the phrase *A-NA* GIŠ.ḪUR *ḫandan* argued that GIŠ.ḪUR in the case of festival texts (and supposedly in the one instance of the phrase in an economic text, 8.1.I l. c. 1′–2′) meant an additional copy that was perhaps intended for use as a more practical version of the library copy.

Present discussion bifurcates over the materiality of GIŠ.ḪUR. For van den Hout (2020, 189), GIŠ.ḪUR is primarily a concept, referring to an "official, state-issued and legally authentic document," which is usually, but not exclusively, written on clay. For Cammarosano et al. (2019, 136–37), GIŠ.ḪUR designates a concrete object, namely a "wax-covered wooden writing board" of any type, regardless of contents. Support for both arguments can be found in the evidence. The best evidence for van den Hout's proposal GIŠ.ḪUR = "(official) document" comes from the myriad of attestations of the phrase *A-NA* GIŠ.ḪUR *ḫandan* 'prepared according to the GIŠ.ḪUR' at the end of festival texts, as well as the other uses of the term in clearly authoritative contexts. Tthe objection in Cammarosano et al. 2019, 137 fn. 154 that the GIŠ.ḪUR in the scapegoat ritual KUB 17.18+//KUB 60.161 are not authoritative can be overcome if the GIŠ.HUR are understood as authoritative from the ritual practitioner's perspective, namely that the documents are intended to be a binding description of the patient's *latti-* 'portion', i.e., the evil fate assigned to him, which are attached to the sacrificial animals for return to the gods. Cammarosano's proposal GIŠ.ḪUR = "wax board" is supported by ample archaeological and philological evidence that waxed wooden tablets existed and were in regular use in Anatolia, a land naturally rich in both substances, as well as the fact that some terms prefixed with GIŠ.ḪUR sometimes appear with just GIŠ. The proposal of van den Hout that the forms ^{GIŠ}*gulzattar* in Kp 14/95 rev. 4 and Kp 15/8+ obv. i 25 are haplographies or abbreviations is now overturned by the additional attestations with GIŠ in KBo 55.181 6′; KpT 1.39 obv. i 40; KpT 1.41 obv. i 15; and Bo 3289 rev. iv 1: thus, some *gulzattar* were certainly written on wax, a position that van den Hout (pers. comm.) now accepts in light of the Kayalıpınar evidence.

Nevertheless, both van den Hout's and Cammarosano's interpretations also have some weaknesses, which is only to be expected due to the intransigence of the data. For van den Hout's argument, one must be very clear about what is understood by "authoritative" in a diplomatic context. An incautious reading could confuse the term with "official." Probably all Hittite clay tablets that have been found so far are official, that is, produced by the office of the Hittite chancery. But it seems that very few of the tablets that have been found are authoritative, i.e., effective legal instruments. Only sealed tablets such as the land-grants, the Bronze Tablet, and other tablets preserving evidence of once having sealed bullae attached can confidently be placed into the "authoritative" category (on the relative scarcity of preserved sealed documents in the Hittite world, see Balza 2012). The scarcity of assuredly authoritative documents makes it impossible to describe what a GIŠ.ḪUR looked like in van den Hout's interpretation. No document has yet been discovered that proclaims itself a GIŠ.ḪUR, neither is there any written evidence from, e.g., an investigation or court proceeding, of a document being rejected for not being a GIŠ.ḪUR, nor a document being denied GIŠ.ḪUR status because it was not sealed (though this may have been so obvious to the ancient users that it required no comment). In effect, van den Hout is still missing the final, positive proof to seal what is a highly plausible argument.

Two criticisms may also be leveled against the argument GIŠ.ḪUR = "wax board." First, there are at least two instances of GIŠ.HUR modifying *ṬUPPU*/***tuppi***- 'clay tablet': first as a determinative in $^{\text{GIŠ.ḪUR}}$***tuppi***- in KUB 13.2 rev. iii 22//KUB 31.86 rev. iv 7, and second as an earlier GIŠ.ḪUR being referred to later by *ṬUPPU* in KUB 21.86 obv. 17–20. Cammarosano et al., not unaware of the problem, tried to account for this (*op. cit.*, 137) by arguing that *ṬUPPU*/***tuppi*** was a generic term for writing tablet of any material in Hittite. His argument rests on the existence of *ṭuppu* of non-clay materials (see list of CAD Ṭ *s.v. tuppu* A 1 h [p. 147]), which outside of Ḫatti are usually written *ṭuppu ša* … "tablet of …-(material)," including three instances of *ṭuppu ša* DUḪ.LÀL/*iškūrim* "tablet of wax" (Old Assyrian: AKT 5 11, 21–22; AKT 6b 468 12–13; Ugarit: RS 19.53 23). In Hittite texts, where the only attested non-clay tablets are made of metal, the formula is written *ṬUP-PU* ZABAR/KÙ.SI$_{22}$/KÙ.BABBAR, etc. (see CAD Ṭ *loc. cit.* [p. 148]). By analogy one would expect to find **ṬUP-PU* DUḪ.LÀL in Hittite texts if it existed (and if the normal Sumerogram/Akkadogram ^{GIŠ}LE.U$_5$/^{GIŠ}*LĒʾU* were not used). But neither **ṬUP-PU* DUḪ.LÀL 'wax tablet' nor *^{GIŠ}*ṬUP-PU* '(wood) tablet' are attested. It could be argued, with Veenhof 2010, 100 as cited by Cammarosano et al. (*op. cit.*, 135 fn. 138), that some *ṬUPPU* without modifiers in Hittite texts were actually waxed wooden tablets, as might have been the case in the Old Assyrian context, but there is no positive evidence for this. Indeed, if it were common that a *ṬUPPU* referred to a non-clay tablet, one would expect to find an instance where a bare *ṬUPPU* was later anaphorically revealed to be made of wood or wax. The examples with GIŠ.ḪUR must be excluded, since these beg the question of the material of the term; what is needed to prove Cammarosano's argument that *ṬUPPU* could refer to a non-clay tablet is a positive instance of *ṬUPPU*/***tuppi*** resumed by ^{GIŠ}LE.U$_5$/^{GIŠ}*LĒʾU*, *^{GIŠ}*ṬUP-PU*, or **ṬUP-PU* DUḪ.LÀL.

The second criticism of Cammarosano's argument is that if the Hittites already had available to them an inherited Sumerogram/Akkadogram ^{GIŠ}LE.U$_5$/^{GIŠ}*LĒʾU*, for waxed wooden tablets, why did they create, or rather adapt to a novel use, another Sumerogram? And, if a Sumerogram was needed, why did they not create something more obvious like *^{GIŠ}DUB, or *$^{\text{(GIŠ)}}$DUB DUḪ.LÀL? Cammarosano et al. did offer a scenario (*op. cit.*, 136) addressing these questions in which *gulzattar*, a native Luwian word that etymologically means 'drawing' (the interpretation of the term as a Sumerogram GUL-*zattar* = **kwanzattar*, proposed by Waal 2014 and Waal 2019 but rejected by Yakubovich 2013–14 and Melchert 2016, is avoided here, while acknowledging with van den

Hout 2020a, 197–204, that the spelling and etymology have little impact on the meaning of the word), was in the pre-Hittite period already extended to mean 'object on which things are drawn', i.e., a waxed wooden tablet. At some point in Hittite cuneiform, the inner-Anatolian development of *gulzattar* 'drawing' > *gulzattar* 'drawn surface' was extended via etymological analogy to GIŠ.ḪUR. Later, GIŠ.ḪUR then became a determinative meaning "wax board," applicable to any of the wax-covered wooden script carriers available in Anatolia (*gulzattar*, *gurta-*, *parzaki(š)*, *gaštarḫaida-*). While there is nothing against such a scenario, it is unparalleled in Hittite cuneiform.

In short, both van den Hout's and Cammarosano's arguments are just a new philological discovery away from being proven or disproven. No attempt will be made to adjudicate between them here. Instead, a few minor philological comments may be offered as contributions to the discussion. Regarding the reading of GIŠ.ḪUR, in earlier literature (e.g., Laroche 1963, 246; Starke 1990, 459–60), *gulzattar* was taken as the only reading of free-standing GIŠ.ḪUR. This was rejected by both Cammarosano and van den Hout, who adduced the supposedly variable gender of GIŠ.ḪUR, as well as the multiplicity of terms determined by GIŠ.ḪUR, as evidence that GIŠ.ḪUR could have multiple readings. The gender argument can, in my opinion, be dispensed with: GIŠ.ḪUR is neuter everywhere. There is a single apparent attestation of common gender in IBoT 2.131 obv. 21′: $^{\text{ḪUR.SAG}}$*liḫšaš* $^{\text{GIŠ.ḪUR}}$*šiyanteš* *ŠA* ^{D}*pirwa ḫarzi* "Mount Liḫša holds the sealed (documents) of Pirwa," where the participle *šiyanteš* can only be common gender. Previous editions read the GIŠ.ḪUR in this passage as a free-standing noun, but there are two objections to this. First, while not an inviolable rule, one would expect a plural marker if GIŠ.ḪUR were free-standing. Second, and more persuasively, the handcopy and the 3D-scan of the tablet show that there is a negligible amount of space between the GIŠ.ḪUR and *šiyanteš*, in contrast to the clear and meaningful word-spacing shown elsewhere in IBoT 2.131. Thus, *šiyanteš* should be read in obv. 21′ as either a substantivized participle or an adjective with an elided head noun, in both cases translated 'sealed (documents)', and GIŠ.ḪUR read as a determinative. Since the noun underlying a determinative does not have to agree with the determined word, and since there is no other example of GIŠ.ḪUR in the common gender, the argument for variable gender in the underlying word(s) can be removed: the noun underlying GIŠ.ḪUR is neuter. Also, *šiyant-* can be added to list of words determinable by GIŠ.HUR.

The variety of words determined by GIŠ.ḪUR is similarly no argument against reading behind it a single word. GIŠ.ḪUR is a free-standing noun is Mesopotamian cuneiform and therefore must have originally been mapped onto a free-standing noun in Anatolia. Apparently, the Anatolian noun behind GIŠ.HUR was semantically broad enough to develop into a determinative within Hittite cuneiform. Once this occurred, the application of the determinative to a range of nouns in the same semantic class is entirely expected, and in fact the definitive behavior of determinatives in cuneiform script. The question then is whether *gulzattar* was this original Anatolian noun.

On the one hand, there is good evidence supporting a reading GIŠ.ḪUR = *gulzattar*. The strongest evidence in favor of the equation is the fact that among the list of script carriers (*gaštarḫaida-*, *gulzattar*, *gurta-*, *parzaki(š)*, ^{GIŠ}LĒ.U$_5$/^{GIŠ}*LĒʾU*, *ṬUPPU*/*tuppi*, GIŠ.HUR) only GIŠ.ḪUR and *gulzattar* can modify other script carriers. As recognized by van den Hout, both GIŠ.ḪUR and *gulzattar* can qualify or be referred to as *ṬUPPU*/*tuppi* 'clay tablet'. The two examples of *gulzattar* immediately following *ṬUPPU*, namely *ṬUP-PA*$^{\text{ḪI.A}}$*=ma=aš gulzattar*$^{\text{ḪI.A}}$ (KUB 58.7 obv. ii 23′) and *ṬUP-PA*$^{\text{ḪI.A}}$*=ma* ^{GIŠ}*gulzattarri*$^{\text{ḪI.A}}$ (KBo 55.181 6′), parallel the determinative use of GIŠ.ḪUR in $^{\text{GIŠ.ḪUR}}$*tuppiaz* in KUB 13.2 rev. iii 21–22//KUB 31.86 rev. iv 6–8, as well as the anaphoric use of *ṬUPPU* for earlier GIŠ.ḪUR in KUB 21.38 obv. 17–20. A further piece of evidence for equating GIŠ.HUR and *gulzattar* comes from the duplicate lines *nu* $^{\text{GIŠ.ḪUR}}$*gulzattar uwanzi* (KUB 50.6+ rev. iii 18) and [*n*]*u* GIŠ.ḪUR$^{\text{ḪI.A}}$ *uwan*[*zi* (KUB 49.93 7) (both edited van den Hout 1998, 184–85), where $^{\text{GIŠ.HUR}}$*gulzattar* is directly replaced by GIŠ.ḪUR$^{\text{ḪI.A}}$. To my knowledge this is the only example of GIŠ.ḪUR directly substituting for one of the other terms for script carrier, suggesting that at least in this case, the terms were identical.

There are also a number of instances in which *gulzattar* are used in the same way as GIŠ.ḪUR, including appearing in many situations with connotations of authority (authority used here in the general sense, and not necessarily van den Hout's technical sense of a "authoritative," i.e. sealed, document). In four examples from Kayalıpınar, ^{GIŠ}*gulzattar* are brought from Ḫattuša laying down regulations on the celebration of various rites. These are (see editions of Cammarosano 2018): KpT 1.36 obv. i 13–15; KpT 1.36 obv. i 33–34; KpT 1.39 obv. i 40–41; KpT 1.41 obv. i 15, all of which have some variation of the formula ^{GIŠ}*gulzattar* ^{URU}GIDRU-*za*/^{URU}KÙ.BABBAR-*za udaš* "He brought a *gulzattar* from Ḫattuša." Cammarosano would rightly see these as perfect examples of wooden writing boards used for long-distance communication. But the authority implied for the ^{GIŠ}*gulzattar* by the capital-to-province direction and the courier-delivery of the records (KpT 1.36 obv. i 33–34 and KpT 1.41 obv. i 15) could equally be emphasized. A similar connotation of authority for the *gulzattar* might be encountered in KUB 42.100+ obv. i 35–37:

> *ŠA* ^{m}NIR.GÁL ^{GIŠ}*kurtaza* 12 EZEN$_4$ ITU^{KAM} 1 EZEN$_4$ Ú.BAR$_8$ [DÙ-*anza*] ^{36} EZEN$_4$ *zēni=ma UL* DÙ-*anza Š*[*A*] É *tuppašš=a kue* ^{37} *gulzatar*$^{\text{ḪI.A}}$ *nu* EZEN$_4$ Ú.BA[R$_8$] DÙ-*anza* EZEN$_4$ *zēni=ma* [*UL* DÙ-*anza*]
>
> "On/by means of the *gurta*-(s) of Muwatalli [are recorded] twelve Festivals of the Month (and) one Spring Festival, but the Fall Festival is not recorded. Also, regarding the *gulzatar* o[f] the É *tuppaš*, the Sprin[g] festival is recorded, but the Fall Festival [is not recorded]."

Here, the *gurta*- from the reign of Muwatalli are compared to the *gulzattar* of the É *tuppaš*, which perhaps stood for the current central administration (see *Lexical Commentary s.v.* É(.GAL) *tuppaš*). Although the earlier records had presumably the greater authority due to their antiquity, that the current *gulzattar* were consulted indicates they also bore authority on the matter.

On the other hand, there is evidence that GIŠ.ḪUR and *gulzattar* could refer to separate objects. In KBo 11.1 obv. 21, one finds *IŠ-TU*(?) GIŠ.ḪU]R$^{\text{ḪI.A}}$ ⸌*gulzattanazz*[*i=y*]*a*. Previously transliterated as a determinative (see Cammarosano et al. 2019, 139 fn. 178, with transliteration, translation, and discussion), the *gulzattar* is in fact separated from the GIŠ.ḪUR$^{\text{ḪI.A}}$ by a conspicuous space. The attachment of the enclitic coordinating conjunction *-a*/*-ya* to ⸌*gulzattanaz* suggests a noun pair: "from(?) the GIŠ.ḪU]R$^{\text{ḪI.A}}$ [a]nd from the *gulzattar*(-s)." Moreover, if the GIŠ.ḪUR is taken as a determinative, it would be the only instance (to my knowledge) of a determinative GIŠ.ḪUR taking a plural marker ḪI.A, as opposed to having the plural marker appear at the end of the determined word: GIŠ.ḪUR...ḪI.A. The relevant clauses from KBo 11.1 obv. 21–22 should probably thus read: *nu IŠ-TU*(?) GIŠ.ḪU]RḪI.A ⩤*gulzattanazz*[*i=y*]*a* 22 *kuit* DUTU-*ŠI kinun wemiškimi n=at ēššaḫḫi* "What(ever) I, His Majesty, now find [on the GIŠ.ḪU]RḪI.A [a]nd the ⩤*gulzattar*(-s), that I will do."

Perhaps the gravest complication to a GIŠ.ḪUR = *gulzattar* equation is the fact that fully spelled out determinatives usually only occur in Old Hittite (see discussion of GIŠ*ta-a-ru* in HEG T/D *s.v. taru- (tāru-)* [p. 230]) or in Sumerograms spelled out in Akkadian (see Wilhelm 1988, 102 for list of examples). The numerous New Hittite examples of GIŠ.ḪUR*gulzattar* would therefore be highly unusual. One could argue that the transition of GIŠ.ḪUR from free-standing noun to determinative was an ongoing process even in New Hittite and therefore, analogous to Old Hittite, the "determinative-ness" of the word had not yet fully taken hold.

In conclusion, the argument of van den Hout's GIŠ.ḪUR = [(ORIGINAL) DOCUMENT] versus Cammarosano's GIŠ.ḪUR = [WAX BOARD] cannot be settled by the current data. In van den Hout's favor is the fact that an abstract meaning for the GIŠ.ḪUR/*gulzattar* better fits the original Mesopotamian meaning as well as the etymology: a drawing or plan. In Cammarosano's favor is the fact that cuneiform determinatives are almost always concrete objects or materials: mountains and rivers, people and animals, silver and gold, and perhaps waxed wooden tablets. This point in fact highlights what is in my opinion the essential problem posed by GIŠ.ḪUR, namely how and why it came to be used as a determinative in the Anatolian cuneiform tradition. Since almost every other determinative in Hittite cuneiform was inherited from Mesopotamia, explaining why the Hittites invented a determinative use for GIŠ.HUR represents to me *the* outstanding problem of the term. The two other non-standard Hittite determinatives, namely SI 'horn' for objects made of horn and ḪUR.SAG 'mountain (region)' for named mountains (found also in texts from Alalaḫ and Ugarit), fall into preexisting categories. GIŠ.ḪUR requires a new determinative category, [WRITTEN OBJECTS], of which it is the only member. While the recent theories of van den Hout and Cammarosano better account for the use of GIŠ.ḪUR as a determinative, the strangeness of this fact has not yet been fully explored. It is likely the phenomenon will remain unexplained until new data is discovered, perhaps in the archives of provincial Anatolia.

(TÚG/GADA)GÚ(.È.A) *ḪURRI*

For "Hurrian shirts/tunic" in general, see Klengel – Klengel 2009, who list the variety of colors and materials attested for the garment. As noted by Baccelli et al. 2014, 122, "the 'Hurrian shirt/tunic' seems to be one of the most fashionable garments among the ancient Near Eastern sovereigns ...." Goetze (1955, 54) suggested that a Hurrian tunic might be depicted on the Theben tomb (TT86) of Men-kheper-re-seneb I, a high official under the reigns of Thutmose III and Amenhotep II, where it is worn by the figures of "the Prince of Tunip" and "the Prince of Kadesh" (see Plate IV in Davies and Davies 1933). The depicted garment is a close-fitting, full-length tunic with a collarless, keyhole neckline with facing, and wrist-length sleeves.

GÚ.ḪAL

In addition to commentary of HVP (p. 500 fn. 1), where a connection to Akk. *guḫaṣṣu, ǧuḫalṣu* (CAD G *s.v.* [p. 123] ‘braided wire or torque’) is suggested, see now Weeden 2011, 239, where [(UZU)]GÚ.ḪAL appears in various Hittite lexical texts and translations as a gloss for both throat and neck. The term will be provisionally translated here as “neck,” with the understanding that GÚ.ḪAL must have referred to some kind of necklace, specifically one that could bear both *išgaratar* (‘beads/pendants?’) and *bašta*-elements.

GÚ.SES

For the conclusion that the GÚ.SES was, at least in Hittite texts, the bitter vetch (*Vicia ervilia*), see Hoffner 1974, 98. The bitter vetch is native to Anatolia and northern Syria, and serves as an important fodder crop, especially for horses (N. Miller – Enneking 2014, 261). The appearance of large quantities GÚ.SES in the school copying exercise 12.2.1 unfortunately allows no economic conclusions to be drawn due to the by-definition artificial nature of the text.

[(TÚG)]GUZ.ZA

See the discussion of Burgin (forth.[2]), where it is concluded that the cloth was a textile defined in construction by its thick weft and in practice by its use during the 2nd millennium as a blanket or upholstery. No evidence for a meaning “shaggy, wiry” is found for the cloth, precluding the traditional translation *Zottenstoff* in connection with the *Zottenrock* of Mesopotamian visual media. Instead, a connection of the cloth’s name with the color ‘(bright) red’ might be conceived for some periods.

ḪI.ḪI

As already expressed in the translations of the previous editions (HIT, 16: “multicoloured[?], striped[?], patterned[?]”; HVP, 654: “‘meliert’[(?)]”), ḪI.ḪI, despite being included among the color terms of the PTAC (e.g., 11.6.5 obv.[?] 7: 5 [TÚG]BAR.“TE” ŠÀ.BA 1 ḪI.ḪI 1 *ḪAŠ-MAN*. 1 *ḪA-ŠÁR* 1 ZA.GÌN 1 BABBAR), denotes, at least in Mesopotamia, the physical act of “mixing, blending” (Akk. *balālu*) of, e.g., ingredients, metal alloys, and wool sorts. This sense also seems to be present at Ḫattuša in the [TÚG]ḪI.ḪI-*natar* “mixed garment,” where the mixture probably refers to the wool used in their construction, which may be further modified by color adjectives. The concept of “multi-hued, versicolored” is expressed in good Sumerian by GÙN.A (Akk. *barmu;* see discussion of Thavapalan 2020, 79–89). Although the lexeme GÙN.A is extant in Hittite texts (Weeden 2011, 506), and is indeed present in the PTAC in the ritual ingredients list 12.1.1, where it refers to colored stone tokens, the term never modifies garments. Since it is highly improbable that multi-hued garments were completely absent from the storehouses and chests inventoried in the PTAC, the concept was probably expressed by another term, for which ḪI.ḪI is the best candidate (already tentatively HIT, *loc. cit.*, though the connection with the [TÚG]ḪI.ḪI-*na-tar* as the “complemented form” of the adjective should be discarded). In the language of the PTAC, then, ḪI.ḪI underwent a trivial semantic shift or expansion from “mixed, blended” in the physical sense, to a mix or blend of colors.

IGI.DU$_8$.A

The primary analysis of the function of IGI.DU$_8$.A in Hittite texts remains HVP (pp. 249–56, 210–12, 559–60, 564–65; see also recapitulative overviews in the RlA entries of Siegelová 2011–12 and Siegelová 2014). The main problem of interpretation of the term consists of squaring its etymology with it use in the PTAC. As discussed by Wilhelm 1992, 503, the etymology of Sumerian IGI.DU$_8$.A/Akkadian *tāmartu* (CAD T *s.v. tāmartu* 3. "gift, contribution, tribute" [p. 113]) suggests that the term was originally a "Besuchsgeschenk," which seems to fit its role in the Old Babylonian period and at Ugarit and Amarna. At Ḫattuša, however, most attestations of IGI.DU$_8$.A come from the domestic tribute texts of the PTAC, where it is closely associated with the term *MADDATTU* 'tribute'. Reasoning from the near-obligatory inclusion of IGI.DU$_8$.A alongside *MADDATTU*, as well as from the note in 3.1.1.A$_2$ rev. v 9′–11′ that a portion of IGI.DU$_8$.A was short by 25 shekels (thereby indicating the quantity of IGI.DU$_8$.A was prescribed), HVP (p. 212) correctly argued that the IGI.DU$_8$.A of the tribute texts was compulsory. This led HVP to subsequently define the term as "Pflichtgeschenk" (p. 212; in the glossary, p. 655: "Abgabe; Pflichtgeschenk"), with the translation intended to combine the function observed in the texts with resonances of the original or core meaning "Geschenk, Begrüssungsgeschenk" (p. 212) (note that a neutral meaning of IGI.DU$_8$.A as 'gift' was certainly available in Hittite texts, as demonstrated by attestations gathered in Neu 1974, 115–16 of the term interchanging with *ḫenkur/ḫinkuwar*, see also the Hittite-Hurrian bilingual, where, as discussed in Wilhelm 1992, 504–5, the term glosses Hurr. *e/irana/i*, the Hurrian word itself corresponding with *qīštu* (NÍG.BA) "gift" in the Nuzi texts). The analysis of HVP has been generally accepted, with the specific translation "Abgabe; Pflichtgeschenk" followed by some (see HZL no. 288 (p. 234): "Geschenk?, Abgabe(n)?"; Wilhelm 1992, 506: "(Plicht-)Geschenk"; Weeden 2011, 514: "gift payment"; Giorgieri – Mora 2012, 655 fn. 38: "(Pflicht-)Geschenk, Abgabe, Tribut, Spende(?)"), although others, mostly from the Italian tradition, preferred to retain a generic translation of "gift" (Archi 1984, 200: "gift"; Zaccagnini 1989–90, 108: "dono"; Mora 2007, 537: "dono"; Vigo 2010, 291 fn. 17: "the translation 'gift' seems to be the currently acceptable one"). The earlier translation in HIT (p. 261) of IGI.DU$_8$.A as "present, show piece," incorporating the earlier work of Goetze (1956, 33, 37) and others (see HIT, 8, with literature) occasionally resurfaces in reviews of the term (Mora 2006, 135: "'assegnazione occasionale/speziale' e 'dono'"; Alexandrov 2016, 7, following HIT), but has for the most part been superseded.

One of the main arguments of HVP (p. 248) concerning the function of IGI.DU$_8$.A in the Hittite palace economy was that since IGI.DU$_8$.A invariably consisted of the same items as *MADDATTU*, just in smaller amounts, practical differentiation of the two consisted entirely of their intended purpose in the redistribution phase. According to the analysis of HVP (p. 249), *MADDATTU* was destined for more-or-less immediate redistribution, while IGI.DU$_8$.A was set aside as a reserve fund (HVP, 249–50), from which votive gifts (pp. 250–52) and handouts (pp. 253–55) were given. Unfortunately, this idea that IGI.DU$_8$.A went to a reserve fund is difficult to support from the texts. On the function of IGI.DU$_8$.A, see the introductory *Analysis* to 4.1.4.1, a text concerning the manufacture of belts for handouts, where it is argued that the IGI.DU$_8$.A designated not the wool, but was construed with the personal names to indicate the products were "gifts" for the named persons. Reinterpretation of the text group 4.1.4.1–4.1.4.6 in fact removes the only evidence for a direct link between incoming IGI.DU$_8$.A and the outgoing handouts proposed in the system of HVP (pp. 249–50). Thus, following the translations of the Italian tradition cited above, it is held here that the connection between the IGI.DU$_8$.A received as tribute and the IGI.DU$_8$.A being distributed as handouts and votive objects was purely linguistic: both were conceived of as simply "gifts," whether from subjects to ruler in the domestic tribute texts, ruler to subjects in the handout texts, or kings to gods in the votive texts. Further qualification of the gifts as "Pflichtgeschenk" or "gift payment" is therefore unnecessary, if it is understood that the specific connotation of the term could change depending on context.

One may naturally ask why the IGI.DU$_8$.A received alongside tribute were labeled "gifts" at all. Here, the proposal of Liverani 1990, 267–73, that the origins of tribute lay in gifts currying diplomatic favor which over time became compulsory seems pertinent (see further Zaccagnini 1989–90, esp. bibliography in p. 105 fn. 3). It may be hypothesized that the reason why IGI.DU$_8$.A was recorded separately from *MADDATTU* in Hittite domestic tribute records was that it served, at least originally, as a way of "keeping score" for political influence. Whether it still had this function in the texts of the Late New Hittite Kingdom is unclear, but it may be provisionally noted while there was undoubtedly a minimum amount that was expected (per the example from 3.1.1.A$_2$ rev. v 9′–11′), the lack of a perceptible ratio of IGI.DU$_8$.A to *MADDATTU* suggests also there was no maximum, leaving open the possibility that some contributions were more generous than necessary. In this way, Hittite domestic IGI.DU$_8$.A can be compared to the *ŠULMĀNU* that was received from subordinate allied kingdoms, namely a semi-formalized supplement to core tribute (see Giorgieri – Mora 2012, 652–53 on *ŠULMĀNU*; note that contra Alexandrov 2016, 7, there is no evidence that the IGI.DU$_8$.A of the domestic tribute texts was destined for to pockets of individual high officials, as was explicitly the case for much of the *ŠULMĀNU*). An analogous semantic development of IGI.DU$_8$.A seems to have been occurring in Middle Assyrian texts (Llop 2020, 332–33), with the difference that the term there designated formalized gifts from external subordinate rulers, whereas the designation *šulmānu* was retained for gifts between equals (as discussed in *Lexical Commentary s.v.* *ŠULMĀNU*, the Hittite term covered both).

^{LÚ}IŠ

See Weeden 2011, 254–58 for a discussion of ^{LÚ}IŠ (also transliterated ^{LÚ}KUŠ$_7$, ^{LÚ}ŠÙŠ), a professional designation for a chariot warrior, and potentially a chariot driver and high-level official if the term is the Sumerographic equivalent of ^{LÚ}*KARTAPPU* (though see Beal 1992, 368–78 and Bilgin 2018, 191–93 for arguments against the equation).

^{NA_4}KA.GI.NA

See Schuster-Brandis 2008, 424–25 for discussion of ^{NA_4}KA.GI.NA in the Mesopotamian context. An inscription on a weight stone has securely identified ^{NA_4}KA.GI.NA/*ŠADÂNU* as magnetite in Mesopotamia, though Schuster-Brandis (*loc. cit.*) does not exclude the possibility of other iron ores, including hematite and goethite, being subsumed under the same term. Since, AN.BAR (GE$_6$) might now also designate iron ore (see *Lexical*

Commentary s.v.), and since magnetite, hematite, and goethite are macroscopically indistinguishable (Melein 2018, 5–12), then distinction between ^{NA_4}KA.GI.NA/*ŠADÂNU* and AN.BAR (GE$_6$) possibly hinges on the former's magnetism, rather than any difference in appearance.

^{NA_4}KÁ.DINGIR.RA

See Riemschneider 1974, 273 for a discussion of the ^{NA_4}KÁ.DINGIR.RA = ^{NA_4}*pabili* as an artificial stone, probably a variety of enamel or glass. Polvani 1988, 145–48 suggested that the "Babylon-stone" of Hittite sources was probably reddish-brown in color. However, the archaeological discovery of a mold labeled 'Babylon' in Anatolian Hieroglyphs in which could be cast divine figurines of a type found often made from lapis lazuli has led Baykal-Seeher – Seeher 2003 to suggest that Babylon-stone was an artificial glass used as a substitute for lapis lazuli.

KEŠDA

See *Commentary* to 2.7.A obv. 10 for the interpretation of KEŠDA-*ma* as a CLuw. participle form of an underlying *ḫišḫiya-* (= Hitt. *išḫai-/išḫi(ya)-*) or equivalently an unattested CLuw. cognate of Hitt. *ḫamank-/ḫamenk-*. HVP (p. 64 fn. 1) convincingly suggested in discussing 4.2.4 obv. 1 that "KEŠDA … dürfte vielleicht eine spezielle Technik der Fadenverknüpfung wiedergeben (z.B. wirken, filieren, stricken o.ä.)." If so, then KEŠDA and $^{(TÚG)}$*ḫamenkant-* might reflect a similar or even identical fabric treatment.

KI.LÁ NA$_4$

See Siegelová 1988 for a discussion of the KI.LÁ NA$_4$ versus KI.LÁ TI$_8^{MUŠEN}$ weight systems in Hittite. It proved impossible to establish a clear distinction between the two systems, save that the KI.LÁ NA$_4$ weights seemed to be used for finer gradations and lighter weights – no more than 3 minas (4.1.1.2.A obv. 8′) is attested in the PTAC versus the 40 minas (4.1.2.3 obv. ii 6′, 11′) for the KI.LÁ TI$_8$. As such, the set of weight stones found at Kuşaklı-Šarišša (Müller-Karpe 2015), which range from what is interpreted as approximately ½ shekel to 2 minas (see Table 2 in Rahmstorf 2018, 200), probably represent a KI.LÁ NA$_4$ set. It may also be noted that the contemporary Mesopotamian and Syrian weight systems correspond, at least in nomenclature, with the Hittite KI.LÁ NA$_4$ system.

It cannot be ruled out that in the context of the PTAC, in which most if not all related texts were probably written in the same location, that the KI.LÁ NA$_4$/TI$_8$ referred to two specific, tangible weight sets in use in the warehouses named after the shapes of their weights.

KI.LÁ TI$_8^{MUŠEN}$

See Siegelová 1988 for discussion of the KI.LÁ NA$_4$ versus KI.LÁ TI$_8^{MUŠEN}$ weight systems in Hittite. It seems the 'eagle-weights' were flat-bottomed figurines in the form of a stylized eagle (see Siegelová 1988, 326 abb. 1). This is in contrast to the shapeless KI.LÁ NA$_4$ weights (see Rahmstorf 2018, 201, fig. 2), if the Kuşaklı-Šarišša weight set may be identified as such.

^{URUDU}KIN

With HVP (p. 330), the ^{URUDU}KIN 'sickle' in the PTAC is attested as a "Verkörperung eines bestimmtem Wertes" rather than a hand-tool, especially in the context of tribute-lists (*passim*) and as rewards or prizes handed out at the AN.DAḪ.ŠUM-festival in 6.1 rev. B. Singer 2006b, 254 connects this function of the ^{URUDU}KIN with the similar use of the PAD 'ingot', and seems to imply that the PAD *TAYYĀRTU* in 'bent (crescent-shaped?) ingot' in 4.2.1.A$_1$ obv. 10 was an alternate description of the sickle *qua* token of value. Although the ^{URUDU}KIN, along with the ^{URUDU}*PĀŠU* 'adze, axe', were certainly tokens of value, the note in 3.1.1.A$_1$ obv. ii 10′ of the accidental breaking up of an ^{URUDU}*PĀŠU* suggests that their form, and not just their weight, was important. As discussed in the introductory *Analysis* to 3.1.5, the receipt of taxation in the form of premade agricultural implements would be useful for a state based on large agricultural estates, where these tools would have been in constant demand.

KÙŠ.SIG

See Cammarosano 2018, 316 (with earlier literature) for a discussion of the KÙŠ.SIG/SIG.KÙŠ. Current consensus is that the KÙŠ.SIG/SIG.KÙŠ measured somewhat less than a regular ell in length, but more than the *ŪṬU* 'handspan', which was regularly expressed by ½.KUŠ 'half-ell' in both Mesopotamia and Anatolia. Since the unit is unknown in Mesopotamia, the KÙŠ.SIG/SIG.KÙŠ might represent the native Anatolian version of the ell or cubit, which was nominally the distance between the elbow and fingertip, but, as with other anthropic units of measurement, varied widely across cultures, geography, and time.

$^{(GIŠ)}$LE.U$_5$

See Cammarosano 2020, 10–11, 18–19, for a discussion with previous literature of the $^{(GIŠ)}$LE.U$_5$, a pseudo-Sumerogram from Akkadian $^{(GIŠ)}$*lēʾu*. Regardless of its potential connection to GIŠ.ḪUR, it is clear from Mesopotamian usage that the $^{(GIŠ)}$*lēʾu* designated a writing board that was often, though not exclusively, made of wood. The spelling LE.U$_5$$^!$(text: ḪU) in 3.1.1.A$_1$ rev. v 15′ might actually be Akkadographic *LE-ḪU* (-*ḪU* for -*ʾu*) rather than a mistake, given the existence of forms such as *IŠ-TU LE-EḪ-E* (KBo 4.2+ rev. iv 45). Given its appearance immediately after a chariot, it could be that the LE.U$_5$$^!$ in 3.1.1.A$_1$ rev. v 15′ was simply a 'board', not necessarily connected with writing.

LÚ^{MEŠ} KÁ UR.GI$_7$

3.1.6 3′ adds now a fifth attestation of the LÚ^{MEŠ} KÁ(.GAL) UR.GI$_7$ to the previously recognized ABoT 1.6 rev. 15′, KBo 59.104 obv. i 5′, VBoT 9 obv. 4′, and VSNF 12.7 obv. i 11. Unfortunately, little can be said about this obscure group of functionaries: the connection supposed by Otten 1974 (p. 115 fn. 269) with the LÚ^{MEŠ} UR.GI$_7$, a group classed among the animal-imitators in festivals, remains, at a minimum, unproven. Rather, as implied by Pecchioli Daddi 2000, 350, who pointed out the appearance of the ^{LÚ}*ḪAZANNU* – an individual charged with the security functions of Ḫattuša – in the same paragraph as the LÚ^{MEŠ} KÁ UR.GI$_7$ in KBo 59.104 obv. i 1–10, and as is also implied by the group's apparent physical proximity to gates in the dramatic action of ABoT 1.6 rev.$^?$ 13′–15′

and KBo 59.104 obv. i 5–6, it may be suggest that the LÚ^{MEŠ} KÁ(.GAL) UR.GI$_7$ were guards of a specific gate named the "Hound's Gate" located somewhere in Ḫattuša.

LÚ ^{URU}GN

See discussions of CHD P *s.v. pešna-* g 1′-2′ and Weeden 2011, 291–98, where two meanings are recognized: 1.) LÚ ^{URU}GN 'ruler of GN' and 2.) LÚ ^{URU}GN 'person from GN.' When used in the first meaning, LÚ ^{URU}GN probably represented Hittite GN-*aš* (gen.) *pešnaš* (nom.) 'man of GN' (Weeden, *op. cit* 291–92). When used in the second meaning, LÚ ^{URU}GN could gloss two different Hittite constructions: most often so-called 'ethnic adjectives' such as *-umna-*, *-aḫšu-*, and possibly others (Weeden, *op. cit.*, 292–98), but also Hittite GN-*aš pešnaš/antuḫšaš*, 'man/person from GN', as revealed by a handful of instances where the GN is inflected as a Hittite genitive (*ibid.* 292–93). The existence of inflected forms suggests that uninflected forms of the GN in LÚ ^{URU}GN should be treated as stem-forms (also called 'Akkadographic' writings or 'morphological calques'; see discussion of Weeden 2011, 358 with literature), concealing either an underlying genitive (first or second meaning) or an ethnic adjective/genitive (second meaning), with the social standing of the individuals determined by context.

LÚ ^{GIŠ}TUKUL.GÍD.DA

As discussed by d'Alfonso 2010, 78:

> [The LÚ ^{GIŠ}]TUKUL.GÍD.DA in the Late Empire seems to be a rather generic term for high-ranking state dependents. Unlike the TUKUL-men, the TUKUL.GÍD.DA-men had a prominent role in the cultic and administrative spheres and held other state dependents under their control. One might speculate that the title ^{GIŠ}TUKUL.GÍD.DA could refer to the highest rank of ^{GIŠ}TUKUL-men, i.e., those who controlled and directed other ^{GIŠ}TUKUL-men.

LÚ *ṬĒMI*

See Weeden 2011, 31 (with fn. 133), 357 for discussion. In Hittite texts, the word may be written LÚ *ṬĒMI* (according to Otten 1969, 18 this reflects the underlying Akkadian *ša ṭēmi* 'he of the message'; cf. also the discussion of *bēl ṭēmi* in CAD Ṭ *s.v. ṭēmu* [p. 96]), or as a *māršipru*-univerbation ^{LÚ}*ṬĒMU* with the case expressed on the final element (so Wilhelm *apud* Weeden 2011, 31 fn. 133). According to Hoffner 2009, 53, LÚ *ṬĒMI* is the older form, while ^{LÚ}*ṬĒMU* is found in younger texts, which fits the prosopography of 5.7 dating it to reign of Ḫattušili III/Tudḫaliya IV.

LUGAL

While in diplomatic and historical documents LUGAL is used to refer to minor kings, in administrative texts and especially festival/ritual texts, where it is the dominant form, LUGAL can also refer to the Hittite king, alongside ^{D}UTU-*ŠI*. This seems to be the case twice in the PTAC (3.12 obv. l. c. 7′; 10.2.2.1 1′), in both instances perhaps triggered by the following MUNUS.LUGAL.

MÁ

The appearance of the "boat" between a drinking vessel (*tapišana/i-*) and a bowl (*KAPPU*) – all within a chest that appears to be a drinking set for a man and a woman (the king and queen?) – suggests that MÁ 'boat' was also the name of a drinking or serving vessel in Hittite (compare English *gravy boat*).

MÁ.(URU.)URU$_6$

As discussed by Weeden 2011, 302: "the rarity of the Akkadogram *IŠPATU* indicates that the Sumerogram [$^{(KUŠ/GIŠ)}$(É.)MÁ.URU.URU$_6$] is in fact the regular cuneiform designation at Hattusa." Weeden then cites (*loc. cit.*, fn. 1406) the twelve attestations known to him of ^{KUŠ}*IŠPATU* at Ḫattuša. Within the PTAC, the reverse seems to be true: there are five attestations of ^{KUŠ}*IŠPATU* across three texts, versus two attestations of MÁ.URU.URU$_6$ in one text. It is difficult to tell whether this is because the $^{(KUŠ/GIŠ)}$(É.)MÁ.URU.URU$_6$ was a complicated and archaic set of signs (Weeden, *loc. cit.*), or simply because a different set of scribes worked on the administrative texts – or both. The ^{URUDU}MÁ.URU$_6$ in 3.1.1.A$_3$ rev. iv 10′ may be noted as the first attestation of the lemma with an URUDU determinative.

$^{(KUŠ/TÚG)}$MAR.ŠUM

With HVP (p. 696), *MARŠUM* should be treated as a single lemma 'strap, thong' with two optional determinatives based on its material of construction, so that contra CAD M$_1$ *s.v. maršu* C (p. 296), there exists no separate garment *TÚG *MAR-ŠUM* existing only at Boğazköy. For the interpretation instead of ^{TÚG}MAR.ŠUM SAG.[DUL (4.2.9 obv. 7) as a 'thong(ed) head[gear', compare later in the same text 4.2.9 obv. 23: 3 ^{TÚG}SAG.DUL ŠÀ.BA 1 GEŠTU 1 ^{TÚG}MAR.ŠUM SAG.DU[L "3 headgear, of which 1 (is) ear(red) [i.e., with ear-covers], 1 (is) a thong(ed) headge[ar ..." and elsewhere 6.9 obv. 3: SAG.DUL *QADU* MAR.ŠUM "headgear with thongs/straps." Contra HIT and HVP, however, and with CAD M$_1$ *s.v. maršu* A (p. 296), the existence of forms with *QA-DU* MAR.ŠUM (6.9 obv. 3′; 9.2.9 rev.$^?$ 5′; 11.6.3 obv.$^?$ 4′) instead of expected *QA-DU* **MAR-ŠI(M)*, suggest that Hittite texts used the (pseudo-)Sumerographic version of the term known also from lexical lists.

MUG

Since MUG (Akk. ^{SÍG}*mukku*) is used only with wool, the translation "Kämmling" (Engl. "noil") – i.e., the short-fiber wool combed out to be either discarded or used for low-strength fabric – of HVP (p. 664) is more correct than the translation "Werg" (Engl. "oakum, tow") – the equivalent from plant-based fibers such as linen, hemp, and jute – given in HZL no. 22 (p. 102). The fact that dyed noil was intentionally issued from the palace, in, e.g., 4.1.4.1 suggests that it was intended to be used as decoration or batting in the garments under manufacture.

MUL

For MUL as a quality or feature of a belt, compare: 4 ^{TÚG}E.ÍB *MAŠ-LU* SIG$_5$ ŠÀ 1 MU[L (4.1.4.2.A$_1$ rev. r. c. 6′); 14 ^{TÚG}E.ÍB ŠÀ 1 MUL (11.6.1 8); and 1 ^{TÚG}E.ÍB MUL (6.10 8′). HW^2 Ḫ *s.v. ḫašter(a)-* III.3 (p. 437) suggested "Gürtelverzierung$^?$/Gürtelschnalle$^?$ in Sternform" for these passages, whereas HVP (p. 522 fn. 5) suggested an equation MUL = *SUḪUPPU* 'hoop' (AHw *s.v. suḫuppum* I, *šuḫuppu* 'etwa "Reifen"' [p. 1054]), translating the passage from 11.6.1 8 as "14 Gürtel davon 1 (in Form von) Reifen(?)." However, since ŠUḪUB$_2$ = MUL does not seem to be attested elsewhere in Hittite cuneiform, and since the rigid or semi-rigid hoop implied by *šuḫuppu* 'wheel rim, hoop' (the "tread" of a wheel) seems in any case impractical, the interpretation of HW^2 of ^{TÚG}E.ÍB MUL as a "belt (with) star (ornaments)" is preferred here. An analogous construction of [garment] + [ornament] without intervening Akkadographic case marker can be found in GAD.DAM U$_4$.SAKAR 'leggings (with) lunula' (2.7.A obv. 26).

$^{(NA_4)}$MUŠ.GÍR

With HZL no. 342 (p. 264), the otherwise unknown ^{N}[^{A_4}NUNUZ?] MUŠ.SÌR should likely be emended to ^{N}[^{A_4}NUNUZ?] MUŠ.GÍR$^{!}$. Since the SÌR and GÍR signs are so dissimilar, it was probably a hearing rather than a reading mistake on the part of the scribe.

NÍG.GÍD.DA

See CAD U/W *s.v. urāku* (p. 206) for range of uses of this lexeme, ranging from wires for stringing beads, rods of precious metals used to construct tiaras and bracelets, to probes for testing viscosity of molten glass. In Hittite contexts, the NÍG.GÍD.DA could also refer to a weapon, probably a type of spear, javelin, or lance. One is reminded of other weapons consisting of a thin metal rod, such as the Iberian *soliferrum* or the shaft of the Roman *pilum*. In the PTAC, only the 5 NÍG.GÍD.DA AN.BAR G[E$_6$] in 8.1.A rev. v 3, which are listed among knives and swords, could plausibly be considered weapons, with the remaining attestations either ambiguous or assuredly jewelry (NÍG.GÍD.DA KÙ.SI$_{22}$ in 8.1.A obv. ii 29′).

^{NA_4}NÍR

See *Lexical Commentary, s.v.* ^{NA_4}*ḫulali-* for main discussion.

$^{(NA_4)}$NUNUZ

See main discussion in Polvani 1988 *s.v.* $^{(NA_4)}$NUNUZ (pp. 149–59), also *s.v.* $^{(NA_4)}$*ku(wa)-nna(n)-* (pp. 47–59), HED IV *s.v. ku(wa)nna(n)-* (pp. 308–10), and Oreshko 2018, 106–7 (with recent bibliography), where $^{(NA_4)}$NUNUZ = $^{(NA_4)}$*ku(wa)nna(n)-* is equated with 'beads' as well as 'copper' (Oreshko 2018, 106) and/or 'copper ore' (Polvani 1988, 57, HED IV, 308). It is uncontested from its use in texts that $^{(NA_4)}$NUNUZ functioned as both an item and as a substance. However, the exact identity of the substance is unclear. As discussed in the bibliography of HED IV (p. 310), the earliest attempts at identification suggested 'copper ore, azurite', with a connection to Gk. κύανος 'dark blue enamel, lapis lazuli, copper ore (azurite?)' (see also the bibliography in Oreshko 2018, 106 fn. 44). Then, the discovery of the substitution of *ku(wa)nna(n)-* for URUDU$^{ḪI.A}$ in a list of materials in an object description (KUB 17.21 obv. ii 14′–15′ with URUDU$^{ḪI.A}$, vs. rev. iii 22–23 with *ku(wa)nna(n)-*) led to the suggestion that the substance could also designate metallic copper (though cf. suggestion of Polvani 1988, 55, following Limet 1960, 38, where it is argued that the plural determinative in URUDU$^{ḪI.A}$ means in this case a "copper mixture," i.e., copper mixed with minerals, not pure copper). In the most recent assessment of the evidence, Oreshko (2018, 106–7) argued that the old interpretation of $^{(NA_4)}$NUNUZ = $^{(NA_4)}$*ku(wa)nna(n)-* as 'copper ore' is unsupported and based primarily on a desire to connection *ku(wa)nna(n)-* with Gk. κύανος. Oreshko proposed instead that the terms meant only 'copper' or 'beads', and possibly, based on the existence of

Luwian *kwan(n)anal(l)a-* 'bead-cutter; stone engraver', just 'beads' (p. 107). It must be pointed out that the proposal of Oreshko to interpret $^{(NA_4)}$NUNUZ = $^{(NA_4)}$*ku(wa)nna(n)-* exclusively as 'copper' when used as a substance seems impossible given the ample attestations of items made of $^{(NA_4)}$NUNUZ and URUDU in the same text: within the PTAC, see most notably objects made of ^{NA_4}NUNUZ appearing among copper (URUDU) ingots and copper (URUDU) objects in a disbursement for crafting purposes in 5.2 obv. ii 1–2, 5–8, which simultaneously confirms that the substance was different from copper, but also suggests it was a related substance. It is also impossible that $^{(NA_4)}$NUNUZ meant only 'beads', since there are numerous examples of items being made of $^{(NA_4)}$NUNUZ that are not expected to be composed of beads (see, e.g., the drinking vessels made of $^{(NA_4)}$NUNUZ in 4.2.1.A_2 obv. 1′–3′ and 10.2.1.1 obv. 11′). Therefore, the traditional equation still seems preferable, so that $^{(NA_4)}$NUNUZ = $^{(NA_4)}$*ku(wa)nna(n)-* meant not only 'beads', but also a mineral from which it may be presumed beads were archetypically made ("bead stone"). The interchange with URUDU$^{HI.A}$ from KUB 17.21 suggests that this mineral was a kind of copper ore. Whether $^{(NA_4)}$NUNUZ = $^{(NA_4)}$*ku(wa)nna(n)-* ever designated metallic copper, as is suggested by the translation of the term exclusively as "copper" in HED IV and Oreshko 2018, cannot in my opinion be decided on the basis of the present evidence.

As already noted by Polvani and others, a number of copper ores are suitable as for the construction of jewelry, with deep-blue azurite (itself one of the copper carbonate referents of Gr. κύανος, as pointed out by HED IV, 310) and dark-green malachite, into which azurite naturally weathers, being among the most prominent. Although Polvani (1988, 57) avoided identifying $^{(NA_4)}$NUNUZ = $^{(NA_4)}$*ku(wa)nna(n)-* specifically with "azurite-malachite," since that mineral is already comprehended by the term "copper ore," it will be assumed here for purposes of translation that since objects made of blue stone (whether true lapis lazuli or otherwise) are designated by $^{(NA_4)}$ZA.GÌN, objects made of $^{(NA_4)}$NUNUZ were probably of a different color. Without claiming lapidary exactness, dark-green malachite, or possibly a blue-green malachite-azurite mixture, would make a good candidate based on its status as a copper ore and the salience of visual difference from blue stones such as lapis lazuli.

PAD

As discussed by Singer 2006b, 252–57, PAD designates a "chunk" of anything (lit. 'a broken off portion'). The term is applied most commonly to foodstuffs in Sumerian and Akkadian (PAD = *kusāpu, kurummattu*), leading to the basic meaning of 'piece of bread, ration' in these languages (see further in Weeden 2011, 314–15). In Hittite, PAD is applied exclusively to metals, giving the meaning 'chunk (of metal)' = 'bar, ingot'. The PAD was not an exact unit of measurement in Hittite, but according to the evidence examined by Singer (*ibid.* 253), had an average weight "fluctuating between 2.29 and 1.5 minas to an ingot."

^{TÚG}PAD(-*ime*-)

Vigo (2010, 295, fn. 49) suggested for ^{TÚG}PAD(-*ime*-) "a strip, a bolt of untreated fabric (linen?)," while HIT (p. 112) and HVP (p. 338 fn. 1) left the term untranslated. The Hittite reading of PAD is unknown, but if it glosses Akkadian *kasāpu* 'to break off, chip, trim', then with the ending *-ime-* suggesting a Luwian participle *-im(m)a/i-*, the garment could be some sort of "broken off" garment, perhaps formed from trimmings or fabric chunks. The relationship proposed by HVP (*loc. cit.*) between the TÚGPAD(*-ime-*) and the (TÚG) *tap(p)a/išpa-* garments cannot be confirmed, nor ruled out.

SA$_5$

One wonders if SA$_5$, very frequently applied to wooden chests (especially those from Egypt), but also to other wooden objects like chariots (e.g., 3.1.1.A$_1$ rev. v 5′, etc.), might refer to a type of varnish. Varnishing with various binding agents was known in Mesopotamia (Thavapalan 2020, 49–53) and ancient Egypt (Newton – Serpico 2000), where varnish mixed with various pigments was used to preserve and highlight wooden prestige objects.

LÚSAG

See Bilgin 2018, 324–25, 340–45, 431–36 for latest comprehensive discussion of the LÚSAG (or LÚ SAG), a high-level courtier from outside of the royal family who nonetheless had personal access to the Hittite king. Bilgin (p. 341), following Miller 2013, 294–95, does not consider the LÚSAG to have (necessarily) been a eunuch, despite use of the term to designate castrated officials in Mesopotamia from Middle Assyrian times.

SIG$_7$(.SIG$_7$)

See Thavapalan 2020, 65–79 for discussion of SIG$_7$(.SIG$_7$)/*arqu*, a color term that designated especially the pale green of young plants, but also pale yellow. As Thavapalan (pp. 65–66) emphasized, SIG$_7$(.SIG$_7$)/*arqu* designates not just yellowish-green, but yellow *or* green. Per Laroche 1952, 162 fn. 1, SIG$_7$.SIG$_7$ was at least some Hittite texts equivalent to *ḪAṢARTU* 'green'.

SUM (*para* SUM-*uaš*)

The translation of *lalameš ŠA* GIŠPISAN *parā* SUM-*uaš* as "receipt of a chest (containing) handouts" in 6.1 obv. 5 differs from previous interpretations: cf. HIT (p. 26) "Receipt of the chest for delivery"; HVP (p. 333) "Ausgabenbeleg des Behälters der Auslieferung"; CHD P *s.v. parā* 6 a 3′ (p. 124) "Receipt for delivery of a chest: ...." Based on the elliptic structure of the rest of 6.1, where each paragraph is introduced by *lalameš* + container (in gen.) and then followed by a one or two word summary of contents, *parā* SUM-*uaš* in obv. 5 should be understood as describing the contents of the chest, not the chest itself. Thus, instead of a "chest (which is/has been) handed over," *parā* SUM-*uaš* in 6.1 obv. 5 indicates that the objects enumerated in the remainder of the paragraph are '(things) to be given out/handed over' = 'handouts' (see CHD P *s.v. parā* 1 z [p. 113] for the sense of *para pai-* as 'to give out'; see GHL §25.8, p. 331 for the deontic sense of a verbal substantive in free-standing genitive). This interpretation fits well with the overall sense of the text, which records the delivery of items to be distributed during a royal visit to Nerik. The attestation in 6.3, although fragmentary, seems to be of a similar context.

TÚGŠÀ.GA.DÙ

According to CAD Š₁ *s.v.* **šakattû* (p. 158), despite the variety of Sumerographic spellings suggesting the existence of an Akkadian reflex **šakattû*, the TÚGŠÀ.GA.DÙ garment, also spelled TÚGŠÀ.GADA.(DÙ), TÚGŠÀ.GA(.AN).DU/TUM, is a "logogram to be read *nēbeḫu*" (*ibid.* p. 159), a type of belt or sash. In turn, *nēbeḫu* is usually glossed in the lexical lists by TÚGÍB.LÁ (CAD N *s.v. nēbeḫu* [p. 143]). Thus, one interpretation is that TÚGŠÀ.GA.DÙ is a subvariety of TÚGÍB.LÁ "sash." Alternatively, Foster (2010, 134–36) offered the interpretation that the garment was an undershirt or shift, noting (p. 134) that the literal meaning of TÚGŠÀ.GA.DÙ is a "garment worn at the heart/abdomen," i.e., for the upper-body as opposed to the waist or loins. The evidence in Hittite texts is inconclusive, but points towards a garment for the upper body: In KUB 45.32 (CTH 713 "Ritual for Ištar of Tamaninga") rev. iii 6′–10′, the queen holds/wears(?) a TÚGŠÀ.GA.DÙ on her shoulders (rev. iii 6′: TÚGŠÀ.GA.DÙ UZU*pal-ta-ni-iš-*[*ši ḫar-zi*) while dancing for the goddess. In the *MELQĒTU*-list KUB 34.86+ rev.! iv! 6′, TÚGŠÀ.GA.DÙ are listed between matching quantities of shirts (TÚGGÚ.È.A) and belts (TÚGE.ÍB) to be distributed to a group of personnel, suggesting again that the garments were worn on the chest or shoulder region. Since the meaning "belt" (TÚGE.ÍB) and "sash" (TÚGÍB.LÁ) are already covered in Hittite, it is not unlikely the TÚGŠÀ.GA.DÙ was something else. There is no definitive proof against Foster's interpretation of "undershirt, shift," but since the TÚGŠÀ.GA.DÙ are usually described in Hittite texts as decorated (*MAŠ-LU*), sometimes even with gold (9.1.1 rev. iii 26′, rev. iv 42′) they were probably meant to be seen. Goetze's original equation (1955, 54) of TÚGŠÀ.GA.DÙ with (TÚG)*maššia-* should therefore be entertained once more, with the caveat that both are to be translated as "scarf, shawl," i.e., a garment for the neck and shoulders, and not "sash."

ŠAḪ.TUR

The description in 9.1.5 rev.! 14′ of a ŠAḪ.TUR-*anza* associated with EME 'tongues; knife blades' and a GIŠŠUKUR 'spear' suggests that the ŠAḪ.TUR(-*anza*) in this context is some kind of bladed tool, and not a figurine of a piglet. This recalls the KA×U ŠAḪ *ŠA* KÙ.BABBAR "silver 'pig's snout'" in KUB 39.35+ obv. i 6′ (Days 8–9 of the Hittite Funerary Ritual) that is used to dig an irrigation ditch (obv. i 10′: *n=ašta* ŠAḪ *wātar* [*nāi* "the pig [diverts] water"). It may be inferred that the (KA×U) ŠAḪ(.TUR) was a kind of digging tool, perhaps one that reminded the Hittites of the rooting tusks of pigs. The description in 9.1.5 rev.! 14′ suggests that the "piglet" consisted of multiple blades (or tines?) and a GIŠŠUKUR 'spear' (or 'peg': see CAD Š₃ *s.v. šukurru* 3. [p. 235]) that was located behind the "piglet." One could thus imagine a heavy rake, or perhaps even a plough, with the "piglet"/"pig's snout" forming the cutting surface or ploughshare.

URUDUŠEN

As is noted under HZL no. 230 (p. 207, citing Steinkeller 1981 and 1984), the signs PÎSAN/ALAL (ŠID×A) and ŠEN (SU×A) should be combined and both read as ŠEN in texts from Boğazköy. In Hittite texts, the sign ŠEN refers to two different objects. With a the URUDU determinative it designates, in accordance with its Mesopotamian reading, a cauldron or kettle. With the GIŠ determinative it assumes a unique Hittite designation as a kind of gutter or drain (Weeden 2011, 380, who seemingly rejects the general sense of 'tube' proposed HZL no. 230). While the catalog entry in Weeden 2011 (pp. 611–12) did not acknowledge the original designation 'kettle' in Hittite texts, and instead assigned to ŠEN with both ^{URUDU} and ^{GIŠ} determinative the sense 'gutter, drain', all attestations of ^{URUDU}ŠEN in the PTAC are consonant with a meaning 'kettle', and almost none demand an interpretation 'gutter, drain' (see *Commentary* to 5.1 rev. iii 7 for possible exception). Indeed, a translation "hand gutter" or "gutter with a handle" for ^{URUDU}ŠEN ŠU-*TI* in 5.7 rev. iii$^{?}$ 11′ makes no sense (see *Lexical Commentary s.v.* ^{URUDU}ŠEN ŠU-*TI* below). The ^{URUDU}ŠEN-kettle could be very large. In Nuzi, the ^{URUDU}ŠEN (= *ruqqu* 'kettle') weighed 30 minas (Schneider-Ludorff 2009, 507) or even heavier (cf. the manufacture of an ^{URUDU}ŠEN(PÌSAN) *ša* GU$_{4}$ weighing 1 talent, 41 minas in HSS 13.70: 1–3, *loc. cit.*). These dimensions fit well with those of the ^{URUDU}ŠEN in Boğazköy, where in, e.g., 5.7 rev. iii$^{?}$ 5′, the vessel and a few other smaller items are found either manufactured from, or weighing in total, one talent of copper. Thus far, no Hittite reading for ŠEN is available (^{GIŠ}ŠEN = ^{GIŠ}*artaḫḫi-* rejected by Hoffner 1983, 416–17; the proposal $^{\text{(URUDU)}}$ŠEN = *ḫuḫḫurtalla-* by Erkut 1997 is also untenable: see discussion *s.v. ḫuḫḫurtalla-* in the *Lexical Commentary* above).

^{URUDU}ŠEN ŠU-*TI*

Although transparently meaning a "hand-kettle," it cannot be definitely determined whether the ^{URUDU}ŠEN ŠU-*TI* was a kettle for washing the hands, or a kettle that can be held in hand with a handle. The appearance of an *a-sà-lu*$_{4}$ ZABAR *ša* ŠU-*ti* in a text from Emar, translated as "bronze *asallu*-vat with a handle" (Goodnick Westenholz 2000, text no. 14, obv. 9 [p. 39]), suggests the latter.

ŠEŠ(-)*pí-ša-te*(-)

Despite emendation to LÚ$^{\text{MEŠ!?}}$ ⟨^{URU}⟩*pí-ša-te* (5.7 rev. iii$^{?}$ 8′) suggested in CHD P *s.v.* [*pí-ša-te*] (p. 316), the original transliterations of HVP (pp. 278, 280) are more probably correct. Examination of the photo shows that the second attestation in 5.7 rev. iii$^{?}$ 21′ also shows two trailing *Winkelhaken*, indicating a ŠEŠ rather that LÚ presented by the handcopy of KUB 60.1 and transcribed by the CHD P (*loc. cit.*). Furthermore, a ŠEŠ is attested as a recipient of items also in 5.1 obv. ii 6 – a text that, if not an indirect join to 5.7, is identical in style and substance – demonstrating, along with the *A-BU* in 5.7 rev. iii$^{?}$ 21′ and the DUMU^{MEŠ} in rev. iii$^{?}$ 23′, that recipients in the "*ĪDE* texts" could be anonymously identified by kinship terms, not just by town name. The meaning of the (-)*pišate*(-) element remains unknown. One would expect a personal name, but it is improbable that the ^{m} determinative would be twice left out. HVP (p. 278 fn. 2) suggested a derivation from Akkadian *piššatu* 'oil-ration' or *peššû* 'limping, halting', while the CHD P (*loc. cit.*) suggests a connection with the town of ^{URU}*Piššatte*. If (-)*pišate*(-) is not read as a personal name, then ŠEŠ would need to be read more figuratively, following HVP, as 'comrade, companion'. Alternatively, one could speculate that (-)*pišate*(-) modified ŠEŠ as a kinship variety, e.g., "step brother" or "cousin."

ŠU PN

The phrase ŠU PN appears in the PTAC in three forms: ŠU PN (nominative), *ANA* ŠU PN (dative), and *ŠA* ŠU PN (genitive). Most previous editions have translated the nominative and genitive phrases differently (the sole example of the dative form occurs in 4.2.1.A_2, which was not edited by HIT or HVP). For the nominative, HIT rendered literally ŠU PN "hand of ..." with the comment (p. 93) that "the gold has temporarily been turned over to somebody for treatment ... ," referencing earlier Goetze 1956, 37. HVP (p. 85) translated the phrase more interpretatively as "Werk des ... ." Other translations include van den Hout 2006, 86 ("The individual to whom the material is handed out is usually referred to with the expression ŠU PN 'hand of PN'.") and Alexandrov 2016, 8 ("Probably, the term ŠU, literally 'hand', should be regarded as a counterpart of *lalami-*: it is attested with personal names and should be understood as 'handed out to'."). For the genitive, HIT continued a literal translation: *ŠA* ŠU PN "from the hand of ..." (p. 124), whereas HVP (p. 364) explained: "Die Verbindung *ŠA* ŠU ^{m}PN drückt wohl aus, dass die zuvor aufgezählten Gegenstände Sachen aus dem Besitz des Betreffenden darstellen." Concurring with HVP are de Martino – Imparati 1998, 188: "'della mano (*ŠA* ŠU) di qualcuno', in riferimento a oggetti 'appartenenti a qualcuno'," and Singer 2011, 462 fn. 26: "this expression ... probably means 'from the property of PN'."

However, a reanalysis of the data from the PTAC suggests that all variants of ŠU PN should be translated the same: as "(into/of) the responsibility, authority, control, trust of PN." In this sense, the items were not owned per se by the named individual, but rather entrusted to their control for a specific purpose, which was usually described; or as Röllig 2008, 17 proposed for a translation of the same phrase in Middle Assyrian administrative texts (see below): "im verantwortlichen Gebrauch."

For ŠU PN, a series of examples for the term meaning "responsibility, control, trust of PN" and not "(handi)work of PN" can be found. In 2.2 rev. 11–12 a quantity of raw silver is described as ŠU ŠU ^{m}*eḫli*-^{D}30, after which a note is appended: ḪAR$^{ḪI.A}$ DÙ-*zi* "he will make rings." The present-future implies the rings have not yet been made, making it difficult to translate ŠU as Eḫli-Šarumma's "handiwork." In 2.7.A rev. 2: 1 MA.NA KÙ.SI$_{22}$ GAL *ienzi* ŠU ^{m}*eḫli*-^{D}30, Eḫli-Šarruma is removed even further from the manufacture of the objects by the use of a third-person plural: here Eḫlišarruma has only responsibility for the mina of gold, with it being an anonymous group of smiths, the "they," who will manufacture the cup. Perhaps most probative is the attestation 4.2.6 obv.$^{?}$ 3′: [n (GADA) $^{(GIŠ)}$*karn*]*ašša* ŠU $^{LÚ.MEŠ}$*šalašḫaš* MUNUS.LUGAL "[n *karn*]*ašša*-chair(s) (or *karn*]*ašša*-chair [linens]), ŠU of the queen's *šalašḫa*-men," where the queen's *šalašḫa*-men (perhaps "footmen"?) can in no way be taken as the craftsmen of the *karnašša*-chair (or its cloth), but could easily be imagined as tasked with fetching furniture and linens. Finally, the single attestation of *ANA* ŠU PN in 4.2.1.A_2 rev. 12′–13′, where a number of *iron (ore)* pieces are described as *ANA* ŠU $^{m.D}$10-*manadu*, is naturally interpretable as "into the responsibility of Tarḫunta-manadu," while "in/into the handiwork ..." proves awkward.

The genitive construction *ŠA* ŠU PN is far less frequently attested, only appearing twice in the PTAC. That the *ŠA* ŠU PN construction has nothing to do with production is confirmed by 4.2.4 obv. 11, where a number of personal grooming items are described as "*ŠA* ŠU MUNUS.LUGAL," where the queen could in no way be expected to have crafted the various gold and stone-inlaid hair clasps listed. Therefore, in attempting to explain the construction, HVP 364 fn. 2 was correct to make recourse to the oracle text KUB 22.70, the sole set of attestations of the phrase outside of the PTAC. KUB 22.70 concerns various misdeeds in the palace that have aroused the gods' anger. One of the subplots of involves a certain Ammatalla and her son Pallili, who is described as wearing clothes which are "*ŠA* ŠU AMA-*ŠU*." The relevant passages are:

KUB 22.70

1.) obv. 9–10

DUMU ^{f}[*Am*]*matallaš=a=za kuit* TÚG^{MEŠ} *ŠA* ŠU AMA-*ŠU waššan ḫarzi* ^{10} *n=aš INA* É.GAL-*LIM anda weriyanza ēšt*[*a*]

(Is the god angry because ...), "and because the son of [Am]matalla has worn garments *ŠA* ŠU AMA-*ŠU*, and he wa[s] called into the Palace?"

2.) obv. 77–78

^{m}*Pallilišš=a kuit INA* É.GAL-*LIM šarā iyattat* ^{78} TÚG^{MEŠ}*=ma ŠA* ŠU AMA-*ŠU waššan ḫarta*

"And because Pallili came up into the palace, but he had worn the clothes *ŠA* ŠU AMA-*ŠU*."

3.) rev. 31

kī kuit DUMU ^{f}*Ammatalla INA* É.GAL-*LIM anda weriyanza ēšta* TÚG$^{\text{ḪI.A}}$*=ma=za ŠA* ŠU AM[A-*ŠU waš*]*šiškit*

"Concerning this, that the son of Ammatalla was called into the palace, but was [dre]ssing himself *ŠA* ŠU AM[A-*ŠU*]."

4.) rev. 35

namma ^{f}*Ammatallann=a kuit IŠTU* É.GAL-*LIM watar*[*n*]*aḫḫir* TÚG$^{\text{ḪI.A}}$-*wa kue zik u*-[x-x-x-x-x *nu*]*=war=at ANA* DUMU-*KA lē peškiši*

"And then, because they comm[a]nded Ammatalla from the palace: 'which garments you [...], don't be giving them to your son!'"

The first passage, KUB 22.70 obv. 9–10, was translated in Ünal 1978, 57: "und weil der Sohn der [Am]matalla die Kleider seiner Mutter anzog und er (in diesem Zustand) in den Palast hineingerufen worden wa[r?]," whereas Beckman (1997, 205) chose: "Because the son of Ammattalla has dressed himself in garments entrusted to his mother and was summoned to the palace?" While Ünal explained that "die Kleider seiner Mutter" is "Wörtl. 'die seiner Mutter zur Verfügung stehenden Kleider'" (*loc. cit.*, fn. c), he clarified in the commentary to the passage (*ibid.* 107–8) that:

> Die Funktion dieser im hethitischen Bereich sehr seltenen Wendung wäre dann darin zu suchen, daß man hier nicht die männlichen Kleider von Pallili, die natürlich nach dem Familienrecht seiner Mutter Ammatalla gehören können, sondern die (weiblichen) Kleider von ihr hervorheben wollte, um dieser ungewöhnlichen Tat Pallilis Nachdruck zu verleihen.

This, then, is the question upon which the interpretation of the passage rests, and in turn the interpretation of the phrase *ŠU* ŠA PN: was Pallili's crime that he was dressing in woman's clothing, or that he was wearing clothing that did not belong to him or his mother? As Ünal (1978, 108) acknowledged, the act of cross-dressing is nowhere paralleled in Hittite sources (outside of the passage from KBo 6.34 obv. ii 42–53 in the "First Soldier's Oath," where dressing as woman is assumed by the oath-takers as a punishment for breaking the oath). One might therefore presume that a man intentionally dressing in woman's clothing would have been perceived as a deviant act, especially in the presence of the king, where it could be imagined to have a deleterious effect on the king's ritual purity. If so, it is curious that a bigger deal was not made of Pallili's misdeed, who it seems was only required to do penance (*zankilatar*, rev. 33). Moreover, the verb *peške/a-* in rev. 35 suggests that Ammatalla was consciously and habitually allowing her son to wear "her" clothes, which also argues against cross-dressing, since she would presumably not wish to be complicit in a such a compromising act. Rather, combining understanding of ŠU PN from elsewhere in the PTAC as (with Beckman's translation) "entrusted to," it seems that Pallili's was the mundane crime of misappropriating palace and/or temple resources – an occurrence that was frequent enough to have generated a sort of institutional paranoia in the Hittite palace, judging by the lawsuits and instructions preserved. It can be assumed that Ammatalla had been entrusted with the care of a number of garments, possibly belonging the god of Arušna, who was the aggrieved party of KUB 22.70, and she allowed her son to use them, thinking neither the god nor the palace would notice.

Decisive now is the discussion of Röllig 2008, 17, of the same term in Middle Assyrian administrative texts, where *ša* ŠU PN and *ina* ŠU PN are often found contrasted to *ša ēkalli*. Previous interpretations of the term included Saporetti 1970, 503 ("*ša qāt* NP indica l'incaricato responsabile ... ," further (*loc. cit.*): "risulta evidente che sta ad indicare l'incaricato-responsabile, non il proprietario della merce."), AHw *s.v. qātu(m)* B 6) (p. 910) ("Verantwortungs-, Arbeitsbereich"), CAD Q *s.v. qātu* 6. (p. 189) ("authority, possession, custody, charge, care, control, jurisdiction") and Postgate 1988, xiii ("*ša qāt* PN ['in the charge of PN']"). After comparing these, Rölling concluded (*loc. cit.*) for the term that: "Es ist dann – durchaus in Überstimmung mit dem AHw. – mit '(in) der Verfügung' im Sinne von 'im verantwortlichen Gebrauch' zu übersetzen." However, it should be noted that the remark of Rölling (*loc. cit.*) that: "Unter der Maßgabe, dass *ša/ina qāt* 'in der Verfügung...' bedeutet, ist allerdings die von J.N. Postgate postulierte 'ownership' für die Texte des Archivs auszuschließen" seems to contain a misinterpretation of Postgate's position. The quote from Postgate 1988, xiii, is: "Like his father, [Urad-Šerua] was an agent of the palace, as appears from the debt-notes bearing the ownership phrase *ša ēkalli* ('of the palace'), or from texts where the item is *ša qāt* PN ('in the charge of PN')." Here, Postgate claims only that the phrase *ša qāt* PN testifies to Urad-Šerua's condition as an agent of the palace – i.e., as someone to whom the palace would entrust goods – and not that the phrase should be taken as an ownership phrase contrasting with *ša ēkalli*.

$^{\text{(URUDU)}}$ŠU.ŠÈ.LÁ

For reading ŠU.ŠÈ.LÁ instead of previous ŠU.TÚG.LÁ, see Hoffner 2001, 188 fn. 47. With Singer 2011, 464: "A metal vessel named šu-šè-lá (also spelled šu-ša-lá, šu-uš-lá, šuš-lá, šu-lá) is attested in Mesopotamian texts, mainly of the third millennium B.C.E. Its literal meaning is 'what hangs from the hand', which may indicate that it was a vessel with handles." Singer goes on to suggest (pp. 465–66) that the ^{URUDU}ŠU.ŠÈ.LÁ KUR *Aḫḫiyauwā* of 4.2.9 lo. e. 33′ was a kind of *krater* for mixing wine, perhaps of an identical fabrication to those depicted in contemporary Mycenaean art and recovered in excavations, with the accompanying ^{URUDU}UGU *laḫuaš* (also 4.2.9 lo. e. 33′) serving as its ladle.

^{GIŠ}ŠU.TAG.GA

ŠU.TAG.GA is a participle meaning either "touched, anointed" (= Akk. *lapātu*; see ePSD *s.v.* šu tag [TOUCH]) or "decorated, spangled, covered" (= Akk. *za'ānu*; see ePSD *s.v.* šu tag [DECORATE]). As HVP argued (p. 242), SÍG SA$_5$ ^{GIŠ}ŠU.TAG.GA appears to stand in opposition to SÍG SA$_5$ SÙḪ (read here BIR) in 4.1.4.6 obv. 2′, 5′, 10′, 14′. Since BIR means 'strewn', in the sense of 'loose' wool, ^{GIŠ}ŠU.TAG.GA would then be another form or condition of bulk wool. Following HVP (p. 245 fn. 5), one can imagine that ^{GIŠ}ŠU.TAG.GA was a wooden grip or handle (some nominal derivative of *lapātu*) on which the wool was stored, i.e., a 'spool' or 'bobbin'. Alternatively, it is also possible that the wool "covered" (from *za'ānu*) a stick (GIŠ).

ŠUL.PÁT

Previously transliterated as an Akkadogram, evidence from the PTAC suggests that ŠUL.PÁT/*ŠULPATU* should rather be treated as a pseudo-Sumerogram derived from Akkadian, analogous to the doublets NAM.TÚL/*NAMTULLU* and ^{UZU}DIR/^{UZU}*TIRĀNU* in Hittite cuneiform (see Weeden 2011, 12, 380–81). In the PTAC, the form ŠUL.PÁT appears thirteen times, never once in a context appropriate for an Akkadographic st. constr., compared to the single occurrence of ^{GIŠ}*ŠULPATU* (4.2.1.A$_1$ obv. 11). Whereas CAD Š$_3$ *s.v.* *šulpatu* (p. 256) defined the object only as "'(a utensil)'," the association of the ŠUL.PÁT/*ŠULPATU* with drinking equipment (see 5.1 obv. ii, where ŠUL.PÁT are distributed alongside cups and drinking horns to various groups), the relatively small size of the object (see chests containing 107 and 200 ŠUL.PÁT respectively in 2.2 rev. 14 and 8.1.A rev. v 27′), and Akkadian lemma *šulpu* 'stalk, reed', confirm the interpretation in HZL no. 46 (p. 114) $^{\text{(GI/GIŠ)}}$ŠUL.PÁT as '(Trink-)Halm, Röhrchen'.

$^{\text{NA}_4}$TI

See Polvani 1988, 161–63 for $^{\text{NA}_4}$TI 'life/living(?)' stone, which she hypothesized to be named after a reflective or chromatic feature of its surface.

(TÚG) *ḫurliš(š)a-*

With HW^2 Ḫ *s.v.* ^{TÚG}*ḫur/ḫar/mur-lišša-*, and contra HIT (p. 215) and HVP (p. 592), the (TÚG) *ḫurliš(š)a-* is probably not a "Hurrian garment." The coexistence of the writings ^{TÚG}GÚ(.È.A) *ḪURRI* and the (TÚG) *ḫurliš(š)a-* in the same texts (e.g., 4.2.6, 8.1.E, and 8.1.F), and the complete absence of the forms *^{TÚG}GÚ(.È.A) *ḫurliš(š)a-* and *(TÚG) *ḪURRI*, suggest that the designation *ḫurli(š)a-* was not equivalent to *ḪURRI*. The absence of a *TÚG *ḪURRI* likewise also means that the abbreviated forms TÚG *ḫur.* in 3.2.1 obv. 14; rev. 16′ and 11.6.1 5, 11 can be confidently assigned to the (TÚG) *ḫurliš(š)a-*. One wonders if the (TÚG) *ḫurliš(š)a-* was another of the "regional" garments in PTAC, based on a hitherto unattested town *^{URU}*Ḫurliš(š)a*; cf. the town of ^{URU}*Ḫurla* (with HW^2 Ḫ *s.v.* $^{\text{(URU)}}$*ḫurla-* [p. 756]: "^{URU}*Ḫurla* als Stadtname ... wohl von *ḫ.* 'ḫurritisch' zu unterscheiden), which at a minimum suggests there was a stem **ḫurl-* available for geographic names on the Anatolian Plateau.

(TÚG/KUŠ) *kapi(r)t(t)aš(š)amna-*

The new reading of [^{URU}*k*]*a-*pí-ta*-šàm-n*[*a-aš* in the tribute-list 3.1.5.A$_2$ obv. ii(?) 13′ (also [^{URU}*ka-pí-t*]*a-š*[*àm-na-aš* in obv. ii(?) 16′), where the word must absolutely be a geographical name, now demonstrates that the (KUŠ/TÚG) *kapi(r)t(t)aš(š)amna-* was another of the "regional" garments, named after their presumed geographical origins: see also (TÚG) *ikkuwaniya-*, TÚG *karkišili-*, (TÚG) $^{\text{(URU)}}$*kummanni*, (TÚG) *tap(p)a/išpa-*, (TÚG)/^{TÚG}GÚ *wašḫaniya-*, the ubiquitous ^{TÚG}GÚ(.È.A) *ḪURRI*, and possibly (TÚG) *ḫurliš(š)a-*. Note that HW^2 K *s.v.* $^{\text{(TÚG/KUŠ)}}$*kapit(t)ašamna(-)*, ^{TÚG}*kapartaš*[*am-* (p. 116) came to a similar conclusion, but derived the name of the garment from the town of ^{URU}*Ka(p)pitta* plus the verb *šamna(i)-* 'to create'. Independent of the exact match now available with [^{URU}*k*]*a-*pí-ta*-šàm-n*[*a-aš*, the fact that none of the other regional garments use any construction besides TÚG + geographic name recommends against the proposed derivation of HW^2.

The location of ^{URU}*Kapitašamna* cannot be determined. Its appearance as a contributor to the É.GAL ^{URU}*Ša*[*pinuwa*(?) in 3.1.5 obv. ii(?) 10′–13′ unfortunately has no bearing on its geography, since that institution was possibly/probably located in Ḫattuša (see *Lexical Commentary s.v.* É(.GAL) $^{\text{(URU)}}$). The forms of the garment written with *ka-*BAR-*ta-* instead of *kapita-* presumably represent a weakly articulated "r" in the original geographic name, suggesting that they are better read TÚG *ka-pir$_x$-ta-šàm-na*: (see HZL no. 20A for BAR = pir$_x$). As with the other regional garments, little can be said about the qualities or shape of the *kapi(r)t(t)aš(š)amna-*, other than it is frequently associated in lists with GADA/TÚG *ŠU-UḪ-RU* 'grey linen/cloth', ^{TÚG}*tapa/išpa-* 'Tapašpan garment', and ^{TÚG}GÚ *ḪUR-RI* 'Hurrian shirt' (see 8.1.D rev. iv 3′//8.1.E(A$_1$) rev. v$^?$ 9′; 8.1.D rev. iv 8′–11′//8.1.H rev. r. c. 6′–9′//8.1.I rev. r. c. 5′–7′; 4.2.9 obv. 2–3, 20–21; rev. 11′–12′; 3.2.1 obv. 14; 11.1.8 2′).

(TÚG) *tap(p)a/išpa-*

For most recent review of literature on the Tapašpan garment, see Vigo 2010, 294, with fnn. 38, 39. The city of Tapašpa was located somewhere in the north-eastern periphery of the Hittite Kingdom (Corti 2017, 222, 224). The look and construction of the Tapašpa garment remain unknown.

U_4.SAKAR, $^{D}U_4$-*aš* SAKAR

The newly recognized attestation $^{D}U_4$-*aš* SAKAR in 9.1.4.A_1 obv. ii 7′ suggests that the previously hapax $^{D}U_4$-*aš* SAKAR-*za* in 9.1.1 rev. iv 15′ must be taken seriously (cf. HVP, 449 fn. 14: "vielleicht fehlerhaft"; HW^2 A *s.v. armanni-* [p. 325] "vermutlich eine volksetymolog. Verballhornung im Gedanken an die Sonnengottheiten"). As already noted by HVP (*loc. cit.*), examples from outside the PTAC, e.g., KUB 36.89 obv. 6: *kuišš=a* U_4.SAKAR-*aš*, attest to an underlying common gender *a*-stem for U_4.SAKAR. However, the agreement of $^{D}U_4$-*aš* SAKAR-*za* with *šuppešduwaran* in 9.1.1 rev. iv 15′ demonstrates that the example here must be neuter, specifically a Luw. sg. nom.-acc. n. with the *-ša/-za* neuter particle (van den Hout 1984, Melchert 2003, 186–87, Jasanoff 2010, Simon (forth.)). Thus, it seems that Hittite had at least three words for 'lunula': the common gender *i*-stem *armanni-*, the common gender *a*-stem behind U_4.SAKAR-*aš*, and a neuter *t-*, *r-*, *l-*, or *n*-stem behind $^{D}U_4$-*aš* SAKAR-*za*, which based on its appearance in the Inventory of Manninni was probably borrowed from Luwian. Moreover, it cannot be ascertained whether both the common gender and neuter forms of U_4.SAKAR were actually two words, or only those written with the phonetic complement on $^{D}U_4$-*aš*. Although three words for 'lunula' is an unexpected lexicographic result, it is perhaps not surprising, given the profusion of celestial ornaments in Hittite iconography, that the Hittites possessed a developed technical vocabulary for depictions of the moon.

UGU *ḫamenkuaš*

With HVP (p. 588), UGU/*šarā ḫamenkuaš* = "des darüber Verbindens, Spange." Attestations of the word both within the PTAC and elsewhere (e.g., KBo 13.61 rev. 7′) fail to elucidate the exact nature of the item, save that it can have, or be composed of, chainlinks (4-*ŠU kulān*, 8.4 rev. 5′) and consist of a decently substantial amount of metal (20 GÍN KÙ.SI_{22} SIG_5 … [UG]U *ḫa-me-en-ku-aš* DÙ-*zi*, 4.1.1.2.B obv. 9–10). One might therefore imagine a brooch with a short length of chain attached.

URU

The three objects inventoried in the 1.5 obv. 1 were transliterated by HIT (p. 154): URU-*LUM* 'city' and HVP (p. 127): *ṢÚ-LUM* 'brooch'. Against the transliteration of HIT, HVP (p. 127 fn. 1) made the salient criticism that a piece of jewelry or clothing is expected here, and moreover, as indicated by the passage, one with an inside and outside. CHD Š *s.v. šarā* B 3.b (p. 226) supported the transliteration of HIT, and cited the article of Hoffner 1969, 178–80 for existence of "models of cities" as votive objects. However, the CHD missed what is perhaps the most important point of Hoffner's contribution (and of Paul 1967, to which Hoffner's article was responding), namely that these model "cities" were in fact mural crowns, that is, crowns modeled after the crenellations of a city wall. As discussed by Paul 1967, Hoffner 1969, and again Paul 2006, mural crowns were a transcultural eastern Mediterranean phenomenon, attested at least as early as the depiction of Ḫebat and her attendants at Yazılıkaya (Paul 2006, 791), worn primarily by women and goddesses, especially when the latter were held as personifications or protectors of the city. The interpretation of the URU-*LUM* in 1.5 obv. 1 as "mural crowns" thus satisfies both the plain reading of the cuneiform and the critique of HVP requiring a piece of jewelry with a clear inside and outside surface.

^{NA_4}ZA.GÌN DUR$_{10}$

The ^{NA_4}ZA.GÌN "ŠEN" attested twice in 3.1.8.A obv. 3′, 7′ presents a problem of interpretation. There exists a reading of ŠEN as an adjective meaning 'pure', but this is seemingly known only from lexical lists (see CAD E *s.v. ellu* [p. 102]). However, ŠEN also has a value DUR$_{10}$, as in DUR$_{10}$.TAB.BA 'axe' and other bladed tools, at Boğazköy and elsewhere, which in turn invites comparison with ^{NA_4}ZA.GÌN DURU$_5$ '"fresh" lapis lazuli' (CAD Z *s.v. zagindurû* [p. 11]; Schuster-Brandis 2008, 455). It can thus be tentatively reconstructed that the Hittites, no doubt following some submerged peripheral cuneiform tradition, occasionally conflated ŠEN (SU × A) with DURU$_5$ (= A) in writing this variety of lapis lazuli, based on overlapping semantics (both ŠEN and DURU$_5$ can mean pure), orthography, and pronunciation (ŠEN with the above-mentioned value DUR$_{10}$ known to the Hittites, which is close enough to DURU$_5$). The Hittites could also write the variety of lapis lazuli normally as ^{NA_4}ZA.GÌN DURU$_5$ (HZL no. 366 [p. 277]).

ZA.ḪUM

See Burgin (forth.^{2}) for discussion of the LUM vs. LUM-šeššig (= SIG$_4$) in Hittite. To summarize, LUM in all its readings (*lum*, *ḫum*, GUZ, etc.) is written as LUM-šeššig in Sumerograms at Ḫattuša, regardless of whether the Sumerogram uses LUM or LUM-šeššig in Mesopotamian sources. In contrast, LUM (*lum*, *ḫum*, etc.) is written normally in Akkadograms. Thus, forms of the ZA.ḪUM/*SĀḪU* vessel written with LUM-šeššig can be classified as Sumerograms ZA.ḪUM("SIG$_4$"), and those written with the LUM are Akkadograms, *SÀ-ḪU$_5$*. The ZA.ḪUM/*SĀḪU* can be equated with *aššuzeri-* '"good" cup' (HW^2 A *s.v. aššuzeri-* [p. 541], with bibliography).

ZI.KIN.BAR

See CHD Š *s.v.* $^{(URUDU)}$*šepik(k)ušta-, šipikkušta-, šapik(k)ušta-* (p. 397) for discussion of ZI.KIN.BAR and equation with *šepikkušta-*. Note, however, that the CHD's claim that ZI.KIN.BAR/*šepikkušta-* without further qualification means 'stylus' is at a minimum unproven (the cited example from KUB 17.20 obv. ii 22 ends at a break), and that all examples of unmodified ZI.KIN.BAR in the PTAC are interpretable as 'needle, pin'.

ZI.KIN.BAR ^{LÚ}DUB.SAR

See now Cammarosano et al. 2019, 141–43, for images and discussion of the "scribal needle" as a stylus specifically for writing Anatolian hieroglyphs on wax.

Akkadograms

ANKURI(N)NU

See Faist – Vita 2010 for a discussion of this object attested across many cultures and periods in the ancient Near East. If the interpretation in Leichty 1996, 234 of BM 56942, a tablet containing a receipt with a sketched illustration for the manufacture of a silver *iggurru* object (= *i(n)gur(i)nu*, *ankuri(n)nu*?) is correct, then the *ankuri(n)nu* was a kind of elaborate lampstand that could hold multiple lamps. This interpretation is supported in the PTAC by the example from 3.1.1.A_3 obv. iii 9′: 1 ^{URUDU}*ANKURINU ANA* 4 ^{URUDU}*wakšur* "one copper *lampstand* for 4 copper *sixth* vessels," since one of the known uses of the *wakšur* '"sixth" vessel' was as a lamp (see *Lexical Commentary s.v.* $^{\text{(URUDU)}}$*wakšur*).

AŠRU

There seem to be at least three different uses of the term *AŠRU* in the PTAC. The first is in the construction *ANA AŠAR* 'in place of', which in 3.1.3 obv.$^?$ 4′, 9′ seems to record substitute tribute. The second use is in the construction *AŠRA* + participle, e.g., *AŠ-RA* GAR.RA, *AŠ-RA arḫa arriran*, etc. As shown by the examples in CHD P *s.v. peda-* A j 1″ a″, 3 ″b′, the form *AŠ-RA* "used like a d.-l." (p. 343) occurs far too often to be a mistake. Following the suggestion of the CHD P (*loc. cit.*) that *AŠ-RA* is an Akkadian sg. acc., this indicates that the underlying Hittite construction is an "accusative of respect" (GHL § 16.25, p. 248), so that the objects are plated or damaged, etc. with respect to the given number of places or spots. The third use is as free-standing noun, *AŠRU*, in 10.3.12 obv. i 9′: *AŠRU=ma=at* 3 ŠÀ.BA 2 *duwarnan* 'but there are 3 'spots', of which 2 are damaged' (also obv. i 7′: *AŠRU=ma=at* 13 erasure [ ) and 10.3.13 8′: 3 *AŠRU* KÙ.S[I_{22} "3 gol[d] 'spots'." Here, the *AŠRU* seem to be physical features, not just reference points for participles, indicating that they were perhaps a technical term for spots of inlay or plating.

∢BARATITINNU

See HVP (p. 487 fn. 13), with reference to AHw *parattitinnu* (p. 832) "ein Teil des Griffs v[on] Peitschen usw." The item is attested twice at El Amarna in lists of gifts from Tušratta as part of a whip (EA 22 obv. i 4) and part of a fly whisk (EA 25 rev. iii 53), both times adorned with (or composed of?) stone. Judging by 9.1.10.A_2 rev. 11′: 13 *TAPAL ŠA* ^{KUŠ}KIR_4.TAB.ANŠE *∢BARATI*[*TTINNU*] "13 sets of halters (with) *∢BARATI*[*TTINNU*]," the *B/PARATITINNU* could also be components or attachment of a halter. One could therefore imagine a kind of ring or tube made of stone that could gather multiple thongs of leather, as would be found in a whip, whisk, or halter.

$^{\text{NA}_4}$*ḪALTU*

According to Schuster-Brandis 2008, 416, the *ḫaltu*-stone is commonly attested as an amulet stone. The relevant entry in *abnu šikinšu* describes the appearance of the *ḫaltu*-stone as like that of the "neck of a *raqqu*-turtle," which Schuster-Brandis 2008, 416 fn. 752 cautiously suggested might indicate a variety of jasper. If the *ḫaltu*-stone is the MA/MB form of the *ḫaštum*-stone attested in OB texts (Schuster-Brandis, *loc. cit.*), then the spelling $^{\text{N}]\text{A}_4}$*ḪAL-TI* in 8.1.A obv. i 9′ would confirm a contemporary borrowing of the stone name into Hittite cuneiform. It is not impossible that the form ^{NA_4}*ḪALTI* in 8.1.A obv. i 9′ was not an Akkadian sg. gen., but rather an *i*-stem borrowing in Hittite sg. nom.-acc. sg.: ^{NA_4}*ḫalti*.

ḪAPALKI(N)NU

With HED III *s.v.* *(ḫ)apalki-* (p. 117), the Akkadogram *ḪAPALKI(N)NU* is probably "Hurroid," possibly reflecting a borrowing of Hattic *ḫapalki-* '*iron (ore)*' with a Hurrian morpheme *-ni-* or *-nni-* and an Akkadian declension pattern; cf. sg. nom. *ḫapalki(n)nu* in the Mitanni-Akkadian context of EA 22 obv. i 32; rev. iii 7, and the suggestion of Hoffner 1968, 43 that *ḫapalki(n)nu* was the reading behind AN.BAR in the Mitanni-Hurrian context.

ḪAṢARTU

See now Thavapalan 2020, 264–66, who identifies this color as "green." Compare also HW² Ḫ *s.v.* *ḫaḫḫala/i-* (p. 7) 'gelb/grün' (adj. related to $^{(GIŠ)}$*ḫaḫḫal* 'bush, undergrowth') = Akk. *ḪAṢARTU* (= SIG_7.SIG_7 in some Hittite texts, per Laroche 1952, 162 fn. 1).

ḪAṢARTU A.AB.BA

Concerning the unique phrase SÍG *ḪA-ṢAR-TUM* A.AB.BA in 2.7.A obv. 17, at least three alternatives present themselves. The first, and perhaps least probable, follows Goetze 1959, 35 fn. 34, who wrote that "The SÍG *ḪA-ZAR-TUM* A-AB-BA of our text (l. 17) seems to point to the circumstance that this wool was brought from 'the sea'." The second alternative considers that it is the color, not the wool, that is modified by the phrase "(of) the sea." HIT and HVP followed this interpretation, and translated *ḪAṢARTU* A.AB.BA as a shade of purple-blue (HIT, p. 6: "purple of the sea"; HVP, p. 83: "purpurblaue Wolle"), based on the assumption the wool was died with marine purple harvested from the *Murex* snail. This is also problematic, at least superficially, since *ḪAṢARTU* is normally translated as "green" (neither HIT nor HVP commented on the contradiction). Fortunately, as demonstrated by a combination of philological research and experimental archaeology presented in Soriga 2017, "purple-blue" is not the only color available from marine snails. Indeed, according to Soriga (p. 83):

> In contact with air and light, the base of molluscan purple changes colour. It turns from a colourless to a yellow-greenish tint, characteristic of very indigoid reduction, reaching then the blue-violet or magenta hues in accordance with the species and even the gender of the molluscs .... Besides that, the use of different substances as reducing agents used in order to create alkaline conditions and solubilise the indigoids in water may affect the gradation of colour.

The bottom center image of Fig. 10.1 in Soriga 2017, 81 presents a modern example of wool dyed to a yellow-greenish hue using marine purple. If the SÍG *ḪAṢARTU* A.AB.BA in 2.7.A obv. 17 was dyed to a similar color, it could represent wool recently processed with molluscan purple, possibly chemically fixed to stabilize at that stage of color. The third and final alternative is that *ḪAṢARTU* A.AB.BA should be translated as "sea-green," i.e., "yellow/green (like the) sea." To cover both the second and third alternatives, the term will be translated here as "marine green."

ḪAŠMĀNU

See now Thavapalan 2020, 269–84 for this color term, identified as "Amethyst-colored, Red-purple" (with previous literature) against earlier blue-green.

ḪIḪINNU(-)

The appearance twice now of the same sign string in 9.2.4 rev. iii 3′ and 9.2.6 rev.$^{!}$ iv 1′ (both unfortunately ending in a break) adds a new lemma to the Hittite corpus. The *-INNU(-)* ending could suggest an Akkadogram of Hurrian origin (cf. *ḪAPALKI(N)NU*), but no convincing comparisons present themselves.

IŠTU ŠA PN

See Weeden 2011, 350 for discussion of this construction, where two translations "on the side of" and "from (the portion of)" are given. The former, spatial sense tends to occur with action verbs, such as fighting and dancing, while the latter sense is illustrated by the example from KUB 12.12 rev. vi 7–8: *nu IŠ-TU ŠA* ^{D}*LE-LU-RI adanna wēkzi* "(the queen) requests to eat from (the portion) of the goddess Leluri." Occurrences of the *IŠ-TU ŠA* PN construction in the PTAC, where in 4.1.1.1.A_1 (and possibly 4.1.1.6) gold is taken "from the lot of ..." named individuals (see introductory *Analysis* to 4.1.1.1), belong clearly to the second sense.

$^{\text{NA}_4}$*IZZIḪU*

Although both HIT (p. 35) and HVP (p. 398) treated $^{\text{NA}_4}$*IZZIḪU* of 8.1.A obv. i 9′ as a stone or gem, HIT (p. 37) also acknowledged the existence of an *izziḫu*-object, which according to CAD I/J *s.v. izziḫu* "a piece of jewelry" (p. 319) is attested at Qatna. Since the following $^{\text{NA}_4}$*KIB-ŠI* is in sg. gen. and without a number, it makes more sense to translate the $^{\text{NA}_4}$*IZZIḪU* as an object which is made from $^{\text{NA}_4}$*KIBŠU*.

$^{\text{(GIŠ)}}$*KANḪANNU*

See the main discussion under ^{GIŠ}DUB.ŠEN, to which the $^{\text{(GIŠ)}}$*KANḪANNU* is to be equated, superseding the prior suggestion of Güterbock (1971, 7) that "*GANḪAN(NU)* ... might be the same as *gangannu* 'potstand'."

KANNU

See CAD K *s.v. kannu* A (p. 154) 2 "metal potstand or structure to support containers with pointed bottom." See also HW^{2} *s.v.* $^{\text{(GIŠ)}}$*ḫapšalli-* IV.5, where ^{GIŠ}*KANNU* interchanges in Hattic rituals with ^{GIŠ}*ḫapšalli-*, in the latter's sense of "Gestell (Art Serviertisch?)."

KAPPU

See CAD K *s.v. kappu* B (p. 188) "bowl (usually of metal)."

$^{\text{NA}_4}$*KIBŠU*

See Polvani 1988, 125–27. HIT (p. 37) offered the translation of "a stone with a variegated or marbled effect," connecting it to an Akkadian term for a rash (CAD K *s.v. kibsu* [p. 339]). It is still not entirely clear whether the term is an Akkadogram at Boğazköy, since all attestations end in -*ŠI*, which could be interpreted as an Akkadian sg. gen. or a loanword in neuter gender, ending in -*i*-. On the one hand, if ^{NA_4}*kibši* is a loanword, then ^{NA_4}*kab-ši-iš* could be an alternative common gender *i*-stem form borrowed a second time from the same lexeme (perhaps to be read ^{NA_4}*kib*$_{X}$-*ši-iš*). On the other hand, if ^{NA_4}*KIBŠI* is treated as an Akkadogram, then ^{NA_4}*kab-ši-iš* could still be a loanword, just as the Hittite reading.

KUŠARU

No convincing interpretation has thus far been offered for the EZEN$_4$ *KUŠARU* in 4.1.1.1.B rev. iii$^{?}$ 16. Contra HVP (p. 694), *KUŠARU* is almost certainly not to be related to Akk. *kuš(a)ru* 'ingot', which is only attested from NB. Hoffner (1968, 40 fn. 54) earlier suggested that the EZEN$_4$ *KUŠARU* was connected either to the Hittite city of Kuššara (though he noted the lack of gemination made this difficult) or to ^{D}Kušara, i.e., the Canaanite craft-deity Kothar (Ugr. *kṯr*) – which, even more problematically, would be missing the divine determinative.

MADDATTU

As emphasized in Siegelová 2014, 133, the term *MADDATTU* was the regular word for both international and domestic "tribute" in Hittite texts. Understanding of the term has been uncontroversial, aside from the etymology of the underlying Hittite word *arkamma(n)-* (see *Lexical Commentary s.v.* for further discussion), so that the primary analysis of the term *MADDATTU* in Hittite texts remains HVP (pp. 207–211, 246–56, 559–60; see also RlA entries 'Steuer', Siegelová 2011–12, and 'Tribut', Siegelová 2014). Within the PTAC, the term *MADDATTU* appears exclusively with domestic tribute, with items received from foreign kingdoms designated as *ŠULMĀNU* 'gifts'. Two instances of gold *MADDATTU* in 4.1.1.1.A$_1$ obv. 2′, 3′ might represent an exception to this rule, since gold is not expected from domestic sources, but the origins of the tribute are unfortunately lost in the break. Taking into account the domestic context of the term, HVP (p. 212) defined it as it is used in the inventory texts as "Steuer." Note that although Lorenz (2020) implicitly contested the interpretation of Hittite domestic *MADDATTU* as a tax on the supposed grounds that taxable private enterprise was non-existent in the Hittite Kingdom, this criticism is difficult to sustain. The vast majority of the *MADDATTU* encountered in the PTAC comes in the form of locally manufactured goods, mostly agricultural tools and wool or woolen garments, i.e. exactly the type of objects that would be produced by the villages of an agrarian society. Combined with the archaeological evidence that the copper items were produced locally according to a wide range of metallurgical traditions (see discussion in *2.3.2.1 Copper, Tin, and Bronze*), this suggests that most of the domestic *MADDATTU* was skimmed from the local and regional economies that were oriented towards supplying the needs of local populations (already Archi 1984, 200–203). Some forms of the economic activity that lay behind the *MADDATTU* could have been sponsored by the Hittite state (see perhaps 3.1.10, a domestic tribute list of silver bars contributed by local Anatolian towns, interpreted by Floreano 2001, 230–32 as the primary extraction of silver from mines near these villages), but it is hardly imaginable that every copper axe, every tin arrowhead, and every spool of wool received from the dozens of Anatolian villages were produced at the instigation of the Hittite state, much less in state workshops embedded at these otherwise unknown localities.

One point that may be added to the analysis of *MADDATTU* in HVP is that there is evidence that the term could also designate the labor added to palace-supplied raw materials for the production of finished goods. This process, dubbed here as "value-added tribute" (see introductory *Analysis* to 3.2.1 for the main discussion), is best exemplified in the text pairs 3.2.1/4.1.3.1 and 4.1.2.1/4.1.2.2, and was perhaps a way for the palace authorities to process the excess raw materials received through tribute into useable goods. The tribute received from government institutions (2.9.A$_{3}$ obv. ii 8′: *MAN-TA-DU* É.GAL $^{\text{NA}_4}$[KIŠIB; 3.2.4 2′: *MAN-TA-AT* É.[…; possibly 8.3) and professional groups (3.1.6 3′: *MAN-TA-TUM*(?) L]Ú^{MEŠ} KÁ UR.GI$_{7}$; and especially 3.1.12 4′ *MA*]*N-TA-TUM* $^{\text{LÚ.MEŠ}}$SIM[UG.A "tr]ibute (of the) smi[ths") should probably also be interpreted in this way, since it is improbable that tribute produced by them would have come from anywhere but the raw materials acquired from government supply chains.

^{GIŠ}*MAGARRU*, ^{GIŠ}*MUKARRU*

HIT (p. 111) and HVP (p. 487) translated 9.1.10.A$_{2}$ rev. 6′: *QA-DU* ^{GIŠ}*MU-KAR-RU* "with wheels"/"mit Rädern," derived from Akkadian *magarru* (CAD M$_{1}$ *magarru (mugarru)* [p. 32]). However, see now HW^{2} Ḫ *s.v.* ^{GIŠ}*ḫatuli(š)-* (p. 536) for the suggestion that ^{GIŠ}*MU-KAR-RU* is a "wohl akkadisierte Form von heth. ^{GIŠ}*mukar-*, ein Gerät zum Erzeugen von Geräuschen/Lärm"; and further CHD L–N *s.v.* ^{GIŠ}*mukar, mukn-* (implement used as a noise-maker) (p. 323), submeaning c. "implement used in a light carriage," discussing IBoT 1.36 obv. ii 12: ^{GIŠ}*ḫulugannaš=a* ^{GIŠ}*mu-kar* (where the emendation ^{GIŠ}*MU-KAR*⟨*-RU*⟩ proposed in Siegelovà 1984, 133 fn. 9 is also acknowledged). The single appearance of the term in the PTAC in 9.1.10.A$_{2}$: $^{\text{GIŠ!?}}$GIGIR *an-da ap-pa-a-an QA-DU* ^{GIŠ}*MU-KAR-RU* "chariot with appurtenances, with ^{GIŠ}*MUKARRU*" does not allow for a firm decision between a meaning 'wheel' or 'noise maker'. On the one hand, the storage of a chariot with its wheels seems obvious in an inventory of military equipment. On the other hand, one would prefer a plural marker *^{GIŠ}*MUKARRU*^{MEŠ} or a number **QADU* 2 ^{GIŠ}*MUKARRU* if a pair of chariot wheels was meant (also **QADU* 1 ^{GIŠ}*MUKARRU* in the unusual case that only a single wheel was meant). Regardless of the origins and meaning, the form *QA-DU* ^{GIŠ}*MU-KAR-RU* in 9.1.10.A$_{2}$ rev. 6′ must be taken as a mistake for *QA-DU* *^{GIŠ}*MU-KAR-RI*, (cf. proper Akk. declension in *QA-DU TU-TI-IT-TI* in 4.1.1.1.B$_{1}$ rev. iii$^{?}$ 4) since there is no independent attestation for a Sumerogram **MU.KAR.RU.

MAŠADDU

See Civil 1987, 187–88, where it was proposed to combine CAD M$_{1}$ *s.v. mašaddu* "1. 'pole' 2. (an official)" (p. 350), *maššatu* "(a weapon)" (p. 389), and CAD M$_{2}$ *s.v. mešētu* "(mng. unknown)" into a single lemma meaning "pole, lance." The equation with a type of weapon in the Hittite context as a translation for LÚ *MEŠEDI* 'man of the lance' was enthusiastically received by Hoffner 1987, 188–89 (although cf. the skepticism of Beal 1992, 220–24, where the earlier interpretation of this title as "the man-of-the-chariot-pole" [p. 221, with fn. 840] is preferred). Within the PTAC, there occur, in addition to two attestations of the title GAL *MEŠEDI* (5.7 rev.$^{?}$ iii 12′, 25′), two attestations of what seems to be the physical object itself (10.3.7 4′ and 10.3.8 2′). Although a firm decision between a (chariot) pole or a spear is prevented by broken contexts in both texts, the description of furniture in both suggest the former, with the "pole" constituting perhaps a component, e.g., the stem of a table.

MAŠLU

Understanding of the term *MAŠLU* has not advanced much beyond the initial remarks of Goetze 1955, 53 fn. 55, who established that "The meaning of *MAŠLU* is shown by the examples quoted in the text to be not much different from GAR.RA (Hitt. *ḫališšiyant-*) 'set with ...'. It is not used exclusively in speaking of textiles, it also occurs in dealing with metal or woodwork." Goetze's attempt (*loc. cit.*) to equate Hitt. *MAŠLU* with a certain *b/pašlu* applied to garments attested at Amarna, Qatna, and Nuzi was not accepted by the CAD, which elected to interpret the latter as coming from *bašālu* 'to cook, ripen' (see CAD B *s.v. bašlu* 4. "dyed (fabric), stained (ivory)" [p. 140]), while giving Hittite *MAŠLU* its own entry (CAD M_1 *s.v. mašlu* B "trimmed(?)" [p. 380]), where it was identified as an Akkadogram appearing only in Hittite.

In terms of the technique denoted by *MAŠLU*, Holt 1958, 150, in a review of the *Festschrift* containing Goetze 1955, further suggested that the items described as *MAŠLU* with gold were reminiscent of gold embroidery or fabric mixed with gold threads. In contrast, HIT (p. 202) posited that embroidering techniques of the 2nd millennium BC ancient Near East were not practicable with gold filament, and so suggested that *MAŠLU* referred (on cloths) to an ornamental appliqué. HVP (p. 696) gave "verziert, gemustert" in the glossary, but also translated 4.2.4 rev. 9′: *QA-DU* ^{GIŠ}ESI TUR GUŠKIN *MAŠ-LU* as "geschmückt mit kleinen (Intarsien aus) Ebenholz (und) Gold" (p. 67) in the context of decorated ivory objects. In discussing the belt-production text 4.1.4.1, HVP (p. 214) considered that the addition of the smaller amounts of different colored wools to the red-wool base of the belts constituted the act of *MAŠLU* for these belts ("Die Textformulierung deutet wohl an, dass die rote Wolle den Fond, die übrigen Wollsorten dann das Muster bildeten. So muss man in diesem Zusammenhang wohl auch die Bedeutung des Terminus *MAŠLU*, 'gemustert', verstehen."), while admitting (*loc. cit*), that: "Über die Technologie und Art der Verzierung (eingewirktes, gesticktes oder appliziertes Muster?) lässt sich dem Text wenig entnehmen." Following HVP, Klengel – Klengel 2009, 207 concluded: "Die Bezeichnung *MAŠLU* dürfte eine Musterung bzw. Verzierung des Kleidungsstücks anzeigen, d.h. eine meist nicht näher zu bestimmende Ausschmückung durch Farbigkeit oder durch Applikationen, auch aus Metall, wie sie des öfteren in Texten belegt sind."

For the purposes of translation, a neutral 'patterned' (when just cloth), 'embellished' (when with precious metal) will be used following HVP and Klengel – Klengel 2009, with the acknowledgement that the exact technique of patterning, whether embroidering, appliqué, or otherwise, remains unknown. Note that, although garments patterned or embellished with precious metals are not uncommon, the assertion in Vigo 2011, 295 fn. 53 that "*mašlu* ... occurs nearly always next to insertions of gold and silver in the clothing" is demonstrably false, at least in the inventories of the PTAC. Of the fifty-two attestation of *MAŠLU* in the PTAC applied to garments (out of a total of fifty-eight attestations where the object is known), there are five attestation of garments with gold *MAŠLU* (^{TÚG}ŠÀ.GA.DÙ in 9.1.1 rev. iii 26′; rev. iv 42′; ^{TÚG}GÚ(.È.A) *ḪURRI* in

8.4 rev. 15′; 9.1.1 rev. iii 30′–31′; rev. iv 41′), all but one of which come from notably sumptuous stock of the Inventory of Manninni (= 9.1.1), resulting in less than a tenth of *MAŠLU* attestations involving garments also involving metal. This relative rarity was perhaps not necessarily due to an inherent difficulty in producing *MAŠLU*, since the smithing texts attest to the production of precious metal *MAŠLU* for garments: cf. 4.1.1.3, where quantities of silver destined respectively for a belt (rev. B 4) and a *bracelet* (rev. B 7) are described as temporarily absent *A-NA E-PIŠ MAŠ-LU* "for making embellishment(s)" (cf. also the fragmentary *E-P*]*IŠ MAŠ-LU* [in 4.1.4.8 6′).

It may be remarked in closing that a seemingly hitherto unrecognized problem for the interpretation of Hittite *MAŠLU* is the fact that it is inflected nowhere in the PTAC, nor indeed in the entire Hittite corpus according to a search of the lexical card files at the *Hethitologie-Archiv* at the Akademie der Wissenschaften und der Literatur, Mainz: even in the fully Akkadographic phrase *A-NA E-PIŠ MAŠ-LU*, mentioned above, the term remains stubbornly intact. The immutability of the form, combined with the fact that the Akkadogram appears only in Hittite texts, leads one to wonder if a Sumerographic reading should be entertained instead, although with which sign-values is unclear.

(TÚG)*MAYYĀLU*

From Kümmel 1967, 76:

> (TÚG)*MAYYĀLU* hier und an allen bisher bekannten Stellen der Boğazköy-Texte als Akkadogramm nicht "Bett" ... als Möbel, sondern, dem Determinativ entsprechend, das an keiner Stelle außer u. D 24′ [= KUB 17.31 24′] (nicht aber in den Dupll.) fehlt, stets im Sinne von "Bettzeug, Lagerpolster". Zu ähnlich gebrauchtem TÚGNÁ/*šašta-* neben dem Möbel GIŠ*šašta-*/NÁ s. o.

Although the number of attestations of *MAYYĀLU* without a TÚG determinative has increased since Kümmel's analysis, his observation that (TÚG)*MAYYĀLU* nowhere means just 'bed' still holds true. In the PTAC the term rather seems to designate 'bedding, bed supplies' in general. In 8.1.F rev. v 16 the "bedding of the Storm-god of Nerik" (*MAYYĀLU* DIŠKUR URU*Nerik*) seems to serve as a label for the preceding lines: certainly for rev. v 13–15, where the footed bed frame (GIŠNÁ ... 4 GÌR UR.MAḪ) and bed sheets (*lakkušanzani-*) are mentioned, but possibly the entire paragraph beginning with rev. v 5, including the wearable garments of rev. v 11–13. This also seems to be the case in 4.2.9 rev. 2′ and 9′, where (TÚG)*MAYYĀLU* appears at the end of a paragraph after the bed frame and sheets. Outside of the PTAC, the example GIŠNÁ *IŠ-TU* TÚG*MA-IA-LI* "bed(-frame) with bedding" in KBo 15.2+ 10′–11′ confirms that the TÚG*MAYYĀLU* refers to only the cloth components of a sleeping arrangement. The Hittite usage perhaps grew out of the usage of *mayyālu* in Mesopotamia to describe a "divan" (Bottéro 1957, 290), "(Schlaf-)Lager" (AHw 587), or "sleeping place, bed" (CAD M_1 117).

PARĪSU

Naturally, when an Akkadogram ending in *-i* is encountered in a context that demands a nominative, one wonders if the word is actually a borrowing as a Hittite *i-* or a Hittite/Luwian *-i(t)-*stem. In this instance, the awkwardness of transliterating *PA-RI-SI* as *pa-ri-ší*, with the SI-sign taken as the rare *-ší*, argues against such an interpretation. It might be enterained instead that the underlying Hittite word was a free-standing genitive: thus, the 2 *PA-RI-SI* ZABAR in 10.3.5 7′ were "2 bronze (vessels) 'of a *PARĪSU*' (in capacity)." Given the nominal capacity of 30–50 liters, the *PARĪSU* vessel would be an enormous serving vessel or mixing bowl.

SĀḪU

See *Lexical Commentary s.v.* ZA.ḪUM for discussion of the ZA.ḪUM("SIG$_4$")/*SÀ-ḪU$_5$* distinction.

SIKKĀNU

It is generally accepted that ^{NA_4}ZI.KIN is a pseudo-Sumerogram derived from Akkadian *sikkānu* 'stele'. In Hittite texts, ^{NA_4}ZI.KIN was certainly read ^{NA_4}*ḫuwaši-*, but it is unclear whether the same applied to Akkadographic *SIKKĀNU*. The appearance of *SÍ-KÀ-NU* in the context of a statue description in 10.3.1 rev. iii 4′ is at the very least an appropriate context for a *ḫuwaši*-stone (see Cammarosano 2018, 74–86 for comprehensive discussion of the ^{NA_4}*ḫuwaši-* 'cult stela').

ŠULMĀNU

The term *ŠULMĀNU* at Ḫattuša appears to conform to the international Akkadian sense of designating greeting gifts from foreign kingdoms. In the PTAC one encounters gifts from Aleppo (2.1.B 9′: *ŠULMĀNT*]*I*(?) *Ḫalap*), Babylon (2.2 rev. 2: *ŠULMĀNTI* KUR *Kar-*^{D}*Dunia*[*š*), and Ugarit (4.1.1.1.B$_1$ rev. iv$^?$ 5: *Š*]*ULMĀN* ^{URU}*Ugarit*). Since Babylon, in contrast to Ugarit and Aleppo, could in no way be considered as tributary to the Hittites, it is apparent that *ŠULMĀNU* in the Hittite context could designate both voluntary and prescribed gifts. The term *ŠULMĀNU* is also found in the PTAC in the context of a votive object seemingly contributed on the private (i.e., non-royal/governmental) initiative of ^{m}ZAG-ŠEŠ in 10.2.2.4 obv.$^?$ r. c. 5′.

The attestation of *ŠUL-MAN-TI* in 2.2 obv. 3′; rev. 2 (also probably 2.1.B 8′, 9′) yields no recognizable grammatical form, there being no feminine ***šulmāntu*. It is possible that these forms are examples of a *-TI* plural marker (cf. Weeden 2011, 346, with fn. 1599, for interpretation of the *-TI* as an "adjectival(?) plural in nouns") appended to a pseudo-Sumerogram: ŠUL.MAN-*TI*.

ŠŪRU/ŠUḪ(U)RU

Thavapalan 2020, 279–80 (with previous literature) considered *šūru* to be a dark color, perhaps black or gray, but also, based on the usage of Hebrew cognate *šāḥōr* and the dye made from the *šuratḫu*-tree, possibly the color of dark-tanned skin, i.e., dark brown (*op. cit.*, 292–94). As documented in the examples under CAD Š$_3$ *s.v. šūru* (*šuḫru, šurʾu*, fem. *šurʾītu*) (p. 367), in addition to being applied to animal hides, and in at least one instance a person's complexion, *šūru/šuḫ(u)ru* can be applied to high-quality textiles, such as garments given as tithes, cloth used to wrap tin, votive offerings to gods, and gifts to royals, suggesting that a striking or desirable shade of gray could be designated by the term.

TAYYĀRTU

Singer 2006b, 254, proposed to interpret the 6 PAD *TA-IA-AR-TÙ* in 4.2.1.A$_1$ obv. 10 as coming from Akk. *tayyāru* 'turning back', with the possible bent or crescent-shape of the PAD 'bar, ingot' inviting comparison to the URUDUKIN 'sickles' attested elsewhere in the PTAC as tribute. In contrast, CAD T *s.v. tajartu* "(mng. unkn.) Akkadogram in Hitt." (p. 58) suggested a connection with a *tajaru* "(a measuring rod and its measure)" (p. 59) attested at Nuzi.

TUDITTU

As noted by HVP (p. 127 fn. 5), the standard reference for *tudittu* 'toggle-pin' is Klein 1983 (see esp. p. 282 Abb. 2 for illustration), superseding the definition "pectoral" under CAD D *s.v. dudittu (tudittu)* (p. 168). Although CAD T *s.v. tudittu* ("see *dudittu*") (p. 449) declined to update the entry, see analysis of Kouwenberg 2015, 167–68 connecting *tudittu* to *edēdum* 'to become sharp', an etymology that would ill-suit the flatness of a pectoral. In spite of the general absence of toggle-pins in the archaeological record of the Hittite period (Andreas Schachner, Suzanne Herbordt, pers. comm.), it must be assumed based on the textual evidence that either limited numbers were imported or crafted in the Syro-Mesopotamian style, or that the Akkodgram was adapted to refer to local toggle-less garment pins.

UNŪTU

The Akkadogram *UNŪTU* in the PTAC demonstrates the full range of meanings attested for the Akkadian term: a collective sense of "equipment, gear" (*kī=kan Ú-NU-TUM*, 8.1.A obv. ii 16′), an individual sense "tool, utensil" (ŠU.NÍGIN 7 *Ú-NU-TUM* 4.1.1.3 obv. 4), and an abstract sense of "furnishing, trappings" (*Ú-NU-UT* KUŠ NU.GÁL 10.3.14 l. c. 6′). With CAD U and W *s.v. unūtu* (p. 172), it seems the Hittites followed the masculine plural formation *unūtū* (oblique *unūtī*) as attested in peripheral Akkadian (Ras Shamra, Emar, El Amarna, Nuzi) instead of the standard feminine plural *uniātu/unâtu/unêtu.*

ZŪRU

The proliferation of Akkadian lexemes spelled *s/ṣ/zū(r)ru* makes it impossible to identify this object with certainty, be it a "blade" (HIT, p. 156), an "Obsidiangemme" (HVP, p. 127 fn. 4), or possibly a third item (the "4 gold *ZŪRU*" in 1.5 obv. 11 do not obviously suggest either a blade or obsidian gem). Note that the entry in CAD S *s.v. sūru* (or *zūru, ṣūru*) C (p. 416) "(an item of jewelry)," which cites 1.5 obv. 11, can be updated with the attestation from 1.1.A_2 rev. 6.

Divine Names

(D)*walipašu-*

See Pecchioli Daddi 1998, 9–11 for a discussion of this god, who is variously written D*Ulip/wa*$_a$*šu*/D*Walipišu*, and is one of many in the Hattian sphere ending with the morpheme *-šu*. Laroche 1973, 88 considered that the first element of the god's name was derived from Hittite/Luwian *ulip(pa)ni-* 'wolf(?)'. However, as Pecchioli Daddi (*ibid.* 11) pointed out, the attestation of the god in the oldest layer of Hittite texts argues for a Hattic origin; although D*Ulip/wa*$_a$*šu*/D*Walipišu* does not appear in Hattian, see also the onomastics under HEG U *s.v. ulippana-* (p. 42), where the personal name ^{m}*Ulippi* might provide an independent attestation of the missing Hattic element. Notwithstanding the probable Hattian origin of ^{D}*Ulip/wa*$_{a}$*šu*/^{D}*Walipišu*, the appearance of *wa-li-pa-šu-ú* (the plene writing *-šu-ú* leaves little alternative other than a divine name despite the absence of a divine determinative) among a list of theriomorphic rhyta suggests the god had an animal form. Which animal this corresponded to is unclear, and without a connection to Hittite/Luwian *ulip(pa)ni-* 'wolf', there is no hint it was a canid.

^{D}IŠTAR ^{URU}ŠAMUḪI

For the Akkadographic form ^{URU}*ŠAMUḪI* 'the Šamuhean', cf. (^{D}*IŠTAR*) ^{URU}*ŠA-MU-ḪI* in KUB 21.17 rev. iii 2′, 5′. See also *ŠA-MU-ḪI* in 3.2.4 1′, if interpreted correctly.

Geographical Names

^{URU}zitḫara ŠA ^{URU}ḫanḫana

See Corti 2017, 221–23, for a discussion of the "province of Ḫanḫana" (KUR ^{URU}*Ḫanḫana*), which lay to the northwest of Ḫattuša, in which Zitḫara was, next to the eponymous city of Ḫanḫana, a principal settlement. The construction ^{URU}X *ŠA* ^{URU}Y seems to be otherwise unattested, but must refer to Zitḫara's location within the region of Ḫanḫana (HIT, 90). While it is possible that there was more than one town named Zitḫara (cf. the discussion of this passage in Forlanini 2008, 165), Kryszeń (2016, 187) found evidence for the existence of only a single town, apparently located very close to the city of Ḫanḫana.

Personal Names

^{f}KÙ.SI$_{22}$-lia- (^{f}Āškilia-$^{?}$, ^{f}Maralia-$^{?}$)

For the reading ^{f}KÙ.SI$_{22}$-*li-aš*(-)x[, see *Commentary* to 6.5 rev. 6′. Due to its exclusive writing as a Sumerogram at Ḫattuša, the underlying word for 'gold' is currently not known for the Hittite, Hattic, and Luwian languages (for the rejection of the argument of Blažek–Schwarz 2016, 90, that Luw. /*washa-*/ means 'gold', see Sasseville, eDiAna, *s.v.* **u̯esHā-* (= lemma 1353), further Sasseville 2021, 274, fn. 25). Therefore, ^{f}KÙ.SI$_{22}$-*liaš* in 6.5 rev. 6′ is of more than usual interest, because the name represents what is, to my knowledge, the first attestation of the Sumerogram KÙ.SI$_{22}$ 'gold' in the Hittite corpus outside of its usage as a simple noun. Consequently, if ^{f}KÙ.SI$_{22}$-*liaš* could be connected with a known personal name, it would reveal a/the currently unknown reading for 'gold' at Ḫattuša.

Female names ending in *-li(y)a(š)* are exceedingly rare in Hittite. The recent work of Zehnder 2010 on Hittite feminine personal names reveals only two: Maralia(š) (KUB 48.117 obv. 12, to be read contra Zehnder 2010, 330: [^{f}x]-*ra-li-aš* / [^{f}x].RA-*li-aš*, as $^{⸢f⸣}$[*m*]*a*$^{?}$-*ra-li-aš*; cf. Mora 1990, 296, Nr. 2: *ma+ra/i-li-i(a)* BONUS$_{2}$.FEMINA), and Āškiliaš (KBo 18.151 rev. 18′: ^{f}*a-aš-ki-li-aš*). If, for the sake of completeness, female names ending with *-(l)l-* + plene *-ī* are also considered – these being potentially original Luwian stems in *-i(ya)-* (Zehnder 2010, 207, 245) –, then the list expands to include ᶠ*Āllī* (KBo 11.12 obv. i 1: ᶠ⸢*a*⸣*-al-li-i*; KUB 58.96 rev. 7′, KBo 55.41 obv. i 1: ᶠ*al-li-i*), ᶠ*Mallī* (KBo 31.5 obv. ii 9, KBo 31.26 obv. 6: ᶠ*ma-al-li-i*; KBo 5.7 obv. 31: ᶠ*ma-li-*[*iš*; KBo 18.199 rev. r. c. 5′: ᶠ*ma-al-li-*[*iš*?), and ᶠ*Pataḫulī* (KBo 32.224 obv. 2, 7: ᶠ*pa-ta-ḫu-li-i-iš*). One cannot rule out a hitherto-unattested female name ending in *-li(y)a(š)*, but neither is this especially likely: the female names ending in *-li(y)a(š)* are not a natural class, but rather stems ending in *-(l)l(V)-* plus a suffix *-i(ya)-*. Thus, although the number of female names ending in *-(l)l(V)-* + *-i(ya)-* could in theory be large, it would be in any case a smaller number than names formed from the highly productive (male) ethnic or appurtenance suffixes *-el-*, *-ali(ya)-*, *-ili(ya)-*, which seem to be attachable to any nominal base. In practice, only the five names listed above can be considered.

As for which of the five names might stand behind ᶠKÙ.SI₂₂*-liaš*, only one, ᶠ*Pataḫulī(š)*, can be firmly ruled out on etymological grounds. The name was connected by Zehnder (*op. cit.*, 245) with the male names ᵐ*Partaḫulla* and ᵐ*Partaḫulaziti* (ᵐ*Pár-ta-ḫu-la-*LÚ), leading him to reconstruct an onomastic element **pa(r)taḫula*. Alp (1991, 84) suggested that *Partaḫula was a place name, with Partaḫulaziti being thus an example of the ubiquitous Anatolian onomastic formation "man of (the god of) the town GN." Alp's hypothesis is highly probable given the existence of the first element in other towns from the Luwian milieu such as ᵁᴿᵁ*Partanta*, ᵁᴿᵁ*Partiya*, and ᵁᴿᵁ*Partaḫuina* (Forlanini 2017, 251–52, with fn. 125) and the use of the *-ḫula-* element in the form ᵁᴿᵁ*Ḫulašša* '(the place of the *ḫula-*)' as a topographic feature or place name, perhaps meaning 'twist, wind; meander (of a river)' (HED III *s.v. hul(a)-* [p. 361]; Melchert 1993, 71). Alternatively, if **pataḫula* is not accepted as equivalent to **partaḫula*, then it may be derived from *pata-* 'foot' + *ḫul(a)-* 'twist, wind', perhaps indicating a physical deformity. In either analysis, **pataḫul(a)-* is a Luwian compound noun with a different meaning, and hence almost certainly not a word for gold.

For ᶠ*Āllī*, and ᶠ*Mallī*, no etymologies can be established. The former appears to be a *Lallname* (Zehnder *op. cit.*, 46), whereas the latter could be connected to any number of Hitt./Luw. roots with the shape **ma(l)l(a)-*, none of which have an obvious connection to gold.

For ᶠ*Āškilia(š)*, earlier works had assumed the name was a form of the masculine name ᵐ*Āškaliya* (Ünal – Kammenhuber 1974, 173; Tischler 1982, 442), the latter being composed of the Hittite elements *aška-* 'gate' and the onomastic ethnic/appurtenance suffix *-ali(ya)-/-ili(ya)-* (Laroche 1966, 338). However, as discussed by Zehnder (*op. cit.*, 128–29), this equation is less than secure. Besides the change in the second vowel being unexplained (if the name is interpreted as Hittite), the *-ili(ya)-/-ali(ya)-* suffix, as mentioned above, is used almost exclusively for male names. A different explanation for ᶠ*Āškilia(š)*/ᵐ*Āškaliya* was given by Soysal 2000, 105–6, where the pair are interpreted as Hattic names. Soysal's explanation has the advantage of explaining the unstable middle vowel (cf. Tudḫilia/Tudḫaliya, Soysal *op. cit.*, 106 with fn. 38) and is supported by the temporal and cultural horizon of the names (ᶠ*A-aš-ki-li-aš* appears in KBo 18.151 rev. 18′ as a ᴹᵁᴺᵁˢŠU.GI from the time of Ḫattušili I, and ᵐ*Āškaliya* is borne by at least three different individuals in the OH period – see prosopography given in Soysal *op. cit.*, 105). Soysal at the time considered the etymology of ᶠ*Āškilia*/ᵐ*Āškaliya* to be unknown, but noted the existence of non-onomastic forms *a-aš-ka-i-e-li* (KUB 28.47 r. c. 8′) and *a-aš-ka-i-*⌈*e*⌉*-*[*li*] (KUB 28.58 rev. r. c. 2). Later, he tentatively proposed (Soysal 2004, 16 fn. 38) to connect the name with *šakil(i)-*, the Hattic word for 'heart', while proposing that the erstwhile non-onomastic forms were derived from different sources (p. 386: nominalization *aš-kaieli*(?) or *aš-ka-ieli*(?)), neither of which offer a perceptible connection to gold. Instead, what makes **aški-* interesting is the natural comparison to Armenian *oski* 'gold'. Unfortunately, the chances of a direct relationship are slim. According to Martirosyan 2010, 532–33, difficulties in deriving *oski* from the proposed IE root *h_2*eus-*, specifically the absence of a labial glide in the Armenian reflex, require either special explanation (*op. cit,* p. 533: *oski* < **əwoskíya* "with vocalic assimilation and loss of intervocalic -*w*- in pretonic position ..."), or derivation from a substratum word that already begins with **o-*. If **aški-* were the lexeme belonging to this substratum, it would require the reconstruction of a new phonological scenario, not currently recognized among the limited borrowings from Anatolian languages into Armenian (cf. Simon 2013), in which the initial vowel of **aški-* would become **o-* in the intervening centuries before adoption into PArm. A shared borrowing from a third language might be also be considered, and thence a connection to the *Wanderwort* that has been proposed to lay behind Sumerian kù.si$_{22}$/sig$_{17}$ 'gold' (pronounced /kuski/, *vel sim.*, see Borger 2010, 195 no. 745, although the fact that the word is analyzable as kù, the Sumerian base for precious metal, + si$_{22}$/sig$_{17}$, a word for 'yellow, green', casts doubt on its appropriateness as a comparandum); Finno-Ugric **vaś/ske* 'copper, bronze' (Finn. *vaski-* 'copper', Hung. *vas* 'iron'; see Martirosyan 2010, 532 with prev. lit.); and perhaps the Urartian mountain name *Uškiani* (Kunze et al. 2013, 51, with previous literature). However, this only delays the problem of conflicting vowels. If one were to assume that a substrate word */*oski*/ (*vel sim.*) 'gold', without labial glide, was borrowed at the PArm. and PAnat. levels, with regular PAnat. *o* > *a* explaining the vowel divergence, the borrowings would be separated by more than a millennium, during which time the putative substrate word did not change. Thus, despite the superficial similarities, there is currently no plausible scenario of phonological development connecting **aški-* with Arm. *oski-*, and therefore no comparandum supporting a reconstruction **aški-*.

The final option, ^{f}*Maralia(š)* = ^{f}KÙ.SI$_{22}$*-liaš*, is more promising. If KÙ.SI$_{22}$*-(li)-* reflects **mara-(li)-*, then the *hapax* noun *maranti-* is a possible comparandum (CHD L–N *s.v. ma?-ra-an-ti-iš* [p. 191] – note that though the CHD saw the first sign of *ma-ra-an-ti-iš* as either a *ku-* or *ma-* based on the handcopy, the photo shows the *ma-* to be identical to that of the immediately preceding 1-*EN-ma*). In KBo 21.87 obv. 11′ (= KBo 20.103 3′) one finds among a list of votive objects: 1-*E*]*N ŠA* ^{NA_4}TI 1-*EN=ma marantiš* KÙ.SI$_{22}$=*y*[*a* "1] of 'life'-stone, but 1 (is) *maranti-* an[d] gold [." As the CHD (*loc. cit.*) noted for the meaning of *maranti-*: "[o]ther nouns in this position in the context are *laḫma-*, gold, silver, lapis lazuli and wood, which such suggests that this word denotes a valuable material such as wood, ivory, gems or precious metal." Though the sequence *marantis* KÙ.SI$_{22}$=*y*[*a* "*marantiš* an[d] gold" means that the two terms cannot be equivalent, it places *maranti-* in the same semantic field of precious metals and luxury materials. If **mara-* were the base word for gold, it could be imagined that *maranti-* was a related material, such as a naturally occurring gold alloy or iron pyrite. The form is analyzable as **mar(a)-* + *-ant-* with Luw. *i*-mutation (Starke 1990, 582), implying either an adjective or frozen participle, perhaps based on IEW 733 *mer- (2.) 'to flicker, shimmer' ("flimmern, funkeln") (pers. comm. Elisabeth Rieken). The difference in *maranti-* and KÙ.SI$_{22}$ (= **mara(li)-*?, see below) might also be predicated on the linguistic background of the two words, i.e., Luwian and, presumably, Hittite.

In sum, ^{f}*Maralia(š)*, with ^{f}*Āškilia(š)* as a distant second, is the best candidate thus far for the reading behind ^{f}KÙ.SI$_{22}$-*lia(š)*. The existence of other metal names ending in *-il(i)-* in Anatolia, such as Hattic *arz/šili-* 'tin' (Soysal 2006); Luwian **parzil(i)-* 'iron' (Valério – Yakubovich 2010; cf. *Lexical Commentary s.v. parzašša/i-* for possibility that the lexeme might also be iron ore); and perhaps the *Kulturwort* behind Hitt. *šulai-* (gen. *šuliyaš*) 'lead' (HEG S *s.v. sulai-* [p. 1142], with lit.), also opens the possibility that the word behind KÙ.SI$_{22}$ actually ended in *-li-* (the inclusion in a phonetic complement of the initial consonant of an open syllable, i.e., *KÙ.SI$_{22}$-*li-*, being unproblematic), so that the stem was actually **marali-* (or **aškili-*). The question becomes, what language could a hypothetical **mara(li)-* (or **aški(li)-*) be? Hurrian *ḫi(y)ari* (Richter 2012, 145–46) and Akkadian *ḫurāṣu* (CAD Ḫ, 245) are obviously non-cognate. As candidates for the Hattic word for 'gold', **mara(li)-* and **aški(li)-* are naturally suspect, since the continued existence of Hattic speakers, and hence scribes who could make Sumerographic substitutions based on Hattic vocabulary, at Ḫattuša in the Late New Kingdom is unconfirmed.

This leaves Hittite and Luwian, where the words for gold appear to be neuter *n-* or *nt-*stems: see IBoT 2.121 obv. i 16′ (OH) and Bo 3948 obv. ii 13 (NH), for KÙ.SI$_{22}$-*an* as a certain Hitt. sg. nom.-acc. n.; KBo 24.56 l. c. 13′–14′ (NH) as a highly probably sg. nom.-acc. n. One would need to reconstruct the pair **mara(li)-/*marant-* (or **aški(li)-/*aškant-*) 'gold': cf. the apparent Hitt. doublet *ḫarki-/*ḫarkant-* 'silver' (HED III, 171), with the existence of a Luwian *maranti-* (or "Luwoid" if *marantiš* is the sg. nom. c. of an *i*-mutated stem, based on an original Hittite **marant-*) heightening the possibility of an underlying *-ant-* derivative. For the moment, however, it seems best to leave ^{f}KÙ.SI$_{22}$-*liaš* as a data point for future interpretations of the word for 'gold'.

^{m}LU.LIM-*miya-* (^{m}*(Ku)runti*$^{?}$*-miya*)

For the first element ^{m}LU.LIM-*miya-*, compare HKM 60 obv. 12, rev. 22 ^{m}UDU-*šiwalli*, which is probably to be read instead as ^{m}LU.LIM-*walli* (cf. ^{m}*Wattiwali*, ^{m}*Dudduwali* for the onomastic element *-wa(l)li-*). For the onomastic element *-miya*, compare the well-attested $^{m.D}$10-/^{D}IM-/^{D}*Tarḫu(n)-miya* (Maşat Letters). ^{m}*Tarḫu(n)-miya* was explained by Melchert 2013, 46 as "a *Kurzname* with the productive appurtenance suffix *-iya-* < **-iyo-* from ^{m}*Tarḫu-mimma* …," itself meaning "'Tarhunt- (has) favoured' or 'favoured by Tarhunt-'" (*id.*, 47). One might also wish to consider a compound with *mai-/mi(ya)-* as the second member: see EDHIL *s.v. mai-*^{i} / *mi-* "to grow (up); to thrive, to prosper; (midd.) to be born" (p. 540), and CHD L–N *s.v. mai-, miya-, miešš-* (p. 113). Thus ^{m}LU.LIM-*miya* may be translated "favored by the stag (i.e., Kuruntiya)," or perhaps "born/prospered/thriven on account of the stag."

GLOSSARY

Words which are fully reconstructed, even if restored based on a parallel or duplicate, are not included. Half-brackets ⸢ ⸣ are not included in the citations. Question marks in the grammatical classifications indicate uncertainty, e.g., sg. nom.? if the case is unclear. Question marks in parentheses indicate the entire grammatical classification is unclear, e.g., pl. gen.(?). Useful clarifications are also given in parentheses when they would change the meaning of the word significantly, e.g., (NUMUN) ^{GIŠ}ESI 'ebony (seeds)' to clarify that the seeds and not the wood itself is meant. For materials such as precious stones, when the lexical item refers to the thing or substance itself it is left unmarked, but when it modifies another object it is marked as a 'material'.

Note that macrons are as a rule not marked in Hittite lemmas.

Hittite

-a-	'he, she, it' (sent. enclit. pron.)	
sg. nom.	*-aš-*	10.2.1.2 obv. 14′. 10.2.1.3 3′
sg. nom.-acc. n.	*-at-*	1.1.A_1 obv. 14′, 17′. 1.1.A_2 rev. 7. 1.1.A_3 rev. 1′. 2.2 rev. 9. 2.7.A obv. 14. 4.1.1.1.A_1 rev. 20′. 4.1.1.1.B_1 rev. iii$^{?}$ 10, 15. 4.2.1.A_1 obv. 3. 8.1.E(A_3) rev. vi 7. 9.1.4.A_1 obv. i 24′; obv. ii 4. 9.1.8 obv. 12′. 9.2.2 rev.$^{!}$ iii 20′. 10.2.1.1 obv. 2′, 8′. 10.3.7 5′. 10.3.12 obv. i 9′
	-at-	10.3.12 obv. i 7′
	-a]t-	7.4 3′.
sg. acc.	*-an-*	1.1.A_1 obv. 11′, 12′. 2.5 obv. 3′
sg. dat./loc.	*-šši-*	3.1.1.A_1 obv. ii 9′. 3.1.2 obv. l. c. 10′, 13′. 8.1.E(A_3) rev. vi 9. 9.1.1 rev. iii 15′. 9.1.14 obv. r. c. 7′, 10′. 9.1.4.A_1 obv. i 2; obv. ii 19. 9.1.4.A_2 r. c. 6′. 9.2.1 obv. ii 8′. 9.2.9 obv.$^{?}$ 10′. 10.2.1.1 obv. 4′
pl. acc.	*-aš-*	2.2 rev. 8. 9.2.1 rev. iii 7′. 9.2.2 rev.$^{!}$ iii 2′, 10′. 10.2.1.1 obv. 6′. 12.1.4 8′
pl. dat./loc.	*-šmaš-*	2.2 rev. 9
-a/-ma	'but' (contrastive enclitic conjunction, also marks change of subject)	
		1.1.A_1 obv. 14′. 1.1.A_4 rev. 7′. 2.2 obv. 6′; rev. 10′. 2.7.A obv. 8, 14. 2.13 rev.$^{?}$ 2′. 2.15 l. c. 8′. 3.1.1.A_1 obv. ii 9′. 3.1.1.A_3 obv. iii 6′, 12′. 3.1.2 obv. l. c. 6′, 10′, 13′. 4.1.1.1.A_1 rev. 7′, 17′. 4.1.1.1.B_1 obv. ii$^{?}$ 5′; rev. iii$^{?}$ 12. 4.1.1.1.B_2 obv. i$^{?}$ i 6′. 4.1.2.3 obv. ii 9′, 13′; rev. iii 4. 4.1.3.2 rev. 2′, 7′. 4.1.4.9 obv. 3, 7. 4.2.4 obv. 6. 8.1.E(A_2) 5′. 8.1.F rev. v 10. 8.6 l. c. 7′. 8.8.A 5′, 6′. 9.1.5 rev.$^{!}$ 7′, 13′, 15′,

		16′. 9.1.6 obv. 8, 10. 9.1.7 obv. 6′. 9.1.8 obv. 12′. 9.2.1 rev. iii 7′. 9.2.2 rev.$^{!}$ iii 2′. 9.2.3 obv. (ii) 4″. 10.1.2.4 r. c. 2′. 10.1.2.2 4′. 10.2.1.1 obv. 6′. 10.3.10 r. c. 10′. 10.3.12 obv. i 3′, 9′. 11.3.1 12′, 18′. 11.6.1 6
	-ma	10.3.12 obv. 7′
	-ma$^{!}$(text: BA)	9.1.7 obv. 6′
	-m]*a*(-)	4.1.1.7 rev.$^{!?}$ 1. 6.3 obv. 6. 9.2.12 3′. 10.2.1.2 obv. 14′
	-m[*a*$^{?}$(-)	9.1.12 3′
-a/-ya	'and'	
		1.1.A_2 obv. 9′. 1.4 5′. 1.5 rev. 24. 2.7.A obv. 4. 2.12 obv.$^{!}$ ii 7′. 4.1.1.1.A_1 rev. 19′. 4.1.1.1.B_1 rev. iii$^{?}$ 9, 15. 4.1.1.8 r. c. 3′. 5.2 obv. ii 9. 6.3 obv. 5. 8.1.F rev. v 15. 9.1.10.A_1 rev. 4′. 9.2.1 obv. ii 8′. 9.2.3 obv. (ii) 5″. 10.2.1.1 obv. 2′. 10.2.2.1 3′. 10.3.2 obv. i(?) 15″. 10.3.7 5′. 11.6.7 5′. 12.3.3 10′
aḫḫuwatar/aḫḫuwatn-	'ring(?)'	
pl. nom.-acc. n.	*aḫ-ḫu-u-wa-at-ra*	9.1.1 rev. iv 9′
	aḫ-ḫu-wa-at-[*ra*(?)	2.13 rev.$^{?}$ 7′
	aḫ-ḫu-u-w[*a-at-ra*(?)	2.14 13′
	aḫ-ḫu-[*wa-at-ra*(?)	2.4 rev. 1′
abl.	*aḫ-ḫu-wa-ta-na-za*	2.17 obv.$^{?}$ r. c. 3′
see *Lexical Commentary*		
ayakki-	(a shrine or reliquary?)	
sg. nom.-acc. n.	*a-ia-ak-ki*$^{!}$(text: UŠ or ⸢DU⸣]	9.1.5 rev.$^{!}$ 5′
see *Lexical Commentary*		
^{URUDU}*akutalla-*	(a drinking cup)	
broken	^{URUDU}*a-ku-*[*ta-al-la*(-)	3.1.7.A_1 obv. i 11′
see *Lexical Commentary*		
annalla/i-	'former, earlier, older'	
sg. nom.-acc. n.	*an-na-al-la-an*	11.1.7 5′
aniya-	'to produce, make; (w/ *tuppi-*) to write, record'	
pres. pl. 3	*a-ni-ia-an-zi*	2.7.A obv. 15
pret. sg. 3	*a-ni-ia-at*	1.1.A_2 obv. 13′
ptc. sg. nom.-acc. n.	*a-ni-ia-an*	8.1.A rev. vi 2′
	a-ni-ia-an(-)[	4.1.1.7 rev.$^{!?}$ 1
iter. pres. sg. 3	*a*]*n-ni-iš-ke-ez-zi*	1.1.A_2 obv. 2′
see *Lexical Commentary*		
anda	'in, into; inside; in addition'	
	an-da	2.6 2′, 6′. 2.7.A obv. 3, 11, 17, 18, 25. 2.16 obv. i 3′, 10′. 2.17 obv.$^{?}$ r. c. 2′, 14′, 15′. 3.1.1.A_3 obv. iii 7′. 3.1.8.A rev. 14′. 4.1.3.2 rev. 2′. 4.2.1.A_1 obv. 8. 4.2.4 obv. 2. 6.1 obv. 19. 6.2 obv. 9′. 6.3 obv. 4, 5. 8.1.A rev. v 26′. 8.1.C 4′, 5′. 8.1.D obv. i 3′. 8.1.E(A_1) rev. v 6′. 8.1.E(A_2) 7′. 8.1.F obv. ii 15′. 8.1.G obv. r. c. 4′. 9.1.1 rev. iii 15′, 16′, 19′ (2×), 21′, 28′; rev. iv 9′, 13′, 33′, 35′. 9.1.4.A_2 r. c. 4′, 5′, 7′. 9.1.4.A_5 3′. 9.1.6 obv. 4. 9.1.10.B 7′, 8′. 9.2.1

		obv. ii 3′, 5′, 7′, 8′, 9′, 10′, 13′, 14′. 9.2.4 obv. i 11′. 9.2.5 obv. i(?) 11′. 10.1.1.2 rev. iv 8′. 10.2.1.6 2′. 10.3.1 rev. iii 13′. 11.1.8 1′. 11.2.1 6′. 11.3.1 10′
	an-da (*ep-/app-*)	9.1.1 25′; rev. iii 24′, 41′; rev. iv 39′. 9.1.10.A_1 rev. 5′. 9.1.10.A_2 rev. 6′. 10.3.4 7′
	an-da (*išḫuwa-*)	8.1.A obv. ii 14′, 15′
	an-da (*peda-*)	9.1.6 obv. 5
	an-da (*šumra(i)-/šumriya-*)	8.1.F obv. ii 15′
	an-da (*da-*)	4.1.1.2.B rev. 4
	an-da (*dammenk-*)	10.1.1.1 rev.$^{?}$ 9′. 11.2.4 4′
	an-da (*tarna-*)	9.1.6 obv. 4
	an-da (DIB)	1.5 obv. 4, 8. 8.1.A rev. v 20′
	a]*n-da*	8.1.E(A_2) 11′. 10.1.1.2 rev. iv 10′. 10.3.1 obv. ii 10′
	a]*n-da* (*ep-/app-*)	6.1 rev. A 4′
	a]*n-da* (DÙ)	5.1 rev. iii 3
	a]*n-d*[*a*	10.3.1 rev. iii 1′
	an]*-da*	2.16 obv. i 5′
	an-d]*a*	2.16 obv. i 3′. 3.1.8.B 2′. 8.1.D rev. iv 8′. 9.1.10.A_1 obv. 4′
	an-d]*a* (*ep-/app-*)	8.1.G obv. l. c. 3′. 10.1.2.7 10′
	an-d]*a*(?) (*ep-/app-*)	11.7.2 3′
	an-d[*a*	9.1.6 obv. 9. 9.2.2 rev.$^{!}$ iii 26′. 9.2.11 3′
	an-d[*a*(?)	8.1.F obv. ii 9′
	an-[*da*	11.3.1 7′
see also GADA *anda damaššuaš*		
andan	‘in, into; inside’	
	an-da-an (DÙ)	9.1.4.A_1 obv. i 19′. 9.1.7 obv. 7′
andur(ri)a-	‘inner; native, domestic’	
sg. nom.	*an-dur-aš*	9.1.11 obv.$^{?}$ 4′
	a]*n-dur-aš*	6.9 obv. 7
	an-dur-ia-aš	8.1.E(A_1) rev. iv 7′
	an-d]*ur-ia-aš*	6.8 4′
	an-dur-ri-ia-aš	1.1.A_2 rev. 6
	an-tu-u-ri-[*ia-aš*	11.6.3 obv.$^{?}$ 2′
see *Lexical Commentary*		
andurza	‘inside, indoors’ (adv.)	
	an-dur-za	1.5 obv. 1
annutaim(m)a/i-	‘set with *annu(ta)-*’	
sg. nom.-acc. n.	*an-nu-ta-i-m*[*a-a*]*n*	8.4 rev. 18′
	an-nu-ta-i-m[*a-an*	11.3.1 17′
	an-nu-[*ta-i-ma-an*(?)	4.2.10 2′
see *Lexical Commentary*		
apa-	‘that’ (demonstrative pron.)	
sg. nom.-acc. n.	*a-pa-a-at*	4.1.4.9 obv. 7
sg. dat./loc.	*a-pé-da-ni*	1.1.A_1 obv. 17′
	a-pé-e-da-ni	3.1.8.A obv. 5′
(*anda*) *appant-*	‘included; “all inclusive, with appurtenances”’	
ptc. sg. nom.-acc. n.	(*anda*) *ap-pa-a-an*	9.1.1 rev. iii 25′. 9.1.10.A_1 rev. 5′. 9.1.10.A_2 rev. 6′

	(*anda*) *ap-pa-a-a*[*n*	9.1.1 rev. iv 39′
	(*anda*) *ap-pa-a-*[*an*	9.1.1 rev. iii 24′, 41′
ptc. pl. nom.-acc. n.	(*anda*) *ap-pa-an-ta*	8.1.G obv. l. c. 3′
	(*anda*) *ap-pa-an-da*	10.1.2.7 10′. 11.7.2 3′
	(*anda*) *ap-pa-an-d*[*a*	10.3.4 7′
	(*anda*) *ap-pa-an-*[*da*	6.1 rev. A 4′
= (*anda*) DAB-*ant-*		
appanziya-	(?) (perhaps "grabbers"?)	
sg. nom.	*ap-pa-an-zi-ia-aš*	9.2.2 rev.! iii 10′. 9.2.3 obv. (ii) 5″
	ap-pa(?)*-a*]*n-zi-ia-aš*	9.2.2 rev.! iv 1′
	ap-pa-an-zi-[*ia-aš*	9.2.2 rev.! iii 14′
see *Lexical Commentary*		
apupi-	'flood-monster(?)'	
sg. nom.	*a-pu-pí-iš*	2.2 rev. 7
sg. nom.-acc. n.	*a-bu-bi*	4.1.1.3 rev. A 6′
see *Lexical Commentary*		
ar-	'to arrive'	
pres. sg. 3	*a-*[*ri*(?)	12.1.1 r. c. 1′
ar-	'to stand, be placed (mid.)'	
pres. sg. 3	*ar-ta*	10.2.1.1 rev. 6′
	ar-ta-ri	10.2.1.1 obv. 6′; rev. 3′
	ar-t]*a-ri*	10.2.1.1 obv. 9′
ptc. sg. nom.	*a-ra-an-za*	2.3 3
ptc. pl. nom.	*a-ra-an-te-eš*	2.2 rev. 6, 7. 4.1.1.1.A_1 3′, 4′ (2×). 4.1.1.1.B_1 obv. ii? 7′
ara-	'right, proper'	
pl. nom.-acc. n.	*a-*[*a-ra*	8.1.E(A_3) rev. vi 6
	a-[*a-ra*(?)	7.1 rev. 10′
arra-	'to wash'	
pres. sg. 3	*ar-ra-i*	2.7.A rev. 6
see also GADA *arrumaš*		
araḫza	'outside'	
	a-ra-aḫ-za	1.5 obv. 1
araḫzanda	'outside, around the outside'	
	a-ra-aḫ-za-an-da	9.2.2 rev.! iii 11′, 20′. 10.3.13 9′
	a-ra-aḫ-za-an-[*da*	9.2.1 obv. ii 25′
aramni-	'falcon, hawk (*vel sim.*)'	
sg. nom.	*a*]*-ra-am-ni-iš*	9.2.1 obv. ii 10′
	a-r]*a-am-ni-iš*	9.2.1 obv. ii 7′; rev. iii 5′
pl. nom.	*a-ra-am-ni-eš*	10.2.1.3 6′
	a-ra-am-ni-uš	9.1.1 rev. iii 22′
	a-ra-am-[*ni-uš*	9.1.2 rev. iii 2′
see *Lexical Commentary*		
^{LÚ}*araunna-*	(a type of garrison troop)	
pl. dat./loc.	$^{\text{LÚ.MEŠ}}$[*a-ra-u*]*n-na-aš*?	6.1 obv. 20
	A-NA $^{\text{LÚ.MEŠ}}$*a-ra-un-na*	6.1 obv. 3, 8
	A-NA [$^{\text{LÚ.MEŠ}}$]*a-ra-un-na*	6.1 obv. 13

stem (pl. dat./loc.?)	$^{\text{LÚ.MEŠ}}$*a-ra-un-na*	6.1 obv. 17
see *Lexical Commentary*		
arḫa	‘away’	
	ar-ḫa	1.1.A_1 obv. 4′. 4.1.1.1.B_1 obv. ii$^?$ 3′; rev. iv 13. 9.2.2 rev.$^!$ iii 5′. 10.3.2 obv. i(?) 10″, 14″
	a[r-ḫa	10.3.2 obv. i(?) 17″. 12.3.7 4′
	ar-ḫa (*arrira-*)	10.2.1.2 obv. 12′. 10.3.5 9′. 10.3.9 7′
	a]r-ḫa (*arrira-*)	10.3.7 3′. 10.3.9 2′
	a[r-ḫa (*arrira-*)	10.3.6 6′
	ar-ḫa (*ḫarra-*)	9.2.2 rev.$^!$ iii 5′
	ar-ḫa (*išḫuwa-*)	9.1.1 rev. iv 22′. 10.2.1.2 obv. 13′
	a]r-ḫ[a (*išḫuwa-*)	10.2.1.2 obv. 15′
	ar-ḫa (*pippa-*)	9.1.8 obv. 12′
	ar-ḫa (*šargani(ya)-*)	9.1.6 obv. 7′
	ar-ḫa (*da-*)	1.1.A_2 rev. 7. 4.1.1.1.A_1 rev. 5′. 4.1.3.2 rev. 8′
	ar-ḫa (*duwarna-*)	5.2 obv. ii 13. 5.5 rev. iii 5′
	a]r-ḫa (*duwarna-*)	10.3.7 5′
	ar-ḫa (*unḫ-*)	2.5 rev. 10′
	(*peran*) *ar-ḫa*	4.2.12 3′
	(*peran*) *ar-ḫa* (*da-*)	4.1.3.3 4′, 6′
	(*peran*) *ar-ḫ]a* (*da-*)	4.1.3.3 1′
	(*pe(r)an*) *ar-[ḫ]a* (GAR)	9.1.5 rev.$^!$ 11′
	(*šer*) *ar-ḫa* (*iya-*)	4.1.4.1.A_1 obv. i 7′
	(*šer*) *a[r-ḫ]a* (*iya-*)	4.1.4.1.A_1 rev. vi 12′
	(UGU) *ar-ḫa* (DÙ)	11.6.1 7, 8
	ar-ḫ]a(?) (*ḫar(k)-*)	12.3.7 3′
see also GADA EGIR*(-an) arḫa* SUD*-waš*		
arrir(r)ant-	‘scraped’ (ptc. of *arrira-*)	
sg. nom.-acc. n.	(*arḫa*) *ar-ri-ra-an*	10.3.2 obv. i(?) 6″
	(*arḫa*) *ar-ri]-ra-an*	10.3.9 6′
	(*arḫa*) *[a]r-r[i-ra-an*	10.3.2 obv. ii(?) 5′
	(*arḫa*) *ar-ri-ra-a[n*	10.3.5 9′. 10.3.7 3′
	(*arḫa*) *ar-ri-ir-r[a-an*	10.2.1.2 obv. 18′
	(*arḫa*) *a[r-ri-ra-an*	10.3.9 2′, 7′
arkamma(n)-	‘(red-)purple(?); tribute’	
sg. gen.?	*ar-kam-ma-aš*	3.2.5 r. c. 2′
see *Lexical Commentary*; = *ḪAŠMĀNU*?; see also *MADDATTU*		
armanni-	‘crescent moon, lunula’	
sg. nom.	*ar-ma-an-ni-iš*	9.2.2 rev.$^!$ iii 15′, 16′
pl. nom.	*ar-ma-an-ni-eš*	9.1.10.B 5′. 9.2.5 obv. i(?) 10′
	ar-ma-a[n-ni-eš	9.1.1 rev. iii 17′
	ar-ma-[an-ni-eš	9.1.10.A_1 obv. 2′
	ar-ma-an-ni-uš	9.2.2 rev.$^!$ iii 4′
= $^{(\text{D})}$U$_4$(*-aš*).SAKAR?		
armannaim(m)a/i-	‘ornamented with lunulas’	
sg. nom.-acc. n.	*ar-ma-an-na-i-ma-[an*	10.1.2.7 8′
see *Lexical Commentary*		
arni(ia)-x[	(a Hurrian bird name)	
	*ar-ni-ia(-)*x[	12.1.1 r. c. 3′

arnu-	‘make go; bring, transport’	
pres. pl. 3	*ar-nu-an-zi*	4.1.4.9 obv. 8
	ar-nu-w[a-an-zi	4.1.4.9 obv. 1
artal-	‘saw (or similar cutting tool)’	
sg. nom.-acc. n.	*a]r-ta-al*	4.2.11 7′
arumu-x[	(a weight measurement?)	
broken	*a-ru-mu*-x[	12.2.3 5′
	*⟨⟨*a-ru-*[*mu*-x⟩⟩*	12.2.2 8′
	a-r[*u-mu*-x	12.2.2 3′
	a-[*ru-mu*-x	12.2.2 5′, 11′. 12.2.3 7′
see *Lexical Commentary*		
arwanal(l)i-	(a bird name)	
sg. nom.-acc. n.	*ar-wa-na-li*	10.3.3 obv.$^{?}$ 13′
ašanni-	(?)	
pl. nom.	*a-ša-an-ni-eš*	9.1.10.A_2 rev. 3′
see *Lexical Commentary*		
ašandul-	‘garrison’	
pl. dat./loc.	*a-ša-an-du-la-aš*	6.1 obv. 3, 13, 18
	a]-ša-an-d[u-la-aš	6.1 obv. 21
	a-ša-an-du-la-[aš	6.1 obv. 8
ašara-	‘(bright) white’	
sg. nom.	*a-ša-ra-aš*	4.1.3.8 rev. A 2′
	a-ša-r[a-aš	4.1.3.5.A_2 4′
	a-š[a-ra-aš	4.1.3.5.A_2 5′
stem	*a-ša-ra*	4.1.3.4.A_1 rev. l. c. 2′
see *Lexical Commentary*; see also *ḫarki-*, *gaši-*, BABBAR		
^{DUG}*aššauwaš*	‘“good” cup’	
sg. gen.	^{DUG}*aš-ša-u-wa-aš*	9.2.1 rev. iii 6′
see *Lexical Commentary*		
aška-	‘gate; (in adv. abl.) outside’	
pl. dat./loc.	*a-aš-ga-aš*	4.1.1.1.B_2 obv. i$^{?}$ 6′
abl.	*a-aš-ka-az*	4.1.1.1.A_1 obv 13′, 20′
	a-aš-ga-za	4.1.1.1.B_1 rev. iii$^{?}$ 7, 15
see *Lexical Commentary*		
ašku-	(?)	
sg. nom.	**aš*$^{?}$*-*ku-uš*	9.1.11 obv.$^{?}$ 8′
see *Lexical Commentary*		
-(a)šta	(sentence particle)	
	-aš-ta	4.1.1.1.A_1 rev. 18′. 4.1.1.1.B_1 rev. iii$^{?}$ 14, 16. 10.2.1.1 obv. 3′, 5′
	-aš-t]a	10.2.1.1 obv. 6′
aššur		
see under *Geographic Names*		
ašuša-	‘(ear)ring, (ear)hoop’	
sg. nom.	*a-šu-ša-aš*	9.1.5 rev.$^{!}$ 2′, 3′, 6′
	a-šu]-ša-aš	9.1.5 rev.$^{!}$ 8′

pl. acc.	*a-šu-šu-uš*	9.1.5 rev.[!] 7′
see *Lexical Commentary*; see also *ištamaḫura-*, *INṢABTU*, *KAMKAMMATU*, HUB(.BI)/ḪÚB(.BI)		
(-)*a*]*ddannaim(m)a/i-*	(?)	
Luw. pl. nom.	(-)*a*]*d-da-an-na-i-me-en-zi*	9.2.1 rev. iii 19′
see *Lexical Commentary*		
$^{\text{(TÚG)}}$*adupli(t)-*	(a garment)	
sg. nom.-acc. n.	*a-du-up-li*	4.2.9 obv. 2; rev. 14′. 4.2.10 7′
	^{TÚG}*a-tu-up-li*	2.7.A obv. 6
	^{TÚG}*a-d*[*u-up-li*	9.1.6 obv. 17
see *Lexical Commentary*; see also ^{TÚG}GÚ *adupli(t)-*		
awiti-	‘sphinx’	
sg. nom.	*a-ú-i-ti-iš*	5.6 5′. 10.3.3 obv.[?] 11′
	a-ú-wi$_5$*-ti-iš*	9.2.1 obv. ii 11′
	a-wi$_5$*-ti-iš*	9.1.1 rev. iii 15′, 38′
pl. nom.	*a-wi*$_5$*-ti-uš*	9.1.1 rev. iv 17′. 10.1.2.5 2′
stem	*a-ú-i-ti*	4.1.1.3 rev. A 6′
	(*BIBRU*) *a-ú-i-ti*	9.1.4.A$_1$ obv. ii 27
	a-ú-i]*-ti*	9.1.4.A$_1$ obv. ii 28
see *Lexical Commentary*		
au(š)-/u(wa)-	‘to see, look, gaze’	
iter. pres. sg. 3	*uš-ke-ez-zi*	4.1.1.9 9′
iter. ptc. pl. nom.	(EGIR-*pa parza*) *uš-kán-te-eš*	9.1.1 rev. iv 11′
broken	*uš-ká*[*n-*	9.1.4.A$_1$ rev. iv 11′
eḫlipak(k)i-	(colored like *eḫlipak(k)i*-stone)	
sg. nom.-acc. n.	*eḫ-li-pa-ki*	2.7.A obv. 10
$^{\text{(NA}_4\text{)}}$*eḫlipak(k)i-*	(a stone)	
sg. nom.-acc. n.	$^{\text{N]A}_4}$*eḫ-li-pa-ki*	10.1.2.4 l. c. 17′
	$^{\text{N]A}_4}$*eḫ-li-pa-ak-k*[*i*	2.6 5′
material		
sg. gen.	*eḫ-li-pa-ki-ia-aš*	4.2.4 obv. 6
	eḫ-li-pa-ak-ki-ia-aš	4.2.4 obv. 3
	eḫ-li-pa-k[*i*[!?]*-ia-aš*	4.2.5 3′
see *Lexical Commentary*		
epp-/app-	‘to take, seize’	
pres. pl. 3	*ap-pa-an-zi*	12.1.1 r. c. 2′
= DAB; see also (*anda*) *appant-*/DAB*-ant-*		
eš-	‘to be sitting (act.); sit down (mid.)’	
mid. pret. sg. 3	*e-ša-at*	2.9.A$_2$ obv. i 10′. 2.9.A$_3$ obv. i 12′. 2.12 obv.[!] i 2′; obv.[!] ii 3′
	e-[*ša-at*	9.1.4.A$_1$ rev. iv 4′
mid. pret. pl. 3	*e-ša-an-ta-at*	2.12 obv.[!] ii 8′
	e-[*ša-an-ta-at*	2.9.A$_3$ obv. ii 4′
= TUŠ		
eš-/aš-	‘to be’	
pres. sg. 3	*e-eš-zi*	9.2.6 obv. i 18′. 10.3.1 rev. iii 7′
	e*-eš-zi*	10.2.1.3 8′
	e[?]*-eš-zi*	11.1.1 l. c. 4″
	e-eš[?]*-*[*zi*	10.2.1.4 7′
pres. pl. 3	*a-ša-an-zi*	1.5 lo. e. 18; rev. 22

	(*šara*) *a-ša-an-zi*	1.5 obv. 2
pret. sg. 3	*e-eš-ta*	4.1.1.1.A_2 rev. 3′. 4.1.1.1.B_1 rev. iv$^?$ 2. 4.1.3.6 rev. 6′, 14″. 10.3.2 obv. i(?) 6″
pret. pl. 3	*e-še-er*	1.1.A_1 obv. 17′
ed-/ad-	‘to eat’	
iter. pres. sg. 3	*az-zi-ke-*[*ez-zi*	8.1.E(A_3) rev. vi 7
infin.	*a-da-an-na*$^!$	8.1.E(A_3) rev. vi 6
^{TÚG}*e/itriwa-*	“‘feeding’ cloth”(?)	
sg. nom (or gen.?)	^{TÚG}*et-ri-wa-aš*	8.8.B l. c. 1′
	^{TÚG}*et-*[*ri-wa-aš*	8.8.B r. c. 6′
see *Lexical Commentary*		
^{É}*ḫalentu(wa)-*	‘(great) hall’	
pl. gen.	^{É}*ḫa-l*[*i-in-tu-u-wa-aš*	2.2 rev. 8
pl. dat./loc.	^{É}*ḫa-li-in-tu-u-wa-aš*	4.1.1.1.A_1 rev. 5′
	^{É}*ḫa-li-in-tu-u*]*-wa-aš*	4.1.1.1.B_1 obv. ii$^?$ 11′
see *Lexical Commentary*		
^{LÚ}*ḫalipi-*	(a title)	
sg. nom.	^{L}[^{Ú}*ḫa-a-li-pí* *ŠA* KUR.UGU(?)	12.3.1 2′
ḫališši(ya)-	‘to plate, inlay (with metal)’	
pret. pl. 3	(EGIR-*pa*) *ḫa-liš-še-er*	10.3.2 obv. i(?) 4″
infin.	*ḫa-liš-šu-an-zi*	4.1.1.1.B_1 rev. iii$^?$ 13
	(EGIR) *ḫa-liš-šu*]*-wa-an-zi*	4.1.1.1.A_1 rev. 6′
ptc. sg. nom.-acc. n.	*ḫa-liš-ši-an*	9.1.5 rev.$^!$ 7′. 9.2.9 obv.$^?$ 5′
= GAR		
ḫalki-	‘barley; grain’	
pl. acc. (or nom.?)	*ḫal-ki-i-uš*	12.3.1 7′
= ŠE		
$^{(TÚG)}$*ḫamankant-*	‘“bound/tied/knotted” garment’	
sg. nom.-acc. n.	*ḫa-ma-an-kán*	8.1.J rev. v$^!$ 2′
	^{TÚG}*ḫa-ma-an-ká*[*n*	9.1.6 obv. 16
see *Lexical Commentary*; see also KEŠDA(*-m(m)a/i-*)		
ḫamenkuaš	‘of binding’	
see UGU *ḫamenkuaš*		
ḫanda(i)-	‘to prepare; determine, fix’	
ptc. sg. nom.-acc. n.	*ḫa-an-da-a-an*	9.2.4 obv. i 12′
	ḫ]*a*$^?$*-an-da-a-an*	8.1.I rev. l. c. 2′
ḫant-	‘front, forehead, brow’; (on ornament)	
pl. nom.	*ḫa-an-ti-iš*	9.2.2 rev.$^!$ iii 18′
abl.(?)	*ḫa-an-t*[*a-az*(?)	11.2.2 3′
see *Lexical Commentary*; = SAG.(DU.)KI		
ḫandi	‘separate(ly), specially’	
	ḫa-an-di-i	4.1.1.1.A_1 rev. 18′. 4.1.1.1.B_1 rev. iii$^?$ 14′
	ḫa-an-d[*i-i*	2.9.A_2 obv. i 1′
	ḫa-[*an-di-i*	2.9.A_2 obv. i 3′
ḫapalki-	‘iron (or iron ore?)’	
sg. gen.	*ḫa-pal-*⟨*ki*⟩*-ia-aš*	9.1.1 rev. iv 32′
see *Lexical Commentary*; = AN.BAR/*ḪAPALKI(N)NU*; see also *kiklibaim(m)a/i-*, *parzagulliya-*, *parzašša-*		

$^{\text{(GIŠ)}}$*ḫapšalli-*	‘stool, chair (esp. for women)’	
sg. nom.-acc. n.	*ḫ[a-a]p-šal-li*	10.3.5 10′
	^{GIŠ}*ḫa-a]p-šal-li*	10.2.1.2 obv. 12′
= ^{GIŠ}GÌR.GUB?; see also GADA $^{\text{(GIŠ)}}$*ḫapšalliaš*		
ḫapuna-	(a material?)	
sg. gen.	*ḫa-pu-na-aš*	5.7 rev. iii$^{?}$ 10′
see *Lexical Commentary*		
^{TÚG}*ḫapušam(m)a/i-*	‘garment of fulled(?) fabric’	
	^{TÚG}*ḫa-pu-ša-am-[mi(-)*	8.8.B r. c. 3′
	^{TÚG}*ḫa-pu-[ša-am-mi(-)*	8.1.E(A_1) rev. iv 14′
see *Lexical Commentary*		
ḫara(n)-	(an object)	
sg. nom.	*ḫa-ra-an-za*	9.1.1 rev. iii 20′
see *Lexical Commentary*		
ḫarrant-	‘abraded, destroyed’	
sg. nom.-acc. n.	(*arḫa*) *ḫar-ra-an*	9.2.2 rev.$^{!}$ iii 5′
ḫar(k)-	‘to have, hold’	
pres. sg. 3	*ḫar-zi*	4.1.1.1.B_1 rev. iii$^{?}$ 8. 4.2.7 2′. 9.1.4.A_1 obv. i 14′. 10.1.2.7 2′. 10.2.1.1 rev. 2′, 7′. 10.2.1.2 obv. 10′, 13′. 12.2.1 obv. 2′, 3′; rev. 6′, 7′
	ḫar-zi	1.2 rev. 12′
	ḫa]r-zi	10.2.1.1 rev. 1′
	ḫar-[z]i	9.1.4.A_1 obv. i 13′
	ḫar-z[i	12.2.1 rev. 5′
	ḫar-z[i$^{?}$	10.3.14 l. c. 1′
	ḫar$^{!?}$-z[i$^{?}$	9.1.4.A_1 obv. i 7′
	ḫar-[zi	12.2.1 obv. 1′
	ḫa[r-zi	12.2.1 rev. 4′
pres. pl. 3	*ḫar-kán-zi*	4.1.1.1.B_1 rev. iii$^{?}$ 15. 9.2.1 obv. ii(?) 13′; rev. iii(?) 7′
	ḫa]r-kán-zi	2.4 rev. 7′
pret. sg. 3	*ḫar-ta*	1.1.A_1 obv. 13′. 1.1.A_2 rev. 8. 10.3.2 obv. i(?) 9″
pret. pl. 3	*ḫar-ker*	4.1.1.1.B_1 rev. iii$^{?}$ 9
ptc. pl. nom.	(*arḫa*?) *ḫar-kán-te-eš*	12.3.7 3′
^{GIŠ}*ḫariuzzi-*	‘wicker(?) table’	
sg. nom.-acc. n.	^{GIŠ}*ḫa-ri(?)]-uz-zi*	10.3.9 5′
ḫarki-	‘white; white (of the eye)’	
sg. nom.	*ḫar-ki-iš*	10.2.1.2 obv. 3′
sg. gen.	*ḫar-ki-aš*	2.7.A obv. 16
= BABBAR; see also *ašara-*, *gaši-*		
$^{\text{(GIŠ)}}$*ḫa/urnašal(l)a-*	‘(lidded) box’ (pl. tant.)	
pl. nom.-acc. n.	*ḫar/ḫur-na-ša-la*	10.3.12 obv. i 10′
	ḫar/ḫur-na-šal-la	9.2.6 obv. i 6′
	ḫar/ḫur-na]-ša-al-la	10.1.2.1 obv.$^{?}$ l. c. 2
	^{GIŠ}*ḫar/ḫur-na-ša-al-la*	2.7.B rev. 3′
	^{GIŠ}*ḫar/ḫur-na-a[š-ša-al-la*	10.2.2.3 obv.$^{?}$ l. c. 2′
pl. gen.	^{GIŠ}*ḫar/ḫur-na-ša-al-la-aš*	4.2.4 obv. 7
see *Lexical Commentary*; = $^{\text{(GIŠ)}}$*KANḪANNU*, ^{GIŠ}DUB.ŠEN(?)		

ḫarnauwa- — ‘birthing stool’
see MUNUS *ḫarnauwaš*

ḫarpant- — ‘joined, connected (ptc. of *ḫarp-*)’
sg. nom.-acc. n. — *ḫar-pa-a-an* — 8.4 rev. 7′

ḫarwaši- — ‘hidden’
see É *ḫarwašiaš*

ḫašḫašant- — ‘smoothed, planed, polished’ (ptc. of *ḫašḫaš-*)
sg. nom.-acc. n. — *ḫa-aš-ḫ[a-ša]-a-an* — 9.2.4 obv. i 18′
ḫa-aš-ḫ]a-ša-a-an — 9.2.4 rev. iv 7. 9.2.5 obv. i(?) 13′
ḫa-aš-ḫ]a-ša-a-[an(?) — 10.1.2.4 l. c. 2′
pl. nom. — *ḫa-aš-ḫa-ša-an-te-eš* — 9.2.1 rev. iii 22′
ḫ]a-aš-ḫa-ša-an-te-eš — 8.4 rev. 9′

ḫaštai-, *ḫašti-* — ‘bone’
see É.ŠÀ *ḫaštiyaš*

ḫattalla- — ‘club, mace’
pl. nom.-acc. n. — *ḫa-at-tal-la* — 9.1.14 obv. r. c. 5′

ḫati- — (an object of gold)
sg. nom. — *ḫa-a-ti-iš* — 9.2.4 obv. i 15′, 17′

ḫatiwant- — (an object of made of goat horn and stone)
sg. nom. — *ḫa-ti-wa-za* — 11.1.2 l. c. 3′

ḫatiwi- — ‘inventory’
sg. nom. — *ḫa-ti-*wi_5*-iš* — 9.1.9 rev. iv 5′
ḫa-ti-ú-i-iš — 9.1.1 rev. iv 45′
see *Lexical Commentary*

ḫatiwita(i)- — ‘to inventory’
pres. pl. 3 — *ḫa-ti-ú-i-ta-an-zi* — 2.7.A obv. 11
ḫa-ti-[ú-i-ta-an-zi(?) — 10.3.6 8′
ptc. sg. nom.-acc. n. — *ḫa-ti-ú-i-ta-an* — 2.8 obv. 1
ḫa-ti-ú-i-ta-a-an — 2.7.A obv. 18, 24
ḫa-ti-ú-i-ta]-a-an — 2.7.B rev. 4′
see *Lexical Commentary*

^{GIŠ}*ḫatuli-* — (archery equipment component?)
sg. nom. — ^{GIŠ}*ḫa-tu-liš* — 9.1.10.A_2 rev. 7′
see *Lexical Commentary*

ḫazila- — (unit of vol. = approx. 2 liters)
sg. nom. — *ḫa-zi-la-[aš* — 5.7 rev. iii$^?$ 5′
ḫ[a-zi-la-aš — 5.7 rev. iii$^?$ 4′

$^{(\text{NA}_4)}$*ḫekur-* — ‘rock sanctuary’
sg. nom.-acc. n. — $^{\text{NA}_4}$*ḫé-kur* — 3.1.7.A_2 rev. v 4′
sg. gen. — *ŠA ḫé-kur* — 4.1.4.8 9′
see *Lexical Commentary*; see also É.GAL *ḫekur* ^{D}LAMMA

ḫilammar — ‘gatehouse’
sg. gen. — *ḫi-lam-na*$^?$*-aš* — 12.3.6 6′

^{GIŠ}*ḫinapi-* — (a weapon or implement of the Storm-god)
sg. nom. — ^{GIŠ}*ḫi-na-pí-iš* — 7.1 obv. 11′

ḫi(n)k-, ḫaik-	'to give, hand over'	
pret. sg. 3	*ḫi-i]n-ik-ta*	5.1 rev. iii 5
ḫe/inzu	(an attribute of the Storm-god) "(lightning)-bundle(?), goad(?), whip(?)"	
sg. nom.	*ḫi-in-zu*	11.1.9 6′
ḫeš(š)-	'to open'	
pres. sg. 3	*ḫé-e-eš-z[i*	2.5 obv. 4′
	ḫé-e-e[š-zi	4.2.1.A_2 lo. e. 10′
ḫeššamala-	(an ornament or object of precious metal)	
sg. nom.	*ḫe-eš-ša-ma-la-aš*	4.1.1.1.A_1 obv. 12′
sg. nom.-acc. n.	*ḫe-e[š]-ša-ma-li*	9.1.5 rev.! 8′
ḫešḫa-	(part of a drinking vessel)	
sg. dat./loc.	*ḫe-eš-ḫi*	9.1.4.A_1 obv. ii 19. 9.1.5 rev.! 13′
see *Lexical Commentary*		
ḫuḫḫurtalla/i-	'necklace' (pl. tant.)	
pl. nom.-acc. n.	*ḫu-uḫ-ḫur-tal-la*	9.1.10.A_1 obv 4′. 9.1.10.B 7′
	ḫu-uḫ-ḫu-ur-tal-a	10.3.2 obv. i(?) 8″
	ḫu-ḫur-ta-al-la	9.2.1 obv. ii 20′
	ḫu-ḫur(?)]*-ta-al-la*	1.3 4′
	ḫu-uḫ-ḫur(?)*-ta*]*l-la*	9.2.2 rev.! iii 25′
pl. gen.	*ḫu-ḫur*(?)]*-ta-al-la-aš*	9.1.5 obv.! 8
see *Lexical Commentary*		
ḫuittiya-, ḫuet-	'to pull, draw; (with cloth) span, spread, lay out'	
sg. nom.-acc. n.	*ḫu-u-i-it-t[i-ya-an*	10.2.1.2 obv. 9′
broken	*ḫu-u-it-[ti-ia-*	8.1.E(A_3) rev. vi 10
= SUD; see also GADA EGIR*(-an) arḫa* SUD*-uaš*, TÚG UGU SUD*-an*		
^{NA_4}*ḫulali-*	(a stone) 'banded agate(?)'	
sg. nom.-acc. n.	^{NA_4}*ḫu-u-la-li*	9.1.10.B 6′
see *Lexical Commentary*; = ^{NA_4}NÍR		
ḫuli-	'wool(?)'	
sg. nom.	*ḫu-liš*	6.5 rev. 9′
see *Lexical Commentary*		
ḫulliya-	'to strike (down), break (up)'	
pret. pl. 3	*ḫu-ul-li-er*	3.1.1.A_1 obv. ii 10′
	ḫu-ul-l]*i*(?)*-er*	3.1.1.A_1 obv. ii 11′
see *Lexical Commentary*		
^{MUNUS}*ḫulpa-*	(?)	
pl. dat./loc.	$^{MUNUS.MEŠ}$*ḫu-ul-pa-aš*	6.1 rev. B 7
ḫulpanali-	(a garment)	
sg. nom.-acc. n.	*ḫu-ul-pa-na-li*	11.6.1 6
	ḫu-ul]*-pa-na-li*	4.1.4.1.A_1 rev. vi 13′
see *Lexical Commentary*		
ḫu(wa)lpanze/a/ina-	'decorative stud, knob(?)'	
pl. nom.	*ḫu-ul-pa-an-zé-na-aš*	9.1.1 rev. iii 28′
	ḫu-u]*l-pa-an-zi-na-aš*	2.14 11′
	ḫu-ul-pa-a]*n-zi-na-aš*	10.1.2.4 l. c. 9′
	ḫu-ul-pa-an-zi-n]*a*(?)*-aš*	2.14 12′
	ḫu-ul-pa-an-z[i-na-aš(?)	9.2.4 rev. iii 8′

	ḫu-ul-pa-an-za-na-aš	9.2.1 obv. ii 26′
pl. acc.	*ḫu-wa-al-pa-zi-nu-uš*	4.1.1.6 rev. iii 6
	ḫu-wa-al-pa-zi-nu-[*uš*	4.1.1.6 rev. iii 4
broken	*ḫu-ul-*[*pa-an-zi-na-*	9.2.14 5′
ḫulpanzinant-	‘set with studs, knobs(?)’	
sg. nom.-acc. n.	*ḫu-u-ul-pa-zi-na-an*	9.2.2 rev.$^{!}$ iv 2′
	ḫ]*u-ul-pa-an-zi-na-an*	10.3.5 10′
ḫulpanzinaim(m)a/i-	‘set with studs, knobs(?)’	
sg. acc. n.	*ḫu-ul-pa-an-zi-na-i-ma-an*	9.2.1 rev. iii 16′
pl. nom.	*ḫu-ul-pa-an-zi-na-i-me-eš*	9.1.1 rev. iv 34′
	ḫu-ul-pa-zi-na⟨⟨*an*⟩⟩*-i-me-eš*	9.1.1 rev. iv 35′
ḫumant-	‘all, every, entire’	
sg. nom.-acc. n.	*ḫu-u-ma-an*	1.5 obv. 10; rev. 20′. 4.1.4.9 obv. 7
pl. dat./loc.	*ḫu-u-ma-an-da-aš*	3.1.1.A_2 rev. vi 4′
^{TÚG}*ḫunipala(za)-*	(a seat cover?)	
sg. nom.?	^{TÚG}*ḫu-ni-pa-l*[*a-*	6.1 up. e. 1
see *Lexical Commentary*		
ḫuntapiri-	(a type of bird?)	
sg. nom.	*ḫu-un-ta-*[*pí-ri-i*]*š*	9.1.1 rev. iv 32′
$^{\text{(GADA)}}$*ḫu(wa)ndar(a)-*	(a linen cloth)	
sg. nom.(?)	$^{\text{GADA!}}$*ḫu-un-ta-ra-aš*	2.11 obv.$^{?}$ 4′
sg. nom.-acc. n.	^{G}]^{ADA}*ḫu-u-wa-an-tar*	4.1.4.8 7′
pl. nom.-acc. n.	*ḫu-wa-an-ta-*[*ra*	11.1.1 r. c. 10′
	^{GADA}*ḫu-u-wa-an-da-ra*	9.2.6 l. e. 1
	^{GADA}*ḫu-u-wa-an-ta-ra*	9.1.10.A_1 obv. 7′
	^{GADA}]*ḫu-u-wa-an-da-ra*	9.1.10.B 11′
see *Lexical Commentary*		
$^{\text{(DUG)}}$*ḫup(pa)r(a)-*	‘pot, bowl’	
sg. nom.	*ḫu-*[*up-pár*(?)	4.2.1.A_2 obv. 2′
	^{DUG}*ḫu-up-pár*	9.2.11 4′. 10.1.1.2 rev. iv 13′
	ḫu-u-up-pár-aš	11.1.9 4′
$^{\text{(GI/GIŠ)}}$*ḫuppar(al)li-*	(a storage container)	
sg. nom.	*ḫu-up-pár-a*[*l-liš*	2.1.A obv. ii(?) 3′
	ḫ]*u-u-up-pár-al-liš*	8.1.D obv. i 4′
	^{GI}*ḫu-up-pár-al-liš*	2.1.A obv. ii(?) 16′
	^{GI}*ḫu-u-up-pár-al-liš*	2.2 obv. 2′, 8′
	^{G}]^{I}*ḫu-up-pár-al-liš*	2.1.B 7′
	^{GIŠ}*ḫu-u-up-pár-al-liš*	8.1.A rev. v 27′, 28′
	^{G}]^{IŠ}*ḫu-up-pár-liš*	2.2 rev. 3
	^{GIŠ}*ḫu-up-pa-r*[*a-liš*	6.11 3′
	^{GIŠ}*ḫu-up-pá*[*r-al-liš*	4.2.2 obv. 4
ḫupitauwant-	(wearing a *ḫupita*-cap)	
sg. nom.	*ḫu-u-pí-t*[*a-u*]*-w*[*a-an-za*	10.2.1.2 obv. 7′
ḫurišaim(m)a/i-	(an object made of gold/stone)	
pl. nom.	*ḫu-u-ri-ša-i-me-eš*	9.2.1 rev. iii 20′
ḫurli-	(?)	
sg. nom.(?)	*ḫur-li-eš*	10.1.2.8 rev. r. c. 2′
see *Lexical Commentary*		

ḫu(wa)rlu-	(a bracket or mount for overlays?)	
sg. nom.	*ḫur-lu-uš*	2.17 obv.$^?$ r. c. 18′
	ḫ[ur-lu-uš	2.17 obv.$^?$ r. c. 19′
	ḫu-wa-ar-lu-uš	9.1.5 rev.$^!$ 15′
	ḫu-wa-ar-lu-u]š	9.1.5 rev.$^!$ 15′
see *Lexical Commentary*		
ḫu(wa)rtiyal(l)a/i-	(a vessel for infusions/concoctions)	
sg. nom.	*ḫu-u-wa-ar-ti-a[l-li-iš*(?)	11.1.9 7′
see *Lexical Commentary*		
ḫudanni-	(a container or vessel)	
sg. nom.-acc. n.	*ḫu-u-da-an-ni*	9.1.15 5′
see *Lexical Commentary*		
^{DUG}*ḫutuši-*	(a container or vessel)	
sg. nom.	^{DUG}]*ḫu-u-tu-ši-iš*	9.1.1 rev. iv 25′
	^{DUG}*ḫu-u-tu*(?)]*-ši-iš*	9.1.4.A$_1$ obv. ii 42
yarammal(l)a-	(a container)	
pl. nom.-acc. n.	*ia-ra-am-ma-al-la*	2.16 obv. i 6′
	ia-ra]-a-am-m[a-la(?)	2.16 obv. i 4′
iyata(r)-/iyatn-	‘plenty; (in gen.) luxurious(?)’	
sg. gen.	*i-at-na-aš*	4.2.9 obv. 3, 21
	i-ia-at-na-aš	8.1.E(A$_3$) obv. i 3′. 8.8.A 3′. 8.8.B l. c. 3′
	i-i]a-at-na-aš	8.8.B l. c. 8′
	i-ia-a[t-na-aš	8.8.A 7′
see *Lexical Commentary*		
iya-	‘to make; (with *šer arḫa)* “finished” on top’	
pres. pl. 3	*i-en-zi*	2.7.A rev. 2. 4.1.1.1.A$_1$ rev. 11′. 4.1.1.1.B$_1$ rev. iii$^?$ 2, 4
	i-en-[z]i	4.1.1.1.A$_1$ rev. 7′
	i-e[n-zi	4.1.1.1.A$_1$ rev. 9′
pret. pl. 3	*i-e-er*	4.1.1.6 rev. iii 2
ptc. sg. nom.	(*šer arḫa*) *i-ia-an-za*	4.1.4.1.A$_1$ obv. i 7′
	(*šer arḫa*) [*i-i*]*a-*[*a*]*n-za*	4.1.4.1.A$_1$ rev. vi 12′
ptc. sg. nom.-acc. n.	*i-ia-an*	11.3.1 20′, 21′
	UGU *arḫa* DÙ*-an*	11.6.1 7, 8
see *Lexical Commentary*; = DÙ		
ilana-	‘stairs’	
see É *ilanaš*		
intaluzzi-	‘shovel, scoop’	
sg. nom.	*in-ta-lu*]*-uz-zi-iš*(?)	11.1.7 4′
intana-	(adj. modifying linen)	
see GADA *intan(n)a-*		
ipeššar (or: *ipa/i-*^{SAR}, *ipi-*^{SAR}) (an object made of gold)		
	i-pé-eš-šar (or: *i-pí-eš*^{SAR})	10.3.13 5′
see *Lexical Commentary*		
$^{\mathrm{(TÚG)}}$*ipul(li)-*	‘wrap, shroud, cover(?)’	
sg. nom.-acc. n.	^{TÚG}*i-pu-li*	6.5 obv. 7′, 8′, 9′, 10′, 12′, 16′
	^{TÚG}*i-pu*$^!$*-li*	6.5 obv. 15′
	^{TÚG}*i-⟨pu⟩-li*	6.5 obv. 11′

	^{TÚG}*i-p]u-[l]i*	8.1.F rev. vi 9
	^{TÚG}*i-pu-l[i*	6.5 obv. 6′
	^{TÚG}*i-pu-[li*	6.5 obv. 4′
pl. dat./loc.	*i-pu-ul-li-ia-aš*	8.1.A obv. i 5′
broken	*i-p]u-ul-li(-)[*	10.3.13 10′
ipurawar	‘earthworks’ (vb. subst. of *epura(i)-*)	
sg. gen.	*i-pu-r[a-u]-aš*	4.2.9 rev. 30′
	i-pu-ra-u-[aš	4.2.9 obv. 15
see *Lexical Commentary*		
$^{\text{(TÚG)}}$*irḫi-*	(a type of belt)	
sg. nom.	*ir-ḫi-iš*	11.6.1 4
	^{TÚG}*ir-ḫi-iš*	4.1.4.1.A_2 obv. ii 6′. 8.1.E(A_1) rev. v 10′
	^{TÚG}*i]r-ḫi-eš*	4.1.4.5 rev. r. c. 5′
	^{TÚG}*i]r-ḫi-iš*	8.1.D rev. iv 4′
	i]r(?)-ḫi-iš	6.1 rev. A 5′
see *Lexical Commentary*; = ^{TÚG}E.ÍB?		
iššar(a)l(l)ad(d)ar	‘bracelet(?)’ (pl. tant.)	
pl. nom.-acc. n.	*iš-ša-ra-al-la-ad-da-ra*	9.2.2 rev.! iii 19′
pl. gen.	*iš-ša-ra-la-ta-na-aš*	4.1.1.1.A_1 obv. 7′
	iš-šar-la-at-ta-aš	4.1.1.3 rev. B 6
see *Lexical Commentary*		
iššera-	(an object)	
(?)	*iš-še-ra*	9.1.13 5′
see *Lexical Commentary*		
išḫuwant-	‘poured; (w/ *arḫa*) fallen out, removed’ (ptc. of *išḫuwa-*)	
sg. nom.-acc. n.	(*anda*) *iš-ḫu-u-wa-a-an*	8.1.A obv. ii 14′, 15′
	(*arḫa*) *iš-ḫu-u-wa-an*	9.1.1 rev. iv 22′
	(*arḫa*) *i[š]-ḫu-u-wa-[a]n*	10.2.1.2 obv. 13′
	(*arḫa*) *iš-ḫ]u-u-wa-an*	10.2.1.2 obv. 15′
	(*arḫa*) *iš-ḫu-u-wa-[an*	10.3.2 obv. ii(?) 2′
	(*arḫa*) *iš-ḫ[u-u-wa-an*(?)	10.3.2 obv. ii(?) 11′
see *Lexical Commentary*		
iškalla-	‘to tear, split, slit, shear’	
pres. pl. 3	*iš-kal-la-an-zi*	4.1.4.9 obv. 3, 5
^{TÚG}*iškalleššar*	(a ‘slitted’ garment)	
sg. nom.-acc. n.	^{TÚG}*i]š-ga-al-*li_{12}*-eš-šar*	4.2.7 5′
see *Lexical Commentary*		
išgapuzzi-	(a small object)	
sg. nom.-acc. n.	*iš-ga-p[u-uz-zi*	9.2.6 obv. i 12′
see *Lexical Commentary*		
išgar-	‘to stick, bore through; thread (beads) on a string’	
ptc. sg. nom.	*iš-ga-ra-an-za*	10.2.1.1 obv. 4′
ptc. sg. nom.-acc. n.	*iš-ga-ra-a-an*	8.1.A obv. i 8′. 9.2.2 rev.! iii 12′
	iš-g]a-ra-a-an	9.2.4 obv. i 8′
	(EGIR-*an*) *iš-ga-ra-a-an*	9.2.2 rev.! iii 14′. 9.2.4 obv. i 6′. 11.3.1 19′
	(EGIR-*an*) *iš-ga-r[a-a-an*	9.2.4 obv. i 3′
ptc. pl. nom.-acc. n.	*iš-ga-ra-a-an-ta*	11.3.1 12′

išgaratar	'(a type of) bead, pendant(?)'	
sg. nom.-acc. n.	*iš-ga-ra-tar*	8.4 rev. 3′
	iš-g[a-r]a-tar	9.1.10.B 4′
	iš-ga-r[a-tar	11.3.2 r. c. 3′
	iš-ga-[ra-tar(?)	11.6.2 rev. 3′
	iš-[ga-ra-tar	11.3.2 r. c. 2′, 6′
	iš-[ga-ra-tar(?)	9.2.2 rev.$^!$ iii 9′
see *Lexical Commentary*; see also $^{(NA_4)}$NUNUZ		
išgariḫ-	'libation scoop/ladle(?)'	
sg. nom.-acc. n.	*iš-ga-r]i-iḫ*	9.2.9 obv.$^?$ 15′
išpant-	'night'	
see ^{TÚG}GÚ *išpandaš*		
išpatar	'spit, skewer; dress pin(?)'	
sg. nom.-acc. n.	*iš-pa-tar*	9.2.2 rev.$^!$ iii 6′
išpišduwara-		
see *šuppe/išduwara/i-*, *išpeštuwara-*		
ištamaḫura-	'earring'	
pl. nom.	*iš-ta-ma-ḫu-u-ru-uš*	9.1.10.A$_1$ rev. 3′
	iš-ta-ma-ḫu-ru-uš	9.1.1 rev. iv 38′
	iš-ta]-ma-ḫu-ru-uš	9.2.1 obv. ii 16′
see also *ašuša-*, *INṢABTUM*, *KAMKAMMATU*, ḪUB(.BI)/ḪÚB(.BI)		
ištarna	'in the middle, in between' (adv.)	
	iš-tar-na	8.1.A obv. i 6′
iwar	'like, as' (postposition with gen.)	
	i-wa-ar	11.3.1 20′, 21′
ka-	'this' (proximal demonstrative pronoun)	
sg. nom.	*ka-a-aš*	8.1.G obv. r. c. 6′
	ka-[a-aš	8.1.F obv. i 6′
sg. nom.-acc. n.	*ki-i*	1.1.A$_1$ obv. 4′. 1.5 rev. 20. 4.1.1.2.A obv. 6′. 4.1.3.2 rev. 7′. 8.1.A obv. ii 16′
	ki]-i	8.6 l. c. 7′
	ki-[i	1.5 obv. 13
	k[i-i	4.1.1.7 rev.$^{!?}$ 1
sg. acc.	*ku-u-un*	2.7.A obv. 11
sg. dat./loc.	*ke-e-da-ni*	8.1.F obv. ii 14′
	ke-e-[da-ni(?)	11.3.1 21′
pl. nom. (or acc.?)	*ku-u-uš*	11.3.1 13′
pl. nom.-acc. n.	*k]e$^?$-e*	11.3.1 24′
kallaratar	'surplus, overflow'	
sg. dat./loc.	*kal-la-ra-an-ni*	4.1.1.1.B$_1$ rev. iii$^?$ 8
see *Lexical Commentary*; = *ĀTRU* (G vb. adj. sg. nom. of *(W)ATĀRU*); DIRI		
galgalturi-	'cymbal(?)'	
sg. nom.-acc. n.	*gal-gal-tu-u-ri*	2.7.A rev. 4
	gal-gal-tu-[ri	4.1.1.2.A obv. 13′
kalmašu-	(a golden object)	
sg. acc.	*kal-ma-šu-un*	9.2.1 obv. ii 13′

^{GIŠ}*kalmu-*	'crook, lituus'	
sg. nom.-acc. n.	^{GIŠ}*kal-mu-uš*	9.1.4.A_1 obv. i 28′. 10.3.1 rev. iii 10′
$^{\text{(TÚG)}}$*kalup(p)a-*	'gown, dress'	
sg. nom.	*ka-lu-pa-aš*	8.4 rev. 17′
	ka-lu-up-pa-aš	8.4 rev. 12′
	ga-lu-pa-aš	2.15 l. c. 9′
	^{TÚG}*ka-lu-pa-aš*	2.7.A obv. 9
	^{TÚG}*ka-lu-up-pa-aš*	2.7.A obv. 8. 6.13 3′. 9.1.1 rev. iii 39′
	^{TÚG}*ga-lu-up-pa-aš*	9.1.8 obv. 11′
	$^{\text{TÚ]G}}$*ka-lu-pa-aš*	6.8 1′
	^{TÚG}*k]a-lu-pa-aš*	6.9 obv. 12′
	^{TÚG}*ka-lu-up-pa-a[š*	9.2.1 obv. ii 21′
	$^{\text{*TÚG*}}$*ka-lu-p[a-aš*	11.6.4 obv. 7′
	^{TÚG}*ka-lu-[pa-aš*	6.5 rev. 17′
	^{TÚG}*ka-l[u-pa-aš*	10.1.2.1 obv.$^{?}$ r. c. 4′
	^{TÚG}*ka-l[u-up-pa-aš*(?)	9.2.6 obv. i 8′
pl. coll. nom.	^{TÚG}*k]a-lu-up-pa*	9.2.9 obv.$^{?}$ 9′
see *Lexical Commentary*		
kalup(p)ašša/i-	(a kind of fastener)	
sg. nom.	*ka-lu-pa-aš-ši-iš*	8.4 rev. 6′
	ga-lu-pa-aš-ši-iš	1.5 obv. 6
	ka-lu-up-pa-aš-ši-iš	9.1.10.A_1 obv. 5′. 9.2.2 rev.$^{!}$ iii 21′
	ka-lu]-pa-aš-ši-iš	9.1.10.B 9′
see *Lexical Commentary*		
-kan	(sentence particle)	
	-kán	1.1.A_1 obv. 4′, 11′, 12′, 14′, 17′. 1.1.A_2 obv. 4′; rev. 1, 7. 1.1.A_3 rev. 1′. 2.1.A obv. i(?) 2′, 7′. 2.2 rev. 8. 2.5 obv. 3′. 2.7.A obv. 2, 4, 17, 18, 25. 2.9.A_1 obv. i 6′. 2.9.A_3 obv. i 9′, 11′. 2.12 obv.$^{!}$ ii 2′. 2.16 obv. i 5′, 10′. 3.1.1.A_3 obv. iii 6′. 4.1.1.1.A_1 rev. 5′, 20′. 4.1.3.2 obv. 1′; rev. 2′, 7′, 8′, 11′. 4.2.1.A_1 obv. 3. 4.2.2 obv. 3. 4.2.4 obv. 2. 5.1 rev. iii 2, 7. 6.3 obv. 5, 6. 7.4 3′. 8.1.A obv. ii 16′; rev. v 19′; rev. vi 1′. 8.1.E(A_1) obv. ii 7. 8.6 l. c. 7′. 9.1.4.A_1 obv. ii 19, 28. 9.1.5 rev.$^{!}$ 7′. 9.1.6 obv. 7, 10. 9.1.7 obv. 5′. 9.1.8 obv. 12′. 9.2.1 obv. ii 8′. 9.2.2 rev.$^{!}$ iii 2′. 9.2.9 obv.$^{?}$ 10′. 9.2.12 3′. 10.2.1.1 obv. 8′. 10.2.1.2 obv. 14′. 10.2.1.6 2′. 12.1.4 6′
	-kán	11.2.1 5′
	-k]án	1.1.A_2 rev. 3′
	-ká]n	2.16 obv. i 3′
	-ká[n	2.5 obv. 5′. 9.1.4.A_1 obv. i 24′
	-k[án	2.5 obv. 2′. 7.1 rev. 9′. 8.1.F obv. ii 14′. 12.1.4 8′
kangant-	'hanging, pendant; weighing, weighed' (ptc. of *kang-*, *kanki(ya)-*)	
sg. nom.-acc. n.	*kán-ga-an*	2.2 rev. 9
pl. nom.	(*katta*) *ká[n-ga-an-te-eš*(?)	4.2.6 rev.$^{?}$ 6′
kanganuškant-	'caused to hang; weighed out' (iter. ptc. of *kanganu-*)	
sg. nom.-acc. n.	*k]án-ga-nu-uš-kán*	3.1.1.A_2 rev. vi 5′

kanduna-	(part of a bow)	
pl. nom.-acc. n.(?)	*kán-du-na*	2.17 obv.$^?$ r. c. 11′
see *Lexical Commentary*		
$^{\text{(TÚG)}}$*kaparzu-*	(a garment or fabric type)	
sg. nom.-acc. n.	^{TÚG}*ka-pár-zu*	6.5 obv. 9′, 11′
sg. gen.	*ka-pár-zu-wa-*[*aš*$^?$	8.8.B l. c. 3′
	ka-[*pár-zu-wa-aš*$^?$	8.8.A 3′
see *Lexical Commentary*		
kapata-	(an object of gold and stone)	
sg. nom.	](-)*ka-pa-ta-aš*	9.2.5 obv. i(?) 3′
kapina-	‘thread, yarn’	
pl. nom.(?)	*ka-pí-nu-uš*	2.2 rev. 3
$^{\text{(TÚG/KUŠ)}}$*kapittašamna-*		
see (TÚG/KUŠ) *kapi(r)t(t)aš(š)amna-*		
$^{\text{NA}_4}$*kabši-*	(a variegated/marbled stone?)	
material		
sg. nom.	$^{\text{NA}_4}$*kab-ši-iš*	9.2.4 obv. i 4′
see *Lexical Commentary*; = $^{\text{NA}_4}$*KIBŠU*?		
karat-	‘innards, entrails’	
pl. nom.	*ka_4-ra+a*(?)*-ti-iš*	12.3.4 obv. 5
^{URUDU}*garipa-*x[	(a copper object)	
	^{URUDU}*ga-ri-pa-*x[	9.1.8 obv. 13′
$^{\text{(GIŠ)}}$*karnaš(š)a-*	(a variety of chair)	
sg. acc.	^{GIŠ}*kar-na-aš-ša-an*	10.2.1.1 obv. 4′
sg. gen.	^{GIŠ}*kar-na-ša-aš*	11.6.2 l. e. 6
	k]*ar-na-ša-aš*	4.2.9 rev. 5′
sg. dat./loc.	^{GIŠ}*kar-na-ši*	4.1.4.9 obv. 3
pl. coll. nom.	*kar-na-ša*	4.2.9 rev. 7′
	kar-n]*a-aš-ša*	4.2.9 rev. 6′
	$^{\text{(GIŠ)}}$*kar-n*]*a-aš-ša*	4.2.6 obv.$^?$ 3′
see *Lexical Commentary*		
karpant-	‘taken up, lifted, raised’ (ptc. of *karp-*)	
sg. nom.-acc. n.	*kar-ap-pa-an*	9.2.1 obv. ii 13′
	kar-ap-pa-a]*n*(?)	9.2.1 rev. iii 7′
karta(i)-	‘to cut off’	
ptc.?	*kar-t*[*a-*	6.1 rev. A 2′
see also GADA *kartawaš*		
karu	‘already’	
	ka-ru-ú	4.1.1.1.A_1 rev. 6′. 4.1.1.1.B_1 rev. iii$^?$ 2, 5, 10. 4.1.4.9 obv. 3, 4
	ka-ru-ú	1.2 rev. 11′
	k]*a-ru-ú*	2.2 rev. 9
^{TÚG}*karupalani-*	(a garment)	
sg. nom.-acc. n.	^{TÚG}*ka-ru-pa-la-ni*	6.10 7′
	^{TÚG}*ka-r*[*u-pa-la-ni*(?)	10.1.2.6 1′
see *Lexical Commentary*; see also É.GAL *karupaḫi-*		

gaši-	'(off)-white'	
sg. nom.	*ga-ši-iš*	4.1.3.5.A_1 obv.$^{?}$ 2′, 3′, 4′. 6.11 5′
	ga-š]i-iš	4.1.3.5.A_1 obv.$^{?}$ 5′
	ga-ši-i[š	4.1.3.5.A_1 obv.$^{?}$ 1′. 4.1.3.5.A_2 3′
	ga-š[i-iš	4.1.3.5.A_2 1′, 2′
	ga-[ši-iš	4.1.3.5.A_2 6′
stem	*ga-ši*	4.1.3.4.A_1 obv. l. c. 1′, 2′, 3′, 4′, 5′; rev. l. c. 1′, 3′, 4′, 5′, 6′. 4.1.3.4.A_2 rev. l. c. 2′, 3′, 4′, 5′, 6′, 7′, 8′. 4.1.3.8 rev. A 3′, 4′
	g]a-ši	4.1.3.4.A_1 obv. l. c. 6′
	ga-š]i	4.1.3.4.A_1 obv. l. c. 7′
	ga-š[i	4.1.3.4.A_1 rev. l. c. 7′
	ga-[ši	4.1.3.4.A_2 rev. l. c. 9′
	g[a-ši	4.1.3.4.A_2 rev. l. c. 1′. 4.1.3.8 rev. A 1′
see *Lexical Commentary*; see also *ašara-*, *ḫarki-*, BABBAR		
katta	'down(wards)' (preverb)	
	kat-ta (*kang-*)	4.2.6 rev.$^{?}$ 6′
	kat-ta (*parzam(m)a/i-*)	9.2.2 rev.$^{!}$ iii 8′. 11.2.2 7′
kattan	'below (postposition), down(wards)' (preverb)	
	kat-an (*ue-/uwa-*)	6.1 l. e. 1c.
$^{(GADA)}$*gaz(z)arnul-*	'drying swatch'	
sg. nom.-acc. n.	*ga]z-za-ar-n[u-ul*	4.2.10 4′
	^{GADA}*gaz-za-ar-nu-ul*	9.2.9 rev.$^{?}$ 4′
	^{GADA}*ka-za-ar-nu-ul*	6.5 rev. 21′
	$^{G]ADA}$*ga-za-ar-[nu-ul*	11.6.4 rev. 5′
	^{GADA}*g]a-za-ar-n[u-ul*	11.6.4 l. e. 1′
see *Lexical Commentary*		
ki-	'to lie, be placed (mid.)'	
pret. sg. 3	*ki-it-ta-ri*	4.2.4 rev. 5′
kiklibaim(m)a/i-	'made of/plated with metallic iron(?)'	
Luw. pl. nom.	*ki-ik-li-ba-i-me-en-zi*	9.1.1 rev. iv 26′
see *Lexical Commentary*; see also *ḫapalki-*, *parzagulliya-*, *parzašša-*, AN.BAR, AN.BAR GE_6, *ḪAPALKI(N)NU*		
kikpaniš	(a vessel type)	
sg. nom.-acc. n.	*ki-ik-pa-ni-iš*	1.2 rev. 8′. 4.1.1.5 obv. 3
gimra-	'field'	
sg. gen.	*gi-i]m-ra-aš*	8.8.B l. c. 5′
= LÍL; = A.ŠÀ?; see also GÍR *gimraš*		
kinant-	'assorted; choice' (ptc. of *kina(i)-*)	
sg. gen.	*ki-i-na-a-an-ta-aš*	2.7.A obv. 21, 22
	ki-i-na-a-an-da-a[š	2.9.A_2 obv. i 9′
	ki-i-na-a-an-[ta-aš	8.1.D obv. i 11′
	k[i-i-na-a-an-ta-aš(?)	2.15 l. c. 4′
see *Lexical Commentary*		
kingali-	(an object?)	
sg. nom.	*ki-in-ga-liš*	10.3.12 obv. i 21′
$^{(UZU)}$*genu-/ganu-*	'knee, lap, loins'	
sg. nom.-acc. n.	$^{U]ZU}$*ga-nu*	9.1.4.A_1 obv. 2
pl. nom.-acc. n.	*ge-nu-wa*	10.2.1.7 rev.$^{?}$ 5′. 10.3.2 obv. i(?) 5″

pl. dat./loc.	*ge-nu-wa-aš*	10.2.1.1 obv. 8′
see also GADA *genuwaš*		
(𒑱)*kinzalpa-*	(an object or ornament)	
sg. nom.	*ki-in-za-al-pa-aš*	9.1.1 rev. iii 36′
	ki]*-in-za-al-pa-aš*	1.1.A_1 obv. 7′
	ki-i[*n-za-al-pa-aš*	9.1.1 rev. iii 37′
Luw. gen. adj. sg. nom.	𒑱*ki-in-za-al-pa-aš-ši-iš*	9.1.1 rev. iii 5′
see *Lexical Commentary*		
gipeššar	‘cubit, ell’	
sg. nom.-acc. n.	*gi-pé-eš*]*-šar*(?)	10.2.1.4 4′
	gi-pé-eš-ša[*r*	8.7 r. c. 8′
	g[*i-pé-eš-šar*(?)	10.2.1.4 5′
($^{\text{NA}_4}$)(𒑱)*kirinni-*	‘carnelian, porphyry(?)’	
sg. nom.	$^{\text{NA}_4}$*k*]*i-ri-in-ni-eš*	2.14 8′
material		
pl. coll. nom.	*ki-ri-in-na*	8.4 rev. 8′
	𒑱*ki-ri-in-na*	1.5 obv. 7
see *Lexical Commentary*; = $^{\text{NA}_4}$GUG?		
$^{(\text{TÚG})}$*kišam(m)a/i-*	‘combed/carded (wool)’ (garment name or adj.)	
sg. nom.	*ki-ša-me-i*[*š*	11.1.3 6′
	^{TÚG}*ki-ša-me-eš*	2.12 obv.$^{!}$ ii 6′
	^{TÚG}*k*]*i-ša-me-iš*	3.2.2 obv.$^{?}$ 11′
	^{TÚG}*ki-ša-*[*me-iš*	8.1.F obv. ii 18′
sg. nom.-acc. n.	*ki-ša-ma*	4.2.6 obv.$^{?}$ 9′. 11.6.5 obv.$^{?}$ 6
	k]*i-ša-ma*	4.2.6 obv.$^{?}$ 5′
	ki]*-ša-ma*	4.2.6 obv.$^{?}$ 18′
	ki(?)*-š*]*a-ma*	2.11 obv.$^{?}$ 2′
stem	*ki-ša-me*	3.2.1 obv. 14
	^{TÚG}*ki-ša-me*	3.2.1 rev. 17′
abbr.	^{TÚG}*ki-ša.*	11.6.1 5
kitkar	‘at the head of, on top of’ (postposition)	
	ki-it-kar	8.1.F rev. v 12
kui-	‘who’ (interrogative/relative pron.)	
sg. nom.	*ku-iš*	6.1 rev. B 4. 7.1 rev. 5′
sg. nom.-acc. n.	*ku-it*	7.1 rev. 6′. 8.1.E(A_3) rev. vi 8. 8.6 l. c. 7′
	ku-it	1.2 rev. 11′, 12′
sg. dat./loc.	*ku-e-da-ni*	5.1 rev. iii 7
pl. nom.	*ku-i-e-e*[*š*	4.2.10 9′
	ku-i-e-[*eš*	1.1.A_4 rev. 4′
pl. nom.-acc. n.	*ku-e*	2.2 obv. 6′
kuiški	‘whoever’ (indefinite pron.)	
sg. nom.	*k*]*u-iš-ki*	2.5 obv. 4′
sg. nom.-acc. n.	*ku-i*]*t-ki*	8.1.E(A_3) rev. vi 12
kuišša	‘each, every’ (distributive pron.)	
sg. nom.	*ku-iš-ša*	8.1.F rev. vi 4
sg. dat./loc.	*ku-e-d*]*a-ni-ia*	8.1.F rev. vi 5
^{TÚG}*kuku(l)laim(m)a/i-*	(a garment)	
sg. nom.	^{TÚG}*ku-ku-la-i-me-eš*	9.2.9 rev.$^{?}$ 3′
	^{TÚG}*ku-gul-la-*⟨*i*⟩*-me-iš*	11.1.3 5′

pl. nom.-acc. n.	^{TÚG}]*ku-gul-la-a-im-ma*	6.6 rev. 7′
	^{TÚG}*ku-gul-l*]*a-im-ma*	6.7 obv.$^?$ 2
^{DUG}*kukupalla(nt$^?$)-*	(a flask for liquids/ointments)	
sg. nom.-acc. n.	^{DUG}*ku-ku-pa-al-la-an*	10.1.1.1 rev.$^?$ 12′
	^{DUG}*ku-ku-pa-al-l*[*a-an*	10.1.1.1 rev.$^?$ 11′
see *Lexical Commentary*; = ^{DUG}ḪAB.ḪAB, *KU(K)KU(B)BU*		
kula-	'pendant, chain-link'	
sg. nom.	*ku-la-aš*	2.13 rev.$^?$ 3′. 4.2.6 rev. 6′. 8.4 rev. 14′
	ku-u-la-aš	9.1.1 rev. iv 4′, 18′. 9.2.4 obv. i 14′. 9.2.5 obv. i(?) 6′, 7′, 9′
	k]*u-u-la-aš*	9.2.4 obv. i 7′. 9.2.5 obv. i(?) 8′
	ku-[*u-la-aš*	9.2.5 obv. i(?) 8′
kulaim(m)a/i-	'fitted with pendants/links' (Luw. ptc. of *kula-*)	
sg. nom.	*ku-la$^!$-i-mi-iš*	6.5 rev. 17′
Luw. pl. nom.	*ku-la-i-me-en-zi*	9.2.1 obv. ii 16′
kulant-	'fitted with pendants/links' (ptc. of *kula(i)-*)	
sg. nom.-acc. n.	*ku-la-a-an*	8.4 rev. 5′
	ku-u-la-an	9.2.2 rev.$^!$ iii 23′
gul(aš)šant-	'inscribed, marked (down)'	
ptc. sg. nom.-acc. n.	*gul-aš-ša-an*	2.7.A obv. 3, 13. 2.7.B rev. 7′
	g]*ul-aš-ša-an*	2.7.B rev. 2′
see *Lexical Commentary*		
^{NA_4}*kunkunuzi-* material	(a hard rock, e.g., basalt, granite, or diorite)	
sg. nom.	$^{NA_4?}$*k*]*u-un-ku-nu-zi-iš*	4.2.1.A_1 obv. 11
= ŠU.U?		
$^{(GIŠ)}$*kupa-*	(an object made of wood or ivory)	
sg. nom.	*ku-u-pa-aš*	9.2.6 obv. i 5′
	^{GIŠ}*ku-pa-aš*	5.6 4′
	^{GIŠ}*ku-pa-a*[*š$^?$*	9.1.12 7′
^{TÚG}*kureššar*	'a cut of cloth'	
sg. nom.-acc. n.	^{TÚG}*ku-re-eš-šar*	1.1.A_1 obv. 16′
	$^{TÚG!}$*ku-re-eš-šar*	11.6.5 obv.$^?$ 9
	^{TÚG}*ku*]*-re-eš-šar*	4.2.9 rev. 15′
	^{TÚG}*ku*]*-re-eš-ša*[*r*	11.6.4 rev. 3′
kurupšini-	(an animal)	
sg. nom.	*ku-r*]*u-up-ši-ni-iš*	2.2 rev. 6
pl. nom.	*ku-*]*ru-up-ši-ni-uš*	10.1.2.5 3′
see *Lexical Commentary*		
kurutauwant-	'helmeted'	
sg. nom.	*ku-ru-ta-u-wa-an-za*	9.1.4.A_1 obv. i 26′
	ku-ru-ta(?)]*-u-*[*w*]*a-an-za*	9.1.4.A_1 obv. i 11′
$^{(TÚG)}$*kuššati-*	(a garment or cloth type)	
sg. nom.-acc. n.	*ku-uš-ša-ti*	4.2.6 obv.$^?$ 5′, 18′. 6.5 rev. 16. 9.2.9 rev.$^?$ 2′. 10.1.2.6 2′. 11.6.5 obv.$^?$ 6. 11.6.7 5′
	ku-uš-š]*a-ti*	4.2.6 obv.$^?$ 9′
	ku-uš-š[*a-ti*	4.2.7 5′
	^{TÚG}*ku-uš-ša-di*	2.7.A obv. 6. 6.9 obv. 6′. 6.13 7′. 8.1.F obv. i 20′

	^{TÚG}*ku-uš*$^{!}$*-⟨ša⟩-ti*	6.12 7′
	^{TÚ}]^{G}*ku-uš-ša-di*	8.1.E(A_1) rev. v 7′
	^{TÚG}*k*]*u-uš-ša-di*	11.6.6 rev. 11′
	^{TÚG}*k*]*u-uš-š*[*a-ti*	11.6.4 obv. 4′
	^{TÚG}*ku-uš-š*[*a-di*	8.1.E(A_1) obv. iii 8′
	^{TÚG}*ku-u*[*š-ša-di*	4.1.4.7 obv. 4
abbr.	^{TÚG}*ku.*	9.1.1 rev. iv 43′
	^{TÚG}*ku-uš.*	11.6.1 2, 3, 5, 7, 11
see *Lexical Commentary*		
$^{\text{(TÚG)}}$*kušiši-*	(a cloth or garment)	
sg. nom.-acc. n.	*ku-ši-ši*	6.5 rev. 11′
	ku-ši-[*ši*	6.5 rev. 16′
	^{TÚG}*ku-ši-ši*	8.1.D rev. iv 1′. 9.1.6 obv. 1. 11.6.1 7
	^{TÚG}*ku-ši-ši⟨⟨ki⟩⟩*	4.1.1.1.A_1 obv. 9′
	^{TÚG}*k*[*u-ši-ši*(?)	8.1.H rev. r. c. 1′
abbr.	^{TÚG}*ku-ši.*	11.6.1 3
see *Lexical Commentary*		
kuwalma-	(a decorative object made of metal)	
sg. nom.	*ku-wa-al-ma-aš*	2.13 rev.$^{?}$ 5′. 10.3.3 obv.$^{?}$ 10′
	ku-wa-al-maš	8.1.A obv. ii 2′
	ku-wa-al-m[*a-aš*	11.1.1 r. c. 12′
kuwaluti-	(a piece of jewelry made of metal and stone)	
sg. nom.	*ku-wa-lu-ti-iš*	3.1.8.A obv. 15′. 9.1.1 rev. iii 16′
	ku-u-wa-lu-ti-iš	9.2.4 obv. i 15′
	ku-u-wa-lu-ti-⟨iš⟩	9.2.4 obv. i 5′
	k]*u-*u-wa*-lu-ti-iš*	9.2.5 obv. i(?) 11′
	ku-wa-l]*u-ti-iš*	3.1.8.A obv. 17′
kuwapi	'when/where' (interrog./rel. temporal/local adverb)	
	ku-wa-pí	2.12 obv.$^{!}$ ii 2′. 4.1.3.2 rev. 6′. 5.1 rev. iii 2. 6.1 obv. 19
	k]*u-wa-pí*	2.9.A_2 obv. i 10′
	ku]*-wa-pí*	2.10 4′
	ku-w]*a-pí*	5.1 rev. iii 4
^{KUŠ}*kuwar(-)*	(?)	
broken	^{KUŠ}*ku-wa-a*[*r(-)*	9.2.4 rev. iii 9′
laḫḫa-	'(military) campaign'	
sg. dat./loc.	*l*]*a*$^{?}$*-aḫ-ḫi*	8.5 rev. iv(?) 6′
laḫḫura-	'pot stand, offering table(?)'	
sg. nom.	*la-aḫ-ḫu-ra-aš*	2.17 obv.$^{?}$ r. c. 9′
laḫ(ḫ)u(wa)-, *laḫ(ḫ)uwa(i)-* 'to pour, pour out; to empty (a container)'		
pret. pl. 3	(EGIR-*pa*) *la-ḫu-wa-a-er*	5.1 rev. iv 3
see also ^{URUDU}UGU *laḫuaš*		
$^{\text{(GADA/TÚG)}}$*lak(k)ušanzani-* 'bed sheets, bed clothes'		
sg. nom.	^{TÚG}*la-ku-ša-an-za-ni-iš*	4.2.9 rev. 23′
	^{TÚG}*la-ku*]*-ša-an-za-ni-iš*	4.2.9 rev. 9′
	^{TÚG}*l*]*a-ku-ša-*[*a*]*n-za-ni-*[*iš*	4.2.9 rev. 1′
pl. nom.	^{GADA}*la-ak-ku-ša-an-za-ni-eš*	9.1.10.A_2 rev. 10′
	^{GADA}*la-ak-ku-ša-an-za-ni-*[*eš*	9.1.10.A_1 obv. 8′
	^{GADA}*la-ak-*[*ku-ša-an-za-ni-eš*	9.1.10.B 12′

Luw. pl. nom.	*la-ak-ku-ša-an-za-ni-en-zi*	8.1.F rev. v 15
pl. acc.	^{GADA}*la-ak-ku-ša-an-za-ni-uš*	10.3.14 l. c. 9′
broken	$^{\text{TÚG*}}$*la*-ku-ša-a[n-za-ni-*	11.1.3 8′
	la-a]k-ku-ša-an-za-n[i-	11.1.4 5′
see *Lexical Commentary*		
lalami-	'list, accounting receipt'	
sg. nom.	*la-la-meš*	4.1.1.1.B_2 obv. i$^?$ 2′
	la-la-me-eš	4.1.1.1.A_1 obv. 4′, 14′, 15′, 16′. 4.1.1.9 8′. 6.1 up. e. 1; obv. 5, 11, 15
	la-la-m]e-eš	6.1 obv. 19
see *Lexical Commentary*		
lalinaim(m)a/i-	'set/endowed with a *lalini-*'	
sg. nom.	*la-li-na-i-me-iš*	9.2.2 rev.$^!$ iv 21′
	la-[l]i-in-na-i-me-eš	9.2.1 obv. ii 23′
Luw. pl. nom.	*la-li-na-i-me-en-zi*	9.1.1 rev. iv 44′
see *Lexical Commentary*		
(≮)*lalini-*	"tonguelet(?)"	
sg. nom.-acc. n.	*la-li-ni*	8.4 rev. 6′
	≮*la-li-[ni*	1.5 obv. 6
see *Lexical Commentary*		
lammam(m)a/i-	(?)	
sg. nom.	*lam-ma-mi-iš*	9.1.1 rev. iv 26′
	lam-ma-am-mi-iš	9.2.1 rev. iii 21′
Luw. pl. nom.	*lam-ma-me-en-zi*	9.2.1 rev. iii 26′
see *Lexical Commentary*		
lamnia-	'to name, enumerate, assign'	
broken	*lam-ni-ia-[*	10.2.2.1 6′
^{URUDU}*lammuwant-*	(?)	
sg. nom.-acc. n.	^{URUDU}*la-am-mu-wa-an*	3.1.1.A_3 rev. iv 2′
pl. nom.-acc. n.	^{URUDU}*la-am-m]u(?)-wa-an-ta*	3.1.1.A_1 obv. ii 1′
lappanuwant-	'kindled, glowing' (ptc. of *lap(pa)nu-*)	
sg. nom.-acc. n.	*la-ap-pa-nu-wa-an*	9.2.1 obv. ii 14′. 9.2.5 obv. i(?) 2′
lapattašši-	(?)	
sg. nom.(?)	*la-pa-at-ta-aš-ši-eš*	10.1.2.8 rev. r. c. 4′
see *Lexical Commentary*		
≮*lapiya-*	(?)	
sg. nom.	≮*la-pí-ia-aš*	10.1.2.8 rev. r. c. 3′
see *Lexical Commentary*		
le	'not' (prohibitive particle)	
	le]-e	2.5 obv. 4′
(DINGIR) *lulaḫ(ḫ)i-*	'mountain-dweller; (a class of deities)'	
pl. nom.	(DINGIR.ME]Š) *lu-la-ḫi-ú-uš*	10.1.1.2 rev. iv 7
lup/wan(n)i-	'cap, pommel (of a knife, rhyton)'	
sg. nom.	*lu-pa-an-ni-eš*	9.1.1 rev. iii 10′. 9.1.4.A_1 obv. i 27′. 9.1.15 6′. 9.2.4 rev. iv 5, 6. 10.2.1.2 obv. 5′
	lu-wa-an-ni-eš	9.1.10.A_1 rev. 2′
	lu-pa-an-n[i-eš	9.1.1 rev. iii 8′

	lu-ba-an-[*ni-eš*	9.1.1 rev. iii 9′
	lu-pa-[*an-ni-eš*	9.2.4 rev. iv 3
see *Lexical Commentary*		
$^{\text{(TÚG/GADA)}}$*lup/wan(n)i-*	(a headdress) ‘cap (vel sim.)’	
sg. nom.	*lu-pa-an-ni-eš*	6.5 rev. 15′. 9.1.9 rev. iv 2′
	l[*u*]*-pa-ni-iš*	2.7.A obv. 9
	l[*u-up-pa-ni*(?)	4.2.10 3′
	^{GADA}*lu-pa-an-ni-eš*	11.6.2 l. e. 2
	^{TÚG}*lu-pa-an-ni-iš*	6.5 rev. 9′. 8.1.K rev. vi$^?$ 6′
	^{TÚG}*lu-pa-an-ni-eš*	6.5 rev. 12′
	^{TÚG}*lu-up-pa-an-ni*(-)[	11.1.1 r. c. 5′
	^{TÚG}*lu-pa-an-ni-i*[*š*	6.6 obv. 4′. 11.6.4 obv. 8′
	^{TÚG}*lu-pa-an-*[*ni-iš*$^?$	8.8.B r. c. 7′
	^{TÚG}*l*[*u-pa-an-ni-iš*	8.1.K rev. v$^?$ 7′
sg. nom.-acc. n.?	^{TÚG}*lu-pa-ni*	6.3 obv. 2
	^{TÚG}*lu-pa-an-ni*	2.9.A_3 obv. ii 11′. 6.10 9′
	^{TÚG}*l*]*u-p*[*a*]*-an-ni*	6.9 obv. 8′
	^{TÚG}*lu*]*-pa-an-ni*	8.1.F obv. i 16′
	^{TÚG}*lu-pa*]*-an-ni*	6.6 obv. 8′
	^{TÚG}*lu-pa-a*]*n-ni*	6.10 5′
see *Lexical Commentary*		
mallitalli-	‘honey pot(?)’	
Luw. pl. nom.	*ma-al-li-ta-al-li-en-zi*	9.1.1 rev. iv 31′
malwi-	(?)	
sg. nom.	*ma-al-ú-i-iš*	2.17 obv.$^?$ r. c. 2′
	ma-al-wi$_5$*-*iš**	2.17 obv.$^?$ r. c. 1′
$^{\text{NA}_4}$*mamḫuišta-*	(a stone)	
	$^{\text{NA}_4}$*ma-am-ḫu-iš-t*[*a*	2.1.A obv. ii(?) 8′
man	if, when (clause-initial conjunction)	
	ma-a-[*an*(?)	7.1 rev. 15′
mannaiya/i-	(adj. applied to containers) ‘bulging(?)’	
sg. nom.	*ma*$^!$*-an-na-iš*	8.1.F rev. v 5
	ma-an-na-[*iš*	8.1.G obv. r. c. 8′
	ma$^!$*-an-n*[*a-iš*(?)	12.1.3 5′
	ma-a[*n-na-iš*(?)	11.6.1 6
see *Lexical Commentary*		
mannin(n)i-	(a type of necklace)	
sg. nom.	*ma-an-ni-ni-iš*	9.1.1 rev. iii 14′
	ma-an-ni-in-ni-iš	9.2.2 rev.$^!$ iii 3′
pl. nom.	*ma-an-ni-ni-uš*	1.5 obv 8
	ma-a]*n-ni-ni-uš*	9.2.9 obv.$^?$ 8′
broken	*ma-an-*[*ni-ni-*(?)	10.2.1.5 1′
see also *pennati-*		
^{GIŠ}*manzari-*	(a vessel?)	
sg. nom.-acc. n.	^{GIŠ}*ma-an-za-ri*	5.7 rev. iii$^?$ 27′
see *Lexical Commentary*		
^{GIŠ}*marawirali-*	(a container)	
sg. nom.	^{GIŠ}*ma-ra-u-i-ra-liš*	8.1.A rev. v 29′

≮*mariḫši-* 'fuzz(?), lint(?)' (an impurity removed during cloth processing)
inst. *QA-DU*≮*ma-ri-iḫ-*[*ši* 4.1.3.3 10′

$^{\text{NA}_4}$*marruwašḫa-* (a mineral)
$^{\text{N}]\text{A}_4}$*mar-ru-wa-aš-ḫa*-x(-)x[2.1.A obv. ii(?) 5′
see *Lexical Commentary*

maruša- 'dark-colored, black'
Luw. adj. sg. gen. *ma-ru-ša-ša-aš* 2.7.A obv. 16
broken *ma-ru-ša-ša*(-)[2.9.A_2 obv. i 13′
see *Lexical Commentary*

marušam(m)a/i- 'darkened, blackened'
sg. nom. *ma-ru-ša-me-eš* 8.1.E(A_1) rev. iv 2′
ma-r[*u-ša-me-eš* 8.1.E(A_1) rev. iv 5′
pl. nom. *ma-ru-ša-me-iš* 8.1.E(A_1) rev. iv 3′
ma-ru-š]*a-me-iš* 8.1.E(A_1) obv. ii 4
ma-ru-ša-m[*e-iš* 8.1.E(A_1) obv. ii 2
ma-r[*u-ša-me-iš* 8.1.E(A_1) rev. iv 6′
pl. nom.-acc. n. *m*]*a-ru-ša-ma* 4.1.4.8 2′
ma]*-ru-ša-ma* 8.1.E(A_2) 6′
ma-ru-[*ša-ma* 8.1.E(A_2) 9′
see *Lexical Commentary*

maššayašši- (made of *maššia*-cloth?)
sg. nom. *maš-ša-ia-aš-ši-iš* 8.1.F rev. vi 15
see *Lexical Commentary*; see also $^{\text{(TÚG)}}$*maššia-*

$^{\text{(TÚG)}}$*maššia-* 'shawl, scarf(?); (a fabric type(?))'
sg. nom. *maš-ši-aš* 4.1.3.8 rev. B 2′. 6.5 rev. 11′, 14′, 25′
^{TÚG}*maš-ši-aš* 1.5 obv. 9. 2.5 obv. 2′. 3.2.1 rev. 9′. 3.2.5 r. c. 3′. 4.2.9 obv. 1; rev. 11′. 6.1 obv. 2. 6.3 rev. B 1. 6.5 rev. 8′. 8.1.E(A_1) obv. ii 3; obv. iii 6′. 8.1.F obv. i 8′. 8.1.G obv. l. c. 2′. 11.6.2 rev. 9′
$^{\text{TÚ]G}}$*maš-ši-ia-aš* 11.6.6 rev. 7′
$^{\text{TÚG]}}$*maš-ši-aš* 3.2.1 obv. 2. 6.6 rev. 6′
^{TÚG}*m*]*aš-ši-aš* 11.1.7 6′
^{TÚG}*maš*]*-ši-aš* 3.2.1 rev. 4′. 8.1.G obv. r. c. 10′
^{TÚG}*maš-ši-a*[*š* 11.6.1 7
^{TÚG}*maš-*[*ši-aš* 6.6 rev. 6′
stem ^{TÚG}*maš-ši* 3.2.1 obv. 14, 16
$^{\text{TÚ]G}}$*maš-ši* 3.2.1 rev. 13′
$^{\text{TÚG]}}$*maš-ši* 3.2.1 rev. 17′. 6.7 obv.$^{?}$ 1
^{TÚG}*maš-š*[*i* 6.7 obv.$^{?}$ 1
abbr. ^{TÚG}*maš.* 3.2.1 obv. 20
see *Lexical Commentary*; = ^{TÚG}ŠÀ.GA/KA.DÙ?

$^{\text{(TÚG)}}$*mazakanni-* (a garment)
sg. nom. *ma-za-kán*$^{!}$*-ni-iš* 8.4 rev. 14′
^{TÚG}*ma-za-kán-ni-iš* 2.7.A obv. 7
^{TÚG}*ma-za-ga-an-ni-eš* 6.5 rev. 17′
^{TÚG}*ma-za-ga-an-ni-iš* 1.5 obv. 3. 8.1.D rev. iv 4′
^{TÚG}*ma-za-g*[*a-an-ni-iš* 6.12 6′
pl. acc. ^{TÚG}*ma-za-ga-an-ni-uš* 9.1.1 rev. iii 18′

mekki-	'much, many'	
sg. nom.	*me-ek-⟨ka$_4$⟩-eš*	3.1.1.A_1 obv. ii 5′
memiya(n)-	'word, deed, matter'	
broken	*me-mi-ia-an*(-)[	4.1.3.7 rev. 3′
^{TÚG}*mezziluri-*	(a garment)	
sg. nom.-acc. n.	^{TÚG}*me-ez-zi-lu-u-ri*	9.1.8 obv. 10′
mulatar	(?)	
sg. nom.-acc. n.	*mu-la-tar*	11.6.2 rev. 11′
$^{\text{NA}_4}$*mušnuwanti-*	(a stone)	
sg. nom.	$^{\text{NA}_4}$*mu-uš-nu-wa-an-te-eš*	9.1.4.A_1 obv. ii 28
	$^{\text{NA}_4}$*m*]*u-uš-nu-an-te-eš*	10.2.1.1 obv. 13′
	$^{\text{NA}_4}$*mu*]*-uš-nu-wa-an-ti-iš*	8.1.D obv. i 7′
	$^{\text{NA}_4}$*mu-uš-nu-wa-a*[*n-te-eš*	9.1.4.A_1 obv. ii 22
	$^{\text{NA}_4}$*mu-u*[*š-nu-wa-an-te-eš*	2.14 15′. 9.1.4.A_1 obv. ii 18
	$^{\text{NA}_4}$*m*[*u-uš-nu-wa-an-ti-iš*	9.2.9 obv.$^?$ 14′
namma	'then'	
	nam-ma	2.9.A_2 obv. i 1′, 3′. 4.1.1.1.A_1 rev. 18′. 4.1.1.1.B_1 rev. iii$^?$ 14
	na]*m-ma*	4.1.1.2.A obv. 6′
nawi	'not yet'	
	na-wi$_5$	2.7.A obv. 18
	na-a-wi$_5$	2.7.A obv. 11
nu	'and, now' (clause-linking conjunction, usually untranslated)	
	nu	1.5 rev. 27′. 2.17 obv.$^?$ r. c. 19′. 4.1.1.1.B_1 rev. iii$^?$ 10. 4.2.9 obv. 19. 6.1 rev. B 7. 8.1.F rev. v 9. 9.1.5 rev.$^!$ 10′, 14′, 15′. 9.1.6 obv. 2, 4, 8. 9.1.8 obv. 7′, 15′. 9.1.14 obv. r. c. 6′. 9.2.3 obv. (ii) 6″
	nu	9.1.1 rev. iii 39′
	na-aš-kán (= *nu* + *aš* + *kán*)	12.1.4 8′
	na-aš-ta (= *nu* + *ašta*)	4.1.1.1.B_1 rev. iii$^?$ 14, 16
	n]*a-aš-ta* (= *nu* + *ašta*)	4.1.1.1.A_1 rev. 18′
	na-at (= *nu* + *at*)	8.1.E(A_3) rev. vi 7. 4.1.1.1.B_1 rev. iii$^?$ 10, 15
	na-at-kán (= *nu* + *at* + *kán*)	1.1.A_1 obv. 17′. 4.1.1.1.B_1 rev. iii$^?$ 16. 4.1.1.7 rev.$^{!?}$ 2. 4.2.1.A_1 obv. 3
	n]*a-at-kán* (= *nu* + *at* + *kán*)	4.1.1.1.A_1 rev. 20′
	nu-kán (= *nu* + *kán*)	9.1.6 obv. 7. 12.1.4 6′
	nu-w[*a*(-)	7.1 rev. 16′
	nu-wa-ra-at (= *nu* + *war* + *at*)	2.7.A obv. 14
	nu-uš-ma-ša-at (= *nu* + *šmaš* + *at*)	2.2 rev. 9
	nu]*-uš-ši* (= *nu* + (*š*)*ši*)	8.1.E(A_3) rev. vi 9
	nu-za (= *nu* + *za*)	1.1.A_1 obv. 13′
nuḫalim(m)a/i-	(?)	
sg. nom.	*nu-ḫa-li$^?$-i-me-iš*	10.1.2.1 rev.$^?$ l. c. 4
broken	*nu-ḫa-l*[*i-i-ma-*(?)	9.1.14 obv. r. c. 7′
nurima(nt)-	'(set with) pomegranate(s)(?)'	
(?)	*nu-úr-i-ma-an-za*(-)x[	9.2.2 rev.$^!$ iii 23′

see *Lexical Commentary*; see also NURMÛ

$^{(\text{GI})}$*nutaršat(t)ena-*	(a container?)	
sg. nom.-acc. n.	*nu-tar-ša-at-te-na*	11.5.2 rev.$^{?}$ r. c. 1′
	nu-tar-ša-t]*i*(?)*-na*	10.3.10 r. c. 11′
	^{GI}*nu-ta*[*r-ša-at-te-na*(?)	2.15 l. c. 2′
see *Lexical Commentary*		
pai-/pi(ya)-	‘to give’	
pres. sg. 1	*pé-e*[*ḫ-ḫi*(?)	7.1 rev. 12′
pres. sg. 3	*pa-a-i*	10.1.1.1 rev.$^{?}$ 3′
	(EGIR-*pa*) *pa-a-i*	6.1 l. e. 1
pret. sg. 3	*pa-iš*	1.1.A_1 obv. 15′. 1.1.A_3 rev. 4′, 5′, 11′
	p[*a-iš*	1.1.A_3 rev. 2′
	pé-eš-ta	1.2 rev. 11′
	pé-eš-t[*a*	1.3 7′
	pé-eš-[*ta*	1.2 rev. 1′
	pí-iš-[*ta*(?)	1.3 5′
	pé-[*eš-ta*	1.3 2′
pret. pl. 3	*pí-e-er*	4.1.1.1.B_2 obv. i$^{?}$ 3′, 5′
	pí-i-e-er	4.1.1.1.B_1 rev. iii$^{?}$ 13
	pí-[*i*]*-e-er*	4.1.1.1.A_1 rev. 6′
	p]*í-i-e-er*	4.1.1.1.B_1 rev. iv$^{?}$ 4
	pí-i]*-e*$^{?}$*-er*	4.1.1.1.B_1 obv. ii$^{?}$ 13′
ptc. sg. nom.-acc. n.	*p*[*í*]*-ia-an*	2.17 obv.$^{?}$ r. c. 6′
	pí-i[*a-an*	2.17 obv.$^{?}$ r. c. 7′
= SUM, *NADĀNU*		
$^{(\text{TÚG})}$*palaḫša-*	(a head-covering characteristic of ^{D}*IŠTAR* and her attendants)	
sg. nom.	*pa-l*[*a-a*]*ḫ-ša*(-)[*aš*(?)	3.1.8.A obv. 15′
sg. gen.	*ŠA* ^{TÚG}*pa-la-aḫ-ša-aš*	9.1.8 obv. 5′
palḫašti-	‘breadth, width’	
sg. nom.-acc. n.	*pal-ḫa-*[*aš-ti*	10.2.1.4 4′
= DAGAL		
palḫi-	‘broad, wide’	
pl. nom.-acc. n.	*pal-ḫi*	9.2.2 rev.$^{!}$ iii 22′
= DAGAL		
palša-	‘road, path; way, behavior; journey, trip’	
sg. dat./loc.	*p*]*al-ši*	1.1.A_2 obv. 3′
= KASKAL		
^{GIŠ}*palšuwant-*	(a valuable wooden object)	
Luw. sg. nom.-acc. n.	^{GIŠ}*pal-šu-u-wa-an-za*	4.2.4 rev. 4′
	^{GIŠ}*pa*[*l-šu-u-wa-an-za*(?)	4.2.5 2′
baluga-	(a metal object)	
sg. nom.	*ba-lu-ga-aš*	11.1.1 r. c. 8′
broken	*ba-lu-g*[*a-*	11.2.5 3′
see *Lexical Commentary*		
palza(š)ḫa-	‘statue base, pedestal’	
sg. nom.	*pal-za-ḫa-aš*	4.2.1.A_1 obv. 7. 8.1.A rev. v 7, 9. 8.1.C 2′. 9.1.5 rev.$^{!}$ 11′. 10.2.1.1 obv. 6′
	pal-za-ḫa-a-aš	10.2.1.2 obv. 14′
	pal]*-za-ḫa-aš*	8.1.D obv. i 3′
	pal-z[*a-ḫa-aš*	8.1.D obv. i 1′

	pal-za-aš-ḫa-aš	7.4 2′
	pal-za-aš-ḫ[a-aš	10.1.2.2 6′
para	‘forth, out, over to’ (preverb)	
	pa-r[a-a(?)	2.5 rev. 9′
para SUM-*uaš*	‘handout(s), things to be distributed’	
see SUM		
$^{\text{NA}_4}$*paraššu-*	(a stone)	
sg. nom.	$^{\text{NA}_4}$*ba-ra-aš-šu-uš*	9.2.5 obv. i(?) 8′
see *Lexical Commentary*		
paraššuwant-	‘set with *paraššu*-stones(?)’	
sg. nom.	*pa-ra-aš-šu-a-an-za*	10.3.11 l. c. 6′
pargašti-	‘height’	
sg. dat./loc.	*pár-ga-aš-ti*	10.2.1.1 obv. 2′. 10.2.1.3 7′
	pá]r-ga-aš-ti	10.2.1.5 4′
	pár-ga-aš-t]i	10.2.1.3 3′
	pár-ga-aš-t[i	10.2.1.4 2′
𒑱*pariyašši-*	(adj. modifying hide/leather)	
sg. nom.	𒑱*pa-ri-ia-aš-ši-iš*	9.1.11 obv.? 11′
see *Lexical Commentary*		
𒑱*pariyaššaim(m)a/i-*	‘upholstered with *pariyašši*-leather(?)’	
pl. nom.-acc. n.	𒑱*pa-ri-ia-aš-ša-i-ma*	3.1.1.A_1 rev. v 4′
	𒑱*pa-ri-ia-aš-ša]-i-ma*	3.1.1.A_1 rev. v 9′
see *Lexical Commentary*		
$^{(\text{TÚG/GADA})}$*parna-*	(a valuable cloth/linen item)	
sg. nom.	^{GADA}*pár-na-aš*	4.2.6 rev.? 11′
	^{TÚG}*pár-na-aš*	2.12 obv.! ii 4′. 4.2.7 4′. 4.2.9 obv. 17; rev. 24′. 8.1.F rev. v 7. 9.1.1 rev. iii 27′. 9.2.9 rev.? 1′, 6′. 10.1.2.1 rev.? r. c. 4′
	^{TÚG}*pár*!*-n[a-aš*	10.1.2.1 obv.? r. c. 6′
see *Lexical Commentary*		
parta-	(a part of a bedstead) “sideboard(?)”	
sg. nom.	*pár-ta-aš*	9.1.10.B 13′. 9.2.6 obv. i 19′. 11.1.4 4′
	pár-t]a-aš	9.1.10.A_1 obv. 9′
see *Lexical Commentary*		
^{LÚ}*parwala-*	(a functionary)	
pl. dat./loc.	$^{\text{LÚ.MEŠ}}$*pár-wa-la-aš* (LUGAL)	5.2 obv. ii 6
	$^{\text{LÚ.MEŠ}}$*pár-w]a-la-aš* (LUGAL)	5.2 obv. ii 8
	$^{\text{LÚ}]\text{.MEŠ}}$*pár-wa-la-aš*	5.2 obv. ii 17
parza, paršza	‘...-wards’ (indicating direction)	
	(EGIR-*pa*) *pár-za* (*au(š)-/u(wa)-*)	9.1.1 rev. iv 11′
$^{(\text{GIŠ.ḪUR})}$(𒑱)*parzaki-*	‘label(?), bulla(?)’	
sg. nom.	$^{\text{GIŠ.ḪUR}}$*pár-za-kiš*	2.12 obv.! ii 9′
	𒑱*pár-za-k[iš*	2.9.A_3 obv. ii 13′
see *Lexical Commentary*		
parzagulliya-	(a piece of jewelry)	
sg. nom.-acc. n.	*pár-za-gul-li-ia*	9.1.1 rev. iii 3′
see *Lexical Commentary*; see also *parzašša-*		

(𒑱)*parzam(m)a/i-* (?) (Luw. ptc. of *parzai-*?)
sg. nom.-acc. n. (*katta*) 𒑱*pár-za-ma-an* 11.2.2 7′
(*katta*) *pár-z[a-ma-an* 9.2.2 rev.[!] iii 8′
see *Lexical Commentary*

parzašša/i- 'made of iron ore(?)'
pl. nom.-acc. n. *pár-za-aš-ša* 9.1.4.A_1 obv. ii 23
see *Lexical Commentary*; see also *ḫapalki-*, *kiklibaim(m)a/i-*, *parzagulliya-*, AN.BAR, AN.BAR GE$_6$, *ḪAPALKINNU*

paškant- 'stuck, fastened, set up' (ptc. of *pašk-*, *paški(ya)-*)
sg. nom.-acc. n. *pa-aš-kán* 10.2.1.1 rev. 6′
pa-aš(?)]*-kán* 10.2.1.1 rev. 3′

(𒑱)*bašta-* (a decorative element)
sg. nom. *ba-aš-ta-aš* 11.3.2 r. c. 5′
pa-aš-ta-aš 10.3.13 7′
𒑱*pa-aš-ta*[!?]*-aš* 12.3.7 4′
see *Lexical Commentary*

baštaim(m)a/i- 'set with *bašta*-decorations'
sg. nom. *ba-aš-ta-i-mi-iš* 4.1.4.2.A_2 obv. r. c. 12′
b]a-aš-ta-[i-me-iš 4.1.4.1.A_2 obv. ii 2′
ba]-aš-ta-i-me-i[š 4.1.4.1.A_1 obv. ii 14′
ba-aš-ta-i-[mi-iš 9.1.10.B 14′
ba-a[š-ta-i-mi-iš(?) 9.1.10.B 9′
sg. nom.-acc. n. *ba-aš-ta-i-m[a-an* 11.3.2 r. c. 4′
Luw. pl. nom. *ba-aš-ta-i-me-en-zi* 9.1.1 rev. iii 34′

baštant- 'set with *bašta*-decorations'
sg. nom.-acc. n. *ba-aš-ta-a-an* 9.1.6 obv. 2
ba[!]*-a-aš-ta-an* 9.2.2 rev.[!] iii 20′
b[a-aš-ta-a-an 9.2.2 rev.[!] iii 11′

baššu- (a material?)
sg. nom. *ba-aš-šu-uš* 11.2.4 3′
see *Lexical Commentary*

-pat (emphatic particle)
-pá[t 10.3.12 obv. i 22′

$^{(\text{TÚG})}$*patalla-* 'puttee, leg wrapping'
sg. nom.? ^{TÚG}*pa-ta-al-la-[aš*[?] 8.8.B r. c. 5′
see *Lexical Commentary*

$^{(\text{UZU})}$*pattar* 'wing, feather'
sg. nom.-acc. n. *pát-tar* 4.1.1.8 r. c. 6′
= *KAPPU*; see also ^{UZU}*partawar*

paddaniyaš(š)a/i- 'feathered(?); scale corselet(?)'
pl. nom.-acc. n. (*GURSIPU*) *pád-da-ni-ia-ša* 2.8 obv. 3
see *Lexical Commentary*

𒑱*patialli-* 'foot/leg (piece)'
sg. nom. 𒑱*pa-ti-al-li[š]* 10.3.2 obv. i(?) 13″
see *Lexical Commentary*

^{LÚ}*patili-* (a priest)
sg. nom. ^{LÚ}*pa-ti-liš* 4.1.1.1.B_1 rev. iii[?] 11

pellawariya/i-	(a designation of a chest)	
sg. nom.	*pé-el-la-wa-ri-i-iš*	8.1.A rev. v 17′
penki(t)-	‘knob’	
sg. nom.-acc. n.	*pé-en-ki*	3.1.8.A obv. 14′. 8.4 rev. 7′
	pé-en-gi	6.5 obv. 7′, 8′, 9′, 10′, 13′, 14′
	p]*é-en-ki*	8.1.A obv. i 6′
	p]*é-en-gi*	6.5 obv. 6′
	p]*é-*[*e*]*n-ki*	9.2.9 obv.? 10′
	pé-en-g[*i*	6.5 obv. 11′, 15′
	pé-en-[*gi*	6.5 obv. 12′
see *Lexical Commentary*		
penkitaim(m)a/i-	‘set with knobs’	
sg. nom.	*pé-en-ki-ta-im-mi-iš*	8.4 rev. 11′
sg. nom.-acc. n.	*pé-en-ki-ta-i-ma-an*	11.3.1 11′
see *Lexical Commentary*		
(≮)*pennati-*	(a type of necklace)	
sg. nom.	*pé-en-na-ti-iš*	8.4 rev. 14′. 9.2.2 rev.! iii 9′
	pé]*-en-na-ti-iš*	9.1.4.A_1 obv. ii 29
	≮*pé-en-n*[*a-ti-iš*	12.3.7 7′
see also *mannin(n)i-*		
pippant-	‘knocked down, turned over, broken up’ (ptc. of *pippa-*)	
sg. nom.-acc. n.	(*arḫa*) *pí-ip-pa-an*	9.1.8 obv. 12′
peran	‘in front, before’ (preverb and local adverb)	
	pé.-an (*arḫa* GAR)	9.1.5 rev.! 11′
	pé-ra-an	9.1.4.A_1 obv. ii 4. 9.2.1 rev. iii 25′
	pé-ra-an (*arḫa da-*)	4.1.3.3 4′, 6′. 4.2.12 3′
	pé-r[*a-an*	9.2.2 rev.! iii 15′
	pé-r[*a-an*(?)	9.2.11 6′
	p]*é-ra-an*	8.8.A 14′
	pé-r]*a-an*	9.2.6 obv. i 18′
see also *peran ped(d)um(m)/naš*		
peran ped(d)um(m)/naš	(a utensil “for carrying in front”) “fore-carrier”	
sg. gen.	*pé.-an pé-dum-ma-aš*	8.4 rev. 16′
	pé-ra-an pé-du-ma-aš	10.3.12 obv. i 20′
	pé-ra-an pé-e-du-ma-aš	4.2.4 obv. 3, 4
	p]*é-ra-an pé-du-ma-aš*	10.3.12 obv. i 22′
	pé]*-ra-an pé-e-du-ma-aš*	8.1.A obv. i 3′
	pé-ra-a]*n pé-e-du-ma-aš*	2.2 rev. 18
	pé-ra-an p]*é-e-dum-ma-aš*	10.3.11 l. c. 7′
	pé-ra-an pé-du-m[*a-aš*	10.3.12 obv. i 18′
	pé-ra-an pé-[*du-ma-aš*	10.3.10 r. c. 13′
	pé-ra-a[*n pé-du-ma-as*	4.2.5 5′
	pé-r]*a-an píd-du-na-aš*	9.2.1 obv. ii 18′
	pé-ra-a]*n pé-du-na-a-aš*	11.2.4 1′
	pé-ra-an pít-tu-na-a-a[*š*	9.1.1 rev. iii 1′
peri-	(a material) ‘ivory(?)’	
sg. nom.	*pé-e-ri-iš*	9.2.1 obv. ii 10′
see *Lexical Commentary*; = ZU$_9$ (AM.)SI?		

pišate(-)		
see ŠEŠ(-)*pišate*(-)		
peda-	'place, location, spot'	
sg. dat./loc.	*pé-di*	10.3.2 obv. i(?) 15″ (2×); obv. ii(?) 4′
	pé-d]*i*	10.3.2 obv. ii(?) 7′
	pé-[*di*	10.3.2 obv. ii(?) 7′
	p[*é-di*	10.3.2 obv. ii(?) 4′
= *AŠRU*		
peda-	'to take (somewhere), carry, transport'	
pres. sg. 3	*pé-da-i*	6.1 lo. e. 10″
pres. pl. 3	*pé-e-da-an-*[*z*]*i*	4.2.6 obv.$^{?}$ 7′
pret. sg. 3	*pé-e-da-aš*	4.1.1.1.B_1 rev. iii$^{?}$ 11
	pé-da]*-aš*	4.1.1.1.A_1 obv. 12′
pret. pl. 3	*pí-te-er*	1.5 rev. 24, 27. 4.1.1.1.B_1 rev. iv$^{?}$ 17. 8.5 rev. iv(?) 6′
	pé-e-te-er	1.1.A_2 obv. 9′, 10′, 11′. 10.3.2 obv. i(?) 5″, 12″
	pí-i-te-er	1.1.A_2 obv. 3′, 8′
	pé-e-[*t*]*e-er*	5.2 obv. ii 12
	p]*é-e-te-er*	1.1.A_2 obv. 4′
ptc. sg. nom.	(*anda*) *pé-da-*[*an-za*	9.1.6 obv. 5
see also *pe(r)an ped(d)um/naš*		
pittalwant-	'plain, simple, unadorned'	
sg. nom.	*pít-tal-wa-an-za*	9.1.1 rev. iii 40′. 9.1.5 obv.$^{!}$ 4
	pít-tal]*-wa-an-za*	9.1.5 obv.$^{!}$ 2
sg. nom.-acc. n.	*pít-tal-wa-an*	11.3.1 16′
	pít-ta[*l-w*]*a*$^{?}$*-an*	10.3.12 obv. i 12′
pl. nom.-acc. n.	*pí*[*t-ta*]*l-wa-an-ta*	8.4 rev. 10′
	pít-tal-wa-an-t[*a*	1.3 6′
broken	*pít-tal-w*[*a-*	10.3.12 obv. i 3′
$^{(\text{SÍG})}$*pittula-*	'(woolen) loop'	
sg. nom.	^{SÍG}*pít-tu-la-aš*	4.1.3.3 10′. 8.1.D obv. i 8′
	^{SÍG}*pít-t*[*u-la-aš*	4.1.3.2 rev. 10′
sg. acc.	^{SÍG}*pít-tu-la-an*	4.1.3.3 11′
sg. gen.	*pít-tu-la-aš*	2.7.A obv. 6
pulpulumi-	(a metal object)	
sg. nom.	*pu-ul-pu-lu-me-eš*	10.3.5 6′
	pu-ul-pu-l[*u-me-eš*(?)	9.2.4 rev. iii 10′
see *Lexical Commentary*		
purana-	(?)	
pl. nom.-acc. n.	*pu-u-ra-na*	9.1.1 rev. iv 36′
^{LÚ}*purapši-*	(a type of priest)	
sg./pl. gen.	$^{\text{LÚ(.MEŠ)}}$*p*]*u-ra-ap-ši-ia-aš*	4.2.6 obv.$^{?}$ 13′
puri-	'lip, rim, edge'	
sg. nom.	*pu-u-ri-iš*	9.1.4.A_1 obv. ii 20
	pu-u-ri-i]*š*(?)	10.3.4 11′
	pu-u-ri-i[*š*	9.2.9 obv.$^{?}$ 9′. 9.2.10 4′
	pu-u-r[*i-iš*	9.2.10 2′
	pu-[*u-ri-iš*	9.1.4.A_1 obv. ii 30

sg. acc.	*pu-u-ri-in*	9.1.1 rev. iv 21′, 43′. 9.1.4.A_1 obv. ii 25
	pu]-u-ri-in	9.2.1 obv. ii 22′
$^{\text{(GIŠ)}}$*puri-*, *puriya-*	(a wood or wicker holder for vessels) ‘tray(?)’	
sg. nom.	*pu-ri-aš*	8.1.A rev. v 8. 8.1.C 3′
	p]u-ri-ia-a[š(?)	5.2 rev. iii 11′
	^{GIŠ}*pu-u-ri-i[š*	4.1.1.5 obv. 5
puriyaim(m)a/i-	‘rimmed, bordered, edged’ (Luw. ptc. **puriyai-*)	
sg. nom.	*pu-ri-ia-i-mi-iš*	8.1.E(A_1) rev. iv 1′
	pu-ri-ia]-i-mi-iš	8.1.E(A_1) obv. ii 1
(≮)*puriyalla/i-*	(a drinking vessel)	
Luw. sg. nom.-acc. n.	*pu-ri-ia-al-la-an*	2.16 obv. i 7′
sg. dat./loc.(?)	*A-N]A*(?) ≮*pu-ri-al-li*	4.1.1.1.A_1 obv. 13′
puripuli-	(?)	
sg. nom.	*pu-ri-pu-liš*$^?$	6.5 rev. 7′
purulliyašša/i-	‘related to the *purulli*-ritual’	
see SISKUR *purulliyašša/i-*		
$^{\text{(TÚG)}}$*puššaim(m)a/i-*	‘felted-cloth(?)’	
sg. nom.	*pu-uš-[ša-i-me-iš*	11.6.6 rev. 2′
	pu-u[š-ša-i-mi-iš(?)	8.4 rev. 18′
	pu-[uš-ša-i-mi-iš(?)	8.4 rev. 13′
	^{TÚG}*pu-uš-ša-i-me-iš*	8.1.E(A_1) obv. ii 4
	^{TÚG}*pu-uš-š]a-i-mi-iš*	8.1.E(A_1) obv. ii 13
	$^{\text{T]ÚG}}$*pu-u[š-ša-i-me-iš*	8.3 obv. 2′
see *Lexical Commentary*		
^{TÚG}*puwalia-*	(a garment associated with leggings)	
Luw. sg. nom.-acc. n.	^{TÚG}*pu-wa-li-an-za*	11.6.1 9
	^{TÚG}*pu-wa*$^?$*-li*$^?$*-[an-za*	10.1.2.1 rev.$^?$ r. c. 1′
	^{TÚG}*pu-wa-l[i-an-za*	10.1.2.1 obv.$^?$ r. c. 3′
šayu-	(a type of animal)	
sg. nom.	*ša-a-i-ú-uš*	9.1.1 rev. iv 23′. 9.1.4.A_1 obv. ii 34
šakantam(m)a/i-	‘set with appliqué(?)’ (Luw. ptc. of **šakantai-*)	
Luw. sg. nom.-acc. n.	*ša-kán-ta-ma-an-za*	9.1.1 rev. iii 20′, 23′
Luw. pl. nom.	*ša-kán-ta-me-en-zi*	9.1.1 rev. iii 18′
šakantat(t)ar	‘appliqué(?)’ (vb. subst. of **šakantai-*)	
sg. nom.-acc. n.	*ša-kán-ta-tar*	9.1.1 rev. iii 17′
	š]a-kán-ta-tar	9.2.1 obv. ii 2′. 9.2.5 obv. i(?) 10′
	ša-k]án-ta-tar	9.2.4 obv. i 10′
	ša-kán-t]a-tar	9.2.4 obv. i 13′
	ša-kán-t]a(?)*-tar*	9.1.10.B 3′
pl. nom.-acc. n.	*ša-kán-ta-at-ta-ra*	9.2.4 obv. i 9′
	ša-kán-ta-ad-da-ra	9.2.2 rev.$^!$ iii 22′
	ša-kán-t]a-ad-da-ra	9.2.1 obv. ii 19′
	ša-kán-ta-a]d-da-ra	10.3.1 rev. iii 1′
	ša-kán-ta-ad-da]-ra	10.3.1 rev. iii 13′
	ša-kán-ta-a]t(?)*-ta-ra*	9.1.4.A_1 obv. i 9′
^{LÚ}*šalašḫa-*	(an official associated with horses, ‘footman’?)	
pl. gen.	(ŠU) $^{\text{LÚ.MEŠ}}$*ša-la-aš-ḫa-aš*	4.2.6 obv.$^?$ 3′
pl. dat./loc.	*A-NA* $^{\text{LÚ.MEŠ}}$*ša-la-aš-ḫa-aš*	4.1.4.9 obv. 10

^{GIŠ}*šalašturi-*	(a piece of archery equipment)	
sg. nom.-acc. n.	^{GIŠ}*ša-a-la-aš-tu-ri*	9.1.1 rev. iv 28′
	^{GIŠ}*š*[*a-l*]*a-aš-tu-u-r*[*i*	2.18 7′
see *Lexical Commentary*		
^{GIŠ}*šalašturi-* ḪURRI	‘*š.* of the Hurrian fashion’	
sg. nom.-acc. n.	^{GIŠ}*ša-la-aš-du-ri* … ḪUR-RI	2.17 obv.$^{?}$ r. c. 17′
šalli-	‘great, large’	
sg. gen.(?)	*šal-la-ia-aš*	9.1.4.A_1 obv. i 15′. 10.2.1.2 obv. 15′
	sal-l]*a-ia-aš*	10.2.1.2 obv. 2′
= MAḪ		
šaluwa-	(a utensil) ‘skewer(?)’	
sg. nom.	*šal-u-wa-aš*	9.1.8 obv. 13′
	ša] *l*$^{?}$*-u-wa-aš*	4.2.8 5′
see *Lexical Commentary*		
^{LÚ}*ša(n)kunniant-*	‘priest’	
sg. nom.	^{LÚ}*šak-ku-ni-an-za*	5.1 rev. iii 3
šap(a)ra-	(a type of belt?)	
sg. nom.	*ša-pa-ra-aš*	6.5 obv. 11′, 12′, 13′, 14′
	ša-a]*p-ra-aš*	9.2.8.A_1 4′
see *Lexical Commentary*		
šapia-	(a metal vessel)	
sg. nom.	**ša***-pí-a*[*š*	9.1.5 obv.$^{!}$ 7
	ša-p]*í-aš*	9.1.5 obv.$^{!}$ 7
šappi[*š*(-)	(?)	
	ša-ap-pí-i[*š*(-)	4.2.4 obv. 13
see $^{\text{(URUDU)}}$*z/šap(p)iškur-*?		
šapeškur		
see $^{\text{(URUDU)}}$*z/šap(p)iškur-*		
šara	‘up, upwards’ (preverb)	
	ša-ra-a (*da-*)	4.1.1.1.B_1 rev. iii$^{?}$ 10
	ša-ra-a (*wašše-*)	8.1.A rev. v 23′
	š]*a-ra-a* (*eš-/aš-*)	1.5 obv. 2
šarra-	(a wooden article of toiletry used for removing/separating)	
sg. nom.	*šar-ra-aš*	10.3.12 obv. i 4′
šarra -	‘to divide, apportion, split off’	
pres. pl. 3	*šar-ra-an-zi*	4.1.4.9 obv. 8
	šar-[*ra-an-zi*(?)	10.2.2.4 rev.$^{?}$ r. c. 1
vb. subst. sg. gen.	*šar-ru-ma-aš*	8.1.E(A_1) obv ii$^{?}$ 9′
	šar-ru-m[*a-aš*	8.3 obv. 5′
(SÍG) *šarḫanuwam(m)a/i-*	(a kind, quality, or treatment of wool)	
sg. nom.	*šar-*[*ḫa-nu-wa-mi-iš*(?)	8.1.F obv. ii 2′
	SÍG *šar-ḫa-nu-wa-me-*[*eš*	11.6.1 10
	SÍG *šar-ḫa-nu-*[*wa-me-eš*	6.11 4′
	SÍ]G … *šar-ḫa-nu-wa-mi-iš*	8.1.H rev. l. c. 5′
šariyant-	‘embroidered(?), sewed on(?)’ (ptc. of *šari(ya)-*)	
ptc. sg. nom.	*ša-ri-an-za*	6.5 rev. 9′
	ša-ri-ia-an-za	9.1.1 rev. iii 37′

ptc. sg. nom.-acc. n.	*ša-a-ri-ia-an*	9.2.5 obv. i(?) 5′
	ša-[a$^{?}$*]-ri-ia-an*	9.2.2 rev.$^{!}$ iii 18′
ptc. pl. nom.	*ša-ri-ia-an-te-eš*	9.2.1 obv. ii 11′
ptc. pl. nom.-acc. n.	*ša-ri-an-da*	11.3.1 22′
	ša-ri-[ia-an(-)	9.2.14 6′
šariyanni-	‘a (Hurrian-style) coat of scale armor’	
sg. nom.-acc. n.	*ša-ri-ia-[an-ni*(?)	9.1.14 obv. r. c. 2′
^{TÚG}*šarriwašpa-*	“upper garment”	
sg. nom.	^{TÚG}*šar-ri-wa-aš-pa-aš*	2.7.A obv. 7
	^{TÚG}*šar-ri]-wa-aš-ša-pa-aš*	11.6.3 obv.$^{?}$ 5′
	^{TÚG}*ša[r-ri-wa-aš-pa-aš*(?)	6.6 obv. 1′
šarganiant-	‘torn apart(?), destroyed(?)’ (ptc. of *šargani(ya)-*)	
sg. nom.	(*arḫa*) *šar-ga-n[i-an-za*	9.1.6 obv. 7
see *Lexical Commentary*		
šarlanni-	(a piece of jewelry)	
sg. nom.-acc. n.	*šar-la-an-ni*	10.1.2.1 rev.$^{?}$ r. c. 3′
pl. nom.-acc. n.	*šar-la-an-na*	10.3.4 8′
see *Lexical Commentary*		
šarnikzil-	‘compensation, replacement’	
sg. nom.-acc. n.	*šar-ni-i]k-zi-i-el*	1.2 rev. 1′
^{GIŠ}*šarpa-*	‘a (cross-legged?) chair/stool’	
pl. coll. nom.	^{GIŠ}*šar-pa*	5.6 3′. 9.1.5 rev.$^{!}$ 10′, 17′
	$^{\text{GI}]\text{Š}}$*šar-pa*	4.2.1.A_1 obv. 9
pl. dat./loc.	*A-NA* … ^{GIŠ}*šar-pa-aš*	4.1.4.9 obv. 5
see also GADA ^{GIŠ}*šarpaš*		
šaša-	‘ibex, wild goat’	
Luw. pl. nom.	*ša-ša-an-z[i*(?)	10.2.2.4 obv.$^{?}$ r. c. 7′
šaššanna-	‘lamp’	
sg. nom.	*ša-ša-an-na-a[š*	11.1.3 9′
see *Lexical Commentary*		
šašant-	‘lying down, sleeping’ (ptc. of *šeš-/šaš-*)	
sg. nom.	*ša-ša-an-za*	9.1.4.A_1 obv. ii 10, 14
	ša-š]a-an-z[a]	11.2.3 1′
pl. nom.	*ša-⟨ša⟩-an-te-eš*	11.2.4 5′
	ša-ša-an-t[e-e]š	9.1.1 rev. iv 17′
	ša-ša-[an-te-eš	9.1.4.A_2 r. c. 5′
^{TÚG}*šašt(a)-*	‘bed, bedding, bedroll’	
sg. gen.(?)	^{TÚG}*ša-aš-t[a-aš*(?)	11.1.3 12′
šata-	(?)	
	ša$^{?}$*-ta*$^{?}$*-an-zi*	9.2.2 rev.$^{!}$ iii 17′
šekan	(a unit of length) ‘(hand) span’	
sg. nom.-acc. n.	*še-kán*	10.1.1.1 rev.$^{?}$ 8′
	še-kán$^{!}$(text: “ER+1”)	10.1.1.2 rev. iv 2′
	še-e-kán	10.2.1.3 3′, 7′
	š]e$^{?}$*-e-kán*	10.2.1.4 6′

šikki- (or: *šikkiš*?)	(a knife or dagger?)	
sg. nom.	*ši-ik-kiš*	9.1.1 rev. iii 13′
see *Lexical Commentary*		
^{É}*šinapši-*	(a sacred building)	
sg. gen.	^{É}*ši-nap-ši-ia-aš*	10.2.1.7 rev.$^{?}$ 4′
$^{\text{(TÚG)}}$*šepaḫi-*	(a garment) 'shepherd's tunic/cloth'	
sg. nom.	^{TÚG}*še-pa-ḫi-eš*	11.6.2 rev. 7′
	^{TÚG}*še-pa-ḫi-eš* (^{GIŠ}*karnaššaš*)	11.6.2 l. e. 6
	^{TÚG}*še-pa-ḫi-iš*	4.2.9 obv. 8
	^{TÚG}*še-p*]*a-ḫi-iš*	4.2.9 rev. 4′
sg. gen.	(^{TÚG}GÚ *ḪURRI*) *še-pa-ḫi-ia-aš*	4.2.9 obv. 28
	(^{TÚG}GÚ ...) *ši-pá-ḫi-ia-*[*aš*	4.1.4.8 3′
šip(p)anduwa-	'libation vessel'	
sg. nom.	*ši-pa-an-tu-u-aš*	9.1.7 rev. 1
	šìp-pa-an-du-wa-aš	4.2.1.A_2 obv. 3′
	š]*i-pa-an-du-wa-aš*	4.1.1.7 rev.$^{!?}$ 4
	šìp-pa-a]*n-du-w*[*a-aš*(?)	4.2.1.A_2 obv. 9′
	ši-pa-an-d]*u-wa-aš*(?)	10.2.1.1 obv. 12′
= BAL-*uwaš*		
šer	'on, on top of, over, above'	
	še-er	9.2.9 obv.$^{?}$ 10′. 11.2.4 2′, 3′
	še-er (*arḫa iya-*)	4.1.4.1.A_1 obv. i 7′
	š]*e-er* (*arḫa iya-*)	4.1.4.1.A_1 rev. vi 12′
	še-er (*wašše-*)	2.11 obv.$^{?}$ 6′. 8.1.A rev. v 21′
	še-er (GUB)	9.1.4.A_1 obv. ii 35
	še-er (GUL)	10.3.1 rev. iii 4′
= UGU		
šertappila-	(a serving utensil)	
sg. nom.	*še-er-tap-pí-la-aš*	9.1.4.A_1 obv. ii 40
see *Lexical Commentary*		
šittar-, šittara-, šittari-	'(sun) disk'	
sg. nom.-acc. n.	*ši-it-tar*	9.1.1 rev. iv 31′. 9.1.4.A_2 r. c. 6′. 9.1.5 rev.$^{!}$ 3′, 5′
	ši-it-t[*ar*	9.1.5 rev.$^{!}$ 8′
Luw. sg. nom.-acc. n.	*ši-i*]*t*(?)*-tar-za*	7.2 3′
see *Lexical Commentary*; = AŠ.ME?		
šiwašša/i-	(a hairpin or hairpin part)	
sg. nom.	*ši-wa-aš-ši-iš*	4.2.4 obv. 9
šuḫḫa-	'roof'	
sg. gen.(?)	*šu-uḫ-ḫa-aš*	9.1.10.A_2 rev. 5′
šulupašša/i-	'of (the town of) Šulupašši'	
see É.GAL *šulupašša/i-*		
šumra(i)-*/šumriya-*	'to load, fill(?)'	
broken	(*anda*) *šum-r*[*i-*	8.1.F obv. ii 15′
see *Lexical Commentary*		
šunna-	'to fill'	
pret. pl. 3	*šu-un-ner*	1.1.A_2 obv. 4′

šuppi-	'pure, holy, consecrated'	
sg. gen.	*šu-up-pa*(?)-*i*]*a-aš*	9.1.4.A_1 obv. i 18′
šuppe/išduwara/i-, *išpeštuwara-* 'ornament(ation), ornamented cup'		
sg. nom.	*iš-piš-du-wa-ra-a-aš*	8.4 rev. 2′
pl. nom.	*šu-up-pí-iš-du-wa-ri-eš*	9.2.1 obv. ii 18′
	š]*u-up-pí-iš-du-wa-ri-iš*	9.2.1 obv. ii 3′
	šu]*-up-pí-iš-du-wa-ri-iš*	9.2.1 obv. ii 5′
šuppešduwarant-	'ornamented, decorated'	
sg. nom.	*šu-up-pé-eš-du-*⟨*wa-ra*⟩*-an-za*	10.3.12 obv. i 19′
	šu-up-p[*é-eš-d*]*u-wa-ra-an-za*	10.3.12 obv. i 14′
	š]*u-up-pé-eš-du-wa-*[*ra-an-za*	10.3.12 obv. i 15′
	šu-up-pé-eš-du-wa-ra-[*an-za*	10.3.12 obv. i 16′
sg. nom.-acc. n.	*šu-up-pé-eš-du-wa-ra-an*	9.1.1 rev. iv 15′
	šu-up-pé-eš-du-wa-ra-a-an	9.1.1 rev. iv 24′
	š]*u-up-pé-eš-du-wa-ra-*[*an*(-)	10.1.2.4 l. c. 20′
	šu]*-up-pé-eš-*[*du-w*]*a-ra-an*	10.3.1 obv. ii 5′
	šu-up-pé]*-eš-du-wa-ra-an*	10.3.3 obv.[?] 6′
	šu-up-pé-eš-d]*u-wa-ra-a-an*	11.2.5 7′
	šu-u]*p-pé-eš-du-wa-r*[*a-an*	11.5.1 8′
	šu-up-pé-eš-du-wa-[*ra-an*	11.5.1 6′
	šu-up-pé-e[*š-du-wa-ra-an*	11.5.1 5′
pl. nom.	*š*]*u-up-pí-iš-du-wa-ra-an-te-eš*	9.2.1 rev. iii 17′
	šu-up]*-pí-iš-du-wa-ra-an-te-eš*	9.2.1 rev. iii 26′
	šu-up-pí-iš-du-wa-ra-a[*n-te-eš*	9.1.4.A_1 obv. ii 39
šuruḫḫa-	(a tree or its wood)	
sg. gen.?	*šu-ru-uḫ-ḫa-aš*	3.1.1.A_1 rev. v 13′
broken	*šu-ru-uḫ-ḫa*(-)[	8.6 l. c. 2′
$^{\text{(URUDU)}}$*šurzi-*	'snaffle bit'	
sg. nom.-acc. n.	^{URUDU}*šur-zi*	3.1.1.A_1 obv. ii 17′. 3.1.1.A_3 obv. iii 6′, 7′
	$^{\text{URUD}]\text{U?}}$*šur-z*[*i*	5.2 rev. iii 5′
sg. dat./loc.	*QA-DU šur-zi-ia*	9.1.10.A_2 rev. 8′
pl. nom.-acc. n.(?)	^{URUDU}*šur-zi-ia*	3.1.1.A_3 obv. iii 5′
šutari-	(a part of a lyre)	
sg. nom.	*šu-u-ta-ri-iš*	8.1.A obv. ii 11′
see *Lexical Commentary*		
šuwant-	'filled' (ptc. of *šu-*, *šuwa-*)	
sg. nom.	*šu-u-wa-an-za*	2.17 obv.[?] r. c. 3′, 4′
sg. nom.-acc. n.	*šu-u-wa-an*	9.1.5 rev.[!] 4′
da-	'to take, seize'	
pres. sg. 3	*da-a-i*	4.1.3.3 12′
	da(?)]*-a-i*	5.1 obv. i 3′
	(*arḫa*) *d*[*a-a-i*(?)	4.1.3.2 rev. 8′
	(*peran arḫa*) *da-a-i*	4.1.3.3 1′
	(*peran arḫa*) *da-a-*[*i*	4.1.3.3 6′
pres. pl. 3	*d*]*a-an-zi*	6.1 rev. B 8
pret. sg. 1	*da-aḫ-ḫ*[*u-un*(?)	7.1 rev. 11′
pret. sg. 3	*da-a-aš*	1.1.A_1 obv. 10′. 1.5 obv. 14. 12.2.3 1′
	d[*a-a-aš*	1.1.A_1 obv. 13′
	(*arḫa*) *da-a-aš*	1.1.A_2 rev. 7. 4.1.1.1.A_1 rev. 5′

	(*šara*) *da-a-aš*	4.1.1.1.B_1 rev. iii$^{?}$ 10
pret. pl. 1	*da-u-en*	4.1.1.1.B_1 rev. iii$^{?}$ 16
pret. pl. 3	*da-a-er*	3.1.8.A obv. 14′. 3.2.1 lo. e. 21′. 4.1.1.1.B_1 rev. iii$^{?}$ 14. 5.1 rev. iii 7
	(*anda*) *da-a-er*	4.1.1.2.B rev. 4
	d]*a-a-er*	4.1.2.5 rev. 13′
ptc. sg. nom.	*da-an-za*	8.1.E(A_1) obv. ii 8
	d]*a-an-za*	8.1.F rev. vi 14
	da-a-an-[*za*	4.1.1.1.A_1 obv. 13′
	d[*a-a-an-za*	4.1.1.1.A_1 obv. 20′
taḫapši-	‘felt’	
sg. nom.-acc. n.	*ta-ḫap-ši*	2.7.A obv. 5, 6. 9.1.10.A_2 rev. 3′ (2×), 4′. 9.1.11 obv.$^{?}$ 7′, 9′, 10′
	t]*a-ḫap-ši*	9.1.10.A_2 rev. 4′
	ta-ḫap-š] *i*(?)	9.1.11 obv.$^{?}$ 11′
see *Lexical Commentary*		
^{KUŠ}*taḫapši-*	‘(horse) blanket, barding’	
sg. nom.-acc. n.	^{KUŠ}*ta-ḫap-ši*	9.1.1 rev. iii 4′
see *Lexical Commentary*		
tayašša/i-	(descriptor or name of a cup)	
pl. nom.	*ta-ia-aš-ši-uš*	9.1.4.A_1 obv. ii 38
see *Lexical Commentary*		
dai-/tiya-	‘to put, place; (ptc.) set, ornamented’	
pres. sg. 1	*te-eḫ-ḫi*	2.7.A obv. 14
pres. pl. 3	*ti-an-zi*	4.1.4.9 obv. 9
pret. sg. 3	(*anda*) *da-a-iš*	2.7.A obv. 11
	da-a-i[*š*$^{?}$	2.5 rev. 11′
pret. pl. 1	*ti-ia-u-en*	4.1.1.1.B_1 rev. iii$^{?}$ 17
pret. pl. 3	*ti-i-e-er*	1.1.A_2 obv. 9′
ptc. sg. nom.	*ti-an-za*	9.1.5 obv.$^{!}$ 5
ptc. sg. nom.-acc. n.?	*ti-ia-an*(-)[	9.1.5 rev.$^{!}$ 17′
ptc. pl. nom.	*ti-ia-*[*an-te-eš*(?)	11.2.2 6′
ptc. pl. nom.-acc. n.	*ti-an-ta*	10.3.11 l. c. 9′
tak(ka)p(p)i-	(a drinking vessel)	
sg. nom.	*ták-pí-iš*	4.1.1.3 obv. 15
	tág-ga-pí-iš	4.1.1.5 obv. 4
see *Lexical Commentary*		
takš-	‘to join to, add to, unite’	
pret. pl.	*ták-ke-e-eš-šir*	6.2 obv. 3′
takšan	‘together, jointly’ (adv.)	
	ták-ša-an	8.1.F rev. vi 4
$^{\text{(GIŠ)}}$*tallai-/talla-*	‘unguentarium’	
sg. nom.	*ta*] *l-la-aš*	9.1.4.A_1 obv. ii 30
sg. nom.-acc. n.	*tal-la-a-i*	9.1.1 rev. iv 28′. 9.2.4 rev. iv 9
	ta[*l-la-a-i*(?)	10.3.12 obv. i 1′
	^{GIŠ}*tal-l*[*a-a-i*	11.1.8 5′
see *Lexical Commentary*		
damašš-	‘to push, press’	
see GADA *anda damaššuaš*		

(GI)*damalanga-*	(?)	
sg. nom.	(GI)*da-m*]*a-la-an-ga-aš*	4.2.3 l. c. 3′
see *Lexical Commentary*		
dammel-	'unprocessed, unworked'	
pl. nom.	*dam-me-lu-uš*	8.1.E(A_1) rev. iv 3′
see *Lexical Commentary*		
dammenkant-	'stuck on, affixed, attached' (ptc. of *dam(m)e(n)k-*)	
broken	(*anda*) *dam-me-in-*[*kán*(-)	11.2.4 4′
	(*anda*) *dam-me-i*[*n-kán*(-)	10.1.1.1 rev.? 9′
URUDU*d/tam(m)uri-*	(an object made of copper)	
sg. nom.	*dam-mu-ri-iš*	4.1.2.3 obv. ii 8′ (2×), 9′; rev. iii 3, 4
	dam-m[*u-ri-iš*	4.1.2.3 obv. ii 1′, 2′
	da[*m-mu-ri-iš*	4.1.2.3 obv. ii 3′
	U]RUDU*ta-mu-ri-*[*iš*?	4.1.2.4 2′
sg. dat./loc.	*A-NA* … [*dam*]*-mu-ri*	4.1.2.3 rev. iii 6
	A-NA … *dam-mu-ri*	4.1.2.3 obv. ii 12′
	A-NA] … *dam-mu-ri*	4.1.2.3 rev. iii 3
taninumaš	'of putting in order' (vb. subst. sg. gen. of *taninu-*)	
see SISKUR *taninumaš*		
GADA*tanipu-*	'hand towel'	
sg. nom.	G]ADA*ta-ni-pu-ú-*[*u*]*š*	4.2.9 rev. 28′
pl. coll.	GADA*ta-ni-pu-ú*	11.6.2 l. e. 1
see *Lexical Commentary*		
tap(p)a/išpa-		
see (TÚG) *tap(p)a/išpa-*		
dapi-, dapiant-	'all, every, each, all together'	
broken	*da-pí-*[	12.1.4 7′
See also TA.ÀM		
(DUG)*tapišani-*	(a drinking vessel)	
sg. nom.	*t*]*a-pí-ša-ni-iš*	7.1 obv. 13′, 17′
	ta-p]*í-ša-ni-iš*	7.1 obv. 16′
	ta]*-pí-š*[*a*]*-n*[*i-iš*	7.1 obv. 22′
pl. nom.	*ta*]*-pí-ša-ni-eš*	4.2.1.A_1 obv. 10
tapri-	(a seat or stool)	
sg. gen.	*tap-ri-aš*	4.2.9 obv. 29; rev. 24′
taptappa-	'nest(?)'	
sg. nom.	*tap-tap-pa-aš*	10.1.2.1 rev.? r. c. 8′. 10.1.2.2 2′
see *Lexical Commentary*		
tarḫu-, taruḫ-	'to prevail, conquer, win'	
pres. sg. 3	*tar-uḫ-zi*	6.1 rev. B 4
TÚG*tarriyanali-*	'"triple"-cloth' (a type of three-ply fabric, i.e., drill or canvas?)	
sg. nom.	TÚG*tar-ia-na-liš*	11.6.2 l. e. 4
	TÚG*tar-ri-ia-na-liš*	4.2.9 rev. 8′, 22′
	TÚG*tar-ri-i*[*a-na-liš*	4.2.9 rev. 3′
	TÚG*tar-r*[*i-ia-na-liš*	4.2.9 obv. 14
tarna-	'let, release, lay down, deposit; (with *anda*) to braid'	
pret. pl. 1	*tar-nu-me-en*	4.1.3.3 11′

ptc. sg. nom.	(*anda*) *tar-na-an-za*	9.1.6 obv. 4
	(*anda*) *tar-na*(?)-*a*]*n-za*	9.1.6 obv. 9
see *Lexical Commentary*		
tarnatarna-	(a precious metal garment decoration) 'button(?)'	
sg. nom.	*tar-na-tar-na-aš*	9.1.6 obv. 5, 8, 9
	tar-na-tar-na-⸢*a*⸣*-*[*aš*	9.1.6 obv. 12
taršant-	'dried, roasted' (ptc. of *tars-*)	
sg. nom.-acc. n.	*tar-ša-an*	10.1.1.1 rev.$^{?}$ 15′
tarupp-	'to collect, to braid together'	
broken	*ta-ru-up-p*[*a-an*(-)	11.3.1 8′
taruppenza	(?)	
sg. nom.(?)	*ta-ru-up-pé-en-za*	9.2.4 obv. i 10′
see *Lexical Commentary*		
tarzu-	(?)	
sg. nom.-acc. n.	*tar-zu-ú*	11.1.3 4′
see *Lexical Commentary*		
tarzuda-	(?)	
broken	*tar-zu-ú-da-*x[	9.1.5 rev.$^{!}$ 3′
	tar-zu-[*ú-da-*x	9.1.5 rev.$^{!}$ 2′
see *Lexical Commentary*		
tattapalaim(m)a/i-	(adj. modifying drinking vessels)	
sg. nom.	*ta-at-ta-pa-la-i-im-me-eš*	9.2.4 rev. iv 8
	t]*a-at-ta-pa-la-i-*[*im-me-eš*(?)	9.2.10 3′
tattapalant-	(adj. modifying drinking vessels)	
sg. nom.-acc. n.	*ta-at-ta-pa-la-a-an*	9.1.1 rev. iv 24′
tiyalant-	'covered, overlaid' (ptc. of *tiyala(i)-*)	
sg. nom.-acc. n.	*ti-ia-la-an*	4.2.9 obv. 2; rev. 14′. 9.1.8 obv. 7′
	ti-ia-[*l*]*a-*[*an*	4.2.9 obv. 29
	ti-ia-l[*a-an*	4.2.6 obv.$^{?}$ 4′
	ti-i[*a-la-an*	4.2.9 rev. 11′
see *Lexical Commentary*		
tiannaš	'of setting, laying' (sg. gen. of *tiyatar*)	
see GAM-*an tiannaš*		
tiyawara-	(?)	
pl. coll.(?)	*ti-ia-wa-*[*ra*(?)	8.1.A obv. ii 4′
see *Lexical Commentary*		
tiyawa(š)	'of setting, laying' (sg. gen. of *tiyawar*)	
see GAM-*an tiyawa(š)*		
tilipunai(ya)-	(a drinking vessel?)	
pl. nom.-acc. n.(?)	*ti-li-pu-na-a-i-ia*	9.1.4.A_1 obv. ii 24
tit(ta)li(t)-	(a decorative metal edging(?))	
sg. nom.-acc. n.	*ti-it-li*	6.5 rev. 12′, 15′
	ti]*-it-ta-li*	8.1.E(A_1) rev. v 4′
see *Lexical Commentary*		
tittalitaim(m)a/i-	'endowed with a *tit(ta)li(t)-*'	
sg. nom.	*ti-it-ta-li-ta-i-me-eš*	9.1.4.A_1 obv. ii 20

	ti-i]*t-ta-li-ta-i-me-eš*	9.1.1 rev. iv 22′
	ti-it-ta-li-t]*a-i-me-eš*	11.2.3 5′
	t[*i-i*]*t-ta-li-ta-i-me-iš*	9.1.4.A_1 obv. ii 31
	ti-i[*t-t*]*a-li-ta-i-me-eš*	9.2.1 obv. ii 22′
	ti-it-ta-li-[*ta-i-me-iš*	9.1.4.A_1 obv. ii 25
	ti-it-ta-l[*i-ta-i-me-eš*(?)	10.3.4 11′
	ti-it-ta-[*li-ta-i-me-eš*(?)	9.2.5 obv. i(?) 12′
Luw. pl. nom.	*ti-it-ta-li-ta-i-me-en-zi*	9.1.1 rev. iv 43′
see *Lexical Commentary*		
tititina-	(?)	
pl. nom.-acc. n.	*ti-ti-ti-na*	9.1.7 obv. 8′
duwarna-	‘to break’	
pret. sg. 3	*du-wa-ar-na-aš*	5.1 rev. iv 2
pret. pl. 3	(*arḫa*) *du-wa-ar-ni-er*	5.5 rev. iii 5′
	(*arḫa*) *du-wa-ar-ner*	5.2 obv. ii 13
	(*arḫa*) *du-wa-a*]*r-ner*	5.2 rev. iii 4′
ptc. sg. nom.-acc. n.	*du-wa-a*[*r-na-an*	10.3.12 obv. i 13′
	du-wa-a[*r*$^!$(text: *r*[*a*)-*na-an*	10.3.12 obv. i 9′
	(*arḫa*) *du-*[*wa-ar-na-an*	10.3.7 5′
tuḫḫan	(a wooden or metal object)	
sg. nom.-acc. n.	*túḫ-ḫa-an*	10.3.11 l. c. 10′
	túḫ-[*ḫa-an*	4.1.1.3 obv. 14
	tú]*ḫ-ḫa-an*	9.1.12 2′
sg. dat./loc.	*túḫ*$^?$*-ḫa-ni*	9.1.12 3′
^{LÚ}*tuḫ(u)kanti-*	(title of the Hittite crown prince)	
	^{L}]^{Ú}*tu-ḫu-kán-t*[*i*	6.6 obv. 2′
sg. dat./loc.	*A-NA* ^{LÚ}*tu-ḫu-kán-ti*	4.1.1.1.B_1 rev. iii$^?$ 17
tuk(k)anzi-	‘cultivation, breeding’	
sg. nom.-acc. n.	*tu-kán-zi*	1.1.A_2 rev. 8
	tu-uk-kán-zi	1.1.A_1 obv. 13′
see *Lexical Commentary*		
$^{\text{(GIŠ)}}$*tuppa-*	‘(wooden) chest’	
sg. nom.	*du-up-pa-aš*	2.17 obv.$^?$ r. c. 5′
	du-up-p[*a-aš*(?)	11.4.1 5′
	^{GIŠ}*du-u*[*p-pa-aš*(?)	2.16 rev. v 3
	tup-pa-aš	2.2 obv. 4′. 2.17 obv.$^?$ r. c. 3′. 9.2.6 obv. i 2′
	t[*up-pa-aš*	2.17 obv.$^?$ r. c. 2′
	^{GIŠ}*tup-pa-aš*	2.1.A obv. ii(?) 7′, 13′. 2.1.B 4′. 2.2 rev. 16. 2.9.A_3 obv. ii 5′, 12′, 13′. 2.12 obv.$^!$ ii 9′. 4.2.1.A_1 obv. 7, 8. 8.4 rev. 19′. 10.3.12 obv. i 17′
	^{GI}]^{Š}*tup-pa-aš*	4.2.1.A_1 obv. 6. 8.1.A rev. v 10, 14′. 9.2.14 2′
	^{GIŠ}*tu*]*p-pa-aš*	4.2.1.A_1 up. e. 1
	^{GIŠ}*tup*]*-pa-aš*	8.1.D obv. i 6′. 9.1.1 rev. iv 15′
	^{GIŠ}*tup-p*]*a-aš*	8.1.D obv. i 9′
	^{GIŠ}*tup-pa-a*]*š*	8.1.D obv. i 11′
	^{GIŠ}*tup-pa-a*[*š*	2.13 rev.$^?$ 8′
	^{GIŠ}*tu*[*p-pa-aš*	4.2.1.A_1 obv. 3
sg. nom.?	*tup-pa*(-)x(-)[	9.2.7 rev. r. c. 4′
sg. acc.	*tup-pa-an*	2.4 rev. 2′
sg. gen.?	^{GIŠ}*tup-pa-aš*	6.1 obv. 11

pl. dat./loc.?	$^{\text{GIŠ!}}$tup-pa-*aš$^{?}$*	11.2.1 5′
abl.	^{GIŠ}*tup-pa-za*	4.1.1.1.A_1 obv. 4′. 4.1.1.1.B_2 obv. i$^{?}$ 2′, 4′
	$^{\text{GI}]\text{Š}}$*tup-pa-za*	4.1.1.1.A_1 obv. 14′, 15′
	^{GIŠ}*tup-p]a-za*	4.1.1.1.A_1 obv. 16′
stem	^{GIŠ}*tup-pa*	4.2.2 obv. 3. 8.1.D obv. i 7′
	^{GIŠ}*tu]p-pa*	2.2 rev. 1
= $^{\text{GI/GIŠ}}$PISAN; see also É(.GAL) *tuppa-*		
tuppanziya-		
see *appanziya-*		
tuppi-	'clay tablet'	
sg. nom.	*tu]-up-pí-iš*	11.1.3 12′
abl.	*tup-pí-az*	2.7.A obv. 14
= DUB		
$^{\text{(URUDU)}}$*dupiyali-*	"striker" (a sledge or maul(?))	
sg. nom.	*du-pí-ia-l[iš*	9.1.5 rev.$^{!}$ 15′
	du-[pí-ia-liš	11.1.7 4′
	^{URUDU}*du-pí-ia-liš*	5.1 obv. ii 12. 5.2 obv. ii 3
	^{URUDU}*d[u-pí-ia-liš*	5.3 r. c. 7′
see *Lexical Commentary*		
turiya-	'to harness, yoke'	
ptc. pl. nom.	*tu-u-ri-i[a-an-te-eš*(?)	10.2.1.6 3′
ue-/uwa-	'to come'	
pres. sg. 3	(*kattan*) *ú-[ez-zi*(?)	6.1 l. e. 1c.
ulip(a)na-	'wolf'	
sg. nom.	*ú-li-ip-ni-eš*	9.2.1 obv. ii 12′
	ú-l[i-ip-ni-iš	9.1.15 3′
see *Lexical Commentary*; see also $^{\text{(D)}}$*walipašu* under *Divine Names*?		
uluppanni-	(?)	
sg. nom.	*ú-lu-up-p[a-an-ni-iš*	9.1.7 obv. 3′
sg. dat./loc.	*ú-lu-up-pa-an-ni*	9.1.7 obv. 6′
see *Lexical Commentary*		
u(n)ḫ-	'to clear, free, remove'	
pret. sg. 3	(*arḫa*) *u-un-uḫ-da*	2.5 rev. 10′
pret. pl. 3	*u-un-ḫi-er*	2.1.B 9′. 2.2 obv. 4′
see *Lexical Commentary*		
unuwašḫa-	'jewelry'	
sg. nom.	*ú-nu-wa-aš-ḫa-aš*	9.2.1 obv. ii 2′
	ú-n]u-wa-aš-ḫa-aš	9.1.10.A_1 rev. 4′
uppa-	'to send, ship'	
pret. pl. 3	*up-pé-er*	5.1 rev. iv 5
broken	*up-[pí-...*	4.2.12 4′
uraki(t)-	'rod; wire; (a variety of spear)'	
sg. nom.	*ú-ra-ki*	2.17 obv.$^{?}$ r. c. 1′, 2′
see *Lexical Commentary*; = NÍG.GÍD.DA		
urašti-	(a piece of jewelry)	
sg. nom.	*ú-ra-aš-ti-iš*	8.4 rev. 12′. 9.2.6 obv. i 3′

ušimašša/i-	(?)	
pl. nom.-acc. n.	*ú-ši-ma-aš-ša*	10.3.4 5′
see *Lexical Commentary*		
uda-	'to bring (hither), carry, transport'	
pres. sg. 3	*ú-da-i*	4.1.1.1.B_1 obv. ii$^{?}$ 6′
	ú-d[a-i	4.1.1.1.A_1 rev. 2′
pret. pl. 3	*ú-te-er*	1.1.A_2 obv. 5′, 6′, 7′. 1.5 rev. 26. 8.6 l. c. 7′
	(EGIR-*pa*) *ú-te-er*	4.1.1.1.A_1 rev. 6′. 4.1.1.1.B_2 obv. i$^{?}$ 7′
	ú-t]e-e[r	4.1.1.1.B_2 obv. i$^{?}$ 1′
	ú-[te-er(?)	1.5 rev. 27
wak(k)-	'to be missing'	
mid. pres. sg. 3	*wa-*ka_4*-ri*	3.1.1.A_1 obv. ii 15′. 3.1.1.A_3 obv. iii 12′, 16′; rev. iv 13′
	wa]-ka_4*-ri*	3.1.1.A_3 obv. iii 2′
	wa-k]a_4*-ri*	3.1.1.A_1 obv. ii 12′
	wa-ka_4*-r[i*	3.1.1.A_1 obv. ii 9′
	wa-ka_4*-[ri*	3.1.1.A_2 rev. v 11′. 3.1.3 obv.$^{?}$ 5′
	wa-k[a_4*-ri*	3.1.1.A_1 obv. ii 6′
	wa-[ka_4*-ri*	3.1.2 obv. l. c. 10′
	w[a-ka_4*-ri*(?)	3.1.2 obv. l. c. 7′. 3.1.3 obv.$^{?}$ 1′
	wa-ak-ka_4*-ri*	3.1.1.A_1 rev. v 11′. 4.1.1.3 rev. B 5. 10.1.2.8 rev. r. c. 5′
	wa-a]k-ka_4*-ri*	2.8 obv. 4
	wa-ak-ka_4*-[ri*	2.14 12′
	wa-ak-ka_4*-r[i*	10.3.13 6′
	wa-ak-ka_4*-a-r[i*	6.10 6′
	wa-a[k-ka_4*-ri*(?)	9.2.5 obv. i(?) 9′
see *Lexical Commentary*		
wakši(ya)-	'to be (temporarily) absent'	
pret. sg. 3	*wa-ak-ši-at*	4.1.1.1.A_1 rev. 2′. 4.1.1.3 rev. B 3, 7
	wa-ak-ši-ia-a[t	2.2 rev. 5
	wa-ak-š[i$^{?}$*-at*(?)	8.1.A obv. ii 29′
	wa-ak-[ši-ia-at	2.2 rev. 10
see *Lexical Commentary*		
$^{\text{(URUDU)}}$*wakšur-*	(a 'one-sixth'(?)-vessel for liquids)	
sg. nom.	*wa-ak-šur*	1.1.A_1 obv. 7′, 9′. 1.1.A_2 rev. 5. 3.1.1.A_2 rev. v 12′, 15′. 4.1.1.3 rev. A 3′. 10.3.5 8′
	$^{\text{(URUDU)}}$*wa-a]k-šur*	9.2.11 2′
	wa-ak-šu]r	1.1.A_1 obv. 3′
	wa-ak-šu[r	4.1.1.7 rev.$^{!?}$ 6
	wa-ak-š[ur	2.13 obv.$^{?}$ 7′
	wa-a[k-šur	3.1.8.A rev. 7′
	^{URUDU}*wa-ak-šur*	3.1.1.A_3 obv. iii 10′. 5.1 obv. ii 2′; rev. iii 5. 5.2 obv. ii 7. 8.5 rev. iv(?) 1′
	$^{\text{UR]UDU}}$*wa-ak-šur*	3.1.1.A_3 obv. iii 9′. 5.7 rev. iii$^{?}$ 19′
	$^{\text{URUD]U}}$*wa-ak-šur*	3.1.1.A_3 rev. iv 15′. 3.1.4 4′
	^{URUDU}*w[a-ak-šur*	3.1.1.A_3 rev. iv 10′
pl. dat./loc.	*A-NA* 4$^{?}$ ^{URUDU}*wa-ak-šur*	3.1.1.A_3 obv. iii 9′
	A-NA 22 *wa-ak-šur*	3.1.8.A rev. 9′
see *Lexical Commentary*		

walli-	'shorn; smooth'	
sg. nom.	*wa-al-liš*	4.1.4.2.A_2 obv. l. c. 7′. 9.1.1 rev. iv
	wa-al-li-iš	2.7.A obv. 25
pl. dat./loc.	*wa-al-la-ia-aš*	4.2.4 rev. 5′
walipašu-		
see $^{(\mathrm{D})}$*walipašu-* under *Divine Names*		
$^{\mathrm{NA}_4}$*wannantila-*	(a variety of stone)	
sg. nom.?	$^{\mathrm{NA}_4}$*wa-an-na-an-ti-la-aš*	9.1.1 rev. iii 33′
-war-/-wa-	(quotative particle)	
	-wa-	1.5 rev. 22. 2.7.A obv. 14. 12.3.7 6′, 8′, 9′
	-w[a-	7.1 rev. 16′. 12.3.7 5′
	-war-	2.5 obv. 3′. 2.7.A obv. 14. 7.1 rev. 7′
warḫueššar	"shag-cloth(?)"	
sg. nom.-acc. n.	*wa-ar-ḫu-eš-šar*	8.8.B l. c. 7′
	wa-ar-ḫ[u-eš-šar(?)	8.3 obv. 6′
see *Lexical Commentary*		
warpal-	(a bronze object)	
sg. nom.-acc. n.	*wa-ar-pa-[a]l*	9.2.6 obv. i 13′
see *Lexical Commentary*		
$^{(\mathrm{URUDU})}$*warpuwaš*	'wash pail' (lit. a vessel "of washing")	
sg. gen.	*wa-ar-pu-wa-aš*	2.7.A rev. 4
	wa-ar-pu-u-wa-⟨aš⟩	3.1.8.A rev. 7′
	wa-ar-pu-u-wa-[aš	11.1.9 3′
	wa-ar-pu-w[a-aš	4.2.6 rev.$^{?}$ 4′
	^{URUDU}*wa-ar-pu-aš*	4.2.9 obv. 16; rev. 30′
	^{URUDU}*wa-ar-[p]u-aš*	6.1 rev. B 7
see also ^{URUDU}ÁB×A, $^{(\mathrm{URUDU})}$NÍG.ŠU.LUḪ(.ḪA), $^{(\mathrm{URUDU})}$ŠE.NAGA		
waršanaim(m)a/i-		
see GUNNI *waršanaim(m)a/i-*		
waršuwar	'reaping; the harvest' (vb. subst. of *warš-*, *warši(ya)-* 'to sweep, reap')	
sg. gen.	*wa-ar-šu-u-wa-aš*	10.2.2.1 4′
waš(ša)pa-	'cloth, clothing'	
pl. coll.	*wa-aš-ša-pa*	10.2.1.1 obv. 3′
wašḫa-	(a 'sacralized' object)	
sg. nom.	*wa-aš-ḫa-aš*	4.1.1.7 rev.$^{!?}$ 5
wašḫaniya-		
see (TÚG) *wašḫaniya-*		
wašše/a-	'to dress, to clothe, to cover with cloth'	
ptc. sg. nom.	(*šer*) *w[a]-a[š]-ša-an-za*	2.11 obv.$^{?}$ 6′
	(*šer*) *wa-[aš-ša-an-za*	8.1.A rev. v 21′
	(UGU) *wa-aš-ša-an-za*	2.2 obv. 5′, 7′. 8.1.B rev. 8′
	(UGU) *wa-aš-ša-an-[za*	2.1.B 3′. 8.1.D rev. iv 7′
	(UGU) *wa-aš-ša-[an-za*	2.1.B 2′
	(UGU) *wa-aš-š[a-an-za*	2.2 obv. 12′. 8.1.A obv. ii 24′
	(UGU) *wa-aš-[ša-an-za*	2.1.A obv. ii(?) 9′
see also GADA *waššuwaš*		

waši(ya)-	'to buy'	
pret. sg. 3	*wa-ši-at*	1.1.A_1 obv. 6′, 12′. 1.1.A_2 rev. 3, 10. 1.1.A_3 rev. 2′, 11′
	wa-ši-ia-at	1.1.A_3 rev. 4′, 5′
	w]a-ši-at	1.1.A_3 rev. 8′
	wa-š]i-at	1.1.A_4 rev. 2′
	wa-si]-ia-at	1.1.A_4 rev. 5′
	wa-ši-a[t	1.1.A_4 obv. 11′
	wa-ši-ia-a[t	1.1.A_3 rev. 3′
	wa-ši-[at	1.1.A_3 rev. 6′
see also ŠÀM		
^{NA_4}*watar*	'"water"-stone'	
sg. nom.-acc. n.	^{NA_4}*wa-a-tar*	12.2.2 8′
watarma-	(a type of chair?)	
sg. nom.	*wa-tar-ma-aš*	4.2.9 obv. 17
see *Lexical Commentary*		
wilan-/wilna-, wilana-	'clay'	
sg. gen.	*ú-i-l[a-na-aš*	10.1.1.2 rev. iv 7′
see *Lexical Commentary*		
-za	(reflexive particle)	
	-az	5.1 rev. iii 3
	-za	1.3 4′. 2.6 1′. 2.9.A_3 obv. i 9′, 11′. 2.12 obv. ii! 2′. 7.1 rev. 9′. 12.3.7 6′, 8′, 9′
$^{(GIŠ)}$*zaḫurti-*	(a seat, bench, or footrest)	
sg. nom.	*za-ḫ[u]r-ti-iš*	10.2.1.2 obv. 12′
	^{GIŠ}*z]a-ḫur-te-iš*	10.3.9 4′
	^{GIŠ}*za-ḫur-ti-i[š*	10.3.5 12′
	^{GIŠ}*za-[ḫur-ti-iš*(?)	2.18 10′
= ^{GIŠ}*MŪŠABU*		
zaima-, zaimi-, zaimiya-	(an adj. applied to garments)	
sg. nom.(?)	*za-i-ma-aš*	11.1.7 7′
pl. nom.-acc. n.(?)	*za-i-mi-ia*	6.1 obv. 6
see *Lexical Commentary*		
zakkit(ta)r-	(a metal object)	
pl. nom.-acc. n.(?)	*za-ak-ki-it-ra*	9.1.11 obv.? 3′
	za-ak-ki-i[t-ra(?)	9.1.13 4′
see *Lexical Commentary*		
zalḫai-	(a wine vessel)	
sg. nom.-acc. n.	*za-al-ḫa-i*	10.3.3 obv.? 10′
	za-al-[ḫa-i	6.2 rev. 7
zanu-	'to smelt'	
pres. sg. 3	*za-nu-zi*	6.3 rev. A 2
infin.	*za-nu-ma-an-z[i*	2.7.A rev. 3
	za-nu-m[a-an-zi	4.1.1.1.A_1 obv. 5′
$^{(URUDU)}$*z/šap(p)iškur-*	'a shaving razor(?)'	
sg. nom.	*za]-pé-eš-ku-⟨ri⟩-iš*	3.1.4 3′
	^{URUDU}*za-pí-iš-ku-ri-i[š*	3.1.1.A_2 rev. v 7′
sg. acc.	^{URUDU}*za-pí-iš-ku-[r]i-in*	5.2 obv. ii 14

	^{URUDU}*z[a-pí-iš-ku-ri-in*(?)	5.2 obv. ii 15
sg. nom.-acc. n.	*ša-pé-eš-gur*	9.1.4.A_1 obv. ii 2
	za-pé-eš-kur	5.2 rev. iii 12′
	za-pé-eš-gur	10.3.5 5′
	za-a[p-pé-eš-gur(?)	10.3.5 2′

see *Lexical Commentary*

zarat(t)a-	(a container or vessel)	
Luw. sg. nom.-acc. n.	*za-ra-ta-an-za*	4.2.1.A_2 obv. 6′
	za-ra-at-ta-an-za	4.2.1.A_2 obv. 5′

see *Lexical Commentary*

$^{\text{(GADA)}}$*zazzi(t)-*	(a delicate or soft cloth)	
abl.	*za-az-zi-ta-[az*(?)	2.2 obv. 9′

see *Lexical Commentary*

^{KUŠ}*zazu-*
see *zuzazu*

zinnant-	'finished, conluded' (ptc. of *zinna(i)-*)	
sg. nom.-acc. n.	*zi-in-na-an*	9.1.1 rev. iv 14′
	zi-in-na-⟨an⟩	4.1.1.3 rev. B 1
	zi-in-n[a-an(?)	10.3.1 rev. iii 13′

see also GAMRU, QATÛ, TIL

zingi-	(?)	
sg. nom.-acc. n.	*zi-in-gi*	9.1.5 rev.! 13′
	z]i-en-gi	9.1.5 rev.! 13′

see *Lexical Commentary*

^{MUNUS}*zintuḫi-*	(a cultic performer)	
pl. dat./loc.	*A-NA* $^{\text{MUNUS.MEŠ}}$*zi-in-tu-ḫi-aš*	6.1 rev. B 6
zipaddanni-	(a vessel or container for comestibles)	
sg. nom.-acc. n.	*zi-pád-da-an-ni*	12.3.2 8′
zuḫati-	(a cloth or leather gorget)	
sg. nom.-acc. n.	*zu-ḫa-ti*	9.1.11 obv.? 9′

see *Lexical Commentary*

zuzazu-	(?)	
sg. nom.-acc. n.(?)	*zu-za-zu*	9.1.11 obv.? 5′

Sumerograms

Note that Sumerograms are not assigned a case unless one is explicitly marked in the text with a phonetic complement or a preposition. Also note that lexical items such as gold or silver that can modify other objects are further subdivided. For materials such as gold and silver, when the lexical item refers to the thing or substance itself it is left unmarked, but when it modifies another object it is marked as a 'material'. Thus, the word for 'gold' in 1 MA.NA KÙ.SI_{22} '1 mina of gold (bullion)' would be unmarked, but the gold in 1 GAL KÙ.SI_{22} '1 gold cup' would be under 'material' in the KÙ.SI_{22} entry.

A	'water'	
abl.	A-*za*	4.1.4.9 obv. 1
	$A^{\text{MEŠ}}$-*za*	4.1.4.9 obv. 8

A.AB.BA	‘sea’	
sg. dat./loc.	*A-NA* A.AB.BA	12.1.1 r. c. 4′
see also *ḪAṢARTU* A.AB.BA		
A.BÁR	‘lead’	
material		
	A.BÁR	11.3.1 18′
A.DA.GUR	(a cultic vessel)	
	A.DA.GUR	4.1.1.3 rev. A 8′. 9.1.5 rev.$^!$ 11′. 7.3 obv. i 9. 11.4.2 obv. 3′
^{KUŠ}A.GÁ.LÁ	‘(leather) bag’	
	^{KUŠ}A.GÁ.LÁ	2.1.A obv. ii(?) 6′. 2.7.A obv. 5, 6, 25
	*^{KUŠ}*A.GÁ.LÁ	2.5 rev. 8′
	^{KUŠ}A.GÁ.*LÁ*	4.2.1.A_1 obv. 8
	$^{\text{KU}]\text{Š}}$A.GÁ.LÁ	2.1.B 1′
^{KUŠ}A.GÁ.LÁ *ŠA* ^{LÚ}*KARTAPPI* ‘charioteer’s bag’		
	^{KUŠ}A.GÁ.LÁ *ŠA* ^{LÚ}*KAR-TA*[*P-PÍ*	9.2.6 obv. i 11′
A.ŠÀ	‘field’	
	A.ŠÀ	12.3.1 5′, 6′
= *gimra-*?; see also LÍL		
^{URUDU}ÁB×A	‘(copper) wash basin’	
	^{URUDU}ÁB×A	3.1.2 obv. l. c. 9′, 11′
see also $^{\text{(URUDU)}}$*warpuwaš*, $^{\text{(URUDU)}}$NÍG.ŠU.LUḪ(.ḪA), $^{\text{(URUDU)}}$ŠE.NAGA		
AL	‘hoe’	
	AL	10.2.1.1 rev. 7′
ALAM	‘statue, figurine’	
	ALAM	2.13 rev.$^?$ 9′. 9.2.1 rev. iii 5′. 9.2.6 obv. i 8′. 9.2.7 rev. r. c. 8′. 9.2.9 obv.$^?$ 7′. 10.1.1.1 rev.$^?$ 8′. 10.1.1.2 rev. iv 3′, 4′. 10.3.3 obv.$^?$ 5′. 11.2.1 4′
	ALAM (LÚ)	9.1.7 rev. 3. 10.1.1.1 rev.$^?$ 7′, 8′. 10.1.1.2 rev. iv 2′
	ALAM (MUNUS)	10.1.1.1 rev.$^?$ 10′. 10.1.1.2 rev. iv 4′
	ALAM (MUNUS-*TI*)	9.1.1 rev. iv 12′
	A]LAM	9.1.4.A_1 obv. ii 3
	A]LAM (MUNUS)	10.1.1.2 rev. iv 3′
	AL]AM	8.1.A obv. i 18′. 10.2.1.2 obv. 7′. 10.3.1 rev. iii 6′
	AL]AM (MUNUS-*TI*)	9.2.4 obv. i 12′; rev. iii 11′
	ALA]M (MUNUS-*TI*)	10.2.1.1 obv. 8′
	ALA[M	9.1.5 obv.$^!$ 12. 10.3.3 obv.$^?$ 4′
	A[LAM	10.1.1.2 rev. iv 2′
	A[LAM$^?$ ($UZ_6$$^?$)	9.1.5 obv.$^!$ 5
pl.	ALAM$^{\text{ḪI.A}}$	10.1.1.1 rev.$^?$ 6′
	ALAM^{MEŠ}	10.1.1.2 rev. iv 1′
$^{\text{(GU}_4\text{)}}$AMAR	‘calf’	
	AMAR	9.1.4.A_4 l. c. 6′
	(GÚ) AMAR	2.17 obv.$^?$ r. c. 5′. 10.2.2.4 obv.$^?$ r. c. 5′
	(^{URUDU}*ANKURINU*) AMAR	8.1.A rev. vi 4′, 5′
	(*BI-IB-RU*) AMAR	9.1.4.A_1 obv. ii 32
	$^{\text{GU}_4}$AMAR	10.3.3 obv.$^?$ 12′

^{LÚ}AMA.TU	'domestic servant'	
	^{LÚ}AMA.[TU	12.3.3 3′
pl.	^{LÚ}AMA.[TU^{MEŠ}	12.3.3 3′
AN.[…	'iron (or iron ore?) or tin' (broken context)	
material		
	AN.[	12.1.1 r. c. 5′
AN.BAR	'iron (or iron ore?)'	
	AN.BAR	3.1.7.A_1 l. e. 3. 4.1.1.1.B_1 rev. iv? 3. 4.2.2 obv. 1. 11.7.2 4′
	A]N.BAR	4.2.2 obv. 1
	AN.B]AR	4.1.1.1.B_1 rev. iv? 1
	AN.BA[R	11.7.2 4′
sg. gen.	*ŠA* AN.BAR	12.1.2 8′
material		
	AN.BAR	1.1.A_1 obv. 7′. 4.2.1.A_1 obv. 7, 8, 10. 4.2.1.A_2 rev. 12′. 4.2.3 l. c. 1′. 4.2.9 rev. 31′ (2×); lo. e. 32′ (2×). 3.1.12 5′. 8.1.A rev. v 4, 5, 7. 8.1.C 1′. 9.1.1 rev. iii 12′. 9.1.4.A_1 obv. ii 8. 9.1.5 rev.! 14′ (2×). 9.1.11 obv.? 3′, 8′. 9.1.14 obv. r. c. 11′. 10.1.1.1 rev.? 5′, 11′. 10.1.1.2 rev. iv 4′, 5′. 10.3.1 obv. ii 3′. 11.1.7 2′, 4′. 11.7.3 rev.? 5. 12.1.1 r. c. 9′. 12.1.2 3′
	AN.BAR	4.2.1.A_1 obv. 5
	AN.BAR(?)	4.2.3 l. c. 3′
	A]N.BAR	4.2.1.A_1 obv. 2. 11.1.7 2′, 3′. 12.1.1 r. c. 6′
	A]N.BAR	9.1.4.A_1 rev. iii 1′
	A]N?.BAR	9.1.4.A_1 rev. iii 25″
	A]N.BA[R	12.1.1 l. c. 1′, 4′
	AN].BAR	10.3.1 obv. ii 10′
	AN?].BAR	9.1.4.A_1 rev. iii 7′
	AN.BA[R	11.1.9 6′
	AN.B[AR	9.2.4 rev. iv 6
	AN.[BAR	10.1.1.1 rev.? 6′, 7′
	A[N.BAR	4.2.1.A_1 up. e. 1; obv. 4
	AN.BAR (SIG_5)	4.2.1.A_1 obv. 6, 12. 4.2.1.A_2 rev. 12′. 8.1.A rev. v 9. 8.1.D obv. i 3′
	[A]N.BAR SIG_5?	8.1.C 3′
	AN.[BAR (SIG_5?)	8.1.A rev. v 8

see *Lexical Commentary, s.v.* AN.BAR (GE_6); = *ḫapalki-*/*ḪAPALKI(N)NU*; see also *kiklibaim(m)a/i-*, *parzašša-*, *parzagulliya-*, AN.BAR GE_6, AN.BAR (*ŠA*) GUNNI

AN.BAR GE_6	'black iron (or iron ore?)'	
	AN.BAR GE_6	8.1.A rev. v 14′. 8.1.D obv. i 11′. 2.3 1
	AN.BAR] GE_6	12.2.2 3′
material		
	AN.BAR GE_6	2.13 obv.? 4′. 3.1.12 7′. 4.2.2 obv. 2, 3. 4.2.4 obv. 10. 8.1.A obv. i 2′ (2×), 3′, 4′, 11′; rev. v 2, 3, 4, 8, 15′. 8.4 rev. 16′. 9.1.1 rev. iii 8′, 13′, 22′. 9.1.10.A_1 obv. 3′; rev. 2′. 9.1.10.B 5′, 6′. 9.1.4.A_1 obv. ii 7,

		17. 9.2.2 rev.$^{!}$ iii 13′. 9.2.4 rev. iv 5. 9.2.7 obv. l. c. 8′. 11.2.2 4′
	AN.BA]R GE_6	8.1.A rev. v 3
	AN.BAR] G[E_6	8.1.D obv. i 12′
	AN.B[AR GE_6	8.1.D obv. i 2′

see *Lexical Commentary, s.v.* AN.BAR (GE_6); see also *ḫapalki-*, *kiklibaim(m)a/i-*, *parzagulliya-*, *parzašša-*, AN.BAR, AN.BAR (*ŠA*) GUNNI, *ḪAPALKI(N)NU*

AN.BAR (*ŠA*) GUNNI	'iron (or iron ore?) "of the hearth"'	
	AN.BAR *ŠA* GUNNI	4.2.1.A_1 obv. 6
	AN.BAR GU[NNI	4.2.1.A_2 rev. 12′

see *Lexical Commentary*; see also *ḫapalki-*, *kiklibaim(m)a/i-*, *parzagulliya-*, *parzašša-*, AN.BAR, AN.BAR GE_6, *ḪAPALKINNU*

AN.DAḪ.ŠUM	(the spring festival or its eponymous plant)	
	($EZEN_4$) AN.DAḪ.ŠUM	6.1 lo. e. 10″
	(GAL) AN.DAḪ.ŠUM	4.1.1.2.A obv. 20′. 4.1.1.2.B obv. 6
AN.NA	'tin'	
	AN.NA	3.1.5.A_1 obv. i(?) 4′. 3.1.7.A_1 obv. i 4′; lo. e. 16′. 3.1.7.A_2 obv. ii 3′, 5b′, 7b′, 9′, 12′, 15′; rev. iv 2′; rev. v 2′, 3′. 5.2 obv. ii 6. 11.7.2 5′. 12.1.1 r. c. 4′, 6′, 10′
	A]N.NA	3.1.5.A_1 obv. i(?) 1′. 3.1.7.A_2 obv. ii 17′. 12.1.1 l. c. 7′
material		
	AN.NA	8.1.A rev. v 22′. 10.3.3 obv.$^{?}$ 12′, 14′
AN.ZA.GÀR	'fort, tower, fortified post'	
	AN.ZA.GÀR	11.2.5 1′
ANŠE	'donkey'	
	(KUŠ$^{!?}$) ANŠE [	4.1.3.6 obv. 15′

see also DUR ANŠE

ANŠE.GÌR.NUN.NA	'hinny (male horse × female donkey)'	
pl.	ANŠE.GÌR.N[UN.NA^{MEŠ}	12.3.3 2′
ANŠE.KUR.RA	'horse'	
	ANŠ]E.KUR.RA	10.2.1.1 rev. 6′
pl.	ANŠE.KUR.RA^{MEŠ}	12.3.3 9′
	ANŠE.KUR].RA^{MEŠ}	12.3.3 8′
	ANŠE.KUR.R]A^{MEŠ}	10.2.1.6 3′. 12.3.3 7′
inst.	*IŠ-TU* ANŠE.KUR.RA	6.1 rev. B 4
ANŠE.NUN.NA	'mule (female horse × male donkey)'	
pl.	ANŠE.NUN.NA^{MEŠ}	12.3.3 6′, 7′
	ANŠE.[NUN.NA^{MEŠ}	12.3.3 9′
AN.ZA.GÀR	'pillar, tower'	
	AN.ZA.GÀR	3.1.8.A obv. 16′
ARAD	'servant, slave'	
pl.	ARAD^{MEŠ}	12.3.3 5′

AŠ.ME	'sun disk'	
	AŠ.ME	1.5 obv. 13. 3.1.8.A obv. 7′. 4.1.1.1.A_1 rev. 11′. 4.1.1.1.B_1 rev. iii? 1. 8.1.A obv. ii 12′. 8.4 rev. 9′. 9.1.1 rev. iii 17′. 9.1.10.B 4′. 9.2.2 rev.! iii 4′, 8′, 11′, 13′. 9.2.4 obv. i 13′ (2×), 16′. 10.2.1.1 obv. 3′
	AŠ.ME(?)	9.2.2 rev.! iii 2′
	AŠ.[ME(?)	9.2.4 obv. ii 1′
= *šittar-, šittara-, šittari-*?		
NA4AŠ.NU11.GAL	'alabaster'	
	NA4AŠ.NU11.GAL	12.2.2 6′
material		
	NA4AŠ.NU11.GAL	2.3 5. 4.2.4 obv. 5. 9.1.4.A_1 obv. i 27′
	NA4AŠ.NU11.G[AL	9.2.8.A_1 3′
LÚAŠGAB	'leather-worker'	
sg. dat./loc.	*A-NA* LÚAŠGAB	1.1.A_3 rev. 8′
BA.BA.ZA	'barley-mash'	
	BA.BA.ZA	10.1.1.1 rev.? 14′. 10.1.1.2 rev. iv 9′
BABBAR	'white'	
	BABBAR	1.2 rev 3′. 2.2 rev. 17. 2.5 obv. 2′. 2.7.A obv. 25. 3.1.12 10′. 4.1.3.4.A_1 obv. l. c. 1′, 2′, 3′, 4′, 5′; rev. l. c. 2′, 3′, 4′, 5′, 6′, 7′. 4.1.3.4.A_2 rev. l. c. 1′, 2′, 3′, 4′, 7′, 8′, 9′. 4.1.3.5.A_1 obv.? 1′, 2′. 4.1.3.5.A_2 1′, 2′, 3′, 4′, 5′. 4.1.4.1.A_2 obv. i 5′. 4.1.4.7 obv. 5. 4.1.4.8 3′. 4.2.4 obv. 1; rev. 3′. 4.2.6 obv.? 4′, 8′, 14′ (2×), 16′, 19′. 4.2.9 obv. 1, 4, 19, 22 (2×). 6.9 obv. 1′, 2′ (2×), 7′, 10′. 6.1 obv. 2. 6.10 2′, 8′. 6.2 obv. 4′. 6.3 obv. 1; rev. B 2′. 6.5 obv. 3′; rev. 18′, 27′. 6.6 rev. 2′. 8.1.D rev. iv 11′ (2×). 8.1.E(A_1) obv. ii 2, 11; obv. iii 6′, 7′, 10′; rev. iv 4′, 7′, 10′. 8.1.F obv. i 8′; obv. ii 9′; rev. v 15. 8.1.G obv. l. c. 2′, 5′; obv. r. c. 9′. 8.1.H rev. r. c. 9′. 8.1.J rev. v! 5′. 8.8.B l. c. 9′. 9.1.1 rev. iii 31′. 9.2.9 rev.? 1′. 10.3.11 l. c. 2′, 3′, 8′. 11.1.3 6′. 11.6.1 5, 7, 9, 12. 11.6.10 2′. 11.6.5 obv.? 7, 8; rev.? 2″, 3″, 4″. 11.6.6 rev. 2′, 5′, 10′. 11.6.7 3′. 11.6.9 6′. 12.1.1 r. c. 10′
	BABBAR!(text: NA_4)	12.1.1 l. c. 5′
	BABBAR?	6.5 rev. 8′
	BA]BBAR	4.1.3.5.A_1 obv.? 3′
	BABB]AR	4.1.3.4.A_1 rev. l. c. 1′. 4.1.3.5.A_1 obv.? 4′.8.1.F obv. i 8′
	BABB[AR	6.6 obv. 7′. 6.9 obv. 4′. 8.1.E(A_1) obv. iii 6′. 8.8.B r. c. 8′. 10.3.11 l. c. 1′. 11.1.4 2′
	BA[BBAR	4.1.4.1.A_2 obv. i 2′. 8.8.A 9′
gen.	BABBAR-*aš*	4.2.9 rev. 7′. 10.2.2.3 obv.? l. c. 5′. 10.2.2.4 obv.? r. c. 2′
	BABBAR-*TIM*	9.1.8 obv. 10′
= *ḫarki-*; see also *ašara-*, *gaši-*		

BAL	‘to libate, consecrate, make an offering’	
pret. sg. 3	BAL-*aš*	5.1 rev. iii 4
BAL-*uwaš*	‘libation vessel’	
sg. nom.	BAL-*u-wa-aš*	9.1.10.A_1 rev. 4′
sg. gen.(?)	(*ḫuppar*) BA[L-*u-wa-aš*(?)	11.1.9 4′
see *Lexical Commentary*; = *šip(p)anduwa-*		
^{GIŠ}BAL	‘spindle’	
	^{GIŠ}BAL	9.1.1 rev. iv 33′
	^{GIŠ}B]AL	11.5.3 4′
BÁN	(unit of vol. = approx. 8.4 liters)	
	BÁN	1.1.A_2 obv. 4′, 8′ (2×), 9′, 10′. 1.1.A_3 rev. 2′. 5.2 obv. ii 1, 5, 8. 10.1.1.1 rev.? 14′. 12.2.1 rev. 6′
	BÁ]N	1.1.A_2 obv. 7′
= *SŪTU*		
$^{(GIŠ)}$BÁN-*ia*	(a container with a volume of one BÁN)	
	BÁN-*i*[*a*	12.2.1 rev. 3′
	^{GIŠ}BÁN-*ia*	12.2.1 obv. 3′
^{GIŠ}BANŠUR	‘table’	
	^{GIŠ}BANŠUR	9.2.1 rev. iii 8′. 10.2.1.2 obv. 4′. 10.3.5 9′. 10.3.6 5′. 10.3.10 r. c. 8′
	$^{G]IŠ}$BANŠUR	5.6 1′
	^{GIŠ}B[ANŠUR	10.2.1.2 obv. 16′
sg. dat./loc.	*A-NA* … ^{GIŠ}BANŠUR	10.2.1.2 obv. 17′
	A-NA(?) … ^{GIŠ}BANŠUR	10.3.10 r. c. 10′
see also GADA ^{GIŠ}BANŠUR		
^{GIŠ}BANŠUR ÉRIN^{MEŠ}	‘army table’	
	^{GIŠ}B[A]NŠUR ÉRIN^{MEŠ}	5.5 obv. ii 5
	$^{G]IŠ}$BANŠUR ÉRIN^{MEŠ}	5.6 2′
	^{GIŠ}BANŠUR(?)] ÉRIN$^{ME.EŠ}$	10.1.2.3 2′
^{GIŠ}BANŠUR MUNUS.LUGAL	‘(the?) queen’s table’	
	(GADA) ^{GIŠ}BANŠUR MUNUS.LUGAL	4.2.6 obv.? 1′
^{GIŠ}BANŠUR ^{MUNUS}MUḪALDIM	‘cooking woman’s table’	
	^{GIŠ}BANŠUR ^{MUNUS}MUḪALDIM	3.1.1.A_3 rev. iv 12′
^{GIŠ}BANŠUR *ḪURRI*	‘Hurrian(-style) table’	
	^{GIŠ}BANŠUR *ḪUR-RI*	2.17 obv.? r. c. 8′
BAPPIR	‘wort’	
	BAPPIR	10.1.1.2 rev. iv 10′
	BAP]PIR	1.1.A_2 obv. 8′
	BAPP]IR	1.1.A_2 obv. 10′
	BA[PPIR?	12.2.3 1′
^{TÚG}BAR.DUL_8	‘robe’	
	^{TÚG}BAR.DUL_8	8.1.A obv. ii 7′. 9.2.4 rev. iii 6′
$^{(TÚG)}$BAR.SI	‘head band’	
	BAR.SI	8.1.H rev. r. c. 4′. 8.1.I rev. r. c. 3′
	BAR].SI	8.1.D rev. iv 4′

	^{TÚG}BAR.SI	11.6.6 rev. 5′
	$^{(TÚG)}$BAR.S]I(?)	8.1.E(A$_1$) obv. ii 3. 11.1.8 2′
$^{(TÚG)}$BAR."TE"	cloak, mantel	
	BAR."TE"	6.8 5′. 8.1.F obv. ii 5′
	BAR."TE"$^{\langle\langle MEŠ\rangle\rangle}$	6.9 obv. 4′
	^{TÚG}BAR."TE"	3.2.1 rev. 7′; lo. e. 20′. 4.2.6 obv.$^{?}$ 10′. 4.2.9 obv. 26, 31. 6.5 rev. 26′. 6.9 obv. 11′. 8.1.E(A$_1$) rev. iv 9′, 10′. 9.1.11 obv.$^{?}$ 6′. 11.6.5 obv.$^{?}$ 7
	^{TÚG}BAR."TE"$^{\langle\langle MEŠ\rangle\rangle}$	4.2.6 obv.$^{?}$ 6′
	$^{T]ÚG}$BAR."TE"	6.6 rev. 4′
	^{TÚG}BA]R."TE"	4.2.9 obv. 16′
	^{TÚG}BAR]."TE"	1.2 rev. 4′
pl.	^{TÚG}BAR."TE"^{MEŠ}	4.2.6 obv.$^{?}$ 13′. 9.1.8 obv. 8′
	^{TÚG}[BAR."TE"^{MEŠ}	4.2.6 obv.$^{?}$ 18′
see *Lexical Commentary*		
BIL.ZA.ZA	'frog'	
	BIL.ZA.ZA	12.1.1 l. c. 3′ (2×)
BIR	'to scatter, strew; (of wool) loose(?)'	
	BIR	4.1.4.6 obv. 2′, 5′, 10′, 14′
^{GIŠ}BUGIN	'trough' (a container for liquids)	
	^{GIŠ}BUGIN	10.3.6 1′. 11.1.7 3′
^{GIŠ}BÚGIN	'coffer' (a trough-like box for dry substances)	
	^{GIŠ}BÚGIN	8.1.A rev. v 22′. 9.1.8 obv. 14′
	^{GIŠ}BÚGI]N(?) (GÍD.DA)	2.2 obv. 13′, 14′
BÚN	'storm; thunder'	
	(^{D}IŠKUR) BÚN	2.1.A obv. ii(?) 15′
BURU$_5$	'locust, grasshopper'	
	BURU$_5$	8.1.A obv. i 10′
DAB	'to take, seize'	
ptc. sg. nom.-acc. n.	DAB-*an*	4.2.9 obv. 4, 22. 11.6.8 2′
= *epp-/app-*		
(*anda*) DAB-*ant-*	'included; "with all appurtenances"'	
ptc. sg. nom.	(*anda*) DAB-*an-za*	1.5 obv. 8. 8.1.A rev. v 20′
	(*anda*) DA[B-*an-za*	1.5 obv. 4
= (*anda*) *appant-*		
^{GIŠ}DAG	'dais, throne'	
sg. nom.	^{GIŠ}DAG-*iš*	9.1.4.A$_1$ obv. i 2. 9.2.1 rev. iii 9′
DAGAL	'wide, broad; width, breadth'	
	DAGAL	11.6.11 3′
= *paḫašti-*, *palḫi-*		
DÀRA	'ibex'	
	DÀRA	9.1.5 obv.$^{!}$ 3
DIM$_4$	'malt'	
	DIM$_4$	1.1.A$_2$ obv. 8′, 10′

DINGIR	'god'	
sg. acc.!	DINGIR-*LUM*	4.1.1.1.A_1 rev. 12′. 4.1.1.1.B_1 rev. iii? 3
sg. gen.	[*ŠA*] DINGIR-*LIM* (LÚ)	2.1.B 6′
	DINGIR-*LIM* (MUNUS)	2.1.B 6′
sg. dat./loc.	*A-NA* DINGIR-*LIM*	10.2.1.1 obv. 8′
pl.	DINGIR^{MEŠ}	2.2 obv. 9′, 10′
	DINGIR^{ME}]^{Š} (*lulaḫ(ḫ)i-*)	10.1.1.2 rev. iv 7′
pl. dat./loc.	*A-NA* DINGIR^{MEŠ}	4.1.1.1.A_1 rev. 17′. 4.1.1.1.B_1 rev. iii? 12
DIRI	'surplus, remaining, left over'	
	DIRI	12.3.1 7′
	DIRI!	9.1.5 rev.! 15′
see *Lexical Commentary*; = *kallaratar*; *ĀTRU* (G vb. adj. sg. nom. of *(W)ATĀRU*)		
mid. pres. sg. 3	DIRI-*ri*	9.1.5 rev.! 15′
	DIRI-*r*[*i*	4.1.1.3 rev. B 8
DÙ	'to do, make'	
pres. sg. 3	DÙ-*zi*	2.2 rev. 12. 4.1.1.2.A obv. 17′. 4.1.1.2.B obv. 3, 6, 8, 10. 3.1.8.A obv. 13′
	DÙ-*z*[*i*	4.1.1.2.A obv. 20′
pres. pl. 3	DÙ-*an-zi*	5.2 obv. ii 14
	DÙ-*an-z*[*i*	5.3 r. c. 6′
	DÙ-[*a*]*n*-[*zi*	5.2 obv. ii 16
	D[Ù-*a*]*n*-[*zi*	5.2 obv. ii 14
pret. pl. 3	DÙ-*er*	10.3.2 obv. i(?) 9″
	(*anda*) DÙ-*er*	5.1 rev. iii 3
ptc. sg. nom.-acc. n.	DÙ-*an*	9.2.4 rev. iv 4
	(*andan*) DÙ-*an*	9.1.4.A_1 obv. i 19′. 9.1.7 obv. 7′
= *iya-*; see also UGU *arḫa* DÙ		
^{URU}DU$_6$ É.GAL-*LIM*	"tell of the palace"	
	^{URU}DU$_6$ É.GAL-*LIM*	3.1.1.A_3 obv. iii 13′
DUB	'tablet'	
	DUB	9.1.1 rev. iv 45′. 9.1.9 rev. iv 4′
	D]UB	9.1.4.A_1 rev. iv 5′
= *tuppi-*		
$^{\text{(LÚ)}}$DUB.SAR	'scribe'	
pl. gen.	(GAL) DUB.SAR^{MEŠ}	4.1.1.1.B_1 rev. iii? 15
	(GAL) DUB.SA[R^{MEŠ}	2.4 rev. 6′
	(GAL) DUB.[SAR^{MEŠ}	5.7 rev. iii? 16′
see also ZI.KIN.BAR ^{LÚ}DUB.SAR, $^{\text{(GIŠ)}}$*KANḪANNU* DUB.SAR		
^{LÚ}DUB.SAR.GIŠ	'clerk, administrator'	
	DUB.SAR.GIŠ	12.3.2 5′, 6′
sg. gen.	*ŠA* ⟨^{LÚ}⟩DUB.SAR.GIŠ	9.1.1 rev. iv 2′
see *Lexical Commentary*		
^{GIŠ}DUB.ŠEN	'(lidded) box, tablet container'	
	^{GIŠ}DUB.ŠEN	1.5 lo. e. 15. 2.7.A obv. 20. 4.1.1.3 rev. A 9′. 4.2.4 rev. 3′, 4′, 8′. 10.3.3 obv.? 2′
	^{GIŠ}DUB.Š]EN(?)	2.3 7

	^{GIŠ}DUB.ŠE[N	4.2.4 rev. 1′
see *Lexical Commentary*; = $^{\text{(GIŠ)}}$*ḫa/urnašalla-*, $^{\text{(GIŠ)}}$*KANḪANNU*(?)		
$^{\text{(URUDU)}}$DUG	‘pot, vessel’	
	DUG	1.5 lo. e. 18; rev. 19. 3.1.3 obv.? 9′. 9.1.8 obv. 14′
	DU]G?	12.3.5 3′
	DU[G.(...)	4.1.1.4 5′
	^{URUDU}DUG	8.5 rev. iii(?) 6′
	$^{\text{URUD]U}}$DUG	3.1.2 obv. l. c. 12′
	DUG ^{URUDU}x[	2.9.A_3 obv. ii 12′
DUG.GEŠTIN	‘wine vessel’	
	DUG.GEŠTIN	3.1.8.A rev. 2′
DUG.KA.GAG	‘(beer) tankard’	
	DUG.KA.GAG	4.1.1.3 obv. 7
	DUG.K]A.GAG	10.1.1.1 rev.? 15′
	DUG.K]A.GAG(?)	9.2.9 obv.? 13′
see *Lexical Commentary*		
$^{\text{(URUDU)}}$DUG.$^{\text{(LÚ)}}$SAGI(.A)	‘cupbearer’s vessel’	
	DUG.SAGI	4.1.1.3 obv. 6
	DUG.SAGI.A	3.1.2 obv. l. c. 4′
	DUG.SAGI].A	3.1.2 obv. l. c. 2′
	DUG.SAGI.[A	3.1.8.A rev. 3′
	DUG.SAG[I.A	3.1.1.A_3 rev. iv 12′
	DUG.^{LÚ}SAGI.A	4.2.6 rev.? 5′
	^{URUDU}DUG.SAGI.A	4.2.9 lo. e. 32′
	$^{\text{(URUDU)}}$DUG(?)].^{LÚ}SAGI.A	9.1.1 rev. iv 5′
see *Lexical Commentary*		
DÙG.GA	‘good, fine’	
	D]ÙG.GA	2.5 rev. 2′
$^{\text{(GIŠ)}}$DÙG.GAN	‘sheath’	
	DÙG.GAN	6.2 obv. 2′. 8.1.E(A_1) rev. iv 16′. 9.2.4 rev. iv 4
	^{GIŠ}DÙG.GAN	9.1.1 rev. iii 7′
see *Lexical Commentary*		
^{LÚ}DUGUD	‘dignitary, official’	
	^{LÚ}DUGUD	3.1.10 4, 6
see *Lexical Commentary*		
DUḪ.ŠÚ.A	‘yellow, calcite-colored’	
	DUḪ.ŠÚ.A	1.1.A_3 rev. 2′. 2.1.A obv. ii(?) 11′. 2.1.B 3′, 5′. 2.2 obv. 7′, 8′, 11′, 12′. 2.6 4′. 4.1.1.2.B rev. 3. 8.1.A obv. ii 19′, 20′, 21′, 28′; rev. v 18′. 9.1.11 obv.? 4′. 10.3.12 obv. i 6′, 15′. 12.1.1 l. c. 3′, 5′, 8′; r. c. 11′
	DUḪ!.ŠÚ.A	2.2 obv. 5′
	D]UḪ.ŠÚ.A	1.1.A_3 rev. 8′
	DU]Ḫ.Š[Ú.A(?)	12.1.1 r. c. 13′
	DUḪ.Š]Ú.A	8.1.B rev. 2′
	DUḪ.ŠÚ.[A	3.1.8.A rev. 10′
	DUḪ.ŠÚ!.[A	2.2 obv. 6′. 9.2.12 5′
	DUḪ.Š[Ú.A	8.1.A rev. v 30′

	DUḪ.[ŠÚ.A(?)	9.2.14 10′
	D[UḪ.ŠÚ.A	8.1.A rev. v 31′
	D[UḪ.ŠÚ.A(?)	2.1.A obv. ii(?) 1′
see *Lexical Commentary*		
$^{(NA_4)}$DUḪ.ŠÚ.A	‘(a yellow stone); calcite’	
material		
	^{NA_4}DUḪ.ŠÚ.A	6.1 obv. 9
DUMU	‘child’	
	DUMU	8.1.E(A_3) l. e. 2
	DUMU$^?$	1.5 rev. 21
	D[UMU	5.8 1′
pl.	DUMU^{MEŠ}	4.2.7 3′. 5.7 rev. iii$^?$ 23′. 5.8 5′.
DUMU.É.GAL	‘palace servant’	
	DUMU.É.GAL	10.3.3 obv.$^?$ 4′
DUMU.LUGAL	‘prince’ (son of the king, later any male member of the extended royal family)	
	DUMU.LUGAL	1.2 obv. 7″. 5.7 rev. iii$^?$ 11′, 24′
	DUMU.L[UGA]L	5.5 rev. iii 1′
DUMU.MUNUS	‘daughter, girl’	
	DUMU.MUNUS	8.1.E(A_3) rev. vi 8. 12.3.3 10′
	DUMU.MUNUS(?)	8.1.E(A_3) rev. vi 11
sg. dat./loc.	*A-NA* DUMU.MUNUS	1.1.A_1 obv. 6′
DUMU.NITA	‘son, boy’	
pl.	DUMU.NITA^{MEŠ}	1.5 rev. 27
see also ^{KUŠ}E.SIR *zazzapi-* DUMU.NITA		
DUR	‘yarn, twine, wire; cord, string, band’	
	DUR	2.7.A obv. 20
	DU[R	3.1.12 10′
	D[UR	3.1.12 9′
= *ṬURRU*		
DUR ANŠE	“band for a donkey”	
	DUR ANŠE(text: GÌR×PA)	8.8.B r. c. 4′
$^{(TÚG)}$E.ÍB	‘belt’	
	E.ÍB	4.1.4.1.A_1 rev. v 7″. 4.1.4.4 3′, 7′. 8.1.F obv. ii 3′. 11.6.4 obv. 6′
	^{TÚG}E.ÍB	1.1.A_1 obv. 11′, 12′. 1.2 rev. 4′. 4.1.4.1.A_1 obv. ii 4′, 6′. 4.1.4.2.A_1 rev. r. c. 3′, 6′; rev. l. c. 3′. 4.1.4.2.A_2 obv. r. c. 3′, 12′. 4.2.6 obv.$^?$ 5′, 9′, 17′. 6.10 6′, 8′. 6.5 obv. 4′, 6′, 7′, 8′, 9′, 19′, 20′; rev. 8′, 11′, 14′, 25′. 6.9 obv. 7′. 8.1.E(A_1) obv. ii 12; rev. iv 8′. 9.1.1 rev. iii 32′, 35′. 9.1.10.A_1 obv. 9′. 9.1.10.B 14′. 9.1.8 obv. 3′, 10′. 11.6.1 8, 12. 11.6.2 rev. 4′
	^{*TÚG*}E.ÍB	9.2.1 rev. iii 2′
	^{TÚG}⟨E⟩.ÍB	11.7.2 2′
	$^{T]ÚG}$E.ÍB	6.1 19. 6.2 obv. 1′
	$^{TÚ]G}$E.ÍB	11.6.5 obv.$^?$ 5

	^{TÚG}E].ÍB	8.3 obv. 7′
	^{TÚG}E].Í[B	4.1.4.1.A$_2$ obv. ii 2′
	^{TÚG}E.Í]B	4.1.4.1.A$_2$ obv. ii 9′. 4.1.4.2.A$_1$ rev. r. c. 15′. 11.1.7 8′
	^{TÚG}E.Í[B	4.2.9 obv. 24. 6.5 rev. 18′. 8.1.E(A$_1$) rev. iv 13′
	^{TÚG}E.Í[B$^{!}$(?)	1.1.A$_1$ obv. 2′
	^{TÚG}E.[ÍB	4.1.4.2.A$_1$ rev. r. c. 11′. 6.12 1′
sg. gen.	*ŠA* ^{TÚG}E.ÍB	4.1.1.3 rev. B 3, 5
^{TÚG}E.ÍB.GÍR	'belt for (carrying?) a knife'	
	^{TÚG}E.ÍB.GÍR	1.1.A$_1$ obv. 18′. 4.2.9 obv. 6, 25
$^{\text{(TÚG)}}$E.ÍB.KUN	'belt with tail'	
	E.[ÍB.KUN(?)	4.1.4.4 5′
	^{TÚG}E.ÍB.KUN	4.1.4.1.A$_1$ obv. ii 7′. 4.1.4.6 obv. 11′
	$^{\text{TÚ}]\text{G}}$E.ÍB.KUN	4.1.4.1.A$_1$ obv. ii 9′
	^{TÚG}]E.ÍB.KUN	4.1.4.1.A$_1$ obv. ii 2′
	^{TÚG}E.Í]B.KUN	4.1.4.1.A$_1$ obv. ii 1′
	^{TÚG}E.ÍB.K[UN(?)	4.1.4.6 obv. 3′
	^{TÚG}E.Í[B.KUN(?)	4.1.4.6 lo. e. 15′
see *Lexical Commentary*		
^{TÚG}E.ÍB ZAG.TAR	(a type of belt)	
	^{TÚG}E.ÍB ZAG.TAR	4.1.4.2.A$_2$ obv. r. c. 3′
	^{TÚG}E.ÍB ZAG.TAR$^{!}$(text: AN)	4.1.4.2.A$_1$ rev. r. c. 3′
	^{TÚG}E.ÍB ... ZAG.TAR	11.6.1 12
	$^{\text{TÚ}]\text{G}}$E.ÍB ZAG.TAR	4.1.4.2.A$_2$ obv. l. c. 4′
	^{TÚG}E.Í]B ZAG.TAR	11.1.7 8′
	^{TÚG}E.ÍB Z]AG.TAR	6.1 obv. 20
$^{\text{(KUŠ)}}$E.SIR	'shoes'	
	E.SIR	8.4 rev. 18′
	^{KUŠ}E.SIR	7.3 obv i 5. 8.4 rev. 13′. 9.2.9 rev.$^{?}$ 5′. 11.6.3 obv.$^{?}$ 4′
	$^{\text{KU}]\text{Š}}$E.SIR	11.6.4 obv. 10′
	^{KUŠ}E.SI[R	9.2.7 rev. r. c. 5′. 11.1.8 3′
	^{KUŠ}E.[SIR(?)	11.6.2 rev. 5′, 6′
pl.	^{KUŠ}E.SIR$^{\text{ḪI.A}}$	4.2.6 rev.$^{?}$ 7′. 9.1.1 rev. iv 34′
^{KUŠ}E.SIR *zazzapi-* DUMU.NITA (a type or style of boy's shoe)		
sg. nom.	^{KUŠ}E.SIR *za-az-za-pí-iš* DUMU.NITA	9.1.1 rev. iv 7′
^{KUŠ}E.SIR $^{\text{(URU)}}$*Ḫat(t)a/ili*	'Hat(t)a/ilian shoes'	
	$^{\text{KUŠ!}}$E.SIR *ḫa-a[t-ta-li*	2.13 rev.$^{?}$ 4′
	^{KUŠ}E.SIR $^{\text{U}]\text{RU}}$*ḫa-ti-li*	2.14 9′
	^{KUŠ}E.SIR ^{URU}*ḫa-at-ta-l[i*	9.2.6 obv. i 9′
	^{KUŠ}E.SIR ^{URU}[*ḫa-ti-li*(?)	2.9.A$_2$ obv. i 11′
see *Lexical Commentary*		
^{KUŠ}E.SIR ^{URU}*Kašipura*	'Kašipura(-styled) shoes'	
	^{KUŠ}E.SIR ... ^{URU}*k[a-ši]-pu-ra*	8.4 rev. 13′
^{KUŠ}E.SIR LÚ-*LIM*	'men's shoes'	
	^{KUŠ}E.SIR LÚ-*LIM*	9.1.10.A$_2$ rev. 9′

^{KUŠ}E.SIR MUNUS(-*TI*)	'women's shoes'	
	^{KUŠ}E.SIR MUNUS	7.3 obv. i 6
pl.	^{KUŠ}E.SIR$^{\text{ḪI.A}}$ MUNUS-*TI*	9.1.10.A_2 rev. 9′
É	'house, institution'	
	É	12.1.1 r. c. 1′
	É.[	4.1.2.1 obv. (i) 6′. 4.1.4.5 rev. r. c. 1′. 7.2 2′
	É$^?$	2.18 8′
sg. gen.	É-*aš*	12.3.4 obv. 4
see also $^{\text{(GADA/TÚG)}}$*parna-*, ^{D}*IŠTAR* É		
É(.GAL) $^{\text{(URU)}}$…	'palace of …'	
É *Gazzimara*	'palace/house of Gazzimara'	
	É *gaz-zi-ma-ra*	3.2.1 rev. 11′
	É *gaz-z*[*i-ma-ra*	4.1.3.1 6′
É.GAL ^{URU}*Ḫariyaša*	'palace of Hariyaša'	
	É.G]AL ^{URU}*ḫa-a-ri-ia-ša*	3.1.1.A_1 rev. v 2′
É.GAL ^{URU}*Ḫupišna*	'palace of Ḫupišna'	
	É.GAL ^{URU}[*ḫ*]*u-piš-*[*na*	8.1.E(A_3) l. e. 1
É.GAL ^{URU}*Kašaya*	'palace of Kašaya'	
	É.GAL ^{URU}*ka-ša-ia*	5.1 obv. ii 4′
É.GAL ^{URU}*Šapinuwa*	'palace of Šapinuwa'	
	É.GAL ^{URU}*ša-*[*pi-nu-wa*(?)	3.1.5.A_2 obv. ii(?) 10′
É.GAL *Šulupašši*	'palace of Šulupašši'	
	É.GAL *šu-lu-pa-aš-ši*	4.1.4.6 obv. 12′
see *Lexical Commentary, s.v.* É(.GAL) $^{\text{(URU)}}$…		
É *Gazzimara*		
see É(.GAL) $^{\text{(URU)}}$…		
É *ḫarwašiaš*	"hoard(?) house" (a storehouse)	
	É *ḫar-wa-ši-aš*	2.7.A rev. 5
see *Lexical Commentary*		
É *ilanaš*	'staircase'	
	É *i-la-na-aš*	9.1.10.A_2 rev. 5′
É(.GAL) *tuppaš*	"(palace) coffer-house" (a storehouse)	
	É *tup-pa-aš*	3.2.1 rev. 8′
	É.GAL *tup-p*[*a-*	4.1.3.1 5′
see *Lexical Commentary*; see also $^{\text{(GIŠ)}}$*tuppa-*		
É DINGIR-*LIM* (GAL)	'(great) temple'	
	É DINGIR-*L*[*IM*	10.1.1.2 rev. iv 14′
sg. gen.	*ŠA* É DINGIR-*LIM* GAL	10.2.1.7 rev.$^?$ 6′
É GIŠ.KIN-*TI*	'House of the Craftsmen'	
sg. dat./loc.	*A-NA* É GIŠ.KIN-*TI*	4.1.4.9 obv. 7
see *Lexical Commentary*		
É(.GAL) $^{\text{NA}_4}$KIŠIB	"seal house" (a storehouse)	
	É $^{\text{NA}_4}$KIŠIB	2.5 rev. 9′. 2.7.A obv. 14. 2.9.A_1 obv. i 5′. 2.9.A_2 obv. i 8′. 2.9.A_3 obv. ii 6′. 9.1.9 rev. iv 5′
	É] $^{\text{NA}_4}$KIŠIB	2.9.A_2 obv. i 10′
	É $^{\text{NA}_4}$KIŠI[B	2.9.A_2 obv. i 2′, 4′

	É ^{NA_4}KI[ŠIB	1.5 rev. 19. 2.9.A_3 obv. ii 9′
	É ^{N}[^{A_4}KIŠIB	2.9.A_1 obv. i 3′
	É [^{NA_4}KIŠIB	2.9.A_1 obv. i 9′. 2.9.A_2 obv. i 14′
	É.GAL ^{NA_4}[KIŠIB	2.9.A_3 obv. ii 8′
	É.[GAL ^{NA_4}KIŠIB(?)	3.2.4 2′
sg. dat./loc.	*INA* É ^{NA_4}KIŠIB	5.9 3′
	I+NA ⟨⟨*NA*⟩⟩ É$^{!?}$ ^{N}[^{A_4}KIŠIB(?)	8.1.E(A_3) obv. i 5′
É ^{NA_4}KIŠIB GÍD.DA	"long seal house"	
	É ^{NA_4}KIŠIB GÍD.DA	5.5 rev. iii 6′
	(É.GAL) É ^{NA_4}KIŠIB	4.1.4.6 obv. 8′
É ^{NA_4}KIŠIB ŠÀ.TAM	"seal house of the treasury"	
	É ^{NA_4}KIŠIB ŠÀ.TAM	2.5 rev. 9′
see also É(.GAL) $^{(LÚ)}$ŠÀ.TAM		
É(.GAL) $^{(LÚ)}$ŠÀ.TAM	'(palace) treasury'	
	(É.GAL) É ŠÀ.TAM	4.1.4.6 obv. 6′
	É].GAL ^{LÚ}ŠÀ.TAM	4.1.4.5 rev. r. c. 6′.
see also ^{LÚ}ŠÀ.TAM		
É ^{D}UTU-*ŠI*	'household/estate of His Majesty'	
	(É.GAL) É ^{D}UTU-*ŠI*	4.1.4.6 obv. 4′
see *Lexical Commentary*; see also ^{D}UTU-*ŠI*		
É *ABŪSU*	'storehouse'	
see EN É *ABŪSI*		
É-*TUM* GAL/*RABÛ*	"the Great House"	
sg. nom.	É-*TUM RA-BU-Ú*	3.1.1.A_1 rev. v 3′
	É-*TUM RA-B*]*U-Ú*	3.1.1.A_1 rev. v 7′
sg. gen.	É-*TIM* [GAL	4.1.4.4 11′
	É-[*TIM* GAL	4.1.4.4 8′
see *Lexical Commentary*		
É.GAL	'(the) Palace' (the bulding, also the seat of Hittite government)	
	É.GAL	4.1.4.6 obv. 4′, 6′, 8′
	É].GAL	4.1.4.9 obv. 9
	É.GA[L	3.1.1.A_3 rev. iv 3′
sg. gen.	*ŠA* É.GAL-*LIM*	8.1.F obv. i 6′
	ŠA] É.GAL-*LIM*	8.1.F rev. vi 7
sg. dat./loc.	*I+NA* É.GAL-*LIM*	8.1.E(A_1) obv. iii 4′
see also DUMU.É.GAL, ^{URU}DU$_6$ É.GAL-*LIM*		
É.GAL ^{URU}*Ḫariyaša*		
see É(.GAL) $^{(URU)}$...		
É.GAL *ḫekur* ^{D}LAMMA	'rock-sanctuary of ^{D}LAMMA'	
	É].GAL *ḫé-kur* ^{D}LAMMA	3.1.1.A_2 rev. vi 2′
see *Lexical Commentary*; see also $^{(NA_4)}$*ḫekur*		
É.GAL ^{URU}*Ḫupišna*		
see É(.GAL) $^{(URU)}$...		
É.GAL *karupaḫi-*	'palace storehouse; granary(?)'	
sg. dat./loc.	É.GA]L *ka-ru-pa-ḫi*	8.1.E(A_1) obv. ii 15

	É.GAL *k]a-ru-pa-ḫi*	4.1.3.2 rev. 11′
sg. gen.	É.GAL *ka-ru-pa-ḫi-aš*	8.1.E(A_1) obv. ii 7
broken	É?.[GAL *ka-ru-pa-ḫi*(?)	8.3 obv. 8′
	É?.[GA]L(?) *ka-ru-pa-ḫ[i*	4.1.3.2 rev. 9′
see *Lexical Commentary*; see also TÚG*karupalani-*		
É.GAL URU*Kašaya*	'palace of Kašaya'	
see É(.GAL) (URU)...		
É.GAL URU*Šapinuwa*	'palace of Šapinuwa'	
see É(.GAL) (URU)...		
É.GAL *Šulupašši*	'palace of Šulupašši'	
see É(.GAL) (URU)...		
É.GAL *tuppa-*	'palace storehouse'	
see É(.GAL) *tuppa-*		
É.GAL ^{NA_4}KIŠIB	'palace seal-house'	
see É(.GAL) ^{NA_4}KIŠIB		
É.GAL MUNUS.LUGAL	'queen's palace'	
	É.GAL MUNUS.LUGAL	4.1.4.6 lo. e. 16′
É.GAL LÚSANGA	'palace of the priest'	
	É.GAL LÚSANGA	3.1.1.A_3 rev. iv 4′
see also LÚSANGA		
É.GAL LÚŠÀ.TAM		
see É(.GAL) (LÚ)ŠÀ.TAM		
(KUŠ/GIŠ)(É.)MÁ.URU.URU_6		
see MÁ.URU.URU_6		
É.NA_4	'royal funerary structure'	
sg. dat./loc.	*A-NA* É.NA_4	4.1.4.9 obv. 12
see *Lexical Commentary*		
É.ŠÀ	'inner chamber, bedroom'	
	É.ŠÀ	4.2.1.A_2 rev. 11′
sg. gen.	É.ŠÀ-*aš*	9.1.4.A_1 obv. i 18′
	Š]A? É.ŠÀ	7.2 6′
É.ŠÀ *ḫaštiyaš*	'ossuary'	
	É.ŠÀ *ḫa-aš-ti-ia-aš*	10.3.1 rev. iii 6′
see *Lexical Commentary*		
EGIR(-*pa*)	'back, in return; re-, again' (local adv.)	
	EGIR?	9.2.7 obv. l. c. 11′
	EGI]R	8.4 lo. e. 23′
	EGIR-*pa*	9.1.1 rev. iv 11′. 10.3.2 obv. i(?) 9″
	EGIR-**pa**	1.2 rev. 12′
	EGI]R-*pa*	10.3.2 obv. ii(?) 6′
	EGIR (*ḫališši(ya)-*)	2.2 rev. 9
	EGIR-*pa* (*ḫališši(ya)-*)	10.3.2 obv. i(?) 4″
	EGIR-*pa* (*pai-/pi(ya)-*)	6.1 l. e. 1
	EGIR-*pa* (*uda-*)	4.1.1.1.B_2 obv. i? 7′
	EGIR-[*pa*] (*uda-*)	4.1.1.1.A_1 rev. 6′

EG]IR-*pa* (*laḫ(ḫ)u(wa)-*, *laḫ(ḫ)uwa(i)-*) 5.1 rev. iv 3
see also GADA EGIR(*-an*) *arḫa* SUD-*waš*

EGIR(*-an*) — 'behind; afterwards' (local adv.)
EGIR(-*ŠU*) — 8.1.E(A_3) rev. vi 10
EGIR-*an* — 1.4 3′. 4.1.3.8 rev. A 4′ 9.2.1 obv. ii 6′. 9.2.2 rev.! iii 14′, 24′. 9.2.4 obv. i 6′, 7′. 11.3.1 19′.
E]GIR-*an* — 9.2.2 rev.! iii 17′. 9.2.4 obv. i 3′
EGIR-*a*[*n*(-) — 6.3 rev. B 4
EGIR-[*an* — 9.2.5 obv. i(?) 6′
E[GIR-*an*(?) — 9.2.5 obv. i(?) 7′
see also GADA EGIR(*-an*) *arḫa* SUD-*waš*

EGIR-*anda* — 'behind; afterwards' (local adv.)
EGIR-*an-da* — 2.4 rev. 3′. 2.7.A obv. 4. 2.17 obv.? r. c. 6′, 7′. 4.1.1.1.A_1 obv. 12′; rev. 2′, 7′. 4.1.1.1.B_1 rev. iii? 13. 4.1.1.8 r. c. 3′. 4.1.4.7 rev. B 3′. 4.2.12 4′. 5.2 obv. ii 8. 8.1.K rev. vi? 10′. 8.5 rev. iv(?) 6′. 8.6 l. c. 7′. 9.1.5 rev.! 14′. 9.2.12 2′
EGI]R-*an-da* — 4.1.1.1.B_2 obv. i? 3′
EGIR-*a*]*n-da* — 4.1.1.1.B_2 obv. i? 5′
EGIR-*an-d*[*a* — 5.7 rev iii? 27′
EGIR-*an-*[*da* — 4.1.1.1.A_1 obv. 9′
E[GIR-*an-da* — 4.1.1.1.A_1 obv. 7′
see *Lexical Commentary*

EGIR-*zi* — 'last, final, hindmost'
sg. nom. — EGIR-*zi-iš* — 9.1.10.A_2 rev. 4′

EME — (1.) 'tongue'
E]ME — 10.1.2.5 5′. 10.2.1.2 obv. 3′. 11.2.6 2′
(2.) 'blade' (of a knife, sword, spear, etc.)
EME — 4.2.2 obv. 4. 9.1.1 rev. iii 8′, 9′, 10′. 9.1.5 rev.! 14′ (2×). 9.1.10.A_1 rev. 2′. 9.2.4 rev. iv 3, 5, 6
EME [— 3.1.12 8′
EME GÍR — 3.1.12 5′. 8.1.A rev. v 5 (2×)
EME [G]ÍR — 4.2.2 obv. 2
E[ME GÍR — 4.2.2 obv. 1
EME GÍ]R — 8.1.C 1′
EME GÍR.GAL — 8.1.A rev. v 6
EME GÍR.TUR — 8.1.A rev. v 4
EME GÍR ^{LÚ}MUḪALDIM — 3.1.12 6′

EN — 'lord, master'
EN [— 4.2.1.A_2 rev. 13′

EN É *ABŪSI* — 'lord of the storehouse'
EN É *A-BU-US-SI* — 5.7 rev. iii? 18′
EN] É *A-BU-SÍ* — 5.7 rev. iv? 3′

EN ŠU-*TI* — 'craftsman, handworker'
EN ŠU-*TI* — 5.7 rev. iv? 15′
see *Lexical Commentary*

EN *UNŪTI*	'lord of the implements'	
	EN *Ú-NU-TI*	5.1 rev. iii 1
see *Lexical Commentary*		
^{GIŠ}EREN	'cedar'	
material		
	⟨^{GIŠ}⟩EREN	8.1.D obv. i 6′
ÉRIN		
see ^{GIŠ}BANŠUR ÉRIN^{MEŠ}, TÚG ÉRIN^{MEŠ}		
^{GIŠ}ESI	'ebony'	
	^{GIŠ}ESI	5.2 obv. ii 11, 12
material		
	^{GIŠ}ESI	2.14 10′. 2.17 obv.$^{?}$ r. c. 10′. 4.2.4 obv. 7. 8.1.J rev. v$^{!}$ 4′. 9.1.4.A$_1$ obv. i 1′. 9.1.5 rev.$^{!}$ 10′, 17′. 9.1.9 rev. iv 1′. 9.1.10.B 13′. 9.2.6 obv. i 17′. 10.3.3 obv.$^{?}$ 6′. 10.3.10 r. c. 9′, 10′. 11.2.4 2′, 4′, 6′
	$^{\text{GI}]\text{Š}}$ESI	10.1.2.4 l. c. 10′. 11.2.4 7′
	$^{\text{G}]\text{IŠ}}$E[SI(?)	10.1.2.4 l. c. 19′
	^{GIŠ}]ESI	10.3.10 r. c. 3′. 10.3.11 l. c. 3′, 9′
	^{GIŠ}E[SI	2.17 obv.$^{?}$ r. c. 8′. 9.2.6 rev.$^{!}$ iv 5′
	$^{\text{G}]\text{IŠ}}$E[SI(?)	8.1.B rev. 1′
	$^{\text{G}[\text{IŠ}}$ESI(?)	8.1.A obv. ii 18′
inst.	*QA-DU* ^{GIŠ}ESI	4.2.4 rev. 9′
see *Lexical Commentary*		
^{GIŠ}ESI *ḪURRI*	'Hurrian ebony (= *Diospyros Lotus*?)'	
	(NUMUN) ^{GIŠ}ESI *ḪURRI*	2.7.A obv. 5
EZEN$_4$	'festival'	
	EZEN$_4$ (AN.DAḪ.ŠUM)	6.1 lo. e. 10″
	EZEN$_4$ (SAG.UŠ)	4.1.1.1.A$_1$ obv. 20′
sg. dat./loc.	*A-NA* EZEN$_4$ (*KU-ŠA-RU*)	4.1.1.1.B$_1$ rev. iii$^{?}$ 16
	A-NA EZE[N$_4$ (*KU-ŠA-RU*)	4.1.1.1.A$_1$ rev. 20′
$^{\text{(GIŠ)}}$GA.ZUM	'comb'	
	GA.ZUM	8.1.J rev. v$^{!}$ 7′. 10.3.12 obv. i 8′
	^{GIŠ}GA.ZUM	9.2.4 rev. iii 4′
	^{GIŠ}]GA.ZUM	4.2.9 rev. 29′
	$^{\text{(GIŠ)}}$G]A.ZUM	11.5.3 2′
	$^{\text{(GIŠ)}}$GA.ZU]M	11.1.4 6′
$^{\text{(GIŠ)}}$GA.ZUM SÍG	'wool comb'	
	GA.ZUM SÍG	4.2.4 rev. 6′. 10.3.10 r. c. 12′. 10.3.11 l. c. 1′. 10.3.12 obv. i 5′
	G]A.ZUM SÍG	4.2.4 obv. 1
	^{GIŠ}GA.ZUM … SÍG	9.2.6 obv. i 7′
	$^{\text{(GIŠ)}}$GA.ZU]M SÍG	11.5.3 3′
	$^{\text{(GIŠ)}}$GA.ZUM] SÍG	2.2 rev. 17
	^{GIŠ}GA.ZUM S[ÍG(?)	9.2.4 rev. iii 4′
GABA	(1.) 'guard(?) (lit. "breast") of a knife'	
	GABA	6.1 obv. 9. 9.1.1 rev. iii 8′, 10′, 12′, 13′, 14′. 9.1.10.A$_1$ rev. 2′. 9.2.4 rev. iv 3

	GA]BA	9.2.13 5′
GABA ^{URU}*MIZRĪ*	‘Egyptian(-styled) pectoral’	
	GABA ^{URU}*MI-IZ-RI-I*	9.1.1 rev. iv 20′
$^{(\text{TÚG})}$GABA	“breast cloth”	
	GABA	4.2.6 obv.$^{?}$ 17′. 8.8.B l. c. 8′
	^{TÚG}GABA	2.11 obv.$^{?}$ 3′. 3.2.1 rev. 7′. 4.2.6 obv.$^{?}$ 12′. 4.2.9 rev. 13′. 8.1.E(A_1) obv. ii 11; rev. iv 6′ (2×). 8.8.A 7′, 9′. 8.8.B l col. 9′. 11.6.5 obv.$^{?}$ 3
	$^{\text{TÚ}]\text{G}}$GABA	3.2.1 lo. e. 20′
	^{TÚG}]GABA(?)	8.8.A 15′
	^{TÚG}GA]BA	11.6.6 rev. 8′
	^{TÚG}[GABA	8.8.A 8′
$^{(\text{UZU})}$GABA	‘chest, breast; front piece’	
	GABA	9.1.4.A_1 obv. ii 17. 11.2.2 5′
	GA[BA(?)	11.2.2 2′
	^{UZU}GABA	10.2.2.4 obv.$^{?}$ r. c. 3′
	$^{\text{UZ}]\text{U}}$GABA	10.2.2.2 obv.$^{?}$ l. c. 5′
	^{UZU}G[ABA	10.2.2.4 obv.$^{?}$ r. c. 1′
	(^{GI}PISAN) GABA	8.1.A rev. v 17′
sg. gen.	*ŠA* GABA	9.2.1 obv. ii 2′
sg. dat./loc.	*A-NA* ^{UZU}GA[BA$^{?}$	4.1.1.1.A_1 obv. 13′
GADA	‘linen’	
	GADA	2.5 rev. 5′. 2.7.A obv. 10. 4.1.4.1.A_1 rev. v 7′, 7″; rev. vi 5′, 11′. 4.1.4.2.A_1 rev. r. c. 3′, 8′. 4.1.4.4 10′. 4.1.4.5 rev. r. c. 4′. 4.2.6 obv.$^{?}$ 1′. 4.2.7 7′. 4.2.9 rev. 20′. 5.7 rev. iii$^{?}$ 2′. 6.5 obv. 17′; rev. 8′, 11′, 14′, 16′, 17′. 8.1.D rev. iv 3′. 8.1.E(A_1) obv. iii 3′; rev. v 9′. 8.1.F obv. i 4′ (2×), 6′; rev. v 15. 9.1.6 obv. 8. 9.2.6 obv. i 10′. 10.1.2.6 5′. 11.6.1 5, 9. 11.6.6 rev. 5′. 11.6.9 4′ (2×). 9.1.1 rev. iii 26′, 31′
	GADA$^{!}$(text: PA)	6.5 obv. 8′
	G]ADA	4.2.9 rev. 18′
	GA[DA	11.6.3 obv.$^{?}$ 5′
	G[ADA	4.2.9 rev. 26′
sg. dat./loc.	*A-NA* GADA	9.1.1 rev. iv 9′
pl.	GADA$^{\text{ḪI.A}}$	2.7.A obv. 3. 9.1.8 obv. 4′
material		
	GADA	1.1.A_1 obv. 8′, 16′. 2.7.A obv. 20. 4.2.9 obv. 2, 5, 6, 13, 19, 20, 24, 25; rev. 3′, 4′, 11′, 13′, 14′. 4.2.11 2′. 6.3 rev. B 1. 6.10 8′. 6.13 9′. 8.1.E(A_1) rev. iv 8′. 8.1.F obv. i 3′, 4′. 8.1.H rev. r. c. 4′; rev. l. c. 6′. 8.1.I rev. r. c. 3′. 9.1.10.A_1 obv. 9′. 9.2.4 obv. ii 9′. 10.1.1.1 rev.$^{?}$ 13′. 11.6.1 5, 11, 13. 11.6.6 rev. 9′. 11.6.7 2′
	GADA$^{?}$	11.1.5 6′
	G]ADA	8.1.G obv. l. c. 4′
	GA[DA$^{?}$	11.6.11 4′

inst.	*QA-DU* GADA	4.2.6 obv.$^?$ 12′. 6.5 rev. 19′, 28′. 6.9 obv. 2′. 8.1.E(A_1) rev. iv 6′. 8.1.F rev. v 11, 13. 11.6.5 rev.$^?$ 1′. 11.6.6 rev. 8′
	**QA*$^!$*-*DU* GADA	4.2.6 obv.$^?$ 11′
GADA ^{URU}*Alašiya*	‘Alašiyan(-styled) linen’	
	GADA ^{URU}*a-la-ši-ia*	2.7.A obv. 4. 8.1.F obv. i 5′
GADA *anda damaššuaš*	‘linen for “pressing in”’	
sg. gen.	GADA *an-da dam-ma-aš-šu-aš*	4.2.9 rev. 26′
	GADA *an-da dam-m*]*a*(?)-*aš-šu-u-aš*	6.3 obv. 4
	GADA *an-da* ⟨*ta*⟩-*ma-aš-*[*šu-wa-aš*	4.2.6 obv.$^?$ 20′
	GADA *an-da ta-ma-a*[*š-šu-wa-aš*	4.2.6 rev.$^?$ 9′
	GADA *an-d*[*a dam-ma-aš-šu-aš*	6.5 rev. 20′
see *Lexical Commentary*		
GADA *arrumaš*	‘wash linen’	
sg. gen.	GADA *ar-ru-ma-aš*	6.5 rev. 20′
	GADA ⟨*ar*⟩-*ru-ma-aš*	4.2.9 rev. 25′
	GADA *a*]*r-ru-um-ma-aš*	4.2.9 rev. 17′
	GADA *ar-r*]*u-ma-aš*	11.6.4 rev. 4′
	GADA *a*]*r-ru-m*[*a-aš*	10.1.2.6 8′
see also *arra-*		
GADA $^{(GIŠ)}$*ḫapšal(l)iaš*	‘linen for a *ḫapšalli*-chair’	
	G]ADA *ḫa-ap-ša-al-li-a*[*š*	4.2.9 rev. 18′
	GADA *ḫa-a*]*p-ša-li-aš*	4.2.6 rev.$^?$ 11′
	GADA ^{GIŠ}*ḫa-ap-ša-al-li-aš*	6.5 rev. 22′
	GADA ^{GIŠ}*ḫa-ap-ša-al-l*[*i-aš*	6.5 rev. 21′
see also $^{(GIŠ)}$*ḫapšalli-*		
GADA *intan(n)a-*	(an article of linen cloth)	
sg. nom.	GADA *in-ta-na-aš*	9.2.1 rev. iii 4′. 10.1.2.6 4′
	GADA *in-ta-na-*⟨*aš*⟩	4.2.7 6′
	G]ADA *in-ta-an-na-aš*	11.6.2 l. e. 5
	GADA *in-t*[*a-na-aš*	11.1.4 3′
	GADA *in-*[*ta-na-aš*	9.1.1 rev. iii 40′
	in-ta]*-an-na-aš* GADA	4.2.10 5′
GADA *kartawaš*	‘linen for “cutting off”’	
	GADA *kar-ta-u-aš*	4.2.9 rev. 26′
	GADA *kar-ta-u-aš*(?)	6.5 rev. 20′
see also *kartae-*		
GADA *genuwaš*	‘lap linen’	
	GADA *ge-nu-wa-aš*	4.2.9 rev. 27′. 7.3 obv. i 3
	GADA] *ge-nu-wa-aš*	4.2.6 rev.$^?$ 9′
	GADA *g*]*e-nu-wa-aš*	10.1.2.6 7′
GADA *latagga*(-)[	(?)	
	GADA *la-tág-ga*(-)[	11.6.2 l. e. 7
GADA ^{GIŠ}*šarpaš*	‘linen for a *šarpa*-chair’	
	GADA ^{GIŠ}*šar-pa-aš*	11.6.2 l. e. 3
see also ^{GIŠ}*šarpa-*		

GADA *waššuwaš*	'linen for clothing/dressing'	
	GADA *wa-aš-šu-wa-aš*	12.3.7 7′
see also *wašše-*		
GADA ^{GIŠ}BANŠUR	'table linen'	
	GADA ^{GIŠ}BAN[ŠUR	4.2.9 rev. 28′
	(GADA ...) ^{GIŠ}BA[NŠUR	11.6.3 obv.$^{?}$ 7′
pl.	GADA]^{MEŠ} ^{GIŠ}BANŠUR (MUNUS.LUGAL)	4.2.6 obv.$^{?}$ 1′
GADA EGIR*(-an) arḫa* SUD*-uaš*	'linen for "spreading out (on the) back"'	
	GADA EGIR *a]r-ḫa ḫu-u-it-ti-ia-u-wa-aš*	4.2.6 rev.$^{?}$ 10′
	GADA EGIR *ar-ḫa* SUD*-u-aš*	4.2.9 rev. 25′
	GADA] EGIR$^{!}$ *ar-ḫa* S[UD*-u-aš*	4.2.9 rev. 19′
	(GADA ...) EGIR*-an ar-*[*ḫa* SU]D-⟨*u*⟩*-aš*(?)	11.6.3 obv.$^{?}$ 6′
see *Lexical Commentary*; see also *ḫuittiya-*, *ḫuet-*, SUD		
GADA IGI	"eye linen"	
	GADA IGI	4.2.9 rev. 27′. 6.5 rev. 20′. 11.6.1 4, 14
	GADA IGI*-aš*	4.2.7 6′
GADA SIG	'gauze(?)' (lit. "thin linen")	
	GADA SIG	4.2.9 obv. 2, 4. 8.1.E(A$_1$) obv. iii 2′. 8.1.F obv. i 5′
	GADA$^{!}$ SIG	9.2.6 obv. i 10′
GADA SU$_6$	'napkin(?)' (lit. "beard/chin linen")	
	GADA SU$_6$	4.2.4 obv. 1
see *Lexical Commentary*		
GADA (*A-NA*) $^{(GIŠ)}$ŠÚ.A	'chair linen'	
	GADA ^{GIŠ}ŠÚ.A	8.1.K rev. v$^{?}$ 4′
	GADA $^{GI]Š}$ŠÚ.A	11.6.2 l. e. 1
	GADA ^{GIŠ}[ŠÚ.A(?)	4.2.9 rev. 28′
	GADA *A-NA* ^{GIŠ}Š[Ú.A(?)	10.1.2.4 l. c. 12′
see also $^{(GIŠ)}$ŠÚ.A		
GADA ZAG	'shawl(?)' (lit. "shoulder linen")	
	*⟨⟨TÚG⟩⟩*GADA ZAG	6.5 obv. 7′, 12′, 14′, 16′
$^{(TÚG)}$GAD.DAM	'gaiters, leggings(?)'	
	GAD.DAM	2.7.A obv. 26. 4.2.4 obv. 2. 6.9 obv. 4′ (2×), 8′, 11′. 8.1.D rev. iv 5′. 8.1.F obv. ii 6′, 7′. 8.8.B r. c. 8′. 11.6.1 4.
	GA]D.DAM	3.2.2 obv.$^{?}$ 2′. 8.1.G obv. l. c. 5′. 8.2 l. c. 2″
	GAD.DA[M	6.6 rev. 4′. 8.1.G obv. r. c. 3′
	^{TÚG}GAD.DAM	3.2.1 rev. 7′. 4.2.6 obv.$^{?}$ 10′. 4.2.9 obv. 31; rev. 16′. 6.5 rev. 18′, 26′. 6.6 obv. 5′. 6.10 5′. 6.13 4′. 11.6.4 obv. 9′. 11.6.5 obv.$^{?}$ 8
	^{TÚG}GAD.[D]AM	6.10 9′
	^{TÚG}GAD].DAM	6.8 2′
	^{TÚG}GAD.D]AM	6.8 5′
	^{TÚG}GAD.DA[M	3.2.5 r. c. 1′
	^{TÚG}G[AD.DAM	8.1.K obv. ii$^{?}$ 4′
	$^{TÚ[G}$GAD.DAM	3.2.1 lo. e. 20′
	TÚG ⟨⟨1⟩⟩ GAD.DA[M	6.5 rev. 15′
pl.	^{TÚG}GAD.DAM^{MEŠ}	2.7.A obv. 8. 9.1.8 obv. 9′. 11.6.3 obv.$^{?}$ 3′

	^{TÚG}]GAD.DAM^{MEŠ}	8.1.K rev. vi$^{?}$ 7′
	^{TÚG}GAD.[DAM	4.2.9 obv. 26
see *Lexical Commentary*		
^{LÚ}GAD.TAR	(an official) ‘herald(?)’	
	^{LÚ}GAD.TAR	6.1 rev. B 5
see *Lexical Commentary*		
$^{\text{(GIŠ)}}$GAG	‘peg, dowel’	
	GAG	9.1.1 rev. iv 40′. 10.2.1.2 obv. 17′. 11.1.3 3′
	^{GIŠ}GAG	10.3.3 obv.$^{?}$ 13′. 10.3.6 2′
inst.	*QA-DU* GAG	10.3.2 obv. i(?) 7″
$^{\text{(GI/GIŠ)}}$GAG(.Ú).TAG(.GA)	‘arrow’	
	GAG.Ú].TAG.GA	3.1.8.B 6′
	GAG.Ú.T]AG.GA	3.1.8.A rev. 19′
	GAG.Ú.TAG].GA	3.1.8.A rev. 21′
	GA[G.Ú.TAG.GA	3.1.8.B 6′
	^{GI}GAG.TAG	9.1.5 rev.$^{!}$ 2′, 6′
	^{GI}GAG.TAG.GA	3.1.1.A_3 rev. iv 8′, 9′
	^{GI}GAG.TAG.GA$^{!}$(text: TA)	9.1.5 rev.$^{!}$ 7′
	^{GI}GAG.TAG.G]A	3.1.1.A_1 rev. v 18′
	^{GI}GAG.Ú.TAG.GA	2.17 obv.$^{?}$ r. c. 14′, 15′, 16′. 5.7 rev. iii$^{?}$ 8′, 21′, 22′, 23′. 8.5 rev. iv(?) 3′
	^{GI}GAG.Ú.TAG.G[A	5.7 rev. iii$^{?}$ 26′. 9.1.10.A_2 rev. 7′
	^{GI}GAG.Ú.[TAG.GA	5.2 obv. ii 3
	^{GI}GAG.[Ú.TAG.GA	3.1.2 rev. l. c. 4′
	$^{\text{G[I}}$GAG(.Ú).TAG(.GA)(?)	9.1.12 5′
	^{GIŠ}GAG.Ú.TAG.GA	3.1.7.A_2 obv. ii 4′. 8.6 l. c. 6′
	^{GIŠ}GAG.Ú.TAG.G[A	3.1.7.A_2 obv. ii 13′
	^{GIŠ}GAG.Ú.[TAG.GA	3.1.7.A_2 obv. ii 16′
	^{GIŠ}GAG.[Ú.TAG.GA	3.1.7.A_1 obv. i 5′
	$^{\text{G[IŠ}}$GAG(.Ú).TAG(.GA)(?)	5.6 4′
	^{GIŠ}GAG].Ú.T[AG.GA	3.1.7.A_1 obv. ii 18′
GAL	(1.) ‘large’	
	GAL	2.5 obv. 2′, 5′, 6′, 7′. 2.7.A obv. 1, 2, 12. 2.9.A_2 obv. i 3′, 7′. 2.9.A_3 obv. ii 1′, 5′, 12′. 2.12 obv.$^{!}$ ii 4′, 9′. 2.16 obv. i 2′. 3.1.8.A obv. 6′. 3.2.1 obv. 20; rev. 7′, 16′. 4.1.1.3 rev. A 9′. 4.1.4.8 4′. 4.2.1.A_1 obv. 5, 6. 4.2.1.A_2 obv. 5′. 4.2.6 obv.$^{?}$ 14′. 4.2.9 obv. 18; rev. 15′. 5.2 obv. i 10. 6.5 rev. 21′. 6.9 obv. 1′. 8.1.A rev. vi 4′, 5′. 8.1.E(A_1) obv. iii 6′; rev. iv 2′. 8.1.G obv. r. c. 9′. 9.1.14 obv. r. c. 5′. 9.2.3 obv. (ii) 4″. 9.2.9 obv.$^{?}$ 11′. 10.1.1.1 rev.$^{?}$ 2′. 10.2.2.3 obv.$^{?}$ l. c. 9′. 10.3.1 obv. ii 3′. 11.2.6 4′. 11.5.1 7′. 11.6.1 5, 7. 11.6.2 rev. 8′. 11.6.9 4′
	GAL$^{!}$(?)	9.2.4 rev. iii 6′
	GA]L	2.7.B rev. 6′. 2.9.A_1 obv. i 8′. 8.1.G obv. r. c. 9′
	GA[L	8.1.F obv. ii 17′

	GA[L(?)	8.1.E(A_1) obv. ii 16

see also $^{\text{(URUDU)}}$*PĀŠU* GAL, DÍLIM.GAL, DINGIR.GAL, É.GAL, É DINGIR-*LIM* (GAL), GÍR.GAL, $^{\text{(URUDU)}}$KIN.GAL, ^{LÚ}SANGA.GAL, ^{URUDU}ŠEN.GAL, ŠU.NÍGIN.GAL

	(2.) 'overseer, chief'	
	GAL(-*ŠU-NU*)	3.1.8.A rev. 6′
	GAL (*ME-ŠE-DI*)	5.7 rev.$^?$ iii 12′, 25′
	GAL (DUB.SAR^{MEŠ})	2.4 rev. 6′. 4.1.1.1.A_1 rev. 15′. 4.1.1.1.B_1 rev. iii$^?$ 15. 5.7 rev. iii$^?$ 16′
	GAL (^{MUNUS}ŠU.GI SISKUR)	5.1 rev. iii 10
	(3.) 'cup'	
	GAL	1.1.A_1 obv. 5′, 7′, 9′. 1.1.A_2 rev. 5. 1.2 rev. 9′. 1.5 lo. e. 16, 17. 2.2 rev. 4. 2.7.A rev. 2. 2.17 obv.$^?$ r. c. 6′. 3.1.2 obv. l. c. 11′. 4.1.1.1.A_1 7′. 4.1.1.2.B obv. 3, 6, 8. 4.1.1.3 obv. 10, 11, 12, 13. 4.1.1.10 obv.$^?$ 2′. 5.1 obv. ii 7′, 10′; rev. iii 4. 6.1 obv. 17. 8.1.A rev. v 26′. 9.1.4.A_1 obv. ii 38. 9.2.4 rev. iii 5′; rev. iv 8. 10.1.2.7 4′. 11.1.6 l. c. 12′. 11.1.7 2′
	GAL$^?$	4.1.1.8 rev. r. c. 7′
	G]AL	5.1 obv. ii 4′. 9.1.4.A_1 obv. ii 41
	GA]L	4.1.1.6 rev. iii 2. 9.1.5 obv.$^!$ 6′
	GA[L$^?$	4.1.1.10 obv.$^?$ 1′
	^{URUDU}GAL	5.7 rev. iii$^?$ 4′, 13′, 15′, 17′, 28′
	$^{\text{URU[DU}}$GA]L	5.7 rev. iii$^?$ 5′
sg. dat./loc.	*A-NA* GAL	3.1.8.A obv. 14′
pl.	GAL$^{\text{ḪI.A}}$	9.1.7 obv. 4′
	GAL$^{\text{ḪI.[A}}$	9.1.7 obv. 4′
pl. dat./loc.	*A-NA* GAL$^{\text{ḪI.A}}$	2.2 rev. 5
^{URUDU}GAL.GEŠTIN	'wine cup'	
	^{URUDU}GA[L.G]EŠTIN	1.1.A_1 obv. 8′
^{LÚ}GAL	'grandee'	
pl. dat./loc.	*A-NA* $^{\text{LÚ.MEŠ}}$GAL (KUR ^{URU}UGU-*TI*)	5.1 rev. iii 5
GAM	'down, with'	
	GAM	2.9.A_3 obv. ii 3′. 2.12 obv.$^!$ ii 6′. 8.1.A obv. ii 18′. 9.1.14 obv. r. c. 7′. 9.2.9 obv.$^?$ 6′
	GAM(-*ŠŪNU*)	10.1.2.2 6′
	GAM-*an*	4.2.9 rev. 5′. 7.4 3′. 9.1.4.A_1 obv. i 2. 9.2.1 rev. iii 7′. 10.2.1.1 obv. 4′, 6′
= *katta(n)*		
GAM-*an tiannaš*	(a utensil for "setting down")	
sg. gen.	GAM-*an ti-an-na-aš*	10.3.11 l. c. 3′
	GAM-*an ti-an-n]a-aš*	10.3.11 l. c. 4′, 5′, 6′
GAM-*an tiyawa(š)*	(a utensil for "setting down")	
sg. gen.	GAM-*an ti-ia-wa-aš*	4.2.4 obv. 5, 6
	GAM-*an ti-ia-u-wa-aš*	9.1.1 rev. iv 8′
	GAM-*an ti-i]a-u-wa-aš*	2.2 rev. 19
pl. coll.	GAM-*an ti-ia-u-wa*	10.3.12 obv. i 11′

	GAM-*an t*]*i-ia-u-wa*	2.14 4′
see *Lexical Commentary*		
GAM-*ra-*	'lower, inferior'	
abl.	GAM-*ra-za*	10.2.1.2 obv. 11′, 16′. 10.3.2 obv. i(?) 5″, 10″. 10.3.8 1′
	⟨GAM⟩-*ra-za*	10.2.1.2 obv. 9′
GAR	'to plate, inlay (with metal)'	
pret. sg. 3 = *ḫališši(ya)-*	GAR-*ri*	4.2.4 obv. 7. 9.1.4.A_1 obv. i 17′; obv. ii 8
GAR(.RA)	'plated, inlaid (with metal)'	
	GAR	9.1.5 rev.! 9′
	(*peran arḫa*) GAR	9.1.5 rev.! 11′
	GAR.RA	2.7.A obv. 23. 2.14 7′, 10′. 2.17 obv.? 9′, 11′. 4.2.1.A_1 obv. 9, 10. 4.2.4 obv. 7, 8. 5.1 obv. ii 2′, 5′, 6′, 7′. 7.1 obv. 11′, 12′, 14′, 15′, 18′, 19′. 8.1.A obv. i 15′, 16′, 22′, 24′; rev. v 22′. 8.1.F rev. v 14. 8.4 rev. 13′ (2×), 14′. 9.1.1 rev. iii 7′; rev. iv 6′, 7′, 8′, 13′, 25′, 29′, 30′ (2×), 31′, 36′, 40′. 9.1.4.A_2 r. c. 6′, 8′. 9.1.5 rev.! 8′, 9′, 11′, 13′ (2×), 14′; rev. 1, 4, 9. 9.1.9 rev. iv 2′. 9.1.11 obv.? 8′. 9.1.13 3′. 9.1.14 obv. r. c. 10′. 9.2.1 rev. iii 3′. 9.2.6 obv. i 19′. 9.2.12 3′, 4′, 5′. 10.1.2.1 rev.? l. c. 7. 10.2.1.1 obv. 7′; rev. 4′. 10.2.1.2 obv. 2′, 4′, 6′, 7′, 11′ (2×), 16′. 10.2.1.7 rev.? 9′. 10.2.2.2 obv.? l. c. 2′. 10.2.2.3 obv.? l. c. 6′. 10.2.2.4 obv.? r. c. 3′, 4′. 10.3.1 rev. iii 3′, 5′, 6′, 8′, 11′. 10.3.3 obv.? 12′ (2×), 14′. 10.3.5 11′. 10.3.8 3′. 10.3.14 l. c. 5′. 11.1.4 7′. 11.2.4 1′. 11.3.1 15′. 11.3.3 2′. 11.4.1 2′
	GAR.RA+A?	4.2.1.A_1 obv. 9
	G]AR.RA	8.1.A obv. i 23′. 9.1.5 rev.! 5′
	GA]R.RA	10.3.14 l. c. 4′
	GAR].RA	9.1.4.A_1 obv. i 27′. 9.1.13 3′
	GAR.R]A	10.2.1.2 obv. 14′. 10.3.14 l. c. 6′
	GAR.R]A(?)	9.2.2 rev.! iv 3′; obv. ii(?) 13′
	GAR.R[A	7.1 obv. 14′, 19′, 20′. 9.1.10.A_1 rev. 8′. 9.2.4 rev. iv 11. 10.1.2.7 9′
	GAR.R[A??	12.3.3 8′
	GAR.[RA	9.1.9 rev. iv 3′. 9.1.11 obv.? 3′. 9.2.1 rev. iii 10′. 10.2.1.5 5′. 10.3.7 4′. 10.3.8 3′
	G[AR.RA	8.1.A obv. ii 7′
GE_6	'black; (a quality of iron or iron ore)'	
	GE_6	2.3 1. 4.2.2 obv. 2, 3. 4.2.4 obv. 10. 4.2.9 obv. 9. 8.1.A obv. i 2′ (2×), 3′, 4′, 11′; rev. v 3, 4, 8, 14′, 15′. 8.1.D obv. i 11′. 8.4 rev. 16′. 9.1.1 rev. iii 8′, 13′, 22′. 9.1.4.A_1 obv. ii 7, 17. 9.1.10.A_1 obv. 3′. 9.1.10.B 5′, 6′. 9.2.2 rev.! iii 13′. 9.2.4 rev. iv 5. 11.2.2 4′. 12.1.1 l. c. 2′, 5′

	G]E_6	8.1.C 3′
	G[E_6	3.1.12 7′. 8.1.A rev. v 2, 3. 9.1.10.A_1 rev. 2′
GEŠPU	‘fist(-shaped drinking vessels)’	
	GEŠPU	4.2.1.A_2 obv. 2′. 4.2.3 l. c. 5′
GEŠTIN	‘wine’	
	GEŠTIN	8.5 rev. iv(?) 5′. 10.1.1.2 rev. iv 13′
see also ^{URUDU}GAL.GEŠTIN		
GEŠTU	‘ear’	
	(^{TÚG}SAG.DUL) GEŠTU	4.2.9 obv. 23, 30
GIBIL	‘new’	
	GIBIL	2.12 obv.! ii 2′, 7′. 3.1.8.A obv. 10′. 4.1.4.9 obv. 11. 8.1.E(A_1) rev. v 6′
	G]IBIL	4.1.3.7 rev. 2′
GÍD.DA	‘long; length’	
	GÍD.DA	2.2 obv. 13′, 14′. 10.3.10 r. c. 9′. 11.6.11 2′, 3′
	GÍD.DA(-*ŠU*)	8.1.F rev. v 9, 11
see also É $^{\text{NA}_4}$KIŠIB GÍD.DA		
^{GIŠ}GIDRU	‘staff, sceptre’	
	^{GIŠ}GIDRU	5.8 6′
^{GIŠ}GIGIR	‘chariot, cart’	
	^{GIŠ}GIGIR	3.1.1.A_3 rev. iv 4′. 8.6 r. c. 4′, 5′. 9.1.8 obv. 11′. 10.2.1.3 1′
	$^{\text{GIŠ!?}}$GIGIR	9.1.10.A_2 rev. 6′
	^{GIŠ}GIG[IR	3.1.8.B 9′
	^{GIŠ}GI[GIR	3.1.1.A_1 rev. v 5′
	^{GIŠ}[GIGIR	3.1.8.A rev. 4′
sg. nom.	^{GIŠ}GIGIR-*TUM*	3.1.1.A_1 rev. v 3′, 8′
pl. dat./loc.	*A-NA* 3 ^{GIŠ}GIGIR	3.1.8.A rev. 10′
	A-NA 4 ^{GIŠ}GIGIR^{MEŠ}	3.1.8.A rev. 4′
^{GIŠ}GIGIR *ueraš*	‘platform cart(?)’	
sg. nom.	^{GIŠ}GIGIR *ú-e-ra-aš*	3.1.1.A_3 rev. iv 5′
	^{GIŠ}GIGIR *ú-e-r]a-aš*	3.1.1.A_1 rev. v 12′
see *Lexical Commentary*		
^{GIŠ}GIGIR *AŠĀBI*	‘sitting wagon’	
	^{GIŠ}GIGIR *A-ŠA-BI*	4.1.4.9 obv. 2. 8.7 r. c. 11′
	^{GIŠ}GIG]IR *A-ŠA-BI*	12.3.3 9′
	^{GIŠ}GIGI]R *A-ŠA-BI*	3.1.1.A_1 rev. v 5′
	^{GIŠ}GIGIR *A-Š]A-BI*	3.1.1.A_1 rev. v 15′
	^{GIŠ}GIGIR *A-Š[A-BI*	8.7 r. c. 11′
GILIM	‘circlet, headband, garland’	
	GILIM	11.3.1 23′
= *KILĪLU*		
GIM-*an*	‘when’	
	GIM-*an*	2.7.A obv. 14. 7.1 rev. 7′. 12.1.1 r. c. 4′

GÍN	‘shekel’	
	GÍN	1.1.A_1 obv. 11′, 12′. 1.2 rev. 3′, 4′, 5′, 6′, 7′, 8′, 9′, 10′ (2×). 1.5 rev. 26. 2.2 rev. 10, 11, 15. 2.7.A rev. 1, 3. 2.16 obv. i 10′. 3.1.1.A_1 obv. ii 14′, 15′. 3.1.1.A_2 rev. v 10′, 11′. 3.1.2 obv. l. c. 10′. 3.1.3 obv.$^?$ 1′, 5′. 3.1.5.A_1 obv. i(?) 4′. 3.1.5.A_2 obv. ii(?) 14′. 3.1.7.A_1 obv. i 4′, 10′; l. e. 3. 3.1.7.A_2 obv. ii 5b′, 7b′, 9′, 12′, 15′; rev. v 2′, 3′, 4′. 3.2.1 obv. 7, 11, 13, 20; rev. 3′, 10′ (2×), 12′. 3.2.2 obv.$^?$ 4′, 8′, 9′. 4.1.1.1.A_1 obv. 10′, 11′, 13′, 17′; rev. 8′. 4.1.1.1.B_1 rev. iii$^?$ 3, 16; rev. iv$^?$ 3, 6, 10 (2×). 4.1.1.2.A obv. 2′, 3′, 4′, 5′, 7′, 9′, 11′, 15′, 16′, 18′, 23′, 25′. 4.1.1.2.B obv. 1, 2, 4, 9. 4.1.1.3 obv. 7. 4.1.1.6 obv. ii 3′; rev. iii 7. 4.1.1.7 rev.$^{!?}$ 8. 4.1.1.8 rev. r. c. 2′, 4′, 5′, 9′. 4.1.2.5 obv. 2′, 6′. 4.1.3.1 1′, 2′, 3′, 6′, 7′, 8′. 4.1.3.2 rev. 1′, 3′, 5′ (2×). 4.1.3.3 8′ (2×). 4.1.3.8 rev. A 3′, 4′. 4.1.3.4.A_1 obv. l. c. 1′, 2′, 3′; rev. l. c. 3′, 4′, 5′, 6′, 7′. 4.1.3.4.A_2 rev. l. c. 5′, 6′, 7′, 8′. 4.1.3.5.A_2 2′, 3′, 4′. 4.1.4.1.A_1 obv. i 5′, 6′, 10′; obv. ii 7′, 9′, 11′, 13′; obv. iii 5′, 6′; rev. v 6′, 7′, 1″, 2″, 4″ (2×), 5″ (2×), 6″ (2×), 9″ (2×); rev. vi 8′ (3×), 9′ (2×), 10′. 4.1.4.1.A_2 obv. i 2′, 5′; obv. ii 4′, 5′, 7′, 8′. 4.1.4.2.A_1 rev. r. c. 2′, 3′, 4′ (2×), 5′, 7′, 8′ (2×), 10′ (2×), 13′, 14′; rev. l. c. 2′, 9′. 4.1.4.2.A_2 obv. r. c. 1′, 4′, 6′, 8′ (2×), 10′ (3×), 11′. 4.1.4.4 2′, 5′ (2×), 6′, 9′, 10′ (2×), 12′. 4.1.4.5 obv. r. c. 2′, 3′, 4′; rev. r. c. 3′, 4′, 7′. 4.1.4.6 obv. 5′, 10′, 13′ (2×), 14′; rev. 17′. 4.1.4.7 rev. B 1′. 5.2 obv. ii 16; rev. iii 8′. 6.1 lo. e. 9″. 7.1 obv. 14′, 19′. 8.1.A obv. ii 25′, 26′. 8.1.B rev. 5′. 10.3.2 obv. i(?) 7″, 11″. 11.7.2 5′. 12.1.3 2′, 3′. 12.2.2 2′, 3′, 4′, 5′, 6′, 8′, 10′, 11′. 12.2.3 3′, 6′, 7′. 12.3.1 3′
	⟨GÍN⟩	4.1.4.2.A_1 rev. l. c. 5′
	⟨⟨GÍN⟩⟩	12.2.2 7′, 8′
	GÍN$^!$	4.1.4.1.A_1 rev. vi 5′. 4.1.4.6 obv. 9′
	GÍN$^?$	4.1.2.5 rev. 1′
	GÍN$^?$	3.2.1 obv. 3
	G[ÍN	1.2 rev. 4′. 3.1.5.A_2 obv. ii(?) 9′. 3.1.7.A_1 obv. i 14′; obv. ii 4′. 3.2.3 3′. 4.1.1.2.B obv. 5
	G[ÍN(?)	4.1.4.2.A_1 rev. r. c. 5′
	GÍ[N	2.16 obv. i 3′. 3.1.2 obv. l. c. 9′. 3.1.7.A_1 obv. i 1′. 3.1.11.A 2. 3.2.1 rev. 1′. 4.1.1.3 obv. 16. 4.1.4.1.A_1 rev. v 3′. 4.1.4.2.A_1 rev. r. c. 7′. 4.1.4.2.A_2 obv. r. c. 2′. 4.1.4.5 rev. r. c. 3′. 4.1.4.7 rev. B 2′. 12.2.2 7′. 12.2.3 8′
	GÍ]N	2.2 rev. 5. 3.1.7.A_2 obv. ii 3′. 3.2.1 obv. 9. 4.1.1.1.A_1 rev. 8′, 12′. 4.1.1.2.A obv. 1′. 4.1.3.4.A_2 rev. l. c. 9′. 4.1.3.5.A_2 1′, 5′. 4.1.4.1.A_1 obv. i 4′, 9′; obv. ii 3′; rev. v 3′, 4′, 10″; rev. vi 3′. 4.1.4.1.A_2

		obv. ii 7′. 4.1.4.2.A_1 rev. l. c. 1′, 8′, 10′. 4.1.4.4 1′. 4.1.4.5 obv. r. c. 2′, 3′, 4′. 4.1.4.6 obv. 9′. 12.1.3 3′
	G]ÍN	4.1.1.1.A_1 obv. 6′. 4.1.3.1 9′. 4.1.3.4.A_1 obv. l. c. 4′. 4.1.3.4.A_2 rev. l. c. 4′. 4.1.3.8 rev. A 1′. 4.1.4.6 obv. 7′. 12.1.3 4′
	G]ÍN$^{?}$	12.1.3 6′
	G]ÍN$^{!?}$	4.1.1.1.A_1 rev. 11′.
pl.	GÍN.GÍN	4.1.1.6 rev. iii 1. 4.1.1.9 5′. 5.2 rev. iii 2′. 7.3 obv. i 7. 7.4 5′. 9.2.11 7′. 11.7.3 rev.$^{?}$ 3. 12.3.1 8′. 12.3.2 3′, 7′ (2×)
	GÍN$^{?}$.GÍN	4.1.1.4 3′
	G]ÍN.GÍN	7.4 6′
	G]ÍN.GÍN(?)	11.7.3 5
	GÍN.GÍ[N	7.3 obv. i 8
	GÍN.G[ÍN	11.1.6 l. c. 8′. 12.3.1 8′
	GÍN$^{!}$.G[ÍN	7.3 obv. i 9
	G[ÍN.GÍN(?)	11.7.3 rev.$^{?}$ 4, 6
$^{(URUDU)}$GÍR	‘(copper) knife/dagger’	
	GÍR	3.1.1.A_2 rev. v 2′, 3′. 3.1.8.A rev. 12′. 4.1.1.5 obv. 6. 5.3 l. c. 2′. 6.1 obv. 9, 11, 12. 7.1 obv. 19′. 8.1.D obv. i 9′. 9.1.1 rev. iii 6′. 9.2.13 5′. 10.3.5 1′
	GÍR$^{?}$	7.1 obv. 14′. 10.3.5 5′
	G]ÍR	2.16 obv. i 7′
	GÍ]R	3.1.8.A rev. 17′
	GÍ[R	5.3 r. c. 3′. 8.1.A rev. v 10
	(EME) GÍR	3.1.12 5′. 8.1.A rev. v 5 (2×)
	(EME) G]ÍR	4.2.2 obv. 2
	(EME) GÍ]R	8.1.C 1′
	^{URUDU}GÍR	5.2 obv. ii 16, 18 (2×). 6.1 rev. B 1
	$^{URUD]U}$GÍR	5.4 r. c. 9′
	^{URUDU}G[ÍR$^{?}$	5.3 r. c. 10′
pl.	GÍR^{MEŠ}	2.16 obv. ii 9′
GÍR *gimraš*	‘field knife/dagger’	
	GÍR *gi-im-ra-aš*	8.1.D obv. i 10′
	GÍR] *gi-im-ra-aš*	1.3 2′
	GÍR *g[i-im-ra-aš*	8.1.E(A_1) rev. iv 15′
GÍR *kinuḫi(ya)-*	(a type of knife/dagger)	
sg. nom.	GÍR *ki-nu-ḫi-iš*	6.2 obv. 5′. 6.13 5′

see *Lexical Commentary*; see also SAG.DU *kinuḫi(ya)-*

GÍR.GAL	‘sword(blade)’	
	(EME) GÍR.GAL	8.1.A rev. v 6
GÍR KUN	‘knife with attachment (lit. “tail”)’	
	GÍR KUN	3.1.8.A rev. 14′
GÍR LÍL	‘field knife/dagger’	
	GÍR LIL	2.7.A rev. 5
	GÍR ... LÍL	6.1 obv. 12

GÍR ^{LÚ}MUḪALDIM	'cook's knife'	
	GÍR ^{LÚ}MUḪALDIM	1.1.A_1 obv. 7′. 3.1.1.A_1 obv. ii 3′. 3.1.8.A rev. 12′. 5.1 rev. iii 2, 3. 8.1.D obv. i 9′
	(GÍR) … ^{LÚ}MUḪALDIM	3.1.8.A rev. 17′. 3.1.8.B 4′. 6.1 obv. 12
	GÍR ^{LÚ}[MUḪALDIM	8.1.A rev. v 11
	(EME) GÍR ^{LÚ}MUḪALDIM	3.1.12 6′
$^{(URUDU)}$GÍR.TUR	'(copper) small-knife'	
	GÍR.TUR	1.1.A_1 obv. 8′. 1.1.A_2 rev. 5. 1.4 4′. 8.1.A rev. v 4. 9.2.6 obv. i 12′
	(EME) GÍR.TUR	8.1.A rev. v 4
	^{URUDU}GÍR.TUR	8.5 rev. iii(?) 4′
	GÍ[R.TU]R	1.1.A_3 rev. 10′
pl.	^{URUDU}GÍ]R.TUR$^{ḪI.A}$	9.2.8.A_1 2′
see also ^{URUDU}ŠU.KÍN GÍR.TUR		
GÍR ^{URU}*Ḫatta*	'Hattan(-styled) knife'	
	G]ÍR ^{URU}*ḫa-at-ta*	9.2.1 obv. ii 25′
	GÍR ^{URU}*ḫ[a-at-ta*	9.1.1 rev. iii 6′
see also ^{TÚG}E.ÍB.GÍR		
GÌR	'foot, leg; foot of a chest/figurine'	
	GÌR	2.7.A obv. 16, 17. 4.2.9 rev. 2′. 8.1.J rev. v! 1′. 9.1.5 obv.! 2, 3. 10.2.2.2 obv.? l. c. 7′. 10.2.2.3 obv.? l. c. 5′. 10.2.2.4 obv.? r. c. 2′, 4′. 10.3.10 r. c. 4′, 8′, 9′, 10′. 11.6.2 l. e. 7
	G]ÌR	8.1.J rev. v! 10′. 10.3.10 r. c. 6′. 11.4.1 6′. 11.5.1 4′
	GÌ]R	9.1.5 obv.! 6
pl.	GÌR^{MEŠ}	9.1.4.A_1 obv. ii 9, 10, 11, 13, 14, 16, 21, 33. 9.2.1 rev. iii 11′, 12′. 10.3.3 obv.? 11′. 10.3.9 5′
	GÌR$^{?MEŠ}$	9.1.5 obv.! 15
GÌR UR.MAḪ	'lion's foot (of a chest)'	
	GÌR UR.MAḪ	2.7.A obv. 2, 12, 20. 2.9.A_1 obv. i 4′. 4.2.1.A_1 obv. 4. 8.1.F rev. v 14
	GÌR U]R.MAḪ	2.16 obv. i 2′
	GÌR [UR.MAḪ	2.5 obv. 8′
pl.	GÌR^{MEŠ} UR.MAḪ	2.7.B rev. 6′
^{LÚ}GÌR.ARAD	'governor'	
sg. dat./loc.	*A-NA* ^{LÚ}GÌ[R.ARAD	6.4 obv.? 5′
^{GIŠ}GÌR.GUB	'(foot)stool, bench, chair (esp. for women)'	
	^{GIŠ}GÌR.GUB	4.2.1.A_1 obv. 9. 4.2.9 rev. 6′
= $^{(GIŠ)}$*ḫapšalli-*?		
GIŠ(*-ru*) material	'wood(en)'	
	GIŠ	10.2.1.1 obv. 2′, 5′
sg. nom.-acc. n.	GIŠ-*ru*	9.1.1 rev. iv 12′
sg. gen.	*ŠA* GIŠ	10.2.1.1 obv. 6′
pl. nom.-acc. n.	GIŠ$^{ḪI.A}$	8.1.A obv. ii 18′
see also *IṢṢU*		

GIŠ.(BAR.)KÍN	‘covering, overlay’	
	GIŠ.KÍN	9.1.1 rev. iii 29′. 9.1.5 rev.! 9′, 10′, 15′, 16′ (2×). 10.3.14 l. c. 2′, 3′
	GI]Š.KÍN	9.1.5 rev.! 10′. 10.3.14 l. c. 2′
	GIŠ.BAR.KÍN	2.17 obv.? r. c. 12′ (2×), 13′ (2×), 17′, 20′. 9.1.1 rev. iv 13′, 32′. 9.2.7 obv. l. c. 11′. 9.2.8.A$_2$ 9″
	GIŠ.[B]AR.[KÍN](?)	9.2.7 obv. l. c. 12′
	GI]Š.BAR.KÍN	2.17 obv.? r. c. 11′
	GIŠ.BA]R.KÍN	9.2.8.A$_2$ 11″
	GIŠ.BAR].KÍN	9.2.7 obv. l. c. 9′
	GIŠ.BA[R.KÍN(?)	10.3.9 6′
	G[IŠ.BAR.KÍN	2.17 obv.? r. c. 13′
pl.	GIŠ.KÍN$^{\text{ḪI.A}}$	4.2.3 l. c. 3′
	GIŠ.KÍN$^{\text{ḪI.A}}$	9.1.5 rev.! 15′
	GIŠ.KÍN$^{\text{Ḫ[I.A}}$	4.2.1.A$_1$ obv. 11
see *Lexical Commentary*; = *SIḪPU*		
GIŠ.KÍN-*mant-*	‘overlaid, set with an overlay(?)’	
broken	GIŠ.KÍN-*ma-[an-*	2.15 l. c. 8′
GIŠ.ḪUR	(an official document or a wax writing board)	
	GIŠ.ḪUR	4.1.3.2 rev. 2′. 4.2.6 rev.? 8′
sg. dat./loc.	*A-NA* GIŠ.ḪUR	4.1.1.1.B$_2$ obv. i? 6′
pl. dat./loc.	*A-NA* GIŠ.ḪUR$^{\text{ḪI.A}}$	4.1.1.1.A$_1$ obv. 17′
inst.	*IŠ-TU* GIŠ.ḪUR	2.7.A obv. 3, 13
	I]Š-TU GIŠ.ḪUR	2.7.B rev. 7′
	IŠ-TU GIŠ.Ḫ[UR	2.7.B rev. 1′
see *Lexical Commentary*		
GIŠ.INANNA(.GAL)	‘(great) lyre’	
	GIŠ.INANNA.GA[L	10.3.2 obv. ii(?) 3′
	G[IŠ ^{D}INANNA(?)	8.1.A obv. ii 11′
GIŠ.KÍN		
see GIŠ.(BAR.)KÍN		
GIŠ.NÁ	‘bed, bedframe, bedstead’	
	GIŠ.NÁ	4.2.10 8′. 8.1.F rev. v 13. 9.1.10.A$_1$ obv. 8′. 9.1.10.B 12′. 10.3.6 4′
	GI]Š!?.NÁ	11.1.3 2′
	GIŠ.N]Á	4.2.9 rev. 2′. 11.1.4 4′
	GIŠ.N[Á	4.2.9 rev. 23′
	GIŠ.[NÁ(?)	8.1.K rev. v? 4′
GIŠKIM	‘sign, omen’	
sg./pl. gen.	GIŠKIM-*aš*	12.1.1 r. c. 5′
GÚ	‘neck; protome (on a drinking vessel)’	
	GÚ	2.13 obv.? 5′. 9.1.4.A$_1$ obv. ii 22. 9.2.7 obv. l. c. 11′
	⟨⟨GÚ⟩⟩	4.2.1.A$_2$ rev. 14′
	G]Ú?	10.3.2 obv. i(?) 3″
	G[Ú	10.1.1.2 rev. iv 5′

GÚ AMAR	'calf protome'	
	GÚ AMAR	2.17 obv.$^?$ r. c. 5′. 10.2.2.4 obv.$^?$ r. c. 5′
GÚ GU$_4$	'ox protome'	
	GÚ GU$_4$	2.13 obv.$^?$ 4′, 5′. 8.1.A rev. v 24′. 11.2.2 8′
	G]Ú$^?$ GU$_4$	4.2.3 l. c. 4′
GÚ ŠAḪ	'pig protome'	
	GÚ ŠAḪ	9.1.4.A$_1$ obv. ii 37
	G]Ú ŠAḪ	9.1.15 5′
GÚ TI$_8$MUŠEN	'eagle protome'	
	GÚ TI$_8$^{MUŠEN}	8.1.A rev. v 25′. 9.1.1 rev. iv 11′
	GÚ TI$_8$^{MUŠEN}(?)	4.2.1.A$_2$ obv. 1′
	G]Ú TI$_8$^{MUŠEN}	6.2 rev. 3′
GÚ UDU.KUR.RA	'mouflon protome'	
	GÚ UDU.KUR.RA	10.2.2.4 obv.$^?$ r. c. 5′
GÚ UR.MAḪ	'lion protome'	
	GÚ UR.MAḪ	6.1 obv. 17. 9.1.1 rev. iv 22′. 9.1.4.A$_1$ obv. ii 18
	GÚ UR.M[AḪ	9.1.15 4′
	GÚ UR.[MAḪ	8.1.A rev. v 24′
$^{\text{(TÚG/GADA)}}$GÚ(.È.A)	'shirt'	
	GÚ	6.5 rev. 11′. 8.1.F obv. i 5′. 11.2.2 5′
	GÚ.È.A	11.6.3 obv.$^?$ 2′
	^{GADA}GÚ	8.3 obv. 6′. 11.6.11 1′
	^{TÚG}GÚ	4.1.4.8 3′. 4.2.9 obv. 4. 6.1 obv. 7. 6.5 obv. 1′, 3′, 5′ (2×), 17′, 19′; rev. 14′. 6.6 obv. 7′; rev. 2′. 6.9 obv. 2′. 6.13 2′. 8.1.E(A$_1$) obv. ii 5. 8.1.E(A$_2$) 8′, 9′. 8.1.F obv. i 4′; obv. ii 11′, 12′, 13′; rev. v 13. 8.1.H rev. r. c. 2′. 9.2.9 rev.$^?$ 3′. 11.1.7 7′. 11.6.4 obv. 5′. 11.6.6 rev. 4′. 11.6.7 4′ (2×), 5′
	$^{\text{T]ÚG}}$GÚ	11.6.5 6
	$^{\text{TÚ]G}}$[G]Ú(?)	4.2.9 obv. 14
	^{TÚG}]GÚ	6.10 8′
	^{TÚG}G]Ú	8.1.I rev. r. c. 1′. 6.5 rev. 28′
	^{TÚG}G]Ú(?)	11.6.7 10′
	$^{\text{T[ÚG}}$G]Ú	6.5 rev. 24′
	^{TÚG}G[Ú	2.9.A$_3$ obv. ii 10′. 8.1.E(A$_1$) obv. iii 10′; rev. iv 4′. 8.3 obv. 3′. 9.2.4 obv. ii 15′. 10.1.2.1 obv.$^?$ r. c. 2′. 11.1.7 8′
	^{TÚG}G[Ú(.È.A)(?)	10.1.2.6 3′
	^{TÚG}GÚ.È.A	1.1.A$_1$ obv. 8′, 16′. 11.6.6 rev. 3′. 9.1.8 obv. 7′
	$^{\text{TÚ]G}}$GÚ.È.A	1.1.A$_1$ obv. 2′
	^{TÚG}G]Ú.È.A	4.2.6 obv.$^?$ 11′, 22′
^{TÚG}GÚ *adupli(t)-*	'*adupli*-shirt'	
	^{TÚG}GÚ *a-du-*[*up-li*	8.1.G obv. r. c. 5′
	$^{\text{TÚ]G}}$GÚ *a-du-up-l*[*i*	9.1.6 rev. 3′

see also $^{\text{(TÚG)}}$*adupli(t)-*

^{TÚG}GÚ *išpandaš*	'"night" shirt'	
	^{TÚG}GÚ (*QA-DU* GADA) *iš-pa-an-da-aš*	6.5 rev. 19′

^{TÚG}GÚ ^{URU}*Wašḫaniya*	'Wašḫaniyan(-styled) shirt'	
	^{TÚG}GÚ(?) ^{URU}*wa-aš-ḫa-ni-ia*	6.5 rev. 7′
see also (TÚG) *wašḫaniya-*		
$^{\text{(GADA/TÚG)}}$GÚ(.È.A) *ḪURRI*	'Hurrian(-styled) tunic'	
	GÚ.È.A *Ḫ*]*UR-RI*	11.6.3 obv.? 2′
	^{GADA}GÚ *ḪUR-RI*	6.2 obv. 4′
	^{TÚG}GÚ *ḪUR-RI*	2.9.A_1 obv. i 6′. 3.2.1 obv. 14, 17. 4.2.9 obv. 2, 3, 4, 21, 22; rev. 11′. 6.1 obv. 6. 6.3 rev. B 2. 6.5 rev. 24′. 6.9 obv. 10′. 8.1.D rev. iv 12′. 8.1.E(A_1) obv. iii 10′; rev. iv 5′ (2×), 7′. 8.1.H rev. r. c. 10′. 8.4 rev. 15′. 8.8.A 11′. 11.6.2 rev. 10′. 11.6.7 3′. 11.6.8 3′
	^{TÚG}GÚ *ḪUR.*	9.1.4.A_4 l. c. 4′. 11.6.1 2
	^{TÚG}GÚ] *ḪUR.*	8.1.D rev. iv 11′
	$^{\text{T]ÚG}}$GÚ *ḪUR-RI*	4.2.9 obv. 28, 29. 8.8.B l. c. 11′
	$^{\text{TÚ]G}}$GÚ *ḪUR-RI*	8.1.F obv. ii 10′
	^{TÚG}]GÚ [*ḪUR-RI*	4.2.9 obv. 12
	^{TÚG}G]Ú *ḪUR-RI*	3.2.1 rev. 18′. 8.1.H rev. l. c. 1′. 10.1.2.7 9′. 11.6.7 2′. 11.6.10 3′
	^{TÚG}GÚ *Ḫ*]*UR-R*[*I*	8.1.F obv. i 11′
	$^{\text{TÚ[G}}$G]Ú *ḪUR-RI*	8.1.F obv. i 3′
	^{TÚG}GÚ [*ḪUR*]*-RI*	8.1.F obv. i 21′
	^{TÚG}GÚ *ḪUR-R*]*I*	11.1.7 7′
	^{TÚG}GÚ *ḪUR-R*[*I*	1.5 rev. 26. 3.2.1 obv. 2, 14. 4.2.9 obv. 8. 6.8 3′
	^{TÚG}GÚ *ḪU*[*R-RI*	8.8.A 10′. 11.6.8 2′
	^{TÚG}GÚ *ḪU*[*R*!?]*-R*[*I*?	6.9 obv. 2′
	^{TÚG}GÚ *Ḫ*[*UR-RI*	6.5 obv 2′. 11.6.8 4′
	^{TÚG}GÚ *Ḫ*[*UR-RI*(?)	2.15 l. c. 6′
	^{TÚG}G[Ú(?) *ḪUR-RI*(?)	4.2.9 obv. 5
	^{TÚG}GÚ.È.A *ḪUR-RI*	1.5 obv. 12; rev. 23, 25. 2.7.A obv. 23. 4.2.6 obv.? 8′. 8.1.E(A_1) obv. ii 10. 9.1.1 rev. iii 30′; rev. iv 41′
	^{TÚG}]GÚ.È.A *ḪUR-RI*	4.2.6 obv.? 15′
	^{TÚG}GÚ].È.A *ḪU*[*R-RI*	11.6.9 1′
	^{TÚG}GÚ.È.A *ḪUR-*[*RI*	7.3 obv. i 2
see *Lexical Commentary*		
^{TÚG}GÚ(.È.A) *ḪURRI ŠURĪPU*	'Hurrian(-styled) tunic (for) frost/ice'	
	^{TÚG}GÚ.È.A *ḪUR-RI ŠU-RI-PU*	4.2.6 obv.? 4′
	^{TÚG}GÚ *ḪUR-RI* … [*ŠU*]*-RI-PU*	4.2.9 obv. 2
GÚ.ḪAL	"neck" (a type of neck-torc or collar)	
	GÚ.ḪAL	8.4 rev. 8′. 11.3.2 r. c. 2′, 3′, 4′
GÚ.SES	'bitter vetch'	
	GÚ.SES	12.2.1 rev. 4′, 5′
	G]Ú.SES	12.2.1 obv. 4′
	GÚ].SES	12.2.1 obv. 5′
see *Lexical Commentary*		

GU$_4$	'ox'	
	GU$_4$	4.1.1.1.A$_1$ rev. 4′. 9.1.1 rev. iv 21′. 9.1.15 2′. 10.1.2.4 l. c. 15′
	GU$_4$?	10.1.1.1 obv.? 10′. 11.2.2 4′
	(GÚ) GU$_4$	2.13 obv.? 4′, 5′. 4.2.3 l. c. 4′. 8.1.A rev. v 24′. 11.2.2 8′
	(KUŠ) GU$_4$	4.1.3.6 obv. 15′
	(SI) GU$_4$	9.1.1 rev. iv 30′. 9.2.4 rev. iv 11
	(*BIBRU*) GU$_4$	5.2 obv. ii 7. 9.1.4.A$_1$ obv. ii 9
see also $^{(GU_4)}$AMAR		
GU$_4$.MAḪ	'bull'	
	GU$_4$.MAḪ	10.1.1.1 rev.? 6′
	GU$_4$.M]AḪ	4.1.1.1.A$_1$ rev. 4′
	GU$_4$.M[AḪ	2.2 rev. 7
GUB	'to stand'	
med. pres. sg. 3	GUB-*ri*	9.2.1 rev. iii 10′
ptc. sg.	GUB.BA	9.1.5 obv.! 2, 3, 6
	G]UB.BA	9.1.5 obv.! 3
	GUB.B[A	9.1.5 obv.! 5
ptc. sg. nom.	GUB-*a*]*n-za*	10.2.1.1 obv. 2′
	GUB-*za*	9.1.4.A$_1$ obv. ii 13 (2×), 16, 21
	G]UB-*za*	2.8 obv. 2
	GUB-*z*]*a*	9.1.4.A$_1$ obv. ii 9
	GU[B-*za*	9.1.4.A$_1$ obv. ii 33
	G[UB-(*an-*)*za*(?)	11.2.3 2′
ptc. sg. acc.	GUB-*an*	9.1.1 rev. iv 16′. 10.2.1.1 obv. 8′
	GUB-*a*]*n*(?)	9.1.1 rev. iv 17′
ptc. pl. nom.	GUB-*an-te-eš*	9.1.1 rev. iv 10′, 21′. 9.2.1 rev. iii 11′. 10.2.1.1 obv. 5′
	G]UB-*an-te-eš*	9.2.1 rev. iii 13′
	GUB-*a*]*n-te-eš*	9.1.1 rev. iv 11′
	GUB-*a*[*n-te-eš*	9.2.1 rev. iii 12′
	GU[B-*an-te-eš*	9.1.4.A$_1$ obv. ii 35
	GUB-*te-eš*	9.1.4.A$_1$ obv. ii 11
GÙB	'on the left, left side'	
abl.	GÙB-*la-za*	10.3.1 rev. iii 10′
	GÙB-*za*	10.2.1.1 obv. 6′
	GÙB-[*za*(?)	10.1.2.6 10′
^{NA_4}GUG	'carnelian'	
	^{NA_4}GUG	12.2.2 5′
material		
	^{NA_4}GUG	2.4 rev. 4′. 8.1.A obv. i 13′
	^{NA_4}]GUG	8.1.A obv. i 24′
	^{NA_4}G]UG(?)	8.1.A obv. i 10′
	^{NA_4}GU]G	8.1.A obv. i 8′
= (^{NA_4})(∢)*kirinni-*?		
GUL	'to strike, smash'	
ptc. pl. nom.	(*šer*) GUL-*an-te-eš*	10.3.1 rev. iii 4′

GUL-š-	'to engrave, inscribe, mark, draw'	
see *gul(aš)šant-*		
GUN	'talent (i.e., 60 minas)'	
	GUN	5.2 obv. ii 1, 5, 6 (2×), 13. 5.7 rev. iii? 3′; rev. iv? 16′
	G]UN	5.1 rev. iii 12
	GU[N	4.1.2.7 1′. 5.7 rev. iii? 5′
	G[UN	5.7 rev. iii? 9′
GÙN.A	'multi-hued'	
	GÙN.A	12.1.1 l. c. 5′; r. c. 11′
	GÙ[N].A	12.1.1 l. c. 3′
see also ḪI.ḪI		
GUNNI	'stove, hearth'	
sg. gen.	(AN.BAR) *ŠA* GUNNI	4.2.1.A$_1$ obv. 6
GUNNI *waršanaim(m)a/i-*	(a type of stove)	
pl. nom.	GUNNI … *wa-ar-ša-na-i-me-uš*	9.1.4.A$_1$ obv. ii 5
	GUNNI … *wa-ar-ša-na-i-me-u[š*	9.1.4.A$_1$ obv. ii 1
^{URUDU}GUNNI.DU.DU	'portable stove'	
	^{URUDU}GUNNI.DU.DU	3.1.1.A$_2$ rev. v 5′
GURUN	'fruit (decoration)'	
	GURUN	9.2.1 obv. ii 8′, 14′; rev. iii 15′. 10.1.2.1 rev.? r. c. 6′. 10.1.2.2 3′, 4′. 10.1.2.3 3′. 10.3.13 4′. 11.2.5 1′
$^{\text{(TÚG)}}$GUZ.ZA	'scarlet-cloth'	
	GUZ("SIG$_4$").ZA	2.5 rev. 5′
	^{TÚG}GUZ("SIG$_4$").ZA	2.9.A$_1$ obv. i 8′. 4.1.4.9 obv. 1, 5, 6, 10, 11. 5.7 rev. iii? 24′. 6.5 rev. 21′, 22′. 9.1.10.B 11′. 10.1.1.1 rev.? 13′. 10.1.2.6 3′. 11.6.1 6. 11.6.2 l. e. 4. 11.6.11 4′
	^{TÚG}GUZ("SIG$_4$").ZA	3.2.3 2′
	$^{\text{TÚG!(text: 1)}}$GUZ("SIG$_4$").ZA	1.5 lo. e. 16
	*$^{\text{TÚG!}}$*GUZ("SIG$_4$").ZA	11.1.3 7′
	$^{\text{TÚ]G}}$GUZ("SIG$_4$").ZA	11.1.5 6′
	^{TÚG}GUZ("SIG$_4$").Z[A	8.1.F rev. v 6′
	^{TÚG}G[UZ("SIG$_4$").ZA	9.1.10.A$_1$ obv. 7′
see *Lexical Commentary*		
^{DUG}ḪAB.ḪAB	(a flask for liquids/ointments)	
	^{DUG}ḪAB.ḪAB	2.13 obv.? 6′. 8.5 rev. iv(?) 5′
= ^{DUG}*kukupalla(nt?)-*, *KU(K)KU(B)BU*		
ḪAR	'ring'	
	ḪAR	2.16 rev. v 2
	Ḫ]AR	9.1.4.A$_2$ r. c. 5′
	Ḫ[AR	2.16 rev. v 1
pl.	ḪAR$^{\text{ḪI.A}}$	2.2 rev. 12. 4.1.1.1.A$_1$ rev. 9′
ḪAR.GÌR	'foot ring, anklet'	
	ḪAR.GÌR	12.1.4 4′

ḪAR.GÚ	‘neckband, torc’	
	ḪAR.GÚ	3.1.8.A obv. 8′, 17′. 4.1.1.1.A_1 obv. 21′. 7.3 obv. i 7. 8.1.A obv. i 2′. 8.4 rev. 4′. 11.4.2 obv. 5′, 6′
$^{\text{(GIŠ)}}$ḪAR.ŠU	‘arm ring, bracelet’	
	ḪAR.ŠU	1.5 obv. 5. 6.1 rev. A 6″. 8.4 rev. 11′. 11.3.1 2′, 4′, 5′, 6′, 7′, 8′, 10′, 11′ (2×), 14′.
	Ḫ]AR.ŠU	8.1.A obv. i 7′
	^{GIŠ}ḪAR.ŠU	9.1.13 6′
^{GIŠ}ḪAŠḪUR	‘apple(tree)’	
	^{GI}]^{Š}ḪAŠḪUR	12.1.2 7′
	^{GIŠ}ḪAŠ]ḪUR	12.1.2 8′
	^{GIŠ}ḪAŠ]ḪUR	12.1.2 8′
	^{GIŠ}[ḪAŠḪUR	12.1.2 7′
	^{GI}[^{Š}ḪAŠḪUR	12.1.2 8′
ḪI.ḪI	‘multi-hued, variegated’	
	ḪI.ḪI	6.3 rev. B 1. 8.1.F obv. i 21′; obv. ii 5′. 8.1.G obv. r. c. 9′. 8.1.K rev. vi? 9′. 11.6.5 obv.? 7. 11.6.6 rev. 6′. 11.6.10 3′
	ḪI.ḪI(?)	11.6.5 rev.? 4″
see *Lexical Commentary*; see also GÙN.A		
$^{\text{(TÚG)}}$ḪI.ḪI-*na-tar*	‘cloth of mixed construction; (wool-)blend’	
sg. nom.-acc. n.	ḪI.ḪI-*na-tar*	6.13 8′. 8.1.F rev. v 12
	ḪI.ḪI-**na-tar**	6.5 obv. 17′
	ḪI].ḪI-*na-tar*	3.2.2 obv.? 4′. 4.2.6 obv.? 12′, 16′
	ḪI.Ḫ]I-*na-tar*	8.1.F rev. v 6
	^{TÚG}ḪI.ḪI-*na-tar*	8.1.D rev. iv 2′. 8.1.E(A_1) rev. v 8′
	^{TÚ}]^{G}ḪI.ḪI-*na-tar*	11.6.6 rev. 3′
	^{TÚG}ḪI.ḪI]-*na-tar*	8.1.D rev. iv 2′
	^{TÚG}ḪI.ḪI-[*na-tar*	9.1.6 obv. 13
ḪUB(.BI)/ḪÚB(.BI)	‘(ear)ring’	
	ḪUB	1.3 3′, 7′. 4.1.1.3 rev. A 4′. 5.9 1′
	Ḫ]UB	1.3 6′
	ḪUB.BI	1.5 obv. 4. 6.5 rev. 2′, 3′, 4′, 5′. 8.4 rev. 18′. 10.1.2.1 rev.? r. c. 2′. 10.2.1.2 obv. 8′
	ḪUB.BI (LÚ)	9.1.1 rev. iv 37′
	ḪUB.BI (MUNUS-*TI*)	9.1.1 rev. iv 39′
	ḪUB!.BI	9.2.4 obv. ii 7′
	ḪUB.PI(sic!)	12.3.3 8′
	Ḫ]UB.BI (LÚ-*LIM*)	9.2.1 obv. ii 17′
	ḪU]B.BI	9.2.1 obv. ii 24′. 10.3.4 7′
	ḪUB.B]I	9.2.1 obv. ii 4′
	ḪUB.B]I (LÚ-*LIM*)	10.3.4 9′
	ḪUB.B[I	11.3.1 15′
	ḪUB.[BI	9.2.4 rev. iii 12′
	ḪÚB.BI	9.1.10.A_1 rev. 3′
	ḪÚ]B.BI	11.3.3 1′
pl.	ḪUB$^{\text{ḪI.A}}$	8.4 rev. 10′. 9.1.1 rev. iii 2′, 24′

	ḪUB.BI$^{\text{ḪI.A}}$	6.5 obv. 17′; rev. 6′. 6.13 6′. 9.1.10.A$_1$ obv. 6′. 11.3.1 15′, 16′, 17′, 19′
	ḪUB.BI$^{\text{Ḫ[I.A}}$	6.5 obv. 16′
	ḪÚB.BI$^{\text{ḪI.A}}$	9.1.5 obv.$^{!}$ 1
	ḪÚ]B.BI$^{\text{ḪI.A}}$	4.1.1.1.A$_1$ obv. 20′
see also *ašuša*-, *ištamaḫura*-, *INṢABTU*, *KAMKAMMATU*		
^{LÚ}ḪUB.BI	'cultic dancer, acrobat'	
pl. gen.	$^{\text{LÚ.MEŠ}}$ḪU[B.B]I-*aš*	8.1.F rev. vi 17
ḪUR.SAG	'mountain'	
	ḪUR.SAG	9.1.1 rev. iv 18′. 10.1.1.1 rev.$^{?}$ 11′. 10.1.1.2 rev. iv 5′
	Ḫ]UR.SAG	10.1.1.2 rev. iv 5′
	ḪUR.S[AG	10.1.1.2 rev. iv 4′
sg. acc.	(GAL) ḪUR.SAG-*in*	4.1.1.2.A obv. 17′. 4.1.1.2.B obv. 3
see also ^{URUDU}*ḪAṢṢINNU* ḪUR.SAG		
Ì	'oil'	
	Ì	9.1.1 rev. iv 30′
Ì.NUN	'butter oil'	
	Ì.N[UN(?)	12.3.2 8′
$^{\text{(TÚG)}}$ÍB.LÁ	'sash'	
	ÍB.LÁ	8.1.F rev. v 12. 11.6.1 14
	^{TÚG}ÍB.LÁ	1.5 obv. 13. 4.1.4.8 5′. 4.2.9 obv. 5, 24; rev. 14′
^{GIŠ}IG	'door'	
	$^{\text{GI]Š}}$IG(?)	10.1.2.8 rev. r. c. 3
	^{GIŠ}I]G(?)	12.1.2 3′, 4′
	$^{\text{G[IŠ}}$IG(?)	12.1.2 3′
IGI	'eye'	
pl.	IGI$^{\text{ḪI.A}}$	10.2.2.3 obv. l. c. 11′
see also GADA IGI		
IGI-*zi*	'first' (adv.)	
	IGI-*zi*	9.1.1 rev. iv 10′, 21′. 9.1.4.A$_1$ obv. ii 11, 13. 9.1.5 obv.$^{!}$ 5. 9.1.15 2′. 10.3.6 8′. 11.2.3 2′
IGI-*ziya*-	'foremost, first-class'	
sg. nom.	IGI-*zi-aš*	3.2.1 obv. 20
	IGI-*zi-a*[*š*	3.2.1 obv. 1
see also SÍG IGI-*zi-aš* MU^{KAM}-*aš*		
^{LÚ}IGI.DU(-)[	"front-goer"	
sg. gen.	*ŠA* ^{LÚ}IGI.DU(-)[	9.1.4.A$_1$ obv. ii 3
IGI.DU$_8$.A	'gift; gift payment'	
	IGI.DU$_8$.A	2.7.A obv. 2; rev. 5. 2.7.B rev. 6′. 3.1.1.A$_2$ rev. v 3′, 9′. 3.1.1.A$_3$ obv. iii 5′, 7′, 10′, 15′; rev. iv 9′, 11′. 3.1.2 obv. l. c. 5′. 3.1.4 4′. 3.1.5.A$_1$ obv. i(?) 2′. 4.1.4.4 4′, 8′. 4.1.4.5 rev. r. c. 5
	I]GI.DU$_8$A	3.1.8.B 5′
	IG]I.DU$_8$.A	4.1.4.4 11′

	IGI].DU$_8$.A	3.1.1.A$_3$ rev. iv 18′
	IGI.D]U$_8$.A	3.1.1.A$_1$ obv. ii 5′. 3.1.3 rev.$^?$ 9′. 3.1.8.A rev. 18′
	IGI.DU$_8$].A	3.1.5.A$_2$ obv. i(?) 8′
	IGI.D[U$_8$.A	3.1.7.A$_2$ obv. ii 8′. 3.1.8.A rev. 21′
	IGI.[DU$_8$.A	3.1.7.A$_2$ obv. ii 8′
pl. dat./loc.	*A-NA* IGI.DU$_8$.A	3.1.2 obv. l. c. 7′
inst.	*QA-DU* IGI.DU$_8$.A	3.1.1.A$_3$ obv. iii 11′. 3.1.5.A$_1$ obv. i(?) 5′. 3.1.5.A$_2$ obv. i(?) 2′
	Q]*A-DU* IGI.DU$_8$.A	3.1.3 rev.$^?$ 4′
	QA]*-DU* IGI.DU$_8$.A	3.1.5.A$_2$ obv. i(?) 5′
	QA-DU IG]I.DU$_8$.A	3.1.5.A$_1$ obv. i(?) 8′
see *Lexical Commentary*		
^{LÚ}IGI.MUŠEN	'auspex, augur'	
	^{LÚ}IGI.MUŠEN$^?$	5.2 up. e. 1
^{KUŠ}IGI.TAB.ANŠE	'blinders'	
	^{KUŠ}IGI.TAB.ANŠE	9.1.10.A$_2$ rev. 11′
	^{KUŠ}IGI.TAB.A[NŠE	9.1.11 obv.$^?$ 10′
IKU	(1.) 'field'	
	IKU	12.3.2 3′, 7′
	(2.) "acre" (unit of area)	
	IKU	12.3.1 6′
^{GIŠ}ÍLDAG	'poplar'	
	^{GIŠ}ÍLDAG	10.3.3 obv.$^?$ 9′
IM.ŠU.NÍG.RIN.NA	'oven, kiln'	
	IM.ŠU.N[ÍG.RIN.NA	11.4.2 obv. 4′
IN.NU.DA	'straw'	
	I]N.NU.DA	1.1.A$_2$ rev. 10
^{LÚ}IŠ	'charioteer'	
	^{LÚ}I[Š(?)	5.5 rev. iii 7′
see *Lexical Commentary*		
KÁ	'gate, door'	
sg. dat./loc.	*A-NA* KÁ	12.1.1 r. c. 1′
see also LÚ KÁ UR.GI$_7$		
$^{\text{NA}_4}$KÁ.DINGIR.RA	"Babylon-stone" (a glass or enamel)'	
	$^{\text{NA}_4}$KÁ.DINGIR.RA	8.1.D obv. i 6′
	$^{\text{N}]\text{A}_4}$KÁ.DINGIR.RA	12.2.2 4′
	$^{\text{NA}_4}$KÁ.DINGIR.[RA	2.1.B 7′
material		
	$^{\text{NA}_4}$KÁ.DINGIR.RA	9.2.13 6′. 11.1.2 l. c. 2′
	$^{\text{NA}_4}$K]Á.DINGIR.RA	9.1.4.A$_1$ obv. i 12′
	$^{\text{NA}_4}$KÁ.DI]NGIR.RA	9.1.4.A$_1$ obv. i 30′
	$^{\text{NA}_4}$KÁ.DINGIR.R[A	9.2.2 rev.$^!$ iii 7′
	$^{\text{NA}_4}$K[Á.DINGIR.RA	9.2.3 obv. (ii) 4″
see *Lexical Commentary*; = NA$_4$ ^{URU}*Papila*		
$^{\text{NA}_4}$KA.GI.NA	'magnetite (also hematite?)'	
	$^{\text{NA}_4}$KA.GI.NA	12.1.3 4′

	⟨⟨^{NA_4}KA.GI.NA⟩⟩	12.2.2
see *Lexical Commentary*		
KASKAL	'road, path; way, behavior; journey, trip: (with numeral) -times'	
	KASKAL	8.1.C 4′. 8.1.E(A_1) obv. ii 8
	(3) KASKAL	4.1.1.3 rev. B 14
gen.	KASKAL-*NI*	1.1.A_2 obv. 3′, 4′. 1.1.A_3 rev. 5′. 8.4 lo. e. 23′
	] KASKAL-*NI*	8.1.A rev. vi 1′
	KASKA]L-*NI*	8.1.G obv. l. c. 1′
	ŠA KASKAL	8.1.A rev. v 9, 16′, 20′. 8.1.D obv. i 8′, 10′; rev. iv 6′. 8.1.E(A_1) obv. iii 4′. 8.1.J rev. v$^{!}$ 9′
	Š]*A* KASKAL	8.1.J rev. v$^{!}$ 11′
	ŠA KAS[KAL	8.1.D rev. iv 13′
	ŠA [KASKAL	8.1.A rev. v 26′. 8.1.D obv. i 5′, 7′
	Š[*A* KASKAL	8.1.A obv. ii 27′. 8.1.B rev. 7′, 12′
	Š[*A* KASKAL(?)	8.1.I rev. r. c. 3′
	ŠA KASKAL-*NI*	8.1.E(A_3) obv. i 4′. 8.1.F obv. i 7′, 18′; rev. vi 8, 14, 16. 8.1.K rev. vi$^{?}$ 10′. 8.3 obv. 4′
	ŠA KAS[KAL]-*NI*	8.1.F rev. v 16
	Š]*A* KASKAL-*NI*	8.1.F rev. vi 6
	ŠA] KASKAL-*NI*	8.1.H rev. l. c. 7′
	ŠA K]ASKAL-*NI*	8.1.H rev. l. c. 3b′. 8.1.K rev. vi$^{?}$ 5′
	ŠA KASKAL-*N*]*I*	8.1.H rev. l. c. 2′
	ŠA KASKAL-*N*[*I*	8.1.F rev. vi 16
loc.	*I-NA* KASKAL	8.1.E(A_1) obv. ii 15
= *palša-*		
KASKAL-*aḫḫ-*	'to dispatch, set on the road'	
pres. pl. 3	KASKAL-*aḫ-ḫa-an-zi*	6.1 rev. A 8″
KAŠ	'beer'	
	KAŠ	12.3.5 3′
KEŠDA(*-m(m)a/i-*)	'bound, tied, knotted'	
	KEŠDA	4.2.4 obv. 1
Luw. ptc. pl. nom.-acc. n.	KEŠDA-*ma*	2.7.A obv. 10
see *Lexical Commentary*; see also $^{(TÚG)}$*ḫamenkant-*		
KI GUB	'standing (on the) ground'	
	KI GUB	10.2.2.2 obv.$^{?}$ l. c. 4′. 10.2.2.3 obv.$^{?}$ l. c. 7′. 10.2.2.4 obv.$^{?}$ r. c. 2′, 4′
	K]I GUB	10.2.2.2 obv.$^{?}$ l. c. 6′
	KI [GUB	10.2.2.2 obv.$^{?}$ l. c. 7′. 10.2.2.3 obv.$^{?}$ l. c. 5′
KI.LÁ(.BI)(-*ŠU*)	'weight'	
	KI.LÁ	3.1.7.A_2 obv. ii 7b′. 4.1.1.1.A_2 rev. 1′. 8.6 l. c. 8′, 11′. 10.3.2 obv. i(?) 7″, 11″. 12.3.1 3′
	KI.L[Á	3.1.7.A_2 obv. ii 12′. 4.1.1.2.A obv. 5′. 4.2.2 obv. 1
	K[I.LÁ	3.1.7.A_2 obv. ii 15′. 5.2 obv. ii 13
	KI.LÁ.BI	4.1.1.6 rev. iii 8, 9. 4.1.1.9 4′, 6′, 7′. 7.2 5′. 8.6 l. c. 10′
	KI].LÁ.BI	4.1.2.6 1′
	⟨⟨KI].LÁ.BI⟩⟩	4.1.1.9 10a′

	KI.L]Á.BI	4.1.1.9 14′
	KI.L]Á.B[I	7.2 1′
	KI.LÁ.B]I	4.1.2.6 2′, 3′
	KI.LÁ.[(BI)	10.3.12 obv. ii 3′
	KI.L[Á.BI	4.1.1.9 3′
	KI.L]Á.BI-*ŠÚ*	5.2 rev. iii 6′
	KI.LÁ-*ŠU*	3.1.11.A 5. 3.1.11.B 4′. 5.2 obv. ii 9
	KI.[LÁ-*ŠU*	3.1.10 5
	K[I.LÁ-*ŠU*	3.1.10 3, 9
(KI.LÁ) NA$_4$	'stone weight'	
	NA$_4$	4.1.1.1.B$_1$ rev. iv$^?$ 6, 10. 4.1.1.2.A obv. 8′, 16′, 19′. 4.1.1.2.B obv. 2, 5. 4.1.2.5 obv. 6′ (2×), 11′; rev. 10′
	N]A$_4$	4.1.1.1.B$_1$ rev. iv$^?$ 10. 4.1.1.2.A obv. 9′. 4.1.2.5 obv. 9′, 14′
	KI.LÁ NA$_4$	4.1.1.1.A$_1$ obv. 6′, 8′, 10′, 18′, 21′. 4.1.1.1.B$_1$ rev. iv$^?$ 9. 4.1.1.2.B obv. 2, 5. 4.1.1.3 rev. B 9. 4.1.2.5 obv. 5′. 8.1.A obv. ii 22′, 23′
	KI.L[Á$^?$] NA$_4$$^?$	10.1.2.2 1′
	K]I.LÁ NA$_4$	4.1.1.3 rev. B 6. 4.1.2.5 obv. 13′. 8.1.C l. c. 2′, 4′
	KI.L]Á NA$_4$	4.1.2.5 obv. 1′; rev. 3′
	KI.LÁ N[A$_4$	4.1.1.1.A$_1$ obv. 11′. 4.1.1.2.A obv. 10′. 4.1.1.5 up. e. 1; obv. 1
	KI.LÁ N[A$_4$$^?$	3.1.1.A$_3$ rev. iv 1′
	KI.L[Á NA$_4$	4.1.1.1.A$_1$ obv. 17′
	K[I.LÁ NA$_4$	4.1.1.1.A$_1$ obv. 14′. 4.1.1.2.B obv. 7
sg. gen.	(KI.LÁ.BI) *ŠA* NA$_4$$^?$	4.1.1.9 7′
see *Lexical Commentary*		
(KI.LÁ) TI$_8$^{MUŠEN}	'eagle weight'	
	TI$_8$^{MUŠEN}	4.1.2.3 obv. ii 6′, 11′; rev. iii 5. 4.1.2.5 rev. 5′
	TI$_8$]^{MUŠEN}	4.1.2.3 rev. iii 2. 5.3 l. c. 3′
	TI$_8$[^{MUŠEN}	4.1.2.1 obv. (i) 8′
	KI.LÁ TI$_8$^{MUŠEN}	2.2 rev. 11. 3.1.2 obv. l. c. 6′. 3.1.5.A$_1$ obv. i(?) 1′, 4′. 4.1.1.1.A$_1$ rev. 8′, 10′, 11′, 12′, 13′, 14′, 15′. 4.1.1.1.B$_1$ rev. iii 3, 6, 7, 9. 4.1.1.2.A obv. 13′. 4.1.1.2.B obv. 9. 4.1.1.8 r. c. 7′. 4.1.2.3 obv. ii 5′; rev. iii 1. 6.3 rev. A 1
	KI.LÁ! TI$_8$^{MUŠEN}	4.1.2.3 obv. ii 10′
	KI.LÁ TI$_8$[$^{MUŠ]EN}$	4.1.2.3 rev. iii 5
	KI].LÁ TI$_8$^{MUŠEN}	4.1.1.3 rev. B 5
	KI.L]Á TI$_8$^{MUŠEN}	3.1.5.A$_1$ obv. i(?) 7′. 3.1.5.A$_2$ obv. i(?) 4′. 4.1.2.5 rev. 7′
	KI.L]Á *TI$_8$*^{MUŠEN}	4.1.1.1.A$_2$ rev. 6′
	KI.LÁ] TI$_8$^{MUŠEN}	3.1.5.A$_2$ obv. i(?) 1′. 4.1.1.1.B$_1$ obv. ii$^?$ 17′; rev. iv 18
	KI.LÁ T]I$_8$^{MUŠEN}	3.1.7.A$_2$ obv. i 10″. 3.1.5.A$_2$ obv. i(?) 7′. 4.1.1.1.B$_1$ rev. iv$^?$ 19
	KI.LÁ TI$_8$$^{MUŠ]EN}$	4.1.2.5 rev. 6′

	KI.LÁ] TI$_8$^{M}[^{UŠ}]^{EN}	4.1.1.3 rev. B 3
	KI.LÁ TI$_8$^{MUŠE}[^{N}	4.1.1.1.A$_2$ rev. 5′. 4.1.1.1.B$_1$ rev. iii$^?$ 1
	KI.LÁ TI$_8$^{M}[^{UŠEN}	3.1.6 2′. 3.1.7.A$_2$ obv. ii 17′
	KI.LÁ TI$_8$[^{MUŠEN}	3.1.7.A$_2$ obv. ii 3′. 4.1.1.1.A$_2$ rev. 2′. 4.1.4.6 obv. 10′
	KI.[LÁ TI$_8$^{MUŠEN}	4.1.4.6 obv. 14′
see *Lexical Commentary*		
KI.MIN	‘ditto’	
	KI.MIN	1.1.A$_2$ rev. 2, 4. 12.1.1 l. c. 4′ (3×), 5′, 6′, 7′; r. c. 5′ (2×), 6 (2×), 7′, 9′, 10′ (2×), 11′
	K[I.M]IN	12.1.1 r. c. 9′
	KI.M[I]N	12.1.1 r. c. 10′
	KI.M[IN	12.1.1 l. c. 7′; r. c. 6′
KIN	‘ornament, (ritual) equipment’	
sg. acc.	KIN-*an*	5.9 2′
^{URUDU}KIN	‘(copper) sickle’	
	^{URUDU}KIN	5.2 obv. ii 7. 5.7 rev. iii$^?$ 14′. 5.3 r. c. 5′, 8′. 6.1 rev. B 2, 3, 4, 5
	^{URU}]^{DU}KIN	5.8 2′, 4′
	^{URUD}]^{U}KIN	1.4 10′. 5.8 3′, 6′
	^{URUDU}K]IN	5.7 rev. iv$^?$ 18′
	^{URUDU}KI]N	1.4 6′
	^{URUDU}KI]N(?)	8.6 l. c. 11′
	^{URUDU}KI[N	1.4 7′, 9′. 5.7 rev. iii$^?$ 17′
	^{URUDU}K[IN	5.3 r. c. 9′
^{URUDU}KIN.GAL	‘large (copper) sickle’	
	^{URUDU}KIN.GAL	3.1.3 obv.$^?$ 4′. 3.1.5.A$_2$ obv. ii(?) 6′, 8′. 3.1.7.A$_1$ obv. i 12′. 8.6 l. c. 8′
	^{URUD}]^{U}KIN.GAL	3.1.7.A$_1$ lo. e. 17′
	^{URUDU}KI]N.GAL	1.2 rev. 7′
^{KUŠ}KIR$_4$.TAB.ANŠE	‘halter’	
	^{KUŠ}KIR$_4$.TAB.ANŠE	9.1.10.A$_2$ rev. 8′
	^{KUŠ}KIR$_4$.[TAB.A]NŠE	10.2.1.3 2′
	^{KUŠ}KIR$_4$.TAB.A[NŠE	9.1.10.A$_1$ rev. 6′
sg. dat./loc.	*A-NA* ^{KUŠ}KIR$_4$.TAB.ANŠE	3.1.1.A$_3$ obv. iii 7′
sg. gen.	*ŠA* *^{KUŠ}KIR$_4$.TAB.ANŠE*	9.1.10.A$_2$ rev. 11′
KIR$_{14}$	‘nose’	
	KIR$_{14}$	10.3.3 obv.$^?$ 3′
KISLAḪ	‘threshing floor’	
	KISLAḪ	1.1.A$_2$ obv. 12′
sg. gen.	KISLAḪ$^{!?}$-*aš*	12.3.6 6′
^{NA_4}KIŠIB	‘seal’	
inst.	*IŠ-TU* ^{NA_4}KIŠIB	4.1.3.2 rev. 4′
see also É ^{NA_4}KIŠIB		

KÙ.[…	‘silver/gold’ (broken context)	
material		
	KÙ.[	1.5 obv. 7. 4.2.6 rev.$^{?}$ 5′. 9.1.4.A_1 obv. ii 40. 9.1.6 obv. 8. 9.2.8.A_2 8″. 10.2.2.3 obv.$^{?}$ l. c. 1′, 3′. 10.2.2.4 obv.$^{?}$ r. c. 6′
	K[Ù.	1.5 obv. 12. 4.1.1.3 rev. A 7′. 6.2 obv. 4′. 9.1.4.A_1 obv. ii 32, 34, 42. 9.1.10.A_1 rev. 4′. 9.2.8.A_2 9″. 10.2.1.7 obv.$^{?}$ 1′. 11.2.5 1′, 5′
	K[Ù$^{?}$.	9.1.14 obv. r. c. 3′
gen.	*ŠA* K[Ù.	9.2.2 rev.$^{!}$ iii 10′
inst.	*IŠ-TU* KÙ.[	1.5 obv. 3′
	I]*Š-TU* K[Ù$^{?}$.	9.1.4.A_1 rev. iv 6′
KÙ.BABBAR	‘silver’	
	KÙ.BABBAR	1.5 rev. 26. 2.2 rev. 5, 10, 11. 2.4 rev. 5′. 2.16 obv. i 10′. 2.17 obv.$^{?}$ r. c. 2′. 3.1.10 1, 3, 5, 7, 9, 11. 3.1.11.A 4. 3.1.11.B 1′, 3′, 6′. 4.1.1.1.A_1 rev. 8′, 10′, 11′, 12′, 13′, 14′, 15′, 16′, 17′. 4.1.1.1.B_1 rev. iii$^{?}$ 1, 3, 6, 7, 9, 10, 12, 14, 16. 4.1.1.3 obv. 3, 5, 7, 12, 13, 14. 4.1.1.5 up. e. 1; obv. 1. 4.1.1.6 obv. 5′; rev. iii 1, 3, 5. 4.1.1.7 rev.$^{!?}$ 3, 6. 4.1.1.9 6′. 6.1 lo. e. 9″
	K]Ù.BABBAR	4.1.1.1.A_1 obv. 17′; rev. 7′. 4.1.1.3 obv. 10, 11. 4.1.1.9 5′
	KÙ.BAB]BAR	2.8 obv. 1
	KÙ.BAB[BAR	4.1.1.6 rev. iii 7. 4.1.1.8 rev. r. c. 2′. 4.1.1.10 obv.$^{?}$ 4′
	KÙ.[BABBAR	4.1.1.7 rev.$^{!?}$ 8
	KÙ.[BABBAR(?)	4.1.1.7 rev.$^{!?}$ 9
	K[Ù.BABBAR	4.1.1.8 rev. r. c. 4′
material		
	KÙ.BABBAR	1.5 obv. 1; lo. e. 17. 2.13 obv.$^{?}$ 5′. 2.14 13′. 2.16 obv. i 8′. 2.17 obv.$^{?}$ r. c. 2′, 6′ (2×), 20′. 2.18 9′. 2.2 obv. 5′, 6′; rev. 4, 6, 7, 14. 2.3 3. 2.8 obv. 1. 3.1.11.A 1. 4.1.1.1.A_1 rev. 3′, 4′, 11′. 4.1.1.1.A_2 rev. 5′. 4.1.1.1.B_1 rev. iii$^{?}$ 1. 4.1.1.3 obv. 5, 6, 8, 10, 11, 12, 13; rev. A 2′, 3′, 6′, 4′, 6′, 7′, 8′. 4.1.1.5 obv. 2. 4.1.1.7 rev.$^{!?}$ 4, 5. 4.1.3.2 obv. 1′. 4.2.1.A_1 obv. 10. 4.2.4 rev. 7′. 4.2.6 rev.$^{?}$ 4′. 4.2.9 rev. 29′. 5.1 obv. ii 2′, 4′ (2×), 5′, 6′ (2×), 7′ (2×), 8′ (2×), 9′; rev. iii 4, 11. 6.1 obv. 15, 17; rev. A 6″. 6.2 rev. 2′. 6.5 obv. 17′; rev. 2′, 3′, 4′, 5′. 7.1 obv. 11′, 13′, 14′, 16′, 17′, 18′, 19′, 20′. 7.3 obv. i 7, 8, 9, 11. 8.1.A obv. ii 7′; rev. v 24′ (2×), 25′, 26′, 28′. 8.4 rev. 13′, 18′. 9.1.1 rev. iv 3′, 12′, 30′, 31. 9.1.2 rev. iii 2′. 9.1.4.A_1 obv. i 20′, 39″; obv. ii 3, 5; rev. iii 4′. 9.1.4.A_2 r. c. 7′. 9.1.5 rev.$^{!}$ 6′, 7′, 8′, 9′, 10′, 11′, 12′, 13′, 15′, 16′ (3×), 17′; rev. 7. 9.1.7 obv. 4′, 6′. 9.1.8 obv. 14′ (3×). 9.1.10.A_1 rev. 4′. 9.2.12 2′, 3′. 9.2.4 rev. iv 9, 12 (2×), 13. 10.1.1.1 rev.$^{?}$ 8′, 10′ (2×). 10.1.1.2 rev. iv 3′, 5′, 6′ (2×). 10.1.2.1 rev.$^{?}$

		r. c. 2′. 10.1.2.2 4′. 10.1.2.4 l. c. 8′. 10.2.1.1 obv. 1′, 2′, 3′, 5′; rev. 1′, 2′, 4′, 6′, 7′. 10.2.1.2 obv. 11′, 16′. 10.2.1.3 8′. 10.2.1.5 5′. 10.2.1.7 rev.$^?$ 5′, 9′. 10.3.2 obv. i(?) 13″. 10.3.3 obv.$^?$ 3′, 5′, 10′, 11′, 13′. 10.3.13 3′. 10.3.14 l. c. 2′, 3′. 11.1.3 10′, 11′. 11.1.6 l. c. 5′. 11.2.6 3′. 11.3.1 17′. 11.4.2 obv. 2′, 3′, 4′. 12.1.1 l. c. 3′; r. c. 5′, 8′
	KÙ.BABBAR(?)	4.1.4.7 rev. A 1′
	KÙ$^!$.BABBAR	12.1.1 l. c. 5′
	KÙ$^?$.BABBAR	6.2 obv. 4′
	KÙ.BABBAR$^!$	10.2.1.5 3′
	K]Ù.BABBAR	2.14 14′. 2.17 obv.$^?$ r. c. 2′. 4.1.1.1.B_1 obv. ii 5′. 4.2.6 rev.$^?$ 5′. 7.1 obv. 14′, 15′, 21′. 9.1.4.A_1 rev. iii 8′. 9.1.5 obv.$^!$ 6. 9.2.1 10′. 10.3.2 obv. i(?) 10″. 10.3.14 l. c. 3′. 11.4.2 obv. 5′, 6′. 12.3.7 10′
	KÙ].BABBAR	4.1.1.9 4′
	KÙ].BABBAR(?)	10.3.14 l. c. 7′
	KÙ.BAB]BAR	4.1.1.1.A_2 rev. 2′. 10.2.1.1 obv. 7′
	KÙ.BAB]BAR(?)	4.2.12 3′. 10.3.2 obv. i(?) 16″
	KÙ.BAB[BAR	7.4 2′. 4.1.3.2 obv. 3′. 9.2.13 2′. 10.1.2.2 2′. 10.2.1.7 rev.$^?$ 5′. 10.3.3 obv.$^?$ 12′
	KÙ.B[ABBAR	4.1.1.7 rev.$^{!?}$ 5. 9.1.4.A_1 obv. ii 24. 9.1.5 obv.$^!$ 8. 10.3.3 obv.$^?$ 3′
	KÙ.[BABBAR	7.1 obv. 19′
	KÙ.[BABBAR(?)	6.13 5′
	KÙ.[BAB]BAR	10.1.2.5 4′
	K[Ù.BABBAR	4.1.1.5 obv. 3. 10.1.2.2 3′. 10.3.3 obv.$^?$ 10′
	K[Ù$^?$.BABBAR	11.4.2 obv. 2′
	K[Ù.BAB]BAR	9.1.5 rev.$^!$ 11′
	KÙ+BABBAR	2.7.A obv. 19. 12.3.1 8′
	K]Ù+BABBAR	12.3.1 3′
sg. gen.	*ŠA* KÙ.BABBAR	9.1.5 rev.$^!$ 13′. 9.1.8 obv. 15′
inst.	*IŠ-TU* KÙ.BABBAR	2.17 obv.$^?$ r. c. 3′
pl. acc.	KÙ.BABBAR-***uš***	4.1.1.6 rev. iii 2
^{LÚ}KÙ.DÍM	'metalsmith'	
	^{LÚ}KÙ.DÍM	5.5 rev. iii 3′
pl.	$^{LÚ.MEŠ}$KÙ.DÍM	2.7.A rev. 3. 6.1 rev. A 7″
pl. dat./loc.	*A-NA* $^{LÚ.MEŠ}$KÙ.DÍM	2.2 rev. 8. 4.1.1.3 rev. B 5
	A-NA $^{LÚ.MEŠ}$KÙ.D[ÍM	2.2 rev. 4
KÙ.SI$_{22}$	'gold'	
	KÙ.SI$_{22}$	2.2 rev. 15. 2.7.A rev. 1, 2, 3. 2.8 obv. 1. 2.17 obv.$^?$ r. c. 1′. 4.1.1.1.A_1 obv. 2′, 3′, 4′, 13′, 16′, 17′. 4.1.1.2.A obv. 4′, 5′, 6′, 13′. 4.1.1.8 rev. r. c. 5′, 9′. 7.1 obv. 5′, 8′, 9′, 12′. 7.4 5′. 8.1.A obv. ii 25′, 26′. 8.1.B rev. 5′. 9.2.1 rev. iii 23′. 10.1.2.8 rev. r. c. 3′
	K]Ù.SI$_{22}$	4.1.1.1.A_1 obv. 18′. 12.2.3 3′
	KÙ].SI$_{22}$	4.1.1.1.A_1 20′
	KÙ].SI$_{22}$$^?$	4.1.1.10 lo. e. 5′

KÙ.S]I$_{22}$	4.1.1.1.A$_1$ obv. 19′. 7.1 obv. 1′. 8.1.B rev. 10′. 8.1.C l. c. 6′. 9.2.10 1′. 12.2.2 2′
KÙ.S]I$_{22}$(?)	6.3 rev. A 1
KÙ.S[I$_{22}$	7.1 obv. 6′. 7.4 6′
KÙ.[SI$_{22}$	4.1.1.2.A obv. 3′. 8.1.A obv. ii 21′. 9.2.1 obv. ii 27′
KÙ.[S]I$_{22}$	9.1.1 rev. iii 10′
K[Ù.SI$_{22}$	4.1.1.1.A$_1$ obv. 17′. 4.1.1.2.A obv. 7′. 7.1 obv. 3′. 9.2.1 obv. ii 27′. 11.3.1 11′
KÙ.SI$_{22}$ (*QA-DU* URUDU)	4.1.1.1.A$_1$ obv. 6′, 8′, 10′, 11′, 14′, 15′, 21′. 4.1.1.2.A obv. 10
KÙ.SI$_{22}$ (SIG$_5$)	4.1.1.2.A obv. 23′, 25′. 4.1.1.2.B obv. 9
KÙ.SI$_{22}$ (SIG$_5$ *QA-DU* URUDU)	4.1.1.2.A obv. 15′, 18′, 21′. 4.1.1.2.B obv. 1, 4, 7
KÙ.SI$_{22}$ (*ŠULMAN*)	2.1.B 8′

material

KÙ.SI$_{22}$	1.3 3′, 4′, 6′, 7′. 1.5 obv. 4, 5, 6, 7, 11, 13; lo. e. 16. 2.7.A obv. 23. 2.13 obv.$^{?}$ 6′; rev.$^{?}$ 3′, 5′. 2.14 7′, 10′, 12′. 2.16 obv. i 7′ (2×). 2.17 obv.$^{?}$ r. c. 5′, 9′, 11′, 12′, 13′, 17′, 18′, 19′, 22′. 2.18 9′. 3.1.8.A obv. 8′. 4.1.1.3 rev. A 4′. 4.2.1.A$_1$ obv. 9 (2×). 4.2.4 obv. 8, 10; rev. 9′. 4.2.5 4′. 4.2.6 rev.$^{?}$ 6′, 7′. 4.2.7 8′, 9′. 5.1 obv. i 4′. 6.1 obv. 9. 6.5 obv. 6′, 7′, 8′, 10′, 13′; rev. 12′, 15′. 6.13 6′. 7.4 3′. 8.1.A obv. i 5′, 6′, 10′, 16′, 18′, 19′. 8.1.E(A$_1$) rev. v 4′. 8.1.F rev. v 14. 8.4 rev. 2′, 4′, 8′ (2×), 9′, 10′, 11′, 12′, 13′, 14′ (3×), 15′, 16′, 17′, 18′. 9.1.1 rev. iii 2′, 15′, 17′ (2×), 18′, 19′, 20′, 21′, 22′, 23′, 24′, 25′, 26′, 27′, 28′ (2×), 31′ (2×), 32′, 33′, 35′, 36′, 37′, 38′; rev. iv 4′, 6′, 8′, 9′ (2×), 10′, 12′ (2×), 13′ (2×), 15′, 18′ (3×), 20′ (2×), 21′ (2×), 23′, 25′, 26′ (2×), 28′ (2×), 29′, 30′, 32′ (2×), 33′, 35′, 36′ (2×), 37′, 38′, 39′, 40′, 41′ (2×), 42′, 44′. 9.1.4.A$_1$ obv. i 2, 8′, 9′, 16′, 28′, 29′; obv. ii 3, 7, 8, 9, 11, 12, 15, 17, 18, 22, 29, 30, 37, 41. 9.1.4.A$_2$ r. c. 4′, 5′, 6′, 7′, 8′. 9.1.5 rev.$^{!}$ 2′, 3′ (2×), 5′, 8′ (3×), 9′ (2×), 10′ (2×), 13′ (3×), 14′ (2×), 15′, 17′; rev. 1, 3, 9, 12, 14. 9.1.9 rev. iv 2′, 3′. 9.1.10.A$_1$ obv. 2′, 3′ (2×), 4′, 5′, 6′; rev. 3′. 9.1.10.B 3′ (2×), 4′, 5′, 6′, 7′, 8′, 9′ (2×), 10′. 9.1.13 1′, 2′. 9.1.14 obv. r. c. 7′, 10′. 9.1.15 3′, 4′, 5′, 6′. 9.2.1 obv. ii 2′, 3′, 4′, 5′, 6′, 7′ (2×), 8′ (2×), 9′, 10′, 12′, 13′, 14′, 15′, 16′ (2×), 17′, 18′ (2×), 19′, 20′, 24′ (2×); rev. iii 3′, 5′, 6′, 8′, 9′, 10′, 11′, 13′, 16′, 20′, 24′, 27′. 9.2.2 rev.$^{!}$ iii 4′, 6′, 8′, 12′, 13′, 16′, 17′, 18′, 19′, 22′, 23′, 25′, 26′. 9.2.3 obv. (ii) 3″. 9.2.4 obv. i 5′, 7′, 9′, 12′, 13′ (2×), 14′ (2×), 15′ (2×), 16′, 17′; rev. iv 2, 8, 11. 9.2.5 obv. i(?) 3′, 6′ (2×), 9′, 10′, 11′, 12′ (2×). 9.2.6 obv. i 18′, 19′. 9.2.7 obv. l. c. 9′ (2×), 11′, 12′. 9.2.9 obv.$^{?}$ 6′, 7′, 8′, 10′, 11′, 12′, 13′ (2×), 15′. 9.2.10 2′. 9.2.12 4′. 10.1.1.1 rev.$^{?}$ 9′. 10.1.1.2 rev. iv 2′, 6′. 10.1.2.1 obv.$^{?}$ l. c. 2′; rev.$^{?}$ r. c. 8′; rev.$^{?}$ l. c. 5, 7, 8. 10.1.2.4 l. c. 3′, 4′, 22′,

24′. 10.1.2.7 4′, 6′, 7′. 10.1.2.8 rev. r. c. 2′, 3′ (2×), 4′, 6′. 10.2.1.2 obv. 2′, 3′, 4′, 5′, 7′, 8′, 9′, 10′, 11′, 12′ (2×), 13′, 15′. 10.2.2.2 obv.$^{?}$ l. c. 7′. 10.2.2.3 obv.$^{?}$ l. c. 1′, 3′, 4′, 5′, 6′, 9′, 12′. 10.2.2.4 obv.$^{?}$ r. c. 2′, 3′, 4′, 5′, 6′. 10.3.1 rev. iii 3′, 6′, 9′, 11′, 13′. 10.3.2 obv. i(?) 7″, 8″, 11″. 10.3.3 obv.$^{?}$ 7′. 10.3.4 3′, 7, 9′. 10.3.5 11′. 10.3.6 2′. 10.3.7 4′. 10.3.8 2′. 10.3.9 3′, 5′. 10.3.13 4′, 6′. 10.3.14 l. c. 2′, 4′, 5′, 7′. 11.1.1 r. c. 7′. 11.1.2 l. c. 4′. 11.1.3 2′, 3′, 4′. 11.1.4 7′. 11.2.2 2′, 3′, 6′. 11.2.3 3′. 11.2.4 1′, 2′, 3′, 4′. 11.2.5 1′. 11.3.1 4′, 5′, 6′, 7′, 8′, 10′, 11′, 15′, 16′, 19′, 22′. 11.3.2 r. c. 1′, 2′, 3′, 4′, 5′. 11.3.3 1′, 2′. 11.4.1 4′. 12.1.1 l. c. 6′; r. c. 5′. 12.3.3 8′. 12.3.7 4′

KÙ.SI$_{22}$ (*QADU* URUDU)	11.1.3 4′
K[Ù].SI$_{22}$	9.1.1 rev. iii 32′
KÙ.[S]I$_{22}$	2.17 obv.$^{?}$ r. c. 12′. 8.4 rev. 4′. 9.1.5 obv.$^{!}$ 4
K]Ù.SI$_{22}$	2.2 obv. 3′. 4.2.5 2′. 8.1.A obv. i 15′. 8.1.B rev. 4′, 9′. 9.1.1 rev. iv 4′, 7′, 16′, 27′, 34′. 9.1.4.A$_1$ obv. i 14′, 23′. 9.1.9 rev. iv 1′. 9.1.10.A$_2$ rev. 8′. 9.1.13 3′. 9.1.15 2′. 9.2.1 obv. ii 11′; rev. iii 21′. 9.2.4 obv. i 17′. 9.2.5 obv. i(?) 2′, 7′. 9.2.9 obv.$^{?}$ 3′, 5′, 7′. 9.2.14 5′. 10.1.2.1 rev.$^{?}$ l. c. 2. 10.1.2.3 3′. 10.1.2.4 l. c. 18′. 10.1.2.7 11′. 10.2.1.2 obv. 5′, 6′, 9′. 10.2.2.4 obv.$^{?}$ r. c. 2′
KÙ].SI$_{22}$	4.2.6 rev.$^{?}$ 6′. 8.4 rev. 4′. 9.1.1 rev. iv 3′, 6′. 9.2.2 rev.$^{!}$ iii 24′. 9.2.12 5′. 11.2.4 6′. 12.1.1 r. c. 9′
K]Ù.S[I$_{22}$	10.2.1.2 obv. 8′
KÙ].S[I$_{22}$	2.18 5′
KÙ.S]I$_{22}$	4.2.5 5′. 9.1.1 rev. iv 23′. 9.1.4.A$_1$ obv. i 7′, 15′, 31′. 9.1.4.A$_5$ 3′. 9.1.5 obv.$^{!}$ 10, 13; rev.$^{!}$ 18′. 9.2.4 obv. i 11′. 9.2.9 obv.$^{?}$ 2′. 10.1.2.4 l. c. 7′. 10.2.2.2 obv.$^{?}$ l. c. 4′, 7′. 10.2.2.3 obv.$^{?}$ l. c. 6′, 7′. 10.3.1 rev. iii 5′, 8′. 10.3.2 obv. i(?) 13″, 14″, 17″. 10.3.4 6′, 13′. 10.3.8 3′. 11.3.2 r. c. 6′. 11.4.1 2′
KÙ.S]I$_{22}$(?)	10.3.14 l. c. 1′. 11.1.2 l. c. 4′. 12.2.2 2′
KÙ.S]I$_{22}$ ≮ SI[G$_5$	4.2.5 1′
KÙ.S[I$_{22}$	2.16 obv. ii 9′. 2.17 obv.$^{?}$ r. c. 5′, 13′. 4.1.1.1.A$_1$ rev. 8′. 6.2 obv. 2′. 8.1.A obv. ii 5′. 8.1.E(A$_1$) rev. iv 16′. 8.4 rev. 6′, 7′. 9.1.1 rev. iii 4′, 15′, 34′, 39′. 9.1.4.A$_1$ obv. ii 10, 19, 21; rev. iii 26″. 9.1.4.A$_2$ r. c. 4′. 9.1.5 obv.$^{!}$ 6, 8, 11. 9.1.10.A$_1$ obv. 5′. 9.1.10.B 7′. 9.2.1 rev. iii 13′. 9.2.8.A$_1$ 7′. 10.1.2.1 rev.$^{?}$ r. c. 6′. 10.1.2.3 2′. 10.1.2.4 l. c. 13′. 10.2.1.2 obv. 14′. 10.2.2.4 obv.$^{?}$ r. c. 5′. 10.3.1 rev. iii 1′. 10.3.2 obv. i(?) 3″. 10.3.7 6′. 10.3.13 4′, 5′, 8′. 11.3.1 2′. 12.1.1 l. c. 3′
KÙ.S[I$_{22}$$^{?}$	9.2.8.A$_2$ 11″
KÙ.S[I$_{22}$(?)	10.3.2 obv. ii(?) 1′

	KÙ.[SI$_{22}$	6.5 obv. 9′. 9.1.1 rev. iii 14′. 9.1.4.A$_2$ r. c. 6′. 9.1.10.B 4′. 9.2.2 rev.$^{!}$ iii 21′. 10.1.2.1 rev.$^{?}$ r. c. 10′. 12.3.7 10′
	K[Ù.S]I$_{22}$(?)	9.2.7 obv. l. c. 12′
	K[Ù.SI$_{22}$	2.17 obv.$^{?}$ r. c. 1′. 6.5 obv. 14′. 9.1.1 rev. iv 31′. 9.2.2 rev.$^{!}$ iii 3′. 10.3.13 7′
	K[Ù.SI$_{22}$(?)	9.1.4.A$_2$ r. c. 3′
sg. gen.	*ŠA* KÙ.SI$_{22}$	9.2.1 obv. ii 12′
	ŠA [K]Ù.SI$_{22}$	6.2 obv. 2′
inst.	*IŠ-TU* KÙ.SI$_{22}$	10.3.6 6′
see also ^{f}KÙ.SI$_{22}$-*lia-*		
KU$_6$	‘fish’	
	KU$_6$	12.1.1 l. c. 2′ (2×); r. c. 8′
	K]U$_6$	12.1.1 l. c. 1′
	K]U$_6$$^{?}$	12.1.1 r. c. 12′, 13′
KUN	‘tail’	
	KUN	10.2.2.3 obv.$^{?}$ l. c. 9′
^{GIŠ}KUN$_5$	‘ladder, stairs, step-ladder’	
	^{GIŠ}KUN$_5$	11.1.3 11′
KUŠ	(1.) ‘skin, hide, pelt’	
	KUŠ (GU$_4$)	4.1.3.6 obv. 15′
	KUŠ (UDU)	4.1.3.6 obv. 7′; rev. 2′
	KUŠ (UZ$_6$)	4.1.3.6 obv. 13′
	KUŠ$^{!?}$ (ANŠE)	4.1.3.6 obv. 15′
sg. nom.(?)	KUŠ-*aš*	12.3.6 2′, 3′, 4′, 5′, 6′
	KUŠ-*aš*(?)	12.3.6 8′
	K]UŠ-*aš*	12.3.6 7′
	KUŠ-[*aš*	12.3.6 1′
sg. dat./loc.	KUŠ-*e*	12.3.6 4′, 5′, 6′, 7′, 9′
	K[UŠ-*e*	12.3.6 2′, 3′
	(2.) ‘leather; leathern’	
	KUŠ	1.1.A$_3$ rev. 2′. 9.1.11 obv.$^{?}$ 8′, 9′, 10′, 11′; rev.$^{?}$ 2′. 9.2.12 5′
	(DÙG.GAN) KUŠ	9.2.4 rev. iv 4
	(*UNŪT*) KUŠ	10.3.14 l. c. 6′
pl.	(*UNŪT*) KUŠ$^{MEŠ!}$	10.3.14 l. c. 8′
(½.)/(1.) KÙŠ	‘(half)/(full)-ell’	
	½.KÙŠ	10.3.10 r. c. 2′, 9′, 10′. 11.6.11 2′, 3′
	1.KÙŠ	8.1.F rev. v 9 (2×), 11
	½.K]ÙŠ	10.3.10 r. c. 7′
KÙŠ.SIG	‘“thin” ell’	
	KÙŠ.SIG	10.3.10 r. c. 3′
see *Lexical Commentary*		
$^{(GIŠ)}$LE.U$_5$	‘(wooden writing) board’	
	LE.U$_5$$^{!}$(text: ḪU)	3.1.1.A$_1$ rev. v 15′
	^{GIŠ}LE.U$_5$	8.1.A obv. ii 3′
sg. dat./loc.	*A-NA* LE.U$_5$ (*ipurawaš*)	4.2.9 obv. 15

	A-NA LE].U$_5$ (*ipurawaš*)	4.2.9 rev. 30′
see *Lexical Commentary*		
LIBIR	‘old’	
	LIBIR	8.1.A rev. v 7
	LIBIR.RA	2.2 obv. 11′. 4.1.4.9 obv. 11. 4.2.7 7′. 8.1.E(A$_1$) obv. iii 5′. 8.1.F obv. i 20′
	L]IBIR.RA	4.1.3.7 obv. 1
	LIBI]R.RA	4.1.3.7 obv. 3. 8.8.B l. c. 1′
	LIBIR.R[A	4.1.1.9 11′. 8.8.A 1′
	LIBIR.R[A(?)	2.18 1′
sg. nom.	LIBIR-*RU*	9.1.8 obv. 11′
	LIBIR-*R*[*U*	9.1.8 obv. 4′
LÍL	‘field, (in gen.) “earth tone”’	
	LÍL	4.2.9 obv. 4
sg. gen.	LÍL-*aš*	4.2.9 obv. 1, 3, 30, 31. 11.6.2 rev. 11′
	LÍL-[*aš*	4.2.9 obv. 31
= *gimra-*		
LU.LIM	‘stag, deer’	
	LU.LIM	9.2.1 rev. iii 10′
	(*BIBRU*) LU.LIM	9.1.4.A$_1$ obv. ii 12
LÚ	‘man’	
	LÚ	3.2.1 rev. 14′. 4.1.2.1 obv. (i) 10′. 8.1.E(A$_2$) 8′. 12.3.1 4′
	(ALAM) LÚ	9.1.7 rev. 3. 10.1.1.1 rev.$^?$ 7′, 8′. 10.1.1.2 rev. iv 2′
	(ḪUB.BI) LÚ	9.1.1 rev. iv 37′
sg. gen.	*ŠA* LÚ	1.1.A$_3$ rev. 10′
	(ḪUB$^{ḪI.A}$) *ŠA* LÚ	9.1.1 rev. iii 2′
	(ALAM) *ŠA* LÚ	9.1.1 rev. iv 16′
	(^{KUŠ}E.SIR) LÚ-*LIM*	9.1.10.A$_2$ rev. 9′
	(ḪUB.BI) LÚ-*LIM*	9.2.1 obv. ii 17′. 10.3.4 9′
	LÚ-*L*]*IM*	10.3.4 10′
	LÚ-*L*[*IM*	2.14 5′
pl.	LÚ^{MEŠ} [	5.7 rev. iii$^?$ 15′
	LÚ^{MEŠ} É.[	4.1.2.1 obv. (i) 6′
	LÚ^{M}[^{EŠ}] x [	4.1.2.2 obv. 6′
pl. dat./loc.	*A*]-*NA* LÚ^{ME}[^{Š}	4.1.1.9 13′
LÚ ^{URU}GN	‘man from (GN)’	
sg.	LÚ (^{URU}*al-ḫi-ša*)	3.2.1 obv. 15
	LÚ (^{URU}*an-da-mi-ša-ra*)	1.1.A$_2$ rev. 2
	LÚ (^{URU}*an-ga-la-a*)	1.1.A$_2$ rev. 4
	LÚ (^{URU}*a*[*n-zi-la-ta-aš-ši*)	3.2.1 obv. 4
	LÚ (^{URU}*ḫal-la-pí-ia*)	6.1 rev. B 3
	LÚ (^{URU}*ḫu-pa-an-da*)	1.1.A$_3$ rev. 6′
	LÚ (^{URU}*ḫur-la*)	1.1.A$_2$ rev. 8
	LÚ (^{URU}*kal-ma-zi-da-a*)	1.1.A$_2$ rev. 1
	LÚ (^{URU}*ga-pa-as-ta-ra*)	1.1.A$_3$ rev. 3′
	LÚ (^{URU}*ga-pa-aš-t*]*a-ra*)	1.1.A$_3$ rev. 11′
	LÚ (^{URU}*kar-ka$_4$-zi-ia*)	1.1.A$_1$ obv. 11′

	LÚ (^{URU}*ka-aš-ta-ma*)	5.1 obv. ii 5′
	LÚ (^{URU}*ma-ḫu-du-wa*)	1.1.A$_1$ obv. 14′
	LÚ (^{URU}*ma-a-ša*)	5.4 r. c. 3′
	LÚ (^{URU}*šam-ma-na*$^!$)	3.2.1 obv. 18
	LÚ (^{URU}*ša-ak-ka*$_4$*-ma-ḫa*)	5.1 obv. ii 11′
	LÚ (^{URU}*ša*$^?$-x[ )	4.1.3.1 9′
	LÚ (^{URU}*tu-u-ma-an-na*)	5.1 obv. ii 9′
	LÚ (^{URU}*wa-an-na-an-d*[*a*)	1.1.A$_3$ rev. 8′
	LÚ (^{URU}*zi-ku-li-ia*)	1.1.A$_2$ rev. 3
	LÚ (^{URU}*zi-ku-*[*li-ia*)	1.1.A$_3$ rev. 1′
	LÚ ($^{U[RU}$ …)	4.1.3.1 8′
	LÚ ($^{U[RU?}$ …)	3.2.2 obv.$^?$ 10′
	LÚ ($^{UR]U}$*ḫur-la*)	1.1.A$_2$ rev. 10
pl.	LÚ^{MEŠ} (^{URU}*ḫa-ti-ti-eš-pa*)	5.7 rev. iii$^?$ 20′
	LÚ^{MEŠ} (^{URU}*kam-ma-ma*)	5.7 rev. iii$^?$ 22′
	LÚ^{MEŠ} (^{URU}*kaš-ta-ma*)	5.1 obv. ii 2′
	LÚ^{MEŠ} (^{URU}*lu-uk-ka*$_4$*-a*)	5.1 obv. ii 8′
	LÚ^{MEŠ} (^{URU}*ma-a-ša*)	5.7 rev. iii$^?$ 13′
	LÚ^{MEŠ} (KUR ^{URU}*pí-ik-ka*$_4$*-uz-z*[*a*)	5.7 rev. iii$^?$ 29′
	LÚ^{MEŠ} (^{URU}*taḫ*-x[ )	5.7 rev. iii$^?$ 17′
	LÚ^{MEŠ} (^{URU}*ta-*[*a*]*p-pu-*[*t*]*a*)	12.2.1 rev. 7′
	LÚ^{MEŠ} (^{URU}*tar-ku-ma*)	1.4 8′
	LÚ^{MEŠ} (^{URU}*ta-ti-mu-wa*)	1.4 6′
	LÚ^{MEŠ} (^{URU}*tu-um-ma-an-na*)	5.1 obv. ii 7′
	LÚ^{MEŠ} (^{URU}*za-ga-pu-ra*)	5.7 rev. iii$^?$ 16′
	LÚ^{MEŠ} (KUR ^{URU}x[)	5.7 rev. iii$^?$ 6′
	LÚ^{MEŠ} (^{URU}x-x-x[ )	1.1.A$_1$ obv. 16′
	LÚ$^{ME]Š}$ (KUR ^{URU}x[)	5.7 rev. iii$^?$ 4′
	L[Ú^{MEŠ} (^{URU} …)	1.4 10′
	LÚ^{MEŠ}(?) (^{URU}*ḫa-te-e*]*n-zu-wa*)	1.4 3′
	LÚ^{MEŠ} (^{URU}*ká*]*n-ti-eš-ši-iš-ša*)	1.4 7′
	LÚ^{MEŠ} (^{URU}*ša-ra-ḫ*]*a-ad-du*)	1.4 9′
	LÚ^{MEŠ} (^{URU}*ta-aš-t*]*a-re-eš-ša*)	1.4 5′
pl. dat./loc.	*A-NA* LÚ^{MEŠ} (^{URU}*ar-za-u-wa*)	1.1.A$_3$ rev. 6′
	A-NA LÚ^{MEŠ} (^{URU}*ma-a-š*[*a*)	5.4 r. c. 4′
	A-NA LÚ]^{MEŠ} (^{URU}*ma-a-ša*)	5.2 obv. ii 2

see *Lexical Commentary*

LÚ KÁ UR.GI$_7$	'man of the "Hound's Gate"'	
pl.	L]Ú^{MEŠ} KÁ UR.GI$_7$	3.1.6 3′

see *Lexical Commentary*

LÚ ^{GIŠ}TUKUL.GÍD.DA	'man of the long weapon'	
	LÚ ^{GIŠ}TUKUL.GÍD.DA	1.1.A$_1$ obv. 12′

see *Lexical Commentary*; see also ^{GIŠ}TUKUL

LUGAL	(1.) 'king'	
	LUGAL	3.1.2 obv. l. c. 7′. 10.2.2.1 1′
	LUGAL ^{KUR}*i-šu-wa*	4.1.4.9 obv. 6
	LUGAL ^{KUR}*kar-g*[*a-miš*	2.16 obv. ii 6′
	L]UGAL	12.1.1 r. c. 1′

sg. nom.	LUGAL-*uš*	12.1.1 r. c. 4′
sg. gen.(?)	*Š*]*A* LUGAL KUR $^{URU\ D}$10-*ta-aš-š*[*a*	1.1.A_3 rev. 12′
	(2.) (as unmarked gen.) 'royal, kingly, fit for a king'	
	(*lupanni*) LUGAL	2.9.A_3 obv. ii 11′
	($^{LÚ.MEŠ}$*parwala*-) LUGAL	5.2 obv. ii 6, 8
	(GADA SU_6) LUGAL	4.2.4 obv. 1
	(TÚG) LUGAL	10.1.1.1 rev.$^{?}$ 13′
	]x LUGAL	8.7 l. c. 10′
	] LUGAL	3.2.5 l. c. 1′
	L]UGAL	8.7 l. c. 1′

see *Lexical Commentary*

LUGAL-*eznatar*	'kingship'	
sg. dat./loc.	LUGAL-*ez-na-ni*	2.12 obv.$^{!}$ ii 8′
	LUGAL-*ez-na-an-ni*	2.9.A_3 obv. ii 4′. 2.9.A_2 obv. i 10′
	LU]GAL-*ez-na-ni*	9.1.4.A_1 rev. iv 4′
	LU]GAL-[*ez-n*]*a-an-ni*	2.9.$A_{2/1}$ obv. i 12′
	LUGA]L-*ez-na-ni*	2.12 obv.$^{!}$ ii 3′

= LUGAL-*UTTU*

LUGAL-*UTTU*	'kingship; (in gen.) "in the royal style, fit for a king"'	
sg. gen.	LUGAL-*UT-TI*	11.6.2 l. e. 2
	ŠA LUGAL-*UT-TI*	11.3.1 21′

= LUGAL-*eznatar*

LÚGUD.DA	'short'	
	LÚGUD.DA	2.7.A obv. 25. 8.1.E(A_1) obv. iii 3′. 8.1.F obv. i 3′
	LÚGU[D.D]A	8.1.F obv. i 6′

MA.NA	'mina'	
	MA.NA	1.4 2′. 2.4 rev. 5′. 2.7.A rev. 2, 3. 3.1.1.A_1 obv. ii 6′, 9′, 14′. 3.1.1.A_2 rev. v 6′, 8′, 10′, 14′. 3.1.1.A_3 obv. iii 5′, 8′; rev. iv 1′, 3′, 15′. 3.1.2 obv. l. c. 5′, 6′, 9′, 10′, 12′; rev. l. c. 3′. 3.1.3 obv.$^{?}$ 5′. 3.1.5.A_1 obv. ii(?) 3′, 4′, 6′. 3.1.5.A_2 obv. ii(?) 4′, 5′, 9′, 12′. 3.1.6 4′. 3.1.7.A_1 obv. i 1′, 7′, 10′; l. e. 1. 3.1.7.A_2 obv. ii 5a′, 5b′, 9′; rev. iv 2′, 4′; rev. v 3′. 3.1.8.A rev. 3′, 5′, 7′. 3.1.10 3, 5, 7, 9. 3.2.1 obv. 3, 5, 13 (2×), 16, 19; rev. 4′, 6′, 9′, 10′ (2×), 13′, 19′. 3.2.2 obv.$^{?}$ 4′, 12′. 3.2.3 1′, 4′. 4.1.1.1.A_1 obv. 8′, 11′. 4.1.1.1.B_1 rev. iii$^{?}$ 1, 6, 7, 9, 10, 12, 14; rev. iv$^{?}$ 3. 4.1.1.2.A obv. 7′, 8′, 16′, 19′, 21′. 4.1.1.3 obv. 16. 4.1.1.5 obv. 1. 4.1.1.6 obv. ii 3′; rev. iii 3, 5, 7. 4.1.1.7 rev.$^{!?}$ 6, 8, 9. 4.1.1.10 obv.$^{?}$ 4′. 4.1.2.2 obv. 1′, 2′ (2×), 5′. 4.1.2.3 obv. ii 5′, 6′ (2×), 7′ (2×), 10′, 11′ (2×); rev. iii 2 (2×), 5 (2×), 6, 8. 4.1.2.5 obv. 8′, 9′, 10′, 14′. 4.1.2.6 1′, 2′. 4.1.3.1 1′. 4.1.3.2 rev. 1′, 3′. 4.1.3.3 10′. 4.1.4.1.A_1 obv. ii 3′; rev. v 3′, 4′, 6″, 7″, 9″. 4.1.4.1.A_2 obv. i 2′; obv. ii 10′. 4.1.4.2.A_1 rev. r. c. 2′, 4′, 5′, 7′, 11′. 4.1.4.2.A_2 obv. r. c. 2′, 11′. 4.1.4.4 6′. 4.1.4.5 rev. r. c. 8′. 4.1.4.7 rev. B 1′, 2′. 5.2 obv. ii 10, 13, 14, 15, 16; rev. iii

		2′, 3′, 4′. 5.5 rev. iii 7′. 5.7 rev. iii$^{?}$ 9′. 7.1 obv. 5′, 7′, 15′, 16′, 17′, 18′. 8.1.A obv. ii 22′, 25′, 26′. 8.1.B rev. 5′. 8.6 l. c. 8′, 10′, 11′. 10.3.2 obv. i(?) 11″. 11.6.1 6, 9, 10. 11.7.2 4′
	MA.NA	3.1.5.A_2 obv. ii(?) 11′
	MA$^{!}$.NA	3.2.3 3′
	MA.NA$^{!}$(?)	4.1.3.8 rev. A 3′
	M[A].N[A(?)	7.1 obv. 21′
	M[A.N]A	3.1.2 obv. l. c. 3′. 3.1.1.A_3 rev. iv 16′
	M]A.NA	3.1.1.A_3 obv. iii 11′. 3.1.5.A_1 obv. i(?) 5′. 3.1.7.A_1 obv. i 14′. 3.1.8.A rev. 9′. 3.1.11.A 2. 3.2.1 rev. 12′. 3.2.2 obv.$^{?}$ 8′. 4.1.1.1.A_1 obv. 3′; rev. 14′, 16′, 17′. 4.1.1.2.A obv. 15′, 18′. 4.1.1.5 up. e. 1. 4.1.1.6 rev. iii 10. 4.1.1.7 rev.$^{!?}$ 3. 4.1.2.5 obv. 6′. 4.1.4.1.A_1 rev. v 4″, 5″; rev. vi 11′. 4.1.4.2.A_1 rev. r. c. 14′; rev. l. c. 5′. 4.1.4.4 2′. 11.7.2 5′
	M]A$^{?}$.NA	3.1.3 rev.$^{?}$ 1′
	MA].NA	3.1.1.A_3 rev. iv 13′. 4.1.1.1.A_1 rev. 15′. 4.1.1.6 rev. iii 1. 11.7.2 4′
	MA.N]A	3.1.1.A_2 rev. vi 3′. 3.1.1.A_3 obv. iii 12′. 3.1.3 obv.$^{?}$ 1′. 3.1.5.A_1 obv. i(?) 4′. 3.1.7.A_2 obv. ii 15′. 3.1.8.A rev. 10′. 3.1.11.B 4′. 3.2.1 rev. 1′, 3′. 3.2.2 obv.$^{?}$ 6′, 9′. 4.1.1.1.A_1 obv. 2′, 15′, 16′; rev. 10′, 13′, 14′. 4.1.1.1.B_1 rev. iv$^{?}$ 6. 4.1.1.6 obv. ii 5′. 4.1.2.5 obv. 2′. 4.1.4.1.A_2 obv. ii 8′
	MA.N[A	3.1.1.A_3 obv. iii 15′. 3.1.2 rev. l. c. 1′. 3.1.5.A_2 obv. ii(?) 1′, 2′, 7′. 3.1.7.A_2 rev. iv 5′. 3.1.8.B 9′. 3.2.3 5′. 4.1.1.1.A_1 rev. 18′. 4.1.1.3 obv. 1, 3, 5, 7. 4.1.1.5 obv. 8. 4.1.2.6 3′. 7.1 obv. 1′, 12′, 13′
	MA.[NA	3.1.5.A_1 obv. ii(?) 7′. 3.1.5.A_2 obv. ii(?) 8′. 3.1.8.B 3′. 3.1.10 1. 4.1.2.1 obv. (i) 7′. 4.1.4.1.A_1 obv. iii 4′, 7′
	MA$^{!}$.[NA	8.1.B rev. 4′
	M[A.NA	3.1.1.A_1 obv. ii 8′. 3.1.10 11. 3.1.11.B 6′. 4.1.2.2 obv. 4′, 5′. 5.2 obv. ii 17. 7.1 obv. 11′, 20′
gen.	*ŠA* n MA.NA	4.1.2.3 obv. ii 3′, 4′, 8′, 9′, 10′, 11′ (2×), 12′, 13′; rev. iii 3, 4, 7
	ŠA n M[A.N]A	4.1.2.3 rev. iii 7
abbr.	MA.	3.1.7.A_2 obv. ii 7a′; rev. iv 3′; rev. v 2′. 3.2.1 obv. 20 (2×). 4.1.1.2.B obv. 1, 2, 4, 5, 7. 4.1.1.3 obv. 12, 13, 14. 4.1.3.1 2′, 3′, 4′. 4.1.4.3 4′, 5′
	M]A.	4.1.3.1 5′
	M[A.	4.1.4.3 2′, 3′

$^{(GIŠ)}$MÁ	(1.) ‘ship, boat’	
	^{GIŠ}MÁ	9.1.4.A_1 obv. i 16′, 29′
	(2.) ‘boat(-shaped vessel)’	
	MÁ	4.2.1.A_1 obv. 10

see *Lexical Commentary*

MÁ.(URU.)URU$_6$	‘quiver’	
	MÁ.URU.URU$_6$	9.1.5 rev.$^!$ 4′
	^{URUDU}MÁ.URU$_5$	3.1.1.A$_3$ rev. iv 10′
see *Lexical Commentary*; = ^{KUŠ}*IŠPATU*		
MÁ.URU.URU$_6$ *Gasga*	‘Gašgaen quiver’	
	MÁ.URU.UR]U$_6$ *ga-aš-ga*	9.1.5 rev.$^!$ 6′
= ^{KUŠ}*IŠPATU* ^{URU}*Gašga*		
MAḪ	‘great, large’	
	⟨⟨MAḪ⟩⟩	9.1.4.A$_1$ obv. i 15′
= *šalli-*		
MAR	‘spade’	
	MAR	4.2.11 6′
$^{(KUŠ/TÚG)}$MAR.ŠUM	‘(leather/cloth) strap’	
sg. nom.	MAR.ŠUM	11.6.5 obv.$^?$ 5
	MAR].ŠUM	8.1.K rev. vi$^?$ 3′
	MAR.Š]UM(?)	11.6.6 rev. 8′
	^{KUŠ}MAR.ŠUM	9.1.1 rev. iv 35′
	^{KUŠ}MAR.Š[UM	8.1.D obv. i 4′
	$^{KU[Š}$MAR.Š]UM	8.1.C 5′
	^{TÚG}MAR.ŠUM	4.2.9 obv. 7, 10, 23
	$^{T]ÚG}$MAR.ŠUM	4.2.9 obv. 27
	^{TÚG}MAR.[ŠUM	4.2.9 obv. 30
sg. inst.	*QA-DU* MAR.ŠU[M	6.9 obv. 3′
	QA-DU ^{KUŠ}MAR.ŠUM	11.6.3 obv.$^?$ 4′
	QA-DU ^{KUŠ}MAR.Š[UM	9.2.9 rev.$^?$ 5′
see *Lexical Commentary*		
^{LÚ}MÁŠDA	‘commoner, poor man’	
	$^{⟨LÚ⟩}$MÁŠDA	11.6.1 5
MÁŠ.ANŠE	‘animal’	
	MÁŠ.*ANŠE$^?$*	9.1.4.A$_1$ obv. ii 35
MÁŠ.ŠIR	‘he-goat’	
	UDU/MÁŠ].ŠIR	9.1.15 3′
ME	‘hundred’	
see *ME* under *Numerals*		
MU^{KAM}	‘year’	
see SÍG IGI-*zi-aš* MU^{KAM}-*aš*		
MUG	‘noil’	
	MUG	4.1.4.1.A$_1$ obv. i 4′, 5′, 6′, 9′, 10′; obv. ii 11′; rev. v 3′, 4′, 1″, 9″; rev. vi 3′, 8′, 10′. 4.1.4.2.A$_1$ rev. l. c. 2′, 8′, 9′, 10′. 4.1.4.2.A$_2$ obv. l. c. 11′; obv. r. c. 8′. 4.1.4.5 obv. r. c. 2′, 3′, 4′
	M]UG	4.1.4.1.A$_1$ obv. i 11′. 4.1.4.2.A$_2$ obv. l. c. 1′
	MU]G	4.1.4.1.A$_1$ rev. vi 4′, 9′. 4.1.4.5 rev. r. c. 3′, 4′
	MU[G	4.1.4.2.A$_2$ obv. r. c. 6′. 4.1.4.5 rev. r. c. 7′
	M[UG	4.1.4.1.A$_1$ obv. ii 13′; rev. v 2″, 4″, 5″, 6″
see *Lexical Commentary*; = ^{SÍG}*MUKKU*		

^{MUNUS}MUḪALDIM	'female cook'	
see ^{GIŠ}BANŠUR ^{MUNUS}MUḪALDIM		
MUL	"star" (a quality/feature of a belt)	
	MUL	6.10 8′. 11.6.1 8
	MU[L	4.1.4.2.A_1 rev. r. c. 6′
see *Lexical Commentary*		
MUNUS	'woman'	
	(ALAM) MUNUS	10.1.1.1 rev.$^?$ 10′. 10.1.1.2 rev. iv 3′, 4′
	(^{KUŠ}E.SIR) MUNUS	7.3 obv i 6
	(GAD.DAM) MUNUS	11.6.1 4
sg. gen.	(ALAM) MUNUS-*TI*	9.1.1 rev. iv 12′. 9.2.4 obv. i 12′; rev. iii 11′. 10.2.1.1 obv. 8′
	(ALAM) *ŠA* MUNUS-*TI*	9.1.1 rev. iv 16′
	(^{KUŠ}E.SIR) MUNUS-*TI*	9.1.10.A_2 rev. 9′
	(ḪUB.BI) MUNUS-*TI*	1.5 obv. 4. 9.1.1 rev. iv 39′
	(ḪUB.BI) MUNUS$^!$-*TI*	10.3.4 6′
	(TÚG) MUNUS-*TI*	1.5 lo. e. 15
	MUNUS-*TI*	2.13 rev.$^?$ 2′. 2.14 5′. 10.3.4 8′. 11.6.9 5′
pl.	MUNUS^{MEŠ}	12.3.3 11′
MUNUS *ḫarnauwaš*	"woman of the birthing stool"	
sg. dat./loc.	*A-NA* MUNUS *ḫar-na-u-wa-aš*	4.1.1.1.A_1 rev. 16′
	A-NA MUNUS *ḫar-na-wa-aš*	4.1.1.1.B_1 rev. iii$^?$ 11
MUNUS.LUGAL	'queen'	
	MUNUS.LUGAL	2.4 rev. 3′. 2.7.A obv. 11, 13. 2.12 obv.$^!$ ii 7′. 3.1.2 obv. l. c. 5′, 7′. 4.1.1.1.B_1 rev. iii$^?$ 10. 4.1.3.2 rev. 6′. 4.1.4.6 lo. e. 16′. 4.2.4 obv. 11. 4.2.6 obv.$^?$ 1′, 3′. 4.2.12 4′. 6.1 l. e. 1. 6.6 obv. 6′. 7.1 rev. 5′. 8.1.E(A_1) rev. v 6′. 10.2.2.1 1′. 11.3.1 15′
	MUNUS.LU[GAL	4.1.3.2 rev. 4′
sg. dat./loc.	*A*]-*N*[*A*] MUNUS.LUGAL	2.5 obv. 3′
^{UZU}MUR$_7$.GÚ	'shoulder'	
	^{UZU}MUR$_7$.GÚ	10.2.2.2 obv.$^?$ l. c. 5′. 10.2.2.3 obv.$^?$ l. c. 7′
see also GADA ZAG, $^{\text{(UZU)}}$ZAG.UDU		
MURUB$_4$	'middle, midsection'	
	MURUB$_4$	10.2.2.4 obv.$^?$ r. c. 6′
	MURUB$_4$(-*ŠU*)	10.2.2.2 obv.$^?$ l. c. 3′. 10.2.2.4 obv.$^?$ r. c. 3′
	MUR[UB$_4$(-*ŠU*)	10.2.2.2 obv.$^?$ l. c. 2′
MUŠEN	'bird'	
	MUŠEN	9.2.14 4′
pl.	MUŠEN$^{\text{ḪI.A}}$	12.1.1 r. c. 5′
MUŠEN *ḪUR-RI*	'Hurri bird'	
	MUŠEN *Ḫ*[*UR-R*]*I*	10.2.1.2 obv. 8′
$^{(\text{NA}_4)}$MUŠ.GÍR	(a stone)	
	(^{N}[$^{\text{A}_4}$NUNUZ?]) MUŠ.GÍR$^!$(text: SÌR)	3.1.8.A obv. 11′
see *Lexical Commentary*		

NA$_4$	‘stonc’	
	NA$_4$	3.1.8.A obv. 12′. 9.2.4 rev. iii 5′. 9.2.5 obv. i(?) 11′
	NA$_4$	12.2.2 9′
pl.	NA$_4^{\text{ḪI.A}}$	9.2.5 obv. i(?) 3′
	NA$_4$ $^{\text{ḪI.A}}$	4.1.3.2 rev. 4′
material		
	NA$_4$	3.1.8.A obv. 17′. 4.2.4 obv. 8. 8.4 rev. 4′ (2×), 6′, 8′, 11′, 12′ (2×). 9.1.1 rev. iii 11′, 22′, 24′, 27′, 32′; rev. iv 15′, 16′, 18′ (2×), 21′, 22′, 23′, 26′, 32′, 33′, 37′, 39′, 44′. 9.1.4.A$_1$ obv. ii 8, 9, 10, 11, 12, 19, 30. 9.1.5 obv.$^!$ 1, 10. 9.1.10.A$_1$ obv. 4′, 5′, 6′; rev. 3′. 9.1.10.B 4′, 8′, 9′, 10′. 9.1.14 obv. r. c. 7′. 9.1.15 3′, 5′, 6′. 9.2.1 obv. ii 3′, 4′, 5′, 7′ (2×), 8′, 9′, 11′, 16′, 17′, 20′; rev. iii 5′, 6′, 9′, 13′, 20′, 21′, 23′, 27′. 9.2.2 rev.$^!$ iii 8′, 12′, 16′, 17′, 18′, 25′. 9.2.3 obv. (ii) 3″. 9.2.4 obv. i 4′, 5′, 6′, 15′; rev. iv 7. 9.2.7 obv. l. c. 12′. 9.2.9 obv.$^?$ 2′, 3′, 6′, 7′, 8′, 11′. 9.2.10 2′. 10.1.2.1 rev.$^?$ r. c. 6′, 7′; rev.$^?$ l. c. 1, 2. 10.2.1.1 obv. 8′. 10.2.1.2 obv. 5′ (2×), 8′, 10′, 13′. 10.2.2.3 obv.$^?$ l. c. 9′, 12′. 10.2.2.4 obv.$^?$ r. c. 4′. 10.3.1 rev. iii 9′. 10.3.2 obv. i(?) 8″. 10.3.3 obv.$^?$ 7′. 10.3.4 3′, 5′, 6′, 9′, 10′. 11.1.2 l. c. 3′, 4′. 11.2.3 3′. 11.3.1 15′. 11.3.3 1′. 12.1.1 l. c. 2′ (2×), 3′; r. c. 7′ (2×), 10′, 11′ (2×). 12.3.3 8′
	NA$_4$$^?$	12.1.1 r. c. 13′
	N]A$_4$	8.4 rev. 7′. 9.1.1 rev. iii 14′, 20′. 9.2.5 obv. i(?) 5′. 9.2.10 4′. 11.2.5 6′. 12.1.1 l. c. 2′, 3′, 5′; r. c. 7′, 8′, 11′
	N]A$_4$$^?$	10.3.4 2′
	N[A$_4$	9.1.1 rev. iii 21′. 9.1.4.A$_1$ obv. ii 37. 9.2.1 obv. ii 24′, 27′. 9.2.2 rev.$^!$ iii 19′. 10.2.1.2 obv. 15′. 10.3.4 6′, 13′. 12.1.1 r. c. 10′.
	N[A$_4$$^?$	8.4 rev. 10′. 9.2.9 obv.$^?$ 7′. 10.2.1.7 rev.$^?$ 8′. 12.1.1 r. c. 6′
NA$_4$ ^{URU}*Papila* material	‘Babylon-stone’ (a glass or enamel)	
	N]A$_4$ ^{URU}*pa-pí-la*	10.2.1.3 10′
= $^{\text{NA}_4}$KÁ.DINGIR.RA		
^{LÚ}NAGAR	‘woodworker, carpenter’	
	^{LÚ}NAGAR	5.1 obv. ii 10′
pl.	$^{\text{LÚ.MEŠ}}$NAGAR	5.7 rev. iii$^?$ 14′
^{LÚ}NAGAR SIG	‘fine woodworker’	
	^{LÚ}N]AGAR SIG	5.7 rev. iv$^?$ 17′
NAM.RA	'booty, loot'	
	NAM.RA	10.1.1.1 rev.$^?$ 3′
NAM.TÚL	(a part of a harness)	
	NAM.TÚL	9.2.4 rev. iii 7′
	NAM.T]ÚL	4.2.11 4′

pl.	N]AM.TÚL[u]$^{\text{I.ḪI.A}}$	2.12 obv.! ii 11′
= *NAMTULLU*		
NÍ.TE	'body; person, self'	
sg. gen.	*ŠA* NÍ.TE	4.1.4.9 obv. 11
NÍG.ÀR.RA	'fine meal; threshed grain(?)'	
	NÍG.ÀR.RA	1.1.A$_2$ obv. 8′. 12.2.3 2′
^{KUŠ}NÍG.BÀR	'curtain, drape, hide'	
	^{KUŠ}NÍG.BÀR	11.6.1 10, 13
	^{KUŠ}N[ÍG.BÀ]R	8.1.F rev. vi 9
pl.	^{KUŠ}NÍG.BÀR$^{\text{ḪI.A}}$	2.5 obv. 5′
NÍG.BÚN.NA	'turtle'	
	NÍG].BÚN.NA	12.1.1 l. c. 6′
	NÍG.B[ÚN.N]A	12.1.1 l. c. 6′
NÍG.GÍD.DA	'rod, wire; (a type of spear)'	
	NÍG.GÍD.DA	8.1.A obv. ii 29′; rev. v 3, 8, 15′
	NÍ]G.GÍD.DA	8.1.D obv. i 2′
see *Lexical Commentary*; = *uraki(t)-*		
^{GIŠ}NÍG.GUL	'pickaxe'	
	^{GIŠ}NÍG.[GUL	7.1 obv. 21′
^{TÚG}NÍG.LÁM	'splendid garment (esp. for festivals)'	
pl.	^{TÚG}NÍG.LÁM^{MEŠ}	2.16 obv. i 4′. 8.1.E(A$_1$) rev. v 6′
	^{TÚG}NÍG.[LÁM^{MEŠ}	6.1 rev. A 3′
$^{\text{(URUDU)}}$NÍG.ŠU.LUḪ(.ḪA)	'wash basin'	
	NÍG.ŠU.LUḪ	2.7.A rev. 4. 4.1.1.3 obv. 5. 4.1.1.5 obv. 2. 11.1.3 10′
	NÍG.ŠU.LUḪ.ḪA	1.1.A$_1$ obv. 6′
	^{URUDU}NÍG.ŠU.LUḪ.ḪA	3.1.1.A$_3$ rev. iv 11′. 4.2.9 rev. 31′
	^{URUDU}NÍG.ŠU.[LUḪ	1.4 5′
see also $^{\text{(URUDU)}}$*warpuwaš*, ^{URUDU}ÁB×A, $^{\text{(URUDU)}}$ŠE.NAGA		
NINDA	'bread'	
pl.	NINDA$^{\text{ḪI.A}}$	12.3.4 obv. 1, 2, 3, 4, 5, 7
	NINDA.NINDA$^{\text{ḪI.A}}$	12.3.4 obv. 6
$^{\text{NA}_4}$NÍR	(a stone) 'banded agate(?)'	
	$^{\text{NA}_4}$NÍR	2.16 obv. i 9′. 3.1.8.A obv. 2′, 7′, 14′. 12.1.3 3′
	$^{\text{NA}_4}$N]ÍR	3.1.8.A obv. 10
	$^{\text{NA}_4}$NÍ]R?	9.2.13 7′
	$^{\text{NA}_4}$N[ÍR	3.1.8.A obv. 1′
	$^{\text{NA}_4}$NÍ[R! (text: $^{\text{NA}_4}$A.TÙ[N)	9.2.13 5′
	$^{\text{NA}_4}$⟨ZA⟩.TÙ[N (= $^{\text{NA}_4}$NÍ[R)	9.1.14 obv. r. c. 8′
see *Lexical Commentary*; see also $^{\text{NA}_4}$*ḫulali*		
NU.GÁL	'not there, not present'	
	NU.GÁL	2.7.A obv. 16, 17. 2.12 obv.! ii 9′. 4.1.1.1.A$_1$ obv. 16′. 8.1.J rev. v! 1′. 9.1.1 rev. iii 11′. 9.2.1 rev. iii 15′, 23′. 10.3.3 obv.? 8′, 11′. 10.3.4 8′. 10.3.9 4′. 10.3.14 l. c. 6′, 8′. 11.6.6 rev. 5′

	NU.GÁ[L	10.3.4 10′
	N[U.GÁL	9.2.4 rev. iv 4
	N]U$^{?}$.GÁL	10.1.2.8 rev. r. c. 3′
NUMUN	‘seed’	
	NUMUN (^{GIŠ}ESI *ḪURRI*)	2.7.A obv. 5
$^{(NA_4)}$NUNUZ	(1.) ‘bead’	
	NUNUZ	4.2.4 obv. 2. 8.4 rev. 4′. 9.1.10.B 3′, 7′. 9.2.1 obv. ii 15′, 20′
	NU]NUZ	9.1.10.B 3′
	^{NA_4}NUNUZ	2.13 rev.$^{?}$ 6′. 2.14 3′. 5.2 obv. ii 1, 5. 9.2.2 rev.$^{!}$ iii 9′
	^{NA_4}NUNUZ (*kibši*)	3.1.8.A obv. 10′
	^{NA_4}[NUN]UZ	5.2 obv. ii 5
	^{NA_4}NUN[UZ	5.2 obv. ii 1
	^{NA_4}NU[NUZ	5.2 obv. ii 7, 8
	^{N}[^{A_4}NUNUZ?] (MUŠ.GÍR$^{!}$)	3.1.8.A obv. 11′
pl. nom.-acc. n.	^{NA_4}NUNUZ-*ia*	11.3.1 12′
see also *išgaratar-*		
	(2.) “bead-stone” (a copper ore, perhaps malachite)	
material		
	NUNUZ	4.2.1.A_2 obv. 2′, 4′, 5′, 6′. 4.2.3 l. c. 4′, 5′ (2×), 6′. 8.1.A obv. i 5′. 9.2.2 rev.$^{!}$ iii 3′, 12′, 17′. 11.3.1 11′
	NUN[UZ	1.5 obv. 4
	NU[NUZ	4.2.1.A_1 obv. 13. 4.2.1.A_2 obv. 1′, 3′
	^{NA_4}NUNUZ	2.15 l. c. 4′. 9.1.1 rev. iii 25′, 35′. 10.2.1.1 obv. 11′, 12′
	$^{N]A_4}$NUNUZ	4.2.12 2′
	^{NA_4}NUN]UZ	4.2.12 1′
	^{NA_4}NU[NUZ$^{?}$	4.2.12 1′
sg. gen.	*ŠA* NUN[UZ	8.1.B rev. 2′
see *Lexical Commentary*		
PAD	‘bar, ingot’	
	PAD (AN.BAR)	4.2.2 obv. 1
	PAD (KÙ.BABBAR)	3.1.10 1, 3, 5, 7, 9, 11. 3.1.11.A 4. 3.1.11.B 6′
	(URUDU) PAD	5.5 rev. iii 2′, 3′
	PAD (URUDU)	5.2 obv. ii 9. 1.4 4′
	PAD (ZABAR)	6.1 rev. B 6
	PAD (*TAYYĀRTU*)	4.2.1.A_1 obv. 10
	P]AD (KÙ.BABBAR)	3.1.11.B 1′, 3′
see *Lexical Commentary*		
^{TÚG}PAD(-*i-me-*)	(a garment)	
sg. nom.	^{TÚG}PAD-*me-eš*	9.1.10.A_1 obv. 9′
	^{TÚG}PAD-*me-iš*	6.5 obv. 2′, 5′, 10′, 13′
	$^{TÚ]G}$PAD-*me-eš*	9.1.10.A_1 obv. 7′, 12′
	^{TÚG}PAD-*me-e*]*š*	9.1.10.B 11′
pl. nom.	^{TÚG}PAD-*uš*	10.1.1.2 rev. iv 8′
abbr.	^{TÚG}PAD-*i-me.*	11.6.1 5
see *Lexical Commentary*		

$^{(GIŠ)}$PAN	‘bow’	
	PAN	2.5 rev. 6′
	^{GIŠ}PAN	1.1.A_1 obv. 13′, 14′. 2.17 obv.$^?$ r. c. 11′. 3.1.1.A_3 rev. iv 7′. 5.2 obv. ii 3. 5.7 rev. iii$^?$ 8′, 21′, 22′, 23′, 26′. 8.5 rev. iii(?) 2′; rev. iv(?) 4′. 8.7 r. c. 5′, 6′. 9.1.5 rev.$^!$ 8′, 13′. 9.1.10.A_2 rev. 6′
	^{GIŠ}PA[N	5.7 rev. iii$^?$ 19′. 10.3.3 obv.$^?$ 7′
	^{GIŠ}PA[N$^?$	9.2.11 2′
	^{GIŠ}P[AN	3.1.1.A_3 rev. iv 5′
sg. dat./loc.	*A-NA* ^{GIŠ}PAN	9.1.5 rev.$^!$ 9′
^{GIŠ}PAN ^{URU}*Gašga*	‘Gasgaen(-styled) bow’	
	^{GIŠ}PAN ^{URU}*ga-aš-ga*	9.1.5 rev.$^!$ 9′
	^{GIŠ}PAN(?) $^{U]RU}$*ga-aš-ga*	2.18 8′
	^{GIŠ}PAN ^{URU}*g[a-aš-ga*	2.17 obv.$^?$ r. c. 16′
^{GIŠ}PAN.TUR	‘a small (model?) bow’	
pl.	^{GIŠ}PAN.TUR.TUR$^{ME[Š]}$	9.1.5 rev.$^!$ 9′
PAP	(scribal mark for damaged text in *Vorlage*)	
	PAP	9.2.1 rev. iii 15′, 23′
PÌRIG	‘tiger’	
	PÌRIG	1.2 rev. 10′
PÌRIG.TUR	‘leopard’	
	PÌRIG.TUR	9.1.4.A_1 obv. i 15′. 9.2.1 rev. iii 12′
	PÌRIG.T]UR	10.2.1.2 obv. 15′
	(GÚ) PÌRIG.TUR	9.1.4.A_1 obv. ii 22
	(*BIBRU*) PÌRIG.TUR	9.1.4.A_1 obv. ii 21
$^{GI/GIŠ}$PISAN	‘chest, container’	
	^{GI}PISAN	1.5 rev. 22. 2.1.A obv. ii(?) 9′, 11′, 14′. 2.1.B 2′. 2.2 obv. 3′, 5′, 7′, 11′. 2.6 3′, 4′. 2.7.A obv. 1, 2, 11, 12, 16, 17, 18, 20, 21, 22, 23. 2.9.A_1 obv. i 2′, 4′. 2.9.A_2 obv. i 1′, 3′, 5′, 7′, 9′. 2.12 obv. ii$^!$ 4′. 2.16 obv. ii 2′, 5′, 8′. 4.1.1.3 rev. A 5′. 8.1.E(A_3) obv. i 2′. 8.1.F obv. ii 16′; rev. v 5. 8.1.G obv. r. c. 6′, 8′
	$^{G]I}$PISAN	2.1.A obv. ii(?) 4′. 2.1.B 5′. 2.2 obv. 9′, 12′, 15′. 2.9.A_1 obv. i 6′
	$^{G]I}$[PIS]AN	8.8.A 1′
	$^{GI]}$PISAN	9.1.1 rev. iv 20′
	^{GI}PI]SAN	2.2 rev. 2. 8.1.F obv. i 3′
	^{GI}PIS]AN	2.1.B 8′
	^{GI}PISA]N	2.9.A_2 11′. 8.8.B r. c. 1′
	^{GI}[PISAN	2.9.A_1 obv. i 1′
	$^{G[I}$PISAN	8.8.B r. c. 9′
	^{GIŠ}PISAN	2.2 rev. 4. 2.5 obv. 6′, 7′. 2.9.A_3 obv. ii 1′, 3′, 7′, 10′. 2.12 obv. ii$^!$ 10′. 2.13 obv.$^?$ 1′, 3′. 2.15 l. c. 5′, 10′, 12′. 2.17 obv.$^?$ r. c. 1′. 4.2.1.A_1 obv. 2. 4.2.3 l. c. 2′. 6.1 obv. 15. 6.12 4′. 8.1.A obv. ii 8′, 18′, 19′, 20′, 21′, 24′, 28′; rev. v 17′, 18′, 19′, 21′, 23′, 30′, 31′. 8.1.D rev. iv 7′. 8.1.E(A_1) obv. iii 5′. 8.1.F

		obv. i 6′. 8.1.H rev. r. c. 5′. 8.1.I rev. r. c. 4′. 9.1.1 rev. iii 42′. 9.2.6 obv. i 4′. 9.2.9 rev.$^{?}$ 1′
	$^{\text{GIŠ!}}$PISAN	11.6.1 6
	^{GIŠ}PISAN(?)	2.7.A rev. 7′
	$^{\text{G[IŠ]}}$PISAN	2.12 obv.$^{!}$ ii 6′
	^{GIŠ}PI]SAN	2.5 obv. 5′, 8′
	^{GIŠ}PISA]N	2.5 obv. 2′
	^{GIŠ}PISA[N	9.2.4 obv. ii 11′
	^{GIŠ}[PISAN	2.13 rev.$^{?}$ 10′
	$^{\text{GI/GIŠ}}$]PISAN	8.1.E(A_1) rev. iv 1′
	$^{\text{GI/GIŠ}}$PISA]N	2.1.A obv. ii(?) 1′, 3′. 11.7.1 l. c. 3′
	$^{\text{GI/GIŠ}}$PISA]N(?)	8.3 obv. 8′
dat./loc.	*A-NA* ^{GIŠ}PISAN	4.1.1.2.B rev. 3
	A-NA … ^{GIŠ}PISAN	8.1.A obv. ii 17′
gen.	*ŠA* ^{GIŠ}PISAN	6.1 obv. 19
	ŠA ^{GIŠ}PISAN$^{!}$	6.1 obv. 5
	ŠA] ^{GIŠ}PISAN	6.1 rev. A 3′
pl.	^{GI}PISAN$^{\text{ḪI.A}}$	2.5 rev. 11′
	^{GI}PISAN^{MEŠ}	2.2 obv. 6′
SA_5	‘red’	
	SA_5	2.1.A obv. ii(?) 9′, 13′. 2.1.B 2′, 4′, 7′, 8′, 10′. 2.2 obv. 2′, 3′, 8′, 9′, 13′, 14′; rev. 2, 3. 2.5 obv. 5′, 6′, 7′, 8′. 2.6 3′. 2.7.A obv. 1 (2×), 2, 8 (2×), 12, 16, 17, 18, 20, 21, 22, 23. 2.7.B rev. 5′. 2.9.A_1 obv. i 4′, 6′. 2.9.A_2 obv. i 1′, 3′, 5′, 7′, 9′, 11′. 2.9.A_3 obv. ii 1′, 10′. 2.12 obv.$^{!}$ ii 4′. 2.16 obv. i 6′; obv. ii 8′. 3.1.1.A_3 rev. iv 5′; rev. v 5′, 10′, 12′. 4.1.1.3 rev. A 5′. 4.1.3.2 rev. 3′. 4.1.4.1.A_1 obv. ii 3′, 6′; rev. v 2″, 6″, 9″; rev. vi 9′. 4.1.4.1.A_2 obv. ii 5′, 8′. 4.1.4.2.A_1 rev. r. c. 5′, 8′, 14′; rev. l. c. 5′. 4.1.4.2.A_2 obv. r. c. 11′. 4.1.4.4 6′, 10′. 4.1.4.5 obv. r. c. 4′; rev. r. c. 8′. 4.1.4.6 obv. 2′, 5′, 7′, 10′, 14′. 4.2.1.A_1 obv. 4. 4.2.3 l. c. 2′. 4.2.4 obv. 2, 4. 4.2.6 obv.$^{?}$ 6′, 19′, 20′; rev. 2′. 4.2.9 obv. 6, 25. 4.2.10 7′. 6.1 obv. 7. 6.5 obv. 5′, 19′; rev. 10′, 13′, 14′, 17′, 18′, 19′, 20′. 6.6 obv. 5′. 6.9 obv. 11′. 6.12 3′, 8′. 6.13 8′. 8.1.A obv. i 7′; obv. ii 18′, 24′; rev. v 10, 14′, 17′, 19′, 21′, 23′. 8.1.D obv. i 4′, 8′, 9′, 11′; rev. iv 4′, 6′, 7′. 8.1.E(A_1) obv. ii 17; obv. iii 5′; rev. iv 1′; rev. v 1′, 10′, 11′. 8.1.E(A_2) 3′, 10′. 8.1.F obv. i 3′, 4′; obv. ii 7′, 16′; rev. v 10, 11, 13. 8.1.G obv. r. c. 8′. 8.1.H rev. r. c. 5′. 8.1.I rev. r. c. 4′. 8.1.K rev. vi$^{?}$ 2′. 8.3 obv. 8′. 8.4 rev. 19′. 8.8.A 1′. 8.8.B r. c. 1′. 9.1.1 rev. iii 35′, 42′; rev. iv 20′. 9.1.10.A_2 rev. 9′. 9.2.1 rev. iii 2′. 10.3.11 l. c. 1′, 5′, 7′. 10.3.12 obv. i 6′, 16′. 11.1.3 1′. 11.6.5 obv.$^{?}$ 8. 11.6.6 rev. 1′, 8′. 11.6.7 4′. 11.7.1 l. c. 3′. 12.1.1 l. c. 5′; r. c. 7′

	S]A$_5$	2.5 obv. 10′. 2.9.A$_1$ obv. i 7′. 4.1.4.1.A$_1$ obv. ii 6′. 4.1.4.1.A$_2$ obv. ii 1′. 5.5 obv. ii 3. 8.1.A obv. i 13′. 8.1.F obv. i 10′, 20′. 8.1.J rev. v$^!$ 2′, 7′. 9.2.9 rev.$^?$ 6′. 12.1.1 l. c. 2′
	S[A$_5$	2.9.A$_1$ obv. i 2′. 2.15 l. c. 5′. 2.16 obv. ii 2′, 5′. 8.1.E(A$_3$) obv. i 2′. 8.1.F obv. ii 13′. 9.1.6 obv. 11. 11.6.6 rev. 6′
sg. gen.	SA$_5$-*aš*	11.6.5 obv.$^?$ 9
	SA$_5$-*TIM*	9.1.8 obv. 4′
see *Lexical Commentary*		
^{LÚ}SAG	‘courtier’	
	(GADA IGI …) ^{LÚ}SAG	4.2.9 rev. 27′
	^{L}]^{Ú}SAG	5.7 rev. iv$^?$ 8′
see *Lexical Commentary*		
SAG(.DU)	‘head; pommel (of a dagger)’	
	SAG-*SÚ*	9.1.1 rev. iv 29′, 40′
	SAG.DU	6.1 obv. 9. 8.1.A obv. ii 10′. 9.1.4.A$_1$ obv ii. 17. 9.1.4.A$_2$ r. c. 2′. 9.1.5 obv.$^!$ 2. 9.1.10.A$_2$ rev. 5′. 9.2.6 obv. i 20′. 9.2.9 obv.$^?$ 14′. 10.2.2.4 obv.$^?$ r. c. 6′. 11.2.5 5′
	SAG.DU-*SÚ*	9.1.1 rev. iii 11′. 9.1.14 obv. r. c. 6′, 8′, 9′. 9.2.2 rev.$^!$ iii 7′
	SAG.D]U-*SÚ*	9.1.1 rev. iv 13′
	SA]G.DU-*SÚ*	10.1.2.4 l. c. 6′
	SAG.DU-*ŠI*$^{\text{(sic)}}$ (= SAG.DU-*SÚ*$^!$?)	10.2.2.4 obv.$^?$ r. c. 3′
	SAG.D[U	2.15 l. c. 3′. 9.1.5 obv.$^!$ 10
	SAG.[DU	9.2.2 rev.$^!$ iii 6′
	SAG.[DU-*S*]*Ú*(?)	10.3.1 obv. ii 3′
pl.	SAG.DU$^{\text{ḪI.A}}$	9.1.4.A$_2$ r. c. 3′. 11.2.5 6′
	SA]G.DU$^{\text{ḪI.A}}$	9.1.4.A$_2$ r. c. 8′
abl.	SAG.DU-*za*	10.2.1.7 rev.$^?$ 4′
SAG.DU *kinuḫi(ya)-*	‘pommel of a *kinuḫa*-knife’	
sg. nom.	SAG.DU *ki-nu-ḫi-i*[*š*	8.1.A obv. ii 10′
see also GÍR *kinuḫi(ya)-*		
SAG.DU TI$_8$^{MUŠEN}	‘eagle’s head’ (a decorative object)	
	SAG.DU TI$_8$^{MUŠEN}	9.1.5 obv.$^!$ 4
SAG.DU UR.MAḪ	‘lion’s head’ (a decorative object)	
	SAG.DU UR.MAḪ	9.1.1 rev. iv(?) 17′. 9.1.4.A$_1$ obv. ii 19
	S]AG.DU [UR.MA]Ḫ	6.4 obv.$^?$ 4′
	SA]G.DU UR.MAḪ	6.4 obv.$^?$ 7′
	SAG].DU-*SÚ* UR.MAḪ	9.1.9 rev. iv 3′
SAG.(DU.)KI	(an ornament) ‘front(let), brow, forehead’	
	SAG.KI	8.1.E(A$_1$) rev. v 4′
	SAG.DU.KI	9.1.1 rev. iv 44′
= *ḫant-*		

$^{\text{(TÚG)}}$SAG.DUL	(a head covering)	
	SAG.DUL	6.9 obv. 3′. 8.1.F obv. ii 8′. 9.1.1 rev. iv 43′. 11.6.5 obv.$^{?}$ 5
	S]AG.DUL	4.2.6 obv.$^{?}$ 10′
	SAG.DU[L	4.2.9 obv. 23
	SAG.[DUL	4.2.9 obv. 7
	^{TÚG}SAG.DUL	4.2.9 obv. 7, 9, 23, 30. 6.8 4′. 8.1.E(A_1) obv. iii 9′. 8.1.K rev. vi$^{?}$ 3′. 9.1.1 rev. iii 43′. 9.1.8 obv. 8′. 11.6.5 obv.$^{?}$ 4. 11.6.7 6′
	^{TÚG}S]AG.DUL	4.1.4.1.A_1 obv. i 1′. 4.1.4.2.A_2 obv. l. c. 7′
	^{TÚG}SA]G.DUL	6.7 obv.$^{?}$ 3
	^{TÚG}SAG.DU]L	8.1.F obv. i 10′
	^{TÚG}SAG.D[UL	4.2.6 obv.$^{?}$ 5′
	^{TÚG}SAG.[DUL	8.1.E(A_1) rev. iv 7′, 8′. 11.6.6 rev. 9′
SAG.KI		
see SAG.(DU.)KI		
$^{\text{(GIŠ)}}$SAG.KUL	‘bolt, bar (for a chest)’	
	SAG.KUL	2.9.A_3 obv. i 10′
	S]AG.KUL	2.10 5′
	SA]G.KUL	2.9.A_3 obv. i 15′
	SAG.K]UL	2.9.A_3 obv. i 14′
	SAG.KU]L	2.9.A_3 obv. i 8′
	^{GIŠ}SAG.KUL	2.9.A_3 obv. i 12′. 2.10 3′
	^{GIŠ}SAG.KUL$^{!}$(text: KUR)	2.11 5′
SAG.UŠ	‘regular, steady’	
	($EZEN_4$) SAG.UŠ	4.1.1.1.A_1 obv. 20′
$^{\text{(LÚ)}}$SAGI(.A)	‘cup-bearer’	
	^{LÚ}SAGI.A	4.2.10 6′. 4.2.11 8′
see also DUG.$^{\text{(LÚ)}}$SAGI(.A)		
^{LÚ}SANGA	‘priest’	
pl. dat./loc.?	$^{\text{LÚ.MEŠ}}$SANGA	6.1 rev. B 1
see also É.GAL ^{LÚ}SANGA		
^{LÚ}SANGA.GAL	“great priest”	
	^{LÚ}S]ANGA.GAL	5.2 obv. i 10
	^{LÚ}SANGA.GA[L(?)	6.1 rev. B 2
SI	‘horn’	
	SI	5.1 obv. ii 2′, 5′, 6′, 7′. 9.1.5 rev.$^{!}$ 8′
pl.	SI$^{\text{ḪI.A}}$	10.2.2.3 obv.$^{?}$ l. c. 6′. 10.2.2.4 obv.$^{?}$ r. c. 6′
material		
sg. gen.	*ŠA* SI	10.2.1.3 6′
SI GU_4	‘cow horn’	
	SI GU_4	9.1.1 rev. iv 30′
	S]I GU_4	9.2.4 rev. iv 11
SI UZ_6	‘goat horn’	
material		
	SI UZ_6	11.1.2 l. c. 3′

^{GIŠ}SI.GAR	'bolt, bar (for a gate); neck stocks'	
	^{GIŠ}SI.⟨GAR⟩	10.3.13 3′
SIG	'fine, thin'	
	SIG	1.1.A_1 obv. 16′. 2.7.A obv. 7 (2×). 3.2.5 r. c. 4′. 4.1.1.2.B rev. 1. 4.1.4.7 obv. 1. 4.2.9 obv. 2, 4, 19. 6.5 rev. 10′, 27′. 6.6 obv. 3′. 6.9 obv. 6′. 6.13 2′. 8.1.D rev. iv 9′. 8.1.E(A_1) obv. ii 5; obv. iii 7′, 8′; rev. iv 4′. 8.1.F obv. i 9′. 8.1.H rev. r. c. 7′. 8.1.I rev. r. c. 6′. 8.1.K rev. v? 3′. 8.7 l. c. 7′, 9′. 8.8.A 2′. 8.8.B l. c. 4′. 9.1.6 obv. 3. 11.1.4 2′. 11.6.1 3
	SIG?	10.1.2.8 rev. r. c. 6′
	S]IG	1.5 obv. 9. 6.10 7′. 8.1.E(A_1) obv. ii 5
	SI]G	9.1.1 rev. iv 41′
	SI[G	4.2.9 rev. 13′. 8.8.A 4′
see also GADA SIG, ^{LÚ}NAGAR SIG		
SÍG	'wool'	
	SÍG	2.7.A obv. 1 (3×), 17. 2.7.B rev. 5′ (2×). 3.2.1 obv. 3, 5, 7, 9, 11, 13, 16, 19; rev. 6′, 9′, 12′, 19′. 3.2.2 obv.? 9′. 4.1.3.1 2′, 3′, 6′, 7′, 8′, 9′. 4.1.3.2 rev. 1′, 3′, 5′. 4.1.3.3 8′. 4.1.3.4.A_1 obv. l. c. 1′, 2′, 3′, 4′; rev. l. c. 2′, 3′, 4′, 5′, 6′, 7′. 4.1.3.4.A_2 rev. l. c. 3′, 4′, 5′, 6′, 7′, 8′, 9′. 4.1.3.5.A_2 1′, 2′, 3′, 5′. 4.1.3.8 rev. A 1′, 3′, 4′. 4.1.4.1.A_1 obv. ii 3′ (2×); obv. iii 5′; rev. v 6′, 4″, 5″; rev. vi 5′, 8′, 9′. 4.1.4.1.A_2 obv. i 2′, 5′; obv. ii 4′, 5′, 7′ (2×), 8′. 4.1.4.2.A_1 rev. r. c. 2′, 4′, 5′, 7′, 8′, 10′ (2×), 13′, 14′; rev. l. c. 1′, 5′. 4.1.4.2.A_2 obv. r. c. 1′, 4′, 6′, 8′, 10′, 11′. 4.1.4.4 1′, 5′ (2×), 6′, 9′ (2×), 10′, 12′. 4.1.4.5 obv. r. c. 2′, 3′, 4′. 4.1.4.6 obv. 5′, 7′, 9′ (2×), 10′, 13′, 14′. 9.1.8 obv. 8′, 11′
	S[Í]G	4.1.4.1.A_1 rev. v 6″, 9″
	S]ÍG	4.1.3.4.A_1 obv. l. c. 5′. 4.1.3.4.A_2 rev. l. c. 2′. 4.1.3.5.A_2 4′. 4.1.3.8 rev. A 2′. 4.1.4.1.A_1 rev. v 10″. 4.1.4.5 rev. r. c. 8′
	SÍ]G	2.7.B rev. 5′. 4.1.3.4.A_2 rev. l. c. 1′. 4.1.3.5.A_1 obv.? 2′. 4.1.4.1.A_1 rev. v 2″. 4.1.4.4 12′. 4.1.4.6 rev. 17′. 8.1.E(A_3) rev. vi 4.
	SÍ[G	3.2.1 rev. 3′. 4.1.3.2 rev. 5′. 4.1.4.3 4′. 4.1.4.6 obv. 13′
	S[ÍG	3.2.3 1′, 4′. 4.1.3.1 1′. 4.1.4.1.A_1 obv. ii 7′, 9′. 4.1.4.4 2′
material		
	SÍG	4.2.9 obv. 9′. 8.1.H rev. l. c. 4′. 9.2.1 obv. ii 21′
	S]ÍG	8.1.E(A_3) rev. vi 3
	SÍ]G	8.1.E(A_3) rev. vi 2
SÍG IGI-*zi-aš* MU^{KAM}-*aš*	'wool of the first year (= wool of a yearling sheep?)'	
	SÍG IGI-*zi-aš* MU^{KAM}-*a*[*š*	3.2.2 obv.? 6′
	SÍG IGI-*z*[*i-aš* MU^{KAM}-*aš*	3.2.2 obv.? 8′

SÍG *ḪURRI*	‘Hurrian(-styled?) wool’	
	SÍG *ḪUR-RI*	2.7.A obv. 25
see also GA.ZUM SÍG		
SIG$_4$	‘brick; panel, plaque’	
	SIG$_4$	11.5.2 rev.$^?$ r. c. 2′
SIG$_5$	‘good, excellent; (a symbol)’	
	SIG$_5$	4.1.1.2.A obv. 15′, 18′, 21′, 23′. 4.1.1.2.B obv. 1, 4, 7, 9. 4.1.4.1.A$_1$ obv. ii 4′; rev. v 7″. 4.1.4.1.A$_2$ obv. ii 9′. 4.1.4.2.A$_1$ rev. r. c. 6′, 15′. 4.2.1.A$_1$ obv. 6. 4.2.1.A$_2$ rev. 12′. 4.2.12 2′. 8.1.A rev. v 9. 8.1.C 4′. 8.1.D obv. i 3′, 7′. 8.1.E(A$_1$) obv. ii 5, 12. 8.3 obv. 3′. 9.2.4 obv. i 14′
	SIG$_5$$^?$	2.18 4′
	S[I]G$_5$$^?$	4.2.1.A$_1$ obv. 12
	SI[G$_5$	2.14 2′. 4.1.4.4 3′, 7′. 4.2.5 1′. 8.1.E(A$_1$) rev. iv 8′
	SI[G$_5$$^?$	8.4 rev. 1′
	S[IG$_5$	4.1.1.2.A obv. 25′
	⟨⟨SIG$_5$⟩⟩	8.3 obv. 6′, 7′
sg. acc.	SIG$_5$-*in*	10.3.2 obv. i(?) 9″
SIG$_7$	‘ten thousand’	
see Numerals		
SIG$_7$.(SIG$_7$)	‘yellow/green’	
	SIG$_7$	4.1.4.1.A$_1$ rev. vi 5′
	SIG$_7$.SIG$_7$	12.1.1 l. c. 2′, 5′
	SI[G$_7$].SIG$_7$	12.1.1 r. c. 7′
	S]IG$_7$.SIG$_7$	12.1.1 r. c. 11′
see *Lexical Commentary*		
^{LÚ}SIMUG(.A)	‘smith’	
	^{LÚ}[SIMUG	5.2 obv. ii 4
sg. dat./loc.?	*A-N*]*A*(?) ^{L}[^{Ú}]SIMUG	4.1.1.1.B$_2$ obv. i$^?$ 8′
sg. dat./loc.(?)	*A-NA*(?) $^{\text{LÚ(.MEŠ)}}$S]IMUG	10.3.1 rev. iii 7′
pl.	$^{\text{LÚ.MEŠ}}$SIMUG.A	5.7 rev. iii$^?$ 10′
	$^{\text{LÚ.MEŠ}}$SIM[UG.A	3.1.12 4′
^{LÚ}SIPA	‘shepherd’	
	^{LÚ}SIPA	5.1 obv. ii 4′
SISKUR	‘ritual’	
	SISKUR	5.1 rev. iii 3, 10. 6.1 l. e. 1, 1c, 2
	⟨SISKUR⟩	5.1 rev. iii 2
SISKUR *purulliyašša/i-*	‘the *purulli*-offering/ritual’	
broken	SISKUR *pu*-[*ru-ul-li-ia-aš-ši*-(?)	4.2.9 obv. 32
SISKUR *taninumaš*	‘ritual of “putting in order”’	
	SISKUR *ta-ni-nu-ma-aš*	6.1 l. e. 1c
	SISKUR *ta-ni-nu*-[*ma-aš*]	6.1 l. e. 2
SU$_6$	‘beard’	
see GADA SU$_6$		

SUD	'to pull, draw; (with cloth) span, spread, lay out'	
pres. pl. 3	S]UD$^?$-*me-ni*	4.1.3.6 rev. 8′
ptc.sg.nom.-acc.n.	(GAM ^{GIŠ}PISAN) SUD-*an*	2.9.A_3 obv. ii 3′. 2.12 obv.$^!$ ii 6′
ptc. sg. gen.	(GAM-*an*) SUD-*u-aš*	4.2.9 rev. 5′
= *ḫuittiya-*, *ḫuet-*; see also GADA EGIR*(-an) arḫa* SUD-*uaš*, TÚG UGU SUD-*an*		
^{MUNUS}SUḪUR.LÁ/LA_5	'handmaiden, female servant'	
	^{MUNUS}SUḪUR.LÁ	5.7 rev. iv$^?$ 12′
	^{MUNUS}SUḪU]R.LÁ	5.7 rev. iv$^?$ 14′
	^{MUNUS}SUḪ[UR.LÁ	6.12 4′
	^{MUNUS}SUḪUR.LÁ-*an-da-la*(?)*	10.2.1.3 4′
pl.	^{MUNUS}SUḪUR.LA_5^{M}[^{EŠ}	12.3.3 5′
SUM	(1.) 'gift'	
	SUM	2.7.A obv. 9
	(2.) 'to give'	
pres. pl. 3	SUM-*an-z*[*i*	4.1.4.9 obv. 2
pret. pl. 3	SUM-*er*	1.2 rev. 2′. 5.2 obv. ii 6, 8. 5.3 l. c. 1′
vb. subst. sg. gen.	(*para*) SUM-*u-aš*	6.1 obv. 5. 6.3 obv. 3
broken	SUM-x[	4.2.11 3′
	(EGIR-*an-da*) S[UM-	4.1.4.7 rev. B 3′
see *Lexical Commentary*; = *pai-/pi(ya)-*, *NADĀNU*		
SUMUN	'old'	
	SUMUN	8.1.A rev. v 17′
	SUMUN$^?$	4.2.9 obv. 14
see also LIBIR(.RA)		
ŠAḪ	'pig'	
	(GÚ) ŠAḪ	9.1.4.A_1 obv. ii 37. 9.1.15 5′
ŠAḪ.TUR	"piglet" (a digging tool(?))	
sg. nom.-acc. n.	Š]AḪ.TUR-*an-za*	9.1.5 rev.$^!$ 14′
sg. dat./loc.	*A-NA* ŠAḪ.TUR	9.1.5 rev.$^!$ 14′
see *Lexical Commentary*		
ŠÀ	'in, inside, among' (abbr. ŠA.BA or ŠA-*ŠU/ŠÚ*)	
	ŠÀ	1.5 rev. 19. 2.1.B 10′. 2.2 rev. 4, 8. 2.5 rev. 5′, 9′, 11′. 2.7.A obv. 14. 2.9.A_1 obv. i 3′, 5′, 9′. 2.9.A_2 obv. i 2′, 4′, 8′, 14′. 2.9.A_3 obv. ii 6′, 9′. 2.14 3′. 3.1.1.A_2 rev. 2′. 3.1.11.B 3′. 3.2.3 2′. 4.1.1.3 rev. A 5′, 9′. 4.1.4.2.A_1 rev. r. c. 4′, 5′, 6′. 4.1.4.2.A_2 obv. r. c. 4′, 6′, 8′. 4.1.4.5 obv. r. c. 2′, 3′, 4′; rev. r. c. 7′. 4.1.4.7 obv. 2. 4.2.1.A_1 obv. 2, 3, 11. 4.2.1.A_2 rev. 11′. 4.2.11 2′. 4.2.3 l. c. 2′. 4.2.4 obv. 7, 9; rev. 4′, 6′, 7′. 4.2.7 4′, 8′. 8.1.A obv. ii 12′; rev. v 7. 8.1.C 3′. 8.1.D obv. i 7′; rev. iv 5′. 8.1.E(A_3) obv. i 2′; rev. iv 2′. 8.4 rev. 10′, 13′, 19′. 8.7 r. c. 1′. 9.1.1 rev. iv 21′. 9.1.4.A_1 obv. i 23′; obv. ii 7, 9, 13, 16, 21, 26, 33, 41. 9.1.5 rev.$^!$ 4′. 9.1.10.B 3′, 6′. 9.1.11 obv.$^?$ 5′. 9.1.14 obv. r. c. 3′, 5′. 9.1.15 2′. 9.2.1 obv. ii 16′, 24′. 9.2.2 rev.$^!$ iii 6′. 9.2.3 obv. (ii) 3″. 9.2.4 obv. i 13′, 16′; obv. ii 12′. 9.2.9 obv.$^?$

		6′, 13′; rev.$^{?}$ 3′, 7′. 9.2.10 5′. 10.1.1.1 rev.$^{?}$ 6′ (2×), 7′. 10.1.1.2 rev. iv 3′. 10.1.2.1 obv.$^{?}$ r. c. 1′. 10.1.2.2 5′. 10.1.2.4 l. c. 11′, 16′, 22′. 10.3.4 2′, 3′, 6′, 9′. 10.3.5 6′. 11.1.2 l. c. 4′. 11.1.5 2′. 11.1.8 4′. 11.2.4 1′. 11.6.1 5, 8, 9, 12 (2×). 11.7.1 r. c. 6′. 11.7.3 rev.$^{?}$ 4
	ŠÀ⟨⟨BA⟩⟩	9.1.5 rev.$^{!}$ 6′
	Š]À	2.14 5′. 4.1.4.2.A_1 rev. l. c. 2′. 4.1.4.7 obv. 5. 4.2.4 rev. 1′. 4.2.6 rev.$^{?}$ 4′. 8.4 rev. 9′. 9.1.11 obv.$^{?}$ 10′
	Š]À$^{?}$	11.7.3 6
	Š[À	2.2 rev. 14. 2.18 11′. 4.1.4.2.A_1 rev. r. c. 15′
	⟨⟨ŠÀ⟩⟩	10.3.12 obv. i 4′
ŠÀ.BA	'among which, of which' (introduces a subset of a group)	
	ŠÀ.BA	2.17 obv.$^{?}$ r. c. 5′, 6′ (2×), 17′. 3.1.1.A_1 obv. ii 7′. 3.1.8.A obv. 6′, 10′; rev. 4′, 10′, 12′, 17′. 3.1.8.B 4′, 6′. 3.1.11.A 4, 7. 3.2.1 obv. 14, 20; rev.$^{?}$ 10′. 3.2.2 obv.$^{?}$ 9′. 4.1.1.2.B obv. 2, 5. 4.1.2.1 obv. (i) 3′, 8′. 4.1.2.3 obv. ii 8′, 11′, 12′; rev. iii 3, 5, 7. 4.1.4.1.A_1 obv. ii 11′, 12′, 13′; rev. v 2″, 4″, 5″, 6″; rev. vi 10′. 4.1.4.2.A_1 rev. r. c. 13′. 4.2.2 obv. 2. 4.2.6 obv.$^{?}$ 14′, 15′. 4.2.9 obv. 1 (2×), 2, 3, 4, 5, 6, 18, 19, 20, 21, 22, 23, 24, 25, 26, 27; rev. 3′, 4′, 13′, 14′, 15′, 27′. 6.5 rev. 10′, 11′, 13′ (2×), 14′, 16′, 18′ (2×), 23′. 6.13 4′. 8.1.A obv. i 12′; obv. ii 5′; rev. v 2, 6, 8, 15′. 8.1.D obv. i 9′. 8.1.F rev. v 6, 7. 8.1.K rev. vi$^{?}$ 4′, 7′, 9′. 8.8.A 8′. 8.8.B l. c. 8′. 9.1.1 rev. iii 6′, 21′, 22′, 23′, 26′, 27′, 30′, 32′; rev. iv 8′, 10′, 12′, 16′ (2×), 26′, 29′, 30′, 32′, 34′, 37′, 41′, 44′. 9.1.5 obv.$^{!}$ 6, 9, 11; rev.$^{!}$ 9′, 13′, 16′. 9.1.6 obv 1, 3, 6, 11. 9.1.7 obv. 4′. 9.1.8 obv. 6′, 8′, 9′, 15′. 9.1.10.A_1 obv. 3′, 11′. 9.1.11 obv.$^{?}$ 4′, 7′, 9′. 9.1.12 6′. 9.2.2 rev.$^{!}$ iii 22′. 10.1.1.2 rev. iv 7′. 10.1.2.8 rev. r. c. 6′. 10.3.12 obv. i 2′, 6′, 9′, 12′. 11.1.1 r. c. 4′, 7′, 9′. 11.1.7 3′, 6′. 11.3.1 16′, 17′, 20′. 11.5.1 4′, 5′, 7′. 11.6.2 rev. 8′. 11.6.5 obv.$^{?}$ 4, 6, 7, 8. 11.6.6 rev. 4′, 7′, 8′. 12.1.2 7′. 12.3.1 5′
	ŠÀ.BA	9.1.5 rev.$^{!}$ 10′
	ŠÀ.*BA*	4.1.2.3 obv. ii 2′
	Š]À.BA	4.2.9 lo. e. 32′. 8.1.E(A_2) 4′. 8.1.F rev. v 9. 9.1.8 obv. 2′. 11.6.6 rev. 10′. 11.6.9 3′
	Š]À.B[A	10.2.2.4 rev.$^{?}$ r. c. 4. 11.5.1 1′
	ŠÀ].BA	4.1.4.1.A_1 rev. v 1″. 4.2.5 4′. 6.1 obv. 12. 8.8.A 4′
	ŠÀ.B]A	4.1.1.2.A obv. 8′, 16′. 4.1.2.3 obv. ii 6′. 4.1.4.1.A_1 obv. i 5′, 6′, 10′ rev. vi 8′. 9.1.1 rev. iv 21′
	ŠÀ.B[A	4.2.9 obv. 4, 9. 8.1.D obv. i 12′. 8.6 r. c. 9′. 11.6.2 rev. 9′. 11.7.1 r. c. 4′
	ŠÀ.B[A$^{?}$	11.6.4 rev. 2′
	ŠÀ.[B]A	4.1.4.1.A_1 rev. v 9″
	ŠÀ.[BA	11.6.5 obv.$^{?}$ 3

	ŠÀ$^{?}$.[BA	4.2.5 6′
	Š[À.BA	4.2.6 obv.$^{?}$ 13′
ŠÀ-*ŠU*/-*ŠÚ*	‘inside of which’ (introduces contents of a container)	
	ŠÀ-*ŠU*	1.5 lo. e. 15. 2.1.A obv. ii(?) 14′. 2.1.B 5′, 8′. 2.2 obv. 3′. 2.7.A obv. 23. 2.9.A_2 obv. i 11′. 4.2.1.A_1 obv. 5, 6, 7. 8.1.A obv. ii 9′, 19′, 28′; rev. v 18′. 8.1.F obv. i 20′; obv. ii 17′. 9.1.5 rev.$^{!}$ 5′, 9′
	Š]À-*ŠÚ*	4.2.1.A_1 obv. 11
	ŠÀ-*Š*[*U*	2.1.A obv. ii(?) 10′. 8.1.E(A_2) 3′. 10.3.12 obv. i 17′
^{TÚG}ŠÀ.GA/KA.DÙ	‘shawl, scarf(?)’	
	^{TÚG}ŠÀ.GA.DÙ	6.1 obv. 7. 9.1.1 rev. iii 26′; rev. iv 42′. 9.1.10.B 10′. 9.2.7 obv. l. c. 13′
	^{TÚG}Š]À.KA.DÙ	10.3.1 rev. iii 14′
	^{TÚG}ŠÀ.GA.D[Ù	9.1.10.A_1 obv. 6′
	^{TÚG}ŠÀ.GA.[DÙ	2.15 l. c. 7′
see *Lexical Commentary*; = $^{\mathrm{(TÚG)}}$*maššia*-?		
^{LÚ}ŠÀ.TAM	‘treasury official, worker at the palace warehouse’	
	^{LÚ}ŠÀ.TAM	9.1.4.A_1 obv. ii 6
sg. gen.	*ŠA* ^{LÚ}ŠÀ.TAM	9.1.4.A_1 obv. ii 4
see also É(.GAL) $^{\mathrm{(LÚ)}}$ŠÀ.TAM		
$^{\mathrm{(DUG)}}$ŠAB	(a cup or bowl)	
	ŠAB	4.1.1.2.A obv. 11′
ŠÀM	‘sales price’	
	ŠÀM	1.2 obv. 1′; rev. 3′, 4′, 5′, 6′, 7′, 8′
	ŠÀM-*an*	1.2 rev. 1′
	ŠÀ[M-*an*(?)	1.4 3′
	Š[ÀM-*an*(?)	1.5 rev. 25
see also *waši(ya)*-		
ŠE	‘barley; grain’	
	ŠE	1.1.A_1 obv. 13′. 1.1.A_2 obv. 3′, 12; rev. 8. 1.1.A_3 rev. 2′, 4′, 5′, 11′. 12.2.1 obv. 1′, 2′, 3′; rev. 1′, 2′, 6′. 12.3.2 2′
see also *ḫalki*-		
ŠE.NAGA	‘(without ^{URUDU}) soap; (with optional ^{URUDU}) bathtub, washtub’	
	(*NAMADDU*) ŠE.NAGA	4.1.1.3 rev. A 7′
ŠE.NAGA *ḪURRI*	‘Hurrian-styled bathtub/soap’	
	ŠE.NAGA *ḪUR-R*[*I*	2.7.A obv. 26
see also $^{\mathrm{(URUDU)}}$*warpuwaš*, ^{URUDU}ÁB×A, $^{\mathrm{(URUDU)}}$NÍG.ŠU.LUḪ(.ḪA)		
^{URUDU}ŠEN	‘copper kettle, cauldron’	
	^{URUDU}ŠEN	5.1 rev. iii 9, 10. 5.7 rev. iii$^{?}$ 11′, 12′, 17′, 19′, 23′, 24′; rev. iv$^{?}$ 10′
	$^{\mathrm{UR[UDU]}}$ŠEN	5.2 obv. ii 7
	$^{\mathrm{URUD]U}}$ŠEN	5.1 rev. iii 6. 5.7 rev. iii$^{?}$ 15′
	$^{\mathrm{URUDU]}}$ŠEN	5.7 rev. iii$^{?}$ 5′
	^{URUDU}Š]EN	5.1 rev. iii 7
	^{URUDU}ŠE]N	5.7 rev. iii$^{?}$ 10′

	^{URUDU}ŠE[N	4.2.10 5′
see *Lexical Commentary*		
^{URUDU}ŠEN ŠU-*TI*	‘kettle with handle?’	
	^{URUDU}ŠEN ŠU-*TI*	5.7 rev. iii? 11′
see *Lexical Commentary*		
^{URUDU}ŠEN.GAL	‘large (copper) kettle’	
	^{URUDU}ŠEN.GAL	4.1.1.10 obv.? 3′
ŠEŠ	‘brother’	
	ŠEŠ	5.1 obv. ii 6
ŠEŠ(-)*pišate*(-)	?	
	ŠEŠ(-)*pí-ša-te*(-)	5.7 rev. iii? 8′
pl.	(*ABU*) ŠEŠ^{MEŠ}(-)*pí-ša-t*[*e*	5.7 rev. iii? 21′
see *Lexical Commentary*		
ŠID	(1.) ‘number, quantity’	
	ŠID	2.7.A obv. 13
	(2.) ‘to count’	
pret. pl. 1	ŠID-*u-en*	10.1.2.8 rev. r. c. 1′
ŠU	(1.) ‘hand’ (body part)	
	ŠU	4.1.2.1 obv. (i) 1′. 10.1.2.8 rev. r. c. 4′
sg. nom.	ŠU-*aš*	10.3.3 obv.? 5′
sg. gen.	ŠU-*aš*	8.1.D obv. i 8′
pl.	ŠU^{MEŠ}	4.1.1.8 r. c. 6′
abl.	ŠU-*za*	10.2.1.2 obv. 9′, 10′. 10.3.1 rev. iii 10′
	ŠU-*za*	9.1.4.A_1 obv. i 28′
	Š]U-*za*	10.2.1.1 rev. 7′
see also EN ŠU-*TI*, ^{URUDU}ŠEN ŠU-*TI*		
	(2.) ‘responsibility, control’	
ŠU PN	‘(in the) trust/charge of PN’	
sg. nom.	ŠU …	2.2 rev. 11, 12, 16. 2.7.A rev. 1, 2, 6. 3.1.8.A obv. 9′, 12′. 4.1.1.1.A_1 rev. 10′. 4.1.1.1.B_1 rev. iv? 14. 4.1.1.2.A obv. 22′, 24′. 4.1.1.2.B obv. 3, 6, 8. 4.1.1.3 rev. A 5′. 4.1.1.3 rev. B 10, 11. 4.1.3.1 2′. 4.1.3.6 obv. 4′, 6′, 9′, 10′. 4.2.6 obv.? 3′
	⟨ŠU⟩(?)	2.7.A obv. 26
	Š]U …	2.2 rev. 15. 4.1.1.2.A obv. 17′. 4.1.3.6 obv. 12′, rev. 7′
	Š[U …	4.1.1.3 rev. A 9′
	Š[U(?) …	1.5 rev. 24
sg. dat./loc.	*A-NA* ŠU …	4.2.1.A_2 rev. 13′
sg. gen.	*ŠA* ŠU …	4.2.4 obv. 11. 4.2.9 lo. e. 34′
see *Lexical Commentary*		
^{GIŠ}ŠU.ŠÙDUN	‘yoke’	
	^{GIŠ}ŠU.ŠÙDUN	10.3.14 l. c. 7′
	$^{GI]Š}$ŠU.ŠÙDUN	10.3.13 2′. 11.1.1 r. c. 13′
^{MUNUS}ŠU.GI	“Old Woman” (a cult functionary)	
	(GAL) ^{MUNUS}ŠU.GI (SISKUR)	5.1 rev. iii 10

^{URUDU}ŠU.KIN GÍR.TUR	‘sickle(-shaped)-knife’	
	^{URUDU}ŠU.KIN GÍR.TUR	1.1.A_1 obv. 18′
ŠU.NÍGIN	‘total’	
	ŠU.NÍGIN	2.7.A obv. 7. 2.16 rev. v 4. 3.1.1.A_3 rev. iv 3′. 3.1.5.A_2 obv. ii(?) 7′. 3.1.8.A rev. 5′. 3.2.1 rev. 15′. 4.1.1.3 obv. 4, 6, 17. 4.1.1.5 obv. 7. 4.1.1.7 7. 4.1.1.8 r. c. 4′. 4.1.2.5 obv. 6′, 11′. 4.1.3.7 rev. 4′. 4.1.4.2.A_1 rev. r. c. 11′. 4.2.1.A_2 obv. 4′. 4.2.4 obv. 11; rev. 8′. 4.2.6 obv.$^?$ 14′. 8.1.F obv. ii 4′. 9.1.5 rev.$^!$ 4′. 10.1.1.2 rev. iv 12′. 11.3.1 14′. 12.3.4 obv. 7
	Š]U.NÍGIN	11.6.8 4′
	ŠU.NÍ]GIN	4.1.1.2.A obv. 7′
	ŠU.NÍG[IN	5.3 r. c. 11′
	ŠU.NÍ[GIN	4.1.4.3 1′
	ŠU.N[ÍGIN	4.1.1.3 obv. 9
ŠU.NÍGIN.GAL	‘grand total’	
	ŠU.NÍGIN.GAL	10.1.2.1 rev.$^?$ r. c. 5′
	ŠU.N]ÍGIN.GAL	3.1.6 4′
	ŠU.NÍGI]N.GAL	3.1.12 3′
ŠU.NIR	‘(divine) emblem, standard’	
	ŠU.NIR	1.5 obv. 5
= ^{GIŠ}*ŠURINNU*		
ŠU.SI	(1.) ‘finger’ (cult vessel or object)	
	ŠU.SI	10.3.3 obv.$^?$ 10′
	(GAL) ŠU.SI	4.1.1.2.B obv. 8
	ŠU.[SI	8.1.A rev. v 25′
	(2.) ‘finger/inch’ (unit of length)	
	ŠU.SI	10.2.1.1 obv. 2′. 10.3.10 r. c. 9′
	ŠU.S[I	10.3.10 r. c. 2′, 7′
	Š[U.SI	10.3.10 r. c. 3′
$^{\text{(URUDU)}}$ŠU.ŠÈ.LÁ	(a vessel) “krater(?)”	
	ŠU.ŠÈ.LÁ	9.1.5 rev.$^!$ 13′
	^{URUDU}ŠU.ŠÈ.LÁ	4.2.9 lo. e. 33′
see *Lexical Commentary*		
^{GIŠ}ŠU.TAG.GA	?	
	^{GIŠ}ŠU.TAG.GA	4.1.4.6 obv. 7′
see *Lexical Commentary*		
$^{\text{(NA}_4\text{)}}$ŠU.U	(a hard stone) ‘basalt(?)’	
	ŠU.U	2.5 rev. 7′. 2.16 obv. i 9′. 8.1.A rev. v 15′
	^{N}]$^{\text{A}_4\text{(?)}}$ŠU.U	8.3 rev. 2′
	$^{\text{NA}_4}$Š[U.U	12.1.2 4′
= $^{\text{NA}_4}$*kunkunuzi*-?		
$^{\text{(GIŠ/URUDU)}}$ŠUKUR	‘spear, spit, peg’	
	ŠUKUR	2.7.A rev. 5. 2.18 9′. 5.2 obv. ii 3. 5.7 rev. iv$^?$ 5′
	^{GIŠ}ŠUKUR	9.1.5 rev.$^!$ 14′, 16′

	^{URUDU}ŠUKUR	5.7 rev. iii? 15′, 19′
	^{UR}]^{UDU}ŠUKUR	5.8 5′
ŠUL.PÁT	‘(drinking) straw, tube’	
	ŠUL.PÁT	2.2 rev. 14. 2.13 rev.? 1′. 4.1.1.1.A$_1$ rev. 2′. 5.1 obv. i 3′; obv. ii 4′, 6′, 8′ (2×), 9′; rev. iii 11′
	ŠU]L.PÁT	5.1 obv. i 4′
	ŠU[L.PÁT	8.1.A rev. v 27′
pl.	ŠUL.PÁT$^{\text{ḪI.A}}$	4.1.1.1.A$_2$ rev. 4′
see also *Lexical Commentary*; = $^{\text{(GIŠ)}}$*ŠULPATU*		
$^{\text{(GIŠ)}}$ŠÚ.A	‘chair, stool (esp. for men)’	
	^{GIŠ}ŠÚ.A	2.17 obv.? r. c. 10′. 11.6.2 rev. 2′
	^{GIŠ}Š[Ú.A	2.17 obv.? r. c. 10′
sg. nom.-acc. n.	^{GIŠ}ŠÚ.A-*ḫi*	2.17 obv.? r. c. 10′
sg. dat./loc.	*A-NA* … ^{GIŠ}ŠÚ.A	4.1.4.9 obv. 4
see also GADA (*A-NA*) $^{\text{(GIŠ)}}$ŠÚ.A		
TA.ÀM	‘each (following a number or unit of measurement)’	
	TA!(text: ŠA or ⸢TA⸣).ÀM	12.3.2 7′
	TA].ÀM	12.3.2 2′
See also *dapi-*, *dapiant-*		
TAR	‘to cut (off), separate’	
pres. pl. 3	TAR-*an-z*[*i*	5.7 rev. iii? 10′
$^{\text{NA}_4}$TI	‘“life”-stone’	
	$^{\text{NA}_4}$T[I	8.1.D obv. i 6′
see *Lexical Commentary*		
TI$_8^{\text{MUŠEN}}$	‘eagle’	
	TI$_8^{\text{MUŠEN}}$	1.5 lo. e. 17. 9.1.1 rev. iv 6′. 11.2.4 2′, 3′. 11.2.5 5′
	TI$_8$]^{MUŠEN}	4.2.11 5′
	TI$_8^{\text{MU}}$]^{ŠEN}(?)	11.2.3 4′
	(GÚ) TI$_8^{\text{MUŠEN}}$	8.1.A rev. v 25′. 9.1.1 rev. iv 11′
	(*BIBRU*) TI$_8^{\text{MUŠEN}}$	9.1.4.A$_1$ obv. ii 15; rev. iv 3′
see also (KI.LÁ) TI$_8^{\text{MUŠEN}}$, SAG.DU TI$_8^{\text{MUŠEN}}$		
^{GIŠ}TIBULA	(a musical instrument)	
	^{GIŠ}TIBU[LA(?)	2.5 rev. 6′
TIL	(a scribal notation) ‘finished, complete’	
	TIL	4.1.1.5 up. e. 0
see also *zinnant-*, *GAMRU*, *QATÛ*		
TÚG	‘garment’	
	TÚG	1.2 rev. 3′. 2.7.A obv. 7 (3×), 10 (2×), 13. 2.15 l. c. 8′. 3.2.1 obv. 14, 20; rev. 7′, 16′. 3.2.5 r. c. 4′. 4.1.1.2.B rev. 1. 4.1.4.7 obv. 1. 4.2.6 obv.? 14′. 4.2.9 obv. 1, 18, 19. 6.5 obv. 6′, 15′; rev. 3′, 4′, 5′, 6′, 10′, 13′, 16′, 21′, 23′, 27′. 6.6 obv. 3′. 6.9 obv. 1′ (2×), 3′, 6′ (2×), 10. 6.13 2′, 7′, 8′. 8.1.D rev. iv 2′. 8.1.E(A$_1$) obv. iii 6′, 7′ (2×), 8′; rev. iv 2′, 4′, 8′. 8.1.F obv. i 9′; obv. ii 9′, 17′. 8.1.G obv. r. c. 9′. 8.1.H rev. r. c. 7′, 8′. 8.1.K rev. v? 3′. 8.3 obv. 7′.

		8.8.A 4′. 8.8.B l. c. 3′, 4′. 9.1.6 obv. 3, 4, 13, 15. 10.1.1.1 rev.$^{?}$ 13′. 10.1.2.1 obv.$^{?}$ r. c. 1′. 11.1.3 6′. 11.1.4 2′. 11.6.1 3, 5, 7, 8. 11.6.2 rev. 8′. 11.6.5 obv.$^{?}$ 1. 11.6.10 2′
	TÚG (MUNUS-*TI*)	1.5 lo. e. 15
	T]ÚG	8.1.I rev. r. c. 6′
	TÚ]G	3.2.2 obv.$^{?}$ 3′. 4.2.9 obv. 5. 8.8.A 2′, 3′. 11.6.6 rev. 3′
	TÚ[G	4.2.6 rev.$^{?}$ 2′. 11.6.2 obv. 4′
	T[ÚG	6.5 rev. 8′. 11.6.2 obv. 6′
sg. nom.	TÚG-*TUM*	1.1.A_2 rev. 6
pl. nom.	TÚG^{MEŠ}	6.9 obv. 7′. 8.1.H rev. r. c. 6′
	T]ÚG^{MEŠ}	8.1.I rev. r. c. 5′
	TÚG$^{M]EŠ}$	8.1.D rev. iv 8′
	TÚG$^{ḪI.A}$	12.3.7 6′
	TÚG$^{\langle ḪI\rangle.A}$	12.3.7 8′
pl. acc.	TÚG-*TI*	6.1 rev. B 7
(TÚG) *ḫurliš(š)a-*	(a garment in the Ḫurliš(š)an fashion?)	
	ḫur-li-ša	6.10 2′
	ḫur-l[i-ša	11.6.7 6′
	TÚG *ḫur-li-ša*	11.6.5 obv.$^{?}$ 9
	TÚG *ḫur-li-iš-ša*	4.2.6 obv.$^{?}$ 6′
	TÚ]G *ḫur-li-[š]a*	11.6.6 rev. 1′
	TÚG *ḫur-li-š[a*	8.1.F obv. i 10′
	TÚG *ḫur-li-[ša*	8.1.E(A_1) obv. iii 9′
abbr.	*ḫur.*	3.2.1 obv. 14
	TÚG *ḫur.*	3.2.1 rev. 16′
	TÚG (GADA) *ḫur.*	11.6.1 5, 11
see *Lexical Commentary*		
(TÚG) *ikkuwaniya-*	(a garment in the Ikkuwanian fashion)	
	ik-ku-wa-ni-ia	6.5 rev. 23′
	TÚG *ik-ku-wa-ni-ia*	2.9.A_1 obv. i 7′. 8.1.E(A_1) obv. ii 2. 8.1.F rev. v 8
	TÚG *i]k-ku-wa-ni-ia*	8.1.E(A_1) obv. ii 9
	TÚG *ik-k]u-wa-ni-i[a]*	8.3 obv. 5′
	TÚG *ik-ku-w[a]-ni-ia*	2.12 obv.$^{!}$ ii 5′
	TÚG *ik-ku-wa-ni-i[a*	2.9.A_3 obv. ii 2′
	TÚG *ik-[ku-wa-ni-ia*	6.12 2′
(TÚG/KUŠ) *kapi(r)t(t)aš(š)amna-*	(a garment in the Kapitašamnan fashion)	
pl. nom.-acc. n.	*ka-pir$_x$-ta-aš-š[àm-na*(?)	8.1.I rev. r. c. 2′
	TÚG *ka-pir$_x$-ta-aš-šà[m-na*	8.1.H rev. r. c. 3′
	ka-pí-ta-šàm-na	4.2.9 obv. 20; rev. 12′
	ka-pí-it-ta-šàm-na	4.2.9 obv. 2. 8.1.D rev. iv 10′
	ka-p]í-ta-šàm-na	8.8.B l. c. 6′
	(TÚG/KUŠ) *ka-p]í-ta-aš-ša-[am-na*(?)	10.2.1.5 2′
	ka-pí-ta]-šàm-na	9.1.6 obv. 11
	(TÚG) *ka-pí-ta-šàm*(?)*]-na*	11.1.5 2′
	ka-pí-ta-šàm-n[a	8.8.A 5′
	ka-pí-it-ta-šàm-[na	8.1.D rev. iv 9′

	ka-pí-ta-[šàm-na	8.1.H rev. r. c. 8′
	ka-pí-it-[ta-šàm-na	9.2.9 rev.? 2′
	ka-pí-[ta-šàm-na	11.6.2 rev. 12′
	ka-[pí-it-ta-šàm-na	8.1.I rev. r. c. 7′
	k[a-pí-ta-šàm-na	8.1.H rev. r. c. 7′
	KUŠ *ka-pí-it-ta-aš-ša-am-na*	9.1.1 rev. iii 29′
	TÚG *ka-pí-ta-šàm-na*	3.2.1 rev. 15′. 8.1.E(A_1) rev. iv 4′
	TÚG *ga-pí-ta-šàm-na*	8.1.E(A_1) rev. v 9′
	TÚG *ka-pí-i]t-ta-ša-am-na*	6.6 rev. 3′
	TÚG *ka-pí-t[a-šàm-na*	8.1.D rev. iv 3′
	TÚG *k[a-pí-ta-šàm-na*(?)	11.1.8 2′
abbr.	*ka-pí-ta-šàm.*	3.2.1 obv. 14
	ka-pí-ta-š]àm.	4.2.6 obv.? 17′
	TÚG *ka-pí-ta-šàm.*	11.6.1 3
see *Lexical Commentary*; see also ^{URU}*Kapitašamna-*		
TÚG *karkišili-*	(a garment in the Karkišan fashion)	
sg. nom.	TÚG *kar-ki-ši-li-iš*	9.1.11 obv.? 6′
	TÚG *kar-k]i-ši-liš*(?)	8.1.K rev. vi? 8′
	TÚG *kar-ki-ši]-liš*(?)	8.1.G obv. l. c. 7′
(TÚG) $^{(URU)}$*Kummanni-*	(a garment in the Kummannian fashion)	
	kum-man-ni	6.10 4′
	^{URU}*kum-man-ni*	8.8.A 6′
	^{URU}*kum-ma]n-ni*	8.8.B l. c. 7′
(TÚG) *tap(p)a/išpa-*	(a garment in the Tapašpan fashion)	
sg. gen.	*tap-pa-aš-pa-aš*	4.2.6 obv.? 11′
stem	*ta-pa-aš-pa*	4.2.6 obv.? 16′. 6.5 rev. 16′
	ta-pa-aš-[pa	6.5 rev. 13′
	tap-pa-aš-pa	4.2.9 rev. 12′. 9.1.10.A_1 obv. 10′. 9.2.9 rev.? 7′
	TÚG *ta-pa-aš-pa*	6.5 obv. 3′, 4′
	TÚG *tap-pa-aš-pa*	8.1.H rev. r. c. 9′. 9.1.6 obv. 6. 11.6.1 11
	TÚG *tap-pa-a-aš-pa*	8.1.F rev. v 11
	TÚG *tap-pa-[aš-pa*	8.1.K rev. v? 5′
	TÚG *ta-piš-pa*	8.1.D rev. iv 11′
	TÚG *ta]-piš-pa*	8.1.D rev. iv 3′
	TÚG *ta-piš-p]a*	8.1.E(A_1) rev. v 9′
	TÚG *ta-[piš-pa*(?)	8.1.F rev. vi 9
see *Lexical Commentary*		
(TÚG) *wašḫaniya-*	(a garment in the Wašḫaniyan fashion)	
	wa-aš-ḫa-[ni-ia	4.2.7 4′
	wa-aš-ḫa-ni-ia	3.2.1 rev. 16′
	TÚG *w]a-aš-ḫa-ni-ia*	3.2.1 obv. 1
	TÚG *wa-a[š-ḫa-ni-ia*(?)	11.6.1 11
see also ^{TÚG}GÚ *wašḫaniya-*		
TÚG ÉRIN^{MEŠ}	'"army"-cloths'	
	TÚG ÉRIN^{MEŠ}	8.1.F obv. i 21′; rev. vi 13, 15. 11.1.7 6′
	TÚ]G ÉRIN^{MEŠ}	8.1.F rev. vi 15
	TÚG ÉRI]N$^{ME[Š}$	8.1.F rev. vi 17

TÚG UGU SUD-*an*	‘cloth cover’ (lit. a “spread over” cloth)	
sg. nom.	TÚ]G UGU SUD-*an-za*	3.2.2 obv.$^{?}$ 3′
sg. nom.-acc. n.	TÚG UGU SUD-*an*	11.6.1 11
see also SUD		
TÚG ŠA.KIŠ	(?)	
	TÚG ŠA.KIŠ	2.7.A rev. 6
^{GIŠ}TÚG	‘boxwood; box tree’	
material		
	^{GIŠ}TÚG	4.2.4 rev. 6′. 4.2.9 rev. 2′. 4.2.10 8′. 9.1.10.A_1 obv. 8′. 9.1.10.B 12′. 11.1.4 4′
^{GIŠ}TUKUL	‘mace; weapon; (agricultural) tool’	
	^{GIŠ}TUKUL	2.8 obv. 2. 3.1.12 7′. 5.2 rev. iii 3′. 8.1.A rev. v 1. 8.6 r. c. 3′. 12.3.1 7′
	$^{\text{GIŠ!?}}$TUKUL	7.1 obv. 19′
pl. dat./loc.	*A-NA* ^{GIŠ}TUKUL$^{\text{ḪI.A}}$	5.1 obv. ii 12′
see also LÚ ^{GIŠ}TUKUL.GÍD.DA		
TUR	‘small’	
	TUR	1.2 rev. 3′. 2.1.A obv. ii(?) 1′, 4′, 6′, 13′, 14′. 2.1.B 1′, 4′, 5′, 7′. 2.2 obv. 2′, 3′; rev. 1. 2.5 rev. 5′. 2.6 3′, 4′. 2.7.A obv. 20, 21, 22. 2.9.A_2 obv. i 9′. 2.9.A_3 obv. ii 7′, 10′. 2.12 obv.$^{!}$ ii 10′. 2.16 obv. i 4′. 3.1.2 obv. l. c. 9′. 3.1.8.A obv. 6′, 13′, 17′. 3.1.11.A 4. 3.1.11.B 3′. 4.1.1.2.B rev. 3. 4.1.4.8 4′, 8′. 4.2.1.A_2 obv. 6′. 4.2.2 2. 4.2.4 rev. 9′. 4.2.7 7′. 4.2.9 obv. 5. 5.1 rev. iii 2. 6.9 obv. 1′, 10′. 6.10 7′. 8.1.A obv. i 12′; obv. ii 24′, 28′; rev. v 6, 14′, 18′, 19′. 8.1.D obv. i 11′; rev. iv 4′. 8.1.F obv. i 17′. 9.1.4.A_1 obv. ii 3, 26. 9.1.5 rev.$^{!}$ 4′. 9.1.8 obv. 14′, 15′. 9.2.4 obv. i 13′, 16′. 9.2.9 obv.$^{?}$ 9′. 10.1.1.2 rev. iv 3′, 4′. 10.1.2.6 5′. 10.1.2.8 rev. r. c. 6′. 10.2.1.1 obv. 4′, 12′. 10.3.3 obv.$^{?}$ 5′. 10.3.5 8′. 10.3.12 obv. i 17′. 11.1.7 3′. 11.5.2 rev.$^{?}$ r. c. 2′. 11.6.1 8. 11.6.10 2′
	TUR$^{!}$	2.9.A_2 11′
	TUR	11.5.2 rev.$^{?}$ r. c. 2′
	T]UR	8.1.D obv. i 1′
	TU]R	8.1.C 2′
	TU[R	11.6.5 obv.$^{?}$ 1
	T[UR	8.1.A obv. ii 12′
	T[UR$^{?}$	2.1.B 10′. 8.6 r. c. 4′
pl.	TUR.TUR	2.1.B 8′. 2.9.A_3 obv. ii 13′. 2.16 obv. i 6′. 4.2.1.A_1 obv. 4. 9.1.5 rev.$^{!}$ 8′, 10′. 11.6.11 4′
	T]UR.TUR	9.1.5 obv.$^{!}$ 12. 11.4.2 obv. 4′
	TU]R.TUR	9.1.5 obv.$^{!}$ 14
see also $^{\text{(URUDU)}}$GÍR.TUR, ^{GIŠ}PAN.TUR, PÌRIG.TUR, SAḪ.TUR		
TUŠ	‘to be sitting (act.); sit down (mid.)’	
pres. sg. 3	TUŠ-*zi*	9.1.1 rev. iv 17′. 10.3.1 rev. iii 11′
see also *eš-*		

U$_4$.SAKAR, ^{D}U$_4$-*aš* SAKAR	'(divinized) lunula, crescent moon'	
	U$_4$.SAKAR	2.7.A obv. 26. 10.1.2.1 rev.$^?$ l. c. 5
	U$_4$.SAKA[R	11.3.1 23′
	^{D}U$_4$-*aš* SAKAR	9.1.4.A$_1$ obv. ii 7
Luw. sg. nom.-acc. n.	^{D}U$_4$-*aš* SAKAR-*za*	9.1.1 rev. iv 15′
see *Lexical Commentary*		
^{UZU}UBUR	'(female) breast'	
	^{UZU}UBUR	10.2.1.7 rev.$^?$ 5′
UD.NU	(?)	
	UD.NU	11.6.2 rev. 12′
UDU	'sheep'	
	UDU	2.3 1. 10.1.2.4 l. c. 15′. 12.1.1 r. c. 6′, 7′
	(KUŠ) UDU	4.1.3.6 obv. 7′, 9′
	(KUŠ) UDU$^!$(text: 3)	4.1.3.6 rev. 2′
	(KUŠ) UD]U	4.1.3.6 obv. 13′
UDU.KUR.RA	'mouflon, mountain sheep'	
	UDU.KUR.RA	9.1.1 rev. iv 13′. 9.1.5 obv.$^!$ 3. 10.2.1.2 obv. 10′
	UD]U.KUR.RA	9.1.5 obv.$^!$ 11
	(GÚ) UDU.KUR.RA	10.2.2.4 obv.$^?$ r. c. 5′
	(*BIBRU*) UDU.KUR.RA	9.1.1 rev. iv 10′
UDU.ŠIR	'ram'	
	UDU/MÁŠ].ŠIR	9.1.15 3′
UGU	'up, over; upper side'	
	UGU	2.2 obv. 11′. 9.1.5 rev.$^!$ 2
	UGU (*arḫa* DÙ-)	11.6.1 7, 8
	UGU (*ḫamenkuaš*)	6.13 1′. 8.4 rev. 5′
	UG]U (*ḫamenkuaš*)	4.1.1.2.B obv. 10
	UGU (*waššanza*)	2.1.A obv. ii(?) 9′, 11′. 2.1.B 2′, 3′. 2.2 obv. 5′, 7′, 12′. 8.1.A obv. ii 24′. 8.1.D rev. iv 7′
	U]GU (*waššanza*)	8.1.B rev. 8′
	UGU (SUD-)	3.2.2 obv.$^?$ 3′. 11.6.1 11
see also *šara*		
UGU *arḫa* DÙ	'"finished" on top'	
see *šer arḫa iya-*		
UGU *ḫamenkuaš*	'brooch, clasp(?)'	
vb. subst. sg. gen.	UGU *ḫa-me-en-ku-aš*	4.1.1.2.B obv. 10. 8.4 rev. 5′
	UGU *ḫa-mi-en-ku-[aš*	6.13 1′
^{URUDU}UGU *laḫuwaš*	'ladle(?)' (lit. an implement of "pouring over")	
	^{URUDU}UGU *la-ḫu-aš*	4.2.9 lo. e. 33′
UGULA *LIM*	'chief of the thousand'	
	UGULA(?)] *LI-IM*	5.7 rev. iv$^?$ 9′
UMBIN (ZABAR)	'(bronze) pin, hair clasp (*vel sim.*)'	
	UMBIN ZABAR	4.2.4 obv. 12
	U]M[BIN$^?$	4.1.2.4 8′
= *KIRISSU*?		

UR.GI$_7$	'dog'	
	UR.G[I$^?$	11.2.5 6′
sg. gen.	UR.GI$_7$-*aš*	12.3.6 3′
see also LÚ KÁ UR.GI$_7$		
UR.MAḪ	'lion'	
	UR.MAḪ	4.1.1.3 rev. A 7′. 4.2.12 1′. 9.1.1 rev. iii 38′. 9.1.4.A$_2$ r. c. 5′. 9.1.15 6′. 9.2.14 3′. 10.3.3 obv.$^?$ 7′
	U]R.MAḪ	4.1.1.1.A$_1$ rev. 3′. 10.1.2.6 9′. 10.2.2.4 obv.$^?$ r. c. 3′. 10.3.1 rev. iii 11′.
	U[R].MAḪ	9.1.1 rev. iii 36′
	UR.M[AḪ	2.2 rev. 6
	UR.[MAḪ	9.2.1 rev. iii 7′
	(GÌR) UR.MAḪ	2.7.A obv. 2, 12, 20. 2.7.B rev. 6′. 2.9.A$_1$ obv. i 4′. 4.2.1.A$_1$ obv. 4. 8.1.F rev. v 14. 9.1.5 rev.$^!$ 10′.
	(GÌR) U]R.MAḪ	2.16 obv. i 2′
	(GÚ) UR.MAḪ	6.1 obv. 17. 9.1.1 rev. iv 22′. 9.1.4.A$_1$ obv. ii 18
	(GÚ) UR.M[AḪ	9.1.15 4′
	(GÚ) UR.[MAḪ	8.1.A rev. v 24′
	(SAG.DU) UR.MAḪ	9.1.1 rev. iv 17′. 9.1.4.A$_1$ obv. ii 19
	(SAG.DU-*SÚ*) UR.MAḪ	9.1.9 rev. iv 3′
	(*BIBRU*) UR.MAḪ	9.1.4.A$_1$ obv. ii 16
sg. gen.	*ŠA* UR.MAḪ	9.1.7 obv. 3′
ÚR	'limb; penis; lap'	
	ÚR	10.2.2.3 obv.$^?$ l. c. 4′
sg. dat./loc.	ÚR-*ši*	4.1.1.1.B$_1$ rev. iii$^?$ 17
pl.	ÚR^{MEŠ}	10.2.2.4 obv.$^?$ r. c. 6′
URU	(1.) 'city, town'	
sg. dat-loc.	URU-*ri*	10.1.1.2 rev. iv 15′
	(2.) 'mural crown?'	
sg. nom.	URU-*LUM*	1.5 obv. 1
see *Lexical Commentary*		
URUDU	'copper'	
	URUDU	1.4 4′. 3.1.1.A$_1$ obv. ii 6′, 15′. 3.1.1.A$_2$ rev. v 11′, 14′. 3.1.1.A$_3$ obv. iii 5′, 12′; rev. iv 13′. 3.1.2 obv. l. c. 3′, 5′, 6′, 10′, 12′. 3.1.5.A$_1$ obv. i(?) 5′. 3.1.7.A$_2$ obv. ii 7a′. 3.1.8.A rev. 3′, 5′, 7′, 9′, 10′. 4.1.1.1.A$_1$ obv. 16′. 4.1.2.3 obv. ii 5′, 10′; rev. iii 5. 5.1 rev. iii 12. 5.2 obv. ii 1, 5, 6, 9, 13. 5.5 rev. iii 2′, 3′. 5.7 rev. iii$^?$ 5′, 9′, 26′. 9.1.4.A$_1$ obv. ii 2
	URUDU$^?$	3.1.3 rev.$^?$ 1′. 4.2.8 1′
	U]RUDU	3.1.2 obv. l. c. 13′. 3.1.5.A$_2$ obv. ii(?) 15′. 3.1.7.A$_1$ obv. i 15′
	UR]UDU	3.1.8.A rev. 1′
	URUD]U	3.1.1.A$_3$ obv. iii 16′. 4.1.2.3 rev. iii 1
	URUD]U$^?$	3.1.8.A rev. 12′
	URU[DU	3.1.2 rev. l. c. 3′. 3.1.5.A$_2$ obv. ii(?) 5′. 4.1.2.3 rev. iii 8
	UR[UDU	3.1.5.A$_2$ obv. ii(?) 12′

	URUDU (*ŠAL-MU*)	3.1.1.A$_1$ obv. ii 14′; obv. iii 8′, 11′. 3.1.1.A$_2$ rev. v 6′, 8′, 10′. 3.1.1.A$_3$ rev. iv 15′, 16′
	URUD]U (*ŠAL-MU*)	3.1.1.A$_1$ obv. ii 6′
sg. gen.	*ŠA* URUD[U	12.1.2 5′
inst.	*QA-DU* URUDU	4.1.1.1.A$_1$ obv. 6′, 8′, 10′, 11′, 14′, 21′, 23′. 4.1.1.2.A obv. 10′. 4.1.1.2.B obv. 1
	QA-DU [URU]DU	4.1.1.2.B obv. 4
	QA-DU URU[DU	4.1.1.1.A$_1$ obv. 15′
material		
	URUDU	1.2 rev. 5′, 9′, 10′. 1.5 lo. e. 18; rev. 19. 2.5 rev. 3′. 2.7.A rev. 4 (2×), 5. 3.1.1.A$_2$ rev. v 2′, 3′. 3.1.1.A$_3$ obv. iii 14′. 3.1.2 obv. l. c. 2′ (2×), 4′ (2×). 5.7 rev. iii$^{?}$ 6′. 8.5 rev. iii(?) 3′, 5′; rev. iv(?) 2′. 9.1.4.A$_1$ obv. i 2 (2×), 20′; obv. ii 1. 9.1.5 rev.$^{!}$ 2′, 3′. 9.1.7 rev. 3. 9.2.4 rev. iii 11′. 10.2.1.2 obv. 2′, 7′, 12′ (2×), 13′, 14′, 15′. 10.3.1 rev. iii 3′. 10.3.5 2′, 5′ (2×). 12.1.1 l. c. 4′, 7′; r. c. 6′
	URUDU$^{?}$	10.3.5 11′
	U]RUDU	12.1.1 r. c. 10′
	URUD[U	3.1.2 rev. l. c. 2′. 4.2.8 6′. 5.2 obv. ii 2. 10.3.5 4′.
	URU[DU	10.3.5 2′
	URU[DU$^{?}$	10.3.7 1′
^{D}UTU-*ŠI*	"His Majesty" (title of reigning Hittite king)	
	^{D}UTU-*ŠI*	2.12 obv.$^{!}$ ii 2′, 7′. 2.9.A$_3$ obv. i 9′, 11′. 6.1 lo. e. 9″. 7.1 rev. 9′
$^{DUG/URUDU}$ÚTUL	'pot, jar'	
	^{DUG}ÚTUL	9.1.8 obv. 14′. 10.3.5 8′
	^{URUDU}ÚTUL	4.2.9 lo. e. 24′.
UZ$_6$	'goat'	
	(KUŠ) UZ$_6$	4.1.3.6 obv. 13′
	U]Z$_6$$^{?}$	9.1.5 obv.$^{!}$ 5
sg. gen.	*UZ$_6$*-*aš*	12.3.6 6′
ZA.GÌN	'blue'	
	ZA.GÌN	2.7.A obv. 1, 8, 9 (2×), 10. 2.7.B rev. 5′. 3.2.1 obv. 1, 13. 4.1.3.2 rev. 1′, 5′. 4.1.3.3 8′. 4.1.4.1.A$_1$ rev. v 4″, 9″. 4.1.4.1.A$_2$ obv. ii 4′, 7′. 4.1.4.2.A$_1$ rev. r. c. 2′, 4′, 7′, 10′, 13′. 4.1.4.2.A$_2$ obv. r. c. 1′, 4′, 10′. 4.1.4.4 1′, 5′, 9′. 4.1.4.5 obv. r. c. 2′; rev. r. c. 7′. 4.1.4.6 obv. 13′; rev. 17′. 4.2.9 obv. 1, 6, 10, 19, 26, 27. 6.5 rev. 7′, 10′, 13′ (2×), 18′. 6.8 2′. 6.9 obv. 8′ (2×). 6.10 5′, 9′. 6.12 5′. 8.1.E(A$_1$) obv. iii 8′. 8.1.F obv. i 9′, 12′, 16′, 17′; rev. v 10. 8.1.H rev. r. c. 8′. 8.1.I rev. r. c. 7′. 8.1.K rev. vi$^{?}$ 7′. 8.2 l. c. 2″. 9.1.1 rev. iv 43′. 9.1.8 obv. 8′, 11′. 9.2.1 obv. ii 21′, 23′. 10.1.2.1 obv.$^{?}$ r. c. 1′. 11.1.5 2′. 11.1.8 2′. 11.2.2 5′. 11.6.1 8, 9. 11.6.5 obv.$^{?}$ 7. 11.6.6 rev. 4′, 6′, 10′
	ZA$^{!}$(text: ḪA).GÌN	4.2.6 obv.$^{?}$ 19′. 9.1.1 rev. iii 39′. 11.6.6 rev. 2′

	ZA.GÌN!	4.1.4.6 obv. 9′
	ZA.GÌN	11.6.5 obv.? 8
	Z[A.GÌ]N	4.1.4.4 12′
	Z]A.GÌN	8.1.D rev. iv 6′, 10′
	ZA].GÌN	4.2.9 rev. 14′. 9.1.11 rev.? 3′
	ZA.G]ÌN	8.1.E(A_1) rev. v 11′
	ZA.GÌ]N	4.1.4.1.A_2 obv. ii 10′
	ZA.G[ÌN	4.2.9 obv. 18. 6.6 obv. 8′. 11.1.8 4′. 11.6.8 1′, 5′
	ZA.[GÌN	4.2.6 obv.? 16′. 8.1.E(A_3) rev. vi 3
	ZA?.[GÌN(?)	4.2.6 obv.? 12′
	Z[A.GÌN	4.2.9 obv. 21
$^{(NA_4)}$ZA.GÌN	'lapis lazuli, "blue stone"'	
	*^{NA_4}*ZA.GÌN	8.1.A rev. v 19′
	$^{N]A_4}$ZA.GÌN	12.1.3 2′
material		
	ZA.GÌN	8.1.A obv. i 6′; obv. ii 12′. 9.1.1 rev. iii 16′. 9.1.5 obv.! 2, 12. 9.2.9 obv.? 12′. 10.2.2.2 obv.? l. c. 3′, 5′, 7′. 10.2.2.3 obv.? l. c. 4′ (2×), 6′, 7′ (2×). 10.2.2.4 obv.? r. c. 2′, 3′
	Z]A.GÌN	10.2.2.2 obv.? l. c. 2′
	$^{(NA_4)}$ZA.G]ÌN	4.2.5 3′
	ZA.GÌ[N	10.2.1.3 6′
	^{NA_4}ZA.GÌN	3.1.8.A obv. 15′. 4.2.4 obv. 9. 8.1.E(A_1) rev. v 3′. 9.1.1 rev. iii 21′; rev. iv 20′. 9.1.4.A_1 obv. ii 15, 18, 22. 9.2.1 obv. ii 11′, 12′, 14′ (2×), 15′. 9.2.3 obv. (ii) 6″. 9.2.5 obv. i(?) 7′, 9′. 9.2.13 3′. 10.1.1.1 rev.? 7′. 10.3.1 rev. iii 8′. 10.3.11 l. c. 4′. 11.2.2 4′, 5′. 11.2.3 3′. 11.2.4 rev.? l. c. 6′
	$^{N]A_4}$ZA.GÌN	9.2.5 obv. i(?) 12′. 11.2.2 1′
	$^{NA_4]}$ZA.GÌN	3.1.8.A obv. 11′
	^{NA_4}Z]A.GÌN	9.1.4.A_1 obv. ii 27
	^{NA_4}ZA].GÌN	9.1.5 obv.! 4
	^{NA_4}Z[A.GÌ]N	11.2.2 7′
	^{NA_4}Z[A.GÌ]N(?)	2.1.B 1′
	^{NA_4}ZA.GÌ[N	10.2.1.3 4′. 10.2.2.4 rev.? r. c. 3. 12.1.2 2′
	^{NA_4}ZA.G[ÌN	8.1.A obv. ii 9′. 9.2.2 rev.! iii 2′, 11′, 13′, 15′. 10.1.2.4 l. c. 6′
	^{NA_4}Z[A.GÌN	8.1.A obv. ii 13′. 9.1.1 rev. iii 13′. 9.2.13 3′
	^{NA_4}Z[A.GÌN(?)	2.1.A obv. ii(?) 6′
^{NA_4}ZA.GÌN DUR_{10}	'"fresh/pure" lapis lazuli'	
material		
	^{NA_4}ZA.GÌN DU[R_{10}	3.1.8.A obv. 3′
	^{NA_4}ZA.GÌN D[UR_{10}	3.1.8.A obv. 7′
see *Lexical Commentary*		
ZA.ḪUM	(a drinking vessel)	
	ZA.ḪUM("SIG_4")	9.1.7 obv. 7′. 10.2.1.1 obv. 11′
	Z]A.ḪUM("SIG_4")	10.2.1.1 obv. 10′
see *Lexical Commentary*; = *SĀḪU*		

ZABAR	'bronze'	
	ZABAR	6.1 rev. B 6.
	ZA]BAR	11.1.6 l. c. 8′
material		
	ZABAR	1.1.A₁ obv. 3′, 5′, 6′, 7′, 9′ (2×). 1.1.A₂ rev. 5 (2×). 1.1.A₃ rev. 10′. 2.8 obv. 2. 3.1.1.A₂ rev. vi 3′. 4.1.1.4 2′. 4.2.11 6′. 8.1.A rev. v 5. 9.1.1 rev. iii 9′, 10′; rev. iv 40′. 9.1.5 rev.! 14′, 16′. 9.1.7 rev. 1, 2. 9.1.10.A₁ rev. 2′. 9.1.10.A₂ rev. 8′. 9.1.11 obv.? 12′. 9.1.14 obv. r. c. 4′. 9.2.4 rev. iv 3, 6. 9.2.6 obv. i 13′, 14′. 10.3.3 obv.? 8′, 9′. 10.3.5 6′, 7′ (2×), 8′ (2×). 10.3.11 l. c. 10′. 12.1.1 l. c. 4′
	ZABAR!(text: UD.KA.⟨BAR⟩)	9.2.6 obv. i 12′.
	Z]ABAR	9.1.13 4′. 11.1.6 l. c. 9′
	ZA]BAR	12.1.1 l. c. 6′; r. c. 9′, 12′. 12.1.3 5′
	ZA]BAR?	11.7.3 rev.? 4
	ZABA[R	4.2.4 obv. 12. 11.1.6 l. c. 12′
	ZAB[AR	4.2.11 5′, 7′. 11.2.6 2′
	Z[ABAR	1.1.A₁ obv. 7′
	Z[ABAR?	2.8 obv. 3. 10.2.2.2 obv.? l. c. 3′
gen.	*ŠA* ZABAR	10.1.1.1 rev.? 12′. 10.2.1.1 obv. 10′
ZAG	'right, righthand side'	
	ZAG?	10.2.2.3 obv.? l. c. 13′
abl.	ZAG-*za*	9.2.7 rev. r. c. 8′. 10.2.1.1 obv. 5′. 10.2.1.2 obv. 9′
(UZU)ZAG.UDU	'shoulder, side'	
pl.	ZAG.UDU^MEŠ	11.2.2 6′
see also GADA ZAG, ^UZU^MUR₇.GÚ		
ZI	'soul, life; (a model object)'	
	ZI	10.1.1.2 rev. iv 6′. 10.2.1.2 obv. 13′
sg. nom.	ZI-*TUM*	10.1.1.1 rev.? 9′
ZÌ.DA	'flour, meal'	
	ZÌ.DA	12.3.5 2′
ZÌ.DA DUR₅	'wet meal'	
	ZÌ.DA DUR₅	1.1.A₂ obv. 4′, 7′, 9′
	ZÌ.D]A DUR₅	1.1.A₂ obv. 6′
^NA₄^ZI.KIN	'(cult) stele, *ḫuwaši*-stone'	
	^NA₄^ZI.KIN	10.1.1.2 rev. iv 6′
= *SIKKĀNU*		
ZI.KIN.BAR	'needle, pin'	
	ZI.KIN.BAR	2.16 rev. v 6. 7.3 obv. i 8. 9.1.14 obv. r. c. 3′
	ZI.K]IN.BAR	8.1.F rev. vi 3
	ZI.KIN.[BAR	10.3.5 3′
	ZI.K[IN.BAR	9.2.4 obv. ii 3′. 10.1.1.1 rev.? 10′
	Z[I.KIN.BAR(?)	11.1.9 8′
see *Lexical Commentary*		

ZI.KIN.BAR ^{LÚ}DUB.SAR	‘stylus’	
	ZI.KIN.BAR ^{LÚ}DUB.[SAR	9.1.5 obv.$^{!}$ 13
See *Lexical Commentary*		
ZÍZ	‘emmer’	
	ZÍZ	1.1.A$_1$ obv. 15′. 10.1.1.1 rev.$^{?}$ 14′. 10.1.1.2 rev. iv 11′. 12.2.1 obv. 4′
ZU$_9$	‘tooth, tusk’	
	ZU$_9$	10.2.2.3 obv.$^{?}$ l. c. 9′
material		
	ZU$_9$	8.1.J rev. v$^{!}$ 5′, 7′. 9.1.5 rev.$^{!}$ 10′. 11.5.3 2′, 4′
ZU$_9$ (AM.)SI	‘ivory’	
material		
	ZU$_9$ SI	9.1.10.B 13′. 9.2.6 obv. i 5′, 6′, 7′, 8′, 15′, 17′. 10.1.2.4 l. c. 10′. 11.1.4 6′. 11.2.4 5′, 6′. 11.2.6 5′
	Z]U$_9$ SI	11.1.5 3′
	ZU$_9$] SI	11.2.4 2′
	ZU$_9$ S]I	11.2.4 3′
	ZU$_9$ S]I(?)	10.1.2.4 l. c. 21′. 11.1.5 5′
	ZU$_9$ S[I	9.2.14 4′
	Z[U$_9$ SI	9.2.14 3′
	Z[U$_9$ SI(?)	9.2.14 2′
	ZU$_9$ AM.SI	2.2 rev. iv 17. 2.4 rev. 2′. 2.5 rev. 4′. 2.16 obv. i 8′. 2.17 obv.$^{?}$ r. c. 8′, 10′. 4.2.4 obv. 1, 4, 7; rev. 2′, 3′, 6′. 4.2.9 rev. 29′. 5.2 obv. ii 11. 8.1.A obv. ii 6′. 8.1.F rev. v 13. 9.1.1 rev. iv 6′, 8′, 29′. 9.1.4.A$_1$ obv. i 1. 9.1.8 obv. 13′. 9.1.10.A$_1$ obv. 9′. 10.2.1.1 obv. 3′. 10.3.10 r. c. 4′, 12′, 15′. 10.3.11 l. c. 1′, 3′, 5′, 6′, 7′, 8′, 9′. 10.3.12 obv. i 8′, 10′. 11.5.1 3′, 4′. 11.5.2 rev.$^{?}$ r. c. 1′. 11.6.2 l. e. 7
	ZU$_9$ AM$^{!}$(text: ŠU$^{?}$).SI	10.3.10 r. c. 11′
	ZU$_9$ AM.⟨SI⟩	4.2.4 rev. 8′
	ZU$_9$ A[M.SI	2.2 obv. 19
	Z]U$_9$ AM.SI	9.1.10.A$_1$ rev. 5′. 10.3.10 r. c. 13′, 14′, 16′. 11.5.1 5′
	Z]U$_9$ AM.[SI	10.3.10 r. c. 1′
	ZU$_9$ A]M.SI	10.3.11 l. c. 2′
	ZU$_9$ AM].SI	11.5.1 7′
	ZU$_9$ AM.S[I	10.2.1.2 obv. 3′. 10.3.10 r. c. 6′. 11.5.1 2′. 11.5.2 rev.$^{?}$ r. c. 2′, 3′
	ZU$_9$ A[M.SI	2.14 4′. 4.2.8 5′. 4.2.9 rev. 2′. 10.3.10 r. c. 8′. 10.3.12 obv. i 11′
	ZU$_9$ [(AM.)SI	1.5 lo. e. 17. 2.7.B rev. 3′
	ZU$_9$ [AM.SI	4.2.9 rev. 4′
	Z[U$_9$ AM.SI	10.3.12 obv. i 5′
	Z[U$_9$ AM.SI(?)	10.3.10 r. c. 12′
= *peri-*?		

Akkadograms

Note that cases assigned in the following section are based on the assumed underlying Hittite case. An exclamation point is added if the Akkadogram used to indicate the underlying Hittite case is atypical, e.g. s.g. acc.! for *KÍ-RI-SÚM* (instead of expected **KIRISSA*), when the underlying Hittite must have been in sg. (nom.–)acc. Supplemental information on Akkadian forms is given in parentheses, so that, e.g., *A-NA A-ŠAR* is categorized as sg. dat./loc. (st. const.) to indicate that the underlying Hittite is a sg. dat./loc. but the Akkadogram is in status constructus. If the underlying Hittite is unclear, as with verbal constructions such as *MA-LI*, analyzed as a G. stat. sg. 3 from *MALÛ* 'to fill', in which it cannot be determined if the underlying Hittite was a participle or a finite verb, only the Akkadian form is given.

ABU	'father'	
sg. nom.	*A-BU* (ŠEŠ(-)***pišate***)	5.7 rev. iii? 21′
ABŪSU		
see EN É *ABŪSI*		
^{GIŠ}*ADDU*	'throw-stick'	
sg. nom.	^{GIŠ}*AD-DU*	7.1 obv. 12′
ANA	'to, for; (with PNs) from' (Hitt. dat./loc.)	
	A-NA	1.1.A_1 obv. 5′, 6′, 8′, 9′, 11′, 12′, 14′, 19′. 1.1.A_2 obv. 6′, 7′; rev. 7. 1.1.A_3 rev. 4′, 8′. 1.4 4′. 2.2 obv. 4′; rev. 4, 5, 8, 10. 2.15 l. c. 11′. 2.17 obv.? r. c. 11′ (2×), 12′ (3×), 13′ (3×), 19′, 20′. 3.1.1.A_3 obv. iii 7′, 9′. 3.1.2 obv. l. c. 7′. 3.1.3 obv.? 4′. 3.1.7.A_1 obv. i 2′, 5′, 8′; l. e. 2. 3.1.8.A obv. 14′; rev. 4′, 9′, 10′. 4.1.1.1.A_1 obv. 14′, 16′, 17′; rev. 7′, 13′, 16′, 17′, 20′. 4.1.1.1.B_1 rev. iii? 2, 5, 6, 11, 12, 16, 17. 4.1.1.1.B_2 obv. i? 6′. 4.1.1.2.B rev. 3 4.1.1.3 rev. B 4, 5, 8. 4.1.2.3 obv. ii 12′; rev. iii 6. 4.1.3.2 rev. 8′. 4.1.3.7 rev. 1′, 2′. 4.1.4.9 obv. 4, 5, 7, 10, 12. 4.2.1.A_2 rev. 13′. 4.2.9 obv. 15. 5.1 obv. ii 12′; rev. iii 4, 5, 7. 5.2 obv. ii 4; rev. iii 8′. 5.4 r. c. 4′, 5′. 6.1 obv. 3, 8, 13; rev. A 5′, 6″; rev. B 6. 6.2 rev. 3′. 6.3 rev. B 3. 6.4 obv.? 5′. 7.1 obv. 2′, 7′, 9′, 10′; rev. 3′, 8′. 7.2 4′. 8.1.A obv. i 7′; obv. ii 17′. 8.1.K obv. ii? 3′. 8.5 rev. iii(?) 2′, 7′. 9.1.1 rev. iii 9′, 19′; rev. iv 9′. 9.1.5 rev.! 9′, 14′. 9.1.14 obv. r. c. 6′, 8′, 9′. 9.2.1 obv. ii 7′, 11′, 12′. 9.2.2 rev.! iii 1′, 7′. 10.1.2.4 l. c. 12′; r. c. 3′. 10.2.1.1 obv. 8′. 10.2.1.2 obv. 17′. 10.2.1.7 rev.? 3′. 10.2.2.1 3′. 10.3.13 2′. 10.3.14 l. c. 3′. 11.3.1 7′, 10′. 12.1.1 r. c. 1′, 4′
	A-NA(?)	10.3.10 r. c. 10′
	〈*A*〉-*NA*	1.1.A_1 obv. 16′
	A]-*NA*	4.1.1.9 13′.
	A]-*N*[*A*	2.5 obv. 3′
	A-N]*A*	7.1 obv. 4′. 7.3 obv. i 1. 9.1.4.A_1 obv. ii 4
	A-N]*A*(?)	4.1.1.1.A_1 obv. 13′

	A-N[*A*	4.1.4.2.A_1 rev. r. c. 8′. 6.4 obv.$^{?}$ 8′. 7.1 obv. 5′; rev. 1′, 13′. 8.1.E(A_3) rev. vi 8. 9.1.1 rev. iii 18′. 10.3.5 11′. 10.3.11 r. c. 2′. 11.3.1 4′
	A-N[*A*(?)	2.1.B 9′
	A-[*NA*	8.1.E(A_3) rev. vi 5. 10.2.2.1 2′
$^{(\text{URUDU})}$*ANKURI(N)NU*	(a lampstand?)	
sg. nom.	*AN*-[*KU-RI-NU*	8.5 rev. iii(?) 5′
	^{URUDU}*AN-KU-RI-NU*	3.1.1.A_3 obv. iii 9′, 14′
	$^{\text{U}]\text{RUDU}}$*AN-KU-RI-IN-NU*	5.4 r. c. 7′
	$^{\text{UR}]\text{UDU}}$*AN-KU-RI-NU* (AMAR)	8.1.A rev. vi 4′
	$^{\text{URU}]\text{DU}}$*AN-KU-RI-NU* (AMAR)	8.1.A rev. vi 5′
see *Lexical Commentary*		
$^{(\text{KUŠ})}$*ARĪTU*	‘shield’	
sg. nom.	*A*(?)-*RI-TUM*	9.1.15 1′
	^{KUŠ}*A-R*[*I-T*]*UM*	7.1 obv. 20′
	$^{\text{K}[\text{UŠ}}$*A-R*]*I*(?)-*TUM*	7.1 obv. 18′
ARNABU	‘hare’	
sg. gen.	(*ŠĒDU*) *AR-NA-BI*	8.6 l. c. 5′
	(*ŠĒDU*) *AR-NA-A-BI*	9.1.10.A_2 rev. 10′
	(*ŠĒDU*) *AR*-[*NA-BI*	8.7 r. c. 7′
AŠĀBU		
see (*W*)*AŠĀBU*		
AŠḪALU	(a container made of metal, wood, or reed)	
sg. nom.	*AŠ-ḪA-LUM*	4.1.1.7 rev.$^{!?}$ 5
	AŠ]-*ḪA-LUM*	9.2.4 rev. iv 12
AŠRU	‘place; (decorated) spot’	
sg. nom.	*AŠ-RU*	10.3.12 obv. i 9′. 10.3.13 8′
	AŠ-RU	10.3.12 obv. i 7′
sg. nom. (st. const.)	*A-Š*[*AR*	8.4 rev. 20′
sg. acc.	*AŠ-RA*	9.1.1 rev. iv 6′. 9.1.5 rev.$^{!}$ 7′, 8′. 9.1.10.B 5′. 9.2.4 rev. iv 11. 10.3.5 9′. 10.3.14 l. c. 5′, 7′
sg. dat./loc. (st. const.)	*A-NA A-ŠAR*	3.1.3 obv.$^{?}$ 4′
	A-NA] *A-ŠAR*	3.1.3 obv.$^{?}$ 9′
see *Lexical Commentary*; = *peda-*		
ĀTRU		
see (*W*)*ATĀRU*		
BANÛ	‘to make, construct; (vb. adj.) well-made, well-formed’	
sg. nom. (G vb. adj. f.)	*BA-NI-TUM*	4.1.4.7 obv. 2
∢*BARATITTINNU*	(a ring or tube?)	
sg. nom.	*∢**BA-RA-TI-I*[*T-TI-IN-NU*	9.1.10.A_2 rev. 11′
see *Lexical Commentary*		
BIBRÛ	‘rhyton’	
sg. nom.	*BI-IB-RU*	2.17 obv.$^{?}$ r. c. 5′. 4.2.1.A_2 obv. 4′. 9.1.1 rev. iv 20′. 9.1.7 obv. 2′
	B]*I-IB-RU*	9.1.4.A_1 rev. iv 2′
	BI-IB-[*RU*	5.2 obv. ii 1

	BI-I[*B-RU*	5.2 obv. ii 5
sg. nom.!?	*BI-IB-RI*	6.1 obv. 15
pl. acc.	*BI-IB-RI*$^{\text{ḪI.A}}$	2.7.A obv. 18
	BI]*-IB-RI*$^{\text{ḪI.A}}$	6.2 rev. 2′
pl. dat./loc.	*A-NA BI-IB-RI*$^{\text{ḪI.A}}$	2.2 rev. 10
	A-NA B[*I-IB-RI*$^{\text{ḪI.A}}$	4.1.1.1.A$_1$ rev. 7′
BIBRU ***awiti-***	‘sphinx rhyton’	
sg. nom.	*BI-IB-RU* ***a-ú-i-ti***	9.1.4.A$_1$ obv. ii 27
BIBRU AMAR	‘calf rhyton’	
sg. nom.	*BI-IB-RU* AMAR	9.1.4.A$_1$ obv. ii 32
BIBRU GU$_4$	‘ox rhyton’	
sg. nom.	*BI-IB-RU* GU$_4$	5.2 obv. ii 7. 9.1.4.A$_1$ obv. ii 9
BIBRU LU.LIM	‘stag rhyton’	
sg. nom.	*BI-IB-RU* LU.LIM	9.1.4.A$_1$ obv. ii 12
BIBRU PÌRIG.TUR	‘leopard rhyton’	
sg. nom.	*BI-IB-RU* PÌRIG.TUR	9.1.4.A$_1$ obv. ii 21
BIBRU TI$_8$	‘eagle rhyton’	
sg. nom.	*BI-IB-RU* TI$_8$^{MUŠEN}	9.1.4.A$_1$ obv. ii 15
BIBRU UDU.KUR.RA	‘mountain sheep rhyton’	
sg. nom.	*BI*]*-IB-RU* … UDU.KUR.RA	9.1.1 rev. iv 10′
BIBRU UR.MAḪ	‘lion rhyton’	
sg. nom.	*BI-IB-RU* UR.MAḪ	7.1 obv. 6′, 8′. 9.1.4.A$_1$ obv. ii 16
	B]*I-IB-RU* UR.MAḪ	7.1 obv. 3′
BIBRU ^{D}UD-*AM*	‘rhyton of the deified day’	
sg. nom.	*BI-IB-RU* ^{D}UD-*AM*	9.1.4.A$_1$ obv. ii 36
BĒLU	‘lord, master’	
pl. nom.	*BE-LU*$^{\text{ḪI.A}}$	10.3.1 rev. iii 7′
Ē/ĪNU	‘eye’	
see *ŠUR ĒNI*		
ĒPĒŠU	‘to make, do; manufacture’	
sg. dat./loc. (G infin. st. const.)	*A-NA E-PIŠ* (*MAŠ-LU*)	4.1.1.3 rev. B 4
	A-NA E-P]*IŠ* (*MAŠ-LU*)	4.1.4.8 6′
^{LÚ}*EPIŠ* ^{GIŠ}PAN	‘bowyer’	
sg. dat./loc.	*A-NA* … ^{LÚ}*E-PIŠ* ^{GIŠ}PAN	1.1.A$_1$ obv. 14′
GAMRU	‘complete, full, total’	
sg. nom.	*GÁM-RU*	2.2 rev. 14. 8.1.A rev. v 10. 8.1.D obv. i 9′
see also ***zinnant-***, *QATÛ*, TIL		
GURSI(*P*)*PU/KURPIŠU*	‘corselet’	
sg. nom.	*GUR-SÍ-PU*	2.8 obv. 3
sg. nom. (st. const.)	*GUR-SÍ-IP*	7.3 obv. i 4
pl. dat./loc.	*A-NA* … *KUR-PÍ-ŠI*$^{\text{ḪI.A}}$	4.1.1.1.B$_1$ rev. iii? 6
^{DUG}*ḪABANNATU*	(a container or jar)	
sg. nom.	^{DUG}]*ḪA-PA-NA-TUM*	1.2 rev. 5′
	^{DUG}]*ḪA-PA-AN-NA-TUM*	9.1.1 rev. iv 24′

^{NA_4}*ḪALTU*	(a stone)	
sg. gen.	$^{N]A_4}$*ḪAL-TI*	8.1.A obv. i 9′
see *Lexical Commentary*		
ḪAPALKI(N)NU	'iron (or iron ore?)'	
sg. gen.	*ḪA]-PAL-KI-NI*	6.4 obv.$^?$ 4′
	ḪA-PA[L-KI-NI	6.4 obv.$^?$ 7′
see *Lexical Commentary*; = *ḫapalki-*/AN.BAR; see also *kiklibaim(m)a/i-*, *parzagulliya-*, *parzašša-*, AN.BAR GE$_6$, AN.BAR (*ŠA*) GUNNI		
ḪAṢARTU	'green'	
sg. nom.	*ḪA-ŠÁR-TUM*	3.2.1 obv. 3, 13, 19; rev. 6′, 9′, 12′. 4.1.4.2.A_1 rev. l. c. 1′. 4.1.4.5 obv. r. c. 3′. 8.1.H rev. l. c. 5′
	ḪA-ŠÁR-TU[M	4.1.3.3 8′. 4.1.4.1.A_1 rev. vi 8′
	ḪA-ŠÁR-[TUM	4.1.4.2.A_1 rev. r. c. 10′
sg. gen.	*ḪA-ṢAR-TI*	2.7.A obv. 10. 4.2.10 3′. 11.6.9 3′
	ḪA-ŠÁR-DI	6.9 obv. 2′. 8.1.D rev. iv 12′. 8.1.E(A_1) rev. iv 5′
	ḪA-ŠÁR-TI	3.2.1 obv. 2, 5, 7, 11, 16; rev. 3′. 4.1.4.1.A_1 obv. ii 3′; rev. v 6′. 4.2.6 obv.$^?$ 8′. 4.2.9 obv. 1. 6.8 3′, 5′. 8.8.A 4′. 8.8.B r. c. 2′. 8.1.F rev. v. 10′. 8.1.H rev. l. c. 4′. 11.6.6 rev. 2′, 6′
	ḪA-[ŠÁ]R-TI	4.1.4.1.A_1 rev. v 5″
	ḪA-Š[ÁR]-DI	4.1.4.8 1′
	Ḫ]A-ŠÁR-DI	4.1.4.1.A_1 obv. ii 12′
	ḪA]-ŠÁR-TI	2.11 rev.$^?$ 5′
	ḪA-ŠÁR]-DI	4.1.4.5 rev. r. c. 3′
	ḪA-ŠÁR-T]I	8.8.B l. c. 4′
	ḪA-ŠÁR-T[I	3.2.1 obv. 3
	ḪA-ŠÁR-D[I$^?$	8.1.I rev. r. c. 1′
	ḪA-ŠÁR-[TI	8.1.G obv. r. c. 11′. 8.1.H rev. r. c. 2′
	ḪA-ŠÁ[R-TI	4.1.3.2 rev. 1′
	ḪA-Š[ÁR-TI	4.1.4.6 obv. 9′
	ḪA-[ŠÁR-DI	8.1.H rev. r. c. 10′
	ḪA-[ŠÁR-TI	4.1.4.4 9′. 4.2.6 obv.$^?$ 19′
	Ḫ[A-ŠÁR-TI(?)	6.13 3′
	ŠA ḪA-ṢAR-TI	9.1.8 obv. 6′, 9′
abbr.	*ḪA-ṢAR.*	6.6 rev. 6′. 6.7 obv.$^?$ 1
	ḪA-ŠÁR.	3.2.1 rev. 19′. 11.6.5 obv.$^?$ 7
see *Lexical Commentary*		
ḪAṢARTU A.AB.BA	'marine green'	
sg. nom.	*ḪA-ṢAR-TUM* A.AB.BA	2.7.A obv. 17
see *Lexical Commentary*		
$^{(URUDU)}$*ḪAṢṢINNU*	'axe'	
sg. nom.	*ḪA-ṢÍ-NU*	3.1.8.A rev. 15′. 3.1.8.B 3′. 4.1.2.2 obv. 1′, 4′. 9.1.7 rev. 2. 10.3.3 obv.$^?$ 8′
	ḪA-AṢ-ṢÍ-NU	9.1.4.A_2 r. c. 4′
	ḪA-AṢ-Ṣ]Í-IN-NU	1.4 8′
	ḪA-AṢ-ṢÍ]-IN-NU	5.1 rev. iv 2
	ḪA-AṢ-ṢÍ-I[N-NU	11.1.9 5′
	ḪA-AṢ-ṢÍ-[(IN)-NU	7.3 obv. i 10

	ḪA-AṢ-Š[Í-(IN)-NU	7.1 obv. 15′
	ḪA-A[Ṣ-ṢÍ-(IN)-NU	4.1.2.1 obv. (i) 5′, 9′
	^{URUDU}*ḪA-ṢÍ-NU*	1.2 rev. 9′. 2.12 obv.$^{!}$ ii 10′. 8.1.F rev. vi 5
	^{URU}]^{DU}*ḪA-AṢ-ŠÍ-IN-NU*	3.1.1.A_1 obv. ii 13′
	^{URUDU}*ḪA-ṢI-N[U*	8.6 l. c. 1′
	^{URUDU}*ḪA-AṢ-Ṣ[Í-(IN)-NU*	4.1.2.4 1′
^{URUDU}*ḪAṢṢINNU* ḪUR.SAG	'mountain axe'	
sg. nom.	^{URUDU}*ḪA-AṢ-ṢÍ-IN-NU* ḪUR.SAG	1.1.A_1 obv. 9′
ḪAŠMĀNU	'(red-)purple, amethyst'	
sg. nom.	*ḪAŠ-MA-NU*	2.7.A obv. 1. 2.7.B rev. 5′
sg. nom.(?)	*ḪAŠ*$^{!}$*-MA[N(-)*	6.12 5′
	ḪAŠ-M[AN(-)	8.1.E(A_3) rev. vi 2
	Ḫ[AŠ-MAN(-)	6.12 3′
sg. gen.	*ḪAŠ-MA-NI*	8.1.K rev. vi$^{?}$ 6′
	ḪAŠ-M[A-NI	12.3.7 8′
	ḪAŠ-MAN-NI	1.5 obv. 3, 9, 12; rev. 25. 4.2.6 obv.$^{?}$ 4′, 6′, 8′. 4.2.9 obv. 3, 18, 21, 26, 27. 6.3 obv. 2. 6.5 obv. 14′, 16′; rev. 9′, 10′, 12′, 15′, 18′, 23′, 24′, 26′, 27′. 6.6 rev. 4′. 6.9 obv. 2′. 8.1.D rev. iv 2′, 9′. 8.1.E(A_1) obv. ii 3; rev. iv 6′, 11′, 12′; rev. v 2′, 8′. 8.1.H rev. r. c. 7′. 8.1.I rev. r. c. 6′. 9.1.11 rev.$^{?}$ 3′. 11.6.5 obv.$^{?}$ 2, 8. 11.6.6 rev. 3′, 4′, 7′
	ḪAŠ-MAN$^{!}$*-NI*	9.1.11 rev.$^{?}$ 4′
	Ḫ]AŠ-MAN-N[I	4.2.6 rev.$^{?}$ 1′
	ḪA]Š-MAN-NI	6.6 rev. 2′
	ḪAŠ]-MAN-NI	11.6.8 5′
	ḪAŠ-M]AN-NI	9.1.6 obv. 13. 11.6.6 rev. 6′
	ḪAŠ-MAN-N[I	4.2.6 obv.$^{?}$ 10′, 15′
	ḪAŠ-MA[N-NI	8.1.D rev. iv 5′
abbr.	*ḪAŠ-MAN.*	4.1.4.2.A_2 obv. r. c. 6′, 8′. 4.2.6 obv.$^{?}$ 10′. 6.7 obv.$^{?}$ 2. 6.9 obv. 4′ (2×). 8.1.E(A_1) rev. iv 9′. 8.1.F obv. ii 6′. 8.1.G obv. r. c. 10′. 8.8.B l. c. 8′. 9.1.6 obv. 3, 6. 11.6.1 9, 12. 11.6.5 obv.$^{?}$ 7. 11.6.7 7′
	ḪAŠ(?)]*-MAN.*	9.1.4.A_1 rev. iii 3′

see *Lexical Commentary*; = *arkamma(n)-*?

^{LÚ}*ḪATANU*	'in-law, relative by marriage'	
sg. gen.	^{L}]^{Ú}*ḪA-TÁ-NI*	5.2 obv. i 17
ḪIḪINNU(-)	(?)	
sg. nom.	*ḪI-ḪI-IN-NU(-)[*	9.2.4 rev. iii 3′
	ḪI-ḪI-IN-N[U(-)	9.2.6 rev. iv$^{!}$ 1′

see *Lexical Commentary*

ḪURRI	'Hurrian; in the Hurrian-style'	

see under *Geographical Names*

IDÛ	'to know'	
pret./pres. sg. 3	*I-DE*	5.1 obv. ii 3′, 5′, 9′, 10′, 11′; rev. iii 6, 8; rev. iv 4. 5.2 obv. i 3, 11; obv. ii 2′, 9′, 10′, 11′, 12′, 15′. 5.7 rev. iii$^{?}$ 9′, 24′; rev. iv$^{?}$ 8′. 5.3 l. c. 7′, 8′. 5.9 4′

	I-DE$^?$	5.5 obv. ii 1
	I]-*DE*	5.7 rev. iv$^?$ 1′
	I-D[*E*	5.1 rev. iii 13. 5.7 rev. iii$^?$ 18′
	I-[*DE*	5.1 rev. iii 1. 5.4 r. c. 6′. 5.7 rev. iii$^?$ 11′
IKRIBU	'prayer, dedication, votive'	
pl. gen.	*IK-RI-BI*$^{\text{ḪI.A}}$	5.1 obv. ii 12′
INA	'in' (Hitt. dat./loc.)	
	I-NA	1.1.A$_2$ obv. 5′, 8′, 10′. 4.1.3.2 rev. 6′. 8.1.E(A$_1$) obv. ii 15
	I-N]*A*	1.1.A$_2$ obv. 11′
	I+NA	8.1.E(A$_1$) obv. iii 4′. 8.1.E(A$_3$) obv. i 5′
	INA	8.4 rev. 11′. 5.9 3′
INṢABTU	'(ear)ring'	
sg. nom.	*IN-ṢA-AB-TUM*	8.1.A obv. i 4′
see also *ašuša-*, *ištamaḫura-*, *KAMKAMMATU*, HUB(.BI)/ḪÚB(.BI)		
IṢṢU	'wood, tree; (in sg. gen.) wooden'	
sg. nom.	*IṢ-ṢÚ*	9.1.14 obv. r. c. 7′, 10′. 10.3.3 obv.$^?$ 6′, 9′
	I[*Ṣ-ṢÚ*	10.3.3 obv.$^?$ 2′
sg. gen.	*IṢ-ṢÍ*	2.9.A$_3$ obv. ii 7′. 2.12 obv.$^!$ ii 10′. 2.17 obv.$^?$ r. c. 9′. 9.1.1 rev. iv 29′. 9.2.4 rev. iv 9. 10.3.12 obv. i 17′
= GIŠ(-*ru*)		
^{KUŠ}*IŠPATU*	'quiver'	
sg. nom	^{KUŠ}*IŠ-PA-TUM*	9.1.10.A$_2$ rev. 7′
	^{KUŠ}*I*]*Š-PA-TUM*	9.1.4.A$_2$ r. c. 6′
= MÁ.URU.URU$_6$		
^{KUŠ}*IŠPATU* ^{URU}*gašga*	'Gasgaen quiver'	
sg. nom.	^{KUŠ}*IŠ-PA-TUM* ^{URU}*ga-aš-ga*	2.17 obv.$^?$ r. c. 16′
= MÁ.URU.URU$_6$ *gašga*		
^{KUŠ}*IŠPATU* ^{URU}*ḪATTIM*	'Hittite quiver'	
sg. nom.	^{KUŠ}*IŠ-PA-TUM* ^{URU}*ḪAT-TIM*	2.17 obv.$^?$ r. c. 14′
^{KUŠ}*IŠPATU* ^{URU}*ḪURRI*	'Hurrian quiver'	
sg. nom.	^{KUŠ}*IŠ-PA-TUM* ^{URU}*ḪUR-RI*	2.17 obv.$^?$ r. c. 15′
IŠTU	'with; from' (Hitt. abl./inst.)	
	IŠ-TU	1.5 obv. 3. 2.7.A obv. 3. 2.7.B rev. 1′. 2.17 obv.$^?$ r. c. 3′. 4.1.3.2 rev. 4′. 6.1 rev. B 4. 10.2.1.6 5′. 10.3.6 6′
	IŠ$^!$-*TU*	9.2.6 rev.$^!$ iv 15′
	I]*Š-TU*	2.7.B rev. 6′. 9.1.4.A$_1$ rev. iv 6′
	I]*Š-T*[*U*	4.1.2.6 4′
	IŠ-T[*U*	1.1.A$_2$ rev. 10. 9.2.6 rev.$^!$ iv 2′, 17′
IŠTU ŠA PN	'from the lot of …'	
	IŠ-TU ŠA (^{m}*lu*[*pakki*(?))	4.1.1.1.A$_1$ obv. 11′
	IŠ-TU Š[*A* (^{m}…)	4.1.1.1.A$_1$ obv. 10′
	IŠ-T[*U ŠA* (^{m}…)	4.1.1.1.A$_1$ obv. 8′
	IŠ-T[*U ŠA* (^{m}…)(?)	4.1.1.6 obv. ii 2′; rev. iii 3, 5

	I[*Š-TU ŠA* (^{m}…)	4.1.1.1.A$_1$ obv. 6′
	I[*Š-TU ŠA* (^{m}…)(?)	4.1.1.6 rev. iii 1
see *Lexical Commentary*		
ITTI	‘with, by, next to’ (Hitt. abl./inst.)	
	IT-TI	5.4 r. c. 2′
^{NA_4}*IZZIḪU*	(a piece of jewelry?)	
sg. nom.	^{NA_4}*IZ-ZI-ḪU*	8.1.A obv. i 9′
see *Lexical Commentary*		
KAMKAMMATU	‘ring, hoop’	
sg. nom.	*KAM-KAM-MA-TUM*	8.4 rev. 12′. 9.2.9 obv.$^{?}$ 12′. 10.2.1.7 rev.$^{?}$ 4′
see also ***ašuša-***, ***ištamaḫura-***, *INṢABTU*, HUB(.BI)/ḪÚB(.BI)		
KANĀKU	‘to seal’	
sg. nom. (G vb. adj.)	*KÁN-KU*	2.12 obv.! ii 9′
	KÁN-K[*U*	2.9.A$_3$ obv. ii 5′
$^{(GIŠ)}$*KANḪANNU*	‘(lidded) box’	
sg. nom.	*KAN-ḪA-AN-NU*	2.16 obv. i 8′; rev. 5
	$^{(GIŠ)}$*KAN-Ḫ*]*A-AN-NU* DUB.SAR	8.5 rev. iv(?) 5′
	KAN-ḪA-A[*N-NU*	1.5 obv. 9
abbr.	^{GIŠ}*KAN-ḪA-AN.*	4.2.4 rev. 7′
see *Lexical Commentary*; = $^{(GIŠ)}$***ḫa/urnašalla-***, ^{GIŠ}DUB.ŠEN(?)		
$^{(GIŠ)}$*KANḪANNU* DUB.SAR	“scribe’s box” (= tablet container?)	
sg. nom.	$^{(GIŠ)}$*KAN-Ḫ*]*A-AN-NU* DUB.SAR	8.5 rev. iv(?) 5′
KANNU	‘(serving) rack, frame’	
sg. nom.	*KÂ-AN-NU*	11.4.2 obv. 2′
see *Lexical Commentary*		
KAPPU	1. ‘wing, quill, feather’	
pl. gen.? (or nom.!)	*KAP-PÍ*$^{ḪI.A}$	10.3.3 obv.$^{?}$ 11′
= $^{(UZU)}$***pattar***		
	2. (a bowl)	
sg. nom.	*KAP-PU*	4.2.1.A$_1$ obv. 10
	KA]*P-PU*	11.5.1 2′
sg. gen.	*K*]*AP-PÍ*	11.5.1 6′
see *Lexical Commentary*		
$^{(TÚG)}$*KARKU*	“‘(inter)twined’ cloth” (G vb. adj. of *KARĀKU*)	
sg. nom.	*KAR-KU*	8.1.E(A$_1$) rev. iv 11′
	KAR-KU!(text: TÚG)	8.1.F obv. ii 9′
	$^{TÚ]G}$*KAR-KU*	8.8.B r. c. 2′
^{LÚ}*KARTAPPU*	‘charioteer’	
see ^{KUŠ}A.GÁ.LÁ *ŠA* ^{LÚ}*KARTAPPI*		
KAŠĀDU	‘to reach, arrive’	
pret. sg. 3	*I*]*K*$^{?}$*-ŠU-UD*	11.7.1 l. c. 2′
$^{(NA_4)}$*KIBŠU*	(a variegated/marbled stone)	
sg. gen.	*KIB-ŠI*	3.1.8.A obv. 10′
	^{NA_4}*KIB-ŠI*	8.1.A obv. i 9′

	NA₄*KI-IB-ŠI*	10.2.2.3 11′, 13′
see *Lexical Commentary*; = *kabši-*?		
KILĪLU	'circlet, headband, garland'	
sg. nom.	*K*]*I-LI-LU*	11.3.1 22′
	KI-L]*I*(?)-*LU*	4.2.3 l. c. 1′
= GILIM		
KIRISSU	'(metal) pin, hair clasp'	
sg. nom.	*KÍ-RI-SÚ*	4.2.4 obv. 10; rev. 2′
	KÍ-RI-S[*Ú*	4.2.4 obv. 8, 9
	KÍ-RI-SÚM	4.2.4 obv. 8
sg. acc.!	*KÍ-RI-SÚM*	2.7.A rev. 1
= UMBIN (ZABAR)?		
KU(K)KU(B)BU	(a flask for liquids/ointments)	
	KU-UK-KU-U[*B*(-)	2.13 obv.? 2′
= DUG*kukupallan(t?)-*, DUGḪAB.ḪAB		
KURPIŠU		
see *GURSI(P)PU, KURPIŠU*		
KUŠARU	(?)	
sg. nom.	(EZEN₄) *KU-ŠA-RU*	4.1.1.1.B_1 rev. iii? 16
KŪTU	(a container)	
pl. nom.	*KU-UT-T*[*A-TU*(?)	4.1.1.3 obv. 8
LIM	'thousand'	
see Numerals		
]x-*LIPUNTU*	(?)	
pl. nom. (f.)	]x(-)*LI-PU-NA-A-TUM*	9.1.15 4′
MADDATTU	'tribute'	
sg. nom.	*MA-TA-DU*	3.2.1 obv. 5
	MAN-TA-DU	2.9.A_2 obv. i 7′. 2.9.A_3 obv. ii 8′. 2.12 obv.! ii 2′, 7′. 3.1.1.A_1 obv. ii 7′, 17′; rev. v 18′. 3.1.1.A_3 obv. iii 10′; rev. iv 10′, 20′, 23′. 3.1.3 rev.? 8′. 3.1.11.B 4′
	MAN-TA!-[*D*]*U*	3.2.1 obv. 21
	MAN-TA]-*DU*	3.1.11.A 3
	M[*AN*]-*TA-DU*	3.1.1.A_1 obv. ii 13′
	MAN-TA-D[*U*	3.1.4 3′
	MAN-T[*A-DU*	3.1.1.A_2 rev. v 12′. 3.1.1.A_3 obv. iii 14′, 17′
	MAN-[*TA-DU*	3.1.1.A_1 obv. ii 3′
	M[*AN-TA-DU*	2.9.A_3 obv. ii 3′. 3.1.1.A_3 rev. iv 8′
	MAN-TA-AD-DU	4.1.1.1.A_1 obv. 3′
	MAN-[*TA-AD-DU*	4.1.1.1.A_1 obv. 2′
	MAN-TA-TUM	3.1.5.A_1 obv. i(?) 5′. 3.1.7.A_1 obv. i 3′, 9′; obv. ii 11′
	MA]*N-TA-TUM*	3.1.12 4′
	MAN-T]*A-TUM*	3.1.5.A_1 obv. i(?) 2′. 3.1.7.A_2 obv. ii 2′
	MAN-TA-TU]*M*(?)	3.1.7.A_2 obv. i 1′
	MAN-TA-[*TUM*	3.1.5.A_2 obv. ii(?) 15′. 3.1.7.A_2 obv. ii 6′. 3.1.12 1′

	MA-AN-DA-DU	3.2.1 obv. 4
	MA-AN-TA-DU	3.2.1 lo. e. 21′
	M]A-AN-TA-DU	3.1.10 2
sg. nom. (st. const.)	*MAN-TA-AT*	3.2.4 2′. 8.3 obv. 8′
	MA-AN-TA-AT	2.7.A obv. 12
sg. gen.	*MAN-TA-TI*	3.1.1.A_3 obv. iii 5′, 6′
	M]AN-TA-TI	3.1.6 5′
	MAN-TA-AT-TI	2.1.B 4′
	M]A-AN-TA-TI	3.2.2 obv.$^?$ 5′, 7′
	ŠA [MA]N-TA-TI	3.1.1.A_1 obv. ii 11′
see *Lexical Commentary*; see also *arkamma(n)-*		
^{GIŠ}*MAGARRU*, ^{GIŠ}*MUKARRU*	'(chariot) wheel; (a noise maker?)'	
inst.!	*QA-DU* ^{GIŠ}*MU-KAR-RU*	9.1.10.A_2 rev. 6′
see *Lexical Commentary*		
MALÛ	'to fill'	
G stat. sg. 3	*MA-LI*	2.7.A obv. 1. 2.7.B rev. 5′. 8.1.A rev. v 22′
G stat. pl. 3	*MA-LU-Ú*	2.7.A obv. 20
MAŠADDU	1. 'pole; spear, lance'	
sg. gen.	*ŠA ME-Š]E-DI*	10.3.8 2′
	Š]A ME-ŠE-DI	10.3.7 4′
	2. 'bodyguard, household troop'	
sg. gen.	(GAL) *ME-ŠE-D[I*	5.7 rev.$^?$ iii 12′
	(GAL) *ME-[ŠE-DI*	5.7 rev.$^?$ iii 25′
see *Lexical Commentary*		
MAŠLU	'patterned, embellished'	
	MAŠ-LU	1.2 rev. 4′. 1.5 obv. 13; rev. 25. 4.1.1.3 rev. B 4. 4.1.4.1.A_1 obv. ii 4′; rev. v 7″. 4.1.4.1.A_2 obv. ii 9′. 4.1.4.2.A_1 rev. r. c. 6′, 15′. 4.1.4.4 3′, 7′. 4.1.4.8 1′, 2′, 5′, 6′. 4.2.4 rev. 9′. 4.2.6 obv.$^?$ 5′, 9′, 17′. 4.2.9 obv. 4 (2×), 5, 22 (2×), 24. 4.2.11 4′. 6.5 obv. 7′, 12′; rev. 13′, 14′, 24′, 25′. 6.9 obv. 3′, 7′. 8.1.E(A_1) obv. ii 12. 8.1.F rev. v 12. 8.1.G obv. l. c. 7′. 8.1.K rev. vi$^?$ 8′. 8.3 obv. 7′. 8.4 rev. 15′. 8.8.B l. c. 10′, 11′. 9.1.1 rev. iii 26′ (2×), 30′, 31′ (2×); rev. iv 41′ (2×), 42′. 9.1.6 obv. 5. 9.1.8 obv. 10′. 9.1.10.B obv. 10′. 9.1.11 obv.$^?$ 5′, 6′, 12′. 9.2.1 obv. ii 19′. 9.2.4 rev. iii 7′; rev. iv 2. 10.3.1 rev. iii 14′. 11.6.1 4, 12. 11.6.5 obv.$^?$ 5. 11.6.7 3′. 11.6.9 2′
	M]AŠ-LU	4.1.1.3 rev. B 7
	MA]Š-LU	11.6.7 1′
	MAŠ]-LU	4.1.4.8 5′. 8.1.E(A_1) rev. iv 8′. 11.6.8 6′. 11.7.2 2′
	MAŠ-L]U	11.6.8 2′
	MAŠ-L]U(?)	4.2.9 rev. 7′
	MAŠ-L[U	6.2 obv. 1′. 8.1.E(A_2) 4′. 11.6.5 obv.$^?$ 2
	MAŠ-[LU	11.6.2 rev. 10′. 11.6.4 obv. 6′
	MA[Š-LU	9.1.6 obv. 9
	MA[Š-LU(?)	9.1.1 rev. iii 33′. 9.1.11 obv.$^?$ 6′
see *Lexical Commentary*		

(TÚG)*MAYYĀLU*	'bedding, bed supplies'	
sg. nom.	*MA-IA-LU*	8.1.F rev. v 16
	MA-IA-[*LU*	4.2.9 rev. 9′
	MA-I[*A-LU*	4.2.9 rev. 2′
sg. gen.	TÚG*MA-IA-LI*	5.7 rev. iii$^?$ 7′
see *Lexical Commentary*		
MEATU	'hundred'	
see *ME* under *Numerals*		
MEŠEDU		
see *MAŠADDU*		
MIMMA ŠUMŠU	'of all sorts' (lit. "whatever its name")	
	(NA$_4$) *MÌ-MA ŠUM-ŠÚ*	3.1.8.A obv. 12′
	(NA$_4$) *MIM-MA ŠUM-ŠU*	10.1.2.1 rev.$^?$ r. c. 7′
	(NA$_4$?) *MIM-MA ŠUM-ŠU*	10.1.2.7 13′
MIZRI	'Egyptian'	
see KUR *Mizri* under *Geographical Names*		
GIŠ*MUKARRU*		
see GIŠ*MAGARRU*, GIŠ*MUKARRU*		
SÍG*MUKKU*	'noil'	
sg. nom.	SÍG*MU-UK-KU*	4.1.3.2 rev. 7′
= MUG		
GIŠ*MŪŠABU*	(a seat, bench, or footrest)	
sg. nom.	GIŠ*MU-ŠA-B*[*U*	10.3.6 3′
= (GIŠ)*zaḫurti-*		
MUŠĀKILU	(an implement used in eating, lit. "feeder")	
sg. nom.	*MU-ŠA-KI-LU*	9.1.1 rev. iv 28′
NADĀNU	'to give'	
pret. pl. 1	*NI-ID-DI-IN*	12.3.1 5′
pret. pl. 3	*ID-DI-N*[*U*(?)	4.2.8 7′
	(*LI-*)*I*[*D-DI-NU*(?)	4.2.8 4′
= *pai-/pi(ya)-*, SUM		
NAKTAMU	'cover, lid'	
inst.	*QA-DU NA-A*[*K-DAM-MI*(?)	10.3.10 r. c. 11′
NAMADDU	(a measuring vessel)	
sg. nom.	*NAM-MA-AN-D*[*U*	4.1.1.3 rev. A 2′
	NAM-MA-AN-TUM	1.2 rev. 6′
	NAM-MA-AN-TUM (ŠE.NAGA)	4.1.1.3 rev. A 7′
	NA]*M-MA-AN-TUM*	4.1.1.3 obv. 8
	NAM-M]*A*(?)*-AN-TUM*	4.1.1.4 4′
NAMTULLU	(part of a harness)	
sg. nom.	*NAM-TÚL-LU*	4.1.4.8 4′
	NAM-TÚL-L[*UM*	8.8.A 13′
sg. acc.	*NAM*]*-TÚL*^{ul}*-LA*	4.2.11 1′
= NAM.TÚL		

^{MUNUŠ}*NAPṬARTU*	'concubine, wife of the second rank'	
pl. gen. (f.!)	$^{\text{MUNUS.MEŠ}}$*NAP-ṬAR-TU*$_4$*-TI*	5.7 rev. iii$^?$ 25′
NAŠÛ	'to carry, transport'	
G stat. pl. 3	*NA-ŠU-Ú*	8.1.E(A_1) obv. ii 15; rev. v 12′
	NA-Š]*U-Ú*	8.1.E(A_1) rev. v 5′
NURMÛ	'pomegranate'	
sg. nom.	*NU-ÚR-MU*	9.1.1 rev. iii 19′
see also *nurima(nt)-*		
PARĪSU	1. (unit of vol. = approx. 30–50 liters)	
sg. nom.!	*PA-RI-SI*	12.3.2 2′
	PA-RI-S[*I*	12.3.2 2′
abbr.	*PA.*	1.1.A_1 obv. 13′, 15′. 1.1.A_2 obv. 3′ (2×), 12′; rev. 8. 1.1.A_3 rev. 4′, 5′, 11′. 10.1.1.1 rev.$^?$ 14′ (2×), 15′. 10.1.1.2 rev. iv 10′, 11′, 12′. 12.2.1 obv. 1′, 2′, 3′, 4′; rev. 1′, 2′, 3′, 4′, 5′, 6′. 12.2.3 1′, 2′. 12.3.5 2′
	P[*A.*	1.1.A_2 obv. 12′. 12.2.1 obv. 4′
	2. (a vessel)	
sg. gen.? (or nom.!)	*PA-RI-SI*	10.3.5 7′
	PA-RI-S]*I*(?)	10.3.5 11′
see *Lexical Commentary*		
$^{\text{(URUDU)}}$*PĀŠU*	'adze, axe, hatchet'	
sg. nom.	*PA-A-ŠU*	3.1.8.A rev. 15′. 8.5 rev. iii(?) 3′
	$^{\text{URUD]U}}$*PA-A-ŠU*	5.1 obv. ii 2′
	^{URUDU}*PA-A-*[*ŠU*	8.5 rev. iii(?) 1′
$^{\text{(URUDU)}}$*PĀŠU* GAL	'large adze, axe, hatchet'	
sg. nom.	*PA-A-ŠU* GAL	4.2.8 3′, 6′.
	^{URUDU}*PA-A-ŠU* GAL	2.12 obv.! ii 10′. 3.1.1.A_1 obv. ii 8′, 10′, 11′. 3.1.1.A_2 rev. v 9′, 13′
	^{URUDU}*PA-A-ŠU* G]AL	3.1.1.A_1 obv. ii 7′
	^{URUDU}*PA-A-*[*ŠU* GAL	3.1.1.A_3 rev. iv 18′
QADU	'with' (Hitt. inst.)	
	QA-DU	3.1.1.A_3 obv. iii 11′. 3.1.5.A_1 obv. i(?) 5′. 3.1.5.A_2 obv. i(?) 2′. 4.1.1.1.A_1 obv. 6′, 8′, 10′, 11′, 14′, 15′, 21′. 4.1.1.1.B_1 rev. iii$^?$ 4. 4.1.1.2.A obv. 10′, 15′. 4.1.1.2.B obv. 1, 4, 7. 4.1.3.3 10′. 4.2.4 rev. 9′. 4.2.6 obv.$^?$ 12′. 6.5 rev. 19′, 28′. 6.9 obv. 2′, 3′. 8.1.E(A_1) rev. iv 6′. 8.1.F rev. v 11, 13. 9.1.10.A_2 rev. 6′, 8′. 9.2.9 rev.$^?$ 5′. 10.3.2 obv. i(?) 7″. 10.3.10 r. c. 11′, 14′. 11.6.2 rev. 11′. 11.6.3 obv.$^?$ 4′. 11.6.5 rev.$^?$ 1′
	QA*!-DU*	4.2.6 obv.$^?$ 11′
	Q]*A-DU*	3.1.3 rev.$^?$ 4′. 4.1.1.1.A_1 obv. 23′
	QA]*-DU*	3.1.5.A_2 obv. i(?) 5′
	QA-D]*U*	4.1.1.1.A_1 rev. 12′
	QA-D[*U*	6.6 rev. 3′. 11.1.3 4′
	QA-[*DU*	8.1.F obv. ii 8′
	Q[*A-DU*	4.1.1.2.A obv. 21′

QĀPU	(a stone object)	
sg. nom.	*QA-A-PU*	2.1.A obv. ii(?) 4′. 2.1.B 5′
^{GIŠ}*QAPU*-x[	(?)	
sg. nom.	^{GIŠ}*QA-PU*-x[	9.2.12 4′
QATÛ	'to finish, complete'	
G stat. sg. 3 m.	*QA-TI*	8.1.A rev. vi 3′. 9.1.1 rev. iv 46′. 9.1.3 1′. 9.1.9 rev. iv 4′
	QA-T]*I*	10.1.1.2 rev. iv 16′
	QA-T[*I*	3.1.1.A_1 rev. v 7′
	QA-[*TI*	9.1.4.A_1 rev. iv 5′
	Q[*A-TI*(?)	3.1.2 obv. l. c. 8′
= TIL; see also *zinnant-*		
RABÛ		
see É-*TUM* GAL/*RABÛ*		
RĪQU	'empty'	
sg. nom.	*RI-QUM*	9.1.5 rev.$^{!}$ 4′
SĀBĪTU	'alewife, brewster, female tavernkeeper'	
sg. nom.	*SA*$^{?}$*-PÍ-TU*[*M*	5.6 6′
SĀḪU	(a drinking vessel)	
	SÀ-ḪU$_5$	2.8 obv. 1. 7.1 obv. 5′, 9′
see *Lexical Commentary*; = ZA.ḪUM		
SIḪPU	'covering, overlay'	
sg. nom.	*SÍ-IḪ-PU*	9.2.1 obv. ii 7′, 8′, 9′, 10′; rev. iii 13′. 9.2.2 rev.$^{!}$ iii 26′
	S]*Í-IḪ-PU*	10.3.9 3′
= GIŠ.(BAR.)KÍN		
SIKKĀNU	'(cult) stele'	
sg. nom.	*SÍ-KÀ-NU*	10.3.1 rev. iii 4′
see *Lexical Commentary*; = ^{NA_4}ZI.KIN		
SŪTU	(unit of vol. = approx. 8.4 liters)	
sg. nom.	*ŠA-A-DU*	10.1.1.2 rev. iv 11′
= BÁN		
ṢIMITTU	'team (of draft animals)'	
sg. dat./loc.	*A-NA ṢÍ-M*[*I-IT-TI*	10.3.13 2′
ŠA	'of' (Hitt. gen.)	
	ŠA	1.1.A_1 obv. 11′, 12′. 1.1.A_3 rev. 10′. 1.1.A_4 rev. 6′. 2.1.A obv. ii(?) 15′. 2.7.A obv. 2. 2.7.B rev. 5′. 2.8 obv. 2, 3. 3.2.4 1′. 4.1.1.1.A_1 obv. 19′. 4.1.1.3 rev. B 3, 5. 4.1.2.3 obv. ii 3′, 4′, 8′, 9′, 12′, 13′; rev. iii 3, 4, 7. 4.2.1.A_1 obv. 6. 4.2.6 obv.$^{?}$ 3′. 4.2.9 lo. e. 34′. 5.7 rev. iii$^{?}$ 7′. 6.1 obv. 5, 19. 6.2 obv. 2′. 6.9 obv. 5′. 6.11 2′, 7′. 6.13 9′. 8.1.A rev. v 9, 16′, 20′, 26′. 8.1.B rev. 2′. 8.1.D obv. i 5′, 7′, 8′, 10′; rev. iv 6′, 13′. 8.1.E(A_3) obv. i 4′; obv. iii 4′. 8.1.F obv. i 6′, 7′, 18′; rev. v 16; rev. vi 8, 14, 16, 18. 8.1.J rev.

		v$^{!}$ 9′. 8.1.K rev. vi$^{?}$ 10′. 8.3 obv. 4′. 9.1.1 rev. iii 2′; rev. iv 2′, 16′ (2×), 45′. 9.1.2 rev. iii 3′. 9.1.4.A_1 obv. ii 3, 4. 9.1.6 obv. 2. 9.1.7 obv. 3′; rev. 2. 9.1.8 obv. 5′, 6′, 9′, 15′. 9.1.9 rev. iv 4′. 9.2.1 obv. ii 2′. 9.2.6 obv. i 11′. 10.1.1.1 rev.$^{?}$ 5′, 12′. 10.2.1.1 obv. 6′, 9′, 10′. 10.2.1.3 6′. 10.2.1.7 rev.$^{?}$ 6′. 11.3.1 21′. 12.1.2 5′, 8′. 12.2.1 obv. 6′. 12.3.1 6′
	Š]A	1.1.A_3 rev 12′. 4.1.2.3 rev. iii 7. 8.1.F rev. vi 6. 8.1.J rev. v$^{!}$ 11′
	Š[A	2.1.A obv. ii(?) 15′. 4.2.9 obv. 17′. 8.1.A obv. ii 27′. 8.1.B rev. 7′, 12′. 8.1.I rev. r. c. 3′. 10.2.1.1 obv. 10′. 12.3.7 6′
	Š[A$^{?}$	9.2.4 rev. iv 2

ŠĀDU
see *SŪTU*

$^{(URUDU)}$*ŠAGARÛ*	(a metal object, often in pairs)	
	ŠA-GA$_5$-RU-Ú	10.3.5 4′
	^{URUDU}*ŠA-GA$_5$-[RU-Ú*	10.3.6 7′
ŠALMU	‘intact, in good condition, healthy, sound’	
sg. nom.	(URUDU) *ŠAL-MU*	3.1.1.A_1 obv. ii 14′. 3.1.1.A_2 rev. v 6′, 8′. 3.1.1.A_3 obv. iii 8′, 11′, 15′, 16′
	(URUDU) *Š[AL-M]U*	3.1.1.A_1 obv. ii 6′
	(URUDU) *ŠA[L-MU*	3.1.1.A_2 rev. v 10′

ŠAMUḪI
see under *Geographic Names*

ŠAṬĀRU	‘to write, inscribe’	
sg. nom. (G vb. adj.)	*ŠAṬ-RU*	10.2.2.3 obv.$^{?}$ l. c. 8′
	Š]A-AṬ-RU	10.2.2.2 obv.$^{?}$ l. c. 9′
	ŠAṬ]-RU	10.2.2.3 obv.$^{?}$ l. c. 10′
G stat. sg. 3	*ŠA-ṬE$_4$-ER*	10.2.2.1 2′, 3′
	Š[A-ṬE$_4$-ER	10.2.2.1 1′
ŠĒDU	‘net’	
sg. nom.	*ŠE-DU (ARNABI)*	8.7 r. c. 7′
	⟨ŠE⟩-E-TU (ARNABI)	9.1.10.A_2 rev. 10′
	ŠE-E]-DU (ARNABI)	8.6 l. c. 5′
	ŠE-E-D[U	8.6 r. c. 2′
ŠĒRTU	(?)	
sg. dat./loc.	*A-NA ŠE-ER-TE*	5.1 rev. iii 7
^{URUDU}*ŠIRINNATU*	‘horse bit’	
sg. nom.	^{URUDU}*ŠE-RI-NA-TUM*	2.12 obv.$^{!}$ ii 11′
-ŠU	‘his, its’ (3 sg. possessive)	
	-ŠU	2.1.A obv. ii(?) 14′. 2.1.B 5′, 8′. 2.7.A obv. 23. 3.1.11.A 5. 3.1.11.B 4′. 5.2 obv. ii 9. 8.1.E(A_3) rev. vi 10. 8.1.F rev. v 9, 11. 8.6 l. c. 8′, 10′, 11′. 9.1.5 obv.$^{!}$ 2′; rev.$^{!}$ 8′. 9.2.4 rev. iv 4. 10.1.2.1 rev.$^{?}$ r. c.

		7′. 10.1.2.7 13′. 10.2.2.2 obv.? l. c. 3′. 10.3.1 rev. iii 2′. 10.3.2 obv. i(?) 3″. 11.2.2 2′
	-Š[U	2.1.A obv. ii(?) 10′. 9.2.2 rev.! iii 12′
	-Š[U?	10.2.2.4 obv.? r. c. 3′
	-SÚ	3.1.8.A obv. 12′. 5.2 rev. iii 6′. 9.1.1 rev. iii 11′, 13′; rev. iv 29′, 40′. 9.1.4.A_1 obv. ii 17′. 9.1.9 rev. iv 3′. 9.1.14 obv. r. c. 6′, 8′, 9′. 9.2.2 rev.! iii 7′. 9.2.9 obv.? 14′. 10.1.2.4 l. c. 6′. 10.2.2.2 obv.? l. c. 3′
	-S]Ú(?)	10.3.1 obv. ii 3′
ŠUḪRU		
see *ŠŪRU*		
ŠULMĀNU	'(greeting) gift, present'	
sg. nom. (st. const.)	*ŠUL-MAN*	10.2.2.4 obv.? r. c. 5′
	Š]UL-MAN	4.1.1.1.B_1 rev. iv? 5
pl. nom.!?	*ŠUL-MAN-TI*	2.2 rev. 2
	ŠUL-M[AN-TI	2.1.B 8′
pl. acc.	*ŠUL-MAN-T]I(?)*	2.1.B 9′
	ŠUL-MAN-T[I	2.2 obv. 3′
see *Lexical Commentary*		
GIŠŠULPATU	'(drinking) straw, tube'	
sg. nom.!	**GIŠ*ŠU-UL-PA-TI*	4.2.1.A_1 obv. 11
= ŠUL.PÁT		
ŠUMU	'name'	
sg. nom.-acc. n.	*ŠUM-**an***	9.2.4 obv. i 12′
sg. nom.-acc. n. (st. const.)	*ŠUM*	9.1.7 obv. 5′. 10.2.2.2 obv.? l. c. 4′, 6′, 8′. 10.2.2.3 obv.? l. c. 8′, 10′. 10.2.2.4 obv.? r. c. 2′, 4′
	Š[UM	10.2.2.2 obv.? l. c. 9′
	ŠU[M?	11.7.1 r. c. 2′
	ŠU[M?	11.7.1 r. c. 5′
	ŠU]M	10.2.2.1 5′
	ŠUM(-ŠU)	9.2.2 rev.! iii 12′. 9.2.4 rev. iv 4. 10.3.1 rev. iii 2′
= see also *MIMMA ŠUMŠU*		
-ŠUNU	'their, theirs' (3 pl. possessive)	
	-ŠU-NU	3.1.2 obv. l. c. 3′. 3.1.8.A rev. 6′
	-Š[U-NU	3.1.2 obv. l. c. 5′, 12′
	-ŠÚ-NU	10.1.2.2 6′
ŠUR ĒNI	'eyebrow'	
	ŠUR E-NI	10.2.2.3 obv.? l. c. 11′
ŠŪRU, ŠUḪ(U)RU	'dark-brown(?); black, grey(?)'	
	ŠU-U-RU	4.1.3.6 obv. 7′, 9′, 10′, 13′; rev. 2′. 8.1.D rev. iv 3′. 8.1.E(A_1) obv. iii 7′; rev. v 9′
	Š]U-U-RU	4.1.3.6 obv. 6′
	ŠU]-U-RU	8.1.D rev. iv 1′
	ŠU-U]-RU	4.1.3.6 rev. 3′

	ŠU-UḪ-RU	4.2.9 obv. obv. 2, 13, 20. 6.5 obv. 6′, 15′; rev. 3′, rev. 16′. 6.9 obv. 6′. 8.1.K rev. vi$^{?}$ 4′. 9.1.1 rev. iv 9′
	ŠU-[UḪ-R]U	6.5 rev. 8′
	Š]U-UḪ-RU	6.10 4′
	ŠU-UḪ-R[U	6.5 rev. 10′
	ŠU-[UḪ-RU	9.1.6 obv. 15. 11.6.7 2′
	ŠU-UḪ-U-RU	8.1.F obv. i 4′
see *Lexical Commentary*		
^{GIŠ}*ŠURINNU*	'(divine) emblem, standard'	
sg. nom.	^{GIŠ}*ŠU-RE-EN-NU*	9.1.5 rev.$^{!}$ 16′
= ŠU.NIR		
ŠURIPU	'frost, ice'	
see ^{TÚG}GÚ.È.A *ḪURRI ŠURĪPU*		
ŠURUḪTU	(an ornament)	
sg. nom.	*ŠU-RU-UḪ-DU*	9.1.1 rev. iii 11′
	ŠU-RU-U]Ḫ(?)-DU	9.2.13 2′
	ŠU-RU-UḪ-TUM	9.2.4 rev. iv 7
	ŠU-R]U-UḪ-TUM	9.1.1 rev. iv 36′
	ŠU-RU-U]Ḫ-TUM	9.2.6 obv. i 16′
	ŠU-RU-UḪ-TU[M	9.1.1 rev. iii 7′
ŠU'RU	'brow'	
see *ŠUR ĒNI*		
ŠŪŠI	'60'	
see Numerals		
TAMLÛ	'filling, inlay'	
sg. nom.	*TÁM-LU-Ú*	1.3 7′. 10.1.2.7 6′, 7′. 11.1.3 3′
	T]ÁM-LU-U	1.3 1′
	TÁM-LU-[Ú	10.1.2.7 4′
TAPAL	'set, pair' (for coll. no. higher than one; otherwise 1-*NŪTUM*)	
	n] *TA-PAL*	9.1.10.A_2 rev. 10′
	n *T]A-PAL*	1.5 obv. 8. 4.2.10 1′, 8′. 9.1.10.A_2 rev. 11′. 10.3.5 4′
	n *T]A-PAL*(?)	10.1.2.4 l. c. 22′
	n *T]A-[PA]L*	3.1.1.A_1 obv. ii 17′
	n *TA-P]AL*	9.1.4.A_4 l. c. 4′
	n *TA-PA]L*	4.1.4.6 obv. 3′. 10.2.1.3 2′
	n *TA-PA]L*(?)	9.2.9 rev.$^{?}$ 5′
see also respective numbers under *Numerals*		
TAYYĀRTU	(an attribute of PAD 'bar, ingot')	
sg. nom.	(PAD) *TA-IA-AR-TÙ*	4.2.1.A_1 obv. 10
see *Lexical Commentary*		
TUDITTU	'toggle-pin'	
sg. nom.	*TU-TI-IT-TUM*	1.5 obv. 11
	TU-TI-IT-TUM$^{!}$	4.2.1.A_1 obv. 4
	TU-TI-IT-TUM	4.2.1.A_1 obv. 5

inst.	*QA-DU TU-TI-IT-TI*	4.1.1.1.B_1 rev. iii$^{?}$ 4
	QA-D]*U TU-TI-IT*-[*TI*	4.1.1.1.A_1 rev. 12′
see *Lexical Commentary*		
^{LÚ}*ṬĒMU*	'messenger'	
sg. nom.	^{LÚ}*Ṭ*]*E₄*(?)-*MU*	10.3.3 obv.$^{?}$ 4′
sg. gen.	^{LÚ}*ṬE₄-ME* (GAL *MEŠEDI*)	5.7 rev. iii$^{?}$ 12′
ṬURRU	'yarn, twine, wire; string, band'	
sg. nom.	*ṬUR-RU*	2.16 obv. ii 1′. 4.1.4.9 obv. 11. 9.1.1 rev. iii 15′. 9.2.1 rev. iii 24′. 9.2.2 rev.$^{!}$ iii 23′
	Ṭ]*UR-RÚ*	9.2.9 obv.$^{?}$ 11′
	ṬU[*R-R*]*U*	9.1.1 rev. iv 18′
	ṬUR]-*RU*	9.2.1 obv. ii 6′
sg. dat./loc.	*A-NA ṬUR-RI*	8.1.A obv. i 7′
= DUR		
U	'and'	
	Ù	8.1.D rev. iv 8′. 8.1.H rev. r. c. 6′. 8.1.I rev. r. c. 5′
UL	'not'	
	UL	8.1.E(A_3) rev. vi 6. 9.1.13 5′. 9.2.4 obv. i 12′
	Ú-UL	2.7.A obv. 24. 4.1.4.9 rev. 2′. 7.1 rev. 10′. 8.1.A rev. vi 3′. 9.1.1 rev. iv 14′, 46′. 9.1.9 rev. iv 4′. 10.1.1.2 rev. iv 8′. 10.2.2.4 rev.$^{?}$ r. c. 1
	Ú]-*UL*	10.2.2.1 6′
	Ú-U[*L*	7.1 rev. 6′
	Ú-[*UL*(?)	11.3.1 13′
UMMA	'thus'	
	UM-MA	1.5 rev. 21. 4.1.1.1.B_1 rev. iii$^{?}$ 2, 4
UNQU	'ring (for a finger)'	
sg. nom.	*UN-QÚ*	8.1.A obv. i 11′, 13′
	UN-QÚ$^{!}$	8.1.A obv. ii 13′
UNŪTU	'equipment, utensils, furnishings'	
sg. nom.	*Ú-NU-TUM*	4.1.1.3 obv. 4. 4.1.1.7 rev.$^{!?}$ 1, 7. 8.1.A obv. ii 16′. 10.1.1.2 rev. iv 1′
	Ú-NU-TU[*M*	4.1.1.7 rev.$^{!?}$ 3. 4.1.2.4 4′
	Ú-NU-T[*UM*	4.1.1.3 obv. 6. 4.1.2.4 6′
sg. nom. (st. const.)	*Ú-NU-UT*	9.2.4 obv. ii 10′. 8.7 r. c. 9′
	Ú-NU-UT (DINGIR^{MEŠ})	2.2 obv. 10′
	Ú-NU-UT (É $^{\text{NA}_4}$KIŠIB)	9.1.9 rev. iv 5′
	Ú-NU-UT (KUŠ)	10.3.14 l. c. 6′
	Ú-NU-UT (KUŠ$^{\text{MEŠ!}}$)	10.3.14 l. c. 8′
	Ú-NU-UT (^{LÚ}ŠÀ.TAM)	9.1.4.A_1 obv. ii 6
	Ú-NU-U[*T*	9.1.4.A_5 2′
	Ú-[*NU-UT*(?) (URUDU(?))	2.9.A_3 obv. ii 7′
pl. acc.	*Ú-NU-TE*^{MEŠ}	9.1.8 obv. 12′
see *Lexical Commentary*; see also EN *UNŪTI*		
UPNU	'handful (unit of vol.)'	
sg. nom.	*UP-NU*	10.1.1.1 rev.$^{?}$ 14′. 10.1.1.2 rev. iv 9′ (2×)

(W)AŠĀBU	'to sit'	
see ^{GIŠ}GIGIR *AŠĀBI*		
(W)ATĀRU	'to be outsize, surplus'	
sg. nom. (G vb. adj.)	*A-AT-RU*	12.3.4 obv. 6
= *kallaratar*; DIRI		
ZŪRU	(an item)	
sg. nom.	*ṢÚ-Ú-RU*	1.5 obv. 11
	ṢÚ-U-Ú-RU	1.1.A_2 rev. 6
see *Lexical Commentary*		

Divine Names

^{D}*Āla*		
sg. gen.	*ŠA* ^{D}*a-a-la*	10.1.2.8 rev. r. c. 5′
^{D}*Anzili*		
sg. gen.	*ŠA* ^{D}[*an-z*]*i-li*	10.2.1.1 obv. 9′
^{D}*Ḫepat*		
	^{D}*ḫé-pát*	8.1.D rev. iv 8′. 8.1.H rev. r. c. 6′. 8.1.I rev. r. c. 5′
^{D}*Kulitta*		
	^{D}*k*[*u-li-it-ta*(?)	4.1.1.8 rev. r. c. 5′
^{D}*Kumarbi*		
sg. dat./loc.	*A-N*]*A* ^{D}*ku-mar-bi*	7.1 obv. 4′
^{D}*Ninatta*		
	^{D}*ni-n*[*a-at-ta*	4.1.1.8 rev. r. c. 6′
^{D}*Pišašapḫi*		
sg. dat./loc.	*A-NA* ^{D}*pí-ša-ša-ap-ḫi*	7.1 obv. 10′
$^{(D)}$*Walipašu-*		
stem	*wa-li-pa-šu-ú*	10.2.2.4 obv.$^{?}$ r. c. 6′
see *Lexical Commentary*		
^{D}DAG		
sg. dat./loc.	*A-N*]*A* ^{D}DAG	9.1.4.A_1 obv. ii 4
DINGIR GAL	"The Great Deity"	
stem	[D]INGIR GAL	6.1 l. e. 1
^{D}É.A		
sg. dat./loc.	*A-NA* ^{D}É.A	7.1 obv. 9′
^{D}IŠKUR		
	^{D}]IŠKUR(?)	4.1.1.9 8′
sg. gen.	*ŠA* ^{D}IŠKUR	10.1.2.8 rev. r. c. 6′
^{D}IŠKUR BÚN	'Storm-god of thunder'	
sg. gen.	*ŠA* ^{D}IŠKUR BÚN	2.1.A obv. ii(?) 15′
^{D}IŠKUR ^{URU}*Ḫalpa*	'Storm-god of Aleppo'	
	^{D}IŠK]UR ^{URU}*ḫal-pa*	9.2.6 obv. i 17′

^{D}IŠKUR ^{URU}*Nerik*	'Storm-god of Nerik'	
	^{D}IŠKUR ^{URU}*ne-ri-ik*	8.1.F rev. v 16
^{D}LAMMA		
	^{D}LAMMA	3.1.1.A$_2$ rev. vi 2′
^{D}LUGAL-*ma* (^{D}*Šarruma*)		
	^{D}LUGAL-*ma*	4.1.1.2.A obv. 11′. 8.1.D rev. iv 8′
	^{D}[LUGAL-*ma*	8.1.H rev. r. c. 6′
$^{(D)}$U$_4$(-*aš*).SAKAR	'(deified) crescent moon, lunula'	
see under *Sumerograms*		
^{D}UD-*AM*	'(deified) day'	
	(*BI-IB-RU*) ^{D}UD-*AM*	9.1.4.A$_1$ obv. ii 36
^{D}UD.SIG$_5$-*me*- ^{URU}*Azzi*	'(deified) "Good Day" of Azzi'	
sg. nom.	^{D}UD.SIG$_5$-*me-iš* ^{URU}*az-zi*	9.2.1 obv. ii 4′
^{D}UTU	'Sun-god(dess)'	
	^{D}UTU(?)	9.2.8.A$_2$ 10″
sg. gen.	^{D}UTU-*aš*	10.2.1.2 obv. 9′
	⸢$^{D?}$UTU-*aš*(?)⸣ (ALAM)	11.2.1 4′
^{D}UTU $^{(URU)}$PÚ-*na*	'Sun-goddess of Arinna'	
	^{D}UTU PÚ-*na*	3.1.11.A 3. 3.1.11.B 2′
	^{D}UTU ^{URU}PÚ-*na*	4.1.1.9 10′
	^{D}UTU⟨⟨*ŠI*⟩⟩ ^{URU}PÚ-*na*	6.1 rev. A 7″
sg. dat./loc.	*A-N*]*A*(?) ^{D}UTU *a-ri-i*[*n-na*	7.3 obv. i 1
^{D}UTU-*ŠI*		
see under *Sumerograms*		
^{D}*IŠTAR*		
sg. gen.	*ŠA* ^{D}*I*[*ŠTAR*	5.1 obv. ii 12′. 5.7 rev. iii$^{?}$ 7′
^{D}*IŠTAR* AMA MUNUS.LUGAL	"Ištar, mother of the queen"	
	^{D}*IŠTAR* AM[A M]UNUS.L[UGAL(?)	8.1.F rev. vi 1
^{D}*IŠTAR* É	'Ištar of the house'	
	^{D}*IŠTAR* É	5.1 rev. iii 1
sg. gen.	^{D}*IŠTAR* É-*TIM*	5.1 rev. iii 2
^{D}*IŠTAR* LÍL	'Ištar of the field'	
sg. dat./loc.	*A-NA* ^{D}*IŠTAR* LÍL	7.1 obv. 7′
^{D}*IŠTAR* ^{URU}*Katapa*	'Ištar of Katapa'	
sg. dat./loc.	*A-NA* ^{D}*IŠTAR* ^{URU}*ka-ta-pa*	5.1 rev. iii 4
^{D}*IŠTAR* ^{URU}*Lawazantiya*	'Ištar of Lawazantiya'	
	^{D}*IŠTAR* ^{URU}*la-wa-za-an-ti-ia*	5.1 rev. iii 1
	^{D}*IŠTAR* ^{URU}*la*]*-wa-za-an-*[*ti*]*-ia*	8.1.F rev. vi 10
	^{D}*IŠTAR* ^{URU}*la-w*]*a-za-an-ti-ia*	10.2.1.7 rev.$^{?}$ 8′
^{D}*IŠTAR* ^{URU}*Ninuwa*	'Ištar of Nineveh'	
	^{D}*IŠTAR* ^{URU}*ni-nu-wa*	8.1.F rev. vi 2
^{D}*IŠTAR* ^{URU}*ŠAMUḪI*	'Ištar of Šamuha'	
sg. dat./loc.	*A-NA* ^{D}*IŠTAR*(?) ^{URU}*Š*]*A-MU-ḪI*	4.1.1.1.A$_1$ rev. 11′
see *Lexical Commentary*		

^{D}10 ḪI.ḪI-*ašši*	'Storm-god of lightning'	
sg. dat./loc.	*A-NA* ^{D}10 ḪI.ḪI-*aš-ši*	7.1 obv. 2′
^{D}10 $^{\text{(URU)}}$*Šapinuwa*	'Storm-god of Šapinuwa'	
	^{D}10 ^{URU}*ša-pí-nu-wa*	3.1.11.A 6
	^{D}]10 *ša-pí-nu-wa*	3.1.11.B 5′
^{D}10 ^{URU}TÚL-*na*	'Storm-god of Arinna'	
sg. dat./loc.	*A-NA* ^{D}10 ^{URU}PÚ-*na*	6.1 rev. A 6″

Geographical Names

KUR *Aḫḫiyawa-*		
stem	KUR *aḫ-ḫi-ia-u-wa-a*	4.2.9 lo. e. 33′
	KUR *aḫ-ḫ*]*i-ia-u-wa*	2.6 1′
^{URU}*Alašiya-*		
see GADA ^{URU}*Alašiya*		
^{URU}*Alatarma-*		
stem	^{U}]^{RU}*a-la-tar-ma*	10.1.2.8 rev. r. c. 1′
abbr.	^{URU}*a.*	10.1.2.8 rev. r. c. 2′
^{URU}*Alḫiša-*		
demonym		
stem (sg.)	(LÚ) ^{URU}*al-ḫi-ša*	3.2.1 obv. 15
^{URU}*Angala-*		
demonym		
stem (sg.)	(LÚ) ^{URU}*an-ga-la-a*	1.1.A_2 rev. 4
^{URU}*Ankuwa-*		
stem	^{URU}*an-ku-wa*	2.7.A obv. 12
	^{URU}*an-ku-*[*wa*	3.1.8.A rev. 5′
^{URU}*Andamišara-*		
demonym		
stem (sg.)	(LÚ) ^{URU}*an-da-mi-ša-ra*	1.1.A_2 rev. 2
^{URU}*Anzilatašši-*		
stem	^{URU}*an-zi-la-ta-aš-ši*	3.1.8.A rev. 8′
	^{URU}*a*[*n-zi-la-ta-aš-ši*	3.2.1 obv. 4
^{URU}*Arinna-*		
see ^{D}UTU ^{URU}PÚ-*na*, ^{D}10 ^{URU}PÚ-*na*, ^{URU}PÚ-*na*		
^{URU}*Arpa-*		
stem	^{URU}*a*]*r-pa*	3.1.11.A 6
	^{URU}*a*[*r-pa*	3.1.11.B 4′
^{URU}*Arpuzzia-*		
stem	^{URU}*ar-p*[*u*$^{?}$*-u*]*z*$^{?}$*-z*[*i-ia*	3.1.7.A_2 obv. ii 14′
	^{UR}]^{U}*a-ar-pu-uz-zi-ia*	3.1.1.A_1 obv. ii 16′
^{URU}*Aršauna-*		
stem	^{URU}*a*]*r-ša-u-na*	4.1.3.6 obv. 11′, 12′

	^{URU}*ar-š[a-u-na*	4.1.3.6 obv. 9′
^{URU}*Arušna-*		
stem	^{URU}*a-ru-uš⟨⟨uš⟩⟩-na*	4.1.1.1.B_1 rev. iii$^?$ 3
	^{URU}*a-ru-[uš-na*	4.1.1.1.A_1 rev. 12′
^{URU}*Arzauwa-*		
demonym		
stem (pl.)	(LÚ^{MEŠ}) ^{URU}*ar-za-u-wa*	1.1.A_3 rev. 6′
^{URU}*Aštuḫira-*		
stem	^{URU}*aš-t]u(?)-ḫi-ra*	3.1.1.A_1 obv. ii 12′
Āššur	'Assyria; Assyrian'	
stem	*a-aš-šur*	2.2 obv. 15′
^{URU}*Azzi-*		
see ^{D}UD.SIG$_5$-*me-* ^{URU}*Azzi*		
^{URU}*Ḫallapiya-*		
demonym		
stem (sg.)	(LÚ) ^{URU}*ḫal-la-pí-ia*	6.1 rev. B 3
$^{\mathrm{(URU)}}$*Ḫalap*	'Aleppo'	
stem	*ḫa-la-ap*	2.1.B 9′
see also ^{D}IŠKUR ^{URU}*Ḫalpa*		
^{URU}*Ḫanḫana-*		
see ^{URU}*Zitḫara ŠA* ^{URU}*Ḫanḫana*		
^{URU}*Ḫariyaša-*		
See É.GAL ^{URU}*Ḫariyaša*		
^{URU}*Ḫatta-*		
see GÍR ^{URU}*Ḫatta*		
^{URU}*Ḫatta/ili-*		
see ^{KUŠ}E.SIR ^{URU}*Ḫat(t)a/ili*		
^{URU}*Ḫadanta-*		
stem	^{URU}*ḫa-d[a-a]n(?)-ta*	1.1.A_2 obv. 12′
^{URU}*Ḫatenzuwa-*		
demonym		
stem (pl.)	(LÚ^{MEŠ}) ^{URU}*ḫa-te-e]n-zu-wa*	1.4 3′
^{URU}*Ḫadara-*		
stem	$^{\mathrm{U]RU}}$*ḫa-da-ra*	4.1.4.1.A_2 obv. i 4′
	$^{\mathrm{URU]}}$*ḫa-*da-ra**	4.1.4.1.A_2 obv. i 1′
^{URU}*Ḫatitešpa-*		
demonym		
stem (pl.)	(LÚ^{MEŠ}) ^{URU}*ḫa-ti-ti-eš-pa*	5.7 rev. iii$^?$ 20′
^{URU}*Ḫadduna-*		
stem	^{URU}*ḫa-ad-du-na*	3.1.10 8
^{URU}*Ḫattuša-*		
sg. dat./loc.	^{URU}*ḫa-ad-du-ši*	4.1.1.1.A_1 rev. 5′
see also ^{URU}KÙ.BABBAR, ^{URU}*ḪATTI*		

^{URU}*Ḫilammattiya-*		
stem	^{URU}*ḫi-lam-ma-at-ti-ia*	3.1.10 10
^{URU}*Ḫupanda-*		
demonym		
stem (sg.)	(LÚ) ^{URU}*ḫu-pa-an-da*	1.1.A_3 rev. 6′
^{URU}*Ḫupišna-*		
see É.GAL ^{URU}*Ḫupišna-*		
^{URU}*Ḫurla-*		
sg. dat./loc.	*I-NA* ^{URU}*ḫur-la*	1.1.A_2 obv. 8′, 10′
	I-N]*A* ^{URU}*ḫur-la*	1.1.A_2 obv. 11′
demonym		
stem (sg.)	(LÚ) ^{URU}*ḫur-la*	1.1.A_2 rev. 8
	(LÚ) $^{\mathrm{UR]U}}$*ḫur-la*	1.1.A_2 rev. 10
^{URU}*Ḫuwarniya-*		
stem	^{URU}*ḫu-u-wa-ar-n*[*i-ia*	3.1.1.A_3 rev. iv 6′
demonym		
stem (sg.)	(LÚ) ^{URU}*ḫu-u-wa-ar-ni-ia*	5.5 rev. iii 4′
Ikkuwaniya-		
see TÚG *Ikkuwaniya*		
KUR *Išuwa-*	'(the land of) Išuwa'	
demonym		
stem (sg.)	(LUGAL) KUR *i-šu-wa*	4.1.4.9 obv. 6
^{URU}*Kalmazida-*		
demonym		
stem (sg.)	(LÚ) ^{URU}*kal-ma-zi-da-a*	1.1.A_2 rev. 1
^{URU}*Kamama-*		
demonym		
stem (pl.)	(LÚ^{MEŠ}) ^{URU}*kam-ma-ma*	5.7 rev. iii$^?$ 22′
^{URU}*Kantieššišša-*		
demonym		
stem (pl.)	(LÚ^{MEŠ}) ^{URU}*ká*]*n-ti-eš-ši-iš-ša*	1.4 7′
^{URU}*Gapaštara-*		
demonym		
stem (sg.)	(LÚ) ^{URU}*ga-pa-aš-ta-ra*	1.1.A_3 rev. 3′
	(LÚ) ^{URU}*ga-pa-aš-t*]*a-ra*	1.1.A_3 rev. 11′
^{URU}*Kapitašamna-*		
sg. gen.	^{URU}*k*]*a-*pí-ta*-šàm-n*[*a-aš*	3.1.5.A_2 obv. ii(?) 13′
	^{URU}*ka-pí-t*]*a-š*[*àm-na-aš*	3.1.5.A_2 obv. ii(?) 16′
see also $^{\mathrm{(KUŠ/TÚG)}}$*Kapi(r)taš(š)amna-*		
(KUR) $^{\mathrm{(URU)}}$*Karduniya-*	'(the land of) Babylon; Babylonian'	
sg. nom.	^{URU}*kar-*^{D}*du-ni-aš*	11.3.1 12′
	^{URU}*ka*]*r-*^{D}*du-ni-ia-aš*	8.8.B l. c. 2′
	^{URU}*kar-*^{D}*d*[*u-ni-aš*	11.3.1 22′
	^{URU}*kar-*^{D}*d*[*u-ni-ia-aš*	8.8.A 2′
	KUR *kar-*^{D}*du-ni-aš*	6.1 obv. 7

	KUR *kar*!-D*du-ni-a*[*š*	2.2 rev. 2
	KUR *kar*-D*du-n*[*i-*	8.1.B rev. 9′
	KUR *kar*-[D*du-ni-*	8.1.A obv. ii 25′
sg. gen.	*ŠA* KUR *kar*-D[*du-ni-aš*	4.1.1.1.A_1 obv. 19′
	ŠA KUR *k*]*ar*-D*du-ni-*[*aš*	4.1.1.1.A_1 rev. 8′
	ŠA KUR *kar*-D*du*]*-ni-aš*	4.1.1.1.B_1 obv. ii? 18′
KUR *Kargamiš*	'(the land of) Carchemish'	
demonym		
stem (sg.)	(LUGAL) KUR *kar-g*[*a-miš*	2.16 obv. ii 6′
URU*Karkaziya-*		
demonym		
stem (sg.)	(LÚ) URU*kar-*ka_4*-zi-ia*	1.1.A_1 obv. 11′
URU*Kašaya-*		
see É.GAL URU*Kašaya-*		
URU*Kašipura-*		
see KUŠE.SIR URU*Kašipura*		
(URU)*Gašga-*		
see MÁ.URU.URU_5 *Gašga*, GIŠPAN URU*Gašga*, KUŠ*IŠPATU* URU*Gašga*		
URU*Kaštama-*		
demonym		
stem (sg.)	(LÚ) URU*ka-aš-ta-ma*	5.1 obv. ii 5′
stem (pl.)	(LÚMEŠ) URU*kaš-ta-ma*	5.1 obv. ii 2′
URU*Katapa-*		
see D*IŠTAR* URU*Katapa*		
URU*Kašuliya-*		
stem	URU*k*]*a-šu-li-ia*	3.1.10 12
URU*Kawarna-*		
stem	URU*ka-wa-ar-na*	5.1 rev. iii 9
Gazzimara-		
see É (URU)*Gazzimara-*		
URU*Kizzuwatna-*		
sg. gen.?	URU*kiz*x*-zu-wa-a*[*t-na-aš*	3.1.5.A_2 obv. ii(?) 6′
stem	URU*ki*]*-iz-zu-wa-at-na*	3.1.1.A_3 rev. iv 17′
URU*Kuenzuliya-*		
stem	URU*ku-en-z*[*u*]*-li-ia*	3.1.1.A_3 obv. iii 4′
URU*Gullalliya-*		
stem	URU*gu*]*l-lal-li-ia*	4.1.4.2.A_2 obv. l. c. 5′
URU*Kummanni-*		
stem	U]RU*kum-man-ni*	10.2.1.7 rev.? 3′
	URU*ku*]*m-man-ni*	10.2.1.7 rev.? 7′
see also (TÚG) (URU)*Kummanni*		
URU*Kurkuriša-*		
stem	URU*ku-ur-ku-ri-ša*	3.1.1.A_1 rev. v 19′

^{URU}*Landa-*		
stem	^{URU}*la-a-an-da*	4.1.3.6 obv. 5′, 6′
	^{URU}*l[a-a-an-da*	4.1.3.6 obv. 16′
^{URU}*Lakkarwa-*		
stem	^{URU}*la-a]k-kar-wa*	3.1.11.B 2′
	^{URU}*la-ak-kar-[wa*	3.1.11.A 3
^{URU}*Lawazantiya-*		
see ^{D}*IŠTAR* ^{URU}*Lawazantiya-*		
(KUR) $^{\text{(URU)}}$*Lukka-*		
stem	KUR *lu-uk-*ka_4*-a*	8.1.B rev. 10′
	KUR *lu-uk-k[*a_4*-a*	8.1.A obv. ii 26′
	KUR *lu-u]k-*ka_4*-a*	12.1.2 6′
demonym		
stem (pl.)	(LÚ^{MEŠ}) ^{URU}*lu-uk-*ka_4*-a*	5.1 obv. ii 8′
^{URU}*Maḫuduwa-*		
demonym		
stem (sg.)	(LÚ) ^{URU}*ma-ḫu-du-wa*	1.1.A_1 obv. 14′
(KUR) ^{URU}*Maša*		
demonym		
stem (sg.)	(LÚ) ^{URU}*ma-a-š[a*	5.4 r. c. 3′
stem (pl.)	(LÚ^{MEŠ}) ^{URU}*ma-a-ša*	5.7 rev. iii$^?$ 13′
	(LÚ^{MEŠ}) KUR ^{URU}*m[a-a-ša*	5.7 rev. iii$^?$ 6′
stem (pl. dat./loc.)	(*A-NA* LÚ^{MEŠ}) ^{URU}*ma-a-š[a*	5.4 r. c. 4′
	(*A-NA* LÚ]^{MEŠ}) ^{URU}*ma-a-ša*	5.2 obv. ii 2
^{URU}*Mattala-*		
sg. gen.?	^{URU}*ma-at-ta-la-aš*	3.1.2 obv. l. c. 8′
^{URU}*Mizamizana-*		
stem	^{URU}*mi-za-mi-za-na*	3.1.1.A_3 obv. iii 8′
KUR $^{\text{(URU)}}$*Mizri*	'the land of Egypt'	
loc.	*INA* KUR *m-iz-ri*	8.4 rev. 11′
	KUR *mi-iz-ri*	4.2.9 lo. e. 34′. 8.1.A obv. i 7′; rev. v 21′, 23′. 11.7.1 l. c. 3′
	KUR *mi-iz-ri-i*	1.5 obv. 5
	KUR *mi-i]z-ri*	2.11 obv.$^?$ 6′
	KUR *mi-iz-r[i*	8.1.A obv. ii 8′
	KU]R ^{URU}*mi-iz-ri*	2.3 4. 8.1.B rev. 3′
stem	KUR $^{\text{U]RU}}$*mi-iz-ri*	2.3 2
see also *MIZRI/Ī*, GABA ^{URU}*MIZRĪ*		
^{URU}*Nerik*		
stem	^{URU}*ne-ri-ik*	6.1 obv. 4, 8, 14, 18
see also ^{D}IŠKUR ^{URU}*Nerik*		
^{URU}*Ninuwa-*	'Nineveh'	
see ^{D}*IŠTAR* ^{URU}*Ninuwa*		
^{URU}*Paniša-*		
stem	^{URU}*pa-ni-š[a*	4.1.4.1.A_1 rev. v 5′

	^{URU}*p*]*a*$^{!}$-*ni-ša*	4.1.4.1.A_1 rev. v 8′
^{URU}*Papila-*		
see NA$_4$ ^{URU}*Papila*		
^{URU}*Parnašša/i-*		
sg. nom.	^{URU}*pár-na-aš-ši-i*]*š*	3.1.8.B 1′
stem	^{URU}*pár-na-aš-ša*	4.1.4.1.A_1 obv. ii 2′, 5′, 6′, 8′, 10′
	^{URU}*pár-na-aš-ši*	3.1.8.A rev. 13′
^{URU}*Pašura-*		
stem	^{URU}*pa-šu-u-ra*	2.7.A obv. 22
	^{URU}*pa-aš-š*[*u-ra*(?)	2.16 obv. ii 3′
= $^{\mathrm{URU.GIŠ}}$BANŠUR?		
KUR ^{URU}*Pikkauzza-*		
demonym		
stem (pl.)	(LÚ^{MEŠ}) KUR ^{URU}*pí-ik-ka$_4$-uz-z*[*a*	5.7 rev. iii$^{?}$ 29′
^{URU}*Puḫanda-*		
stem	^{UR}]^{U}*pu-ḫa-an-da*	5.4 r. c. 8′
	^{URU}*pu-ḫa-a*[*n-da*	4.1.4.2.A_2 obv. r. c. 9′
^{URU}*Šaḫḫuwiya-*		
stem	^{URU}*ša-aḫ-ḫu-w*[*i$_5$-ia*(?)	3.1.7.A_1 obv. i 13′
^{URU}*Šakkamaḫa-*		
demonym		
stem (sg.)	(LÚ) ^{URU}*ša-ak-ka$_4$-ma-ḫa*	5.1 obv. ii 11′
^{URU}*Šamuḫa-*		
stem	^{URU}*š*]*a-mu-ḫa*	4.1.4.2.A_1 rev. l. c. 12′
see also ^{D}*IŠTAR ŠAMUḪI, ŠAMUḪI*		
^{URU}*Šapla-*		
stem	^{URU}*ša-ap-la*	3.1.1.A_3 rev. iv 19′
^{URU}*Šapinuwa-*		
see É.GAL ^{URU}*Šapinuwa-*, ^{D}10 $^{\mathrm{(URU)}}$*Šapinuwa-*		
^{URU}*Šaraḫaddu-*		
demonym		
stem (pl.)	(LÚ^{MEŠ}) ^{URU}*ša-ra-ḫ*]*a-ad-du*	1.4 9′
^{URU}*Šaripiya-*		
stem	^{URU}*ša-ri-pí-ia*	5.2 obv. ii 12
^{URU}*Šarmana-*		
demonym		
stem (sg.)	(LÚ) ^{URU}*šar-ma-na*$^{!}$	3.2.1 obv. 18
^{URU}*Šarwa*(-)		
stem	^{URU}*šar-w*[*a*(-)	3.1.1.A_3 rev. iv 7′
^{URU}*Šawatta-*		
stem	^{URU}*ša-wa-at-ta*	3.1.1.A_1 rev. v 14′
Šulupašša/i-		
see É.GAL $^{\mathrm{(URU)}}$*šulupašša/i-*		

Tap(p)a/išpa-		
see (TÚG) *tap(p)a/išpa-*		
^{URU}*Tapputa-*		
demonym		
stem (pl.)	(LÚ^{MEŠ}) ^{URU}*ta-[a]p-pu-[t]a*	12.2.1 rev. 7′
^{URU}*Tarkuma-*		
demonym		
stem (pl.)	(LÚ^{MEŠ}) ^{URU}*tar-ku-ma*	1.4 8′
^{URU}*Taštarešša-*		
demonym		
stem (pl.)	(LÚ^{MEŠ}) ^{URU}*ta-aš-t]a-re-eš-ša*	1.4 5′
^{URU}*Tatimuwa-*		
demonym		
stem (pl.)	(LÚ^{MEŠ}) ^{URU}*ta-ti-mu-wa*	1.4 6′
^{URU}*Tetumna-*		
sg. gen.?	^{URU}*te-tu[m-na-aš*(?)	3.1.5.A_2 obv. ii(?) 3′
^{URU}*Tummanna-*		
demonym		
stem (sg.)	(LÚ) ^{URU}*tu-u-ma-an-na*	5.1 obv. ii 9′
stem (pl.)	(LÚ^{MEŠ}) ^{URU}*tu-um-ma-an-na*	5.1 obv. ii 7′
^{URU}*Tuššimna-*		
stem	^{URU}*tu-uš-š[i]-im-na*	3.1.1.A_3 rev. iv 14′
^{URU}*Ugarit*		
stem	^{URU}*ú-ga-ri-it*	4.1.1.1.B_1 rev. iv$^{?}$ 5
	^{URU}*ú-ga-ri-it*$^{!}$	1.5 rev. 24
^{URU}*Urikina-*		
stem	^{URU}*ú-ri-ki-na*	4.1.1.1.B_1 rev. iii$^{?}$ 12
	^{URU}*ú-ri-ki-n[a*	4.1.1.1.A_1 rev. 17′
^{URU}*Walḫu[z-…*		
demonym		
stem (pl.)	(LÚ^{MEŠ} KUR ^{URU}*maša*) $^{\text{U[R]U}}$*wa-al-ḫu-u[z*$^{?}$*-*	5.7 rev. iii$^{?}$ 13′
^{URU}*Wannanda-*		
demonym		
stem (sg.)	(LÚ) ^{URU}*wa-an-na-an-d[a*	1.1.A_3 rev. 8′
^{URU}*Waniya*(-)[		
sg. gen.	*ŠA* ^{URU}*wa-a-ni-ia*(-)[	12.3.1 6′
^{URU}*Wašḫaniya-*		
see ^{TÚG}GÚ ^{URU}*wašḫaniya*, (TÚG) *wašḫaniya*		
^{URU}*Watru-*		
demonym		
stem (pl.)	(LÚ^{MEŠ} KUR ^{URU}*maša*) ^{URU}*wa-a[t*$^{?}$*]-ru*	5.7 rev. iii$^{?}$ 6′
^{URU}*Zagapura-*		
demonym		
stem (pl.)	(LÚ^{MEŠ}) ^{URU}*za-ga-pu-ra*	5.7 rev. iii$^{?}$ 16′

^{URU}*Zarara*(-)...		
stem	^{URU}*za-ra-r*[*a*(-)	3.1.8.A rev. 16′
^{URU}*Zarwiša-*		
stem	^{URU}*za-ar-wi*$_5$*-ša*	4.1.4.1.A$_1$ rev. v 8″; rev. vi 6′
	^{URU}*za-ar-wi*$_5$]*-ša*	4.1.4.1.A$_1$ rev. vi 1′
	^{URU}*za-ar-*[*wi*$_5$*-ša*	4.1.4.1.A$_1$ rev. v 3″
^{URU}*Zi(š)kuliya-*		
stem	^{URU}*zi-iš-k*[*u-li-ia*	3.1.4 2′, 5′
demonym		
stem (sg.)	(LÚ) ^{URU}*zi-ku-li-ia*	1.1.A$_2$ rev. 3
	(LÚ) ^{URU}*zi-ku-*[*li-ia*	1.1.A$_3$ rev. 1′
^{URU}*Zippaššana-*		
stem (	^{URU}*zi-i*[*p-p*]*a-aš*$^{!}$*-ša-na*	5.7 rev. iii$^{?}$ 14′
^{URU}*Zitḫara ŠA* ^{URU}*Ḫanḫana* 'Zithara-of-Ḫanḫana'		
stem (	^{URU}*zi-it-ḫa-ra ŠA* ^{URU}*ḫa-an-ḫa-na*	5.1 obv. ii 3′
see *Lexical Commentary*		
^{URU}Á.ŠÉŠ		
	^{URU}]Á.ŠÉŠ(?)	3.1.8.A obv. 16′
^{URU}DU$_6$ É.GAL-*LIM*	'tell of the palace'	
see under *Sumerograms*		
$^{\mathrm{URU.GIŠ}}$BANŠUR		
see ^{URU}PA.URUDU(.)		
^{URU}KÙ.BABBAR	'Ḫattuša'	
sg. gen.	^{URU}KÙ.BABBAR-*aš*	11.3.1 20′
sg. dat./loc.	^{URU}KÙ.BABBAR-*ši*	1.5 rev. 27
	^{URU}K]Ù.BABBAR-*ši*	4.1.1.1.B$_1$ obv. ii$^{?}$ 3′
	I-NA ^{URU}KÙ.BABBAR-*TI*	1.1.A$_2$ obv. 5′
stem	^{URU}KÙ.BABBAR-*TI*	3.2.2 obv.$^{?}$ 5′
	^{URU}KÙ.BABBAR-*T*[*I*	3.2.2 obv.$^{?}$ 7′
see also ^{URU}*ḫattuša-*, ^{URU}*ḪATTI*		
^{URU}PA.URUDU(.) (mistake for $^{\mathrm{URU.GIŠ}}$BANŠUR?)		
stem	^{URU}PA.URUD[U(.)	4.1.3.1 4′
^{URU}PÚ-*na*	'Arinna'	
stem	^{URU}PÚ-*na*	6.1 rev. B 1; lo. e. 10″
	U]^{RU}PÚ-*na*	6.1 rev. B 2
see also ^{D}UTU ^{URU}PÚ-*na*, ^{D}10 ^{URU}PÚ-*na*		
KUR ^{URU}UGU	'the Upper Land'	
sg. gen.	KUR ^{URU}UGU-*TI*	5.1 rev. iii 5
KUR $^{\mathrm{(URU)}}$*AMURRU*		
sg. gen.	*ŠA* KUR *A-MUR-RI*	2.7.A rev. 2
	ŠA KUR ^{URU}*A-MUR-R*[*I*	2.7.B rev. 6′
^{URU}*ḪATTI*	'Ḫattuša; Hittite, in the Hittite style'	
see ^{KUŠ}*IŠPATU* ^{URU}*ḪATTIM*		

$^{(\text{URU})}$*ḪURRI*	'Hurrian, in the Hurrian style' (nisbe adj.)	
	ḪUR-RI	10.3.5 6′, 10.2.1.2 obv. 5′
	ḪU[*R-RI*(?)	9.1.10.A_2 rev. 3′

see also ^{GIŠ}*šalašturi- ḪURRI*, ^{KUŠ}*IŠPATU* ^{URU}*ḪURRI*, ^{GIŠ}BANŠUR *ḪURRI*, ^{GIŠ}ESI *ḪURRI*, ^{TÚG}GÚ(È.A) *ḪURRI*, ŠE.NAGA *ḪURRI*, SÍG *ḪURRI*

MIZRI/Ī	'Egyptian, in the Egyptian style' (nisbe adj.)	
	MI-IZ-RI	8.1.D rev. iv 7′. 8.1.H rev. r. c. 5′
	MI-IZ-R[*I*	8.1.I rev. r. c. 4′
	MI-IZ-RI-I	8.1.A obv. i 13′
	M]*I-IZ-RI-I*	6.4 obv.? 2′. 8.1.A obv. i 12′
	MI-IZ-RI-[*I*	8.1.A obv. ii 17′
	MI-IZ-R[*I-I*	8.1.A obv. ii 20′

see also KUR $^{(\text{URU})}$*Mizri*, GABA ^{URU}*MIZRĪ*

ŠAMUḪI	'Šamuha; in the Šamuhean style' (nisbe adj.)	
	ŠA-MU-ḪI	3.2.4 1′
KUR $^{\text{URU D}}$10-*tašša-*	'Tarḫuntašša'	
	(LUGAL) KUR $^{\text{URU D}}$10-*ta-aš-š*[*a*(-)	1.1.A_3 rev. 12′

Personal Names

^{m}*Agallu-*		
sg. nom.	^{m}*a-gal-lu-ú-uš*	3.2.1 rev. 8′
stem	^{m}*a-gal-lu-ú*	4.1.3.1 5′
^{f}*Agatti-*		
sg. nom.	^{f}*a-ga-at-ti-eš*	12.3.7 8′
^{m}*Alalimi-*		
stem	^{m}*a-la-li-m*[*i*	3.1.2 rev. l. c. 5′. 5.1 rev. iii 12
	^{m}*a-la-li-*[*mi*	5.8 7′
^{m}*Alamuwa-*		
stem	^{m}*a-la-mu-u-wa*	4.1.1.2.B obv. 11
	^{m}*a-la-m*[*u-u-wa*	4.1.1.2.A obv. 24′
^{m}*Alantalli-*		
sg. gen.	*ŠA* ^{m}*a-la-a*[*n-ta-al-li*(?)	6.13 9′
^{m}*Aliḫešni-*		
sg. nom.	^{m}*a-li-ḫe-eš-ni-iš*	3.1.8.A rev. 11′
^{m}*Alipiḫame-*		
sg. nom.	^{m}*a-li-pí-ḫa-me-e*[*š*	5.7 rev. iii? 25′
^{m}*Ali*-LÚ- (^{m}*Aliziti-*)		
sg. dat./loc.	*A-NA* ^{m}*a-li*-LÚ-*ia*	1.1.A_1 obv. 14′
^{m}*Amuna-*		
stem	^{m}*a-mu-na*	8.1.A rev. vi 5′
^{m}*Ammi*-ŠEŠ- (^{m}*Amminani-*)		
stem	^{m}*am-mi*-ŠEŠ	4.2.12 5′

^{m}*Ammu*-ŠEŠ- (^{m}*Ammunani-*)		
stem	^{m}*am-mu*-ŠEŠ	4.1.3.1 9′
^{f}*Anni-*		
sg. dat./loc.	*A-NA* ^{f}*an-ni-i*	4.1.3.2 rev. 8′
	A-NA(?) ^{f}*a*]*n-ni-i*	4.1.3.3 6′
^{m}*An(n)aru(m)miya-*		
sg. gen.?	^{m}]*an-na-ru-mi-ia-aš*	4.1.3.6 rev. 3′
	^{m}*a-na*(?)]*-ru-um-mi-ia-aš*	4.1.3.7 rev. 3′
^{m}*Apallu-*		
sg. gen.	(*ŠA* ŠU) ^{m}*a-pal-lu-ú*	4.2.9 lo. e. 34′
sg. dat./loc.	*A-NA* ^{m}*a-pal-lu*	1.1.A$_3$ rev. 4′
^{f}*Apadda-*		
stem	^{f}*a-pád-da-a*	6.5 obv. 18′
^{f}*Apatti-*		
sg. nom.?	^{f}*a-pát-ti-i-*[*iš*$^{?}$	4.1.3.4.A$_1$ rev. r. c. 4′
^{m}*Ari*-^{D}UTU-		
sg. nom.	^{m}*a-ri*-^{D}UTU-*aš*	5.5 rev. iii 2′
broken	^{m}*a-ri*-⌜^{D}⌝[UTU-*aš*(?)	4.2.8 2′
^{m}*Arnuwanda-*		
sg. gen.	*ŠA* ^{m}*ar-nu-wa-an-d*[*a*	9.1.9 rev. iv 4′
^{f}*Arumura-*		
stem	^{f}]*a-ru-mu-ra*	5.1 rev. iii 10
^{m}*Ašme*-LUGAL-*ma*- (^{m}*Ašme-Šarruma-*)		
stem	^{m}*aš-me*-LUGAL-*ma*	10.3.1 rev. iii 2′
^{f}*Ašpunawiya-*		
stem	^{f}*aš-pu-na-wi*$_5$*-ia*	2.7.A obv. 9
^{m}*Ašdu*-^{D}LAMMA-		
stem	^{m}*aš-du*-^{D}LAMMA	4.1.4.1.A$_1$ obv. ii 2′
	^{m}*aš-d*[*u*-^{D}LAMMA	4.1.4.1.A$_1$ obv. ii 1′
^{m}*Atta-*		
sg. gen.(?)	(*ŠA*(?)) ^{m}*at-ta-a*	3.2.2 obv.$^{?}$ 10′. 4.2.9 rev. 10′
^{m}*Attaniya-*		
stem	^{m}*at-ta-ni-ia*	3.2.1 rev. 5′
^{m}*Awanda(-)*		
stem?	^{m}*a-wa-an-da*(-)[	1.1.A$_1$ obv. 3′
^{m}*Eḫi-*		
stem	^{m}*e-ḫi*	3.1.8.A rev. 16′
^{m}*Eḫli*-^{D}30- (^{m}*Eḫli-Kušuḫ-*)		
sg. nom.	^{m}*eḫ-li*-^{D}30-*aš*	4.1.1.1.A$_1$ rev. 14′
stem	^{m}*eḫ-li*-^{D}30	2.2 rev. 12. 4.1.1.1.B$_1$ rev. iii$^{?}$ 2, 4, 7; rev. iv$^{?}$ 14
	^{m}*eḫ-li*-$^{D!}$30	2.2 rev. 15
	^{m}*eḫ-li*-^{D}[30	2.7.A rev. 2
	^{m}*eḫ-l*[*i*-^{D}30	2.2 rev. 11
	^{m}*eḫ-li*]-^{D}3[0	4.1.1.1.A$_1$ rev. 8′

^{m}*Eḫli*-LUGAL-*ma*- (^{m}*Eḫli-Šarruma*-)		
stem	^{m}*eḫ-li*-LUGAL-*ma*	5.7 rev. iii$^{?}$ 24′
^{f}*Elwattaru*-		
sg. nom.	^{f}*el-wa-at-ta-r*[*u-uš*	4.1.3.5.A_1 obv.$^{?}$ 4′
^{m}*Ḫakipuili*-		
stem	^{m}*ḫa-ki*]-*pu-i-li*	5.7 rev. iv$^{?}$ 24′
^{m}*Ḫalpašulupi*-		
stem	^{m}*ḫal*]-*pa*$^{?}$-*šu-lu-pí*	4.2.10 9′
^{m}*Ḫalpa*-A.A- (^{m}*Ḫalpamuwa*-)		
stem	^{m}*ḫal-pa*-A.A	3.1.1.A_1 obv. ii 15′
^{m}*Ḫannutti*-		
sg. nom.	^{m}*ḫa-an*]-*nu-ut-ti-iš*	6.4 obv.$^{?}$ 3′
^{m}*Ḫarwanduli*-		
sg. nom.	^{m}*ḫar-wa-an-du-li-iš*	3.1.1.A_3 rev. iv 19′
	^{m}*ḫar-wa*-[*an-du-li-iš*	5.1 rev. iii 11
^{m}*Ḫašiya*-		
stem	^{m}*ḫa-ši-ia*	4.1.4.1.A_1 rev. iii 8″
^{m}*Ḫattušili*-		
stem	^{m}*ḫa-at-tu-ši-li*	10.2.2.4 obv.$^{?}$ r. c. 4′
^{m}*Ḫilašdu*-		
sg. nom.	^{m}*ḫi-la-aš-du-uš*	3.1.10 6
^{m}*Ḫila*-^{D}LAMMA-		
stem	^{m}*ḫi-la*-^{D}LAMMA	3.1.8.A rev. 8′
	^{m}*ḫe-el-la*-^{D}LAMMA	3.2.1 obv. 4
^{f}*Ḫenti*-		
sg. dat./loc..	*A*-[*NA*] ^{f}*ḫé-en-ti-i*	8.1.E(A_3) rev. vi 5
stem?	^{f}*ḫé-en-t*[*i*(-)	6.6 rev. 1′
^{m}*Ḫešmi*-LUGAL (^{m}*Ḫešmi-Šarruma*-)		
sg. nom.	^{m}]*ḫe-eš-mi*-LUGAL-*aš*	5.1 obv. ii 5′
^{m}*Ḫešni*-		
sg. nom.	^{m}*ḫe-eš-ni-i-eš*	5.1 obv. ii 9′
	^{m}*ḫi-iš-ni-i-iš*	5.7 rev. iii$^{?}$ 11′
^{f}*Ḫištayara*-		
sg. nom.	^{f}*ḫi-iš-ta-ia-ra-aš*	4.1.3.5.A_1 obv.$^{?}$ 5′
^{f}*Ḫepat*-IR- (^{f}*Ḫepatuzzi*)		
stem	^{f}*ḫé-pát*-IR	6.9 obv. 9′
^{m}*Ḫuitula*-		
stem	$^{m?}$]*ḫu-i-tu-la-a*	12.3.2 5′
^{m}*Ḫuwameti*-		
sg. nom.	^{m}*ḫ*]*u-u-wa-me-ti-iš*	5.2 obv. ii 9
^{f}*Ḫurma*-		
stem	^{f}*ḫur-ma*	4.1.3.4.A_1 obv. r. c. 5′

^{m}*Yarra*-SUM- (^{m}*Yarrapiya*-)		
sg. nom.	^{m}*ia-ar-ra*-SUM-*aš*	5.2 obv. ii 11
stem	^{m}*ia-ar-ra-pí-ia*	4.1.4.1.A_1 obv. ii 6′
	^{m}*ia-a[r-ra-pí-i]a*	4.1.4.1.A_1 obv. ii 8′
	^{m}*i[a-ar-ra-pí-i]a*	4.1.4.1.A_1 obv. ii 10′
	^{m}*ia-ar-ra-pí-i]a*	4.1.4.1.A_1 obv. ii 5′
^{f}*Yarawiya*-		
sg. gen.	^{f}*ia-ra-wi*$_5$*-aš*	2.7.A obv. 21
^{m}*Izzummiziti*-		
	^{m}*iz-zu-ú-u[m-mi*-LÚ	4.1.3.1 3′
^{m}*Kammaliya*-		
stem	^{m}*kam-ma-li-ia*	5.1 obv. ii 8′. 8.1.A rev. vi 4′.
^{m}*Kannuwari*-		
nom.	^{m}*kán-nu-wa-ri-š(a-an)*	6.1 obv. 10
^{m}*Kapiuwa*-		
stem	^{m}*ka-pí-u-wa*	2.7.A rev. 6
^{m}*Karanuwa*-		
stem	^{m}*ka]-ru-nu-wa*	12.3.1 2′
^{m}*Kaššu*-		
sg. dat./loc.	*A-NA* ^{m}*kaš-šu-ú*	4.1.1.1.B_1 rev. iii$^?$ 5
	A-NA ^{m}*k[aš-šu-ú*	4.1.1.1.B_1 rev. iii$^?$ 2
^{m}*Gaštanili*-		
sg. nom.	^{m}*ga-aš-ta-ni-li-iš*	3.1.1.A_2 rev. v 4′
^{m}*Kawarnaili*-		
stem	^{m}*ka-wa-ar-na-i-li*	5.1 obv. ii 6′
^{f}*Kiki*-		
sg. nom.	^{f}*ki-ki-i[š*	4.1.3.4.A_1 rev. r. c. 3′
^{m}*Kida*-		
stem	^{m}*ki-i-da*	5.1 obv. ii 5′
^{m}*Kukkunni*-		
sg. nom.	^{m}*ku-uk-k]u-un-ni-iš*	4.1.4.1.A_1 rev. v 3″
^{m}*Kunni*-		
sg. nom.	^{m}(-)*k]u-un-ni-eš*	3.1.1.A_1 obv. ii 4′
stem	^{m}*ku-un-ni*	4.1.3.6 obv. 6′, 10′, 12′
	^{m}*k]u-un-ni*	4.1.3.6 obv. 5′, 16′
	^{m}*ku]-un-ni*	4.1.3.6 obv. 2′
	^{m}*ku-un-n[i*	4.1.3.6 obv. 17′
^{m}*Kurakura*-		
sg. nom.	^{m}*ku-ra-ku-ra-aš*	5.1 rev. iii 4
^{m}*Kuwayanu*-		
sg. nom.	^{m}*ku-wa-ia-nu-uš*	4.1.2.2 obv. 3′
stem?	^{m}*ku-[wa-ia-nu*	4.1.2.1 obv. (i) 1′
^{m}*Kuwalana*-^{D}LAMMA-		
stem	^{m}*ku-wa-la-na*-^{D}LAMMA	3.2.1 obv. 15

^{f}*Kuwari-*		
sg. nom.	^{f}*ku-wa-a-ri-iš*	4.1.3.5.A_1 obv.$^{?}$ 3′
^{m}*Lullu-*		
sg. nom.	^{m}*lu-ul-lu-uš*	4.1.1.1.B_1 rev. iii$^{?}$ 11
^{m}*Lupakki-*		
sg. dat./loc.	*(IŠTU) ŠA* ^{m}*lu-[pa-ak-ki*(?)	4.1.1.1.A_1 obv. 11′
^{m}*Makarduwa-*		
sg. nom.	^{m}*ma-kar-du-wa-aš*	3.2.1 rev. 11′
^{m}*Malaš-Inar-*		
sg. dat./loc.	^{m}*ma-la-aš-i-na-ri*	12.3.2 6′
^{f}*Malli-*		
sg. nom.?	^{f}*ma-al-li-[iš*$^{?}$	4.1.3.4.A_1 rev. r. c. 5′
^{f}*Manattawiya-*		
sg. nom.	$^{*\langle\langle m\rangle\rangle *f}$*ma-na-at-ta-wi*$_5$*-ia-aš*	12.3.7 5′
^{m}*Manninni-*		
sg. gen.	*ŠA* ^{m}*ma-an-ni-in-ni*	9.1.1 rev. iv 45′. 9.1.3 2′
^{m}*Maraššanta-*		
sg. nom.	^{m}*ma-ra-aš-ša-an-ta-aš*	5.4 r. c. 6′
stem	^{m}*ma-ra-aš-ša-an-da*	4.1.4.2.A_2 obv. r. c. 9′
^{m}*Mariyanni-*		
stem	^{m}*ma-ri-an-ni*	8.1.E(A_3) l. e. 3
^{m}*Maša*-A.A- (^{m}*Mašamuwa-*)		
sg. dat./loc.	*A-N]A* ^{m}*ma-a-ša*-A.A	1.1.A_2 rev. 4
stem	^{m}*ma-ša*-A.A(?)	5.8 2′
	^{m}*ma-a-ša-*[A.A(?)	5.8 8′
^{m}*Mašidu-*		
stem	^{m}*ma-ši-du*	4.1.3.1 6′
^{m}*Minzana-*		
stem	⟨^{m}⟩*mi-in-za-na*	4.1.3.6 obv. 4′
^{f}*Muḫunawiya-*		
stem	^{*f*}*mu-ḫu*$^{?}$*-na-wi*$_5$-[*ia*(?)	8.1.E(A_3) l. e. 2
^{m}*Muršili-*		
stem	^{m}*mur-ši-li*	10.2.2.3 obv.$^{?}$ l. c. 8′
	^{m}*mur-ši-l[i*	10.2.2.2 obv.$^{?}$ l. c. 8′
	^{m}*mur-ši-[li*	10.2.2.2 obv.$^{?}$ l. c. 6′
	^{m}*mur-š[i-li*	10.2.2.2 obv.$^{?}$ l. c. 4′
^{m}*Mutta-*		
sg. dat./loc.	*A-NA* ^{m}*mu-ut-ta*	4.1.1.3 rev. B 8
stem	^{m}*mu-ut-ta*	4.1.1.3 rev. B 10
^{m}*Mutarki-*		
sg. dat./loc.	*A-NA* ^{m}*mu-tar-ki*	1.1.A_2 obv. 6′, 7′
^{m}*Muwala-*		
sg. nom.	^{m}*mu-u-wa-la-a-aš*	4.1.4.2.A_1 rev. r. c. 9′

	^{m}*mu-u-w[a-la-a-aš*	4.1.4.2.A_1 rev. r. c. 12′
^{m}*Muwalanni-*		
sg. nom.	^{m}*mu-u-wa-la-an-ni-iš*	4.1.3.1 8′
^{m}*Nanni-*		
sg. nom.	^{m}*na-an-ni-iš*	3.1.1.A_3 rev. iv 7′
^{f}*Nikalmati-*		
sg. nom.?	^{f}*ni-kal-m[a*$^{!}$*-ti-iš*$^{?}$	2.14 6′
^{m}*Nikri-*^{D}10*-up-* (^{m}*Nikri-Teššup-*)		
sg. nom.	^{m}*ni-ik-ri-*^{D}10*-up-aš*	1.5 obv. 14
^{m}*Neri-*		
sg. dat./loc.?	*A-NA*(?)] ^{m}*né-ri*	4.2.8 4′
stem	^{m}*ne-ri*	4.1.1.3 rev. B 12
^{m}*Nerikka-*DINGIR-*LIM-* (^{m}*Nerikkaili-*)		
sg. gen.	^{m}*né-ri-ik-*ka_4-DINGIR-*L[IM*	10.2.2.1 5′
	^{m}*né-ri-ik-k]*a_4-DINGIR-*LIM*	10.2.2.1 2′
	^{m}*n]e-ri-i[k-*ka_4-DINGIR-*L]IM*	6.4 obv.$^{?}$ 5′
stem?	^{m}*ne-ri-i[k-*ka_4-DINGIR-*LIM*	6.6 rev. 5′
^{m}*Nuḫati-*		
stem	$^{m?}$*nu-ḫa-ti*	5.1 obv. i 6′
	^{m}*nu*(?)]*-ḫa-ti*	5.7 rev. iv 26′
^{m}*Pal[la*(-)		
broken	^{m}*pal-l[a*(-)	4.1.4.1.A_2 obv. ii 9′
^{m}*Palla-*		
sg. dat./loc.	*A-NA* ^{m}*p]al-la-a*	4.1.1.1.A_1 obv. 5′
	A-NA ^{m}*pal-la]-a*	4.1.1.1.A_1 obv. 22′
stem	^{m}*pal-la-a*	4.1.1.3 rev. B 11
^{m}*Pallanza-*		
sg. nom.	^{m}*pal-la-an-za-aš*	3.1.10 4
stem	^{m}*pa-a]l-la-an-za*	5.7 rev. iv$^{?}$ 13′
^{f}*Parminza-*		
stem	^{f}*pár-mi-in-z[a*	4.1.3.4.A_1 obv. r. c. 1′
^{m}*Padutti-*		
sg. dat./loc.	*A-NA* ^{m}*pa-du-ut-ti-ia*	1.1.A_2 rev. 7
^{m}*Piya-*		
sg. nom.	^{m}*p]í-ia-aš*	12.2.1 rev. 6′
^{m}*Piḫana-*		
sg. dat./loc.	*A-NA* ^{m}*pí-ḫa-ni*	1.1.A_1 obv. 12′
^{m}*Piḫašdu-*		
sg. nom.	^{m}*pí-ḫa-aš-du-uš*	3.2.1 rev. 14′
stem	^{m}*pí-ḫa-aš-du*	4.1.3.1 4′
^{f}*Piḫawiya-*		
sg. dat./loc.	*A-NA* ^{f}*pí-ḫa-*wi_5*-i[a*	1.1.A_1 obv. 8′

^{m}*Piḫa*-A.A- (^{m}*Piḫamuwa-*)		
sg. nom.	^{m}*pí-ḫa*-A.A-*aš*	5.2 obv. ii 12
sg. dat./loc.	*A-NA* ^{m}*pí-ḫa*-A.A	5.2 obv. ii 4
^{m}*Piḫašša*-A.A- (^{m}*Piḫaššamuwa-*)		
stem	^{m}*pí-ḫa-aš-ša*-A.A	5.7 rev. iii$^{?}$ 12′
^{m}*Piḫa*-LÚ- (^{m}*Piḫaziti-*)		
stem	^{m}*pí-*[*ḫ*]*a*-LÚ	12.2.1 obv. 3′
	^{m}]*pí-ḫa*-LÚ	12.2.1 rev. 3′
^{m}*Piḫa*-^{D}10- (^{m}*Piḫa-Tarḫunta-*)		
stem	^{m}*pí-ḫa*-^{D}10	5.1 rev. iii 1
^{m}*Pikku-*		
sg. dat./loc.	*A-NA* ^{m}*p*]*í-ik-ku*	1.1.A_3 rev. 3′
^{m}*Pidumili-*		
sg. dat./loc.	*A-NA* ^{m}*pí-du-mi-li*	5.4 r. c. 5′
^{m}*Pipinili-*		
sg. nom.	^{m}*pí-pí-ni-l*[*i-iš*	12.2.1 rev. 1′
	^{m}*pí-p*]*í-n*[*i-l*]*i-iš*	12.2.1 obv. 1′
^{m}*Pulli-*		
stem	^{m}*pu-ul-l*[*i*	4.1.4.4 4′, 8′, 11′
^{m}*Pulliya-*		
sg. nom.	^{m}*p*]*u*$^{?}$*-ul*$^{?}$*-li-ia-aš*	3.1.1.A_3 obv. iii 4′
^{m}*Pulpulumi-*		
stem	^{m}]*pu-ul-pu-lu-mi*	3.1.8.A rev. 16′
^{m}*Pupuli-*		
sg. nom.	^{m}*pu-pu-liš*	4.1.1.1.A_1 rev. 19′. 4.1.1.1.B_1 rev. iii$^{?}$ 9, 15
stem	^{m}*pu-pu-*li_{12}	2.7.A obv. 26
	^{m}*pu-pu-*[li_{12}	4.1.1.3 rev. A 5′
Anat. hieroglyph.	PU-PU-LI_x("SÀ")	9.1.9 rev. iv 6′
^{m}*Šaggana-*		
stem	^{m}*šag-ga-na*	5.1 obv. ii 10′, 11′
^{m}*Šalikka-*		
sg. nom.	^{m}*ša-li-ik-*ka_4*-aš*	5.2 obv. ii 2
^{m}*Šalwini-*		
sg. nom.	^{m}*šal-*wi_5*-ni-eš*	12.3.7 6′
^{m}*Šadduwa*-LÚ (^{m}*Šadduwaziti-*)		
stem	^{m}*ša-ad-du-wa*-LÚ	4.1.4.2.A_2 obv. r. c. 7′
^{m}*Šippa*-LÚ (^{m}*Šippaziti-*)		
stem	^{m}*ši-ip-pa*-LÚ	5.1 rev. iii 3
^{m}*Šuna*-DINGIR-*LIM* (^{m}*Šunaili-*)		
sg. nom.	^{m}*šu-na*-DINGIR-*LIM-iš*	10.1.1.1 rev.$^{?}$ 4′
	^{m}*šu-n*[*a*-DIN]GIR-*LI*[*M-i*]*š*	12.2.1 obv. 2′
	^{m}*š*[*u-n*]*a*-DINGIR-*LIM-i*[*š*	12.2.1 rev. 2′
stem	^{m}*šu-na*-DINGIR-*LIM*	6.1 obv. 10

^{m}*Šuppiluliuma-*		
stem	^{m}*šu-up-pí-lu-li-u-ma*	9.1.10.A_2 rev. 5′
	^{m}*šu-up-p*]*í-lu-li-u-ma*	9.1.13 7′
^{m}*Taki*-LUGAL-*ma-* (^{m}*Taki-Šarruma-*)		
sg. nom.	^{m}]*ta-ki*-LUGAL-*ma-aš*	5.2 obv. ii 4
	^{m}*ta-k*]*i*-LUGAL-*ma-aš*	5.4 r. c. 10′. 5.5 rev. iii 1′
^{m}*Talmi-*^{D}10(*-up-aš*) (^{m}*Talmi-Teššub-*)		
sg. nom.	^{m}*tal-mi-*^{D}[10(*-up-aš*)	1.5 rev. 20
^{m}*Taparami-*		
stem	^{m}*ta-pa-ra-mi*	3.1.8.A rev. 18′
	^{m}*ta-pa-r*[*a-mi*	3.1.8.A rev. 17′
	^{m}[*ta-pa-ra-mi*	3.1.8.B 5′
^{m}*Tarzu-*		
sg. nom.	^{m}*tar-zu-ú-uš*	3.1.1.A_3 rev. iv 6′
^{m}*Tatta-*		
sg. dat./loc.	*A-NA* ^{m}*ta-at-ta(-)*	6.3 rev. B 3
^{m}*Dadamaru-*		
stem	^{m}*da-da-ma-ru*	1.2 rev. 2′
^{f}*Tawanti-*		
sg. nom.	^{f}*ta-wa-an-ti-i*[*š*	4.1.3.5.A_1 obv.$^{?}$ 2′
^{m}*Titti-*		
sg. dat./loc.	*A-NA* ^{m}*ti-it-ti*	4.1.3.7 rev. 2′
^{m}*Tulla-*		
nom.	^{m}*túl-la-a-aš*	3.1.8.A rev. 14′. 3.1.8.B 2′
^{m}*Tulpaʾi-*		
stem	^{m}*tul-pa-aḫ*$^{?}$*-i*	1.5 rev. 21
^{m}*Dunia(-)*		
stem	^{m}*du-ni-ia*(-)x[	7.1 rev. 4′
^{m}*Dunwa*-LUGAL-*ma-* (^{m}*Dunwa-Šarruma-*)		
stem	^{m}*du-un-wa*-LUGAL-*ma*	4.1.1.2.A obv. 12′. 5.1 rev. iii 2
^{m}*Tutḫaliya-*		
sg. nom.	^{m}*t*]*u-ut-ḫa-li-aš*	6.4 obv.$^{?}$ 8′
	^{m}*tu-u*]*t-ḫa-li-*[*aš*	6.4 obv.$^{?}$ 1′
stem	^{m}*du-ut-ḫa-li-ia*	10.2.2.3 obv.$^{?}$ l. c. 10′
	^{m}*tu-*[*ut-ḫa-l*]*i-ia*	9.2.4 rev. iv 4
	^{m}]*tu-ut-ḫa-li-ia*	5.1 rev. iii 11
	^{m}*tu*]*-ut-*[*ḫ*]*a-li-ia*	4.1.4.1.A_1 obv. i 2′
	^{m}*tu-ut*(?)]*-ḫa-li-ia*	9.1.5 lo. e. 1′
	^{m}*tu-ut-ḫ*[*a-li-ia*	9.1.4.A_1 rev. iv 7′
^{m}*Tuttu-*		
	1. Tuttu EN *ABUSI*	
sg. nom.	^{m}*tu-ut-tu-uš*	5.7 rev. iii$^{?}$ 18′
	2. Tuttu ^{LÚ}I[Š(?)	
stem	^{m}*tu-ut-tu*	5.5 rev. iii 7′

^{m}*Tuwatta*-LÚ- (^{m}*Tuwattaziti-*)		
stem	^{m}*tu-u-wa-at-ta*-LÚ	4.1.3.1 7′
^{m}*Uḫḫa*-x-x[		
sg. dat./loc.	*A-NA* ^{m}*uḫ-ḫa-a*-x-x[	1.1.A_1 obv. 5′
^{m}*Urḫilina-*		
stem?	^{m}*úr-*[*ḫi-li-na*(?)	5.5 rev. iii 3′
^{m}*Urkatpuraya-*		
stem	^{m}*úr-kat-pu-ra-ia*	4.1.3.6 obv. 9′
^{m}*Uttikiyapi-*		
sg. nom.	^{m}*u*]*t-ti-ki-ia-pí-iš*	12.2.1 rev. 5′
	^{m}*ut-ti-ki-ia-*[*pí-iš*	12.2.1 obv. 5′
^{m}*Wanni-*		
stem	^{m}*wa-an-ni*	4.1.3.6 rev. 7′
^{m}*Warkumi-*		
sg. nom.	^{m}*wa-ar-ku-mi-iš*	3.1.1.A_1 obv. ii 12′
^{m}*Warpa*-LÚ- (^{m}*Warpaziti-*)		
stem	^{m}*wa-ar-pa*-LÚ	3.2.1 obv. 18
^{f}*Wašti-*		
sg. nom.	^{f}*wa-aš-ti-iš*	1.5 obv. 10
^{m}*Wattiḫaḫla-*		
stem	^{m}*wa-at-ti-ḫa-aḫ-la*	5.1 obv. ii 4′
^{f}*Wattiya-*		
sg. gen.	^{f}*wa-at-ti-ia-a*[*š*	5.7 rev. iii$^{?}$ 28′
^{f}*Zamuwatti-*		
sg. dat./loc.	*A-NA* ^{f}*za-mu-wa-at-ti*	2.2 obv. 4′
^{f}*Zapate*[*n-*		
	^{f}*za-pa-ti-e*[*n-*	4.1.3.4.A_1 obv. r. c. 2′
^{m}*Zikkuwa-*		
sg. nom.	^{m}*zi-ik-ku-wa-aš*	3.1.8.A rev. 6′
^{m}*Zuw*[*a-*		
broken	^{m}*zu-w*[*a*(-)	4.1.4.1.A_2 obv. ii 6′. 9.1.4.A_1 rev. iv 10′
^{m}*Zuwali-*		
stem	^{m}*zu-wa-li*	3.1.8.A obv. 9′, 12′
^{m}*Zuzu-*		
sg. nom.	^{m}*zu-zu-u*[*š*	5.2 obv. ii 9
	^{m}*zu-zu-*[*uš*	5.2 obv. ii 4
	^{m}*zu*]*-zu-u*[*š*	5.2 rev. iii 7
^{m}*Zuzuli-*		
stem	^{m}*zu-zu-li*	4.1.1.1.A_1 obv. 5′. 4.1.1.2.B obv. 3
	^{m}*zu-zu-li*$_{12}$	3.1.2 obv. l. c. 8′. 10.1.1.1 rev.$^{?}$ 3′, 5′
	^{m}*zu-zu-l*[*i*	4.1.1.1.A_1 obv. 22′
	^{m}*zu-zu-u*[*l-li*	2.7.A rev. 1
	^{m}*zu-zu-*[*li*	4.1.1.2.B obv. 8

	^{m}*zu-z[u-li*	4.1.1.1.A_1 rev. 10
	^{m}*[zu-zu-li*	4.1.1.2.A obv. 22′. 4.1.1.2.B obv. 6
^{m}AMAR.MUŠEN-*na*-		
stem	^{m}AMAR.MUŠEN-*na*	5.1 obv. ii 10′
$^{m.D}$AMAR.UTU-		
sg. nom.	$^{m.D}$AMAR.UTU-*aš*	3.1.8.A rev. 11′
stem	$^{m.D}$AMAR.UTU	5.2 rev. iii 10′
^{m}DINGIR^{MEŠ}-SUM-		
stem	^{m}DINGIR]^{MEŠ}-SUM	5.2 up. e. 1
$^{m.D}$GE$_6$-LÚ-		
stem	$^{m.D}$GE$_6$-L[Ú	3.1.10 8
^{m}EN-LUGAL-*ma*- (^{m}*Ewri-Šarruma*)		
stem	^{m}EN-LUGAL-*ma*	6.6 rev. 5′
$^{m.D}$IŠKUR-*walḫuwar*		
stem	$^{m.D}$IŠ]KUR$^{?}$-*wa-al-ḫu-w[a-ar*	5.7 rev. iii$^{?}$ 13′
^{m}KI-^{D}UTU-		
nom.	^{m}KI-^{D}UTU-*u[š*	5.7 rev. iii$^{?}$ 20′
	^{m}K[I-^{D}UTU-*uš*	5.7 rev. iii$^{?}$ 22′
stem	^{m}KI-^{D}UTU	5.7 rev. iii$^{?}$ 9′
^{f}KÙ.SI$_{22}$-*lia*- (^{f}*Āškilia*-$^{?}$, ^{f}*Maralia*-$^{?}$)		
sg. nom.	^{f}KÙ.SI$_{22}$-*li-aš*	6.5 rev. 6′
see *Lexical Commentary*		
^{m}LU.LIM-*miya*- (^{m}*(Ku)runtimiya*-$^{?}$)		
sg. dat./loc.	*A-NA* ^{m}LU.LIM-*mi-ia*	1.1.A_1 obv. 11′
see *Lexical Commentary*		
^{m}NIR.GÁL- (^{m}*Muwatalli*-)		
sg. gen.	*ŠA* ^{m}NIR.GÁL	2.8 obv. 2
stem	^{m}NIR.GA]L(?)	10.2.2.1 3′
	⟨^{m}⟩NIR.GÁ[L	9.1.7 obv. 5′
^{m}SIG$_5$-LÚ-		
	$^{m(?)}$S]IG$_5$-LÚ	3.2.4 2′
^{m}ŠEŠ-*zi*- (^{m}*Nanizi*-)		
sg. nom.	^{m}ŠEŠ-*zi-iš*	3.1.1.A_3 obv. iii 8′
^{m}UR.MAḪ-LÚ- (^{m}*Walwaziti*-)		
sg. nom.	^{m}U]R.MAḪ-LÚ-*iš*	2.4 rev. 6′
stem	^{m}UR.MAḪ-LÚ	4.1.1.1.A_1 rev. 15′. 4.1.1.1.B_1 rev. iii$^{?}$ 9. 12.2.1 rev. 4′
	^{m}U]R.MAḪ-L[Ú	12.2.1 obv. 4′
	^{m}[U]R.MAḪ-LÚ	5.7 rev. iii$^{?}$ 20′
	^{m}UR.[M]AḪ-LÚ	5.7 rev. iii$^{?}$ 16′
^{m}UR.SAG(-)		
sg. dat./loc.	*A-NA* ^{m}UR.SAG(-)	1.1.A_1 obv. 19′
^{D}UTU-*ŠI*		
see Sumerograms		

^{m}ZAG-ŠEŠ- (^{m}*Bentešina-*)		
stem	^{m}ZAG-ŠEŠ	10.2.2.4 obv.? r. c. 5′
$^{m.D}$10-*manadu-* (^{m}*Tarḫuntamanadu-*)		
stem	$^{m.D}$10-*ma-na-du*	4.2.1.A$_2$ rev. 13′
	$^{m.D}$10-*ma-n[a-du*	5.5 rev. iii 6′
$^{m.D}$10-*timara-* (^{m}*Tarḫuntatimara-*)		
sg. nom.	$^{m.D}$10-*ti-ma-ra-aš*	1.1.A$_1$ obv. 13′
$^{m.D}$10-PAB-		
stem	$^{m.D}$10-PAB	2.2 rev. 16. 5.2 rev. 15′
$^{m.D}$10-SUM- (^{m}*Tarḫuntapiya-*)		
sg. nom.	$^{m.D}$10-SUM-*aš*	5.1 rev. iii 6. 5.2 obv. ii 10
	$^{m.D}$]10-SUM-[*aš*	4.2.1.A$_2$ lo. e. 8′
$^{f.D}$30-IR- (^{m}*Armauzzi-*)		
stem	$^{f.D}$30-IR	12.3.7 9′
$^{m.D}$30-SUM-*ia-* (^{m}*Armapiya-*)		
sg. dat./loc.	*A-NA* $^{m.D}$]30-SUM-*ia*	1.1.A$_3$ rev. 1′
stem	$^{m.D}$30-SUM	4.1.4.2.A$_2$ obv. r. c. 5′

Numerals

½	'one half'	
	½	4.1.4.1.A$_1$ rev. vi 8′ (2×), 9′, 10′ 4.1.4.2.A$_2$ obv. r. c. 8′ (2×), 10′. 4.1.4.5 obv. r. c. 2′, 3′, 4′: rev. r. c. 3′. 5.2 obv. ii 1, 5, 8. 10.1.1.2 rev. iv 9′. 10.3.10 r. c. 3′. 12.2.2 2′, 3′, 5′, 6′, 10′, 11′. 12.2.3 3′, 5′, 6′, 7′ (2×)
	⟨⟨½⟩⟩	12.2.2 8′
1	'one'	
	1	1.1.A$_1$ obv. 2′, 3′, 7′, 9′ (3×), 11′, 12′, 13′, 14′, 16′, 18′ (2×). 1.1.A$_2$ obv. 3′; rev. 5, 6. 1.1.A$_3$ rev. 5′, 10′, 11′. 1.2 rev. 3′, 4′ (2×), 6′ (2×), 7′, 9′, 10′ (2×). 1.4 4′, 5′, 7′. 1.5 obv. 3, 9, 11, 13; lo. e. 15, 16, 17; rev. 19, 25, 26. 2.1.A obv. ii(?) 3′, 4′, 7′, 9′, 13′, 14′, 16′. 2.1.B 1′, 2′, 5′. 2.2 obv. 2′, 3′, 5′, 7′, 8′; rev. 11, 17. 2.4 rev. 2′. 2.5 rev. 7′. 2.6 3′, 4′. 2.7.A obv. 2, 5, 6 (2×), 7 (2×), 8, 9 (2×), 10 (2×), 12, 16, 17, 18, 20, 21, 22, 23, 25; rev. 2, 3, 4 (×3), 5 (2×), 7′. 2.7.B rev. 3′. 2.8 obv. 1. 2.9.A$_1$ obv. i 1′, 2′, 4′. 2.9.A$_2$ obv. i 1′, 3′, 5′, 7′, 9′. 2.9.A$_3$ obv. ii 5′, 7′, 10′, 12′. 2.12 obv.! ii 4′, 9′, 10′. 2.13 obv.? 1′, 2′, 3′, 4′, 5′, 6′ (2×); rev.? 1′, 2′, 5′, 8′, 10′. 2.14 5′. 2.15 l. c. 2′, 5′, 8′, 12′, 13′. 2.16 obv. i 6′, 7′; obv. ii 2′, 5′, 8′; rev. v 3, 5, 6. 2.17 obv.? r. c. 10′. 3.1.1.A$_1$ obv. ii 11′; rev. v 5′, 15′. 3.1.1.A$_2$ rev. v 5′, 7′. 3.1.1.A$_3$ obv. iii 2′, 9′; rev. iv 2′, 5′, 10′, 12′. 3.1.2 obv. l. c.

	rev. v 9′ (2×). 8.1.F obv. i 2′, 4′, 10′, 21′; obv. ii 16′; rev. v 5, 9 (2×), 11 (2×), 12, 13; rev. vi 5, 9 (2×). 8.1.G obv. r. c. 1′, 2′, 8′, 9′. 8.1.H rev. r. c. 2′, 3′, 4′, 5′, 7′, 8′, 9′ (2×), 10′. 8.1.I rev. r. c. 2′, 3′, 4′. 8.1.J rev. v! 7′. 8.1.K obv. ii? 4′, 5′; rev. v? 5′, 7′, 8′; rev. vi? 7′. 8.2 r. c. 1′. 8.4 rev. 2′, 4′, 5′, 6′ (2×), 8′, 11′, 13′ (2×), 14′, 16′, 17′. 8.5 rev. iii(?) 5′ (2×), 6′. 8.7 r. c. 2′. 8.8.A 4′. 8.8.B r. c. 9′. 9.1.1 rev. iii 6′, 26′, 40′; rev. iv 8′, 12′, 23′, 26′, 32′ (2×), 42′. 9.1.4.A_1 obv. ii 36; rev. iii 27″. 9.1.5 obv.! 2, 3 (2×), 4, 7, 13, 14; rev.! 2′ (2×), 3′ (3×), 4′, 5′, 6′, 9′ (2×), 10′, 11′, 13′ (2×), 15′, 16′ (2×). 9.1.6 obv. 2, 4, 11, 13, 15. 9.1.7 obv. 1′, 2′, 3′; rev. 1, 2, 3. 9.1.8 obv. 3′, 6′, 8′, 10′, 11′, 15′. 9.1.10.A_1 obv. 9′; rev. 3′. 9.1.10.A_2 rev. 1′, 3′, 7′. 9.1.11 obv.? 5′ (2×), 6′ (2×), 7′, 8′, 9′ (3×), 10′ (2×), 11′, 12′; rev.? 3′. 9.2.13 3′. 9.2.2 rev.! iii 25′. 9.2.6 obv. i 19′. 9.2.7 obv. l. c. 13′; rev. r. c. 6′. 9.2.9 obv.? 6′, 15′; rev.? 1′, 2′. 10.1.1.1 rev.? 6′, 7′, 8′, 10′, 11′ (2×), 12′, 13′, 14′ (2×). 10.1.1.2 rev. iv 4′, 6′ (2×), 8′, 9′, 10′ (2×), 13′. 10.1.2.1 obv.? r. c. 3′, 5′; rev.? r. c. 1′. 10.1.2.2 2′. 10.1.2.6 1′, 11′. 10.2.1.1 obv. 5′. 10.2.1.3 3′, 7′. 10.2.1.7 rev.? 5′. 10.2.2.3 obv.? l. c. 2′; obv.? r. c. 4′. 10.2.2.4 obv.? r. c. 5′, 6′. 10.3.2 obv. i(?) 11″. 10.3.3 obv.? 2′, 3′, 4′, 5′ (2×), 10′ (2×), 12′. 10.3.5 2′, 9′. 10.3.9 5′. 10.3.10 r. c. 10′. 10.3.11 l. c. 1′; r. c. 1′. 10.3.12 obv. i 6′, 10′, 17′, 20′. 10.3.13 3′, 4′, 7′. 11.1.3 4′, 11′. 11.1.7 2′, 3′ (2×). 11.1.8 5′. 11.1.9 6′, 7′, 9′. 11.2.2 8′. 11.4.2 obv. 2′, 4′. 11.5.1 7′. 11.5.2 rev.? r. c. 1′. 11.6.1 5 (2×), 7 (2×), 8 (2×), 11 (3×), 13. 11.6.2 obv. 4′; rev. 2′, 10′, 11′, 12′; l. e. 7 (2×). 11.6.3 obv.? 6′. 11.6.4 rev. 4′. 11.6.5 obv.? (5×). 11.6.6 rev. 1′, 2′ (3×), 3′, 4′ (3×), 6′ (4×), 7′, 10′ (2×). 11.6.7 1′, 3′, 7′. 11.6.8 1′, 3′. 11.7.2 4′. 12.1.1 l. c. 3′ (2×), 5′ (6×), 6′ (3×), 7′ (3×); r. c. 6′, 7′, 8′, 9′ (2×), 10′ (3×), 11′ (2×). 12.1.2 1′. 12.1.3 1′, 2′, 3′, 5′. 12.1.4 3′, 4′, 5′. 12.2.3 1′, 2′ (2×). 12.3.3 4′. 12.3.7 7′
1	2.5 rev. 8′
1!	4.1.1.8 r. c. 7′. 4.2.6 obv.? 8′. 6.5 rev. 12′
1?	4.1.1.1.A_1 rev. 7′. 4.1.4.2.A_1 rev. r. c. 1′. 5.7 rev. iii? 26′. 8.4 rev. 12′. 9.1.13 5′. 11.6.5 obv.? 2. 12.3.3 10′
n+]1	2.2 rev. 4. 3.2.1 obv. 3; rev. 12′, 15′, 16′ (2×), 17′. 4.1.1.3 obv. 7. 4.1.1.4 5′. 4.1.4.1.A_1 rev. v 6″, 7″. 4.2.8 6′. 4.2.9 obv. 6. 5.2 rev. iii 4′. 5.3 l. c. 2′. 5.7 rev. iv? 10′. 6.9 obv. 11′. 8.1.E(A_1) rev. v 8′. 9.1.6 obv. 16. 9.2.11 4′, 7′. 10.1.1.1 rev.? 9′, 10′. 10.1.1.2 rev. iv 2′. 10.2.1.1 obv. 10′
n+]1?	4.1.2.4 6′

		1[+n	4.1.4.7 obv. 2. 4.2.5 4′. 4.2.6 obv.? 11′. 9.1.1 rev. iv 37′. 8.1.J rev. iv! 1′, 3′, 7′. 9.1.4.A_1 obv. ii 41
	sg. dat./loc.	1-*e-da-ni*	9.1.5 rev.! 7′, 15′ (2×). 9.1.6 obv. 7. 9.1.7 obv. 5′
		1-*e-da-ni*	9.1.6 obv. 10
		1-*e-da-*[*ni*(?)	11.3.1 23′
		A-NA 1	8.5 rev. iii(?) 7′. 9.1.1 rev. iii 9′
		A-NA 1[+n	8.5 rev. iii(?) 2′
	coll.	1-*e*	9.1.5 rev.! 16′
1-EN		'one' (Akk. *išten*)	
		1-EN	2.14 5′. 2.15 l. c. 1′. 2.17 obv.? r. c. 1′, 2′, 3′, 5′, 6′, 8′, 9′, 10′, 17′. 4.1.1.2.A obv. 8′. 4.2.10 3′, 4′, 5′, 7′. 4.2.11 2′. 4.2.7 4′, 7′. 9.1.1 rev. iii 4′, 13′, 14′, 17′, 20′, 21′, 23′, 27′, 32′, 37′, 38′, 40′, 42′; rev. iv 6′, 11′, 15′, 16′, 20′, 21′, 22′, 28′, 30′, 31′, 33′. 9.1.4.A_1 obv. i 15′; obv. ii 8, 9, 10, 13, 14, 16, 18, 19, 21, 33, 34; rev. iv 3′. 9.1.4.A_2 r. c. 6′. 9.1.4.A_3 4′. 9.1.6 obv. 8. 9.1.10.A_1 obv. 2′, 3′, 6′, 7′, 9′; rev. 4′. 9.1.10.A_2 rev. 3′. 9.1.10.B 3′, 5′, 6′, 10′, 11′. 9.1.14 obv. r. c. 2′, 3′. 9.1.15 3′, 4′, 5′, 6′. 9.2.2 rev.! iii 8′, 11′, 13′, 15′, 23′. 9.2.4 obv. i 10′, 15′; obv. ii 2′, 9′, 11′, 14′; rev. iii 6′, 9, 10′; rev. iv 8, 9, 12, 13. 9.2.5 obv. i(?) 9′. 9.2.6 obv. i 2′, 3′, 4′, 5′, 11′, 12′, 13′, 15′. 9.2.7 rev. r. c. 4′, 7′. 10.1.2.4 l. c. 11′, 13′. 10.1.2.8 rev. r. c. 4′, 6′. 10.2.1.2 obv. 12′, 19′. 10.3.5 5′. 10.3.6 1′, 3′, 5′. 10.3.9 6′. 10.3.14 l. c. 3′. 11.1.1 r. c. 4′. 11.1.4 3′. 11.2.4 7′. 11.6.3 obv.? 7′. 11.6.9 5′
		1]-EN	2.17 obv.? r. c. 18′. 9.1.10.A_1 obv. 5′. 9.1.10.B 14′. 9.2.4 rev. iv 5
		1-E]N	4.2.10 7′. 9.1.4.A_1 obv. i 20′; obv. ii 2. 9.1.10.A_1 obv. 10′. 9.2.2 rev.! iii 2′. 10.3.5 12′. 11.2.3 2′
		1-E]N(?)	9.2.4 rev. iv 6
		1-E[N	2.17 obv.? r. c. 17′, 20′. 9.1.1 rev. iii 15′. 9.1.4.A_1 obv. i 23′. 9.2.2 rev.! iii 22′. 9.2.4 obv. ii 13′. 10.1.2.4 l. c. 5′, 16′. 11.1.4 6′. 11.7.4 rev. r. c. 2′, 3′, 4′, 5′, 6′
		1-[EN	4.2.11 2′
	sg. dat./loc.	*A-NA* 1-EN	2.17 obv.? r. c. 12′, 13′ (2×), 20′. 9.1.1 rev. iii 19′. 9.1.14 obv. r. c. 6′, 8′, 9′. 9.2.1 obv. ii 7′, 11′, 12′. 10.2.1.2 obv. 17′. 10.3.14 l. c. 3′
		A-NA 1-E]N	9.2.1 obv. ii 8′, 9′
		A-NA 1-E[N	2.17 obv.? r. c. 12′. 10.1.2.4 r. c. 3′
		A-N[*A* 1-EN	9.1.1 rev. iii 18′
1-NU		'one set'	
		1-NU	4.2.1.A_1 obv. 9. 4.2.11 4′. 6.6 obv. 1′, 7′. 8.4 rev. 3′, 8′, 10′ (2×), 18′ (2×). 8.8.B r. c. 4′. 9.1.5 rev.! 17′. 9.1.10.B 7′, 11′, 12′ (2×). 9.2.3 obv. (ii) 3″, 4″. 9.2.4 obv. ii 7′; rev. iii 4′, 5′, 7′, 12′. 9.2.6 obv. i 6′; l. e. 2. 10.1.2.1 rev.? r. c. 2′. 10.1.2.4 l. c. 8′; r. c.

		2′. 10.3.4 9′. 10.3.14 9′. 11.3.2 r. c. 2′, 3′. 11.5.1 4′. 11.6.1 10
	1-*NU*(-)[	6.7 obv.$^{?}$ 3. 9.1.7 rev. 1. 9.1.13 3′
	1]-*NU*	4.1.1.6 rev. iii 9. 11.3.2 r. c. 4′
	1-*N*]*U*	8.8.A 5′, 6′
	1-*N*[*U*	8.4 rev. 21′. 11.2.4 1′
1-*NŪTUM*	'one set'	
sg. nom.	1-*NU-TUM*	1.1.A_1 obv. 8′. 1.5 obv. 4, 7, 12. 2.7.A obv. 8 (2×). 3.2.4 1′. 4.1.1.3 rev. A 4′. 4.1.4.8 4′. 4.2.10 2′. 8.1.F rev. v 15. 8.4 rev. 7′. 8.8.A 10′. 8.8.B r. c. 6′. 9.1.1 rev. iii 3′, 14′, 31′; rev. iv 7′, 39′. 9.1.8 obv. 6′, 10′. 9.1.10.A_1 obv. 4′, 7′, 8′; rev. 6′, 7′. 9.1.11 obv.$^{?}$ 8′. 9.2.1 obv. ii 20′, 24′. 9.2.2 rev.$^{!}$ iii 3′, 19′. 10.2.1.2 obv. 8′. 10.3.2 obv. i(?) 8″. 11.1.1 r. c. 2′, 6′, 9′, 11′, 12′. 11.1.7 5′. 11.3.1 15′, 16′, 17′, 18′, 20′, 21′. 11.6.2 rev. 5′, 6′. 11.6.3 obv.$^{?}$ 2′. 12.3.3 8′
	1-*NU-TUM*$^{?}$	4.2.9 obv. 32
	1]-*NU-TUM*	5.6 3′. 10.3.5 3′
	1-*N*]*U-TUM*	8.8.A 13′. 9.1.1 rev. iv 35′. 9.1.10.A_1 obv. 6′. 10.2.1.2 obv. 8′
	1-*NU-T*]*UM*	1.1.A_1 obv. 16′. 9.1.10.A_1 obv. 8′. 11.6.3 obv.$^{?}$ 4′
	1-*NU-TU*[*M*	9.1.1 rev. iv 41′. 11.3.1 20′
	1-*NU-T*[*UM*	8.4 rev. 9′. 9.1.8 obv. 1′, 8′
	1-*NU-T*[*UM*(?)	12.1.4 1′
sg. gen.	1-*NU-TI*	9.1.8 obv. 7′, 9′. 11.6.3 obv.$^{?}$ 8′
	1]-*NU-TI*	11.6.3 obv.$^{?}$ 3′
	1-*NU-TIM*	9.1.7 obv. 8′. 10.2.1.6 4′. 11.1.8 2′, 3′
	1-*NU-T*]*IM*	7.3 obv. i 2, 5, 6
	1-*NU-TI*[*M*	12.1.4 2′
1-*ŠU*	'once'	
	1-*ŠU*	1.5 obv. 6. 9.1.6 obv. 2
	1-*Š*]*U*$^{?}$	1.5 obv. 6
	1-*ŠÚ*	8.1.F rev. v 12. 9.1.5 rev.$^{!}$ 13′
1.KÙŠ see (1.)KÙŠ under Sumerograms		
2	'two'	
	2	1.1.A_1 7′, 8′ (2×), 13′. 1.1.A_2 obv. 2′, 8′, 10′; rev. 5. 1.1.A_3 rev. 4′, 5′. 1.2 rev. 3′, 5′. 1.4 2′, 4′, 9′. 1.5 obv. 5; lo. e. 17; rev. 22, 27. 2.1.A obv. ii(?) 11′. 2.1.B 3′. 2.2 obv. 9′; rev. 1, 6, 7, 16. 2.5 rev. 4′. 2.7.A obv. 6, 7, 10; rev. 5. 2.8 obv. 3. 2.9.A_3 obv. ii 13′. 2.12 obv.$^{!}$ ii 6′. 2.13 obv.$^{?}$ 5′. 2.14 3′. 2.15 l. c. 3′, 9′. 2.16 rev. v 2. 2.17 obv.$^{?}$ r. c. 5′, 6′, 12′, 13′ (2×), 17′. 3.1.1.A_1 obv. ii 6′; rev. v 3′, 8′. 3.1.1.A_2 rev. v 9′, 15′. 3.1.1.A_3 obv. iii 10′; rev. iv 10′, 11′. 3.1.2 obv. l. c. 10′. 3.1.3 obv.$^{?}$ 9′. 3.1.7.A_1 obv. i 12′. 3.1.7.A_2 obv. ii 9′, 15′; rev. iv 4′. 3.1.8.A rev. 1′, 3′. 3.1.8.B 10′. 3.2.1 rev. 4′, 7′ (2×), 9′, 13′, 16′;

lo. e. 20′. 3.2.3 3′. 4.1.1.1.A_1 rev. 4′. 4.1.1.1.B_1 rev. iii$^?$ 9; rev. iv$^?$ 10. 4.1.1.2.B rev. 1. 4.1.1.3 obv. 2, 5 (2×), 6, 8, 13, 14, 15, 16; rev. A 1′, 2′, 3′, 7′, 8′. 4.1.1.5 obv. 5. 4.1.1.7 rev.$^{!?}$ 5 (2×). 4.1.2.3 obv. ii 7′. 4.1.3.2 rev. 3′. 4.1.3.3 8′. 4.1.4.1.A_1 obv. i 5′; obv. ii 6′ (2×); rev. v 3′, 4′; 4″, 5″, 9″. 4.1.4.2.A_1 rev. r. c. 4′, 7′. 4.1.4.2.A_2 obv. r. c. 11′, 12′. 4.1.4.3 2′, 4′. 4.1.4.9 obv. 3. 4.2.1.A_1 obv. 8, 11. 4.2.4 obv. 8; rev. 6′ (2×). 4.2.6 obv.$^?$ 5′, 10′, 12′, 14′, 17′, 18′; rev.$^?$ 5′, 9′. 4.2.9 obv. 1 (2×), 2 (3×), 3, 4, 5 (2×), 6, 7 (2×), 9, 10, 14 (2×), 16 (2×), 18, 21, 24, 25, 26, 27, 30, 31; rev. 4′, 12′, 14′, 15′, 17′, 22′, 25′, 26′ (2×), 27′. 5.1 obv. ii 6′, 7′, 10′. 5.2 obv. ii 3, 7 (2×), 18. 5.4 r. c. 5′. 5.5 rev. iii 3′, 4′. 5.7 rev. iii$^?$ 14′, 21′, 23′ (2×). 6.1 obv. 6, 12, 17; rev. B 6. 6.3 rev. B 2. 6.5 rev. 6′, 8′, 11′, 12′, 14′, 15′, 16′, 17′, 18′ (2×), 20′ (2×), 25′. 6.9 obv. 2′, 6′, 7′ (2×). 6.11 6′. 6.13 2′, 3′, 4′. 7.1 obv. 1′, 5′, 7′, 15′. 7.3 obv. i 4. 7.4 2′. 8.1.A obv. ii 3′, 8′, 17′, 19′, 20′, 21′, 26′ (2×), 29′; rev. v 6, 18′, 25′. 8.1.D rev. iv 1′. 8.1.E(A_1) obv. ii 2, 3, 5; obv. iii 8′, 9′; rev. iv 2′, 3′ (2×), 4′ (2×), 6′ (2×), 9′, 10′, 12′ (2×); rev. v 2′. 8.1.F obv. i 4′, 9′, 19′; obv. ii 5′, 7′, 8′; rev. v 7, 9, 13. 8.1.G obv. r. c. 3′, 9′, 10′. 8.1.H rev. r. c. 1′. 8.1.K obv. ii$^?$ 6′. 8.3 obv. 3′, 6′. 8.4 rev. 13′, 19′, 20′. 8.6 r. c. 4′, 5′. 8.7 r. c. 9′. 8.8.B r. c. 3′, 5′. 9.1.1 rev. iii 8′, 17′, 18′, 22′, 23′, 29′, 33′, 35′, 36′, 39′; rev. iv 6′, 10′, 16′, 17′, 26′, 28′, 31′, 32′, 38′, 43′. 9.1.4.A_1 obv. ii 7, 11, 13, 22, 26, 27, 37, 38, 40. 9.1.4.A_2 r. c. 4′, 5′. 9.1.5 obv.$^!$ 11, 12; rev.$^!$ 6′, 7′, 10′ (2×), 16′ (3×). 9.1.6 obv. 1, 17. 9.1.8 obv. 11′, 13′, 14′ (3×), 15′. 9.1.9 rev. iv 2′. 9.1.10.A_1 rev. 3′. 9.1.10.A_2 rev. 3′. 9.1.10.B 5′. 9.1.11 obv.$^?$ 2′, 5′, 7′; rev.$^?$ 2′. 9.1.14 obv. r. c. 5′. 9.1.15 2′. 9.2.1 rev. iii 5′, 8′, 10′, 12′. 9.2.14 3′. 9.2.2 rev.$^!$ iii 22′, 23′, 24′. 9.2.3 obv. (ii) 4″, 6″. 9.2.4 obv. ii 1′, 3′, 5′, 12′; rev. iii 8′; rev. iv 11. 9.2.6 obv. i 8′, 12′, 13′, 18′. 10.1.1.1 rev.$^?$ 8′, 10′, 13′. 10.1.1.2 rev. iv 2′, 4′, 5′, 7′, 11′. 10.1.2.1 obv.$^?$ r. c. 4′; rev.$^?$ l. c. 6. 10.1.2.8 rev. r. c. 4′. 10.2.1.1 obv. 10′. 10.2.1.2 obv. 4′, 16′. 10.2.2.3 obv.$^?$ r. c. 3′. 10.3.2 obv. ii(?) 3′, 15′. 10.3.3 obv.$^?$ 12′, 14′. 10.3.5 7′, 8′. 10.3.7 2′. 10.3.10 r. c. 9′. 10.3.12 obv. i 6′, 9′. 11.1.1 r. c. 8′. 11.1.3 3′, 5′, 9′, 10′. 11.1.6 l. c. 1′. 11.1.9 8′. 11.2.3 3′. 11.3.1 2′, 4′, 5′, 6′, 7′, 10′, 11′ 4.1.4.4 10′. 11.4.1 5′. 11.5.1 5′. 11.6.1 3 (3×), 5 (2×), 6, 7, 12. 11.6.2 obv. 6′; rev. 3′, 4′; l. e. 3, 6. 11.6.4 obv. 6′, 8′, 9′. 11.6.5 obv.$^?$ 5, 6 (2×), 8 (2×), 9; rev.$^?$ 3″. 11.6.6 rev. 5′. 11.6.7 4′ (2×), 5′. 11.6.8 2′, 6′. 11.6.10 2′. 12.1.1 r. c. 2′. 12.3.2 7′. 12.3.3 3′, 5′

	2	10.3.2 obv. i(?) 11″
	2!	3.1.7.A$_1$ obv. i 1′. 6.9 obv. 1′
	2?	5.7 rev. iii? 24′
	n+]2	2.5 rev. 5′. 4.1.1.8 r. c. 9′. 4.1.4.1.A$_1$ obv. ii 4′. 4.1.4.2.A$_1$ rev. l. c. 9′. 6.9 obv. 10. 9.2.13 4′. 10.3.10 r. c. 4′. 12.3.2 8′
	2[+n	8.1.J rev. iv! 4′. 11.1.1 r. c. 7′
nom.-acc. n.	2-*e*	4.2.4 obv. 6
dat./loc.	*A-NA* 2	2.17 obv.? r. c. 12′, 13′. 4.1.1.1.A$_1$ rev. 13′. 4.1.1.1.B$_1$ rev. iii? 6. 4.1.4.9 obv. 4, 5
	A-NA! 2	10.3.1 rev. iii 9′
2^{KAM}	‘second’	
	2^{KAM}	9.1.1 rev. iv 45′. 9.1.4.A$_1$ rev. iv 5′. 9.1.9 rev. iv 4′
2-*ŠU*	‘twice’	
	2-*ŠU*	4.1.2.3 obv. ii 11′. 8.8.B l. c. 1′
	2-*ŠÚ*	8.4 rev. 7′
2-*Ú*	‘second’	
	2-*Ú*	4.1.1.2.A obv. 8′, 16′, 19′. 4.1.1.2.B obv. 2, 5. 4.1.2.2 obv. 2′, 5′. 4.1.2.3 obv. ii 6′; rev. iii 2, 6. 9.1.1 rev. iii 23′. 9.1.5 rev.! 10′
	2]-*Ú*(?)	6.1 l. e. 1c.
2 *TAPAL*	‘two sets’	
	2 *TA-PAL*	3.1.1.A$_3$ obv. iii 7′. 4.2.6 rev.? 7′. 8.4 rev. 9′, 10′, 15′. 9.1.1 rev. iii 24′; rev. iv 3′. 9.1.8 obv. 8′. 9.1.11 obv.? 10′. 10.1.1.1 rev.? 13′. 10.3.5 10′. 10.3.6 4′, 7′. 11.3.1 17′. 12.3.3 6′.
	2! *TA-PAL*	6.5 obv. 7′
	2 *TA*!-*PAL*	9.2.6 obv. i 14′
	2 *TA*-[*PAL*	4.2.10 8′
	2 *T*[*A-PAL*	9.1.1 rev. iv 34′
abbr.	2 *TA.*	2.15 l. c. 6′. 3.1.7.A$_1$ obv. i 11′. 4.1.4.1.A$_1$ obv. ii 7′. 9.1.5 rev.! 10′
	2 *TA.*!	10.1.2.1 obv.? r. c. 2′
2 ½	‘two and a half’	
	2 ½	10.3.10 r. c. 2′
3	‘three’	
	3	1.1.A$_2$ obv. 4′, 9′, 12′; rev. 8. 1.2 rev. 4′, 8′. 1.5 obv. 1, 5, 13; lo. e. 18; rev. 23 (2×). 2.4 rev. 5′. 2.5 rev. 6′. 2.7.A obv. 7. 2.9.A$_3$ obv. i 10′, 12′. 2.11 obv.? 5′. 2.13 rev.? 9′. 2.15 l. c. 10′. 2.17 obv.? r. c. 12′. 3.1.1.A$_2$ rev. v 1′, 8′, 10′, 13′. 3.1.1.A$_3$ rev. iv 4′. 3.1.5.A$_2$ obv. ii(?) 9′. 3.1.8.A obv. 15′; rev. 7′ (2×). 3.1.8.B 3′. 3.2.1 obv. 14, 20. 4.1.1.1.A$_1$ obv. 12′, 18′. 4.1.1.1.B$_1$ rev. iii? 6, 7, 14. 4.1.1.2.A obv. 8′. 4.1.1.3 rev. A 6′; rev. B 14. 4.1.2.5 obv. 6′. 4.1.3.6 obv. 13′. 4.1.4.1.A$_1$ obv. i 6′, 10′; obv.

		ii 3′, 11′, 13′. 4.1.4.2.A_1 rev. r. c. 2′, 3′. 4.1.4.2.A_2 obv. r. c. 2′, 3′. 4.1.4.3 3′, 5′. 4.1.4.5 rev. r. c. 8′. 4.2.2 obv. 1. 4.2.4 obv. 8. 4.2.6 obv.? 17′, 19′. 4.2.9 obv. 1, 3, 4, 6, 10, 18, 20, 21, 23, 24, 26; rev. 8′, 13′ (2×), 27′. 4.2.10 3′. 5.1 obv. ii 2′. 5.2 obv. ii 1, 2, 5, 6, 17. 5.7 rev. iii? 13′, 15′, 17′, 22′. 6.1 obv. 2, 12; rev. B 1. 6.5 rev. 6′, 14′, 23′, 26′. 6.9 obv. 4′. 6.13 2′, 7′. 7.1 obv. 9′, 13′. 7.3 obv. i 11. 8.1.A obv. ii 22′; rev. v 1, 8, 24′. 8.1.B rev. 5′. 8.1.C 3′. 8.1.E(A_1) rev. iv 7′. 8.1.F obv. ii 2′, 6′, 13′; rev. v 10. 8.1.J rev. v! 5′. 8.1.K rev. v? 6′; rev. vi? 4′. 8.5 rev. iii(?) 3′, 4′. 8.8.B r. c. 7′, 8′. 9.1.1 rev. iii 1′, 26′, 39′; rev. iv 16′, 21′, 36′, 44′. 9.1.4.A_1 obv. ii 7, 16, 21, 24, 32. 9.1.4.A_3 3′. 9.1.5 obv.! 6, 10; rev.! 8′, 9′ (2×), 13′ (2×). 9.1.6 obv. 6. 9.1.8 obv. 2′, 4′. 9.1.12 4′. 9.1.14 obv. r. c. 5′. 9.2.1 obv. ii 21′; rev. iii 6′, 7′, 15′. 9.2.2 rev.! iii 9′, 16′. 9.2.3 obv. (ii) 6″. 9.2.4 obv. i 5′; rev. iii 3′; rev. iv 7. 9.2.7 rev. r. c. 2′. 9.2.9 obv.? 8′; rev.? 6′. 10.1.1.1 rev.? 5′, 14′. 10.1.2.7 13′. 10.2.2.4 5′. 10.3.2 obv. i(?) 16″; obv. ii(?) 16′. 10.3.3 obv.? 9′. 10.3.5 9′. 10.3.10 r. c. 2′, 3′, 7′, 10′. 10.3.11 l. c. 3′. 10.3.12 obv. i 9′. 10.3.13 5′, 8′. 10.3.14 l. c. 2′. 11.1.8 4′. 11.1.9 3′, 4′. 11.3.1 11′, 23′. 11.4.2 obv. 3′. 11.6.1 2, 3, 4 (2×), 7, 9, 12, 14. 11.6.2 rev. 7′; l. e. 6. 11.6.5 obv.? 8; rev.? 4″. 11.6.8 5′. 11.7.3 rev.? 2. 12.2.3 8′. 12.3.2 3′, 7′. 12.3.7 7′
	⟨⟨3⟩⟩	4.2.1.A_1 obv. 10
	3?	9.1.5 rev.! 10′. 11.1.7 1′
	n+]3	3.2.1 rev. 17′
	3[+n	8.1.J rev. iv! 5′
gen.	*ŠA* 3	4.1.2.3 obv. ii 3′, 8′, 12′; rev. 3
	ŠA *3*	4.1.2.3 rev. iii 7
dat./loc.	*A-NA* 3	2.17 obv.? r. c. 19′. 3.1.8.A rev. 10′. 11.3.1 7′, 10′
3-*ŠU*	'thrice'	
	3-*ŠU*	4.1.2.1 obv. (i) 4′. 4.1.2.2 obv. 2′, 5′
	3-*Š*]*U*	4.1.2.3 obv. ii 7′
3 *TAPAL*	'three sets'	
	3 *TA-PAL*	4.1.4.6 obv. 5′. 8.4 rev. 13′. 9.1.1 rev. iv 36′, 41′. 9.1.8 obv. 9′. 11.3.1 16′, 19′
	3 *TA-PA*[*L*	9.1.1 rev. iv 35′
	3 *TA-P*[*AL*	4.1.4.6 obv. 7′
abbr.	3 *TA.*	11.6.1 6
	*3 *TA.**	2.13 rev.? 4′
3 ½	'three and a half'	
	3 ½	11.6.11 2′, 3′. 12.2.2 3′, 4′, 5′, 6′, 7′. 12.2.3 3′
	3 ⟨⟨½⟩⟩ (or: 3 ½⟨.KÙŠ⟩?)	11.6.11 1′
	⟨⟨3 ½⟩⟩	12.2.2 8′, 9′

4		'four'	
		4	1.1.A_1 obv. 7′, 12′. 1.1.A_2 obv. 4′. 1.1.A_3 rev. 2′. 1.5 obv. 11. 2.2 rev 6, 7. 2.3 3. 2.4 rev. 1′. 2.5 rev. 5′. 2.7.A obv. 19. 2.14 3′. 2.16 rev. v 1. 2.17 obv.$^{?}$ r. c. 2′, 5′, 15′, 16′ (2×), 17′. 3.1.1.A_2 rev. v 8′. 3.1.2 rev. l. c. 3′. 3.1.3 obv.$^{?}$ 5′. 3.1.5.A_1 obv. ii(?) 6′. 3.1.7.A_2 obv. ii 8′, 9′. 3.1.8.A obv. 14′; rev. 14′. 3.1.8.B 8′. 3.2.1 obv. 3. 4.1.1.1.A_1 obv. 17′; rev. 3′, 4′ (2×). 4.1.1.1.B_1 obv. ii$^{?}$ 7′. 4.1.1.2.A obv. 3′, 7′. 4.1.1.3 obv. 13; rev. A 6′ (2×), 7′. 4.1.1.7 rev.$^{!?}$ 6. 4.1.1.9 4′. 4.1.2.3 obv. ii 2′, 3′, 4′; rev. iii 6, 7. 4.1.4.1.A_1 obv. iii 1′; rev. v 3′, 7″. 4.1.4.2.A_1 rev. r. c. 6′, 7′; rev. l. c. 2′. 4.1.4.6 obv. 9′, 13′ (2×). 4.2.4 rev. 6′. 4.2.6 obv.$^{?}$ 1′, 13′; rev.$^{?}$ 11′. 4.2.9 obv. 5, 19, 22; rev. 3′, 4′, 26′. 5.1 obv. ii 7′. 5.2 rev. iii 2′. 5.3 r. c. 9′. 5.7 rev. iii$^{?}$ 19′ (3×). 6.5 rev. 10′, 13′, 20′ (2×), 28′. 6.12 5′. 6.13 7′. 8.1.A obv. i 12′; obv. ii 22′ (2×), 25′. 8.1.B rev. 5′. 8.1.D rev. iv 5′, 6′. 8.1.E(A_1) obv. ii 10; obv. iii 7′; rev. iv 3′, 8′; rev. v 11′. 8.1.E(A_2) 4′, 5′. 8.1.F rev. v 9, 14. 8.1.K rev. v$^{?}$ 3′. 8.4 rev. 12′, 19′. 8.8.B l. c. 3′. 9.1.1 rev. iii 22′, 29′, 30′, 34′; rev. iv 13′, 21′, 30′, 44′. 9.1.4.A_1 obv. ii 1, 9 (2×), 10. 9.1.4.A_1 obv. ii 12, 13, 14, 15, 16, 21, 33, 41. 9.1.5; obv.$^{!}$ 2, 3, 5; rev.$^{!}$ 7′, 9′, 11′, 15′. 9.1.6 obv. 4. 9.1.7 obv. 7′. 9.1.8 obv. 5′. 9.1.13 6′. 9.1.14 obv. r. c. 4′. 9.2.1 obv. ii 16′, 27′; rev. iii 11′, 12′. 9.2.4 obv. ii 15′; rev. iii 5′. 10.1.2.4 l. c. 12′. 10.1.2.6 3′. 10.1.2.7 4′. 10.1.2.8 rev. r. c. 6′. 10.2.1.1 obv. 11′. 10.2.2.2 obv.$^{?}$ l. c. 7′. 10.2.2.3 obv.$^{?}$ l. c. 5′; obv.$^{?}$ r. c. 1′. 10.2.2.4 obv.$^{?}$ r. c. 2′, 4′, 7′. 10.3.2 obv. i(?) 13″. 10.3.3 obv.$^{?}$ 8′. 10.3.5 6′. 10.3.10 r. c. 8′. 10.3.12 obv. i 16′. 10.3.14 l. c. 7′. 11.1.7 4′. 11.3.1 8′. 11.6.1 14. 11.6.2 obv. 5′, 7′. 11.6.6 rev. 5′. 11.6.7 6′. 11.7.1 r. c. 3′. 11.7.2 2′. 11.7.3 rev.$^{?}$ 6′. 12.1.2 7′, 8′. 12.2.1 obv. 3′, 4′; rev. 3′, 4′, 6′. 12.3.2 3′
		4$^{?}$	2.18 9′. 3.2.1 obv. 11. 6.13 9′. 9.1.5 obv.$^{!}$ 7. 10.3.3 obv.$^{?}$ 10′. 11.3.1 19′
		⟨4⟩	5.2 obv. ii 14
		n+]4	2.16 obv. i 3′. 3.1.11.A 4. 4.1.3.4.A_1 rev. l. c. 4′, 5′, 6′. 4.1.3.4.A_2 rev. l. c. 6′, 7′, 8′
		4[+n	1.5 lo. e. 15. 2.17 obv.$^{?}$ 11′. 8.1.J rev. iv$^{!}$ 2′
	gen.	*ŠA* 4	4.1.2.3 obv. ii 4′, 9′, 13′; rev. iii 4
		Š]*A* 4	4.1.2.3 rev. iii 7
	dat./loc.	*A-NA* 4	2.17 obv.$^{?}$ r. c. 11′ (2×). 3.1.1.A_3 obv. iii 9′. 3.1.8.A rev. 4′
4-*ŠU*		'four times'	
		4-*ŠU*	8.4 rev. 5′

4-Ú	'fourth'	
	4-Ú	4.1.2.2 obv. 2′. 4.1.2.3 obv. ii 7′
4 TAPAL	'four sets'	
	4 TA-PAL	3.1.1.A_3 obv. iii 5′. 4.1.4.6 obv. 11′; lo. e. 15′. 9.1.1 rev. iii 31′; rev. iv 37′. 9.2.6 obv. i 4′.
abbr.	4 TA.	11.6.1 13
4 ½	'four and a half'	
	4 ½	10.3.10 r. c. 9′, 10′
5	'five'	
	5	1.1.A_2 obv. 8′, 12′. 1.2 rev. 9′. 1.5 lo. e. 16. 2.7.A obv. 7. 2.13 obv.? 7′. 3.1.1.A_2 rev. v 14′. 3.1.1.A_3 rev. iv 18′. 3.1.5.A_2 obv. ii(?) 1′. 3.1.7.A_2 rev. v 3′. 3.1.8.A obv. 6′. 3.1.9 2′. 3.2.1 obv. 14. 4.1.1.1.A_1 obv. 11′. 4.1.1.1.B_1 rev. iii? 1. 4.1.1.8 r. c. 5′. 4.1.2.5 obv. 11′. 4.1.3.4.A_1 obv. l. c. 3′. 4.1.3.5.A_2 2′, 3′, 4′. 4.1.4.1.A_1 rev. vi 5′. 4.1.4.7 rev. B 1′. 4.1.4.9 obv. 6. 4.2.2 obv. 2. 4.2.6 obv.? 18′. 4.2.9 obv. 4, 6, 21, 24 (2×), 26, 30. 5.2 obv. ii 7 (2×). 5.4 r. c. 8′. 5.7 rev. iii? 28′. 6.5 rev. 16′. 7.1 obv. 11′, 12′. 8.1.A obv. ii 5′; rev. v 3, 4, 25′. 8.1.E(A_1) obv. iii 2′, 3′, 6′, 8′; rev. iv 8′; rev. v 10′. 8.1.F obv. i 5′, 6′; obv. ii 9′, 17′; rev. iv 5′; rev. v 9. 8.1.K rev. v? 4′; rev. vi? 9′. 8.3 obv. 7′. 8.4 rev. 4′. 8.7 r. c. 6′. 9.1.1 rev. iv 30′. 9.1.5 rev.! 4′ (2×). 9.1.6 obv. 3, 5. 9.1.7 obv. 4′. 9.1.10.A_2 rev. 7′. 9.2.2 rev.! iii 6′, 21′. 9.2.6 obv. i 7′. 10.1.1.1 rev.? 14′, 15′. 10.1.2.1 obv.? r. c. 1′. 10.3.3 obv.? 13′. 11.1.4 1′. 11.1.9 5′. 11.6.1 2, 5, 6, 9, 12 (2×), 14. 11.6.3 obv.? 5′. 11.6.4 obv. 7′. 11.6.5 obv.? 7. 12.3.1 8′
	5!	11.1.1 r. c. 5′
	5?	4.1.3.2 rev. 9′. 8.1.F rev. vi 13
	n+]5	10.1.2.1 rev.? r. c. 8′
5 TAPAL	'five sets'	
	n+]5 TA-PAL	9.1.10.A_2 rev. 8′
abbr.	5 TA.	11.6.1 2
6	'six'	
	6	1.5 lo. e. 16. 2.5 rev. 2′. 2.7.A rev. 6. 2.9.A_3 obv. ii 6. 2.16 obv. i 10′. 2.17 obv.? r. c. 13′. 3.1.7.A_1 obv. i 7′; l. e. 1. 3.1.8.A obv. 17′; rev. 17′. 3.1.8.B 4′. 3.2.1 obv. 14, 20 (2×). 3.2.2 obv.? 4′, 11′, 12′. 4.1.1.1.B_1 rev. iii? 3. 4.1.1.3 obv. 6. 4.1.2.6 3′. 4.1.3.4.A_1 obv. l. c. 2′. 4.1.4.1.A_2 obv. i 2′. 4.1.4.2.A_1 rev. r. c. 5′, 7′, 8′ (2×), 14′. 4.1.4.2.A_2 obv. r. c. 2′. 4.1.4.7 obv. 2. 4.2.1.A_1 obv. 10. 4.2.1.A_2 obv. 6′. 4.2.4 obv. 2; rev. 4′. 4.2.7 7′. 4.2.9 obv. 25. 5.1 obv. ii 8′, 12′. 5.2 obv. ii 11, 14. 5.5 rev. iii 7′. 6.12 8′. 7.3 obv. i 7, 9. 8.1.A rev. v 4, 5.

		8.1.C 1′. 8.1.E(A_1) obv. ii 4; rev. iv 13′. 8.1.F obv. ii 12′; rev. v 11. 9.1.1 rev. iii 17′, 38′; rev. iv 17′, 18′, 20′, 34′. 9.1.5 rev.$^{!}$ 10′, 14′ (2×). 9.1.6 obv. 8, 9. 9.2.4 obv. i 17′. 9.2.5 obv. i(?) 6′. 9.2.8.A_1 8′. 9.2.9 rev.$^{?}$ 4′, 7′. 9.2.11 2′. 10.3.11 r. c. 5′. 10.3.12 obv. i 4′. 11.1.3 7′, 8′. 11.1.6 l. c. 12′. 11.2.5 3′. 11.3.2 r. c. 2′, 6′. 11.4.2 obv. 6′. 11.6.1 9, 11, 12. 11.6.2 rev. 8′; l. e. 4. 11.6.6 rev. 9′
	6$^{?}$	2.15 l. c. 11′. 7.3 obv. i 9. 9.1.10.B 7′. 9.2.9 rev.$^{?}$ 7′. 11.6.5 obv.$^{?}$ 1
	6$^{!?}$	10.3.12 obv. i 18′
	n+]6	6.6 obv. 4′. 9.2.4 obv. i 15′
6-*ŠU*	‘six times’	
	6-*ŠÚ*	8.1.F rev. v 8
6 *TAPAL*	‘six sets’	
	6 *TA-PAL*	3.1.1.A_1 rev. v 12′. 8.1.F rev. v 6. 10.3.12 obv. i 8′
7	‘seven’	
	7	1.1.A_1 obv. 11′. 2.12 obv.$^{!}$ ii 6′. 2.13 rev.$^{?}$ 7′. 2.14 13′. 2.15 l. c. 7′. 2.16 rev. v 4. 2.18 2′. 3.1.1.A_2 rev. v 3′. 3.1.4 1′. 3.2.2 obv.$^{?}$ 3′. 4.1.1.1.B_1 rev. iv$^{?}$ 10. 4.1.1.2.A obv. 21′. 4.1.1.3 obv. 4, 14. 4.1.1.7 rev.$^{!?}$ 7. 4.1.2.3 obv. ii 12′, 13′; rev. iii 3. 4.1.4.1.A_1 obv. iii 2′, 5′, 6′. 4.1.4.2.A_1 rev. r. c. 10′ (2×); rev. l. c. 3′. 4.2.4 obv. 11; rev. 8′. 4.2.7 6′. 4.2.9 obv. 4, 5, 19, 27; rev. 13′, 15′. 5.2 obv. ii 16. 5.7 rev. iii$^{?}$ 19′. 8.1.A obv. ii 25′; rev. v 7. 8.1.C 2′. 8.1.D obv. i 1′. 8.1.E(A_1) obv. iii 6′; rev. iv 7′. 8.1.F obv. i 8′; rev. vi 15. 8.1.K obv. ii$^{?}$ 2′. 8.6 l. c. 11′; r. c. 7′. 9.1.1 rev. iii 27′; rev. iv 29′. 9.1.6 obv. 3. 9.1.10.B 4′. 9.1.14 obv. r. c. 4′. 9.2.1 obv. ii 7′; rev. iii 24′. 9.2.5 obv. i(?) 10′. 9.2.6 obv. i 1′. 10.1.1.2 rev. iv 4′. 10.3.10 r. c. 13′. 11.6.1 10. 11.6.9 4′. 12.1.1 l. c. 2′ (2×), 3′
	7$^{?}$	11.2.2 4′. 11.6.9 4′
dat./loc.	*A-NA* 7	4.1.2.3 rev. iii 6
7 *TAPAL*	‘seven sets’	
	7 *TA-P*[*AL*	9.1.1 rev. iii 44′
8	‘eight’	
	8	1.1.A_1 obv. 7′. 3.1.1.A_1 obv. ii 7′. 3.1.1.A_3 obv. iii 5′, 8′. 3.1.2 obv. l. c. 5′. 3.1.7.A_2 obv. ii 7a′. 3.1.10 9. 3.1.12 6′. 3.2.1 obv. 5, 11. 4.1.1.2.A obv. 9′. 4.1.1.9 6′. 4.1.1.10 obv.$^{?}$ 4′. 4.1.2.3 obv. ii 1′. 4.1.4.4 9′, 10′ (2×). 4.1.4.5 rev. r. c. 3′, 4′. 4.2.9 rev. 11′, 16′. 5.7 rev. iii$^{?}$ 15′. 8.1.A obv. i 2′; obv. ii 6′. 8.1.E(A_1) obv. iii 2′. 8.1.F obv. i 5′; obv. ii 18′. 8.5 rev. iii(?) 3′. 8.6 l. c. 11′. 9.1.1 rev. iii 16′, 21′; rev. iv 8′. 9.1.5 rev.$^{!}$ 2′. 9.2.1 obv. ii 9′; rev. iii 13′. 9.2.6 obv. i 10′. 10.1.1.2 rev. iv 2′. 10.1.2.1

		rev.? r. c. 3′. 10.2.1.1 obv. 3′. 10.3.4 2′, 6′. 10.3.14 l. c. 5′. 11.3.2 r. c. 3′. 11.6.1 3, 8, 14
	8?	3.1.2 obv. l. c. 3′. 4.1.4.4 9′.
	n+]8	3.2.1 obv. 19
8 *TAPAL*	‘8 sets’	
	8 *TA-PAL*	11.3.1 15′
abbr.	8 *TA.*	11.6.1 4
9	‘nine’	
	9	2.7.A rev. 1. 3.1.2 obv. l. c. 6′. 4.1.1.2.A obv. 2′. 4.1.1.3 obv. 10. 4.1.1.10 obv.? 3′. 4.1.2.3 obv. ii 11′; rev. iii 2. 4.1.4.2.A_2 obv. r. c. 1′; rev. r. c. 2′. 4.1.4.8 5′. 4.2.5 4′. 4.2.9 obv. 2. 5.2 obv. ii 10. 5.7 rev. iii? 15′. 6.12 6′. 8.1.F obv. i 21′; obv. ii 3′, 11′. 8.1.G obv. r. c. 7′. 9.1.1 rev. iii 32′. 9.1.6 obv. 8. 9.1.10.A_2 rev. 10′. 9.1.14 obv. r. c. 3′. 9.2.1 obv. ii 8′ (2×). 10.3.10 r. c. 8′, 9′. 11.1.5 2′. 11.6.5 obv.? 8
	n+]9	4.1.2.5 obv. 8′
9 *TAPAL*	‘nine sets’	
	9 *TA-PAL*	3.1.1.A_3 obv. iii 6′. 9.1.1 rev. iii 30′
10	‘ten’	
	10	1.2 rev. 10′. 2.8 obv. 2. 2.11 obv.? 3′. 2.17 obv.? r. c. 1′, 2′. 3.1.2 obv. l. c. 10′. 3.1.5.A_2 obv. ii(?) 11′. 3.1.7.A_2 rev. iv 2′; rev. v 3′. 3.1.8.A rev. 15′. 3.1.8.B 3′. 3.2.1 obv. 7; rev. 6′, 9′. 3.2.3 3′. 4.1.1.1.B_1 rev. iii? 16; rev. iv? 6. 4.1.1.2.A obv. 15′, 16′, 18′, 23′, 25′. 4.1.1.2.B obv. 1, 2, 4. 4.1.1.3 obv. 16. 4.1.1.6 obv. ii 3′; rev. iii 1. 4.1.2.1 obv. (i) 4′. 4.1.2.2 obv. 5′. 4.1.2.3 obv. ii 7′. 4.1.2.5 obv. 6′, 9′. 4.1.4.1.A_1 obv. ii 9′; rev. vi 8′, 9′. 4.1.4.2.A_1 rev. r. c. 5′. 4.1.4.4 5′. 4.2.1.A_2 rev. 12′. 4.2.7 9′. 5.2 obv. ii 15, 16; rev. iii 3′. 5.3 r. c. 1′. 5.7 rev. iii? 8′. 6.5 rev. 21′. 6.12 3′, 10. 7.1 obv. 14′. 8.1.A rev. v 5. 8.1.F obv. i 20′; obv. ii 5′. 8.1.G obv. r. c. 5′. 8.5 rev. iii(?) 2′; rev. iv(?) 5′. 8.6 r. c. 2′. 8.7 r. c. 7′, 12′. 8.8.A 4′. 8.8.B l. c. 4′. 9.1.1 rev. iii 21′. 9.1.10.B 3′. 9.2.1 rev. iii 2′. 9.2.9 obv.? 13′. 11.1.6 l. c. 8′. 11.5.3 3′. 11.6.1 9. 12.2.1 obv. 4′; rev. 4′. 12.3.1 3′, 8′
	10?	4.1.4.4 5′. 4.1.1.5 obv. 6. 4.1.1.6 obv. ii 5′. 4.2.8 3′. 9.1.6 obv. 12. 9.2.7 rev. r. c. 5′. 10.1.2.1 obv.? r. c. 7′
	n+]10	1.2 rev. 9′. 3.1.8.A obv. 8′; rev. 15′
	n+1]0	10.1.1.2 rev. iv 11′
	10[+n	4.2.8 3′. 8.1.F rev. iv 2′. 10.1.1.2 rev. iv 3′. 11.6.2 obv. 1′
dat./loc.	*A-NA* 10	9.2.2 rev.! iii 7′

11	'eleven'	
	11	1.5 lo. e. 15. 2.5 obv. 6′. 2.7.A obv. 26. 2.16 obv. i 8′. 3.1.8.A obv. 10′. 4.1.3.3 8′. 4.1.4.1.A_1 rev. v 9″. 4.1.4.5 rev. r. c. 7′. 4.2.7 8′. 4.2.9 obv. 19. 8.1.D obv. i 7a′. 9.1.1 rev. iii 10′; rev. iv 40′. 9.1.8 obv. 13′. 9.1.10.A_2 rev. 9′. 9.2.2 rev.[!] iii 26′. 9.2.4 obv. i 14′. 9.2.9 rev.[?] 3′. 10.1.1.2 rev. iv 14′. 10.1.2.8 rev. r. c. 3′. 10.3.5 8′. 11.3.2 r. c. 5′. 11.6.1 12
	1]1[?]	11.3.2 r. c. 5′
12	'twelve'	
	12	1.1.A_1 obv. 7′. 1.5 obv. 9. 2.2 rev. 15. 2.17 obv.[?] r. c. 10′. 3.1.1.A_1 obv. ii 14′. 3.1.1.A_3 obv. iii 14′. 3.1.5.A_1 obv. i(?) 4′. 3.1.5.A_2 obv. ii(?) 9′. 3.1.8.A rev. 12′. 3.1.9 1′. 3.1.10 5. 4.1.2.3 obv. ii 8′. 4.1.4.1.A_1 rev. v 6″. 4.1.4.1.A_2 obv. i 5′; obv. ii 4′ (2×), 5′ (2×). 4.1.4.2.A_2 obv. r. c. 8′. 4.2.1.A_2 obv. 4′. 8.1.E(A_1) rev. iv 2′. 8.4 rev. 14′. 9.1.1 rev. iv 18′ (2×). 9.2.1 obv. ii 10′. 9.2.2 rev.[!] iii 18′. 11.1.7 6′. 11.6.2 l. e. 4. 12.3.1 6′
	12[?]	4.1.1.1.A_1 obv. 13′. 10.1.1.1 rev.[?] 6′
	n+]12	1.5 obv. 9. 4.1.3.1 7′
12 *TAPAL*	'twelve sets'	
	12 *TA-PAL*	9.2.4 obv. ii 6′
abbr. (dat./loc.)	*A-NA* 12 *TA.*	3.1.7.A_1 obv. i 8′
13	'thirteen'	
	13	3.1.1.A_3 obv. iii 1′. 3.1.8.B 9′. 3.2.1 rev. 10′. 4.1.4.1.A_2 obv. i 2′. 6.5 obv. 7′, 8′, 9′, 10′, 11′, 12′, 13′, 14′, 15′. 8.1.A rev. v 24′. 9.2.4 obv. i 16′. 10.1.2.4 r. c. 4′. 10.3.12 obv. i 7′. 11.4.2 obv. 5′. 11.6.2 rev. 12′. 11.6.8 4′. 12.2.1 obv. 3′; rev. 3′
	[n+]13	2.9.A_1 obv. i 8′
13 *TAPAL*	'thirteen sets'	
	13 *TA-PAL*	9.1.10.A_2 rev. 11′. 11.3.1 14′
14	'fourteen'	
	14	3.1.7.A_2 obv. ii 7b′; rev. iv 3′. 3.1.10 9. 3.2.1 obv. 16. 4.1.1.3 obv. 11. 4.1.2.3 obv. ii 9′. 4.1.3.8 rev. A 4′. 4.1.4.1.A_1 rev. v 9″. 4.1.4.2.A_2 obv. r. c. 10′ (2×). 4.1.4.6 rev. 17′. 5.1 rev. iii 5. 5.2 obv. ii 12. 8.1.A rev. v 26′. 8.1.D rev. iv 5′. 8.1.F rev. v 7. 9.1.1 rev. iii 43′. 9.2.9 rev.[?] 1′. 10.1.1.2 rev. iv 3′. 10.2.1.2 obv. 17′. 11.6.1 8. 11.6.2 l. e. 1. 12.2.1 rev. 6′
dat./loc.	*A-NA* 14	4.1.2.3 obv. ii 12′
	A-NA] 14	4.1.2.3 rev. iii 3
15	'fifteen'	
	15	2.7.A rev. 3. 3.1.1.A_2 rev. v 10′. 3.1.7.A_1 obv. i 4′. 3.1.8.A obv. 6′, 7′. 4.1.1.3 obv. 12. 4.1.1.8 r. c. 2′.

		4.1.3.2 rev. 1′. 4.1.3.8 rev. B 2′. 4.2.2 obv. 2. 5.2 obv. ii 15. 8.1.A obv. ii 4′. 8.5 rev. iii(?) 1′. 9.1.5 rev.! 7′. 9.1.6 obv. 6. 9.1.10.B 4′. 9.2.4 obv. ii 4′. 9.2.6 obv. i 7′. 10.1.2.1 rev.? r. c. 6′. 11.1.3 7′. 11.1.7 7′
	15?	9.1.1 rev. iii 20′. 9.1.5 rev.! 1′
	n+]15	4.1.3.1 4′. 4.1.4.1.A_1 rev. v 6′
16	‘sixteen’	
	16	2.9.A_3 obv. ii 10′. 3.1.5.A_2 obv. ii(?) 4′. 3.1.8.A obv. 11′. 3.1.12 7′. 4.1.3.2 rev. 3′. 8.1.A obv. ii 12′; rev. v 15′. 8.1.D obv. i 10′. 8.1.F obv. ii 4′. 8.4 rev. 3′, 12′. 9.1.5 rev.! 1′. 9.1.10.B 3′. 9.2.2 rev.! iii 6′, 10′. 10.3.11 r. c. 3′. 12.2.1 rev. 5′
	16?	2.17 obv.? r. c. 14′
	1[6	12.2.1 obv. 5′
17	‘seventeen’	
	17	3.1.7.A_2 obv. ii 5b′. 3.1.10 7. 4.1.1.1.A_1 rev. 8′. 8.1.E(A_1) obv. iii 7′. 9.2.6 obv. i 8′
17	‘seventeen-times’	
	17-⟨*ŠU*⟩	9.1.10.A_1 obv. 5′. 9.1.10.B 9′
18	‘eighteen’	
	18	3.1.1.A_1 obv. ii 3′. 3.1.7.A_1 obv. i 14′. 3.1.7.A_2 obv. ii 5b′. 3.1.10 3, 5. 4.1.1.6 rev. iii 8. 4.1.4.2.A_2 obv. r. c. 4′, 6′. 8.1.A rev. v 6. 8.4 rev. 14′. 8.8.B l. c. 8′. 9.2.4 obv. i 13′
	1]8	3.1.10 11
	n+]18	9.2.4 obv. i 16′
19	‘nineteen’	
	19	3.1.5.A_1 obv. ii(?) 1′, 4′. 3.1.7.A_1 obv. i 10′. 11.1.3 6′. 11.5.2 rev.? r. c. 2′. 11.6.1 9
19 *TAPAL*	‘nineteen sets’	
	n+]19 *TA-PAL*	8.8.A 12′
20	‘twenty’	
	20	1.5 rev. 26. 2.12 obv.! ii 5′. 2.17 obv.? r. c. 1′. 3.1.1.A_3 rev. iv 1′, 5′, 7′. 3.1.3 obv.? 5′. 3.1.7.A_2 rev. iv 3′; rev. v 4′. 3.1.11.B 6′. 3.2.1 obv. 13 (2×), 20 (2×); rev. 1′, 3′, 10′, 19′. 3.2.2 obv.? 4′, 8′, 9′. 4.1.1.1.A_1 obv. 10′. 4.1.1.2.B obv. 9. 4.1.1.3 obv. 5, 7. 4.1.1.6 obv. ii 3′; rev. iii 7 (2×). 4.1.1.7 rev.!? 9. 4.1.2.3 rev. iii 5. 4.1.2.6 2′. 4.1.3.1 1′, 6′. 4.1.3.3 10′, 11′. 4.1.3.6 obv. 7′. 4.1.3.8 rev. A 3′. 4.1.4.1.A_1 obv. ii 7′. 4.1.4.1.A_2 obv. ii 1′, 8′. 4.1.4.2.A_1 rev. r. c. 2′, 3′, 5′. 4.1.4.4 2′, 6′. 4.1.4.7 obv. 4. 4.2.2 obv. 1. 5.2 obv. ii 13, 16. 5.7 rev. iii? 26′. 6.12 3′. 7.1 obv. 19′. 8.1.E(A_2) 8′. 8.5 rev. iv(?) 1′. 8.7 r. c. 6′, 8′. 9.1.4.A_1 obv. ii 35. 9.1.5 rev.! 5′, 7′. 9.2.6

		obv. i 9′. 10.1.1.1 rev.? 15′. 11.6.1 11. 12.2.1 obv. 1′, 2′. 12.3.4 obv. 5, 6
	20?	4.1.1.5 up. e. 1; obv. 1. 4.1.4.1.A_2 obv. ii 10′. 4.1.4.3 5′. 4.1.2.6 1′
	⟨⟨20⟩⟩	3.1.8.A rev. 19′
	2]0	2.9.A_3 obv. ii 2′. 12.2.1 rev. 1′, 2′
	n+]20	3.1.8.B 6′. 4.1.4.1.A_1 rev. vi 5′. 7.4 5′
	20[+n	3.1.7.A_1 l. e. 1. 4.1.4.1.A_1 rev. v 9″. 4.1.4.5 rev. r. c. 8′. 11.6.2 obv. 3′
20 *TAPAL*	'twenty sets'	
	n+]20 *TA-PAL*	9.1.10.A_2 rev. 9′
21	'twenty-one'	
	21	3.1.8.A rev. 7′. 4.1.2.7 1′. 4.1.4.2.A_1 rev. r. c. 13′. 9.1.1 rev. iii 6′. 10.3.12 obv. i 2′
	21(?)	8.1.F rev. v 10′
	2]1	4.1.4.6 obv. 5′
22	'twenty-two'	
	22	4.2.1.A_1 obv. 6. 8.4 rev. 2′. 9.1.1 rev. iv 28′
dat./loc.	*A-NA* 22	3.1.8.A rev. 9′
23	'twenty-three'	
	23	4.1.4.2.A_1 rev. l. c. 5′. 4.2.12 2′. 9.1.6 obv. 1
	n+]23(?)	2.5 rev. 6′
dat./loc.	*A-NA* 23	3.1.7.A_1 l. e. 2
24	'twenty-four'	
	24	3.1.8.A rev. 12′. 4.1.1.3 obv. 3. 4.1.1.7 rev.!? 6. 4.1.2.3 rev. iii 5. 4.1.4.4 12′. 4.1.4.6 obv. 10′, 14′. 4.1.4.7 obv. 1
	24!	4.1.4.2.A_1 rev. r. c. 11′
	2]4	10.3.12 obv. i 15′
	n+]24	4.1.4.1.A_1 rev. v 7′
25	'twenty-five'	
	25	3.1.5.A_2 obv. ii(?) 11′, 14′. 3.2.3 4′. 4.1.3.2 rev. 5′. 4.1.3.7 obv. 4. 4.1.4.2.A_2 obv. r. c. 11′. 10.3.12 obv. i 3′, 13′. 11.6.9 2′
	25	4.2.1.A_1 obv. 8
	25!	3.1.1.A_2 rev. v 11′
26	'twenty-six'	
	26	3.1.7.A_1 l. e. 3. 4.1.3.2 rev. 5′. 8.1.A obv. i 13′
	2]6	4.1.2.3 obv. ii 8′
27	'twenty-seven'	
	27	3.1.1.A_1 rev. v 1′. 4.1.1.2.A obv. 7′. 8.1.D obv. i 4′. 8.1.G obv. l. c. 2′
28	'twenty-eight'	
	28	4.1.4.1.A_1 obv. ii 12′. 8.1.A obv. ii 9′. 8.8.A 8′. 10.1.2.3 3′. 11.7.2 5′. 12.3.4 obv. 3
	2]8	3.1.1.A_1 obv. ii 15′

29	‘twenty-nine’	
	29	2.2 rev. 11. 3.1.7.A_1 obv. i 1′. 9.1.1 rev. iv 4′. 9.2.6 obv. i 10′. 11.1.1 r. c. 10′
	2]9	10.3.12 obv. i 14′
30	‘thirty’	
	30	2.2 rev. 10. 2.9.A_1 obv. i 7′. 3.1.2 obv. l. c. 9′. 3.1.3 obv.$^{?}$ 1′. 3.1.5.A_2 obv. ii(?) 4′. 3.1.7.A_2 obv. ii 12′; rev. v 2′. 3.1.11.A 2. 3.2.1 rev. 12′. 4.1.1.1.B_1 rev. iv$^{?}$ 3. 4.1.1.3 obv. 13. 4.1.1.6 rev. iii 5, 10. 4.1.1.7 rev.$^{!?}$ 8. 4.1.1.8 r. c. 4′. 4.1.2.1 obv. (i) 9′. 4.1.2.5 obv. 2′. 4.1.3.1 2′, 3′, 5′. 4.1.4.1.A_2 obv. ii 7′. 4.1.4.7 rev. B 2′. 4.2.1.A_1 obv. 12. 4.2.6 rev.$^{?}$ 6′. 9.1.1 rev. iii 2′, 19′. 10.1.1.2 rev. iv 12′. 10.2.2.3 obv.$^{?}$ r. c. 2′. 11.2.6 4′
	30$^{?}$	5.7 rev. iii$^{?}$ 21′
	30[+n	8.1.F rev. iv 3′
31	‘thirty-one’	
	3]1	4.1.1.6 rev. iii 3
32	‘thirty-two’	
	32	12.3.4 obv. 1
33	‘thirty-three’	
	33	3.1.1.A_2 rev. v 12′. 10.1.2.8 rev. r. c. 2′. 11.1.2 l. c. 4′
	n+]33	2.18 7′
33 ½	‘thirty-three and one half’	
	33 ½	12.2.2 2′
34	‘thirty-four’	
	34	9.2.1 obv. ii 18′. 10.1.2.5 2′
35	‘thirty-five’	
	35	3.1.1.A_2 rev. v 2′. 4.1.1.9 5′. 4.1.3.2 rev. 3′
	35$^{?}$	3.1.10 1
	3]5$^{?}$	4.1.1.3 obv. 1
	3]5$^{!?}$	8.6 l. c. 8′
36	‘thirty-six’	
	36	3.1.2 obv. l. c. 12′. 12.3.4 obv. 2
37	‘thirty-seven’	
	37	2.7.A obv. 4. 9.2.4 obv. i 13′
38	‘thirty-eight’	
	38	3.1.2 obv. l. c. 9′. 3.1.10 3, 11. 9.1.1 rev. iii 28′. 8.1.B rev. 4′
	3[8	8.1.A obv. ii 21′
39	‘thirty-nine’	
	39	3.1.10 7. 8.1.E(A_1) obv. iii 1′. 8.1.F obv. i 4′; obv. ii 19′
	39$^{(sic)}$	4.2.1.A_2 obv. 5′

40		‘forty’	
		40	3.1.1.A_3 rev. iv 15′. 4.1.1.10 obv.$^{?}$ 2′. 4.1.2.2 obv. 2′ (2×), 5′. 4.1.2.3 obv. ii 6′, 11′; rev. iii 2. 5.7 rev. iii$^{?}$ 22′. 6.12 7′. 8.1.A rev. v 22′. 8.1.F obv. i 3′. 8.6 l. c. 10′. 9.1.5 rev.$^{!}$ 8′. 11.7.3 rev.$^{?}$ 4
		40$^{!}$	9.1.10.A_2 rev. 6′
		40$^{?}$	2.2 rev. 12. 3.1.1.A_3 rev. iv 16′
42		‘forty-two’	
		42	3.1.5.A_2 obv. ii(?) 2′. 4.1.1.10 obv.$^{?}$ 2′. 9.1.6 obv. 3. 10.1.2.1 rev.$^{?}$ l. c. 5
42		‘forty-three’	
		43	2.17 obv.$^{?}$ r. c. 11′
46		‘forty-six’	
		46	4.1.2.1 obv. (i) 5′. 4.1.2.2 obv. 4′. 8.8.A 7′. 9.2.13 4′. 11.6.2 rev. 9′
47		‘forty-seven’	
		47	10.1.1.2 rev. iv 1′
48		‘forty-eight’	
		48	3.1.5.A_2 obv. ii(?) 7′. 10.1.2.4 l. c. 3′
49		‘forty-nine’	
		49	4.1.2.3 obv. ii 10′
50		‘fifty’	
		50	3.1.1.A_2 rev. v 6′. 3.1.1.A_3 rev. iv 9′. 3.1.2 rev. l. c. 2′. 4.2.1.A_1 up. e. 1
55		‘fifty-five’	
		55	4.2.1.A_2 rev. 12′
56		‘fifty-six’	
		56	3.1.12 5′
57		‘fifty-seven’	
		57$^{?}$	8.1.D obv. i 9′. 10.3.12 obv. i 1′
59		‘fifty-nine’	
		59	3.1.5.A_1 obv. ii(?) 7′. 3.2.2 obv.$^{?}$ 2′
60		‘sixty’	
		60	6.12 1′
		ŠU-ŠI	4.1.2.1 obv. (i) 7′. 4.2.1.A_1 obv. 7. 5.7 rev. iii$^{?}$ 9′, 23′
		ŠU-ŠI	3.2.3 2′
		1 *ŠU-Š*[*I*	12.3.2 9′
	sg. nom.	*Š*]*U-ŠI-aš*	8.6 l. c. 6′
62		‘sixty-two’	
		ŠU-ŠI 2	4.1.3.6 rev. 2′
64		‘sixty-four’	
		ŠU-ŠI 4	3.2.1 obv. 13. 4.1.2.2 obv. 1′. 10.1.2.2 5′

65	‘sixty-five’	
	ŠU-ŠI 5	11.1.1 r. c. 3′
66	‘sixty-six’	
	ŠU-ŠI 6	4.2.1.A_1 obv. 6. 10.1.2.4 l. c. 22′
67	‘sixty-seven’	
	ŠU-ŠI 7	2.13 rev.$^{?}$ 6′. 2.17 obv.$^{?}$ r. c. 8′
68	‘sixty-eight’	
	ŠU-ŠI 8	10.3.12 obv. i 5′
70	‘seventy’	
	70	6.12 2′. 8.6 l. c. 8′; r. c. 3′. 8.7 r. c. 3′. 10.3.10 r. c. 12′. 11.1.2 l. c. 2′
	70$^{?}$	11.6.5 rev.$^{?}$ 2″
72	‘seventy-two’	
	72	3.1.1.A_3 obv. iii 15′. 10.1.2.1 rev.$^{?}$ l. c. 4
74	‘seventy-four’	
	74	10.1.2.2 4′
	74	11.2.5 1′
	70+4$^{?}$	12.3.4 obv. 4
78	‘seventy-eight’	
	n+]78	4.1.3.1 2′, 3′
80	‘eighty*	
	80$^{(sic)}$	8.8.B l. c. 9′
	80(?)	7.1 rev. 2′
81	‘eighty-one’	
	81	8.1.A rev. v 8, 10. 8.1.D obv. i 9′. 10.3.12 obv. i 12′
82	‘eighty-two’	
	82	8.8.A 9′
83	‘eighty-three’	
	83	4.1.3.8 rev. B 1′
87	‘eighty-seven’	
	87	2.17 obv.$^{?}$ r. c. 16′
90	‘ninety’	
	90$^{?}$	3.2.3 1′. 6.1 obv. 19. 11.7.3 rev.$^{?}$ 3
91	‘ninety-one’	
	91	10.1.2.1 rev.$^{?}$ r. c. 9′
92	‘ninety-two’	
	92	4.1.2.1 obv. (i) 2′. 4.1.2.2 obv. 4′
	9]2	4.1.2.3 obv. ii 5′
94	‘ninety-four’	
	94	12.3.2 4′
96	‘ninety-six’	
	9]6$^{!}$	3.1.5.A_2 obv. ii(?) 12′

99	‘ninety-nine’	
	99	3.1.3 rev.$^{?}$ 8′. 9.1.5 rev.$^{!}$ 6′
100	‘one hundred’	
	1 *ME*	3.1.7.A_2 obv. ii 6′. 5.2 obv. ii 3. 8.7 r. c. 5′. 6.1 lo. e. 9″. 9.1.12 6′. 12.3.3 2′, 6′, 7′, 9′ (2×)
	1] *M*[*E*]	3.1.1.A_1 obv. ii 13′
dat./loc.	*A-NA* 1 *ME*	3.1.7.A_1 obv. i 5′
104	‘one hundred four’	
	1 *ME* 4	11.1.7 8′
107	‘one hundred seven’	
	1 *ME* 7	2.2 rev. 14
108	‘one hundred eight’	
	1+n] *ME* 8	9.2.9 rev.$^{?}$ 4′
109	‘one hundred nine	
	1+n] *ME* 9	10.1.2.6 5′
120	‘one hundred twenty’	
	1 *ME* 20	9.2.5 obv. i(?) 8′
127	‘one hundred twenty-seven’	
	1 *ME* 27	2.17 obv.$^{?}$ r. c. 15′
128	‘one hundred twenty-eight’	
	1 *ME* 28	4.1.2.2 obv. 1′
130	‘one hundred thirty’	
	1 *ME* 30	11.6.1 6
131	‘one hundred thirty-one’	
	1 *ME* 31	9.2.5 obv. i(?) 7′
133 ½	‘one hundred thirty-three and one half’	
	1 *ME* 33 ½	12.2.2 10′
	*⟨⟨1 *ME* 33 ½⟩⟩*	12.2.2 12′
134	‘one hundred thirty-four’	
	1 *ME* 34	3.1.5.A_2 obv. ii(?) 5′
141	‘one hundred forty-one’	
	1 *ME* 41	10.3.5 5′
150	‘one hundred fifty’	
	1 *ME* 50	3.1.7.A_2 obv. ii 13′
	1 *ME* 50[(+n)	8.6 r. c. 6′
153	‘one hundred fifty-three’	
	1 *ME* 53	3.1.8.A rev. 5′
166	‘one hundred sixty-six’	
	1 *ME ŠU-ŠI* 6	10.3.12 obv. i 11′
170	‘one hundred seventy’	
	1 *ME* 70	2.12 obv. ii$^{!}$ 5′
178	‘one hundred seventy-eight’	
	1 *ME* 78	8.1.A obv. ii 13′

179	'one hundred seventy-nine'	
	1 *ME* 79	8.1.A rev. v 19′
182	'one hundred eighty-two'	
	1 *ME* 82(?)	8.1.A obv. ii 28′
188	'one hundred eighty-eight'	
	1 *M*[*E*] 88	3.1.1.A_1 obv. ii 8′
190	'one hundred ninety'	
	1 *ME* 90	5.3 r. c. 4′
	1] *ME* 90(?)	9.2.1 obv. ii 26′
192	'one hundred ninety-two'	
	1 *ME* 92	2.12 obv. ii$^{!}$ 4′
	1 *ME* [92	2.9.A_3 obv. ii 1′
195	'one hundred ninety-five'	
	1 *ME* 95$^{?}$	10.1.2.1 rev.$^{?}$ r. c. 5
199	'one hundred ninety-nine'	
	1 *ME* 99	10.1.2.2 3′
	1] *ME* 99	3.1.1.A_1 obv. ii 14′
200	'two hundred'	
	2 *ME*	3.1.1.A_3 rev. iv 3′. 3.1.7.A_2 obv. ii 5a′. 3.1.12 10′. 8.1.A rev. v 27′. 8.5 rev. iv(?) 4′
210	'two hundred ten'	
	2$^{?}$ *ME* 10	12.3.4 obv. 7
240	'two hundred forty'	
	2 *ME* 40[+n	3.2.1 rev. 18′
340	'three hundred forty'	
	3 *ME* 40	4.1.3.2 rev. 10′
380	'three hundred eighty'	
	3 *ME* 80	4.1.3.7 rev. 4′
469	'four hundred sixty-nine'	
	4 *ME ŠU-ŠI*	3.1.6 4′
496	'four hundred ninety-six'	
	4 *ME* 96	3.1.5.A_2 obv. ii(?) 8′
500	'five hundred'	
	5 *ME*	3.1.2 rev. l. c. 4′. 5.6 4′
930	'nine hundred thirty'	
	9 *ME* 30	2.17 obv.$^{?}$ r. c. 14′
1000	'one thousand'	
	1 *LI-IM*	3.1.12 3′
dat./loc.	*A-NA* 1 *LI-IM* [n *ME*	3.1.7 obv. i 2′
see also UGULA *LIM*		
1000 ½	'one thousand and one half'	
	1 *LI-IM* ½	12.2.2 11′

1100	‘one thousand, one hundred’	
	n *LI-I*]*M* 1 *ME*	3.1.7.A_2 obv. ii 1′
1150	‘one thousand, one hundred fifty’	
	n *LI-I*]*M* 1 *ME* 50	3.1.7 obv. ii 16′
1570	‘one thousand, one hundred seventy	
	n *LI-I*]*M*(?) 5 *ME* 70[+n	3.1.9 3′
1800	‘one thousand, eight hundred’	
	1 *LI-IM* 8 *ME*	3.1.1.A_3 rev. iv 8′
2000	‘two thousand’	
	2 *LI-IM*	3.1.12 8′
2160	‘two thousand, one hundred sixty’	
	2 *LI-IM* 1 *ME ŠU-Š*[*I*	3.1.7.A_2 obv. ii 10′
2200	‘two thousand, two hundred’	
	2 *LI-IM* 2 *ME*	3.1.12 8′
3000	‘three thousand’	
	3 *LI-IM*	9.1.12 5′
	3 *LI-*[*IM*	8.6 r. c. 8′
17160	‘seventeen thousand, one hundred sixty’	
	1 SIG_7 7 *LI-IM* 1 *ME ŠU-ŠI*	9.1.10.A_2 rev. 7′

Non-Lexical *Glossenkeile*

The following attestations are non-lexical *Glossenkeile*, i.e., those not used to mark a foreign word (see Pisaniello 2020 for latest research on the use of *Glossenkeile* in Hittite, although the triple *Glossenkeile* of 8.1.A obv. ii 5′, 6′ are explicitly excluded from analysis [*op. cit.*, 125 fn. 15]). The function and purpose of the non-lexical *Glossenkeile* in the PTAC cannot in most cases be determined, although some sort of editorial notation may be suspected. In 2.2 rev. 12, for example, a “quadruple” *Glossenkeil* marks where the duplicate text from 4.1.1.1 ends, representing a potentially new use for the *Glossenkeil* not recognized in Pisaniello 2020. Note also that the “triple” and “quadruple” forms of *Glossenkeile* are newly recognized here. That the triple *Glossenkeil* is a valid form is confirmed by the attestation of the same in KUB 32.61+ obv. i 55′ (CTH 628 – *(ḫ)išuwa-* Festival), where it is affixed to the word *luiššar* (attestation pointed out to me by Daniel Schwemer, pers. comm.). The quadruple *Glossenkeil* form attested in 2.2 rev. 12 is without parallel, and is perhaps to be interpreted instead as two double *Glossenkeile* without any space in between.

≮	double *Glossenkeil*	
	KÙ.S]I_{22} ≮ SI[G_5	4.2.5 1′
	≮ ŠÀ.B[A	11.7.1 r. c. 4′
	≮ ŠU.NÍGIN	4.2.6 obv.$^{?}$ 14′
	≮ *ŠU*[*M*$^{?}$	11.7.1 r. c. 2′
	≮ **ŠU*[*M*$^{?}$*	11.7.1 r. c. 5′
	≮ 2 [	10.2.2.3 obv.$^{?}$ r. c. 3′
	≮ 12 ^{TÚG}GUZ(“SIG_4”).ZA	11.6.2 l. e. 4
	≮ x[	11.7.1 r. c. 1′

𒑱*	triple *Glossenkeil*	
	𒑱* ŠÀ.BA	8.1.A obv. ii 5′
	⟨⟨𒑱⟩⟩* 8 ZU$_9$ AM.SI	8.1.A obv. ii 6′
	𒑱* ŠÀ.BA	4.1.4.1 A_1 rev. vi 10′
𒑱𒑱	quadruple$^?$ *Glossenkeil*	
	𒑱𒑱	2.2 rev. 12

Broken or Illegible Forms

a-x-x-*an-zi*(?)	2.2 rev. 1
𒌋*a-ar*-[	10.1.2.2 5′
𒑱$^?$*an*-[	9.2.9 rev.$^?$ 6′
ar-x-[x]-x	11.6.3 obv.$^?$ 6′
𒑱*ar*-x[	4.1.1.1.A_1 obv. 15′
(GAM-*an*) *ar*-[	7.4 3′
ar-[	10.1.2.1 rev.$^?$ r. c. 9′
ḫa-an-x[	11.2.2 3′
ḫar-ša-ni-x(-)[	9.2.7 rev. r. c. 6′
ḫar-[	3.1.1.A_1 obv. ii 2′
ḫu-u-da-x[	9.1.1 rev. iii 27′
ḫu-u-x-x[	8.1.E(A_3) rev. vi 9
ḫu-x[	11.7.1 r. c. 3′
iš-ga-[	10.1.2.3 1′
iš-kum-ma-n[*a*(-)	8.7 r. c. 10′
e-x-*man*-x[	10.2.1.3 9′
kar-ka-x[	9.2.4 obv. ii 5′
kat-x-x[	9.1.4.A_3 3′
gi-nu-x[	2.15 l. c. 2′
ki-pu-[	9.1.1 rev. iii 14′
ku-lu-x[	2.2 rev. 3
ku-u[*š*-	12.2.3 4′
pal-ḫa-x[	9.2.9 obv.$^?$ 4′
pár-du-uš-x[	9.1.10.A_1 rev. 7′
b[*a*-	9.2.4 obv. ii 2′
pu-u-x[	9.2.7 rev. r. c. 2′
ša-aḫ-ḫu-[	9.2.4 obv. ii 4′
šar-la-x[	9.2.4 obv. ii 8′
ši-ta-x	4.1.4.9 obv. 11
šu-x[-*i*]*a*	9.1.1 rev. iii 21′
da-an-[	10.3.11 r. c. 4′
ta-li-x[	9.1.14 obv. r. c. 4′
ta$^!$-*ma*-[	2.13 obv.$^?$ 3′
tar-x[	9.1.4.A_3 4′
ú-i-i[*a*-	10.1.1.2 rev. iv 7′
ú-i-x(?)	10.2.2.3 obv.$^?$ l. c. 3′
ul-x[	11.3.1 16′
ú-wa-ma-x[	11.1.1 r. c. 11′
za-ar-x[	9.1.4.A_4 l. c. 6′

zi-ia-x[	3.1.8.B 8′
x-ḫu?-ul-x[	11.6.11 5′
x-x-[l]i?-za(-)⸢ni?⸣-en-ni	5.7 rev. iii? 7′
x[x]x x-na-im-m[a	8.4 rev. 7′
x[x]x-ra-an-za	5.2 obv. ii 10
x-wa-x[-x]-ru	5.7 rev. iii? 6′
x-wa-ti-x[	9.1.12 4′
^{DUG}x[	12.1.4 5′
^{DUG}[	2.13 obv.? 6′. 3.1.8.A rev. 1′
GADA a[p-	4.2.9 obv. 13
GADA x x x[	11.6.1 13
GA[DA	8.1.K obv. ii? 2′. 11.6.8 6′
GA[DA?	6.10 4′
G[ADA?	11.6.4 rev. 4′
^{GI}x[	4.1.1.3 rev. A 1′
^{GIŠ}kat-x[	3.1.1.A_1 rev. v 12′
^{GIŠ}x[	2.5 rev. 7′. 5.6 3′. 9.2.6 obv. i 5′, 18′. 4.1.1.3 obv. 2. 4.1.3.2 obv. 1′. 12.1.4 3′. 10.1.2.4 l. c. 12′. 10.2.1.7 rev.? 7′
^{GIŠ}[	8.6 r. c. 7′. 3.1.7.A_1 l. e. 2. 2.6 3′. 10.1.2.4 l. c. 11′. 11.5.3 3′. 11.2.4 2′
$^{GIŠ?}$[	9.1.4.A_1 rev. iii 27″. 8.7 r. c. 3′
$^{GI[Š}$	11.7.1 r. c. 6′. 7.1 obv. 10′
$^{G[IŠ?}$	11.2.4 3′
IN?-[	9.2.2 rev.! iii 1′
KUR [	4.1.1.1.A_1 obv. 14′
^{KUŠ}ku-wa-a[r-	9.2.4 rev. iii 9′
^{KUŠ}ku-ša-x[	6.11 6′
^{KUŠ}ša-x[	9.1.11 obv.? 7′
^{KUŠ}x[	9.1.10.A_2 rev. 1′
^{KUŠ}[	2.5 obv. 6′. 10.2.1.6 4′
^{LÚ}x[	5.5 rev. iii 2′
^{NA_4}na-ap-[	9.1.5 rev.! 6′
^{NA_4}[x-x]-ta-ri-an-z[a]	8.4 rev. 6′
^{NA_4}MUNUS?(-)[	2.1.A obv. ii(?) 7′
^{NA_4}x x x x	12.2.2 7′
⟨⟨^{NA_4}x x x x⟩⟩	12.2.2 9′
^{NA_4}x[	9.2.6 obv. i 16′. 2.2 obv. 2′. 12.2.2 13′. 12.1.3 2′. 9.2.13 1′
$^{NA_4?}$x[	10.2.1.7 rev.? 7′
^{NA_4}[	3.1.8.A obv. 11′. 10.1.2.5 1′. 9.1.14 obv. r. c. 6′, 9′
$^{N[A_4}$	9.2.3 obv. (ii) 6″. 12.1.3 3′
$^{N[A_4?}$	12.1.3 6′
^{SÍG}x-x[	4.1.3.7 obv. 4; rev. 4′
^{TÚG}ḫa-x-x[	9.2.6 l. e. 2
$^{TÚG!}$iš?-[	10.1.2.1 obv.? r. c. 5′
$^{TÚG?}$lu-pár(-)x[	11.1.7 1′
^{TÚG}x x x[	11.1.1 r. c. 6′
^{TÚG}x x[	6.10 1′

^{TÚG}x[	9.2.4 obv. ii 14′. 8.1.G obv. r. c. 2′, 10′. 8.1.K rev. v$^{?}$ 6′. 5.7 rev. iii$^{?}$ 2′. 10.1.2.6 3′. 4.2.9 obv. 25; rev. 4′, 16′. 6.5 rev. 28′. 11.1.2 l. c. 4′
^{TÚG}[	9.2.6 l. e. 1. 8.1.E(A$_1$) rev. iv 2′. 8.1.G obv. r. c. 1′. 8.1.K obv. ii$^{?}$ 5′. 4.1.1.3 rev. A 6′. 4.2.9 obv. 10, 27. 1.5 rev. 23. 11.6.9 2′. 2.15 l. c. 13′. 11.6.3 obv.$^{?}$ 8′. 10.1.1.1 rev.$^{?}$ 13′
$^{\text{TÚ}]\text{G}[}$	4.2.9 obv. 14
$^{\text{TÚ}[\text{G}}$	8.1.E(A$_1$) rev. IV 9′. 8.1.F obv. ii 19′. 11.6.1 14. 6.5 obv. 3′. 11.6.7 1′. 3.2.5 r. c. 4′. 11.6.6 rev. 1′
$^{\text{T}[\text{ÚG}}$	4.2.9 obv. 6; rev. 15′. 6.9 obv. 8′. 9.1.6 obv. 1. 11.6.1 3
$^{\text{T}[\text{ÚG?}}$	8.1.G obv. r c. 9′
^{URUDU}*ku-n*[*a-*	3.1.9 2′
^{URUDU}x[	1.1.A$_1$ obv. 8′. 5.4 r. c. 8′. 5.3 r. c. 7′. 3.1.4 1′
^{URUDU}[	5.4 r. c. 7′
$^{\text{URU}[\text{DU}}$	5.4 r. c. 5′. 4.2.9 obv. 16. 5.8 6′. 3.1.9 1′
Z[*U-*	9.2.4 rev. iii 5′
^{D}*a-la*-x[	7.4 4′
^{D}x-x[	7.1 obv. 18′
^{D}x(-)[	6.1 rev. A 5′
^{D}x[	9.1.7 rev. 2. 7.1 obv. 17′
^{D}[	4.1.1.8 rev. r. c. 9′. 7.2 4′. 11.2.1 2′ (2×), 4′.7.1 rev. 14′
KUR *aš*-[	8.1.E(A$_3$) rev. vi 4
KUR x[	12.3.3 11′
K[UR(?)	3.2.4 1′
^{URU}*a*[*n*$^{?}$-x-*š*]*a-an*	2.9.A$_{2/3}$ obv. i 7′
^{URU}*a-wa-n*[*a-*	3.1.5.A$_1$ obv. ii(?) 5′
^{URU}*a*-[	4.1.3.2 rev. 6′
^{URU}*ḫa*-[	2.16 obv. ii 4′
^{URU}*ḫi-en*-[	3.1.1.A$_1$ obv. ii 4′
^{URU}*ga*$^{?}$-[	4.1.4.1.A$_2$ obv. ii 3′
^{URU}*ka-ta*-[	2.16 obv. ii 7′
^{URU}*lu-li*-x[	3.1.7.A$_2$ rev. iv 1′
^{URU}*mu-un-na*-[	3.1.7.A$_1$ obv. i 6′
^{URU}*ša*-[	3.1.5.A$_2$ obv. ii(?) 10′
^{URU}*taḫ*-x[	5.7 rev. iii$^{?}$ 17′
^{URU}*du*-[	3.1.10 2
^{URU}*du*$^{?}$-x[	4.1.3.1 8′
^{URU}*z*[*a-*	3.1.8.A rev. 18′
^{URU}x-x-x[	1.1.A$_1$ obv. 16′
$^{\text{URU!?}}$[ ]x x[	12.2.1 obv. 6′
^{URU}x[	3.1.5.A$_1$ obv. ii(?) 2′, 8′. 8.7 r. c. 4′
$^{\text{URU?}}$x[	3.1.3 obv.$^{?}$ 8′
^{URU}[	2.5 rev. 4′; 3.1.7.A$_1$ lo. e. 18′. 4.1.3.1 7′
$^{\text{UR}[\text{U}}$	4.1.4.2.A$_1$ rev. r. c. 9′
$^{\text{UR}[\text{U?}}$	11.7.3 rev.$^{?}$ 1
$^{\text{U}[\text{RU}}$	4.1.1.1.A$_1$ rev. 16′. 3.1.8.A rev. 11′
^{m}*a-ki-i*-x-x	12.3.4 obv. 1

^{m}*a-li-*[	4.1.2.4 5′
$^{m?}$*al*-x[	5.8 9′
*^{m}⟨⟨*a*[*t*]⟩⟩**at-t*[*i-*	3.1.6 5′
^{m}*a-*[	1.1.A$_4$ rev. 6′
^{f}*am*-x[	4.2.7 3′
^{m}*eḫ/uḫ*-x-x-*na*-x[	4.1.4.5 rev. r. c. 5′
^{m}*ḫa-i*-x[	5.1 obv. ii 10′
^{m}*ka*-x[	5.8 4′
^{m}*la*-x[	1.1.A$_1$ obv. 9′
^{m}*ma*-x[	4.1.3.1 2′
^{f}*mu*-x[	5.1 rev. iii 9
^{f}*na-aḫ-*[	4.1.3.4.A$_1$ obv. r. c. 6′
^{m}*ba*-x[	9.1.4.A$_1$ rev. iv 9′
^{m}*pí*-x[	1.4 4′
^{f}*pí-pí-*[	4.1.3.4.A$_1$ obv. r. c. 4′
^{m}*ša-še-ta*-x-x-x-*na-ši*	12.3.4 obv. 2
^{f}*ša-*[	4.1.3.5.A$_1$ obv.$^{?}$ 1′
^{m}*ši-en-me-ik*$^{?}$-[	5.4 r. c. 9′
^{m}*šu-*[	4.1.3.7 rev. 1′
^{m}*da-ú-la*-x	12.3.4 obv. 3
^{f}*u-ra*-x[	4.1.3.4.A$_1$ obv. r. c. 3′
^{m}*ut*-x[	5.8 3′
^{f}*wi$_5$-*[	6.11 7′
^{m}*za*-x[	3.1.8.A rev. 9′
$^{m.D}$UT[U-	9.1.4.A$_1$ rev. iv 8′
$^{f.D}$x[	6.8 2′. 4.1.3.4.A$_1$ rev. r. c. 2′
^{m}x[-x]-*ru-z*[*i*(-)	3.1.1.A$_3$ rev. iv 13′
^{m}x[-x-x-]x-*pí*	3.2.1 obv. 12
$^{m.D}$x-[x-x]	1.1.A$_1$ obv. 6′
^{f}x[	6.5 obv. 8′
^{m}x[	4.1.1.1.B$_1$ rev. iii$^{?}$ 2. 5.7 rev. iii$^{?}$ 23′. 3.2.1 obv. 21
^{m}[x-]x-*ti-wa*	3.2.1 obv. 6
^{f}[	6.9 obv. 5′. 6.5 obv. 6′, 7′, 10′, 13′. 4.1.3.4.A$_1$ obv. r. c. 5′, 7′
^{m}[	5.7 rev. iii$^{?}$ 14′. 3.1.10 10. 1.5 rev. 21

Acephalic Forms

(x) x-*a*]*d-du-wa-ra-la*	9.1.4.A$_1$ obv. i 1
x-*ad-d*]*u-wa-ra-a*[*l-la*	9.2.14 8′
x-(x-)*z*]*u-u*[*l-*	9.1.14 obv. r. c. 1′
x]-*šu-u-wa-aš*	11.1.9 2′
-a]*m-mar-ri*	4.1.3.3 12′
-ḫ]*a-na*	5.5 obv. ii 2
-ḫ]*u*$^{?}$*-un-na*	10.1.2.7 12′
-i]*a-an-zi*	4.1.1.1.A$_1$ obv. 19′
-i]*a-aš-ša*	10.1.2.1 rev.$^{?}$ l. c. 8′
-i]*a-aš-šu*	10.2.1.5 3′

-l]a-aš-[š]i-iš	2.16 obv. i 10′
-l]i-ia-aš	4.1.1.1.B_1 rev. iv$^{?}$ 8
-l]i-ia	4.1.1.1.B_1 rev. iv$^{?}$ 7
-n]a-a-aš	4.2.9 rev. 29′
-n]u-wa-an-zi	3.1.1.A_3 obv. iii 3′
-p]í-in-za-an-ta-aš	3.1.1.A_1 rev. v 16′
-r]i-ia-za	1.2 rev. 10′
(-)š]i-an-da	10.3.4 12′
-t]i-wi_5-en-zi	6.10 3′
-u]z$^{?}$-zi-iš	8.5 rev. iv(?) 2′
-w]a-na-x-aš	4.2.7 1′
-w]a-aš-ša	10.2.1.6 5′
-z]i-l[a]-x x x	9.1.5 obv.$^{!}$ 1
-z]i$^{?}$-wa-na-aš	3.1.3 obv.$^{?}$ 8′
]-a-az-ḫa	4.2.11 3′
]-a-i	5.1 obv. i 3′
]-an-ni-en-zi	6.9 obv. 14′
](-)a-ša-an$^{?}$-x[	4.1.4.1.A_1 rev. v 1′
](-)ḫi$^{?}$-lam(-)x	12.3.6 6′
]-ḫu-*da*-iz-zi	10.2.1.3 9′
]-im-ma	4.1.2.5 obv. 7′
]-i-ma-an-za	11.4.1 1′
]-i-me-en-zi	9.2.1 rev. iii 27′
]-la-aš-ši-[i]š	2.16 obv. i 9′
]-li-ia	4.1.1.1.B_1 rev. iv$^{?}$ 12
]-li-ia-aš	4.1.1.1.B_1 rev. iv$^{?}$ 11
]-ma-aš-ša-an	2.4 rev. 8′
]-ri-ia-ia	1.3 5′
]-ša-an-zi	9.2.1 rev. iii 18′. 10.1.2.4 l. c. 5′
]-ša-iz$^{?}$-zi	10.2.1.3 11′
]-ša-ra-i$^{!?}$-me-eš	4.2.11 4′
]-ši-ia-an	10.2.1.3 13′
](-)ši-tar	10.3.13 1′
](-)šu-ma-an-na-aš	8.6 l. c. 3′
]-ta-an-ni-iš	9.1.5 rev.$^{!}$ 16′
](-)tar(-)b[a-	9.1.10.B 2′
]-ul-li-iš-x[	4.1.3.2 obv. 2′
](-)wa-al-li-i	6.1 l. e. 2
]-za-aš-ši-iš	3.1.1.A_1 rev. v 10′
]-zi-za	11.1.2 l. c. 3′
]x-a$^{!}$-a-aš	4.1.1.6 obv. ii 4′
]x-aḫ-ḫi	8.5 rev. iv(?) 6′
]x-al-pí-na-[	4.1.4.1.A_1 rev. v 2′
]x-an-na	11.6.11 5′
]x-an-ni-ia	11.1.2 l. c. 5′
]-*⟨⟨x-aš-ša⟩⟩*	12.2.2 7′
]x-aš-ša	12.2.2 8′
]x-eš-ša-na-aš	5.9 2′
]x-ia-aš	9.1.4.A_1 obv. i 29′
]x(-)i-ia-an-zi	4.1.1.1.B_1 rev. iv$^{?}$ 16

]x-*i-me-en-zi*	11.2.5 4′
]x-*in-ni-an-za*	2.14 2′
]x-*da*$^{?}$-*kán-ta*	1.1.A_1 obv. 17′
]x-*kán*	9.2.4 obv. i 19′
]x-*ku-un-nu*(-)[	5.2 rev. iii 9′
]x-*lal-li-ia*	4.1.4.2.A_2 obv. l. c. 5′
]x-*li-ia-an-zi*	9.1.4.A_2 r. c. 3′
]x-*man*-x[	10.2.1.3 10′
]x-*na-im-ma*	4.1.1.3 rev. B 12
]x-*nu-ú*-x	8.4 rev. 11′
]x-*pal*	10.1.2.4 l. c. 22′
]x-*pa-am-ma*	11.2.5 3′
]x-*pí-na*	4.1.3.6 obv. 1′
]x-*pu-ri-in*	9.1.5 obv.$^{!}$ 5
]x-**pu*(-)*ši-an-da-at/la*(?)*	10.2.1.3 4′
]x-*ra-i-me-eš*	11.2.5 2′
]x-*ru*-x-*ú-ša-aš-ša*[*r*$^{?}$	7.4 1′
]x-*ši-i-mi-iš*	8.1.A obv. i 17′
]x-*še-ša-an-zi*	9.2.4 rev. iv 10
]x-*da-an-te-eš*	9.1.4.A_1 obv. i 21′
^{NA_4}x(?)]-x-*ta-ri-an-za*	11.1.2 l. c. 2′
]x-*ta-wa-na-aš*	8.6 l. c. 9′
]x-*ti-an-na-aš*	9.1.6 rev. 4′
]x-*uz-zi-iš*	11.1.7 4′
]x-*wa-an-ta*	3.1.1.A_1 obv. ii 1′
]x-*wa-ar*	4.1.3.6 rev. 6′
]x-*wa-liš*	8.1.K rev. vi$^{?}$ 8′
]x-*wa-ra-a-an*	11.2.5 7′
]x(-)*za-z*[*i*$^{?}$	5.9 5′
]x-**li*$^{?}$-*it**-*ta-aš*	3.1.7.A_2 obv. i 8″
.R]A	12.3.3 3′, 4′
]^{MEŠ}-*TIM*	10.2.1.2 19′
]x-KUR-*aš*	8.1.E(A_3) rev. vi 4
-*A*]*K-DU*	2.5 rev. 7′
-*Š*]*UM*	10.2.1.6 4′
-*D*]*A-NI-TI*	5.3 l. c. 5′
-*Z*]*I-TUM*	1.5 obv. 10
-*TU*]*M*$^{?}$	11.4.1 4′
]-*IN-NA-IA-TI*	5.1 obv. i 2′
]-*EN-NU-Ú*	4.1.1.9 3′
]-*KU-TUM*	8.5 rev. iv(?) 4′
]-*KUM*	8.1.J rev. v$^{!}$ 3′
]-*NU-TI*	8.4 rev. 3′
]x-*IN-NU*	9.1.10.A_2 rev. 3′
]x-*LUM*	4.1.4.2.A_2 obv. l. c. 2′
]x-*RI-A-AM*	8.6 l. c. 2′
]x(-)*RI-QUM*	8.6 l. c. 4′
]x-*UT-TI*	4.1.3.6 rev. 14″
]x-*ZA-AL-LU*	11.5.2 rev.$^{?}$ r. c. 3′
]x-*ZA-KI-IN-NI*	5.1 obv. i 5′

]x-x-*TUM*	10.3.1 rev. iii 8′
^{T}]^{ÚG}x[	4.1.4.7 obv. 6
^{URU}x-x-x-*l*]*i-na-aš*	3.1.5.A$_1$ obv. i(?) 6′
^{URU}...(-)*š*]*a*$^?$*-an-ta-ra*	4.1.4.2.A$_1$ rev. l. c. 4′
^{URU}...(-)*ša*$^?$*-a*]*n-ta-ra*	4.1.4.2.A$_1$ rev. l. c. 7′
^{URU}...]-*ḫa-aš*	3.1.1.A$_3$ rev. iv 22′
^{URU}...]-*ḫa-*da-ra**	4.1.4.1.A$_2$ obv. i 1′
^{URU}...]-*za-na*	3.1.11.A 6
^{URU}...]x-*ḫa-da-ra*	4.1.4.1.A$_2$ obv. i 4′
^{URU}x-x]x-*li-na-aš*	3.1.5.A$_1$ obv. i(?) 3′
^{m}]x-*la*-x	4.1.4.1.A$_2$ obv. ii 3′
^{m}x.L]Ú	2.2 rev. 8
^{m}...-*l*]*i-ma*	12.2.1 obv. 6′
^{m}...-*u*]*z-zi-ni-iš*	3.1.1.A$_3$ rev. iv 19′
^{f}(-)*w*]*a*$^?$*-na*$^?$*-ti-wa-li-i*[*š*	4.1.3.5.A$_1$ obv.$^?$ 6′
^{m}...-*z*]*i-zi-iš*	4.1.4.1.A$_2$ obv. i 3′
^{m}...-LUGAL]-*ma*	1.2 obv. 7″
^{m}...]-*ia-aš*	4.1.4.1.A$_1$ rev. v 5′
^{m}...(?)]-*ia-aš*	11.7.3 rev.$^?$ 1
^{m}...]-*me*-LUGAL-*ma*	9.1.4.A$_1$ obv. i 19′
^{m}...]-*ú-i-iš*	4.1.4.1.A$_1$ rev. vi 6′
^{m}...]-*u-ma-aš*	4.1.4.5 rev. r. c. 1′
^{m}...]-*up-pí-ta-ru-wa*	4.2.6 rev.$^?$ 8′
^{m}...]-*wa*-LÚ	4.1.1.2.A obv. 12′
^{f}...]-IR	5.7 rev. iv$^?$ 12′
$^{\text{m/f}}$...](-)^{D}LAMMA	6.9 lo. e. 13
^{m}...]-LUGAL-*ma-aš*	2.14 6′
^{m}...]x-*nu*	5.9 4′
^{m}...]x-*pí-ru-wa*	12.3.1 4′
^{m}...]x-*ra*	5.1 rev. iii 9
^{m}...]x-*ri-iš*	3.1.1.A$_1$ rev. v 14′
^{m}...]x-*uš*	5.1 rev. iii 8
^{m}...]x-DINGIR-*LIM*	5.1 obv. ii 3′
$^{\text{m/f}}$...]x(-)^{D}LAMMA	6.8 6′
^{m}x x x]-*ut-ti-iš*	3.1.1.A$_3$ obv. iii 13′

BIBLIOGRAPHY

Adams, Robert McCormick

1974 "Historic Patterns of Mesopotamian Irrigation Agriculture." In *Irrigation's Impact on Society*, edited by Theodore E. Downing and McGuire Gibson, 1–6. Anthropological Papers of the University of Arizona 25. Tucson: University of Arizona Press.

Akdoğan, Rukiye

2010 *Hethitische Texte in Transkription. Ankara Arkeoloji Müzesinde Bulunan Boğazköy Tabletleri II (ABoT 2).* Dresdner Beiträge zur Hethitologie 32. Wiesbaden: Harrassowitz.

2016a *Hethitische Texte. Bo 4658–Bo 5000. Teil 1: Transkriptionen.* Dresdner Beiträge zur Hethitologie 46/1. Wiesbaden: Harrassowitz.

2016b *Hethitische Texte. Bo 4658–Bo 5000. Teil 2: Autographien.* Dresdner Beiträge zur Hethitologie 46/2. Wiesbaden: Harrassowitz.

Akkemik, Ünal, Hülya Caner, Grace A. Conyers, Matthew J. Dillon, Nurgül Karlıoğlu, Nicholas K. Rauh, and Lawrence O. Theller

2012 "The Archaeology of Deforestation in South Coastal Turkey." *International Journal of Sustainable Development and World Ecology* 19/5: 1–11.

Alexandrov, Boris

2016 "Accounting Texts from Boğazköy in Current Hittitological Research." *Comptabilité(S)* 8. Accessed 02/10/20. journals.openedition.org/comptabilites/2010.

Alp, Sedat

1983 *Beiträge zur Erforschung des hethitischen Tempels. Kultanlagen im Lichte der Keilschrifttexte.* Türk Tarih Kurumu Yayınları 6/23. Ankara: Türk Tarih Kurumu.

1990 "Die Verpflichtungen *šahhan* und *luzzi* in einem Maşat-Brief." *Orientalia* 59/2: 107–13.

1991 *Hethitische Briefe aus Maşat Höyük.* Türk Tarih Kurumu Yayınları 6/34. Ankara: Türk Tarih Kurumu.

1998 "Zur Datierung des Ulmitešup-Vertrages." *Altorientalische Forschungen* 25: 54–60.

Alparslan, Metin and Meltem Doğan-Alparslan

2011 "Symbol der ewigen Herrschaft: Metall as Grundlage des hethitischen Reiches." In *Anatolian Metal V*, edited by Ünsal Yalçın, 79–84. Der Anschitt 24. Bochum: Deutsches Bergbau-Museum.

Arbuckle, Benjamin S.

2014 "The Rise of Cattle Cultures in Bronze Age Anatolia." *Journal of Eastern Mediterranean Archaeology & Heritage Studies* 2/4: 277–97

Archi, Alfonso

1973a "L'organizzazione amministrativa ittita e il regime delle offerte cultuali." *Oriens Antiquus* 12: 209–26.

1973b "Bureaucratie et communautés d'hommes libres dans le système économique hittite." In *Festschrift Heinrich Otten*, edited by Erich Neu and Christel Rüster, 17–24. Wiesbaden: Harrassowitz.

1977 "Il 'feudalismo' ittita." *Studi Micenei ed Egeo-Anatolici* 18: 7–18.

1983 *Keilschrifturkunden aus Boghazköi. Heft LII. Hethitische Orakeltexte und Texte verschiedenen Inhalts.* Keilschrifturkunden aus Boghazköi 52. Berlin: Akademie-Verlag.

1984 "Anatolia in the Second Millennium B.C." In *Circulation of Goods in Non-Palatial Context in Ancient Near East*, edited by Alfonso Archi, 195–206. Roma: edizioni dell'Ateneo.

1989–90 "Funzioni economiche del tempio ittita." *Scienze dell'Antichità* 3–4: 119–25.

Arnaud, Daniel

1985–87 *Recherches au Pays d'Aštata: Emar.* 2 vols. Emar VI: Les textes sumériens et accadiens. Paris: Editions Recherches sur les Civilisations, 1985–87.

1991 *Textes syriens de l'âge du bronze récent.* Aula orientalis: Supplementa 1. Barcelona: Editorial AUSA.

Artzi, Pinhas

1963 "The Glosses in the El Amarna Tablets." *Sefer Bar Ilan* 1: 24–57. English summary: XIV–XVII.

Baccelli, Giulia, Benedetta Bellucci, and Matteo Vigo

2014 "Elements for a Comparative Study of Textile Production and Use in Hittite Anatolia and in Neighbouring Areas." In *Prehistoric, Ancient Near Eastern and Aegean Textiles and Dress*, edited by Mary Harlow, Cécile Michel, and Marie-Louise Nosch, 97–142. Oxford: Oxbow Books.

Bachhuber, Christoph

2012 "The Anatolian Plateau." In *A Companion to the Archaeology of the Near East*, edited by Dan T. Potts, 575–95. Oxford: Wiley-Blackwell.

Bachmann, Martin, and Sırrı Özenir

2004 "Das Quellheiligtum Eflatun Pınar." *Archäologischer Anzeiger* 2004/1: 85–122.

Balza, Maria Elena

2012 "Sealed Tablets from Ḫattuša." *Studia Mediterranea* 23: 77–110.

Barjamovic, Gojko, Thomas Hertel, and Mogens Trolle Larsen

2012 *Ups and Downs at Kanesh. Chronology, History and Society in the Old Assyrian Period.* Old Assyrian Archives Studies 5. Leiden: Nederlands Instituut voor het Nabije Oosten.

Barsacchi, Francesco

2017 *Le feste ittite del tuno: edizione critica di CTH 631.* Studia Asiana 12. Firenze: Firenze University Press.

Bayburtoğlu, Bülent, and Selahattin Yıldırım

2008 "Gold and Silver in Anatolia." In *Anatolian Metal IV*, edited by Ünsal Yalçın, 43–51. Der Anschnitt 21. Bochum: Deutsches Bergbau-Museum.

Baykal-Seeher, Ayşe and Jürgen Seeher

2003 "Götterbilder aus Babylonstein? Eine hethitische Gußform aus Boğazköy-Ḫattuša." *Istanbuler Mitteilungen* 53: 99–111.

Beal, Richard

1988 "The ^{GIŠ}TUKUL-institution in Second Millennium Hatti." *Altorientalische Forschungen* 15: 269–305.

1992 *The Organisation of the Hittite Military.* Texte der Hethiter 20. Heidelberg: Winter.

2003 "Assuring the Safety of the King During the Winter (1.79) (KUB 5.4 + KUB 18.53 and KUB 5.3 + KUB 18.52)." In *The Context of Scripture. Volume 1: Canonical Compositions from the Biblical World*, edited by William W. Hallo and K. Lawson Younger, Jr., 207–11. Leiden; New York; Köln: Brill.

2014 Review of *Hittite Votive Texts*, by Johan de Roos. *Journal of Near Eastern Studies* 73/2: 341–45.

Beckman, Gary

1982 "The Hittite Assembly." *Journal of the American Oriental Society* 102: 435–42.

1983 *Hittite Birth Rituals.* Studien zu den Boğazköy-Texten 29. Wiesbaden: Harrassowitz.

1984 Review of *Beiträge zur Erforschung des hethitischen Tempels: Kultanlagen im Lichte der Keilschrifttexte*, by Sedat Alp. *Journal of the American Oriental Society* 104/3: 583–84.

1988 "Herding and Herdsmen in Hittite Culture," in *Documentum Asiae Minoris Antiquae. Festschrift für Heinrich Otten zum 75. Geburtstag*, edited by Erich Neu, 33–44. Wiesbaden: Harrassowitz.

1992 "Hittite Administration in Syria in Light of the Texts from Ḫattuša, Ugarit, and Emar." In *New Horizons in the Study of Ancient Syria*, edited by Mark W. Chavalas and John L. Hayes, 41–49. Malibu: Undena.

1995a "Hittite Provincial Administration in Anatolia and Syria: the View from Maşat and Emar." In *Atti del II Congresso Internazionale di Hittitologie*, edited by Onofrio Carruba, Mauro Giorgieri, and Clelia Mora, 19–37. Studia Mediterranea 9. Pavia: Gianni Iuculano Editore.

1995b “Royal Ideology and State Administration in Hittite Anatolia.” In *Civilizations of the Ancient Near East, vol. 1*, edited by Jack M. Sasson, John Baines, Gary Beckman, and Karen S. Robinson, 529–43. New York: Scribner’s Sons.

1997 “Excerpt from an Oracle Report.” In *The Context of Scripture. Volume 1. Canonical compositions from the biblical world*, edited by William W. Hallo and K. Lawson Younger, 204–6. Leiden: Brill.

1999a *Hittite Diplomatic Texts.* 2nd edition. Writings from the Ancient World 7. Atlanta: Society of Biblical Literature.

1999b “The City and the Country in Hatti.” In *Landwirtschaft im Alten Orient. Ausgewählte Vorträge der XLI. Rencontre Assyriologique Internationale Berlin, 4.–8.7.1994*, edited by Horst Klengel and Johannes Renger, 161–69. Berliner Beiträge zum Vorderen Orient 18. Berlin: Reimer.

2005 “The Limits of Credulity.” *Journal of the American Oriental Society* 125: 343–52.

Beckman, Gary and Harry A. Hoffner, Jr.

1985 “Hittite Texts in American Collections.” *Journal of Cuneiform Studies* 37: 1–60.

Beckman, Gary, Trevor R. Bryce, and Eric H. Cline

2011 *The Ahhiyawa Texts.* Writings from the Ancient World 28. Atlanta: Society for Biblical Literature.

Benveniste, Émile

1962 *Hittite et Indo-Européen. Études comparatives.* Bibliothèque archéologique et historique de l’institut français d’archéologie d’Istanbul 5. Paris: Maisonneuve.

Berman, Howard

1982 Review of *Hethitische Orakeltexte, Keilschrifturkunden aus Boghazköy, 49,* and *Hethitische Orakeltexte, Keilschrifturkunden aus Boghazköy, 50,* by Alfonso Archi. *Journal of Cuneiform Studies* 34: 118–26.

Berthon, Rémi

2017 “The contribution of zooarchaeology to the knowledge of Hittite economy.” In *Innovation versus Beharrung: Was macht den Unterschied des hethitischen Reichs im Anatolien des 2. Jahrtausends v. Chr.? Internationaler Workshop zu Ehren von Jürgen Seeher, Istanbul, 23–24. Mai 2014,* edited by Andreas Schachner, 175–84. Byzas 23. Istanbul: Deutsches Archäologisches Institut.

Bilgin, Tayfun

2018 *Officials and Administration in the Hittite World.* Studies in Ancient Near Eastern Records 21. Berlin: De Gruyter.

Bin-Nun, Shoshana

1973 “The Offices of GAL MEŠEDI and *tuhkanti* in the Hittite Kingdom.” *Revue hittite et asianique* 31: 7–25.

Bittel, Kurt
1958 "b. Ausgewählte Kleinfunde aus J–K/20." In *Vorläufiger Bericht über die Ausgrabungen in Boğazköy im Jahre 1957*, by Kurt Bittel, Peter Neve, Franz Fischer, Thomas Beran, and Heinrich Otten, 21–35. *Mitteilungen der Deutschen Orient-Gesellschaft* 91: 1–84.
1979 *Die Hethiter*. München: Beck.

Black, Jeremy
2001 "Amethyst." *Iraq* 63: 183–86.

Blažek, Václav
2012 "Hittite *wakšur*." In *Proceedings of the 23rd Annual UCLA Indo-European Conference*, edited by Stephanie W. Jamison, H. Craig Melchert, and Brent Vine, 17–28. Bremen: Hempen.

Blažek, Václav and Michael Schwarz
2016 *The Early Indo-Europeans in Central Asia and China. Cultural Relations as Reflected in Language*. Innsbruck: Institut für Sprachen und Literatur der Universität Innsbruck, Bereich Sprachwissenschaft.

Bloch, Marc
1961 *Feudal Society*. Translated by L.A. Manyon. Chicago: University of Chicago Press.

Boehmer, Rainer Michael
1972 *Die Kleinfunde von Boğazköy: aus den Grabungskampagnen 1931–1939 und 1052–1969*. Boğazköy-Ḫattuša 7. Berlin: Mann.

Bordrueil, Pierre, Daniel Arnaud, and Béatrice André-Salvini
1991 *Une bibliothèque au sud de la ville. Les textes de la 34e campagne (1973)*. Ras Shamra–Ougarit 7. Paris: Éditions Recherche sur les civilisations.

Börker-Klähn, Jutta
1994 "Ahnengalerie und letzte Dienste derer von Ḫattuša." In *Cinquante-Deux Reflexions sur le Proche-Orient Ancien: offertes en hommage à Léon De Meyer*, edited by Hermann Gasche, Michel Tanret, Caroline Janssen, and Ann Degreave, 355–67. Mesopotamian History and Environment, Occasional Publications 2. Leuven: Peeters.

Bottema, Sytze and Henk Woldring
1984 "Late Quaternary Vegetation and Climate of Southwest Turkey II." *Paleohistoria* 26: 123–49.
1990 "Anthropogenic Indicators in the Pollen Record of the Eastern Mediterranean." In *Man's role in the shaping of the Eastern Mediterranean Landscape*, edited by Sytze Bottema, Geertje Entjes-Nieborg, and Willem van Zeist, 231–64. Rotterdam: Balkema.

Bottema, Sytze, Henk Woldring, and Burhan Aytuğ
1993 "Palynological Investigations on the Relations Between Prehistoric Man and Vegetation in Turkey: The Beyşehir Occupation Phase." *Proceedings*

of the 5th Optima Congress, Sept. 1986, 315–28. Istanbul: İstanbul Üniversitesi, Fen Fakültesi.

Bottéro, Jean

1949 "Les Inventaires de Qatna." *Revue d'Assyriologie et d'Archéologie Orientale* 43: 1–40.

1957 *Archives royales de Mari VII: Textes économiques et administratifs.* Archives royales de Mari 7. Paris: Imprimerie Nationale.

Bryce, Trevor

2011 "Hittite State and Society." In *Insights into Hittite History and Geography*, edited by Hermann Genz and Dirk Paul Mielke, 85–97. Leuven: Peeters.

Burgin, James M.

2019 *Functional Differentiation in Hittite Festival Texts: An Analysis of the Old Hittite Manuscripts of the* KI.LAM *Great Assembly.* Studien zu den Boğazköy-Texten 65. Wiesbaden: Harrassowitz.

2022 "A Hands-Off Administrator? The Absence of the King, but Presence of the Crown Prince, in the Hittite Palace-Temple Administrative Corpus." *Die Welt des Orients* 52/1: 112–35.

(forth.[1]) "Hittite Ration Lists Revisited: the Old and Middle Hittite Ration Text Corpus." In *Proceedings of the 10th International Congress of Hittitology, August 28–September 1, 2017, Chicago.* Chicago Hittite Dictionary Supplements. Chicago: Oriental Institute.

(forth.[2]) "The ^{tug_2}guz-za/^{tug_2}GUZ.ZA at Hattuša and Beyond." *Altorientalische Forschungen.*

Burgin, James M. and Theo van den Hout

2016 Weihgaben. B. Bei den Hethitern. RlA 15: 32–35.

Cammarosano, Michele

2012 "Hittite Cult Inventories – Part Two: The Dating of the Texts and the Alleged 'Cult Reorganization' of Tudḫaliya IV." *Altorientalische Forschungen* 39/1: 3–37.

2013 "Hittite Cult Inventories – Part One: The Hittite Cult Inventories as Textual Genre." *Die Welt des Orients* 43: 63–105.

2014 "Rejoicing in the Gods: the Verb *dušk-* and Hittite Cheese Fighting." In *Proceedings of the Eighth International Congress of Hittitology, Warsaw, 5–9 September 2011*, edited by Piotr Taracha, 138–70. Warsaw: Agade.

2018 *Hittite Local Cults.* Writings from the Ancient World 40. Atlanta: Society for Biblical Literature.

2019 "Kultinventare aus Kayalıpınar (Šamuḫa)." In *Keilschrifttafeln aus Kayalıpınar 1. Textfunde aus den Jahren 1999–2017*, edited by Elisabeth Rieken, 47–110. Documenta Antiqua Asiae Minoris 1. Wiesbaden: Harrassowitz.

2021 *At the Interface of Religion and Administration: The Hittite Cult Inventories.* With a contribution by Adam Kryszeń. Studien zu den Boğazköy-Texten 68. Wiesbaden: Harrassowitz.

Cammarosano, Michele, Katja Weirauch, Feline Maruhn, Gert Jendritzki, Patrick L. Kohl

2019 "They Wrote on Wax. Wax Boards in the Ancient Near East." *Mesopotamia* 54: 121–80.

Cancik-Kirschbaum, Eva

1999 "[lú]*sāpi'u/sēpû*. Eine akkadische Berufszeichnung aus dem Bereich der Textilherstellung." In *Munuscula Mesopotamica. Festschrift für Johannes Renger*, edited by Barbara Böck, Eva Cancik-Kirschbaum, and Thomas Richter, 79–93. Alter Orient und Altes Testamentum 267. Münster: Ugarit-Verlag.

Carruba, Onofrio

1970 Review of *Hethitische Gerichtsprotokolle (StBoT 4)*, by Rudolf Werner. *Oriens Antiquus* 9: 83–87.

Christiansen, Birgit

2006 *Die Ritualtradition der Ambazzi. Eine Philologische Bearbeitung und entstehungsgeschichtliche Analyse der Ritualtexte CTH 391, CTH 429 und CTH 463.* Studien zu den Boğazköy-Texten 48. Wiesbaden: Harrassowitz.

Christman-Franck, Lisbeth

1971 "Le rituel des funérailles royales hittites." *Revue hittite et asianique* 29: 61–111.

Çinaroğlu, Aykut and Elif Genç

2003 "Alaca Höyük ve Alaca Höyük hitit baraji kazilari, 2002." *Kazi Sonuçlari Toplantisi* 25/1: 279–88

Civil, Miguel

1987 [Note brève]. *Revue d'Assyriologie et d'archéologie orientale* 81: 187–88.

Cohen, Yoram

2002 *Taboos and Prohibitions in Hittite Society.* Texte der Hethiter 24. Heidelberg: Winter.

Cordani, Violetta

2016a "Two Interesting Mentions of Iron Objects in Hittite Texts." *Mesopotamia* 51: 1–9.

2016b "The Development of the Hittite Iron Industry. A Reappraisal of the Written Sources." *Die Welt des Orients* 46: 162–76.

2017 *Lettere fra Egiziani e Ittiti.* Testi del Vicino Oriente Antico, Letterature dell'Asia Minore 5. Torino: Paideia.

Cornelius, Friedrich

1972 "Das Hethiterreich als Feudalstaat." In *Gesellschaftsklassen im Alten Zweistromland und in den angrenzenden Gebieten; XVIII. Rencontre assyriologique internationale, München, 29. Juni bis 3. Juli 1970*, edited by Dietz Otto Edzard, 31–34. München: Verlag der Bayerischen Akademie der Wissenschaften.

Cornil, Pierre and René Lebrun

1976 "Fragments hittites relatifs à l'Égypte." *Orientalia Lovaniensia Periodica* 67: 83–108.

Corti, Carlo

2017 "The North: Hanhana, Hattena, Ištahara, Hakpiš, Nerik, Zalpuwa, Tummana, Pala and the Hulana River Land." In *Hittite Landscape and Geography*, edited by Mark Weeden and Lee Z. Ullmann, 219–38. Handbuch der Orientalistik 1/121. Leiden: Brill.

2020 "The Grain of the King. Agricultural Landscape of the Hittite Festival and Land Management in Late Bronze Age Anatolia and the Northern Levant." In *Cult, Temple, Sacred Spaces. Cult Practices and Cult Spaces in Hittite Anatolia and Neighbouring Cultures*, edited by Susanne Görke and Charles W. Steitler, 231–51. Studien zu den Boğazköy-Texten 66. Wiesbaden: Harrassowitz.

d'Alfonso, Lorenzo

2005 *Le procedure giudiziare ittite in siria. (XII sec. a.C.).* Studia Mediterannea 17. Pavia: Italian University Press.

2010 "'Servant of the King, Son of Ugarit, and Servant of the Servant of the King'. RS 17.238 and the Hittites." In *Pax Hethitica. Studies on the Hittites and their Neighbours in Honour of Itamar Singer*, edited by Yoram Cohen, Amir Gilan, and Jared L. Miller, 67–86. Studien zu den Boğazköy-Texten 51. Wiesbaden: Harrassowitz.

d'Alfonso, Lorenzo and Alvise Matessi

2021 "Extracting Cohesion: Fiscal Strategies in the Hittite Staple Economy." In *Ancient Taxation. Mechanics of Extraction in Comparative Perspective*, edited by Jonathan Valk and Irene Soto Marín, 128–59. Institute for the Study of the Ancient World Monographs. New York: New York University Press.

d'Alfonso, Lorenzo, Yoram Cohen, and Dietrich Sürenhagen (editors)

2008 *The City of Emar among the Late Bronze Age Empires: History, Landscape, and Society (Proceedings of the Konstanz Emar Conference, 25.–26.04.2006).* Alter Orient und Altes Testament, 349. Münster: Ugarit-Verlag.

Dalley, Stephanie

1980 "Old Babylonian Dowries." *Iraq* 42: 53–74.

D'Altroy, Terence and Timothy Earle

1985 "Staple finance, wealth finance and storage in the Inka political economy." *Current Anthropology* 26/2: 187–206.

Daues, Alexandra

2012 "Zum Bedeutungsspektrum von heth. *kuwapi*." *Historische Sprachforschung* 125: 90–111.

Davies, Nina M. and Norman de Garis Davies
1933 *The Tombs of Menkkheperrasonb, Amenmosĕ, and Another (nos. 86, 112, 42, 226).* Theban Tomb Series – Memoir, 5. London: Egypt Exploration Society.

Dardano, Paola
2018 "Semitic Influences in Anatolian Languages." In *Change, Continuity, and Connectivity. North-eastern Mediterranean at the turn of the Bronze Age and in the early Iron Age,* edited by Łukasz Niesiołowski-Spanò, Marek Węcowski, 345–75. Philippika 118. Wiesbaden: Harrassowitz.

de Martino, Stefano
2008 "Relations Between Ḫatti and Alašiya, According to Textual and Archaeological Evidence." In *Ḫattuša–Boğazköy. Das Hethiterreich im Spannungsfeld des Alten Orients. 6. Internationales Colloquium der Deutschen Orient-Gesellschaft, 22–24 März 2006 in Würzburg,* edited by Gernot Wilhelm, 247–63. Colloquium der Deutschen Orient-Gesellschaft 6. Wiesbaden: Harrassowitz.
2013 "The Wives of Šuppiluliuma I." In *New Results and New Questions on the Reign of Šuppiluliuma I,* edited by Stefan de Martino and Jared L. Miller, 65–80. Firenze: Elite.
2022 "Hatti: From Regional Polity to Empire." In *Handbook of the Hittite Empire. Power Structures,* edited by Stefano de Martino, 205–70. Empires through the Ages in Global Perspective 1. Oldenbourg: De Gruyter.

de Martino, Stefano and Fiorella Imparati
1998 "La 'mano' nelle più significative espressioni idiomatiche ittite." In *do-ra-qe pe-re. Studi in memoria di Adriana Quattordio Moreschini,* edited by Luciano Agostininani, Maria Giovanna Arcamone, Onofrio Carruba, Fiorella Imparati, and Riccardo Rizza, 175–89. Pisa: Istituti editoriali e poligrafici internazionali.

de Roos, Johan
1989 "*KBo* 33.216. A Votive Text of Tuthalias IV." *Journal of Ancient Civilizations* 4: 40–48.
2007 *Hittite Votive Texts.* PIHANS = Uitgaven van het Nederlands Instituut voor het Nabije Oosten te Leiden 109. Leiden: Nederlands Instituut voor het Nabije Oosten.

del Monte, Giuseppe
1986 *Il trattato fra Muršili II di Ḫattuša e Niqmepa' di Ugarit.* Orientis antiqui collectio 18. Rome: Centro per le antichita e la storia dell'arte del Vicino Oriente.
1995a "I testi amministrativi da Maşat Höyük/Tapika." *Orientis Antiqui Miscellanea* 2: 89–138.
1995b "Bier und Wein bei den Hethitern," in *Studio Historiae Ardens. Ancient Near Eastern Studies Presented to Philo H.J. Houwink ten Cate on the Oc-*

casion of his 65th Birthday, edited by Theo P.J. van den Hout and Johan de Roos, 211–24. Leiden: Nederlands Historisch-Archaeologisch Instituut te Istanbul.

del Monte, Giuseppe and Johann Tischler

1978 *Die Orts- und Gewässernamen der hethitischen Texte.* Répertoire géographique des textes cunéiformes 6. Wiesbaden: Reichert.

Dercksen, Jan

1992 Review of *Innāya dans les tablettes paléoasyriennes*, by Cécile Michel. *Bibliotheca Orientalis* 49: 790—800.

2004a *Old Assyrian Institutions.* PIHANS = Uitgaven van het Nederlands Instituut voor het Nabije Oosten te Leiden, 98. Leiden: Nederlands Instituut voor het Nabije Oosten.

2004b "Some Elements of Old Anatolian Society in Kaniš." In *Assyria and Beyond. Studies Presented to Mogens Trolle Larsen*, edited by Jan G. Dercksen, 137–77. PIHANS = Uitgaven van het Nederlands Instituut voor het Nabije Oosten te Leiden, 100. Leiden: Nederlands Instituut voor het Nabije Oosten.

2005 "Metals According to Documents from Kültepe-Kanish Dating to the Old Assyrian Colony Period." In *Anatolian Metal III*, edited by Ünsal Yalçın, 17–34. Der Anschnitt 18. Bochum: Deutsches Bergbau-Museum.

2007 "On Anatolian Loanwords in Akkadian Texts from Kültepe." *Zeitschrift für Assyriologie* 97/1: 26–46.

Devecchi, Elena

2015 *Trattati internazionali ittiti.* Testi del Vicino Oriente antico, Letterature dell'Asia Minore 4. Brescia: Paideia.

2019 "A Reluctant Servant: Ugarit under Foreign Rule during the Late Bronze Age." In *A Stranger in the House – The Crossroads III: Proceedings of an International Conference on Foreigners in Ancient Egyptian and Near Eastern Societies of the Bronze Age held in Prague, September 10–13, 2018*, edited by Jana Mynářová, Marwan Kilani, and Sergio Alivernini, 121–36. Prague: Charles University.

2022 "The Governance of Subordinated Countries." In *Handbook of the Hittite Empire. Power Structures*, edited by Stefano de Martino, 271–312. Empires through the Ages in Global Perspective 1. Oldenbourg: De Gruyter.

Diakonoff, Igor

1967 "Die hethitische Gesellschaft." *Mitteilungen des Instituts für Orientforschung* 13/3: 313–66.

1968 "Проблемы экономики: О структуре общества Ближнего Востока до середины 2 тыс. до н. З. = Problemy èkonomiki: O strukture obščestva Bližnego Vostoka do serediny II tys. do n. è. [Problems of Economics: On the Structure of Society in the Near East to the Middle of the 2nd Millennium BC]." 2 parts. *Vestnik Drevneĭ Istorii* 1968/3: 3–27, 1968/4: 3–40.

1969 "Editor's Preface." In *Ancient Mesopotamia*, edited and translated by Igor M. Diakonoff, 1–16. Moscow: Nauka Publishing House.

1969 "Agrarian Conditions in Middle Assyria," translated by G.M. Sergheyev. In *Ancient Mesopotamia*, edited and translated by Igor M. Diakonoff, 204–34. Moscow: Nauka Publishing House.

1969 "The Rise of the Despotic State in Ancient Mesopotamia." Translated by G.M. Sergheyev. In *Ancient Mesopotamia*, edited by Igor M. Diakonoff, 173–203. Moscow: Nauka Publishing House.

1982 "The Structure of Near Eastern Society Before the Middle of the 2nd Millennium." *Oikumene*, 3: 7–100.

Dietrich, Manfried and Oswald Loretz

1964–66 "Der Vertrag zwischen Šuppiluliuma und Niqmaddu: Eine philologische und kulturhistorische Studie." *Die Welt des Orients* 3: 206–45.

Diffey, Charlotte, Reinder Neef, and Amy Bogaard

2017 "The Archaeobotany of Large-scale Hermetic Cereal Storage at the Hittite capital of Hattusha." In *Innovation versus Beharrung: Was macht den Unterschied des hethitischen Reichs im Anatolien des 2. Jahrtausends v. Chr.? Internationaler Workshop zu Ehren von Jürgen Seeher, Istanbul, 23–24. Mai 2014*, edited by Andreas Schachner, 175–202. Byzas 23. Istanbul: Deutsches Archäologisches Institut.

Diffey, Charlotte, Reinder Neef, Jürgen Seeher, and Amy Bogaard

2020 "The Agroecology of an Early State: New Results from Hattusha." *Antiquity* 94/377: 1204–1223.

Dörfler, Walter, Reinder Neef, and Reiner Pasternak

2000 "Untersuchungen zur Umweltgeschichte und Agrarökonomie im Einzugsbereich hethitischer Städte." *Mitteilungen der Deutschen Orient-Gesellschaft* 132: 367–80.

Dörfler, Walter, Christa Herking, Reinder Neef, Reiner Pasternak, and Angela von den Driesch

2011 "Environment and Economy in Hittite Anatolia." In *Insights into Hittite History and Archaeology*, edited by Hermann Genz and Dirk Paul Mielke, 99–124. Leuven: Peeters.

Durand, Jean-Marie

2009 *La Nomenclature des Habits et des Textiles dans les textes de Mari. Matériaux pour le Dictionnaire de Babylonien de Paris, Tome I.* Archives Royales de Mari 30. Paris: CNRS Éditions.

Düring, Bleda S.

2011 *The Prehistory of Asia Minor: From Complex Hunter-Gatherers to Early Urban Societies.* Cambridge: Cambridge University Press, 2011.

Earle, Timothy

2002 *Bronze Age Economics: The Beginnings of Political Economies.* Boulder, Colorado: Westview Press.

2011 "Redistribution and the Political Economy: The Evolution of an Idea." *American Journal of Archaeology* 115/2: 237–44.

Eastwood, Warren, Neil Roberts, and Henry Lamb

1998 "Paleoecological and Archaeological Evidence for Human Occupance in Southwest Turkey: The Beyşehir Occupation Phase." *Anatolian Studies* 48: 69–86.

Edel, Elmar

1994 *Die Ägyptisch-hethitische Korrespondenz aus Boghazköi in babylonischer und hethitischer Sprache.* 2 vols. Opladen: Westdeutscher Verlag.

Eichner, Heiner

1992 "Chapter 3. Anatolian." In *Indo-European Numerals*, edited by Jadranka Gvozdanović, 29–96. Trends in Linguistics Studies and Monographs 57. Berlin: De Gruyter.

Emre, Kutlu

1993 "The Hittite Dam of Karakuyu." In *Essays on Anatolian Archaeology*, edited by H. I. H. Prince Takahito Mikasa, 1–42. Bulletin of the Middle Eastern Culture Center in Japan 7. Wiesbaden: Harrassowitz.

Erkut, Sedat

1997 "Hethitisch *ḫuḫurtalla-* und seine eventuelle sumerische Entsprechung ^{GIŠ}PISÀN." *Archivum Anatolicum* 3: 111–15.

Fairbairn, Andrew

2005 "Crop Storage at Kaman-Kalehöyük. Some Preliminary Observations." *Kaman-Kalehöyük* 14 = *Anatolian Archaeological Studies* 14: 129-135.

Fairbairn, Andrew and Sachihiro Omura

2005 "Archaeological Identification and Significance of É.SAG (agricultural storage pits) at Kaman-Kalehöyük, Central Anatolia." *Anatolian Studies* 55: 15–23.

Faist, Betina and Juan-Pablo Vita

2010 "angurinnu." *Nouvelles Assyriologiques Brèves et Utilitaires (N.A.B.U.)* 2010/1: 6–8.

Fijałkowska, Lena

2015 "Politics and Socials Needs in 2nd Millennium Syrian Sale Formularies: the Case of Emar." In *Sale and Community Documents from the Ancient World. Individuals' Autonomy and State Interference in the Ancient World. Proceedings of a Colloquium supported by the University of Szeged. Budapest 5-8.10.2012, Trieste*, edited by Éva Jakab, 29–40. Graeca Tergestina, Storia e civiltà 2. Trieste: EUT Edizioni Università di Trieste, 2015.

Forlanini, Massimo

2008 "The Central Province of Hatti: an Updating." In *New Perspectives on the Historical Geography and Topography of Anatolia in the II and I Millenium* (sic) *B.C.*, edited by Karl Strobel, 145–88. Eothen 16. Firenze: LoGisma.

2017 "South Central: The Lower Land and Tarḫuntašša." In *Hittite Landscape and Geography*, edited by Mark Weeden and Lee Z. Ullmann, 239–52. Handbuch der Orientalistik 1/121. Leiden: Brill.

Foster, Benjamin

2010 "Clothing in Sargonic Mesopotamia: Visual and Written Evidence." In *Textile Terminologies in the Ancient Near East and Mediterranean from the Third to the First Millennia BC*, edited by Cécile Michel and Marie-Louise Nosch, 110–45. Oxford: Oxbow Books.

Frangipane, Marcella

2010 "Different Models of Power Structuring at the Rise of Hierarchical Societies in the Near East: Primary Economy Versus Luxury and Defense Management." In *Development of Pre-state Communities in the Ancient Near East: Studies in Honour of Edgar Peltenberg*, edited by Diane Bolger and Louise C. Maguire, 79–86. Oxford: Oxbow Books.

2012 "The Evolution and Role of Administration in Anatolia: A Mirror of Different Degrees and Models of Centralisation." In *Archivi, depositi, magazzini presso gli ittiti: nuovi materiali e nuove ricerche*, edited by Maria E. Balza, Mauro Giorgieri, and Clelia Mora, 111–26. Studia Mediterranea 23. Genova: Italian University Press.

Frangipane, Marcella and Enrica Fiandra

2007 "Chapter VII: Arslantepe: A Complex Administrative System before Writing." In *Arslantepe* Cretulae*: An Early Centralised Administrative System Before Writing*, by Marcella Frangipane, Piera Ferioli, Enrica Fiandra, Romina Laurito, and Holly Pittman, 415–68. Arslantepe 5. Rome: Edizioni Centra Internazionle di Richerche Archeologiche, Antropologiche e Storiche.

Frantz-Szabó, Gabriella

1980–83 "Kulitta, Ninatta und." RlA 6: 303–4.

Freu, Jacques

2008 "Quatre-vingts ans d'histoire hittite (1320–1240 av. J.-Chr.)." In *L'apogée du nouvel empire hittite*, edited by Jacques Freu and Michel Mazoyer, 13–286. Les hittites et leur histoire 3. Paris: L'Harmattan.

Friberg, Jöran

1987–90 "Mathematik." RlA 7: 531–85.

Friedrich, Johannes

1959 *Die hethitischen Gesetze*. Documenta et Monumenta Orientis Antiqui 7. Leiden: Brill.

Ganshof, François-Louis

1957 *Qu'est-ce que féodalité?* 3é ed. rev. et augm. Bruxelles: Office de publicité.

1961 *Was ist das Lehnwesen?* Darmstadt: Wissenschaftliche Buchgesellschaft.

Garelli, Paul

1967 "Le problème de la 'féodalité' assyrienne du XVe au XIIe siècle av. J.-C." *Semitica* 17: 5–21.

Gaspa, Salvatore

2018 *Textiles in the Neo-Assyrian Empire. A Study of Terminology.* Studies in Ancient Near Easter Records 19. Berlin: De Gruyter.

Gates, Marie-Henriette

1997 "Archaeology in Turkey." *American Journal of Archaeology*, 101: 241–305.

2001 "Potmarks and Kinet Höyük and the Hittite ceramic industry." In *La Cilicie: espaces et pouvoirs locaux (2e millénaire av. J.-C. – 4e siècle ap. J.-C.),* edited by Éric Jean, Ali M. Dinçol, and Serra Durugönül, 137–57. Istanbul: Institut français d'études anatoliennes Georges Dumézil.

Genz, Hermann

2003 "Früheisenzeitliche Keramik von Büyükkale in Boğazköy/Hattuša." *Istanbuler Mitteilungen* 53: 113–29.

2010 "Anatolien als Landbrücke in der späten Bronzezeit? Kommentare zu den hethitischen Fernbeziehungen aus archäologischer Sicht." In *Interkulturalität in der Alten Welt. Vorderasien, Hellas, Ägypten und die vielfältigen Ebenen des Kontakts*, edited by Robert Rollinger, Birgit Gufler, Martin Lang, and Irene Madreiter, 13-22. Philippika. Marburger altertumskundliche Abhandlungen 34. Wiesbaden: Harrassowitz.

Gerçek, N. İlgi

2012 "The Kaška and the Northern Frontier of Ḫatti." PhD diss., University of Michigan.

Gilan, Amir

2007a "Formen der Transaktion im hethitischen 'Staatskult' - Idee und Wirklichkeit." In *Geschenke und Steuern, Zölle und Tribut*, edited by Hilmar Klinkott, Sabine Kubisch, and Renate Müller-Wollermann, 293–322. Culture and History of the Ancient Near East 29. Leiden: Brill.

2007b "'Ist denn der Sinn von Menschen und Göttern irgendwie verschieden?' – Zur Ökonomie, Religion (und Herrschaft) im hethitischen Anatolian." In *Das Heilige und die Ware. Zum Spannungsfeld von Religionen und Ökonomie*, edited by Martin Fitzenreiter, 57–65. Internet-Beiträge zur Ägyptologie und Sudanarchäologie 7. Düsseldorf: Golden House Publications.

Giorgadze, Gregor

1987 "Two Forms of Non-Slave Labour in Hittite Society." *Labor in the Ancient Near East*, edited by Marvin A. Powell, 251–55. New Haven: American Oriental Society.

1991 "The Hittite Kingdom." In *Early Antiquity*, edited by Igor M. Diakonoff, 266–85. Chicago: University of Chicago Press.

1998 "Zum Kauf und Verkauf von Grund und Boden in der hethitischen Gesellschaft." *Altorientalische Forschungen*, 25: 54–60.

Giorgieri, Mauro

2011 "Das Verhältnis Assyriens zum Hethiterreich." In *Assur – Gott, Stadt und Land*, edited by Johannes Renger, 169–90. Colloquium der Deutschen Orient-Gesellschaft 5. Wiesbaden: Harrassowitz.

2012 "*anaḫi, anaḫiti*: luvio o hurrico?" In *Interferenze linguistiche e contatti culturali in Anatolia tra II e I millennio a. C. Studi in onore di Onofrio Carruba in occasione del suo 80° compleanno*, edited by Paola Cotticelli Kurras, Mauro Giorgieri, Clelia Mora, and Alfredo Rizza, with collaboration of Federico Giusfredi, 139–52. Studia Mediterranea 24. Genova: Italian University Press.

Giorgieri, Mauro and Clelia Mora

2012 "Luxusgüter als Symbole der Macht: Zur Verwaltung der Luxusgüter im Hethiter-Reich." In *Organization, Representation, and Symbols of Power in the Ancient Near East. Proceedings of the 54th Rencontre Assyriologique Internationale at Würzburg 20–25 July 2008*, edited by Gernot Wilhelm, 647–65. Winona Lake: Eisenbrauns.

Giusfredi, Federico

2011 "Zwei hethitische Fragmente." *Nouvelles Assyriologiques Brèves et Utilitaires* 2011/2: 30–33.

2020 "On the Old Assyrian *tuzzinnum*." In *talugaeš witteš. Ancient Near Eastern Studies Presented to Stefano de Martino on the Occasion of his 65th Birthday*, edited by Michele Cammarosano, Elena Devecchi, and Maurizio Viano, 215–24. Kasion 2. Münster: Zaphon.

Glatz, Claudia

2009 "Empire as Network: Spheres of Material Interaction in Late Bronze Age Anatolia." *Journal of Anthropological Archaeology* 28: 127–41.

2011 "The Hittite State and Empire from Archaeological Evidence." In *The Oxford Handbook of Ancient Anatolia*, edited by Sharon Steadman and Gregory McMahon, 877–99. Oxford: Oxford University Press.

2020 *The Making of Empire in Bronze Age Anatolia. Hittite Sovereign Practice, Resistance, and Negotiation.* Cambridge: Cambridge University Press.

Glatz, Claudia and Roger Matthews

2005 "Anthropology of a Frontier Zone: Hittite-Kaska Relations in Late Bronze Age North-Central Anatolia." *Bulletin of the American Schools of Oriental Research* 339: 47–65.

2009 "The Historical Geography of North-central Anatolia in the Hittite Period: Texts and Archaeology in Concert." *Anatolian Studies* 59: 51–72.

Glatz, Claudia and Aimée Plourde
2011 "Landscape Monuments and Political Competition in Late Bronze Age Anatolia: An Investigation of Costly Signaling Theory." *Bulletin of the American Schools of Oriental Research* 361: 33–66.

Glocker, Jürgen
2011 "Ališarruma, König von Išuwa." *Altorientalische Forschungen* 38/2: 254–76.

Goedegebuure, Petra
2014 *The Hittite Demonstratives: Studies in Deixis, Topics and Focus.* Studien zu den Boğazköy-Texten 55. Wiesbaden: Harrassowitz.

Goetze, Albrecht
1933 "Kleinasien." In *Kulturgeschichte des alten Orients, Abs. III, Lfg. 1,* edited by Albrecht Alt, Arthur Christensen, Albrecht Goetze, Adolf Grohmann, Hermann Kees, and Benno Landsberger. Handbuch der Altertumswissenschaft 3.1.3. München: Beck.
1947 "The Priestly Dress of the Hittite King." *Journal of Cuneiform Studies 1/2:* 176-185.
1955 "Hittite Dress." In *Corolla Linguistica. Festschrift Ferdinand Sommer zum 80. Geburtstag am 4. Mai 1955,* edited by Hans Krahe, 48–62. Heidelberg: Winter.
1956 "The Inventory Text IBoT I 31." *Journal of Cuneiform Studies* 33: 32–38.
1957 "Kleinasien." 2. neubearbeite Auflage. In *Kulturgeschichte des alten Orients, Abs. III, Lfg. 1,* edited by Albrecht Alt, Arthur Christensen, Albrecht Goetze, Adolf Grohmann, Hermann Kees, and Benno Landsberger. Handbuch der Altertumswissenschaft 3.1.3. München: Beck.
1964 "State and Society of the Hittites." In *Neuere Hethiterforschung,* edited by Gerold Walser, 22–33. Wiesbaden: Steiner.

Gordin, Shai
2010 "*Scriptoria* in Late Empire Period Ḫattusa: The Case of the É GIŠ.KIN.TI." In *Pax Hethitica. Studies on the Hittites and their Neighbours in Honour of Itamar Singer,* edited by Yoram Cohen, Amir Gilan, and Jared L. Miller, 158–77. Studien zu den Boğazköy-Texten 51. Wiesbaden: Harrassowitz.

Gorny, Ronald
1995 "Hittite Imperialism and Anti-Imperial Resistance as Viewed from Alishar Höyük." *Bulletin of the American Schools of Oriental Research* 299–300: 65–89.

Grandet, Pierre
2013 "The Ramesside State." In *Ancient Egyptian Administration,* edited by Juan Carlos Moreno García, 831–99. Handbuch der Orientalistik 1/104. Leiden: Brill.

Groddek, Detlev

2006 *Hethitische Texte in Transkription. KUB 60.* Dresdner Beiträge zur Hethitologie 20. Wiesbaden: Harrassowitz.

2007 *Hethitische Texte in Transkription. IBoT 4.* Dresdner Beträge zur Hethitologie 23. Wiesbaden: Harrassowitz.

2011 *Hethitische Texte in Transkription. KBo 57.* Dresdner Beiträge zur Hethitologie 36. Wiesbaden: Harrassowitz.

2012a *Hethitische Texte in Transkription. KBo 48.* Dresdner Beiträge zur Hethitologie 38. Wiesbaden: Harrassowitz.

2012b *Hethitische Texte in Transkription. KBo 58.* Dresdner Beiträge zur Hethitologie 39. Wiesbaden: Harrassowitz.

2014 *Hethitische Texte in Transkription. KBo 59.* Dresdner Beiträge zur Hethitologie 44. Wiesbaden: Harrassowitz.

2015 *Hethitische Texte in Transkription. KBo 46.* Dresdner Beiträge zur Hethitologie 57. Wiesbaden: Harrassowitz.

Groddek, Detlev, and José Virgilio Garciá Trabazo

2005 *Hethitische Texte in Transkription. KUB 58.* Dresdner Beiträge zur Hethitologie 18. Wiesbaden: Harrassowitz.

Groddek, Detlev, Albertine Hagenbuchner, and Inge Hoffmann

2002 *Hethitische Texte in Transkription. VSNF 12.* Dresdner Beiträge zur Hethitologie 6. Wiesbaden: Harrassowitz.

Guichard, Michaël

2005 *La vaisselle de luxe des rois de Mari. Matériaux pour le Dictionnaire de Babylonien de Paris, tome II.* Archives Royales de Mari 31. Paris: Éditions Recherche sur les Civilisations.

Gurney, Oliver R.

1958 "Hittite Kingship." In *Myth, Ritual, and Kingship*, edited by Samuel Henry Hooke, 105–21. Oxford: University Press.

1961 *The Hittites.* 3rd edition. Baltimore: Penguin Books.

1983 "The Hittite Title *tuhkanti-*." *Anatolian Studies* 33: 97–101.

1997 "The Annals of Ḫattušili III." *Anatolian Studies* 47: 127–39.

Güterbock, Hans G.

1954 "Authority and Law in the Hittite Kingdom." *Journal of the American Oriental Society*, Supplement 17: 16–24.

1957 Review of *Hethitiches Wörterbuch. Kurzgefasste kritische Sammlung der Deutungen hethitischer Wörter*, by Johannes Friedrich. *Oriens* 10: 350–62.

1962 "Rituale für die Göttin Ḫuwaššanna." *Oriens* 15: 345–51.

1964 "Lexicographical Notes II." *Revue hittite et asianique* 22/74: 95–113.

1967 "The Hittite Conquest of Cyprus Reconsidered." *Journal of Near Eastern Studies* 26: 73–81.

1970 "Some aspects of Hittite festivals." In *Actes de la XVIIe Rencontre Assyriologique Internationale. Université Libre de Bruxelles 30 juin–4 juillet 1969,* edited by André Finet, 175–80. Ham-sur-Heure: Comité belge de recherches en Mésopotamie.

1971 "Ivory in Hittite Texts." *Anadolu* 15: 1–7.

1973 "Einige seltene oder schwierige Ideogramme in der Keilschrift von Boğazköy." In *Festschrift Heinrich Otten*, edited by Erich Neu and Christel Rüster, 71–88. Wiesbaden: Harrassowitz.

1974 "The Hittite Palace." In *Le Palais et la Royauté*, edited by Paul Garelli, 305–14. Rencontre Assyriologique Internationale 19. Paris: Geuthner.

1975 "Hieroglyphensiegel aus dem Tempelbezirk." In *Boğazköy V. Funde aus den Grabungen 1970 und 1971*, edited by Kurt Bittel, Hans G. Güterbock, Peter Neve, Heinrich Otten, and Ursula Seidl, 44–75. Abhandlungen der Deutschen Orient-Gesellschaft 18. Berlin: Mann.

1983 "Hethitische Götterbilder und Kultobjekte." In *Beiträge zur Altertumskunde Kleinasiens. Festschrift für Kurt Bittel*, edited by Rainer M. Boehmer and Harald Hauptmann, 203–17. Mainz: von Zabern.

Güterbock, Hans G. and Theo van den Hout

1991 *The Hittite Instruction for the Royal Bodyguard.* Assyriological Studies 24. Chicago: Oriental Institute.

Haas, Volkert

1988 "Das Ritual gegen den Zugriff der Dämonin ᴰDÌM.NUN.ME und die Sammeltafel KUB XLIII 55." *Oriens Antiquus* 27: 85–104

1994 *Geschichte der hethitischen Religion.* Handbuch der Orientalistik 1/15. Leiden: Brill.

2007 "Notizen zu den Ritualen der Frau Allaituraḫi aus Mukiš." *Altorientalische Forschungen* 34: 9–36.

Haase, Richard

1966 "*Einführung in das Studium keilschriftlicher Rechtsquellen.* Rezension von G. Cardascia." *IVRA* 17: 325–28.

1968 "Herrscher und Beherrschte im Hatti-Reich." *Recueils de la Société Jean Bodin,* 23: 87–100.

1983 "Die ländliche Gemeinschaft im Hethiterreich." In *Les Communautés rurales, Deuxième partie: Antiquité = Rural Communities, Second Part: Antiquity*, by Société Jean Bodin pour l'histoire comparative des institutions, 187–205. Paris: Desain et Tolra.

Hallo, William W.

1990 "The Limits of Skepticism." *Journal of the American Oriental Society* 110: 187–99.

Hallock, Richard T.

1940 *The Chicago Syllabary and the Louvre Syllabary AO 7661.* Assyriological Studies 7. Chicago: University of Chicago Press.

Harmanşah, Ömur, Peri Johnson, Ben Marsh, and Müge Durusu-Tanrıöver

2017 "Lake-Places, Local Hydrology, and the Hittite Imperial Projects in the Ilgın Plain: Yalburt Yaylası Archaeological Landscape Research Project 2015–2016 Seasons." In *The Archaeology of Anatolia Volume II. Recent Discoveries (2015–2016)*, edited by Sharon R. Steadman, Gregory McMahon, 302–320. Newcastle upon Tyne: Cambridge Scholars Publishing.

Haroutunian, Hripsime

2002 "Bearded or Beardless? Some Speculations on the Function of the Beard among the Hittites." In *Recent Developments in Hittite Archaeology and History: Papers in Memory of Hans G. Güterbock*, edited by Harry A. Hoffner, Jr. and K. Aslıhan Yener, 43–52. Winona Lake: Eisenbrauns.

Hawkins, J. David

2011 "VI. The Seals and the Dynasty." In *Die Siegel der Grosskönige und Grossköniginnen auf Tonbullen aus dem Nişantepe-Archiv in Ḫattuša*, by Suzanne Herbordt, Daliah Bawanypeck, and J. David Hawkins, 85–102. Boğazköy-Ḫattuša 23. Mainz: von Zabern.

2013 "Gods of Commagene: The Cult of the Stag-God in the inscriptions of Ancoz." In *Diversity and Standardization: Perspectives on social and political norms in the ancient Near East*, edited by Eva Cancik-Kirschbaum, Jörg Klinger, and Gerfrid Müller, 65–80. Berlin: Akademie Verlag.

Hazenbos, Joost

2007 "Der Mensch denkt, Gott lenkt. Betrachtungen zum hethitischen Orakelpersonal." In *Das geistige Erfassen der Welt im Alten Orient. Sprache, Religion, Kultur und Gesellschaft*, edited by Claus Wilcke, after the preliminary studies of Joost Hazenbos and Annette Zgoll, 95–110. Wiesbaden: Harrassowitz.

2011–13 "Šulupašša/i." RlA 13: 289.

Heinhold-Krahmer, Susanne

2019a "I. Einleitung." In *Der "Tawagalawa-Brief." Beschwerden über Piyamaradu. Eine Neuedition*, edited by Susanne Heinhold-Krahmer and Elisabeth Rieken, 1–22. Untersuchungen zur Assyriologie und vorderasiatischen Archäologie 13. Berlin: De Gruyter.

2019b "VIII. Zur Datierung von VAT 6692 in die Regierungszeit von Ḫattušili III. (ca. 1265–1237)." In *Der "Tawagalawa-Brief." Beschwerden über Piyamaradu. Eine Neuedition*, edited by Susanne Heinhold-Krahmer and Elisabeth Rieken, 366–76. Untersuchungen zur Assyriologie und vorderasiatischen Archäologie 13. Berlin: De Gruyter.

Heltzer, Michael

1969 "Problems of Social History." In *Syria nel tardo bronzo*, edited by Mario Liverani, 31–36. Roma: Ipocan.

Herbordt, Suzanne
2005 *Die Prinzen- und Beamtensiegel der hethitischen Grossreichszeit auf Tonbullen aus dem Nişantepe-Archiv in Hattusa.* Boğazköy-Ḫattuša 19. Mainz: von Zabern.
2019 "Die Tempelinventare aus der Oberstadt von Boğazköy/Hattusa: hethitische Tempelanlagen als Kultstätten und Wirtschaftseinheiten." In *Ancient Near Eastern Temple Inventories in the Third and Second Millennia BCE: Integrating Archaeological, Textual, and Visual Sources. Proceedings of a conference held at the LMU Centre for Advanced Studies, November 14–15, 2016*, edited by Jean M. Evans and Elisa Roßberger, in cooperation with Paola Paoletti, 175–87. Münchener Abhandlungen zum Alten Orient 4. Gladbeck: PeWe-Verlag.

Herbordt, Suzanne and Alwo von Wickede
2021 *Kleinfunde aus der Oberstadt von Hattusa. Das zentrale Tempelviertel und die Tempelviertel am Königs- und Löwentor.* Boğazköy-Ḫattuša 29. Wiesbaden: Harrassowitz.

Hoffmann, Ingeborg
1984 *Der Erlaß Telipinus.* Texte der Hethiter 11. Heidelberg: Winter.
2004 "Ein Kamm mit sieben Zinken. Hethitisch *šalašturi* und Verwandtes." In *Šarnikzel. Hethitologische Studien zum Gedenken an Emil Orgetorix Forrer (19.02.1894–10.01.1986)*, edited by Detlev Groddek and Sylvester Rößle, 379–83. Dresdner Beiträge zur Hethitologie 10. Dresden: Technische Universität Dresden.

Hoffner, Harry A. (Jr.)
1968 "A Hittite Text in Epic Style." *Journal of Cuneiform Studies* 22: 34–45.
1969 "The 'City of Gold' and the 'City of Silver'." *Israel Exploration Journal* 19: 178–80.
1974 *Alimenta Hethaeorum. Food Production in Hittite Asia Minor.* American Oriental Series 55. New Haven: American Oriental Society.
1978 Review of *Hethitisches Wörterbuch. Zweite, völlig neubearbeitete Auflage. Lieferung 1*, by Johannes Friedrich and Annelies Kammenhuber. *Bibliotheca Orientalis* 35: 242–46.
1983 Review of *Hethitisches Wörterbuch. Zweite, völlig neubearbeitete Auflage. Lieferungen 4 und 5*, by Johannes Friedrich and Annelies Kammenhuber. *Bibliotheca Orientalis* 40: 407–17.
1987 "A Hittite Note on *mešedi, mešettu(m)*." *Revue d'Assyriologie et d'archéologie orientale* 81: 188–89.
1989 "The First Volume of A. Kammenhuber's Hittite Dictionary." Review of *Hethitisches Wörterbuch. Zweite, völlig neubearbeite Auflage auf Grunde der edierten hethitischen Texte. Lieferung 8*, by Johannes Friedrich and Annelies Kammenhuber. *Journal of the American Oriental Society* 109: 87–95.

1995 "Legal and Social Institutions of Hittite Anatolia." In *Civilizations of the Ancient Near East, vol. 1*, edited by Jack M. Sasson, John Baines, Gary Beckman, and Karen S. Robinson, 555–69. New York: Scribner's Sons.

1997 *The Laws of the Hittites: A Critical Edition.* Documenta et Monumenta Orientis Antiqua 23. Leiden: Brill.

2001a "Some Thoughts on Merchants and Trade in the Hittite Kingdom." In *Kulturgeschichten: Altorientalistische Studien für Volkert Haas zum 65. Geburtstag*, edited by Thomas Richter, Doris Prechel, and Jörg Klinger, 179–89. Saarbrücken: Saarbrücker Druckrei und Verlag.

2001b "Alimenta Revisited." In *Akten des IV. Internationalen Kongresses für Hethitologie: Würzburg, 4.–8. Oktober 1999*, edited by Gernot Wilhlem, 199–212. Studien zu den Boğazköy-Texten 45. Wiesbaden: Harrassowitz.

2002 "The Treatment and Long-Term Use of Persons Captured in Battle according to the Maşat Corpus." In *Recent Developments in Hittite Archaeology and History: Papers in Memory of Hans G. Güterbock*, edited by Harry A. Hoffner Jr., and K. Aslıhan Yener, 61–72. Winona Lake: Eisenbrauns.

2007 "On Higher Numbers in Hittite." *Studi Mediterranea ed Egeo-Anatolici* 49: 377–85.

2009 *Letters from the Hittite Kingdom.* Edited by Gary Beckman. Writings from the Ancient World 15. Atlanta: Society of Biblical Literature.

Hollenstein, Daria and Geraldine Middea

2016 "The Faunal Remains from the Square Building Horizon in the Valley West Sarıkale, Boğazköy-Ḫattuša, Turkey (16th/15th Century BC)." In *Ausgrabungen und Forschungen in der westlichen Oberstadt von Ḫattuša I*, edited by Andreas Schachner and Jürgen Seeher. Boğazköy-Ḫattuša 24. Berlin: De Gruyter.

Holt, Jens

1958 "A propos de la Corolla Linguistica: quelques problèmes des études hittites." *Bibliotheca Orientalis* 15: 148–57.

Hongo, Hitomi

2003 "Continuity or Changes: Faunal Remains from Stratum IId at Kaman-Kalehöyük." In *Identifying Changes: The Transition from Bronze to Iron Ages in Anatolia and Its Neighbouring Regions. Proceedings of the International Workshop, Istanbul, November 8–9, 2002*, edited by Bettin Fischer, Hermann Genz, Éric Jean, and Kemalettin Köroğlu, 257–69. Istanbul: Türk Eskiçağ Bilimleri Enstitüsü.

Hopf, Maria

1992 "Plant remains from Boğazköy, Turkey." *Review of Palaeobotany and Palynology* 73: 99–104.

Houwink ten Cate, Philo H. J.

1973 Review of *Les noms des Hittites*, by Emmanuel Laroche. *Bibliotheca Orientalis* 30: 252–57.

1994 "Urhi-Tessub revisited." *Bibliotheca Orientalis* 51: 233–59.

Hrůša, Ivan

2010 *Die akkadische Synonymenliste* malku = šarru. *Eine Textedition mit Übersetzung und Kommentar.* Alter Orient und Altes Testament 50. Münster: Ugarit-Verlag.

Hüser, Andreas

2002 *Hethitische Anlagen zur Wasserversorgung und Entsorgung.* Kuşaklı-Sarissa 3. Rahden/Westf.: Leidorf.

Hutter, Manfred and Sylvia Hutter-Braunsar (eds.)

2019 *Economy of Religions in Anatolia: From the Early Second to the Middle of the First Millennium BCE. Proceedings of an International Conference in Bonn (23rd to 25th May 2018).* Alter Orient und Altes Testament 467. Münster: Ugarit-Verlag.

Hütteroth, Wolf-Dieter

1982 *Türkei.* Wissenschaftliche Länderurkunden 21. Darmstadt: Wissenschaftliche Buchgesellschaft.

Hütteroth, Wolf-Dieter and Volker Höhfeld

2002 *Türkei.* Darmstadt: Wissenschaftliche Buchgesellschaft.

Ikram, Salima

2003 "A Preliminary Study of Zooarchaeological Changes between the Bronze Age and Iron Ages at Kinet Höyük, Hatay." In *Identifying Changes: The Transition from Bronze to Iron Ages in Anatolia and Its Neighbouring Regions. Proceedings of the International Workshop, Istanbul, November 8–9, 2002*, edited by Bettin Fischer, Hermann Genz, Éric Jean, and Kemalettin Köroğlu, 283–94. Istanbul: Türk Eskiçağ Bilimleri Enstitüsü.

Imparati, Fiorella

1974 *Una Concessione di Terre da Parte di Tudḫaliya IV.* Revue hittite et asianique 32. Paris: Klinkcsieck.

1979 "Une reine de Hatti vénère la déesse Ningal." In *Florilegium Anatolicum: Mélanges offerts à Emmanuel Laroche*, 169–76. Paris: de Boccard.

1980–83 "Lehenswesen s. a. Feudalismus, *ilku*. A. Bei den Hethitern," RlA 6: 543–47.

1982 "Aspects de l'organization de l'État Hittite dans les documents juridiques et administratifs." *Journal of the Economic and Social History of the Orient* 25: 225–67.

1991 "Autorità centrale e istituzioni collegiali nel regno ittita." In *Esercizio del potere e prassi della consultazione. Atti dell'VIII Colloquio internazionale romanistico-canonistico (10–12 maggio 1990)*, edited by Americo Ciani and Giovanni Diurni, 161–81. Utrumque ius 21. Rome: Libreria editrice vaticana.

1997 "Observations on a Letter from Maşat Höyük." *Archivum Anatolicum* 3: 199–214.

1998 "Die Organisation des hethitischen Staates." In *Geschichte des Hethitischen Reiches*, by Horst Klengel, with contributions of Fiorella Imparati, Volkert Haas, and Theo van den Hout, 320–87. Handbuch der Orientalistik 1/34. Leiden: Brill.

Jakob, Stefan

2003 *Mittelassyrische Verwaltung und Sozialstruktur: Untersuchungen.* Cuneiform Monographs 29. Leiden: Brill.

Jakob-Rost, Liane

1963 "Zu den hethitischen Bildbeschreibungen (II. Teil)." *Mitteilungen des Instituts für Orientforschung* 9: 175–239.

1966 "Beiträge zum hethitischen Hofzeremoniell (IBoT 1 36)." *Mitteilungen des Instituts für Orientforschung* 11: 165–225.

Jasonoff, Jay

2010 "The Luvian 'Case' in -ša/-za." In *Ex Anatolia Lux: Anatolian and Indo-European Studies in Honor of H. Craig Melchert*, edited by Ronald Kim, Norbert Oettinger, Elisabeth Rieken, and Michael Weiss, 167–79. Ann Arbor; New York: Beech Stave Press.

Jean, Eric

2001 "Le fer chez les hittites." In *Aux origines de la metallurgie du fer. Actes de la 1ère Table ronde internationale d'archéologie. L'Afrique et le bassin méditerranéen. Muséum d'Histoire Naturelle Genève, 4–7 juin 1999*, edited by Jean-Paul Descœudres, Eric Huysecom, Vincent Serneels, and Jean-Louis Zimmermann. *Mediterranean Archaeology* 14: 163–88.

Jin Jie

1994 *A Complete Retrograde Glossary of the Hittite Language.* PIHANS = Uitgaven van het Nederlands Instituut voor het Nabije Oosten te Leiden, 71. Leiden: Nederlands Historisch-Archaeologisch Instituut te Istanbul.

Jursa, Michael

2010 *Aspects of Economic History of Babylonia in the First Millennium BC.* Münster: Ugarit-Verlag.

Kammenhuber, Annelies

1969 "Das Hattische." In *Altkleinasiatische Sprachen*, with contributions of Johannes Friedrich, Erica Reiner, Annelies Kammenhuber, Günter Neumann, and Alfred Heubeck, 428–546. Handbuch der Orientalistik 1/2/1–2/2. Leiden: Brill.

1970 Review of *Das Gelübde der Königin Puduḫepa an die Göttin Lelwani*, by Heinrich Otten and Vladimir Souček. *Zeitschrift für Assyriologie* 60: 221–23.

1976 *Orakelpraxis, Träume und Vorzeichenschau bei den Hethitern.* Texte der Hethiter 7. Heidelberg: Winter.

Kemp, Barry J.
2006 *Ancient Egypt: Anatomy of a Civilization.* 2nd edition. London; New York: Routledge.

Kempiński, Aharon and Silvin Košak
1977 "Hittite Metal 'Inventories' (CTH 242) and their Economic Implications." *Tel Aviv: Journal of the Institute of Archaeology of Tel Aviv University* 4: 87–93.

Kestemont, Guy
1974 *Diplomatique et droit international en asie occidentale (1600–1200 av. J.C.).* Publications de l'Institut Orientaliste de Louvain 9. Louvain-la-Neuve: Institut orientaliste.

Klein, Harald
1983 "Tudittum." *Zeitschrift für Assyriologie* 73/2: 255–84.

Klengel, Horst
1965 "Die Rolle der 'Ältesten' (LÚ.MEŠ ŠU.GI) im Kleinasien der Hethiterzeit." *Zeitschrift für Assyriologie* 57: 223–35.
1974 "'Hungerjahre' in Ḫatti." *Altorientalische Forschungen* 1: 165–74.
1975 "Zur ökonomischen Funktion der hethitischen Tempel." *Studi Micenei ed Egeo-Anatolici* 16: 181–200.
1982 "Naturbedingungen und Produktivkraftentwicklung im alten Vorderasien." *Ethnographisch-Archäologische Zeitschrift*, 23: 33–44.
1986 "The Economy of the Hittite Household (É)." *Oikumene* 5: 23–31.
1988 "Aspetti dello sviluppo dello stato ittita." In *Stato Economia Lavoro nel Vicino Oriente antico: Atti del convegno promosso dal Seminario di orientalistica dell'Ist. Gramsci Toscano*, 183–94. Milano: Franco Angeli.
1990 "Hattuša: Residence and Cult-Centre." In *Towns as Regional Economic Centre in the Ancient Near East (10th International Economic History Congress)*, edited by Erik Aerts and Horst Klengel, 45–50. Leuven: Leuven University Press.
1998 *Geschichte des hethitischen Reiches.* Handbuch der Orientalistik 1/34. Leiden: Brill.
2003 "Einige Bemerkungen zur Struktur des hethitischen Staates." *Altorientalische Forschungen* 30: 281–89.
2005 "Studien zur hethitischen Wirtschaftsgeschichte: Einleitende Bemerkungen." *Altorientalische Forschung* 32: 3–23.
2006 "Studien zur hethitischen Wirtschaft, 2: Feld- und Gartenbau." *Altorientalische Forschungen* 33: 3–21.
2007 "Studien zur hethitischen Wirtschaft, 3: Tierwirtschaft und Jagd." *Altorientalische Forschungen* 34: 154–73.
2011 "Handel mit Lapislazuli, Türkis und Karneol im alten Vorderen Orient." In *Anatolian Metal V*, edited by Ünsal Yalçın, 69–77. *Der Anschnitt* 24. Bochum: Deutsches Bergbau-Museum.

Klengel, Evelyn and Horst Klengel

2009 "'Hurritische Hemden' in der keilschriftlichen Tradition." *Altorientalische Forschungen* 36: 205–8.

Klinger, Jörg

1996 *Untersuchung zur Rekonstruktion der hattischen Kultschicht.* Studien zu den Boğazköy-Texten 37. Wiesbaden: Harrassowitz.

2008 "Zalpa, Nerik und Ḫakmiš. Die Bedeutung der nördlichen Peripherie Zentralanatoliens in hethitischer Zeit." In *Ḫattuša–Boğazköy. Das Hethiterreich im Spannungsfeld des Alten Orients. 6. Internationales Colloquium der Deutschen Orient-Gesellschaft, 22–24 März 2006 in Würzburg*, edited by Gernot Wilhelm, 277–90. Colloquium der Deutschen Orient-Gesellschaft 6. Wiesbaden: Harrassowitz.

2011 "Ein Einblick in die bisherigen Texfunde." In "Archäologische Forschungen am Oymaağaç Höyük/Nerik (?) in den Jahren 2007–2010," by Rainer M. Czichon, Jörg Klinger, Peter Breuer, Jacob Eerbeek, Sherry Fox, Elena Marinova-Wolff, Henning Marquardt, Harald von der Osten-Woldenburg, Silvio Reichmuth, Simone Riehl, and Theodor Johannsen, 220–24. *Mitteilungen der Deutschen Orient-Gesellschaft* 143: 169–250.

2015 "Šuppiluliuma II. und die Spätphase der hethitischen Archive." In *Saeculum. Gedenkschrift für Heinrich Otten anlässlich seines 100. Geburtstags*, edited by Andreas Müller-Karpe, Elisabeth Rieken, and Walter Sommerfeld, 87–111. Studien zu den Boğazköy-Texten 58. Wiesbaden: Harrassowitz.

2018 "Prestigeobjekte am hethitischen Hof – und warum es sie doch gegeben hat." In *Anatolian Metal VIII. Eliten–Handwerk–Prestigegüter*, edited by Ünsal Yalçın, 205–217. *Der Anschnitt* 39. Bochum: Deutsches Bergbau-Museum.

2022 "Hittite Economics." In *Handbook of the Hittite Empire. Power Structures*, edited by Stefano de Martino, 605–47. Empires through the Ages in Global Perspective 1. Oldenbourg: De Gruyter.

Kloekhorst, Alwin

2010 "Initial stops in Hittite (with an excursus on the spelling of stops in Alalaḫ Akkadian)." *Zeitschrift für Assyriologie* 100: 197–241.

2020 "The Phonetics and Phonology of the Hittite Dental Stops." In *Hrozný and Hittite. The First Hundred Years. Proceedings of the International Conference Held at Charles University, Prague, 11–14 November 2015*, edited by Ronald I. Kim, Jana Mynářová, and Peter Pavúk, 147–75. Leiden: Brill.

Korbel, Günther

1985 *Die spätbronzezeitliche Keramik von Norşuntepe.* Hannover: Institut für Bauen und Planen in Entwicklungsländern.

Korošec, Viktor

1972 "Einige Beiträge zur gesellschaftlichen Struktur nach hethitischen Rechtsquellen." *Gesellschaftsklassen im Alten Zweistromland und in den angrenzenden Gebieten; XVIII. Rencontre assyriologique internationale, München, 29. Juni bis 3. Juli 1970*, edited by Dietz Otto Edzard, 105–111. Munich: Verlag der Bayerischen Akademie der Wissenschaften.

Košak, Silvin

1978 "The inventory of Manninni (CTH 504)." *Linguistica* 18: 99–123.

1982 *Hittite Inventory Texts. (CTH 241–250).* Texte der Hethiter 10. Heidelberg: Winter.

1986 "The Gospel of Iron." In *Kaniššuwar. A Tribute to Hans G. Güterbock on his Seventy-fifth Birthday (May 27, 1983)*, edited by Harry A. Hoffner and Gary Beckman, 125–40. Assyriological Studies 23. Chicago: Oriental Institute.

1994 Review of *Keilschrifturkunden aus Boghazköi, Heft LX: Texte verschiedenen Inhalts*, by Horst Klengel. *Zeitschrift für Assyriologie* 94: 288–90.

Kouwenberg, N. J. C. (Bert)

2015 "Sargon's *tūdittum*, or How to Make Fools of Your Enemies." In *Cahit Günbattı'ya Armağan = Studies in Honour of Cahit Günbattı*, edited by İrfan Albayrak, Hakan Erol, and Murat Çayır, 165–70. Anakara Üniversitesi Yayınaları 476, Dil ve Tarih-Coğrafya Fakültesi Eskiçağ Dilleri ve Kültürleri Bölümü Sumeroloji Anabilim Dalı Yayınları 417. Ankara: Ankara Üniversitesi Basımevi.

Kozal, Ekin and Mirko Novák

2007 "Geschenke, Tribute und Handelswaren im Hethiterreich. Eine archäologische Bestandsaufnahme am Fallbeispiel Ḫattuša." In *Geschenke und Steuern, Zölle und Tribute: Antike Abgabenformen in Anspruch und Wirklichkeit*, edited by Hilmar Klinkott, Sabine Kubisch, and Renate Müller-Wollermann, 323–46. Leiden: Brill.

Kryszeń, Adam

2016 *A Historical Geography of the Hittite Heartland.* Alter Orient und Altes Testament 437. Münster: Ugarit-Verlag.

Kronasser, Heinz

1966 *Etymologie der hethitischen Sprache. Band 1.* Wiesbaden: Harrassowitz.

1967 "Heth. *we-/wa- : ḫu-*." In *Beiträge zur Indogermanistik und Keltologie. Julius Pokorny zum 80. Geburtstag gewidmet*, edited by Wolfgang Meid, 45–49. Innsbrucker Beiträge zur Kulturwissenschaft 13. Innsbruck: Sprachwissenschaftliches Institut der Universität Innsbruck.

Kudrinski, Maksim

2016 "Hittite heterographic writings and their interpretation." *Indogermanische Forschungen* 121: 159–75.

Kümmel, Hans Martin

1967 *Ersatzrituale für den hethitischen König.* Studien zu den Boğazköy-Texten 3. Wiesbaden: Harrassowitz.

Kunze, René, Arsen Bobokhyan, Ernst Pernicka, and Khachtur Melksetian

2013 "Projekt Ushkiani. Untersuchungen der Kulturlandschaft um das prähistorische Goldrevier von Sotk." *Veröffentlichungen des Landesamtes für Denkmalpflege und Archäologie Sachsen-Anhalt* 67: 49–88.

Kuzucuoğlu Catherine

2015 "The Rise and Fall of the Hittite State in Central Anatolia: How, When, Where, Did Climate Intervene?" In *La Cappadoce méridionale de la Préhistoire à l'époque byzantine. 3e Rencontres d'archéologie de IFEA, Istanbul 8–9 novembre 2012*, edited by Dominique Beyer, Olivier Henry, and Aksel Tibet, 17–41. Istanbul: Institut français d'études anatoliennes.

Lackenbacher, Sylvie

1995 "Une correspondance entre l'administration du pharaon Merneptah et le roi d'Ougarit." In *Le Pays d'Ougarit autour de 1200 av. J.-C.: Historie et archéologie. Actes du Colloque International; Paris, 28 juin-1er juillet 1993*, edited by Marguerite Yon, Maurice Sznycer, and Pierre Bordreuil, 77–83. Ras Shamra-Ougarit 11. Paris: Éditions recherche sur les civilisations.

2001 "Une lettre d'Égypte (nº 1)." In *Études ougaritiques: I. Travaux 1985–1995*, edited by Marguerite Yon and Daniel Arnaud, 239–48. Ras Shamra-Ougarit, 14. Paris: Éditions recherche sur les civilisations.

2002 *Textes akkadiens d'Ugarit. Textes provenant des vingt-cinq premières campagnes*. Littératures anciennes du Proche-Orient 20. Paris: Éditions du Cerf.

Landsberger, Benno and Oliver R. Gurney

1958 "Practical Vocabulary of Assur." *Archiv für Orientforschung* 18: 328–41.

Laroche, Emmanuel

1952 "Quelques valeurs rares du syllabaire Hittite." *Revue d'Assyriologie et d'archéologie orientale* 46: 161–63.

1956 "Catalogue des Textes Hittites." *Revue hittite et asianique* 14/58–59: 33–38, 68–116.

1957a "Catalogue des Textes Hittites." *Revue hittite et asianique* 15/60: 30–89.

1957b "Études de vocabulaire VI." *Revue hittite et asianique* 15/60: 9–29.

1958 "Catalogue des Textes Hittites." *Revue hittite et asianique* 16/62: 18–64.

1961 Review of *Hethitische Totenrituale*, by Heinrich Otten. *Bibliotheca Orientalis* 18: 83–84.

1966 *Les noms des Hittites*. Études linguistiques 4. Paris: Klincksieck.

1973 "Études de linguistique anatolienne." *Revue hittite et asianique* 31: 83–99.

1982 "Pouvoir central et pouvoir local en Anatolie hittite." In *Les Pouvoirs locaux en Mésopotamie et dans les régions adjacentes: colloque organisé par l'Institut des Hautes Études de Belgique 28 et 29 janvier 1980*, edited by André Finet, 138–43. Bruxelles: Institut des hautes études de Belgique.

Lebrun, René

2008 "Les missions des scribes hittites durant la seconde moitié du XIIIe s. av. J.-C." *Res Antiquae* 5: 365–69.

Lehner, Joseph W.

2015 "Cooperation, the Craft Economy, and Metal Technology during the Bronze and Iron Ages in Central Anatolia." PhD diss., University of California Los Angeles.

Lehner, Joseph W. and Andreas Schachner

2017 "The Organization of Metal Production at Hattuša: A First Assessment." In *Overturning Certainties in Near Eastern Archaeology: A Festschrift in Honor of K. Aslıhan Yener*, edited by Çiğdem Maner, Mara T. Horowitz, and Allan S. Gilbert, 403–435. Culture and History of the Ancient Near East 90. Leiden: Brill.

Lehnhardt, Enrico

2021 "The Introduction of Iron in the Old World as a Research Problem." In *Time and Materiality: Periodization and Regional Chronologies at the Transition from Bronze to Iron Age in Eurasia (1200-600 BCE)*, edited by Elke Kaiser and Wolfram Schier, 19–60. Prähistorische Archäologie in Südosteuropa 31. Rahden/Westf.: Leidorf.

Leichty, Erie

1996 "angurinnu." In *Festschrift für Hans Hirsch zum 65. Geburtstag gewidmet von seinen Freunden, Kollegen und Schülern* (= *Wiener Zeitschrift für die Kunde des Morgenlandes* 86), edited by Arne A. Ambros and Markus Köhbach, 233–34. Wien: Institut für Orientalistik.

Limet, Henri

1960 *Le travail du métal au pays de Sumer, au temps de la IIIe dynastie d'Ur.* Paris: Société d'Edition "Les Belles Lettres."

Liverani, Mario

1972 Review of *Ancient Mesopotamia: Socio-Economic History*, by Igor Diakonoff. *Oriens Antiquus* 11: 226–29.

1973 "Memorandum on the approach to historiographic texts." *Orientalia* 42: 178–94.

1975 "Communautés de village et palais royal dans la Syrie du IIème millénaire." *Journal of the Economic and Social History of the Orient* 18: 146–64.

1978 "Sulle tracce delle comunità rurali. In margine ai lavori della Société J. Bodin." *Oriens Antiquus* 17: 63–72.

1990 *Prestige and Interest: International Relations in the Near East ca. 1600–1100 B.C.* Padova: sargon srl.

1996 "Economic and Socio-Political Developments." In *History of Humanity, Volume II, From the Third Millennium to the Seventh Century B.C.*, edited by Ahmed H. Dani and Jean-Pierre Mohen, 126–41. New York: Routledge.

2004 "Shunashura, or: on reciprocity (reprint and translation of "Storiografia politica hittita - I. Šunaššura, ovvero: della reciprocità." *Oriens Antiquus* 12 (1973): 267–97)." In *Myth and Politics in Ancient Near Eastern Historiography*, by Mario Liverani, edited and introduced by Zainab Bahrani and Marc Van De Mieroop, 53–84. London: Equinox.

2004 "Telipinu, or: on solidarity (reprint and translation of "Storiografia politica hittita - II. Telipinu, ovvero: della solidarietà." *Oriens Antiquus* 16 (1977): 105–31)." In *Myth and Politics in Ancient Near Eastern Historiography*, by Mario Liverani, edited and introduced by Zainab Bahrani and Marc Van De Mieroop, 27–52. London: Equinox.

Llop, Jaume

2020 "Tributes and Taxes in the Middle Assyrian Documentation." In *Economic Complexity in the Ancient Near East. Management of Resources and Taxation (Third – Second Millennium BC)*, edited by Jana Mynářová and Sergio Alivernini, 327–40. Prague: Charles University.

Lorenz, Jürgen

2013 "'Lange Jahre' und Lebenszeit bei den Hethitern." In *Time and History in the Ancient Near East: Proceedings of the 56th Rencontre Assyriologique Internationale at Barcelona 26–30 July 2010*, edited by Lluís Feliu, Jaume Llop, Adelina Millet Albà, and Joaquin Sanmartín, 169–80. Winona Lake: Eisenbrauns.

2017 "Sahhan und luzzi." In *Private and State in the Ancient Near East. Proceedings of the 58th Rencontre Assyriologique Internationale at Leiden 16– 20 July 2012*, edited by Rients de Boer and Jan G. Dercksen), 193– 202. Winona Lake: Eisenbrauns.

2020 "Empire Period Hatti – Tax Heaven in the Late Bronze Age." In *Economic Complexity in the Ancient Near East. Management of Resources and Taxation (Third – Second Millennium BC)*, edited by Jana Mynářová and Sergio Alivernini, 437–43. Prague: Charles University.

Lorenz, Jürgen and Simona Lamante

2015 "KUB 27.68+. Ein Inventar zum Kult von Nerik." *KASKAL* 12: 245–66.

Lorenz, Jürgen and Elisabeth Rieken

2007 "Auf dem Weg der Stadt *Šāššūna* … ." In *Tabularia Hethaeorum. Hethitologische Beiträge Silvin Košak zum 65. Geburtstag*, edited by Detlev Groddek and Maria Zorman, 467–86. Dresdner Beiträge zur Hethitologie 25. Wiesbaden: Harrassowitz.

2011 "Zur Bedeutung und Etymologie von hethitisch *ū(n)ḫ-*." *Historische Sprachforschung* 124: 84–95.

Lorenz, Jürgen and Ingo Schrakamp

2011 "Hittite Military and Warfare." In *Insights into Hittite History and Archaeology*, edited by Hermann Genz and Dirk Paul Mielke, 125–52. Colloquia Antiqua 2. Leuven, Paris, Walpole, MA: Peeters.

Maner, Çiğdem

2017 "Searching for Ḫupišna. Hittite Remains in Ereğli Kara Höyük and Tont Kalesi." In *Places and Spaces in Hittite Anatolia I: Hatti and the East. Proceedings of an International Workshop on Hittite Historical Geography in Istanbul, 25th–26th October 2013*, edited by Metin Alparslan, 101–14. İstanbul: Türk Eskiçağ Bilimleri Enstitüsü.

Mankowski, Paul V.

2000 *Akkadian Loanwords in Biblical Hebrew*. Winona Lake: Eisenbrauns.

Marazzi, Massimiliano

1994 "Ma gli hittiti scrivevano veramente su 'legno'?" In *Miscellanea di studi linguistici in onore di Walter Belardi*, edited by Palmira Cipriano, Paolo Di Giovine, and Marco Mancini, 131–60. Roma: Il Calamo.

2007 "Sigilli, sigillature e tavolette di legno: alcune considerazioni alla luce di nuovi dati." In *Belkıs Dinçol ve Ali Dinçol'a Armağan. VITA: Festschrift in Honor of Belkıs Dinçol and Ali Dinçol*, edited by Metin Alparslan, Metlem Doğan-Alparslan, and Hasan Peker, 465–74. Istanbul: Ege Yayınları.

2008 "Messa a coltura e procedure di gestione e controllo dei campi nell'Anatolia hittita: caratteristiche della documentazione e stato della ricerca." In *The Management of Agricultural Land and the Production of Textiles in the Mycenaean and Near Eastern Economies*, edited by Massimo Perna and Francesco Pomponio, 63–88. Studi egei e vicinorientali 4. Paris: De Boccard.

Marston, John

2012 "Agricultural Strategies and Political Economy in Ancient Anatolia." *American Journal of Archaeology* 116/3: 377–403.

Marti, Lionel and Grégory Chambon

2019 "Identifying Weights in Cuneiform Texts from Mari and Assyria: Management and Circulation of Silver." In *Weights and Marketplaces from the Bronze Age to the Early Modern Period*, edited by Lorenz Rahmstorf and Edward Stratford, 51–66. Kiel, Hamburg: Wachholtz Verlag.

Martirosyan, Hrach

2010 *Etymological Dictionary of the Armenian Inherited Lexicon*. Leiden Indo-European Etymological Dictionary Series 8. Leiden: Brill.

Marx, Karl

1939–41 *Grundrisse der Kritik der politischen Ökonomie (Rohentwurf). 1857–1858, Anhang 1850–1859*. Edited by the Marx-Engels-Lenin-Institut, Moskau. Moskau: Verlag für fremdsprachige Literatur.

Mascheroni, Lorenza M.

1979 "Un'interpretazione dell'inventario KBo XVI 83 + 26 e i processi per malversazione alla corte di Ḫattuša." In *Studia Mediterranea. Piero Meriggi dicata*, edited by Onofrio Carruba, 353–71. Pavia: Aurora Edizioni.

Matessi, Alvise
2021 "The Ways of an Empire: Continuity and Change of Route Landscapes across the Taurus during the Hittite Period (ca. 1650–1200 BCE)." *Journal of Anthropological Archaeology* 62, 101293.

Maxwell-Hyslop, Kathleen Rachel
1974 "Assyrian Sources of Iron. A Preliminary Survey of the Historical and Geographical Evidence." *Iraq* 36, 1/2: 139–54.
1980 "A Note on the Jewellery Listed in the Inventory of Manninni (CTH 504)." *Anatolian Studies* 29: 85–90.

Melchert, H. Craig
1983 "Pudenda Hethitica." *Journal of Cuneiform Studies* 36: 137–45.
1984 *Studies in Hittite Historical Phonology.* Zeitschrift für Vergleichende Sprachforschung 32. Göttingen: Vandenhoeck & Ruprecht.
1993 *Cuneiform Luvian Lexicon.* Chapel Hill: Published by the author.
1994 *Anatolian Historical Phonology.* Leiden Studies in Indo-European 3. Leiden: Rodopi.
1999a "Hittite *karzan-* 'basket of wool'." In *Studi e testi II*, edited by Stefano de Martino and Fiorella Imparati, 121–32. Eothen 10. Firenze: LoGisma.
1999b "Hittite *tuk(kan)zi-* 'cultivation, breeding'." *Ktema* 24: 17–23.
1999c "Two Problems of Anatolian Nominal Derivation." In *Compositones Indogermanicae in Memoriam Jochem Schindler*, edited by Heiner Eichner, Hans Christian Luschützky, and Velizar Sadovski, 365–75. Praha: Enigma Corp.
2003a *The Luwians.* Handbuch der Orientalistik 1/68. Leiden: Brill.
2003b "Hittite Nominal Stems in *-anzan-*." In *Indogermanisches Nomen. Derivation, Flexion, und Ablaut*, edited by Eva Tichy, Dagmar S. Wodtko, and Britta Irslinger, 129–39. Bremen: Hempen.
2013 "Naming Practices in Second- and First-Millennium Western Anatolia." In *Personal Names in Ancient Anatolia*, edited by Robert Parker, 31–49. Proceedings of the British Academy 191. Oxford: Oxford University Press, 2013.
2016 "Formal and Semantic Aspects of Hittite *Gul(aš)ša-* 'Fate'." In *Studies in Honour of Ahmet Ünal Aramağanı*, edited by Sedat Erkut and Özlem Sir Gavaz, 355–59. Istanbul: Arkeologji ve Sanat Yayınları.
2017 Addenda and Corrigenda to Harry A. Hoffner and H. Craig Melchert. *Grammar of the Hittite Language (GHL). Reference Grammar.* Accessed 01/10/20. *eisenbrauns.org/books/supplements/Addenda_Corrigenda_GHL.pdf*
(forth.) *A Dictionary of Cuneiform Luvian.* Ann Arbor; New York: Beech Stave.

Melein, Martine Marieke
2018 *Iron Oxide Rock Artefacts in Mesopotamia c. 2600–1200 BC. An interdisciplinary study of hematite, goethite, and magnetite objects.* Oxford: Archaeopress.

Mellink, Machteld
1977 "Archaeology in Asia Minor." *American Journal of Archaeology* 81: 289–321.

Menabde, Eduard Akakievich
1965 *Хеттское общество: экономика собственность, семья и наследование.* Тбилиси: Издат. Мецниереба.

Michel, Cécile and Klaas R. Veenhof
2010 "The Textiles Traded by the Assyrians in Anatolia (19th–18th centuries BC)." In *Textile terminologies in the ancient Near East and Mediterranean from the third to the first millennia BC*, edited by Cécile Michel and Marie-Louise Nosch, 210–71. Oxford: Oxbow Books.

Mielke, Dirk Paul
2006 *Die Keramik vom Westhang.* Kuşaklı-Sarissa 2. Rahden/Westf.: Leidorf.
2007 "Red Lustrous Wheelmade Ware from Hittite Contexts." In *The Lustrous Wares of Late Bronze Age Cyprus and the Eastern Mediterranean, Papers of a Conference, Vienna 5th–6th of November 2004*, edited by Irmgard Hein, 155–68. Contributions to the Chronology of the Eastern Mediterranean 13, Österreichische Akademie der Wissenschaften. Wien: Verlag der Österreichischen Akademie der Wissenschaften.
2011 "Hittite Cities: Looking for a Concept." In *Insights into Hittite History and Archaeology*, edited by Hermann Genz and Dirk Paul Mielke, 153–94. Leuven: Peeters.
2016 "Produktion und Distribution von Keramik im Rahmen der hethitischen Wirtschaftsorganisation." In *Wirtschaft als Machtbasis. Beiträge zur Rekonstruktion vormoderner Wirtschaftssysteme in Anatolien: drittes wissenschaftliches Netzwerk der Abteilung Istanbul des Deutschen Archäologischen Instituts*, edited by Katja Piesker, 155–86. Byzas 22. Istanbul: Deutsches Archäologisches Institut.
2017a "From 'Anatolian' to 'Hittite'. The Development of Pottery in Central Anatolia in the 2nd Millennium BC." In *Innovation versus Beharrung: Was macht den Unterschied des hethitischen Reichs im Anatolien des 2. Jahrtausends v. Chr.? Internationaler Workshop zu Ehren von Jürgen Seeher, Istanbul, 23–24. Mai 2014*, edited by Andreas Schachner, 121–44. Byzas 23. Istanbul: Deutsches Archäologisches Institut.
2017b "Hittite Settlement Policy." In *Places and Spaces in Hittite Anatolia I: Hatti and the East. Proceedings of an International Workshop on Hittite Historical Geography in Istanbul, 25th–26th October 2013*, edited by Metin Alparslan, 13–27. İstanbul: Türk Eskiçağ Bilimleri Enstitüsü.
2022 "Hittite Pottery: Research, Corpus and Social Significance." In *Handbook of the Hittite Empire. Power Structures*, edited by Stefano de Martino, 649–90. Empires through the Ages in Global Perspective 1. Oldenbourg: De Gruyter.

Miller, Jared

2004 *Studies in the Origins, Development and Interpretation of the Kizzuwatna Rituals.* Studien zu den Boğazköy-Texte 46. Wiesbaden: Harrassowitz.

2008 "Setting up the Goddess of the Night Separately." In *Anatolian Interfaces: Hittites, Greeks and their Neighbours*, edited by Billie Jean Collins, Mary Bachvarova, and Ian Rutherford, 67–72. Oxford: Oxbow Books.

2010 "Six Rituals 'Edited' in the Manner of Arusna." In *VII. Uluslarası Hititoloji Kongresi Bildirileri. Çorum 25–31 Ağustos 2008 = Acts of the VIIth International Congress of Hittitology. Çorum, 25–31 August 2008*, edited by Aygül Süel, 503–14. Ankara: T. C. Çorum Valiliği.

2013 *Royal Hittite Instructions and Related Administrative Texts.* Writings from the Ancient World 31. Atlanta: Society of Biblical Literature.

Miller, Naomi

2009 "From Food and Fuel to Farms and Flocks: The Integration of Plant and Animal Remains in the Study of Ancient Agropastoral Economies at Gordion, Turkey." *Current Anthropology* 50: 915–24.

2010 *Botanical Aspects of Environment and Economy at Gordion.* Philadelphia: University of Pennsylvania Museum of Archaeology and Anthropology.

Miller, Naomi and Dirk Enneking

2014 "*Bitter Vetch* (Vicia ervilia): Ancient Medicinal Crop and Farmers' Favorite for Feeding Livestock." In *New Lives for Ancient and Extinct Crops*, edited by Paul E. Minnis, 254–68. Tucson: The University of Arizona Press.

Miller, Naomi and John Marston

2012 "Archaeological Fuel Remains as Indicators of Ancient West Asian Agropastoral and Landscape Use Systems." *Journal of Arid Environments* 86: 97–103.

Müller, Uwe

2005 "Norşun Tepe and Lidar Höyük. Two Examples for Cultural Change During the Early Iron Age." In *Anatolian Iron Ages 5*, edited by Altan Çilingiroğlu, Gareth Darbyshire, 107–14. London: British Institute of Archaeology Ankara.

Müller-Karpe, Andreas

1994 *Altanatolisches Metallhandwerk.* Offa-Bücher 75. Neumünster: Wachholtz Verlag.

2015 "Archäologische Beiträge zur Kenntnis hethitischer Maße und Gewichte." In *Saeculum. Gedenkschrift für Heinrich Otten anlässlich seines 100. Geburtstags*, edited by Andreas Müller-Karpe, Elisabeth Rieken, and Walter Sommerfeld, 147–60. Studien zu den Boğazköy-Texten 58. Wiesbaden: Harrassowitz.

2017 *Sarissa: Die Wiederentdeckung einer hethitischen Königsstadt.* Darmstadt: von Zabern.

Mora, Clelia

1983 "Il ruolo politico-sociale di *pankus* e *tulijas*: revision di un problema." In *Studi orientalistici in ricordo di Franco Pintore*, edited by Onofrio Carruba, Mario Liverani, and Carlo Zaccagnini, 159–84. Studia Mediterranea 4. Pavia: GJES.

1990 *La glittica anatolica del II millennio A.C.: Classificazione tipologica. I sigilli a iscrizione geroglifica. Primo supplemento.* Pavia: Iuculano.

2006 "Riscossione dei tributi e accumulo dei beni nell'impero ittita." In *Fiscality in Mycenaean and Near Eastern Archives. Proceeedings of the Conference held at Soprintendenza Archivistica per la Campania, Naples, 21–23 October 2004*, edited by Massimo Perna, 133–46. Studi egei e vicinorientali 3. Paris: De Boccard.

2007 "I testi ittiti di inventario e gli archive di *cretule.* Alcune osservazioni e riflessioni." In *Tabularia Hethaeorum. Hethitologische Beiträge Silvin Košak zum 65. Geburtstag*, edited by Detlev Groddek and Maria Zorman, 535–50. Dresdner Beiträge zur Hethitologie 25. Wiesbaden: Harrassowitz.

2012 "The Enigma of the 'Westbau' Depot in Ḫattuša's Upper City." In *Archivi, depositi, magazzini presso gli Ittiti: nuovi materiali e nuove ricerche / Archives, Depots and Storehouses in the Hittite World: New Evidence and New Research (Proceedings of the Workshop held in Pavia, June 18, 2009)*, edited by Maria Balza, Mauro Giorgieri, and Clelia Mora, 59–76. Studia Mediterranea, 23. Genoa: Italian University Press.

Mora, Clelia and Matteo Vigo

2012 "Attività femminili a Ḫattuša. La testimonianza dei testi d'inventario e degli archivi di *cretulae.*" In *Centro Mediterraneo Preclassico. Studi e Ricerche III. Studi vari di egeistica, anatolistica e del mondo mediterraneo*, edited by Natalia Bolatti-Guzzo, Silvia Festuccia and Massimiliano Marazzi, 173–223. Serie Beni culturali 20. Napoli: Suor Orsola Benincasa nell'Università.

Moran, William L.

1992 *The Amarna Letters.* Baltimore: John Hopkins.

Morris, Ian and Joseph G. Manning

2005 "Introduction." In *The Ancient Economy: Evidence and Models*, edited by Joseph G. Manning and Ian Morris, 1–46. Stanford: Stanford University Press.

Mouton, Alice

2007 *Rêves hittites: Contribution à une histoire et une anthropologie du rêve en Anatolie ancienne.* Culture and History of the Ancient Near East 28. Leiden: Brill.

Neef, Reinder
2001 "Getreide im Silokomplex and der Poternenmauer (Boğazköy) – erste Aussagen zur Landwirtschaft." In *Die Ausgrabungen in Boğazköy-Ḫattuša 2000*, by Jürgen Seeher, *Archäologische Anzeiger* 2001/3: 335–41.

Nakamura, Mitsuo
2002 *Das hethitische* nuntarriyašḫa-*Fest*. PIHANS = Uitgaven van het Nederlands Instituut voor het Nabije Oosten te Leiden, 94. Leiden: Nederlands Instituut voor het Nabije Oosten.

Neu, Erich
1980 "Die hethitischen Verben des Kaufens und Verkaufens." *Die Welt des Orients* 11: 76–89.
1982 "Studie über den Gebrauch von Genetivformen auf *-u̯as* des hethitischen Verbalsubstantivs *-u̯ar*." In *Investigationes Philologicae et Comparative. Gedenkschrift für Heinz Kronasser*, edited by Erich Neu, 116–48. Wiesbaden: Harrassowitz.
1983a *Glossar zu den althethitischen Ritualtexten*. Studien zu den Boğazköy-Texten 26. Wiesbaden: Harrassowitz.
1983b Review of *Hethitisches etymologisches Wörterbuch, Lieferung 3*, by Johann Tischler, with contributions of Günther Neumann. *Indogermanische Forschungen* 88: 302–7.
1993 "Zu den hethitischen Ortspartikeln." Bojan Čop Septuagenario in Honorem Oblata = *Linguistica* 33: 137–52.

Neve, Peter
1969 "Der Große Tempel und die Magazine." In *Boğazköy IV: Funde aus den Grabungen 1967 und 1968*, edited by Kurt Bittel, 9–19. Abhandlungen der Deutschen Orient-Gesellschaft 14. Berlin: Mann.

Newton, Maryanne and Peter Ian Kuniholm
2004 "A Dendrochronological Framework for the Assyrian Colony Period in Asia Minor." Türkiye Bilimler Akademisi Arkeoloji Dergisi 7: 165–76.

Newton, Richard and Margaret Serpico
2000 "Adhesives and Binders." In *Ancient Egyptian Materials and Technology*, edited by Paul T. Nicholson and Ian Shaw, 475–94. Cambridge: Cambridge University Press.

Nougayrol, Jean
1955 *Le palais royal d'Ugarit III: Textes accadiens et hourrites des archives est, ouest et centrales*. Mission de Ras Shamra 6. Paris: Klincksieck.
1956 *Le palais royal d'Ugarit. IV: Textes accadiens des archives sud (archives internationales)*. Mission de Ras Shamra 9. Paris: Klincksieck.
1970 *Le palais royal d'Ugarit VI: Textes en cunéiformes babyloniens des archives du grand palais et du palais sud d'Ugarit*. Mission de Ras Shamra 12. Paris: Klincksieck.

Nougayrol, Jean, Emmanuel Laroche, Charles Virolleaud, and Claude F.-A. Schaeffer

1968 *Ugaritica V: Nouveaux textes accadiens, hourrites et ugaritiques des archives et bibliothèques privées d'Ugarit; Commentaires des textes historiques (première partie).* Mission de Ras Shamra 16. Paris: Geuthner.

Oppenheim, A. Leo

1956 *The Interpretation of Dreams in the Ancient Near East, with a Translation of an Assyrian Dream-Book.* Transactions of the American Philosophical Society 46/3. Philadelphia: American Philosophical Society.

Oettinger, Norbert

1981 Review of *Hethitisches etymologisches Glossar, Lieferung 2,* by Johann Tischler, with contributions of Günter Neumann. *Zeitschrift der Deutschen Morgenländischen Gesellschaft* 131: 386–88.

Oreshko, Rotislav

2018 "Anatolian Linguistic Influences in Early Greek (1500–800 BC)? Critical Observations Against Sociolinguistic and Areal Background." *Journal of Language Relationship / Вопросы языкового родства* 16/2: 93–118.

Otten, Heinrich

1954–56 "Zum hethitischen Gewichtssystem." *Archiv für Orientsforschung* 17: 128–31.

1958 *Hethitische Totenrituale.* Berlin: Akademie-Verlag.

1971 *Ein hethitisches Festritual. (KBo XIX 128).* Studien zu den Boğazköy-Texten 13. Wiesbaden: Harrassowitz.

1975 *Puduḫepa: Eine hethitische Königin in ihren Textzeugnissen.* Akademie der Wissenschaften und der Literatur, Mainz. Abhandlungen der Geistes- und Sozialwissenschaftlichen Klasse. 1975, No. 1. Wiesbaden: Steiner.

1988 *Die Bronzetafel aus Boğazköy.* Studien zu den Boğazköy-Texten Beiheft 1. Wiesbaden: Harrassowitz.

1989 "Tiergefässe im Kult der späten hethitischen Grossreichszeit." In *Anatolia and the Ancient Near East. Studies in Honor of Tahsin Özgüç,* edited by Kutlu Emre, Barthel Hrouda, Machteld Mellink, and Nimet Özgüç, 365–68. Ankara: Türk Tarih Kurumu.

Otten, Heinrich and Vladimir Souček

1965 *Das Gelübde der Königin Puduḫepa an die Göttin Lelwani.* Studien zu den Boğazköy-Texten 1. Wiesbaden: Harrassowitz.

Özgüç, Nimet

1980 "Seal Impressions from the Palaces at Acemhöyük." In *Ancient Art in Seals,* edited by Edith Porada, 61–100. Princeton: Princeton University Press.

Özgüç, Tahsin

2003 *Kültepe. Kaniş/Neşa: The Earliest International Trade Center and the Oldest Capital City of the Hittites.* Ankara: The Middle East Culture Center in Japan.

Pare, Christopher
(forth.) "Chapter 2. The Near East." In a monograph to be published by Archaeopress, Oxford.

Parkinson, William and Michael Galaty
2007 "Primary and Secondary States in Perspective: An Integrated Approach to State Formation in the Prehistoric Aegean." *American Anthropologist* 109: 113–29.

Pasternak, Rainer
1998 "Übersicht über die Ergebnisse der archäobotanischen Arbeiten in Kuşaklı 1994–1997 und ein Interpretationsansatz zu den Befunden." In *Untersuchungen in Kuşaklı 1997*, by Andreas Müller-Karpe, 160–70. *Mitteilungen der deutschen Orient-Gesellschaft* 130: 93–174.
2000 "Archäobotanische Arbeiten 1999: Die Bearbeitung eines Massenfundes von Gersten im Nordflügel des Gebäudes C." In *Untersuchungen in Kuşaklı 1999*, by Andreas Müller-Karpe, *Mitteilungen der Deutsche Orient-Gesellschaft* 132: 348-351.
2012 "Vorbericht über die archäobotanischen Arbeiten in Ḫattuša 2009–2011." In *Die Ausgrabungen in Boğazköy-Ḫattuša 2011*, by Andreas Schachner, 110–14. *Archäologischer Anzeiger* 1/2012: 85–137.

Paul, Shalom M.
1967 "Jerusalem: A City of Gold." *Israel Exploration Journal* 17: 259–63.
2006 "Jerusalem of Gold – Revisited." In *"I Will Speak the Riddle of Ancient Times." Archaeological and Historical Studies in Honor of Amihai Mazar on the Occasion of His Sixtieth Birthday*, edited by Aren M. Maeir and Pierre de Miroschedji, 787–94. Winona Lake: Eisenbrauns.

Payne, Annick
2015 *Schrift und Schriftlichkeit: die anatolische Hieroglyphenschrift.* Wiesbaden: Harrassowitz.

Pecchioli Daddi, Franca
1982 *Mestieri, professioni e dignità nell'Anatolia ittita.* Incunabula Graeca 79. Roma: Edizioni dell'Ateneo.
1998 "Gli dei del pantheon hattico: i teonomi in *-šu*." *Studi Micenei ed Egeo-anatolici* 40/1: 5–27.
2000 "Un Nuovo ritual di Muršili II." *Altorientalische Forschungen* 27: 344–58.
2006 "The System of Government at the Time of Tuthaliya IV." In *The Life and Times of Hattušili III and Tuthaliya IV. Proceedings of a Symposium Held in Honour of J. de Roos, 12–13 December 2003, Leiden*, edited by Theo van den Hout, 121-25. PIHANS = Uitgaven van het Nederlands Instituut voor het Nabije Oosten te Leiden 103. Leiden: Nederlands Instituut voor het Nabije Oosten.
2010 "The Hittite Word *talla-*." In *Investigationes Anatolicae. Gedenkschrift für Erich Neu*, edited by Jörg Klinger, Elisabeth Rieken, and Christel Rüster,

197–203. Studien zu den Boğazköy-Texten 52. Wiesbaden: Harrassowitz, 2010.

Pisaniello, Valerio
2020 "Glossenkeil and Indentation on Hittite Tablets" *Altorientalische Forschungen* 47/1: 123–42.

Polvani, Anna Maria
1988 *La terminologia dei minerali nei testi ittiti (parte prima).* Eothen 3. Firenze: Elite.

Popko, Maciej
1995 *Religions of Asia Minor.* Translated by Iwona Zych. Warsaw: Academic Publications Dialog.

Powell, Marvin
1987–90 "Masse und Gewichte." RlA 7: 457–517.

Postgate, J. Nicholas
1988 *The Archive of* Urad-Šerūa *and his Family: A Middle Assyrian Household in Government Service.* Pubblicazioni del Progetto "Analisi ellettronica del cuneiforme," Corpus Medio-Assiro, 1. Roma: Roberto Denicola.
2000 "Assyrian Felt." In *Donum natalicium: studi presentati di Claudio Saporetti in occasione del suo 60° compleanno*, edited by Paola Negri Scafa, Paolo Gentili, 213–17. Roma: Borgia.
2007 "The ceramics of centralization and dissolution: a case study from Rough Cilicia." *Anatolian Studies* 57: 141–50.
2014 *Bronze Age Bureaucracy. Writing and the Practice of Government in Assyria.* Cambridge: Cambridge University Press.

Przeworski, Stefan
1939 *Die Metallindustrie Anatoliens in der Zeit von 1500–700 v.Chr.: Rohstoffe, Technik, Produktion.* Leiden: Brill.

Puhvel, Jaan
1996 "Signet of Steel." *Archivum Anatolicum* 2: 61–66.
2012 "Hittite *dammeli-*: Jurare in Verba Magistri?" *Journal of Cuneiform Studies* 64: 83–86.

Radner, Karen
2007 "Abgaben an den König von Assyrien aus dem In- und Ausland." In *Geschenke und Steuern, Zölle und Tribut*, edited by Hilmar Klinkott, Sabine Kubisch, and Renate Müller-Wollermann, 213–30. Culture and History of the Ancient Near East 29. Leiden: Brill.

Rahmstorf, Lorenz
2018 "Ökonomische Integration durch Gewichtsnutzung im bronzezeitlichen Anatolien." In *Anatolian Metal VIII. Eliten–Handwerk–Prestigegüter*, edited by Ünsal Yalçın, 195–203. *Der Anschnitt* 39. Bochum: Deutsches Bergbau-Museum.

Rainey, Anson F.

2015 *The El-Amarna Correspondence. A New Edition of the Cuneiform Letters form the Site of El-Amarna based on Collations of all Extant Tablets.* 2. vol., edited by William Schneidewind and Zipora Cochavi-Rainey. Handbuch der Orientalistik 1/110. Leiden: Brill.

Reiter, Karin

1997 *Die Metalle im Alten Orient unter besonderer Berücksichtigung altbabylonischer Quellen.* Alter Orient und Altes Testament 249. Münster: Ugarit-Verlag.

Richter, Jana

2016 "Spätbronzezeitliche Bebauung: das Silo." In *Archäologische Forschungen am Oymaağaç Höyük/Nerik 2011–2015*, by Rainer M. Czichon, Jörg Klinger, Pavol Hnila, Dirk Paul Mielke, Herbert Böhm, Christoph Forster, Carol Griggs, Martin Kähler, Günther Karl Kunst, Monika Lehmann, Brita Lorentzen, Sturt Manning, Kathryn Marklein, Henning Marquardt, Silvio Reichmuth, Jana Richter, Corinna Rössner, Burhan Sadıklar, Katherine Seufer, Robert Sobott, Irene Traub-Sobott, Harald von der Osten-Woldenburg, Melanie Weber, Horst Wolter, Mehmet Ali Yılmaz, 38–42. *Mitteilungen der Deutschen Orient-Gesellschaft* 148: 5–141.

Richter, Thomas

2012 *Bibliographisches Glossar des Hurritischen.* Wiesbaden: Harrassowitz.

2016 *Vorarbeiten zu einem hurritischen Namenbuch. Erster Teil: Personennamen altbabylonischer Überlieferung vom Mittleren Euphrat und aus dem nördlichen Mesopotamien.* Wiesbaden: Harrassowitz.

Rieken, Elisabeth

1999 *Untersuchungen zur nominalen Stammbildung des Hethitischen.* Studien zu den Boğazköy-Texten, 44. Wiesbaden: Harrassowitz.

2013 "Die Numeruskongruenz nach Kardinalzahlen im Hethitischen." *Indogermanische Forschungen* 118: 321–38.

2021 "Anatolische Fruchtbarkeit, urindogermanische Männer und die Wurzel **men-* 'hervorragen'." In *lyuke wmer ra. Indo-European Studies in Honor of Georges-Jean Pinault*, edited by Hannes A. Fellner, Melanie Malzahn, and Michaël Peyrot, 462–76. Ann Arbor: Beech Stave.

Rieken, Elisabeth and Ilya Yakubovich

2020 "Ein lydisches Schmuckstück." In *Maiores philologiae pontes. Festschrift für Michael Meier-Brügger zum 70. Geburtstag*, edited by Matthias Fritz, Tomoki Kitazumi, and Marina Veksina, 215–23. Ann Arbor: Beech Stave.

Riemschneider, Kaspar K.

1957 "Hethitisch 'gelb/grün'." *Mitteilungen des Instituts für Orientforschung* 5: 141–47.

1958 "Die hethitischen Landschenkungsurkunden." *Mitteilungen des Instituts für Orientforschung* 6: 321–81.

Roberts, Neil

2017 “The Land of the Hittites: Airs, Waters and Places.” In *Hittite Landscape and Geography*, edited by Mark Weeden and Lee Z. Ullmann, 17–27. Handbuch der Orientalistik 1/121. Leiden: Brill.

Röllig, Wolfgang

2008 *Land- und Viehwirtschaft am unteren Ḫābūr in mittelassyrischer Zeit.* Berichte der Ausgrabung Tell Šēḫ Ḥamad/Dūr-Katlimmu (BATSH) 9. Wiesbaden: Harrassowitz.

Rosenkranz, Bernhard

1965 “Ein hethitischer Wirtschaftstext.” *Zeitschrift für Assyriologie und vorderasiatische Archäologie* 57: 237–48.

Rost, Liane

1953 “Ein hethitisches Ritual gegen Familienzwist.” *Mitteilungen des Instituts für Orientforschung* 1: 345–79.

1961–63 “Zu den hethitischen Bildbeschreibungen (I. Teil).” *Mitteilungen des Instituts für Orientforschung* 8: 161–217.

Roszkowska-Mutschler, Hanna

2007 *Hethitische Texte in Transkription: KBo 44.* Dresdner Beträge zur Hethitologie 22. Wiesbaden: Harrassowitz.

Rößle, Sylvester

1998 “Heth. *karza* ‘Gerät des Webens’ und *kazzarnul* ‘eine bestimmte Tuchart’.” *Münchner Studien zur Sprachwissenschaft* 58: 111–28.

Rüster, Christel and Gernot Wilhelm

2012 *Landschenkungsurkunden hethitischer Könige.* Studien zu den Boğazköy-Texten Beiheft 4. Wiesbaden: Harrassowitz.

Rutherford, Ian

2004 “Women Singers and the Religious Organisation of Hatti. On the Interpretation of CTH 235.1&2 and Other Texts.” In *Offizielle Religion, locale Kulte und individuelle Religiosität*, edited by Manfred Hutter and Sylvia Hutter-Braunsar, 377–94. Alter Orient und Altes Testament 318. Münster: Ugarit-Verlag.

Sahlins, Marshall

1972 *Stone Age Economics.* New York: Aldine De Gruyter.

Sakuma, Yasuhiko

2009 “Hethtische Vogelorakeltexte.” PhD diss., University of Würzburg.

Saporetti, Claudio

1970 “Sulla frase *še’um in sūti ša bēt ḫiburni ša ekalli.*” *Orientalia* 39: 500–3.

Sasseville, David

2021 *Anatolian Verbal Stem Formation. Luwian, Lycian and Lydian.* Brill’s Studies in Indo-European Languages and Linguistics 21. Leiden: Brill

Schachner, Andreas

1999 *Von der Rundhütte zum Kaufmannshaus: Kulturhistorische Untersuchungen zur Entwicklung prähistorischer Wohnhäuser in Zentral-, Ost- und Südostanatolien.* Oxford: Oxford University Press.

2006 "Auf welchem Fundamenten? Überlegungen zum Stand der Erforschung der hethitischen Architektur." In *Strukturierung und Datierung der hethitischen Archäologie: Voraussetzungen – Probleme – Neue Ansätze. Internationaler Workshop Istanbul, 26–27. November 2004,* edited by Dirk Paul Mielke, Ulf-Dietrich Schoop, and Jürgen Seeher, 149–66. Byzas 4. Istanbul: Deutsches Archäologisches Institut.

2009 "Das 16. Jahrhundert v. Chr. – eine Zeitenwende im hethitischen Zentralanatolien." *Istanbuler Mitteilungen* 59: 9–24.

2011a *Hattuscha: Auf der Suche nach dem sagenhaften Großreich der Hethiter.* München: Beck.

2011b "Von einer anatolischen Stadt zur Hauptstadt eines Großreichs – Entstehung, Entwicklung und Wandel Hattušas in hethitischer Zeit." *Mesopotamia* 46: 79-101.

2015 "Die Ausgrabungen in der Unterstadt von Ḫattusa (2009–2014): erste vorläufige Ergebnisse." In *Sacred Landscapes of Hittites and Luwians. Proceedings of the International Conference in Honour of Franca Pecchioli Daddi. Florence, February 6th–8th 2014,* edited by Anacleto D'Agostino, Valentina Orsi, and Giulia Torri, 67–82. Studia Asiana 9. Firenze: Firenze University Press.

2017a "Hattusa and its Environs: Archaeology." In *Hittite Landscape and Geography,* edited by Mark Weeden and Lee Z. Ullmann, 37–49. Handbuch der Orientalistik 1/121. Leiden: Brill.

2017b "Motor oder Bremse? Die Rolle der hethitischen Hauptstadt Hattuša für die Transformation des hethitischen Reichs." In *Innovation versus Beharrung: Was macht den Unterschied des hethitischen Reichs im Anatolien des 2. Jahrtausends v. Chr.? Internationaler Workshop zu Ehren von Jürgen Seeher, Istanbul, 23–24. Mai 2014,* edited by Andreas Schachner, 219–37. Byzas 23. Istanbul: Deutsches Archäologisches Institut.

2022a "Geographical Prerequisites versus Human Behavior: Settlement Geography, Rural Economy, and Ideological Aspects of Anthropogenic Relations with the Natural Environment during the Second Millennium BC in Central Anatolia." In *Handbook of the Hittite Empire. Power Structures,* edited by Stefano de Martino, 159–202. Empires through the Ages in Global Perspective 1. Oldenbourg: De Gruyter.

2022b "Building for King and Country: Architecture as a Symbol of the Hittite Empire." In *Handbook of the Hittite Empire. Power Structures,* edited by Stefano de Martino, 421–66. Empires through the Ages in Global Perspective 1. Oldenbourg: De Gruyter.

Schachner, Andreas and Hartmut Wittenberg

2012 "Zu den Wasserspeichern in Boğazköy/Hattuša und der Frage ihrer Befüllung." In *Wasserwirtschaftliche Innovationen im archäologischen Kontext: Von den prähistorischen Anfängen bis zu den Metropolen der Antike*, edited by Florian Klimscha, Ricardo Eichmann, Christof Schuler, and Henning Fahlbusch, 245–56. Rahden/Westf.: Leidorf.

Schloen, David

2001 *House of the Father as Fact and Symbol: Patrimonialism in Ugarit and the Ancient Near East.* Winona Lake: Eisenbrauns.

Schneider-Ludorff, Helga

2009 "Metallgefäße aus Nuzi nach den schriftlichen Quellen." In *General Studies and Excavations at Nuzi 11/2, in Honor of David I. Owen on the Occasion of his 65th Birthday, October 28, 2005*, edited by Gernot Wilhelm, 491–530. Studies on the civilization and culture of Nuzi and the Hurrians. Bethesda, Md.: CDL Press.

Schoop, Ulf-Dietrich

2003 "Pottery Traditions of the Later Hittite Empire: Problems of Definition." In *Identifying Changes: The Transition from Bronze to Iron Ages in Anatolia and Its Neighbouring Regions. Proceedings of the International Workshop, Istanbul, November 8–9, 2002*, edited by Bettin Fischer, Hermann Genz, Éric Jean, and Kemalettin Köroğlu, 167–78. Istanbul: Türk Eskiçağ Bilimleri Enstitüsü.

2005 *Das anatolische Chalkolithikum. Eine chronologische Untersuchung zur vorbronzezeitlichen Kultursequenz im nördlichen Zentralanatolien und den angrenzenden Gebieten.* Remshalden: B. A. Greiner.

2009 "Indications of Structural Change in the Hittite Pottery Inventory at Boğazköy." In *Central-North Anatolia in the Hittite Period: New Perspectives in Light of Recent Research Acts of the International Conference held at the University of Florence (7–9 February 2007).* Edited by Giulia Torri, Carlo Corti, and Francesca Pecchioli Daddi, 145–67. Studia Asiana 5. Rome: Herder.

2011 "Hittite Pottery: A Summary." In *Insights into Hittite History and Archaeology*, edited by Hermann Genz and Dirk Paul Mielke, 241–73. Leuven: Peeters.

Schuster-Brandis, Anais

2008 *Steine als Schutz- und Heilmittel. Untersuchung zu ihrer Verwendung in der Beschwörungskunst Mesopotamiens im 1. Jt. v. Chr.* Alter Orient und Altes Testament 46. Münster: Ugarit-Verlag.

Schwemer, Daniel

2005/2006 "Lehnbeziehungen zwischen dem Hethitischen und dem Akkadischen." *Archiv für Orientforschung* 51: 220–34.

2016 "Quality Assurance Managers at Work: The Hittite Festival Tradition." In *Liturgie oder Literatur? Die Kultrituale der Hethiter im transkulturellen Vergleich. Akten eines Werkstattgesprächs an der Akademie der Wissenschaften und der Literatur Mainz, 2.–3. Dezember 2010*, edited by Gerfrid G. W. Müller, 1–29. Studien zu den Boğazköy-Texten 60. Wiesbaden: Harrassowitz.

2022 "Religion and Power." In *Handbook of the Hittite Empire. Power Structures*, edited by Stefano de Martino, 355–418. Empires through the Ages in Global Perspective 1. Oldenbourg: De Gruyter.

Seeher, Jürgen

2000 "Getreidelagerung in unterirdischen Großspeichern: Zur Methode und ihrer Anwendung im 2. Jahrtausend v. Chr. am Beispiel der Befunde in Hattuša." *Studi Micenei ed Egeo-Anatolici* 42/2: 261–301.

2001 "Die Zerstörung der Stadt Ḫattuša." In *Akten des IV. Internationalen Kongresses für Hethitologie. Würzburg, 4.–8. Oktober 1999*, edited by Gernot Wilhelm, 623–34. Wiesbaden: Harassowitz.

2006a "Die hethitischen Ostteiche." In *Ergebnisse der Grabungen an den Ostteichen und am mittleren Büyükkale-Nordwesthang in den Jahren 1996–2000*, edited by Jürgen Seeher, 1–23. Boğazköy-Berichte 8. Mainz: von Zabern.

2006b "Der althethitische Getreidekomplex." In *Ergebnisse der Grabungen an den Ostteichen und am mittleren Büyükkale-Nordwesthang in den Jahren 1996–2000*, edited by Jürgen Seeher, 45–84. Boğazköy-Berichte 8. Mainz: von Zabern.

2009 "Der Landschaft sein Siegel aufdrücken – hethitische Felsbilder und Hieroglypheninschriften als Ausdruck des herrscherlichen Macht- und Territorialanspruchs." *Altorientalische Forschungen* 36: 119–39.

2010 "After the Empire: Observations on the Early Iron Age in Central Anatolia." In *ipamati kistamati pari tumatimis. Luwian and Hittite Studies presented to J. David Hawkins on the Occasion of his 70th Birthday*, edited by Itamar Singer, 220–29. Monograph Series of the Institute of Archaeology 28. Tel Aviv: Tel Aviv University.

2012 "Natürliche und künstliche, unbewusste und beabsichtige Landmarken: Menschliche Wahrnehmung und herrscherliche Betonung der Besetzung von Landschaft und Territorien." In *Manifestation von Macht und Hierarchien in Stadtraum und Landschaft*, edited by Felix Pirson, 25–42. Byzas 13. Istanbul: Deutsches Archäologisches Institut.

2017 "Die Besiedlung des Mittleren und Unteren Plateaus in hethitischer Zeit." In *Büyükkaya II. Bauwerke und Befunde der Grabunskampagnen 1952–1955 und 1993–1998*, edited by Jürgen Seeher, 32–87. Boğazköy-Ḫattuša 27. Berlin: De Gruyter.

Sideltsev, Andrej and Marina Molina

2015 "Enclitic *-(m)a* 'but', Clause Architecture and the Prosody of Focus in Hittite." *Indogermanische Forschungen* 120/1: 209–53.

Siegelová, Jana

1984 "Gewinnung und Verarbeitung von Eisen im hethitischen Reich im 2. Jahrtausend v.u.Z." *Annual of the Náprstek-Museum* 12: 71–178.

1986 *Hethitische Verwaltungspraxis im Lichte der Wirtschafts- und Inventardokumente.* 3 volumes. Praha: Národní muzeum v Praze.

1988 "Ein Adlergewicht in den Sammlungen des Britischen Museums." In *Documentum Asiae Minoris Antiquae. Festschrift für Heinrich Otten zum 75. Geburtstag*, edited by Erich Neu, 317–26. Wiesbaden: Harrassowitz.

1993 "Metalle und Metallurgie in den hethitischen Texten." RlA 8: 112–19.

1994 "Anwendung von Kupfer und Bronze in Anatolien anhand der hethitischen Texte." In *Handwerk und Technologie im alten Orient: Ein Beitrag zur Geschichte der Technik im Altertum. Internationale Tagung Berlin, 12.–15. März 1991*, edited by Ralf-Bernhard Wartke, 119–24. Mainz: von Zabern.

2001 "Der Regionalpalast in der Verwaltung des hethitischen Staates." *Altorientalische Forschungen* 28/2: 193–208.

2005 "Metalle in hethitischen Texten." In *Anatolian Metal III*, edited by Ünsal Yalçın, 35–40. *Der Anschnitt* 18. Bochum: Deutsches Bergbau-Museum.

2008 "Metals in Hittite records." In *Ancient Mining in Turkey and the Eastern Mediterranean*, edited by Ünsal Yalçın, Hadi Özbal, and A. Günhan Paşamehmetoğlu, 43–56. Ankara: Atılım University.

2011 "Geschenk oder Geschäft? Wovon zeugt die ägyptisch-hethitische Korrespondenz." In *Times, Signs and Pyramids: Studies in Honour of Miroslav Verner on the Occasion of His Seventieth Birthday*, edited by Vivienne Gae Callender, Ladislav Bareš, Miroslav Bárta, Jiri Janak, and Jaromír Krejčí, 323–34. Prague: Faculty of Arts, Charles University of Prague.

2011–12 "Steuer. E. Bei den Hethitern." RlA 13, 175–77.

2014 "Tribut. D. Bei den Hethitern." RlA 14, 133–34.

2015 "Die hethitische Königin und die Wirtschaft der Krone." In *Saeculum. Gedenkschrift für Heinrich Otten anlässlich seines 100. Geburtstags*, edited by Andreas Müller-Karpe, Elisabeth Rieken, and Walter Sommerfeld, 239–50. Studien zu den Boğazköy-Texten 58. Wiesbaden: Harrassowitz.

2019 "Naturalabgaben für den Kult und für Kulteinrichtungen des hethitischen Reiches." In *Economy of Religions in Anatolia: From the Early Second to the Middle of the First Millennium BCE. Proceedings of an International Conference in Bonn (23rd to 25th May 2018)*, edited by Manfred Hutter and Sylvia Hutter-Braunsar, 103–12. Alter Orient und Altes Testament 467. Münster: Ugarit-Verlag.

Siegelová, Jana and Hidetoshi Tsumoto
2011 "Metals and Metallurgy in Hittite Anatolia." In *Insights into Hittite Archaeology and History*, edited by Hermann Genz and Dirk Paul Mielke, 275–300. Colloquia Antiqua 2. Leuven: Peeters.

Simon, Zsolt
2013 "Die These der hethitisch-luwischen Lehnwörter im Armenischen. Eine kritische Neubetrachtung." *International Journal of Diachronic Linguistics and Linguistic Reconstruction* 10: 97–135.
2020 "Die hurritischen Lehnwörter im Keilschriftluwischen." In *Loanwords and Substrata in Indo-European Languages. Proceedings of the Colloquium held in Limoges (5th–7th June, 2018)*, edited by Romain Garnier, 411–26. Innsbruck Beiträge zur Sprachwissenschaft 164. Innsbruck: Institut für Sprachen und Literaturen der Universität Innsbruck.
(forth.) "Once Again on the Distribution of Cuneiform Luwian =ša/za." To appear in *Journal of Cuneiform Studies*.

Singer, Itamar
1983–84 *The Hittite KI.LAM Festival.* Studien zu den Boğazköy-Texten 27–28. Wiesbaden: Harrassowitz.
1984 "The AGRIG in the Hittite Texts." *Anatolian Studies* 34: 97–127.
1985 "The Battle of Nihriya and the End of the Hittite Empire." *Zeitschrift für Assyriologie* 75: 100–123.
1991 "A Concise History of Amurru." In *Amurru Akkadian: A Linguistic Study, vol. 2*, by Shlomo Izre'el, 135–95. Atlanta: Scholars Press.
1996 *Muwatalli's Prayer to the Assembly of Gods through the Storm-God of Lightning (CTH 381).* Atlanta: American School of Oriental Research.
1999 "A Political History of Ugarit." In *Handbook of Ugaritic Studies*, edited by Wilfred G.E. Watson and Nicolas Wyatt, 603–33. Handbuch der Orientalistik 1/39. Leiden: Brill.
2006a "The Failed Reforms of Akhenaton and Muwatalli II." *British Museum Studies in Ancient Egypt and Sudan* 6: 37–58.
2006b "Ships Bound for Lukka: A New Interpretation of the Companion Letters RS 94.2530 and RS 94.2523." *Altorientalische Forschungen* 33: 242–62.
2007 "Who were the Kaška?" *Phasis* 10/2: 166–81.
2008 "A Hittite-Assyrian diplomatic exchange in the Late 13th Century BCE." *Studi Micenei ed Egeo-Anatolici* 50/2: 713–20.
2009 "'In Hattuša The Royal House Declined'. Royal Mortuary Cult in 13th Century Hatti." In *Central-North Anatolia in the Hittite Period: New Perspectives in Light of Recent Research Acts of the International Conference held at the University of Florence (7–9 February 2007)*, edited by Giulia Torri, Carlo Corti, and Francesca Pecchioli Daddi, 169–93. Studia Asiana, 5. Rome: Herder.

2010 "Purple-dyers in Lazpa." In *Anatolian Interfaces: Hittites, Greeks and their Neighbours,* edited by Billie Jean Collins, Mary Bachvarova, and Ian Rutherford, 21–44. Oxford: Oxbow Books.

2011 "Aḫḫiyawans Bearing Gifts." In *The Calm before the Storm. Selected writings of Itamar Singer on the end of the Late Bronze Age in Anatolia and the Levant,* 459–66. Writings from the Ancient World Supplements 1. Atlanta: Society for Biblical Literature.

2013 "Between Scepticism and Credulity: In Defence of Hittite Historiography." In *Diversity and Standardization: Perspectives on Social and Political Norms in the ancient Near East,* edited by Eva Cancik-Kirschbaum, Jörg Klinger, and Gerfrid Müller, 173–214. Berlin: Akademie Verlag.

Skaist, Aaron

1998a "The Chronology of Legal Texts from Emar." *Zeitschrift für Assyriologie* 88/1: 45–71.

1998b "A Hurrian Term at Emar." In *General Studies and Excavations at Nuzi 10/2,* edited by David I. Owen and Gernot Wilhelm, 169–71. Studies on the Civilization and Culture of Nuzi and the Hurrians 9. Bethesda, Md.: CDL Press.

Sommer, Ferdinand and Adam Falkenstein

1938 *Die hethitisch-akkadische Bilingue des Ḫattušili I. (Labarna II.).* Abhandlungen der Bayerischen Akademie der Wissenschaften, Philosophisch-historische Abteilung, Neue Folge 16. München: Beck.

Soriga, Elena

2017 "Mari(ne) Purple: Western Textile Technology in Middle Bronze Age Syria." In *Treasures from the Sea. Sea Silk and Shellfish Purple Dye in Antiquity,* edited by Hedvig Landenius Enegren and Francesco Meo, 79–95. Ancient Textiles Series 30. Oxford: Oxbow Books.

Souček, Vladimír

1959 "Die hethitischen Feldertexte." *Archív Orientální* 27: 5–43.

1963 "Randnotizen zu den hethitischen Feldertexte." *Mitteilungen des Instituts für Orientforschung* 8: 368–82.

1979 "Soziale Klassen und Schichten in der hethitischen Tempelwirtschaft." *Archív Orientální* 47: 78–82.

1988 "Zur Struktur der hethitischen Gesellschaft." *Šulmu* 1: 329–35.

Soysal, Oğuz

2000 "Analysis of a Hittite Oracular Document." *Zeitschrift für Assyriologie* 90: 85–122.

2004 *Hattischer Wortschatz in hethitischer Textüberlieferung.* Handbuch der Orientalistik 1/78. Leiden: Brill.

2006 "Das hethitische Wort für 'Zinn'." *Historische Sprachforschung* 119: 109–116.

2009 "On Recent Cuneiform Editions of Hittite Fragments (I)." *Journal of the American Oriental Society* 129/2: 295–306.

2016 "On Recent Cuneiform Editions of Hittite Fragments (III)." *Journal of the American Oriental Society* 136/2: 417–38.

(forth.) *Unpublished Bo-Fragments in Transliteration.* Chicago Hittite Dictionary Supplements 4. Chicago: Oriental Institute.

Soysal, Oğuz and Başak Yıldız Gülşen

2019 *Unpublished Bo-Fragments in Transliteration. (Bo 6151 – Bo 9535).* Chicago Hittite Dictionary Supplements 3. Chicago: Oriental Institute.

Stalin, Joseph

1972 "Dialectical and Historical Materialism." In *The Essential Stalin: Major Theoretical Writings, 1905–52*, edited by Bruce Franklin. Garden City, N.Y.: Anchor Books.

Starke, Frank

1977 *Die Funktionen der dimensionalen Kasus und Adverbien im Althethitischen.* Studien zu den Boğazköy-Texten 23. Wiesbaden: Harrassowitz.

1990 *Untersuchung zur Stammbildung des keilschrift-luwischen Nomens.* Studien zu den Boğazköy-Texten 31. Wiesbaden: Harrassowitz.

1996 "Zur 'Regierung' des hethitischen Staates." *Zeitschrift für Altorientalische und Biblische Rechtsgeschichte* 2: 140–82.

Steinkeller, Piotr

1981 "Studies in Third Millennium Paleography, 2. Signs ŠEN and ALAL." *Oriens Antiquus* 20: 243–49.

1984 "Studies in Third Millennium Paleography, 2. Signs ŠEN and ALAL: Addendum." *Oriens Antiquus* 23: 39–41.

2004 "The Function of Written Documentation in the Administrative Praxis of Early Babylonia." In *Creating Economic Order: Record-Keeping, Standardization, and the Development of Accounting in the Ancient Near East*, edited by Michael Hudson and Cornelia Wunsch, 65–88. Bethesda, Maryland: CDL.

Stol, Marten

1996 "Quelques nombres en écriture cunéiforme." *Nouvelles Assyriologique Brèves et Utilitaires (N.A.B.U.)* 1996/3: 65.

Struve, Vasilii

1934 "Проблема зарождения, развития и разложения рабовладельческих обществ древнего Востока." Известия Государственной Академии истории материальной культуры 77. Ленинград: ИГАИМК.

1969 "The Problem of the Genesis, Development and Disintegration of the Slave Societies in the Ancient Orient." In *Ancient Mesopotamia*, edited and translated by Igor M. Diakonoff. Moscow: Nauka Publishing House.

Symington, Dorit

1991 "Late Bronze Age Writing-Boards and their Uses: Textual Evidence from Anatolia and Syria." *Anatolian Studies* 41: 111–24.

Tani, Nicoletta

1999 "Osservazioni sui processi ittiti per malversazione." In *Studi e testi II*, edited by Stefano de Martino and Fiorella Imparati, 167–72. Eothen 10. Firenze: LoGisma.

Taracha, Piotr

2003–05 "Pfeil und Bogen. A. II. In Anatolien." RlA 10: 458–61.

2007 "The Capital Hattuša and Other Residential Cities of Hittite Great Kings." In *Belkıs Dinçol ve Ali Dinçol'a Armağan. VITA: Festschrift in Honor of Belkıs Dinçol and Ali Dinçol*, edited by Metin Alparslan, Metlem Doğan-Alparslan, and Hasan Peker, 755–59. Istanbul: Ege Yayınları.

2017 "Hittite ^{É}*ḫalentuwa-* Revisited." *Altorientalische Forschungen* 44: 101–10.

Taş, İlknur

2014 *Hethitische Texte in Transkription. Bo 8264–Bo 8485.* Dresdner Beiträge zur Hethitologie 43. Wiesbaden: Harrassowitz.

2017 "Aspekte von Kultinventaren im Licht des unveröffentlichten Textes Bo 8359." In *Private and State in the Ancient Near East. Proceedings of the 58th Recontre Assyriologique Internationale at Leiden, 16–20 July 2012*, edited by Rients de Boer and Jan G. Dercksen, 291–95. Winona Lake: Eisenbrauns.

Tenney, Jonathan S.

2011 *Life at the Bottom of Babylonian Society: Servile Laborers at Nippur in the 14th and 13th Centuries B.C.* Leiden: Brill.

Thames, John Tracy, Jr.

2020 *The Politics of Ritual Change. The* zukru *Festival in the Political History of Late Bronze Age Emar.* Harvard Semitic Monographs 65. Leiden: Brill.

Thavapalan, Shiyanti

2020 *The Meaning of Color in Ancient Mesopotamia.* Culture and History of the Ancient Near East 104. Leiden: Brill.

Tischler, Johann

1982 "Beiträge zur hethitschen Anthroponymie." In *Serta Indogermanica: Festschrift für Günter Neumann zum 60. Geburtstag*, edited by J. Tischler, 439–54. Innsbrucker Beiträge zur Sprachwissenschaft 40. Innsbruck: Institut für Sprachwissenschaft der Universität Innsbruck.

1988 Review of *Hethitische Briefe und Texte verschiedenen Inhalts. Keilschrifturkunden aus Boghazköi 57*, by Alfonso Archi. *Zeitschrift der Deutschen Morgenländischen Gesellschaft* 138/2: 376–78.

2013 Review of *Hethitisches Wörterbuch. Zweite, völlig neubearbeite Auflage auf der Grundlage der edierten hethitischen Texte. Band III: Ḫ, Lieferungen 18 und 19*, edited by Johannes Friedrich, Annelies Kammenhuber. *Zeitschrift für Assyriologie* 103: 252–54.

2016 *Hethitische Texte in Transkription. KUB 56 und 57.* Dresdner Beiträge zur Hethitologie 49. Wiesbaden: Harrassowitz.

Torri, Giulia

2009 "The Old Hittite Textual Tradition in the 'Haus am Hang.'" In *Central-North Anatolia in the Hittite Period. New Perspectives in Light of Recent Research. Acts of the International Conference Held at the University of Florence (7–9 February 2007)*, edited by Franca Pecchioli Daddi, Giulia Torri, and Carlo Corti, 207–22. Studia Asiana 5. Roma: Herder, 2009.

2016a "The Goldsmith Zuzu(l)li and the Find-spots of the Inventory Texts from Ḫattuša." *Altorientalische Forschungen* 43: 147–56.

2016b "Landowners and Renters at Ḫattuša." In *Antike Wirtschaft und ihre kulturelle Prägung. The Cultural Shaping of the Ancient Economy*, edited by Kerstin Droß-Krüpe, Sabine Föllinger, and Kai Ruffing, 37–46. Philippika – Altertumskundliche Abhandlungen 98. Wiesbaden: Harrassowitz.

Torri, Giulia and Francesco G. Barsacchi

2018 *Hethitische Texte in Transkription. KBo 13.* Dresdner Beiträge zur Hethitologie 51. Wiesbaden: Harrassowitz.

Trémouille, Marie-Claude

2006 "Un exemple de continuité religieuse en Anatolie. Le dieu Šarrumma." In *Pluralismus und Wandel in den Religionen im vorhellenistischen Anatolien. Akten des religionsgeschichtlichen Symposiums in Bonn (19.–20. Mai 2005)*, edited by Manfred Hutter and Sylvia Hutter-Braunsar, 191–224. Alter Orient und des Alten Testaments 337. Münster: Ugarit-Verlag.

Trigger, Bruce

1996 *A History of Archaeological Thought.* Second Edition. Cambridge: Cambridge University Press.

Ünal, Ahmet

1974 *Ḫattušili III. Teil I. Ḫattušili bis zu seiner Thronbesteigung. Band 1: Historischer Abriß.* Texte der Hethiter 3. Heidelberg: Winter.

1977 "M. Ö. II. Binyıl Anadolu'sunda Doğal Âfetler / Naturkatastrophen in Anatolien im 2. Jahrtausend v. Chr." *Belleten* 41: 423–46/447–72.

1978 *Ein Orakeltext über die Intrigen am hethitischen Hof. (KUb XXII 70 = Bo 2011).* Texte der Hethiter 6. Heidelberg: Winter.

1989 "Drawings, Graffiti and Squiggles on the Hittite Tablets – Art in Scribal Circles." In *Anatolia and the Ancient Neart East. Studies in Honor of Tahsin Özgüç*, edited by Kutlu Emre, Barthel Hrouda, Machteld Mellink, and Nimet Özgüç, 505–13. Ankara: Türk Tarih Kurumu.

1994 "The Textual Illustration of the 'Jester Scene' on the Sculptures of Alaca Höyük." *Anatolian Studies* 44: 207–18.

1999 "A Hittite Mycenaean Type B Sword from the Vicinity of Kastamonu, Northwest Turkey." In *Essays on Ancient Anatolia*, edited by H. I. H. P. Takahito Mikasa, 207–226. Bulletin of the Middle Eastern Culture Center in Japan 11. Wiesbaden: Harrassowitz.

2003 "Word Play in Hittite Literature?" In *Hittite Studies in Honor of Harry A. Hoffner Jr. on the Occasion of His 65th Birthday*, edited by Gary Beckman, Richard Beal, and Gregory McMahon, 377–88. Winona Lake: Eisenbrauns.

Ünal, Ahmet and Annalies Kammenhuber

1974 "Das Althethitische Losorakel KBo XVIII 151." *Zeitschrift Für Vergleichende Sprachforschung* 88: 157-80.

Valério, Miguel and Ilya Yakubovich

2010 "Semitic Word for 'Iron' as Anatolian Loanword." In *Исследования по Лингвистике и Семиотике. Сборник статей к юбилею Вяч. Вс. Иванова* = Issledovanija po Lingvistike i Semiotike. Sbornik stateĭ k jubileju Vjač. Vc. Ivanova [Studies in Linguistics and Semiotics. A Collection of Articles for the Anniversary for Vyacheslav V. Ivanov], edited by Tatyana M. Nikolaeva, 108–16. Moscow: Languages of Slavonic Culture.

van den Hout, Theo

1984 "Einige luwische Neutra auf *-ša/-za* in überwiegend junghethitischen Texten." *Zeitschrift für vergleichende Sprachforschung* 97: 60–80.

1987–90 "Maße und Gewichte. Bei den Hethitern." RlA 7: 517–27.

1990 Review of *Keilschrifturkunden aus Boghazköy. Heft LVII: Hethitische Briefe und Texte verschiedenen Inhalts*, by Alfonso Archi. *Bibliotheca Orientalis* 47: 423–32.

1991 "Hethitische Thronbesteigungsorakel und die Inauguration Tudhalijas IV." *Zeitschrift für Assyriologie* 81: 274–300.

1995 *Die Ulmitešub-Vertrag. Eine prosopographische Untersuchung*. Studien zu den Boğazköy-Texten 38. Wiesbaden: Harrassowitz.

1998 *The Purity of Kingship: An Edition of CTH 569 and Related Hittite Oracle Inquiries of Tudḫaliya IV*. Documenta et Monumenta Orientis Antiqui 25. Leiden: Brill.

2001 "Bemerkungen zu älteren hethitischen Orakeltexten." In *Kulturgeschichten: Altorientalische Studien für Volkert Haas zum 65. Gerburtstag*, edited by Thomas Richter, Doris Prechel, and Jörg Klinger, 423–40. Saarbrücken: Saarbrücker Druckerei und Verlag.

2002 "The (Divine) Stone-House and *Ḫegur* Reconsidered." In *Recent Developments in Hittite Archaeology and History: Papers in Memory of Hans G. Güterbock*, edited by Harry A. Hoffner, Jr. and K. Aslıhan Yener, 73–91. Winona Lake: Eisenbrauns.

2005 "On the Nature of the Tablet Collections at Ḫattuša." *Studi Micenei ed Egeo-Anatolici* 47: 277–89.

2006 "Administration in the Reign of Tuthaliya IV and the Later Years of the Hittite Empire." In *The Life and Times of Ḫattušili III and Tutḫaliya IV:*

Proceedings of a Symposium Held in Honor of J. de Roos, 12–13 December 2003, edited by Theo van den Hout, 77–106. PIHANS = Uitgaven van het Nederlands Instituut voor het Nabije Oosten te Leiden 103. Leiden: Nederlands Instituut voor het Nabije Oosten.

2010a "^{LÚ}DUB.SAR.GIŠ = 'Clerk'?" In *Studi di Ittitologia in onore di Alfonso Archi*, edited by Rita Francia and Giulia Torri. *Orientalia* 79: 255–67.

2010b "Object Description; Catalog No. 63." In *Visible Language. Inventions of Writing in the Ancient Middle East and Beyond*, edited by Christopher Woods, 107–8. Oriental Institute Museum Publications 32. Chicago: Oriental Institute.

2012 "Administration and Writing in Hittite Society." In *Archivi, depositi, magazzini presso gli Ittiti: nuovi materiali e nuove ricerche / Archives, Depots and Storehouses in the Hittite World: New Evidence and New Research (Proceedings of the Workshop held in Pavia, June 18, 2009)*, edited by Maria Balza, Mauro Giorgieri, and Clelia Mora, 41–58. Studia Mediterranea, 23. Genoa: Italian University Press.

2016 "A Brief Note on the Syntax of Writing in Hittite." In *Audia fabulas veteres. Anatolian Studies in Honor of Jana Součková-Siegelová*, edited by Šárka Velhartická, 426–37. Culture and History of the Ancient Near East, 79. Leiden: Brill.

2020a *A History of Hittite Literacy. Writing and Reading in Late Bronze-Age Anatolia (1650–1200 BC)*. Cambridge: Cambridge University Press.

2020b "Hittite Society, Economy, and Rituals." *Orient: Journal of the Society of Near Eastern Studies in Japan* 55: 3–11.

2022 "Elites and the Social Stratification of the Ruling Class in the Hittite Kingdom." In *Handbook of the Hittite Empire. Power Structures*, edited by Stefano de Martino, 313–54. Empires through the Ages in Global Perspective 1. Oldenbourg: De Gruyter, 2022.

van Gessel, Ben H.L.

1998 *Onomasticon of the Hittite Pantheon*. 3 vols. Handbuch der Orientalistik 1/33. Leiden: Brill.

Van Lerberghe, Karel

1979 "An Enigmatic Cylinder Seal Mentioning the *UŠÛM*-Tree in the Royal Museum of Art and History, Brussels." In *On Trees, Mountains, and Millstones in the Ancient Near East*, by Marten Stol and Karel Van Lerberghe, 31–49. Leiden: Ex Oriente Lux.

van Zeist, Willem, Henk Woldring, and Dick Stapert

1975 "Late Quaternary Vegetation and Climate of Southwestern Turkey." *Paleohistoria* 17: 55–143.

Veenhof, Klaus R.

1972 *Aspects of Old Assyrian Trade and its Terminology*. Studia et Documenta ad Iura Orientis Antiqui Pertinentia 10. Leiden: Brill.

2010 "Ancient Assur: The City, its Traders, and its Commerical Network." *Journal of the Economic and Social History of the Orient* 53 (2010): 39–82.

Vigo, Matteo

2008 "'Tradurre e non tradire' il problema delle integrazioni. Il caso di KBo XII 39." In *Traduzioni di tradizioni e tradizioni di traduzione. Atti del quarto incontro "Orientalisti" (Pavia, 19–21 aprile 2007)*, edited by Benedetta Bellucci, Elio Jucci, Alfredo Rizza, and Bianca Maria Tomassini Pieri, 191–248. Milan: Qu.A.S.A.R S.r.l.

2010 "Linen in Hittite Inventory Texts." In *Textile terminologies in the ancient Near East and Mediterranean from the third to the first millennia BC*, edited by Cécile Michel and Marie-Louise Nosch, 290–322. Ancient Textiles Series 8. Oxford: Oxbow Books.

2018 "On the Terminology of Some (Job) Titles in Hittite Texts." In *What's in a Name. Terminology related to the Work Force and Job Categories in the Ancient Near East*, edited by Agnés Garcia-Ventura, 271–314. Alter Orient und Altes Testament 440. Münster: Ugarit-Verlag.

2019 "Staple and Wealth Finance and the Administration of the Hittite Empire." In *Economy of Religions in Anatolia: From the Early Second to the Middle of the First Millennium BCE. Proceedings of an International Conference in Bonn (23rd to 25th May 2018)*, edited by Manfred Hutter and Sylvia Hutter-Braunsar, 141–51. Alter Orient und Altes Testament 467. Münster: Ugarit-Verlag.

Virolleaud, Charles

1957 *Le palais royal d'Ugarit II: Textes en cunéiformes alphabétiques des archives est, ouest et centrales.* Mission de Ras Shamra 7. Paris: Klincksieck.

1965 *Le palais royal d'Ugarit V: Textes en cunéiformes alphabétiques des archives sud, sud-ouest et du petit palais.* Mission de Ras Shamra 11. Paris: Klincksieck.

Vita, Juan Pablo

2010 "Textile Terminology in the Ugaritic Texts." In *Textile terminologies in the ancient Near East and Mediterranean from the third to the first millennia BC*, edited by Cécile Michel and Marie-Louise Nosch, 323–37. Ancient Textiles Series 8. Oxford: Oxbow Books.

von den Driesch, Angela and Joachim Boessneck

1981 *Reste von Haus- und Jagdtieren aus der Unterstadt von Boğazköy-Ḫattuša. Grabungen 1958–1977. Grabungen 1958–1977.* Boğazköy-Ḫattuša 11. Berlin: Mann, 1981.

von den Driesch, Angela and Nadja Pöllath

2003 "Changes from Late Bronze Age to Early Iron Age Animal Husbandry as Reflected in the Faunal Remains from Büyükkaya/Boğazköy-Ḫattuša." In *Identifying Changes: The Transition from Bronze to Iron Ages in Anatolia and Its Neighbouring Regions. Proceedings of the International Workshop, Istanbul, November 8–9, 2002*, edited by Bettina Fischer, Hermann Genz,

Éric Jean, and Kemalettin Köroğlu, 295–99. İstanbul: Türk Eskiçağ Bilimleri Enstitüsü.

2004 *Vor- und frühgeschichtliche Nutztierhaltung und Jagd auf Büyükkaya in Boğazköy-Ḫattuša, Zentralanatolien.* Boğazköy-Berichte 7. Mainz: von Zabern.

von Schuler, Einar

1956 "Die Würdenträgereide des Arnuwanda." *Orientalia (Nova Series)* 25: 209–240.

1957 *Hethitische Dienstanweisungen für höhere Hof- und Staatsbeamte. Ein Beitrag zum antiken Recht Kleinasiens.* Archiv für Orientforschung, Beiheft 10. Graz: Weidner.

1964 "Staatsverträge und Dokumente hethitischen Rechts." In *Neuere Hethiterforschung*, edited by Gerold Walser, 34–53. Wiesbaden: Steiner.

1965a *Die Kaškäer: Ein Beitrag zur Ethnographie des alten Kleinasiens.* Berlin: De Gruyter.

1965b "Sonderformen hethitischen Staatsverträge." In *Anadolu Arastirmalari. Helmuth Bossert'in Hatırasına Armağan* (Fs. H. Th. Bossert), 445–64. Istanbul: Istanbul University.

1976–80 "Kaškäer." RlA 5: 460–63.

Waal, Willemijn

2011 "They Wrote on Wood. The Case for a Hieroglyphic Scribal Tradition on Wooden Writing Boards in Hittite Anatolia." *Anatolian Studies* 61: 21–34.

2014 "Changing Fate: Hittite *gulš-*/GUL-*š-*/^{d}*Gulšeš*/^{d}GUL-*šeš*, Cuneiform Luwian *gulzā(i)-*/GUL-*zā(i)-*, Hieroglyphic Luwian REL-*za-* and the *Kuwanšeš* Deities." In *Proceedings of the Eighth International Congress of Hittitology, Warsaw, 5–9 September 2011*, edited by Piotr Taracha, 1016–1033. Warsaw: Agade.

2015 *Hittite Diplomatics.* Studien zu den Boğazköy-Texten 57. Wiesbaden: Harrassowitz.

2017a "A New Interpretation of the Hititte Expression *šarā ar-*." In *Hittitology Today: Studies on Hittite and Neo-Hittite Anatolia in Honor of Emmanuel Laroche's 100th Birthday = L'hittitologie aujourd'hui: Études sur l'Anatolie hittite et néo-hittite à l'occasion du centenaire de la naissance d'Emmanuel Laroche*, edited by Alice Mouton, 71–80. Rencontres d'archéologie de l'IFÉA 5. Istanbul: Institut Fançais d'Études Anatoliennes Georges - Dumézil.

2017b "Anatolian Hieroglyphs on Hittite Clay Tablets." In *Studies in Iconography and Cultures of the Ancient Near East in Honour of F. A. M. Wiggermann*, edited by David Kertai and Olivier Nieuwenhuyse, 297–307. Alter Orient und Altes Testament 441. Münster: Ugarit-Verlag.

2019 "Fate Strikes Back: New Evidence for the Identification of the Hittite Fate Dieties and its Implications for Hieroglyphic Writing in Anatolia." *Journal of Cuneiform Studies* 71: 121–32.

Waetzoldt, Hartmut

1972 *Untersuchungen zur neusumerischen Textilindustrie.* Studi economici e tecnologici 1. Roma: Centro per le antichità e la storia dell'arte del Vicino Oriente.

1980–83 "Leinen (Flachs)." RlA 6: 583–94.

Weber, Max

1999 "The Social Causes of the Decay of Ancient Civilizations." In *Essays in Economic Sociology,* by Max Weber, edited by Richard Swedburg, 138–53. Princeton: Princeton University Press.

Weeden, Mark

2011 *Hittite Logograms and Hittite Scholarship.* Studien zu den Boğazköy-Texten 54. Wiesbaden: Harrassowitz.

Wegner, Ilse

1981 *Gestalt und Kult der Ištar-Šawuška in Kleinasien.* Alter Orient und Altes Testament 36. Kevelaer: Butzon & Bercker.

2004 *Hurritische Opferlisten aus hethitischen Festbeschreibungen. Teil III: Das Glossar.* Corpus der Hurritischen Sprachdenkmäler I/3-3. Roma: Istituto di Studi sulle Civiltà dell'Egeo e del Vicino Oriente.

Werner, Rudolf

1967 *Hethitische Gerichtsprotokolle.* Studien zu den Boğazköy-Texten 4. Wiesbaden: Harrassowitz.

Westenholz, Joan Goodnick

2000 *Cuneiform Inscriptions in the Collection of the Bible Lands Museum Jerusalem. The Emar Tablets.* In collaboration with Jun Ikeda, Shlomo Izre'el, Marcel Sigrist, Itamar Singer, and Masamichi Yamada. Cuneiform Monographs 13. Groningen: Styx Publications.

Wilhelm, Gernot

1988 "Neue akkadische Gilgameš-Fragmente aus Ḫattuša." *Zeitschrift für Assyriologie* 78: 99–121.

1992 "Hurritisch *e/irana/i* 'Geschenk'." In *Sedat Alp'a Armağan = Festschrift für Sedat Alp. Hittite and Other Anatolian and Near Eastern Studies in Honour of Sedat Alp,* edited by Heinrich Otten, Ekrem Akurgal, Hayri Ertem, and Aygül Süel, 501–6. Anadolu Medeniyetlerini Araştırma ve Tanıtma Vakfı Yayınları 1. Ankara: Türk Tarih Kurumu.

1997 *Keilschrifttexte aus Gebäude A.* Kuşaklı - Sarissa 1/1. Rahden/Westf.: Leidorf.

2007 "Ausgewählte Textfunde der Kampagne 2006." *Archäologischer Anzeiger* 2007/1: 86–90.

2015 "The Sacred Landscapes of Sarissa." In *Sacred Landscapes of Hittites and Luwians. Proceedings of the International Conference in Honour of Franca Pecchioli Daddi. Florence, February 6th–8th 2014,* edited by Anacleto

D'Agostino, Valentina Orsi, and Giulia Torri, 93–99. Studia Asiana 9. Florence: Firenze University Press.

Wilkinson, Tony J.

2003 *Archaeological Landscapes of the Ancient Near East.* Tucson: University of Arizona Press.

Wiseman, Donald J.

1953 *The Alalakh Tablets.* Ankara: British Institute of Archaeology.

1954 "Supplementary Copies of Alalakh Tablets." *Journal of Cuneiform Studies* 8: 1–30.

1959 "Ration Lists from Alalakh IV." *Journal of Cuneiform Studies* 13: 50–59.

Wittenberg, Hartmut

2017 "Capture and Management of Ground and Stratum Water in the Hittite Empire – Technology and Cultural Significance." In *Innovation versus Beharrung: Was macht den Unterschied des hethitischen Reichs im Anatolien des 2. Jahrtausends v. Chr.? Internationaler Workshop zu Ehren von Jürgen Seeher, Istanbul, 23–24. Mai 2014*, edited by Andreas Schachner, 163–73. Byzas 23. Istanbul: Deutsches Archäologisches Institut.

Wright, Nathan J., Andrew S. Fairbairn, J. Tyler Faith, and Kimiyoshi Matsumura

2015 "Woodland Modification in Bronze and Iron Age Central Anatolia: An Anthracological Signature for the Hittite State?" *Journal of Archaeological Science* 55: 219–30

Yakar, Jak

2000 *Ethnoarchaeology of Anatolia. Rural Socio-Economy in the Bronze and Iron Ages.* Monograph series (Tel Aviv University) 17. Jerusalem: Emery and Claire Yass Publ. in Archaeology.

2011 *Reflections of Ancient Anatolian Society in Archaeology: From Neolithic Village Communities to EBA Towns and Polities.* Istanbul: Homer Kitabevi.

Yakubovich, Ilya

2013–14 "The Luwian Deity Kwanza." *Aramzd* 8: 282–97.

Yalçın, Ünsal

2005 "Zum Eisen der Hethiter." In *Das Schiff von Uluburun: Welthandel vor 3000 Jahren. Katalog der Ausstellung des Deutschen Bergbau-Museums Bochum vom 15. Juli 2005 bis 16. Juli 2006*, edited by Ünsal Yalçin, Cemal Pulak, and Rainer Slotta, 493–502. Veröffentlichungen aus dem Deutschen Bergbaumuseum 138. Bochum: Deutsches Bergbau-Museum.

2016 "Zinn für die Königin. Ein Barrenfragment aus Alacahöyük und seine Deutung." In *From Bright Ores to Shiny Metals. Festschrift for Andreas Hauptmann on the Occasion of 40 Years Research in Archaeometallurgy and Archaeometry*, edited by Gabriele Körlin, Michael Prange, Thomas Stöllner, and Ünsal Yalçin, 69–74. Der Anschnitt, Beiheft 29. Rahden/Westf.: Leidorf.

Yalçın, Ünsal and Hadi Özbal
2009 "Ein neues Zinnvorkommen in Kayseri-Hisarcık – Ein Vorbericht." *Türkiye Bilimler Akademisi Arkeoloji Dergisi* 12: 117-122.

Yamada, Masamichi
1993 "'ARANA-Documents' from Emar." *Orient* 29: 139–46.
2017 "The Arana Documents from Emar Revisted." *Orient* 52: 121–33

Yasur-Landau, Assaf
2005 "Mycenaean, Hittite and Mesopotamian Tables 'with Nine Feet'." *Studi Mediterranea ed Egeo-Anatolici* 47: 299–307.

Yener, K. Aslıhan
2015 *The Domestication of Metals: The Rise of Complex Metal Industries in Anatolia.* Leiden: Brill.

Yener, K. Aslıhan, Fikri Kulakoğlu, Evren Yazgan, Ryoichi Kontani, Yuichi S. Hayakawa, Joseph W. Lehner, Gonca Dardeniz, Güzel Öztürk, Michael Johnson, Ergun Kaptan, and Abdullah Hacar
2015 "New Tin Mines and Production Sites Near Kültepe in Turkey: A Third-millennium BC Highland Production Model." *Antiquity* 89 (345): 596–612.

Yıldırım, Tayfun abd Aslı Kısa
2015 "Çorum/Resuloğlu 2014 yılı kazıları." *Çorum Kazı ve Araştırmalar Sempozyumu* 5: 97–104.

Yıldırım, Tayfun, Nimet Demirci Bal, Gonca Dardeniz
2021 "Symbolism in 13th-century BC Hittite Metallurgy: The Kastamonu-Kınık (Turkey) Metal Hoard, Again." *Journal of Near Eastern Studies* 80: 31–57.

Zaccagnini, Carlo
1973 *Lo scambio dei doni nel Vicino Oriente durante i secoli XV–XIII.* Orientis Antiqui Collectio, 11. Rome: Centro per le antichità e la storio dell'arte del Vicino Oriente.
1981 "Modo di produzione asiatico e Vicino Oriente antico. Appunti per una discussione." *Dialoghi di archeologia*, NS 3/3: 3–65.
1989 "Asiatic Mode of Production and Ancient Near East, Notes Towards a Discussion." In *Production and Consumption in the Ancient Near East*, edited by Carlo Zaccagnini, 1–126. Budapest: Chaire d'Egyptologie de l'Université Eötvös Loránd de Budapest.
1989–90 "Dono e tributo come modelli istituzionali di scambio: Echi e persistenze nella documentazione amministrativa vicino-orientale del Tardo Bronzo." *Scienze dell'antichità. Storia archeologia antropologia* 3–4: 105–110.

Zawadzki, Stefan
2006 *Garments of the Gods: Studies on the Textile Industry and the Pantheon of Sippar According to the Texts from the Ebabbar Archive.* Orbis Biblicus et Orientalis 218. Göttingen: Vandenhoeck & Ruprecht.
2013 *Garments of the Gods, vol. 2: Texts.* Orbis Biblicus et Orientalis 260. Göttingen: Vandenhoeck & Ruprecht.

Zehnder, Thomas
2010 *Die hethitischen Frauennamen: Katalog und Interpretation*. Dresdner Beiträge zur Hethitologie 29. Wiesbaden: Harrasswitz.
Zimansky, Paul
2007 "The Lattimore Model and Hatti's Kaska Frontier." In *Settlement and Society: Essays Dedicated to Robert McCormick Adams*, edited by Elizabeth Stone, 157–72. Los Angeles: Cotsen Institute of Archaeology.
Zinko, Christian
2001 "Bemerkungen zu den hethitischen *s*-Stämmen." In *Anatolisch und Indogermanisch = Anatolico e indoeuropeo. Akten des Kolloquiums Indogermanischen Gesellschaft, Pavia 22.–25. September 1998*, edited by Onofrio Carruba and Walter Meid, 411–25. Innsbruck: Institut für Sprachen und Literaturen der Universität Innsbruck.
Zubieta Lupo, Valeria
2020 "Foreign Medical Knowledge in Ḫattuša." In *Hrozný and Hittite: The First Hundred Years. Proceedings of the International Conference Held at Charles University, Prague, 11–14 November 2015*, edited by Ronald I. Kim, Jana Mynářová, Peter Pavúk, 603–17. Culture and History of the Ancient Near East 107. Leiden: Brill.

LIST OF CITED TEXTS

The following texts received some form of commentary or treatment in this volume. Simple citations, where no new information is added, are excluded. References to commentary pertaining to the text as a whole are in-line with the root entry. References to treatment of specific lines are broken down by obv./rev. and column. Passages receiving general commentary are in normal font. Passages receiving transliteration and translation are cited in **bold**, while those receiving only translation are cited in *italics*. Numbers in parentheses ( ) after a table, e.g., Table 34 (244), refer to the page on which the table containing the cited text begins, not necessarily the actual page on which the text appears.

Studien zu den Boğazköy-Texten

Herausgegeben im Auftrag der Akademie der Wissenschaften und der Literatur, Mainz, von Elisabeth Rieken und Daniel Schwemer

65: James M. Burgin

Functional Differentiation in Hittite Festival Texts

An Analysis of the Old Hittite Manuscripts of the KI.LAM Great Assembly

2019. XII, 232 pages, hc
170x240 mm
ISBN 978-3-447-11247-5 *€ 68,– (D)*

This book investigates how the clay tablet record of the Hittite festival tradition interfaced with the reality of Hittite festival performance. Previous studies of Hittite festival texts have assumed that the main festival action was recorded in a more or less neutral, objective fashion, i. e. recording what was essential to the festival as a whole.

Through an examination of the so-called 'outline' festival texts, as well as a new study of the four Old Hittite manuscripts of the KI.LAM Great Assembly – one of the spectacular highpoints of the Hittite festival calendar – it is argued instead that the Hittite festival texts recorded the multiple perspectives, based on their specialized needs, of the cultic actors tasked with correct performance of the rites. The multi-perspective hypothesis of Hittite festival texts leads to a reassessment of the Hittite festival corpus as it is preserved. Instead of interpreting Hittite festival texts as products of scholastic learning or documentation, the texts are shown to be, at least in origin, the working documents of expert practitioners produced in the planning and production of festival performances. This interpretation of multiple, functionally-specialized perspectives for the Hittite festival texts carries implications for the festival corpus as a whole.

66: Susanne Görke, Charles W. Steitler (Eds.)

Cult, Temple, Sacred Spaces

Cult Practices and Cult Spaces in Hittite Anatolia and Neighbouring Cultures
Proceedings of the First International HFR Symposium, Mainz, 3–5 June 2019

2020. XVI, 376 pages, 3 diagrams,
61 ill., 2 maps, 27 tables, hc
170x240 mm
ISBN 978-3-447-11486-8
⊙E-Book: ISBN 978-3-447-39035-4 *each € 88,– (D)*

In June 2019, the project "Corpus der hethitischen Festrituale" (HFR) invited renowned international scholars to a symposium discussing recent developments in ancient Near Eastern studies regarding the interpretation of philological and archaeological sources from Anatolia and adjacent areas in the 2nd mill. BCE. The symposium focused on questions concerning the archaeology of temples and other sacred places, differentiation of sacred spaces according to written sources, the organization of festivals with a focus on spatial aspects, participation in festivals, and possibilities of interpretation thanks to insights into the cult practices of areas such as Northern Syria, the Levant, Mesopotamia or Egypt.

The first section includes studies examining rituals and their temple contexts in Egypt, the Levant, Assyria and Babylonia, providing comparative insights for understanding the Hittite festivals. An archaeological section offers new analyses of existing temple finds as well as a presentation of recent discoveries of sacred architecture in both Anatolia and the Levant. The remainder of the volume consists primarily of Hittitological philological studies of sacred space, analyzing the significance of various places, such as rivers, *loci numinosi*, roofs, the movement from one place to another within ritual practices, special terminology and characteristics of various festivals, the economic aspects of Hittite festivals and their ideological background in Hittite kingship and the king's connection to festivals.

Studien zu den Boğazköy-Texten

Herausgegeben im Auftrag der Akademie der Wissenschaften und der Literatur, Mainz, von Elisabeth Rieken und Daniel Schwemer

67: Giulia Torri

The *Haus am Hang* at Ḫattuša

A Late Hittite State Scriptorium and Its Tablet Collections

2021. XVI, 306 pages, 13 ill., 32 tables, hc
170x240 mm
ISBN 978-3-447-11621-3
⊙E-Book: ISBN 978-3-447-39136-8 *each € 78,– (D)*

During the first excavations in Lower City of Ḫattuša, conducted by H. Winckler and Th. Makridi in 1907, Makridi discovered a palace built east of the main Temple. The building was later named *Haus am Hang* (House on the Slope, HaH) because it leaned on the terraces leading up to the royal palace on Büyükkale. Several fragments of clay tablets in cuneiform script were discovered within and around the building during this period and in the following archaeological investigations until the 1960s. These text fragments exemplified the various text typologies produced by Hittite scribes.
Giulia Torri's research focuses on this collection of texts in search of the original criteria for its organization inside the building and provides a new approach in outlining the cultural environment in which the Hittite texts were produced: As a first step, the range of information about the discovery and the find-spots of the fragments is analyzed and contextualised (Part I). In the second part the texts, classified according to their content as administrative texts, chancellery texts, and texts of the scribal tradition, are collected, studied, and compared with their duplicate versions from other locations, with the aim of showing how the Hittite scribes composed and preserved them in this area of the Lower City (Part II).

68: Michele Cammarosano

At the Interface of Religion and Administration: The Hittite Cult Inventories

With a contribution by Adam Kryszeń

2021. XX, 264 pages, 1 ill.,
1 map, 15 tables, hc
170x240 mm
ISBN 978-3-447-11731-9
⊙E-Book: ISBN 978-3-447-39197-9 *each € 68,– (D)*

The so-called cult inventory texts report on the state of religious festivals, rites, cult objects, and cult supplies in a number of provincial towns and villages under Hittite control, thereby documenting the interaction between the central administration and local settlements. As such, they do not concern the official "state cults," but rather a variety of rites and customs, which in part preserve local traditions. Because of its nature and size, this corpus is unique in the ancient Near East, and is relevant to the comparative history of religions and centre-periphery studies. Within Anatolian studies, the corpus is especially relevant to the study of historical geography, regional and local Hittite panthea, religious iconography, the production and logistics of cult supplies, and the participation of village communities in rites and festivals.
Expanding upon a comprehensive edition of 450 cuneiform tablets and the pertinent database "Hittite local cults," the volume provides an in-depth overview of the text genre; a study of the material, palaeographic, orthographic, and linguistic aspects of the manuscripts; a thorough investigation into the geography of the local cults as well as into the local panthea and cult calendar; and finally critical editions of a representative selection of original texts.